ILLUSTRATED
DICTIONARY
OF
ESSENTIAL
KNOWLEDGE

ILLUSTRATED DICTIONARY OF ESSENTIAL KNOWLEDGE
was edited and designed by The Reader's Digest Association Limited, London.

First edition Copyright ©1995
The Reader's Digest Association Limited, Berkeley Square House, Berkeley Square, London W1X 6AB.
Copyright © 1995 Reader's Digest Association Far East Limited.
Philippines Copyright © 1995 Reader's Digest Association Far East Limited.

Printed in Belgium

ISBN 0 276 42153 1

The typeface used in this book is Janson Text.

READER'S DIGEST

ILLUSTRATED DICTIONARY
OF
ESSENTIAL
KNOWLEDGE

Published by The Reader's Digest Association Limited

LONDON • NEW YORK • SYDNEY • CAPE TOWN • MONTREAL

The *Illustrated Dictionary of Essential Knowledge* is the perfect antidote to dry works of reference – it contains the kind of information that people feel they *ought* to know, selecting nuggets of essential knowledge from the morass of information with which we seem to be bombarded daily. Reflecting the culture of today, the book provides a diverse and lively guide to all those disparate subjects which well-informed people want to understand and discuss – from Leonardo da Vinci to junk bonds. The range of the book is vast; the academic gravitas of Aristotle or quantum mechanics is balanced by the fun of James Bond or *Blind Date*. It travels lightly through the arts, business, food and drink, geography, history, music, philosophy, politics, science and sport. Its 23 thematic chapters contain some 6000 clear, concise entries brought to life by more than 800 colour photographs, pictures and diagrams that capture key moments and explain essential facts.

The *Illustrated Dictionary of Essential Knowledge* excludes obscure or highly technical information; its editors have also rejected subjects which were considered too obvious or too

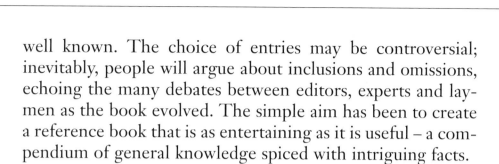

well known. The choice of entries may be controversial; inevitably, people will argue about inclusions and omissions, echoing the many debates between editors, experts and laymen as the book evolved. The simple aim has been to create a reference book that is as entertaining as it is useful – a compendium of general knowledge spiced with intriguing facts.

HOW TO USE THE BOOK

Within each of the 23 sections, entries appear in alphabetical order. The pronunciation of difficult words is explained clearly, without resort to accents or strange symbols. Cross-references to other entries in the same section appear in SMALL CAPITAL LETTERS; if prefaced by a ▷ symbol, they appear in a different section and should be looked up in the comprehensive index. The index also lists a host of subsidiary subjects which are referred to in the course of main entries. A 🎙 symbol at the end of an entry prefaces an offbeat, sometimes amusing sidelight on a subject – that Coco Chanel made the sun tan fashionable, for example, or that Dover's famous White Cliffs are composed of billions of shells.

CONTENTS

WORDS, PHRASES AND THE ENGLISH LANGUAGE................9

ENGLISH LITERATURE................31

WORLD LITERATURE................61

MYTHS AND LEGENDS................75

IDEAS, BELIEFS AND RELIGION................91

ART AND DESIGN................117

ARCHITECTURE AND ENGINEERING................153

HUMAN SOCIETY................169

BRITISH HISTORY................187

WORLD HISTORY................219

POLITICS, GOVERNMENT AND THE LAW................259

BUSINESS AND ECONOMICS................289

FILMS, ENTERTAINMENT AND THE MEDIA 307

MUSIC, SONG AND DANCE 335

SPORT AND LEISURE 361

FOOD AND DRINK 389

PLACES AND LANDSCAPES OF BRITAIN 397

NATIONS AND PLACES OF THE WORLD 425

THE EARTH AND THE ENVIRONMENT 463

THE LIVING WORLD 477

MEDICINE, HEALTH AND THE HUMAN BODY 493

SCIENCE, SPACE AND MATHEMATICS 521

TECHNOLOGY AND INVENTION 549

INDEX 567   ACKNOWLEDGMENTS 607

WORDS, PHRASES AND
THE ENGLISH LANGUAGE

Our ability to use language defines us as human, and forms the basis of all our relationships. It is the principal means we have for expressing our feelings and exchanging ideas. But language is also a fascinating subject in its own right, a complex structure of sounds and symbols, rules of grammar, newborn words and dying words, and phrases and proverbs with layers of significance much deeper than their literal meaning.

!?* mnemonic Hobson's choice

catch-22

¶ A PARLIAMENT OF ROOKS

&

Q.E.D

gilding the lily

flash in the pan

non sequitur

«áâäãåàæ

faux pas (FOH-PAA)

CYRILLIC RUSSIAN ALPHABET

abbreviation Shortened form of a word or phrase, used mainly in writing, and often having full stops to indicate missing letters. *Adj.* is the abbreviation of adjective, *UK* or *U.K.* of United Kingdom, and *ft* of feet. (Compare CONTRACTION.)

abstract noun Noun referring to an idea or quality rather than to an actual thing. *Happiness*, *parenthood* and *cause* are abstract nouns, but *field*, *leather* and *pen* are CONCRETE NOUNS.

accent Way in which words are pronounced in a particular region or by a particular social class. It also refers to DIACRITICAL MARKS such as the ACUTE ACCENT and GRAVE ACCENT, which adjust the way letters are pronounced in some languages. The word can also refer to the emphasis or stress placed on a particular syllable in a word. For example, *inflammable* has an accent on its second syllable.

Achilles' heel Small flaw or weakness that causes problems or puts one in danger: *He would win the decathlon easily if he could do better in the high jump, which is his Achilles' heel*. The phrase alludes to the vulnerable spot of the Greek warrior ▷ACHILLES.

acid test Any crucial or decisive test. The phrase derives from the practice of checking the amount of gold in a sample of metal by testing it with acid that will dissolve base metals but not gold.

acronym Word formed by combining the initial letters or syllables of a name or phrase, and pronouncing it as if it were an ordinary word. Examples include NATO, from North Atlantic Treaty Organisation, and radar, from *r*adio *d*etection *a*nd *r*anging. (Compare INITIALISM.)

active VOICE, or verb form, indicating that the subject of the sentence performs the action of the verb. For example, the sentence *The choir sang the hymn* is active (or 'in the active voice'). The counterpart of active is PASSIVE, as in the sentence *The hymn was sung by the choir*.

acute accent Mark (´), placed above a vowel, either to adjust the way it is pronounced, as in *glacé* or *flambé*, or to indicate that it should be stressed, as in *Márquez*. (Compare CIRCUMFLEX; GRAVE ACCENT.)

AD Abbreviation used to indicate a specific year after the birth of Jesus Christ. In formal writing, AD precedes the year, as in *He was born in AD 371*. It stands for *anno Domini*, a Latin phrase meaning 'in the year of the Lord'. Instead of AD, non-Christians sometimes use CE, which stands for 'Common Era'. (Compare BC.)

adage Short saying or proverb, especially a traditional and very old one. An example is *He who laughs last laughs longest*.

ad hoc An arbitrary arrangement, action, decision or committee that deals with an irregular or one-off situation: *No trains were running, so we made an* ad hoc *decision to hire a car*. The phrase is Latin in origin, meaning literally 'towards this'.

adjective Word that modifies a noun or noun phrase. In the sentence *He built a red brick house* both *red* and *brick* are adjectives. Adjectives that can have varying degrees of intensity are called GRADABLE ADJECTIVES.

ad lib Freely, undirected, without restrictions: *Experienced jazz musicians are often at their best when playing* ad lib. As a verb, *ad-lib* means to improvise: *I left my speech at home and had to* ad-lib. The term is a contraction of the Latin *ad libitum*, meaning 'as desired'.

ad nauseam To a tedious extreme, to a sickening extent: *He spoke* ad nauseam *about his hobby*. The phrase comes from Latin, and means 'to the point of nausea'.

adverb Word that modifies a verb, an adjective or another adverb, as *delightfully* does in these three sentences: *she dances delightfully*; *her dancing is delightfully innocent*; *she dances delightfully slowly*. Although adverbs often end in *-ly*, as in *quickly*, *immediately* or *extremely*, they do not always do so: *fast*, *soon* and *very* are adverbs too. Adverbs typically answer such questions as *How? Where? When?*

agreement Compatibility of GENDER, NUMBER, CASE and PERSON among words in a sentence or clause. In the sentence *She is still in her twenties*, the subject pronoun *she* is feminine, singular, and third-person, and agrees with the verb *is* (third-person singular), and the possessive adjective *her* (feminine and third-person singular). Sometimes, agreement is disregarded, as when a plural noun is seen as a single quantity, as in *Ten miles is a long walk*.

allusion Indirect reference to someone or something without specifically identifying it, as in *He made an allusion to his time in prison when he said he had been out of circulation for several years* or *The headmaster's speech was full of Classical allusions*.

alma mater School, college or university that one attended as a student. The Latin phrase means 'a cherishing mother'.

ambiguity The quality of having more than one possible interpretation. Both these sentences are ambiguous: *The peasants are revolting*; *Visiting aunts can be a bore*.

ampersand The sign &, representing the word *and*, as in *Gross & Co*.

anagram Word or phrase formed by reordering the letters of another word or phrase. The words *pots*, *tops*, *spot*, *stop* and *opts* are all anagrams of one another, and *one hug* is an anagram of *enough*.

analogy Similarity or comparison made between otherwise dissimilar things: *The lecturer drew an analogy between his daughter's make-up and the courtship displays of the animal kingdom*. The term also describes the extension of an existing pattern or model. For example, young children sometimes say *teached* rather than *taught*, by analogy with the word *reached*.

annus mirabilis Extraordinary or very important year: *1989 was an* annus mirabilis *for her: her twins were born, she won £1 million on the Pools and she was acquitted at the murder trial*. The phrase originally referred to 1588, the year of the Spanish Armada, when great disasters were predicted but never happened. It was also used for 1759, when English forces won a string of battles in the Seven Years' War. The phrase is Latin and means 'wondrous year'.

anonymous Having an unknown name or of unknown origin. When used as an attribution, the word is often abbreviated to 'Anon'.

ante- Prefix, from Latin, meaning 'before', as in *antenatal* or *anteroom*. (Compare POST-; PRE-.)

anti- Prefix, from Greek, meaning 'against' or 'opposed to', as in *anticlimax*, *anticlockwise* and *antihero*. (Compare PRO-.)

antithesis The juxtaposition of sharply contrasting ideas, using a careful balance of words or phrasing, as in *More haste, less speed*. The word also refers to a direct opposite, as in *Despair is the antithesis of hope*.

antonym Word having the opposite sense from another word. *Hot* is the antonym of *cold*, and *slowly* is the antonym of *quickly* or *fast*. (Compare SYNONYM.)

aphorism Brief, pithy statement expressing a truth or an opinion: *Time is money. Blood is thicker than water.*

apostrophe Punctuation mark ('), used to indicate possession in a noun – *a teacher's pet, the Peasants' Revolt* – or to indicate a missing letter or letters in a CONTRACTION – *isn't, we'll, fish 'n' chips.*
🖐A 'greengrocer's apostrophe' is an apostrophe incorrectly used as a plural, a fault of some greengrocers' signs: *Potato's 15p a pound, Strawberry's £1 a punnet.*

apposition Noun or noun phrase positioned directly after another to help to explain it. For example, in the sentence *Gooch, the England Captain, played a captain's innings*, the noun phrase *the England Captain* is in apposition to the noun *Gooch*. In an apposition, the two nouns or noun phrases should always be interchangeable.

apropos (A-pro-POH) Term derived from French, meaning 'with reference to' or 'concerning'. It is sometimes used with the preposition *of*, but can also stand without it, as in *Apropos your suggestion, I think we should wait and see what happens before making a final decision.*

aqua- Prefix derived from Latin, meaning 'water', as in *aquarium, Aqualung* and *aqua-sports*. HYDRO- is a similar prefix meaning water, but originating from the Greek.

arch- Prefix derived from Greek, meaning 'first', or 'main', as in *archangel, archbishop* and *archetypal.*

archaism Word or expression widely used in earlier times which now sounds very old-fashioned, such as *doth, perchance, yonder* and *wench.*

-archy Suffix, from Greek, meaning 'form of government', as in *monarchy, oligarchy* and *patriarchy.*

argot (AR-go) Special and often secret vocabulary used by a particular group, class or profession. In former times, it was common for criminals to use a kind of secret slang, and some members of the Mafia still use their own argot.

article Word used before a noun to indicate how widely it applies. *A* and *an* are indefinite articles and do not define a specific thing: *Pass me a chair*, for example, refers to any chair. *The* is the definite article and is used to specify a particular object: *Pass me the chair.*

au fait **(OH FAY)** Fully informed, skilled or familiar: *Are you* au fait *with the rules of cricket?* The phrase is French in origin, meaning literally 'to the point'.

Aunt Sally Scapegoat or WHIPPING BOY that is often made the target of criticism or ridicule: *New teaching methods have been made an Aunt Sally for the increasing lack of discipline in the classroom.*
🖐The original Aunt Sally was a fairground game involving a wooden head of an old woman smoking a pipe placed on a pole. Members of the public paid to throw sticks at her. If they hit her nose or knocked the pipe out of her mouth, they won a prize.

auto- Prefix, from Greek, meaning 'oneself', as in *automatic, autograph, autobiography* and *auto-pilot.*

auxiliary verb A verb that helps (or 'modulates') the main verb in a sentence. *May, could* and *did* are auxiliary verbs in the sentences *He may run faster, He could run faster* and *Did he run faster?*

avant-garde **(AV-on-gard)** The group considered most modern in a given field, especially among artists or writers. The term is also used as an adjective, which usually implies a sense of being daring or radical: *The* avant-garde *poetry of the 1960s seems curiously tame today.* The term is French in origin, and refers to the vanguard or front troops of the army.

back-formation Word created accidentally, on the mistaken assumption that it is an earlier and more basic form of an existing word. For example, *burgle* and *laze* are back-formations of *burglar* and *lazy.*

BC Abbreviation for 'before Christ', written after a date to indicate that the year is being counted backwards from the birth of Jesus Christ: *Aristotle was born in 384 BC and died in 322 BC.* Non-Christians sometimes use BCE instead, standing for 'before the Common Era'. (Compare AD.)

bene- Prefix, from Latin, meaning 'well', 'good' or 'kind', as in *benefit, benevolent* and *benediction.* The prefix with the opposite meaning is MALE-.

bête noire **(BETT NWAAR)** Person or thing that one particularly dislikes or avoids: *She is my best friend but her husband is my* bête noire. The plural is *bêtes noires*, pronounced in the same way as the singular. The term is French in origin, meaning literally 'black beast'.

beyond the pale Totally unacceptable, unreasonable or unbearable: *Simon's behaviour last night was really beyond the pale.* The original Pale was an area surrounding Dublin which was under English control in the 12th to 16th centuries. People living outside it were considered to be dangerous and uncivilised.

biblio- Prefix derived from the Greek *biblion*, meaning 'book', as in the words *bibliography* and *bibliophile.*

bilingual Capable of speaking two languages fluently, or something which involves two languages: *She is bilingual in Hindi and English; a bilingual Bible.*

bio- Prefix, from the Greek for 'life', as in *biography, biology* and *biodegradable.*

blue blood Noble birth, aristocratic descent: *She mixes in high society and pretends to have blue blood, but her father was a fishmonger.* The term is a direct translation of the Spanish *sangre azul*: in Spain, a pale complexion used to be considered a sign of pure breeding – unmixed by Moorish stock from the long Arab occupation of Spain. Such fair skin showed up the bluish veins on the wrist or temples, and so the idea of blue blood developed as a mark of nobility.

bona fides **(BOH-ner FYE-deez)** Good faith, or honest intention: *We stupidly accepted the* bona fides *of the man who sold us a Caribbean holiday for £300.* When used as an adjective, without the 's', the phrase also means authentic: *It is a* bona fide *Van Gogh.* The term is Latin for 'good faith'.

bon mot **((BON MOH)** Witty remark, such as an EPIGRAM, occurring in conversation: *The music critic's* bon mot *about 'the survival of the fattest' was a bit unfair on most of today's opera stars.* The plural is *bons mots* and is pronounced in the same way as the singular. The term is French in origin, and means literally 'good word'.

brackets See PARENTHESES; SQUARE BRACKETS.

burning one's boats (or burning one's bridges) Committing oneself to a course of action that it will be impossible to back out of later. The idea behind the phrase is drawn from ancient warfare: by burning its boats, an invading army would be destroying its own means of retreat, and would fight more bravely in the knowledge that safety lay only in victory. (Compare CROSSING THE RUBICON.)

11

capital letters See UPPER CASE.

caret Mark used by editors in the shape of an upside-down V or Y, placed in the text to indicate to the typist or printer where new material is to be inserted. The name comes from Latin and means literally 'there is lacking'.

carte blanche Unlimited power or permission to act as one thinks best: *The department store gave me* carte blanche *to choose any coat I liked, after I was stuck in one of their lifts all night.* The term is French in origin, meaning literally 'white card' or 'blank paper' – that is, a document allowing the bearer to write in whatever terms or conditions he wished.

case The relationship of a noun or pronoun to other words in a sentence. In English, nouns are either in the basic case (*James, dog, ladies*) or the POSSESSIVE (*James's house, dog's bone, ladies' dresses*). Pronouns can be in the subjective, objective or possessive case. In the sentence *He admitted that his conscience was troubling him,* the pronoun *he,* as subject of the verb, is in the subjective case; *his* is in the possessive case; and *him,* as the object of the verb, is in the objective case.

catch-22 Situation in which your apparent options tend to cancel each other out, leaving you the loser no matter which way you turn: *Starting a career in PR is a catch-22 situation – they won't offer you a job unless you have experience, but you can't get experience until you have a job.* The term comes from Joseph Heller's novel ▷CATCH-22.

cause célèbre Interesting public matter, such as a trial or scandal, arousing much discussion and taking of sides: *The minister's habitual visits to the casino became a nationwide* cause célèbre *only when his debts were revealed.* The plural is *causes célèbres,* pronounced in the same way as the singular. The phrase is French for 'famous case'.

cedilla (si-DILL-uh) Mark (¸) shaped rather like a comma, placed beneath a letter in some languages to adjust the way it is pronounced. For example, a cedilla placed beneath the letter 'c' in French words indicates that it should be pronounced as 's', as in *garçon.*

centi- Prefix, from Latin, meaning 'hundred' or 'hundredth', as in *centipede* (an insect which was traditionally thought to have a hundred feet) and *centimetre* (a hundredth of a metre).

COLLECTIVE NOUNS

A collective noun refers to a group of people, animals or things regarded as a unit, such as *family, assembly, team* or *orchestra.* Over the centuries, writers have delighted in coining witty, apt or colourful collective nouns; for example *a parliament of rooks* or *an exaltation of larks,* though not all of them are in standard current use.

BENCH OF BISHOPS

CHARM OF GOLDFINCHES

CHOIR OF ANGELS

CLUTCH OF EGGS

DIGEST OF LAWS

DRAY OF SQUIRRELS

GAGGLE OF GEESE

KINDLE OF KITTENS

LODGE OF BEAVERS

MURDER OF CROWS

MURMURATION OF STARLINGS

MUSTER OF PEACOCKS

NEST OF HORNETS

PLUMP OF WATERFOWL

POD OF WHALES

PRIDE OF LIONS

SCHOOL OF PORPOISES

SHOWER OF BLESSINGS

SKULK OF FOXES

UNKINDNESS OF RAVENS

WISP OF SNIPE

---

cf. Abbreviation of the Latin word *confer,* which directs the reader to compare the item under discussion with a related item, as in *For another example of Dickens' delight in children's parties cf. p. 37.*

chacun à son goût (SHAK-uh ah son GOO) French expression meaning literally 'each to his own taste'.
The Latin poet Terence (*c.*190-159 BC) expressed a similar idea in one of his comedies: *Quot homines tot sententiae* meaning 'so many men, so many opinions'.

chrono-, chron- Prefix or COMBINING FORM from Greek, meaning 'time', as in *chronology* and *synchronise.*

circum- Prefix, from Latin, meaning 'around', or 'on all sides', as in *circumnavigate* and *circumstance.*

circumflex Mark (ˆ) placed above a vowel in certain languages which slightly alters the way it is pronounced, for example, in the French words *tête* and *château.*

circumlocution Use of long-winded and roundabout language, often as a means of avoiding spelling out an unwelcome piece of information. (See also EUPHEMISM.)

clause Group of words containing both a SUBJECT and a PREDICATE, and typically forming part of a COMPLEX SENTENCE or COMPOUND SENTENCE. The sentence *I will come if I can* contains two clauses: *I will come* (main clause) and *if I can* (subordinate clause). (Compare PHRASE.)

cliché Expression that is used so often and so automatically that it has lost its freshness and descriptive power, and sounds boring or insincere. *Green as grass, shining example* and *bright as a button* are all clichés.

cloud-cuckoo-land An idealised fantasy world: *Stop living in cloud-cuckoo-land for once, and be realistic.* The term is a translation of the name for an imaginary city, floating in the air, in the play The ▷BIRDS by Aristophanes.

colloquialism Informal word or expression typical of speech rather than writing, as in *Who does she think she is?* and *She should get her act together.* (Compare SLANG.)

colon Punctuation mark (:) used to introduce a list, an explanation or an example, as in *Here's what you will need to bring: a tent, a sleeping bag, a compass, a Primus stove and five days' rations.*

combining form Word or part of a word used to form new words by combining with others. In *multipurpose,* 'multi-' is a combining form, and in *psychology,* both 'psycho-' and '-logy' are combining forms.

comma Punctuation mark (,) used to separate ideas or elements within a sentence, as in *If you hurry, you should be in time to meet the deadline* and *Your rations should include apples, powdered milk and sliced bread.*

comme il faut (KOM eel FOH) Socially correct or in keeping with accepted standards: *Calling the bishop 'Bish' is hardly* comme il faut, *but she was drunk at the time.* It is a French phrase, meaning 'as it should be'.

common noun Noun referring either to a concept or to all of the members of a class of things, rather than to a named individual: *information*, *book* and *child* are common nouns. (Compare PROPER NOUN.)

comparative Form of an adjective or adverb indicating a greater or more intense degree of the quality, for example the use of 'older' in *He is thought to be the older of the two brothers*. (Compare SUPERLATIVE.)

complement The part of a sentence that 'completes' or gives more information about the subject or object, usually in the form of an adjective or noun phrase. In the following sentences, the adjective 'drunk' and the noun phrase 'managing director' are known as subject complements: *George is drunk. Gillian becomes managing director next week*. In the following sentences, they are called object complements: *A single shot of whisky makes George drunk. The company appointed Gillian managing director*. (Compare OBJECT; PREDICATE; SUBJECT.)

complex sentence Sentence that has at least one SUBORDINATE CLAUSE in addition to its MAIN CLAUSE, such as *There I met an old man* (main clause) *who wouldn't say his prayers* (subordinate clause).

compos mentis Sane, of sound mind: *The psychiatrist testified that the accused was* compos mentis, *and therefore fit to stand trial*. The phrase is Latin in origin, meaning 'having control of one's own mind'. The opposite is *non compos mentis*.

compound sentence Sentence that has at least two MAIN CLAUSES, often joined by a conjunction such as *and* or *or*; for example, *So I took him by the left leg and threw him down the stairs*. (Compare COMPLEX SENTENCE and SIMPLE SENTENCE.)

concordance Index listing every occasion on which individual words are used in a particular text, such as the Bible or Shakespeare's plays.

concrete noun NOUN which refers to a real object rather than to an idea or quality. *Dog* and *milk* are concrete nouns but *fear* and *beauty* are ABSTRACT NOUNS.

conjunction 'Joining' word or part of speech that connects other words, phrases or sentences. There are three main types: co-ordinating conjunctions such as *and*, *but* and *so* which join two or more similar elements; correlative conjunctions such as *either . . . or* which are used in pairs; and

subordinating conjunctions such as *when*, *if* and *before* which link a SUBORDINATE CLAUSE to the rest of the sentence.

connotation Sense of a word or expression, apart from its literal meaning and including its emotional suggestions and personal associations. For most people, the word *heat* has connotations of pleasurable warmth and love, though for some it may have frightening or stifling connotations.

consonant Letter of the alphabet or speech sound that – unlike a VOWEL – is made by obstructing the air stream with the tongue, teeth, throat or lips.

contra- Prefix, from Latin, meaning 'against', 'opposite' or 'counter-', as in *contradict*, *contravene* and *contraflow*.

contraction Shortened form of a word or phrase, formed by leaving out or fusing some of the sounds or letters, such as *we'd* for *we would*, *shan't* for *shall not*, *flu* for *influenza*, and *pram* for *perambulator*. The omitted letters are sometimes replaced by apostrophes. Contractions are often, though not always, informal in use. (Compare ABBREVIATION; ELLIPSIS.)

corollary Conclusion or inference drawn from a previously proven idea, but not actually proved itself, such as *He did not know about the robbery, so as a corollary someone else must have called the police*.

cosmo- Prefix, from the Greek, meaning 'world' or 'universe', for example in *cosmology*, *cosmonaut* and *cosmopolitan*.

count noun (also countable noun) Noun that can occur in the plural or be preceded by a number or by *a* or *an*: *dog* and *child* are count nouns. Many words can be either count nouns or MASS NOUNS, depending on the way they are used in a sentence: Compare the use of the noun *fear* in the sentences *A fear of the dark is only one of my many irrational fears* (count noun) and *She seems devoid of fear when she steps into the ring* (mass noun).

coup de grâce (KOO duh GRASS) Final blow or finishing stroke, either literally (as when killing a fatally wounded person or animal to prevent further suffering) or figuratively, as in *The financial scandal delivered the* coup de grâce *to the politician's declining career*. The plural is *coups de grâce*, pronounced in the same way as the singular. The term is French in origin, meaning literally 'stroke of mercy'.

creole In linguistics, a mixed tongue developed from two other languages, usually as the result of conquest or colonisation – especially combinations of English, French and Portuguese with African languages. Creoles keep the grammar of the local language but add the vocabulary of the foreign one, eventually forming their local mother tongue. (Compare PIDGIN.)
♣Creole also refers to the language and culture of French descendants in Louisiana and other southern states of America.

crossing the Rubicon Taking a step or making a decision on which there is no going back, and which marks the start of a chain of events: *By rejecting the offered compromise, my ex-partner has crossed the Rubicon, and our differences will now be settled in court*. The Rubicon is the ancient name of a river in northern Italy, believed to be the present-day Fiumicino, which Julius Caesar was prohibited from crossing. In 49 BC, however, he forded the river with his army, effectively declaring war on Rome.

cross-reference Indication in one part of a book, index or other text, directing the reader to consult another part which contains related information, as in *The entry on Wordsworth contains a cross-reference to the Lake Poets*. In this book, cross-references are indicated by small capital letters.

cuneiform (KEW-ni-form) Writing system used in the ancient Middle East, consisting of wedge-shaped symbols or letters drawn on a soft clay tablet with a sharpened reed. The tablet was baked in a kiln to harden it. Originally derived from PICTOGRAMS, the symbols were later used to represent words, syllables and phonetic elements. Earliest examples were written from top to bottom, but around 3000 BC scribes found that they could write better by turning the tablets and writing from left to right in horizontal rows.

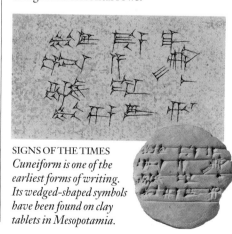

SIGNS OF THE TIMES
Cuneiform is one of the earliest forms of writing. Its wedged-shaped symbols have been found on clay tablets in Mesopotamia.

TRUE HUMILITY *The phrase 'curate's egg' derives from this cartoon of 1895 – Bishop: 'I'm afraid you've got a bad egg, Mr Jones!' Curate: 'Oh no, my Lord, I assure you! Parts of it are excellent!'*

curate's egg Something that is actually bad although claimed by some – out of sensitivity or some other reason – to have both good and bad parts. The phrase derives from a *Punch* cartoon in which a nervous young curate at a bishop's table is given what is obviously a bad boiled egg but fearful of giving offence tells his host that 'parts of it are excellent'.

♟This term is often misused. It correctly refers to something which is in fact completely bad or which cannot be redeemed, and not to something which has both good and bad qualities.

curriculum vitae (c.v.) Résumé or short account of one's education, work experience, achievements and interests, as compiled and submitted when applying for a job. A curriculum vitae should be concise – one side of paper should usually be enough. It should also be relevant to the job being applied for. Any previous work experience should be listed in reverse chronological order, since a prospective employer will be most interested in recent jobs. The phrase is Latin in origin, meaning 'the course of one's life'.

cutting the Gordian knot Solving a problem by taking prompt and extremely bold or unconventional action, as in *Faced with intolerable financial difficulties, the directors cut the Gordian knot by declaring the company bankrupt.* The phrase is based on a supposed incident that occurred in ancient history. The Gordian knot was an enormous and intricate knot tied with rope made of bark by King Gordius of Phrygia in the 4th century BC. According to an oracle, whoever could undo the knot was destined to reign over a large empire in Asia Minor. Alexander the Great apparently took up the challenge by simply hacking through the knot with his sword in 334 BC.

dangling participle Form of MIS-RELATED CONSTRUCTION in which a PARTICIPLE, especially a PRESENT PARTICIPLE, is linked not to the word intended but to some empty word such as *it* or *there*, as in the sentence *Having no umbrella, there was nothing to do but take shelter from the rain.* A better version would be *Having no umbrella, we had to take shelter from the rain*, where the participle *having* is linked to the subject *we* instead of simply 'dangling'.

dark horse Unfamiliar competitor or quiet newcomer whose abilities remain unknown or untested. *Although he was a dark horse during the opening rounds of his first Wimbledon, McEnroe was a household name by the time he reached the semi-finals.* The phrase derives from horse racing: the betting public might be 'in the dark' regarding the speed, stamina, or jumping ability of an unfamiliar runner – a dark horse – and therefore uncertain about the odds.

dash Punctuation mark (–) used to indicate a break in thought, to introduce a summing up, or to mark off a PARENTHESIS, as in *Then she hit me – what for? Demand and supply – there you have economics in a nutshell. Very few of the football players – three, to be exact – were reselected by the coach.* The dash can also serve some of the functions of a COLON, such as introducing an explanation: *She went to college with one clear intention – to find a husband.*

deci- Prefix, from Latin, meaning 'a tenth', as in *decibel, decimal* and *decilitre.*

declarative sentence Sentence that 'declares' something or makes a statement; the most common form of sentence. *He is making a speedy recovery* and *We leave at midnight* are declarative sentences. (Compare IMPERATIVE; INTERROGATIVE.)

de facto (day FAC-toe) Phrase referring to a state of affairs that exists but which is not officially recognised. *He is* de facto *army commander, even though he is formally ranked*

The Cyrillic alphabet is used in various Eastern European languages, such as Russian and Bulgarian. Its name is derived from its supposed inventor, St Cyril, who was a 9th-century Macedonian missionary.

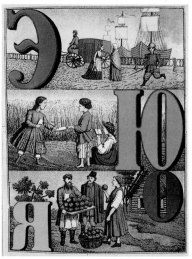

SLAVIC SCRIPT *The alphabet known as Cyrillic developed out of Greek.*

only second-in-command. The phrase is Latin in origin, meaning literally 'from the fact'. (Compare DE JURE.)

defining clause Another name for RESTRICTIVE CLAUSE.

definite article The word *the*. Unlike the INDEFINITE ARTICLE *a*, it indicates that a particular item is being referred to by the noun or noun phrase which follows it.

déjà vu The strange feeling of 'I've been here before' when it is impossible for this to be the case. It is French for 'already seen'.

de jure (day-JOOR-ay) By legal right, in keeping with the law, officially: *Even though too old even to sign his own name, the King was still* de jure *ruler of the country, and had to be consulted.* The phrase is Latin in origin, meaning literally 'according to the law'.

demi- Prefix, from French, meaning 'half' or 'less than full status', as in *demigod*. (Compare SEMI-.)

demonstrative pronoun Pronoun that specifies or points out the person(s) or thing(s) referred to; specifically, *this*, *that*, *these* and *those* when used independently, rather than directly before a noun, as in the sentence *He likes those, but she prefers these.*

denotation The literal sense or basic dictionary meaning of a word or expression, without its CONNOTATIONS. The denotation of the word *modern* is 'belonging to or characteristic of recent times'. While the denotation stays the same, however, the connotations will be positive for some people and negative for others.

de rigueur (duh-ri-GERR) Socially compulsory, required by custom or fashion: *It is no longer* de rigueur *to wear a suit and tie to the opera.* It is a French phrase, and means literally 'of strictness'.

derivative Word formed by adding a prefix or suffix to another word. *Importation*, for example, is a derivative of *import*. It also refers to a word's origin and historical development, or ETYMOLOGY.

determiner Word placed in front of a noun or noun phrase in order to limit its meaning. The words *the*, *all*, *that* and *their* are determiners in the following phrases: *the brilliant, award-winning biologist*; *all things bright and beautiful*; *that interesting new magazine*; *their computer operator.* (Compare ADJECTIVE; ARTICLE.)

de trop (duh TRO) French expression which means 'superfluous' or 'unwanted': *We felt decidedly* de trop *having to share a table with a honeymoon couple.*

deus ex machina (DAY-uss eks MACK-een-uh) Person or thing brought in unexpectedly to resolve a problem, especially to untangle the plot of a play. The phrase is a Latin translation of a Greek term, meaning literally 'god out of a machine'. It refers to the practice in ancient drama of using stage machinery to bring in an actor representing a god to resolve a difficult situation.

devil to pay An IDIOM used to warn that trouble is on the way: *There'll be the devil to pay when father finds out what you've done.* The original version shows how its meaning has changed: *the devil to pay and no pitch hot* suggests a lack of preparation for some important task – that is, the sailors' task of sealing with tar the seam (known as 'the devil') between the planks of a wooden sailing ship.

diacritical marks Marks used in writing and printing to adjust the way in which a letter is pronounced, as in the French words *tête* and *garçon*. See also ACUTE ACCENT; CEDILLA: CIRCUMFLEX; DIAERESIS; GRAVE ACCENT; TILDE; UMLAUT.

diaeresis Mark (¨) placed over a vowel to indicate that it should be independently pronounced, as in the words naïve, Noël, and Brontë. (See also UMLAUT.)

diminutive Suffix or word conveying the idea of small size, youthfulness, unimportance, or else of affection. The words *piglet* and *kitchenette* are diminutives, and so are their suffixes *-let* and *-ette*.

diphthong (DIF-thong) Complex speech sound beginning with one vowel sound and moving to another within a single syllable; for example the sound *oy* in *boy*, which involves a shift between the two sounds *aw* and *ee*. The word also refers to the fused letters æ and œ (also called ligatures), as in the old-fashioned spelling of *amœba*.

direct object Person, thing or set of circumstances directly affected by the action of a verb. In English, the direct object almost always follows the verb. It may consist of a simple noun or pronoun, a phrase or a clause. In the sentence *I cannot understand her*, the direct object is the pronoun *her*. In the sentence *I cannot under-*

stand why she gave me so many roses, the direct object is the entire clause *why she gave me so many roses.* (Compare INDIRECT OBJECT.)

direct speech Speech or writing quoted exactly in its original words. When written, direct speech is usually enclosed in quotation marks, as in *The suspect said: 'I swear it wasn't me!'* (Compare INDIRECT SPEECH.)

'Don't look a gift horse in the mouth' Proverb advising that one should accept gifts without inspecting them too closely, let alone criticising them. It refers to the practice of inspecting a horse's teeth to find out its age – the shorter the teeth, the older the horse, since chewing wears the teeth down. Someone buying a horse would obviously inspect its mouth – hence the expression 'from the horse's mouth' as an assurance of reliable information.

'Don't spoil the ship for a ha'p'orth of tar' Proverb or MAXIM advising against false economy. Its origin lies in farming rather than seafaring: *ship* is here a dialect version of *sheep*, and the allusion is to the old practice of treating a sheep's cuts and grazes with tar. If the farmer or shepherd neglected this simple and cheap treatment, the sheep might die.

double entendre (DOOB'L on-TOND-ruh) Word or expression having two different meanings, especially when one of them is indelicate or bawdy, as in many saucy jokes and funny headlines: *Cricket captain bowls a maiden over. Rival nudist clubs meet to air their differences.* In French, the phrase means 'double understanding', though the French no longer use the term.

double negative Use of two negative or near-negative expressions, such as *not* or *barely*, in a sentence. When used correctly it conveys a positive sense, as in *I'm so happy that I can't not burst out singing* or *She's hardly unenthusiastic.* Double negatives intended to convey a negative meaning – as in *I'm so drunk I can't hardly stand up* or *You don't know nothing about it* – are considered wrong in modern English, though not in all other languages or earlier English.

dys- Prefix, from Greek, meaning 'bad', as in *dysentery*, *dyslexia* and *dysfunctional*.

eating humble pie Admitting one's mistakes, or apologising for them, often in humiliating circumstances: *The boastful physicist was forced to eat humble pie when a student pointed out a simple error in his calculations.* The phrase is based on a clever play on words. A humble pie was formerly one made from the offal of a deer – its 'humbles', 'umbles' or 'numbles', in earlier English. Since this was the cheapest, least desirable meat, it would be eaten by poor or humble people, though the two words spelt humble are unrelated in origin.

e.g. Abbreviation of the Latin phrase *exempli gratia*, meaning 'for example' and used to introduce an example or list of examples: *With this new diet, your breakfast is restricted to tropical fruit – e.g. mangoes, guavas and papayas.* (Compare I.E.)

ego- Prefix, from Latin, meaning 'I' or 'myself', as in *egotism, egomania* or *ego-trip*.

ellipsis Omission from a sentence of a word or phrase that is implied by the context, as in *Know what I mean?* for *Do you know what I mean?* or *Alan cannot and Beryl will not play bridge* for *Alan cannot play bridge and Beryl will not play bridge.* Faulty ellipsis is a common error of grammar or style, as in *Alan has never and Beryl will never play bridge.* The correct form is *Alan has never played and Beryl will never play bridge.*
🖉Ellipsis also refers to the 'dot-dot-dot' punctuation mark (. . .) used to indicate that something is missing from a quoted passage: *I felt, in Keats's words, 'like stout Cortez . . . upon a peak in Darien'.*

enfant terrible (on-FON teh-REEB'L) Person of unconventional ideas or behaviour, who causes dismay to the established members of his group or profession: *Ken Russell used to be the* enfant terrible *of the British film industry, but he seems to have mellowed in recent years.* The plural is *enfants terribles*, pronounced in the same way as the singular. The term is French in origin, meaning literally 'terrible child'.

epigram Brief, pithy statement or striking observation, often with a witty twist, such as Oscar Wilde's remark: *Work is the curse of the drinking classes.*

epitaph Inscription on a tombstone or monument in memory of the person or people buried there.

epithet Adjective or phrase used to characterise a person or thing, or as a nickname or substitute title. *Lionheart*, for example, was an epithet for Richard I.

eponymous Referring to the person after whom something such as a book or a city is named: *The* eponymous *hero of the film 'Ben Hur' was played by Charlton Heston.*

ersatz German word used to refer to an imitation or substitute, particularly an inferior one, as in *ersatz coffee*.

Esperanto Artificial language invented in 1887 by the Polish linguist Dr Ludwig Lazarus Zamenhof, and intended as an international language. It is based on words familiar in many European languages, and its grammar is very regular.

esprit de corps (ess-PREE duh KOR) Spirit of fellowship, or feeling of mutual support or team spirit among the members of a group: *So strong was their* esprit de corps *that the party of mountaineers remained cheerful even when they were snowed in for a week.* The phrase is French in origin, meaning literally 'spirit of body' or 'platoon spirit'.

esprit d'escalier (ess-PREE dess-kal-YAY) Reply thought of after it is too late. From the French for 'staircase wit' – a witty remark that occurs to you only as you are walking down the staircase to leave. (Compare PARTING SHOT.)

ethno- Prefix, from Greek, meaning 'people', 'race' or 'ethnic', as in *ethnology, ethnography* and *ethnocentric*.

etymology The origin and historical development of a word, or the study of word origins, as in *You can trace the etymology of the word 'scrupulous' back to the Latin word for a rough stone.*

eu- Prefix, from Greek, meaning 'good', as in *euphemism, euphonious* and *eugenics*.

euphemism Bland or neutral term or expression used in place of one that might give offence: *pass away* is a euphemism for *die* and *ethnic cleansing* for *genocide*. (See also CIRCUMLOCUTION.)

exclamation mark Punctuation mark (!), used after a command, an exclamation of surprise, an INTERJECTION or an abrupt and emphatic statement, such as *Ouch!* or *Life discovered on Mars!*

ex gratia (eks GRA-shia) Given purely as a favour, without any legal necessity, as in *an ex gratia payment*. The phrase is Latin for 'from kindness', or 'as a favour'.

expletive Any exclamation or oath, especially one considered to be blasphemous or obscene, whether currently or formerly, such as *Damn!* or *Heavens above!* Nowadays, any obscene word can be loosely referred to as an expletive.

fait accompli (FET-a-COM-plee) Established fact or performed action that cannot be reversed: *The publication of the rumour is a* fait accompli *– all we can do now is to issue a denial and try to limit the damage.* The plural is *faits accomplis*, pronounced in the same way as the singular. The term is French, meaning 'accomplished fact'.

false colours See SAILING UNDER FALSE COLOURS.

faux pas (FOH PAA) Social blunder, mistake of etiquette or failure of tact, as in *She committed the* faux pas *of mistaking the duchess for her maid.* The plural is also *faux pas*, and is pronounced in the same way as the singular. The term is French, meaning literally 'false step'.

feet of clay Phrase used of a highly regarded person revealed to have a character weakness or flaw: *The vicar's arrest for burglary revealed him to have feet of clay.* It probably comes from a passage in the Book of Daniel. King Nebuchadnezzar had dreams of a huge statue with a gold head, silver arms, and so on, down to feet of iron and clay. Daniel interpreted the dream to mean that a future kingdom would be divided, and would eventually crumble like the clay that supported the statue.

figure of speech Expression in which the words are used for the sake of emphasis or dramatic effect rather than for their literal meaning. LITOTES, SIMILES and HYPERBOLES are figures of speech, as are METAPHORS such as *the last flickering flames of consciousness before sleep*.

flash in the pan Something that suddenly seems to have great interest, appeal or promise, but that soon loses it and returns to obscurity, as in *His dramatic improvement in last term's exams turned out to be a flash in the pan – this term, he almost failed.* The original flash in the pan occurred in the old flintlock gun. The loose gunpowder, carefully measured and placed in the gun's 'flashpan', was meant to be ignited by a spark from the flint. If the gunpowder was damp or insufficient, however, it would fizzle or flash rather than explode effectively.

Fourth Estate Term referring to journalism or to journalists generally, regarded as a power in the land. In France before the French Revolution, the three 'Estates of the Realm' were citizens with political rights: the Church, the nobility and the people, as represented in the British parliament by the Lords Spiritual, the Lords Temporal and

---

GRAPHOLOGY: WHAT HANDWRITING REVEALS

Graphology is the study of handwriting and is sometimes used to analyse personality. Graphologists believe that handwriting is a form of 'brain-writing', in which the unconscious mind is conveyed to the fingers and reveals itself on paper.

SIZE

Large writing This usually denotes ambition or 'thinking big'. People in show business often have large writing.

Small writing This indicates modesty or a feeling of inferiority; alternatively, the writer may be objective and scientific.

WIDTH

Narrow writing People with narrow writing are often disciplined and inhibited. They may be mean and restricted in view.

Broad writing Those with broad writing tend to be uninhibited, and to like travel. They may also be rash and uncontrolled.

SLANT

Left slant A left-hand slant is typical of people who are shy and retiring. They tend to stay in their shell, hide their emotions and adopt a passive attitude.

Right slant Writing that leans to the right suggests an outgoing personality – an ability to mix with other people.

SPACING

Wide spacing People who leave large spaces between words are often ill-at-ease in company, and can be stand-offish.

Narrow spacing Small spaces between words can indicate a gregarious personality. But they also suggest that the writer chooses friends discriminatingly.

---

the Commons. The reference to a Fourth Estate was supposedly first made by the writer and politician Edmund Burke in the late 18th century, as a joking comment on the power of the press.

full stop (in American English, period) Punctuation mark (.), used to end a sentence, and often to indicate an abbreviation, as in *Co.* and *i.e.*

future perfect See PERFECT.

future tense See TENSE.

gender Classification of nouns, pronouns, and sometimes adjectives, as 'masculine', 'feminine' and 'neuter', as in the pronouns *he*, *she* and *it*. In English, nouns referring to male and female creatures are of the obvious gender, and inanimate objects are normally neuter. Countries, ships and other vehicles may be feminine.

generalisation Sweeping statement or broad conclusion about an entire group of people or things, that may be true of many of the items but is probably not true of all, such as *The Swedes are extraordinarily good at playing tennis* and *The more trees a London neighbourhood has, the richer its residents are.*

geo- Prefix, from Greek, meaning 'the Earth', as in *geology* and *geography*.

gerund Form of a verb, ending in '-ing' in English, that functions as a noun in a sentence. For example, the word *walking* is a gerund in the sentence *Walking in the woods alone can be dangerous at night*. The POSSESSIVE case is linked with the gerund in sentences such as *Jane's talking in class was annoying* . (Compare PRESENT PARTICIPLE.)

gilding the lily Trying to improve something that is already beautiful or perfect: *Dyeing her naturally blonde hair would just be gilding the lily*. The phrase is often taken to be a quotation from Shakespeare, but the words he actually used in *King John* were: 'To gild refined gold, to paint the lily . . . is wasteful and ridiculous excess.'

glossary List of words with accompanying definitions, rather like a short specialised dictionary. A glossary is often included at the end of a textbook to explain the difficult or technical terms used throughout it. (Compare LEXICON.)

gobbledegook (also officialese) Needlessly complicated and unclear speech or writing, as used by some officials. It often includes an excessive use of bureaucratic or technical JARGON.

Gordian knot See CUTTING THE GORDIAN KNOT.

gradable adjective Adjective that can occur in varying degrees of intensity and that can be modified by such adverbs as *more*, *most*, *extremely* and *slightly*. The adjectives *happy*, *complex* and *enthusiastic* are gradable because a person can be more happy, extremely happy, less happy and so on. 'Absolute' adjectives such as *perfect*, *unique*, *dead* and *pregnant* are not gradable: it is illogical, for example, to speak of something as being 'more unique' or 'slightly dead'. Adverbs are also classified as gradable or nongradable. (See also COMPARATIVE; SUPERLATIVE.)

-gram Suffix, from Latin and Greek, meaning 'writing', as in *diagram*, *anagram* and *telegram*.

grammar Analysis and classification of the elements of a language, such as the pronunciation and meaning of words, and the system of rules for using it.

-graph- Prefix or suffix, from Greek, meaning 'draw' or 'write', as in *autograph* and *geography*.

grave accent (**GRAAV**) Mark (`), placed above a vowel, either to adjust the way it is pronounced, as in *Sèvres*, or to indicate that it needs to be sounded out in its own right, as in the poetic use of *agèd*. (Compare ACUTE ACCENT; CIRCUMFLEX.)

grist to the mill Something that can be turned to one's advantage, or something that should prove useful even though it may not appear particularly promising at first: *As a comedy writer, he almost welcomes life's setbacks since they are all grist to the mill*. The image is of an old grain mill, such as a watermill, which treats anything presented to it as grist or grain, and grinds it regardless.

guttural CONSONANT that is produced in the throat or in the back of the mouth, for example the sounds 'k' and 'g' in the words *keg* and *gawky*.

haemo- Prefix, from the Greek for 'blood', as in *haemorrhage* and *haemophilia*.

hetero- Prefix, from Greek, meaning 'different', as in *heterogeneous, heterodoxy* and *heterosexual.* (Compare HOMO-.)

hiding one's light under a bushel Being excessively modest about one's talents or unadventurous in developing them: *She's a fine actress, but she hides her light under a bushel, always keeping in the background and never auditioning for major roles.* The phrase is an allusion to Jesus's call, in the Sermon on the Mount, for open practice of one's faith: '*Neither do men light a candle, and put it under a bushel, but on a candlestick*' (Matthew 5:15). The bushel was a vessel used to measure out corn.

hieroglyphs Characters used in the writing system of ancient Egypt, in which pictures of people or things were used to represent words or sounds. (See IDEO-GRAM; PICTOGRAM.)

Hobson's choice Apparent choice in which all options turn out to be the same: *Henry Ford offered his customers a Hobson's choice by telling them they could have any colour of car they liked, as long as it was black.* The original Hobson's choice was offered in Shakespeare's time by a Cambridge stable-keeper called Hobson. He hired out his horses in strict rotation, forcing clients to take the one next in line.

hocus-pocus Nonsense words uttered by a magician when performing a trick, or pompous phrases used by officials to avoid giving a straight answer. A likely origin for the term is mimicking, perhaps by mocking Protestants, of the Roman Catholic Mass, in which the phrase *Hoc est corpus* occurs, meaning 'This is the body'.

hoi polloi The common people, the masses. The phrase is used dismissively by those who consider themselves superior: *If hoi polloi keep picnicking in the square, we'll have to lobby the council to introduce admission control.* The phrase is Greek, meaning 'the many', and should therefore not be preceded by 'the' in an English sentence.

hoist with one's own petard Caught out by one's own scheming, or being the victim of one's own cleverness: *To avoid speaking to her fellow traveller, Mary pretended to speak only German. She was hoist with her own petard when he broke into perfect German.* The expression means literally 'blown up by one's own small bomb'.

homo- Prefix, from Latin and Greek, meaning 'same' or 'equal', as in *homogenise* and *homosexual.* (Compare HETERO-.)

homograph Word that has the same spelling as another, but a different meaning and origin, such as *sewer* (a drain) and *sewer* (a person who sews) or *lead* (to show the way) and *lead* (the metal). Some homographs have the same pronunciation as each other, in which case they may also be called homonymous. *Bear* (the furry mammal) and *bear* (to carry) are HOMONYMS, as are *bill* (an invoice) and *bill* (a duck's beak).

homonym Word that has the same pronunciation and spelling as another word, but a quite different meaning and origin; for example, *row* (a line) and *row* (to use oars) are homonyms.

homophone Word having the same pronunciation as another, but a different meaning and origin, and usually a different spelling. *Pear* and *pair* are homophones.

hydro-, hydr- COMBINING FORM, often a prefix, from the Greek for 'water', as in *hydroelectric* or *dehydrate.* (Compare AQUA-.)

hyper- Prefix, from Greek, meaning 'too much' or 'excessive', as in *hyperactive* and *hypersensitive.* (Compare HYPO-.)

hyperbole (hye-PER-ber-lee) Figure of speech consisting of an exaggerated expression, such as *I could sleep for weeks* or *This book weighs a ton.* (Compare LITOTES.)

hyphen Punctuation mark (-) used to link associated words into a compound, as in *self-love* or *mother-in-law*, and to split a word that runs over at the end of a line.

hypno- Prefix, from Greek, meaning 'sleep', as in *hypnosis* and *hypnotherapy.*

hypo- Prefix, from Greek, meaning 'under' or 'low', as in *hypodermic* (under the skin) and *hypothermia* (low body temperature). (Compare HYPER-.)

ibid. Abbreviation of the Latin word *ibidem*, meaning 'in the same place'. It is used in footnotes to refer to the book, chapter, article or page cited just before. (Compare IDEM and LOC. CIT.)

idée fixe (EE-day FEEKS) Set idea or obsession, often mistaken but impossible to remove: *She had an* idée fixe *that her house was going to burn down.* The term is French, and means 'fixed idea'.

idem Latin term meaning 'the same', used in footnotes to indicate a reference previously mentioned. Sometimes the abbreviation *id.* is used. (Compare IBID; LOC. CIT.)

ideogram (also ideograph) Sign or symbol used in Chinese and some Japanese writing to represent an idea or object without indicating pronunciation; also, any symbol used in writing, other than letters of the alphabet and punctuation marks, such as %, £, $, @. (Compare PICTOGRAM.)

idiolect The unique speech or language patterns of an individual person.

idiom Common phrase or traditional expression, often informal, whose meaning cannot be derived from the meanings of the individual words. *Under the weather* (feeling poorly) and *round the bend* (mad) are examples of idioms.

i.e. Abbreviation of the Latin phrase *id est*, meaning 'that is', used to specify or explain the term preceding it: *As from tomorrow the new rules apply, i.e. no going out during the week, and no staying out after 10 o'clock on weekends.* (Compare E.G.)

illiteracy Inability to read or write.

imperative Grammatical form or MOOD of a verb used in expressing commands or requests. In the following sentences, the verbs *save, leave* and *be* are imperative (or 'in the imperative'): *Save me from such indignity! Leave that alone! Be ready by midnight.* (Compare INDICATIVE; SUBJUNCTIVE.)

impersonal verb A verb that expresses an action or state without ascribing it to a particular subject, as in *It snowed.* Some verbs can be used either personally or impersonally, such as *looks* or *seems* in *Joseph looks/seems ill* (personal) and *It looks/seems as if Joseph is ill* (impersonal).

in camera In private or in secret; specifically, in a judge's private chambers rather than in open court: *The trial was held in camera, since it involved issues of state security.* The phrase is Latin in origin, and means 'in the chamber'.

indefinite article The word *a* or *an*, the article that introduces a noun or noun phrase without specifying the particular individual or item referred to, as in *a jar; an urn.* The choice of *a* or *an* is determined by the sound rather than by the letter following it: hence *an hourglass*, but *a unicorn.* (Compare DEFINITE ARTICLE.)

indefinite pronoun Pronoun that stands in for an undefined or unidentified person or thing, as in *anyone; some; nobody.*

independent clause See MAIN CLAUSE.

indicative Grammatical form or MOOD of a verb which indicates that the action or condition mentioned is factual or probable, in contrast to the SUBJUNCTIVE, where it is only supposed. In the following sentences, the verb *was* is indicative (or 'in the indicative') in the first, whereas the verb *were* in the second is subjunctive: *She was delayed and missed her train. If she were delayed, she would have telephoned to say that she'd missed her train.* (Compare IMPERATIVE.)

indirect object Object indirectly affected by the action of a TRANSITIVE VERB, usually as if the word *to* or *for* were placed in front of it. In the sentence *She gave me a withering look*, the pronoun *me* is the indirect object, whereas the phrase *a withering look* is the DIRECT OBJECT.

indirect speech (also reported speech) Speech or writing reported in different words from those originally used. It is typically introduced by a verb such as *say* or *tell*, and sometimes by *that*, and involves changes in person or tense, as in *The suspect then swore that he had not committed the crime.* (Compare DIRECT SPEECH.)

Indo-European Family of languages that includes most European tongues (notably excluding Finnish and Hungarian), as well as many languages of India and Iran. Two of the many sub-families are the Germanic, to which English belongs, and the Romance languages, which include French, Spanish and Italian.

in extremis On the verge of death, or in very serious difficulties: *The victim lay in* extremis, *trapped in no-man's-land. The company is* in extremis, *and will go under unless the bank agrees to a further loan.* The phrase is Latin, meaning literally 'in the last'.

infinitive Basic form of a verb, as it appears in a dictionary, without any INFLECTION to indicate tense, number or the like. The forms *walk, fly* and *be* are infinitive (or 'infinitives' or 'in the infinitive'), unlike *walking, flew* and *were*. In English, the word *to* often marks a verb as infinitive: *to walk, to fly, to be.*

in flagrante delicto In the very act of committing an offence; red-handed: *The police caught the forger* in flagrante delicto *as*

he sat operating his printing press. The phrase is Latin in origin, meaning 'with the crime still blazing'. It is often used of people found in the act of having sex.

inflection Changes in the form of a word according to its different grammatical functions within a sentence. English has only a few inflections left, notably those indicating the past tense of verbs by means of a different ending, as in *walked* or *walking*; those indicating the plural (*-s* or *-es*) and possessive (*-'s* or *-s'*) of nouns, as in *his girlfriend's parents*; those affecting pronouns, as in *he, him, his*; and those in irregular verbs and nouns, such as *shrink, shrank, shrunk,* and *mouse, mice*.

infra dig Informal contraction of the Latin phrase *infra dignitatem*, meaning 'beneath one's dignity', as in *The dean considers it* infra dig *to say hello to any student.*

initialism Abbreviation of a phrase formed by the initial letters of each word, but not pronounced as a single word. Examples include BBC for *British Broadcasting Corporation* and OTT for *over the top*. (Compare ACRONYM.)

in loco parentis Acting in the role of parents, or having the responsibilities or duties of a parent: *The housemaster at a boarding school acts* in loco parentis. The phrase is Latin for 'in a parent's place'.

innuendo An indirect suggestion, often intended as a veiled insult or accusation, as in the remark *Not everyone would be able to believe your story.*

inter- Prefix, from Latin, meaning 'between', 'among' or 'together with', as in *interbreed, interval, international* and *intercity*. (Compare INTRA-.)

inter alia Among other things: *Several European currencies surged as a result,* inter alia *the guilder and the French franc.* The term is Latin in origin. It is often used to mean 'among other people' as well, though strictly speaking that should be *inter alios*.

interjection An exclamation. Interjections are often single words or brief phrases that can stand alone as complete utterances, such as *Oh! Gosh! Never!*

interrogative Word, construction or sentence asking a question, for example, *How are you feeling? Where were you born?* or *Will we be leaving before dawn?* (Compare DECLARATIVE SENTENCE; IMPERATIVE.)

in the doldrums Gloomy, down in the dumps, feeling depressed and lazy: *I'm always in the doldrums in winter, when nature seems fast asleep.* It can also be used of economic conditions: *The housing market will remain in the doldrums until interest rates come down.* The phrase originated as a reference to equatorial seas, where ships were often becalmed.

in toto Altogether, totally, completely: *The repairs will cost an estimated £2300, in toto – that includes parts, labour and VAT.* The phrase is Latin, meaning 'as a whole'.

intra- Prefix, from Latin, meaning 'inside' or 'within', as in *intravenous, intramural,* and *intra-uterine*. (Compare INTER-.)

intransitive verb Verb that does not take a direct object. The verbs *wonder* and *die* are intransitive, as is *despair: My teachers despair (of me).* Many verbs can be transitive or intransitive, depending on how they are used in a sentence; compare the verb *argue* in the sentences *My teachers always argue their case energetically* (transitive) and *You always argue!* (intransitive). An intransitive verb cannot occur in the PASSIVE voice. (Compare TRANSITIVE VERB.)

inverted commas Another term for QUOTATION MARKS.

in vino veritas Latin phrase or proverb, suggesting that people speak the truth when they are drunk. The literal meaning is 'in wine there is truth'.

ipso facto By the very fact or deed; as a logical result of the fact itself; by definition: *A foreigner is,* ipso facto, *unable to vote.* The phrase is Latin for 'by the fact itself'.

irony Use of words to convey a meaning opposite to that of their literal or surface meaning: *Their love affair is one of the great secrets of Hollywood.* Irony is a major ingredient of sarcasm, a biting kind of ridicule: *Thank you for all your support – your silence was a great help!*

irregular verb (also strong verb) Verb that changes its whole form, rather than simply adding *-ed* or *-d*, when forming the past tense and past participle: *I drew, I have drawn* and *I went, I have gone.* (Compare REGULAR VERB.)

italics Slanted typeface, as in *This example is printed in italics*, in contrast to the ordinary upright (Roman) typeface of the rest of this sentence. Italics have many uses – to

give emphasis or stress to certain words, to indicate words in a foreign language, or to mark book titles, newspapers or films.
🖋 In typing and handwriting, underlining usually takes the place of italics.

ivory tower Institution or way of life secluded from reality and often devoted to abstract intellectual concerns rather than practical everyday matters: *The professor lived in an ivory tower and had no idea of what was going on in the outside world.*

jargon Specialised or technical language used by a particular group, often of members of a profession, such as lawyers, stockbrokers, or doctors. For those who use it, jargon may be an efficient shorthand for communicating complex ideas. To outsiders, however, it often seems incomprehensible, elitist and manipulative. An objectionable use of jargon would occur, for example, if a doctor warned a patient that his diet may cause 'epidermal seborrhoea' – referring to nothing more than an oily skin. (See SLANG; VOGUE WORD.)

***je ne sais quoi* (jher nuh say KWAA)** Quality that one notices clearly but cannot define or identify properly: *She has a certain* je ne sais quoi *that makes me distrust her.* The phrase is French and means literally 'I do not know what'.

***joie de vivre* (JWAH duh VEEV'R)** High spirits, zestfulness, carefree enjoyment of life: *His* joie de vivre *makes him the life and soul of the party.* The phrase is French in origin, meaning literally 'joy of living'.

laconic Using few words, terse: *President Coolidge's laconic style was admired at the time, but it would fall flat nowadays with televised election debates.* The term is derived from the ancient Greek name for the Spartans or Laconians, who were famous for their brevity of speech.

lexicon Dictionary, especially of an ancient language such as Latin; also, a specialised vocabulary used by a particular profession or interest-group, as in *Computer experts use a lexicon which is incomprehensible to outsiders.* (Compare GLOSSARY.)

ligature See DIPHTHONG.

lingua franca Language adopted as a means of communication between people who speak different mother tongues: *English is increasingly the* lingua franca *of those associated with the international art world.*
🖋 The original Lingua Franca was a medieval PIDGIN composed of a mixture of Italian, French and other tongues, and was used by traders in Mediterranean ports.

linguistics The science or study of language and its structure, including PHONETICS, SEMANTICS and SYNTAX.

litho-, -lith- COMBINING FORM, sometimes used as a prefix, from Greek, meaning 'stone', as in *lithograph* and *Neolithic*.

litotes (lye-TOH-teez) Figure of speech consisting of a deliberate understatement, typically by denying the opposite, for example: *We weren't exactly sweet-smelling after our three-day hike.* (Compare HYPERBOLE.)

loc. cit. Abbreviation of the Latin phrase *loco citato*, meaning 'in the place mentioned'. It is used in footnotes to refer to a book, article or page previously cited.

logo (also logotype) Symbol or name used to identify a company, magazine or product. The symbol of Pegasus, the flying horse, is the logo of Reader's Digest.

lower case Small letters, the common form of the letters of the alphabet, as opposed to capital letters. (Compare UPPER CASE.)

macro- Prefix, from Greek, meaning 'large', as in *macroeconomics* and *macrocosm*. (Compare MICRO-.)

magnum opus Masterpiece or great work, especially the single greatest work of a writer, artist or composer: *Beethoven's 9th Symphony is the composer's* magnum opus. The term is Latin for 'great work'.

main clause (also independent clause) Clause – particularly in a complex sentence – that can stand alone as a full sentence. In the sentence *When snow falls, children rush out to play*, the main clause is *children rush out to play*. (Compare SUBORDINATE CLAUSE.)

malapropism Humorous misuse of a word that sounds similar to the intended word: *an allegory on the banks of the Nile* in place of *an alligator* is an example from Mrs Malaprop in ▷SHERIDAN'S play *The Rivals*.

male-, mal- Prefix, from Latin, meaning 'bad' or 'badly', as in *maladroit, maladministration* and *malediction*. (Compare BENE-.)

mass noun (also uncountable noun, noncountable noun) Noun referring to an object or substance that has no clear limits. It cannot usually occur in the plural or be preceded by *a* or *an*. *Milk* and *information* are mass nouns. Many words can be either mass nouns or COUNT NOUNS, depending on the way they are used, as with *wine* in the sentences *Have a glass of wine* (mass noun) and *We stock more than two thousand different wines* (count noun).

maxim Brief summing-up of some general truth, guiding principle or rule of conduct, such as *Do as you would be done by* or *It ain't necessarily so.* (See also MOTTO.)

mega- Prefix, from Greek, meaning 'a million' or 'very large', as in *megaton, megawatt* and *megaphone*.

metaphor Figure of speech in which one thing is compared to another, without the use of *like* or *as* to make the comparison obvious. The effect can vary greatly from the extremely evocative, as in *The road through the village was a ribbon of moonlight*, to the overused cliché, as in *He is in the twilight of his life.* (Compare SIMILE.)

metonymy Figure of speech in which an idea is referred to by a related and usually more specific term, such as *the Crown* to refer to the monarchy or *treading the boards* for acting. (Compare SYNECDOCHE).

-metry Suffix, from Greek, meaning 'measuring', as in *geometry* and *symmetry*.

micro- Prefix, from Greek, meaning 'small', as in *microbe, microdot* and *microscopic*. (Compare MACRO-).

misnomer Incorrect or unsuitable term for a person or thing: *It would be a misnomer to call her handsome – 'pretty' or 'beautiful' might be more appropriate.*

misrelated construction Verb or phrase linked by the SYNTAX of the sentence to a noun other than the one intended. For example, *While strolling along the pavement, a loose flagstone sent her sprawling*, which suggests that a flagstone was strolling along. In *As prime minister, I would like to ask you about your cabinet reshuffle* it sounds as if the speaker is the prime minister. Correct wording would be *While strolling along the pavement, she was sent sprawling by a loose flagstone* and *I would like to ask you, as prime minister, about your cabinet reshuffle.* (See also DANGLING PARTICIPLE).

mixed metaphor Sequence of METAPHORS or SIMILES drawn from clashing fields of comparison and producing a ridiculous effect, as in the sentences: *By sitting on the fence you are just burying your head in the sand* and *That prospect is the one oasis of hope in the sea of economic gloom.*

mnemonic (neh-MONN-ick) Rhyme, formula or device used as an aid to memory. For example, the colours of the rainbow can be recalled by the sentence *Richard of York gave battle in vain.* The initial letters of the words in the sentence prompt the names of the colours in their correct order: red, orange, yellow, green, blue, indigo, violet.

modifier (also qualifier) Word, phrase or clause that describes or defines the sense of another word or phrase. The modifier of a noun is an adjective – for example, *green* in *the green door.* An adverb modifies a verb, adjective, or another adverb, as in *desperately seeking Susan.*

modus operandi Manner in which a thing operates or a person works: *The company's* modus operandi *was to poach customers from its rivals. The artist's* modus operandi *is to make sketches abroad and then come home to paint.* The phrase is Latin for 'way of working'.

modus vivendi Living arrangement or practical compromise between people or groups with different interests or habits: *She's not the housemate I'd have chosen, but we've found a* modus vivendi. *The Republicans'* modus vivendi *with the Nationalists could not last, and the coalition government collapsed.* The phrase is Latin for 'way of living'.

mono- Prefix, from Latin, meaning 'one', as in *monorail, monopoly,* and *monotonous.*

mood Form of a verb indicating the speaker's attitude towards either the utterance or the person addressed, such as whether the action mentioned is true or doubtful, and whether the listener is meant to react (as to a command) or simply absorb information (as from a statement). In English, the indicative mood is used for factual statements (*The fence is blue*), the subjunctive for wishes and doubts (*If the fence were blue*), the imperative for commands (*Paint the fence blue*), and the interrogative for questions (*Is the fence blue?*).

-morph- COMBINING FORM, from Greek, meaning 'shape', as in *morphology, endomorph* and *amorphous.*

mot juste The most suitable word or expression for the occasion: *'Elated' is the* mot juste *for her reaction to the news.* The phrase means 'exact word' in French.

motto Word, phrase, or short sentence, typically expressing some belief or ideal and sometimes accompanying a coat of arms, as in *Dieu et mon droit* 'God and my right' – the motto of the British monarchy. The word also refers to a MAXIM adopted as a guide to conduct, such as *give and take* or *If a thing is worth doing, it's worth doing well.*

Mrs Grundy (or Mother Grundy) Prudish and narrow-minded person, always ready to criticise the morals and behaviour of others. The original Mrs Grundy was a character mentioned (though not actually appearing) in Thomas Morton's play *Speed the Plough* (1798).

multi- Prefix, derived from Latin, meaning 'many' or 'much', as in *multinational* and *multifaceted.* (Compare POLY-).

Murphy's Law The principle humorously adopted by engineers and scientists, stating 'If anything can go wrong, it will'.

nailing one's colours to the mast Stating one's policy openly, or making a clear commitment to pursue a particular goal: *The third candidate nailed his colours firmly to the mast, and announced that he would raise taxes if elected.* The phrase is of nautical origin. The 'colours' of a ship are its flags, which in battle would be lowered to surrender. By nailing them to the mast, the captain would make surrender impossible, and so announce his intention to fight to the death. (Compare SAILING UNDER FALSE COLOURS.)

NB Abbreviation of the Latin phrase *nota bene,* meaning 'note well', used to emphasise or draw attention to an important point under discussion.

neo- Prefix, originating from the Greek for 'new' or 'revived', as in *Neolithic* and *neo-Nazi.* (Compare PALAEO-.)

neologism Newly coined word or phrase, or a familiar word used in a new sense. Recent neologisms include *greenhouse effect, yuppie* and *toy boy.*

Newspeak Language that is full of ambiguities, jargon and propaganda, especially as used by bureaucrats and politicians. The original Newspeak was a language invented by George Orwell in his novel ▷NINETEEN EIGHTY-FOUR.

noblesse oblige (NOH-BLESS oh-BLEEZH) Honourable or generous behaviour of the kind supposedly required of the nobility. It is often used with IRONY to imply obligation: *Oh yes, I take Aunt Myrna out to lunch every few weeks* – noblesse oblige, *you know.* The phrase is French, and means literally 'nobility obliges'.

nom de plume False name or pseudonym adopted by an author. 'Mark Twain' was the *nom de plume* of the American writer Samuel Langhorne Clemens, and the thriller-writer Ruth Rendell also writes under the *nom de plume* Barbara Vine. The term means 'pen name' in French, though the French themselves now prefer *nom de guerre,* 'war name'.

nonce word Word invented for a specific occasion and not intended for use anywhere else, such as the adjective 'sloeblack' used by Dylan Thomas to describe the sea at night in his play *Under Milk Wood.*
🔎 'Nonce' is a corrupted form of the 12th-century phrase *for then anes,* meaning literally 'for the once'.

nonrestrictive clause (also nondefining clause) RELATIVE CLAUSE that gives some extra information about the noun it refers to, but does not define it or crucially limit it. Nonrestrictive clauses can be left out without drastically affecting the meaning of the sentence. They are often introduced by *which* or *who* and are usually placed between commas in the sentence, as in *The family, which is the basic unit of society, is gradually losing its appeal* or *Mr Jones, who lives next door to my parents, is emigrating.* (Compare RESTRICTIVE CLAUSE).

non sequitur Irrelevant remark lacking a logical connection with what has just been said, or a false deduction incorrectly derived from given information: *Born in Glasgow, he was fascinated by aeroplanes from an early age.* The Latin phrase means literally 'it does not follow'.

noun Part of speech that refers to a person, place, thing or idea. Nouns may be common nouns (referring to things or concepts), such as *information* or *infinity;* or proper nouns (names), such as *Mary,* or *Scotland.* They may be concrete nouns (referring to material things), such as *dog, book* and *milk;* or abstract nouns (referring to qualities or ideas), such as *happiness, beauty* or *cause.* They may be singular, as in *dog, fly* and *child;* plural, as in *dogs, flies* and *children;* or MASS NOUNS, as in *air* and *noise.* Within sentences, nouns may function as SUBJECTS, OBJECTS, or COMPLEMENTS. (See also COLLECTIVE NOUNS panel, GERUND, COUNT NOUN and POSSESSIVE.)

noun phrase Phrase that functions as a noun in a sentence. In the sentence *The whole family, including the dog, sat down and watched the video of our holiday*, there are two noun phrases: *The whole family, including the dog* and *the video of our holiday*.

nouveau riche Person who has recently become rich – often regarded as an upstart lacking in taste or social graces. The plural is *nouveaux riches*, pronounced in the same way as the singular: *The* nouveaux riches *are moving into our area in droves, with their ghastly flashy cars and their ridiculously expensive and pretentious parties*. The term is French for 'new rich'.

nuance Subtle variation of meaning. For example, the verbs *to prevaricate* and *to dissemble* have a nuance that distinguishes them from the blunter verb *to lie*.

number Way in which a word varies according to whether it refers to one thing or to many (that is, whether it is singular or plural). In English, NOUNS, VERBS and PRONOUNS may vary in number: *ox*, *has* and *it* are singular; *oxen*, *have* and *them* are plural. (See also AGREEMENT; PERSON.)

object Part of a sentence or clause that receives or is affected by the action of a verb. In the sentence *She gave me roses*, the noun *roses* is the DIRECT OBJECT, directly affected by the action, and the pronoun *me* is the INDIRECT OBJECT, being indirectly on the receiving end of the action. An object may consist of a single noun or pronoun, or of a phrase or clause such as *three presents including a necklace* in the sentence *On my twenty-first birthday, she gave me three presents including a necklace*. (Compare COMPLEMENT; PREDICATE; SUBJECT.)

omni- Prefix, from Latin, meaning 'all' or 'totally', as in *omnivorous* and *omnipotent*.

onomatopoeia (ON-er-MAT-er-PEE-er) Words whose sound suggest their meaning, for example *buzz*, *crackle*, *whoosh* or *squelch*. Poets often use onomatopoeic words to great effect, to evoke a particular sound or association with a noise.

on tenterhooks Anxious, in suspense, waiting uneasily for news: *We were on tenterhooks until the doctor phoned to assure us that the operation had been a success*. In weaving or clothmaking, a tenter was a frame over which new cloth would be stretched taut and held in place by hooked nails, or tenterhooks. By association, tense people were said to be on tenterhooks.

Oxford English Dictionary Standard work of reference for the English language. The first edition was completed in 1928 after 70 years in preparation. The current version was published in 1989 in 20 volumes and contains almost half a million entries and 2 million quotations giving the earliest uses of each meaning of a word.

oxymoron Figure of speech in which a dramatic effect is achieved by using two contradictory words together, such as *sweet sorrow*, *a militant pacifist*; *a cheerful pessimist*; *a profoundly superficial answer*. The term is Greek and means 'pointedly foolish'.

***pace* (PAA-chay)** Way of expressing polite disagreement with someone's views, or of saying 'whatever so-and-so may say' or 'with all due respect to', as in Pace *Dr Webb, I don't believe she's really ill*. The word *pace* is Latin and means 'with peace to'.

palaeo-, paleo- Prefix, from Greek, meaning 'old' or 'ancient', as in *palaeontology* and *Palaeolithic*. (Compare NEO-.)

palindrome Word or expression that reads the same backwards and forwards, such as the words *reviver* and *Otto*, and the sentences *Evil rats on no star live* and *Able was I ere I saw Elba*.

pan- Prefix, from the Greek, meaning 'all' or 'everywhere', as in *pantheism*, *panacea*, and *Pan-African*.

paradox Statement that seems absurd or self-contradictory but turns out to have a striking truth or wisdom about it, such as *You have to be cruel to be kind* and *nonconformists tend to think alike*.

paragraph Division of written text, usually marking a change of theme or topic. A paragraph may consist of a single sentence, but usually contains several sentences that develop the central idea into a fairly self-contained unit. Each paragraph is marked off by beginning on a separate line, often indented from the margin.

paraphrase Different and often shorter version of a spoken text or written passage, expressing the same ideas but using more easily understood words to clarify the meaning. For example, the sentence *Her intellectual faculties are exceptional* could be paraphrased as *She is very bright*.

parentheses (also brackets) The punctuation marks ( ), used to mark off secondary material in a sentence, such as a phrase that explains or qualifies something without altering the grammatical structure of the sentence, as in *Grandma Iris (she is actually my great-aunt) still rides a motor-bike*. The singular is parenthesis. (See also PARENTHESIS; SQUARE BRACKETS.)

parenthesis Phrase or clause within a sentence, typically marked off by dashes or PARENTHESES, that qualifies or explains something without affecting the grammatical structure of the sentence. The words between the dashes form a parenthesis within the sentence *That's without doubt the best wine – and I've tried thousands – that I've ever tasted*.

par excellence To the highest degree, supremely, serving as an outstanding example of its kind, as in *The show house is an example of energy efficiency* par excellence. The term is French in origin, meaning literally 'by way of excellence'.

parsing The analysing of a SENTENCE into its various PARTS OF SPEECH, with an explanation of their forms, functions and relationships.

participle Form of a verb that combines with an AUXILIARY VERB to indicate a certain tense, to indicate the passive voice, or to form an adjective. In the following sentences, *affecting* is the present participle, and *affected* is the past participle of the verb *affect*: *The noise was affecting my concentration. My concentration was affected by the noise. He is an affected young man, but he can certainly write an affecting love story*. (See also DANGLING PARTICIPLE; MISRELATED CONSTRUCTION.)

parting shot (also Parthian shot) Final sneer or cutting remark at the close of an argument. The phrase is an allusion to the battlefield tactics of the ancient Parthians, an Asian people, whose warriors would turn in the saddle while retreating and shoot a volley of arrows at the pursuing enemy. (Compare ESPRIT D'ESCALIER.)

part of speech Category or type of word, classified according to its function within a sentence and its relations to other words. The main traditional parts of speech are ADJECTIVE, ADVERB, ARTICLE, CONJUNCTION, INTERJECTION, NOUN, PREPOSITION, PRONOUN and VERB.

passé Out of date, no longer in fashion, as in *His views on women not working outside the home are very* passé. The term is French in origin, and means literally 'past' or 'passed'.

passim Term used in footnotes and indexes to indicate that the word or subject under discussion is found very often within the reference cited. For example, the footnote *For his striking use of similes, see the story 'Mrs Harris' pp.13-18* passim means that similes occur throughout pages 13 to 18. The term is Latin for 'throughout'.

passive VOICE, or verb form, indicating that the action of the verb is done to (rather than by) the subject. For example, the sentence *The hymn was then sung by the cantor* is passive, or 'in the passive', since the subject (the hymn) undergoes rather than performs the action of the verb (the singing). The counterpart of the passive is the ACTIVE, as in the sentence *The cantor then sang the hymn.* The passive is often used when the person or thing responsible for an action is unknown: *My car was stolen.*

past participle Participle used to indicate a past or completed action, or the PASSIVE voice, and usually ending in -*ed* or -*d: The storm has broken. The curfew was lifted.* (Compare PRESENT PARTICIPLE.)

past perfect See PERFECT.

past tense See TENSE.

-path- COMBINING FORM, from Greek, meaning 'disease' or 'feeling', as in *pathology* and *sympathy*.

patois (PAT-WA) SLANG or JARGON belonging to a particular group, especially a gang or underclass; a regional dialect; or Jamaican English, CREOLE or any other mixed language. (Compare ARGOT.)

pecking order Hierarchy of power or importance in any group or organisation: *The scriptwriter ranks very low in the Hollywood pecking order.* The phrase came from the behaviour of chickens, where weaker or less aggressive individuals submit meekly to the pecking of stronger ones.

per capita Per person: *In some countries the* per capita *income is less than $100 a year.* The phrase is Latin, meaning 'by heads'.

perfect Kind of tense form known as an 'aspect' used to indicate that an action has been completed. In English, perfect tenses always include a form of the verb *to have* and the PAST PARTICIPLE. *They have finished* is in the 'present perfect'; *They had finished* is in the 'past perfect', or 'pluperfect'; and *They will have finished* is in the 'future perfect'. (Compare PRETERITE; PROGRESSIVE.)

periodic sentence COMPLEX SENTENCE in which the main clause or main point appears at the end, producing the effect of a climax after a build-up; for example, *Even though they needed our help, instead of welcoming us they resented our arrival.*

per se In itself, as such, through its own nature: *I've nothing against the proposal* per se *– it's just that the details need thinking through.* The phrase is Latin in origin, meaning literally 'by itself'.

person Form of a pronoun or verb that distinguishes the speaker 'first person', the person addressed 'second person', and the person or thing spoken about 'third person'. In combination with NUMBER (singular or plural), person determines the word's INFLECTION. For example, for personal pronouns and the present-tense verb *to be*, the first person singular is *I am*, and the third person plural is *they are*.

personal pronoun Pronoun that indicates the person or people, thing or things, being spoken about. Its form depends on PERSON, NUMBER, GENDER and CASE. For example, *she* is first person, singular, feminine, subject; and *them* is third person, plural, any gender, object. The other personal pronouns include *I, you, he, it* and *us* and are sometimes considered to include POSSESSIVE PRONOUNS such as *his, her, our, your, my, its* and *theirs*.

persona non grata Unwelcome or unacceptable person, especially a diplomat whose presence is no longer acceptable in a foreign country: *The cultural attaché was accused of spying and declared* persona non grata. *I'm* persona non grata *at the Frasers' after criticising her poetry in public.* The phrase is Latin for 'unacceptable person'.

petro-, petr- Prefix, from Greek, meaning 'stone' or 'rock', as in *petrify, petroleum,* and *petrology*.

-phile Suffix, from Greek, meaning 'love', as in *Anglophile* and *bibliophile*.

-phobia Suffix, from Greek, meaning 'fear' or 'irrational hatred', as in *claustrophobia, Francophobia* and *hydrophobia*.

-phon- COMBINING FORM, from Greek, meaning 'sound' or 'speaking', as in *stereophonic* and *Anglophone*.

phonetic alphabet Set of letters and symbols used to represent the sounds of speech in writing. The term also refers to the radio operator's code for identifying letters of the alphabet by words such as Foxtrot for F, Oscar for O and Tango for T.

phonetics Science or study of speech sounds, including the way they are produced by the voice.

phrase Group of connected words within a sentence, typically having a SUBJECT or a PREDICATE, but not both. In the sentence *A litter of piglets trotted towards the fence*, the words *a litter of piglets* is a NOUN PHRASE, and *towards the fence* is an adverb phrase.

pictogram (also pictograph) Picture used to represent a word or idea, as in HIEROGLYPHS. Pictograms are the oldest form of writing known. (Compare IDEOGRAM.)

pidgin Simplified language based on two or more other tongues, and generally developed in colonial times as a means of communication between foreigners and indigenous people. Pidgin often sounds comical to speakers of one of the original languages – for example when an English-speaker hears Prince Philip described as *number one fellah bilong Missis Queen*.
🔹Pidgin English was originally a form of Anglo-Chinese used by 17th-century traders; curiously, the term 'pidgin' is believed to have been a Chinese corruption of the word 'business'.

pig in a poke A purchase made sight unseen. The phrase goes back to the old market custom of selling live piglets in a sack or 'poke'. A dishonest trader might sneak a stray cat or dog into the sack, and the unwary buyer might be 'sold a pup'; the buyer who opened the sack to check its contents might 'let the cat out of the bag'.

pleonasm REDUNDANCY through the use of more words than necessary, as in *ancient old man*. (Compare TAUTOLOGY.)

pluperfect See PERFECT.

plural A word that indicates that more than one object or person is being spoken about is said to be plural (or 'a plural' or 'in the plural'). In English, nouns, pronouns and verbs may be plural; for example, each of the words in the sentence *Doctors cure themselves* is plural. Most nouns form the plural by adding -*s* or -*es: cows, calves, dairies;* others have irregular plurals such as *oxen, fungi* and *geese;* others are always plural (*cattle*) or the same in the singular and the plural (*deer, sheep*). (Compare SINGULAR. See also NUMBER and AGREEMENT.)

plus ça change, plus c'est la même chose
Expression coined by the French writer Alphonse Karr, meaning 'The more things change, the more they are the same'. It is often quoted as simply *plus ça change*.

poly- Prefix, from Greek, meaning 'many' or 'much', as in *polygamy*, *polyglot* and *polygon*. (Compare MULTI-.)

portmanteau word (also blend) Word formed by fusing the sounds and meanings of two different words, such as *Chunnel* (from *channel* and *tunnel*) and *chortle* (from *chuckle* and *snort*). The second example was coined by Lewis Carroll, who was also responsible for the term 'portmanteau word'. In *Through the Looking-Glass*, Humpty Dumpty describes such blends as 'like a portmanteau – there are two meanings packed up into one word' – just as a portmanteau bag consists of two thinner cases hinged together at the back.

possessive Case, or form, of a noun or pronoun indicating possession or association. Nouns usually form the possessive by adding an apostrophe if plural, or *'s* if singular or an irregular plural: *It is to the students' credit rather than the teacher's; the children's toys.*

possessive pronoun Pronoun indicating possession; specifically the pronouns *mine*, *hers*, *his*, *its*, *ours*, *yours*, *theirs* and *whose*. The adjectival forms, *my*, *her*, *his*, *their*, *our*, *your* and *its* are also sometimes referred to as possessive pronouns, but are correctly called possessive adjectives. (Compare PERSONAL PRONOUN.)

post- Prefix derived from Latin, meaning 'after' or 'behind', as in *postgraduate* and *posterior*. (Compare ANTE-; PRE-.)

pre- Prefix derived from Latin, meaning 'before', as in *prefix*, *pre-date* and *pre-Victorian*. (Compare ANTE-; POST-.)

predicate Part of a sentence that indicates something about the subject. The predicate includes the main verb and all its modifiers. In the following sentence, only the first word is the subject, and all the rest is the predicate: *You can hardly expect me to dance with delight at the news.* (Compare COMPLEMENT; OBJECT.)

prefix Letter or letters attached to the beginning of a word to modify the meaning, such as 'dis-', 'pro-' and 're-' in the examples *disallow*, *pronoun* and *regroup*. Most prefixes are COMBINING FORMS – that is, they can be combined with other words or combining forms to create new words. (Compare SUFFIX.)

preposition Part of speech indicating the relationship of a noun or pronoun to another word or words nearby. Common English prepositions are *to*, *for*, *in*, *on*, *with*, *at*, *by* and *from*, as in *We spoke to the guard* and *Could you run an errand for me?* An old schoolroom rule used to forbid the use of prepositions at the end of a sentence. However, this rule is often ignored if the alternative leads to a clumsy sentence. Except in very formal contexts it is just as correct to say *That is the guard we spoke to*, as it is to say *That is the guard to whom we spoke*.
♣ When Sir Winston Churchill's secretary changed a sentence of his to ensure it did not end with a preposition, Churchill is said to have written beside it: 'This is the kind of English up with which I will not put!'

present participle Participle consisting of the *-ing* form of the verb, typically indicating a present or continuing action: *The drought is/was ravaging the woodlands.* (Compare PAST PARTICIPLE; GERUND.)

present perfect See PERFECT.

present tense See TENSE.

preterite (PRETT-er-it) The past tense, or a verb in the past form, indicating a completed action or condition. In the sentence *Tom stole a pig*, the verb *stole* is said to be in the preterite.

prima facie (PREE-mah FAY-see) At first sight; on the face of it; before a more detailed inspection: *It seems* prima facie *that she died of a heart attack. There is* prima facie *evidence of insider trading.* The phrase is Latin, meaning 'on first appearance'.

pro- Prefix taken from Latin, and having many meanings, including 'in favour of', as in *pro-American*, and 'serving in place of', as in *pronoun* and *proconsul*. (Compare ANTI-.)

proactive Taking actions so as to try and determine a course of events, rather than waiting for something to happen and then merely reacting to it.

progressive (also continuous) Kind of tense form known as an 'aspect' that indicates that an action or process is continuing. In English, it consists of a form of *be* and the *-ing* form of the verb, as in *She will be giving a recital* and *The cat is sleeping on the chair.* (Compare PERFECT.)

pronoun Word that serves in place of a noun or noun phrase that has been mentioned before or that can be understood from the context. For example, by substituting the pronouns *she*, *it* and *mine* for the various noun phrases, the sentence *The princess modelled her story on my story* could be reduced to *She modelled it on mine.* (See DEMONSTRATIVE PRONOUN; INDEFINITE PRONOUN; PERSONAL PRONOUN; POSSESSIVE PRONOUN; REFLEXIVE PRONOUN; RELATIVE PRONOUN.)

proper noun (or proper name) Noun referring by name to an individual person, animal, country or book, for example, and typically spelt with a capital first letter. *Mary*, *Beethoven* and *Scotland* are proper nouns. (Compare COMMON NOUN.)

pro rata In proportion: *The liquidator distributed all remaining assets* pro rata *to the creditors.* The term is a shortened version of the Latin phrase *pro rata parte*, meaning 'according to the calculated share'.

proverb Short, memorable, widely known saying, expressing a traditional piece of wisdom or advice, such as *More haste, less speed*, *A bird in the hand is worth two in the bush*, or *Spare the rod and spoil the child*. Sometimes, several proverbs convey a single idea in their different ways, as in *Beauty is only skin deep*, *All that glitters is not gold*, and *Don't judge a book by its cover*. Sometimes one proverb appears to contradict another, as in *Too many cooks spoil the broth* and *Many hands make light work*; or *Look before you leap* and *He who hesitates is lost*; or *Out of sight, out of mind* and *Absence makes the heart grow fonder*. But they do not invalidate each other: in different contexts, both are true of human experience.

pseudo- Prefix, taken from the Greek, meaning 'false', as in the words *pseudonym* and *pseudo-intellectual*.

pseudonym False or adopted name, especially the 'pen name' or NOM DE PLUME of an author. 'Saki', for example, was the pseudonym of the writer H.H. Munro.

pulling out all the stops Putting all one's energies into pursuing a goal. The phrase is based on organ playing, and refers to the great effort and dexterity required to manipulate the many stops (knobs) while playing.

pun Play on words, based either on juggling different senses of the same word or on substituting one word for another that

IN THE WARS *Pyrrhus, King of Epirus, defeats the Romans at Ausculum in 279 BC. However, he suffered such heavy losses in his 'victory' that he was unable to avert eventual defeat by the Romans.*

sounds alike: *My moustache makes it quite a strain to drink soup.* Many newspaper headlines and advertisements attempt to use puns for comic effect: *Cemetery in grave financial difficulties.*

purple passage (or purple prose). Passage of speech or writing that is full of flowery language, long sentences and extravagant METAPHORS.

Pyrrhic victory Victory that involves such great losses for the victor as to be almost as bad as defeat. The phrase is based on a supposed remark by Pyrrhus, a Greek king of the 3rd century BC. After defeating the Roman army in a battle, but suffering severe losses to his own army, he is believed to have said: 'We cannot afford another victory like that.'

QED Abbreviation of the Latin phrase *quod erat demonstrandum*, meaning 'which was to be demonstrated'. It is used when the proof of a proposition has just been successfully completed.

qua Preposition used when explaining in what role a person or organisation is carrying out an action. It means roughly 'in the capacity of' or 'by virtue of being': *Mr Green,* qua *father, was inclined to overlook his eldest daughter's prank, but* qua *headmaster he felt obliged to punish it.*

quasi- Prefix, from Latin, meaning either 'slightly', as in *quasi-scientific,* or 'similar to but not really the same as', as in *quasi-intellectual* or *quasi-victory.*

question mark Punctuation mark (?), used after a direct question: *How are you feeling? Has the meeting started yet?* Informally, it can also be used to indicate doubt: *If we invited her to the party would she arrive on time?* (See also INTERROGATIVE; RHETORICAL QUESTION.)

quid pro quo Something given in exchange, compensation, in return or received, as in *He never does anyone a favour without calculating what he can expect as a* quid pro quo. The plural is *quid pro quos.* The phrase is Latin in origin, meaning literally 'something for something'.

quixotic (kwik-SOT-tik) Adjective meaning enthusiastic and well-meaning, but given to unreachable ideals. The word derives from the hero of Cervantes' novel ▷DON QUIXOTE, who was a romantic idealist, and is often misused to mean 'gallant but absurd' or 'dangerously foolish'.

quotation marks (also inverted commas) Punctuation marks (' ') or (" "), used to mark the beginning and end of dialogue, quoted words, definitions and titles. When quoted material appears within a quotation, the quotation marks switch from single to double, or vice versa: *She told the typist, 'Every time I write "salt" you type "slat".'*

q.v. Abbreviation of the Latin phrase *quod vide,* meaning 'which see'. It is used to refer the reader to the item mentioned, which is discussed under its own heading elsewhere, as in *Headaches can sometimes be caused by tension* (q.v.) *in the neck.*

raison d'être (RAY-zon DETT'R) The central purpose of a person or object's existence; the point of living or being: *Wine-tasting seems to be his entire* raison d'être, *so it's no wonder he feels suicidal when he has a cold. She was devastated when the company made her redundant, as work is her* raison d'être. The term is French in origin, meaning literally 'reason to be'.

rat-race Term meaning the struggle for power, promotion or survival in urban society, and often used in the context of work or earning a living. It may have originated from experiments into animal behaviour in which rats try to find their way out of a maze, or run or walk continuously on a treadmill.

re Preposition used in formal writing to introduce the subject for discussion. It is Latin in origin, meaning 'concerning', 'about', 'with reference to', and is frequently used in business letters: *re your request for three weeks' credit.*

received pronunciation See RP.

red herring False clue or trail; a distraction; something that draws attention away from more important matters. The original phrase was *to draw a red herring across the path.* Foxhunting hounds were traditionally trained to ignore distracting scent-trails – or to avoid being 'thrown off the scent' – by having a smoked herring (reddish in colour) dragged across the countryside.

redundancy In grammar, unnecessary repetition or excessive wordiness in speech or writing. The phrase *freedom and liberty* displays redundancy. (Compare PLEONASM; TAUTOLOGY.)

reflexive pronoun Pronoun, typically ending in *-self,* that refers to a previously mentioned noun or pronoun, as in *I hurt myself. The candidates voted for themselves. The cat licked itself clean.*

reflexive verb TRANSITIVE VERB whose subject and object refer to the same person or thing, and that takes a reflexive pronoun as its object, as in *She prides herself on her complexion.* In many cases reflexive use is optional: one can say *We enjoyed ourselves at the concert* (reflexive) or *We enjoyed the concert* (non-reflexive).

regular verb (also weak verb) Verb that follows the standard pattern of inflection when forming its past tense and PAST PARTICIPLE, by simply adding *-ed* or *-d,* as in *talk* and *hope*, which become *I talked, I have talked* and *I hoped, I have hoped*. (Compare IRREGULAR VERB.)

relative clause SUBORDINATE CLAUSE that functions like an adjective to describe the noun it follows. The clause beginning 'who' is a relative clause in the sentence *Bianca is the woman who lives in the tower in the middle of the forest.*

relative pronoun PRONOUN that relates one part of a sentence to another, such as *who, whom, whose* and *which*. In *He was the famous stuntman who climbed the tower which belongs to a life assurance company*, *who* and *which* are relative pronouns.

reported speech See INDIRECT SPEECH.

resting on one's laurels Relying on one's past achievements instead of maintaining one's efforts: *If the champion rests on his laurels and doesn't train properly, he will be beaten by his young opponent.* The opposite is *looking to one's laurels*, which means protecting one's reputation or leading position by taking care not to underestimate the task ahead or the competition facing one: *He'd better look to his laurels, because his young opponent seems very sharp.* The original laurels were wreaths presented as marks of honour in antiquity. The tradition of giving champions laurel wreaths was carried on until quite recently in motor racing.

restrictive clause (also defining clause) RELATIVE CLAUSE, often introduced by *that* rather than *which*, that defines or specifies the noun it modifies, and is a crucial part of the meaning of the sentence. In the sentence *The family that prays together stays together*, the clause *that prays together* is called a restrictive clause. (Compare NON-RESTRICTIVE CLAUSE.)

rhetoric The study or use of style in literature and public speaking, especially to persuade or influence listeners. It can also refer to high-flown but empty or insincere language, as sometimes used by politicians.

rhetorical question Question that is posed in order to make a point rather than to elicit an answer: *You don't really expect me to accept that story, do you?* or *Where have good manners gone?*

ringing the changes Repeating something that is familiar or routine in a slightly different way each time so as to seem original: *His poems are clever but not really varied, always ringing the changes on the theme*

RHYMING SLANG – THE LANGUAGE OF COCKNEYS

Rhyming slang is a humorous and often complicated form of SLANG, associated with Cockneys and other Londoners. A word is replaced by another word or phrase that rhymes with it – as for example, *brown bread* for *dead*, *mince pies* for *eyes*, *trouble and strife* for *wife*. Sometimes only the first word of the phrase is used, as in *china* for *friend* (from *china plate* for *mate*) or else the phrase is modified, as in *titfer* (from *tit for tat*) meaning *hat*.

What's the use of me making Rosy when you go straight off to have a pig's ear down the rub-a?

Adam an' Eve	believe
apples an' pears	stairs
Barnet Fair (*Barnet*)	hair
butcher's hook (*butcher's*)	look
daisy roots (*daisies*)	boots
dolly mixtures	pictures
Gipsy Rosie Lee (*Rosy*)	tea
Gregory Peck	cheque
heavenly bliss	kiss

Hickory Dickory dock (*dickery*)	clock
Jack Jones (*on my Jack*)	alone
Joanna	piano
loaf of bread (*loaf*)	head
pig's ear (*pig's*)	beer
plates of meat	feet
rub-a-dub-dub (*rub-a*)	pub
whistle and flute (*whistle*)	suit

'Take a butcher's at me whistle!' Pearlies – Pearly kings and queens – were Cockney costermongers and their wives who wore clothes covered in pearl buttons.

---

of homesickness. The original and literal sense of the phrase still refers to a pattern or sequence of ringing church bells.

risqué Slightly rude, indecent or improper, saucy: *None of your risqué jokes tonight, please – Aunt Myrna will be present.* The term is French, meaning literally 'risked'.

Romance languages Group of INDO-EUROPEAN tongues descended from Latin, which include French, Spanish and Italian.

root Word or word-element, often Latin or Greek, which forms the core or basis of other words. For example, the element *nov*

(from the Latin *novus*, 'new') is the root of such words as *novelty, novice* and *renovate*; and the form *soph* (from the Greek *sophia*, 'wisdom') is the root of such words as *sophisticated* and *philosophy*. The word 'root' can also be used to refer to a STEM.

RP (received pronunciation) The form of English pronunciation that is typically associated with the English upper middle class. Today it is widely considered the most neutral, socially acceptable and standard English accent. It is sometimes referred to as BBC English, the Queen's English or Oxford English, though these terms can also suggest a rather pompous (or 'plummy') pronunciation.

RSVP Abbreviation of the French phrase *répondez s'il vous plaît*, which literally means 'reply if you please'. It is written or printed at the end of formal letters and invitations, and demands a response.

runes The letters of an ancient alphabet used in northern Europe before the Roman alphabet took over in the Middle Ages. ♣Runes were used for charms. *Run* is an Old English word meaning 'secret'.

running the gamut Covering the entire range of something: *She accused me of running the gamut of deadly sins, from sloth to gluttony.* The original gamut was the entire series of musical notes, a contraction of the medieval Latin *gamma* and *ut*, the names of the highest and lowest notes of the scale.

running the gauntlet Facing criticism or disgrace: *After yet another home defeat, Rangers have once again had to run the gauntlet of their supporters.* The phrase comes from a military punishment in which the victim had to run between two lines of men who beat him with sticks or ropes. ♣The word *gauntlet* comes from a Swedish term meaning 'passageway'. The spelling was influenced by the word *gauntlet* meaning 'a glove', as in THROWING DOWN THE GAUNTLET, but the phrase is otherwise unrelated to it.

run-on sentence Sentence, considered faulty in standard grammar, in which two or more independent main clauses are linked without an appropriate conjunction or punctuation mark, as in the sentence *The fog was thick he could not drive home.* Inserting *and* or a semicolon after *thick* would remedy things, but a comma would be insufficient.

sacred cow Person, object, institution or idea held in such high regard as to be above criticism: *The theory of monetarism became a sacred cow in our department in the 1980s.* The phrase comes from the sacred status of the cow in Hindu society as laid down in religious texts.

sailing under false colours Taking on a false name or identity, or pretending to believe in a policy, in order to hide one's real purpose: *A private investigator often has to sail under false colours in order to gain the confidence of informers.* The phrase harks back to the days of sailing ships, when a pirate ship or a warship might fly a false flag, or 'false colours', to trick an approaching vessel. Similarly, revealing one's true colours, or showing oneself in one's true colours, means revealing one's real nature or purpose at last – in the same way as the pirate ship or warship might hoist its real flag just before attacking. (Compare NAILING ONE'S COLOURS TO THE MAST.)

sang-froid (SAHN-FRWAA) Well-controlled feelings, calm behaviour, self-control, self-possession: *She showed admirable* sang-froid *when her ex-husband tried to gatecrash the wedding ceremony.* The term is French, meaning literally 'cold blood'.

savoir-faire Ability to say or do the correct thing in any given situation, particularly in social terms: *For a teenager he has great* savoir-faire. The term is French in origin, meaning literally 'knowing to do'.

scapegoat See WHIPPING BOY.

semantics The study or science of word meaning, including changes of meaning over time and the way that words or sentences convey sense. ♣The word is often used to refer to a difference in the meaning of words, particularly in an argument: *You're talking about a gut reaction and I'm talking about instinct – it all comes down to semantics.*

semi- Prefix, from Latin, meaning 'half', as in *semitone*, *semidetached* and *semifinals*. (Compare DEMI-.)

semicolon Punctuation mark (;) used to separate two MAIN CLAUSES in a sentence, such as *Human effort arranges the pieces on the board; blind fate decides the outcome.* A COMMA would be insufficient, since the two clauses are grammatically independent (see RUN-ON SENTENCE). A full stop would be possible but less satisfactory, since the ideas within the two clauses are closely linked.

sentence A complete and independent unit of expression, consisting of a group of words or occasionally a single word, and typically containing a SUBJECT and a PREDICATE. The three expressions *Help!* and *How are you?* and *Rumour has it that the chairman will resign tomorrow* are all sentences. (See also COMPLEX SENTENCE, COMPOUND SENTENCE, DECLARATIVE SENTENCE and SIMPLE SENTENCE.)

shibboleth Word or phrase used by members of a group as a sign of solidarity, such as a slogan or catchphrase that excludes outsiders. It is also used of a traditional belief or policy accepted unquestioningly by a group, as in *By getting rid of some of its old socialist shibboleths, the Labour Party widened its electoral appeal.* The word is Hebrew in origin, meaning 'an ear of corn', and was a password used by the Gileadites to identify enemy Ephraimites, who always pronounced the 'sh' sound as 's'.

short shrift Brief and unsympathetic treatment, or abrupt dismissal: *The management gave short shrift to the strikers' demands.* The word *shrift* is an old term for confession in church, and short shrift originally referred to the brief time in which a condemned prisoner could make his confession before being executed.

sibilant Hissing sound in speech, specifically the English CONSONANT sounds 'sh', 's', 'z'and 'zh', as in the sentence *She sells leisurewear.*

sic Latin word meaning 'thus' which is used in a quoted passage of writing to indicate that an odd or incorrect word, spelling, phrase or statement has been accurately quoted, as in *The lecture is entitled 'The Revival* (sic) *of the Fittest'. Her diary refers to 'the storm of 31 November* (sic) *last year'.* 'Sic' usually appears in italics, either in parentheses or in square brackets.

simile (SIM-i-lee) Figure of speech in which one thing is compared to another by the use of words such as *like*, *as*, or *similar to*. The effect is sometimes vivid, as in *He squatted there like an unexploded bomb, glaring at me.* However, a simile can degenerate into cliché: *My mother's bright as a button during the day, and sleeps like a log at night.* (Compare METAPHOR.)

simple sentence Sentence that has only one MAIN CLAUSE and no SUBORDINATE CLAUSES, such as *She gave them some soup without any bread.* (Compare COMPLEX SENTENCE and COMPOUND SENTENCE.)

sine qua non (SEE-nay kwaa NON) Essential condition or element: *An outgoing personality is a* sine qua non *for success in public relations.* The plural would be *sine qua nons.* The phrase is Latin in origin, meaning literally 'without which not'.

singular A word that indicates that a single person or thing is being spoken about is said to be singular (or 'a singular' or 'in the singular'). Each of the words in the sentence *She is a surgeon* is singular. (Compare PLURAL; see NUMBER; AGREEMENT.)

slang Casual or informal language used among people familiar with one another or from a similar group. Slang is considered to be inappropriate for conventional speech or writing. It is often colourful and fairly short-lived. The words *hassles* and *hang-ups* are slang terms that communicate meaning more directly than formal wording such as *pressing demands* and *personal anxieties*. (Compare COLLOQUIALISM; see ARGOT; JARGON; RHYMING SLANG panel.)

slogan Short phrase, typically expressing some principle, purpose or boast, as used in political or advertising campaigns, such as *Not in my back yard* and *Probably the best lager in the world*.

sold down the river Cheated, betrayed, or deserted, as in *He promised to keep quiet about the accident, but when the police arrived we realised that we'd been sold down the river*. The phrase comes from the days of slavery in North America. The farther south a slave was sent, the hotter and more unbearable the conditions became.

solecism (SOL-i-sizm) Error or unconventional use of grammar, such as the failure of AGREEMENT as in the sentence: *The delivery of letters and parcels have been delayed by the flooding*.

sotto voce (SOT-oh VO-chay) Very softly, as if to avoid being overheard: *She warned me, sotto voce, not to mention our hosts' imminent divorce*. The phrase is Italian in origin, meaning literally 'under the voice'.

split infinitive Phrase, such as *to boldly go* or *to quickly and easily fix*, in which the infinitive form of a verb is separated from the word *to* by another word or words, usually an adverb. To split an infinitive is still widely regarded as poor style, but it sometimes adds vividness.

square brackets (also brackets) Punctuation marks [ ] used within PARENTHESES for a second stage of subordinate information: *Follow the B3212 as far as Princetown (about 6 miles [10km] from Yelverton)*. They are also used within quotations to surround material that is not part of the original, as in *The mayor's promise was to 'aid [us] if necessary and compensate [us] if possible'*.

status quo Existing state of affairs or present condition. The term is Latin in origin, meaning literally 'state in which'.
🔹*Status quo ante* means 'in the previous state of affairs', and *in status quo* means 'in the same state (as before)'.

stealing someone's thunder Gaining the praise or profits that really belong to someone else, by claiming his efforts, idea or invention as one's own, as in *I did most of the research, but the project director stole my thunder by publishing the report under his own name*. The phrase apparently goes back to the 18th century, when an English playwright, John Dennis, invented a machine to make the noise of thunder during a storm scene in a play. A similar machine was later used in a performance of Shakespeare's *Macbeth*, and Dennis complained that the management had 'stolen his thunder'.

stem Main, unchanging part of a word to which a prefix or suffix may be added. For example, the stem of the verb *raise* is *rais-*, allowing for the words *raising*, *raised* and *raises*. (Compare ROOT.)

SPOONERISMS

William Spooner, warden of New College, Oxford, from 1903 to 1924, was well known for transposing the initial sounds of words when speaking, with bizarre results. He is said to have once described the Lord as a 'shoving leopard', and to have announced a hymn as 'Kinquering kongs their titles take'. Some colourful 'spoonerisms' are, however, probably apocryphal. These include the claim 'There's nothing to beat a ride on a well-boiled icicle', and the rebuke to an undergraduate: 'You have hissed my mystery lectures and tasted a whole worm. You were fighting a liar in the quadrangle, and you will leave Oxford immediately by the town drain'.

PUZZLING DON *During a speech, Spooner supposedly asked: 'Which of us has not felt in his bosom a half-warmed fish?'*

---

stet Word written in the margin, often by an editor, to indicate to the typist or printer that a correction made to the text should be ignored. The word is usually accompanied by a line of dots under the word or phrase referred to. It comes from Latin, and means 'let it stand'.

still waters run deep Proverb pointing out that a quiet exterior may conceal a profound thinker or great depths of character, just as the deepest lake or river may have the smoothest surface.

strong verb An IRREGULAR VERB.

sub- Prefix, from Latin, meaning 'under', as in *subnormal*, *subzero* and *submarine*.

subject Part of a sentence or clause that indicates what it is about. The subject may be a noun, pronoun, noun phrase, or clause, and usually introduces the verb. In the sentence *We resent your suspicions*, the pronoun *we* is the subject. Sometimes the subject is only implied, as *you* is in the sentence *Go and fetch your coat*. (Compare COMPLEMENT; OBJECT; PREDICATE.)

subjunctive Grammatical form or MOOD of a verb used in some formal commands or in discussing doubtful or hypothetical situations. In the following sentences, the verbs *have*, *save*, *be* and *were* are in the subjunctive: *I suggested that she have a good night's rest. God save the Queen. Far be it from me. If I were you, I'd resign. I wish I were dead*. Nowadays the subjunctive is used less often in English. (Compare IMPERATIVE; INDICATIVE.)

subordinate clause (also dependent clause) Clause that cannot stand alone as a full sentence, but instead forms part of a COMPLEX SENTENCE, functioning in the same way as a noun, adverb or adjective. In the sentence *When the wind blows, the cradle will rock*, the clause *When the wind blows* is a subordinate clause. (Compare MAIN CLAUSE; see also RELATIVE CLAUSE.)

substantive Noun, pronoun, word or group of words acting as a noun.

suffix Letter or set of letters attached to the end of a word or STEM that modifies the meaning. In the words *feverishness* and *raising*, *-ish* and *-ness* are suffixes to the word *fever*, and *-ing* is a suffix to the stem *rais-*. (Compare PREFIX and COMBINING FORM.)

sui generis (SOO-ey JEN-eris) Unique, individual or in a class of its own: *Clancy's* *madcap comedy act is* sui generis, *following no tradition and having no imitators.* The phrase is Latin and means 'of its own kind'.

superlative Form of an ADJECTIVE or ADVERB indicating the greatest or most intense degree of the quality concerned. *Greatest* and *most intense* are the superlative forms of *great* and *intense*.

When only two items are being compared, the COMPARATIVE should be used and not the superlative: *He is the taller of the twins*, not *He is the tallest of the two*.

sword of Damocles An ever-present danger, a constantly worrying threat of disaster: *Until the Fraud Squad completes its investigation, I feel I'm under the sword of Damocles.* The phrase goes back to an ancient legend in which an envious court flatterer called Damocles was invited to a feast by the ruler of Syracuse. Damocles was seated beneath a deadly sword suspended by a single horsehair from the roof – a symbol of the ever-present uncertainty and danger of the life that he coveted.

The phrase *hanging by a thread*, as in *The victim's life is still hanging by a thread*, probably alludes to the same story.

syllable Basic unit of the sound of a word, usually containing one vowel sound and one or more consonants. The word *basic* has two syllables (ba-sic), and the word *containing* has three (con-tain-ing).

sym-, syn- Prefix, from Greek, meaning 'together', or 'same' as in *symphony*, *sympathy* and *syndicate*.

synecdoche (si-NEK-der-kee) Figure of speech in which a part of something is used to refer to the whole, or vice versa. In the phrase *All hands on deck*, sailors are referred to by means of only their hands. (Compare METONYMY.)

synonym Word having a meaning identical or very similar to that of another in the same language. The noun *container* is a synonym of *receptacle*, and the verbs *mix*, *blend* and *mingle* are roughly synonymous. The opposite is ANTONYM.

synopsis Brief or condensed review of a subject or text; a summary: *I haven't time to read the whole report, but if you prepare a synopsis, I'll read that.* (See also PARAPHRASE.)

syntax The way in which words are arranged to form phrases and sentences, and the system of rules for acceptable sentence structure. In English, word order

is very important (*Jack loves Jill* does not mean the same as *Jill loves Jack*) but in Latin it is less so, because its greater use of different word endings to indicate meaning allows a more flexible sentence structure. (Compare GRAMMAR.)

tautology Unnecessary repetition of a thought or idea through the use of different words or ideas. *Both species share the same ancestor in common* is tautological several times over. *Advance planning* also involves a tautology, as planning is necessarily done in advance. (Compare PLEONASM.)

telegraphese Abbreviated style of writing developed to save money when sending telegrams charged by the word. Evelyn Waugh's novel *Scoop* contains such extreme examples as *News exyou unreceived*.

tense Form of a verb indicating the time of the action or condition referred to ('past', 'present', or 'future'). For example, *I sing* refers to a current action and is therefore in the present tense, *I sang* refers to something that has already happened and is in the past tense, and *I shall sing* refers to something yet to occur and is future tense. Tense also includes the 'aspect' of the verb – that is, whether the action is considered complete (PERFECT) or continuing (PROGRESSIVE). Aspect allows for the formation of compound tenses such as the past progressive (*I was singing*) and the future perfect (*I shall have sung*). (See PRETERITE.)

terra firma Solid ground or dry land: *A round-the-world yachtsman must feel very relieved to get back on* terra firma. The phrase is Latin for 'firm ground'.

tête-à-tête A private conversation between two people: *It's time we had a tête-à-tête to decide what to do about Uncle Cyril's proposed visit.* The term is French in origin, meaning literally 'head to head'.

thesaurus Book of SYNONYMS systematically arranged for easy use as a word finder. The first serious English thesaurus, compiled by Peter Mark Roget, was published in 1852, and modern editions of it are still published today.

throwing down the gauntlet Issuing a challenge: *By rejecting the offered pay rise, the trade union members threw down the gauntlet to the management.* The original challenge involved was to a duel. The gauntlet was the protective glove worn as part of a soldier's armour in the Middle Ages. Throwing one's gauntlet at the feet of a rival knight

was a standard way of challenging him to one-to-one combat. (Compare RUNNING THE GAUNTLET.)

tilde (TIL-da) Mark (˜) placed above a letter to adjust the way it is pronounced. A tilde is often placed above the letter 'n' in Spanish to indicate that it should be pronounced in a slightly nasal way, similar to the 'ny' in the English word *canyon*, as in *mañana* or *señorita*.

topic sentence Main sentence in a paragraph, often the first sentence, conveying the central idea of the paragraph.

tour de force Brilliant display of strength or skill; an outstanding deed, work of art or performance: *His paintings are all wonderful, but 'Aunt Myrna in Tears' strikes me as a* tour de force *that surpasses everything else in the exhibition.* The term is French, meaning 'turn of strength' or 'feat of skill'.

ENDURING SYMBOL *Francis Barraud's painting of a terrier called 'Nipper', entitled* His Master's Voice, *provided the name for the famous record label as well as its trademark.*

trademark Name or symbol used to identify a product. Trademarks are officially registered and legally restricted so that only the owner or manufacturer may use them. For example, *Reader's Digest* and *The Digest*, and the LOGO of Pegasus, the flying horse, are registered trademarks of The Reader's Digest Association, Inc.

trans- Prefix, from Latin, meaning 'across', 'over', 'beyond' or 'through', as in *translate*, *transplant*, *trans-Siberian*, *transcend* and *transparent*.

transitive verb Verb that needs a direct object to complete its meaning, or that can occur in the PASSIVE voice. The verbs *solve* and *use* are transitive, as is *betray*: *He betrayed his country. His country was betrayed by him.* Many verbs can be transitive or intransitive depending on the way in which they are used: compare the use of *yell* in the following sentences: *My teachers regularly yell abuse at me* (transitive) and *My teachers regularly yell at me* (intransitive). (Compare INTRANSITIVE VERB.)

transliteration Conversion of one alphabet into another in order to represent a foreign language: *A better transliteration of the Chinese name 'Peking' would be 'Beijing'*.

ultra- Prefix, from Latin, which means 'beyond' or 'too much', as in *ultraviolet*, *ultraconservative* and *ultramodern*.

umlaut Mark (¨), used particularly in German. It is placed over the vowels 'a', 'o' and 'u' to lengthen and flatten the sound. In English, an umlaut is often replaced by an 'e' written after the vowel, as when *Göring* is written *Goering*. (See also DIAERESIS.)

uncountable noun See MASS NOUN.

understatement Restrained speech or writing in which claims are given less importance than they deserve: *He was quite pleased when he inherited two million pounds*. It can be used as a sort of reverse emphasis: *Compared with his peers, Einstein was quite bright*. (See also LITOTES.)

upper case Capital letters, the larger and less common form of the letters of the alphabet, as used at the start of sentences or proper names. The 'M' and 'C' are upper case in the sentence *My dog bit Charlotte's leg*. (Compare LOWER CASE.)
🐾 The terms 'upper case' and 'lower case' come from the early days of printing when type was stored in a case, with capital letters at the top and small letters at the bottom.

verb Part of speech that represents an action. The words *run, raise, think and become* are all verbs. The form that a verb takes is determined by such factors as NUMBER, PERSON, TENSE, MOOD and VOICE. (See AUXILIARY VERB; GERUND; IMPERATIVE; IMPERSONAL VERB; INFINITIVE; INFLECTION; INTRANSITIVE VERB; IRREGULAR VERB; PARTICIPLE; REFLEXIVE VERB; REGULAR VERB; SUBJUNCTIVE; TRANSITIVE VERB.)

verbatim Using exactly the same words, word-for-word: *a verbatim report of her speech*. The term comes from the Latin *verbum*, meaning literally 'word'.

vernacular Ordinary language of the people of a region. It refers to informal everyday speech rather than strictly correct or formal written language.

vice versa With the reverse order or meaning, conversely: *The gangster arranged for his rival to be assassinated, and* vice versa. The phrase is Latin in origin, meaning roughly 'the position being changed'.

vis-à-vis (VEEZ-a-VEE) In relation to, or regarding: *Could we have a quick talk this morning* vis-à-vis *your holiday plans?* The term is French in origin, meaning literally 'face to face'.

viz. Abbreviation of the Latin word *videlicet*, meaning 'it is permitted to see' or 'plainly', used to introduce an item or list of items previously referred to, as in *The novelist Henry James derived little benefit from the three most noted teachers of the day,* viz. *Leavis, Holloway and Hough.*

vogue word Word that rises quickly into fashion, appearing widely in newspapers, on radio and television and in the conversation of people trying to sound up-to-date. Vogue words may be old terms used in a new sense, such as *syndrome* and *parameter*, or new words such as *interface* and *clone*. (Compare JARGON.)

voice Form of a verb indicating the relationship between the subject of a sentence and the action expressed by the verb. In the sentence *The liquidators auctioned the stock*, the verb *auctioned* is in the active voice, whereas in *The stock was auctioned by the liquidators*, the verb is in the passive voice.

SACRED BEAST *White elephants were treated with awe as long ago as the 6th century. A manuscript illustration shows Abraha, viceroy of Yemen, whispering his grandson's name into the animal's ear to bring the child luck.*

volte-face (VOLT-FASS) Turn-around, reversal, 'U-turn' or complete change in policy or belief: *In yet another* volte-face, *the government has bowed to pressure and devalued the pound*. The plural can be either *volte-face* or *volte-faces*, and is pronounced in the same way as the singular. The word came into English from French, which adopted it from an Italian term meaning 'turn-face'.

vowel Speech sound produced by a relatively unobstructed air stream and made with an open or partially open mouth, or a letter of the alphabet representing such a sound: 'a', 'e', 'i', 'o', 'u' and sometimes 'y' as in *rhythm*. (Compare CONSONANT.)

weak verb A REGULAR VERB.

weasel words Words or phrases with a vague meaning – such as *efficiency* or *not in the public interest* – as used in official statements to avoid specific commitments. The idea behind the term is the supposed ability of a weasel to suck out the contents of an egg while leaving the shell intact.

whipping boy Person who gets blamed for the mistakes of others, especially those more powerful: *Poor Henry is always the whipping boy when the financial manager has to explain his own bungling*. The phrase goes back to an old aristocratic practice of transferring the punishment intended for a nobleman to an innocent playmate or fellow pupil. Compare AUNT SALLY.
🐾 A person who carries the blame for others is also termed a *scapegoat*. This term comes from the Israelite practice of confessing sins over the head of a goat which was then released into the wilderness to carry them away – literally an (e)scape(d) goat.

white elephant Large or impressive possession that costs more to maintain than it is worth, or an expensive project that turns out to be a failure: *This new heating system is a white elephant – it's already cost more in repairs than we can ever save in fuel costs*. In ancient Siam (now Thailand), elephants with a pale hide were highly valued and their owners were required to pamper them. According to tradition, such an elephant might be presented by the king to a courtier who had offended him. What appeared a generous gift turned out to be a harsh punishment, given the cost of feeding and housing the animal.

zeugma (or syllepsis) Figure of speech in which a single word is used to apply to two or more others, either wrongly or in different ways: *She left in high dudgeon and a taxi.*

ENGLISH LITERATURE

The literature of the English-speaking world is a treasure house of stories, plays and poems. The works of Chaucer and Shakespeare, of Keats and Dickens, mould us and mark us; in the 19th century, American writers such as Edgar Allan Poe and Mark Twain began to add their contribution. In modern times, writers from Australia, Africa, Asia and the Caribbean have enriched our literary heritage still further.

BEATRIX POTTER CLASSICS

WILLIAM SHAKESPEARE

EDITH SITWELL

Achebe, Chinua (1930-) Nigerian novelist and academic who writes about the effects of colonialism on African society and the conflict between modern and traditional values. His first novel *Things Fall Apart* (1958), which depicts a tribal society's first contact with Europeans, attracted considerable attention. Achebe won the Nobel prize for literature in 1989.

Addison, Joseph (1672-1719) Essayist, poet and politician, and a close friend of the writers Jonathan SWIFT and a former schoolfellow, Sir Richard Steele. He is best known for his elegant articles in the two periodicals *The Tatler* and *The Spectator*, which he and Steele cofounded.
♙ Today's *Spectator* was launched in 1828.

Alcott, Louisa May (1832-88) American author known for LITTLE WOMEN, *Little Men* and other books for and about children. She began writing when young – to help support her family – and later became a campaigner for women's votes.

Alice's Adventures in Wonderland Children's book by Lewis CARROLL, published in 1865 and written for Alice Liddell, the daughter of a friend. Alice enters Wonderland by following the White Rabbit down his hole, and has many strange adventures there. She meets the Mad Hatter and the March Hare, the grinning CHESHIRE CAT and the Queen of Hearts, who shouts, 'Off with her head!' when Alice makes a mistake at croquet. The book was highly successful and was followed in 1872 by THROUGH THE LOOKING-GLASS.
♙ The book has been interpreted in many different ways, from being a satire on the court of Queen Victoria or academic pedantry at Oxford, to mocking the legal system or exploring the unconscious mind.

Amis, Kingsley (1922-) British novelist and poet who achieved fame with the publication of the satirical novel *Lucky Jim* in 1954 and has written prolifically ever since. The hero of *Lucky Jim* is Jim Dixon, a university lecturer who takes an uncompromising stand against all forms of pretension. Although Amis was hailed as an ANGRY YOUNG MAN and has written in a variety of styles, his comic novels are the best known of his works. His later writings reflect an increasingly pessimistic attitude to the world. His son, Martin Amis (1949-), is also a writer, whose novels include *The Rachel Papers*, *Money*, *London Fields* and *Time's Arrow*.

Anglo-Saxon See OLD ENGLISH.

Angry Young Men Term applied in the 1950s to a group of British writers and dramatists whose work was known for its radical views and rejection of the status quo. They included the satirist Kingsley AMIS and playwright John OSBORNE.

Animal Farm Novel by George ORWELL published in 1945 as a satire on Stalin's USSR. Animals, led by pigs, take over a farm to escape human tyranny but are soon suffering worse treatment under their new masters than they experienced from man.

Anne of Green Gables Much-loved novel for children by the Canadian author L.M. Montgomery, published in 1908. An elderly couple ask an orphanage for a young farm hand, but much to their surprise a boisterous, red-haired 11-year-old girl called Anne turns up.

Antony and Cleopatra Tragedy by SHAKESPEARE, thought to have been written in 1606-7. It dramatises the ill-fated love of the Roman general Mark Antony for Cleopatra, queen of Egypt, and his ensuing struggle between duty and desire.

Archer, Jeffrey (1940-) Popular novelist and former MP who wrote his first bestseller, *Not a Penny More, Not a Penny Less*, after losing a fortune in a bad investment. Later works include *Kane and Abel* and the play *Beyond Reasonable Doubt*.

Arnold, Matthew (1822-88) Poet, critic and school reformer much concerned with what he saw as the narrow materialism and ignorance of 19th-century British society. Two of Arnold's best-known poems are *Dover Beach* and *The Scholar Gypsy*.
♙ The poet's father, Thomas Arnold, was a well-known headmaster of Rugby school.

Asimov, Isaac (1920-) Russian-born American scientist and prolific science fiction writer who, with his contemporary Ray Bradbury, first made the genre respectable. He won fame with early works such as *I, Robot* (1950) and the *Foundation* trilogy (1951-3), and coined the term 'robotics'.

'A thing of beauty is a joy for ever' First line of *Endymion*, a long verse ▷ALLEGORY by John KEATS, dealing with the quest for beauty in art and in life.

Atwood, Margaret (1939-) Canadian poet, critic and novelist whose witty and accessible works often explore complex female themes. Her novels include *The Edible Woman* (1969), *Life Before Man* (1979), *Bodily Harm* (1981), *The Handmaid's Tale* (1986) and *Cat's Eye* (1989).

Auden, W.H. (1907-73) Poet who wrote prolifically in a wide range of styles. His use of ordinary speech rather than high-flown 'poetic' language influenced many other poets in Britain and the USA.

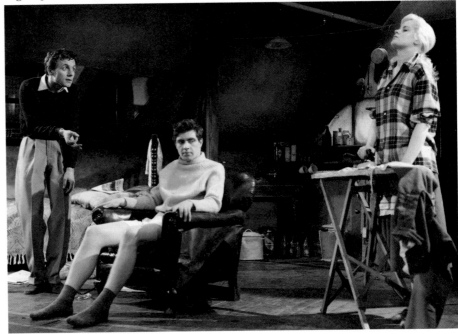

ANGRY YOUNG MAN *Jimmy Porter (Alan Bates, centre) chafes at the restraints of marriage in the original production of John Osborne's* Look Back in Anger *at the Royal Court Theatre (1956).*

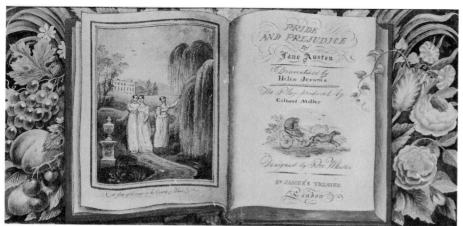

SCENE CHANGE *Pride and Prejudice – one of Jane Austen's best-loved novels – was adapted for the stage in 1936. The English artist Rex Whistler designed the sets, including this drop curtain.*

Auden was the leading figure among the radical writers of the 1930s and went to Spain to support the Republicans during the Spanish Civil War. In 1939 he emigrated to the USA with Christopher ISHERWOOD, but eventually returned to Britain to become professor of poetry at Oxford University. His later poetry became increasingly Christian.

Augustan writers Group of 18th-century British writers – including Pope and Swift – who modelled themselves on Virgil, Ovid and other authors of the reign of Emperor ▷AUGUSTUS.

Austen, Jane (1775-1817) One of the finest English novelists, known for her witty and sensitive portrayal of middle-class social life and relationships of the late 18th and early 19th centuries. Her works include PRIDE AND PREJUDICE, EMMA and *Northanger Abbey*. Jane Austen never married; but she shows deep insight into the character of her heroines, who come to recognise and eventually marry the right suitor.
♪Jane Austen described her work as a 'little bit (two Inches wide) of Ivory on which I work with so fine a brush, as produces little effect after much labour'.

Baldwin, James (1924-87) Harlem-born writer and activist who wrote about the condition of black Americans in works such as *Go Tell It On The Mountain* (1953) and *Another Country* (1962).

Ballard, J.G. (1930-) British novelist and short-story writer, born in Shanghai. He is known for science fiction and fantasy writing, and for the novel *Empire of the Sun*, which was based on his childhood experiences of China during World War II.

Barrie, J.M. (1860-1937) Scottish novelist and playwright, best known for his play PETER PAN, about a boy who never grows up.

Beerbohm, Sir Max (1872-1956) Comic writer and caricaturist who used his light, witty touch to make fun of the institutions and personalities of the day, including writers such as Rudyard Kipling and H.G. Wells, whose style he mimicked. His novel about Oxford life in the 1890s, *Zuleika Dobson*, is still popular.

Beggar's Opera, The Satirical low-life opera in ballad form by the 18th-century English playwright John Gay. It tells the story of the highwayman Macheath who marries Polly Peachum, the daughter of one of his criminal clients. Mr Peachum, furious at the bad match, informs on Macheath, who is arrested and taken to Newgate prison where he falls for the warder's daughter Lucy.
♪In the 1920s the German playwright Bertold Brecht and composer Kurt Weill collaborated on a modern version called *The Threepenny Opera*.

Belloc, Hilaire (1870-1953) British writer and Liberal politician who was born in France. Belloc is best known for his volumes of humorous children's verse, *Cautionary Tales* and *A Bad Child's Book of Beasts*, which contains such verses as:
I shoot the Hippopotamus
With bullets made of platinum,
Because if I use leaden ones
His hide is sure to flatten 'em.

Bellow, Saul (1915-) American novelist born in Canada of Jewish emigrants from Russia. His novels include *The Adventures of Augie March*, the story of a boy growing up and moving from the USA to Paris, and *Herzog*, about an intellectual whose wife leaves him and who then becomes obsessed with communicating his thoughts in letters to the living and the dead. Bellow received the Nobel prize for literature in 1976.

Benchley, Peter (1940-) Popular novelist who wrote the best-selling book ▷JAWS, about a man-eating great white shark which terrorises the inhabitants of a small American resort on Long Island.

Bennett, Alan (1934-) Actor and playwright who, with Jonathan Miller, Peter Cook and Dudley Moore, was responsible for the satirical revue *Beyond the Fringe* in 1960. Bennett went on to write comic and serious plays, including the series *Talking Heads* and the television drama *An Englishman Abroad*, based on a real meeting between the actress Coral Browne and the spy Guy Burgess in Moscow.

Bennett, Arnold (1867-1931) Writer whose novels depict everyday life among the lower middle classes of provincial Midlands towns. They include *Anna of the Five Towns*, *The Old Wives' Tale* – about two sisters, one who marries an unadventurous shop assistant and remains in her home town, while the other elopes to Paris with an unscrupulous commercial traveller who deserts her – and *Riceyman Steps*, the story of Henry Earlforward, a mean second-hand bookseller living in Clerkenwell, London.

WEIGHTY WIT *Although best known for jovial nonsense verses, Hilaire Belloc was deeply religious and held firm political views – a seriousness reflected in David Low's 1930s cartoon.*

Beowulf (BAY-uh-wolf) Epic poem in Old English; the earliest long work of literature in English. *Beowulf* survives in a 10th-century manuscript, but may be much older. It tells how the hero Beowulf slays the monster Grendel and Grendel's mother, and of Beowulf2's battle with a dragon, in which he is mortally wounded.

Betjeman, Sir John (1906-84) Poet who wrote about British institutions, manners and social life in a gently mocking style, but often with a more serious message below the surface. Betjeman was appointed poet laureate in 1972. Well-known poems include 'A Subaltern's Love-song', which begins 'Miss J. Hunter Dunn, Miss J. Hunter Dunn/Furnish'd and burnish'd by Aldershot sun', and 'Slough', which starts:
  Come, friendly bombs, and fall on Slough
  It isn't fit for humans now,
The poet apologised for the lines when the town was indeed bombed in World War II.

'Big Brother is watching you' Slogan appearing on posters throughout the fictional dictatorship in George Orwell's novel NINETEEN EIGHTY-FOUR. Big Brother is the unseen head of the ruling party.
🖉 The term 'Big Brother' is used to refer to any ruler or government seen as invading the privacy of individuals.

Biggles Hero of a series of children's books written in the 1930s-70s by Captain W.E. Johns. Biggles – short for Major James Bigglesworth, DSO, MC – is a daring British airman who flies adventurous missions with his two companions Algy

---

BRITISH PLUCK *Biggles keeps his cool, and his stiff upper lip, in yet another mission against the Germans. The books are still in print, and remain popular.*

and Ginger. Some of the earlier Biggles books have been criticised for jingoism and insulting references to foreigners.

Billy Bunter Fat schoolboy-hero of stories by 'Frank Richards' – pseudonym of the writer Charles Hamilton – first published in the children's magazine *Magnet*. Bunter attends the public school Greyfriars, where his notorious greed and craftiness continually get him into trouble often leading to anguished cries such as 'Yaroooh, you rotters! Oh, crikey!'

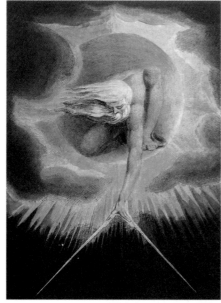

CREATIVE ENERGY *Blake's engraving* The Ancient of Days *(1794) was the frontispiece to his poem 'Europe'. It shows God measuring the Universe with a pair of compasses.*

Billy Liar Comic novel by Keith Waterhouse, published in 1959. Billy is a young undertaker's clerk who uses fantasy, make-believe and downright lying to escape the dullness of his family and home town.

Black Beauty Children's classic written by Anna Sewell and popular ever since its publication in 1877. It describes the experiences of a black mare which suffers at the hands of several cruel masters before eventually finding a kind owner.

Blake, William (1757-1827) Visionary English poet and one of the most important early figures in ▷ROMANTICISM. An engraver by trade, Blake illustrated and printed most of his works himself. They brought little reward during his lifetime, but he is now considered one of Britain's greatest poets. Many of Blake's works contain ▷ALLEGORY and symbolism that makes them difficult to understand, but verses such as 'The Lamb', 'The TYGER' and 'Jerusalem', which opens 'And did those feet in ancient time/Walk upon England's mountains green?', are widely known and loved.

blank verse Unrhyming verse, usually with five stresses per line which is very close to the natural rhythm of speech. It is the commonest form of English dramatic verse perfected in the works of Shakespeare and his contemporaries.

Bleak House Novel by Charles DICKENS, published in 1852-3 in monthly instalments. The story revolves around a lawsuit which drags on for decades and almost destroys the lives of the central characters. Such suits, which were common in Dickens's day, frequently ruined the litigants, while benefiting the greedy lawyers.

Bloomsbury Group Influential group of writers, artists and intellectuals who met at the Bloomsbury home of the novelist Virginia WOOLF and her artist sister Vanessa Bell during the early years of the century. The members included the writers E.M. FORSTER and Lytton Strachey, the economist John Maynard ▷KEYNES, the painter Duncan Grant and the art critic Roger Fry. They were devoted to friendship, conversation, art, and the rejection of Victorian standards of morality.

Blyton, Enid (1897-1968) Best-selling children's author known for her 'NODDY', 'Famous Five' and 'Secret Seven' series.
🖉 Enid Blyton's books have been accused of racism and sexism; new versions exclude such characters as the 'naughty Golliwog'.

Booker prize Name by which Britain's oldest major literary award – the Booker McConnell Prize for Fiction – is generally known. It was founded in 1969 and the prize of around £20 000 is awarded annually to a novel in English published within the last 12 months. The selection is made by a panel of literary figures who publish their shortlist before the award is made. Their choice is frequently the subject of public debate. Well-known winners include V.S. Naipaul, Iris Murdoch, William Golding and Salman Rushdie.

Boswell, James (1740-95) Scottish lawyer and writer, best known for his biography of his friend Samuel JOHNSON, which was published in 1791. 'Boswell' has become a general term for a biographer, as

LITERARY SISTERS *This group portrait of Charlotte, Emily and Anne Brontë was painted by their brother Branwell. A ghostly smudge marks the place where he humbly erased himself from the scene.*

in 'James Joyce found his Boswell in Richard Ellmann'. It can also sometimes mean simply a devoted admirer.

Brave New World Futuristic novel by the British author Aldous Huxley, published in 1932. It is set in a time when society is governed by science, and solutions have supposedly been found to all human problems. The main character is an intellectual, Bernard Marx, who in his travels encounters 'Savages' who still lead lives of unscientific disorder. Marx returns to London accompanied by a Savage, and the book ends with a debate on human freedom versus scientific determinism.
The book's title comes from Shakespeare's play The TEMPEST in which Miranda, brought up alone on an island, catches her first glimpse of a man other than her father. 'O brave new world,' she exclaims, 'that has such people in it.'

Brer Rabbit Wily animal character from black American folklore used by the 19th-century American author Joel Chandler Harris in his 'Uncle Remus' tales.
'Brer' is a dialect version of 'brother'.

Brontë, Charlotte, Emily and Anne Three daughters of a Yorkshire clergyman who were all novelists. They lost their mother in early childhood but, with their brother Branwell (1817-48), lived a rich imaginative life, inventing fantasy worlds, writing stories and poems, and producing their own miniature magazine. In later life Charlotte (1816-55) became a teacher and governess, and went on to write novels including the romantic tale JANE EYRE. Emily (1818-48), who also worked as a governess, is known both for her poems and for WUTHERING HEIGHTS – a tragic masterpiece set on the Yorkshire moors, which she loved passionately. Anne (1820-49) was the author of two novels – *Agnes Grey* and *The Tenant of Wildfell Hall*. Branwell, who showed great early promise both as a writer and a painter, became an alcoholic and an opium addict. Tragically, he, Emily and Anne died of tuberculosis during 1848-9.

Brooke, Rupert (1887-1915) Poet best known for his light verse and romantic view of rural England. Brooke wrote a sequence of war poems before his death; he died of blood poisoning on his way to the

Dardanelles. His sentiments are often idealistic and patriotic, as in these lines from 'The Soldier':
    If I should die, think only this of me;
    That there's some corner of a foreign
    field
    That is forever England.

Brookner, Anita (1928-) Novelist and former art historian who began writing fiction in middle age. Her heroines are innocent romantics who find to their cost that in life – unlike literature – there are few happy endings. Her novel *Hôtel du Lac* won the 1984 Booker prize.

Browning, Elizabeth Barrett (1806-61) Poet and wife of the poet Robert BROWNING. Elizabeth Barrett is known for her works *Aurora Leigh* and *Sonnets from the Portuguese*, one of which begins 'How do I love thee? Let me count the ways.'
The Brownings' romantic courtship inspired the play *The Barretts of Wimpole Street* by Rudolf Besier.

Browning, Robert (1812-89) Romantic poet whose many works include 'The Pied Piper of Hamelin' and 'My Last Duchess'. In 1846 Browning eloped with the poet Elizabeth Barrett and took her to live in Italy, where he remained until her death.

Buchan, John (1875-1940) Author of action stories such as *The Thirty-Nine Steps* and *Greenmantle*, featuring Richard Hannay and other similar heroes. His books contain vivid descriptions of landscapes from the Cotswolds and Scotland to Canada and South Africa – all of which he knew from first-hand experience. Buchan also worked in the foreign service, and became governor-general of Canada.

Bunyan, John (1628-88) Puritan preacher and writer of religious works such as THE PILGRIM'S PROGRESS. In 1660 he was arrested for preaching without a licence and imprisoned for 12 years in Bedford jail.

Burgess, Anthony (1917-93) Prolific novelist born and brought up in Manchester (as John Anthony Burgess Wilson) but later living on the Continent. Burgess began writing in middle age after a period of colonial service in Malaysia and Borneo. His best-known novel is ▷A CLOCKWORK ORANGE, which deals with man's capacity to choose evil of his own free will, and which was made into a film by Stanley Kubrick in 1971. Burgess's other works include *The Malayan Trilogy* and three humorous novels about a minor poet called Enderby.

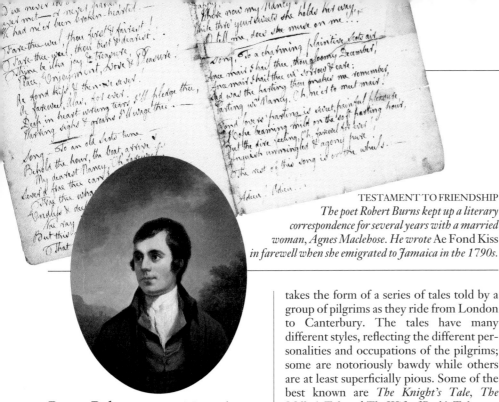

TESTAMENT TO FRIENDSHIP
The poet Robert Burns kept up a literary correspondence for several years with a married woman, Agnes Maclehose. He wrote Ae Fond Kiss *in farewell when she emigrated to Jamaica in the 1790s.*

Burns, Robert (1759-96) Poet who rose from a poor farming background to become one of Scotland's greatest writers of verse, known particularly for poems in the Scottish dialect such as 'To a Mouse', 'A Red, Red Rose', 'John Anderson, my Jo', and the well-known 'Auld Lang Syne'.
🖌 Some of his lines have become proverbial such as 'The best-laid schemes o' mice an' men/ Gang aft a-gley' (often go astray).
🖌 Burns's birthday, January 25 (Burns Night), is celebrated with whisky and haggis by Scots the world over.

Butler, Samuel (1835-1902) Author best known for the satirical fantasy *Erewhon* (an anagram of 'nowhere') which is set in a topsy-turvy land where none of the normal rules apply: for example, crime is considered an illness and illness a crime.

Byron, Lord George Gordon (1788-1824) English poet known for his sexual exploits and rebelliousness as well as for his verse. He was a leading figure in romanticism, although both his life and works were attacked for immorality – particularly his long satirical poem *Don Juan*. Byron had a deep love of Greece and in 1824 joined the Greek struggle against the occupying Turks. Before he saw active combat, however, he died from a fever.
🖌 The epithet 'Mad, bad, and dangerous to know' was applied to Byron by the novelist and socialite Lady Caroline Lamb, who had a passionate affair with him.

Canterbury Tales, The Greatest work of the medieval English poet Geoffrey CHAUCER. Written in the late 14th century in Middle English, the 17 000-line poem takes the form of a series of tales told by a group of pilgrims as they ride from London to Canterbury. The tales have many different styles, reflecting the different personalities and occupations of the pilgrims; some are notoriously bawdy while others are at least superficially pious. Some of the best known are *The Knight's Tale, The Miller's Tale* and *The Wife of Bath's Tale*.

Carey, Peter (1943-) Australian writer whose novel *Oscar and Lucinda* (1988) won the Booker prize. Other works include *Bliss* (1981) and *Illywhacker* (1985).

Carroll, Lewis Pseudonym of the writer, mathematician and Oxford don, Charles Lutwidge Dodgson (1832-98), author of the children's classics – ALICE'S ADVENTURES IN WONDERLAND, THROUGH THE LOOKING-GLASS and the mock-heroic nonsense poem The HUNTING OF THE SNARK.

Carter, Angela (1940-1992) Writer of ▷MAGIC REALISM whose books include *Nights at the Circus* (1984) and *Wise Children* (1991). She scripted the film *The Company of Wolves* (1984) – based on one of her stories.

TELLERS OF TALES *Chaucer's pilgrims prepare for the ride to Canterbury, in a detail from an engraving by William Blake. At the centre of the party are the jovial Host and the Prioress.*

Cartland, Barbara (1901-) One of the world's most prolific authors, with some 600 romantic novels to her name and a worldwide readership of over 650 million. She is known for her professional approach, dictating her novels into a tape recorder at the rate of about 23 a year.

Catch-22 Satirical war novel by the American author Joseph Heller, published in 1961. 'Catch-22' is a provision in army regulations which stipulates that a soldier's request to be relieved from active duty can be accepted only if he is mentally unfit to fight. Any soldier, however, who has the sense to ask to be spared the horrors of war is obviously mentally sound, and therefore must stay to fight.
🖌 A 'Catch-22 [situation]' means a predicament in which the alternatives are equally undesirable and mutually exclusive, leaving no means of escape.

Catcher in the Rye, The Novel by the American author J.D. Salinger, published in 1951. It relates the experiences of Holden Caulfield, a sensitive and idealistic but sceptical youth who runs away from boarding school to New York, and attacks the phoniness of the adult world.

Cavalier poets A group of witty and sophisticated 17th-century poets, including Robert Herrick and Richard Lovelace, who were strong supporters of Charles I in the English ▷CIVIL WAR.

Celtic Twilight Name given to the Irish literary revival of the late 19th and early 20th centuries, involving writers such as W.B. YEATS, Sean O'CASEY and J.M. SYNGE. The term comes from a collection of Yeats's stories published in 1893.

Chandler, Raymond (1888-1959) American writer of detective fiction, who only began writing at the age of 44. He is known for his dry, ironic style and for creating Philip Marlowe – a tough, witty and eccentric private detective. Chandler's most successful books include *The Big Sleep, Farewell, My Lovely* and *The Long Goodbye*, all of which have been filmed.

Charge of the Light Brigade, The Poem written by TENNYSON in 1854, about a disastrous British cavalry charge in the Crimean War, in which nearly 250 soldiers were killed or wounded. The poem contains the lines:

Theirs not to make reply,
Theirs not to reason why,
Theirs but to do and die.

Chaucer, Geoffrey (*c.*1343-1400) One of the greatest English poets and the most renowned of those who wrote in Middle English. Although Chaucer came from a middle-class background and was the son of a wine merchant, he married into the aristocracy and held several positions in the service of the Crown and at the court of John of Gaunt, where his literary talents were highly appreciated. As a diplomat Chaucer travelled abroad to France and Italy, and his work was much influenced by Italian literature, particularly the works of ▷DANTE and ▷BOCCACCIO. Some of Boccaccio's stories are retold in Chaucer's best-known work, The CANTERBURY TALES.

CHESHIRE CAT *John Tenniel's line drawings created the popular view of Alice and of other Lewis Carroll characters. He never drew from life, claiming that he could remember his observations.*

Cheshire cat Cat with an enormous grin encountered by Alice in ALICE'S ADVENTURES IN WONDERLAND by Lewis CARROLL. The cat tends to disappear, leaving only its smile hanging in the air.

Chesterton, G.K. (1874-1936) English journalist, poet, novelist and playwright. His best-known works include *The Man Who Was Thursday* and the Father Brown detective stories, such as *The Innocence of Father Brown*, which tell of an unassuming Roman Catholic priest with remarkable powers of deduction.

Christie, Dame Agatha (1890-1976) Writer of thrillers and detective fiction, and creator of Hercule POIROT, a precious and plump Belgian detective, and Miss MARPLE, an elderly spinster with a flair for solving mysterious crimes. Agatha Christie wrote nearly 70 detective novels, many of which have been filmed, including *Murder on the Orient Express* and *Death on the Nile*.
🕭 Agatha Christie's play *The Mousetrap* is the world's longest-running show, having played in London continuously since 1952.
🕭 In 1926, Agatha Christie created her own personal mystery: she disappeared for ten days, prompting nationwide concern, when she heard of her husband's love affair.

Christmas Carol, A Novel by DICKENS, published in 1843, about the spiritual conversion of the miser Ebenezer Scrooge. Following the appearance of the ghosts of Jacob Marley and of the Christmases Past, Present and Future, Scrooge becomes a reformed character. He gives money to the poor and delights the young family of his ill-used clerk Bob Cratchit by sending a Christmas turkey to his home.

Clarissa Extremely long tragic novel running to more than 1 million words in letter form, written around 1747 by the British author Samuel Richardson (1689-1761). The title character is a beautiful and virtuous young woman who is ill treated by her family and abducted by a rakish suitor, Lovelace. He keeps her captive and then drugs and rapes her, after which she dies.

Coleridge, Samuel Taylor (1772-1834) Leading poet, philosopher and critic of English ▷ROMANTICISM. During the 1790s Coleridge became a close friend of the poet William WORDSWORTH and his sister Dorothy. For a while they lived close together in Somerset, where Coleridge wrote some of his greatest poems, including KUBLA KHAN and The RIME OF THE ANCIENT MARINER. For much of his life he suffered from ill health and opium addiction. In his later years he turned increasingly to writing criticism.

'Come live with me and be my love' Opening line of *The Passionate Shepherd to His Love*, by the 16th-century poet Christopher MARLOWE. The shepherd paints a sensuous picture of rustic pleasures in order to woo his lady.
🕭 The poet John DONNE wrote a pastiche of Marlowe's poem called *The Bait*, which exposes the snares that could lie in wait for an unwary maiden.

Conrad, Joseph (1857-1924) Novelist and short-story writer, born in the Ukraine to Polish parents and whose real name was Teodor Jozef Konrad Nalecz Korzen-

ALL MY OWN WORK *Agatha Christie is shown here at her home in Wallingford, Berkshire, in 1950, surrounded by her novels. In all, she published 82 books in a literary career spanning half a century.*

iowski. Both his mother and father died when he was young, and at the age of 14 he began a seafaring career aboard a French ship. He later became master of a British vessel and, in 1886, a British citizen. His experiences at sea and abroad in southeast Asia and the Belgian Congo (now Zaire) inspired much of his writing. English was Conrad's third language, but novels such as *Chance* and *Lord Jim*, and the novella HEART OF DARKNESS have established him as a 20th-century master. His works deal with themes of human weakness and the devastating effects of corrupted idealism.

Cookson, Catherine (1906–) One of Britain's most popular novelists ever. She has written more than 80 books and sold more than 85 million copies worldwide. In addition, her books continue year after year to top the public library lending records. They are frequently set in the northeast of England, where she was born, and concentrate on unglamorous working-class family life and historical adventures.

Catherine Cookson has also written under the pseudonym Catherine Marchant.

cummings, e e (1894-1962) American poet who spurned the use of many conventions of standard written English, including capital letters. His poetry is often ironic in tone, and covers subjects as disparate as love and public institutions.

Dahl, Roald (1916-90) British writer who became known in the 1960s for collections of macabre short stories such as *Kiss, Kiss*, and for children's tales of fantasy such as *Charlie and the Chocolate Factory* – a world best seller which tells the story of a boy who wins a tour around a bizarre sweet-making plant – and its sequel *Charlie and the Great Glass Elevator*.

Some adults consider Dahl's books gruesome, but his brand of surreal, naïve horror appeals to children.

David Copperfield Novel by Charles DICKENS, published in instalments during 1849 and 1850, and largely based on events in Dickens's own life. The story begins with the birth of David Copperfield and follows his experiences as he is sent away to school and then to work while still very young. Gradually David grows to manhood, eventually achieving fame as an author and marrying first a child-bride Dora and then, after her death, the loyal and good Agnes.

Part of Dickens's purpose in writing his grim account of David's boyhood was to expose the cruel conditions of child labour he had witnessed in Britain.

CHARLES DICKENS: CREATOR OF CHARACTERS

Dickens had a great gift for bringing to life the characters in his novels. Few were based directly on real people (though the novelist himself provided the model for David Copperfield), but readers have always responded as if they were reading about flesh and blood people. The plight of Little Nell in the instalments of *The Old Curiosity Shop* aroused such public emotion that Dickens was flooded with letters begging him to let her live, and he admitted that the story was breaking his own heart.

'God bless us every one!'
Tiny Tim
A Christmas Carol

'It's always best on these occasions to do what the mob do.'
'But suppose there are two mobs?' suggested Mr Snodgrass.
'Shout with the largest,' replied Mr Pickwick.
Pickwick Papers

'Bah! . . . Humbug!'
Ebenezer Scrooge
A Christmas Carol

in came little Bob, the father . . . his threadbare clothes darned up and brushed, to look seasonable; and Tiny Tim upon his shoulder.
Bob Cratchit
A Christmas Carol

the solemn presence . . . on every side, of Death – filled her with deep and thoughtful feelings, but with none of terror or alarm.
Little Nell
The Old Curiosity Shop

'Oliver Twist has asked for more!'
Mr Bumble
Oliver Twist

Uriah, with his long hands slowly twining over one another, made a ghastly writhe from the waist upwards.
Uriah Heep
David Copperfield

Defoe, Daniel (1660-1731) Writer of a large number of political and religious tracts, and also books including *A Journal of the Plague Year, Moll Flanders* and ROBINSON CRUSOE, which combine factual detail with highly imaginative writing.

🕯Because of his mastery of sustained story-telling in prose, Defoe is sometimes called the first true English novelist.

Dickens, Charles (1812-70) One of Britain's greatest novelists, and author of such works as A CHRISTMAS CAROL, DAVID COPPERFIELD, GREAT EXPECTATIONS, PICKWICK PAPERS and OLIVER TWIST. Dickens wrote 20 novels, many as serials in magazines which became very popular as a result. His writing combines humour, warmth, sentiment and often pathos to paint a detailed picture of life in Victorian times, including suffering and injustice, which he worked hard to expose. Dickens's novels are notable for their memorable characters such as Uriah Heep, Scrooge and Mr Micawber. (See box, left.)

Doctor Dolittle Main character in a series of children's books written by Hugh Lofting (1886-1947). Doctor Dolittle is a kind and eccentric doctor who looks after animals and is able to talk to them.

Dr Faustus, The Tragical History of Play written by Christopher MARLOWE in the late 16th century but based on a tale dating from medieval times. ▷FAUST, a scholar and magician, pledges his soul to the devil in return for 24 years of life during which his wishes will be fulfilled. These include calling up the spirit of Helen of Troy, reputedly the most beautiful woman in history, whom Faust addresses with the words 'Was this the face that launched a thousand ships . . . ?' The final scene is a harrowing portrayal of Faust's torment as the hour of his death approaches.

Dr Jekyll and Mr Hyde Novel by Robert Louis STEVENSON, published in 1886. The well-intentioned experiments of the good scientist Dr Jekyll periodically turn him into the sadistic Mr Hyde.

🕯Dr Jekyll and Mr Hyde provide a literary example of a dual personality, and the two characters are often used as symbols of the good and evil sides of an individual.

Donne, John (1572-1631) English poet and Dean of St Paul's Cathedral in London. Donne is known for witty and passionate love poetry, for sermons and holy poems, and for his use of intricate metaphors, as in *A Valediction Forbidding Mourning,* where the souls of two lovers are compared with the legs of mathematical compasses. (See METAPHYSICAL POETS.)

Doyle, Sir Arthur Conan (1859-1930) Writer of historical and detective fiction, and creator of the character Sherlock HOLMES who solves crimes by brilliant deductions from tiny pieces of evidence. Doyle's best-known works include *A Study in Scarlet* and *The Hound of the Baskervilles*.

Drabble, Margaret (1939-   ) Novelist known for books mainly about the lives of middle-class women. Her works include *A Summer Birdcage* and *The Radiant Way*.

Dryden, John (1631-1700) Poet, dramatist and critic known for his biting satire and works on public, political and religious topics. These include the tragedy *All For Love* (1677), the comedy *Marriage à la Mode* (1673), which are still performed, and the poem *Absalom and Achitophel*. Much of Dryden's work was inspired by several Classical authors, and he made many translations from Greek and Latin. In 1668 he became poet laureate.

du Maurier, Daphne (1907-89) Writer of historical romances and novels concerned with family history and mysteries about the past. Her books include *Jamaica Inn, Frenchman's Creek* and *Rebecca* – a

---

PICNIC AT POLKERRIS COVE *Daphne du Maurier wrote much of* Rebecca *at Menabilly, her house near this Cornish beach which she used as the model for the fictional Manderley.*

20th-century Gothic novel about a young woman whose husband Max de Winter is obsessed by memories of his dead first wife, Rebecca. It is largely set in the house they shared, hauntingly beautiful Manderley.

🕯The film of *Rebecca* (1940), which starred Laurence Olivier, was Alfred Hitchcock's first Hollywood production.

Eliot, George Pseudonym of Mary Ann Evans (1819-80), author of *The Mill on the Floss, Silas Marner, Adam Bede, Middlemarch* and other books, and generally regarded as one of the greatest English novelists. Her works deal with moral issues in human relationships – often between incompatible individuals – and the conflict between duty and social convention on the one hand and personal feelings on the other.

🕯George Eliot lived for many years with the writer G.H. Lewes but was never able to marry him because he could not obtain a divorce from his estranged wife.

Eliot, T.S. (1888-1965) American-born author, who settled in Britain in 1914. Eliot wrote poems, plays and essays, and urged the use of ordinary language and images from everyday life in poetry. He was much concerned with the emptiness of modern life and the need for a revitalisation of religion. Among his best-known works are the poems *The Love Song of J. Alfred Prufrock*, The WASTE LAND and *Four Quartets*, and the play *Murder in the Cathedral*, about the death of Thomas Becket. He won the Nobel prize for literature in 1948.

🕯In 1981 a collection of Eliot's comic poems, *Old Possum's Book of Practical Cats*, was turned into the musical *Cats* by Andrew Lloyd Webber.

Emma Novel by Jane AUSTEN, published in 1816 and regarded by many as her best work. The heroine, Emma Woodhouse, is a talented and attractive young woman who is, however, just a little too pleased with herself and a little too keen to meddle in the lives of others. Her actions upset many people and nearly cause disaster on several occasions. However, Emma eventually learns her lesson and is rewarded by marriage to the chivalrous Mr Knightley.

Everyman Early 16th-century morality play. As death approaches, Everyman finds himself deserted by old associates Fellowship, Kindred, Cousin, and Goods, and therefore reliant on Good Deeds and Knowledge, who speaks the lines:

> Everyman, I will go with thee and be thy
>   guide,
> In thy most need to go by thy side.

Faerie Queene, The Long and complex poem in six books by the 16th-century English poet Edmund SPENSER. It takes the form of an ▷ALLEGORY, with the Faerie Queene representing both the monarch, Elizabeth I, and the abstract idea of Glory. Various knights, representing virtues, set out on adventures in her name.

Fall of the House of Usher, The Horror story by Edgar Allan POE, published in 1840. It describes the macabre deaths of the last two members of the Usher family, and the spectacular destruction of their ancestral mansion.

Falstaff Endearing, fat rogue who appears in several of Shakespeare's plays, notably *The Merry Wives of Windsor* and *Henry IV*. Falstaff is a lover of wine, women and song. Although he is a coward, he often tells tales of his supposed bravery.

Fanny Hill Sexually explicit mid-18th-century novel by John Cleland (1709-89), originally published as *Memoirs of a Woman of Pleasure*. It enjoyed great success, and although Cleland was summonsed for indecency he was discharged.

Far from the Madding Crowd Novel by Thomas HARDY, published in 1874. It tells the story of farmer Bathsheba Everdene and her three suitors – the good-hearted Gabriel Oak, the dashing Sergeant Troy and the wealthy Farmer Boldwood.
🗝The title comes from a line in GRAY'S ELEGY which says of those buried in the country churchyard: 'Far from the madding crowd's ignoble strife/ Their sober wishes never learned to stray.'

Faulkner, William (1897-1962) American author of powerful, symbolic novels, mostly set in the southern states of the USA. His books include *As I Lay Dying*, which he wrote in six weeks, *Absalom, Absalom!* and *The Sound and the Fury*. He won the Nobel prize for literature in 1949.

Fielding, Henry (1707-54) Lawyer and author with a witty style and a humane, tolerant outlook. Fielding's best-known books are the comic novel *Joseph Andrews* and the ▷PICARESQUE adventure tale TOM JONES. His work helped to establish the position of the novel in English literature and paved the way for later writers such as Dickens and Thackeray.

Fitzgerald, F. Scott (1896-1940) American author of novels and short stories about fashionable life in the Jazz Age of the

HIGH SOCIETY *F. Scott Fitzgerald and his wife Zelda lived the American Dream and experienced the glamorous life they wrote about.*

1920s, such as *This Side of Paradise* and *The Diamond as Big as the Ritz*. His best-known work is *The Great Gatsby*, about the destructive passion of the millionaire Jay Gatsby for his former mistress Daisy Buchanan. During the 1920s Fitzgerald was one of several American writers, including Ernest Hemingway, to live in Paris.

Fleming, Ian (1908-64) Journalist and author who worked in Naval Intelligence during World War II, and afterwards wrote thrillers featuring the suave, sophisticated British secret agent James ▷BOND. The first of 12 Bond novels, *Casino Royale*, was published in 1953. Fleming is also remembered for his *Chitty-Chitty-Bang-Bang* series of children's stories.

Forster, E.M. (1879-1970) Novelist, short-story writer, critic and member of the BLOOMSBURY GROUP. In his novels, Forster considered plots to be somewhat incidental; he was more interested in characterisation and themes. He championed the values of individualism, imagination and sincerity against narrow-mindedness and prejudice of all forms.
🗝Several successful films have been made from Forster's novels, including David Lean's A PASSAGE TO INDIA and the Merchant/Ivory productions of *A Room with a View* and *Howards End*.

Forsyte Saga, The Sequence of three novels by John Galsworthy (1867-1933), dealing with the affairs of the large and prosperous Forsyte family. The story is continued in a second trilogy, *A Modern Comedy*, and in various other shorter pieces.
🗝*The Forsyte Saga* was made into a celebrated BBC television serial in 1967.

Forsyth, Frederick (1928-) Best-selling author of suspense thrillers including *The Day of the Jackal* and *The Odessa File*. His books are known for the accuracy of their research, down to the smallest detail, and their meticulous and compelling plots.

'for whom the bell tolls' Phrase from a sermon by the 17th-century poet and divine, John DONNE, in which he expresses a view of human brotherhood: 'Any man's death diminishes me, because I am involved in mankind; and therefore never send to know for whom the bell tolls; it tolls for thee.' The sermon begins with the words 'No man is an island'.
🗝Ernest HEMINGWAY used the words 'for whom the bell tolls' as the title of a novel set during the Spanish Civil War.

Fowles, John (1926-) Schoolteacher who turned to writing in the 1960s and made his name with disturbing psychological novels such as *The Collector* and *The Magus*. One of his most experimental works, *The French Lieutenant's Woman*, offers two different endings; a film version (1981) starred Meryl Streep and Jeremy Irons.

Frankenstein Gothic novel by Mary Shelley, wife of the poet Percy Bysshe Shelley, published in 1818. The title character, Dr Victor Frankenstein, makes a man-like monster from parts of corpses, and brings it to life by electricity. Horrible to look at but capable of human emotion, the creature is eaten up by loneliness and begs for a mate. When Frankenstein refuses, it unleashes vengeance.
🗝The monster itself is often incorrectly referred to as Frankenstein.

Frost, Robert (1874-1963) American nature poet known for such works as 'Mending Wall', 'The Road not Taken' and 'Stopping by Woods on a Snowy Evening', which contains the lines:
> The woods are lovely, dark and deep.
> But I have promises to keep,
> And miles to go before I sleep.

Gaskell, Mrs Elizabeth (1810-65) Novelist who wrote about social issues and relationships in books such as *Mary Barton*, a love story set against desperate poverty in Manchester in the 1840s, and *Cranford*, which sketches provincial life.

'Gather ye rosebuds while ye may' First line of the 17th-century poem *To the Virgins, to Make Much of Time* by Robert Herrick (1591-1674). The poem urges young people to make the most of life – in particular, of love – while they can.

Globe Theatre Octagonal theatre in Southwark, London, where William SHAKESPEARE acted and many of his plays were produced. The thatched roof caught fire in 1613 and the building was destroyed. It was rebuilt the following year but demolished 30 years later. In 1989 the foundations of the Globe were unearthed and a reconstruction of the theatre started on a site nearby.

Golding, William (1911-93) Writer who made his name in the 1950s with LORD OF THE FLIES, a novel about a group of boys stranded on a deserted island, where the law of the jungle quickly asserts itself. Many of Golding's other novels, such as *Pincher Martin*, also deal with people in isolated or extreme positions, who battle to survive without the normal supports of civilisation. His novel *Rites of Passage* won the Booker prize in 1980, and Golding won the Nobel prize for literature in 1983.

Goldsmith, Oliver (*c.*1728-74) Irish writer known for the novel *The Vicar of Wakefield*, about the good-hearted Dr Primrose who battles to save his family from debt and dishonour, and the play *She Stoops to Conquer*, a comedy based on the misunderstandings that arise when some travellers mistake a private home for an inn. The great Shakespearean actor/manager David Garrick said of Goldsmith: '[He] wrote like an angel, but talk'd like poor Poll.'

Graves, Robert (1895-1985) British poet, novelist and critic. His books include an autobiography of his early life and experiences in World War I, *Goodbye to All That*; two novels set in ancient Rome, *I, Claudius* and *Claudius the God*; and works about mythology, including *The White Goddess* and *Greek Myths*.

Gray's Elegy Popular name for the poem *Elegy Written in a Country Church-Yard* by Thomas Gray (1716-71). The poem begins by considering the lives of those who lie buried in the village churchyard and then turns into a meditation on death. It contains many well-known lines, such as 'Full many a flower is born to blush unseen,/And waste its sweetness on the desert air'.

Great Expectations Novel by Charles DICKENS, published in monthly instalments from 1860 to 1861. The story concerns a young man, Pip, who develops grandiose ambitions when he starts to receive anonymous gifts of money. Pip is in love with the beautiful Estella but she has been brought up by her aunt Miss Havisham to break men's hearts. Pip left his friends and embarked on a new life in London. However, when he discovers that the source of his money is the ex-convict Abel Magwitch whom Pip helped many years before, Pip returns home mortified and repentant.

Greene, Graham (1904-91) One of the greatest British novelists of the 20th century, also known for his short stories, essays, plays and other writings. Greene joined the Roman Catholic Church in 1926 and elements of Catholic doctrine – such as sin, damnation and redemption – are central to many of his novels. He wrote a large number of these, including *Stamboul Train*, a thriller which takes place on the Orient Express, *The Honorary Consul* which is set in South America, and *The Heart of the Matter*, whose main character, a police officer in West Africa, is driven to dishonesty and eventual suicide by a combination of good motives and treacherous circumstances. Greene classed some of his works as 'entertainments', including one of his best-known novels, *Brighton Rock* – a story set against the background of gang warfare in Brighton. A young and vicious criminal, 'Pinkie', commits murder and marries the innocent Rose to stop her testifying against him. However, Pinkie is pursued by a friend of the victim and is eventually killed. Greene's other books include *The Quiet American*, *Our Man in Havana*, *The Comedians* and *Travels with my Aunt*. Greene's novel *The Third Man* was originally written as a screenplay. It was filmed in 1949 and starred Orson Welles.

Grossmith, George and Weedon Two brothers who together wrote the comic and hugely popular *The Diary of a Nobody* which pokes fun at the genteel pretensions of its hero, the clerk Charles Pooter. It was published first as a column in *Punch* in the 1890s and later in novel form.

Gulliver's Travels Satire on human folly by Jonathan SWIFT, published in 1726. Lemuel Gulliver is shipwrecked on the island of Lilliput, where the inhabitants are just six inches tall but take themselves and their petty squabbles very seriously – a satire on contemporary English politics and self-importance. Gulliver then travels to

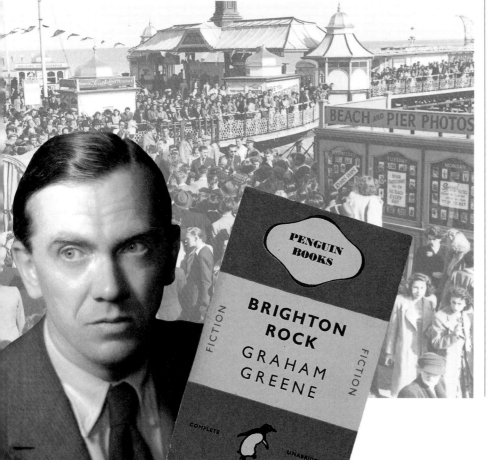

MORAL NARRATIVE *A convert to Roman Catholicism, Graham Greene dealt with good and evil in his novels.* Brighton Rock *(1948 film still, background) is a stark portrayal of human brutality.*

ALAS, POOR YORICK *Laurence Olivier as the prince laments an old friend in one of the most moving scenes from* Hamlet. *Olivier also directed this 1947 film version of William Shakespeare's tragedy.*

Brobdingnag, a land of giants, and to Laputa where the professors are so involved with projects such as extracting sunshine from cucumbers that practical matters are quite forgotten. His last encounters are with noble, intelligent horses called Houyhnhnms and brutish, degraded men called Yahoos. Gulliver finally returns home and finds himself unable to tolerate even his own family.

Hamlet Tragedy by William SHAKE-SPEARE, written around 1599-1601. Before the play opens, the king of Denmark has been murdered by his brother, Claudius, who has taken the throne and married the queen, Gertrude. The ghost of the dead king visits his son, Prince Hamlet, and urges him to avenge the murder. Hamlet, tormented by this revelation, appears to be mad and cruelly rejects Ophelia whom he loved. Using a troupe of visiting players to act out his father's death, the prince prompts Claudius to expose his guilt. Hamlet then kills Ophelia's father Polonius in mistake for Claudius, and Claudius tries but fails to have Hamlet killed. Ophelia drowns herself in grief, and her brother Laertes fights a duel with Hamlet. The play ends with the death by poison of the main characters and the arrival of Fortinbras, prince of Norway, who assumes control.

🔖 Hamlet's dilemma is often seen as typical of those whose thoughtful nature prevents quick and decisive action.

🔖 *Hamlet* contains several fine examples of ▷SOLILOQUY, such as 'TO BE OR NOT TO BE' and Hamlet's earlier speech lamenting his mother's hasty remarriage and Claudius' reign which opens 'O! that this too too solid flesh would melt'. Much-quoted lines include 'Neither a borrower nor a lender be', 'Something is rotten in the state of Denmark', 'Brevity is the soul of wit', 'To sleep: perchance to dream: ay, there's the rub;' 'The lady doth protest too much, methinks,' and 'Alas, poor Yorick'.

Hardy, Thomas (1840-1928) Writer of novels, short stories and poems, many set in the West Country – 'Wessex'. His best-known works are the novels FAR FROM THE MADDING CROWD, *Jude the Obscure*, *The Mayor of Casterbridge* and *Tess of the D'Urbervilles*. Hardy's main theme is the struggle of the individual against the impersonal, and sometimes hostile, forces of nature and fate that determine events. Although their endings are often tragic, Hardy's books are full of humour and human sympathy.

He wrote more than 900 poems dealing with deeply personal subjects, including reminiscences of his first wife, Emma.

Hawthorne, Nathaniel (1804-64) American author best known for *The Scarlet Letter*, a novel about the brutal treatment meted out to an adulterous wife in 17th-century Boston. His children's stories, such as *Tanglewood Tales*, are also well known.

Heaney, Seamus (1939-) Irish poet who writes unsentimentally about nature in both its destructive and creative aspects, the relationship of man to the earth, and various social and political issues, particularly those connected with Ireland.

Heart of Darkness Novella by Joseph CONRAD, published in 1902. The narrator Marlow tells of a journey upriver in Africa to find a successful ivory dealer called Mr Kurtz, who is ill. When he finds Kurtz, Marlow discovers that hideous barbarism and corruption underlie the dealer's achievements. At the end, in bitter self-recrimination, Kurtz dies uttering the words 'The horror! The horror!'

🔖 The novel's theme inspired the Vietnam war film epic ▷APOCALYPSE NOW.

Hemingway, Ernest (1899-1961) American novelist and short-story writer known for tough, masculine subjects and an economical prose style. In such books as *A Farewell to Arms*, *The Sun Also Rises*, *Death in the Afternoon*, *For Whom the Bell Tolls* and *The Old Man and the Sea* he glorified heroic male exploits such as bullfighting, boxing, soldiering, safari hunting and game fishing – many of which he took part in himself. Hemingway also wrote collections of short stories such as *Men without Women*, and worked as a war correspondent. He won the Nobel prize for literature in 1954. In 1961 he shot himself after a long illness.

Henry IV, Parts 1 and 2 Two historical dramas by William SHAKESPEARE, written *c.*1597. Part 1 deals with the 15th-century rebellion of the Percys against the Crown, which was defeated by the king and Prince Hal, the prince of Wales, at Shrewsbury in 1403. In the course of the battle, Hal kills Harry Hotspur, the valiant eldest son of Henry Percy, the earl of Northumberland. A lighter subplot in the play concerns the riotous exploits of Hal, his friend Falstaff, and their underworld associates. In Part 2, Henry IV is obliged to put down another rebellion, while at the same time Hal and Falstaff continue their comic escapades. Towards the end, the king dies and Hal is crowned Henry V. Burdened with affairs of state, he leaves behind his former way of life and harshly rejects Falstaff's friendship, disowning him with the words, 'I know thee not, old man'.

Henry V Historical play by William SHAKESPEARE, written in 1599. The new king, Henry V, is advised that he has a claim to the French throne and wages war on France. After his rousing and patriotic speech – designed to increase his soldiers' comradeship, and which includes the line 'We few, we happy few, we band of brothers' – the English win a great victory at Agincourt. The play ends with peace re-established and Henry courting Katherine of France.
♣Films of *Henry V* include a 1944 version, starring Laurence Olivier, and a 1989 version directed by Kenneth ▷BRANAGH in which he also played the title role.

Hiawatha, The Song of (1855) Epic poem by Henry Longfellow based on the legendary American Indian hero. It has a distinctive pulsating rhythm and begins:
By the shore of Gitche Gumee,
By the shining Big-Sea-Water,
Stood the wigwam of Nokomis . . .

Holmes, Sherlock Fictional English detective created by the writer Sir Arthur Conan DOYLE. Holmes's extraordinary powers of memory, observation and deduction enable him to solve the most baffling crimes from minute pieces of evidence. Holmes smokes a pipe, wears a deerstalker hat and cloak, takes opium and cocaine, and plays the violin. His arch-enemy is Professor James Moriarty. His companion and foil is Dr John Watson with whom he shares rooms at 221b Baker Street, London. Watson records Holmes' accomplishments but can hardly keep pace with his brilliant mind.
♣Sherlock Holmes is said to be based on Dr Joseph Bell, an eminent Edinburgh surgeon under whom Doyle, who practised medicine for some years, had studied.
♣The expression 'Elementary, my dear Watson' has become associated with Sherlock Holmes, but in fact these exact words never appear in any of Doyle's stories.

Hopkins, Gerard Manley (1844-89) Poet and Jesuit priest who used inventive and beautiful language to express the divinity he saw in man and nature. Two of Hopkins's best-known poems are *The Windhover*, which compares the mastery of a falcon riding the wind with the majesty of Christ, and *Pied Beauty* which begins 'Glory be to God for dappled things'.

Housman, A.E. (1859-1936) English poet best known for his collection of ballad-like verses *A Shropshire Lad*. They look back with nostalgia at a vision of country life which Housman calls 'the land of lost content', and deal with poignant themes of friendship, love, loss and death.

Huckleberry Finn, The Adventures of Novel by the American author Mark TWAIN, published in 1884 and the sequel to TOM SAWYER. 'Huck' Finn runs away from his father and travels down the Mississippi river on a raft with his friend Jim, a runaway slave. When Jim is captured, Huck helps him escape. The novel takes the form of an adventure story but is deeply concerned with issues such as slavery. The lessons Huck learns about life are its main theme.

Hughes, Ted (1930-) British poet known for works – such as the poem sequence *Crow* – which deal with the darker, more violent side of nature, including the human unconscious. Hughes was married to the writer and poet Sylvia PLATH, who later committed suicide. He was made poet laureate in 1984.

Hunting of the Snark, The Mock-heroic nonsense poem by Lewis CARROLL, published in 1867. Despite attempts by critics to interpret its apparent absurdity, he insisted there was no hidden meaning.

Isherwood, Christopher (1904-86) British novelist best known for his books *Mr Norris Changes Trains* and *Goodbye to Berlin*, which are largely based on his own experiences of living in Berlin in the early 1930s. He was an intimate friend and associate of the poet W.H. AUDEN.

'I wandered lonely as a cloud' First line of one of William WORDSWORTH's best-known poems. Wordsworth did not give the poem a title, but it is often referred to as 'Daffodils'. It begins:
I wandered lonely as a cloud
That floats on high, o'er vales and hills,
When all at once I saw a crowd,
A host, of golden daffodils.

Jabberwock Monster created by Lewis CARROLL in his semi-nonsense poem 'Jabberwocky' in THROUGH THE LOOKING-GLASS. In chapter VI of the book, Humpty Dumpty gives a partial explanation of the meaning of the first four lines:
Twas brillig, and the slithy toves
Did gyre and gimble in the wabe;
All mimsy were the borogoves,
And the mome raths outgrabe.

James, Henry (1843-1916) American writer who moved to Europe in his early thirties and eventually settled in Britain, where many of his best-known books were written. His novels include *Washington Square* and *The Bostonians*, both of which deal with the position of women in society, and *The Portrait of a Lady* and *The Ambassadors*, which are about Americans living in Europe. James's other works include *What Maisie Knew*, which describes adult corruption from a child's point of view, and the ghost story *The Turn of the Screw*, in which a governess becomes convinced that evil powers are threatening her young charges. The latter was made into a spine-chilling opera by Benjamin Britten in 1954.
♣James's prose is known for long, convoluted sentences and occasional obscurity.

James, P.D. (1920-) Crime writer who created the superior and poetic detective Adam Dalgleish in books such as *A Taste For Death* (1986). At one time, earlier in her career, James worked with the forensic science department at the Home Office.

Jane Eyre Romantic novel by Charlotte BRONTÉ, published in 1847. It describes how Jane, an orphan, becomes governess at Thornfield Hall and eventually marries its intense, brooding master, Mr Rochester.

Jerome, Jerome K. (1859-1927) English humorist remembered for writing *Three Men in a Boat*, a whimsical account of three friends' chaotic progress along the Thames between Kingston and Oxford.
♣Jerome's initial 'K' stands for 'Klapka'.

Johnson, Samuel (1709-84) Writer, wit, critic and lexicographer, best known for his *Dictionary of the English Language*, published in 1755. In it, Johnson defines more than 40 000 words and includes over 100 000 quotations illustrating their usage. The book remained the standard reference work until publication of the *Oxford English Dictionary* began in 1884.
♣A few entries in Johnson's dictionary contain his own eccentric interpretations – as for example: *lexicographer*, 'a writer of dictionaries, a harmless drudge'.
♣His devoted friend, the Scottish writer James Boswell, published his classic biography *Life of Samuel Johnson* in 1791.

Jonson, Ben (1572-1637) Dramatist and poet who was a contemporary of Shakespeare. His first success came with the comedy *Every Man in his Humour*, performed in 1598, and based on the medieval theory that certain humours, or liquids in the body determined a person's dominant temperament. This was followed the next year by *Every Man out of his Humour* and by a series of other comedies and satires. The best known are *Volpone* – about a wealthy man who exploits his relatives through feigning illness – and *The Alchemist*, which deals with the comings and goings of lowlife thieves and tricksters.

Joyce, James (1882-1941) Dublin-born author who left Ireland as a young man to escape what he saw as the narrowness of Irish society and the overwhelming influence of the Roman Catholic Church. Joyce lived in Paris, Trieste and Zurich, but the works for which he is known are all set in Ireland. His early books include the short-story collection *Dubliners* and the autobiographical novel *A Portrait of the Artist as a Young Man*, which chronicles the struggle of young Stephen Dedalus to establish himself as a poet. Stephen also appears in Joyce's best-known book, the controversial ULYSSES, which presents the events of a single day in Dublin. Both *Ulysses* and Joyce's other mature novel *Finnegans Wake* are known for their passages of ▷STREAM OF CONSCIOUSNESS writing.

Julius Caesar Tragedy by William SHAKESPEARE, probably written in 1599. It deals with the assassination of Julius Caesar and its aftermath, and is largely based on historical fact. The assassination is the work of a group of influential Romans – including Cassius and Brutus – who mistrust Caesar's ambitions. After the murder, an army is raised against them, Brutus's wife commits suicide, and Brutus and Cassius kill themselves after defeat at Philippi.

Jungle Book, The Collection of short stories for children by Rudyard KIPLING, published in 1894 and followed by *The Second Jungle Book*. Many of the stories feature Mowgli, a boy who is brought up by wolves and educated in the ways of the jungle by animals such as Baloo, the brown bear, and Bagheera, the black panther.
⚘ Mowgli and his friends are now, perhaps, best known to thousands of youngsters through Walt Disney's 1967 delightful animated film version of *The Jungle Book*.
⚘ *The Jungle Book* was the inspiration behind the Wolf Cubs, the junior division of the Boy Scouts, founded in 1916.

Keats, John (1795-1821) English poet who was one of the leading literary figures of ▷ROMANTICISM. Keats died of tuberculosis in Rome at the age of just 25, by which time he had written a number of great poems inspired by nature, art and mythology, and dealing with themes such as artistic creation and the relationship between art and life. The best known include ODE ON A GRECIAN URN, 'Ode to a Nightingale', 'To Autumn', *Hyperion*, and *Endymion*, which contains the line, 'A THING OF BEAUTY IS A JOY FOR EVER'. His work is known for its beauty and sensuousness. Keats is also remembered for his doomed love affair with Fanny Brawne, and for his many letters.

Keneally, Thomas Michael (1935-) Australian novelist whose book *Schindler's Ark* (1982), based on a true account of Polish Jews saved by a German industrialist during World War II, won the Booker prize. Steven ▷SPIELBERG turned it into a powerful film, *Schindler's List* (1994).

King James Bible The best-known English translation of the ▷BIBLE, sometimes referred to as the 'Authorised Version'. Commissioned by King James I, it was published in 1611 after three and a half years' work by nearly 50 experts. It had no rival among the English Protestant faiths until the late 19th-century Revised Version; the Roman Catholic Church continued to use the Latin Vulgate. The King James Bible is still widely used and much loved for its fine use of language.

King Lear Tragedy by William SHAKESPEARE, written in about 1605. It is based on a legendary British king who in old age unwisely hands over his kingdom to his two elder daughters, Goneril and Regan. The daughters turn on him, reducing him to poverty and, eventually, to madness. Lear's youngest daughter Cordelia, whom the king at first spurned, remains faithful to him and helps to raise an army against his enemies. She and Lear are captured, however, and she is hanged. Lear dies with her in his arms.
⚘ Many familiar lines come from *King Lear*, including: 'Nothing will come of nothing'; 'As flies to wanton boys, are we to the gods;/ They kill us for their sport'; and 'How sharper than a serpent's tooth it is/ To have a thankless child'.

Kipling, Rudyard (1865-1936) British author of poems, short stories and novels, many dealing with the British Empire, particularly the Indian Raj. Kipling was born in India, where he returned as an adult and worked as a journalist. He also travelled to the USA, and to South Africa during the Boer War. In 1907 he became the first English writer to receive the Nobel prize for literature. Kipling's best-known works are the children's books *Just So Stories*, The JUNGLE BOOK and *Kim*, and poems such as 'Mandalay', 'If' and 'Gunga Din'.

THE MIGHTY FALLEN *The great tiger Shere Khan is finally slain by Mowgli in the* Jungle Book *story 'Tiger! Tiger!' Rudyard Kipling began writing the stories in 1892 when he was living in the USA. They were based on his childhood memories of India and experiences he had there as a journalist during the 1880s.*

'Kubla Khan' Poem written by Samuel Taylor COLERIDGE in 1797, about the legendary palace built by the Chinese emperor ▷KUBLAI KHAN in Xanadu. The words of the poem are said to have come to Coleridge in a dream he had after taking opium. However, he was interrupted by 'a person . . . from Porlock' and the end of the poem was lost. The first and last few lines are best known:

> In Xanadu did Kubla Khan
> A stately pleasure-dome decree;
> Where Alph, the sacred river, ran
> Through caverns measureless to man
> Down to a sunless sea
> . . .
> Weave a circle round him thrice;
> And close your eyes with holy dread,
> For he on honey-dew hath fed,
> And drunk the milk of Paradise.

Kyd, Thomas (1558-94) Elizabethan dramatist best known for *The Spanish Tragedy*, a bloodthirsty play about political intrigue and revenge, set in Spain after the Spanish defeat of the Portuguese in 1580.
🔖 *The Spanish Tragedy* is thought to have influenced Shakespeare's tragedy HAMLET.

Lady Chatterley's Lover Novel by D.H. LAWRENCE, written in the 1920s but not published in full in Britain until 1960, because of its explicit sexual descriptions and strong language. It concerns a passionate love affair between Lady Chatterley, the wife of an intellectual but invalid land-owner, and the gamekeeper Oliver Mellors. Lady Chatterley becomes pregnant with Mellors's child, and despite the scandal she decides to turn her back on respectable society rather than deny her love.
🔖 In 1960 Penguin Books were prosecuted for publishing *Lady Chatterley's Lover*. They were acquitted, after which ▷CENSORSHIP laws were relaxed in Britain.

'Lady of Shalott, The' Poem by TENNYSON, based on medieval legend. It tells of a lady shut up in a tower on a river island. She is under a curse, and may only look at the world outside in a mirror. One day, hearing Sir ▷LANCELOT approach, she rushes to the window – and brings down the curse upon herself. She knows that death is near, leaves the tower and floats downstream in a boat, singing a last lament until she arrives – dead – at ▷CAMELOT.

Lake poets Group of 19th-century Romantic poets whose work is associated with the Lake District. They include Samuel Taylor COLERIDGE, Robert SOUTHEY and William WORDSWORTH.

Lamb, Charles (1775-1834) British author remembered for the children's book *Tales from Shakespeare* (1807), which he wrote with his sister Mary.

Langland, William (*c.*1330-86) Author of PIERS PLOWMAN, a medieval verse ▷ALLEGORY. Little is known about Langland's life, but he is thought to have been born in the west Midlands – possibly Ledbury in Hereford and Worcester – and to have lived in London, where he was probably a minor churchman.

Larkin, Philip (1922-85) Writer of complex satirical and melancholy poems about modern life, incorporating themes such as old age and death. Larkin delighted in breaking taboos, but his writing can also be sincere and moving. He was head librarian of the Brynmor Jones Library at Hull University from 1955 until his death.

Lawrence, D.H. (1885-1930) Poet, novelist and short-story writer much concerned with human passions and sexuality, and the stultifying effects of social convention. He began writing poems and short stories at an early age, and made his name with the semi-autobiographical novel *Sons and Lovers* (1913) while still in his twenties. At about the same time, Lawrence fell in love and eloped with a married woman, Frieda Weekley. In 1914 she obtained a divorce and they were married. Years of travelling followed, in Europe, Ceylon, Australia, the USA and Mexico. Despite the disruption, poor health and a difficult relationship with Frieda, Lawrence wrote many novels now considered classics, including *The Rainbow*, WOMEN IN LOVE and LADY CHATTERLEY'S LOVER.

Lear, Edward (1812-88) Writer of humorous and nonsense verse for children, including 'The OWL AND THE PUSSY-CAT', 'The Jumblies', 'The Pobble Who Has No Toes' and 'The Dong with a Luminous Nose'. His *Book of Nonsense* (1846) popularised the limerick – a light, humorous five-line verse. Lear was also a talented artist, and illustrated many of his own rhymes.

Le Carré, John Pseudonym of the writer David Cornwell (1931-), the author of thrillers and spy novels such as *The Spy Who Came in from the Cold; The Honourable Schoolboy; Tinker, Tailor, Soldier, Spy; Smiley's People* and *The Little Drummer Girl*. Le Carré is known for the intricacy of his plots and for creating the intellectual British spy master George Smiley, who features in many of his books.

Lessing, Doris (1919-) Novelist and short-story writer who grew up in Southern Rhodesia (now Zimbabwe) but moved to Britain in 1949. Her first novel, *The Grass is Singing*, was set in Rhodesia and published in 1950. Since then she has written novels and stories dealing with themes ranging from politics and feminism to madness. They include *The Golden Notebook*, a long novel about a woman writer struggling with a creative block and other personal crises, and the novel sequence *Children of Violence* – the life story of heroine Martha Quest, ending in the year 2000.

'Let us go then, you and I' First line of the poem *The Love Song of J. Alfred Prufrock* by T.S. ELIOT. The title is ironic, and Eliot deliberately uses unromantic images to reflect the nature of modern existence. The poem continues:

> When the evening is spread out against the sky
> Like a patient etherised upon a table.

limerick Humorous nonsense jingle, usually consisting of two long rhyming lines followed by two short rhyming lines and a longer final line that rhymes with the first two or, more strictly, ends on the same word as the first line. Limericks often begin, 'There was a . . .', as in this one by Edward LEAR:

> There was an Old Man with a beard,
> Who said, 'It is just as I feared! –
> Two owls and a hen,
> Four larks and a wren,
> Have all built their nests in my beard!

Little Women Novel by Louisa May ALCOTT, published in two parts in 1868-9. It follows the fortunes of four sisters – Jo, Meg, Beth and Amy March – as they grow up in 19th-century New England.

Lolita Novel by the Russian-born writer Vladimir ▷NABOKOV, published in 1955. It tells the story of a middle-aged professor of English, Humbert Humbert, and his sexual obsession with Lolita, his precocious adolescent stepdaughter.

Longfellow, Henry Wadsworth (1807-82) American poet who wrote popular works such as The Song of HIAWATHA, 'The Village Blacksmith' and the ballad 'The Wreck of the Hesperus'.

Lord of the Flies Novel by William GOLDING, published in 1954. It tells the story of a group of schoolboys who are stranded on an island after a plane crash. Two of the boys, Ralph and Piggy, try to get the group to cooperate in establishing a rational, ordered society. However, their authority is soon challenged and a reign of terror begins under a boy called Jack. Piggy and another boy are killed before the boys are finally rescued.

🖉 William Golding wrote *The Lord of the Flies* in response to *The Coral Island*, a novel by R.M. Ballantyne in which three shipwrecked children have a series of exciting but innocent adventures.

🖉 'Lord of the flies', Beelzebub in Hebrew, is a name for the devil.

Lord of the Rings, The Fantasy novel by J.R.R. TOLKIEN, published in three volumes between 1954 and 1955. It is a sequel to his earlier novel *The Hobbit*, published in 1937. Four HOBBITS, Frodo, Sam, Merry and Pippin, set out on a dangerous mission to prevent the evil Sauron from obtaining a golden ring which will give him power to control the world. The Hobbits' mission is aided by the Elves and by the good wizard Gandalf, but on several occasions they almost lose their lives in doing battle with the fearsome Orcs, Ringwraiths and other agents of Sauron. Eventually the ring is destroyed, Sauron falls and a benevolent human ruler established in his place.

Macbeth Tragedy by SHAKESPEARE, dating from about 1606 and based on historical events of the 11th century. The Scottish nobleman Macbeth, encouraged by the prophecy of three witches and by his ambitious wife, murders the king, Duncan, and usurps the throne. To maintain his ill-gotten position, Macbeth is driven to increasingly desperate measures, and arranges the murders of his friend Banquo and the family of his enemy Macduff. At the end, Lady Macbeth loses her mind and dies, and Macbeth is killed in battle by Macduff.

🖉 Many lines from *Macbeth* have become familiar expressions: 'the milk of human kindness'; 'Is this a dagger which I see before me?'; the witches' chant 'Double, double, toil and trouble'; 'Out, damned spot!'; and 'Lay on, Macduff – Macbeth's challenge to his rival to fight to the death, often misquoted as 'Lead on, Macduff'.

🖉 Within theatrical circles, superstition precludes any mention of the title 'Macbeth'; it is always called 'The Scottish Play'.

Maclean, Alistair (1922-87) Best-selling Scottish author of adventure tales and thrillers set in exotic locations. His books include *The Guns of Navarone*, *Ice Station Zebra*, the Western *Breakheart Pass* and *Where Eagles Dare*. Many of Maclean's novels have been made into films.

MacNeice, Louis (1907-63) Writer of poems and plays in a variety of styles, often satirical and in colloquial language. He was associated with the literary group that included W.H. AUDEN. Christopher ISHERWOOD, and Stephen SPENDER in the 1920s and 1930s, but did not share their left-wing political views.

Malory, Sir Thomas (*d*.1471) English author, known for the medieval romance *Le* MORTE D'ARTHUR. Little is known about Malory's life and identity, except that he wrote *Le Morte D'Arthur* in prison and may have been a former knight from Warwickshire who was charged with crimes including rape and assault around 1450.

Man for All Seasons, A Play by the British dramatist Robert Bolt (1924-), about Sir Thomas ▷MORE, who was beheaded in 1535 for refusing to recognise Henry VIII instead of the pope as the head of the Church in England.

Mansfield, Katherine (1888-1923) New Zealand author known for her fine short-story writing and her original and experimental style. She settled in London in 1908 and her stories first appeared in several weekly magazines. She published various collections, notably *In a German Pension*; *Bliss, and Other Stories*; and *The Garden Party, and Other Stories*. Her reputation grew as her health deteriorated; she died from tuberculosis. Several works were published after her death, including her poetry and many of her letters.

Marlowe, Christopher (1564-93) Poet and playwright whose style of blank verse influenced Shakespeare's early plays. Marlowe was quick-tempered, irreligious and apparently involved in crime. He died after a brawl in a Deptford tavern while awaiting trial for blasphemy; it has been suggested that he was murdered by his criminal accomplices who were afraid of exposure in Marlowe's evidence. Marlowe's best-known works are tragedies such as *Tamburlaine the Great*, *The Jew of Malta* and DR FAUSTUS, in which bold, ruthless individuals take on the fates, eventually bringing about their own destruction. However, Marlowe was also capable of sensuous love poetry such as *The Passionate Shepherd to his Love*, which begins 'COME LIVE WITH ME AND BE MY LOVE'.

Marple, Miss Elderly spinster and keen knitter who is a successful amateur detective in many of Agatha CHRISTIE's crime novels. Her keen insight into human nature helps her to draw parallels between the behaviour of people in her village, St Mary Meads, and the unknown criminal.

Marvell, Andrew (1621-78) One of the English METAPHYSICAL POETS, known for witty political satire and for lyrics such as *To His Coy Mistress* – an elegant argument against lovers delaying their pleasure. It contains memorable lines such as:

But at my back I always hear
Time's wingèd chariot hurrying near:

Maugham, (William) Somerset (1874-1965) British short-story writer, novelist and playwright. Many of Maugham's works are set abroad and based on the writer's own travels in China, the Pacific Islands, India, southeast Asia and Mexico. 'Rain', one of his best-known short stories, deals with an encounter between a prostitute and a missionary on the island of Samoa. Maugham's novels include *The Moon and Sixpence*, based on the life of the artist Paul Gaugin in Tahiti; *Cakes and Ale*, whose main character is the cheerful wife of a distinguished writer; and the autobiographical novel *Of Human Bondage*.

Melville, Herman (1819-91) American novelist and poet best known for the symbolic sea tales MOBY DICK and *Billy Budd* – about the sentencing and execution of a young sailor after he accidentally kills one of the crew. In his writing, Melville drew on several adventurous years at sea, including time spent on a whaling ship.

Merchant of Venice, The Play by SHAKESPEARE, written between 1596 and 1598. A Venetian merchant, Antonio, borrows money from Shylock, a Jew, to help his friend Bassanio to woo Portia. If Antonio fails to repay the money on time he is to forfeit a pound of his flesh. Bassanio marries Portia, but Antonio's ships are wrecked and he cannot repay the debt. Portia, disguised as a lawyer, appeals to Shylock to have mercy on Antonio, but he refuses. She concedes the moneylender's right to Antonio's flesh but points out that the agreement does not permit him to spill a single drop of blood. Outwitted, Shylock gives up the case and, as punishment for conspiring against the life of a Venetian, he is required to become a Christian and leave his money to his runaway daughter Jessica.

🖉 Although Shakespeare's play reflects the anti-Semitic attitudes of his time, it also contains a moving speech in which Shylock asserts his common humanity: 'I am a Jew,' he says. 'Hath not a Jew hands, organs, dimensions, senses, affections, passions?'

Metaphysical poets Group of English poets of the 17th century including John DONNE and Andrew MARVELL. Their work often uses intricate scholarly arguments and elaborate comparisons to make its point.
♠ ▷METAPHYSICS is a speculative branch of philosophy that examines such issues as life and death, reality, knowledge, time and space, and the interplay between them.

Middle English Form of English written and spoken from c.1150 to 1500. Its basis was the Germanic language Old English – also called Anglo-Saxon – with the addition after the Norman Conquest of 1066 of a large number of Norman French words. It had no standard system of spelling and there were five main dialects in Middle English: East Midland, West Midland, South Eastern, South Western and Northern. Much literature of the time was written in the two Midlands dialects, and it was a London version of East Midlands that developed into modern English.

Midsummer Night's Dream, A Comedy by William SHAKESPEARE, written around 1595. Four lovers spend a night in a wood outside Athens, where the fairy king and queen, Oberon and Titania, have had an argument. To punish Titania, Oberon gets the sprite Puck to drop the juice of a magic herb on her eyes while she sleeps so that she will fall in love with the first thing she sees when she wakes. This turns out to be the weaver Bottom wearing an ass's-head mask for a play rehearsal. Puck also uses the herb on the human lovers who unfortunately set eyes on the wrong partners first. When Titania and Oberon are reconciled, Oberon releases the human lovers from the spell.
♠ Well-known lines from the play include 'Ill met by moonlight, proud Titania', and 'Lord, what fools these mortals be!'

Miller, Arthur (1915-) American dramatist known for realistic and often tragic plays about modern life. His works include *Death of a Salesman*, about an ordinary man's inability to face up to what he sees as his own failure, *All My Sons*, which deals with the emotional effects of war, and *The Crucible*, which deals with the 17th-century Salem witch trials, but refers by implication to the anticommunist witch-hunts of the McCarthy era in the USA.
♠ Arthur Miller was the third husband of the film actress Marilyn Monroe.

Milne, A.A. (1882-1956) British author known for his 1920s children's books WINNIE-THE-POOH and *The House at Pooh*

Corner which feature the little boy Christopher Robin – modelled on Milne's own son – and toy animals such as the bear Winnie-the-Pooh, the donkey Eeyore, Rabbit, Piglet, Owl, Tigger, Kanga and Roo. Milne also wrote two books of children's verse, *When We Were Very Young* and *Now We Are Six*.

Milton, John (1608-74) Poet considered to be one of the greatest ever to write in English along with Chaucer and Shakespeare. Milton's best-known poem is PARADISE LOST, which he dictated after he went blind. It describes in epic form the events of the Book of Genesis surrounding the Fall of Man. Milton later wrote a sequel, *Paradise Regained*, about Christ's triumph over Satan's temptation in the wilderness. His other well-known works include *Lycidas* – an elegy on the death of a friend – and *Samson Agonistes*, which describes the last days of Samson after he had been taken prisoner. Milton supported parliament in the English Civil War and became Oliver Cromwell's Latin secretary. He was an outspoken campaigner for liberty and justice, writing many tracts on subjects ranging from divorce to the freedom of the press and of religion.

Mitty, Walter Title character in the 1930s short story *The Secret Life of Walter Mitty* written by the American humorist James THURBER. Walter Mitty is a repressed and henpecked man who takes refuge in romantic or fantastic daydreams.
♠ A Walter Mitty character is someone who lives in a fantasy world.

Moby Dick Symbolic novel by the American writer Herman MELVILLE, published in 1851. The central character, Captain Ahab, sets off on an obsessive quest for revenge on the great white whale Moby Dick, which had cost him a leg on an earlier encounter. The story is narrated by the young sailor Ishmael who begins the book with the much-quoted sentence, 'Call me Ishmael'. For both men, the voyage, on the ship *Pequod*, becomes as much a journey of self-discovery as a whaling expedition. While Ishmael discovers compassion and love, Ahab becomes enveloped by the dark, destructive forces represented by the whale.

Modest Proposal, A Satirical pamphlet written by Jonathan SWIFT in 1729, suggesting the eating of children as a way of solving social problems in Ireland. It was written in outrage at government policy towards Ireland and at the appalling conditions in which the Irish peasantry lived.

Molesworth, Nigel Schoolboy narrator in humorous children's books from the 1950s written by Geoffrey Willans and illustrated by Ronald Searle. In books such as *Down with Skool* and *Whizz for Atomms* Molesworth records the antics of a dubious assortment of masters and boys such as the 'weedy' Fotherington-Thomas, the sadistic headmaster Grimes, and Sigismund the Mad Maths Master.

Morrison, Toni (1931-) American novelist whose richly detailed novels explore life among rural blacks in the deep South. They include *Song of Solomon* (1977), *Tar Baby* (1981) and *Beloved* (1987) – a factually based account of infanticide which won the 1988 Pulitzer prize.

Morte D'Arthur, Le Series of stories about King Arthur and the Knights of the Round Table, written by Sir Thomas MALORY and published in 1485 by the English printer William Caxton. Malory's book brought together a diverse assortment of French and English legends, turning them into the great tales of quests, chivalry and romance that still colour the popular view of the Middle Ages.
♠ Malory's *Morte D'Arthur* has inspired many other works of art, including poems by Tennyson, the paintings of the ▷PRE-RAPHAELITE BROTHERHOOD, the children's book *The Sword in the Stone*, the film *Excalibur* and the musical *Camelot*.

Murdoch, Iris (1919-) Novelist, playwright and philosopher known for novels concerned with individuals' inner lives and with complex moral and psychological issues such as good and evil, religious belief and sexuality. Her best-known books include *Under the Net* and *The Black Prince*, which are both narrated by a male in the first-person; *The Bell*, which is set in a lay religious community; *A Severed Head*, about marriage and infidelity; and *The Sea, The Sea*, a love story, which won the Booker prize in 1978.

Naipaul, V.S. (1932-) Novelist and travel writer born in Trinidad but resident in Britain since 1950. Naipaul's early books were comedies about Trinidadian life but his later works take a deeper view, probing issues of personal and national identity, politics and alienation. His best-known novels are *A House for Mr Biswas*, whose main character was modelled on Naipaul's own father, and *A Bend in the River*, set in the turbulent times that follow independence in an African state. *A Bend in the River* won the Booker prize in 1979.

ENGLISH LITERATURE

Nash, Ogden (1902-71) American poet known for outrageous rhymes such as 'A bit of talcum/ Is always walcum' and 'Candy/ Is dandy/ But liquor/ Is quicker'.

Nicholas Nickleby Novel by Charles DICKENS, published in instalments during 1838 and 1839. When his father dies, Nicholas, his mother and sister are left penniless. Nicholas becomes an usher at Dotheboys Hall – a school for boys run by the cruel Mr Wackford Squeers. Nicholas runs away with a half-witted boy, Smike, and finds better employment. Smike dies of consumption, however, and turns out to have been the son of Nicholas's miserly uncle Ralph, who kills himself in remorse. Nicholas ends up happily married and Squeers is transported to Australia.

Nineteen Eighty-Four Novel by George ORWELL, published in 1949. The book is set in the imaginary totalitarian state of Oceania, whose population is controlled in word, deed and thought by the Party, the menacing but unseen Big Brother, the Thought Police and all-pervading propaganda. The main character, Winston Smith, tries to stand up for truth and humanity but is broken by the system. Orwell wrote the book as a general warning against totalitarianism and the loss of individual freedom, but it has also been interpreted by some as referring specifically to Stalin's USSR.
🔖The terms 'Newspeak' and 'Double-speak' were coined in the novel to refer to types of propaganda. Doublespeak, for example, uses slogans such as 'Freedom is Slavery' and 'War is Peace'.

Noddy Character in a children's book invented by Enid BLYTON in 1949 after she had seen a sketch by the Dutch artist Harmsen van der Beek. Noddy books, featuring such characters as Big-Ears the Brownie and Mr Plod the Policeman, have been best sellers ever since. But they have also been attacked for racism and naiveté.

O'Casey, Sean (1880-1964) Irish playwright who wrote tragicomedies about the dangers and beliefs behind Irish patriotism, the comedy of everyday life and the realities of poverty. His best-known plays are *Juno and the Paycock* and *The Plough and the Stars*.

ode On a Grecian Urn Poem by John KEATS, written in 1819. The scenes of rural life depicted on the urn lead Keats to consider the difference between art, which endures, and human experience, which is portrayed in art but is always fleeting.

FREE THINKER *George Orwell reacted against his public-school education by championing the individual against the establishment.*

Old English Germanic language with genders and cases, also called Anglo-Saxon, which was spoken and written from 700 AD to *c*.1150. At least four dialects were used – Northumbrian, Mercian, Kentish and West Saxon. The best-known Old English poetry, including BEOWULF, is contained in four manuscripts from the late 10th and early 11th centuries. The earliest known work is the *Hymn of Creation*, composed in the late 7th century by Caedmon, an illiterate Northumbrian cowherd.

Oliver Twist Novel by Charles DICKENS, published in instalments during 1837 and 1838. Oliver is born in a workhouse where his parentage is unknown and where the children are cruelly treated. He runs away to London and falls in with a group of thieves led by Fagin. The members of the band – which includes a young pickpocket known as the 'Artful Dodger' and the burglar Bill Sikes – try to force Oliver to join them, but after a disastrous expedition he is taken in by the kindly Mrs Maylie. However, an evil man called Monks continues to pursue him. The plot becomes more violent and several deaths occur. Eventually Monks's motives are revealed, the evil characters are punished and Oliver is adopted by one of his benefactors.
🔖A film of *Oliver Twist* was made in 1948, and a musical, ▷OLIVER, in 1960.

O'Neill, Eugene (1888-1953) American playwright known for dramas such as his great trilogy *Mourning Becomes Electra*, *The Iceman Cometh*, about a group of hopeless alcoholics and their fantasies, and *A Long Day's Journey into Night*, a domestic tragedy partially based on O'Neill's own family background. O'Neill won the Nobel prize for literature in 1936.

Orton, Joe (1933-67) Dramatist known for black comedies such as *Entertaining Mr Sloane*, *What the Butler Saw* and *Loot* – a grotesque farce involving stolen money hidden in the coffin of the hero's mother.
🔖Orton's death was as macabre as one of his plots: he was murdered by his homosexual lover, who then committed suicide.

Orwell, George Pseudonym of the writer Eric Blair (1903-50). Orwell was interested in political and social issues, and in his writings he defended the liberty of the individual against all forms of oppression. He identified with the working classes and took various lowly jobs – experiences which he drew on in *Down and Out in Paris and London* and in *Keep the Aspidistra Flying*. After a journey in 1936 he wrote a heartfelt account of poverty and hardship in the north of England, entitled *The Road to Wigan Pier*. Orwell fought for the Republicans in the Spanish Civil War and afterwards wrote an account of it in *Homage to Catalonia*. The best known of all his works are the 1940s satirical novels ANIMAL FARM and NINETEEN EIGHTY-FOUR, both of which deal with political oppression and the evils of totalitarianism.

Osborne, John (1929-) Dramatist associated with the group of writers known as the ANGRY YOUNG MEN in the 1950s. His plays are realistic portrayals of ordinary life, often containing impassioned social criticism. His best-known work, *Look Back in Anger*, was written in 1956 and inspired a trend for social realism in British drama. The play concerns an ill-matched couple, Jimmy and Alison Porter, the conflicts that tear them apart, and their eventual imperfect reconciliation.

Othello Tragedy by William SHAKE-SPEARE, probably written between 1602 and 1604. Othello, a Moor, has command of the Venetian forces in Cyprus. However, the villain Iago cunningly convinces Othello that Desdemona, his beautiful and faithful wife, has committed adultery with Cassio, a lieutenant. Consumed by jealousy, Othello murders Desdemona by smothering her in bed. When he realises his error and Iago's malice, he kills himself.

Owen, Wilfred (1893-1918) British poet who served in World War I. His verses describe the suffering of soldiers in the trenches; among his most famous poems is 'Anthem for Doomed Youth'. Owen was killed a week before the armistice. His poems were not popular at the time, but he is now highly regarded as a war poet.

SAILING AWAY *Writing nonsense verse such as 'The Owl and the Pussy-Cat' was an escape for Edward Lear, who suffered from depression.*

Owl and the Pussy-Cat, The Children's nonsense poem written by Edward LEAR in 1867 for the daughter of a friend. It begins with the lines:

> The Owl and the Pussy-Cat went to sea
> In a beautiful pea-green boat,
> They took some honey, and plenty of money,
> Wrapped up in a five-pound note.

Paradise Lost Epic poem written by John MILTON, between about 1658 and 1663, and consisting of 12 books containing more than 10 000 lines. The poem deals with the temptation and disobedience of Adam and Eve in the Garden of Eden, and the Fall of Man which follows. It also describes the rebellion and punishment of Satan and his cohorts, and foretells the coming of the Messiah, who will redeem mankind.

Parker, Dorothy (1893-1967) American satirist and acid wit who wrote poems, short stories, film scripts and reviews. She once said of the late Katharine Hepburn in a Broadway play 'She ran the whole gamut of the emotions from A to B.' Other well-known lines include 'Men seldom make passes/ At girls who wear glasses.'

Passage to India, A Novel by E.M. FORSTER, published in 1924 and set in India at the time of the British Raj and in which Forster examines the complex interaction of the two cultures. The events revolve around the strange experience of a young English woman, Adela Quested, in the Marabar caves. The experience – never fully explained – leads her to accuse Aziz, an Anglophile Indian, of rape. Eventually she withdraws the charge, but Aziz and many other Indians are left angry and embittered, and the British community is divided.

Pepys, Samuel (1633-1703) Civil servant who kept a diary from January 1, 1660, to May 31, 1669, in which he recorded such events as the Great Fire of London, the Restoration and the Great Plague, as well as giving an extraordinarily frank account of his private and social life. The diary was written in a shorthand code and was not published until 1825. A complete and unexpurgated version appeared in the 1970s and 1980s, occupying 11 volumes.

Peter Pan Play by the Scottish writer J.M. BARRIE, first performed in 1904. The title character is a little boy who lives in a place called Never Never Land where children never grow up. Peter Pan, accompanied by the fairy Tinkerbell, persuades Wendy and her two brothers to leave their parents, the Darlings, and their faithful canine nurse, Nana, and fly from their Kensington home to Never Never Land. There, they have various adventures and finally vanquish the pirates and their leader, evil Captain Hook.

Pickwick Papers Novel by Charles DICKENS, published in 1836-7. It has a loose plot and purports to be a record of the proceedings of the Pickwick Club – a group of eccentrics who use words in unusual ways and entertain one another with tales of their adventures. The main characters are Mr Pickwick, the club chairman, and his cheerful servant Sam Weller.

Piers Plowman One of the greatest poems in Middle English, written by William LANGLAND between the 1360s and

EASTERN EPIC *David Lean's lavish 1985 film version of* A Passage to India *followed Forster's novel closely. When the book was published, in 1924, the author was accused of anti-British bias.*

1380s. Three different versions exist, all telling of a series of visions which the narrator has while asleep. The visions concern various virtues and vices at large in the world, and the search for spiritual truth and redemption from sin through Christ.

♣ Langland's poem contains serious criticism of the medieval Church and other institutions of the time.

Pilgrim's Progress, The Spiritual ▷ALLEGORY by the English author and preacher John Bunyan (1628-88), published in two parts in 1678 and 1684. In Part I the author sees in a dream the character Christian carrying a burden and reading a book which tells him of the imminent destruction of the city in which he lives. Christian sets off on a pilgrimage, passing through the Slough of Despond, the Valley of Humiliation and other treacherous regions until he comes at last to the Celestial City. Part II deals with a similar pilgrimage made by Christian's wife, Christiana, and their children, who had at first refused to go with him.

Pinter, Harold (1930-) British dramatist known for plays in which inconsequential small talk between the characters gradually builds up an atmosphere of tension and menace. His works include *The Birthday Party*, about the mysterious persecution of an unemployed pianist by two characters who arrive from nowhere, and *The Caretaker*, which follows the shifting relationships and balance of power between two brothers and a tramp who accompanies them home. Pinter has also written scripts for films such as *The Servant* and *The French Lieutenant's Woman*, which was adapted from the novel by John FOWLES. His 1993 play *Moonlight* deals with a dying man who wants to see his sons – but they refuse to visit.

♣ Harold Pinter is married to the writer Antonia Fraser, who is known for her historical biographies and detective stories.

Plath, Sylvia (1932-63) American writer known for poems dealing with troubled states of mind such as depression and despair, from which she suffered herself. She also wrote one novel, *The Bell Jar*, an autobiographical account of a young woman's life after she leaves university, including a description of her mental breakdown and recovery. Sylvia Plath's death was the result of a suicide attempt – one of several she made – which some believe was never intended to succeed.

♣ Sylvia Plath was the wife of the current poet laureate, Ted HUGHES.

Poe, Edgar Allan (1809-49) American writer of stories and poems dealing with the macabre and mysterious. His best-known works are the story The FALL OF THE HOUSE OF USHER and the poem 'The Raven', in which a man mourning his lost lover is visited by a raven that tells him he will see her 'nevermore'.

poet laureate Title conferred for life on a British poet who is appointed the official poet of the royal household. The poet laureate is expected to compose verses for such occasions as royal birthdays, coronations and military victories. The tradition of court entertainers, including poets and musicians, goes back to ancient times, but the first official laureateship was not conferred until 1668, when John Dryden received the title. Since then, several other major poets have held the position, including Wordsworth and Tennyson. Ted Hughes received the title in 1984.

♣ The salary – originally £200 and a butt of wine – is now a token amount.

♣ Since 1985 a poet laureate has also been appointed in the USA.

Poirot, Hercule (PWA-roe) Plump but dapper Belgian detective hero who appears in many Agatha CHRISTIE's crime novels. He has an obsession with precision, tidiness and symmetry and sports a neatly waxed moustache, patent leather shoes and a monocle. In solving crimes Poirot relies on his 'little grey cells', and he particularly detests being mistaken for a Frenchman.

Pope, Alexander (1688-1744) British poet who tried to introduce the forms of Classical Latin verse into English. Pope's best-known works include the mock-heroic poem *The Rape of the Lock*, based on a real incident in which the playful theft of a snippet of hair from a young lady set two families at odds, and the more serious philosophical poems *An Essay on Man* and *An Essay on Criticism*. The latter contains many familiar lines including 'A little learning is a dang'rous thing', 'To err is human, to forgive, divine' and 'Hope springs eternal in the human breast'.

Potter, Beatrix (1866-1943) Author and illustrator of small-format children's books about human and animal characters such as the mischievous Peter Rabbit, his adversary Mr McGregor, the hedgehog-washerwoman Mrs Tiggywinkle, and the rivals Mr Tod the fox and Mr Brock the badger. The books are set in the Lake

COUNTRY CHARM *Beatrix Potter grew up in London but always loved the English countryside which she came to know during childhood holidays. The latter part of her life was spent farming and writing at Sawrey in the Lake District.*

District, which Potter knew and loved, and where she eventually settled. Many of her characters were based on real people.

Pound, Ezra (1885-1972) American poet who came to Europe and helped to establish ▷MODERNISM. He had a flair for languages and his verses, particularly his *Cantos*, reflect influences from many cultures. During World War II, he supported Mussolini and was later accused of treason by the USA. The charge was dropped when Pound was judged insane; he spent the next 14 years in an asylum.
🔖 Pound helped T.S. ELIOT to edit his poem *The Wasteland*.

Powell, Anthony (1905-) British novelist best known for his 12-book sequence *A Dance to the Music of Time* (1951-76) which follows the interweaving threads in the lives of a number of characters at all levels of London society.

Pre-Raphaelite Brotherhood (PRB) Group of writers and artists founded in 1848. Harking back to the spirit of the Middle Ages, the writers adopted a deliberately literary and archaic style. The most influential poet was Dante Gabriel ROSSETTI. (See also ▷PRE-RAPHAELITE BROTHERHOOD in 'Art and Design'.)

Pride and Prejudice Novel by Jane AUSTEN, published in 1813. The story concerns an upper-middle-class Hertfordshire family consisting of the foolish Mrs Bennet, her wryly humorous husband and their five daughters. After a complex succession of proposals, refusals, engagements and even an elopement, three of the daughters end up happily married.
🔖 The book's opening sentence is well known: 'It is a truth universally acknowledged, that a single man in possession of a good fortune, must be in want of a wife.'

Priestley, J.B. (1894-1984) Prolific English novelist and dramatist, and popular wartime broadcaster. His works include the psychological mystery drama *An Inspector Calls* and the farce *When We Are Married*.

Pygmalion Play by George Bernard SHAW, first performed in 1913. To win a bet, Professor Henry Higgins – a specialist in English phonetics – trains an ill-spoken Cockney flower girl, Eliza Doolittle, to speak and behave like a lady. Eventually her training is complete and Eliza successfully mixes in high society without giving away her origins. Higgins wins his bet, but Eliza eventually rebels and asserts her right to

control her own life. In Classical mythology ▷PYGMALION was a Cypriot king who fell in love with a sculpture he created.
🔖 The 1957 musical ▷MY FAIR LADY was based on Shaw's play, however, it emphasises a romantic attraction between Eliza and Higgins that Shaw only hints at.

Pym, Barbara (1913-80) British novelist known for her tragicomic satirisation of middle-class life. Among her best-known books are *Excellent Women*, *Less Than Angels, A Glass of Blessings* and *Quartet in Autumn*.

Rattigan, Terence (1911-1977) English dramatist known for well-crafted plays about emotional suffering and troubled human relationships, such as *The Winslow Boy*, *The Browning Version*, *Separate Tables* and *The Deep Blue Sea*. He was knighted in 1971.

KING ON CRUTCHES *The actor Antony Sher created a menacing Richard III in the Royal Shakespeare Company's 1984-5 production of the play. Sher exaggerated Richard's hunched back to symbolise his moral deformity, and played him as a cripple, dragging himself about on crutches. The costume enhanced the spidery silhouette.* Richard III *completed the series of plays begun with the* Henry VI *dramas, giving a vivid account of 63 turbulent years of English history.*

Restoration comedy Style of comic drama developed in England around the time of the restoration of the monarchy in 1660. In reaction to the puritanism of the Commonwealth era, the humour was bawdy, the plots complex and the morals questionable or non-existent. Examples include William Wycherley's *The Country Wife* (1675), Willliam Congreve's *The Way of the World* (1700) and George Farquhar's *The Beaux' Stratagem* (1707).

revenge tragedy Type of tragedy popular in late Elizabethan and Jacobean England. It deals with a quest for vengeance or retribution in return for a wrong – usually murder. Well-known revenge tragedies include *The Spanish Tragedy* by Thomas KYD, Christopher MARLOWE's *The Jew of Malta* and John WEBSTER's

The Duchess of Malfi. The greatest of all, however, is Shakespeare's HAMLET, which contains many typical elements – such as ghosts, madness, graveyard scenes, poisoning, and a conclusion in which the main characters come to an unpleasant end.

Richard III Historical drama by William SHAKESPEARE, written around 1591. The play portrays the ruthless pursuit of the crown by the hunchback Richard of Glou-

cester. When the king, Edward IV, is close to death, Richard starts to claw his way to the throne by having his brother murdered and then cynically marrying the Prince of Wales's widow Anne. When Edward dies, Richard eliminates his opponents one by one, is proclaimed king and decrees the deaths of his young nephews, the Princes in the Tower. Eventually, however, his enemies – led by Henry Tudor (later Henry VII) – defeat him at Bosworth.
🔖 Some of the best-known lines from *Richard III* are: 'My horse, my horse, my kingdom for a horse!' and 'Now is the winter of our discontent/ Made glorious summer by this sun of York.'
🔖 The Richard III Society was set up in 1924 to try to restore the king's reputation which the members maintain Shakespeare had distorted and unfairly destroyed.

Rime of the Ancient Mariner, The
Supernatural poem by Samuel Taylor COL-
ERIDGE, published in 1798. An old sailor
stops a stranger and tells him of a voyage
during which he shot an albatross. A curse
fell upon the ship, which was becalmed, and
the rest of the crew were struck dead. The
mariner drifted alone until he caught sight
of some water snakes and spontaneously
'blessed them unaware', breaking the spell.
The mariner now wanders about telling his
story and teaching reverence for life. Some
of the poem's best-known lines are 'Water,
water, everywhere/ Nor any drop to drink'.
🐾 Albatrosses are known for accompanying
ships at sea, and an old superstition holds
that killing one brings a lifetime of bad luck.
🐾 The expression an 'albatross round one's
neck' refers to any problem or burden that
has to be borne.

Ring a Ring o'Roses Nursery rhyme sung
in a children's game. The children hold
hands and dance around in a ring until
reaching the last line, when they pretend to
sneeze and fall down. The words are
believed by many to date from the ▷GREAT
PLAGUE, with the 'roses' being the red spots
and the 'pocketful of posies' the herbs
which were supposed to ward off the illness.
'A-tishoo! a-tishoo!' is said to imitate the
cold symptoms which came before 'we all
fall down' – and die. However, there is no
evidence to confirm this, and the earliest
printed version dates only from the 1800s.

Robbins, Harold (1916-) Best-selling
American novelist known for books such as
Never Love a Stranger and *The Carpetbaggers*, the latter of which sold more than 6
million copies.

Robinson Crusoe Adventure tale by
Daniel DEFOE, published in 1719 as a true
story. It is based on the real-life experience
of the sailor Alexander Selkirk, who spent
five years alone on an island before being
rescued in 1709. Defoe's novel vividly
describes how Crusoe is shipwrecked, but
ingeniously clothes himself, grows crops,
domesticates wild animals and builds a
house and a boat. Eventually he acquires a
companion and servant, Friday, whom he
saves from cannibals. After 28 years Crusoe
is finally rescued by a passing English ship.
🐾 *Robinson Crusoe* was an instant success and
inspired many works such as *Swiss Family
Robinson* and Defoe's own sequel *The Farther Adventures of Robinson Crusoe*.

Romeo and Juliet Romantic tragedy by
William SHAKESPEARE, written around
1595. The action is set in Verona where

A SAIL! A SAIL! *A ghostly ship approaches, bringing hope to the
Ancient Mariner and his becalmed shipmates. Terror sets in
when they realise that the vessel is sailing without wind.*

bitter hatred divides the powerful Montague
and Capulet families. Romeo (a young Montague) and Juliet (a Capulet) fall in love and
are secretly married. However, Romeo is
banished for duelling and he and Juliet have
just one night together. Juliet's parents are
meanwhile planning her marriage to Count
Paris. In desperation she consults the friar
who married her and arranges to take a
potion which makes her appear dead while
the friar sends a message to Romeo. It fails to
reach him; he hears only that Juliet is dead.
He returns and drinks poison at her side. She
wakes and, finding him dead, kills herself
with her dagger. When the two families
realise what has happened, they vow to end
their tragic feud.
🐾 When Juliet utters the well-known exclamation 'Romeo, Romeo! Wherefore art
thou Romeo?' she is lamenting Romeo's
name because it ties him to the Montague
family. 'Wherefore' means 'why'.
🐾 The 1957 musical *West Side Story* transferred the tale of Romeo and Juliet onto the
streets of New York.

Rossetti, Dante Gabriel (1828-82)
Poet, painter and founder of the PRE-
RAPHAELITE BROTHERHOOD. His best-
known poems include 'The Blessed Damozel', in which a young woman in heaven
yearns for her earthly lover, and the sonnet
sequence *The House of Life*, which deals with
themes of love, death and art. (See also
▷ROSSETTI in 'Art and Design'.)
🐾 In remorse at the death of his wife
Elizabeth in 1862, Rossetti buried several
of his poems with her. Seven years later,
however, he had her coffin exhumed and
published the retrieved manuscripts.
🐾 Rossetti's sister, Christina, wrote children's poetry and religious verse.

Rushdie, Salman (1947-) English
novelist born in India of Muslim parents.
He won the Booker prize in 1981 for

Midnight's Children, which
deals with the independence
of India and its separation
from Pakistan at midnight on
August 14, 1947. Rushdie's
▷MAGIC REALISM – his technique of mingling fact, fiction
and fantasy, had serious consequences when he applied it to
Muslim beliefs in his 1988
novel *The Satanic Verses*. Rushdie's alleged blasphemy outraged Muslim fundamentalists
and a death sentence – or *fatwa*
– was declared on him by the
Iranian leader Ayatollah
Khomeini. As a result Rushdie
went into hiding and could make only
irregular, unannounced appearances in
public. His plight became the focus of
campaigns by fellow writers and supporters
of civil liberty in Britain.

**Sackville-West, Vita (Victoria)
(1892-1962)** English writer and friend of
the novelist Virginia WOOLF. She married
the diplomat Harold Nicolson in 1913 and,
though both partners had homosexual love
affairs, the marriage survived. The main
character of Virginia Woolf's *Orlando* – a
beautiful youth who lives for 400 years, as
both man and woman – was modelled on
Vita Sackville-West.
🐾 Vita Sackville-West was also an accomplished gardener. The grounds she created
at ▷SISSINGHURST in Kent attract thousands of visitors every year.

Saki Pseudonym of the writer Hector
Hugh Munro (1870-1916), who specialised
in short stories with macabre plots, often
involving ferocious animals. Munro was
born in Burma, but his mother died when
he was very young and he was brought up in
Devon by two unmarried aunts. His books
include *Reginald*, *The Chronicles of Clovis* and
Beasts and Superbeasts.

Salinger, J.D. (1919-) American
novelist and short-story writer best known
for his classic novel about the turmoil of
adolescence, The CATCHER IN THE RYE. In
other works such as *Franny and Zooey*, *Raise
High the Roof-Beam, Carpenters* and *Seymour: an Introduction* Salinger describes the
experiences of various members of the
eccentric Glass family.

Sassoon, Siegfried (1886-1967) British
writer known for his war poetry and
memoirs. Sassoon fought with distinction
in World War I until 1917 when disgust
with the war leaders led him to refuse

further service. He published two volumes of anti-war poetry: *The Old Huntsman* and *Counter-Attack*. After the war Sassoon turned to religious poetry, and to semi-autobiographical works such as the well-known *Memoirs of a Fox-Hunting Man*.

Sayers, Dorothy L. (1893-1957) British author of meticulously researched crime novels featuring the erudite amateur detective Lord Peter Wimsey and, in later books, the woman investigator Harriet Vane. Her best-known books include *Strong Poison, Murder Must Advertise, The Nine Tailors* and *Busman's Honeymoon*, in which Wimsey and Harriet finally marry. Sayers also wrote a number of religious plays, and made an acclaimed translation of ▷DANTE's *Divine Comedy*.

Scott, Sir Walter (1771-1832) Scottish author of historical novels, ballads and romantic poetry based mainly on tales and legends of the Scottish border region. His works include *The Lay of the Last Minstrel*, a love story in verse, and the adventure tales *Waverley* and ▷ROB ROY, both set during the Jacobite rebellions in Scotland. *Ivanhoe* is set in medieval England. Scott is considered to be the inventor of the historical novel and also, by some, of the short story.
Scott's tragic novel *The Bride of Lammermoor* – in which the heroine is driven mad and provoked to commit murder by the appalling cruelty of her family – provided the inspiration for Gaetano Donizetti's opera *Lucia di Lammermoor*.

Seuss, Dr Pseudonym of the American children's author and illustrator Theodor Seuss Giesel (1904-91). Initially Giesel worked as a cartoonist and then as a film animator in Hollywood, but in the 1930s he began to produce children's picture books with comic rhymes. His best-known books are a series for young readers, beginning with *The Cat in the Hat*.

sex-and-shopping novels Popular works of fiction, generally written for and by women, in which glamorous characters indulge in steamy romantic affairs and spend vast sums of money. Typical examples include Judith Krantz's novel *Princess Daisy*, Shirley Conran's *Lace* and Jackie Collins's *Hollywood Wives*. An earlier example is Jacqueline Susann's 1968 novel *The Valley of the Dolls*, which sold more than 28 million copies.

Shaffer, Peter (1926-) British playwright. His works include *The Royal Hunt of the Sun*, which deals with the conquest of Peru, and *Equus*, a play about the relationship between a youth obsessed with horses and a psychiatrist who tries to help him. In *Amadeus* Schaffer dramatised – and exaggerated – the rivalry between the composer Mozart and his contemporary Salieri.
An Oscar-winning film of ▷AMADEUS was released in 1984.

Shakespeare, William (1564-1616) English poet and dramatist, generally considered the greatest writer in the English language for his insights into human nature and for his poetic brilliance. Shakespeare was born in Stratford-upon-Avon, and was the eldest son of the glove seller John Shakespeare and his wife Mary Arden. In 1582 he married Anne Hathaway, who was eight years older and already pregnant. A daughter, Susannah, was born in 1583 and twins, Hamnet and Judith, two years later. Some time in the late 1580s or early 1590s Shakespeare became established as an actor and playwright in London. In 1594 he became a partner in a group of actors called Lord Chamberlain's Men, and from that time on almost all his work was written for that company. From 1599, Shakespeare and his colleagues occupied the GLOBE THEATRE in Southwark. They soon became London's leading theatrical company and in 1603 received royal patronage, after which they were known as the King's Men. Shakespeare's success eventually enabled him to buy a large house and retire to Stratford, where he died. His earliest-known works date from the late 1580s and early 1590s and include the three *Henry VI* plays, RICHARD III, The TAMING OF THE SHREW and the narrative poems *Venus and Adonis* and *The Rape of Lucrece*. These were followed between the mid-1590s and about 1600 by comedies such as A MIDSUMMER NIGHT'S DREAM, The MERCHANT OF VENICE, *Much Ado About Nothing* and TWELFTH NIGHT; the tragedies ROMEO AND JULIET and JULIUS CAESAR; the historical plays *Richard II*, HENRY V and HENRY IV, PARTS 1 AND 2; and a sequence of more than 150 sonnets. Between 1600 and 1607 Shakespeare produced the great tragedies HAMLET, OTHELLO, KING LEAR and ANTONY AND CLEOPATRA, and the 'problem plays' *Troilus and Cressida* and *Measure for Measure*. In the last years of his life Shakespeare wrote the romances

PRECIOUS RELICS *Modern editions of Shakespeare's plays are largely based on the First Folio, which was brought out in 1623 and contains what is probably the only authentic portrait of the bard. Earlier printings of the plays – such as the 1597* Romeo and Juliet *– were often much less accurate.*

Cymbeline, The Winter's Tale and The TEMPEST, and is thought to have collaborated with other authors on *Pericles* and *Henry VIII*.

It has been argued that Shakespeare's plays could have been written by a group of Elizabethan authors or by other, individual authors such as Francis Bacon or Christopher Marlowe. However, few experts take these theories seriously.

'Shall I compare thee to a summer's day?'

First line of a sonnet by William SHAKESPEARE, and followed by the line 'Thou art more lovely and more temperate'. The poet argues that, unlike the beauty of nature which must come to an end, his beloved's 'eternal summer shall not fade' because it will be immortalised in his poem, which ends:

> So long as men can breathe, or eyes can see,
> So long lives this, and this gives life to thee.

Shaw, George Bernard (1856-1950)

Irish dramatist and critic. Shaw moved to London as a young man and became an influential member of the socialist Fabian Society and a renowned public speaker. He wrote novels, criticism, political tracts and more than 50 plays including *Arms and the Man, Man and Superman, Major Barbara, Heartbreak House* and *Saint Joan*. PYGMALION – the tale of a Cockney flower girl who with the help of elocution lessons becomes a high society lady – was the basis for the 1956 musical ▷MY FAIR LADY. Shaw's plays are known for their wit and for their social and moral concerns, which he often spelled out in lengthy prefaces. His other works include *The Intelligent Woman's Guide to Socialism and Capitalism* and *The Perfect Wagnerite* – a political interpretation of the operas of Richard Wagner. Shaw won the Nobel prize for literature in 1925.

Shaw and Winston Churchill disliked each other but enjoyed exchanging insults. On one occasion Shaw sent the statesman two tickets for the first night of his new play with a note saying, 'Bring a friend – if you have one'. Churchill returned the tickets, asking instead for tickets for the second night – 'if there is one'.

Shelley, Percy Bysshe (1792-1822)

English poet and a leading figure in ▷ROMANTICISM. Shelley held radical views and fought all his life for causes such as vegetarianism, republicanism and free love. As a student, he was expelled from Oxford for publishing an atheistic pamphlet, and he later lost custody of his children because of his anti-religious views. In 1818 Shelley went to live in Italy where he composed many of his best-known works. Four years later he was drowned in a boating accident off the Italian coast on his way home from visiting his friend Lord BYRON, who was also living in Italy. Shelley's best-known poems include the political fables *Queen Mab, Prometheus Unbound* and *The Mask of Anarchy*; an elegy on the death of John KEATS entitled *Adonais*; and the lyrical poems 'Ode to the West Wind' and 'To a Skylark'. One of his most popular poems is the sonnet 'Ozymandias' in which he describes a magnificent statue from antiquity, lying shattered but bearing the still-legible inscription:

> 'My name is Ozymandias, king of kings:
> Look on my works, ye Mighty, and despair!'

Shelley's private life was as unconventional as his beliefs. He eloped with his first wife, Harriet Westbrook, when she was just 16. Despite having two children, he left her within a few years for Mary Wollstonecraft Godwin, another 16-year-old and daughter of the philosopher William Godwin. For some years Shelley and Mary lived as a ménage à trois with Mary's stepsister Claire, who was also Byron's lover. When Harriet drowned herself in 1816, Shelley married Mary, who wrote FRANKENSTEIN.

SOCIAL ENGINEERING *In the 1964 film* My Fair Lady, *which was based on George Bernard Shaw's* Pygmalion, *Eliza Doolittle (Audrey Hepburn) discovers that being a lady has its drawbacks – mainly in the form of Professor Henry Higgins (Rex Harrison).*

Sheridan, Richard Brinsley (1751-1816) English playwright born in Dublin. He wrote light social comedies such as *The Rivals* – known for the character Mrs Malaprop who habitually uses the wrong word, so creating a malapropism; at one point she exclaims, 'If I reprehend any thing in this world, it is the use of my oracular tongue, and a nice derangement of epitaphs!'. Sheridan's other comedies include *The School for Scandal* and *The Critic*.

Sidney, Sir Philip (1554-86) English poet, sportsman, soldier and courtier, regarded because of his varied accomplishments as the archetypal Renaissance Man. Sidney is known for the collection of sonnets *Astrophel and Stella* and for his generous patronage of other writers, including Edmund SPENSER.
♟ Sidney's descendants still live at his stately home, Penshurst Place, in Kent.

Sir Gawain and the Green Knight
Anonymous 14th-century poem from the northwest Midlands. Sir Gawain, in response to a challenge, sets off to find a mysterious 'Green Knight'. On the way Gawain is entertained at a castle where he behaves faultlessly except for a single act of dishonesty motivated by fear for his life. He eventually finds the Green Knight who asks Gawain to attack him with an axe, on condition that he has the right to return the blow a year and a day later. Gawain beheads the knight but he survives and rides away. When Gawain shows up on the appointed day to meet his death, the Green Knight spares him, but inflicts a slight wound as token punishment for his one failing. (See also ▷GAWAIN in 'Myths and Legends'.)

Sitwell, Dame Edith (1887-1964) English poet who used the rhythms of jazz and dance music in verses such as the sequence *Façade* (1923), which was later set to music by Sir William Walton. She also wrote poems about the horror of war, such as 'Still Falls the Rain', which deals with the

ECCENTRIC PRESENCE *Edith Sitwell's stature as a writer has been disputed, but for many years her theatrical appearance exemplified the romance of literary life.*

Blitz on London during World War II. ♟ Edith Sitwell was a familiar public figure, noted for her eccentric and flamboyant medieval-style clothing.

Southey, Robert (1774-1843) English poet, friend of Wordsworth and Coleridge and a pioneer of ▷ROMANTICISM. Southey wrote ballads, including 'The Inchcape Rock', and narrative poems. In 1813 he was made poet laureate. In his later years Southey turned increasingly to writing histories of nations and wars.

Spark, Muriel (1918-) Edinburgh-born author known primarily as a novelist, although she also wrote poems, plays and criticism. Many of her books contain elements of fantasy, the macabre or the supernatural. Spark's best-known book is *The Prime of Miss Jean Brodie*, a novel about a schoolmistress who leads her teenage protégées onto dangerous moral ground. It was filmed in 1969 with Maggie Smith in the leading role.

Spender, Stephen (1909-) English poet and critic whose *Twenty Poems* (1930), *Vienna* (1934) and *The Still Centre* (1939) reflect his early left-wing views. Other works include translations of European literature, an autobiography *World Within World* (1951) and *Journals 1939-83* (1985).

Spenser, Edmund (*c.*1552-99) English poet, considered one of the greatest of the Elizabethan age. His first important work was a series of seasonal verses, *The Shephearde's Calendar*, which was dedicated to Sir Philip Sidney. This was followed by the poem for which he is best known, a long moral and political ▷ALLEGORY entitled The FAERIE QUEENE. It was published in six books between 1590 and 1596, and glorified the reign of Elizabeth I. His other works include *Amoretti*, in which he wooed his second wife, and *Epithalamion*, which celebrated their marriage.
♟ In *The Faerie Queene* Spenser developed a new form of poetic stanza that became known as the Spenserian stanza.

Steinbeck, John (1902-68) American author of novels and short stories mainly about the lives of the rural working class in the western USA. His books include *Of Mice and Men*, a study of the relationship between two travelling labourers, *Cannery Row*, and *East of Eden*, a family saga about the conflict between good and evil. The best known is *The Grapes of Wrath* – the tale of a family from the American Dust Bowl who, displaced by drought and bankruptcy, set off for California in search of a better life. Steinbeck received the Nobel prize for literature in 1962.

Sterne, Laurence (1713-68) Innovative Irish-born author who became famous after writing the eccentric comedy TRISTRAM SHANDY. Sterne also wrote sermons and a chronicle of his travels abroad entitled *A Sentimental Journey*. His witty, original books are highly regarded for their humane outlook, tolerance and warmth.

Stevenson, Robert Louis (1850-94) Scottish novelist and essayist who wrote some of the best-known tales of adventure and romance in the English language, including TREASURE ISLAND, *Kidnapped* and DR JEKYLL AND MR HYDE, as well as the well known *A Child's Garden of Verses*. Many of Stevenson's most memorable characters are complex mixtures of good and evil, and his books often leave the reader uncertain about the distinction between right and wrong.
♟ Stevenson's life was colourful: he married an American woman ten years his senior and they eventually settled in Samoa. His last book, *Weir of Hermiston*, was left unfinished when he died.

Stoker, Bram (Abraham) (1847-1912) Irish writer remembered for his thriller ▷DRACULA, the classic vampire tale.

Stoppard, Tom (1937-) English dramatist born in Czechoslovakia. His plays are comedies which satirise social and theatrical conventions at the same time as tackling moral issues. The best known include *Rosencrantz and Guildenstern are Dead*, a fantasy woven around a scene from *Hamlet*; *Jumpers*, a satire on academic philosophy; and *Travesties*, a farce bringing together James Joyce, Lenin and Tristan Tzara, the founder of ▷DADA art, in Zurich during World War I. In his play *Arcadia*, a female historian and a male academic visit a country estate and uncover a 180-year-old dangerous liaison.

Streetcar Named Desire, A Play written by Tennessee WILLIAMS in 1947. Blanche DuBois, a faded Southern belle with pretensions to gentility, visits her married sister in New Orleans. Blanche's airs and graces soon arouse the hostility of her brutal and inarticulate brother-in-law, Stanley Kowalski, with tragic consequences.
🔊 The play was filmed in 1951 with Vivien Leigh playing Blanche and Marlon Brando playing her brother-in-law.

Sumer is icumen in Early English song celebrating summer's arrival. Both words and music date from the 13th century.

Swallows and Amazons Children's novel by the British author Arthur Ransome (1884-1967), the first in a series of 12 books about children's holiday adventures. The 'Swallows' and the 'Amazons' are two families of children on boating holidays in the Lake District. They are rivals at first but soon become firm friends and go on to solve a mystery together.
🔊 Most of the characters in *Swallows and Amazons* were based on real people, including the children of friends, and even Ransome himself.
🔊 Ransome's novels are known for their meticulous descriptions of outdoor activities such as boating and fishing, which were passionate interests of his.

Swift, Jonathan (1667-1745) Anglo-Irish satirist, poet and Anglican cleric, who used his sharp wit to attack ignorance, vice and folly wherever he found it – particularly in high places. His books include *A Tale of a Tub* – a satire on religious extremism – and GULLIVER'S TRAVELS, which ridicules many aspects of life from politics to science, philosophy and, in the end, humanity itself. Swift also wrote essays and pamphlets on issues that aroused his indignation, such as the treatment of Ireland, which he satirised in A MODEST PROPOSAL. Although never well-off, he gave a third of his income to charity and another third towards the founding of a Dublin hospital for the insane. The last years of his life were dogged by ill health, probably caused by the inner-ear disorder Ménière's disease.
🔊 Swift's personal life is still something of a mystery. For many years he was close to Esther Johnson – addressed as 'Stella' in his journals and letters – and although it seems their relationship was not sexual, they may have married secretly. He was also pursued by Esther Vanhomrigh – 'Vanessa' – until her jealousy of Stella led Swift to break off all contact with her.
🔊 Swift is sometimes referred to as 'Dean Swift', in reference to his position as Dean of St Patrick's in Dublin from 1713.

Swinburne, Algernon Charles (1837-1909) English author and critic, whose early works such as the lush and erotic *Poems and Ballads* (1866) both enthralled and shocked his Victorian public. His finest poems such as 'Ave Atque Vale', a farewell to the French poet Baudelaire, and 'The Triumph of Time', the lament of a rejected lover, express eloquent sympathy for the suffering of others.

Synge, John Millington (SING) (1871-1909) Irish dramatist known for plays about peasant, life including the tragedy *Riders to the Sea* (1904), about a mother's loss of her six sons, and *The Playboy of the Western World* (1907), in which a young stranger arrives in a village and talks his way into the affections of the local women.
🔊 Synge's forthright language – in particular his use of the word 'shift' (meaning a petticoat) – caused a riot when *The Playboy of the Western World* was first performed in Dublin in 1907.

Taming of the Shrew, The Comedy by William SHAKESPEARE, probably written around 1592. The 'shrew' is Katherina, or Kate, a woman of violent moods and rude outbursts. She meets her match in the spirited Petruchio who marries and reforms her by giving her a taste of her own medicine. At the end of the play she is sufficiently 'tamed' by Petruchio to make a speech in which she urges wives to submit to their husbands.
🔊 Cole Porter's musical comedy *Kiss Me, Kate* is based on *The Taming of the Shrew*.

Tempest, The Magical romantic play by William SHAKESPEARE, written in about 1611. Prospero, the usurped Duke of Milan and a magician, has had to bring up his daughter Miranda on an island where they are alone except for the monster-slave Caliban and various spirits, such as Ariel. The play opens as Prospero, who is concerned about the young Miranda's future, creates a tempest which shipwrecks a young man, Ferdinand, together with the false Duke of Milan and his confederates, on the island. Miranda and Ferdinand fall in love and the others are delivered into Prospero's hands. He forgives them on condition that his dukedom is restored. At the end of the play, Prospero renounces magic and prepares to return to Italy.

STAKED OUT *Gulliver is tied down by the Lilliputians after a shipwreck brings him to their land. Although it is often regarded as an adventure tale, Swift's book is a bitter attack on human folly.*

Tennyson, Alfred, Lord (1809-92)

The most renowned poet of the Victorian age, known for his lyrical, musical poems on subjects ranging from mythology and religion to personal relationships and contemporary events. He was made poet laureate in 1850 and received a peerage in 1884. Tennyson's best-known works include The LADY OF SHALOTT; The CHARGE OF THE LIGHT BRIGADE; *In Memoriam*, a sequence of verses mourning the death of his friend Arthur Hallam; and *Idylls of the King*, a retelling of the legend of King Arthur. Tennyson's last poem, 'Crossing the Bar', symbolises death as a sea voyage that begins by crossing the harbour bar:

Sunset and evening star,
And one clear call for me!
And may there be no moaning of the bar,
When I put out to sea.

Thackeray, William Makepeace

(1811-63) English writer born in India. He wrote essays, articles and novels including VANITY FAIR – a social satire about the lives of two women, Becky Sharp and Amelia Sedley, at the time of the Napoleonic Wars of the late 18th and early 19th centuries.

Thomas, Dylan (1914-53)

Welsh writer of poetry and prose about the country life of his youth and his own experiences. His work is known for verbal inventiveness and vivid portraits of landscapes and people. Thomas was a meticulous craftsman and revised his work to fit strict poetic forms. His writings include the poems 'Fern Hill', 'And Death Shall Have No Dominion' and 'Poem in October', and the 1954 radio drama UNDER MILK WOOD.

Thomas's heavy drinking probably contributed to his early death during a lecture tour of the USA.

Thomas, the Tank Engine

The main character in a series of 26 picture books for children, by the Reverend W. Awdry. Thomas has various adventures with other trains such as Gordon and Henry, under the watchful eye of the Fat Controller.

Through the Looking-Glass

Children's book by Lewis CARROLL, published in 1872 and the sequel to ALICE'S ADVENTURES IN WONDERLAND. In a dream, Alice walks through the looking-glass and enters a world of absurdity where she encounters bizarre characters such as Tweedledum and Tweedledee, Humpty-Dumpty and the red and white queens.

Through the Looking-Glass contains the nonsense poems 'Jabberwocky' (see JABBERWOCK) and 'The Walrus and the Carpenter'.

PORTRAIT OF THE ARTIST *Augustus John painted Dylan Thomas as a young man. The poet's flamboyant personality and brilliance as a speaker later won him a large public following.*

Thurber, James (1894-1961)

American humorist whose stories and essays, many of which appeared in *The New Yorker*, often explore the dilemma of a naive hero in trendy society. He was also known for his charming sketches of lugubrious dogs.

Tintern Abbey

Poem by William WORDSWORTH, written in 1798 but inspired by a visit to the abbey five years before. The poem describes Wordsworth's changing feelings for nature in boyhood, youth and adulthood.

'To be, or not to be'

Opening line of one of the most celebrated speeches in English literature. It comes from Shakespeare's play HAMLET, and occurs in a ▷SOLILOQUY in which the prince considers suicide as a way out of his dilemma. Ultimately, he rejects it because of fears about 'what dreams may come' – that is, the possibility of damnation and eternal torment – and concludes, 'Thus conscience doth make cowards of us all'.

Tolkien, J.R.R. (1892-1973)

English scholar and critic, and author of the fantasy novels *The Hobbit* and The LORD OF THE RINGS trilogy. Hobbits, a race of small people with large, furry feet, who appear in both works, are home-loving, peaceable and live underground in the fictional world of Middle Earth. Tolkien, who attracted a cult following in the 1960s, created complete mythologies of his own, influenced by a deep knowledge and love of Old English literature as well as Norse mythology.

Tom Brown's Schooldays

Children's book by the author and Liberal politician Thomas Hughes (1822-96), published in 1857. It describes the experiences of a typical schoolboy, Tom Brown, at the public school of Rugby under the headmastership of Thomas Arnold, father of the poet Matthew Arnold. The book expresses Hughes's belief in 'muscular Christianity' – the doctrine that physical activity and competitive games could develop Christian virtues such as courage and self-discipline.

The book's school bully, Harry Flashman, later became the anti-hero of a series of comic novels by George Macdonald Fraser (1925-).

Tom Jones

▷PICARESQUE novel by Henry FIELDING, published in 1749 and generally considered Fielding's greatest work. It follows the adventures of the title character from the time that he is found abandoned as a tiny baby, through childhood and youth, and into manhood and the discovery of his true identity. The book upholds the values of innocence and kindness while ignoring conventional morality, which Fielding saw as hypocritical, as for example by openly describing Tom's sexual encounters.

Tom Jones was one of the first novels to be written in English and its style had a major influence on the development of fiction.

Tom Sawyer, The Adventures of

Children's book by Mark TWAIN, published in 1876. The hero is a wily, independent boy who engages in a series of anarchic escapades. In one episode, Tom tricks his friends into whitewashing a fence for him by pretending it is a great privilege and making them pay to take over the job. On another occasion, Tom and his friends disappear for so long that they are presumed dead, finally returning to find their own funeral in progress.

Tom's best friend is Huckleberry Finn, a character who reappears as the hero of The Adventures of HUCKLEBERRY FINN.

Townsend, Sue (1946-)

English writer known for the comic novel about adolescence, *The Secret Diary of Adrian Mole, aged 13¾*, and its sequels, and the satirical *The Queen and I*.

Treasure Island

Adventure tale by Robert Louis STEVENSON, originally published as a magazine serial (1881-2). A young boy, Jim Hawkins, lives with his mother who keeps the Admiral Benbow inn. An old pirate comes to stay at the inn but drops down dead when he receives the dreaded 'black spot' – a sign that his enemies are closing in. Among the old pirate's papers Jim finds a map of buried treasure and sets off with two associates on the schooner *Hispaniola* to look for the hoard. However, among the ship's crew are the villainous pirate and his men who are after the hoard for themselves. With great daring, and the help of his friends, Jim foils their plans and gains the treasure.

Tristram Shandy Rumbustious, experimental novel by Laurence STERNE, published in nine volumes between 1759 and 1767. The story is narrated, with lengthy digressions, by the title character who in the process pokes fun at the plotting, structure and even typography of the novel form – still very new at the time. *Tristram Shandy* has been seen as a precursor of ▷STREAM OF CONSCIOUSNESS writing.

Trollope, Anthony (1815-82) English writer best known for his 'Barchester Chronicles', a series of novels dealing with provincial middle-class life in the imaginary county of Barsetshire. They include *The Warden*, concerned with infighting behind the scenes in a charitable hospital, and *Barchester Towers*, in which the diocese of Barchester is subjected to a clerical power struggle. Both the Barchester books and Trollope's 'Palliser' novels have been made into television series.
♣As well as writing, Trollope had a successful career as a civil servant in the Post Office. He is credited with introducing the pillar-box to Britain.

Twain, Mark Pseudonym of the American writer Samuel Langhorne Clemens (1835-1910). Twain won acclaim in 1869 with *The Innocents Abroad*, an account of a voyage to the Mediterranean which satirises both European and American pretensions. His best-known books are the children's novels *The Adventures of* TOM SAWYER and *The Adventures of* HUCKLEBERRY FINN. In later works such as *A Connecticut Yankee in King Arthur's Court* Twain's satire became increasingly biting.
♣As a young man Twain worked on a Mississippi steamboat. His pen name comes from a call used in taking river soundings meaning 'two fathoms deep'.
♣Twain is well known for witty sayings, such as 'The report of my death was an exaggeration' and 'A classic is something that everybody wants to have read and nobody wants to read'.

Twelfth Night Comedy written by William SHAKESPEARE around 1601. The twins Sebastian and Viola are separated in a foreign land after a shipwreck. Viola disguises herself as a young man and is employed in the service of Duke Orsino, a bitter man who has been rejected by his beloved Olivia. Olivia falls for the disguised Viola, Sebastian returns and one confusion follows another before, finally, Sebastian marries Olivia and the duke marries Viola.
♣Much of the humour in the play is provided by lesser characters such as the pompous steward Malvolio and Olivia's uncle Sir Toby Belch.

'Tyger, The' Poem by William BLAKE, from his collection *Songs of Experience*. It praises the beauty and power of the tiger, including its terrible capacity for destruction, as a reflection of the Creator's spirit. The poem opens with the question:

> Tyger! Tyger! burning bright
> In the forests of the night,
> What immortal hand or eye
> Could frame thy fearful symmetry?

Ulysses Controversial novel, experimental in form, written by the Irish author James JOYCE and published in Paris in 1922, although not in England until 1936 because of obscenity laws. *Ulysses* deals with the experiences of a small number of Dublin characters as they go about their business on June 16, 1904 – a date now known as Bloomsday. In themselves the events are ordinary, everyday occurrences, but Joyce describes them in terms of episodes from Homer's ▷ODYSSEY. The main characters are a middle-aged Jewish advertisement salesman Leopold Bloom (representing Homer's hero Odysseus), a young poet Stephen Dedalus – to whom Bloom acts as a father-figure – and Leopold's wife Molly.
♣*Ulysses* introduced ▷STREAM OF CONSCIOUSNESS into English writing and greatly influenced the modern novel.

Uncle Tom's Cabin Novel by the American author and antislavery campaigner Harriet Beecher Stowe, describing the grim realities of slave life in the Southern states. It was serialised in 1851-2 and was considered by some – including Abraham Lincoln – to have contributed to the American Civil War by arousing antislavery sentiment in the North. The title character is a pious, loyal slave who is eventually beaten to death by the cruel overseer of the plantation.

Under Milk Wood Dramatic evocation of the seaside town of Llareggub by the Welsh writer Dylan THOMAS, bringing to life such characters as the church organist Organ Morgan, the salty old sea-dog Captain Cat and the twice-widowed Mrs Ogmore-Pritchard. It was written for radio in 1954, and then adapted for the stage.

Vanity Fair Novel by William Makepeace THACKERAY, published in instalments during 1847 and 1848 and intended as a satire on social behaviour and attitudes. It contrasts the lives and characters of two young women – the worldly-wise orphan Becky Sharp and the protected, kind-hearted Amelia Sedley. They meet at Miss Pinkerton's academy for young ladies and go on to marry soldiers. Amelia's husband is killed at Waterloo, and Becky's husband leaves her when he discovers she is unfaithful. Eventually both women face life alone.

THE ROOT OF ALL EVIL... *Money – and the lack of it – rules the lives of all the characters in* Vanity Fair. *For Becky Sharp, it is the key to social climbing, however disreputable its source.*

Vidal, Gore (1925-) Novelist, essayist and satirist, best known for *Myra Breckinridge* (1968) and historical fiction including *Burr* (1973) and *Lincoln* (1984).

Walcott, Derek (1930-) West Indian poet and playwright, born in St Lucia, whose works combine elements such as Creole vocabulary and classical mythology. His best-known poem is *Omeros* (1989), based on Homer's ▷ODYSSEY. Walcott won the Nobel prize for literature in 1992.

Waste Land, The Poem by T.S. ELIOT, published in 1922 and considered one of the major works associated with ▷MODERNISM. The poem deals despairingly with the state of post-World War I society, which Eliot saw as sterile and decadent. Numerous references to religious imagery, mythology and literature of the past are used ironically to point out the comparative emptiness of Eliot's time. The poem begins:

April is the cruellest month, breeding
Lilacs out of the dead land, mixing
Memory and desire, stirring
Dull roots with spring rain.

Water Babies, The Fantasy children's novel by Charles Kingsley (1819-75), published in 1863. Tom, a young chimney-sweep, falls into a river and is transformed into a 'water baby'. In his new existence he learns all about underwater life and is instructed by Mrs Doasyouwouldbedoneby and Mrs Bedonebyasyoudid.

Waugh, Evelyn (1903-66) English novelist known for his social satire and black humour. Waugh's first novel *Decline and Fall*, based on his unhappy experiences as an assistant schoolmaster, was an immediate success. It was followed by several other comic works including *A Handful of Dust*, *Scoop* – a hilarious account of an incompetent journalist's attempts to cover a civil war in Africa – and *The Loved One*, a grotesque satire on California-style death. In 1930 Waugh converted to Roman Catholicism. More serious works include *Brideshead Revisited* – the saga of a decadent family, turned into a popular television series in 1981 – and *The Ordeal of Gilbert Pinfold* which deals with faith, redemption and madness. Waugh also wrote travel books and about his experiences in the Balkans and Crete during World War II – in the 'Sword of Honour' trilogy.
🔥 Waugh's satirical style has been continued by his son, the journalist Auberon.

Webster, John (c.1580-1634) English playwright generally considered, after Shakespeare, to be the greatest of the Jacobean period. His dark, bloodthirsty revenge tragedies *The White Devil* (c.1612) and *The Duchess of Malfi* (c.1613-14) are still frequently performed.

Wells, H.G. (1866-1946) Prolific English author, and one of the first to write science fiction. His first book, *The Time Machine*, is partly set in a distant future age when the human race is divided into the subterranean workers, the Morlocks, and the decadent class of the Eloi. Wells's other fantasies include *The Island of Doctor Moreau*, *The Invisible Man* and *The War of the Worlds* – a tale about Martians invading the Earth which caused panic when an adaptation by Orson Welles was broadcast by radio in the USA in 1938. Wells wrote more than 100 books in all, including works on politics and history, and comic

novels such as *The History of Mr Polly*, in which a shopkeeper plots a daring escape from his dreary existence.

West, Dame Rebecca (1892-1983) British writer and feminist, born Cecily Isabel Fairfield. At 19, she adopted the name Rebecca West from Henrik Ibsen's play *Rosmersholm*. Her writing is tough-minded and stylish, and includes journalism, politics and history as well as novels. She conducted a love affair with the novelist H.G. WELLS, and had a son by him.

Whitman, Walt (1819-92) American poet best known for his collection *Leaves of Grass*, in which he tried to express the young, independent spirit of the USA. He revised the book continually throughout his lifetime and it eventually grew from 12 poems to more than 150. Like all Whitman's work, it celebrates nature and upholds the values of individualism, freedom and brotherhood.

Who's Afraid of Virginia Woolf? Tragicomic play by the American dramatist Edward Albee (1928-), first produced in 1962. It concerns the events of a single, tense evening during which an alcoholic academic couple play a series of mutually destructive games while supposedly entertaining their guests.
🔥 The 1966 film of the play starred Richard Burton and Elizabeth Taylor.
🔥 The title is a literary play on words sung by the 'heroine' to the tune of *Who's Afraid of the Big, Bad Wolf*.

Wife of Bath One of the pilgrims in Geoffrey Chaucer's CANTERBURY TALES. She is a robust, colourful character who has had five husbands – all now dead – and is sometimes seen as an early feminist. The Wife of Bath launches a spirited attack on chastity and female submissiveness.

Wilde, Oscar (1854-1900) Irish writer known for his wit, brilliant conversation and extreme aestheticism – the view that art should be judged solely by standards of beauty and that issues such as morality are irrelevant. Wilde wrote poems, fairy tales such as *The Happy Prince*, and a single novel, *The Picture of Dorian Gray*. His best-known works are comic plays such as *Lady Windermere's Fan*, *An Ideal Husband* and *The Importance of Being Earnest*. Wilde also wrote a tragedy, *Salomé*, which was later turned into an opera by Richard Strauss. Wilde led a flamboyant life and made enemies among the establishment. In 1895 he was bankrupted by a lawsuit and imprisoned for homo-

sexuality. He later described his experience of prison in *The Ballad of Reading Gaol*. After his release in 1897, Wilde went to live in Paris where he remained up to his death.
🔥 His witty lines are legion; he defined the cynic as 'A man who knows the price of everything and the value of nothing' and fox-hunting as 'the unspeakable in full pursuit of the uneatable'.

Wild Swans Epic account of 20th-century China, by the writer Jung Chang (1952-). Published in 1991, the book depicts, in moving detail, the lives of her grandmother, her mother and herself against the repressive backdrop of her homeland.

'William' books Series of children's books by Richmal Crompton (1890-1969), about the escapades of an 11-year-old schoolboy (William Brown) and his gang, the Outlaws. His parents vainly attempt to civilise him but he remains chronically unable to stay out of trouble.

Williams, Tennessee (1911-83) American playwright known for psychological dramas such as *The Glass Menagerie*, A STREETCAR NAMED DESIRE and *Cat on a Hot Tin Roof*. His plays deal with small

STUDIED POSE *Oscar Wilde's sharp wit was renowned in London's literary salons. 'The man who can dominate a London dinner-table can dominate the world,' he pronounced.*

OSCAR WILDE.
NEW YORK.

groups of characters who battle against the odds, handicapped by their personal inadequacies and desperate circumstances. Undercurrents of violence and sexual tension are never far below the surface.

Wilson, Angus (1913-91) Writer of social satires in which middle-class life is disrupted by unforeseen and, occasionally, bizarre events. His books include *Hemlock and After*, and *Anglo-Saxon Attitudes*, in which mysteries from the past come back to haunt a middle-aged historian.

Wind in the Willows, The Animal story for children by Kenneth Grahame (1859-1932), published in 1908. The book started out as a series of tales told to Grahame's son, featuring the highly strung, conceited and irresponsible Toad and his riverside companions Rattie, Mole and Badger – characters partly based on friends of Grahame's and partly on the rural gentry.
🔖A musical, *Toad of Toad Hall*, was adapted from the book by A.A. Milne in 1930.

Winnie-the-Pooh Much loved children's book by A.A. MILNE, published in 1926. The main characters are Christopher Robin

MAKING TRACKS *The familiar outlines of Pooh and Piglet, drawn by E.H. Shepard. The Pooh books made Shepard almost as well known as the author, A.A. Milne (left).*

– a little boy modelled on Milne's own son – his toy bear Winnie-the-Pooh (a 'bear of very little brain') and other toy animal characters including Piglet, Owl, Tigger and the doleful donkey Eeyore. The appeal of the book is based on whimsical illogicality and episodes of comic misunderstanding. On one occasion, for example, Pooh and Piglet are alarmed by the increasing numbers of footprints as they circle a tree in pursuit of a creature called a 'Woozle', not realising that they are making the tracks themselves. Other adventures involve an attempt to catch a large and frightening 'heffalump' by building a trap.

Wodehouse, P.G. (1881-1975) Comic writer known for novels and short stories about the foppish, helpless aristocrat Bertie Wooster and his manservant Jeeves, a master of British understatement and reserve. He also wrote humorous school stories about an immaculately dressed and extremely dignified youth, Rupert Psmith.

Women in Love Novel by D.H. LAWRENCE, published in 1920. The story revolves around two sisters, Ursula and Gudrun Brangwen, and their respective lovers, Rupert Birkin (a self-portrait of Lawrence) and Gerald Crich. While Ursula and Birkin eventually get married and find mutual fulfilment, the relationship between Gerald and Gudrun becomes increasingly destructive. Lawrence considered *Women in Love* to be his finest book but, at the time, one reviewer called it 'an epic of vice'.
🔖The acclaimed 1969 film version of the book contained a notorious nude wrestling match between Alan Bates and Oliver Reed.

Woolf, Virginia (1882-1941) English novelist, and a leading figure in ▷MODERNISM. She came from a well-known intellectual family and with her brothers and her sister – the artist Vanessa Bell – she held meetings of friends at her home in Bloomsbury, from which the BLOOMSBURY GROUP was born. In 1912 she married the writer and left-wing political thinker Leonard Woolf and together they set up the Hogarth Press. Virginia Woolf's principal novels were *Mrs Dalloway*, *To the Lighthouse* and *The Waves* – all of which use experimental techniques such as ▷STREAM OF CONSCIOUSNESS writing to give expression to the inner lives of characters. Woolf was also an outstanding journalist and critic, and her witty feminist essay *A Room of One's Own* is particularly well known. She suffered from recurrent periods of depression and mental illness, and finally drowned herself in the River Ouse in Sussex.

🔖Woolf dedicated *Orlando*, a historical novel and her most commercially successful work, to her friend Vita SACKVILLE-WEST.

Wordsworth, William (1770-1850) English poet whose work played a major role in the development of ▷ROMANTICISM in English literature. His writing expresses a mystical view of life in which nature and the human spirit are closely connected. Wordsworth grew up in Cumbria, and the Lake District countryside inspired many of his poems, such as 'The Prelude', 'Intimations of Immortality' and 'Resolution and Independence'. He was a close friend of the poet Samuel Taylor Coleridge, and in 1798 they published a joint volume, *Lyrical Ballads*, which included such poems as The RIME OF THE ANCIENT MARINER and TINTERN ABBEY. He was made poet laureate in 1843.
🔖Wordsworth lived with his sister Dorothy and wife, Mary, at Dove Cottage, now a museum, in Grasmere.

Wuthering Heights Romantic novel by Emily BRONTË, published in 1847. It tells the story of the passionate but troubled relationship between Catherine Earnshaw and the brooding Heathcliff, a homeless youth taken in by her family. Heathcliff overhears Catherine say that it would degrade her to marry him, and he leaves the house in a fury. Three years later Heathcliff returns, seeking vengeance. A series of disasters ensue; most notably, Catherine – now married to the feeble Edward Linton – dies in childbirth. The story ends with Heathcliff's death – which he greets as a reunion with his beloved Catherine.
🔖Wuthering Heights is the name of the Earnshaws' home on the Yorkshire moors.

Yeats, William Butler (1865-1939) Irish poet and playwright influential in the revival of Irish literature in the late 19th and early 20th centuries, and in the founding of an Irish national theatre. His early works were romantic and based on Irish history and legend. Later on, however, Yeats's style became starker and his mature poems – such as 'Sailing to Byzantium', 'The Tower' and 'The Second Coming' – are dominated by themes of historical change, old age and death. He was a senator of the Irish Free State from 1922 to 1928, and won the Nobel prize for literature in 1923.
🔖Yeats died in the south of France but his body was brought back to Ireland in 1948. His epitaph comes from one of his poems:
    Cast a cold eye
    On life, on death.
    Horseman, pass by!

WORLD LITERATURE

Works of prose, poetry and drama from around the globe have become part of our heritage. The passionate Anna Karenina is not just Russian; she is an archetypal tragic heroine. The name Don Juan is synonymous with cruel seduction everywhere. In our children's imagination, fictional characters from many nations – Cinderella, Hansel and Gretel, Babar – jostle for attention.

COLETTE

THE GUTENBERG BIBLE

LEO TOLSTOY

'Abandon all hope, ye who enter here' Inscription above the gateway to hell in the 'Inferno' section of Dante's 14th-century masterpiece, The DIVINE COMEDY.

Aeneid (**Ee-NEE-id**) Latin epic poem in 12 books written by VIRGIL, a Roman poet of the 1st century BC. It traces the origin of the Romans back to the adventures of the Trojan prince Aeneas after the fall of Troy in the mid 13th century BC.

Aeschylus (EES-ki-luss) (525-456 BC) Classical Greek dramatist who is believed to have introduced dialogue into Greek tragedy and is known for the grand style of his works. Only seven of his estimated 90 plays survive, including the ORESTEIA.

Aesop's *Fables* Collection of animal tales with a strong moral point, such as *The Boy Who Cried Wolf* and *The Fox and the Grapes*. By tradition, the fables are attributed to 'Aesop' – a legendary Greek storyteller of the 6th century BC.

FRONT-LINE FRIENDSHIP *A moment of camaraderie amid the horrors of trench warfare is caught in a still from the 1930 film of E.M. Remarque's novel* All Quiet on the Western Front.

SLOW AND STEADY WINS THE RACE *The persistent tortoise outstrips the dallying hare in one of Aesop's best-loved fables, illustrated above in a 1912 watercolour by Charles Folkard.*

aesthetes (or aesthetic movement) Writers and artists of the late 19th century who devoted themselves to beauty and style above all else. They were influenced by the ▷PRE-RAPHAELITES and adopted the motto ▷'ART FOR ART'S SAKE'. They included Oscar ▷WILDE, W.B. ▷YEATS in his younger days and the French writer Villiers de l'Isle-Adam, who once said, 'Live? Our servants will do that for us'.

allegory Use in literature or art of apparently realistic characters, objects or events to stand for abstract qualities or ideas. An allegory can also be any work with such a double meaning. Bunyan's The ▷PILGRIM'S PROGRESS, for example, uses a physical journey to represent the spiritual search of a man as he travels through life.

All Quiet on the Western Front Novel about the horrors of World War I by the German author Erich Maria Remarque, published in 1929. In an understated style it describes the experiences of soldiers who seem to have no life beyond the trenches.

Andersen, Hans Christian (1805-75) Danish writer known for collections of fairy tales such as *The Emperor's New Clothes* and *The Ugly Duckling*. The tales are based on Danish folklore but also clearly bear the stamp of Andersen's own personality and sometimes rather morbid outlook.

Anna Karenina Tragic novel by Leo TOLSTOY, written between 1873 and 1877. Anna, a beautiful woman trapped in an unhappy marriage, falls passionately in love with a young army officer, Vronsky. She leaves her husband who forbids her ever to see her son again. In the end, her life becomes intolerable and she throws herself under a train.
🕯*Anna Karenina* begins with one of the most celebrated sentences in literature: 'All happy families are like one another; each unhappy family is unhappy in its own way.'

Antigone Tragedy by the Greek dramatist SOPHOCLES. It concerns the punishment of Antigone – daughter of Oedipus and Jocasta – for performing funeral rites for her brother Polynices in defiance of her uncle Creon. In the end she kills herself to escape being walled up alive. (See also ▷ANTIGONE in 'Myths and Legends'.)

Arabian Nights, The (or *The Thousand and One Nights*) Collection of folk tales from Indian, Persian and Arabian sources. One of the best-known versions is the English translation made by the explorer Sir Richard Burton between 1885 and 1888. The tales purport to be those told by Scheherazade to her husband – a king who was in the habit of executing his wives after a single night because his first wife had been unfaithful. Each night Scheherazade would begin a tale so riveting that the king would spare her one more night in order to hear the end – but then she would begin the next tale, and delay her fate once more.

Aristophanes (*c.*448-380 BC) Classical Greek dramatist whose satirical comedies dealt with issues of Athenian life. His 11 surviving plays include The BIRDS, The CLOUDS, The FROGS and LYSISTRATA.

Around the World in Eighty Days Novel by the French writer Jules VERNE, published in 1873. An Englishman, Phileas Fogg, and his French valet, Passepartout, set out to win a bet by proving that they can circle the world in a mere 80 days, travelling part of the way by hot-air balloon. Verne wrote his novel after hearing about actual journeys made by two Americans in the 1870s, one of which took exactly 80 days. After the book was published, others started trying to beat the record, which tumbled to just 54 days in Verne's lifetime.

Astérix French hero of a series of children's cartoon books started in 1959, with text by René Goscinny and illustrations by Albert Uderzo. Astérix and his friend Obelix are ancient Gauls fighting to defend their Brittany village from the Romans. In the English version, characters such as Getafix the druid and Cacofonix the bard help them to trounce the Romans time after time. Other comic names include Vitalstatistix the chief and centurion Armisurplus.

Babar the Elephant Main character in a series of children's books by the French author and illustrator Jean de Brunhoff and his son Laurent. In the first book, published in 1931, Babar, after being orphaned by a hunter, finds a home in the city, where he becomes a celebrity. His cousins Arthur and Celeste join him, but eventually all three elephants return to the forest and Babar and Celeste are chosen as King and Queen of the elephants.

Bacchae, The (or *The Bacchants*) Tragedy by the Classical Greek dramatist EURIPIDES. Pentheus, the king of Thebes, refuses to recognise the young god Dionysus and imprisons him because of the disturbance his cult is causing. Eventually Pentheus is torn to pieces by Dionysus' followers, the Bacchae, who include his own mother.

ballad Traditional poem or song – originally an accompaniment to a dance – which tells the story of an event from history or legend. Examples include *Sir Patrick Spens* and *Barbara Allen*. Most ballads have short rhyming verses with a repeated refrain.

Balzac, Honoré de (1799-1850) French novelist, author of a series of 91 books and stories known as *La Comédie*

UP, UP AND AWAY *Poster advertising the 1956 film of* Around the World in Eighty Days, *starring David Niven as Phileas Fogg and the comic Cantinflas as his valet Passepartout.*

Humaine (*The Human Comedy*) that give a wide-ranging picture of contemporary French society and earned Balzac a reputation as one of the world's greatest novelists.

Baudelaire, Charles Pierre (1821-67) French poet best known for the collection *Les Fleurs du Mal* (*The Flowers of Evil*) in which he employs exquisite imagery and compelling rhythms to describe evil, decadence and the quest for love and beauty.

Beauvoir, Simone de (1908-86) French feminist, writer and long-time partner of the philosopher Jean-Paul ▷SARTRE. Her books include *The Second Sex*, *The Mandarins* and several volumes of autobiography.

Beckett, Samuel (1906-89) Irish novelist, poet, dramatist and critic with a despairing yet humorous outlook on life. He settled in Paris during the 1930s and wrote many of his works in both French and English. In the 1950s he became a leading figure in the THEATRE OF THE ABSURD with the success of his play WAITING FOR GODOT. Beckett was awarded the Nobel prize for literature in 1969.

Birds, The Greatest comedy of the Greek dramatist ARISTOPHANES. Two Athenians persuade the birds to build a city ('Cloud-cuckooland') in the sky to intercept the smoke from sacrifices, which nourishes the gods. As a result, the birds and their two human friends can demand whatever they wish from the gods.

black comedy Type of cynical humour developed in the 20th century, particularly in the THEATRE OF THE ABSURD. It represents a view of life in which human striving is futile, beliefs and values are arbitrary, and events are governed by chance. Samuel Beckett's WAITING FOR GODOT and Joe ▷ORTON's *Loot* are black comedies.

Blixen, Karen (1885-1962) Danish writer, known for her short stories and for *Out of Africa* – an autobiographical account of a coffee-farming venture in Kenya which ended in failure. Blixen wrote under various pseudonyms, including Isak Dinesen.

AT HOME IN AFRICA *Karen Blixen, outside her farmhouse in Kenya, holds the son of her servant Farah (left). Bankruptcy and personal tragedy eventually forced her to return to Denmark, where she made her name as a writer.*

Boccaccio, Giovanni (bo-KACH-io) (1313-75) Italian writer and humanist of the Middle Ages. His best-known work, The DECAMERON, influenced Chaucer, Shakespeare and many other writers.

Borges, Jorge Luis (BOR-khez) (1899-1986) Argentinian writer of poems, short stories and essays, including the collections *Fictions* (1944), *The Aleph* (1949), and *Labyrinths* (1953) which brought him fame. His works are concerned with theoretical and philosophical issues and often mix reality and imagination. Borges was an exponent of MAGIC REALISM.

Brecht, Bertolt (1898-1956) Experimental German writer known for plays with a Marxist message, including *Mother Courage*, set in the Thirty Years' War, and *The Threepenny Opera* – an adaptation of the English 17th-century ▷BEGGAR'S OPERA.

Brothers Karamazov, The Novel by Fyodor DOSTOYEVSKY, published in 1880 and generally considered his finest work. It deals with the complex psychological and ethical issues involved in the trial of one of four brothers for the murder of their father.

Camus, Albert (kaa-MOO) (1913-60) French existentialist writer born in Algeria. His works, which include the two highly acclaimed novels *The Plague* and *The Outsider*, explore the dark, irrational side of human nature. He received the Nobel prize for literature in 1957.

Candide Satirical novel by the French writer and philosopher VOLTAIRE. It was published in 1759, and describes a series of calamities that befall the naive young Candide and his tutor Dr Pangloss, who parodies the philosophy of ▷LEIBNIZ by maintaining, against all evidence, that all is for the best in the best of all possible worlds.

catharsis Term used by ▷ARISTOTLE to describe the purifying effect of releasing the emotions of pity and terror which he believed was the purpose of TRAGEDY.

Catullus, Gaius Valerius (*c.*84-*c.*54 BC) Roman poet known for love lyrics addressed to 'Lesbia', a married society woman whose real name was Clodia.

Cervantes, Miguel de (1547-1616) One of Spain's greatest writers, best known for his masterpiece DON QUIXOTE which satirised chivalry and chivalric literature. Cervantes only took up writing after losing the use of his left hand in battle.

CLASSIC CHEKHOV *Three Sisters by Anton Chekhov is one of the masterpieces of the Russian stage and is regularly performed all over the world. This 1902 edition of the play is housed in Moscow's Chekhov Museum.*

Chekhov, Anton Pavlovich (1860-1904) Russian dramatist and short-story writer best known for his four plays *The Seagull, Uncle Vanya, The Cherry Orchard* and *Three Sisters* – a comedy about three women brought up in the countryside and their longing for Moscow. Chekhov first wrote comedy sketches while studying medicine in Moscow from 1879 to 1884. Although humorous, his later work often depicts characters whose lives are frustrated or empty, and who take refuge in dreams, memories or illusions.

Cicero, Marcus Tullius (106-43 BC) Orator, writer and statesman of ancient Rome. His speeches to the Senate are renowned for their ornate style and his letters provide a picture of Roman life at the time. ♟His prose has yielded Latin tags such as *O tempora! O mores!* ('What times! What customs!') and *cui bono?* ('to whose profit?').

Cinderella One of the world's most popular fairy tales, loved for its rags-to-riches optimism and for the magical transformations that enable Cinderella to go to the ball despite the meanness of her stepmother and ugly stepsisters. More than 600 variations of the tale have been identified, including a Chinese story of the 9th century – hundreds of years earlier than the first Western versions. ♟*Cinderella* has inspired numerous works of art including a sparkling opera by Rossini and a much-loved ballet by Prokofiev.

Classicism In literature, any style of writing based on the principles and forms used by Classical Greek and Roman authors, such as those laid down by ▷ARISTOTLE in his *Poetics*. It is sometimes contrasted with ROMANTICISM, which concentrates on imagination and feeling rather than form and style. Classicism flourished during the 17th and 18th centuries when writers such as Voltaire and Molière in French, Swift and Dr Johnson in English, and Goethe and Schiller in German all based their work on Classical models.

Clouds, The Comedy by the Greek dramatist ARISTOPHANES. A farmer sends his son to study under Socrates so that he can learn to outwit his creditors in argument. The strategy proves highly successful until the son turns his newly acquired skills against his own parents.

Colette, Sidonie Gabrielle (1873-1954) French novelist known for her sensitive handling of nature and childhood. Her novel *Gigi* – a version of the ▷PYGMALION legend – was turned into a prize-winning musical film in 1958 starring Leslie Caron.

FEMININE INTUITION *Sidonie Gabrielle Colette was a dancer and mime artist before turning to writing. Her work often reflects her deep sympathy for women and children.*

FIGURES OF FUN *Of all the spectacles on offer in ancient Rome, comedy was probably the most popular. It took many forms, from low farce to satire with a serious message. The actors wore stiff linen masks like those shown in this mosaic to create instantly recognisable stock characters on stage.*

comedy Type of literature which treats its subject matter humorously and which usually has a happy ending. The plot is often unbelievable and the characters are usually ordinary people rather than the kings and heroes of TRAGEDY. Western comedy grew out of ancient Greek fertility rituals in which certain well-known people were publicly ridiculed. Later it became unacceptable to mock individuals and instead stock characters or 'types' were used. In modern times, SATIRE, BLACK COMEDY, FARCE and THEATRE OF THE ABSURD have tended to dominate the comic form.

courtly love Idealised form of love in medieval ROMANCE literature, supposed to exist between a knight and the lady whom he served. The essence of courtly love was an almost religious devotion which uplifted and ennobled the knight and inspired him to great deeds. In theory the love was spiritual and unfulfilled.
There is still much debate as to whether courtly love existed in real life or whether it was just a convention of the poets.

Crime and Punishment Novel by the Russian author Fyodor DOSTOYEVSKY, published in 1866. A poor young student, Raskolnikov, kills an elderly pawnbroker for money. Afterwards, his conscience begins to torment him so that he eventually confesses and then begins the slow path to repentance and atonement. The book was Dostoyevsky's first great novel.

Cyrano de Bergerac Comic swashbuckling play by the French dramatist Edmond Rostand (1868-1918), nominally based on the life of a 17th-century soldier and writer. Cyrano is cursed with a long nose which makes him unattractive to women. However, his literary gifts succeed in wooing a beautiful woman on behalf of a handsome but inarticulate friend.
The story has been been filmed in the USA and France, most recently in 1990 with Gérard Depardieu in the leading role.

Dante Alighieri (1265-1321) Greatest and most influential Italian writer of the Middle Ages. His early life was spent in Florence where as a child he fell in love with 'Beatrice' who figures in his writing. She was also a child, and appears to have done no more than acknowledge him from time to time. For Dante, however, the experience was a spiritual revelation that affected him for the rest of his life. When Beatrice died in 1290 Dante was devastated and turned to philosophy and writing for consolation. Between 1290 and 1294 he wrote his first great work *La Vita Nuova* (*The New Life*) – about his love for Beatrice. Later, he was forced to take up a life of wandering because of political intrigue in Florence. He died in Ravenna, shortly after finishing The DIVINE COMEDY.

Decameron Collection of stories put together around 1350 by the Italian writer Boccaccio. The tales are presented as being told by ten young people who leave Flor-

LITERARY LOVER *José Ferrer gave an eminent performance as the long-nosed, lovelorn Cyrano de Bergerac in the 1950 American film version of Edmond Rostand's romantic play.*

ence in 1348 to escape an outbreak of the plague. Confined together in the hills above the city, they each tell a story a day to amuse one another. The story-telling continues for ten days, making a total of 100 tales, encompassing both comedy and tragedy. The *Decameron* or 'Ten Days' Work' inspired Italian literature for several centuries afterwards.
Chaucer used some of Boccaccio's stories in his ▷CANTERBURY TALES.

dénouement (day-NOO-mon) Point at the end of a book or play when all the intricacies of the plot are untangled for the reader or audience. It usually occurs during or shortly after the climax.
Dénouement is a French word that means 'untying' or 'unknotting'.

Divine Comedy, The Finest work of the medieval Italian writer DANTE ALIGHIERI, completed shortly before his death in 1321. There are three sections, *Hell*, *Purgatory* and *Heaven*, each dealing with a vision of a different supernatural realm. In the first two sections Dante, guided by the Roman poet VIRGIL, meets the souls of pagans and sinners. At the end of *Purgatory* he enters the Earthly Paradise where he finds his beloved Beatrice, who becomes his guide to heaven, which Virgil, a pagan, cannot enter. The poem, noted for its symbolism and allegory, influenced writers such as ▷MILTON, ▷BYRON and T.S. ▷ELIOT.
In the Middle Ages, any work that started off badly but ended well could be called a comedy. Thus *The Divine Comedy*, although a serious work, is a comedy because it begins in hell and ends in heaven.

Doll's House, A Play by Henrik IBSEN, first performed in 1879. The main character, Nora Helmer, is a sheltered, pampered woman. When she finally realises that in eight years of marriage her husband has treated her more as a doll than an adult, she leaves him to establish a life of her own.

Don Juan (DON HWAAN or DON JEW-un) Cruel aristocratic Spanish seducer who features in some 200 literary works, including a satirical poem by ▷BYRON as well as Mozart's opera *Don Giovanni* (its name in Italian). In the basic version of the story, the Don kills an elderly man after attempting to rape his daughter. Later, a memorial statue is erected to the old man, and Don Juan mockingly invites the statue to dinner. The invitation is accepted, and the tale ends with the old man returning from the dead to drag the unrepentant libertine off to hell.

***Don Quixote* (DON QUICK-suht or DON kee-HOH-tee)** Satirical novel by the Spanish writer Miguel de CERVANTES, published in two parts in 1605 and 1615. The title character is a poor country gentleman whose mind becomes deranged by reading too many knightly ROMANCES. Obsessed with the idea of reviving the age of chivalry, he climbs into a rusty suit of armour, mounts his old horse Rosinante and sets off with his fat friend Sancho Panza as his squire. Together they have a series of absurd adventures including an incident where Don Quixote attacks windmills, believing they are giants.

🔖 The expression 'tilting at windmills' means taking on an imaginary enemy.

🔖 A 'quixotic' person is idealistic to the point of impracticality.

Dostoyevsky, Fyodor Mikhailovich (1821-81) One of the greatest Russian novelists and short-story writers of the 19th century. As a young man he was arrested for belonging to a socialist group and underwent a mock execution in which he was reprieved at the last minute. While in prison, Dostoyevsky experienced a religious conversion, and his earlier political views were replaced by an outlook based on spiritual and humanitarian values. His books, including CRIME AND PUNISHMENT and The BROTHERS KARAMAZOV, are known for their insight into human psychology and for their philosophical depth.

dramatis personae List of the characters appearing in a play (as opposed to a cast list, which gives the actors' names). Literally, 'the persons of the drama'.

Dumas, Alexandre (doo-MAH) (1802-1870) French novelist and playwright best known for the historical adventure tales *The Count of Monte Cristo* and *The Three Musketeers* – the exploits of Athos, Porthos, Aramis and their friend D'Artagnan.

🔖 Dumas's son Alexandre (1824-95) was also a writer. His play *La Dame aux Camélias* inspired Verdi's opera *La Traviata*.

Electra Name of two surviving Greek tragedies: one by SOPHOCLES, the other by EURIPIDES. According to Greek legend, ▷ELECTRA's mother Clytemnestra murdered her father Agamemnon. In order to avenge his death, Electra persuaded her brother Orestes to kill their mother and her mother's lover, Aegisthus.

🔖 The psychoanalyst Sigmund Freud coined the phrase 'Electra complex' to refer to the early romantic attraction he believed girls experience towards their fathers.

KNIGHT IN RUSTY ARMOUR *Proud and upright, Don Quixote on his mare Rosinante sets off in search of great deeds and chivalry in an 1868 painting by Honoré Daumier.*

elegy Reflective poem, particularly one mourning someone's death or a sad event. ▷MILTON's *Lycidas* and ▷GRAY'S ELEGY are well-known examples. In Classical times, an elegy was any poem written in alternating lines of six stresses and then five stresses – a form used for love poetry and comic verse as well as serious subjects.

epic Long poem about the larger-than-life achievements of a great hero from history or legend, such as Achilles in Homer's ILIAD, Aeneas in Virgil's AENEID or the knight Roland in *The Song of Roland*. The stories told in epics are often part of a people's national identity, but they can deal with the destiny of all mankind, as in Milton's ▷PARADISE LOST.

🔖 'Epic' can also be used to refer to any work on a grand scale, such as Cecil B. De Mille's film *The Ten Commandments* or Tolstoy's novel WAR AND PEACE.

epistolary novel Novel written as a series of letters, sometimes interspersed with entries from journals. The French 18th-century novel *Les Liaisons Dangereuses* and Samuel Richardson's ▷CLARISSA are well-known examples of this literary form.

eulogy Formal written or spoken tribute to someone's accomplishments or character; particularly a speech made to honour a person who has recently died – for example, Mark Antony's speech in honour of Brutus, 'This was the noblest Roman of them all', from ▷JULIUS CAESAR.

🔖 To eulogise something is to praise it extravagantly and at length.

Euripides (480-406 BC) Greek tragic playwright known for the splendour of his verses, his interest in extreme states of mind such as madness and passionate love, and his sympathetic portrayal of women and everyday people. His plays appear to question the Greek myths and even the existence of the gods, and were disapproved of by more conventional members of Greek society. The BACCHAE, *Electra* and *Medea* are among Euripides' 19 surviving plays.

farce Type of low comedy based on ridiculous situations, exaggerated characters and over-the-top buffoonery. The French playwright Georges Feydeau (1862-1921) was among the best-known writers of farce.

🔖 The word comes from the Latin *farcire* meaning 'to stuff', because originally farces were inserted as brief comic interludes in otherwise serious dramas.

Figaro Wily rogue who appears in two comic and openly anti-aristocratic dramas by the 18th-century French dramatist Beaumarchais: *The Barber of Seville* and *The Marriage of Figaro*. Both have been made into operas, the first by ▷ROSSINI and the second by ▷MOZART.

fin de siècle French for 'end of century'. Spirit of effete refinement that affected late 19th-century writers such as the AESTHETES and SYMBOLISTS.

Flaubert, Gustave (floh-BAIR) (1821-1880) French novelist and story writer known for his careful style, precise choice of words and exact descriptions. His best-known work is the novel MADAME BOVARY. The book is set in Normandy where Flaubert spent most of his life.

Frogs, The Comedy by the Greek dramatist ARISTOPHANES. Dionysus, the god of drama, has to judge a poetic contest in the underworld between the two great tragic playwrights AESCHYLUS and EURIPIDES in order to decide which to bring back to Athens. Despite Euripides' cleverness and daring, the god decides that Aeschylus would prove a wiser ruler.

Genji, The Tale of Early 11th-century novel generally regarded as one of the greatest works of Japanese literature. It was written by the novelist and diarist Shikibu

HIGH GOTHIC *Quasimodo climbs the bell-tower in the 1939 film version of the great Gothic novel* The Hunchback of Notre Dame. *Charles Laughton played the monster with a heart of gold.*

Gothic novel Work of fiction concerned with supernatural, macabre or grotesque events, often set in a wild, haunted or isolated location. The genre became established in the 18th century, and was closely associated with ROMANTICISM. It acquired the name 'Gothic' because originally such novels were set in medieval times, but by the beginning of the 19th century the historical element had become less important than the extraordinary.
🔖 Gothic novels include The HUNCHBACK OF NOTRE DAME and ▷FRANKENSTEIN.

Grass, Gunter (1927-) German novelist, poet and playwright whose striking first novel *The Tin Drum*, written in 1959, established his literary reputation as the voice of his generation. The book is a colourful exaggeration of his experiences of creeping pre-war Nazification, the war and post-war years. Serious moral and socialist convictions underlie the fantasy of this and later works, such as the novella *Cat and Mouse*, or his epic novel *Dog Years*.

Grimm, The Brothers Two German linguists and scholars, Jakob (1785-1863) and Wilhelm (1786-1859) Grimm, who collected popular German folktales. Their three-volume work *Grimm's Fairy Tales* contains more than 200 traditional stories including such perennial favourites as HANSEL AND GRETEL, *Snow White and the Seven Dwarfs* and *Rumpelstiltskin*.

Gutenberg Bible (c.1455) Named after the German printer Johann ▷GUTENBERG, the Bible is thought to be the first book in the West printed with movable metal type.

THE BIBLE IN PRINT *Some 40 copies remain today of the so-called Gutenberg Bible which was printed at Mainz in the mid-15th century. Its coloured decorations were added by hand.*

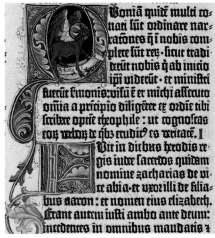

Murasaki, probably to entertain the Empress Akiko whom she served. Its 54 chapters chronicle the romances of the fictional Prince Genji and provide fascinating insights into Japanese court life.

genre Class or category of literature with a specific form, such as the novel or short story. In Classical times, the three great genres were EPIC, LYRIC and dramatic poetry (the last divided into TRAGEDY and COMEDY), and the rules for each were very strict. Until the 18th century genres were sharply distinguished but later writers have produced more mixed works.

Gide, André (JEED) (1869-1951) French writer of novels and journals about the inner conflict between his Protestant upbringing and his intense longing for personal freedom. His homosexuality and communist politics made him a highly controversial writer. His novels include *The Immoralist* (1902) and *Strait is the Gate* (1909). He won the Nobel prize in 1947.

Goethe, Johann Wolfgang von (GER-tuh) (1749-1832) German writer, scholar and statesman whose works include the autobiographical novel *The Sorrows of Young Werther* and the two-part drama *Faust* – a philosophical treatment of the ▷FAUST legend, which ends with Faust's redemption. His early writing was Romantic in style but, after a visit to Italy in the 1780s, he drew on Classical models in his later works. Goethe wrote outstanding lyric poetry, spoke six languages and was knowledgeable about the theatre, science, philosophy and even the occult.

Gorky, Maxim (1868-1936) (Real name Alexei M. Peshkov) Russian writer best known for his three autobiographical books, *Childhood*, *In the World* and *My Universities*. He supported the Russian Revolution, and in 1934 became the first president of the Soviet Writers' Union. He protected persecuted writers, which may have led to his death – said to have been engineered by his political enemies.

Hansel and Gretel Traditional German fairy tale, first printed by the Brothers GRIMM in the early 19th century. Two small children emerge victorious from a sequence of terrible ordeals including abandonment by their parents and capture by a witch who intends to eat them – proving that true innocence can triumph even in the most desperate circumstances.

Heidi Children's novel by the Swiss author Johanna Spyri, published in 1881. Heidi, a little orphan, leads an idyllic life in the Alps with her grandfather until she is kidnapped and taken to town to be the companion of a rich, crippled child, Clara Sesemann. Heidi's country manners create havoc in the Sesemann household and eventually she is allowed to return to the mountains. Clara goes with her and learns to walk.
🔔*Heidi* has been translated into many languages, filmed three times, and turned into a cartoon series for television. Two sequels were written in the 1950s.

Hesse, Herman (1877-1962) German novelist and poet. His books include *Steppenwolf* (1927), which explores the split personality of an artist, and *The Glass Bead Game* (1943), which envisages a future Utopia. He won the Nobel prize in 1946.

Homer Greek epic poet who wrote in the 8th century BC, and is traditionally assumed to have composed the ILIAD and the ODYSSEY – although this is disputed by many scholars. Almost nothing is known about Homer's life, except that he probably lived in Ionia in Asia Minor and may have come from a poor family. According to legend he was blind. The poems attributed to him were clearly put together from a wide variety of sources and were probably not written down until about the 6th century BC. The surviving versions date from the 5th to 4th centuries BC, and almost certainly contain substantial alterations from the originals. In antiquity, Homer was considered the greatest of all poets, and his influence ever since has been immense.

Horace (65-8 BC) (Full name Quintus Horatius Flaccus) Latin poet, the son of a freed slave, and one of the most frequently quoted Classical authors. He is known for his vivid portrayal of Roman society and for his humane point of view.
🔔The expression *carpe diem*, meaning 'seize the day' comes from Horace, as does the line *Dulce et decorum est pro patria mori* 'It is sweet and fitting to die for one's country' – used ironically in a poem about World War I by Wilfred Owen.

Hugo, Victor (1802-85) French novelist, poet, dramatist and the leading figure in French ROMANTICISM. He was also involved in politics, and was a keen upholder of republican ideals. Hugo is best known for his poetry and for the novels *Notre Dame de Paris* (published in English as The HUNCHBACK OF NOTRE DAME) and *Les Misérables*, on which the long-running musical was based.

Hunchback of Notre Dame, The Gothic novel by the French writer Victor HUGO, published in 1831. It is set in the Middle Ages and tells the story of Quasimodo, a deformed bellringer at Notre Dame Cathedral in Paris, who falls in love with a beautiful gypsy girl, Esmeralda.

Ibsen, Henrik (1828-1906) Norwegian dramatist and poet, considered to be the founder of modern drama. He wrote many powerful plays concerned with social, political and psychological themes. A DOLL'S HOUSE, *Ghosts* and *Hedda Gabler*, for example, have become modern classics.

COUP DE GRÂCE *Achilles lunges forward to deal a mortal blow to the Trojan hero Hector. The scene from Homer's epic* Iliad *was painted on a 5th-century BC Greek vase.*

Iliad Epic Greek poem attributed to HOMER but possibly the work of many hands. It survives on papyrus fragments dating from the 5th to 4th centuries BC, from which the modern version is taken. The *Iliad* tells the story of the ▷TROJAN WAR – Ilios was the Greek name for Troy.

PLAY OF PASSIONS *More than a century after it was written, the violent emotions of* Hedda Gabler *can still disturb a modern audience. Theatregoers of the 1890s were shocked and outraged by Ibsen's forthright portrayal of destructive human relationships and suffering in marriage.*

imagery Figurative language used to convey a mental picture of an object or to represent some aspect of it. Homer's expression 'the wine-dark sea' is an example of visual imagery because it creates an impression of the water's colour. In the Bible the image of 'the Lamb' is used in reference to Christ in order to express the abstract ideas of mildness and sacrifice. Imagery often makes use of ▷METAPHORS, ▷SIMILES and other ▷FIGURES OF SPEECH.

Ionesco, Eugène (1912-94) Romanian-born French playwright, who was influential in establishing the THEATRE OF THE ABSURD. His works are known for their bizarre comedy and use of symbolism. They include *The Bald Prima-Donna* – an often farcical study of an empty marriage – and *Rhinoceros*, which was based on Ionesco's own experience of Nazism.

Juvenal (*c.*60-*c.*130) (Full name Decimus Junius Juvenalis) Latin poet known for his 16 brilliant *Satires* attacking the affectation, greed and corruption of Roman society. His work has had a powerful influence on satirists ever since.
🔔 The expression *Mens sana in corpore sano* 'A sound mind in a sound body' comes from one of Juvenal's satires.

Kafka, Franz (1883-1924) Czech novelist and short-story writer. His writing – in German – depicts the terrors and frustrations of modern life in terms of surreal, nightmarish events afflicting characters who are lonely, tormented or victimised. Kafka's works include *The Trial*, a novel in which a man unaccountably finds himself under arrest, and the short story The METAMORPHOSIS, whose main character wakes up as a giant insect.

Kazantzakis, Nikos (1885-1957) Greek writer best known for the colourful novels *Zorba the Greek* and *The Last Temptation of Christ*. The latter caused an uproar when it was filmed in 1988 because it contains a scene in which Christ is tempted by a vision of life as an ordinary man, as he is dying on the Cross.

La Fontaine, Jean de (1621-95) French poet known for his elegant *Fables*, adapted from AESOP'S FABLES and other sources. His moral tales, told in verse, remain popular because of his colourful characterisations of mankind, beast and nature.

Little Red Riding-Hood European fairy tale first printed in French in the late 17th century. This version ends with the wolf

MY, WHAT BIG TEETH YOU HAVE ... *Little Red Cap encounters the Big Bad Wolf in an illustration by Arthur Rackham for a 1900 edition of the Grimm brothers'* Fairy Tales.

swallowing the little girl and carries an explicit warning that young girls should take care whom they trust. The first version with a happy ending was the German tale *Little Red Cap* published by the Brothers GRIMM in the early 19th century.

Lorca, Frederico García (1898-1936) One of Spain's greatest modern dramatists and poets, and one of the few writers in any language to produce outstanding verse tragedy in this century. His best-known plays are *Blood Wedding* and *The House of Bernarda Alba*, both of which deal with passion, violence and emotional repression in Andalusian culture. Lorca was shot by Nationalist partisans at the outbreak of the Spanish Civil War.

lyric Type of poetry which is written to express the subjective thoughts, feelings or impressions of a single speaker. It is distinguished from EPIC and narrative verse, which tells a story, and from dramatic verse, which has parts for different speakers.
🔔 In ancient Greece, such poems were usually sung to the lyre, which is why the words of songs are often referred to as lyrics.

Lysistrata Bawdy comedy by the Greek poet ARISTOPHANES. The women of Athens and Sparta, sick of the warring of their menfolk, refuse to sleep with their husbands until they make peace.

Mabinogion, The Collection of medieval Welsh tales derived from Celtic, Norman and French sources. The four main stories deal with the Welsh hero Pryderi.

Madame Bovary Novel by the French writer Gustave FLAUBERT, published in 1857. The main character, Emma Bovary, is obsessed with dreams of passion and romance which remain unfulfilled in her loveless marriage. She has two unhappy affairs and then falls deeply into debt. When her creditors threaten to tell her husband, she commits suicide.

magic realism Term applied to works written in a realistic style about events that include imaginary and fantastic elements alongside the credible and everyday. Exponents of magic realism include ▷RUSHDIE, BORGES and MÁRQUEZ.

Mallarmé, Stéphane (1842-98) French SYMBOLIST poet who tried to describe a world of abstract ideals lying beyond physical reality. His works include *L'Après-Midi d'un Faune (The Afternoon of a Faun)* which inspired a TONE POEM by the composer Debussy and a ballet by Nijinsky.

Mann, Thomas (1875-1955) German novelist and short-story writer whose books deal with artistic creation and the moral and intellectual struggles of individuals trying to come to terms with the world around them. His masterpieces include *The Magic Mountain* and *Death in Venice*. He won the Nobel prize in 1929. Mann opposed the Nazi regime and became a US citizen in 1940.

Márquez, Gabriel García (1928-) Colombian writer known for books and short stories that combine realistic characters and details with mysterious and magical events. His works include the fine novel *One Hundred Years of Solitude*, about the Buendía family, and *Love in the Time of Cholera*. In 1982 he received the Nobel prize for literature.

masque (or mask) Lavish courtly entertainment of the 16th and 17th centuries, popular in Italy, France and England. It usually took the form of a procession or pageant, with costumed amateurs acting out a dramatic poem or ALLEGORY to the accompaniment of music and dancing.

Maupassant, Guy de (1850-93) French short-story writer and novelist. He was encouraged to write by Flaubert and Zola and produced some 300 stories on subjects from peasant life to high society.

Metamorphoses Poem by the Roman writer OVID, composed around AD 2-8 and generally considered to be his masterpiece. It takes the form of a series of tales from Classical and near-eastern mythology which all involve miraculous transformations, or metamorphoses. The poem begins with the development of chaos into order, the birth of the gods and the history of mankind, and ends with Julius Caesar becoming a god.

Metamorphosis, The Short story by the Czech writer Franz KAFKA, written in 1915. It is a tale of psychological terror, in which Gregor Samsa, a salesman, suddenly finds himself transformed into a giant insect.

meter The rhythmic pattern of poetry created by the mixing of stressed and unstressed syllables in a single line. The unit of poetic meter is known as a 'foot' and can have various forms such as the *iamb* (an unstressed syllable followed by a stressed one, as in to-DAY), the *trochee* (a stressed syllable followed by an unstressed one, as in NEV-er) or the *dactyl* (a stressed syllable followed by two unstressed ones, as in YES-ter-day). Poetry with one foot per line is known as monometer; with two feet per line as dimeter; with three feet per line trimeter; and so on. One of the best-known forms is iambic pentameter, which has five iambs in every line – the meter used in the plays of Shakespeare. Up until the 19th century strict metrical rules were generally applied to Classical literature and to European poetry. Romantic and modern poets have adopted a freer approach.

miracle play Form of medieval religious drama based on Bible stories or episodes from the lives of saints. In the past the term also included the MYSTERY PLAYS.

mock-heroic Work that satirises the conventions of the heroic or EPIC style of writing by using it to describe trivial events or low-life characters. Alexander ▷POPE's poem *The Rape of the Lock* is an example.

modernism Literary movement associated with writers of the first half of the 20th century such as Marcel PROUST, Ezra ▷POUND, Virginia ▷WOOLF and James ▷JOYCE. Its main features were experimentation, rejection of 19th-century attitudes and values, and an interest in the unconscious processes of the mind, inspired in part by the theories of Sigmund ▷FREUD. One of modernism's most important contributions was the STREAM OF CONSCIOUSNESS technique, where a character's inner thoughts are told within the story.

TALENT TO AMUSE *Admired by theatregoers of all classes, Molière single-handedly created a new style of 17th-century French comedy.*

Molière Pen name of the French playwright, actor and director Jean-Baptiste Poquelin (1622-73), known for social satires such as *The Misanthrope* and *Tartuffe*. Molière began his theatrical career at the age of 21 by forming an acting troupe called L'Illustre Théâtre which was first based in Paris and then toured the provinces during 1645-58. Molière returned to Paris and won acclaim as an actor and playwright entertaining city and court audiences alike. He wrote 30 comedies, all showing his profound understanding of human nature and French society of the time.

mystery plays Cycles of dramas enacting events from the Bible, performed annually by members of craftsmen's guilds in many parts of Europe from medieval times until as late as the 17th century. Mystery plays developed out of dramatised Bible stories presented in church at Christmas, Easter and other festivals, and were one of the earliest forms of popular theatre. The Oberammergau Passion Play from Bavaria is a mystery play. The ▷CHESTER mystery plays are performed every five years.

Nabokov, Vladimir (1899-1977) Russian-born novelist, poet and literary critic who wrote his early books in Russian under the name of V. Sirin. Nabokov left Russia in 1919 and lived the rest of his life in the West. After 1940 all his novels were written in English. Nabokov is known for his original story-telling techniques and inventive language in such novels as ▷LOLITA and *Pale Fire*.

Name of the Rose, The Intellectual suspense novel set in the 14th century, by the Italian writer and philosopher Umberto Eco (1932-). It was first published in 1981 and became an international bestseller in spite of containing difficult philosophical argument and passages of untranslated Latin. The main character is an English Franciscan friar, William of Baskerville, who with his young novice Adso sets out to solve a frightening series of murders in a rambling Benedictine abbey in Italy. The book was filmed in 1986, with Sean Connery in the leading role.

narrative Writing which tells a story or describes a sequence of events. The word can also be used as an adjective to refer to the quality of telling a story. Narrative poetry, for example, includes medieval ROMANCES about King Arthur and his knights, and Virgil's AENEID which tells of the founding of Rome.

narrator The speaker in a poem, novel or short story. Sometimes the narrator is named and it is clear that the work is written from his point of view, as in Herman Melville's ▷MOBY DICK, where the speaker is identified in the first sentence: 'Call me Ishmael.' Often there appears to be no narrator, but even then it cannot be assumed that the author is speaking directly to the reader; instead there is said to be an 'implied narrator'.

Nibelungenlied (*The Song of the Nibelungs*) Medieval German epic written around 1200 but based on much older sources. The first part deals with the hero Siegfried's wooing of the Burgundian (Nibelung) princess Kriemhild, his subduing of the warrior-queen Brunhild, and his eventual murder by the Burgundians. In the second section Kriemhild marries Attila the Hun and with his help wreaks vengeance on her own people for Siegfried's death – a historical event that has been dated to the 5th century. Similar legends are related in the Scandinavian SAGAS.
♪Richard ▷WAGNER's opera cycle *The Ring of the Nibelungs* is based on the *Nibelungenlied* and the Scandinavian sagas.

nonsense verse Humorous poetry which is absurd or illogical, or based on comic made-up words. These lines from Lewis Carroll's poem *The Walrus and the Carpenter* are a typical example:
'The time has come,' the Walrus said,
'To talk of many things:
Of shoes – and ships – and sealing-wax –
Of cabbages – and kings –
Of why the sea is boiling hot –
And whether pigs have wings.'

novel Extended work of prose fiction. Its early roots are found in ancient Egyptian literature from around 1200 BC, and in

Latin writing from the first and second centuries AD. There is also a long history of story-telling in Arabic and Japanese literature from the 11th century. The modern novel, however, developed in the 18th century out of the work of English writers such as Defoe, Fielding and Richardson. Since then the novel has become the most prominent form of literature with dozens of specialist categories such as science fiction, crime, fantasy and romance.

novella Compact story which hinges on a single episode or event and which has an unexpected, but logical, twist at the end – such as the tales in Boccaccio's DECA-MERON or Joseph ▷CONRAD's *Heart of Darkness*. The term is also loosely used to refer to any short novel or long short-story.

ode Formal poem expressing lofty thoughts or profound emotions. Public odes, such as those by the ancient Greek poet Pindar, have a stately, ceremonial tone and were written for important occasions. Private odes, such as those of HORACE and John ▷KEATS, deal with personal emotion and intense inner experience.

Odyssey Ancient Greek epic attributed to HOMER, and considered one of the greatest works of literature ever constructed. It follows on from the ILIAD and tells of the Greek king ▷ODYSSEUS' ten-year voyage home to Ithaca after the Trojan War. His many strange adventures on the way include encounters with a one-eyed Cyclops called Polyphemus, the enchantress Circe and the goddess Calypso, who keeps him as her lover for eight years. Eventually, Odysseus arrives back in Ithaca where his wife Penelope is faithful despite her many suitors. With the help of his son Telemachus, Odysseus slays the suitors and resumes his kingship.
♨ Figuratively, an odyssey is any long, difficult journey.

Oedipus Rex (also known as *Oedipus Tyrannus*) One of the finest tragedies of the Greek playwright SOPHOCLES. It dramatises the downfall of King Oedipus who unwittingly kills his father and marries his mother. (See also ▷OEDIPUS in 'Myths and Legends'.)

Omar Khayyám (*c.*1048-1123) Persian poet and mathematician, remembered for his *Rubáiyát*, a collection of four-line verses, or *ruba'is*, that became enormously popular in the 19th century when they were translated into English by Edward Fitzgerald. This translation – which is poetic rather than strictly accurate – is still the best-known form of the *Rubáiyát*, opening with the celebrated lines, 'Awake! for Morning in the Bowl of Night/ Has flung the Stone that puts the Stars to Flight'.

Oresteia Sequence of three plays by AES-CHYLUS, recounting the tragic legend of the royal family of Atreus. King Agamemnon is compelled to sacrifice his daughter Iphigenia, which prompts his own murder by his wife Clytemnestra. She, in turn, is killed by her son Orestes who is required by Apollo to avenge his father. Orestes is pursued by the ▷FURIES, tried by the goddess Athena and acquitted.

Ovid (43 BC-*c.*AD 17) One of the wittiest and most accomplished Roman poets, known for his compilation of myths, the METAMORPHOSES, and for poems about love, including the *Ars Amatoria* (*Art of Love*) and *Remedia Amoris* (*Remedy for Love*). The erotic *Ars Amatoria* helped to bring about his exile to the Black Sea.

parody In literature, a work that mimics or exaggerates another work or a style of writing in such a way as to make it appear ridiculous. ARISTOPHANES used parody in *The Frogs*, mimicking the style of Aeschylus and Euripides. CERVANTES imitated the medieval chivalric style in *Don Quixote*.

A FLASK OF WINE, A BOOK OF VERSE – AND THOU *Edmund Dulac captured the sensuality and romance of the East in his illustrations for a 1909 edition of Omar Khayyám's* Rubáiyát.

Pasternak, Boris (1890-1960) Russian writer known for his poems and for the novel *Doctor Zhivago*, which was banned in the Soviet Union for almost 40 years. Pasternak initially supported the revolutionary movement in Russia, but became increasingly critical of its conformism and inhumanity during the Stalinist era. In 1958 he was expelled from the Soviet Writers' Union and compelled to turn down the Nobel prize for literature.

pastoral Work or passage that portrays scenes of rural life, usually in an idealised manner. Many of the shorter poems of the Latin poet Virgil fall into this category, as does William Shakespeare's *As You Like It*.

personification Embodiment of an abstract quality or idea as a character in a drama, poem or novel; or the attribution of human qualities to an inanimate object. It is a very common technique found in many languages and periods.

Petrarch (1304-74) (Full name Francesco Petrarca) Italian Renaissance poet who combined Classical scholarship with Christian and humanist beliefs. He is known for his love poems to 'Laura', written in the SONNET form which takes his name. Petrarch inspired many English imitators including the poets Henry Surrey (1517-47) and Thomas Wyatt (1503-42).

picaresque Literary term used to describe a satirical novel with a rogue hero, such as Henry ▷FIELDING's *Tom Jones*. The form originated in 16th-century Spain; *pícaro* is Spanish for 'rogue'.

Pirandello, Luigi (1867-1936) Italian writer chiefly known for his two plays, *Henry IV* and *Six Characters in Search of an Author*, which deal with the nature of madness and identity. He anticipated later dramatists such as BRECHT and Jean Anouilh, and won the Nobel prize in 1934.

poetry Any type of literature with a rhythmic structure, or METER. Poetry is often divided into regular stanzas with a set pattern of rhymes. As well as RHYME, it may make use of assonance, alliteration and ▷ONOMATOPOEIA. Poetry often employs heightened, figurative or imaginative language in order to convey its meaning. Some form of poetry exists in almost every language and culture.

Proust, Marcel (1871-1922) French novelist known for his 12-volume masterpiece *A la Recherche du Temps Perdu*, which

was first translated into English as REMEMBRANCE OF THINGS PAST. Proust was an important figure in literary MODERNISM, particularly in his exploration of the workings of human memory and the influence of the past on present experience.

Pushkin, Alexandr (1799-1837) Russian poet, novelist and playwright, regarded as one of the founders of Russian literature. His works include *Eugene Onegin*, a novel in verse, which was turned into an opera by Tchaikovsky. His historical drama *Boris Godunov* was also made into an opera, by Mussorgsky. Pushkin was exiled from Moscow in 1820 for his political verse. He returned six years later, but was still subject to censorship. He was fatally wounded in a duel over his wife in 1837.

Rabelais, François (*c.*1494-*c.*1553) French satirist known for his humanitarian outlook and earthy humour. He was a former monk with a deep religious faith but he delighted in all forms of comedy, including obscenity and bawdy farce. His masterpieces, *Gargantua* and *Pantagruel* – named after two giants who are the main characters – provide a scathing portrait of French Renaissance society.

realism Broad term for literature that attempts to give a close impression of real life by means of accurate descriptions, believable events and characters with understandable motives. In particular, it is applied to 19th-century novels by writers such as Zola, Dickens and Tolstoy.

Remembrance of Things Past English translation of the semi-autobiographical novel *A la Recherche du Temps Perdu* by the French writer Marcel PROUST, published in 12 volumes between 1913 and 1927. It deals with the narrator's discovery of his vocation as a writer, and is known for its insights into the workings of human memory. In one episode, the smell of madeleine cakes vividly evokes a childhood experience.

rhyme Use in poetry of words that echo one another's sounds for two main purposes: to create a musical effect and to structure the verse by marking line endings and emphasising rhythm. Rhyme helps to stress the meaning of verse and makes it easier to remember and recite accurately.

romance Courtly adventure tale about great deeds of chivalry or love, of a type popular in the Middle Ages; alternatively, a love story. Literature of the first type frequently involves magical or mystical

events, such as a sighting of the Holy Grail or encounters with mythical beasts.
🎙Shakespeare's plays *The Tempest* and *The Winter's Tale* are called romances because they involve strange adventures culminating in a fantastical happy ending.

Romance of the Rose French poem of the 13th century about COURTLY LOVE, and one of the most influential works of the Middle Ages. Parts of the poem were translated into Middle English in the 14th century, possibly by Geoffrey Chaucer.

romanticism Revolutionary artistic movement beginning in the late 18th and early 19th centuries. It stressed the value of personal emotion and imagination, and freedom from the strict rules of form that dominated 18th-century literature. It also expressed a new view of nature, seen as being spiritually connected with mankind, and a source of inspiration. Romantic writers include ▷WORDSWORTH and ▷BLAKE in English, SCHILLER and GOETHE in German, and Victor HUGO in French.

sagas Ancient epics from Scandinavia and Iceland, composed in the Dark Ages but not written down until around the 12th to 13th centuries. They are a mixture of history and legend, and recount the deeds of heroes, kings, great families and characters from pagan Norse mythology. Many of the stories are brutal, painting a picture of a fierce, warrior society dominated by superstition and long, bitter feuds.

Sand, George (SAH'N) (1804-76) Pen name of the French writer Amandine-Aurore Lucille Dupin. She separated from her husband Baron Dudevant in 1831, adopted a man's name, wore trousers and began a literary career in Paris. Her works, which include *Indiana* (1832), *The Devil's Pool* (1846) and *The Little Fairy* (1848), were popular and dealt with themes ranging from romance to women's emancipation and idealised country life. She had an affair with the poet Alfred de Musset and a lengthy relationship with ▷CHOPIN.

Sappho (*c.*612-*c.*580 BC) Greek poet known for passionate love poems written for her female followers on the island of Lesbos. Only fragments of her work have survived, but it was greatly revered in the ancient world.
🎙Sappho's admirers on Lesbos gave rise to the word 'lesbian' and 'sapphism'. Popular but discredited legend has it that she drowned herself because her love for the boatman Phaon remained unrequited.

satire Work or type of writing that ridicules human vice and folly, particularly among the rich and powerful. Two early satirists were the Latin poets JUVENAL and HORACE, who used their verses to criticise Roman society. The 17th and 18th centuries in France and England were a great age of satirical writing and produced such masterpieces as Voltaire's CANDIDE and Jonathan Swift's ▷GULLIVER'S TRAVELS.

Satyricon Novel-like account of low-life society in ancient Rome by the first-century Latin author Petronius, who was probably a close friend of the emperor Nero. Manuscripts of the work were often hidden as it was considered pornographic, and only small sections have survived.

Schiller, Friedrich von (1759-1805) German poet and playwright, influential in German ROMANTICISM. His works are concerned with the issue of human freedom. Schiller's best-known work is his ode *To Joy*, which Beethoven set to music in the last movement of his Ninth Symphony.

Seneca (*c*.4 BC-AD 65) (Full name Lucius Annaeus Seneca; also known as Seneca the Younger) Roman writer of Latin tragedies based on Greek myths, such as *Oedipus*, *Medea* and *Agamemnon*, and for philosophical works advocating the beliefs of the ▷STOICS. Seneca was an adviser to the emperor Nero but was forced to commit suicide after being accused of conspiring to assassinate him.

short story Tale which aims at conveying a single impression of emotion or focuses on a single event. The author Edgar Allan ▷POE is generally regarded as the father of the modern short story and was one of the first to set out its principles. After him the form was developed in Russia and France by writers such as Gogol, TURGENEV, CHEKHOV, FLAUBERT and MAUPASSANT.

Simenon, Georges (1903-89) Prolific Belgian writer who created the celebrated detective Maigret in a series of crime novels which achieved international acclaim and were adapted for television.

Singer, Isaac Bashevis (1904-91) Polish-born author of novels and short stories in both Yiddish and English. He emigrated to the United States as a young man, but in works such as *The Magician of Lublin* and *The Spinoza of Market Street* he recorded the colourful, lively way of life of Polish Jews before the Holocaust. He won the Nobel prize for literature in 1978.

Sleeping Beauty, The Fairy tale about the Princess Aurora who falls asleep by magic for a hundred years, until woken by the kiss of a handsome prince. The earliest version of the tale dates from the 14th century and features an ungentlemanly prince who rapes the sleeping princess so that she wakes to find herself pregnant.

soliloquy Speech in which a character in a play reveals his thoughts while alone on the stage, as in Hamlet's much-quoted ▷'TO BE, OR NOT TO BE' speech.

Solzhenitsyn, Alexandr (1918-) Russian writer and dissident. He was exiled to Siberia during the 1940s and 1950s for criticising Stalin. Works such as *One Day In The Life of Ivan Denisovich* and *The Gulag Archipelago* draw on that experience. He received the Nobel prize for literature in 1970. Four years later, Solzhenitsyn was expelled from the Soviet Union and settled in the United States. He regained his Russian citizenship in 1990 and moved back to Russia in 1994.

sonnet Poem of 14 lines, divided either into one section of eight lines and one of six – the form favoured by PETRARCH – or into three sets of four lines and one of two – as used by Shakespeare. The poem often airs a proposition – commonly on the subject of love – which is developed to a logical or witty conclusion. The earliest sonnets were written in the Middle Ages by poets such as Petrarch and DANTE. Milton and Wordsworth and the French poet Ronsard also used the form.

Sophocles (*c*.496-406 BC) Classical Greek dramatist, known for his theatrical innovations, his range of styles and his ability to create rounded characters in tragedies such as ANTIGONE, ELECTRA and OEDIPUS REX. He wrote more than 120 dramas, of which only seven have survived.

Stendhal Pseudonym of the French novelist Henri Beyle (1783-1842). His work was an important influence on the development of the novel in France and is known for combining romance and passion with deep psychological analysis as in *Le Rouge et Le Noir (The Red and the Black)*.

stream of consciousness A narrative technique which gives an impression of the way thoughts, perceptions and emotions flow through the mind of a character. Virginia ▷WOOLF is one exponent; parts of James ▷JOYCE's novel *Ulysses* and all of his book *Finnegans Wake* are also examples.

BOLD WRITER *August Strindberg formed his own theatre companies so that he could stage his unconventional and visionary plays.*

Strindberg, August (1849-1912) Swedish playwright and novelist, known for pioneering psychological realism in the theatre. He had an unhappy childhood and three disastrous marriages, leading to a passionate dislike of women which influenced some of his best-known plays, including *Miss Julie* and *The Father*.

Sturm und Drang (Storm and Stress) Late 18th-century movement in German literature and music, associated with the beginning of ROMANTICISM. It rejected conventional ideas about literary form and structure and emphasised the passionate, heroic side of human nature.

Swiss Family Robinson, The Adventure story by a Swiss pastor, Johann David Wyss, published in 1812-13. The book was strongly influenced by ▷ROBINSON CRUSOE, and tells how a shipwrecked family – very like Wyss's own – manages to survive and even prosper on an uninhabited island. The book was later enlarged in a French edition by Mme de Montolieu.

symbolists Group of late 19th-century French poets including MALLARMÉ, Verlaine and Rimbaud, who rejected realism in favour of abstraction and attempts to portray spiritual and philosophical truths symbolically. They were influenced by mysticism as well as by musical techniques such as Richard Wagner's leitmotifs.

theatre of the absurd Type of drama developed in the 1950s and 1960s by writers such as Samuel BECKETT, Eugène IONESCO and Harold ▷PINTER. By 'absurdity' they meant a view of life that was contradictory, meaningless, and ruled by chance or by forces too mysterious to understand. Some of the best absurdist plays are comedies, such as Beckett's WAITING FOR GODOT.

Tintin Boy reporter-detective and hero of a series of Belgian comic-strip adventure stories by Hergé – the pseudonym of the author and illustrator Georges Remi (1907-83). Together with his dog Snowy and friends such as the eccentric Professor Calculus and short-tempered Captain Haddock, Tintin visits South America, flies to the moon, dives for treasure and even gets involved in Balkan politics.

Tolstoy, Count Leo (1828-1910) Russian writer, regarded as one of the world's finest novelists for his epic masterpieces WAR AND PEACE and ANNA KARENINA. His works paint a vivid portrait of 19th-century Russian society, covering a vast sweep of characters and events. Tolstoy inherited a large estate, where he worked hard to improve the lot of the peasants. After a spiritual crisis in middle age, however, he concentrated on religious works such as the short story *The Death of Ivan Ilyich*.

tragedy Drama dealing with the death or downfall of a noble character, usually as the result of some error of judgment or crime against the natural order, as when Oedipus kills his father and marries his mother. Tragedy is considered the most elevated form of drama. Ancient Greek dramatists believed it should provoke CATHARSIS.
🔱The word 'tragedy' comes from the Greek for 'goat song' as the form developed from choral songs which accompanied goat sacrifices to the god Dionysus.

tragi-comedy Drama that combines elements of both tragedy and comedy. In the most common form an essentially tragic plot is given a happy – or at least not fatal – ending, as in Shakespeare's *Measure for Measure*. Alternatively, the wit and lightness of a comedy may be overshadowed by unexpectedly serious developments, as in Shakespeare's *Much Ado About Nothing*.

troubadours Travelling poet-musicians who flourished in southern France and northern Italy during the 12th to 14th centuries. Their songs about chivalry and love influenced European poetry and introduced the concept of COURTLY LOVE.

DIVINE INTERVENTION *Leo Tolstoy spent the second half of his life obsessed by evangelism and condemned his great works as worthless. He lived the life of a peasant until his death.*

Turgenev, Ivan (1818-83) Russian novelist whose works include the play *A Month in the Country*, and the great novel *Fathers and Sons* which deals with revolutionary aspirations and nihilist philosophy. He spent his later life in Western Europe where his work was admired for its poetic realism and fine characterisation.

Verne, Jules (1828-1905) French author of adventure tales including AROUND THE WORLD IN EIGHTY DAYS, and science fiction such as *Journey to the Centre of the Earth* and *Twenty Thousand Leagues Under the Sea*. His books were based more on imagination than on scientific knowledge, but some of them anticipated inventions such as space travel and television.

POWER OF THE PEN *A front-page letter from Emile Zola (below, painted by Edouard Manet) helped to secure justice for Alfred Dreyfus, a Jewish army officer falsely accused of treason.*

Villon, François (1431-c.1463) Medieval French poet known for his turbulent life which included several periods of imprisonment and a death sentence that was commuted to banishment. His poem *Le Testament* contains the celebrated refrain: *Mais où sont les neiges d'autan?* ('Where are the snows of yesteryear?').

Virgil (70-19 BC) (Full name Publius Vergilius Maro) Greatest poet of ancient Rome, known for his epic AENEID, which tells how the Trojan hero Aeneas founded Rome after the war with the Greeks. Virgil also wrote lyric pastoral poems known as the *Eclogues* and *Georgics*.

Voltaire Pseudonym of the French writer, philosopher and wit François-Marie Arouet (1694-1778). His works express the spirit of the Age of Enlightenment and uphold the values of reason, toleration and justice. Voltaire's best-known books include the satire CANDIDE, which makes fun of the optimistic philosophy of ▷LEIBNIZ, and the *Philosophical Dictionary* in which he expressed his views on morality, faith, art, science and justice.

Vulgate Latin translation of the BIBLE made from Greek by Saint Jerome in the 5th century, and the oldest surviving translation of the complete Bible. It was adopted as the official Bible of the Roman Catholic Church in the 16th century.

Waiting for Godot Play by Samuel BECKETT, produced in French in 1953 and in English two years later. Two tramps, Vladimir and Estragon, spend the entire play waiting for a mysterious character called Godot, who never appears. *Waiting For Godot* was a milestone in the development of THEATRE OF THE ABSURD.

War and Peace Sweeping novel by the Russian writer Leo TOLSTOY, published in 1869 and considered by many to be the greatest novel ever written. It recounts the histories of several Russian families during the Napoleonic Wars.

Zola, Emile (1840-1902) French novelist whose principal work *Les Rougon-Macquart* comprises 20 novels written between 1871 and 1893. The books deal with two branches of the same family – the Rougons and the Macquarts – and paint a vivid picture of middle and working-class life in 19th-century France. Zola is also remembered for his open letter *J'accuse* ('I accuse'), which criticised the French government over the ▷DREYFUS AFFAIR.

MYTHS AND LEGENDS

At the edge of our knowledge of the Universe lies the shadowy realm of myth and legend. It embraces narratives of gods and men set in the remote past, earthly heroes whose exploits have captured the popular imagination, as well as spells and stories passed down through generations in the form of folklore. In every culture, this is the world of the human imagination, inventing fantastical tales and conjuring up symbols to represent fundamental truths and mysteries of life.

TAROT CARDS

DRUIDS AT STONEHENGE

UFOs AT SALEM, MASSACHUSETTS

ABOMINABLE ENCOUNTER *Peering from the pages of a 1950s Italian magazine, a fanciful Yeti watches over two unsuspecting explorers.*

Abominable Snowman Shaggy man-beast, also known as the Yeti, said to live in the Himalayas. According to local folklore, the Yetis were the offspring of a monkey king who married an ogress. Despite reported sightings and discoveries of extraordinary tracks, there is still no firm evidence of the existence of the Abominable Snowman or its Western counterpart, Bigfoot, which has been reported in various locations throughout America.

Achilles Greatest Greek warrior in the TROJAN WAR, and the hero of Homer's ▷ILIAD. When he was an infant, his mother Thetis tried to protect Achilles by bathing him in the magical River Styx to make him immortal, but the heel by which she held him remained vulnerable. During the siege of Troy, Achilles quarrelled with Agamemnon and withdrew his army, but he eventually returned to slay the Trojan hero Hector, whose corpse he dragged in the dust behind his chariot. Later, Achilles was fatally wounded in the heel by an arrow from the bow of Hector's brother Paris.
🜚 The phrase 'Achilles' heel' is sometimes used to describe a strong person's one significant weakness.

Adonis In Greek mythology, a beautiful youth who was loved by Aphrodite. He was killed by a wild boar when hunting, but allowed to return from the underworld for six months every year so that he and Aphrodite could be reunited.
🜚 A young man considered as handsome as a Greek god may be called an Adonis.

Aeneas (ee-NEE-ers) Trojan warrior in Greek mythology. A son of Aphrodite and the hero of Virgil's ▷AENEID. After the fall of Troy, Aeneas fled with his father and son and was shipwrecked at Carthage in northern Africa. Dido, the queen of Carthage, fell in love with him, and burned herself to death on a funeral pyre when he left her. After many trials, Aeneas arrived in what is now Italy. Rome was said to have been founded by his descendants.
🜚 Because he carried his father Anchises out of the ruins of defeated Troy, Aeneas represents filial devotion.

Agamemnon King of Mycenae who led the Greeks against Troy in the TROJAN WAR. While he was away, his wife Clytemnestra took a lover called Aegisthus, and they murdered Agamemnon when he returned home. The guilty pair were killed by Agamemnon's son Orestes, encouraged by his sister Electra.

alchemy A combination of magic and scientific experiment that was widely practised during the Middle Ages, and the forerunner of modern chemistry. Alchemy arose from the search for the 'philosopher's stone' that would turn base metals such as lead into gold, and for the 'elixir of life' that would bring eternal youth. However, the alchemists' true goal lay beyond the material world; they believed that perfecting metals would provide the key to perfecting the human spirit too. Alchemy is thought to have originated in Egypt during the 2nd century BC, but it did not reach its height in Europe until the Middle Ages. For reasons of secrecy, alchemical formulae were usually written in an obscure code.

GODDESS OF LOVE AND BEAUTY *A bronze head of Aphrodite, from the 2nd century BC, portrays the Greek ideal of feminine beauty.*

Amazons In Greek mythology, a group of female warriors who lived near the Black Sea. They had their right breasts burnt off in order to use a bow and arrow more efficiently in war. THESEUS took captive an Amazon named Hippolyta, and they had a son called Hippolytus.
🜚 Any strong, aggressive woman is sometimes called an Amazon.

ambrosia Food of the gods in Greek mythology. Those who ate it were said to become immortal.
🜚 Particularly delicious food is sometimes referred to as ambrosia.

Antigone (an-TIG-o-nee) In Theban legend, the daughter of King OEDIPUS. After the abdication of Oedipus, her two brothers, Polynices and Eteocles, became joint sovereigns of Thebes and agreed to govern in alternate years. After his first year, Eteocles refused to give up the throne, and the two brothers fought and killed each other. Although burial of the dead was a religious obligation among the Greeks, the new Theban king, Creon, forbade the burial of Polynices because he was considered to be a traitor. Because Antigone buried him, she was ordered to be buried alive, but she committed suicide.
🜚 Antigone is the heroine of the tragedy of the same name by Sophocles.

Aphrodite (AFF-rer-DYE-tee) (Roman name Venus) Greek goddess of love and beauty, the mother of Eros and Aeneas. In the JUDGMENT OF PARIS, Paris chose Aphrodite as the most beautiful goddess, over Hera and Athena. Aphrodite was believed to have been born out of the foam of the sea, and is often pictured rising from the water, notably in the painting *Birth of Venus* by Sandro ▷BOTTICELLI.

Apollo Greek and Roman god of music, prophecy, medicine and the Sun. Apollo represents order and civilisation, and is sometimes contrasted with Dionysus who represents the relaxation of inhibitions. Apollo was worshipped at the DELPHIC ORACLE, where a priestess gave forth his predictions. Zeus was his father, and Artemis was his sister.

apple of discord In Greek mythology, an apple that was thrown into a banquet of the gods by the goddess Discord, who had not been invited. The apple had 'For the Fairest' written on it, and it was to resolve the conflicting claims of Aphrodite, Athena and Hera that the JUDGMENT OF PARIS was made.

Argonauts In Greek mythology, the companions of JASON in the quest for the Golden Fleece. Their ship was the *Argo*. ⚓*Naut* means 'sailor' in Greek, and is the root of the word nautical.

Artemis (Roman name Diana) Greek virgin goddess of hunting and the Moon; daughter of Zeus and sister of Apollo.

Arthur, King Legendary English king who was born out of wedlock and raised by the wizard MERLIN. When he was only a boy, Arthur gained the throne by withdrawing the magic sword EXCALIBUR from a stone, after many men had tried and failed. Arthur established his court at Camelot, where he gathered around him the knights of the ROUND TABLE. Other characters associated with the legends of Arthur are his wife Queen GUINEVERE, and his treacherous nephew Modred. When a love affair between Guinevere and Sir LANCELOT was discovered, Modred exploited the scandal to start a civil war, and caused Arthur's downfall at the Battle of Camlann. Mortally wounded, Arthur sailed to the mysterious isle of AVALON, promising to

ARTHURIAN LEGEND *The Round Table was designed to avoid disputes over which knight should preside at its head. Excalibur, the magic sword, was directly linked to King Arthur's fate, and as he lay dying the king asked Sir Bedivere to return it to the Lady of the Lake (right).*

return whenever his people needed him. The legends of Arthur may have been based on a 6th-century Celtic chieftain of the same name, who united the squabbling, regional kings of Britain and led them to victory against the Saxons. In Somerset, Cadbury Castle has been identified with CAMELOT, and Glastonbury may be the isle of Avalon where Arthur is said to be buried.

astral body In occult belief, an exact – though non-material – copy of the physical body. It is capable of separating itself, and remains attached to the physical body by a seemingly endless cord. At death the cord is severed and the astral body is freed from the limitations of the flesh.

astral projection Experience of seeming to leave one's body and observing it from outside. Occultists believe that this occurs when the ASTRAL BODY leaves the physical body. People who claim to have had an 'out-of-body experience' have talked of a

sense of well-being, vitality and buoyancy. The experience usually occurs involuntarily, and can happen whether the subject is conscious or unconscious. The natural habitat of the astral body is said to be a kind of 'fourth dimension' called the astral plane, and its experiences there may sometimes be remembered as dreams.

astrology Study of the relative position of the planets and stars, in order to predict their supposed influence on human actions. The principles were laid down by Babylonian priests around 3000 BC. Having observed that the Sun, Moon and five known planets seemed to move around the Earth along a track passing through 12 constellations, they divided the track into 12 segments, or signs of the Zodiac. Each month, as the Earth moves in its annual orbit, the Sun appears to rise in a different segment. To cast a horoscope, an astrologer must know the date, time and place of a person's birth. The sign in which the Sun was rising, as well as the positions of the planets, are also considered in the horoscope reading. Astrology became discredited with the discoveries of astronomers such as ▷GALILEO, but many still believe that there is some truth in it.

Athena (Roman name Minerva) Greek goddess of war, wisdom and the arts. At birth she sprang fully grown and fully armed out of the forehead of her father Zeus. Athena was one of the goddesses slighted by the JUDGMENT OF PARIS; as Paris was a Trojan prince, Athena gave her help to the Greeks in the TROJAN WAR. Athena was the patron goddess of Athens, which was named after her. The greatest of her temples was the Parthenon.

Atlantis Lost continent first described by the Greek philosopher Plato more than 2000 years ago. Atlantis was said to have been a marvel of prosperity and advanced engineering, enjoyed by a just and peaceful society, until it became corrupted by its wealth. The gods then directed earthquakes and floods against Atlantis until it was swallowed up by the sea. This legend may simply have been a moral fable invented by Plato, but historians still argue about the continent's possible existence and geographical position. Some scientists think Plato's Atlantis may have been based on the Minoan civilisation of Crete, destroyed around 1500 BC by a series of natural disasters. Archaeological discoveries suggest that the island of Santorini, 70 miles (112 km) north of Crete, may have been Atlantis itself.

Atlas In Greek mythology, son of one of the TITANS, famous for his strength. He refused hospitality to PERSEUS, who, using the head of MEDUSA, turned him into stone. He became the Atlas mountains, forced to support the heavens for ever.
♣ Since the 16th century, pictures of Atlas and his burden have been used as decoration on maps. Accordingly, the word atlas is used for a book of maps.

Augean stables Stables belonging to King Augeas which figured in the Greek myth of the Labours of HERCULES. They housed a large herd of cattle, and had not been cleaned for several years. Hercules was ordered to clean them in a day. He achieved his task by diverting the course of two rivers so that they flowed through the stables.
♣ To 'clean the Augean stables' is to clean up a large amount of filth or moral corruption, or to accomplish any distasteful job.

Avalon Mythical isle where King ARTHUR was taken as he was dying; it was ruled over by Arthur's half-sister, an enchantress called Morgan le Fay. Avalon has often been associated with Glastonbury in Somerset, England.

Bacchus (Greek name Dionysus) Roman god of wine, ecstasy and fertility, whose followers were called bacchants (priests) and bacchantes (priestesses). In the 2nd century BC the worship of Bacchus was banned in Rome, but it was readmitted as a mystery cult under the empire.
♣ In art, Bacchus is often depicted eating a bunch of grapes, surrounded by SATYRS.
♣ A 'bacchanalian' party or feast is marked by unrestrained drunkenness. The name recalls the Roman festivals called Bacchanalia, held in honour of Bacchus, which usually culminated in drunken orgies.

ball lightning Mysterious luminous globes said to appear during electrical storms. Witnesses claim that the balls can either explode on contact with objects or burn their way through them. Although ball lightning has won the credence of many scientists, its physical composition still remains a mystery.

Bermuda Triangle Area of the north Atlantic lying between Florida, Bermuda and Puerto Rico where numerous aircraft and ships and their crews and passengers are said to have vanished. Most experts now believe that many of the so-called unexplained disappearances either never occurred, or can be explained rationally.

Blarney Stone Block of rough limestone set high in the battlements of 15th-century Blarney Castle in County Cork, Ireland. According to an Irish legend, those who kiss the Blarney Stone receive a gift of eloquence that enables them to obtain anything they want through persuasion. Visitors have to lie on their backs, leaning out over a sheer drop, in order to kiss it.
♣ Blarney can be used as an expression to describe flattery designed to gain a favour.

Bluebeard Villain of European folk tales, who murdered his wives and kept their bodies in a locked room in his castle. The legend of Bluebeard may have been based on the career of Comorre the Cursed, a 6th-century Breton chief, but it also became interwoven with that of the mass-murderer Gilles de Rais, who was executed at Nantes in 1440. Bluebeard appears in Charles Perrault's *Contes du Temps* of 1697.

Book of the Dead Ancient Egyptian texts concerned with the guidance of the soul in the afterlife. Containing spells, incantations and rituals, they were placed in the tombs of the dead to help them rise again, pass safely through the dangers of the underworld, and achieve eternal happiness in the next life. They were adapted from Pyramid Texts (*c.*2350-2175 BC) written by priests for dead pharaohs, and Coffin Texts (*c.*2160-1580 BC) written for nobles. Simple versions were available to the poor, while the wealthy bought elaborate, illustrated versions. The use of these texts continued into the 1st century BC.

Brünnhilde (broon-HILL-der) A VALKYRIE in Norse mythology who loved the hero Sigurd. When he deceived her, she had him killed and then committed suicide.
♣ The characters of Brünnhilde and Sigurd appear in Wagner's *Ring of the Nibelung*, a cycle of four operas based on a 12th-century German poem.

Brutus In British mythology, the founder and first king of Britain. According to Geoffrey of Monmouth's 12th-century *History of the Kings of Britain*, Brutus and his

EGYPTIAN RITUAL *A papyrus from a Book of the Dead of 1310 BC depicts the ritual of 'Opening the Mouth', designed to restore the faculties of the embalmed body and help it to pass into the afterlife.*

Trojan settlers killed the last remaining GIANTS who lived on the island, after which Britain was named after Brutus.

Camelot In British legend, the capital of the kingdom of King ARTHUR.
🕯Cadbury Castle in Somerset, an isolated Iron Age hill-fort, is the site most often identified with Camelot. Archaeological evidence confirms that during the 6th century AD the fort was occupied by a powerful British warrior chieftain. However, local folklore advances alternative sites at Camelford in Cornwall and Winchester in Hampshire as the original Camelot.

Cassandra In Greek mythology, daughter of Priam, king of Troy. To win Cassandra's love, Apollo gave her the gift of prophecy; however, when she rejected his advances he ordained that nobody would believe her predictions.
🕯A Cassandra is a prophet of doom, especially one whose prophecies go unheeded.

centaur Creature in Greek mythology with the upper part of a human being and the lower body and legs of a horse, representing animal desires and barbarism. Centaurs were often depicted being ridden by Eros the Greek god of love – an allusion to their lustful nature.

Cerberus Three-headed dog in Greek mythology who guarded the entrance to HADES, the underworld.

Ceres (SEER-eez) Roman name for DEMETER, the goddess of agriculture.

Charon (KAAR-on) Ferryman in Greek mythology who carried the souls of the dead across the River STYX and into HADES, the underworld. The Greeks used to put coins in the mouths of the dead as his fee.

chimera Fire-breathing she-monster in Greek mythology, usually represented with the head of a lion, the body of a goat and the tail of a serpent.

Circe (SUR-see) Sorceress in Greek mythology, who turned the followers of ODYSSEUS into swine. Helped by a magic herb, Odysseus resisted Circe's magic and forced her to restore his men. Enamoured of Odysseus, Circe persuaded him to stay for a year on her island, before giving him directions to his home in Ithaca.

clairvoyance Supposed psychic ability of 'second sight' which enables someone to see or know things that are out of the natural range of human perception, such as ghosts, objects that are far away, and past and future events.

Classical mythology Collection of myths about the origin and history of the Greeks and Romans. The Romans adopted a vast part of their mythology, such as the system of gods, from the Greeks, but gave the gods Roman names. Works recounting these myths include the *Aeneid* by the Roman poet ▷VIRGIL, and the *Iliad* and *Odyssey* by the Greek author ▷HOMER.

corn circles Circular formations that began to materialise in British cornfields in the 1980s, mainly in Wiltshire and Hampshire. The crops are flattened into precise circles and patterns. Theories regarding their creation range from UFOs to rampaging hedgehogs, but in September 1991, two artists called Doug Bower and Dave Chorley admitted that they had made many of the more elaborate circles. Some scientists believe that others may be caused by electrically charged whirlwinds.

Cupid Roman name of Eros, the young and beautiful god of love who inspired physical desire. When his mother Venus grew jealous of PSYCHE's beauty, she ordered Cupid to make Psyche fall in love with the ugliest of men, but instead he fell in love with her himself.
🕯Cupid is often depicted as a cherub shooting an arrow at someone to make them fall in love – a favourite device of Victorian valentine cards and rococo art.
🕯The term 'Cupid's bow' refers to the top of the upper lip, because it resembles the shape of Cupid's double-curved bow.

Cyclopes Savage one-eyed giants in Greek mythology. Their leader Polyphemus, son of POSEIDON, imprisoned ODYSSEUS in his cave and ate some of his men. The survivors blinded Polyphemus in his drunken sleep with a hot poker, and escaped by clinging to the bellies of his sheep when they were let out of his cave to graze. Odysseus incurred the undying hatred of Poseidon, who burdened his journey home with difficulties.

Daedalus Legendary Greek inventor who built the LABYRINTH in which the MINOTAUR was kept. He was later imprisoned in it by Minos, king of Crete, for revealing the secret of the Labyrinth. Daedalus escaped with his son Icarus by making wings. Icarus, however, flew too close to the Sun; the wax that held his wings together melted, and he fell to Earth.

Damocles, sword of Subject of a story about a sycophantic but envious courtier called Damocles and a Greek ruler called Dionysus the Elder. To show Damocles what it felt like to be a king Dionysus held a magnificent banquet and seated Damocles under a sword that was suspended from the ceiling by a single hair.
🕯Figuratively speaking, a sword of Damocles is an impending danger that may strike at any moment, causing much anxiety.

Delphic Oracle The most influential ORACLE of the ancient Greeks, the shrine at which Apollo answered questions about the future. The Temple of Apollo at Delphi was built over a volcanic chasm on Mount Parnassus, where a priestess inhaled the sulphurous fumes, entered into a trance and acted as the medium for Apollo's prophetic messages. These messages were so ambiguous that a priest had to interpret them.

Demeter (Roman name Ceres) Greek goddess of corn, agriculture and fruitfulness. PERSEPHONE, her daughter by Zeus, was taken to the underworld by HADES to be his bride. Demeter was so forlorn that she neglected the crops and brought about the first winter. Zeus arranged for Persephone to be returned to her mother, but she had to spend some part of every year underground, when winter would commence again.

Devil Supreme embodiment of evil and the archenemy of God, also known as Beelzebub, Lucifer, Old Nick, Satan and the Prince of Darkness. Satan has been depicted in many ways: as a man with horns, goat hoofs and a pitchfork, and as an angel with large bat wings. In the early books of the Old Testament, it was God who inflicted punishment on men, while one of his officials – known as 'the satan', Hebrew for 'adversary' – acted as a prosecutor. In the New Testament and in later times, the image of Satan grew increasingly monstrous, until he was eventually blamed for all sin and evil. The story of the fall from heaven of Lucifer is told in the Book of Isaiah, in the Old Testament. Belief in the Devil was largely abandoned among theologians as a result of the ▷ENLIGHTENMENT.
🕯John Milton's epic poem ▷PARADISE LOST tells of the rebellion and punishment of Lucifer, a proud, arrogant and tragic figure who believes that it is 'better to reign in hell than serve in heaven'.

Diana Roman name of Artemis, goddess of hunting, wild animals, childbirth, fertility and the Moon.

SUN WORSHIP *Modern Druids believe that the standing stones of Stonehenge symbolise the human journey through life, and their summer solstice ceremony represents the change from darkness to light.*

Dido In Roman mythology, the founder and queen of Carthage in North Africa. She fell in love with the Trojan hero AENEAS when he was shipwrecked on the coast of Carthage, but committed suicide when he deserted her.

Dionysus Greek name for BACCHUS, the god of wine and revelry.

divination Art of predicting future events and giving supernatural guidance, using intuition or occult techniques such as ASTROLOGY, CLAIRVOYANCE, palmistry, ▷RUNES and TAROT CARDS. The ancient Greeks regularly consulted ORACLES, including the DELPHIC ORACLE.

Dracula, Count Bloodthirsty nobleman of the Middle Ages who was born in Transylvania (now a part of Romania) in about 1430. Dracula was nicknamed Vlad the Impaler because he skewered his victims on stakes. Dracula was the inspiration for a novel by English author Bram Stoker, published in 1897, and many ▷DRACULA FILMS. In Stoker's novel a VAMPIRE remained 'un-dead' until laid to rest by having a wooden stake driven through its heart – the eventual fate of Count Dracula.
🗡Crucifixes, garlic and holy water supposedly help to keep vampires at bay.

VAMPIRE FEAST *In the* Dracula *film of 1958, actor Christopher Lee dons the vampire's cloak; the actress Melissa Stribling is his victim.*

dragon Imaginary fire-breathing beast that figures in mythology and tales of chivalry, usually as a winged serpent with glaring eyes, flared nostrils, sharp teeth and talons. To Christians the dragon was a symbol of the Devil, and slaying the beast symbolised the triumph of Christ over evil. Many saints were depicted as dragon slayers, including ST GEORGE. In heraldry the dragon symbolised strength, and in Chinese mythology it was a benevolent beast.

Druids Priesthood of pre-Roman Celtic religion in Gaul and Britain, whose rites are said to have involved human sacrifice. They seem to have had knowledge of astronomy, and claimed to have prophetic powers. They believed that the soul was immortal. It was once thought that the Druids built Stonehenge and other stone circles as their temples. However, although the Druids may have used Stonehenge, archaeology shows that the circle was finished around 1550 BC – some 1200 years before the earliest-known Druids.
🗡The name Druid means 'knowing the oak tree' and may refer to their rituals which took place in sacred oak groves.

Eldorado Mythical 'Golden Land' in South America said to belong to El Dorado, a 'Golden Man' who covered himself with gold dust. The Golden Land was thought to exist in the area of the Orinoco and Amazon rivers, but centuries of exploration, including two expeditions led by Sir Walter ▷RALEIGH, failed to locate it.
🗡Figuratively, Eldorado is a place of fabulous wealth, or an opportunity to obtain it.

Elysian Fields In Greek mythology, the place where the souls of the righteous go after death. According to Homer, it is a beautiful region at the end of the Earth.

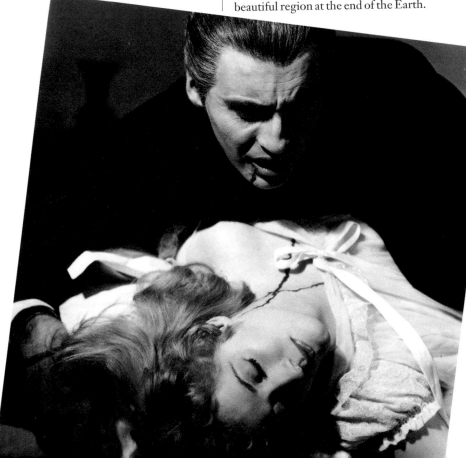

🐚 Figuratively, the Elysian Fields are a place or condition of ideal happiness.

🐚 The French translation of Elysian Fields, 'Champs Élysées', is the name of the principal boulevard in Paris.

Eros (EAR-os) (Roman name CUPID) Greek and Roman god of love, associated with all beautiful things. Eros was both playful and cruel, and he fired arrows that produced physical desire in his victims.

ESP Abbreviation for extrasensory perception, the supposed reception of information through other means than the five senses of seeing, hearing, smelling, touching and tasting. It is often referred to as the 'sixth sense'. Types of ESP include CLAIRVOYANCE and telepathy.

Excalibur King ARTHUR's magical sword, said to symbolise both destruction and fertility. In one version of the legends of Arthur, the future king proved his right to rule by pulling Excalibur out of a stone, which no other man could do. In another version, he received the sword from the Lady of the Lake – who lived in the middle of a lake. As Arthur lay dying he asked Sir Bedevere, one of his knights, to return Excalibur to the lake, where an arm rose up out of the water to receive it.

FAKE FAIRY *More than 50 years after Elsie Wright took her famous 'photographs' of fairies in 1917, she admitted they were a hoax.*

fairies Supernatural beings found in the folklore of many countries; often mischievous, they are capable of assisting or harassing humans. Hundreds of kinds of fairies have been described, varying in size, character and magical powers. They are said to covet human babies, and cradle-snatching is their chief vice. In place of the stolen baby they leave a changeling – a fairy child or a piece of wood carved to look like a child. The Christian Church once thought that fairies were fallen angels, or the souls of babies who had died unbaptised.

🐚 Oberon and Titania were introduced by Shakespeare as the King and Queen of Fairyland in *A Midsummer Night's Dream*.

Fates, The Three Greek and Roman goddesses who governed human fate. They are Clotho, the spinner of man's destiny; Lachesis, the weaver of chance; and Atropos, who cuts the thread of life with her scissors when death comes.

Faust Legendary scholar, magician and practitioner of astrology, who sold his soul to the Devil in exchange for youth, knowledge and power. A 'real' Faust lived in 16th-century Germany – a charlatan who boasted that he could perform miracles because he was in league with the Devil. The writers Christopher Marlowe and Johann Wolfgang von Goethe wrote plays about Faust. In Marlowe's ▷DR FAUSTUS, Faust ends up being dragged to hell to face an eternity of torment; in ▷GOETHE's version, however, Faust is finally redeemed.

🐚 A 'Faustian' bargain is one in which a person sells his soul for huge tangible material gain.

Fisher King King in Arthurian legend who presided over the Grail castle where the HOLY GRAIL was kept; he is also known as the Grail King. The Fisher King had been severely wounded yet was incapable of dying. His land was in desolation and the crops would not grow. According to a prophecy, he could be healed only when an innocent fool arrived in the court and asked him why he was ill. An innocent knight called PARSIFAL found the castle, and eventually asked the necessary question.

Flying Dutchman Dutch phantom ship which, according to legend, was doomed to roam the seas until Judgment Day. Old records show that a real ship of that name set sail from Amsterdam in 1680, but was caught in a gale near the Cape of Good Hope. Because the captain defied God by persisting in his attempt to round the Cape, he was condemned to roam the seas forever, luring other ships to their destruction. Many reports of a ship fitting the Flying Dutchman's description have been dismissed as mirages, but the similarity of detail given by witnesses cannot be explained.

🐚 The Flying Dutchman legend inspired Wagner to write his opera *Der Fliegende Holländer*. He wrote it after a rough North Sea crossing in 1839, which took three weeks instead of the expected eight days.

Friar Tuck One of ROBIN HOOD's legendary 'merry men', a fighter with whom Robin had a trial of strength. The pair met by a river at Fountain Dale, Nottinghamshire, where the friar agreed to carry Robin over the water, but dropped him into the stream. He joined the outlaws only after a ferocious and indecisive battle with them.

Furies, The (Greek name Erinyes) Three hideous female goddesses in Classical mythology – winged monsters called Tisiphone, Alecto and Megaera, with snakes in their hair. They pursued evildoers, and their main duty was to destroy those who had murdered their own kin. When KRONOS castrated his father (Heaven), his father's blood fell upon the Earth and she conceived and bore the Furies.

Gaia The 'earth goddess' of Greek mythology. The daughter of Chaos, she was both mother and wife of Uranus, by whom she produced the CYCLOPES and the TITANS. (See also ▷GAIA HYPOTHESIS in 'The Earth and the Environment'.)

FOUL AVENGERS *The three Furies shriek for the blood of Orestes because he killed his mother Clytemnestra. It was his tragic duty to kill her after she murdered his father Agamemnon.*

Galahad, Sir Young knight in the tales of King ARTHUR. The son of Sir LANCELOT and the model of a perfect Christian knight, Galahad marked the end of the worldly values of chivalry and the beginning of the spiritual quest for the HOLY GRAIL. His exceptional purity enabled him to have a vision of Heaven in which he found the Grail, after which he died in ecstasy.

Gawain, Sir A knight of the ROUND TABLE famous for his courage and courtesy, and a nephew of King ARTHUR. Gawain failed in his quest for the HOLY GRAIL but proved his honour, as recounted in the 14th-century poem ▷SIR GAWAIN AND THE GREEN KNIGHT.

giants Colossal beings who feature in myths, legends and folk tales around the world. Because ancient peoples found dinosaur bones, massive Stone Age monuments and strangely shaped rocks, they believed that a race of giants once existed. In folklore, these giants were often slow-witted, and were easily defeated by heroes such as ODYSSEUS – who escaped from Polyphemus, leader of the CYCLOPES – and BRUTUS, who killed GOG AND MAGOG. In Greek mythology, the Giants' War was a revolt against ZEUS that was easily quashed with the help of HERCULES. The giants of Scandinavian myths were more formidable; dubbed 'the voracious ones', they represented the unbridled forces of nature and were ascribed superhuman powers.

Glastonbury Market town in Somerset and traditional site of King Arthur's isle of AVALON. Bones discovered in the graveyard of Glastonbury Abbey in 1191 are said to be those of King Arthur and Guinevere. According to legend, Christ himself visited Glastonbury as a boy, and later so did Joseph of Arimathea, who brought with him the HOLY GRAIL and began the conversion of Britain to Christianity. The Grail is said to rest below the spring on Glastonbury Tor. Because of its mystical past, Glastonbury has become a focus for hippie and New Age culture.

Godiva, Lady Heroic English noblewoman of the 11th century. While Godiva was virtuous and charitable, her husband – Earl Leofric of Mercia – was a tyrant who imposed severe taxes on his people. According to legend, Leofric agreed to change his ways if his modest wife would ride naked through Coventry on market day. She accepted the challenge. One account says that Godiva covered her nakedness with her long hair; a later version says that the people of Coventry stayed indoors and that only one man, later known as Peeping Tom, looked into the streets, and was struck blind.

Gog and Magog Two mythical giants in British legend, statues of which now stand in London's Guildhall. According to legend, they were the last survivors of a race of British giants conquered by BRUTUS and his Trojan warriors.

Golden Fleece In Greek mythology, the fleece of the winged ram Chrysomallus. It hung on a sacred oak tree at Colchis, south of the Caucasus mountains, and was guarded by a dragon. It was stolen by JASON and the Argonauts.

Gorgons Three frightful sisters in Greek mythology – Stheno, Euryale and MEDUSA. They had glaring eyes, huge teeth, and snakes for hair, and anyone who looked at them was turned to stone by their gaze. The Gorgons figure chiefly in the story of PERSEUS, who looked only at Medusa's reflection in a polished shield while he cut off her head.

Graces Three goddesses in Greek mythology who personified and bestowed the qualities of grace, charm and beauty. The daughters of Zeus, they were named Aglaia (the radiant), Thalia (the flowering) and Euphrosyne (joy).

Green Man Woodland spirit, also known as Jack-in-the-Green, who was an important figure in springtime festivities throughout Europe. Dressed from head to foot in green branches, he represented new life in plants and trees. The Green Man is depicted in medieval churches as a sinister mixture of man and tree, and he can still be seen on some British pub signs.

gremlins Mischievous spirits in the lore of British and American airmen. Gremlins were blamed for causing mechanical problems in military aircraft during World War II. They supposedly drank petrol, and were said to have the ability to raise and lower airfields beneath novice pilots as they came in to land.

Grim Reaper Figure commonly used to represent death, and taking the form either of a cloaked skeleton, or of Father Time wielding his scythe.

Guinevere Wife of King ARTHUR. In some versions of the legends of Arthur, she had a love affair with Sir LANCELOT.

Arthur's treacherous nephew Modred used this affair to start a civil war, which led to the end of Arthur's reign and of the fellowship of the ROUND TABLE.

Hades (Roman name Pluto) Greek name for both the god of death and the gloomy underworld which he ruled. Charon, the ferryman, carried the souls of the dead across the River Styx into Hades, where a three-headed dog called Cerberus guarded the entrance. When souls drank from the River Lethe, they forgot their former lives. PERSEPHONE spent each winter with the god Hades as his queen.
⚲Hades later became associated with the ▷HELL of Christianity.

Halloween The eve of All Saints' Day on October 31, which used to be called Samhain Eve in the Celtic calendar. The Celts believed that the dead walked the Earth on that night, and could only be placated by gifts of food from the living. The Christian Church incorporated Samhain into its own calendar by calling it All Saints' Day, but pre-Christian beliefs remained, and the living dead were joined by witches and demons. Halloween is now the night of 'trick or treat', when children in fancy dress go from door to door demanding gifts.

Harpies Vicious monsters in Greek mythology, often depicted as birds of prey with women's faces and breasts. In the story of JASON, the Harpies were sent by the gods to punish the blind King Phineus, by stealing his food at every meal.
⚲Figuratively, a harpy is a fierce, grasping hag or a merciless sponger.

Hector A prince of Troy in Greek mythology – eldest son of Priam, and the bravest of the Trojan warriors. At the end of the TROJAN WAR, Achilles killed Hector, tied him to his chariot, and dragged his body across the battlefield.

Helen of Troy In Greek mythology, the most beautiful woman in the world. She was daughter of the mortal LEDA and the god Zeus. She married Menelaus, king of Sparta, and her abduction by Paris led to the TROJAN WAR. The playwright Christopher Marlowe referred to Helen's face as 'the face that launched a thousand ships'; referring to the fact that the entire Greek army sailed to Troy to recover her.

Hephaestus (heh-FYE-stus) (Roman name Vulcan) Greek god of fire and blacksmith of the gods. He was lamed by being flung out of Olympus after interfering in a quarrel between his parents Hera and Zeus. According to some stories, Hephaestus was married to APHRODITE, in others to one of the three GRACES. According to the account in Homer's *Odyssey*, when Aphrodite was unfaithful Hephaestus trapped her and her lover Ares in an invisible net, and the gods came to laugh at them.

Hera (Roman name Juno) Greek goddess who protected women and marriage, and was the wife of Zeus. Hera is best known for her jealousy and animosity towards the many mortal women with whom her husband fell in love.

Hercules (Greek name Heracles) One of the greatest heroes of Classical mythology – a son of ZEUS and supposedly the strongest man on Earth. To atone for slaughtering his family in a fit of madness – inflicted on him by Hera – he was set 12 seemingly impossible tasks by Eurystheus, the ruler of Tiryns. Called the Labours of Hercules, the 12 tasks were: to kill the Nemean Lion; to kill the many-headed HYDRA; to catch the Arcadian stag; to kill the Erymanthian boar; to clean the AUGEAN STABLES; to kill the vicious flock of Stymphalian birds; to catch the Cretan bull given to Minos by POSEIDON; to catch the man-eating horses of Thrace; to seize the girdle of the queen of the AMAZONS; to catch the cattle of the monster Geryon; to catch the golden apples of the Hesperides nymphs; and to fetch the three-headed dog CERBERUS who guarded the entrance to Hades. After successfully completing his labours and surviving many other adventures, Hercules was rewarded with immortality.
⚘Any extraordinary effort or task can be described as 'herculean'.

Hermes (Roman name Mercury) Messenger of the gods who flew with great swiftness, aided by the wings he wore on his sandals and cap. He was a son of Zeus and the father of Pan.
⚘The wand of Hermes – a caduceus – is the symbol of physicians, with wings at the top and serpents twined about the staff.

Holy Grail Sacred cup said to have been used by Jesus at the Last Supper. It became an object of quest for the knights of the ROUND TABLE, including Sir GALAHAD and PARSIFAL. In one story, it was kept in the Grail castle of the crippled FISHER KING. According to legend, the Grail is said to rest beneath the spring on Glastonbury Tor.
⚘A grail can be any esteemed object which people strive at length to attain.

Hydra In Greek mythology, a many-headed water snake that lived in the marshy plain of Lerna in new Argos. As one of his 12 Labours, HERCULES was sent to kill the Hydra, but as soon as he cut off one of its heads two grew in its place. His charioteer had to help by burning the roots of each head.

Icarus Son of DAEDALUS in Greek mythology, who melted the wax of his wings by flying too near the Sun.

Jason Greek hero and leader of the ARGONAUTS. Jason was heir to a kingdom in Greece, but his uncle Pelias had seized the throne and would only let it go in return for the magical GOLDEN FLEECE at Colchis. Jason set sail and obtained the fleece with the help of Medea – a Colchian princess as well as a sorceress – who fell in love with him. Medea helped Jason to escape from her father, the king, by killing and cutting up her brother and throwing his body into the sea. While the distraught king was gathering up the remains of his son for burial, Jason and Medea fled. The couple returned to Greece and successfully toppled the usurper, King Pelias. They married and raised a family, but Jason later decided to divorce Medea and marry another princess. Enraged, Medea killed their children and the princess. Jason was crushed to death when the stern of his ship, the *Argo*, fell on him.

Judgment of Paris Incident that ultimately caused the TROJAN WAR. When the goddess Discord threw the Apple of Discord marked 'For the Fairest' among the gods, it was claimed by Aphrodite, Athena and Hera. Zeus asked the Trojan prince Paris to decide which goddess was the most beautiful and each of them tried to bribe him: Athena with military power, Hera with political power, and Aphrodite with the most beautiful woman in the world. Paris gave the apple to Aphrodite, who as his reward led him to Helen, afterwards known as HELEN OF TROY. Helen was already the wife of the Greek king of Sparta, but Paris abducted her. The Greeks, helped by the slighted Hera and Athena, waged war on Troy to recover Helen. Trojan civilisation was destroyed in the process.

Juno Roman goddess who is usually associated with HERA.

Jupiter Roman name of ZEUS.

Kronos In Greek mythology, chief of the TITANS – the gods who were children of Heaven and Earth, and who ruled before the Olympians. Because Heaven kept his offspring imprisoned within the body of Earth, who groaned with the burden, Kronos castrated his father with a sickle to separate Heaven from Earth and free himself and his siblings. Kronos married his sister Rhea, who had six children: Hestia, DEMETER, HADES, HERA, POSEIDON and ZEUS. Because of a prophecy that one of his children would overthrow him, Kronos tried to swallow them as they were born. They survived, however, and his son Zeus eventually dethroned him. The Romans identified Kronos with their god SATURN.

Labyrinth Vast maze which according to Greek mythology was built at Knossos by the craftsman DAEDALUS, on the orders of King Minos of Crete, to hide the monstrous MINOTAUR. The hero Theseus killed the Minotaur, and used a thread which he played out to retrace his route out of the maze. Daedalus escaped from the labyrinth with his son Icarus by making artificial wings and flying over the walls.
⚘Figuratively, a labyrinth can be any intricate construction or problem.

Lancelot, Sir Greatest and most tragic of the heroes of the knights of the ROUND TABLE. Lancelot was torn between his loyalty to King Arthur and his love for Arthur's wife, Queen Guinevere. When their affair was openly denounced it led to civil war, and Arthur was fatally wounded at the Battle of Camlann. Heavy with grief, Lancelot became a hermit and eventually died of a broken heart.
⚘Lancelot is a prominent character in Malory's *Le Morte d'Arthur*, where the knight's tragic love for his queen prevents him finding the HOLY GRAIL.

Leda and the swan Story from Greek mythology about the rape of Leda, a queen of Sparta, by Zeus, who had taken the form of a swan. As a result of the rape, HELEN OF TROY hatched from a white egg.
⚘The rape of Leda has frequently been portrayed in art, and W.B. Yeats wrote a poem entitled *Leda and the Swan*.

leprechauns Fairy shoemakers of Irish folklore who resemble elves and bury hoards of gold. If caught, a leprechaun can be forced to reveal his hidden treasure.

Little John Second in command of the Merry Men who followed ROBIN HOOD. Little John was given his nickname in ironic reference to his large stature: he overpowered Robin in a fight with clubs at their first meeting.

MONSTER HOAX *The 'surgeon's photograph' of the Loch Ness Monster fooled experts for 60 years until 1994, when it was revealed that the serpent-like neck was a plastic model on a toy submarine.*

Loch Ness Monster Large aquatic creature, nicknamed Nessie, said to live in Scotland's Loch Ness. The first sighting was made in AD 565 by St Columba, but only after a newspaper article in 1933 did the creature become world famous. In 1934, a London gynaecologist called R.K. Wilson supposedly took a photograph of Nessie's swan-like neck, which resembled that of an extinct marine reptile called a plesiosaur. This has since been exposed as a hoax mounted by Marmaduke Wetherell, a film producer and big game hunter. Large, unidentified shapes have been picked up on sonar equipment, but there is still no undisputed proof of Nessie's existence.

mandrake Narcotic plant with purplish flowers from the family *Solanaceae*, once used as an anaesthetic and as an aphrodisiac. Dogs were often used to uproot the plant because the long, forked root was said to embody a demon, and pulling it from the ground would make the demon shriek so horribly that anyone hearing it would die.

Mars Roman name for the Greek god Ares, the god of war, farmers and herdsmen, the son of Zeus and Hera, and the lover of Aphrodite.
♣ The fourth planet from the Sun is named Mars, probably because of its reddish tinge.

May Day Festival of rebirth and renewal once held on the first day of May throughout Europe. May Day has its origins in the Celtic festival of Beltane, when the return of summer was celebrated.

DUGONG AHOY *The source of mermaid legends may be sailors' accounts of marine mammals called dugongs or sea cows.*

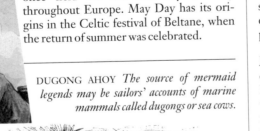

Medea Sorceress who fell in love with JASON and used magic to help him and the Argonauts obtain the Golden Fleece.

Medusa In Greek mythology, the best known of three GORGONS whose gaze turned people to stone. The hero PERSEUS killed her with the aid of Athena. While fighting Medusa he avoided her stare by looking only at her reflection in his polished shield. From the blood of the slain Medusa sprang the winged horse PEGASUS.

Mercury Roman name of HERMES, messenger of the gods, who flew with great swiftness. He was the patron of travellers.
♣ The planet nearest the Sun is named Mercury because of its swift motion.

Merlin Wizard who acted as adviser to King Arthur, said to have been fathered by a demon. He may have been founded upon a real-life Celtic bard and seer – named Myrddin – who lived in the land of the northern Welsh in the 5th or 6th century AD. There are many legends about Merlin; one tells how he used magic to transport Stonehenge from Ireland.
♣ The legend of Merlin was the inspiration for T.H. White's *The Once and Future King*, on which the film *The Sword in the Stone* was based.

mermaid Mythical sea creature with a woman's body and a fish's tail. Mermaid legends are very old, and are remarkably similar whatever their country of origin. Mermaids are seductive SIRENS, personifying the beauty and treachery of the sea. They are said to lull sailors to sleep with their sweet singing and then carry them away beneath the waves. Belief in the existence of a race of merfolk was widespread among seamen until the late 19th century. To see a mermaid was considered a portent of danger and disaster.

Midas King of Phrygia in Greek mythology, who was granted one wish by the god Dionysus – that everything he touched would turn to gold. He regretted his request when his food became inedible metal and he turned his daughter into a golden statue. On the instruction of Dionysus, he bathed in the river Pactolus to rid himself of his golden touch.
♣ A person who easily acquires riches is sometimes said to have the 'Midas touch'.

Midsummer Eve Night of June 23 when in Celtic times great sacrificial bonfires were lit in honour of the Sun. Even in recent centuries, rural folk lit bonfires and men and beasts passed through the embers to ward off disease and bad luck. It was also a time when witches and evil creatures were believed to be active, and when girls practised simple magic to discover the identity of their future husbands.

Minerva Roman name of ATHENA, goddess of war, wisdom and the arts.

Minotaur Monster in Greek mythology with a human body and a bull's head. It was born to Pasiphaë, the queen of Crete, after she mated with a sacred bull. King Minos ordered DAEDALUS to construct the LABYRINTH in which to keep the monster, and every year seven young men and seven maidens were sent from Athens to be its prey. To stop the slaughter, Theseus volunteered to fight the Minotaur. As he went through the maze he unwound a ball of thread and, after killing the Minotaur, used the thread to find his way out.

Morpheus God of sleep and dreams in Greek and Roman mythology.
♣ Someone who is 'in the arms of Morpheus' is asleep.
♣ The narcotic morphine was named after the god Morpheus.

Muses Nine goddesses in Greek mythology, all daughters of Zeus. Each Muse presided over a different art or science: Calliope (epic poetry), Clio (history), Erato (love poetry), Euterpe (lyric poetry), Melpomene (tragedy), Polyhymnia (hymns), Terpsichore (dance), Thalia (comedy), and Urania (astronomy).

♣ To this day, writers, artists and musicians often speak of their muse as a source of inspiration. By analogy, a muse can also be a real person, such as Beatrice Portinari, who inspired the Italian poet Dante.

Narcissus Beautiful youth in Greek mythology who fell in love with his own reflection. Because he was unable to tear himself away from the image, he wasted away and turned into the narcissus flower.
♣ In psychology narcissism is the excessive admiration of oneself.

Nemesis Greek goddess of retribution, who punished the wicked as well as anyone she deemed to be too fortunate.
♣ Anything that brings about a person's downfall is described as their nemesis.

Neptune Roman god of fresh water, who became a sea god when the Romans identified him with the Greek god Poseidon. He is portrayed as a bearded giant, holding a three-pronged spear, or trident.
♣ The planet Neptune, cold and dimly lit, is the eighth planet from the Sun.

Norse mythology The mythology of Scandinavia, which also became widespread in Germany and Britain until the establishment of Christianity. People and places in Norse mythology include: BRÜNN-HILDE, ODIN, THOR, TROLLS, Valhalla, the VALKYRIES and the WORLD TREE.

Nostradamus (1503-66) Latinised name of Michel de Nôtredam, a French astrologer and physician who wrote a strange

collection of obscure rhymed prophecies. The first edition was published in 1555, and the ambiguity of the verses has fired the imaginations of Nostradamus enthusiasts ever since. In recent times his followers have credited Nostradamus with foretelling the outbreak of World War II and many other significant events.

nymphs Young and beautiful female spirits of nature in Classical mythology who lived in forests, caves, seas, rivers and springs. They liked dancing and music and were companions of the SATYRS.
♣ Any young, beautiful or seductive woman may be referred to as a nymph.

Odin Father and leader of the gods in Norse mythology. Odin sacrificed one of his eyes to obtain wisdom, hung himself upon the WORLD TREE, and acquired a magic drink called the Mead of Inspiration, in order to bestow the gifts of wisdom and poetry upon mankind. Odin was the god of battle and of the dead. His messengers, the Valkyries, escorted the souls of heroic slain warriors to his realm of Valhalla, where there was eternal joy and feasting.
♣ Wednesday is named after Odin's Germanic name, Woden.

Odysseus (oh-DISS-ee-uhs) (Roman name Ulysses) King of Ithaca and a Greek leader in the TROJAN WAR. He helped bring about the fall of Troy by conceiving the ruse of the TROJAN HORSE. He is also the central character of the ▷ODYSSEY in which Homer recounts the adventures of Odysseus involving CIRCE, the CYCLOPES, SCYLLA AND CHARYBDIS, and the SIRENS. Odysseus returned home after an absence of 20 years, and killed the suitors who were pressing his wife PENELOPE to marry again. Odysseus may have been a real chieftain around whom legends gathered.
♣ The novel ▷ULYSSES by James Joyce is based on the legend of Odysseus.

Oedipus (EE-di-puhs) Tragic king in Greek mythology, who unknowingly killed his father and married his mother. Warned by Apollo that his son would kill him, King Laius of Thebes left his newborn son on a mountainside, but the infant was found and raised by the king and queen of Corinth. Ignorant of his true ancestry, Oedipus left Corinth when the DELPHIC ORACLE predicted that he would kill his father and marry his mother. He killed Laius in a chance encounter on the way to Thebes. He also defeated a SPHINX that had been troubling the city, and was made the new king of Thebes. Oedipus married his

ENCHANTING SEAS *A Greek vase from the 5th century BC shows how Odysseus was lashed securely to the mast of his ship, so that he could listen to the song of the sirens without falling under their spell.*

mother Jocasta, not knowing her true identity; when he learned the truth he blinded himself and Jocasta hanged herself.
♣ In psychology, an ▷OEDIPUS COMPLEX is a boy's sexual desire for his mother.

Olympus, Mount Legendary home of the gods, and an actual mountain in Greece on the borders of Thessaly and Macedonia. The Greek gods were known as Olympians.

oracle Greek shrine at which a deity was consulted about the future. An oracle was also the priest through whom the prophecy was given, as well as the prophecy itself.

Orpheus and Eurydice (yoo-RID-i-see) Orpheus was a great poet and musician in Greek mythology, and Eurydice was his wife. Orpheus sang so beautifully with his lyre that he attracted wild animals, trees and even stones. When Eurydice was killed by a snake, Orpheus went to the underworld and begged HADES to let Eurydice return to Earth. Hades agreed on one condition – that Orpheus should go on ahead of her and not look back until they had reached the Earth again. Orpheus could not resist looking, and so he lost her for ever.

Pan Shepherd god of the Greek countryside who had the legs, ears and horns of a goat, and was the son of Hermes. He wandered through woodland glades playing his reed panpipes, and was believed to be the source of frightening noises in the wilderness at night, which could cause sudden panic among herds and men.
♣ The word *panic* comes from the god Pan.

Pandora In Greek mythology, the first mortal woman, created by HEPHAESTUS. To punish mankind for PROMETHEUS' theft of fire, Zeus sent Pandora to Earth with a box containing a few blessings, but many more evils, such as war and sickness. When she opened the box the evils flew out, to plague mankind; only hope remained.
♣ The phrase 'a Pandora's box' means any source of great suffering or trouble, often unsuspected at first.

Paris In Greek mythology, the son of Priam, king of Troy. He made the crucial JUDGMENT OF PARIS and then abducted the Greek queen who became known as HELEN OF TROY. These events led to the TROJAN WAR, in which Paris killed Achilles by piercing his heel with an arrow.

Parnassus Mountain in Greece, north of the Gulf of Corinth. One of its peaks was revered as the abode of Apollo and the MUSES, while the other belonged to Bacchus. The DELPHIC ORACLE lived on its south side. Because of its link with the Muses, Parnassus is known as the mythological home of poetry and music.

Parsifal A simple country boy who became a knight in King Arthur's court. When he left home his mentor Gurnemanz instructed him never to ask any questions. He searched for the castle of the wounded FISHER KING where the HOLY GRAIL was kept, and when he found it, obediently refrained from asking the Fisher King why he was ill. This question would have healed the Fisher King, and Parsifal would then have become his successor as the new grail king. Only after many years did Parsifal return to ask the vital question.

Pegasus Winged horse in Greek mythology, that sprang from the blood of the dying MEDUSA. The hero Bellerophon tamed Pegasus and tried to fly to heaven, but was thrown off. Pegasus created Hippocrene, the fountain of the MUSES, when he struck his hoof on Mount Helicon.

Penelope Wife of ODYSSEUS in Greek mythology. Penelope remained true to her husband while he was away fighting in the TROJAN WAR, even though she was harassed by suitors pressing her to remarry. To stall for time, she promised to choose someone after she had finished weaving a robe for her father-in-law, but she unravelled her work every night. When her trick was discovered, she agreed to give herself to whoever could bend Odysseus's mighty bow – a bow which only he could string. When a man she did not recognise accomplished the task, Penelope realised that her husband had returned, in disguise.

Persephone In Greek mythology, the daughter of Zeus and Demeter, who was abducted by HADES and taken to the underworld. Demeter, the goddess of the harvest, grieved and neglected the crops, creating the first winter. Zeus ordered Hades to return Persephone, but because she had eaten in the underworld, she had to spend a third of every year there.

Perseus Greek hero and a son of Zeus, who killed the Gorgon MEDUSA. Anyone who looked at a Gorgon was turned to stone, but Hermes and Athena helped Perseus by giving him winged shoes, a magical sword, and a polished shield. He swooped down on Medusa from the air and used the shield as a mirror to cut off her head without looking at it directly.

phoenix A mythical bird that lived in Arabia and burned itself to death every 500 years. The roots of this story first appeared in Greek literature, in an account of Egypt given by ▷HERODOTUS around 430 BC. When the phoenix was nearing death, it built a nest of sweet spices and sang while the sun ignited it. A worm arose from the ashes and grew into the new phoenix.
♣ A phoenix can also be a person or thing that has been restored to a new existence from destruction, downfall or ruin.

SHADOW DANCE *A sinister figure sets the pace on the cover of this 1934 edition of Robert Browning's poem 'The Pied Piper of Hamelin'.*

Pied Piper of Hamelin German folk tale from the Middle Ages about a town that was infested with rats, until a mysterious piper lured them into a river with his music. When the townspeople refused to pay the piper his fee, he used his strange music to lure their children away. The legend may be based on a folk memory of a medieval epidemic of ergotism, caused by a hallucinogenic fungus that grows on grain, which apparently caused crowds of people to dance from town to town until they were exhausted. However, a more likely basis for the legend is the children's ▷CRUSADE.

Pluto Roman name of HADES, god of the underworld and ruler of the dead.
♣ The planet Pluto is the ninth and normally the farthest known true planet from the Sun. However, because of its elliptical orbit, Pluto will be closer to the Sun than Neptune until the year 2000.

poltergeist Mischievous household spirit that manifests itself by moving objects and making noises, named from the German term *polter* meaning noise, and *geist* meaning spirit. In many cases a particular person is said to be the focus of the disturbance, often an adolescent with emotional troubles. Some parapsychologists believe that the disturbances may be caused by an involuntary form of psychokinesis – the supposed ability to move objects using psychic powers.

Poseidon Greek name for NEPTUNE, the god who ruled the sea. Poseidon could command the waves, provoke storms and cause springs to flow.

Prester John Legendary Christian monarch of the Middle Ages, believed to rule a kingdom in central Asia. His name means 'Priest John', and he is thought to be descended from the Magi. In the Middle Ages many journeys were made to try to find Prester John's country in the hope that he would help Europe's kings to fight against Islam. From the mid-14th century the search focused on Ethiopia, a Christian country cut off from Europe.

Priam Aged king of TROY at the time of the TROJAN WAR. He was the father of 50 children, including HECTOR and PARIS. When the Greeks sacked the city, Priam was killed by Neoptolemus, son of Achilles.

Prometheus One of the TITANS in Greek mythology. When Zeus denied man the use of fire, Prometheus stole fire from HEPHAESTUS and brought it to Earth to save mankind. Zeus punished mankind by sending PANDORA to Earth with a box of evils. He also ordered Prometheus to be chained to a rock while an eagle preyed upon his liver. Every day his liver grew back and was eaten again by the eagle. Prometheus was eventually rescued by Hercules.
🔖 Aeschylus wrote a play called *Prometheus Bound*, and Shelley wrote a long poem entitled *Prometheus Unbound*.
🔖 Prometheus has become a symbol of lonely and valiant resistance to authority.

Psyche Beautiful girl in Roman mythology. Venus was so jealous of her beauty that she ordered her son Cupid to make Psyche fall in love with someone ugly. But Cupid himself fell in love with Psyche; he visited her every night in the dark and ordered her never to try to see him. One night Psyche lit a lamp to look at Cupid while he was asleep, but he awoke and fled. While Psyche searched for him, Venus

GREENWOOD LIFE *Medieval outlaws such as Robin Hood's band were forced to gang together and survive by poaching and robbery.*

treated her cruelly and set her many harsh tasks. Eventually Jupiter made Psyche immortal, and she and Cupid were married.

Pygmalion Legendary king of Cyprus who fell in love with a statue he had made of his ideal woman. Aphrodite brought it to life so that he could marry her. George Bernard Shaw's play ▷PYGMALION adapts this theme.

Robin Hood Folk hero of English ballads, who stole from the rich and gave to the poor. His 'merry men' included FRIAR TUCK and LITTLE JOHN; his sweetheart was Maid Marian. The first known literary reference to Robin is in William Langland's *The Vision of Piers Plowman* (1377), in which a chaplain boasts that he can recite ballads about 'Robyn Hode' – ballads with which he expected his audience to be familiar. The first collection of such ballads was published at the end of the 15th century and titled *A Lytell Geste of Robyn Hode*. The legends of Robin Hood vary, but all of them stress his skill as an archer. Some say that he was born Robert Fitz-Ooth, Earl of Huntingdon, in Locksley, Nottinghamshire, in 1160. He was outlawed for some unknown offence, and his traditional haunts were Sherwood Forest in Nottinghamshire and Barnsdale Forest in Yorkshire. There is no firm evidence that Robin existed; he may have been an idealised figure created by the peasants.
🔖 Robin Hood's grave is said to be in the park of Kirklees Hall, Yorkshire. Legend has it that Robin was killed by a prioress when he sought refuge at a nunnery.

Romulus and Remus Twin brothers in Roman legend and founders of the city of Rome. They were sons of the god Mars and a VESTAL VIRGIN called Rhea Sylvia.

Because Rhea had been violated by Mars, her sons were set adrift in a boat and left to die. They drifted ashore and were suckled by a she-wolf. Romulus killed Remus in a quarrel over the site for the city of Rome. Romulus ruled for 40 years, then vanished in a storm and became a god.

Round Table, Knights of the Fellowship of the knights of King ARTHUR, who included Sir GALAHAD, Sir GAWAIN, Sir LANCELOT and PARSIFAL. Among their adventures was the quest for the HOLY GRAIL. The Round Table was first described in 1155 by the poet Robert Wace who held that Arthur devised the table to promote equality among the knights.
🔖 A table said to be the Round Table hangs in the Castle Hall in Winchester, but this dates only from the 13th century.

St George Saint of the Christian Church, who may have been a high-ranking officer in the army of the Roman Empire in Asia Minor in about AD 300. In early Christian belief, the legendary slaying by St George of a dragon symbolised the triumph of Christ over the Devil.
🔖 St George is the patron saint of England and Portugal. In England, St George's Day is celebrated on April 23. It seems likely that Edward III made him patron saint of England when he founded the Order of the Garter in St George's name in the mid-14th century.

CHRISTMAS HAMPER *A card from the early 1900s shows a jovial Santa. A generous saint has become a symbol of Christmas.*

Santa Claus Legendary character based on St Nicholas – patron saint of children – whose gifts of gold to poor children led to the European custom of exchanging gifts on December 5, the eve of his feast day. Early Dutch settlers in America took this custom with them; Santa Claus is an American corruption of *Sinter Klaes*, the Dutch form of St Nicholas. The old custom is still maintained in Germany and the Netherlands, but elsewhere Santa Claus has become a central figure in Christmas celebrations. By the 1890s, the English Father Christmas, originally a character in village folk plays, had become firmly linked to Santa Claus, and now the two figures are thought of as being one and the same.

🜍 The first association of a reindeer with St Nicholas was in 1821 in an American publication called *The Children's Friend*.

Saturn Roman god of agriculture, identified with the Greek Titan called KRONOS. He established a Golden Age, in which all people were equal and harvests were plentiful. Saturn's festival – the Roman Saturnalia – took place in December and was a time of merrymaking and debauchery.

🜍 Saturday is named after Saturn, and the sixth planet from the Sun bears his name.

satyrs Forest gods or demons in Greek mythology who were part-man and part-goat, with horns, pointed ears and the tail of a horse. They were called fauns by the Romans. Satyrs were pleasure-loving, fond of wine and joined in wild dances with the NYMPHS. They were companions of Dionysus, the god of wine and revelry.

Scylla and Charybdis (SILL-er; ka-RIB-dis) In Greek mythology, Scylla was a six-headed sea monster who lived on a rock on one side of a narrow strait, while Charybdis was a whirlpool on the other side. When ships passed close to Scylla's rock in order to avoid Charybdis, she would seize and devour their sailors.

🜍 To be 'caught between Scylla and Charybdis' is to be forced to choose between two equally unpleasant options.

sirens Evil sea nymphs in Greek mythology who, by their sweet singing, lured sailors to destruction on the rocks surrounding their island. When ODYSSEUS encountered the sirens, he ordered his crew to plug their ears with wax and to bind him to the mast of his ship, so that he could listen to their song without peril.

🜍 A siren is a dangerous or alluring woman; a 'siren song' is an irresistible distraction.

Sisyphus In Greek mythology, king of Corinth. He offended Zeus, who condemned him to push a huge boulder up a steep hill eternally.

Sphinx Monster of Greek and Egyptian mythology. In Greek mythology, the Sphinx had the head and breasts of a woman, the body of a lion, and the wings of

a bird. In the story of OEDIPUS it waylaid travellers on the roads near the city of Thebes, carrying away and devouring anyone who could not answer its riddle: 'What creatures walk on four legs in the morning, on two legs at noon, and on three legs in the evening?' Oedipus finally gave the correct answer: human beings, who crawl on all fours as infants, walk upright in maturity, and use a walking stick in old age. The Egyptian sphinx was usually portrayed as a lion with a pharaoh's head, like the huge stone statue at Giza in Egypt.

Stonehenge Great circle of stones standing on England's Salisbury Plain, and the focus of several romantic legends. The 12th-century chronicler Geoffrey of Monmouth wrote that the massive stones were brought from Africa to Ireland by a race of giants, then moved to Wiltshire in the 6th century by the wizard MERLIN. The 17th-century antiquary John Aubrey suggested that the DRUIDS built Stonehenge as a temple. Although the Druids may have used Stonehenge for ceremonies, archaeology shows that it was built some 1200 years before the Druids had established themselves in Britain. Stonehenge was constructed in three stages by generations of prehistoric people between about 3000 and 1550 BC, using bluestones from the Prescelly Mountains in southwest Wales and sarsen stones from the Marlborough Downs, set in upright pairs arranged in concentric circles; some pairs were topped

by lintels. Opinion differs as to whether Stonehenge served as a temple, a royal palace, or an observatory – used to study the Sun and Moon, predict eclipses and create a seasonal calendar for harvests and festivals. (See also STONEHENGE in 'Places and Landscapes of Britain'.)

Styx In Greek mythology, the river which flowed seven times around the underworld of HADES, and across which Charon ferried the souls of the dead. Its waters were thought to be poisonous.

Tantalus King in Greek mythology who offended the gods by divulging their secrets to mortals. They punished him with everlasting thirst and hunger. He stood up to his chin in a river in HADES, but each time he bent to quench his thirst the water receded. Similarly the boughs above him, heavy with fruit, were always just out of reach.

🜍 The ordeal of Tantalus is the origin of the word 'tantalise', meaning to tease or torment by exciting a hope and then disappointing it, or to keep out of reach something that is much desired.

Tarot cards Elaborately decorated cards of unknown origin that are used for fortune-telling or DIVINATION. There were traditionally 78 cards in the pack – 56 divided into four suits and 22 trump cards with symbolic pictures. There is no standard design for Tarot symbols, and there are many ways of interpreting them.

TAROT SPREAD *A selection of Tarot cards depicting the Knight of Wands, Death, The Magician, The Sun and the Four of Pentacles. The four suits of Swords, Cups, Wands and Pentacles tell of everyday issues concerning conflicts, emotions and prosperity. The symbolic trump cards contain a wealth of occult lore.*

Tell, William Legendary 14th-century hero of Switzerland, famous for his skill as an archer. Because he refused to salute Gessler, the steward of a tyrannical Austrian ruler, Tell was sentenced to shoot with his crossbow and arrow an apple resting on his son's head. After accomplishing this, Tell killed Gessler and led an uprising that established the independence of Switzerland. The first written account of the legend dates from 1474.

Theseus Legendary hero of Athens who killed the MINOTAUR.

Thor God of thunder and lightning in Norse mythology who had three magic weapons: a hammer which returned to him after it was thrown, iron gloves which helped him to throw the hammer, and a belt which increased his size and strength.
🕯 Thursday is named after Thor.

Titans Greek gods of enormous size and strength who were the children of Heaven and Earth. The youngest Titan, KRONOS, overthrew his father and became king of the gods, until he in turn was overthrown by his own son ZEUS. Other Titans included ATLAS and PROMETHEUS.
🕯 The terms titan and titanic are used to describe a powerful person or thing.

Tristan and Iseult (Iz-OOLT) Two tragic lovers in the medieval legends of England, Ireland and Germany. After being wounded by a poisoned spear, Tristan was nursed back to health by Iseult the Fair – the king of Ireland's beautiful daughter. Tristan brought her back to England to be the bride of his uncle, King Mark of Cornwall, but on the journey home, the couple accidentally drank a love potion which had been prepared for Mark and Iseult on their wedding night. They fell deeply in love, and although Iseult married King Mark, the lovers were discovered and fled into the forest where they lived happily for four years, until Iseult decided to return to Mark, who banished Tristan. Years later, Tristan was wounded in battle and sent for Iseult to heal him – telling his messenger to hoist a white sail on the returning ship if Iseult was on board, a black sail if not. As the ship approached, Tristan's jealous wife lied and told him it had a black sail, whereupon Tristan died of grief. Iseult, on hearing the news, died soon afterwards.

Trojan horse In Greek mythology, a large, hollow horse made of wood used by the Greeks to win the TROJAN WAR. Greek soldiers hid inside the horse, which was left outside the gates of Troy, masquerading as a harmless offering to the gods. The Trojans ignored a priest called Laocoon who warned against bringing the horse into the city, saying that he was 'wary of Greeks even when they are bringing gifts'. The soldiers emerged at night to open the city gates to their awaiting army.

Trojan War Great war fought between the Greeks and the Trojans, the story of which is told in Homer's ▷ILIAD. According to the legend, the ten-year siege of Troy was brought on by an incident known as the JUDGMENT OF PARIS, which led to HELEN – the beautiful wife of a Greek king – being abducted by PARIS, a Trojan prince. The Greeks sailed to Troy to recover her, under the leadership of their legendary king AGAMEMNON. Their greatest warrior, ACHILLES, killed the Trojan warrior HECTOR. The Greeks achieved a final victory through the device of the TROJAN HORSE and burned Troy to the ground. The *Iliad* was not based purely on legend and imagination; an actual war did take place around 1200 BC, 400 years before the poem was written.

trolls In Norse mythology, mischievous dwarfs or giant ogres who lived in caves and mountains. They were skilled at working metals and notorious for stealing.

Troy Ancient city inhabited by the Trojans, and site of the TROJAN WAR. Troy was believed to be a mythical city until the 19th-century German archaeologist Heinrich Schliemann used clues from Homer's epic poem, the ▷ILIAD, to find the lost city. Its Roman name is Ilium and its ruins can still be seen in the western part of Turkey.

UFOs Abbreviation for 'Unidentified Flying Objects' – a modern phenomenon that was first reported in 1947 when Kenneth Arnold in the American state of Washington saw from his private aircraft some silvery disc-like objects. He described them as looking like 'pie plates'. The term 'flying saucers' was coined in the headlines next day, and hundreds of sightings poured in from around the world. Some people thought that UFOs were interplanetary space vehicles and that the world's governments were involved in a cover-up; 'men in black' were said to turn up after sightings to intimidate witnesses and destroy evidence. Most scientists still dismiss UFOs as illusions caused by natural phenomena.

Ulysses Roman name of the Greek hero ODYSSEUS, king of Ithaca.

unicorn Mythical and heraldic animal resembling a small white horse with one spiralled horn growing out of its forehead.

STRANGE OBJECTS IN THE SKY *'Flying saucers' photographed over Massachusetts in 1952. Reports from all over the world still continue to compound an intriguing 20th-century mystery.*

THE SIGNS OF THE ZODIAC

Astrologers believe that the most important clue to people's characters is in their birth sign – the sign of the Zodiac in which the Sun was rising when they were born. For a full character analysis, the exact positions of the Moon and planets at the moment of birth are also taken into account when casting a person's horoscope.

ARIES
Mar 22-Apr 20

TAURUS
Apr 21-May 21

GEMINI
May 22-June 22

CANCER
June 23-July 23

LEO
July 24-Aug 23

VIRGO
Aug 24-Sept 23

LIBRA
Sept 24-Oct 23

SCORPIO
Oct 24-Nov 22

SAGITTARIUS
Nov 23-Dec 22

CAPRICORN
Dec 23-Jan 19

AQUARIUS
Jan 20-Feb 19

PISCES
Feb 20-Mar 21

According to medieval writing, the horn represented the Gospel of Truth. The unicorn was an untameable beast that could only be captured by a young virgin. It supports the British royal coat of arms, along with its traditional enemy, the lion.
⚜ The source of the unicorn legends may be unusual whales called narwhals; the male of the species has a single spiralled tusk.

Valkyries In Norse mythology, fierce battle-maids of the god ODIN. They rode into battle and selected those who were destined to die, then conducted the souls of these heroes to Valhalla, the hall of the slain.

vampires Living corpses who leave their coffins at night to feed on human blood. Their appearance in central European folklore in the Middle Ages may have originated when graves left empty by grave-robbers led people to believe that the dead could rise at night. The most notorious vampire is Count DRACULA.
⚜ Vampire bats in South America feed on the blood of living mammals at night.

Venus Roman name of APHRODITE, goddess of love and beauty.
⚜ The second planet from the Sun is named Venus, possibly because it is one of the most beautiful sights in the night sky.

Vestal Virgins Six maidens who tended the sacred flame of Vesta, the Roman goddess of the hearth and home.

Vulcan (Greek name HEPHAESTUS) Roman god of metalworking and fire, and the blacksmith of the gods.

werewolves Men who, according to ancient superstition, could assume the form and characteristics of a wolf. The term lycanthropy (from the Greek *lukos* meaning wolf and *anthropos* meaning man) is used to describe both this supernatural ability and the insanity afflicting a person who imagines himself to be some kind of animal.

will-o'-the-wisps English fairies that played tricks on people crossing the marshes at night. Their lights flickered alluringly above the water, inviting wayfarers to follow them to certain death in the deep bogs. The lights were in fact caused by burning marsh gas (methane) given off by rotting vegetation.
⚜ The phrase will-o'-the-wisp is used to describe any illusory human hope or aim.

witchcraft Magical practices of a witch. While some modern authorities believe that witchcraft was a figment of medieval imagination, others argue that it can be traced back to pagan religions. A revival of witchcraft in England was provoked by several books, including Gerald Gardner's *Witchcraft Today* (1954). Along with the infamous magician Aleister Crowley (the 'Beast'), Gardner produced a manual of rituals called the *Book of Shadows*, still used by present-day covens, who refer to their religion as 'Wicca', an Old English word for 'witch'. It is basically a fertility cult involving ritual nudity and ceremonial magic.

witches Men and women who practise magic and occult pursuits. In Europe during the 15th, 16th and 17th centuries, superstitious belief in the Devil led to the torture and execution of around 200 000 people accused of witchcraft, most of them solitary old women. Witch-hunting was a favourite activity of Puritans during the 17th century; the notorious witch-finder Matthew Hopkins hanged 60 witches in Essex in one year. English and Scottish laws against witchcraft were repealed in 1736.
⚜ The last official witch-burning in Britain took place in 1722, after Janet Horne allegedly turned her daughter into a pony.

World Tree Tree of life and knowledge in Norse mythology, also known as Yggdrasil. An evergreen ash tree, it bound heaven, earth and hell together with its roots and branches. The god ODIN hung himself from the World Tree for nine days in order to acquire wisdom.

Zeus (Roman name Jupiter) Chief of the Greek gods, and father and ruler of mankind. Zeus defeated the TITANS and dethroned his father KRONOS to assume domination of the Universe. He lived on Mount OLYMPUS and ruled by power rather than by righteousness. He fathered many children both by goddesses and by mortal women.

Zodiac A band of the sky along which the Sun, Moon and principal planets appear to move. In ASTROLOGY this band is divided into 12 segments, or signs of the Zodiac, which are named after constellations.

IDEAS, BELIEFS AND RELIGION

Belief in some power beyond the world we inhabit is as old as the human race. Different religions have given this belief enduring substance, and spawned a rich diversity of ritual and ceremony. While theologians debate religious truths, great philosophers attempt to understand our physical world, grappling with logic in their search for knowledge and certainty.

BERTRAND RUSSELL

ORTHODOX
CHRISTIAN ICON

THE KORAN

BUDDHIST MONKS
AT MANDALAY

Abraham According to the Old Testament, the founder of the Hebrew nation. Around 1800 BC he settled with his family in Canaan, where God told them they would become a mighty race. God tested Abraham's faith by asking him to sacrifice his son Isaac. However, as Abraham raised a knife to kill the boy, an angel appeared and told him to spare Isaac: Abraham's obedience had proved his faith.

♟ Abraham is also honoured in Islam as one of the great prophets.

absolution Forgiveness of sins when the penitent has made a full confession and truly repents. In the Roman Catholic and Orthodox Churches, it is performed by an ordained priest in the sacrament of PENANCE; in the Protestant and Anglican Churches it is included in the EUCHARIST.

Adam and Eve According to the Bible, the first man and woman, ancestors of all mankind. The Book of Genesis tells how God created Adam by breathing life into 'the dust of the ground', and later created Eve from Adam's rib. God intended the couple to live in the Garden of Eden but they were tempted by the serpent to eat the forbidden fruit of the Tree of Knowledge and expelled. This was the Fall of Man and the beginning of ORIGINAL SIN, which Christians believe all humans inherit.

agnosticism Claim that it is impossible to know something, particularly whether or not God exists. The word was coined by the 19th-century British philosopher Thomas Huxley from the Greek *a*, 'not', and *gnosis*, 'knowledge'.

♟ It is logically possible for an agnostic to believe in God, if he admits that his belief is a matter of faith and not of knowledge.

ANGELIC VISITOR *Mary modestly turns away as she learns from Gabriel that she is to become the mother of Jesus. In Botticelli's* Annunciation, *the window frames a Renaissance townscape.*

Allah Muslim name for God. (See ISLAM.)

Amish North American Protestant sect which migrated from Switzerland, France and Germany in the 18th and 19th centuries. The Amish adhere strictly to the word of the Bible, and are known for their austere way of life, which uses no modern machinery, cars, phones or electric lights.

Anabaptists Radical Protestant group that arose out of the ▷REFORMATION, and later gave rise to the BAPTIST CHURCHES. The name Anabaptist means 'rebaptiser' and refers to the sect's insistence that a convert baptised in infancy must be baptised again as an adult. The Anabaptists advocated strict adherence to the Bible, and the separation of Church and State, maintaining that true Christians shold not hold government office or bear arms.

Anglican Communion Family of Churches with the same basic doctrine as the Church of England, and all accepting each other's sacraments and ministry. Every ten years, bishops meet at the Lambeth Conference in London.

animism Belief that spirits are active in nature and that animals, plants and even rocks have souls. Celtic religion was animistic, as are many African traditions.

annunciation In the New Testament, the appearance of the archangel Gabriel to the Virgin Mary to tell her that she would be visited by the Holy Spirit, as a result of which she would conceive and bear Jesus.

SIMPLE LIVING *The Amish of Pennsylvania live frugally, and dress plainly and alike. Men wear broad-brimmed black hats in winter and straw hats in summer, and a beard without a moustache.*

Antichrist In Christianity, a false messiah who will appear shortly before the end of the world. According to the First Epistle of John, he will attract followers but eventually be vanquished by Jesus.

apocalypse Type of Jewish and Christian scripture which claims to reveal secrets, especially concerning the future, and which generally gives hope to persecuted groups. The best known of these is St John's Book of Revelation in the New Testament, which prophesies the end of the world. The word comes from the Greek for 'unveiling'.
🔥Figuratively, an apocalypse is any cataclysmic event marked by violence and destruction, as in the title of the Vietnam War film *Apocalypse Now*.

Apocrypha Writings accepted by some churches, but not all, as part of the BIBLE. Roman Catholics, for example, include some 14 more books in the Old Testament than are recognised by Jews and Protestants. Various early Christian writings have also been proposed as additions to the New Testament but have not so far been accepted by any of the Christian Churches.

a posteriori Statement whose truth or falsity would have to be discovered by observation – *The Earth is round*; *unicorns do not exist* – or an argument based on INDUCTIVE REASONING. By contrast, statements and arguments that are independent of observation are called A PRIORI.

apostles Twelve men chosen by Jesus Christ to follow him and spread his teachings after his death. They included Peter, James, John, Thomas, Matthew and Judas Iscariot, who betrayed Jesus to the Roman authorities. Paul, although not one of the original 12, is often also considered an apostle because of his crucial role in the spread of Christianity.
🔥The Apostles' Creed is a statement of Christian faith traditionally supposed to have been composed by Jesus's apostles. However, the earliest known version dates from the 3rd century AD.

apostolic succession Belief that there is an unbroken line of succession from Christ through the 12 APOSTLES to the bishops of the present-day Church. The apostles founded the first churches at sites such as Alexandria, Jerusalem and Rome, and these churches claimed primacy over all churches that were established afterwards. Rome later claimed authority over all the others, based on its link with St Peter, whom Roman Catholics consider the first pope.

appearance and reality Since at least the 6th century BC, thinkers have puzzled about the nature of reality and how – or if – we can know it, given that every one of our five senses can deceive us. One response to the problem is IDEALISM, which claims that nothing exists except in the mind, while SCEPTICISM argues that nothing can be known for sure. The question of how we gain our knowledge of the external world is one of the major concerns of EPISTEMOLOGY.

a priori Statement that is necessarily true, requiring no verification by experience. It is true or false by virtue of the meaning of the words or the laws of logic, such as: *All kittens are cats* or *Three is greater than two*, or alternatively, any argument which is based on DEDUCTIVE REASONING.

SAINTLY THOUGHTS *Thomas Aquinas, philosopher and saint, is depicted by Fra Bartolommeo in the habit of a Dominican friar.*

Aquinas, St Thomas (*c.*1225-74) Medieval philosopher and theologian who compiled a comprehensive summary of all the important ideas of his day. Aquinas was influenced by ARISTOTLE, whose theories he adapted to Christian theology, arguing that reason and faith are compatible. The result was a coherent set of beliefs which are still the basis of Roman Catholic teachings.

Arianism Doctrine based on the views of Bishop Arius, a 4th-century theologian who held that Christ, although divine, is subordinate in status to God the Father, having been created by Him. The Arians were persecuted by the orthodox Church, and Arianism largely died out by the 6th century.

Aristotle (384-322 BC) Ancient Greek philosopher. He was a pupil of PLATO, but developed his ideas in a more methodical and scientific way. Aristotle devised a comprehensive system of thought embracing logic, ethics, aesthetics, metaphysics, politics and science, much of which is still studied and taught today. His method was analytical and systematic, questioning everything and always looking for the essential principles in every area of knowledge. His ideas dominated European thought at least until the ▷RENAISSANCE. (See also ▷ARISTOTLE in 'Science, Space and Mathematics'.)
🔥Aristotle was tutor to Alexander the Great and acquired considerable political prestige in the Greek world.

Ark of the Covenant Portable wooden chest constructed by the Israelites in the time of Moses to house the TEN COMMANDMENTS. It was thought to provide protection and divine guidance for the Jewish nation, and was sometimes taken into battle. Eventually the Ark was placed in the Temple of Jerusalem, but it is now lost.
🔥Every Jewish synagogue contains a cabinet known as an Ark, housing the TORAH. The scrolls are considered sacred, and a symbol of divine presence.

Armageddon In the Book of Revelation, the site of the final battle between good and evil, which will herald the end of the world and the DAY OF JUDGMENT.

asceticism Spiritual discipline practised in many religions including Christianity, Hinduism and Buddhism, which attempts to conquer the desires of the body so that the spirit can be freed and purified. It often involves fasting, self-inflicted pain (such as flagellation), self-imposed discomfort (such as sleeping on cold floors or not washing), and nearly always avoidance of sex.

atheism Non-belief in, or denial of the existence of a god or gods. Reasons for atheism vary from the view that the world is so full of injustice and suffering that it cannot be governed by a benevolent deity, to scientific arguments that the idea of a creator does not help to explain the existence of the Universe. Many Greek philosophers were atheists, although this could be dangerous – SOCRATES was forced to take poison because of his atheistic teachings. The Roman pagans accused the early Christians of atheism, since they denied the traditional gods. Atheism was long suppressed in Christian Europe and North America but it was not a criminal offence.

Augustine, St (354-430) One of the greatest bishops of the early Christian Church, born in North Africa to a pagan father and a Christian mother. Augustine originally followed the Manichean religion which accorded God and Satan equal power but converted to Christianity after a series of dramatic spiritual crises. He was a powerful thinker, and developed the doctrines of the Fall of Man, original sin and predestination – which scholars have claimed still show some Manichean influence. As Bishop of Hippo, near Carthage, he became known for his vigorous defence of the teachings of the Orthodox Church against the many heresies of the time.

🕮 Augustine described his spiritual journey in his *Confessions*, which contains the prayer, 'Oh Lord, make me chaste . . . but not yet.'

ayatollah Learned leader and teacher among SHI'A Muslims, and the nearest Islamic equivalent to a Christian priest. In 1979 the revolution in Iran overthrew the shah and replaced him with a religious regime, headed by the Ayatollah ▷KHOMEINI.

Ayer, A.J. (1910-89) English philosopher known for his book *Language, Truth and Logic* (1936) which set out the principles of LOGICAL POSITIVISM. He argued that, as METAPHYSICS is meaningless, philosophy should concentrate on criticism and analysis. He was knighted in 1970.

Baal Powerful warrior-god in the biblical land of Canaan, and a rival of the Israelite God YAHWEH (Jehovah). The first commandment given to Moses, 'thou shalt have no other gods before me', was particularly aimed at discouraging Baal-worship.

🕮 The Baal cult was taken to Carthage in North Africa by the Phoenicians. Many Carthaginian names, such as Hannibal, take 'bal' as the last syllable in honour of the god.

Bahaism Religious movement that developed out of Islam in the late 19th century. It preaches the oneness of God, reconciliation among different faiths, and the unity of mankind. Prejudice of any type is strongly opposed, and social justice is stressed alongside spiritual development.

baptism (or christening) Rite or SACRAMENT that initiates a person into the Christian community. Baptism usually occurs soon after birth, although in some denominations such as the BAPTIST CHURCHES it is reserved for adult converts and involves complete bodily immersion. In the early Church it was often administered shortly before death, to absolve the

JESUS BAPTISED *John, forerunner of Jesus Christ, baptises him in the River Jordan, set by Piero della Francesca in an Italian landscape.*

person's sins. The first Christian emperor, Constantine, was accused by pagan enemies of choosing Christianity because baptism offered the chance to wash away the guilt of executing several members of his family.

Baptist Churches Group of evangelical Protestant Churches which baptise by immersion but only those old enough to make a personal confession of faith. They adhere strictly to the Bible, and each congregation governs itself.

🕮 Baptist Churches are strong in the USA, especially among black communities.

bar mitzvah Jewish ceremony marking an adolescent boy's coming of age at 13, after which he is considered a full member of the congregation. A bat mitzvah is performed for girls at the age of 12 in some synagogues. The words are Hebrew for 'son of the Commandments' and 'daughter of the Commandments'.

belief Opinion or point of view which is based on varying degrees of evidence. One extreme of belief is FAITH, which is not based on evidence and may even contradict the evidence. The other is KNOWLEDGE, which is often defined as justified, true belief. Religious belief generally involves strong personal and moral commitments. Belief that the sun will rise tomorrow morning, however, requires only a generalisation based on past experience.

Benedict, St (*c.*480-*c.*547) Italian monk and founder of Christian monasticism in the West. He studied in Rome but as a young man went to live in a cave as a hermit. After three years he emerged to do good

works. He soon gathered a devoted following and began to found small religious communities, culminating in the establishment of the first Benedictine monastery at Monte Cassino near Naples. His book *The Rule of St Benedict* established the basic principles of European monasticism, stressing manual labour, scholarship and teaching as well as spiritual discipline.

🕮 The Benedictines became one of the most prosperous monastic orders, contrasting with the austerity of the Franciscans, who taught that monks should be poor.

Bentham, Jeremy (1748-1832) English political thinker and philosopher. He established the foundations of UTILITARIANISM – the theory that society should try to provide the greatest happiness of the greatest number. Bentham's work was further developed by John Stuart MILL.

Berkeley, George (1685-1753) Irish bishop and EMPIRICIST philosopher who shocked conventional opinion by arguing that material objects exist only in our perceptions of them – in Berkeley's words 'to be is to be perceived'. To get round the problem of appearing to claim that ordinary objects stopped existing the moment no one was looking at them, he argued that God was always there to perceive them.

🕮 Samuel ▷JOHNSON was highly indignant at Berkeley's argument about the nonexistence of material objects. In annoyance, he lashed out violently with his foot against a large stone and exclaimed, 'I refute it *thus*.'

Bhagavad Gita (The Song of the Lord) Sanskrit poem, dating from around 300 BC, expressing the basic ideas of Hinduism, and forming part of the epic *Mahabharata*. It takes the form of a dialogue between Lord Krishna and the prince Arjuna, in which Krishna reveals the eternal cycle of reincarnation and the many paths to NIRVANA or spiritual liberation.

Bible Sacred text of the Christian religion. It comprises the Old Testament, a collection of Hebrew and Aramaic scriptures written up to about the 2nd century BC, and the New Testament, written within a century of Jesus's death. The books of the Old Testament record the history of the Jewish people and their relationship with God. The New Testament includes the four Gospels relating the life of Jesus, the Acts of the Apostles, the letters of St Paul, and the Book of Revelation.

🕮 The best-known versions of the Bible include the Latin ▷VULGATE and the English ▷KING JAMES BIBLE. There are also

BUDDHA'S WAY *The Wheel of Becoming shows the six states of existence into which Buddhists believe humans are continually reborn. Following Buddha's teaching, monks such as those at Mandalay seek to break free from the cycle of reincarnation by meditation.*

some editions with notorious misprints, such as the 'Wicked Bible' of 1631 in which the seventh commandment was printed 'Thou shalt commit adultery'.

The sacred scriptures of Judaism correspond roughly to the Old Testament of the Christian Bible and are sometimes referred to as the Hebrew Bible.

Boethius, Anicius (*c.*480-524) Roman senator and philosopher who acted as minister in Italy to the Ostrogoth king Theodoric, after the Roman Empire had fallen. He was later imprisoned without trial and condemned to death. While awaiting execution, Boethius wrote *The Consolation of Philosophy*, in which Philosophy appears to him in human form and proves that true happiness comes from virtue and does not depend on earthly fortune.

Book of Common Prayer Service book of the Church of England, introduced by its main author Thomas ▷CRANMER in 1549. It has been revised many times, and was suppressed by the Catholic Mary I (1553-8) and by Oliver Cromwell during the Commonwealth and Protectorate (1649-60). The Act of Uniformity (1662) enforced its use in all Anglican churches.

A modern replacement, *The Alternative Service Book*, introduced in 1980, is often used in Anglican churches today. It has been both criticised and praised for its use of contemporary English.

Brahma One of the three central deities of HINDUISM, together with Shiva and Vishnu. Brahma is considered to be the creator of the cosmos.

Brahman Supreme power or eternal spirit of the universe in Hinduism, from which everything originates and to which it all, eventually, returns.

Members of the traditional priestly caste, the highest in Hindu society, are known as Brahmans or Brahmins. In everyday usage, a Brahman can also mean anyone belonging to an elite group in society.

Buddha Name meaning 'Enlightened One', applied to the Indian prince and mystic Gautama Siddhartha (*c.*563-*c.*483 BC), the founder of BUDDHISM. He was born in northern India in a region that is now part of Nepal, and at about 30 gave up all worldly possessions and ambitions to live a life of contemplation and spiritual devotion. He is said to have achieved ENLIGHTENMENT while sitting under a bodhi tree – or holy fig tree – after which he spent the rest of his life travelling and teaching a philosophy of compassion and spiritual insight.

Many other Buddhas are also revered in Buddhism. Mahayana Buddhism also venerates *bodhisattvas* – those who have reached enlightenment but who forego NIRVANA and choose to continue living in the world to work for the good of all beings.

Buddhism Religion based on the teachings of Gautama Siddhartha, or the BUDDHA. It teaches that suffering is part of existence, but that spiritual liberation can be achieved through overcoming all desires, even for one's own existence. It has many similarities to Hinduism, but offers the hope of NIRVANA and freedom from the cycle of death and rebirth to all, rather than a select few. Buddhism is a peaceable religion, stressing meditation, compassion and good works. There is no worship of a supreme god. It has several branches – including Mahayana, Theravada and ZEN. There are more than 300 million Buddhists worldwide, mainly in central and Southeast Asia, Tibet and Japan.

Calvinism Christian doctrine based on the views of the 16th-century Protestant reformer John ▷CALVIN. It emphasises obedience to God, strict adherence to the Bible, the importance of faith and the doctrine of predestination, according to which some people are born destined for salvation, the remainder for damnation.

Cathars Members of a medieval Christian sect who believed that the material world was evil, and that spiritual salvation required the giving up of all physical pleasures. They included the Albigensians of southern France. They were considered heretical by the Church, and were brutally suppressed during the 13th century.

Catholic Church Shorter name for the Roman Catholic Church. The term is also sometimes used to refer to any Church which is governed by bishops, such as the Church of England or the Russian or Greek Orthodox Churches.

cause and effect An apparently simple idea which has caused philosophers much difficulty ever since David HUME pointed out that there is no logical connection between events and the things that are supposed to cause them. The assertion that a spark 'causes' gunpowder to explode is based merely on the fact that one event has always followed the other in the past. Immanuel KANT, however, later contended that cause and effect is a fundamental principle of human thought.

Chanukkah (or Hanukkah) Eight-day Jewish festival beginning on the 25th day of the month of Kislev, which falls in December, also called the Feast of Lights or Feast of Dedication. It commemorates the rededication of the Temple of Jerusalem after the Jewish defeat of the Syrians in the 2nd century BC. Candles are lit in the home and presents given to children.

Christ Saviour or MESSIAH prophesied in the Old Testament. Christians believe that he was Jesus of Nazareth; Jews that he has not yet appeared on Earth. Muslims do not believe in a messiah, but only in prophets, among whom they number both Jesus and MUHAMMAD.

Christianity Worldwide religion based on the teachings and example of JESUS CHRIST. It developed out of Judaism, retaining many of the Hebrew scriptures and beliefs, but differing in that it acknowledges Jesus as the Christ or MESSIAH and accepts the law of love and compassion that he brought. The central doctrines of Christianity are that God is a Trinity composed of the Father, the Son (Jesus) and the Holy Spirit; that the path to salvation is through Jesus Christ; and that at the end of the world Jesus will return to judge both the living and the dead. After Christ's death, the religion was spread by his APOSTLES and their followers, and rapidly developed in the Roman and Greek worlds. In 315 it was declared the official religion of the Roman Empire by the Emperor ▷CONSTANTINE. After a period of decline during the Dark Ages, it revived spectacularly in medieval times and has remained the major European religion ever since. Christianity's three principal branches are the ROMAN CATHOLIC and ORTHODOX Churches and

PROTESTANTISM. Although differences in doctrine have led to many splits and disputes, Christianity in its various forms is practised by more than 1300 million people throughout the world.

Christian Science Movement devoted to spiritual healing, founded as the Church of Christ, Scientist by Mary Baker Eddy in Boston in 1879. Its basis is that sickness only seems real and that sin and disease can be healed through prayer to God. Followers generally reject orthodox medical treatment, relying on prayer instead. The Christian Science movement operates worldwide, and publishes a daily newspaper, the *Christian Science Monitor*.

Christmas Central Christian festival held on December 25 to celebrate the birth of Jesus Christ. The date was probably agreed on as a compromise with pagan cults which also had festivals around the same time. Non-Christian midwinter celebrations are still evident in traditions such as the decorated tree, the evergreen holly and ivy, feasting, partying and giving presents.
🕯Christmas is also sometimes called 'Yule', from the Old English word *geol*, a time of traditional midwinter feasting.

church Place of Christian worship, and – usually with a capital 'C' – the name for the community of Christians. From early on the Church had a hierarchy of bishops, priests and other officials and was based on areas such as the cities and provinces of the Roman Empire. The Orthodox, Roman Catholic and Anglican Churches retain this basic structure, but others such as the Baptist, Congregationalist and Presbyterian Churches are less hierarchical and give more power to individual congregations.

Church of England The established Church in England, formed in the 16th century after Henry VIII broke away from the Roman Catholic Church and denied the authority of the pope. It combines both Catholic and Protestant elements and is headed by the British monarch in place of the pope. Under the monarch come the archbishops of Canterbury and York, and under them 44 bishops each of whom presides over a diocese containing a number of local parishes. The Church of England's doctrines and practices, known as Anglicanism, are very broad and encompass both 'high' and 'low' versions. High Anglicanism – or Anglo-Catholicism – is much closer to Rome and retains many rituals of Catholicism, while low Anglicanism keeps ceremony to a minimum and emphasises the

importance of scripture. The Church of England is the leading member of the worldwide ANGLICAN COMMUNION.

Communion, Holy See EUCHARIST.

confession Public or private admission of sin, required before PENANCE and ABSOLUTION can be administered in the Roman Catholic and Orthodox Churches. In the Anglican and Protestant Churches, it is a regular part of the EUCHARIST.

confirmation Christian SACRAMENT marking the admission of the baptised to full membership of a church. It is usually performed at adolescence, although adult confirmation is becoming popular.

Confucianism Ancient Chinese philosophy based on the teachings of the sage Confucius (551-479 BC). It emphasises social order and responsibility; respect for parents, elders and authorities; and the veneration of ancestors. Confucius was chief minister of the state of Lu (now Shandong Province) and was deeply concerned with ethics, piety, duty and the stability of the state. In his philosophy, ethics and politics were inseparable. He sought to relieve the suffering of the poor through government reform, and drew up a code of behaviour for the honourable civil servant (or 'mandarin') which has been influential in China ever since. Religious concepts such as God and Heaven were viewed by Confucius only as a way of inspiring correct behaviour.
🕯China's leader Mao Zedong said: 'I have hated Confucius since I was eight.'

SAYINGS OF THE SAGE

The Chinese sage Confucius was more concerned with the management of society than with religion. A collection of his sayings called the *Analects* includes the words of advice: 'If you would divine the future, study the past'; 'What you do not want done to yourself, do not do to others'; and 'Repay injury with justice, and kindness with kindness'.

LASTING IDEAS *Confucian thought still influences many societies, even those that are under communist rule.*

Congregationalism Christian movement that rejects the hierarchy of the Anglican and Catholic Churches, allowing each church to be independent and to elect its own minister. It began in England in the 16th century, but persecution drove many followers to Holland and America.

consubstantiation Doctrine of some Protestant Churches that the bread and wine of the EUCHARIST coexist with the body and blood of Christ, unlike Roman Catholics who believe they become one and the same (TRANSUBSTANTIATION).

Coptic Church Main Christian Church of Egypt and the Sudan, which refused to convert to Islam after the Arab conquest. It separated from the ORTHODOX CHURCH in the 5th century and adheres to the belief that Jesus was wholly divine and not partly human – the 'Monophysite' doctrine.

Counter Reformation Reforms made by the Roman Catholic Church in response to the REFORMATION. Some of the beliefs criticised by reformers, such as veneration of the saints and acceptance of the authority of the pope, were reaffirmed, but others were rejected. The JESUITS emerged as leaders of the Counter Reformation, which culminated in a general redefinition of Roman Catholic doctrine at the Council of ▷TRENT (1545-63). (See also ▷COUNTER REFORMATION in 'World History'.)

crucifixion Common and cruel form of execution for non-citizens in the Roman Empire. The victim was bound or nailed to a wooden cross, often after a beating, then left to die. In particular, the Crucifixion refers to the death of JESUS CHRIST on the cross at Calvary *c.*AD 30. The cross became the central symbol of Christianity.

Dalai Lama Traditional ruler and Buddhist spiritual leader in Tibet and Mongolia, believed by his followers to be the reborn *bodhisattva* Avalokitshvara (see BUDDHA). After the death of a Dalai Lama, the search begins for a new incumbent, who shows signs of being the same spirit reborn. ⚲The current Dalai Lama, forced into exile in India after the Chinese suppression of Tibetan nationalism in 1959, continues to work for the freedom of Tibet.

damnation Condemnation of the souls of the wicked to eternal torment in HELL. The precise grounds for damnation have been the subject of much debate in Christianity, but traditionally anyone who dies in a state of SIN is considered to be damned.

AGONY ON THE CROSS *For six hours Jesus hung crucified, a crown of thorns mocking the kingship claimed for him by his followers. Christ's ordeal is vividly portrayed by the artist Diego Velásquez.*

David and Goliath Old Testament story in which David, a shepherd boy, slays the mighty Philistine Goliath with a sling, and later becomes king of the Israelites. ⚲Michelangelo's statue ▷DAVID portrays him just before his fight with Goliath.

Day of Judgment Christians believe that at the end of the world Christ will return in glory, and the dead will rise up and be miraculously reunited with their bodies for final judgment to be passed on them. The good will be separated from the evil, and taken up into Heaven to live with God. ⚲Early Christians expected the world to end soon after Jesus's death. When it did not, the Church introduced the idea of individual judgment immediately after death. ⚲The Day of Judgment is also one of Islam's most basic beliefs, and Jews look forward to a Day of YAHWEH which will inaugurate the Kingdom of God.

SCROLLS OF MYSTERY *For 1000 years, caves in the arid cliffs above the Dead Sea were the hiding place of scrolls apparently made by a sect known as the Essenes, who followed a monastic type of Judaism. Discovered by chance by a shepherd boy in 1947, the scrolls have cast new light on the relations between Judaism and early Christianity.*

Dead Sea Scrolls Ancient texts discovered at Qumran, near the Dead Sea, in 1947. Some are copies of Old Testament books dating back 1000 years earlier than previously known versions. They are believed to be the scriptures of the Essenes, a Jewish sect living an ascetic, communal way of life in desert locations.

deductive reasoning Logical and indisputable derivation of a conclusion from a PREMISE, as in: *If Sue is older than Tom and Tom is older than James, then Sue must be older than James.* Mathematics is based on deductive reasoning, but most ordinary thinking and much of science relies on less certain INDUCTIVE REASONING.

deism Belief that God or a supreme being exists but does not actively intervene in the Universe or in human affairs. It was at its strongest in Britain in the 17th and 18th centuries, when scientifically minded thinkers sought to establish reasonable grounds for belief in God, without falling back on the idea of divine revelation. It contrasts with THEISM – belief in a personal God directly involved with mankind.

Derrida, Jacques (1930-) French philosopher associated with the theory of 'deconstruction' – the attempt to take apart an idea or system to show what has been excluded. He argues that language creates our idea of reality and refers to itself rather than to anything in the real world. Instead of searching vainly for truth, Derrida says philosophy should 'deconstruct' the way meaning is created in words. His views are controversial because they suggest that distinctions between fact and fiction, good and evil, and truth and falsity are no more than semantic differences or word games.

Descartes, René (1596-1650) French philosopher, mathematician and a founder of RATIONALISM – a school of thought which tries to explain how knowledge can be derived from reasoning alone. Descartes wanted to discover which aspects of human knowledge are absolutely certain and cannot be doubted. To do this, he began by imagining that an evil demon was deliberately trying to mislead him and that he had to doubt everything. But the one thing he could not doubt was the fact that he was thinking and, consequently, that he existed to be able to do the thinking. This enabled him to reach his celebrated conclusion, *Cogito, ergo sum* – 'I think, therefore I am', on which he built a systematic philosophy which included several proofs of the existence of God. (See also ▷DESCARTES in 'Science, Space and Mathematics'.)

determinism Belief that the way events occur is fixed in advance, either by some supernatural plan of God or by the laws of nature. The concept appears to undermine ideas such as FREE WILL, morality, justice and responsibility. Many philosophers, however, have tried to find ways of reconciling human freedom with the belief that there are causes for our behaviour. The problem is difficult for religious believers who maintain that God knows everything, including the future, since this implies that the future is fixed. On the other hand, they also want to say that people are responsible for their actions and are free to choose between good and evil.
🕯Modern physics ceased to be deterministic in the early 20th century, with the development of ▷QUANTUM MECHANICS, which suggests that, at the most fundamental level, the behaviour of matter cannot be predicted with any certainty.

devil Malevolent spirit or supernatural being responsible for causing suffering and for tempting people to commit evil acts. The idea is common to many religions, including Islam, Hinduism, Buddhism, Judaism and Christianity. The concept of the Devil as the embodiment of evil and the archenemy of God is also found in many faiths. The Devil is called SATAN by Jews and Christians, IBLIS by Muslims and Mara by Buddhists. (See also ▷DEVIL in 'Myths and Legends'.)

dialectic Term used in philosophy to describe theories or methods based on dialogue or competition between opposing points of view. It is mainly applied to SOCRATES' method of arriving at knowledge by a process of questioning, and to HEGEL's view of the way ideas develop through contradiction between thesis and antithesis, resulting in a synthesis. MARX applied the process to the material world; his theory of class conflict that results in the overthrow of capitalism has been called 'dialectical materialism'.

Diaspora The dispersal of the Jewish people from Jerusalem and Judea, after the Assyrian conquest of 722 BC, the Babylonian conquest of 586 BC and the disastrous revolts of AD 70 and 135 against the Roman rulers. These led to the destruction of the TEMPLE OF JERUSALEM and finally to the expulsion of Jews from their holy city. From the Middle East, the Jews spread over other areas such as North Africa and Europe, but maintained their religion and identity despite opposition and persecution, especially from Christians.
🕯The term Diaspora is used to refer to all Jews now living outside Israel, or the dispersion of any once homogenous people.

NEW TONGUE *One reason for the impact of René Descartes was that he wrote his* Discourse on Method *in French rather than in Latin, the traditional language of philosophy.*

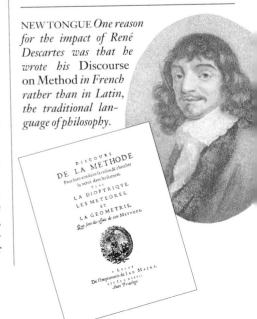

dogma Unproved, and often unprovable, theory or doctrine which has to be accepted as true without question. The term is often applied to the teachings of the Roman Catholic Church, which are pronounced on by the pope and which all Catholics are bound to accept.

Druze Faith that broke away from mainstream ISLAM in the 10th and 11th centuries to become a new religion in Jordan, Syria and Lebanon. Followers reject many traditional Islamic teachings and await the return of the Muslim religious leader al-Hakim, who died in 1021.
⚲The Druze militia was one of the principal factions in the Lebanese civil war during the 1980s.

dualism System of thought which, in some manner, divides everything into two categories, or which has as a basic principle an important opposition, such as 'the world as it exists' as opposed to 'the world as it is perceived'. In philosophy, it usually refers to the idea that a person has both a physical body as well as an independent, non-material mind or soul. In religion, dualism refers to faiths that place good and evil, spirit and matter, or God and the Devil in absolute opposition. (Compare MONISM.)

Easter Christian festival commemorating the resurrection of Jesus after his Crucifixion. On Maundy Thursday the Last Supper is recalled; Good Friday commemorates the Crucifixion; and the festival ends with Easter Sunday. The penitential season of Lent is a preparation for Easter. Palm Sunday, the Sunday before Easter, commemorates Jesus's entry into Jerusalem, when people laid palm leaves in his path as a sign of homage.
⚲Easter Sunday is the first Sunday after the full moon on or after March 21. In the ORTHODOX CHURCH it falls slightly later.

Ecclesiastes Book of the Old Testament, conventionally held to be the work of Solomon, known for its philosophical tone and for reflections on life such as 'Vanity of vanities; all is vanity', 'To every thing there is a season' and 'The race is not to the swift, nor the battle to the strong'.

ecumenism Movement that promotes cooperation and understanding among Christian Churches and their eventual re-unification. Its main achievements so far have been the establishment of the World Council of Churches in 1948 and the encouragement of closer ties and joint services between similar denominations.

Elijah Old Testament prophet said to have lived in the 9th century BC. He opposed the worship of idols and the false god BAAL, for which he incurred the wrath of Queen Jezebel, who tried to kill him. According to the Bible, he ascended directly to Heaven in a chariot of fire.

empiricism Philosophical view that knowledge arises from experience and observation rather than from pure reason or innate ideas, as RATIONALISM claims. It adopts a sceptical attitude, refusing to take anything for granted or to rely on conventional authorities, such as the Bible or popular belief. Empiricism became a powerful force in Britain in the 17th and 18th centuries as a result of the work of philosophers such as BERKELEY, HUME and LOCKE, and was closely related to the development of experimental science.

Engels, Friedrich (1820-95) Revolutionary German political thinker. He collaborated with Karl MARX on *The Communist Manifesto* of 1848, and wrote a number of other works influential in developing the theory of ▷COMMUNISM.

enlightenment In Eastern religions such as HINDUISM and BUDDHISM, a state of spiritual insight that brings liberation from the cycle of reincarnation. It is closely tied to the concept of NIRVANA.

Enlightenment Intellectual movement of the 18th century which promoted rational scientific enquiry and advocated religious toleration, social reform, progress and the elimination of tyranny. Major figures of the Enlightenment included ▷DIDEROT, HUME, KANT, LOCKE, ROUSSEAU and ▷VOLTAIRE.

Epicureanism Philosophy developed by the Greek thinker Epicurus (342-270 BC) and his followers. It was based on the belief that the greatest good is pleasure – in the sense of cultivated enjoyment of life, especially the joys of friendship, rather than sensual indulgence. Epicurus was an atheist, and taught that there is nothing to fear in death, which is merely a disappearance, a state of nothingness.
⚲The word epicure now means one who enjoys good food and good living.

Epiphany Christian festival celebrated on January 6, the 'twelfth day of Christmas' and the last day of the Christmas festival. It commemorates the visit of the Magi who were said to have been guided by a star to the infant Jesus in Bethlehem.

episcopacy System of Church government based on bishops, as in the Roman Catholic, Anglican, Orthodox and Lutheran traditions. The word comes from the Latin *episcopus* 'bishop', which in turn comes from the Greek word for an overseer.
⚲Churches belonging to the ANGLICAN COMMUNION other than the Church of England are known as the Episcopal or the Episcopalian Churches.

epistemology Branch of philosophy concerned with knowledge and where it comes from. Traditionally, the two main positions on the issue were RATIONALISM, which claimed that knowledge is somehow 'built in' to the human mind, and EMPIRICISM, which maintained that it is a result of experience. Since KANT, however, this distinction has broken down, and modern philosophers such as WITTGENSTEIN have concentrated more on analysing the meaning of statements rather than deciding whether they constitute knowledge.

Erasmus, Desiderius (*c.*1466-1536) Dutch priest and Renaissance scholar who encouraged a form of HUMANISM which laid stress on free will and taught that people should think for themselves in spiritual matters. Erasmus urged reforms to make the Roman Catholic Church less worldly. He was, however, repelled by the violence that accompanied the REFORMATION when it came.

ethics Branch of philosophy that deals with morality. It attempts to define the difference between good and evil in the world, right and wrong in human actions, and virtue and wickedness in people.

Eucharist Central SACRAMENT in the Christian religion, also known as the MASS, Holy Communion or Lord's Supper. It re-enacts the Last Supper in which Jesus blessed the bread and wine before giving them to his disciples, saying, 'This is my body; this is my blood.' Unlike Protestants, Roman Catholic and Orthodox Christians believe that by a repeated miracle the bread and wine actually become the body and blood of Christ (TRANSUBSTANTIATION). Lutherans believe that Jesus is present in the spirit but not in the flesh – CONSUBSTANTIATION – and members of Reformed Churches accept his presence in a symbolic way only.
⚲In the Roman Catholic and Orthodox Churches, children celebrate their first communion at the age of seven or eight; in the Anglican Churches, the first communion is usually taken after CONFIRMATION.

evangelist Preacher or missionary (usually Protestant) who spreads the Christian message. The GOSPEL writers Matthew, Mark, Luke and John are sometimes referred to as the four Evangelists.

evil Force or power working against mankind, God or the gods. In ancient Greek thought and in Buddhism there is little concern for the origin of evil, which is generally seen as the result of human ignorance and error. In Christianity, Judaism and Islam, however, the DEVIL, SATAN or IBLIS is widely perceived to be a central, intelligent source of evil.

excommunication Exclusion from membership of a Church because of a serious challenge to its teaching or authority. In Roman Catholic tradition this means damnation unless it is later revoked. In medieval times the threat of excommunication was often wielded by the pope as an instrument of political power.

existentialism Movement in 20th-century philosophy, theology and literature, based on the view that people are entirely free and therefore responsible for what they make of themselves. With this responsibility comes anguish or dread. One of the most influential existentialist philosophers was the French thinker and writer Jean-Paul SARTRE, who summed up his views in the maxim, 'Existence precedes essence' – that is, humans spring up in the world undefined and without a fixed nature or 'essence'. There is no divine plan, nor any fixed values, by which they can guide themselves; they are 'condemned to be free'.

Exodus Journey of MOSES and the ancient Israelites out of slavery in Egypt around 1200 BC, as told in *Exodus*, the second book of the Old Testament. According to the Bible, the Red Sea parted to let the Israelites cross, after which they wandered in the desert for 40 years before reaching Canaan, the land they believed was promised to them by God.

exorcism The casting out of demons or evil spirits believed to have 'possessed' a person or place. Among the ancient Israelites, mental conditions such as schizophrenia and epilepsy were often considered to be a sign of demonic possession and were treated by ritual exorcism. Jesus Christ performed many exorcisms, and in the early Church there was a standard office of Exorcist. Exorcisms are still occasionally performed by Roman Catholic and some Protestant Churches.

RICH SYBOLISM *A ladder – which represents levels of consciousness to freemasons – rises among many other masonic symbols, including Classical columns and the mason's tools.*

faith Belief that is not based on scientific evidence. It is one of the three great virtues – together with hope and charity (or love) – listed by St PAUL in the New Testament.
Faith is not always possible, even for the devout. Doubting Thomas could not believe that Jesus had risen from the dead without seeing Him and touching His wounds, and St Mark prayed: 'Lord, I believe; help thou mine unbelief'.
Martin LUTHER argued that faith alone, regardless of any good works, was the true path to salvation.

Fall of Man In Christianity, the expulsion of Adam and Eve from the Garden of Eden after they disobeyed God, and the suffering handed down to future generations as a result – the doctrine of ORIGINAL SIN. Christians believe that Jesus was sent to redeem the human race from its fallen state. In Judaism there is no concept of original sin; the consequence of Eden is the challenge to choose between good and evil.
In Islam, the devil IBLIS is considered responsible for the Fall, and so guilt is not passed on to all mankind.

fatwah Edict issued by a Muslim religious leader. The term came to prominence in the West in 1989 when the Ayatollah ▷KHOMEINI issued a fatwah offering a considerable cash reward to any Muslim who assassinated the writer Salman ▷RUSHDIE, after the publication of his novel *The Satanic Verses*, which was deemed to have grossly insulted the Islamic faith.

first principles Underlying assumptions or basic ideas on which a theory or system of thought is founded. Modern science, for example, is based on the belief that nature obeys regular laws, and theology assumes, or rests on, a belief in God.

Francis of Assisi, St (1181-1226) Italian monk and founder of the Franciscan Order. He was born Giovanni Bernadone, into a wealthy family. After serious sickness and a religious dream, he gave away all his property and devoted himself to helping the poor. He took the name Francis from the nickname of his youth 'Il Francesco' 'The Little Frenchman' – given to him because he spoke French. Francis' simplicity, goodness and love of all living things soon won him a band of devoted followers. Franciscans still live by his rules, taking vows of chastity, poverty, obedience, and giving up all personal property.

DEVOUT FLOCK *A love of nature led St Francis to preach to the birds. He is the patron saint of animals and the modern ecology movement.*

freemasons Secret men's society that developed out of the medieval stonemasons' ▷GUILD. Members are now men who meet together in 'lodges' to practise rituals and ceremonies said to date back centuries, and to work for charity. The movement is non-religious, requiring only a belief in some form of supreme being.
The masons' secrecy has led to accusations that they favour one another in business and professional life, and that the police force is largely dominated by them.
Freemasons in England and in the secret Italian lodge P2 are still being questioned over the murder of the Italian banker Roberto Calvi, who was found hanging under London's Blackfriars Bridge in 1982.

free will Human capacity to choose, think and act voluntarily. Christians, Jews and Muslims believe that God has given the human race free will, to choose between good and evil. (Compare DETERMINISM.)

fundamentalism Conservative and often zealous religious movement seeking to preserve and strengthen the basic doctrines of a faith, and stressing their literal truth. In Christianity, it usually takes the form of reaffirming beliefs such as the Virgin Birth and the Resurrection of Jesus. Islamic fundamentalists desire the religious organisation of society and the state.

fuzzy logic New branch of thought that rejects conventional 'black or white' logic in favour of a flexible approach that can accommodate shades of grey, ambiguity and contradictions, making it more akin to Far Eastern philosophies. Its chief exponent, American academic Bart Kosko, claims that binary logic, which demands that things be right or wrong, 1 or 0, sacrifices accuracy for convenience, as many of the 20th century's greatest mathematicians and philosophers have proved that almost nothing is certain, including long-established laws of logic and science.

Genesis First book of the Old Testament, describing the creation of the world, the expulsion of ADAM AND EVE from the Garden of Eden, the story of Noah and the Flood, and the founding of the Hebrew nation under ABRAHAM.
♘ *Genesis* is Greek for 'creation'.

Gnostics Members of a 2nd-century Christian sect who believed that spirit and matter are completely opposed, and that the material world is evil. Combining aspects of philosophic paganism and Christianity, they produced secret texts on subjects such as alchemy and magic, and were considered heretical by the Church.

God In religions with one god, such as Christianity, Judaism and Islam, God is the supreme being or power, and creator of the Universe. Even in systems with many gods, there is usually one primary deity more powerful than the rest, such as BRAHMA in Hinduism, ▷ZEUS in Classical Greek belief and Jupiter in ancient Rome. Many different views of God exist, generally based on attributes such as goodness, wisdom, perfection, power, justice, completeness and love. Since Classical times various attempts have been made to logically prove or disprove the existence of God or the gods, but without success.

DECISION FOR CHRIST *Converted himself at a revival meeting at the age of 16, Baptist preacher Billy Graham's worldwide 'crusades' are credited with bringing millions to Christianity.*

Good Friday The most sacred day of the Christian calendar, known as Great Friday in the ORTHODOX Church. It falls on the Friday before EASTER Sunday and commemorates the Crucifixion of Jesus.
♘ Hot cross buns, marked with a cross, are traditionally eaten on Good Friday.

Good Samaritan In one of the parables of Jesus, a man from Samaria was the only person to stop and help a Jew who had been attacked and left to die at the roadside. The man's kindness was particularly admirable because Samaritans were supposedly despised by Jews.
♘ The Samaritans are a nationwide organisation that offers free telephone counselling to people who are in a state of emotional distress or suicidal despair.

Gospels Biblical message of Christian salvation, in particular the four books of the New Testament, which record the life, teachings and miracles of Jesus Christ. Their authorship is unknown, but they are traditionally attributed to the four Evangelists – Matthew, Mark, Luke and John – and were probably put together from the spoken tradition of the apostles within a century of Jesus's death. Together with the letters, or epistles, of St Paul, they form the central Christian scriptures.
♘ The word 'gospel' derives from the Anglo-Saxon *god-spell*, which literally meant 'news' or 'tidings'.

grace In Christianity, love, protection and favour bestowed by God as an unmerited gift which leads to salvation. According to the New Testament, it is freely given to those who have faith. Whether grace could be increased by doing good works or purchasing INDULGENCES was one of the major issues of the REFORMATION. Martin Luther argued, against the Roman Catholic Church, that salvation was by faith alone. However, there is now little difference between the Churches, most Christians accepting that faith without deeds is empty.
♘ 'Grace' is also a short blessing or prayer said before a meal.
♘ In Britain, 'grace-and-favour' refers to something – usually a residence – lent or let free of rent by the Crown.

Graham, Billy (1918-) American Baptist evangelist noted for the mass rallies held in the course of his worldwide tours. His preaching, writing and radio and television broadcasts have made him known to millions, and he became the friend of several US presidents.

guru Hindu religious teacher who gives personal instruction to a disciple. Sikhs also have gurus, whom they consider semidivine and directly inspired by God. The word comes from the Sanskrit *guruh*, meaning 'venerable'.
♘ In general usage, a guru can be any leader or sage who inspires some sort of following.

Hare Krishna movement Common name for the International Society for Krishna Consciousness, a Hindu cult founded in the United States in 1953, to spread the message that human happiness can be found only through greater love of God or KRISHNA. Disciples wear saffron robes, chant a mantra, or sacred phrase, and shave their heads except for a topknot – which they believe Krishna will use to pluck them up to Heaven on the last day.

Hegel, Georg Wilhelm Friedrich (1770-1831) German philosopher who argued that mind or spirit, rather than matter, is the basic reality. History, according to Hegel, shows a gradual unfolding of the universal Mind (or World Spirit), and proceeds by means of a DIALECTIC. By this he meant that every idea or state of affairs (which he called a 'thesis') is sooner or later confronted by its opposite (or 'antithesis'). Eventually, a combination (or 'synthesis') of the two arises, which then becomes a new thesis, giving rise to a new antithesis and so on. The task of philosophy, according to Hegel, is to demonstrate the rationality of what exists. Hegel's philosophy was an important influence on many other thinkers, including Karl MARX.

Hell In Christianity, the place where the souls of the damned are sent after judgment. It was traditionally thought of as a place of eternal punishment, but in modern theology Hell is more often seen as the state of separation from God.
🕯The Jewish Hell is called Gehenna and the Islamic Hell Johannam.

heresy Belief or doctrine opposed to orthodox teaching, especially of a religion. Religions or beliefs considered heretical by the Christian Church have included the ANABAPTISTS, the GNOSTICS and ARIANISM. Although heretics have been savagely persecuted by the Church in the past – particularly by the ▷INQUISITION – the strongest punishment used today is EXCOMMUNICATION. In Islam, however, the penalty for heresy is still death.

Hinduism Indian religion that aims at liberating the spirit from the material world through the purification of desires and the surpassing of personal identity. Hindu writings go back to around 1200 BC, but there is no single founder, sacred text or set of doctrines. Instead, emphasis is placed on right living, or *dharma*, and spiritual development throughout life. Although some Hindus believe in one God and some in none, most worship a number of deities, of whom the most important are BRAHMA, SHIVA and VISHNU. All Hindus, however, share a belief in KARMA and reincarnation. There are about 500 million Hindus in the world. Traditionally, Hinduism was linked to the Indian ▷CASTE SYSTEM, a rigid social hierarchy which governs every aspect of an individual's life, from birth to death.

Hobbes, Thomas (1588-1679) English political philosopher known for his book *Leviathan*, which advocates absolute government as the only means of achieving order; otherwise, he said, life is 'solitary, poor, nasty, brutish, and short.' He proposed a social contract under which the ruled agree to obey the ruler if he in turn provides social peace.

holism View that whole systems – such as living beings or societies – are more than the sum of their parts and cannot be explained simply by examining and evaluating their components. Holists believe that people and events can be understood only within a social or historical context.
🕯Holistic medicine, such as ▷HOMEOPATHY, aims to treat the 'whole person' – body, mind and spirit.

Holy Communion See EUCHARIST.

Holy Spirit (also Holy Ghost) Third person of the divine TRINITY believed in by Christians. The Holy Spirit is often described as the creative power or breath of God, responsible for miracles such as the conception of Jesus by the VIRGIN MARY.
🕯The Church's missionary work and miraculous experiences such as speaking in tongues and prophesying are said to be inspired by the Holy Spirit.
🕯The Holy Spirit is described in the Bible as descending in the form of a dove, and is often represented this way in art.

humanism Cultural movement of the ▷RENAISSANCE, inspired by the rediscovery of Classical authors and an optimistic belief in the glory and accomplishments of the human race. Humanism is also a 20th-century philosophy which rejects religious belief, claiming that people are capable of achieving happiness and behaving morally without any divine guidance.

Hume, David (1711-76) Scottish philosopher whose *Treatise of Human Nature* (1740) is a central text of British EMPIRICISM. His ideas were based on the work of BERKELEY and LOCKE, but went much further. Starting from a sceptical point of view, he questioned all claims to knowledge including the idea of CAUSE AND EFFECT, which he argued lacked logical justification. He concluded that all knowledge had to be based either on perceptions of the senses or on logical relationships between ideas.

JUNGLE TEMPLE *The 12th-century temple at Angkor Wat in the Cambodian jungle was dedicated to the god Vishnu – one of Hinduism's principal gods, together with Shiva (bottom) and Brahma.*

hypothesis Any PROPOSITION that has yet to be proved or disproved. In logic, hypotheses form the basis for argument and reasoning. In science, they give rise to predictions that can be tested in experiments before being put forward as a theory.

Iblis The Devil in ISLAM. Like SATAN, he is said to have rebelled against God and to have been banished from Heaven. In Muslim belief, Iblis is responsible for the disobedience of ADAM AND EVE in the Garden of Eden, and so there is no doctrine of ORIGINAL SIN. The KORAN suggests that, even in Hell, Iblis remains the servant of God and that he will eventually be saved.

I-Ching (Book of Changes) Chinese book of wisdom dating from 1000 BC, based on Taoist and Confucianist principles. It attempts to explain nature and human fortune as a constant cycle of change, and can be used as an oracle to give advice.

iconoclasm Rejection or destruction of religious images, often on the grounds that they are forbidden by the second commandment ('thou shalt not make unto thee any graven image'). In the 8th and 9th centuries many images and icons were destroyed with the blessing of the pope. During the REFORMATION, however, the Roman Catholic Church itself became a victim of iconoclasm, and lost many religious images. The word 'iconoclasm' comes from Greek words for 'image breaking'.

idealism In philosophy, any view that the material world is in some way dependent on the mind that perceives it. Idealist thinkers do not necessarily deny that material objects exist, but claim that they cannot be known to exist independently of the human mind. BERKELEY, HEGEL and KANT were all idealist thinkers. Idealism is opposed by REALISM and MATERIALISM.

idolatry Worship of images or idols as if they were divine. The term has often been misapplied to people who merely make use of sacred images in order to worship some unseen power.
♣The Islamic faith forbids the representation of living creatures in art because of the danger of idolatry – hence the rich abstract designs found in mosques.

imam In Islam, either a prayer leader in a mosque or an important Muslim scholar. Although it is not a priestly office, among Shi'a Muslims imams are religious leaders believed to have been appointed by God and to have special spiritual powers.

Immaculate Conception Roman Catholic doctrine that the VIRGIN MARY was conceived and born without sin, a matter of dispute for centuries but established as DOGMA in 1854. It is rejected by both Protestants and the Orthodox Church because it is not supported by the Bible.
♣Mary's conception of Jesus is often wrongly referred to as the 'Immaculate Conception'. The correct term for this is the VIRGIN BIRTH.

inductive reasoning Type of reasoning that uses individual observations to build up general rules – for example: *If every raven that has ever been seen is black, it is reasonable to conclude that all ravens are probably black.* The result is not absolutely certain and could be disproved by a single observation of a white raven. However, it is a reasonable assumption at the time. Modern science is based on this type of thinking. (Compare DEDUCTIVE REASONING.)

indulgence In the Roman Catholic Church, forgiveness of sin granted after repentance, which is believed to reduce the amount of time to be spent in PURGATORY after death. The idea was abused in medieval times when spiritual merit was openly bought and sold for money. Disgust at this system was a principal factor leading to LUTHER's break with Rome and the beginning of the REFORMATION.

infallibility Roman Catholic doctrine that the Church is assisted by the HOLY SPIRIT and cannot be mistaken when teaching on matters of faith and morals. At a Vatican Council in 1869-70 this authority was partially extended to the pope himself. Protestants deny that any human pronouncement is infallible.

Islam Religion founded in the 7th century by the prophet MUHAMMAD, and based on the teachings of the KORAN. It acknowledges one God – the same as that worshipped by Jews and Christians – called Allah in Arabic. Islam means 'submission to the will of God', and followers are known as MUSLIMS. In Islam, there is no distinction between spiritual and secular life, and believers are expected to obey Shari'a – the religious law, as laid down in the Koran and the sayings of Muhammad, supplemented by agreements among Muslims over the centuries. Religious observances centre on the 'Five Pillars of the Faith': reciting the creed ('There is no God but God, and Muhammad is His prophet'), praying five times a day facing MECCA, giving alms to the poor, fasting during RAMADAN, and

making a pilgrimage to Mecca at least once. The public place of worship is the MOSQUE. There are around 700 million Muslims in the world. Islam is the dominant faith in the Arab nations, in some countries of central Asia and southeastern Europe, as well as in Malaysia and Indonesia. In many Muslim countries Islamic FUNDAMENTALISM is a powerful political force.

Jainism Indian religion which dates back to the 6th century BC, and shares many elements with HINDUISM and BUDDHISM. The religion has no deity and is monastic, like Buddhism. Jains believe in reincarnation and aim at spiritual development as the way to liberation from the cycle of birth and death. They are strict vegetarians and strive to follow a practice of non-violence towards all living creatures.

Jehovah The name of God as translated by 15th and 16th-century Western scholars from the consonants YHWH – the written Hebrew form. The Hebrews, who spoke of Him as *Adonai* 'Lord', considered His proper name too holy to be pronounced. Modern scholars prefer to use YAHWEH.

Jehovah's Witnesses Group founded as the International Bible Students' Association in 1872 by the American Charles Taze Russell (1852-1916), who believed that the SECOND COMING of Jesus and the MILLENNIUM were imminent. They insist on using Jehovah as a name for God, reject the doctrine of the TRINITY and consider Jesus as God's agent who will come to establish a divine kingdom on Earth. There are nearly 5 million members worldwide who refuse to bear arms or obey any law that goes against the Bible. There are no clergy.
♣Jehovah's Witnesses are known for vigorous door-to-door missionary work, during which they distribute copies of their magazine *The Watchtower*.

Jesuits Members of the Society of Jesus (SJ), the largest and most influential Roman Catholic religious organisation, founded by St Ignatius of Loyola in 1534 and approved by the pope in 1540. They spearheaded the COUNTER REFORMATION and have a long tradition of missionary and scholarly work. In recent years they have been influential in modernising the Roman Catholic Church.

Jesus Christ (*c.***6 BC-***c.***AD 30)** Prophet believed by Christians to be the Son of God, the second person of the Holy TRINITY and the Christ or MESSIAH sent by God to save mankind. According to the New Testament, Jesus was conceived by the VIRGIN MARY through the power of the Holy Spirit, making him both human and divine. He was born in Bethlehem but raised in Nazareth by Mary and her husband Joseph. After baptism by John the Baptist in the River Jordan he chose 12 disciples with whom he travelled throughout Palestine preaching the coming of the kingdom of God, teaching a gospel of love and compassion, healing the sick and performing miracles. He attracted many followers but also made enemies by failing to observe Jewish laws and for turning the moneylenders out of the Temple. Jesus was betrayed by Judas Iscariot, condemned by the Roman governor Pontius Pilate at the insistence of the Jewish population, and crucified at Calvary. Christians believe that he rose again from the dead and that he will return to Earth at the SECOND COMING to save those who believe in him.

🙎Muslims consider Jesus a great prophet, second only to MUHAMMAD, and in Judaism he is generally acknowledged as a religious teacher, or rabbi.

Judaism Traditional religion of the Jews, based on the teachings of the Hebrew Scriptures (roughly the same as the Christian OLD TESTAMENT), the TALMUD and other religious commentaries. It involves belief in one God, creator of the world and liberator of His chosen people, the Jews, whom He delivered from slavery in the EXODUS from Egypt. ABRAHAM is considered the founder of Judaism, around

1800 BC, and MOSES, with whom God renewed His covenant around 1200 BC, is one of its major prophets. Followers believe that a MESSIAH will appear in the future to gather all the Jews together again in the Promised Land, and to rebuild the great TEMPLE OF JERUSALEM. The faith is taught by RABBIS and through family life, which is central to Jewish culture and religion. Jewish law – or TORAH – lays down strict ritual observances in many areas of life, particularly regarding the SABBATH and the preparation of kosher food. In recent times, the Reform and Liberal movements in Judaism have relaxed some of the rules observed by Conservative or Orthodox Jews.

🙎Jews have their own calendar based on the lunar cycle. Their festivals include CHANUKKAH, PASSOVER, ROSH HASHANAH, and YOM KIPPUR.

Kant, Immanuel (1724-1804) German philosopher who, in *The Critique of Pure Reason* and other works, set out views which attempted to bridge the gap between EMPIRICISM and RATIONALISM. Kant was concerned that conventional METAPHYSICS had failed to resolve issues such as the existence of God, the immortality of the soul and the operation of FREE WILL. He maintained that the first step to answering such questions was to investigate the limits of human understanding and reasoning – a type of investigation he called a 'critique'. In the end, Kant concluded that we cannot ever know a 'thing-in-itself', but only as it

appears to the human mind. Kant also argued that 'right action' could not be based on intuition or desire but must conform to a law of reason, the Categorical Imperative, which urges people to behave as they would wish everyone else to.

🙎Kant led a simple life, never leaving his home town of Königsberg in Prussia. The townspeople could allegedly set their clocks by his punctual afternoon walks.

karma In Eastern religions such as HINDUISM and BUDDHISM, the principle that all good and bad actions have consequences that will affect one throughout life, and even in future lives.

🙎By extension, 'karma' is sometimes loosely used to mean fate or destiny.

Kierkegaard, Soren (1813-55) Danish philosopher and religious writer who defended Christianity. His work concentrates on the emotions of fear and loneliness which he believed to be part of true religion.

🙎Kierkegaard is regarded as a forerunner of EXISTENTIALIST thinkers.

knowledge Something which has been defined as justified true BELIEF, and which is studied in the branch of philosophy known as EPISTEMOLOGY. Because knowledge is clearly different from 'feeling sure' about what exists or about the course of events, most philosophical debate on the subject centres on the nature of TRUTH and on what counts as appropriate evidence for claiming to know something.

Koran (or Qur'an) Islamic sacred book, held by believers to be the word of God as revealed to MUHAMMAD by the archangel Gabriel. Its central message is belief in one God, the obedience due to Him, and His involvement in history from the creation to the Last Judgment. It also lays down religious principles that form the basis of Islamic law, or Shari'a.

🙎The Koran contains many parallels with the Old Testament. It also venerates Jesus as a prophet, or messenger of God, but maintains that God saved him from dying on the cross.

Krishna In HINDUISM, an incarnation of the god VISHNU in human form. He was supposedly a great ruler and was known for amorous encounters with milkmaids. He plays a leading role in the BHAGAVAD GITA.

Lao-Tzu (also Lao Zi or Lao Tan) Ancient Chinese philosopher of the 6th century BC – but possibly a legendary figure. His thought is said to have provided

HOLY WALL *Judaism's holiest site, the Western Wall in Jerusalem, is a remnant of Herod's Temple. Lamentation by the Jews over its ruin and their long exile earned it the name of 'Wailing Wall'.*

HOLY SCRIPTURE *Islamic tradition forbids the representation of human and animal figures, so the adornment of manuscripts like this 15th-century Koran is based on geometric shapes and plant motifs.*

the inspiration for TAOISM and for the *Tao Te Ching* (*The Way of Power*) – a series of philosophical meditations compiled some 300 years after his supposed lifetime. Much of Lao-Tzu's teaching appears to complement the ideas of CONFUCIANISM.

Leibniz, Gottfried (1646-1716) German RATIONALIST philosopher, mathematician and optimist who, like SPINOZA, developed an entire system of philosophy by deduction from FIRST PRINCIPLES. According to Leibniz the Universe consists of an infinite number of independent units ('monads') which God has placed in harmony with one another in 'the best of all possible worlds'.
♪Leibniz is satirised as Dr Pangloss in ▷VOLTAIRE's book, *Candide*.

liberation theology Belief that Christ's message was one of liberation and preferential treatment for the poor, and that the Church should campaign for worldwide economic and political justice. It originated in the 1960s within a radical branch of the Roman Catholic Church in Latin America. In the 1980s Pope Jean Paul II accused its followers of wrongly supporting violent revolution and Marxist class-struggle.

Locke, John (1632-1704) English philosopher, regarded as one of the founders of EMPIRICISM. Locke rejected the view of RATIONALISM – that some ideas are innate in the human mind – and insisted that knowledge is based on experience alone. A newborn baby's mind, he said, is a *tabula rasa*, or 'blank slate', until experience begins to 'write' on it. As a political philosopher, Locke opposed the ▷DIVINE RIGHT OF KINGS and maintained that the legitimacy of governments should depend on the consent of the governed, and that the role of government is only to safeguard the liberty and rights of the individual.

♪Locke's views were influential in the French Revolution and in the drawing up of the American Constitution.

logic Branch of philosophy dealing with the principles of reasoning. Classical logic, as developed in ancient Greece, is concerned with the rules for deriving valid conclusions from a set of propositions (DEDUCTIVE REASONING). Logic today has become more abstract and mathematical. (See also FUZZY LOGIC and SYLLOGISM.)

logical positivism Philosophical movement of the first half of the 20th century, influenced by the early works of AYER, RUSSELL and WITTGENSTEIN. It insisted that a statement is meaningful only if it can be logically or experimentally tested. Statements such as 'God exists' are meaningless as there is no way to test them. 'The Moon is made of green cheese' is meaningful (although false) because it can be tested.

Luther, Martin (1483-1546) German priest whose criticism of the Roman Catholic Church initiated the REFORMATION, which led to the rise of PROTESTANTISM. As professor of Biblical Exegesis at the University of Wittenburg he compiled a list of Ninety-Five Theses which attacked the Church for selling INDULGENCES, and argued that faith alone is sufficient for salvation. He denied the authority of the pope and other aspects of Catholic doctrine, including TRANSUBSTANTIATION, and wrote many books and pamphlets.

Lutheran Church Protestant denomination with a large following in Germany and Scandinavia. It accepts the teachings of Martin LUTHER and stresses the importance of 'justification' (being made righteous) by God's grace, which is received through faith alone. The Church is non-hierarchical and grants autonomy to each individual congregation.
♪Lutherans are known for their choral and organ music. J.S. ▷BACH wrote much of his music for Lutheran worship.

Machiavelli, Niccolò (1469-1527) Italian statesman and political philosopher whose principal work *The Prince* (1513) argues that to win and maintain power, rulers should not be constrained by Christian morality – that a noble end can justify ruthless means. Critics called him a dangerous cynic, admirers claimed he was a pragmatic realist. He was the first to base his political thought on the study of human nature, observed during 23 years on the council of the Florentine republic.

Marcuse, Herbert (1898-1979) Radical German-born American philosopher whose Marxist writings were influenced by Hegel and Freud. He believed that Western societies are not free, and that the masses are only kept docile by the technology that permits widespread possession of material goods.

Marx, Karl (1818-83) German thinker concerned with theories of economics and history. His views were based on the philosophy of HEGEL, but replaced Hegel's IDEALISM with a form of MATERIALISM. His systematic study of class struggles and belief in the DIALECTICAL development of history have been enormously influential. Marx is best known for the theory that violent proletarian revolution will eventually topple capitalism and bring about a just and classless society. (See also ▷MARX in 'Business and Economics'.)
♨Marx's *Das Kapital* and *The Communist Manifesto* – the latter written in collaboration with ENGELS – were highly influential in the development of ▷SOCIALISM and ▷COMMUNISM. However, many political systems going by the name ▷MARXISM bear little relationship to Marx's own ideas.

Mary Magdalene, St Woman mentioned in the New Testament Book of Luke, from whom Jesus exorcised seven evil spirits. She is generally identified with a repentant prostitute also described by Luke. She accompanied Jesus's mother Mary at the Crucifixion, and is said to have been the first to meet the risen Christ.

Mass Central liturgical rite in the Roman Catholic, Orthodox and some Anglican Churches; also known as the EUCHARIST. It commemorates Christ sharing bread and wine with his disciples at the Last Supper.
♨The word 'Mass' comes from the Latin *Missa*, used in dismissing communicants after the service.

materialism In philosophy, the position that nothing exists except physical objects and forces that are perceptible and measurable. Materialists deny the existence of spirit, soul or mind as a separate type of reality, and they look for physical explanations of all phenomena – for example, by explaining thoughts or emotions in terms of chemical reactions in the brain.
♨▷MARXISM is a form of materialism in which almost every aspect of culture is seen in terms of economic forces.

Mecca Birthplace of MUHAMMAD in about AD 570, in present-day Saudi Arabia, and revered as Islam's holiest place. Forced in 622 to flee from Mecca to Medina, Muhammad returned to the city in triumph a few years later. The Koran decrees that every Muslim, whose health and means permit them to, should make a pilgrimage, or *hadj*, to Mecca once in their lifetime, after which they can take the title *Hadji*.

Messiah The promised 'anointed one', saviour, or 'Christ', foretold by the Old Testament prophets. Christians believe that JESUS CHRIST was the Messiah, although he himself never explicitly claimed the title. In Judaism, the Messiah has yet to appear. When he does, Jews believe he will gather them all together in the Holy Land, after which the dead will be resurrected for the DAY OF JUDGMENT.

metaphysics Branch of philosophy dealing with the ultimate nature of reality and the fundamental principles on which other systems of thought are based – such as the assumption in science that nature obeys regular laws, or in theology that God exists. Metaphysics has often been criticised for its hypothetical nature and for dealing in theories that can be neither supported nor disproved by any form of evidence. Some views, such as LOGICAL POSITIVISM, have argued that metaphysical statements are totally meaningless.
♨The word 'metaphysics' means literally 'after physics'; it originated from a speculative work by ARISTOTLE, which followed his book on physics.

Methodism Largest non-Anglican Protestant Church in Britain, begun by the breakaway Anglican preacher John WESLEY and his brother Charles in the 18th century. It appeals directly to the Gospels and stresses the freely given grace of God which leads to salvation. The Church is regulated by an annual Conference, and emphasises the social and individual responsibility of Christians.

Mill, John Stuart (1806-73) English philosopher and economist, who refined UTILITARIANISM – the pursuit of 'the greatest happiness of the greatest number' – by arguing that some types of pleasure were higher than others. His book *On Liberty* is a classic endorsement of liberal government, stressing freedom of belief, speech and behaviour; arguing for individual responsibility; and advocating a severe restriction on the powers of the state.
♨Mill was allegedly learning Greek by the age of three; by eight he was reading Plato.

millennium According to some Christian groups, including SEVENTH-DAY ADVENTISTS and JEHOVAH'S WITNESSES, a period of 1000 years during which Jesus and his followers will reign over the Earth after the battle of ARMAGEDDON. The doctrine is based on the Book of Revelation, but has never been adopted by any of the more traditional Christian Churches.

Mithraism Cult in the Roman Empire during the first centuries of the Christian era, and found as far afield as Germany and Britain. It was based on worship of the

ISLAM'S SACRED ROCK *Every year some 2 million Muslims pour into Mecca to make seven circuits of the Kaaba – a black-draped stone cube said to have been the first place where Allah was worshipped.*

WAGONS ROLL WEST *In 1847, in one of the epic treks of American history, Brigham Young led his persecuted Mormons 1500 miles (2400 km) from Illinois to the valley of the Great Salt Lake, Utah.*

Persian god Mithras, who was believed to have come from the Sun and to have slain a bull whose blood fertilised the Earth. The cult was popular in the Roman armies, and in the 3rd century AD, it was one of the main rivals to Christianity.

monasticism Devotion of one's life entirely to God and to spiritual development. It usually involves separation from the world and residence in a monastery or convent. In Christianity, it is practised by monks and nuns in the Roman Catholic, Orthodox and some Anglican Churches. Followers take vows of poverty, chastity and obedience, for example, and are committed to a rigorous regime of prayer and work. Some orders are extremely strict, such as the silent Trappists; others, such as the Benedictines, do teaching and missionary work. Some other faiths, such as BUDDHISM, also have versions of monasticism.

monism View that reality consists of only one basic substance, generally either mind (thoughts, emotions, perceptions, intuitions and all other inner experiences) or matter (physical objects and forces). MATERIALISM and IDEALISM are both monist theories. Monism is opposed by DUALISM, which maintains that there are two basic substances, and by PLURALISM, which maintains that there are many.

Montesquieu, Charles (1689-1755) French political philosopher of the ENLIGHTENMENT. His major work, *The Spirit of Laws*, set out the theory of separation of powers – the view that states should have separate legislative, executive and judicial powers. Montesquieu influenced the Founding Fathers of the United States and many countries' constitutions.

Moonies Common name for members of the Unification Church, founded in 1954 by the Korean religious leader Sun Myung Moon. Moon offers a new interpretation of the Bible and claims to have had direct revelations from God. Church members live in strictly disciplined communal groups and some revere Moon as a MESSIAH.
🕯The Unification Church has been accused of brainwashing and splitting up families. Meanwhile, followers accuse their opponents of kidnapping members and indoctrinating them against the movement.

Mormons Members of the Church of Jesus Christ of Latter-Day Saints, founded in 1830 by the American religious leader Joseph Smith. Smith claimed that a new book of the Bible, the Book of Mormon, was revealed to him by an angel and that Jesus would return to America to build a New Jerusalem. After Smith's death, the Mormons moved west under the leadership of Brigham Young and founded a new capital at Salt Lake City in Utah. They have distinctive religious practices such as marriages for eternity and baptism of the deceased. There are some 6 million members worldwide.
🕯In the past the Mormons were controversial for practising polygamy, but this is no longer officially sanctioned by their Church.

mortal sin In the Roman Catholic Church, a sin so grave that the soul is completely cut off from God's grace. Traditionally, mortal sins include murder, suicide, bestiality and crimes against the HOLY SPIRIT, such as despair. However, even these, to be mortal, must be committed with full knowledge of the consequences and as a deliberate act of will. Someone who has committed a mortal sin and dies unrepentant is considered damned to Hell. Lesser misdemeanours are VENIAL SINS.

Mosaic law In JUDAISM, the law – or TORAH – believed to have been passed down to the Israelites through God's revelation to Moses. It offers spiritual guidance and includes the TEN COMMANDMENTS.

Moses Prophet and leader of the ancient Israelites. According to the Old Testament, Moses was born in the 13th century BC in Egypt, where the Israelites were living as slaves. While he was still an infant, the ruling pharaoh ordered all male Hebrew children to be slain. Moses' mother placed him in a basket of rushes and hid him in a marsh, where he was found and adopted by the pharaoh's daughter. As a man, Moses was commanded by God to bring the Israelites out of bondage, and he led his people out of Egypt on the journey that became known as the EXODUS. Moses received the TEN COMMANDMENTS from God on Mount Sinai, after which he and his people wandered in the wilderness for 40 years. Just as they came in sight of the 'Promised Land' of Canaan, Moses died – according to tradition, at the age of 120.

mosque Islamic place of worship, prayer and meeting. In many mosques, the faithful are called to prayer by a *muezzin*, or crier, from the top of a minaret. Although Muslims believe that daily prayers can be said anywhere, most try to attend the communal service at their mosque at noon on Fridays. (See also ▷MOSQUE in 'Architecture and Engineering.')
🕯The tradition in many Islamic countries of fine, decorated carpets comes from the use of prayer mats in mosques.

Muhammad (or Mohammed) (c.AD 570-632) Founder and chief prophet of ISLAM. He was born in MECCA, where he became familiar with both Judaism and Christianity. Initially a wealthy merchant, he was convinced by religious revelations that he was the last great prophet in the line of MOSES and JESUS, and that he had been chosen to spread the divine message in its final form. As a result of persecution he fled Mecca in 622 with a few followers – a journey known as the Hegira. They settled at Yathrib, renaming it Medina ('city of the prophet'), and set up a form of religious rule. A few years later Muhammad reconquered Mecca and began to spread Islam across the Arab world. His teachings are recorded in the KORAN, which Muslims believe was dictated to him by the archangel Gabriel in a series of visions.

mullah Title given to a learned and devout Islamic scholar, or one who executes Islamic law. The word is a corruption of the Arabic word for 'master'.
In fundamentalist Islamic states such as Iran, mullahs often have considerable political influence.

Muslim Follower of ISLAM – literally one who has 'surrendered' to God. The majority of Muslims belong to the orthodox SUNNI branch or to the more fundamentalist SHI'A (or Shiite) group, but there are many smaller branches, including SUFISM.

mystery religions Ancient Greek and Roman religious cults which grew up around various pagan gods and goddesses. Initiation was by secret rites, and held out the promise of life after death. One of the best-known cults was that of the fertility goddess ▷DEMETER at Eleusis in Greece, where rituals were enacted in caverns.

mysticism Religious belief based on personal spiritual experience or alleged union with God, or with some other divine being or principle. Most of the world's great religions have mystical traditions, in which direct contact with the supernatural is said to be achieved by practices such as meditation, rhythmic chanting, fasting or going into trances. Noted Christian mystics include Thomas a Kempis, Julian of Norwich and St AUGUSTINE.

naturalism Philosophical view that there is no need to go beyond the natural world in explaining anything – that, for example, society can be studied in a similar way to the climate. Instead of seeing life as part of a

divine plan, naturalists argue that it is the result of certain physical and chemical conditions. Similarly, they see ethics and morality as codes developed to ensure survival by means of social cooperation.

natural theology Attempt to base religious thought on a rational foundation; the belief that knowledge of God and the divine order can be based on observation of the natural world, without the need for revelation. One example is the so-called 'argument from design', according to which the natural world shows such intricate and beautiful design that it could not have arisen accidentally but must have been created. The medieval thinker St Thomas AQUINAS offered five proofs of God based on general facts about the world. However, there are logical problems with all of them.

Newman, John Henry (1801-90) English poet and priest, and one of the founders of the OXFORD MOVEMENT. As a Church of England theologian he composed a number of tracts, one of which – Tract 90 – claimed that the principles of the Anglican Church were consistent with Roman Catholicism. It provoked a reaction that brought the Oxford Movement to an end and eventually led to Newman's conversion to Roman Catholicism in 1845. In 1879 he was made a cardinal.

New Testament Second section of the Christian BIBLE, dealing with the life of JESUS CHRIST and its aftermath. It contains the four GOSPELS of Matthew, Mark, Luke and John; the Acts of the APOSTLES; the Epistles of St PAUL and others; and the Book of Revelation.

Nicene Creed Fundamental statement of belief recited in the Roman Catholic and Orthodox Churches, as well as in many Protestant Churches, beginning: 'I believe in One God, the Father Almighty, Creator of Heaven and Earth . . . ' It was the outcome of a council of bishops called in AD 325 by Emperor Constantine at Nicea (now in Turkey), to settle disagreements over Christian doctrine.

Nietzsche, Friedrich (1844-1900) Radical German philosopher and linguist. He vigorously rejected all philosophy since SOCRATES, appealing instead to early Greek thought and its dual view of human nature, embodied in the distinction between ▷APOLLO (representative of reason) and ▷DIONYSUS (representative of emotion and instinct). Nietzsche rejected the accepted moral values of Christianity and

condemned it as a religion suitable only for the weak. In place of its 'slave morality' he asserted the self and the idea of the Superman or 'Overman' (Übermensch) – an ideal superior being, free from conventional notions of right and wrong, who would be supremely creative in representing the goal of human evolution.

nihilism Radical type of MATERIALISM which rejects all moral values in the name of science and popular revolution. It arose in Russia, inspired by Bazarov, the hero of Ivan ▷TURGENEV's masterpiece, the novel Fathers and Children (1862). Philosophers have generally rejected nihilism on the grounds that it is impossible to do away with all values, and that one can argue against something only by proposing something else in its place.

nirvana In Buddhism and other Indian religions, the highest state of blessedness, in which the individual is freed from all desires and attachments, as well as from the cycle of reincarnation. After his enlightenment, the BUDDHA is said to have attained partial nirvana – complete nirvana not being possible until after death.
'Nirvana' is sometimes used inaccurately to refer to heaven, paradise or simply bliss.

Nonconformists Protestant groups – also known as Free Churches or Dissenters – who broke away from the Church of England in the 17th century, rejecting the authority of bishops and the influence of Roman Catholic forms of worship. After 1662 the term was used in reference to those refusing to accept the Act of Uniformity, which required adherence to the Prayer Book in all Churches. Today the term is applied to any Protestant denomination which does not belong to an established or national Church.

Ockham (or Occam), William of (c.1285-c.1349) English philosopher and theologian who wrote extensively on logic and politics. He was excommunicated in 1328 and exiled to Bavaria after supporting the Franciscans on the issue of monastic poverty, which the pope opposed.
Ockham is remembered for the philosophical principle – 'Ockham's razor' – that the simplest explanation is the best one; in his own words, 'a plurality is not to be posited without necessity'.

Old Testament Christian term for the first part of the Bible. It consists of 39 books (which correspond to the 24 books in the Hebrew scriptures) or 51 including the

ROLE MODEL
Nazis corrupted the 'Superman' ideal proposed by Friedrich Nietzsche (right) – and chose to ignore the fact that Nietzsche condemned nationalism and praised Jews.

APOCRYPHA recognised by the Roman Catholic Church. It records the history of the Jews, their relationship with God and their prophets' sayings. Christians believe its prophecies were fulfilled by JESUS CHRIST, as told in the NEW TESTAMENT.

Opus Dei International Roman Catholic society founded in Spain in 1928 and approved by the Holy See in 1950, to promote Christian ideals in modern life. In 1982 it was elevated in status, and its leader was placed on the same level as heads of religious orders, although the organisation does not have the autonomy of such orders. It has sometimes been controversial for its secrecy and political involvement, especially in Spain where Opus Dei was used to bolster General Franco's regime.

ordination Initiation into the Christian priesthood. It is considered a solemn sacrament that confers spiritual powers, such as the power to consecrate the EUCHARIST and to give Communion and ABSOLUTION.
♪ Traditionally ordination was reserved for men, but since the 1970s many Churches of the ANGLICAN COMMUNION have extended it to include women. In 1994 the General Synod of the Church of England, after parliamentary approval, formally altered Church law to allow women's ordination, in the face of extreme opposition from some conservative Church members.

PARADISE LOST *The serpent's wiles tempt Adam and Eve to eat the forbidden fruit of the Tree of Knowledge – the act of disobedience which gave rise to the concept of original sin.*

HOLY ICON *In Eastern, or Orthodox, Christianity, icons or paintings on wood were revered as taking on the sacredness of the subjects they portrayed, such as the Madonna and Child.*

original sin In Christianity, the corruption of ADAM AND EVE as a result of their tasting the forbidden fruit of the Tree of Knowledge. This led to the FALL OF MAN, since all humans are said to have inherited the sin of Adam. Christians believe that Jesus atoned for original sin and that those who believe in him and accept BAPTISM are redeemed from it. Muslims reject the doctrine of original sin, as they believe that the Devil, IBLIS, was responsible for the disobedience of Adam and Eve.

Orthodox Church (or Eastern Orthodox Church) Group of Churches forming one of the three main branches of Christianity, together with Protestantism and Roman Catholicism. They include the Russian and Greek Orthodox Churches and other smaller East European and Balkan Churches recognising the supremacy of the patriarch of Constantinople. They broke away from the Roman Catholic Church in 1054, after centuries of disagreement over ritual and doctrine, particularly on relations between the three persons of the Holy TRINITY. Orthodox worship centres on the celebration of the EUCHARIST, although six other SACRAMENTS (or 'mysteries') are also recognised – baptism, confirmation, penance, last rites, ordination and marriage. Clergy below the rank of bishop are allowed to marry. There are 130 million adherents.
♪ The word 'orthodox' comes from the Greek words meaning 'correct belief'.

Oxford Movement Theological tendency within the Church of England which urged closer ties with the Roman Catholic

Church and the restoration of Catholic ceremonies and rituals in Anglican services. It was begun in 1833 by John NEWMAN – who later became a Roman Catholic cardinal – and other theologians associated with Oxford University. Although the movement itself was short-lived, its influence remains strong in Anglo-Catholicism.

paganism Term first used by early Christians to describe the beliefs of all non-Christians. The word comes from the Latin for 'country-dweller'. These days it is usually applied to beliefs that are not part of a world religion such as Christianity, Judaism, Buddhism or Islam.

Paine, Thomas (1737-1809) Radical English political philosopher known for his pamphlet *Common Sense*, which argued for American independence, and for *The Rights of Man* – a defence of the French Revolution, democracy and republicanism, which prompted a charge of treason and his escape to France. He wrote *The Age of Reason* as a defence of DEISM, but it led to accusations of atheism because of its attack on Christianity. He died in poverty in New York.

pantheism Belief that God and the natural world are the same thing, as found in HINDUISM, some forms of BUDDHISM and the philosophy of the Greek STOICS, HEGEL and SPINOZA.

paradigm Prevailing framework of theories on which scientists base their work. If a fundamental theory is proved wrong, it may cause a scientific revolution; for example, Einstein transformed Newtonian physics.

paradise Place or state of pure happiness. In Christianity, paradise has been identified with both Heaven and the Garden of Eden, which is sometimes called the 'earthly paradise'. The Islamic paradise is concerned with sensual pleasures.
♪ The word 'paradise' comes from an ancient Persian term for a walled garden.

Parsees Followers of the Persian religion of ZOROASTRIANISM, who settled in India in the 10th century. They now live mainly in the area around Bombay, and since the 19th century have modernised and reformed the faith, mainly as a result of Western education and missionary influence.

Passover (or Pesach) Jewish festival at the beginning of spring, commemorating the deliverance of the first-born on the eve of the EXODUS of the ancient Israelites from Egypt. During Passover –

which lasts for eight days, except for Reform Jews and in Israel where it is seven days – a form of unleavened bread called *matzo* and other kosher foods are eaten.
♁ Jesus was crucified at Passover.

Paul, St (c.3-c.67) Early Christian theologian and APOSTLE to the non-Jewish communities of the Mediterranean and Near East. Paul (formerly Saul) was a Jew from Tarsus (now in Turkey) who had trained as a rabbi and was an opponent of the early Christians until around AD 35, when he had a vision on the road to Damascus. He later became an energetic Christian leader who preached Christianity to all, not only the Jews. He was allegedly crucified by Emperor Nero. Thirteen Epistles (letters) to various Christian communities are attributed to Paul and form part of the New Testament.

penance Repenting for one's sins, or acts performed to make up for them. After CONFESSION in the Roman Catholic and Orthodox Churches, penance usually involves being asked to say so many 'Hail Marys' or 'Our Fathers'. Today, fasting, pilgrimage and good works such as giving alms are also performed as penance.

Pentecost In Judaism, the feast of Shavuot held in May or June to commemorate Moses receiving the Ten Commandments. Christians celebrate Pentecost seven Sundays after EASTER in remembrance of the descent of the HOLY SPIRIT on Jesus's disciples at the time of the Jewish feast, enabling them to 'speak in tongues'.
♁ In the Church of England, Pentecost is often called Whitsun or Whit Sunday, from the tradition of clothing the newly baptised in white robes on the day.

Pentecostalism Breakaway Christian movement – also known now as the charismatic movement – started in the United States in 1901, in reaction to what was considered the rigidity of traditional services. Worship is seen as a joyful occasion, involving singing, chanting and invoking the HOLY SPIRIT in activities such as healing, prophesying and speaking in tongues. Pentecostalists take the Bible literally and are zealous missionaries.

Peter, St Foremost of Christ's APOSTLES, originally a fisherman called Simon, but renamed Peter (meaning 'rock') by Jesus. Just before the Crucifixion, Peter denied being a follower of Jesus three times, as Jesus had predicted he would. He became the leader of the early Christians so

beginning the APOSTOLIC SUCCESSION and fulfilling another of Christ's prophecies – 'Upon this rock I will build my Church'. Peter died at the foot of the Vatican Hill, in Rome, near the site of ▷ST PETER'S BASILICA, named after him.
♁ Peter is often depicted holding the keys to the kingdom of Heaven. By Roman Catholic tradition, he was the first POPE.

phenomenology Philosophical approach that studies concrete personal experiences as subjectively described without making judgments about whether this reflects 'reality'. It was developed by the German thinker Edmund Husserl in the early 20th century, and became a major force in modern continental philosophy.

Plato (c.428-c.348 BC) Ancient Greek philosopher, considered one of the most important figures in Western philosophy. He was a pupil of SOCRATES and became the teacher of ARISTOTLE. Plato's writings take the form of dialogues in which Socrates conducts discussions with other thinkers on subjects such as politics, ETHICS, KNOWLEDGE and METAPHYSICS. Plato is best known for his theory (which probably had nothing to do with Socrates) that abstractions such as truth or the good – which he called 'forms' or 'ideas' – exist in a realm beyond the physical world. Unlike individual material objects which are perceived with the senses, forms can be grasped only by reason – which is why philosophy is so important. In his *Republic*, Plato suggested that the ideal state would be one ruled by the 'philosopher-king'.

pluralism Theory that reality is composed of many different basic types of substance; the opposite of MONISM.

Plymouth Brethren Strict Protestant sect founded in Plymouth, Devon, in 1830. Members follow a simple, devout way of life and look forward to the SECOND COMING and the MILLENNIUM.

polytheism Belief in more than one god. Ancient Greek and Roman religion was polytheistic, as are some types of HINDUISM. Usually the various gods govern particular places or aspects of life – in Greece, ▷ATHENA protected Athens and was the goddess of wisdom, while ▷APHRODITE ruled love and ▷PLUTO the underworld. Monotheism is belief in one God.

pope Bishop of Rome and head of the Roman Catholic Church, also known as the Holy Father, Vicar of Christ or Roman

Pontiff. According to Roman Catholic doctrine, all popes are direct successors of the apostle St PETER through APOSTOLIC SUCCESSION. In the past, popes have had extensive political power and influence. Today, however, their authority is mainly restricted to spiritual affairs. (See also ▷AVIGNON PAPACY in 'World History'.)
♁ New popes are chosen by a convocation – a meeting of cardinals in the Sistine Chapel. Crowds wait for white smoke from the chimney, signalling a successful ballot.

Popper, Sir Karl (1902-94) British philosopher, born in Austria. He argues that it is impossible to prove a theory, since however many observations support it, a vital exception may have been overlooked. However, finding a single exception is enough to disprove – or falsify – a theory. Scientists must therefore look for contradictions and exceptions. If they find them, they must revise their theories; if they do not, their theories become stronger. Popper contends that science progresses in an orderly, logical manner as theories are exposed to the possibility of refutation. He is also known for his criticism of ▷MARXISM and other totalitarian systems of government (which he traces back to Plato).

positivism Philosophical view that the only genuine knowledge is that based on science and factual observation. It rejects the attempts of theology and metaphysics to understand things – such as the purpose of life – that lie beyond the physical world. LOGICAL POSITIVISM was popular in the first half of the 20th century.

premise In logic, a PROPOSITION forming the basis of an argument or from which a conclusion is drawn. The classical SYLLOGISM has a major premise and a minor premise. Logic is not concerned with the truth or falsity of premises, only with the logical relationship between them.

Presbyterianism Version of CALVINISM found in English-speaking Reformed Churches, which refers essentially to a form of Church government. Ministers are democratically elected and a system of Church courts oversees the conduct of the congregation. The Presbyterian Church is the established Church in Scotland and is also a powerful influence in Northern Ireland. In England, it is now part of the United Reformed Church.

prophet Person who brings a message from God to the people. Old Testament prophets such as Isaiah preached virtuous living, true worship of God and the future coming of an ideal ruler. They were frequently unpopular for condemning immorality and idol worship.

🕯In some non-Christian faiths, including Islam, Jesus is revered as a prophet, although he is not accepted as the MESSIAH.

proposition In philosophy, an assertion, supposition or any idea that can be expressed, whether true, false or still hypothetical. After a proposition has been put forward it is scrutinised and if found to be true, it may give rise to a new theory. Propositions are the building blocks of LOGIC and science.

Protestantism One of the three main branches of Christianity, alongside Roman Catholicism and the Orthodox Church. Although foreshadowed by earlier developments, it arose in the 16th century as part of the REFORMATION initiated by Martin LUTHER as a reaction against the Roman Catholic Church. The Protestants viewed Catholicism as corrupt, riddled with superstition, and more concerned with wealth and power than with spirituality. They rejected the authority of the pope and urged a return to the teachings of the Bible and the spirit of the early Church. In many groups more democratic forms of Church government were established. Protestant Churches stress prayer, conscience and personal commitment to God rather than ritual and reliance on priests.

🕯Protestant Churches range from those of the ANGLICAN COMMUNION, which have hierarchies of priests and bishops and administer the same SACRAMENTS as the Roman Catholic Church, to extreme Puritan sects such as the QUAKERS, who have no formal structure, do not have to acknowledge the Scriptures and take none of the sacraments. Between these are denominations such as the Baptists, Congregationalists, Lutherans, Methodists and Presbyterians.

purgatory In Roman Catholic belief, a place of suffering and punishment where the souls of the dead are purified before being admitted to Heaven, where they are at last united with God.

🕯Purgatory is not mentioned anywhere in the Bible, but Catholics argue that praying for the dead is an ancient Christian practice, and one which implies that their souls must somehow be suffering.

Puritanism Extreme form of PROTESTANTISM, originating in England in the 16th century. Its followers believed that the Church of England had not gone far enough in rejecting Roman Catholic dogma and ritual. The movement included the PRESBYTERIAN and other NONCONFORMIST Churches. Persecution drove many Puritans to the Netherlands and the United States in the early 17th century.

🕯Among the Puritans were the Pilgrim Fathers who travelled to America on the ▷MAYFLOWER and who founded the first settlements in New England.

Quakers Unofficial name for the Society of Friends, a Protestant sect founded in the mid 17th century by the English religious leader George Fox. They have no priesthood or formal structure and do not take SACRAMENTS. Instead, they practise simplicity of life and worship, and stress the importance of the inner voice of the spirit. Worship, which takes place in meeting houses that are open to all, is conducted in silence until someone is moved by the spirit to speak. The movement is strongly pacifist, and committed to social reform.

rabbi In JUDAISM, a teacher and leader of a congregation, usually associated with a particular synagogue. Rabbis are responsible for the religious education and welfare of the community, and may also conduct religious services. In some synagogues women can become rabbis, and there are also some part-time rabbis.

Rama An incarnation of the Hindu god VISHNU, and hero of the epic Sanskrit poem *Ramayana*, which tells of Rama's triumph over the demon Ravana who had abducted Rama's wife Sita. Episodes from the poem are often depicted in Hindu art.

Ramadan Holy ninth month in the Islamic calendar, corresponding roughly to the Christian season of Lent. It includes a commemoration of the Night of Power, when it is believed MUHAMMAD received his revelation from the archangel Gabriel. During Ramadan, Muslims fast from dawn to dusk as a form of purification.

Rastafarianism West Indian religious movement. It developed out of the views of Marcus Garvey (1887-1940), who urged black people to return to Africa to escape oppression. Rastafarians recognise ▷HAILE SELASSIE, who became Emperor of Ethiopia in 1930, as their Messiah, and view Ethiopia as their 'promised land'. They follow a distinctive way of life involving strict dietary rules, smoking cannabis, wearing distinctive knitted hats called 'toms' and styling their hair in long 'dreadlocks'.

SILENT WORSHIP *The simple oak panelling and benches at Brigflatts in Cumbria are typical of the meeting houses in which George Fox told his followers to 'tremble at the word of the Lord' – the phrase which gave Quakers their name.*

REVOLT FROM ROME *Statues and other ornaments of the Roman Catholic Church were among the targets of the zealots of the Reformation, who attacked and condemned them as objects of superstition.*

rationalism Philosophical movement of the 17th and 18th centuries, according to which pure reasoning, rather than observation, is the source of knowledge. DESCARTES, LEIBNIZ and SPINOZA were all rationalist thinkers. They were opposed by EMPIRICISM, which stressed the importance of discovering truth through experience.

realism In modern philosophy, the view that opposes IDEALISM in maintaining that material objects exist independently of human observers. Applied to medieval philosophy, realism is the belief that abstractions such as truth and beauty have an independent existence rather than simply being qualities of individual objects.

reductionism View that entities of one kind are combinations of entities of a simpler kind and can be explained or defined in terms of the simpler entities. For example, if society is no more than a collection of individuals, psychology can explain it, and sociology is irrelevant.

Reformation Movement against the corruption and worldliness of the 16th-century ROMAN CATHOLIC CHURCH, foreshadowed by events from the 12th century onwards, but set in motion by Martin LUTHER in the early 16th century. It spread rapidly to many countries, and resulted in the establishment of PROTESTANTISM and numerous new Churches which rejected the authority of the pope. (See also REFORMATION in 'British History'.)

reincarnation Belief that after death some part of a person's identity – usually the soul – is reborn in a new human or animal body. It is one of the basic teachings of BUDDHISM and HINDUISM, and has also appeared in some Western beliefs.

Roman Catholic Church Worldwide body of Christians who recognise the spiritual authority of the POPE, which is often referred to simply as the Catholic Church. It emphasises the authority of the pope and bishops to teach on matters of faith and morality, and recognises seven SACRAMENTS: baptism, confirmation, eucharist, confession, marriage, holy orders and the anointing of the sick. Roman Catholics also venerate saints and the VIRGIN MARY, and pray to them to plead with God on their behalf. Roman Catholicism is the largest Christian denomination in the world, with more than 900 million followers.

🖎 The Roman Catholic Church does not recognise divorce, but will on certain grounds grant an annulment – official recognition that no valid marriage existed.

🖎 The Roman Catholic Church is controversial for its persistent opposition to abortion and any form of artificial contraception.

Rosh Hashanah Two-day Jewish New Year festival. It takes place at the first new moon after the autumn equinox, in late September or early October, and marks the start of a period of evaluation and prayer concluding eight days later with YOM KIPPUR, the Day of Atonement.

Rousseau, Jean-Jacques (1712-78) French philosopher, and a leading figure of the ENLIGHTENMENT. He believed that people are naturally good but are corrupted by society's false values. He also developed the idea of the general will, and argued that conformity with it had to be the guiding principle of government. Essentially concerned with the notion of freedom, Rousseau began his masterpiece *The Social Contract* (1762) with the words 'man is born free, and everywhere he is in chains'.

🖎 Rousseau's ideas were an important influence on ▷ROMANTICISM and on the ▷FRENCH REVOLUTION.

Russell, Bertrand (1872-1970) British philosopher and mathematician, known for his work in logic and the theory of knowledge. His *Principia Mathematica* (written with A.N. Whitehead) set out to show how mathematics is based on LOGIC. Russell tutored WITTGENSTEIN at Cambridge University, although they later disagreed. In 1950 Russell was awarded the Nobel prize for literature, mainly in tribute to his *History of Western Philosophy*. Russell was critical of religion, which he believed had hindered human progress.

PIPE OF PEACE *A prominent pacifist in both world wars, the philosopher Bertrand Russell became a leading figure in the Campaign for Nuclear Disarmament (CND) in the 1960s.*

Sabbath Seventh day of the week, reserved in Judaism and Christianity for rest and worship. It recognises the seventh day of creation when, according to GENESIS, God rested, and also the fourth of the TEN COMMANDMENTS: ' . . . Six days shalt thou labour . . . But the seventh day is the sabbath . . . in it thou shalt not do any work.' Jews observe the Sabbath (or Shabba, from the Hebrew word for 'rest') from nightfall on Friday until nightfall on Saturday. Most Christians celebrate the Sabbath on Sunday – possibly because Jesus was supposed to have risen from the dead on a Sunday. However, some so-called 'Sabbatarian' sects such as the SEVENTH-DAY ADVENTISTS observe Saturday as the Sabbath. In ISLAM Friday is regarded as the holy day, although it is not a day of rest.

sacrament Christian ritual considered as an outward sign of inner grace. There are seven sacraments in the Catholic and Orthodox Churches: BAPTISM, PENANCE, EUCHARIST or Holy Communion, CONFIRMATION, ORDINATION, marriage, and last rites. Many PROTESTANT faiths acknowledge only baptism and communion as sacraments, and some – such as the QUAKERS – not even these.

saint In the Roman Catholic and Orthodox Churches, saints are venerated and invoked to intercede with God on behalf of those who pray to them. Other Christian Churches recognise saints but do not permit veneration or invocation. Buddhism and Islam also acknowledge many saints to whom prayers are addressed.

salvation In Christianity, a state of union or closeness to God, and deliverance from evil – the reverse of DAMNATION. Jesus promised salvation to all who followed him, but this has not prevented disagreements among Christians as to who was saved, and whether salvation has to do with good works on Earth or only with faith. The idea of salvation is also found in other faiths, including ISLAM and BUDDHISM.

Salvation Army Christian mission, originally the Christian Revival Association, founded by William Booth in 1865 to minister to the poor of London, and now one of the biggest voluntary social work agencies in the world. The Salvation Army is organised in military fashion and is renowned for its work with the destitute and homeless, rousing brass bands, and for its collections in pubs.
♟Bernard SHAW wrote about the Salvation Army in his play *Major Barbara*.

Sartre, Jean-Paul (1905-80) French philosopher, novelist and a leading proponent of EXISTENTIALISM, as outlined in his philosophical essay *Being and Nothingness* (1943). His main concern was the nature of human existence and the freedom of human beings to create their own destiny.

Satan In Jewish and Christian belief, a fallen angel who opposes God and tempts people to commit evil – also identified as Lucifer or the DEVIL. In the early books of the Old Testament, Satan is simply an opponent or adversary. In later books and in the New Testament he is increasingly identified as the personification of evil and the archenemy of Christ.

scepticism Philosophical approach of rigorously doubting and questioning what others claim to know. It was used by DESCARTES, who hoped that if he was as critical as possible about everything people normally claimed to know, he would eventually discover something that could not be doubted. Sceptics, however, say there is no such thing as certain knowledge.

Scientology Movement founded in the 1950s by the American philosopher and science-fiction writer L. Ron Hubbard, which claims to increase spiritual awareness. Its use of dianetics, a form of psychotherapy, has been denounced as unscientific, and the sect has been criticised for seeking to influence vulnerable young people.
♟Tom Cruise, John Travolta and Lisa Marie Jackson (née Presley) are among Scientology's 8 million members.

Second Coming According to the New Testament, the future return of Jesus to Earth to judge the living and the dead and to bring about the final triumph of good over evil. The APOSTLES appeared to believe this would occur soon after their own time. Since then, many groups have propounded the imminence of Christ's appearance; they include JEHOVAH'S WITNESSES and SEVENTH-DAY ADVENTISTS.

Seventh-Day Adventists Christian denomination founded in 1863 in the USA. Adventists worship on Saturdays, abstain from alcohol and tobacco and practise adult baptism by total immersion. They believe that the SECOND COMING is imminent.

Shakers Members of the United Society for Believers in Christ's Second Appearing, which stemmed from a group of radical English QUAKERS. In 1744 the English visionary Ann Lee and eight followers emigrated to America, where they and a number of converts won respect for their orderly and prosperous communities and for their simple but beautiful artefacts, especially their furniture.
♟The name 'Shaker' refers to dancing designed to induce visionary experience.

HELPING THE POOR *William Booth, founder and first general of the Salvation Army, tirelessly campaigned to ease the sufferings of the poor and homeless. 'Sally Army' trademarks remain its military titles, brass bands and its journal* – The War Cry.

Shi'a Second-largest branch of the Islamic faith, influential mainly in Iran, Iraq and the Indian subcontinent. Adherents are known as 'Shi'ites' and follow the teachings of MUHAMMAD's cousin Ali. Shi'a Islam has its own system of law and theology, and emphasises FUNDAMENTALISM and the political role of Islam more than the main SUNNI branch.
♣One sect of Shi'ite Muslims are the Ismailis, who broke away after a schism in the 11th century under an IMAM known as the Aga Khan.

Shinto Religion of Japan. It goes back to ancient times but has little established theology. Instead, it stresses the forces of nature, which are seen as divine gifts to mankind. Natural objects are believed to symbolise gods, and the purpose of worship is seen as purification. Followers prefer to pray and place shrines in natural surroundings. The religion is officially recognised but has not been state-supported since it was disestablished after World War II.
♣Most Japanese follow both Shinto (which is concerned with the here and now) and Buddhism (for the afterlife).

Shiva (or Siva) One of the three major gods of HINDUISM, along with Brahma and Vishnu. He rules over creation and destruction, and symbolises fertility, often being represented by a phallic symbol, or lingam. Shiva is called the Lord of the Dance and is also often depicted dancing.

Sikhism Indian religion founded by the religious teacher Guru Nanak (1469-c.1539). The name 'Sikh' means disciple. Sikh belief is a combination of Hinduism and Islam, but rejects ritual in favour of meditation and simple devotion. The religion recognises a single god or creator of the Universe, and it is felt that closeness to God comes only through grace. There is considerable tension between Sikhs and Muslims, particularly in the Punjab.
♣All Sikhs take the surname Singh (Sanskrit for 'lion'). Sikh men carry ceremonial daggers and wear their hair uncut and wound up under a turban.

sin Evil that stems from actions that offend a deity. In Christianity, mankind is believed to inherit the ORIGINAL SIN of Adam and Eve, redemption from which can come only through faith and the grace of God. Roman Catholicism distinguishes between MORTAL SIN, which leads to damnation, and VENIAL SIN, which is punished in PURGATORY. In the Anglican, Roman Catholic and Orthodox Churches, sin is atoned for in collective or individual CONFESSION, but in the Reformed Churches it is considered purely a matter between the conscience of the individual and God.

Socrates (*c.*469-399 BC) Ancient Greek philosopher, generally considered the father of Western philosophy and one of its greatest minds. He conducted his speculations by means of question-and-answer discussion (DIALECTIC), and had a devoted following of wealthy young men. Socrates wrote nothing himself, but many of his dialogues are mentioned in the writings of PLATO, his pupil. Socrates, who preached ATHEISM, was primarily concerned with ETHICS and KNOWLEDGE, arguing that virtue is the same as knowledge and vice the result of ignorance. He was also an outspoken opponent of political tyranny.

Solomon Jewish king and lawgiver of the 10th century BC. He was the son of DAVID and built the first TEMPLE OF JERUSALEM. He is credited with vast wisdom and wealth, and many wives.
♣The Biblical Song of Solomon, once thought to be his work, is now thought to date from about the 3rd century BC.

♣The 'Judgment of Solomon' involved two women claiming to be the mother of a baby. Solomon decreed that the child be cut in half. When one woman said that she would rather it be given to the other, he knew that she was the real mother.

sophists Group of Greek philosophers and teachers of public speaking in the 5th century BC. They felt that genuine knowledge was impossible to achieve, and were accused by SOCRATES and PLATO of being more interested in winning arguments than in pursuing truth.
♣The term 'sophistry' refers to the use of devious or cunning argument.

Spinoza, Benedict de (1632-77) Dutch philosopher who developed a notoriously difficult system of thought set out like a series of mathematical proofs. It was founded on a form of PANTHEISM which identified God with nature, but denied the immortality of the soul and the personal nature of God. Spinoza argued that good and evil are relative terms. He also rejected FREE WILL, arguing that 'self determination' – acting in accordance with one's nature – is the only true freedom.

SEVEN DEADLY SINS *The sins seen in the Middle Ages as incurring eternal damnation were shown by Hieronymus Bosch as (clockwise from top) gluttony, sloth, lust, pride, anger, envy and covetousness.*

Stoics Ancient philosophers who advocated calm acceptance of the natural order, including death, and the overcoming of all passions, both pleasurable and painful. Stoicism was started by the Greek philosopher Zeno around 308 BC, but was later taken up in ancient Rome, notably by the writer and philosopher ▷SENECA.

🔦 The word 'stoic' comes from the Greek *stoa*, meaning a portico, after the porch of a building in Athens where Zeno taught.

Sufism Mystical sect in ISLAM, dating from the 8th century AD, which developed chiefly in Iran. Sufis live in religious communities and devote themselves to spiritual development and the search for God – often by means of chanting, music, dancing and controlled breathing. They also do charitable and educational work.

Sunni Larger of the two main branches of ISLAM, the second being SHI'A. Members recognise the first four caliphs, or leaders, as the true successors of Muhammad, and base their teachings on the KORAN and traditional Muslim law (Sunna).

syllogism Formal logical argument composed of two statements – the major and minor PREMISES – and a conclusion derived from them by DEDUCTIVE REASONING. A classic example is: *All men are mortal* (major premise); *Socrates is a man* (minor premise); therefore *Socrates is mortal* (conclusion).

Talmud Compilation of Jewish traditions, law and commentary. The rules of the Talmud are strictly followed by Orthodox Jews, but more freely interpreted in Reform and Liberal synagogues.

Taoism Ancient Chinese school of thought dating from around the 3rd century BC. It is based on the idea of *Tao* 'The Way' – an indefinable principle believed to govern the Universe – and stresses the need for harmonious interaction with the environment. Taoists aim at personal tranquillity and detachment, and at living in harmony with *Tao*. The main Taoist texts include the *Tao te Ching* attributed to LAO-TZU and the I-CHING.

Temple of Jerusalem Place of worship built by King SOLOMON in the 10th century BC for the ancient Israelites. It housed the ARK OF THE COVENANT containing the TEN COMMANDMENTS, but was destroyed in 587 BC by Nebuchadnezzar. A later temple built on the same site was also destroyed. The Western Wall in Jerusalem (also known as the Wailing Wall) was part of the

DEATH OF A PHILOSOPHER *Condemned to death for 'corrupting' the youths of Athens by his teaching, Socrates calmly drinks the deadly hemlock and dies philosophically consoling his friends.*

second Temple, destroyed by the Romans in AD 70. Jews believe the Temple will be rebuilt when their Messiah comes.

Ten Commandments (or Decalogue) Fundamental laws of JUDAISM, which are said to have been handed down by God to Moses on Mount Sinai. Slightly different commandments are given in the Books of Exodus and Deuteronomy, but the basic ten are usually accepted as being: I. I am the Lord thy God; thou shalt have no other gods before me. II. Thou shalt not make unto thee any graven image. III. Thou shalt not take the name of the Lord thy God in vain. IV. Remember the Sabbath day, to keep it holy. V. Honour thy father and thy mother. VI. Thou shalt not kill. VII. Thou shalt not commit adultery. VIII. Thou shalt not steal. IX. Thou shalt not bear false witness against thy neighbour. X. Thou shalt not covet thy neighbour's house. Thou shalt not covet thy neighbour's wife, nor his manservant, nor his maidservant, nor his ox, nor his ass, nor anything that is thy neighbour's.

theism Belief in the existence of God or the gods, particularly in a personal, all-powerful, all-knowing creator. Theism is the basic foundation of such faiths as Christianity, Islam and Judaism.

Theosophical Society Esoteric religious movement founded in 1875 by the spiritualist Madame H.P. Blavatsky. Many of her ideas were based on Eastern religion, but she developed them further into a complex system of her own. Two years after its founding the Society moved to India, where its headquarters remain. After Madame Blavatsky's death, Annie ▷BESANT took over the leadership.

torah Term which can embrace all Jewish literature, laws, customs, ceremonies and religious teachings. In a more limited sense Torah refers only to the Pentateuch (the first five books of the Old Testament); the whole Jewish Bible is normally called the Tanakh or sometimes the Miqra.

transubstantiation Roman Catholic doctrine that the bread and the wine of the EUCHARIST, or Holy Communion, are miraculously transformed after consecration 'in substance' (although not in appearance) into the body and blood of Christ. Other denominations believe either that Jesus's body and blood are only symbolically present, or that they are present together with the bread and wine (CONSUBSTANTIATION). In the Orthodox Church, Christ is believed to be present in the congregation and the church building as well as in the bread and wine.

Trinity, Holy Central Christian doctrine that God, although one, exists in the form of three 'persons'; Father, Son and Holy Spirit. Disputes about the exact relationship of the three to one another caused the split between the Orthodox and Roman Catholic Churches in the 11th century.

truth One of the most basic philosophical concepts, but without a simple, agreed definition. The common sense view that truth somehow corresponds with reality (the correspondence theory) raises problems about the nature of reality and what constitutes KNOWLEDGE. The coherence theory is equally problematic, maintaining that only complete understanding can provide truth – everything else is merely an approximation. Another approach is the 'pragmatic' theory, according to which truth is simply the point of view that is most useful in the long run.

Unitarians Christian sect that grew out of PROTESTANTISM. It rejects the central Christian doctrines of the TRINITY and the divinity of Christ, but recognises the importance of Jesus as a religious teacher.

United Reformed Church Church that was formed in 1972 by a merger between the English Presbyterian and Congregationalist Churches.

Utilitarianism Theory of ethics developed by the British philosopher Jeremy BENTHAM in the 18th century and further refined by John Stuart MILL. Its basis is the principle that actions are morally good insofar as they promote human happiness, and bad insofar as they promote pain or suffering. Versions of utilitarianism are still highly influential in moral philosophy.

venial sin In Roman Catholicism, a sin not as grave as a MORTAL SIN. It therefore does not automatically deprive the soul of salvation.

Virgin Birth Christian belief that JESUS did not have a human father, but was conceived by the VIRGIN MARY through the power of the HOLY SPIRIT.

Virgin Mary Mother of Jesus. According to the New Testament, she miraculously conceived while still a virgin and betrothed to Joseph, after the HOLY SPIRIT had visited her. She is revered throughout Christianity for her humility and maternal love, particularly by Roman Catholics who believe strongly in her mercy and her power to plead on their behalf with God. The Roman Catholic Church also teaches the doctrine of the IMMACULATE CONCEPTION – that Mary herself was born free from all stain of ORIGINAL SIN.
🔥One of the most familiar Roman Catholic prayers – known as a 'Hail Mary' – begins 'Hail Mary, full of grace, the Lord is with thee, Blessed art thou among women . . .'

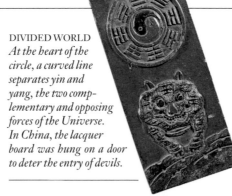

DIVIDED WORLD
At the heart of the circle, a curved line separates yin and yang, the two complementary and opposing forces of the Universe. In China, the lacquer board was hung on a door to deter the entry of devils.

Vishnu Hindu god known as the 'Preserver', and considered the embodiment of goodness and mercy. He is said to have appeared several times on Earth, including incarnations as KRISHNA and RAMA.

Voodoo Folk religion of Haiti and some other Caribbean islands, as well as some parts of Africa. It arose in the 17th century on slave plantations and contains both Roman Catholic elements and West African beliefs. Voodoo rituals involve animal sacrifice and the conjuring of spirits.
🔥Myths of zombies – mindless human beings who can be controlled by witchcraft and kept as slaves – are part of Voodoo legend and superstition.

Wesley, John (1703-91) English clergyman and founder of METHODISM. He travelled the country on horseback, preaching in the open air. He made enormous numbers of converts, particularly among labourers, miners and factory workers at huge public meetings of up to 30 000 people. He insisted that Methodism should stay within the Church of England, but it broke away four years after his death.
🔥Wesley's brother Charles was a well-known writer of hymns; his works include 'Hark the Herald Angels Sing'.

Wittgenstein, Ludwig (1889-1951) One of the most influential philosophers of the 20th century. He was born into a wealthy Austrian family, but spent much of his life in Britain. He studied under Bertrand Russell at Cambridge, where he later became professor of philosophy. Wittgenstein's early work attempted to apply strict logical criteria to language and was a major influence on LOGICAL POSITIVISM. Later he became interested in the variety and flexibility of language, and its power to shape our view of reality.
🔥In the 1920s 'to avoid having friends for the sake of . . . money' Wittgenstein gave away all his inheritance. He had several menial jobs before returning to philosophy; during World War II he worked as a porter at Guy's Hospital in London.

Yahweh Hebrew name of God deduced by modern scholars from the four consonants YHWH (the 'Tetragrammaton') which are written in Judaism but considered too sacred to be spoken. (See also JEHOVAH.)

yin and yang In Chinese and Japanese thought, two principles or qualities eternally in opposition. Yin represents femininity, darkness, coldness, passivity and the Earth; while yang represents masculinity, light, heat, activity and Heaven. Each contains a tiny fragment of the other and everything in nature is in a constant state of flux between the two.

yoga Technique used in Indian religious traditions to achieve mental tranquillity and detachment from worldly concerns. The type most frequently practised in the West is hatha yoga, based on physical postures. Other sorts of yoga focus more on breathing and meditation.

Yom Kippur (or Day of Atonement) Most solemn holy day in the Jewish year, which occurs ten days after ROSH HASHANAH. It commemorates the creation of the world, and the bond between God and the Jewish people. It is traditionally observed by fasting, prayer, repentance and silent reflection in a synagogue.

Zen Buddhism School of BUDDHISM taken to Japan from China in the 12th century. The goal of Zen is a state of deep insight known as satori. This is said to be achieved by a combination of meditation, study with a Zen master and the contemplation of riddles, or *koans*, such as 'What is the sound of one hand clapping?' Precise skills such as calligraphy and archery are also taught as a path to spiritual insight.
🔥Zen was influential among Japanese samurai warriors because of its emphasis on discipline and self-control.
🔥As an aid to meditation followers of Zen have constructed gardens of great simplicity and beauty – often consisting simply of raked gravel, a few rocks and some moss.

Zoroastrianism Persian religion founded by the prophet Zoroaster (or Zarathustra), who lived around 1000 BC. It teaches that the world is the site of a cosmic battle that is continually raging between good and evil. Eventually the good god Ahura Mazda will defeat the powers of evil.
🔥The Magi who came from the East to present gifts of gold, frankincense and myrrh to the infant Jesus in Bethlehem were probably Zoroastrian priests.

ART AND DESIGN

Art is the visual expression of civilisation: every age is
remembered for its artistic legacy. Painters and sculptors inspire
awe and delight in their quest to express themselves
and reflect the human condition. Photographers chronicle social
change as they capture moods and moments. Designers
shape and colour our everyday world, influencing the clothes
we wear and the homes we live in. Without them all
our lives would be dull and grey.

LE MOULIN DE LA GALETTE (1876) BY RENOIR

SIMPLE STYLE
*This sketch
design by Giorgio
Armani shows
his concern with
comfort as well as
elegance and his
unstructured,
understated tailoring.*

abstract art Painting and sculpture that explores form and colour, conveying an emotion or idea without using recognisable images. Wassily KANDINSKY's *Blue Rider* (1911) was one of the first abstract paintings.

acrylic Water-soluble synthetic paint which can be used thickly or thinly and allows an artist to combine the techniques of oil and watercolour paintings.

Adams, Ansel (1902-84) American photographer known for his black and white landscapes of America's western states – especially for his pictures of Yosemite National Park. Adams accentuated the tonal contrast in his photographs, giving them more depth and drama.

Amies, Hardy (AY-miss) (1910-) English couturier who has designed clothes for Queen Elizabeth II since 1950. He was also one of the first people to produce designer menswear for the mass market.

Angelico, Fra (c.1400-55) Celebrated Florentine painter known for his FRESCOES of religious subjects. His simple but realistic style made an important contribution to the flowering of RENAISSANCE art.

Annigoni, Pietro (1910-) Italian painter best known for his portraits of world leaders. His pictures of Queen Elizabeth II made him a household name in Britain. Annigoni's highly realistic style is complemented by his use of the same traditional techniques employed by the great painters of the Renaissance.

Arbus, Diane (1923-71) American photographer, best known for her stark portraits of bizarre or freakish subjects, such as midgets, transvestites and manic children with guns.

Armani, Giorgio (1935-) Italian fashion designer who has enjoyed enormous success with his modern but classic collections for men and women. He has shops in most of the world's major cities.

Art Deco Style of decoration, design and architecture popular in the late 1920s and the 1930s. Unlike the flowing forms of the earlier ART NOUVEAU movement, Art Deco used bold geometric shapes and man-made materials such as steel, glass and plastic. Art Deco designers were strongly influenced by CUBISM. (See also ▷ART DECO in 'Architecture and Engineering'.)
🕯Art Deco got its name from the first major exhibition of decorative arts after World War I – the *Exposition Internationale des Arts Décoratifs*, held in Paris in 1925.

BOLD MOVES *This 1925 headscarf shows the strong geometric forms of Art Deco which broke away from the gentle curves of Art Nouveau.*

art for art's sake Phrase meaning that art is justified simply by its beauty and does not have to serve any political, religious or economic purpose.
🕯*Ars gratia artis*, which is a loose translation of 'art for art's sake,' is the Latin motto of the film company MGM.

NATURAL GRACE *Alfonse Mucha's* Poster of a Girl *(1899) shows the flowing lines and sinuous forms which typify Art Nouveau.*

Art Nouveau Style of design and architecture popular during the 1890s which often incorporated stylised plants and the sinuous, flowing lines of the human body. It formed part of the late 19th-century reaction against the decline of craftsmanship following the Industrial Revolution and attempted to create a new form of art that broke free from tradition and history. Art Nouveau was largely inspired by the ARTS AND CRAFTS MOVEMENT – especially the work of William MORRIS. Its principal exponents included Aubrey BEARDSLEY, Charles Rennie MACKINTOSH, and René LALIQUE. (See also ▷ART NOUVEAU in 'Architecture and Engineering'.)

Arts and Crafts Movement Social and aesthetic movement in England during the late 19th century, inspired by John RUSKIN and Augustus ▷PUGIN, which sought to reassert the value of handmade objects in the face of ever-increasing mass-production. William MORRIS and Charles ▷VOYSEY led the movement, which aimed to produce objects that were individual, functional and decorative. The Arts and Crafts Movement influenced the development of ART NOUVEAU and eventually the BAUHAUS, particularly in the United States, where it flourished until World War I. (See also ▷ARTS AND CRAFTS MOVEMENT in 'Architecture and Engineering'.)

Ashley, Laura (1926-85) British designer who originally made furnishing materials in the 1950s. She later expanded into clothing design and manufacture in the 1960s. The Laura Ashley style is characterised by Romantic English designs – often with a 19th-century rural feel – and the use of natural fabrics.

Bacon, Francis (1909-92) Self-taught Irish-born artist, widely regarded as the greatest postwar British painter. His best-known work includes grotesque studies of *Figures at the Base of a Crucifixion* and dramatic portraits of screaming, tortured popes, which convey a sense of unease and alarm to the viewer.

Bailey, David (1938-) British photographer whose naturalistic style of fashion photography did much to promote British fashion in the 1960s. Bailey discovered the model Jean Shrimpton.

BAROQUE GLORY
Bernini's carved stone angel in the Church of St Andrea della Fratte in Rome shows the genre's typically flowing line and theatrical pose.

baroque Dramatic and decorative style of art and architecture that originated in Italy in the late 16th century. It spread to France, and then to Germany and Austria, where it lasted into the 18th century. Its curved lines, ornate decoration and flamboyant compositions create a theatrical effect, as seen in the works of RUBENS and BERNINI. The works of POUSSIN and CARRACCI show how the baroque also drew on the Classical tradition. It is typified by the LOUIS QUARTORZE STYLE and the work of LE BRUN. The baroque succeeded MANNERISM and was followed by the ROCOCO style of art. (See also ▷BAROQUE in 'Architecture and Engineering'.)

bas-relief Three-dimensional effect on carvings created by cutting out the background so that figures appear raised. 'Bas-relief' is French for 'low-relief'.

Bauhaus Probably the most influential school of design and architecture of the 20th century. It was founded at Weimar, in Germany, in 1919 by the architect Walter ▷GROPIUS; the school sought to mix modern technology with architecture and the decorative arts. Bauhaus designers attempted to produce functional and well-made designs – carrying on some of the earlier ideals upheld by the ARTS AND CRAFTS MOVEMENT – that could be successfully mass-produced. In 1933 the school was closed down by the Nazis, but its ideas continued to be influential, especially in the USA. (See also ▷BAUHAUS in 'Architecture and Engineering'.)

Beardsley, Aubrey (1872-98) British illustrator whose stylised black and white ART NOUVEAU drawings reflect the decadence of the times. He belonged to an aesthetic movement which included Oscar Wilde and James Whistler.

Beaton, Sir Cecil (1904-80) British photographer and designer known for his portraits of politicians, royalty and other famous people. He designed many film and stage shows, including Oscar-winning sets and costumes for the films *Gigi* and ▷MY FAIR LADY.

Bellini, Giovanni (c.1430-1516) Italian painter known for his atmospheric and luminous landscape paintings. His style strongly influenced the next generation of artists, among whom were his best-known pupils Titian and Giorgione.

Bernini, Giovanni Lorenzo (1598-1680) Italian sculptor, painter and architect who was the leading exponent of BAROQUE art. In sculpture, his skill in portraying gesture, facial expression and movement in draperies was, and probably still is, unequalled. (See also ▷BERNINI in 'Architecture and Engineering'.)

Biba Shop that epitomised the 'Swinging Sixties' in Britain. Started by Barbara Hulanicki and her husband in 1964, Biba had black and gold wallpaper, throbbing music and London's most eye-catching salesgirls. It introduced cheap new fashions in striking colours, such as olive, aubergine and gold. The business closed in 1975.

Biedermeier (BEE-der-my-er) Style of decoration and solid, comfortable-looking furniture which flourished in Austria, Scandinavia and Germany from the 1820s until the 1840s. It was the Continental equivalent of REGENCY, and its functional pieces resembled many of those inspired by the French Empire style.

Birth of Venus Painting by Sandro BOTTICELLI depicting the goddess Venus standing nude on a giant shell emerging from the foam of the sea. The painting was probably commissioned in 1484 by a member of the ▷MEDICI family.

PORTRAIT OF AN ARTIST *Cecil Beaton, photographer of royalty, celebrities and haute couture, captured in front of the camera in 1937.*

Blake, Peter (1932-) British painter who played a major role in the development of POP ART in Britain. He uses scraps from comics, pin-ups and advertisements to create pictures with an almost sentimental atmosphere. One of his best-known works is the cover of the Beatles' album *Sgt. Pepper's Lonely Hearts Club Band* (1967).

bohemian Term describing the lifestyle of artists and intellectuals who disregard conventional social standards and values. The expression, which became particularly fashionable at the end of the 19th century, was derived from the popular French belief that gypsies originally came from Bohemia, in central Europe. It was extended to apply to anyone who led an unconventional life, and especially to the dissolute artists of Paris, such as Henri TOULOUSE-LAUTREC and Amedeo MODIGLIANI.

Bonnard, Pierre (BON-arr) (1867-1947) French POST-IMPRESSIONIST painter and lithographer noted for his strong designs, use of brilliant colour and dazzling depiction of light. Apart from his paintings, Bonnard produced work for posters, decorative panels, stained glass and furniture.

Bosch, Hieronymus (*c.*1450-1516) Flemish artist widely regarded as the world's greatest painter of fantasy. His obsessive and often horrific work, full of bizarre imagery, as in *The Garden of Earthly Delights* (*c.*1500-10), is often considered to be a precursor of SURREALISM. It was also the first convincing visual depiction of evil and of human fears.

Botticelli, Sandro (BOT-ti-CHEL-lee) (*c.*1445-1510) Italian artist whose flowing draughtsmanship and religious and mythological paintings greatly influenced the Renaissance art of Florence. He was supported by the ruling Medici family, who probably commissioned his BIRTH OF VENUS. Botticelli also painted frescoes in the Sistine Chapel.

Boucher, François (BOO-shay) (1703-70) Decorative painter whose work typifies the ROCOCO style. He depicted mythological scenes in a romantic yet erotic style, and also painted landscapes, portraits and scenes of gallantry. Boucher was influenced by Veronese, Rubens and Watteau – under whom he originally worked.

UNEARTHLY VISION *The depiction of hell in Bosch's masterpiece* The Garden of Earthly Delights *brims over with grotesque images.*

Braque, Georges (BRAAK) (1882-1963) French POST-IMPRESSIONIST painter who joined the FAUVISTS in 1906 and was a close friend of Dufy and Picasso. Braque and Picasso developed CUBISM, a new approach to painting which profoundly influenced MODERN ART.

Bruegel, Pieter the Elder (BROY-gul) (c.1530-69) Flemish painter known for his amusing but sensitive pictures of peasant life, which often show scenes of drunkenness, gluttony and lechery but also include a moral message. His best-known works include *Hunters in the Snow* (1565), *The Wedding Banquet* and *The Peasant Dance* (both c.1568). His sons, Jan and Pieter the Younger, were also painters.

Burne-Jones, Sir Edward (1833-98) British PRE-RAPHAELITE painter known for his dreamy, romantic style and use of greeny-yellow tones. He was greatly influenced by Dante Gabriel Rossetti and William Morris, for whose firm he designed tapestries and stained glass.

Byzantine Style of painting and design developed in the ▷BYZANTINE EMPIRE from 330 to 1453. The Orthodox Church imposed strict constraints on art, and paintings depicted religious scenes in formal and often two-dimensional designs, with simple, stylised figures or ICONS using rich colour and gold leaf. (See also ▷BYZANTINE in 'Architecture and Engineering'.)

Calder, Alexander (1898-1976) American sculptor, painter and illustrator of children's books. Calder was originally an engineer, and his mobiles, such as *Antennae with Red and Blue Dots* (1960), are the product of marrying engineering with sculpture. His work often has an element of wit, and has inspired jewellers, painters and even wallpaper designers.

Canaletto, Antonio (1697-1768) Venetian painter known for his views of Venice and London. Canaletto was a master of light and shadow, and his extraordinarily detailed paintings, almost photographic in their realism, were both influential and popular, especially in England.

Caravaggio, Michelangelo (1573-1610) Italian painter who has become as noted for his turbulent life as for the vivid realism of his works and his rejection of idealism in his religious paintings. His mastery of light in portraiture and still life influenced Velásquez and Rembrandt. Caravaggio was imprisoned several times for violent assault. In 1606 he killed a man and spent the last four years of his life in exile in Naples, Malta and Sicily.

caricature Comic picture of a person with at least one feature exaggerated, but not to the extent that the likeness is lost. The first great artist to use caricature was Annibale CARRACCI in c.1600. William HOGARTH popularised caricatures in the 1730s, after which James GILLRAY in England and Honoré Daumier in France used them as a political weapon in satirical cartoons.

Carracci (ka-RAA-chee) Family of Bolognese painters, including Lodovico and his cousins Agostino and Annibale (1560-1609) – the greatest of the Carraccis. The family revived the Renaissance style of Raphael and set up a celebrated teaching academy. Annibale's most renowned work is the set of mythological paintings he produced for the Farnese Gallery in Rome.

Cartier-Bresson, Henri (1908-) French pioneer of photojournalism who took great care in composing and framing his photographs of people at a 'decisive moment'. He said: 'To me, photography is the simultaneous recognition, in a fraction of a second, of the significance of an event as well as a precise organisation of forms which give the event proper expression.'

cartoon In fine art, a cartoon is a preparatory sketch, usually the same size as the painting to be made from it; LEONARDO DA VINCI's cartoons are well-known examples.

Cassatt, Mary (1845-1926) American painter known for her pictures of mothers with their children, as in *The Bath* (1892). She worked mainly in France with the Impressionists and befriended Edgar Degas.

Cellini, Benvenuto (1500-71) Florentine sculptor and goldsmith. His bronze figure *Perseus* (1545-54) is possibly the finest piece of MANNERIST sculpture.
🕯Cellini's life story is generally believed to be the first true autobiography.

Cézanne, Paul (1839-1906) French painter and a member of the IMPRESSIONIST group. However, his reputation as the most important and influential painter of the 19th century is based largely on his POST-IMPRESSIONIST work. Cézanne's most celebrated works include *The Card Players* (c.1892), studies of Mont Sainte-Victoire, and still life paintings of fruit. He believed that colour and tone should be thought of together, not as separate entities. Cézanne's belief, in later life, that all forms could be reduced to cones, spheres or cylinders, led directly to the development of CUBISM and ABSTRACT ART.

ART AND DESIGN

PAINTING BY PLANES The Lake at Annecy, *painted in the summer of 1896, is evidence of Cézanne's study of the interlocking forms which make a picture, and displays his skilful use of colour.*

Chagall, Marc (sha-GAL) (1887-1985) Russian-born artist known for his brilliant use of colour and for painting recognisable objects floating in space or in unusual juxtapositions. Chagall's works of fantasy influenced the SURREALIST movement.

Chanel, Gabrielle 'Coco' (1883-1970) French fashion designer who revolutionised women's fashion in the 1920s and 1930s. She was noted for designing the 'little black dress', classic tailored ladies' suits and perfumes – especially *Chanel No. 5*. Chanel started a vogue for costume jewellery, which she also designed.
🔖 It was Coco Chanel who first made a suntan fashionable, after a holiday on the Duke of Westminster's yacht in 1927.

Chippendale, Thomas (1718-79) English cabinet-maker whose book of furniture designs, *The Gentleman and Cabinet Maker's Director* (1754), made him a household name. His elaborate and ornate work was usually in the ROCOCO style. Designs by Chippendale incorporating Chinese motifs are often called 'Chinese Chippendale'.

Cimabue (CHEEM-a-BOO-ay) (c.1240-1302) Italian artist who is generally acclaimed as the cofounder of MODERN ART – together with GIOTTO, whom he possibly taught. Cimabue began the breakaway from BYZANTINE art's stereotypical forms by giving his figures character and a three-dimensional appearance.

Classicism Approach based on the culture and art of ancient Greece and Rome, which emphasises the importance of proportion and simplicity of form. The influence of Classical art can be detected in Romanesque art. Classicism never entirely disappeared in Europe: it was revived in Florence during the 15th century, when it ultimately gave rise to the RENAISSANCE, and again in the second half of the 18th century, when it became known as NEO-CLASSICISM. (See also ▷CLASSICISM in 'World Literature'.)

Claude, Lorrain (1600-82) French pastrycook who went to Italy where he became the pupil of the landscape painter Agostino Tassi. By the end of the 1630s Claude's vast atmospheric and contrived Classical landscapes, seascapes and port scenes had become extremely popular. Although often compared with his contemporary Nicolas Poussin, Claude was more inspired by the work of late MANNERIST landscape artists – and in turn his work influenced J.M.W. Turner.

Constable, John (1776-1837) Leading English Romantic painter whose natural and fresh-looking views of the British countryside and rural landmarks are among the most familiar of all landscape paintings. Constable's paintings appear to be spontaneous likenesses of the scene, but are in fact skilfully contrived. His style greatly influenced French Romantic painters. Some paintings previously attributed to Constable are now known to have been painted by his son Lionel (1828-87).

ENGLISH IDYLL *With bold strokes and fresh colours, Constable captured unspoiled landscapes. Much of his best work, such as* The Hay Wain *(1821), was done in his native Suffolk.*

UNPOSED SCENE *The Rehearsal (1875) demonstrates Degas's interest in movement, space and the effect of light and shade on the human form – supplied here, as so often, by ballet dancers.*

Corot, Jean Baptiste Camille (KORR-oh) (1796-1875) French landscape painter who enjoyed enormous success in the latter half of his career, when he softened his Classical pictures with an evocative, slightly fuzzy style using soft grey-green tones. Corot's work had great influence on the IMPRESSIONISTS.

Cubism Art movement which analysed the geometry and structure of objects rather than their ordinary appearance. It developed out of PRIMITIVE ART, FAUVISM and Paul CÉZANNE's earlier attempts to replace IMPRESSIONISM with a less aesthetic and more intellectual approach to form and colour. The creators of Cubism were Pablo PICASSO and Georges BRAQUE. Their first exhibition was held in 1907 in Paris. After 1912 Picasso and Braque were joined by artists such as GRIS, Delaunay and Léger who took Cézanne's ideas much further by trying to express the concept of an object – often by superimposing several different views of it in one picture. Cubism opened the way for ABSTRACT ART.

Cuyp, Aelbert (KOYP) (1620-91) Versatile Dutch painter who specialised in river scenes and landscapes with animals. The soft glowing light and atmosphere of idyllic peace in his landscapes made his work popular and influential in England during the 18th and 19th centuries.

Dada Early 20th-century art group which intended to shock with its iconoclastic approach to art. It was the forerunner of SURREALISM. An example of Dadaist art is Marcel Duchamp's *Mona Lisa* (1919) – with a beard and moustache, and an obscene caption. Artists associated with the group include Max ERNST and Hans Arp.
🕯 'Dada' is a French word for a child's hobbyhorse, and was chosen at random.

Dali, Salvador (1904-89) Spanish SURREALIST painter. Influenced by psychoanalytic theories of the unconscious, he painted dream-like visions in a meticulous, photographic style. Among his best-known images are limp pocket-watches and oversized ants in harshly lit landscapes.
🕯 Dali's eccentricities included shaving off half his waxed moustache and calling his autobiography *Diary of a Genius* (1967).

David A marble statue 18 ft (5.5m) high by MICHELANGELO, depicting the young David just before his battle with Goliath. The exquisitely proportioned hero reflected Florentine civic pride, and remains a great symbol of the RENAISSANCE.

David, Jacques-Louis (da-VEED) (1748-1825) French painter who was a leading exponent of NEO-CLASSICISM. During the French Revolution he dominated French art and created powerful propaganda. His best-known paintings are the *Death of Marat* (1793), and the massive *Coronation of the Emperor Napoleon* (1805-7).

Degas, Edgar (DE-gah) (1834-1917) French painter and sculptor who was one of the first members of the IMPRESSIONIST movement. His favourite subjects included ballet dancers, young women bathing, and café scenes. He was chiefly concerned with depicting movement and often used pastels to create fluid and lively drawings.

Delacroix, Eugène (dell-a-KRWAH) (1798-1863) Leading Romantic painter in France. His brilliant use of colour, freedom of style and contemporary subject matter influenced many artists, including the Impressionists, and persuaded others to abandon neo-Classicism for Romanticism. His great rival was INGRES.

Dior, Christian (1905-57) French fashion designer who introduced a glamorous era for women in Europe and North America with his 'New Look' in 1947: dresses and outfits with narrow shoulders and long, flared skirts.

Dix, Otto (1891-1969) German painter who drew on his experiences during World War I and the Great Depression to give his pictures a bitter realism. He was persecuted and branded as a 'degenerate' by the Nazis. After World War II, Dix painted large allegorical and religious works in a more EXPRESSIONIST style.

Donatello (c.1386-1466) The greatest Florentine sculptor before Michelangelo. His work includes wood and marble carving as well as bronzes, and shows Renaissance artists' renewed interest in Classical ideals and their concern to represent the human figure in a realistic manner. Donatello influenced many artists, including Bellini and Masaccio.

Duccio di Buoninsegna (doo-CHEE-oh) (c.1255-c.1318) Italian painter whose work gave a new aura of humanity to the stern beauty of BYZANTINE art. His masterpiece, the *Maestà* (1308-11) at Siena Cathedral, displays his outstanding craftsmanship, his use of rich and subtle colour and an innovative composition.

Dufy, Raoul (doo-FAY) (1877-1953) French painter and designer of textiles and ceramics. He was influenced by Henri Matisse and FAUVISM. Dufy's work uses simple forms and bright colours, and is usually light-hearted and decorative.

Dürer, Albrecht (DOO-rur) (1471-1528) German painter, designer and engraver who created expressive and extremely detailed woodcuts and copper engravings. Dürer was greatly influenced by the Italian Renaissance and was responsible for introducing many of its ideas to his fellow artists in northern Europe. In turn, the northern realism of his work had an influence on Italian art.

Egyptian art Egyptian wall paintings and hieroglyphic picture writing provide a vivid account of life in ancient Egypt more than 3000 years ago. The ancient Egyptians' strong belief in an afterlife means that most art is found in tombs or on monuments. Features are shown from the most interesting angle or in the most characteristic light, with little resemblance to their actual form; for example, people's eyes and torsos are normally portrayed from the front while the rest of their faces and their legs are shown in profile. Egyptian art's clear lines and perfect forms, devoid of detail, influenced the development of art in ancient Greece.

Elgin Marbles Ancient Greek friezes removed from the Parthenon in Athens by the Earl of Elgin, between 1801 and 1803. Elgin's action has been strongly criticised since: he claimed that he was saving important works of art from destruction by the Ottoman Turks. In 1816 the marbles were bought from Elgin for the nation, and are housed in the British Museum.
🔊 In 1983 the Greek government asked for the marbles to be returned. The British Museum refused on the grounds that they are the marbles' legal custodians.

El Greco (1541-1614) (Real name Domenicos Theotocopoulos) One of the greatest artists of the Spanish school, best known for his religious paintings. El Greco (Spanish for 'The Greek') was born in Crete, but he moved to Italy and then settled in Spain in 1577. Although he was allegedly the last pupil of Titian, his work is much more obviously influenced by Tintoretto, Raphael, Dürer, Michelangelo and MANNERISTS such as Parmigianino. His ecstatic and passionate style was highly individual: he painted elongated figures in a stylised BYZANTINE manner. *The Burial of Count Orgaz* (1586) shows how El Greco's use of livid blues, greens, yellows and pinks gives his work an eerie appearance.

Elizabethan style Term applied to any decorative object or piece of furniture made in England during the reign of Elizabeth I (1558-1603). Furniture, usually made from oak, tended to be massive, squat and richly carved with a mix of Gothic and Renaissance motifs. Pottery and metalwork were usually very simple. (See also ▷ELIZABETHAN in 'Architecture and Engineering'.)

engraving Art of making a design on a printing block or plate. Strictly speaking, engraving refers only to designs cut into metal plates, usually made from copper, zinc, pewter or steel. This type of engraving is called 'intaglio' (Italian for 'cut into'). Mezzotints and aquatints are both types of intaglio. Engraving is also used as a generic term that covers etchings, woodcuts, linocuts and even potato cuts.

Epstein, Sir Jacob (1880-1959) American-born British sculptor whose portraits and figure groups frequently caused uproar. His monumental, aggressive, CUBIST style was often deemed obscene, but his portrait busts were widely admired.

Ernst, Max (1891-1976) German painter and sculptor of the surrealist school, and cofounder of the DADA movement. He was also one of the leading exponents of collage and photomontage.

Expressionism Early 20th-century art movement that developed from IMPRESSIONISM and aimed to convey expressions of emotion rather than mere representations of the physical world. Expressionist artists such as VAN GOGH, KOKOSCHKA, MUNCH and some FAUVIST artists exaggerated line and colour to heighten the emotional impact of their work.

Fabergé, (Peter) Carl (1846-1920) Russian goldsmith and jeweller who made a range of exquisite decorative objects such as tea services, cigarette cases and statuettes. Most famous of all are his gold and enamel eggs, encrusted with precious stones and containing miniature figures or trinkets.

HAPPY EASTER *Tsar Nicholas II presented this Fabergé egg to the Empress Alexandra Feodorovna in 1897. The golden coach fits inside.*

Fauvism Style of art that grew out of EXPRESSIONISM and used violent, contrasting colours in flat, distorted patterns. A critic first used the term *Les Fauves* (the wild beasts) to refer to a group of artists at the 1905 Paris autumn Salon who used shocking colours and peculiar patterns. The 'group' – their work was hung in the same room – included Henri MATISSE and Maurice Vlaminck. The Fauvists were later joined by Raoul DUFY and Georges BRAQUE. The style ended in 1908, when CUBISM and the influence of Pablo PICASSO became dominant.
🔊 The Die Brücke group – active in Dresden, Germany, from 1905 to 1913 – grew out of Expressionism and had many similarities to Fauvism.

Florentine Term applied to art that flourished in the city-state of Florence, Italy, during the Renaissance. Under the lavish patronage of the ▷MEDICI family, Florence replaced nearby Siena as the world's foremost centre of art. Florentine painters included GIOTTO, LEONARDO DA VINCI, MICHELANGELO and RAPHAEL.

Fragonard, Jean Honoré (1732-1806) French ROCOCO artist who painted decorative romantic and gallant scenes in clear, pastel colours. Like his teacher François BOUCHER, Fragonard painted in an erotic style: in *The Swing* (1769), one of his best-known works, he shows the legs and under-clothes of a young woman as she swings exuberantly through the air.

fresco Picture painted onto a freshly plastered wall or ceiling. *Buon fresco* – painting onto damp plaster – has proved to be one of the most durable forms of decoration. Painting onto dry plaster, known as *fresco secco*, was normally reserved for repairing an existing fresco. The great era of *buon fresco* began in Italy with GIOTTO at the end of the 13th century and ended in 1770 with the death of TIEPOLO. There have been sporadic revivals of the technique, most notably by the Mexican muralist Diego RIVERA.

Freud, Lucian (1922-) British painter and grandson of the psychoanalyst Sigmund Freud. His early work is remarkably intense and expressive, his nudes are often unsettling, and his portraits, including those of his friend Francis Bacon, are either painted close-up or set in barren interiors.

Frink, Dame Elisabeth (1930-93) British sculptor best known for her bronze horses, dogs, angular birds and menacing, oversized heads wearing goggles.

Gainsborough, Thomas (1727-88)

British landscape and portrait painter. He was influenced by many artists, but especially by Van Dyck, whose style he often copied as in his portrait *The Blue Boy* (1770). Gainsborough had superb technical skill, using long brush strokes and extremely thin oil paint and, unusually for an 18th-century artist, he never employed a 'drapery man' to fill in the background of his canvases. He used his ability for capturing a flattering likeness of his sitters to vie for royal favour with his great rival Joshua REYNOLDS. Gainsborough was one of the founding members of the Royal Academy in 1768.
🎣 The open-sided upholstered armchairs seen in many Gainsborough paintings became known as 'Gainsborough chairs'.

Gauguin, Paul (GO-gan) (1848-1903)

French POST-IMPRESSIONIST painter who, together with Cézanne and Van Gogh, had a great influence on the development of MODERN ART. Gauguin abandoned his family and his respectable job in a Paris bank to paint. He spent most of the 1890s in Tahiti, where he developed his own style of imaginative symbolism, using very bright colours and simple, flat, rather distorted forms. Gauguin's rejection of naturalism and Impressionism and his attention to the expressive power of primitive art inspired many artists, including the NABIS.

🎣 Gauguin's life has been the subject of several novels, most notably Somerset Maugham's *The Moon and Sixpence*.

Gaultier, Jean-Paul (1952-)

Innovative designer whose witty creations often mix the traditional with the strikingly new. He formed his own company in 1976 and became the 'enfant terrible' of French fashion, designing costumes for the pop star Madonna and creating skirts for men.

Georgian

Term for a variety of decorative styles popular in Britain from 1714 until about 1800. The first 16 years of the Georgian period were influenced by BAROQUE excess. Clothes were extravagant in their use of fabric, and furniture was ornate, with richly carved surfaces. Around 1730, the French ROCOCO style took hold, and its distinctive 'C' and 'S' curves were seen in mirror frames, fireplaces, wallpapers, textiles, fabric design and ceiling mouldings. Late Georgian style coincided with the reign of George III (1760 to 1820). It reflected the new influence of CLASSICISM following the rediscoveries of Herculaneum (in 1709) and Pompeii (in 1748). The work of Robert ▷ADAM and Thomas CHIPPENDALE was typical of the period. After the 1780s, under French influence, furniture makers such as HEPPLEWHITE and Sheraton used clear, elegant lines and

AT EASE *Gainsborough's relaxed picture of* Mr and Mrs Andrews *combines skilful portraiture with a reassuring view of peaceful countryside.*

rare woods from all over the world. The Georgian era was an age of superb craftsmanship funded by the immense wealth of Britain's new merchant classes, which saw an extravagant increase in the use of ceramics, porcelain, silver, copper, brass, and pewter. (See also ▷GEORGIAN in 'Architecture and Engineering'.)

Ghent Altarpiece, The

Large decorated altarpiece painted by VAN EYCK in about 1432 for Ghent Cathedral in Belgium. It consists of 20 painted panels in two rows. The upper row depicts *Christ the King* flanked by the Virgin and St John the Baptist, while the lower row depicts the *Adoration of the Lamb*. The name Hubert van Eyck appears on the altarpiece alongside his brother's. Art historians still debate the importance of Hubert's contribution, but almost nothing is known about him.

Ghiberti, Lorenzo (1378-1455)

Italian sculptor, goldsmith, writer, architect and designer who was a major figure in the transition between GOTHIC and RENAISSANCE art. He is best remembered for his bronze sculpted doors of the baptistery in

ART GALLERIES AND MUSEUMS OF THE WORLD

Bavarian State Art Gallery (Alte Pinakothek)	Munich	14th to 19th-century European paintings including a large Rubens collection.
British Museum	London	Largest museum in Britain, which houses a vast collection of 14th to 19th-century prints and drawings and the Elgin Marbles.
Burrell Collection	Glasgow	19th-century French and Impressionist paintings, Chinese bronzes and medieval tapestries.
Getty Museum	Los Angeles	World's richest art gallery. Greek and Roman antiquities, pre-20th-century European art (including Van Gogh's *Irises*) and 19th to 20th-century American photographs, housed in a reconstruction of a Roman villa.
Guggenheim Museum	New York City	European and American post-Impressionist and modern art housed in a building designed by Frank Lloyd-Wright.
Hermitage	St Petersburg	Largest collection of art in the world – mainly 16th to 19th-century European and Russian works.
Louvre	Paris	14th to 19th-century European paintings and sculpture, including Leonardo da Vinci's *Mona Lisa*, and Egyptian, oriental, Roman and Greek antiquities, including the *Venus de Milo*.
Metropolitan Museum of Art	New York City	Wide range of European and American paintings, furniture and decorative objects, including period room reconstructions.
Musée d'Orsay	Paris	Former railway station housing 19th and early 20th-century art, including Manet's *Olympia*.
Museum of Modern Art (MOMA)	New York City	Modern art from 1880 onwards, including Van Gogh's *Starry Night*, Picasso's *Guernica* and some of Monet's *Waterlilies*.
National Gallery (includes National Portrait Gallery)	London	Collection of 14th to 20th-century European paintings, including Constable's *Hay Wain* and Turner's *Fighting Téméraire*. The Sainsbury wing opened in 1991. The National Portrait Gallery provides a visual history of Britain's best-known people from the 16th century onwards.
Prado	Madrid	12th to 19th-century Spanish and European art including the largest collection of paintings by Velásquez and Bosch.
Rijksmuseum	Amsterdam	15th to 19th-century Dutch and European paintings. Finest collection of Rembrandts in the world, including *The Night Watch*.
Tate Gallery	London	British paintings from 1500 onwards including several rooms devoted to Turner. Also large exhibitions of modern paintings, sculpture and drawings from all over the world.
Uffizi	Florence	13th to 18th-century Italian and European art making up the greatest collection of Renaissance paintings in the world. Botticelli, Leonardo da Vinci, Raphael, Michelangelo and Rubens all have rooms devoted to them. The Botticelli room contains *Primavera* and *The Birth of Venus*.
Victoria and Albert Museum	London	World's largest collection of decorative art from all periods of history and from all over the world. Commonly known as the 'V & A'.
Vienna Art Museum (Kunsthistorisches)	Vienna	15th to 20th-century European paintings including the largest museum collection of Bruegels.

Florence Cathedral which depict scenes from the Old and New Testaments. Michelangelo said the latter were worthy to be the gates of paradise. Uccello and Donatello both trained in Ghiberti's workshop .
♣ Ghiberti's *Commentaries* – incomplete and written throughout his life – give a fascinating account of his own career and of Italian art history.

Giacometti, Alberto (1901-66) Swiss sculptor, painter and poet of highly individual works. He joined the SURREALISTS in the 1930s, and made witty 'still-life' sculptures such as *The Palace at 4am* (1932-3). After 1945 he created tall, spidery 'thin men' sculptures in bronze.

Gill, Eric (1882-1940) Prolific and eccentric British engraver, illustrator, sculptor and typographer. Gill became a Roman Catholic in 1913 and was inspired by medieval religious attitudes to art, mysticism, and his socialist beliefs. He is best remembered for his plain square-cut typeface – 'Gill Sans Serif' – which became a symbol of ▷MODERNISM in the 1930s and is still widely used today.

Gillray, James (1757-1815) English artist whose savagely witty but often coarse caricatures lampooned people such as Napoleon I, George III and other contemporary personalities. His vicious satires were inspired by William HOGARTH.

Giorgione (jaw-gee–OH-nee) (*c.*1477-1510) Venetian who was the first artist to clearly portray people's mood or character in his portraits. He was enormously influential – despite the fact that he did not leave a single signed and dated painting. Giorgione mostly painted religious works commissioned by churches, but he is best known for his smaller oil paintings which depict scenes in an evocative and poetic style. *The Tempest* (date unknown), for example, creates a powerful sense of the heat and tension of an approaching storm.

Giotto (JOTTO) (*c.*1266-1337) Florentine artist who, with CIMABUE, is widely regarded as the founder of Western painting because of the way his realistic and expressive style broke away from the more stylised BYZANTINE tradition. Giotto was also one of the first artists to create the illusion of space and volume by the use of perspective. His powerful religious frescoes can be found in Padua, Assisi and Florence. Giotto greatly influenced the next generation of Florentine artists which heralded the dawn of the Renaissance.

Glaser, Milton (1929-) American graphic designer whose work uses a great diversity of styles and has covered everything from labels and packaging to corporate identity, shopfittings and magazine design. His new designs for *Paris Match* and *Esquire* magazines, among others, gained him international recognition.
🪶 Glaser's best-known design is I❤NY.

Goya, Francisco de (1746-1828) Spanish artist considered one of the world's greatest portrait painters. He gave an extraordinary insight into the character of his sitters and had an unusual freedom of style inspired by Velásquez. Goya was also an outstanding draughtsman, and his etchings record the political, social and religious climate of his time with intense realism – as in the *Disasters of War* series (1810-20) which record the horrors of the Napoleonic wars. He influenced 19th-century French painters, especially Édouard Manet.
🪶 In his later years, Goya, who was profoundly deaf from 1794, produced the so-called 'Black Paintings' – dark, grim visions of human fear and cruelty.

Grandma Moses (1860-1961) American NAÏVE artist who painted endearing and intimate scenes of farms and country life. She was completely self-taught, and did not start painting until her late seventies. Her 100th birthday was declared 'Grandma Moses Day' in New York State.

SPANISH BEAUTY *The clarity and strength of Goya's style shines out in this lively portrait of the beautiful Dona Isabel de Porcel.*

Grand Tour Extended educational tour of Continental Europe taken by fashionable and wealthy young men, particularly the British, during the 18th century. Some tours could last as long as five years, while the young men (often accompanied by their tutors) viewed the Continent's scenery, art, architecture, and Classical antiquities. It was usual to paint and draw and to buy and bring back other works of art.

graphic arts Term that applies to any form of drawing or engraving, or any piece of art that depends more on line than on colour for its effect.

Gris, Juan (GREES) (1887-1927) Spanish artist who turned to CUBISM under the influence of Picasso. He helped define the style and developed a personal version where each work began as 'flat coloured architecture'. He also designed costumes and stage sets for ▷DIAGHILEV.

Guardi, Francesco (1712-93) Best-known member of a family of artists who worked in Venice. Guardi is usually remembered for his views of Venice which, unlike the minutely detailed studies of his contemporary Canaletto, capture the atmosphere of the city in a free and evocative style. Guardi's brother, Giovanni, and his brother-in-law Giambattista Tiepolo were also important painters.

Habitat Chain of stores which brought modern furniture and interior design to the British general public. The chain, founded in the 1960s by Terence Conran, was the first to offer a complete range of stylish but practical domestic products at low prices. Conran's functional, attractive and often brightly coloured designs of furniture, ceramics and textiles have won many awards.

Hals, Frans (*c.*1580-1666) Dutch portrait painter whose lively domestic scenes and portraits, such as the much-reproduced *The Laughing Cavalier* (1624), show genius in catching a subject's fleeting expression. Hals often painted *alla prima* – painting onto canvas without preliminary drawing or underpainting. Hals's formal commissioned civic group portraits, which he painted later in his life, are more reflective and show greater insight than he demonstrated in his earlier, more showy style.

Hamnett, Katherine (1948-) British fashion designer, best known for her enormous T-shirts emblazoned with controversial political and social statements which were particularly popular in the 1980s.

TOP TABLE
Hepplewhite's 18th-century design for a pier table marries an elegant, ornamental style with functionality.

Hepplewhite, George (*d.*1786) English cabinet-maker who became well known two years after his death when his book of furniture designs, *Cabinet-Maker and Upholsterer's Guide*, was published. The neo-Classical designs combine elegance with utility. However, little is known of Hepplewhite's life, and no piece of furniture can definitely be ascribed to him.

Hepworth, Dame Barbara (1903-75) One of the first British abstract sculptors. Like Henry MOORE, she made no preliminary models and carved directly into wood and stone. Hepworth also used bronze towards the end of her life. She belonged to a group of English artists living at ▷ST IVES in Cornwall, and was married to the abstract painter Ben NICHOLSON. She died tragically – in a fire at her studio.

Hicks, David (1929-) British interior designer famous for 'the mix' – old and new ideas combined in a simple but grand style. His early work used bold juxtapositions of bright colours and unusual arrangements of objects. He also creates 'tablescapes' – displays of objects on a table.

hieroglyphs Egyptian pictorial script, in use from about 3000 BC to AD 300. The word *hieroglyph* is Greek for 'sacred carving'; hieroglyph writing was originally used in temples and on tombs. The symbols, which were usually arranged from right to left, could represent either the actual object shown, or else separate consonants spelling out the sound of a complete word. Hieratics were a simplified form of hieroglyphs for faster writing with a brush and ink on the smooth surfaces of wood or papyrus. Hieroglyphs and hieratics used the same stylised forms which appear in all Egyptian art.
🪶 A cartouche – a defined oval or oblong area containing hieroglyphs – showed the name of a royal or divine personage.

Hilliard, Nicholas (*c.*1547-1619)
English painter noted for his miniatures.
He used his training as a goldsmith to make
elaborate jewelled cases for his small and
intricate pictures. Hilliard also painted
full-scale portraits, including several of
Elizabeth I. His linear, shadowless and
meticulously detailed style was based on
the exquisite miniatures of Hans HOLBEIN.
Hilliard's best-known miniature is of an
Elizabethan nobleman entitled *Young Man
Among Roses* (*c.*1587).

Hockney, David (1937-) Bradford-
born painter, etcher, set-designer and
film-maker who became the best-known
British artist of his generation. Hockney,
now resident in California, usually uses
acrylic paint in strong, light colours in his
portraits or paintings. His early work,
which had a flat, naïve style incorporating
bold, simple forms, was associated with POP
ART. Many of his paintings explore the
effect of light on reflecting objects, such as
water and glass, and some have a frank
homosexual content. Among his best-
known works are *A Bigger Splash* (1967) and
The Rake's Progress (1961-3). Hockney has
also designed opera productions and
experimented with photomontage. He has
even created artworks with fax machines.

BIG HEAT, COOL WATER *The sunshine and
swimming pools of California inspired David
Hockney to paint* A Bigger Splash (1967).

Hogarth, William (1697-1764) One of Britain's most original and influential painters and engravers. Hogarth began painting small portrait groups, called conversation pieces. He then invented the genre for which he is best remembered – moral narrative – using paintings to tell a story and expose the follies of the age, as in *A Rake's Progress* (1733-5).

Holbein the Younger, Hans (c.1497-1543) German artist and one of the greatest north European portrait painters. He originally worked in the workshop of his father – Hans Holbein the Elder (c.1465-1524). Holbein the Younger's pictures were remarkable for their realism; he painted his subjects' faces or costumes in minute detail, and captured their characters with relentless accuracy. Holbein gained an international reputation as a portrait artist, and in 1532 he settled in London where he became court painter to Henry VIII.

Hopper, Edward (1882-1967) American painter best known for his depictions of city scenes, such as cinemas, shops and offices. His pictures, which often feature carefully placed solitary figures, convey an eerie sense of loneliness and melancholy.

Hunt, William Holman (1827-1910) English painter and cofounder of the PRE-RAPHAELITE BROTHERHOOD. Hunt was the only member of the group to remain faithful to its ideals. This can be seen in his best-known paintings, such as his two versions of *The Light of the World*.

icon Image of a saint, religious figure or sacred event which is used as an object of Christian devotion. Icons are usually painted in oils on wood in a two-dimensional BYZANTINE style. Examples date back to the 5th century AD, and the style has remained virtually unchanged. Icons still play an important part in the Greek and Russian Orthodox churches.
🕯In 8th-century Byzantium and in 16th-century Europe there was a reaction against icons by iconoclasts, or 'image-breakers', who believed that icons were idolatrous.

Impressionism Movement in 19th-century painting from which MODERN ART evolved. The Impressionists abandoned traditional methods of composition, drawing and perspective in favour of painting more spontaneously to capture a particular moment. The artists aimed to achieve greater naturalism, and preferred to paint outdoors – where they were fascinated by changing colour and light. They often used primary colours and small brush strokes to simulate reflected light. The artists who exhibited in the eight Impressionist exhibitions from 1874 to 1886 were MONET, DEGAS, PISSARRO, MORISOT, RENOIR and SISLEY.
🕯The movement's name was coined by a critic – in a derisive sense – from the title of Monet's work *Impression: Sunrise* (1872).
🕯A key factor in the development of Impressionism was the manufacture of paint in tubes which enabled artists to leave their studios and work outdoors.

Ingres, Jean (ANG-ruh) (1780-1867) French painter who specialised in painting portraits, religious and historical scenes. Ingres's draughtsmanship and style led him to champion NEO-CLASSICISM against the increasingly popular wave of ROMANTI-CISM, led by DELACROIX, with its emphasis on colour. Ingres was influenced by the work of Raphael, as can be seen in one of his best-known paintings *The Bather* (1808), which shows a rear view of a naked woman just after she has had her bath.

Issigonis, Sir Alec (1906-88) British car engineer and designer, born in Turkey. He is remembered for designing three cars: the Morris Minor of 1948, the Mini of 1959 and the Morris 1100 of 1962. All combined innovative though quite simple technology (such as rubber or hydraulic suspension) with skilful use of space. The enduring Mini has been particularly popular; it remains both cheap and fashionable.

Japonism Vogue for Japanese art in mid 19th-century Europe, soon after it started arriving in the West. The simplified forms, flat areas of colours and unusual perspective of Japanese prints, especially those of the master Hokusai, greatly influenced Impressionist artists such as Whistler and Van Gogh, as well as later exponents of ART NOUVEAU such as Aubrey Beardsley.

John, Augustus (1878-1961) British painter remembered as much for his rebellious and passionate character as for his bold and colourful portraits and drawings of gypsy life. His sister was Gwen JOHN.

John, Gwen (1876-1939) Painter whose work was little appreciated during her lifetime but who is now regarded as one of the most important British female artists. She was very different from her exuberant brother, Augustus JOHN. She often painted timid, introspective studies of young girls, on a small scale and in muted colours. John spent most of her life living in Paris, where she studied with James Whistler and was the mistress of the sculptor Auguste Rodin.

Johns, Jasper (1930-) American artist often regarded as the father of POP ART, and one of the outstanding figures of post-World War II art. In his bold, flat paintings and sculptures Johns uses collage, metal, plastic and bronze as well as paint. His themes include flags, targets, numbers and letters, and he casts everyday objects such as lightbulbs and beer cans in bronze.

STARS AND STRIPES *Jasper Johns' Three Flags (1958), a three-dimensional work made from encaustic (coloured wax fixed with heat) on canvas, was sold for $1 million in 1980.*

ART AND DESIGN

SLEEPING BEAUTIES *The Young Girl (1912-13) is classic Klimt: a languid, erotic scene rendered in rich, jewel-like colours. His decadent life and paintings scandalised Austria's art establishment.*

Kandinsky, Wassily (1866-1944)
Russian-born painter and pioneer of ABSTRACT ART. He had been influenced by ART NOUVEAU and FAUVISM before painting his first purely abstract picture, *Blue Rider*, in 1911. Kandinsky was interested in the relations between colour, music, philosophy and religion. His work did not really become influential until he was teaching at the BAUHAUS school of design from the early 1920s until 1933.

Karsh, Yousouf (1908-)
Armenian-born photographer whose sharp and extraordinarily detailed portraits appear to give great insight into the characters of subjects such as Winston Churchill, Jawarharlal Nehru and Pablo Picasso.

kinetic art
Painting and sculpture that incorporates real or apparent movement, often using an optical illusion, artificial lighting or a motor. Alexander CALDER's mobiles are an example of kinetic art.

Klee, Paul (clay) (1879-1940)
Swiss painter and etcher, and one of the 20th century's most original artists. His style is characterised by precise draughtsmanship combined with free fantasy. Klee described some of his small, exquisitely painted abstract pictures as 'taking a line for a walk'. His wit, inspired use of colour and complete lack of pretentiousness make some of his works appear almost childlike.

Klein, Calvin (1942-)
American fashion designer best known for his figure-hugging underwear ranges (with his name printed on the waistbands) and for his 'designer' jeans and casual sportswear.

Klimt, Gustav (1862-1918)
Austrian decorator and painter known for his sensuous pictures of women painted against brilliant, bejewelled backgrounds and for his mosaics and murals. His best-known work is *The Kiss* (1908), which shows a couple embracing amid a myriad of colours and gold. His work influenced Egon Schiele and Oskar Kokoschka. Klimt was a founder of the Vienna Sezession – the Austrian equivalent of ART NOUVEAU.

Kneller, Sir Godfrey (1646-1723)
German-born artist who settled in England in 1674 and quickly became the country's leading portrait painter. His best-known works are 42 portraits known as the 'Kit Cat' series (1702-17), portraying the members of a London Whig club.

Kokoschka, Oskar (1886-1980)
Austrian artist and writer and one of the major EXPRESSIONIST painters of the 20th century. His imaginative and vivid style was influenced by the work of Gustav Klimt. Kokoschka is best known for his brightly coloured and rather restless portraits, allegorical pictures, and urban landscapes often painted from a curiously high viewpoint.

Lagerfeld, Karl (1938-)
One of the most prolific and successful modern fashion designers. He was born in Germany but has spent most of his working life in France and Italy. His best-known work has been for the CHANEL fashion house, whose classic designs he has wittily updated.

Lalique, René (1860-1945)
French jeweller and glassmaker who was one of the leading exponents of ART NOUVEAU and ART DECO. He began designing perfume bottles for Coty in 1907, and from 1910 he concentrated on glassware, creating a huge range – from figurines and vases to commercial perfume bottles.

Landseer, Sir Edwin (1802-73)
English artist known for his paintings of animals and for his sculptures – in particular the four lions round Nelson's column in London's Trafalgar Square (1859-66). His best-known painting is *The Monarch of the Glen* (1850), which depicts a majestic stag standing against rugged Scottish scenery. Landseer's sentimental pictures of animals were extremely popular, and were especially admired by Queen Victoria.

Larson, Gary (1950-)
American cartoonist with an off-beat sense of humour, best known for his *The Far Side* series which appears in nearly 2000 daily and Sunday newspapers worldwide. Far Side collections published in book form have sold more than 21 million copies worldwide.

BIZARRE HUMOUR *Gary Larson's surreal cartoons, which often feature animals in everyday human situations, expose the absurdity of life in a modern urban environment.*

To Ernie's horror, and the ultimate disaster of all, one more elephant tried to squeeze on.

Last Supper, The Fresco painted by LEONARDO DA VINCI in *c*.1497 depicting the moment when Jesus reveals to his disciples that one of them will betray him.
♪ For *The Last Supper*, Leonardo applied oil paint straight onto plaster, which resulted in rapid deterioration. The fresco has been periodically restored since the 16th century, and it needs continual upkeep.

Lauren, Ralph (1939-) American clothes designer whose Polo label ranges from classic semi-formal 'Ivy-League' styles to native American designs.

Lawrence, Sir Thomas (1769-1830) English portrait artist who became the most fashionable painter of his day when he was only 20, after painting George III's wife, Queen Charlotte, in 1789.

DECAYED MASTERPIECE *Da Vinci's mural of* The Last Supper *has been badly damaged, partly by several clumsy attempts at restoration.*

EASTERN INFLUENCE *Bernard Leach learned the potter's art in Japan, and produced simple stoneware from his pottery in St Ives, Cornwall.*

Leach, Bernard (1887-1979) Generally considered the greatest and most influential British potter. Leach studied ceramics in Japan for 12 years and on his return to Britain in 1920 he established a pottery in St Ives, Cornwall. His work always has a simple, almost austere, practical quality.

Le Brun, Charles (1619-90) Chief designer of the LOUIS QUATORZE style. He ran the Gobelins factory, the European centre of tapestry-making, from 1663 and was director of the French Academy. Le Brun's elegant and decorative CLASSICISM

exerted an influence on French art for generations. He oversaw the interior decoration of the Palace of Versailles and designed several rooms, including the *Galerie des Glaces* 'Hall of Mirrors' (1679-84).

Lely, Sir Peter (1618-80) The most influential portrait painter in England in the second half of the 17th century. Lely was of Dutch origin, but he settled in London in the early 1640s. He was influenced by VAN DYCK, whom he emulated when he became principal painter to Charles II in 1661. Lely ran a highly organised studio that produced hundreds of BAROQUE portraits, capturing the fashionable and decadent languor of Charles II's court during the ▷RESTORATION.

Leonardo da Vinci (1452-1519) Italian artist and possibly the most versatile genius who ever lived. The illegitimate son of a Florentine lawyer, Leonardo was the embodiment of what came to be called Renaissance man – one skilled in a wide

range of activities. His fields of research included anatomy, botany, hydraulics, engineering, mathematics and philosophy, as well as sculpture and painting. Very few of Leonardo's paintings, however, were completed. He left *The Adoration of the Magi* (1481) unfinished in Florence and went to Milan, where he produced his most famous early work, the LAST SUPPER (*c.*1497). In *c.*1503 he painted the enigmatic MONA LISA – the world's most famous portrait. Leonardo experimented with different techniques and mediums and perfected a subtle method for differentiating light and shade known as SFUMATO. His notebooks contain sketches of flowers and animals, studies of human anatomy, and architectural and technical drawings, including a design for a ▷HELICOPTER. His influence on the development of art, and on other artists of his age such as Michelangelo and Raphael, was immense.

Liberty, Sir Arthur Lasenby (1843-1917) Promoter of ART NOUVEAU and founder of Liberty's store in London's Regent Street, a large department store which pioneered the importing of foreign decorative goods. The store commissioned many lasting designs, especially of textiles – the so-called 'Liberty prints'.

Lichtenstein, Roy (1923-) American artist who became one of the leading exponents of POP ART in the 1960s. He is best known for his large pictures based on advertising imagery and strip cartoons. Many of his paintings imitate the coarse dots used in some printing processes.

Louis Quatorze (ka-TORZ) French style of furniture and decoration popular in France from the 1640s to about 1715. It closely mirrored the taste of King ▷LOUIS XIV and his finance minister Jean-Baptiste Colbert, and tempered richness with Classical restraint. It was a grand, masculine, militaristic style, taking many motifs from ancient Rome – such as shields, eagles, and palms. Sumptuously gilded furniture made in the BAROQUE style was created in the royal workshops to adorn many palaces, including ▷VERSAILLES.

Louis Quinze (KANZ) Main style of interior design and furnishings in France from about 1720 to 1750, named after Louis XV. It was an elegant, light-hearted and feminine style, using nature's curves – a reaction to the ostentatious LOUIS QUATORZE style. However, it encompassed the elaborate ROCOCO style which, during the mid 18th century, spread through Europe.

Louis Seize (SEHZ) French style of design and decoration profoundly influenced by the renewed interest in CLASSICISM prompted by the discovery of the ancient cities of Pompeii and Herculaneum. It began in the 1750s, some 20 years before ▷LOUIS XVI came to the throne, and lasted until the outbreak of the French Revolution in 1789. It rejected ROCOCO excesses, using Classical motifs such as key patterns and caryatids, and straighter, more elegant lines. It coincided with the late GEORGIAN period in Britain.

Lowry, L.S. (1887-1976) English artist known for his highly original paintings of stick-like figures in almost monochromatic industrial, urban landscapes. The earliest date from the 1920s and most are set in and around his home town Salford in Lancashire, where he spent most of his life.

Mackintosh, Charles Rennie (1868-1928) Scottish designer and architect who was one of the most notable exponents of ART NOUVEAU. Mackintosh combined the languid curves of Art Nouveau with the crisp rectangular forms that were to characterise the work of many 20th-century

STRAIGHT AND NARROW *This ladder-back chair by Mackintosh is on view in Hill House, Helensburgh, of which he was the architect.*

architects. He is known for his modern interiors and rectilinear, often inlaid furniture – especially high-backed chairs. He had little influence in Britain but was highly regarded in Austria, Germany and Italy, where artists were abandoning Art Nouveau for a clearer style. Some of his designs are still made. (See also ▷MACKINTOSH in 'Architecture and Engineering'.)

Magritte, René (1898-1967) Belgian SURREALIST painter. Rather like Salvador Dali, whom he befriended in Paris during the late 1920s, Magritte developed a meticulous, dream-like, almost photographic style. His paintings can be both witty and disturbing, and often incorporate outsized objects – an apple or a comb might fill a room. Among the bizarre images he created were a burning tuba, a steam train emerging from a fireplace and bowler-hatted men floating in midair.

Manet, Édouard (man-AY) (1832-83) French artist who is widely regarded as the precursor of IMPRESSIONISM, although he was not a member of the movement. His style was inspired by his study of Velásquez, Goya and Hals, and he was essentially an academic painter with traditional motivations, who resented being seen as the leader of the Impressionists. Manet developed a style that relied on the opposition of light and shadow, with as little halftone as possible. He avoided idealising his subjects, and painted without detailed preliminary studies. Although this gave Manet's work an immediacy and freshness, it provoked bitter attacks from the critics who thought he was merely ignorant or inept. One of Manet's famous paintings, *Déjeuner sur l'herbe* (1863) – which portrays two naked women having a picnic with two fully clothed men – scandalised traditionalists and was rejected by the French Academy or 'Salon' – the only public art exhibition in Paris. However, his *Olympia* (1863), a reclining female nude, was accepted. In the 1870s, partly influenced by his friend and sister-in-law Berthe Morisot, Manet began to use lighter, softer colours and adopted a looser technique. It was only towards the end of Manet's life that the critics began to respect his work.

Mannerism Style of art prevalent in Italy, France and Spain from *c.*1520 to 1600 – between the High RENAISSANCE and the emergence of the BAROQUE. Italian Mannerists such as Francesco PARMIGIANINO exaggerated the styles of Michelangelo and Raphael to create striking and theatrical visual effects, using heightened colour and

POND-LIFE *The characteristics of a typical Lowry painting, from smoking factory chimneys to dogs and stick-like figures at work and play, are all represented in his 1950 urban landscape* The Pond.

distorted scale and perspective. The Mannerist painters used elongated or over-muscular figures to give a greater sense of movement and expression. The work of EL GRECO is often described as Mannerist.
🔖 The term derives from the Italian *maniera* which means 'contrived expressiveness'.

Mantegna, Andrea (man-TAIN-ya) (c.1431-1506) Italian early Renaissance artist who was greatly influenced by DONATELLO. He studied Greek and Roman archaeology, which is reflected in his use of Classical architecture and sculptural forms. Mantegna was the first artist to paint a *sotto in sù* (Italian for 'from below upwards') – an illusion achieved by dramatic foreshortening in which the ceiling appears to be open to a sky where figures seem to float above the viewer. This technique later became popular in BAROQUE decoration. Mantegna, his brother-in-law Giovanni Bellini and Albrecht Dürer had a profound influence on each other's work. Mantegna was one of the first Italian artists to experiment with ENGRAVING.

Martini, Simone (c.1284-1344) Pupil of the Sienese painter DUCCIO. Martini's graceful use of outline and the decorative richness of his religious and courtly paintings influenced many Italian artists. The grand and elegant style of his best-known work, the *Annunciation* (1333), is reminiscent of Byzantine and French Gothic art.

Masaccio (ma-SARCH-ee-oh) (1401-c.1428) Florentine artist whose understanding of light, form and realistic perspective built on the art of GIOTTO. His innovations gave his work a much greater degree of realism, in keeping with the intellectual approach developed by his contemporaries – ▷BRUNELLESCHI (in architecture) and DONATELLO (in sculpture). Masaccio's frescoes in the church of Santa Maria del Carmine in Florence were an inspiration to many artists, including Michelangelo, who emulated their grand, realistic and heroic style in his ceiling frescoes in the Sistine Chapel.

Matisse, Henri (1869-1954) French artist whose simple, bold and colourful work profoundly influenced 20th-century painting and design. Early in his career Matisse was influenced by Impressionism and worked with BONNARD and Édouard Vuillard. However, it was the paintings of Cézanne which inspired him to create his own style of highly coloured neo-Impressionism. Matisse was also greatly influenced by the bright pigments and complex, intertwined forms of near eastern decorative art. By 1905 his use of bright, pure colours and simple designs – such as *Luxe, Calme et Volupté* (1904) – had made him the leading exponent of FAUVISM. Although he admired the Cubists, Matisse never joined them. His career culminated in the huge murals of the *Dance* (1932-3), based on paintings on the same theme created in 1909-10, and his well-known 'cut-outs' – collages of coloured paper which he created towards the end of his life, when he was crippled with arthritis.
🔖 Matisse wrote in his autobiographical *Notes of a Painter* (1908): 'What I dream [of] is an art of balance, purity and serenity . . . something like a good armchair in which to rest from physical fatigue.'

MOULD-BREAKER *Manet's depiction of female nakedness with fully clothed men in* Déjeuner sur l'herbe *flouted artistic conventions, shocked the critics, but led to the birth of Impressionism.*

medium Term for the method and materials used in art. For example, painting is a different medium from sculpture, and acrylic paint is a different medium from oil paint. A work of art using more than one medium – collage and paint, for example – is described as mixed media. The term can also refer to water, oil, turpentine or varnish added to paint for an effect.

Memling (or Memlinc), Hans (c.1430-94) Flemish painter known for his serene but restrained religious paintings, such as the *Donne Triptych* (c.1477). Memling is usually thought of as a painter of devotional works, but he also painted sensitive portraits of great integrity for his Italian patrons and for wealthier inhabitants of Bruges, where he lived all his life.

Michelangelo Buonarroti (1475-1564) Italian painter, sculptor, architect, and poet who was one of the greatest artists of all time. Michelangelo grew up and trained in Florence, but he created his first major sculptures in Rome, a PIETÀ (1499) and *Bacchus* (1496-7). Back in Florence, he completed his famous sculpture of DAVID in 1504. Pope Julius II asked Michelangelo to paint the ceiling of the Sistine Chapel. Working almost totally unaided and lying on his back on precarious planking, Michelangelo took four years (1508-12) to paint the ceiling's Old Testament scenes – including *The Creation of Adam*, *The Deluge* and *The Drunkenness of Noah*. The ceiling, which combined Classical Renaissance heroic forms with Christian themes, inspired awe in his contemporaries. Later,

between 1536 and 1541, Michelangelo painted the *Last Judgement* on the Sistine Chapel's altar wall. At the age of 71, he was appointed chief architect of ▷ST PETER'S BASILICA. Just before he died, when he was 89, he was still writing poetry and finishing the moving and stylised *Rondanini Pietà*.

♣ Michelangelo had deep religious convictions, and he often said that his tireless work was inspired by the glory of God.

♣ Michelangelo's most challenging commission was a tomb for Pope Julius II. He worked on it for nearly 40 years, during which the design was changed many times. The striking figures of *Slaves* (1513-16) – now in the Louvre, Paris – were intended for the tomb, but were judged unsuitable. The final version was completed in 1545, but *Moses* was the only figure made by Michelangelo himself.

♣ Together with Leonardo da Vinci and Raphael, Michelangelo changed the status of artists – hitherto thought of as mere craftsmen. In fact, while still in his thirties, he was called *il divino* 'the divine', because of his remarkable talent.

Millais, Sir John Everett (1829-96)

English painter who was one of the founders of the PRE-RAPHAELITE BROTHERHOOD. As he became more successful, he softened the brightly coloured and detailed style so typical of paintings of the Pre-Raphaelites, and began producing more

IN HIS OWN IMAGE The Creation of Adam, *one of Michelangelo's ceiling frescoes in the Sistine Chapel, is one of the best-known and most memorable images of the Renaissance.*

sentimental paintings. By the end of his career he had become a highly respected portrait painter and was in constant demand among English society's leading figures. Millais was appointed president of the Royal Academy in 1896.

🕯 Millais's best-known painting, *Bubbles* (1886), was used for several years to advertise the soap made by A. & F. Pears Ltd.

Millet, Jean François (mill-AY) (1814-75) French artist whose paintings of rustic peasant life such as *The Winnower* (1846) and *The Sower* (1850) are grimly realistic. But he achieved immense popular success with his more sentimental pictures, such as *The Angelus* (1857-9) – in which two peasants are standing in the middle of a field, praying in the evening light.

Miró, Joan (mee-ROH) (1893-1983) One of the leading Spanish SURREALIST painters, along with Salvador Dali. His work tended towards abstract art; his best-known pictures have brightly coloured amoeba-like forms in apparent movement against a dark background. Miró also worked in ceramics, and used the medium to create enormous wall decorations for Harvard University (1950) and the UNESCO building in Paris (1955-8).

Miyake, Issey (1939-) Japanese fashion designer who worked in Paris in the 1960s before opening the Miyake Design Studio in Tokyo in 1971. The cut of his clothes is inspired by traditional Japanese forms, but the richness and subtlety of his fabrics sets his designs apart.

modern art Term which has two distinct meanings. In everyday language it refers to IMPRESSIONISM and later artistic styles such as POST-IMPRESSIONISM, CUBISM, ABSTRACT ART, SURREALISM and POP ART, which all broke away from the traditions of CLASSICISM. However, art historians use the term when referring to art created as long ago as the 13th century. Artists such as CIMABUE and GIOTTO have often been called 'the fathers of modern art' because they were among the first to start the break away from the long-established traditions of BYZANTINE art – a move which eventually led to the Renaissance.

Modigliani, Amedeo (1884-1920) Italian artist who spent most of his career in Paris. He is best known for his dramatic nudes and portraits, which often depict dark, almond-eyed women with elongated oval faces. Modigliani took a great interest in primitive African sculpture. Although he was well known in bohemian circles in Paris, he gained wider recognition only after his early death from tuberculosis.

🕯 The handsome Modigliani was also well known for his dissolute and amorous lifestyle and his addiction to alcohol and drugs.

Mona Lisa (La Gioconda) Celebrated portrait, supposedly of a Florentine official's wife, painted by LEONARDO DA VINCI between about 1503 and 1507, which is sometimes thought to be a self-portrait. The painting was one of the few works that Leonardo completed. It broke new ground by portraying the subject's features with more naturalism and subtlety than had previously been achieved.

🕯 The painting was stolen from its place in the Louvre, Paris, in 1911, and was not recovered until two years afterwards.

STYLISED BEAUTY *Modigliani painted sensual nudes and portraits of friends including his mistress Jeanne Hébuterne. He often elongated people's features – reflecting his interest in primitive art.*

HARMONIOUS ORDER *For Mondrian, the geometrical forms of works such as his* Composition *(1921) were the essence of painting.*

Mondrian, Piet (1872-1944) Dutch artist who was one of the most important purely abstract painters. He was greatly influenced by CUBISM and he sought what he described as 'pure reality' – a harmonised sense of order without expression. His paintings became increasingly geometric – many of them consisted of different sized rectangles of flat, primary colour framed by black lines. During the last four years of his life he lived in New York where his work found a more lively rhythm, influenced by his love of jazz – shown in works such as *Broadway Boogie-Woogie* (1942-3).

Monet, Claude (1840-1926) French painter who was the leading IMPRESSIONIST. In 1859, Monet went to study art in Paris where he met Pissarro, Sisley, Renoir, Cézanne and Whistler. Monet was greatly influenced by Manet, whom he met in 1866 and by JAPONISM: from 1890 Monet started creating a Japanese-inspired water garden at his home in Giverny, northwest of Paris. He then began to concentrate on painting series of pictures of the same subject viewed at different times of the day in different lights, such as *Haystacks* (from 1890), *Poplars* (from 1891), *Rouen Cathedral* (1892-5), *The Thames* (1899-1904) and, most famous of all, *Waterlilies* (1895-1926). After 1916 he painted a series of *Waterlilies* for the state, which are now kept in the Orangerie in Paris. These enormous canvases, filled with vibrant pools of colour almost devoid of form, are considered by many as the ultimate Impressionist works.

🕯Monet is often considered the most dedicated Impressionist painter. Throughout his life, even in old age when his eyesight was severely impaired, he strove to paint an impression of what he saw at a given moment, capturing a particular light and the shifting colours it created, without worrying about the conventional representation of an object's form. 'Forget what you have before you: only think, here is a little square of blue, here an oblong of pink . . . and paint it just as it looks to you,' he told students.

monochrome Any painting, drawing or print executed in only one colour.
🕯Art executed only in neutral shades of grey is termed *grisaille*.

montage Picture made by combining ready-made images – often by sticking one over another. Montage differs from collage in that each element is chosen for its subject matter, whereas in collage material is used simply for its overall visual effect, as in Matisse's 'cut-outs'. From about 1911 montage was used by CUBISTS who used newspaper clippings and menus in their pictures; Max ERNST produced haunting SURREALIST montages using engravings from cheap illustrated novels and from catalogues. Photomontage – using cut-out photographic images, often mixed with other media – is now a widespread form of montage and has made a considerable impact on commercial art since the 1920s.

CALM REFLECTIONS *As Monet's* Waterlilies *series (1895-1926) progressed, the shapes and colours gradually became less defined. Some regard these paintings as the starting point of abstract art, while others think of them as the ultimate Impressionist works – pure and spontaneous visual impressions of a movement.*

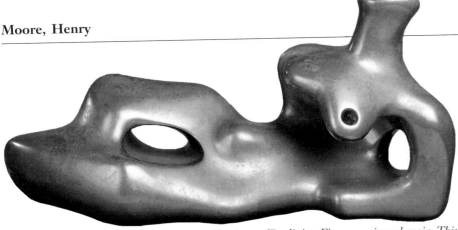

STRANGE FIGURE *Henry Moore returned to the theme of* Reclining Figure *again and again. This example, from 1939, shows the daring way he hollowed out solid forms to create internal shapes.*

Moore, Henry (1898-1986) Widely regarded as Britain's greatest sculptor, known for his simple, hollowed out or pierced human forms. Works such as the famous *Reclining Figure* (1929) display his interest in the relationship between the human form and the landscape. Along with Barbara HEPWORTH, Moore favoured direct carving into blocks of wood or stone – without making preparatory models. He was greatly influenced by the simplicity of form in African and Mexican art, and his own work became so simplified that it was sometimes considered to be ABSTRACT ART. In 1940 he was appointed an official war artist, after his drawings of figures sheltering from air raids became popular.

Moreau, Gustave (1826-98) French artist and leading SYMBOLIST painter. He created fabulous mythological and Biblical scenes in a detailed style, often layering on bright oil colours to give an encrusted, bejewelled appearance, as in *The Unicorns* (c.1855). In contrast, his watercolours,

which were often swiftly executed, can appear almost abstract. During the last six years of his life, Moreau taught at the *École des Beaux Arts* in Paris, where he influenced students such as Henri Matisse.

Morisot, Berthe (1841-95) French artist and the first woman IMPRESSIONIST, known for her paintings of quiet scenes of women and children. She was influenced by her early teacher Jean Baptiste Corot, but in 1868 she met Édouard Manet who became her mentor and whose brother, Eugène, she married. She in turn encouraged Manet to abandon his use of black paint and to adopt the bright primary colours used by the emerging band of Impressionists; the result directly inspired and shaped Impressionism. After 1885 her work was strongly influenced by Renoir.

Morris, William (1834-96) English craftsman, painter, designer, poet and left-wing political activist who was one of the great Victorian reformers. He first made his name as a painter linked to the PRE-RAPHAELITE BROTHERHOOD and as the driving force behind the ARTS AND CRAFTS MOVEMENT. In 1861 Morris set up a decorating company that produced only hand-made goods, to combat the new phenomenon of mass-production in the wake of the Industrial Revolution. The carpets, tapestries, carvings, textiles, wallpaper, stained glass and furniture he designed, with his friend Edward Burne-Jones, are some of the finest examples of 19th-century decorative art. In 1890 he founded the Kelmscott Press, with the aim of improving book design and printing. He designed ornamental borders for his books and created several new typefaces. Many of Morris's fabric and wallpaper designs are still reproduced today.

Morris summed up his aesthetic philosophy in the following way: 'Have nothing in your home that you do not know to be useful or believe to be beautiful.'

PATTERN WITH A PURPOSE *The hand-made products of William Morris's south London company, such as this* Wey *cotton textile print, combined decorative beauty with traditional craftsmanship.*

FLORAL COMFORT *William Morris designed this reclining chair in c.1865. The chintz upholstery dates from 1891.*

mosaic Design made by setting small pieces of marble, glass or ceramic into cement or plaster. The small pieces are known as *tesserae* (from the Latin for 'squares'), and are often irregular in shape. Mosaic is one of the oldest known forms of decoration; the earliest known example is Sumerian, from around 3000 BC. Most early mosaics were used to cover floors, but with the rise of Christianity mosaics were widely used for murals to decorate the walls of Byzantine churches. After the 13th century, mosaics were largely superseded by frescoes, although a few artists such as Paolo Uccello continued the tradition.

Muir, Jean (1933-) British fashion designer known for her classic and supremely simple dresses and ladies' suits. Her restrained clothes are usually made in brown, grey, dark blue or black fabrics.

Munch, Edvard (MUNK) (1863-1944) Norwegian artist known for his disturbing and often depressing paintings and drawings, such as *The Scream* (1893), one of his best-known works. The influence of SYMBOLISM and the work of Van Gogh and Gauguin led Munch to use simplified forms and evocative blocks of colour to represent his main themes of love, solitude, despair, illness and death. While working in Germany, from 1892 to 1908, he became an influential forerunner of EXPRESSIONISM, from which abstract art eventually developed. Munch suffered a nervous breakdown in 1908, after which his work became more optimistic.

Munnings, Sir Alfred (1878-1959) British artist who specialised in painting sporting scenes with horses. He was a controversial president of the Royal Academy (1944-9), and launched frequent attacks on what he felt were the shortcomings of modern art.

Murillo, Bartolomé (1618-82) Spanish painter known for his rather sentimental scenes of peasant children and for his devotional pictures, including several versions of *The Immaculate Conception*. He was also an excellent portrait painter. Following the departure of Velásquez for Madrid in 1623, Murillo became Seville's leading painter and enjoyed greater popularity. In the 18th century, he was widely regarded as one of the greatest painters ever, and his work had widespread influence.

Mytens, David (c.1590-1647) Dutch painter who came to London in 1618 and dominated court portraiture from 1625 to

CRY FOR HELP *Munch painted* The Scream *(1893) after a moment of personal crisis in which he became aware of a 'great cry' in nature. It has come to symbolise the loneliness of modern life.*

1632, when Van Dyck arrived. He painted elegant portraits of James I and Charles I, but his masterpiece is the portrait *The First Duke of Hamilton* (1629).

Nabis Small group of French artists founded by Pierre BONNARD and Édouard Vuillard which was active during the 1890s. The group was influenced by JAPONISM and by Paul Gauguin's advice to paint in pure, flat colours. The Nabis believed that painting should go further than imitating reality and should stress the artist's subjective perceptions. The Nabis produced work for theatre design, posters, book illustrations as well as stained glass.
🔖 The name of the group is derived from a Hebrew word, and means 'prophets'.

naïve art Childlike painting which uses bright colours and an often enchanting simplification of form and perspective. Naïve art has never been a coherent movement, unlike PRIMITIVE ART, but is created by untrained artists living in sophisticated society. Among the leading exponents of the genre are GRANDMA MOSES, Henri ROUSSEAU and Beryl Cook.

Nash, Paul (1889-1946) British painter, designer and book illustrator, known for his beautiful and lyrical pictures of the English landscape. As an official war artist during both world wars, he often used SURREALISM to create a sense of mystery and threat, as in *Totes Meer* (*Dead Sea*, 1940-1) in which the waves are the wings of crashed aircraft.

naturalism Style which attempts to make an accurate copy of nature without stylising it in any way. The meaning is often confused with that of REALISM.

neo-Classicism Movement that dominated European art and architecture in the late 18th and early 19th centuries. It was a reaction to the heaviness of BAROQUE and the frivolity of ROCOCO. It was also inspired by the rediscoveries of Herculaneum (1709) and ▷POMPEII (1748); neo-

Nicholson, Ben (1894-1982) British abstract artist who produced geometric paintings inspired by Mondrian and CUBISM. He is best known for his carved white plaster abstract reliefs, in which rounded and rectangular shapes give a sense of space. Nicholson was married to the sculptor Barbara HEPWORTH.

O'Keeffe, Georgia (1887-1986) American watercolourist best known for her paintings of natural objects and land-

SUBLIME SHOT *Norman Parkinson's fashion photographs nearly always evoked a world of cool glamour populated by sophisticated ladies.*

GEOMETRIC TENSION *Ben Nicholson's elegant linking of rectangular forms, as seen in his* Painting *(1937), depends on a carefully worked out balance of shape, line and colour.*

Classicism sought to revive the simplicity and grandeur of ancient Greek and Roman CLASSICISM and deliberately imitated Roman and Greek art. It was a philosophical and intellectual movement which affected all European countries, but had especially strong associations with the French Revolution. Among the great neo-Classical artists were the French painters INGRES and DAVID, the German painter Anton Mengs and the British architect Robert ▷ADAM. As the 19th century progressed, neo-Classicism was superseded by ROMANTICISM, which moved away from the rigid rules and limitations of the Classical tradition and towards subjective experience. (See also ▷NEO-CLASSICISM in 'Architecture and Engineering'.)

scapes. O'Keeffe's typically stark paintings of bleached bones, plants and the desert, show her strong sense of design, although they are almost abstract.

Op Art (Optical Art) Any sculpture or painting which creates optical effects or illusions. For example, the work of British artist Bridget Riley uses static black and white stripes in swirling or geometric patterns which appear to move and change shape as you look at them.

Orphism Form of CUBISM, dating from 1912, which used vivid colours and geometric shapes. It was a precursor of ABSTRACT ART, and had a strong influence on Paul KLEE and Wassily KANDINSKY.

Palmer, Samuel (1805-81) English landscape painter whose mystical, intense pastoral scenes were influenced by the visionary art of William ▷BLAKE. He specialised in watercolour and ink drawings, and his best work depicted the countryside near his home in Shoreham, Kent.

Parkinson, Norman (1913-90) British photographer known for his glamorous and lively fashion shots and his elegant and attractive celebrity portraits. He was also a competent reportage photographer, and worked for many magazines including *Vogue*, *Life*, and *Harper's Bazaar*.

Parmigianino, Francesco (1503-40) Italian painter and etcher, who produced some of the most distinctive and elegant work of the early MANNERISTS. In 1523 he moved from Parma to Rome, where the work of Raphael and Michelangelo inspired Parmigianino to produce graceful and powerful work, as shown in his masterpiece from that period, *The Vision of St Jerome* (1526-7). Parmigianino often elongated posture and gesture to make his subjects more expressive, as in the so-called *Madonna with the Long Neck* (c.1535), whose subject appears to be almost swooning.

pastels Soft-coloured sticks made of dried pigment and chalk bound by gum and used to make sharp, vivid lines or areas of soft, bright colour. Pastel was a favourite medium of 18th and 19th-century French artists, and was used with particular flair by Degas and other Impressionists. Different colours can be easily merged or built up in layers to create a rich and varied effect. Pastels have a tendency to smudge unless they are treated with a fixative.

In everyday usage, 'pastel colours' are soft shades of blue, pink, green and yellow.

pastiche Unashamed, often witty imitation or use of another's work. Some artists may also create a pastiche by copying and combining parts of other works of art in an original way.

patina Surface colour and finish which builds up on furniture or metal through a combination of age, usage and polishing. On metals such as bronze or copper, the greenish or brown colour on the surface is the result of oxidisation.

perspective The representation of three-dimensional objects on a two-dimensional plane. It is based on the premise that objects of the same size look smaller and closer together the further away they are from the viewer. The vanishing point – a point on the horizon at which all parallel lines appear to converge is essential to the whole theory of perspective. The more accomplished use of perspective by Western artists in the 15th century gave Renaissance art its new sense of realism.

'Aerial perspective' refers to the use of colour to create perspective: in a landscape,

for example, warm reds and browns would be used in the foreground, greens in the middle distance and cool blues and purples in the background.

Perugino (*c*.1445-1523) Italian painter who had a great influence on high RENAISSANCE artists, and much later on the PRE-RAPHAELITE BROTHERHOOD. His pupil Raphael learnt from the harmony of his style and the clarity of his composition. Perugino's frescoes can be seen in the Sistine Chapel, but his most important works were for altarpieces.

Picasso, Pablo (**1881-1973**) Spanish painter, sculptor, graphic artist and designer, who became the most renowned artist of the 20th century. Picasso was a child prodigy, producing exquisite Classical drawings by the age of ten. He lived in Barcelona where he developed his 'Blue period' (1901-4), which reflects the influence of Toulouse-Lautrec in its colour and form as well as its subject matter – the poor and down-and-outs. In 1904 he moved to Paris and stayed there until 1945. The 'Rose period' that followed this move is warmer but more enigmatic than the Blue. In 1907, influenced by the work of Cézanne and primitive African and ancient Iberian art, Picasso produced the *Demoiselles d'Avignon* (1907) – an early Cubist work. The style of CUBISM was developed by Picasso and Georges Braque over the next seven years. Picasso's output was prolific and he experimented with different ideas – from using more decorative elements to producing works of almost Classical poise

and weight. He also produced collage and sculpture. One of his most famous works, *Guernica* (1937), was painted in response to the Spanish Civil War and was a devastating attack on man's cruelty and folly. Picasso's creativity and a quirky playfulness in his approach gave a freedom to 20th-century art which is still apparent in contemporary artists.

Piero della Francesca (*c*.1410-92) Italian painter who, with his contemporary Masaccio, was a pioneer of linear PERSPECTIVE. He was a mathematician as well as a painter, uniting science and art in keeping with Renaissance ideals. The solemn grandeur and monumental, simplified forms of Piero della Francesca's religious and secular scenes later influenced the development of CUBISM in the 20th century.

pietà Italian word meaning 'pity', generally applied to paintings or sculptures of the Virgin Mary holding the dead Christ on her lap. The best-known example is MICHELANGELO's marble pietà, which can be seen in St Peter's, Rome.

Piper, John (**1903-92**) British painter, designer and print-maker. In the 1930s he was one of the leading British abstract artists, but by the start of World War II he had turned to a form of neo-ROMANTICISM. Piper was an official war artist from 1940 to 1942 and some of his most enduring works are evocative paintings of bomb damage. After the war, Piper designed large stained-glass windows for Coventry Cathedral and Liverpool Metropolitan Cathedral.

ANGUISH OF WAR *Picasso's* Guernica *(1937) was inspired by the vicious aerial bombing of the town of that name in the Spanish Civil War.*

Pissarro, Camille (1830-1903) One of the leading French IMPRESSIONISTS, who exhibited at all eight of the Impressionist exhibitions. Born in the West Indies, he moved to Paris where he studied with Corot and met Monet. He painted atmospheric views of Montmartre in Paris, and of Norwood in London, where he lived from 1870 to 1872 and where he studied the work of Turner and Constable. Pissarro often adapted the art of his contemporaries into his own paintings, such as the POINTILLISM of Seurat. As the teacher of Cézanne and Gauguin, he was an important influence on 20th-century art.

pointillism Technique of painting with small dots of pure colour which, observed from a distance, are intended to fuse without losing the intensity of colour. The neo-Impressionists Georges SEURAT and Paul Signac were its chief exponents, but they called the technique 'divisionism'.

Pollock, Jackson (1912-56) American painter generally thought of as an important initiator of 'action painting', or abstract Expressionism. This involves dripping, throwing or pouring paint onto a canvas so that the unconscious takes control and produces the work of art. Pollock, however, maintained that he *could* control the work, and that the result was 'no accident'. He was initially influenced by SURREALIST and Native American art as well as Chinese calligraphy. His technique involved taping enormous canvases to the floor and pouring paint over them in all directions. Pollock's art combines simplicity with 'pure painting', and his larger works have a monumental quality.

Pop Art Movement which began in the mid-1950s and reached its peak in the 1960s in both Britain and the USA, although it is still active today. It mocks 'serious' art and takes its images from the media, advertising, popular culture and everyday life – as in the work of Peter BLAKE and Roy LICHTENSTEIN. Ordinary consumer objects, such as Andy WARHOL's *100 Campbell's Soup Cans* (1962), are also popular subject matter. Jasper JOHNS is considered to be the father of the movement.

post-Impressionism Term coined in 1910 when an exhibition called 'Manet and the post-Impressionists' was mounted in London. It was dominated by MANET, VAN GOGH, GAUGUIN and CÉZANNE. The term covers movements such as neo-Impressionism, SYMBOLISM, EXPRESSIONISM, FAUVISM, POINTILLISM and the NABIS. Post-Impressionists shared a belief in the importance of subject matter and a return to a more formal conception – as opposed to an Impressionist's spontaneous recording of a moment or scene.

Poussin, Nicolas (1594-1665) French painter who worked mainly in Italy but who profoundly affected French Classical painting. He was also a philosopher, and his highly disciplined work was based on his theory that the moral content of a painting should be enhanced by its intellectual content. He also thought that colour should be subservient to the overall vision. Poussin often sought to convey the innocence and dignity of the past. His emphasis on formal values and draughtsmanship strongly influenced Charles le Brun who, in turn, shaped French art for generations.

Pre-Raphaelite Brotherhood (PRB) Group formed in 1848 by several English painters – Dante Gabriel ROSSETTI, his brother Michael, Sir John MILLAIS, Holman HUNT, Thomas Woolner and Frederic Stephens. They wanted to return to the purity of art before Raphael, whose work they considered overpraised and insincere. The group used bright colours, complex symbolism and elaborate detail. Their realistic treatment of religious subjects caused great indignation, and the group's motives were attacked by critics. However, in 1851 they became widely acclaimed after John RUSKIN defended them, praising their aims and efforts. The group broke up in 1853, but Rossetti founded a second partnership in the late 1850s, with William MORRIS and Edward BURNE-JONES. (See also ▷PRE-RAPHAELITE BROTHERHOOD in 'English Literature'.)

primitive art Painting, decoration and sculpture created by untrained artists living in an unsophisticated or 'primitive' society, such as the tribal masks produced by African peoples.

Quant, Mary (1934-) British fashion designer whose name is synonymous with the 'Swinging Sixties'. She made cheap and cheerful geometric designs in bright colours and is best known for her revolutionary design – the miniskirt.

ACTION ART *For Jackson Pollock, the process of painting was more important than the final result – massive abstract canvases without any formal composition such as* Guardians of the Secret *(1943).*

CHEEKY COUTURE *Mary Quant (centre) pictured in 1967 with some of the bold designs that revolutionised fashion for young women.*

quattrocento (KWAT-tro-CHEN-toh) Italian word for 'four hundred'. It refers to the 15th century or 1400s – the start of the RENAISSANCE.

Raphael (1483-1520) (Real name Raffaello Sanzio) The youngest of the three great Italian painters of the high RENAISSANCE – he was 31 years younger than Leonardo da Vinci and eight years younger than Michelangelo. Raphael was a pupil of Perugino, and in 1504 he went to Florence to study the work of Leonardo and Michelangelo. He moved to Rome in 1508 where he worked relentlessly to emulate the two great masters. Raphael painted several frescoes in the Vatican which show high Renaissance art at its peak, joining beauty, serenity and poise in perfect harmony. In 1514 he was appointed architect in charge of St Peter's, as well as of Rome's town planning. Raphael's later style was simpler and more monumental, but retained the vitality and warmth of his earlier work. His depiction of feminine beauty was particularly influential in NEO-CLASSICISM.
Raphael was the first artist to become a close friend of princes and cardinals; he was buried in Rome's ▷PANTHEON at the request of Pope Leo X.

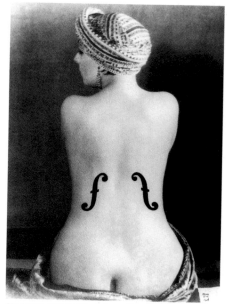

SEEING THINGS *Man Ray explored many photographic techniques to create surreal images such as* Le Violon d'Ingres *(1924).*

Ray, Man (1890-1976) American painter, photographer, sculptor and film-maker, who was one of the leading figures in the DADA movement. He is best known for his black and white art photography and for his imaginative SURREALIST work.

A LIFE IN PICTURES *Rembrandt painted a series of searchingly honest self-portraits over a period of 40 years. This example, from c.1665, reveals his sadness as a despairing, bankrupt, lonely old man.*

realism Nineteenth-century French art movement dedicated to depicting life as it really was, and was therefore close to NATURALISM – copying nature without stylising it. Realist painters, such as MILLET, rebelled against the idealised images of formal art and produced uncompromisingly honest pictures. Artists painted candid scenes of everyday life, inspired by contemporary writers such as Gustave Flaubert and Honoré de Balzac.

Regency Period in Britain from 1800 to 1830, typified by elegant, lavish and exotic furnishings, fashion and architecture. It takes its name from the flamboyant Prince of Wales (George IV from 1820), who patronised the arts and, from 1811, acted as Regent because of George III's bouts of mental illness. (See also ▷REGENCY in 'Architecture and Engineering'.)

Rembrandt van Rijn (1606-69) Dutch artist, draughtsman and etcher who was one of the greatest artists of all time. His prodigious output included at least 600 paintings, 300 etchings and 1500 ink and wash drawings. His reputation was established in 1632 with *The Anatomy Lesson of Dr Tulp*, a group portrait of the Amsterdam Guild of Surgeons. His most celebrated work, *The Night Watch*, a group portrait of volunteer militia, was painted in 1642. Just as his fortunes changed, his wealthy wife Saskia died, and his finances collapsed. Although he painted landscapes, Biblical, mythological and historical pictures and scenes from everyday life, Rembrandt is mainly remembered as a remarkably sensitive portrait painter who endowed his sitters with great inner dignity, but at the same time his pictures provide an uncanny insight into their character.

Renaissance

Renaissance French term meaning 'rebirth' which refers to the renewal of Classical ideals in literature, art and architecture that took place from the late 14th to the end of the 16th centuries. The early Renaissance, or QUATTROCENTO, was ushered in by GIOTTO and MASACCIO during the 15th century and was centred on Florence. The high Renaissance lasted from 1500 to about 1527. It was dominated by Leonardo, Michelangelo and Raphael, whose mastery of technique, faithfulness to nature and elimination of superfluous detail produced paintings of such serenity and harmony that they still have the power to inspire awe. The high Renaissance gave way to greater expressiveness – already inherent in the work of Michelangelo and Raphael – in the form of MANNERISM.

♫ The blossoming of the arts that occurred during the Renaissance was based on the rediscovery of the art and literature of ancient Greece and Rome. The Renaissance is seen as marking the transition from the ▷MIDDLE AGES to modern times.

Renoir, Pierre Auguste (1841-1919) French artist who trained as a porcelain painter and became one of the leading IMPRESSIONISTS. Renoir's sensuous use of light and colour, the voluptuous nudes in his later works and the vitality and warmth of his style make him one of the best-loved of all the Impressionists. His early paintings typically depict bright, sun-filled scenes with light glinting on water and people by the river or at festivities. He almost always painted outside, or away from his studio, and often worked with Claude Monet. Renoir gradually came to use lighter tones, and his paintings were increasingly made up of patches of light and shadow. In paintings such as *The Umbrellas* (*c.*1881-4) and *The Bathers* (*c.*1884-7) he began to concentrate more on form and on the pinks and reds of flesh tones. Other well-known works include *The Theatre Box* (1874) and *Le Moulin de la Galette* (1876). Renoir produced almost 6000 paintings, and worked right up to his death, even though he was crippled with arthritis.

Restoration Style of English furnishing from *c.*1660 to 1700 which was inspired by the Restoration of Charles II to the English throne in 1660. This introduced a new way of life for the wealthy – the result of the Continental habits and attitudes adopted by the royalists who had been in exile. These new fashions might have been restricted to the court had it not been for the Great Fire of London in 1666, which destroyed 10 000 homes that had to be replaced and refurnished. Lighter, more elegant furniture, including wing chairs, day beds and reclining chairs, was often made in walnut instead of oak, and given generous curves and intricate carving. The BAROQUE detail found in Restoration furnishings reflects the influence of the French court, particularly the decorative style of French palaces such as Versailles.

HAPPY CROWD *Renoir captures the exuberant, relaxed mood of Parisians at play in the sun in his picture* Le Moulin de la Galette *(1876).*

DEEP IN THOUGHT *This 1880 sculpture, one of several that Rodin made of* The Thinker, *shows his skill at modelling the human form.*

Reynolds, Sir Joshua (1723-92) British painter who, unlike most artists of the time, came from an educated background: his friends included such figures as Dr Johnson, Oliver Goldsmith, Edmund Burke and David Garrick. Reynolds, a prolific and versatile painter, was inspired by the Old Masters, especially Van Dyck and Rembrandt. He combined Classical allusion with competent painting, especially in his portraits. His learned writings, particularly his *Fifteen Discourses on the Rules of Art* (1769-90), his enthusiasm and his social standing made a major contribution to raising the status of art in Britain.

Rivera, Diego (1886-1957) Mexican painter who was the leading light in the rebirth of Mexican mural art, and who is best known for his works inside and outside public buildings. After producing early CUBIST work in France, he returned to Mexico in 1921 where he was influenced by traditional and Aztec art. Inspired by strong socialist principles, his murals are dominated by figures of peasants and workers.

Rockwell, Norman (1894-1978) American artist and illustrator, known for his warm-hearted paintings of rural and small-town life in the United States.

rococo Decorative, light and frivolous style of painting and decoration which developed in early 18th-century France as a reaction to the heavier style of the BAROQUE and LOUIS QUATORZE period. The main exponents of rococo painting were BOUCHER, FRAGONARD and WATTEAU. The rococo style was fashionable throughout Europe until about 1760, when it was succeeded by NEO-CLASSICISM, but it remained popular in Germany, where it mingled with the baroque style in churches and palaces. Rococo designs are characterised by scrolls, asymmetrical curves and motifs taken from nature, such as rocks, shells and flowers. (See also ▷ROCOCO in 'Architecture and Engineering'.)
🖋 The term rococo derives from the French *rocaille*, which means 'rockwork' and *coquillage*, which means 'shellwork'.

Rodin, Auguste (1840-1917) French sculptor who re-established the place of sculpture in mainstream art. Rodin is known for his 'unfinished' sculptures – 'fragments', such as a highly polished pair of hands emerging from an unworked block of marble – which echo some of Michelangelo's work. Rodin's vision and creativity can be seen in the *Gate of Hell* (1880-1917), a bronze door of nearly 200 parts. Although the door was never finished, its many elements were an endless source of inspiration for Rodin; various versions of his two noted sculptures, *The Thinker* and *The Kiss*, were part of the door's original design. Rodin successfully combined realism and symbolism to produce naturalistic but grand figures.
🖋 By far the largest collection of Rodin's work is at the Musée Rodin, in Paris.

Romanticism Movement in late 18th and early 19th-century art, literature and music which arose in reaction to the Industrial Revolution and to the previously unquestioned adherence to reason and tradition. Romanticism strove to express man's feelings, his innate powers of creativity, his spontaneity and his relationship with the natural world. In the visual arts, TURNER, CONSTABLE, ▷BLAKE and DELACROIX were among its best-known exponents.

Rossetti, Dante Gabriel (1828-82) English painter, poet and cofounder of the first PRE-RAPHAELITE BROTHERHOOD in 1848. After the group broke up in the 1850s, Rossetti founded another. He then produced medieval dream-world paintings dominated by heavy-lidded, sensuous women – the model for which was usually Jane, the wife of William Morris. (See also ▷ROSSETTI in 'English Literature'.)

Rothko, Mark (1903-70) American abstract painter who portrayed soft-edged rectangles of intense, almost luminous colour which seem to float on a solid background of harmonising or contrasting deep hues. His very large canvases were meant to create a sense of awe in the viewer.

PRISONER OF LOVE *Dante Gabriel Rossetti's passion for Jane, the wife of his friend William Morris, inspired him to paint her as* La Pia de Tolomei *– a woman imprisoned by her suspicious husband.*

Rousseau, Henri (1844-1910)

French amateur painter known for his meticulous and often fanciful works of NAÏVE ART. These large, detailed pictures of exotic subjects painted in a precise but unsophisticated manner have a haunting, dreamlike quality. He is best known for jungle scenes in which wild animals prowl sedately through lush foliage.

🔖 Rousseau's job as a goods inspector in the Paris customs-house earned him the nickname of *Le Douanier* (the customs officer.)

Rubens, Sir Peter Paul (1577-1640)

Flemish painter, scholar and draughtsman known for his grand, colourful and dramatic style. His vast canvases are full of vitality and vigour and often depict fleshy women or cherubs in glowing colours. Rubens went to Italy in 1600 and became the court painter in Mantua. In Italy he studied and was greatly influenced by the works of Titian, Michelangelo, Carracci and Caravaggio. He returned to Antwerp in 1608 and became court painter to the Spanish governors of the Netherlands. The success of two triptychs – the *Raising of the Cross* (1610) and the *Descent from the Cross* (1611-14) – led to Rubens being deluged with commissions. He produced hundreds of works – landscapes, hunting scenes, portraits, and religious and mythological pictures – through his own extraordinary energy and his highly organised studio, where one of his assistants was Van Dyck. Rubens' dominance meant that hardly any European artists of the 17th century were left untouched by his influence.

LEGENDARY TRIO *The term 'Rubenesque', describing plumply sensuous women, stems from paintings such as* The Three Graces *(1639).*

PRIMITIVE DREAM *Rousseau's untutored style, as seen in* The Jungle – Tiger Attacking a Buffalo *(1908), was very influential. His dreamlike clarity of vision prefigured the surrealist movement.*

Ruskin, John (1819-1900)

English writer and eminent art critic who was himself a talented draughtsman and watercolourist. Ruskin was a celebrated figure during his lifetime, and his criticism and writings on the philosophy of art were highly influential. He viewed art as an expression of morality, and believed that social problems could be solved through art. His highly spirited defence of the PRE-RAPHAELITE BROTHERHOOD single-handedly secured its success, and his praise of Turner established the artist as the leading landscape painter of the day. In 1878 Ruskin made an astounding attack on James WHISTLER, and lost the resulting lawsuit.

St Laurent, Yves (1936-)

French designer of glamorous and well-cut clothes. St Laurent became head designer at the major fashion house, Christian Dior, at the age of 21. Five years later he opened his own couture house and designed the 1960s 'rich hippy' look, which was strongly influenced by gypsy and North African motifs. By the 1970s, Yves St Laurent had become a household name, selling perfumes and ready-to-wear clothes as well as couture.

Sargent, John Singer (1856-1925)

American portrait painter who studied in Paris, where he developed his 'loaded brush' technique, involving long, fluent brush strokes of pure colour. In 1884, his 'erotic' painting of *Madame Gautreau* caused such a scandal that he moved to London. There he became the most celebrated portrait painter of Edwardian society, sometimes ironically conveying his sitters' sense of their own grandeur. He was an official war artist during World War I.

Schiele, Egon (SHE-luh) (1890-1918)

Austrian draughtsman and EXPRESSIONIST painter, influenced by Gustav Klimt. Known for his stark, angular nudes, Schiele outraged his contemporaries and was briefly imprisoned for distributing indecent drawings. Much of his work reflected his fascination with Sigmund Freud's psychoanalytical studies. Schiele died in the great influenza epidemic of 1918, just as he was achieving public recognition.

Schwitters, Kurt (1887-1948)

German ABSTRACT painter, poet and sculptor, and a leading member of the DADA group. He developed a type of collage art he called *Merz*: pictures and sculptures made with everyday materials, such as bus tickets, newspapers, lino and wire. Schwitters also created three *Merzbau*, structures the size of a house made of the same material.

sepia Brown pigment made from the ink-like secretions of cuttlefish which was sometimes applied to early photographs. The term can refer to any brown ink or wash.

Seurat, Georges (1859-91) Leading French neo-Impressionist painter who invented POINTILLISM – a technique that involves the use of small dots of pure colour. His most famous paintings, such as *Bathers at Asnières* (1884), *La Grande Jatte* (1886) and the unfinished *The Circus*, have great clarity and stillness.

The life and work of Seurat is the subject of Stephen Sondheim's 1984 musical *Sunday in the Park with George*.

SHIMMERING DOTS *Seurat's mastery of pointillism – as in* La Grande Jatte *(1886) – produced stunning effects of light and shade.*

sfumato Italian term, meaning 'smoky', that refers to a subtle blending of tones which makes the transition from light to dark imperceptible. Leonardo da Vinci invented the technique, which was one of the distinctive innovations of the Renaissance. He said that light and shade should blend 'without borders or lines, in the manner of smoke'.

Sickert, Walter Richard (1860-1942) Painter regarded as one of the most important of British IMPRESSIONISTS, although much of his work has sombre tones and colours. He was profoundly influenced by his friends James Whistler and Edgar Degas. Sickert's studio became a centre for aspiring young artists, especially those of the Camden Town Group in London, which he founded in 1911. His most important paintings are based on the themes of urban life and the music hall.

Sienese Europe's leading school of art during the 13th and 14th centuries, which flourished in Siena, Italy. The most important artists of the Sienese school, such as DUCCIO and MARTINI, drew much of their inspiration from Byzantine and French Gothic art. The school was superseded by the neighbouring FLORENTINE school.

Signac, Paul (1863-1935) French neo-Impressionist painter, who became the leading exponent of POINTILLISM after the death of Georges Seurat in 1891.

Sisley, Alfred (1839-99) Painter of the IMPRESSIONIST school, born in France of English parents. The influence of his friendship with Monet and Renoir shows in his carefully composed landscapes, painted with delicate, patch-like brushwork. Sisley lived in France, but during four visits to England he painted at Hampton Court and in south London. His paintings did not sell well during his lifetime.

Smith, Paul (1946-) British menswear designer who began to put his mark on classic fashions in the 1970s, persuading many young men to buy his designer clothes. Smith's loose-fitting suits are made from high-quality, natural fabrics. His brightly coloured casual clothes and accessories often have original and amusing details.

ART AND DESIGN

Spencer, Sir Stanley (1891-1959)
Eccentric British painter known for his realistic, if naïve, religious paintings and portraits – many of them nude. Spencer imagined Biblical scenes, such as the resurrection of the dead and Christ carrying the cross, taking place in his native village of Cookham, Berkshire. Many of his later paintings have sexual overtones which he intended to be both erotic and repellent.

lilies symbolised purity, for example. Still life developed as an art form in the late 16th century with artists such as Caravaggio producing *memento mori* – reminders of the fleetingness of life – in the form of skulls, hourglasses and spluttering candles. In the 18th century, still lifes lost all symbolic meaning, and became simple depictions of everyday objects. Those of Chardin and, later, Cézanne are particularly well known.

for Coventry Cathedral. He was also one of the leading portrait painters of his day; his sitters included Somerset Maugham, Lord Beaverbrook and Sir Winston Churchill – who hated the painting so much that Lady Churchill eventually burned it.

symbolism Art movement whose prime aim was to express ideas and moods through symbols. It began in the 1880s as an intellectual alternative to the purely visual and aesthetic approach of IMPRESSIONISM. Artists such as GAUGUIN used allegorical symbols and large areas of flat, bright colour heavily outlined in black to create abstract and decorative depictions of his emotions and thoughts.
♟In a more general sense, symbolism is the visual representation of an idea, such as a lamb being used to represent the holiness of Christ, or a dog implying fidelity.

ECCENTRIC VISION The Resurrection, Cookham *(1923-7), with its depiction of holy events taking place in humdrum surroundings, reflects Stanley Spencer's curiously oblique spirituality.*

Staël, Nicholas de (1914-55) Russian painter who worked mainly in France. Although he was influenced by the abstract painter Braque, Staël insisted that he himself was not an abstract painter – merely a non-figurative one. His paintings usually consist of blocks of subtly varied colour, but the work he produced after 1952 is more representational, and contains some recognisable features or images.

Stern, Irma (1894-1966) South African painter who studied in Germany before returning to South Africa, where she introduced European influences and became a celebrated artist. Her vibrant, warm colours and distinctive brush strokes are similar to those of Van Gogh.

Stieglitz, Alfred (1861-1946) American photographer and New York gallery owner who played a key role in promoting modern art to the American public. He mounted major exhibitions of works by artists including Matisse, Rodin, Rousseau and Picasso. He was married to the American watercolourist Georgia O'KEEFFE.

still life Depiction of inanimate objects – especially flowers and fruit – in painting, drawing or photography. In early Christian art, still lifes were only used symbolically –

Stubbs, George (1724-1806) British painter and engraver, best known for his studies of horses. Stubbs had no formal training as an artist, but began to paint portraits in order to earn a living while studying anatomy. His work is remarkable not only for its beauty, but also for its accuracy. *Mares and Foals in River Landscape* (1763-8) and *Horse Attacked by a Lion* (1770) are among his best-known works.

surrealism Movement in art and literature which began in France and reached its height in the 1920s and 1930s. Surrealists sought to express the contents of the subconscious and the process of thought, merging DADA and CUBIST elements with the fantastic imagery of artists such as BOSCH and GOYA. Leading surrealists such as MIRÓ, DALI and MAGRITTE often depicted deliberately distorted objects, unlikely combinations of mundane objects, or a mixture of the banal and the bizarre.

Sutherland, Graham (1903-80) British official war artist whose etchings and paintings of World War II show disturbing scenes of desolation. After the war Sutherland created some important religious paintings and designs, notably a *Crucifixion* (1946) for St Matthew's, Northampton, and a huge tapestry, *Christ in Glory* (1962),

tapestry Hand-woven fabric with a non-repetitive pattern woven in silk or wool. The Aubusson factories near Limoges, France, began making tapestries in the early 16th century and are best known for making scenes of La Fontaine's fables. The Gobelins factory near Paris was unrivalled in the 17th and 18th centuries, when it produced BAROQUE tapestries for Louis XIV, designed by Charles LE BRUN. Both centres remain active. The term 'tapestry' is often incorrectly used in reference to embroidery – as in the ▷BAYEUX TAPESTRY – or upholstery.
♟Needlepoint differs from tapestry in that the needlework covers the canvas and is not integral to the fabric. Appliqué work is the sewing or arranging of different pieces of fabric to another one to form a design.

tempera Medium used in painting made from ground pigment bound with egg and water. Tempera gives a quick-drying, bright result that can be worked over with oil glazes to enhance its colour and sheen. It was often used on wooden panels prepared with gesso – a thin layer of plaster of Paris.

Tenniel, Sir John (1820-1914) British illustrator best known for his cartoons for the satirical magazine *Punch* and his witty engravings for Lewis Carroll's book ▷ALICE'S ADVENTURES IN WONDERLAND.

Ter Borch, Gerard (1617-81) Dutch painter and a contemporary of Rembrandt and Hals. He is known for his small individual and group portraits and for his detailed interior scenes of well-to-do Dutch family life. His figures often seem delicate, while his painting of materials is exquisite.

Thornhill, Sir James (1675-1734)

The only important British BAROQUE painter. He competed successfully against the many Italian artists of the time, to paint grand works on a huge scale for St Paul's Cathedral, Queen Anne's bedroom at Hampton Court, and Greenwich Hospital. His success, and the honours bestowed upon him, were greater than those of any other painter until the advent of Sir Joshua Reynolds. Thornhill was both the teacher and father-in-law of William Hogarth.

♠ Thornhill set a price of £5 per square yard for the painting of the ceiling at Greenwich Hospital – however, he eventually accepted the still sizable sum of £3.

Tiepolo, Giovanni Battista (Giambattista) (1696-1770)

Last in the line of great Venetian decorative artists which included Veronese and Tintoretto. Tiepolo became renowned as a decorator of buildings throughout Europe. His most celebrated FRESCOES, of skies filled with floating figures painted in clear pastel colours, can be seen on the ceilings of Würzburg Palace, Germany.

Tiffany, Louis Comfort (1848-1933)

American ART NOUVEAU designer and interior decorator. Inspired by William MORRIS, Tiffany decorated many public buildings, including several rooms in the White House, in a curious mixture of Moorish, BYZANTINE and ▷ROMANESQUE styles. His hallmark was his handmade, iridescent glass, which he called *favrile*. He also made lampshades from leaded mosaics of opaque, tinted glass and produced goblets and glasses in flowing shapes resembling different plants and flowers.

♠ Tiffany's father founded the New York jewellers Tiffany & Co, featured in the film *Breakfast at Tiffany's*.

LIGHT WORK *A 'Wisteria' leaded glass and bronze table lamp, designed by Tiffany in 1902.*

Tintoretto (1518-94)

(Real name Jacopo Rubusti) Venetian painter known for his vast religious works. On the walls of his studio was the motto 'The colour of Titian and the drawing of Michelangelo': he aimed to combine these, adding a MANNER-IST sense of drama and movement.

♠ The name Tintoretto came from his father's profession as a dyemaker (*tintore*).

Titian (c.1488-1576)

(Real name Tiziano Vecellio) One of the greatest painters of the Venetian school, who dominated the scene for nearly 60 years. His mastery of the use of colour and the freedom of his brush strokes, together with his search for greater expressiveness, greatly influenced the BAROQUE style. The richness and sensuality he gave to fabrics as well as to human flesh influenced artists such as Rubens, while his poetic treatment of Classical scenes inspired artists such as Poussin.

♠ Like all Venetian artists Titian was first and foremost a master of colour: Michelangelo, looking at some of his work, is reported to have said 'Pity he can't draw'.

♠ 'Titian hair' is golden red or auburn. The term derives from the fact that Titian often gave his subjects auburn hair.

tone

Although the hue of a colour may remain the same, the tone can be changed to make it darker or lighter by the addition of either black or white pigment. Any shade of grey or any other colour that is not pure, or 'solid', can be called a half-tone.

Toulouse-Lautrec, Henri de (1864-1901)

French painter and graphic artist best known for his paintings of Parisian low-life and his bold designs for posters. He did not belong to a particular art movement, but was strongly influenced by Degas and by JAPONISM. His subject matter reflects his lifestyle: he painted prostitutes, their clients, dancers and café scenes with great insight and detachment. Toulouse-Lautrec was less interested in light or colour than in form and movement, which he captured with bold lines and large, flat areas of colour. His style and technique – using oil paints thinned with spirit on cardboard – influenced the new arts of lithography and poster-making.

♠ Toulouse-Lautrec suffered two accidents in his childhood which stunted the growth of his legs, leaving him a dwarf.

triptych

Painting, usually a religious altarpiece, consisting of three hinged panels. The subject matter varies, but triptychs often portray the Madonna or the Crucifixion in the centre panel and patron saints on the side panels. Some triptychs were owned privately and show the owner's coat of arms when the side panels are folded shut. A painting with only two panels is called a diptych and one with more than three panels is a polyptych.

trompe l'oeil (tromp-LOY)

French term for something that 'deceives the eye'. It usually refers to the creation of a three-dimensional illusion on a flat surface by using perspective – such as a false window with views painted on a solid wall. It is also used to refer to a depiction so realistic that the viewer is tricked into believing that the object is real, such as a fly on a frame.

♠ One form of trompe l'oeil, first successfully used by MANTEGNA and popular in the BAROQUE period, was *sotto in sù* – extreme foreshortening which creates the impression that figures are floating in space.

PUBLICITY WITH PANACHE *Toulouse-Lautrec designed this bold image for Aristide Bruant, a satirical nightclub singer.*

ART AND DESIGN

Turner, Joseph Mallord William (1775-1851) One of the greatest and most original of British landscape painters, who first exhibited in the Royal Academy at the age of 15. After a visit to Italy and Switzerland he produced oil paintings suffused with pale, brilliant light which Constable described as 'tinted steam'. Critics either loved or hated Turner's work. His reputation was secured only after he gained the support of John RUSKIN. In paintings such as *The Fighting Téméraire* (1838) and *Rain, Steam and Speed* (1844) Turner took ROMANTICISM to its height as he used nature to express man's emotions. In these works his representations of the effects of light and air count for more than the subject matter itself. Turner was strongly influenced by Dutch seascapes and the contrived Classical landscapes of CLAUDE.

DRAMATIC TURMOIL *Turner was fascinated by water, moody skies and rapid movement, as seen in* Rain, Steam and Speed *(1844).*

🕯When Turner died, he left 300 paintings and 20 000 watercolours and drawings to the nation on the condition that they were kept and displayed together. His wishes were ignored for over a century until 1987, when the Clore Gallery was opened at the Tate Gallery, London, to house a permanent exhibition of Turner's work.

Uccello, Paolo (1397-1475) Florentine painter who had a decorative, elegant and courtly style, and used brilliant colours and sinuous lines. Under the influence of Donatello, he developed a fascination for perspective which is particularly apparent in *The Flood* (*c*.1445) and his masterpiece, *The Battle of San Romano* (*c*.1455).

Utrillo, Maurice (1883-1955) French artist who began painting as therapy for his addiction to drink and drugs. His calm, almost monochromatic 'townscapes' have an eerie sense of solitude and were often painted from postcards. He sometimes mixed sand or plaster into his paint to capture the effect of the crumbling walls of the Montmartre quarter in Paris. He did his best work between 1908 and 1916.

Van Dyck, Sir Antony (van DIKE) (1599-1641) Flemish artist renowned for his portrait paintings. He originally worked as an assistant to Rubens, but quickly became independent – displaying a less robust and more introspective style than his master. Van Dyck was most popular in England, where he became court painter to Charles I whose portrait he painted several times, and who awarded him a knighthood. The portraits Van Dyck painted during the period he lived in England – from 1632 until his death – convey his extraordinary sensitivity to the individuality of each sitter. His work influenced many other British portrait painters for several generations.

Van Eyck, Jan (van IKE) (*c*.1390-1441) Flemish painter whose realism and extraordinary attention to detail has possibly never been matched. He had an enormous

influence on 15th-century art in northern Europe. Among his best-known master-pieces are the *Portrait of Giovanni Arnolfini and Giovanna Cenami* (1434) (popularly known as the *Arnolfini Marriage*) and the *Adoration of the Lamb* (1432) – one of the scenes on the GHENT ALTARPIECE.

🔔 For many years Van Eyck was incorrectly credited with the invention of oil painting. In fact, he simply refined existing techniques with remarkable skill.

Van Gogh, Vincent (van GOFF) (1853-90)

Dutch POST-IMPRESSIONIST painter who was one of the greatest and most influential artists of the 19th century. He began to paint only in 1880 after being dismissed from the mission where he preached in Belgium. He lived in poverty and was largely self-taught, although he was influenced by the flat, colourful designs of JAPONISM. After meeting Degas, Gauguin, Seurat and Toulouse-Lautrec in Paris in 1886, Van Gogh began to use vivid colours and experiment with different brush strokes. In 1888 he moved to Arles, in southern France, where he painted some of his greatest pictures, including *Sunflowers* (1888), *Bedroom at Arles* (1888-9) and *Starry Night* (1889). In letters to his brother, Theo, Van Gogh conveyed the thrill and struggle of using paint to express exactly what he felt. He suffered from loneliness and depression, and after a quarrel with Gauguin, he cut off part of one ear. Soon afterwards he went into an asylum where, during lucid periods, his paintings became even more intense. Van Gogh shot himself on July 27, 1890, and died two days later. His work had an enormous influence on SYMBOLISM, FAUVISM, EXPRESSIONISM and SURREALISM, and opened the way for the development of abstract and most other forms of modern art.

🔔 Van Gogh is believed to have sold only two paintings during his lifetime, including one to his brother. In 1990, however, his *Dr Gachet* (1890) sold for a record $82.5 million (£49.1 million).

Vasarély, Victor (1908-)

Hungarian-born French painter and sculptor who pioneered OP ART. His paintings combine variations of circles, squares and triangles, sometimes with gradations of pure colour, to create undulating abstract images.

Vasari, Giorgio (1511-74)

Italian painter and architect best known as a critic and biographer. His book *Lives of the Most Eminent Italian Painters, Sculptors and Architects* (1550) is still an essential work for art scholars of the Renaissance period. His

INSPIRING FLOWERS *Van Gogh's free brush strokes express his turbulent emotions:* Sun-flowers *(1888) was painted with exhilaration.*

most successful architectural achievement was the Uffizi Palace in Florence, which is now a major art museum.

Velásquez, Diego Rodriguez de Silva y (1599-1660)

Spanish artist who raised the art of portraiture to new levels and became court painter to King Philip IV of Spain. He was much affected by two visits to Italy, where he painted a portrait of the pope as well as his only known female nude, the *Toilet of Venus* (c.1650). On his return to Spain, he produced even more vivid paintings of a richness and brilliance not seen before. In his celebrated group portrait *Las Meniñas* (*The Maids of Honour*) (1656), a fleeting moment at court is captured with an almost photographic quality. Velásquez was greatly influenced by Titian and Rubens.

Venus de Milo

Statue of the Greek goddess Venus, found on a beach on the Greek island of Milos in 1820 and now in the Louvre, Paris. Probably dating from c.100 BC, it embodied the Greek ideal of female beauty – feminine and elegant yet sturdy. Although the arms are missing, the soft appearance of the flesh and the heavy texture of the falling drapery contribute to the statue's enduring beauty.

Vermeer, Jan (1632-75)

Dutch painter born in Delft, where he spent most of his time dealing in art. Virtually forgotten for two centuries, Vermeer is now rated as one of the greatest Dutch masters. He often painted quiet domestic scenes, such as

people absorbed in sewing or reading, with the aid of a camera obscura – a darkened chamber in which a clear image of the scene outside is received through a small opening or via a lens and mirrors. Although precise, Vermeer's paintings seem almost mellow and often have a cool silvery light, created by using subtle tones of yellow and blue. His best-known works are *The Maid with the Milk Jug* (c.1658), *View of Delft* (c.1662), *A Lady at the Virginals with a Gentleman* (c.1662) and *The Lacemaker* (c.1665).

Veronese, Paolo (1528-88)

Venetian MANNERIST painter who specialised in large-scale, decorative scenes of great pomp and extravagance. The sumptuous colours and ingenious illusions of space in his pictures reveal the influence of Titian and Michelangelo. Veronese fell foul of the Inquisition in 1573, when he painted a version of the Last Supper which showed, among other things, disciples picking their teeth. He was forced to rename it *Feast in the House of Levi*, but his spirited defence broke new ground in gaining recognition of the artist's right to give his subjects a personal interpretation.

Versace, Gianni (1946-)

Italian fashion designer whose clothes are among the most expensive and exclusive in the world. Versace is known for combining incongruous fabrics such as leather and silk and for his skill in cutting material on the bias, or diagonally across the weave.

Victorian style

Term applied to several different styles of architecture, furniture and furnishings in Britain during the reign of Queen Victoria (1837-1901). At the beginning of the period, the lingering designs of the REGENCY style became more elaborate, curved and detailed, taking on a ROCOCO feel, and Augustus ▷PUGIN's designs for buildings and furniture breathed life into the ▷NEO-GOTHIC movement. However, it was the onset of mass production and the new prosperity of the middle classes, caused by the Industrial Revolution, that really determined the style of the mid-Victorian era. Houses were filled with increasingly ornate and heavy furniture, covered with an array of bric-a-brac and framed photographs. At the ▷GREAT EXHIBITION of 1851, more interest was shown in technical advances than in design. Only later did attention begin to focus on Japanese artefacts – which slowly led to less clutter. In the late Victorian period, under the influence of William Morris and the ARTS AND CRAFTS MOVEMENT, decoration became much more restrained.

QUIET STUDY *Whistler called this picture* Arrangement in Gray and Black *in order to stress its careful balance of tone and form, but it is usually known as* Portrait of the Artist's Mother *(1871)*.

Warhol, Andy (1928-87)

(Real name Andrew Warhola) Controversial American artist of Czech origin best known for his contribution to POP ART. Warhol often used stencils to create outsized depictions of everyday objects, such as dollar bills and Coca-Cola bottles. He also made multiple images printed by the silk-screen process – using the faces of celebrities such as Elizabeth Taylor or everyday objects, as in *100 Campbell's Soup Cans*, varying only the colours and adding no other detail. Production of these series was handled by 'The Factory', a group of admirers who also starred in Warhol's avant-garde films. These included *Sleep*, which shows a man sleeping for six hours; *The Chelsea Girls*, set in New York's Chelsea Hotel; and *Empire*, a static view of the Empire State Building which lasts for eight hours.

🖋 Warhol is also known for declaring that 'In the future, everybody will be famous for 15 minutes' – a recognition of the increasing power of the mass media.

Watteau, Jean-Antoine (1684-1721)

French artist whose style of painting was so innovative that the French Academy created a new category for his work: *fêtes galantes* (countryside parties). His wistful and dreamlike paintings create a fantasy world where love reigned supreme. He was greatly influenced by Rubens, and his own work and ideals had a significant effect on the development of ROCOCO art.

POP ICON *The repetition and false colours of Andy Warhol's silk-screened* Marilyn Monroe *(1967) are deliberately dehumanising.*

Wedgwood, Josiah (1730-95)

British master potter, inventor, philanthropist and industrialist. He is best known for jasperware – matt-finished, tinted (especially 'Wedgwood blue') pottery with white decoration in relief – and Queens ware – strong, cream-coloured pottery used for plates and other tableware. Wedgwood's shrewd business sense led him to pioneer sales catalogues for the public, and with instantly recognisable colours and styles his name soon became a trademark. Many of his original designs are still in production.

Westwood, Vivienne (1941-)

Unconventional fashion designer who has based her collections on themes such as fetishes, pirates and folk dress. Many of her designs, such as see-through dresses and enormously high platform shoes, were derided at first, but quickly appeared in the high street in less extreme guises.

Whistler, James Abbott McNeill (1834-1903)

American-born painter who studied in Paris, where he was influenced by the simplicity of JAPONISM. After moving to London, he specialised in portraits and landscapes dominated by one or two colours. One of his best-known portraits is of his mother (1871).

🖋 Whistler's *Nocturne in Black and Gold: The Falling Rocket* (1877) so disgusted John RUSKIN that he accused the artist of 'flinging a pot of paint in the public's face'. Whistler successfully sued him, but won damages of only a farthing; the cost of the action forced Whistler to move to Venice, where he sold his etchings to earn a living.

🖋 Whistler was quite as witty as his friend Oscar Wilde. Admiring one of Whistler's remarks, Wilde said: 'I wish I had said that!' to which Whistler immediately retorted: 'You will, Oscar, you will!'

woodcut

Print made by gouging out sections from a flat block of wood, leaving untouched parts raised. These are inked, so that paper pressed against the block picks up the design in reverse. A similar technique in which the design itself is cut away – so that they appear white against a black background – is known as wood engraving.

🖋 Among the greatest exponents of woodcutting was Albrecht DÜRER.

Zoffany, Johann (1733-1810)

German painter who trained in Italy and attracted the attention of George III when he came to London in 1761. He was a founder-member of the Royal Academy and was known for his portraits of famous contemporary actors, including David Garrick.

ARCHITECTURE AND ENGINEERING

From the basic human need for shelter and the desire to honour deities there has sprung a rich diversity of buildings, from private homes and office blocks to cathedrals and palaces. Buildings reflect the lives and culture of the people who build and use them. The skills of the engineer underpin the architect's vision, bringing about a marriage of function and beauty.

THE PARTHENON, ATHENS

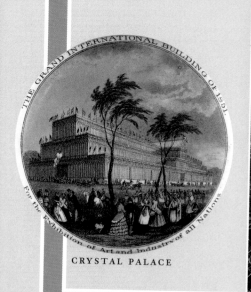

CRYSTAL PALACE

FALLINGWATER
BY FRANK LLOYD WRIGHT

Aalto, Alvar (1898-1976) Finnish architect and designer, celebrated for his simple and elegant bent-plywood furniture. One of his finest buildings is the Finlandia concert hall in Helsinki (1962-75).

abbey Church and dwelling house of monks or nuns, similar to a monastery or convent, and presided over by an abbot or an abbess. Monastic architecture developed in the 6th century under the influence of St Benedict at Monte Cassino, Italy. Many monasteries can still be seen in Continental Europe, but in England very few survived the ▷DISSOLUTION OF THE MONASTERIES in the 1530s. The best-preserved ruins in England are Fountains Abbey in North Yorkshire, a Cistercian abbey.

Abercrombie, Sir Patrick (1879-1957) British architect and town planner, who made his name in 1916 with a scheme for replanning Dublin. He later produced designs for other major cities, including one for the rebuilding of London after the bombing of World War II.

acropolis Highest part of a fortified Greek city or citadel which comprises its principal temples and public buildings. The Acropolis at Athens, which is crowned by the remains of the PARTHENON, is the supreme example.

Adam, Robert (1728-92) First architect to design and execute buildings and contents as a unit, from the structure down to the fireplaces, door handles and furniture. Adam worked with his three brothers to create a style of architecture that has become associated with their name. His delicate interpretation of NEO-CLASSICISM aimed 'to transfuse the beautiful spirit of antiquity with novelty and variety'. ▷SYON HOUSE in Middlesex (1760-9) and Kenwood House, overlooking Hampstead Heath in North London (1767-9), are among the best-known Adam buildings.

adobe Sun-baked brick, made from mud and reinforced with chopped straw, used for building in Latin America (especially Mexico), Spain and other parts of Europe. It is still sometimes used for constructing large as well as small buildings.

Akashi-Kaikyo Bridge Steel bridge under construction since 1988 between Honshu and Shikoku islands in Japan. At 2½ miles (4 km) long, it will become by far the world's longest suspension bridge when it is completed. Its six-lane highway is scheduled to open in 1998.

Alberti, Leon Battista (1404-72) Italian RENAISSANCE architect whose treatise *De Re Aedificatoria* (*On Building Matters*, 1485) was the first printed book on architecture. The only buildings Alberti designed in their entirety are the churches of San Sebastiano (1460 onwards) and San Andrea (1470) in Mantua, Italy.

Alhambra, The Citadel-palace built in Granada by the Muslim rulers of Spain between 1238 and 1391. Set on a dramatic ridge, the Alhambra is one of the most celebrated architectural achievements of Muslim Spain. Part of it is a castle, and the whole area is enclosed by high walls. It was created as an evocation of the paradise described in the ▷KORAN, with water flowing in channels and small fountains, through buildings, gardens and terraces, collecting in many basins and pools.

amphitheatre Round or oval arena, open to the sky and surrounded by tiered seating on all sides. Amphitheatres, built in ancient Rome, were adapted from Greek theatres, to make them suitable for holding gladiatorial combats, wild animal hunts, sports events and other public entertainments. They could even be filled with water to stage sea battles. The largest to have survived is the Colosseum in Rome, built in *c*.AD 80 to hold 50 000 spectators.

Angkor Ruined city in Cambodia, centred on a vast complex of Hindu and Buddhist temples dating from the 9th century AD. The main building, Angkor Wat – a stepped pyramid with five ornate towers, set in a large moated rectangle – was built by King Suryavarman II in the 12th century. Reliefs covering its walls depict scenes from the mythology of ▷HINDUISM. The city covers 75 square miles (190 km²). ▷Angkor was abandoned in the 15th century. It was unknown to the West until 1860, when natives led a French naturalist through the Cambodian jungle to the city.

Anglo-Saxon English architectural style used from the 5th century AD until the ▷NORMAN CONQUEST in 1066. Surviving stone buildings have thick, heavy walls, triangular arches and decorative strips of stone to simulate timber framework. The best example of an Anglo-Saxon building is Earls Barton Tower in Northamptonshire.

aqueduct Stone or brick channel with elevated sections designed to move water from one place to another – usually a city. Aqueducts were a Roman invention, and 11 major aqueducts were in use in Rome alone. However, the longest was in Carthage, stretching for 87.6 miles (141 km). One of the best-preserved aqueducts is the Pont du Gard in Provence, France.

WATER CARRIER *The Pont du Gard – a three-tiered Roman aqueduct built in AD 19 – transported water from a source in Uzès to Nîmes in Provence, France. It was engineered with extraordinary precision: over a distance of 30 miles (50 km) the water dropped only 55 ft (17 m).*

arch Curved structure which redistributes the pressure and weight of the material above it to its supports at either end. The two main forms are the ROMANESQUE or NORMAN arch, which is rounded, and the GOTHIC arch, which is pointed. During construction, arches are supported by wooden frameworks. Triumphal arches, which celebrate great victories, were first built in Roman times; more recent examples include the Arc de Triomphe in Paris and ▷MARBLE ARCH in London.

Art Deco Style that influenced architecture during the 1920s and 1930s, using straight lines and regular curves as a modern return to Classical styles and as a reaction to the organic curves of ART NOUVEAU. Some cinemas provide good examples, with their slabs of bright, flat colours, shiny metals and strong geometric patterns. In the USA, development of the style led to the design of skyscrapers such as the Chrysler Building in New York. (See also ▷ART DECO in 'Art and Design'.)

Art Nouveau Decorative style that used swirling lines and writhing plant forms, popular in Europe between 1890 and 1914. Well-known examples are the ornate entrances to many Parisian Métro stations. Charles Rennie MACKINTOSH and Antoni GAUDÍ were among the leading architectural exponents of the style. (See also ▷ART NOUVEAU in 'Art and Design'.)

Arts and Crafts Movement British movement originating in the late 19th century whose members – most notably William ▷MORRIS – advocated a return to functional designs and individual craftsmanship in the face of increasing mass production. Its influence can be seen in the work of Norman SHAW, Charles VOYSEY and Edwin LUTYENS, especially in their domestic architecture. (See also ▷ARTS AND CRAFTS in 'Art and Design'.)

Arup, Sir Ove (1895-1988) British engineer who pioneered the imaginative use of REINFORCED CONCRETE. As a consultant he collaborated closely with the architects of important buildings such as the SYDNEY OPERA HOUSE – for which he also designed the roof shells – and the POMPIDOU CENTRE in Paris. One of his best-known structures is the penguin pool at Regent's Park Zoo in London.

atrium Large open space inside a building, usually topped by a glass roof to provide light. An atrium was originally the open inner court of a Roman house.

POINT OF STYLE *The distinctive Art Deco form of the Chrysler Building, completed in 1930, soars 1046 ft (319 m) above New York.*

baroque Grand, flamboyant style that originated in Rome in the early 17th century and spread through Europe over the next 100 years. Its fusion of architecture, painting and sculpture created ostentatious, lavishly decorated buildings of theatrical grandeur. Its direct appeal to the emotions was exploited by church and state, and can be seen in BERNINI's churches and fountains in Rome, the interiors of VERSAILLES, Wren's ST PAUL'S CATHEDRAL and Vanbrugh's ▷BLENHEIM PALACE. It was succeeded by the ROCOCO style. (See also ▷BAROQUE in 'Art and Design'.)

Barry, Sir Charles (1795-1860) British architect who helped to popularise NEO-CLASSICISM. His most celebrated building however is the NEO-GOTHIC Houses of Parliament (1837-52) for which he designed the overall plan, commissioning Augustus PUGIN to do most of the external and internal decoration. He also designed the Travellers' Club and Reform Club in London, in RENAISSANCE style.

basilica Roman assembly hall, usually rectangular with rows of columns on each side of the central nave and two or more aisles at the sides. This plan was adopted by early Christian churches, and was recently revived at the world's largest church, the Basilica of Our Lady of Peace at Yamoussoukro, in the Ivory Coast.

battlements Parapet with a series of rectangular notches for defence, also known as crenellation. The defenders could stand behind the high parts and fire arrows and bullets through the notches.

DECORATIVE WELCOME *Hector Guimard's Art Nouveau designs for some of the Paris Métro stations featured cast-iron supports with 'organic' forms and curvaceous, top-heavy calligraphy.*

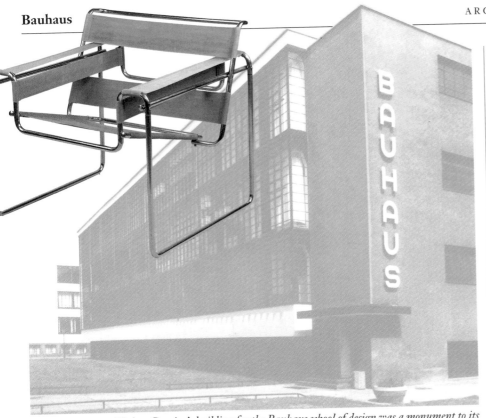

SEAT OF DESIGN *Walter Gropius's building for the Bauhaus school of design was a monument to its own philosophy: its furniture, such as this 'Wassily' chair, by Marcel Breuer, was created there.*

Bauhaus School of architecture and applied arts founded in Weimar, Germany, in 1919 by the architect Walter GROPIUS. Its purpose was to create a closer relationship between design, craft and industry. Its influence became worldwide. (See also ▷BAUHAUS in 'Art and Design'.)

Bernini, Giovanni Lorenzo (1598-1680) Italian architect, sculptor and exponent of the BAROQUE. He designed the piazza in front of ST PETER'S, Rome, and many of the city's churches and fountains. (See also ▷BERNINI in 'Art and Design'.)

bridge There are five main designs of bridge. (i) A beam bridge is a simple slab of reinforced concrete or a steel girder supported at each end. (ii) An arch bridge spans a river or gorge from side to side in a curve, so that the weight pushes down and outwards to its supports. The world's longest single spans are those of (iii) suspension bridges, in which the bulk of the load is carried by cables supported by giant towers and anchored to the ground on each bank. (iv) Cantilever bridges have two projecting arms which meet or are joined together by a central span, and are supported on piers and anchored by counterbalancing posts. (v) Bascule bridges, such as London's Tower Bridge, have hinged sections which can be raised to let tall vessels pass.

Brown, 'Capability' (1716-83) (Real name Lancelot Brown) British landscape gardener and architect, who rejected the traditional formal garden design of his day and manipulated the landscape to create an illusion of informality. He planted clumps of trees and built serpentine lakes and winding roads to such effect that the results looked natural. Among his works are the grounds at ▷BLENHEIM PALACE (1763 onwards), ▷LONGLEAT (1757) and Warwick Castle (1749-50).
🔔 Brown was dubbed 'Capability' because he invariably observed that a client's site had great 'capabilities for improvement'.

Brunel, Isambard Kingdom (1806-59) British engineer whose masterpiece is the Clifton Suspension Bridge (1829-62) at Bristol. As engineer to the Great Western Railway from 1833, Brunel introduced broad gauge (7ft; 2.13m) track and designed all the line's tunnels, bridges and viaducts. At sea, Brunel revolutionised steam travel in 1838 with the ocean-going paddle steamer *Great Western*. His *Great Britain*, launched in 1843, was the first iron-built, ocean-going ship with a screw propeller. In 1853-8 Brunel built the enormous and sophisticated liner *Great Eastern*, which later laid the first telegraph cable across the Atlantic. He was the son of the engineer Sir Marc Isambard BRUNEL.

Brunel, Sir Marc Isambard (1769-1849) French-born British architect and engineer who in 1818 invented the tunnelling shield, which made it practicable to build TUNNELS under water or in soft earth. The earliest use of the shield – a giant iron casing that could be pushed along to protect workers at the tunnelling face – was to build the first tunnel under the River Thames, from Wapping to Rotherhithe, between 1825 and 1843.

Brunelleschi, Filippo (1377-1446) Florentine architect who was one of the leading exponents of RENAISSANCE architecture. He drew on Classical models for their methods of construction as well as for aesthetic reasons. His masterpiece is the enormous yet elegant dome of Florence Cathedral (1420-36), which has a unique structure of an inner and an outer shell.

Burlington, Lord (1694-1753) English aristocrat who became an influential patron, as well as a renowned architect, after being inspired by a ▷GRAND TOUR around Europe. He championed the Classical PALLADIAN style that flourished among his followers in England for 50 years. His best-known work is Chiswick House, London (*c.*1723), based on PALLADIO's Villa Rotonda near Vicenza, Italy.

buttress Brick or stone structure which projects from or is built against an external wall to give it extra strength, or in order to

HISTORIC LINKS *Isambard Kingdom Brunel stands before the enormous launching chains of the* Great Eastern *(1858) – the world's largest and most sophisticated liner of its time.*

counteract the outward thrust of a roof, vault or arch. Flying buttresses, which elegantly arch away from the wall they support, are a feature of GOTHIC cathedrals and churches and enabled their architects to build wide, soaring VAULTS.

Byzantine Early Christian style of architecture which developed after AD 330 in Constantinople. Byzantine churches have round arches, massive domes, intricate spires and MINARETS; inside ▷MOSAIC is often used extensively. The masterpiece of Byzantine architecture is the HAGIA SOFIA in Istanbul. (See also ▷BYZANTINE in 'Art and Design' and ▷BYZANTINE EMPIRE in 'World History'.)

Campbell, Colen (1676-1729) Scottish architect whose three-volume book *Vitruvius Britannicus* (1715-25), illustrating his own and other British architects' work, influenced Lord Burlington and helped to initiate the PALLADIAN style in England. His best-known works are Burlington House, London (1718-19), and Mereworth Castle, Kent (*c.*1722-5).

canals The earliest canals are thought to have been built around 4000 BC in Iraq. Work on the GRAND CANAL in China, the world's oldest man-made waterway still in use, started in AD 540.
🦆 The great breakthrough in canal building came with the invention of the lock on China's Grand Canal in AD 984. By flooding or draining a section of water between two watertight gates, vessels can move from one level to another, allowing them to climb or descend gradients.

castle There have been fortified buildings or settlements, such as ▷MAIDEN CASTLE, from prehistoric times, but the first true castles were built in Europe during the Middle Ages. Early castles consisted of a fortified timber stockade, or 'keep', raised on a circular mound called a 'motte', encircled by a ditch. Inside the castle a courtyard or 'bailey' was enclosed by a CURTAIN WALL with battlements on top. The entrance was guarded by a barbican, or gatehouse. Wherever possible, castles were built in a place that offered natural defences, such as a hill or the bank of a river. By the end of the Middle Ages, artillery had been invented which was capable of breaking down their walls and castles lost their defensive role. By the end of the 15th century the castle had evolved into the French *château* and the German *Schloss*, designed more as an impressive dwelling place than as a defensive stronghold.

COLUMNS AND THE CLASSICAL ORDERS

Classical architects designed buildings according to three main styles, or 'orders', each of which had its own mathematical rules for harmony and balance.

The Doric order was the simplest; Ionic columns were slimmer, with scrolled capitals and ornate bases; and the Corinthian order had a motif based on acanthus leaves.

DORIC   IONIC   CORINTHIAN

cathedral Main church of a diocese, in which the *cathedra*, the bishop's chair or throne, is placed. Some cathedrals are known as minsters – from the Old English term *mynster* meaning 'monastery church'.

Channel Tunnel Anglo-French project to link Britain with the Continent by a tunnel under the English Channel which links Cheriton, near Folkestone, to Sangatte, near Calais. Work, which began in 1987, took longer than planned, and the tunnel was eventually opened in 1994. There are three tunnels: two 24 ft (7.6 m) diameter single-track railway tunnels – one for each direction – and a central service tunnel. The tunnels are 31 miles (50 km) long, and lie 130 ft (40 m) beneath the sea-bed.
🦆 The first serious proposal for a Channel tunnel was made to Napoleon Bonaparte in 1802 by his chief engineer Albert Mathieu. The tunnel was to have a cobbled passage for horse-drawn carriages. Work was started, but soon abandoned for lack of funds.

church Early churches were built on the BASILICA plan, with a nave, aisles and a high altar in the apse of the east end, so that the congregation faced in the direction of the land of Jesus's birth and crucifixion. The Greek cross plan has four arms of equal length, and was the model used for BYZANTINE churches. In northern Europe, the Latin cross design, with one arm longer than the others, was used from the 11th century onwards. The nave occupied the longer arm and a dome or spire was commonly placed over the intersection.

Classical Architectural style based on the buildings of ancient Greece and Rome. Classical architecture emphasises simplicity of form and proportion, following several distinct 'orders', and makes extensive use of columns with decoration, especially FLUTING. The great Classical revival of the RENAISSANCE was partly inspired by the rediscovery of *De Architectura* (*On Architecture*) by Vitruvius, a Roman architect in the 1st century BC. It is the only Classical treatise on the subject to survive. (See also ▷CLASSICISM in 'Art and Design'.)

concrete Cement mortar mixed with broken brick, shingle, gravel or stones to make a strong building material. In and around Rome, the Romans added *pozzolana* (a volcanic ash) to make an extremely strong – and lasting – form of concrete. The use of concrete declined after the fall of the Roman Empire, although it was still used throughout Europe in the building of durable castle walls and for cathedral foundations. It gained popularity again after it was 'rediscovered' in the 18th century. (See also REINFORCED CONCRETE.)

READY MADE *This pot lid celebrates the Crystal Palace – the first ever prefabricated building, assembled from factory-made parts in 1850-1.*

Crystal Palace World's first major prefabricated building of iron and glass, built for the ▷GREAT EXHIBITION of 1851 in London's Hyde Park. It was designed by Sir Joseph Paxton, and it took only six months to build. The Crystal Palace covered 19 acres (7.7 ha) and its 300 000 panes of glass were held up by thousands of iron columns and girders. After the Great Exhibition the palace was re-erected at Sydenham, in south London, but it was destroyed by fire on a winter's night in 1936.

STAGE BY STAGE *The Eiffel Tower took almost 18 months to build and was the tallest building in the world. It was intended to be temporary.*

curtain wall Wall that carries no load, built on a framework of timber, concrete or steel. Such walls are a common feature of castles and also of skyscrapers, where the frame carries the weight of the building and the curtain wall keeps the weather out.

dams There are two basic types of dam: gravity dams and arch dams. Both can be used to hold back a body of water and so prevent floods and provide irrigation or water for human consumption, or to generate hydroelectric power. Gravity dams are simply earth or concrete embankments which depend on their own weight to resist the force of the water. Arch dams curve towards the body of water which they contain, resisting and redistributing the pressure of the water against each bank, in much the same way as an ARCH does in a building. Some dams are hybrid structures, combining both types.
⚫The earliest known dams, uncovered in Jerusalem and Jordan, date from *c.*3200 BC.

Decorated Style in English GOTHIC architecture used between about 1250 and 1380, following the EARLY ENGLISH period. Buildings in this style abound in decorative mouldings, lavish flowing TRACERY, and often incorporated S-shaped curves. The cathedrals at Bristol, Exeter and Wells contain notable examples of the style.

Durham Cathedral The outstanding example of NORMAN (or Romanesque) architecture in England. The nave is 201 ft (61 m) long, with a ceiling 155 ft (47 m) high at the central crossing. The cathedral was largely built between 1093 and 1133, and its ceiling is believed to have the first ribbed VAULT built in Europe.
⚫Durham Cathedral houses the tomb of the Venerable Bede (AD 735), a scholar, theologian and important early historian.

dykes Embankments used to reclaim land from the sea or to prevent flooding. A dyke along a river bank may be called a levée.

Early English The earliest phase of the GOTHIC style in England, lasting from the late 12th to the late 13th centuries. Early English churches were built very high, symbolising mankind reaching heavenwards, and had lancet (slender, pointed) windows, pointed arches and simple TRACERY. The best surviving examples of Early English architecture are SALISBURY CATHEDRAL (1220-66) and Wells Cathedral (*c.*1180-1239). Early English was followed by the DECORATED style.

Eiffel Tower Paris's most prominent landmark was built in 1887-9 for the Paris Exhibition by the celebrated French engineer Gustave Eiffel. It is made of wrought

10 Aout 1887   8 Octobre 1887   15 Mars 1888   10 Juillet 1888

iron sections bolted together, and is 985 ft (300 m) high. It was the world's tallest building until the EMPIRE STATE BUILDING was completed in 1931.

Elizabethan Style of English architecture built mainly during the reign of ▷ELIZABETH I (1558-1603). Features of Elizabethan buildings include large leaded oriel (upper-storey, bay) windows, multiple chimneys, gables and turrets, panelled interiors and ceilings decorated with moulded plasterwork. Elizabethan houses are often built on an E or H plan. (See also ▷ELIZABETHAN STYLE in 'Art and Design'.)

Ely Cathedral Building which spans NORMAN and GOTHIC styles, as it dates from the 11th century and was added to well into the 14th century. Its magnificent 14th-century octagonal main LANTERN is supported by 63 ft (19 m) long corner posts.

Empire State Building The most celebrated skyscraper in New York City which opened in 1931. It is 1250 ft (381 m) high, has 102 floors, and took just under 14 months to build. The top of the building bends about 3 ft (1 m) in high winds; it is crowned by a 222 ft (68 m) television aerial.

fluting Vertical grooves in the surface of a column which help to emphasise its height.

HIGH-TECH TERMINAL *Sir Norman Foster's design for Stansted Airport (1991) illustrates his use of modern engineering techniques to produce supremely functional buildings.*

folly Building with no practical purpose erected purely for decorative effect – usually providing a focal point in a garden or landscaped parkland. Follies were fashionable during the 18th and 19th centuries among wealthy and eccentric landowners. They ranged from fake medieval ruins to Classical temples and Gothic towers.

Forth Rail Bridge Double cantilever bridge that crosses the Firth of Forth in Scotland. It is 361 ft (110 m) high, and its total length is about 1½ miles (2.5 km). The bridge, opened in 1890, took seven years to build, during which 57 workmen died and a further 461 were injured.

🎙A team of 16 painters used to be employed full-time painting the Forth Rail Bridge to prevent rust. A new type of paint means that the bridge is now painted less frequently, but never-ending tasks are still said to be 'like painting the Forth Bridge'.

Foster, Sir Norman (1935-) Innovative British architect who specialises in carefully engineered HIGH-TECH buildings that are a complete departure from previous historical styles. Among his most acclaimed buildings are The Sainsbury Centre for the Visual Arts in Norwich (1974-8), the Hong Kong and Shanghai Bank in Hong Kong (1979-86) and Stansted Airport Terminal (1981-91).

Fuller, Richard Buckminster (1895-1983) American inventor, engineer and architect. Among his many inventions was the geodesic dome – a lightweight hemispherical structure composed of interlocking tetrahedrons (four-faced sections) which could cheaply cover a large area.

14 Octobre 1888   *14 Novembre 1888*   *12 Février 1889*   *31 Mars 1889*

gable Upper, triangular part of a wall at the end of a pitched, or sloping, roof. Among the several types of decorative gables are 'crowstepped' gables with stepped sides, and the more common Dutch gables with curved sides.

gallery Long room, often hung with pictures and used for entertainment, in ELIZABETHAN and JACOBEAN houses. In a church, a gallery is an upper storey overlooking the main aisle. The word also describes a platform or mezzanine floor supported by pillars or brackets and overlooking a large room, such as a minstrel's gallery.

gargoyle Grotesque animal or human face, often decorating rainwater outlet spouts projecting from the parapet of a medieval church or cathedral. Hideous gargoyles seem to have been carved at the whim of the mason, although they were often believed to have the function of driving away the devil.

STRANGE CHURCH *Antoni Gaudí's peculiar openwork spires (1903-26) at the Sagrada Familia in Barcelona are part of one of the most eccentric creations of Art Nouveau.*

Gaudí, Antoni (1852-1926) Spain's greatest architect and leading exponent of ART NOUVEAU. His most celebrated work is the Sagrada Familia, or Holy Family, a large church in Barcelona, which had already been started when Gaudí took over in 1883. He transformed it from a NEO-GOTHIC design to a highly imaginative vision of fantastic forms and twisted shapes, decorated with fragments of multi-coloured ceramics. Its extraordinary bell towers are known as the Gaudí towers. The church is still unfinished. Gaudí also designed many eye-catching houses in Barcelona, including the Casa Batlló and the Casa Milá, with their undulating stonework, intricate balconies, and walls studded with fragments of coloured glass.

Georgian Style of British architecture during the reigns of George I, II and III, from 1714 to about 1800. It is sometimes taken to include the REGENCY period, from about 1800 to 1830. Georgian architecture is usually restrained, with an emphasis on elegance, scale and proportion rather than decoration. The classic example of Georgian style is the terraced town house, with large sash windows divided into small panes, which lends such dignity to many of Britain's cities especially ▷BATH. (See also ▷GEORGIAN in 'Art and Design'.)

Gibbons, Grinling (1648-1721) Woodcarver born of English parents in Rotterdam, who settled in England in about 1670. He became Master Carver in Wood to the Crown after the diarist John Evelyn introduced him to Charles II. ST PAUL'S CATHEDRAL, ▷WINDSOR Castle, and several English stately homes have fine examples of his carving.

Gibbs, James (1682-1754) Scottish architect whose highly individual style was influenced by Christopher Wren and by Italian architecture. His work is a fusion of BAROQUE, PALLADIAN and EARLY ENGLISH. Among his commissions were several major churches in London including St Mary-le-Strand (1714-17) and his masterpiece St Martin-in-the-Fields (1720-6). His last building was the cylindrical Radcliffe Library in Oxford (1737-48).

Golden Gate Bridge Suspension bridge that crosses the strait connecting San Francisco Bay with the Pacific Ocean. Fast-running tides, fogs and storms hampered the building of the bridge – which was rammed by a cargo boat while half-completed. It was opened in 1937, and had the world's longest span (4200 ft; 1280 m) until the Verrazano Narrows Bridge in New York opened in 1964 (4258 ft; 1298 m).

golden section A particular proportion generally considered to be pleasing to the eye. The golden section, or golden mean, is based on a division of a line into two unequal parts in which the ratio of the smaller part to the larger is the same as that of the larger part to the whole; the proportions are 1:1.618. The concept goes back at least as far as the ancient Greek mathematician ▷EUCLID, and greatly influenced RENAISSANCE architects and artists.
🗝The golden section is alleged to have a mystical quality based on a hidden harmony naturally in tune with the Universe.

Gothic Style of architecture which flourished in Europe from the 12th to the 15th centuries. It is characterised by pointed arches, ribbed VAULTS, flying BUTTRESSES and lofty cathedrals with huge windows, such as Wells Cathedral and NOTRE DAME. In England, the Gothic style divided into three styles: EARLY ENGLISH, DECORATED and PERPENDICULAR.
🗝The style takes its name from the ▷GOTHS who invaded Italy from the north in the 4th and 5th centuries AD. The Italians used the term to describe their church architecture, with its great height and elaborate embellishment.

DELICATE TOUCH *Grinling Gibbons's lime-wood carved panel (c.1692) at Petworth, in Sussex, illustrates his exquisite craftsmanship.*

Gothic Revival See NEO-GOTHIC.

Grand Canal Waterway in China started in the 6th century AD as a series of short sections linked to stretches of navigable rivers. By 1327 a canal 1107 miles (1781 km) long had been created. More than 5 million labourers worked on the project, and about 2 million of them died of exhaustion or through accidents. The canal, the world's longest, is still in use.

SNAKING BARRIER *The building of the Great Wall of China was begun by Qin Shi Huangdi, the first emperor of China – who also commissioned an army of some 7000 life-sized terracotta soldiers and clay horses to guard his tomb.*

Great Wall of China Wall built as a means of keeping out nomadic invaders from the north. It first came into being in about 217 BC, but most of the present wall dates from the Ming Dynasty (1368-1644). The wall winds from Shanhaiguan, on the Yellow Sea near Beijing, to Jiayuguan, 1500 miles (2400 km) to the west in central northern China, and covers 4000 miles (6400 km) at an average height of 23 ft (7 m).

Gropius, Walter (1883-1969) German-born architect who founded the BAUHAUS school in 1919. He was influenced by ▷EXPRESSIONISM and the work of William ▷MORRIS, and felt that the Bauhaus should

be a meeting place of all arts and crafts teaching. Gropius emigrated to the USA before World War II and founded his own firm The Architects' Collaborative (TAC), a cooperative which created clean, elegant and functional designs. His work had a lasting effect on American design.

Hagia Sofia BYZANTINE church in Istanbul built between AD 532 and 537. It was formerly used as a mosque but is now a museum. Its monumental, richly decorated interior is crowned by a colossal dome 107 ft (33 m) in diameter. Hagia Sofia is the outstanding architectural achievement of the Byzantine Empire.

Hawksmoor, Nicholas (1661-1736) Baroque architect who, as WREN's assistant, helped to design St Paul's Cathedral and worked with VANBRUGH on ▷CASTLE HOWARD and ▷BLENHEIM PALACE. His own projects which display striking Gothic and Classical elements include six London churches and All Souls' College, Oxford.

high-tech Style of architecture which uses steel and glass and shows off functional elements such as ventilation ducts and lifts, in celebration of modern technology. Among examples are the POMPIDOU CENTRE in Paris and the Lloyd's building in London, both by Richard ROGERS.

Humber Bridge World's longest single-span suspension bridge. Its span of 4626 ft (1410 m) crosses the River Humber estuary near Hull. It was opened in 1981.

International Modern Style of architecture developed early in the 20th century by Walter GROPIUS and the BAUHAUS movement, Frank Lloyd WRIGHT and, later, Ludwig MIES VAN DER ROHE. It is typified by cube-shaped buildings with almost no decoration and large windows.

Islamic architecture Style which developed from BYZANTINE and early Greek architecture in Islamic countries of the present-day Middle East from the 7th to the 16th centuries. Its features include horseshoe arches, tunnel vaults, domed spaces, courtyards and dazzling decoration using stone carving, ▷MOSAIC, glazed tiles, and painting. The earliest surviving example of Islamic architecture is the Dome of the Rock MOSQUE (685-705) in Jerusalem. One of the most impressive is the ALHAMBRA palace in Granada, Spain.

Jacobean Style of English architecture during the reign of King ▷JAMES I (1603-25). It is similar to the ELIZABETHAN style, with the addition of Dutch curved GABLES, extravagantly ornamented plasterwork ceilings and carved woodwork: Hatfield House in Hertfordshire and the market hall at Chipping Camden are fine examples. Towards the end of the reign, Inigo JONES introduced the PALLADIAN style.

Jekyll, Gertrude (1843-1932) (JEE-kul) English garden designer whose natural-looking creations were inspired by the cottage gardens of her childhood Surrey. She stressed the importance of colour, and said that she sought to use plants to 'form beautiful pictures'. Jekyll worked closely with Sir Edwin LUTYENS.

Jones, Inigo (1573-1652) English architect who introduced the Italian Renaissance style to England after a visit to Italy, where he developed a great admiration for the work of Andrea PALLADIO. He was Surveyor of the King's Works from 1615 to 1642, during which time he designed the Queen's House at Greenwich (1616-19 and 1630-5) and his masterpiece, the Banqueting House (1619-22) in Whitehall. Both these buildings broke dramatically with traditional Jacobean architecture. He also designed the plan for London's ▷COVENT GARDEN market.

Kremlin Citadel in Moscow, enclosing a complex of princely residences and churches fortified in the 15th century, and now Russia's seat of government. Its architecture is a mixture of styles, dominated by BYZANTINE and RENAISSANCE buildings. Tsar ▷IVAN THE GREAT brought Italian architects to Russia to rebuild the Kremlin in the 15th century. The Cathedral of the Assumption (1475-9) and especially that of Archangel Michael (1505-8), with its traditional medieval onion-shaped domes surmounting Renaissance façades, show the composite style at its best. The octagonal Ivan the Great bell tower houses 21 bells, the largest of which weighs 64 tons.
🔦 Kremlin is the Russian word for 'citadel'.

lantern Small turret with windows crowning a dome or roof. Lanterns are usually circular or polygonal.

Leaning Tower of Pisa Celebrated Italian bell tower, or campanile, begun in 1174, which started to lean before it was even finished due to weak foundations and subsidence. The 179 ft (55 m) high tower has been tilting ever since, and the top now leans about 17 ft (5 m) to one side. In 1993, for the first time in 800 years, the bells were silenced because of fears that vibration would topple the tower. In the same year the tilt reversed by a few millimetres, after lead weights were placed on the ground floor of the tower.
🔦 The tower's architect, Bonanó Pissanó, tried to compensate for the incline by building the upper storeys at an opposing angle, in the hope of balancing the building.

Le Corbusier (1887-1965) (Real name Charles Édouard Jeanneret) Swiss-born French architect who influenced 20th-century buildings with his philosophy that a house should be a 'machine for living in' and that architecture was the 'magnificent play of masses brought together in light'. Inspired by ▷CUBISM, Le Corbusier

devised an innovative system of calculating proportions to design individual buildings and entire cities. He advocated the use of concrete, standardised building elements and prefabrication. Among his best-known buildings are the Unité d'Habitation (1946-52) – a concrete block of flats in Marseilles, France – and the Chapel of Notre Dame du Haut (1951-5), in Ronchamp, France, which has a roof shaped like a ship's hull.
🔦 The architect adopted the name Le Corbusier because of his likeness, when wearing glasses, to a crow – in French, *corbeau*.

lich gate Covered wooden gateway at the entrance to a churchyard, providing a resting place for a coffin before a funeral.
🔦 *Lich* or *lych* is a Saxon word for 'corpse'.

listed buildings In Britain, buildings of special architectural or historic interest which are protected by law, so that alterations to them are restricted. These include all buildings built before 1700 if they are in anything like their original condition; most of those built between 1700 and 1840; and some of special merit built after 1840. Very few are given the special status of Grade I; most are Grade II, or Grade II* for the more important buildings.

Liverpool Catholic Cathedral Strikingly original place of worship resembling a giant bell tent. It was designed in 1960-7 by

Sir Frederick Gibberd (1908-84) in the INTERNATIONAL MODERN style. Built from reinforced concrete on a circular plan, it has the altar at the centre, with the congregation assembled around it. A 2030 ton stained glass LANTERN above the altar allows light to flood into the interior.

Lloyd's building See Richard ROGERS.

Lutyens, Sir Edwin Landseer (1869-1944) British architect whose traditional approach made him the Edwardian establishment's favourite builder. Early in his career he was heavily influenced by the ARTS AND CRAFTS MOVEMENT and specialised in designing romantic country houses for the wealthy. Munstead Wood, in Surrey, was commissioned in 1896 by the famous garden designer Gertrude JEKYLL. Later Lutyens designed a number of public buildings and the Cenotaph in Whitehall, London, a national monument to those who died in the two world wars. His masterpiece was the plan for New Delhi, which included the Viceroy's House (now Presidential Palace) (1912-31).

McAdam, John Loudon (1756-1836) Scottish engineer who devised a durable road surface composed of stones and gravel laid down to form a dense, firm base. Later, engineers added tar to bind the stones together, calling the surface 'tarmacadam' or 'tarmac' after him.

CROWNING GLORY *Le Corbusier's Chapel of Notre Dame, which dominates the crest of a hill in Ronchamp, France, is often cited as one of the most important buildings of the 20th century.*

Mackintosh, Charles Rennie (1868-1928) Leading British exponent of ART NOUVEAU, whose designs for the Glasgow School of Art (1896-9 and 1906-9), and its interior furnishings, won him international admiration. His unusual design for the Willow Tearoom (1911) in Glasgow is also widely acclaimed. After leaving Scotland in 1914, Mackintosh designed less; he devoted himself to painting from 1923 and produced exquisite watercolours. (See also ▷MACKINTOSH in 'Art and Design'.)

Mies van der Rohe, Ludwig (1886-1969) German-born architect who, with Le Corbusier and Frank Lloyd Wright, was one of the key figures of modern architecture. In 1938 Mies left Germany, where he had been a director of the BAUHAUS school, for the USA. He believed that 'less is more', and produced simple, clean-cut designs. He pioneered the use of steel and glass in skyscrapers remarkable for their elegant proportions. The Seagram Building in New York (1954-8) and the Lake Shore Drive Apartments in Chicago (1948-51) are examples of his work.

minaret Tall tower linked to a MOSQUE from which a *muezzin*, or crier, calls Muslims to prayer. Minarets may be square or cylindrical in shape, and some have a series of projecting balconies.

monastery See ABBEY.

mosque Muslim place of worship. Many mosques are simple assembly halls for daily worship. Friday mosques, however, are designed to hold large numbers of people for prayers on Friday (the Muslim holy day) and have inspired some of Islamic architecture's masterpieces. Examples include the Holy Mosque in Mecca (built around the Kaaba, a sacred stone), the Dome of the Rock in Jerusalem and the London Central Mosque in Regent's Park. Most large mosques are built around a large courtyard containing a fountain for ritual washing. The *mihrab*, a special niche in the wall facing Mecca, shows Muslims which way to face when praying. Many mosques are richly decorated with calligraphic designs, which turn quotations from the ▷KORAN into dazzling abstract patterns. (See also ▷MOSQUE in 'Ideas, Beliefs and Religion'.)

Nash, John (1752-1835) British architect who became the favourite of the Prince Regent, later ▷GEORGE IV. He was the leading exponent of PICTURESQUE architecture, and specialised in grandiose, STUCCO façades. Nash's prolific output encompassed a range of styles, including Classical and castellated Gothic. He was the master architect of the REGENCY, with his plans for London's Regent Street, Carlton House Terrace and Regent's Park. Notable works include All Souls Church, Langham Place, London (1822-5); parts of ▷BUCKINGHAM PALACE (1825-30); and the rebuilding of ▷BRIGHTON's Royal Pavilion in an extravagant oriental style (1815-21).

neo-Classicism Revival of the CLASSICAL style in Europe from the late 18th century to the early 19th century. It was inspired by the rediscoveries of the Roman cities of Herculaneum (1738) and ▷POMPEII (1748), and employed the simpler ideals and forms of the ancient Greeks and Romans as a reaction against the ornate style of the ROCOCO period. At the start of the revival, buildings were solid and severe, with restrained decoration and massive spaces and forms. By the end of the period, the design was more attractive, with more elaborate decoration and less austere forms. Robert ADAM was the leading British exponent of the style. (See also ▷NEO-CLASSICISM in 'Art and Design'.)

neo-Gothic or Gothic Revival. Re-awakening of interest in GOTHIC architecture in the mid 19th century, based on the fashionable romantic nostalgia for medieval Europe. The decoration of the Houses of Parliament (1844-52) by Augustus PUGIN and St Pancras Station (1868-74) and the Albert Memorial (1863-72) in London by Sir George Gilbert SCOTT are among the best examples of the style.

Norman English version of ROMANESQUE architecture which flourished from the 11th century to about the mid 12th century. Typical features include round arches, tunnel vaulting, Classical columns and geometrical ornamentation. Norman churches often have square, flat-topped towers rather than spires. DURHAM CATHEDRAL is an outstanding Norman building.

Notre Dame Name given to many French cathedrals, but particularly associated with the cathedral of Paris which is one of France's most distinguished examples of GOTHIC architecture. It was built from 1163 to 1345 on the Île de la Cité, an island in the River Seine. The cathedral's monumental structure – 425 ft (130 m) long, 155 ft (47 m) wide and 115 ft (35 m) high – can accommodate up to 9000 worshippers. Notre Dame is supported by enormous flying BUTTRESSES, and has sunk several feet under its own weight since it was built.

obelisk Tall, four-sided shaft of stone that tapers to a point. The first obelisks were built by the Egyptians to flank the entrances to tombs and temples.
🕯 Cleopatra's Needle on London's Embankment, brought to England in 1878, is one of a pair of Egyptian obelisks. The other is in Central Park, New York. The obelisk at the Place de la Concorde in Paris was presented by Mohammed Ali Pasha to King Louis-Philippe in 1831.

Palladian Classically inspired architecture in the manner of Andrea PALLADIO . The style was brought to England by Inigo JONES in the 17th century and developed by Colen CAMPBELL and Lord BURLINGTON during the 18th century. In Britain, Palladian architecture was the precursor of NEO-CLASSICISM.

Palladio, Andrea (1508-80) Italian architect whose extensive study of antique design, *The Four Books of Architecture* (1570), influenced architecture throughout Europe. His work was inspired by CLASSICAL models, and his formula for the ideal villa, with Classical PORTICOS and airy colonnades, was a major influence on English and American architecture.

GOTHIC GRANDEUR *Notre Dame, standing on an island in the Seine, is one of the oldest French Gothic cathedrals, dating from 1163.*

Panama Canal Link between the Atlantic and Pacific oceans across the Isthmus of ▷PANAMA. The 51 mile (82 km) canal, which saves ships the long journey round Cape Horn, took 33 years to build and opened in 1914.
🕯 The canal was planned by Ferdinand de Lesseps, who also built the SUEZ CANAL.

Pantheon Circular domed temple to all the gods, rebuilt in Rome by the Emperor Hadrian in AD 120-4 from an earlier building of *c*.27 BC. The diameter of the building, 142 ft (43 m), is the same as its height, and its entrance is through an impressive portico with Corinthian columns. The monumental dome inspired a great deal of ▷RENAISSANCE architecture, in particular BRUNELLESCHI's dome for Florence cathedral. The Pantheon, now a Roman Catholic church, contains many tombs, including that of the artist ▷RAPHAEL.

pargetting Ornamental patterning on external walls, formed with special tools on damp plaster. Pargetting is commonly found on half-timbered 16th and 17th-century houses throughout East Anglia.

Parthenon Temple dedicated to the goddess Athena, built on the ACROPOLIS in Athens between 447 and 438 BC. It was seen by the Greeks as the architectural ideal with its perfect combination of austerity and grace. The temple is 228 ft (69.5 m) long and 101 ft (31 m) wide. The Parthenon later served as a Christian church then an Islamic mosque before being used as an ammunition store by Turkish occupiers in the 17th century. It was badly damaged by an explosion in 1687, when it was bombarded by Venetian forces besieging Athens. Many friezes and sculptures such as the ▷ELGIN MARBLES were taken from the building in the 19th century.

pediment In Classical architecture, a low-pitched GABLE on the façade which is placed above a PORTICO, door or window.

Perpendicular Last phase of English GOTHIC architecture, following the DECORATED style and lasting from *c*.1340 to *c*.1530. Buildings in this style often have rib or fan vaulting, slender columns, and large windows divided by prominent mullions, or vertical ribs, and mock battlements. Gloucester cathedral is a fine example.

Picturesque Style of English architecture and landscape gardening in the late 18th and early 19th centuries, during the REGENCY period. It combined freedom and formality, asymmetry and mixed forms and textures. One example is the castellated Gothic style of John NASH. The Picturesque style influenced European architecture more than any other English style.

Pompidou Centre HIGH-TECH building built in Paris in 1971-7 which houses a modern art gallery as well as a centre for

CLASSIC BEAUTY *The Parthenon's superb proportions have influenced architects ever since it was built in the 5th century BC, when it housed a massive gold and marble statue of the goddess Athena.*

industrial design. Richard ROGERS and the Italian architect Renzo Piano created the controversial, six-storey structure by 'turning the building inside out'. Functional services such as staircases and escalators are visible from outside, to increase the amount of display space. The building is sometimes referred to as the Centre Beauborg, the name of the piazza which it overlooks.
🕭 The Pompidou Centre is named after Georges Pompidou, President of France from 1969 to 1974.

portico Roofed entrance, usually in the centre of the façade of a church, house or temple. It may be open or partly enclosed, and often has columns and a pediment, or a low pitched gable.

post-modernism Mid 20th-century stylistic reaction to the BAUHAUS movement and the INTERNATIONAL MODERN style, which tries to create a link between modern technology and the past by reintroducing colour, ornament and sculpture. By combining older styles, post-modernist architects have sought to create more appealing and evocative buildings than their immediate predecessors.

prefabrication System in which standardised sections of a building are mass-produced in a factory and assembled on site. The CRYSTAL PALACE was an early example. Prefabricated houses became a necessity in Britain after World War II, to provide a

cheap and quick replacement for housing destroyed by bombing raids. The same principle is extended to much larger buildings when large panels of reinforced concrete are used.

prestressed concrete Extremely strong form of REINFORCED CONCRETE made by pouring CONCRETE over stretched steel cables within a mould. When the concrete has set it stops the cables from returning to their normal length after the mould has been removed. The tension created compresses the concrete and enables it to resist enormous stresses. Prestressed concrete is often used to make slender bridges.

Pugin, Augustus (1812-52) British architect who became an ardent medievalist after converting to Roman Catholicism in 1834. He studied GOTHIC architecture and wrote several influential books promoting its virtues. He is most noted for the exterior and interior NEO-GOTHIC decoration of the Houses of Parliament in London, built between 1844 and 1852.

pyramids Colossal monuments built by the ancient Egyptians to house their ▷PHARAOHS' tombs. Pyramids date from around 2660 BC. The shape of the pyramid is thought to symbolise a staircase to the sun, so that the king could climb to heaven.
🕭 The Great Pyramid of King Cheops, at Giza, near Cairo, rises 450 ft (137 m) above the ground. It is built from 2.3 million

blocks of stone weighing an average of 2.5 tons, and was originally covered with polished limestone slabs. The pyramids at Giza are the only one of the Seven Wonders of the Ancient World to survive.
⚒ The term pyramid is also applied to artificial hills with flat tops built by the ancient peoples of South America.

'Queen Anne style' British style of red brick town architecture, popular in the 1870s and 1880s. Despite the name, it was not a revival of the style of Queen ▷ANNE's reign (1702-14); it retains certain features but also draws on English and Flemish domestic buildings of both the 17th and 18th centuries. It is characterised by Dutch GABLES, white timber sash windows, grouped chimneys, steep tiled roofs, terracotta ornament, doors and (often bay) windows with individual PEDIMENTS and Classical decorative details. The leading exponents of the style were Norman SHAW and W.E. Nesfield (1835-88).
⚒ Queen Anne furniture *does* date from Queen Anne's reign. The elegant designs typically have cabriole legs (curved with an ornamental foot) and walnut veneer. The style was brought to Britain by French and Dutch Huguenot craftsmen fleeing persecution by Catholics in their own countries.

Regency Early 19th-century style of British architecture and design which marks the concluding phase of the GEORGIAN period. Named after the fashionable Prince Regent, later King George IV, the Regency style is one of lavishness combined with elegance – a kind of NEO-CLASSICISM with added flourishes such as exterior STUCCO work and wrought iron, roofed balconies. The elegance of John NASH's terraces around Regent's Park in London are typical of the period. Regency architecture was also influenced by the PICTURESQUE approach, exemplified by Nash's celebrated Royal Pavilion in Brighton which incorporates Chinese and Indian architectural styles. (See also ▷REGENCY in 'Art and Design'.)

reinforced concrete Strong and versatile building material made from a mesh of thin steel rods embedded in CONCRETE. It can support very heavy loads – a property exploited to the full in the construction of domes and bridges. PRESTRESSED CONCRETE is even stronger.

Renaissance Renewal of Classical ideals in architecture, literature and art which took place in Europe from the late 14th century to the end of the 16th century.

Renaissance buildings have arches borne on slender columns, graceful decoration and layers of massive stone blocks with accentuated deeply indented joints. In architecture the style is typified by the work of BRUNELLESCHI and ALBERTI, and the term generally refers to the Italian Renaissance style – even though its influence spread from Italy throughout Europe. (See also ▷RENAISSANCE in 'Art and Design'.)

Repton, Humphry (1752-1818) British landscape gardener who initially followed the naturalism of 'Capability' BROWN but later created more formal landscapes, with straight paths and flower beds. He frequently collaborated with the architect John NASH, creating a setting for a house that gave panoramic views over the garden.

Rheims Cathedral One of the finest French GOTHIC churches. Work started in 1211, and most of the cathedral was finished 100 years later. Its 176 windows contain some of the world's most beautiful stained glass, including the celebrated rose window 40 ft (12 m) in diameter.
⚒ The baptism of King Clovis in Rheims Cathedral in AD 406 started a royal tradition; many French kings were subsequently consecrated there.

INSIDE OUT *Richard Rogers's use of external pipes and ducts at the Lloyd's building, in the City of London, is intended to reduce the maintenance and servicing costs.*

rococo Style of decoration using elegant fanciful forms inspired by nature. It also used elements of the NEO-GOTHIC style – particularly in England. From France, where it originated in the early 18th century, its influence quickly spread to Germany and Austria extending the preceding BAROQUE period and refining its vigour with great technical mastery. (See also ▷ROCOCO in 'Art and Design'.)

Rogers, Sir Richard (1933-) British architect of HIGH-TECH buildings whose major work, the Lloyd's building in London (1978-86), won him critical acclaim as well as scorn for its unconventionality. The building has heating and ventilation pipework on the exterior in a maze of polished aluminium, stainless steel and smooth grey concrete. Rogers also co-designed the POMPIDOU CENTRE in Paris.

Romanesque Style of architecture common in western Europe from the 11th century to about the mid 12th century, named after the Roman architecture from which it is derived. Romanesque buildings typically have Classical columns, round arches, tunnel vaulting and fantastical decoration. In England, the Romanesque style is called NORMAN. It was followed by the GOTHIC style.

Roman roads The Romans built roads that sliced across the terrain in a series of straight lines. These roads were so well constructed – with an earth base, then a layer of small stones in mortar, topped by a layer of solid material covered by stone slabs – that some, such as the Appian Way from Rome to Capua, are still in use 2300 years later. England's many Roman roads include Watling Street, now followed by the A2 from Dover to London, the A5 from London to Telford, and Ermine Street, which heads north on the A10 from Ware.
⚒ The total distance covered by Roman roads by the end of the 3rd century AD was 53 000 miles (85 000 km) – more than twice the circumference of the Earth.

St Paul's Cathedral Crowning achievement of the English architect Sir Christopher WREN, built between 1675 and 1710 to replace the old St Paul's which was destroyed in the ▷GREAT FIRE OF LONDON in 1666. The first cathedral in England to remain under the control of its creator from start to finish, it is the second largest church in Britain after WESTMINSTER ABBEY. The height from the floor of the nave to the top of the cross above the lantern (in the main dome) is 365 ft (111 m).

St Peter's Basilica Europe's largest church, in the ▷VATICAN CITY. It is linked with the martyrdom of St Peter the apostle, who is said to have been crucified at the foot of the Vatican Hill, in Rome. A BASILICA built on the site in AD 324 was demolished in 1505 to make way for the present building, which was built in the RENAISSANCE and BAROQUE styles between 1506 and 1624. Twenty popes and ten architects, including the aged ▷MICHELANGELO, worked on the building. BERNINI added the monumental entrance piazza flanked by colonnades in the 17th century. St Peter's dome, which was designed by Michelangelo and finished by his assistants, is 452 ft (137 m) high.

Salisbury Cathedral Rare example of an EARLY ENGLISH cathedral built as a harmonious whole. It was built between 1220 and 1258, although its magnificent spire – at 404 ft (123 m) the tallest in England – was added in about 1305.

Scott, Sir George Gilbert (1811-78) Leading practitioner of NEO-GOTHIC architecture. He restored hundreds of churches, but was often criticised for 'over-restoring' them. As well as new churches, he built the Albert Memorial (1863-72) and St Pancras Station (1868-74), which are both in London, and Glasgow University (1867-70).

Sears Tower World's tallest office building, completed in Chicago in 1974. It has 110 storeys and is 1454 ft (443 m) high.

Shaw, Norman (1831-1912) British architect known for his designs in the 'QUEEN ANNE STYLE'. His best-known buildings are Old Swan House, Chelsea (1875-7), and New Scotland Yard (1887-1907), on London's Victoria Embankment. He also co-designed Bedford Park, in west London (1877-80), the first garden suburb.

Stephenson, George (1781-1848) Britain's first railway engineer, who was put in charge of the Stockton to Darlington railway in 1821 – it opened in 1825 with Stephenson's *Locomotion* engine pulling the first passenger train. Stephenson then built the Liverpool to Manchester railway, which opened in 1830 and incorporated 73 bridges and the first deep railway cutting. His son Robert STEPHENSON was also a noted engineer. (See also George ▷STEPHENSON in 'Technology and Invention'.)
⚓In 1829 George Stephenson's engine *The Rocket* won a prize for maintaining an average speed of 29 mph (46 km/h).

Stephenson, Robert (1803-59) George STEPHENSON's son who helped his father with the construction of the Stockton to Darlington railway line. Robert Stephenson was appointed engineer in charge of the London to Birmingham line which opened in 1838, and also designed various railway lines overseas. His other work includes the tubular rail bridge (1845-50) over the Menai Straits, which links north Wales with Anglesey.

stucco Durable smooth finish for exterior walls made from a mixture of cement, sand and lime. The term also describes the REGENCY vogue for using plaster to imitate exterior stonework.

Suez Canal Waterway stretching 100 miles (162 km) across Egypt linking Port Said on the Mediterranean Sea to Suez on the Red Sea, saving ships the long journey around Africa's Cape of Good Hope. It was planned by the French engineer and diplomat Ferdinand de Lesseps (1805-1894) and opened in 1869. The canal was financed by an Egyptian company, and the British government subsequently bought a major share in its ownership.
⚓The Egyptian government forcibly nationalised the canal in 1956, sparking off the ▷SUEZ CRISIS. It was closed by Egypt during the ▷SIX-DAY WAR in 1967, and only reopened in 1975. More than 20 000 vessels a year now pass through the canal.

Sydney Harbour Bridge World's widest and heaviest steel arch bridge which was opened in 1932 and took eight years to build. The bridge's arch spans 1650 ft (503 m) and it carries two railway tracks, an eight-carriageway road, a footpath and a cycleway on a deck 160 ft (49 m) wide.

STEALING THE SHOW *At the opening ceremony of the Sydney Harbour Bridge, a monarchist protester charged on horseback past the premier of New South Wales to cut the ribbon.*

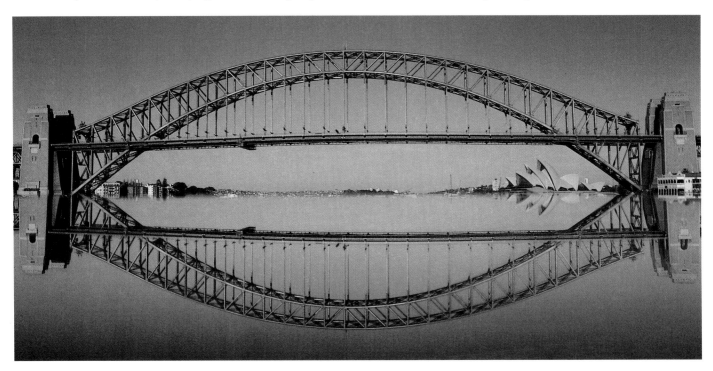

Sydney Opera House Australia's most renowned building, set on a promontory in Sydney Harbour. It houses five halls – for music, drama and exhibitions – three restaurants and six bars in its ten concrete 'shells'. The ambitious design, by Danish architect Jørn Utzon (1918-), won a competition in 1957 but proved impossible to carry out. Ove ARUP solved the problems, and the building was eventually completed in a much-altered form in 1973. The roof, covered by over 1 million tiles, weighs more than 20 000 tons.

Taj Mahal Mausoleum at Agra, in northern India, widely regarded as one of the world's most beautiful buildings. It was completed in 1653 by the Mogul emperor Shah Jahan in memory of his favourite wife, Mumtaz Mahal. A large onion-shaped dome is flanked by four smaller domes and four minarets. An ornamental pool reflects the entire composition, which is a superb melding of Islamic and Hindu styles in white marble.
The mausoleum's marble façade is inlaid with semiprecious stones but hides a structure built out of common rubble.

Telford, Thomas (1757-1834) Scottish engineer noted for building canals and the trunk road from Shrewsbury to Holyhead, which includes the spectacular suspension bridge (1826) over the Menai Straits. Telford built 1200 bridges and more than 1000 miles (1600 km) of roads in Britain.
The New Town of Telford, in Shropshire, is named after the engineer.

tracery Ornamental stonework in the upper part of a window or arch first used in the GOTHIC windows of RHEIMS CATHEDRAL at the beginning of the 13th century. The dividing ribs are known as mullions (vertical) and transoms (horizontal).

Trans-Siberian Railway Longest railway line in the world. It was largely built between 1891 and 1904, and runs from Moscow to Nakhodka on the Sea of Japan – a distance of 5864 miles (9436 km). Another branch goes through Mongolia and across China to the capital, Beijing.

Tudor Style of architecture in Britain mainly associated with the late GOTHIC period (1485-1558). ▷HAMPTON COURT PALACE is one of the finest examples of Tudor architecture, with its imposing gatehouses, battlemented parapets and ornate chimneys all built from red brick.
The whitewashed walls and exposed timbers of Elizabethan domestic architec-

MONUMENTAL LOVE *The Taj Mahal, one of India's most-visited sites, is a stunning memorial to a Mogul emperor's beloved wife. It took an army of 20 000 workers more than 12 years to complete.*

ture were widely copied in English houses built in the 1920s and 1930s, in a style known as 'mock Tudor'.

tunnels Shallow tunnels can be built by the 'cut and cover' method of digging a deep trench which is then covered over. Deeper tunnels have to be made by tunnelling underground, using picks and shovels or mechanical drills. The tunnelling shield invented by Marc Isambard BRUNEL was a major technical advance, enabling tunnels to be driven through soft soil as well as under rivers or the sea-bed. The shield protects the tunnellers, and prevents the tunnel walls collapsing. After it has been pushed along, support rings are installed. Modern tunnels, such as the CHANNEL TUNNEL, are excavated by enormous tunnelling machines called 'moles', which also incorporate a protective shield.
The longest tunnel in the world is the Seikan rail tunnel, which runs more than 33 miles (53 km) under the Tsugaru Straits between the Japanese islands of Honshu and Hokkaido. The longest road tunnel runs 10 miles (16 km) through the St Gotthard Pass in Switzerland.

underground railways The first underground rail link was London's Metropolitan Railway from Farringdon Street to Paddington, which opened in 1863. Steam trains carried more than 9 million passengers during its first year – despite the sulphurous fumes. London's first 'tube' line, deep enough to avoid the foundations

of buildings, opened in 1890. Budapest opened an underground line in 1896, Boston in 1897, Paris in 1900, New York in 1904 and Moscow in 1935. The first fully automated system, the Bay Area Rapid Transit (BART), was completed in San Francisco in 1974. London's underground network is the largest of any city.

Vanbrugh, Sir John (1664-1726) Leading English architect of the BAROQUE style, whose masterpiece is ▷BLENHEIM PALACE (1705-16) – built for John Churchill, the first Duke of Marlborough. Vanbrugh was also a successful dramatist, and Blenheim reflects a sense of theatrical magnificence – a palatial mansion arranged around three sides of an immense courtyard.

vault Arched roof used for spanning large spaces. It was employed extensively by the Romans in aqueducts, amphitheatres, warehouses and public baths. The basic 'barrel' or 'tunnel' vault, springing from a series of rounded arches, was much used in ROMANESQUE or NORMAN architecture. The use of the pointed arch in GOTHIC architecture from the 12th century onwards led to the 'ribbed vault', a fine skeleton of stone ribs forming the arches, with the spaces between the ribs filled in by thin stonework. Vaulting reached a peak of sophistication with the 'fan vault', the supreme example of which is at King's College Chapel, Cambridge (1446-1515), where the stone looks almost as intricate and delicate as lacework.

Venturi, Robert (1925-) American architect and writer, regarded as the father of POST-MODERNISM. He reacted against the purity of the INTERNATIONAL MODERN style, seeking to give his buildings at least a degree of complexity and adornment. He is best known in England for the Sainsbury Wing at London's National Gallery, completed in 1991.

Versailles Spectacular palace and gardens built largely by King ▷LOUIS XIV of France near Paris. Work on the building started in 1668, and the royal court moved there in 1682. The magnificent BAROQUE apartments include the 240 ft (73 m) long *Galerie des Glaces*, or Hall of Mirrors, where the Treaty of Versailles which ended World War I was signed in 1919.

Victorian Period during the reign of Queen Victoria (1837-1901) which saw the revival of many architectural styles – Classical, rococo and, in particular, Gothic. Victorian building design usually exaggerated the styles it revived, as with the NEO-GOTHIC work of SCOTT and PUGIN. Buildings were massive and the ornamentation often flamboyant. Designs were also influenced by the Industrial Revolution and advances in engineering which allowed many parts to be factory-made, as in the prefabricated CRYSTAL PALACE. Other notable Victorian architects were Sir Charles BARRY and Sir Joseph Paxton. (See also ▷VICTORIAN STYLE in 'Art and Design'.)

Voysey, Charles (1857-1941) British architect and interior designer who built many houses in accordance with the aims of the ARTS AND CRAFTS MOVEMENT, breaking away from formal and ornate late VICTORIAN architecture. His houses have an informal, cosy quality created by the use of low elevations, steeply sloping roofs, white STUCCO walls and little or no ornament. Voysey also designed furniture, fireplaces and decorative details such as wallpaper and textiles.

wattle-and-daub Popular method of building walls in the Middle Ages: timber framework was covered with interlaced twigs, or wattles, and daubed with a mixture of clay reinforced with cow dung and horsehair, before being roughly plastered.

Westminster Abbey Earliest example of NORMAN architecture, started under Edward the Confessor around 1048. His original church has all but disappeared under a series of later alterations. The existing abbey was finished in about 1740.

FITTING IN WITH NATURE *Frank Lloyd Wright's Fallingwater in Pennsylvania was designed to echo the natural contours of the land, making the house become part of the surrounding landscape.*

Among its points of interest are Henry VII's Chapel (1503-9) which houses the king's tomb and Poet's Corner where many poets, including Chaucer and Byron, are buried. The honour of burial in the abbey is conferred by the dean of Westminster.
⚲ Most of England's kings and queens have been crowned at Westminster Abbey.

World Trade Center Tallest office block in New York, its twin square towers dominating the southern tip of Manhattan. Built by the architect Minoru Yamasaki between 1962 and 1976, the towers are 1350 ft (411 m) high.

Wren, Sir Christopher (1632-1723) English architect whose masterpiece is ST PAUL'S CATHEDRAL, London (1675-1710). In his role as surveyor general of the king's works he built 52 other churches in the City of London alone. Wren also devised a plan for the radical replanning of London after the ▷GREAT FIRE of 1666, but it was not adopted. His other buildings include the Greenwich Observatory.

Wright, Frank Lloyd (1867-1959) American architect and one of the most influential figures in 20th-century architecture. Wright built houses in what he called an 'organic style' – that is, appearing to grow from the ground rather than just sitting on it. His most celebrated house, Fallingwater, Pennsylvania (1936-9), was built over a waterfall. He also designed New York's Guggenheim Museum, in the form of a continuous corkscrew.

York Minster Largest GOTHIC church in England, built between 1220 and 1480. It is renowned for its magnificent original stained glass, which includes the celebrated Great East Window – the largest area of stained glass in the world.
⚲ York Minster was ravaged by a fire caused by lightning in 1984. The roof of the south transept and the entire vault were destroyed and the rose window was badly damaged.

ziggurat Ancient Assyrian or Babylonian temple shaped like a stepped pyramid with the top sliced off to allow space for a shrine, with ramps giving access to each level. The earliest ziggurats were built by the Sumerians around 3000 BC.
⚲ The fabled Tower of Babel was a giant ziggurat designed to reach the heavens.

WREN'S MASTERPIECE *St Paul's Cathedral, widely regarded as one of London's finest buildings, houses memorials to national heroes such as Kitchener, Wellington and Nelson.*

HUMAN SOCIETY

A brain that evolved far beyond the instinctive responses of
other animals enabled our ancestors to create complex
languages and organise themselves into settled communities.
Societies across the globe have developed in diverse ways
according to their history and culture, but all have
an elaborate web of family ties and distinctive rituals that
mark an individual's progress through life.

ETON COLLEGE

SIGMUND FREUD

MASAI, KENYA

Aboriginals First human inhabitants of Australia, some 750 000 of whom were living there when European settlers arrived in 1788. The term can also refer to the earliest known inhabitants of any region. Australia's Aboriginals were nomadic HUNTER-GATHERERS who migrated from southern Asia at least 50 000-60 000 years ago. Although most Aboriginals now live in cities or towns, a few, mostly in the Northern Territory, have returned to the bush to lead a life close to that before European contact. Land rights remain a dominant issue; Aboriginals own 12 per cent of Australia but have claimed more.
🎵 Australian Aboriginals have a rich spiritual life based on 'Dreamtime', or 'Dreaming', a golden age at the beginning of creation, when plants, animals and humans came into existence. Although about 600 languages were once spoken (two-thirds of which are now extinct) and there are wide cultural differences, the 265 000 Australian Aboriginals have a strong sense of unity.

Afrikaners Descendants of Dutch, German and French settlers in South Africa. Their forebears arrived at the Cape in the 17th century and were originally known as ▷BOERS. They make up about 60 per cent of South Africa's white population and speak Afrikaans, a language derived from Dutch. From 1948 to 1994, Afrikaners dominated South Africa's government, and their leaders were responsible for developing the policy of ▷APARTHEID.

Afro-Caribbean Person from the West Indies who is originally of African descent. Many Afro-Caribbeans emigrated to the United Kingdom from Jamaica, Trinidad and other islands in the 1950s, encouraged by the British government to help fill a shortage of labour. There are more than half a million people of West Indian background in Britain today, about half of whom live in Greater London.
🎵 The annual Notting Hill Carnival, held in London at the end of August, is Britain's major Afro-Caribbean celebration.

age of consent Minimum age below which it is a criminal offence to have sexual intercourse. In Britain, the age of consent for heterosexual intercourse is currently 16; homosexual men can consent when they have reached the age of 18. In most developed nations the age of consent falls between 15 and 18, and in some parts of the world homosexuality is completely illegal.
🎵 Although Britain's 16-year-olds can legally have heterosexual sex, they need parental consent to marry before they are 18.

INSTRUMENT MAKERS *Aboriginals in northern Australia put the finishing touches to a didgeridoo – the traditional long, hollowed-out wooden tube which produces a deep note when blown.*

Aleut Native of the Aleutian islands, off western Alaska. Aleuts have a similar lifestyle to the INUIT people, but they speak a different language and follow a different religion – Russian Orthodox Christianity.

A levels National examinations taken at secondary school in England, Wales and Northern Ireland, usually at the age of 17 or 18, two years after GCSEs. The 'A' stands for Advanced, and in the past they were preceded by 'O' (for Ordinary) level tests. In Scotland, pupils take five 'Highers' instead of A levels, and have the opportunity to follow these with a year of specialised Sixth Year Studies.

alienation Feeling of separation or isolation from other people, or from society as a whole. Karl Marx used the term to describe the effects of capitalism, which he believed dehumanised people and deprived them of creative and fulfilling work. More recently, the term has been used by psychologists to refer to feelings of powerlessness and lack of purpose in modern society.

American Indian Term applied to the indigenous peoples of North and South America by European explorers who mistakenly believed they had reached India. Many American, or 'Red', Indians now prefer to be called NATIVE AMERICANS.

androgyny Having both male and female characteristics, in appearance and behaviour. The word is a compound of the Greek *andros* 'man' and *gyne* 'woman'. Entertainers have sometimes cultivated deliberately androgynous images; among them are the rock musicians David ▷BOWIE and Boy George. Androgyny is not usually connected to hermaphroditism – the condition of having both male and female sexual characteristics.

animal rights Campaigning issue which holds that animals have the right to protection from cruel or unnatural treatment. Most groups such as the animal welfare organisation, the RSPCA, lobby peacefully against the abuse of animals in a range of areas such as drug trials, cosmetic tests, battery farming, hunting, the fur trade and zoos. But the issue has prompted violent 'direct action' by some sections of the Animal Liberation Front; extremists have been prosecuted for vandalising laboratories and intimidating scientists.

anthropology Study of the origin and development of mankind and of societies. The latter is known as cultural anthropology, and embraces other disciplines such as archaeology, linguistics and ethnography (the study of different societies, based on first-hand observation).

anti-Semitism Persecution, discrimination or prejudice against the JEWS and their religion. Hostility against the Jews has existed in Europe since the days of the Roman Empire, but became particularly strong in the Middle Ages, when they were accused of murdering Christ. Many countries expelled Jews or barred them from certain professions, so forcing them to make a living by moneylending, banking and trade. Their prosperity often attracted envy and their distinctive way of life made them easy targets. From the time of the ▷CRUSADES, the Jewish communities of Europe suffered massacres known as pogroms, but the most extreme form of anti-Semitism was the Nazi ▷HOLOCAUST of 1933-45, in which approximately 6 million Jews were systematically murdered.
🎵 Anti-Semitism remains a feature of extreme right-wing groups such as the British National Party, the French National Front and the German neo-Nazis.

antisocial personality Term applied to a person who appears to have no conscience or concern for others, and who habitually resorts to lying, stealing and violence. Antisocial behaviour, which was previously known as psychopathy, begins in childhood or adolescence, and often leads to a life of delinquency, addiction and crime.

🔑 People who dislike social gatherings should be referred to as 'asocial', 'unsocial' or 'unsociable', rather than 'antisocial'.

aptitude test Test designed to measure someone's potential for achievement, rather than what they already know or can do. General-aptitude tests – such as intelligence tests – measure a broad range of abilities, while special-aptitude tests can measure just one type of ability, such as eye-hand coordination or mathematical skill. They are mostly used in career guidance.

Arabs Group of Arabic-speaking SEMITIC PEOPLES who started to migrate from the Arabian peninsula in c.3500 BC, and are now spread throughout the Middle East and North Africa. Most Arabs are ethnically CAUCASOID in origin, but in some areas they have intermarried with local populations. Some Arab tribes, known as Bedouins, are nomads, but the majority live more settled lives. About 95 per cent of the world's 250 million Arabs are ▷MUSLIMS.

🔑 Arab rulers conquered Spain in the 8th century AD, and were expelled in the 15th century. They left behind masterpieces of architecture such as the ▷ALHAMBRA.

arranged marriage Selection of marriage partner by parents, relatives or a professional matchmaker rather than by the couple themselves. The union is seen as an alliance of families based on property and social status rather than affection. Love remains the desired result, however, and many prefer the system, arguing that arranged marriages are stronger and more successful than love matches. The practice is still common in many societies; in the West it was widespread among royalty and the aristocracy until World War I.

🔑 In Britain, an arranged marriage is legal only if both partners consent freely and are of marriageable age.

Aryans Nomadic group held to be the linguistic forefathers of Indo-Europeans. They are thought to have moved from central Asia and eastern Europe into India and western Europe from 2000 BC. In ▷NAZISM, Aryans were wrongly hailed as a Germanic blond, blue-eyed master race.

assimilation Process of being absorbed into a culture, as when settlers or refugees take on the customs and traditions of their host country. The United States is sometimes called a 'melting pot' because it has assimilated so many immigrant groups.

baby boom Sudden increase in the birth rate, as happened in Britain and the USA after World War II and again during the 1960s, following a period of sustained prosperity. People born during a baby boom are sometimes called 'baby boomers'.

Bantu Language spoken by about 60 million related peoples of central and southern Africa, including the Kikuyu, ZULU, XHOSA, and Matabele. Studies of the 500-odd Bantu languages and their ORAL TRADITIONS suggest a common origin in Cameroon or Nigeria. In this century, many Bantu speakers have become urbanised.

behaviourism School of psychology based on the study of observable behaviour. It ignores subjective experiences, such as feelings and thoughts, because they cannot be observed directly or assessed scientifically. Behaviourism was developed just before World War I by the American psychologist J.B. Watson, who was influenced by Ivan Pavlov's discoveries about animal CONDITIONING. The theory was refined by B.F. SKINNER, who said that most behaviour was shaped by learning how to win rewards and avoid punishment.

🔑 Behaviour therapy involves learning new patterns of behaviour in order to confront and overcome problems such as phobias, compulsions, and habits such as smoking.

betrothal Engagement or promise to be married. In many Western countries, it is often an informal event, and the couple may have been living together as man and wife for years. In other cultures, a handfasting ceremony, at which the engaged couple join hands, counts as official permission for them to sleep together.

black consciousness Movement begun in the United States during the 1950s with the aim of giving black people living in a white-dominated society a sense of pride in their culture and history. In order to raise black consciousness, campaigners promoted important aspects of black identity, from music to literature and religion. Leading figures in raising black consciousness included ▷MALCOLM X, Martin Luther ▷KING and in South Africa, Steve Biko. (See also ▷CIVIL RIGHTS MOVEMENT in 'World History'.)

HUMAN SOCIETY

BLACK LEADER *Malcolm X addresses a 1961 rally in the USA. His views moved from total rejection of white culture to a more multi-racial approach which led to his murder by radical Black Muslims.*

blue-collar Term applied to manual jobs or labourers, as opposed to WHITE-COLLAR office workers. It refers to the blue overalls and shirts traditionally worn by mechanics, factory labourers and other people who work with their hands.

blue-stocking Educated or academic woman, often with little interest in appearance, fashion, gossip and other supposedly 'feminine' concerns. The phrase arose in the 1750s when a group of London women held intellectual meetings to which some men wore blue worsted stockings, rather than formal black silk.

body language Non-verbal communication by means of subconscious gestures, movements and physical attitudes. People's body language may contradict their spoken message, confusing the observer or betraying their true feelings. A man may sound friendly, but convey hostility by standing with his hands on his hips, or a liar may give himself away by covering his mouth, in some way, with his hand, as he speaks. Such behaviour owes much to our animal origins, as zoologist Desmond Morris has explained in his popular 'man watching' books and TV series.
🔖 One guilty sign that officials look for as travellers go through customs is licking the lips – a response to inner tension.

bonding Forming of close emotional relationships – in particular, that between a mother and baby, which normally starts to happen during the very first hours of life. For this reason, newborn infants are given immediately to their mothers.
🔖 Activities which have high levels of male participation, such as playing football or spending evenings in the pub, are sometimes jokingly called 'male bonding'.

brainwashing Indoctrination aimed at fundamentally altering a person's attitudes and beliefs so that he or she unquestioningly accepts a particular political or religious point of view. Techniques such as isolation, deprivation of food or sleep, hypnosis, constant repetition and even physical torture may be used to break down resistance and increase dependence on the brainwasher.

breadline Minimum income needed to sustain a person or family. In Britain, state benefits are supposed to stop people falling below the breadline.
🔖 In 1994-5 income support for a typical couple with two children under the age of 11 was £113.05 a week, excluding housing costs. This figure is meant to allow for some

non-essential goods, but has still been widely criticised as too low.
🔖 The original breadlines were food queues organised by charities in the United States to feed the destitute.

bride price Money or goods given by a bridegroom or his family to the bride's family. Bride prices are most common in cultures with extended families, where the bride becomes part of her husband's family. By paying it, the groom's family compensates the bride's family for the loss of a potential labourer and gains control of any children born of the marriage. In other traditions, the bride's family pays a dowry to the groom, to defray the cost of supporting her. This is probably the origin of the modern Western custom that the bride's parents pay for the wedding.

Britons Pagan Celtic people who inhabited Britain before the arrival of the Romans in the 1st century AD. They lived in tribes and spoke Gaelic and Celtic languages. The name 'Briton' is thought to derive from the Latin *pritani* 'painted people', used by the Romans to describe the tribesmen's tradition of painting their bodies with woad, a blue vegetable dye.

care in the community Policy of discharging people with mental, physical or behavioural problems from hospitals, and reintegrating them into society once their condition is under control. Introduced in Britain some 60 years ago, it became widespread in the 1980s, when many psychiatric patients were encouraged to administer their own medication under the supervision of their GPs or in 'supported accommodation', instead of being treated in hospital.

caste system Rigid social framework in which the status of a person's family determines almost every aspect of life, from permitted diet and dress to education and choice of marriage partner. It is impossible to improve one's standing by effort or by marriage. The world's most elaborate caste system is found in India, where hereditary social divisions are based on the precepts of ▷HINDUISM. *Brahmins* (priests) are holy men with the highest status. Below them are *ksatriyas* (landowners and warriors), *vaisyas* (farmers and merchants) and *sudras* (labourers). In addition there is a vast underclass of *harijans* (previously called 'untouchables'), who are only allowed to make a living by performing menial tasks – collecting the rubbish or cleaning the streets, for example.

caucasoid Group of peoples – often referred to as 'white' – which includes large population groups in Europe, north Africa, southwest Asia and the Indian subcontinent. They have also displaced native peoples from many parts of the world – notably the Australian ABORIGINALS and the NATIVE AMERICANS. Caucasoid, or caucasian, people vary greatly in appearance, with skin tones ranging from pink to olive and hair colours from blond to black.

DIRTY WORK *India has long had a strict caste system. This woman, carrying cow dung which she has collected and dried to sell as fuel, belongs to the lowest rank, which were once called 'untouchables'.*

ARTISTIC LICENCE *D.H. Lawrence's tale of rustic adultery, censored for 30 years because of its robust language, became an instant best-seller in 1960, after a British court lifted the ban.*

censorship Restriction on the free expression or exchange of ideas and information. In order to suppress dissent, authoritarian regimes censor unfavourable news while giving wide publicity to other, more optimistic information. Freedom of expression is a prized asset in most democracies, which generally censor only to suppress extremely violent, obscene or racially abusive material, or to protect military secrets and state security.
🎙Modern technology has made censorship increasingly difficult. Electronic communications such as computer modems, satellite telephones and television stations can easily bypass the censors. Even if there is no free press in a country, photocopiers and fax machines make it possible to produce alternative news sheets.

census Population survey carried out by governments at regular intervals in order to obtain the statistical information they need for efficient government. Censuses date from ancient times: the very title of the Old Testament book of Numbers refers to the counting of the children of Israel to assess their military capability. The ▷DOMESDAY BOOK, a tax survey conducted by William I in 1085-6, provided the first census information in the British Isles. Regular censuses have been held in Britain since

1801, usually at ten-yearly intervals. They have evolved from being simple headcounts to providing detailed information about the age, occupation, lifestyle and ethnic origin of the population.
🎙The New Testament relates how Joseph and Mary had to travel to Bethlehem in order to register for a census ordered by the Roman emperor Augustus. As a result, Jesus was born in a manger instead of at their home in Nazareth.

Chomsky, Noam (1928-) American linguist whose analysis of the structure and grammar of language has produced revolutionary theories. He proposed that mankind shares a single fundamental grammar which is 'transformed' by a series of rules into all the different languages of the world. Noting the remarkable speed with which infants grasp the abstract rules of sentence construction, Chomsky suggested that humans have an instinctive, genetically programmed ability to learn languages. The existence of a universal grammar which is common to all human tongues appears to support this theory.
🎙Chomsky campaigned vigorously against US involvement in the Vietnam War, and is a well-known voice of the American left.

class Position in society as measured by birth, education, occupation, income, wealth and place of residence. In Britain, accent is also an indication of class. Unlike the rigid CASTE SYSTEM, it is usually possible to move from one class to another by personal achievement or marriage. Britain is widely seen as one of the West's most classbound societies, but the distinctions are blurring, with both the upper class and the working class increasingly resembling the middle class. The aristocracy is no longer viewed in quite the same light as it once was.
🎙British analysts grade social status on a six-point scale: Grade A (upper middle class) represents top management and professionals; B (middle class) is middle management; C1 (lower middle class) is clerical, supervisory and junior management; C2 (skilled working class) is skilled manual workers; D (working class) covers semi- and unskilled manual workers; and E comprises casual workers and state pensioners.

clause 28 Controversial part of Britain's Local Government Bill (1988), which prohibits local authorities from 'promoting' homosexuality. It also makes it illegal for state schools to promote 'the acceptability of homosexuality as a pretended family relationship'. It has failed to produce any prosecutions – partly because the wording of the clause is too vague for lawyers to be confident of winning their case.

collective unconscious Memories and mental patterns that are shared by members of a single culture, or, more broadly, by all human beings. The psychologist Carl JUNG proposed the theory to explain recurring delusions in patients with different backgrounds, common themes in dreams, and the existence of universal ideas (or 'archetypes') which appear as similar myths in disparate cultures.

Comte, Auguste (1798-1857) French philosopher who founded the science of SOCIOLOGY – a term he invented. Comte believed that human society obeyed laws in the same way as the natural world, and so could be studied scientifically, which was the goal of his philosophy of ▷POSITIVISM.

conditioning Process by which a person or animal comes to associate a certain object, sight, sound or state of affairs (known as the 'stimulus') with a pleasant or painful experience (the 'reinforcer'), so producing a particular response whenever the stimulus is present. In so-called classical conditioning, the response is usually involuntary, as when the Russian scientist

Ivan Pavlov (1849-1936) taught dogs to salivate at the sound of a bell they had learned to associate with food. In 'operant' conditioning, as developed by B.F. SKINNER, the response takes the form of voluntary behaviour; it aims at obtaining a reward or avoiding a punishment. For example, a mouse may be trained to press a lever to obtain food or avoid an electric shock.

Conditioning is sometimes used to modify human behaviour. Alcoholics may be given a drug that induces nausea whenever they drink. Eventually they associate the taste of alcohol with being sick, and so find it easier to give up drinking.

cult Organisation which focuses on ritual, magic or other religious observances. Many African and Oceanic peoples, for example, have ancestor cults, in which dead ancestors are revered as divine and ceremonies are organised to invoke their aid. A cult is also a religious group held together by a dominant individual. The term is often used derogatorily by members of mainstream faiths to refer to fringe groups.

Religious cults in the West have often caused controversy. For example, members of the Unification Church – popularly known as ▷MOONIES – have been accused of brainwashing and extorting money from adherents.

In 1978 more than 900 cult followers of the Reverend Jim Jones committed mass suicide in Guyana, and in 1993 members of

David Koresh's Branch Davidian sect set fire to their compound at Waco, Texas, rather than surrender to US government agents. Eighty bodies were eventually recovered from the ruins.

culture The attitudes, customs, beliefs and values that distinguish one group of people from another. Culture is transmitted from generation to generation through language, objects, rituals, institutions and many other aspects of daily life. For anthropologists, the key aspects of culture – using language, making artefacts and regulating behaviour – are what distinguishes humans from other animals.

'Culture shock' is a form of stress affecting people who have to adapt suddenly to an unfamiliar society. It is often experienced by refugees and immigrants.

debutante In Britain, a young woman of aristocratic background or aspirations who attends a series of social events and formal balls. This process, known as 'coming out', supposedly marks a girl's debut, or appearance, in high society, and introduces her to a carefully vetted group of friends. Until 1958, the season reached its climax when the 'debs' were presented to the sovereign at Buckingham Palace.

Whether or not they 'come out' officially, aristocratic young women are often labelled as 'debs', and the 'suitable' men who court them are known as 'debs' delights'.

defence mechanism Unconscious response which protects someone from a worrying or unpleasant experience or memory. Anger or violence could be a defensive response to fear, upset or embarrassment. Similarly, a person who feels guilty about something may produce reasons to justify his or her behaviour or blame someone else.

discrimination In Britain, there are laws against discrimination on the basis of sex or ethnic group at work and in education, housing and social facilities. Other areas remain controversial – such as whether homosexual couples should be allowed to adopt children. (See also RACISM.)

Many British employers now monitor the ethnic origins of their employees. Some follow equal opportunity programmes to try to counter racial and sex discrimination. Such programmes include 'affirmative action' or 'positive discrimination' to meet the needs of specific groups. However, despite concerted efforts to achieve equality, and many cases successfully being taken to court, discrimination still remains in many areas of society.

divorce In Britain, the courts only grant divorce applications if they are satisfied that the marriage has irretrievably broken down. Adultery is the most commonly given reason: other grounds for divorce include desertion and 'intolerable behaviour' – which could mean anything from persistent nagging, drunkenness or violence. It is also possible for the partners to agree to dissolve the marriage after two years of living apart. There are two stages to divorce: first, the judge issues a decree *nisi* (Latin for 'unless'), which declares that the marriage has broken down – unless the parties change their minds within six weeks, after which the marriage can be dissolved by a 'decree absolute'. Jews and Muslims must go through religious divorce procedures as well as obtaining a civil divorce.

In Britain some two in five marriages are likely to end in divorce, and there were about five times as many divorces in 1991 as there were 40 years previously.

Durkheim, Emile (1858-1917) French social scientist and one of the first to develop SOCIOLOGY. He argued that the beliefs, attitudes and behaviour of individuals in any society were shaped by a 'collective conscience' – ideas and values shared by all of its members, and often expressed in the form of religion. His writings, including a classic work on *Suicide* (1897), are still widely studied.

SOCIAL GRACES *Under expert supervision, the debutantes of 1927 practise the low curtsey they are to perform for George V at Buckingham Palace to mark their 'coming out' into high society.*

BRITAIN'S EDUCATION SYSTEM

In Britain, education is compulsory from the age of 5 to 16. Most children move from primary to secondary schools at the age of 11; in Scotland they transfer to 'high schools' at 12 years old. At the age of 16, pupils sit the General Certificate of Secondary Education (GCSE) in England, Wales and Northern Ireland; in Scotland, they take the Scottish Certificate of Education (SCE) Standard Grade. About 65 per cent of all students have some form of further education, but fewer than 13 per cent go on to higher education, such as university. More than 80 per cent of British schools are co-educational and a growing number are 'opting out' from Local Education Authority (LEA) control to become self-governing, funded directly by the government. National Vocational Qualifications (NVQs), which can usually be obtained in the course of everyday work, were introduced in the 1980s and provide five national grades of competence for a wide range of skills.

City Technology Colleges are funded jointly by the government and private sponsors. Set up in the 1980s to widen the choice of secondary schooling, they stress technology, science and business studies.

Colleges of Further Education prepare students of 16 and over for GCSEs, A (Advanced) levels and NVQs at various levels. They may also offer higher education courses.

Colleges of Higher Education teach students, who must have at least two A levels, to degree level and beyond.

Comprehensive schools (high schools in Scotland) teach nine out of ten secondary students. Pupils are drawn from a geographical area, and taught in mixed ability classes up to school leaving age. Many comprehensives also have sixth forms, up to the age of 18, enabling students to gain more GCSEs, A levels, or, in Scotland, Highers at 17 and the Certificate of Sixth Year Studies (CSYS) at 18.

Grammar schools have entrance exams and stream pupils (aged 11 to 18) according to ability. Most have been replaced by comprehensives, or become public schools.

Independent schools are fee-paying and range from small kindergartens to large boarding schools.

Open University offers degree courses to all. Students attend residential summer schools and learn at home via TV and radio programmes and correspondence tuition.

Private preparatory schools, or 'prep' schools, prepare fee-paying pupils from the age of seven or eight for the entrance exams to independent or public schools.

Public schools teach 13 to 18-year-olds, who often board. Fees can be more than £10 000 a year. About 1 in 14 children attend independent or public schools.

Sixth Form Colleges teach mainly academic subjects to 16 to 19-year-olds. Tertiary colleges are similar, but also offer vocational courses.

Universities teach students – who should have two or three A levels – degree and postgraduate courses. Students and staff may carry out important research work. In 1992, all polytechnics and some higher education colleges gained university status, but many still offer vocational courses.

---

ego (Latin for 'I') The 'self' or centre of a person's conscious identity and experience. The Austrian psychoanalyst Sigmund FREUD believed that there were three regions of the human mind: the unconscious ID, the rational ego and the moral SUPEREGO. In this theory the ego's task is to mediate among three contending forces – the demands of the outside world, the instinctual desires of the pleasure-seeking id and the moral strictures of the superego. It also has to control functions such as memory and problem solving.
♣ In common usage, ego means someone's self-importance or sense of superiority. For example: 'His ego is enormous – he is convinced that he is a genius at everything'.

elitism Power and privilege being held by a small group of people, or the belief in such a minority's superiority and right to dominate society. Several social and political theories are based on the concept of elitism – some claim that it is a beneficial way of organising society, others that it is inevitable for some groups to rise to the top. Elitist theories often conflict with the ideals of equality and democracy.

empty-nest syndrome Sense of loss and purposelessness experienced by many parents when their children have grown up and leave home. Mothers without careers, who have devoted their lives exclusively to raising a family, tend to suffer most.

endogamy Social rule or custom which requires people to marry within a particular group. Traditional Hindus, for example, should marry within their own CASTE, and in ancient Egypt, royalty practised brother-sister marriage to keep the line 'pure'. Marriage outside a designated group – EXOGAMY – is much more common.

equality In democratic society, equality – fair treatment, irrespective of race, sex or religion – takes several forms, including equal rights to justice and a fair trial (equality before the law), the right to be considered for a job purely on the grounds of qualifications and ability (equality of opportunity), and equal rights to vote and to stand for public office (political equality). The equal sharing of goods and resources between all citizens has, in theory, been one of the main goals of all communist states.
♣ Britain's Equal Opportunities Commission was set up in 1975 to ensure equal pay and employment opportunities for all. The commission claims that despite its efforts, women still earn an average of 20 per cent less than men for doing similar work.

Eskimo One of the three ethnic groups of native peoples of Alaska, Canada, Greenland and Siberia. The other two are the ALEUT and the INUIT.

Establishment Term applied to certain individuals and institutions – such as the Church, parliament, OXBRIDGE and the civil service – which enjoy social, economic and political ascendancy or privileges in society. The Establishment has always tended to be conservative, for its interests usually lie in maintaining the status quo.

ethnic cleansing Euphemism for driving ethnic minorities out of an area, either by physically removing them or by killing them. The term was often used in the early 1990s to refer to the Serbian government's policy of creating exclusively Serb areas in the former ▷YUGOSLAVIA.

ethnicity Identity with, or membership of, a particular racial, national or cultural group, and observance of that group's customs. Gypsies, Chinese, Asians and the Welsh are all ethnic groups.

ethnocentrism Belief that the values and standards of other cultures should be compared with one's own. Ethnocentrism usually implies that one's own culture is somehow superior to all others and it is often manifested as prejudice, discrimination or RACISM.

HUMAN SOCIETY

175

eugenics Attempt to improve or influence a race or the entire human species by selective reproduction. The term was first used by the 19th-century scientist Francis Galton, who believed that society should discourage people with hereditary diseases from having children, while helping those with high intelligence to have large families. The idea fell into disrepute after the 1930s, when the Nazis implemented a eugenics programme to boost the blond, blue-eyed 'Aryan' race and destroy 'sub-human' people such as Slavs and Jews. Medicine was used in attempts to further the ends of political extremism; doctors carried out gruesome medical experiments and collaborated in mass murder.

New developments in medicine and ▷GENETIC ENGINEERING, which make it possible to detect and cure abnormalities in human foetuses or choose the sex of a child, have made eugenics a controversial subject once again.

euthanasia Act of inducing a painless death at the request of someone who is terminally ill or critically injured to prevent further, needless suffering. In Britain, passive euthanasia (refusal to prolong life artificially) is legal if the person is in a condition to make the decision, or otherwise at the doctor's and family's discretion. Active euthanasia – deliberately causing death, perhaps by administering drugs – is murder, even if it is carried out at the patient's insistence. The Voluntary Euthanasia Society campaigns to make active euthanasia legal in certain circumstances.

The word euthanasia is derived from the Greek for 'good death'.

exogamy Social requirement to marry outside a particular group or groups. Almost all societies are exogamous to some extent, in that marriage to close relatives is usually forbidden. Some require members to choose partners from other clans or tribes.

extrovert Someone whose motives and actions are directed outward – towards other people or the outside world, rather than being concerned with their own inner life. Extroverts are said to have a sociable, outgoing and expressive personality, while INTROVERTS are considered to be quieter, more contemplative and reserved.

Eysenck, Hans Jürgen (1916-) German-born British psychologist who provoked a furore in the 1970s by claiming that IQ (intelligence quotient) is linked to race as well as genes. Eysenck also wrote a best-selling book, *Know Your Own IQ*.

DOCTOR OF THE MIND *At the age of 80, Sigmund Freud boards an aircraft for the first time. The house in Hampstead, north London, where he spent his last years is now a museum. Among the displays is the celebrated rug-draped couch where his patients lay for consultations.*

feminism Social and political movement aimed at securing equal rights for women in all spheres of life. It follows the tradition of the ▷SUFFRAGETTES, who campaigned for votes for women in the early 20th century. The many forms of feminism, range from straightforward campaigning for sexual equality to outright and often strident rejection of the male and all aspects of language and society that reflect male domination. 'Women's Lib', as it was popularly termed, was at its zenith in the early 1970s and provoked a post-feminist backlash. However, feminist approaches to literary criticism, the social sciences, history and theology are well-established branches of those disciplines.

Among the more popular and influential feminist writers have been Simone de Beauvoir (who wrote *The Second Sex*), Germaine Greer (*The Female Eunuch*), Betty Friedan (*The Feminine Mystique*) and Kate Millet (*Sexual Politics*).

free association Psychological technique of exploring a person's UNCONSCIOUS mind or investigating thought processes. Words are read out one by one to someone, who is asked to say the first thing that comes to mind. A psychiatrist or psychoanalyst then interprets the responses as a way of understanding the person's thought patterns. INKBLOT TESTS are similar, but use visual rather than verbal stimuli.

Freud, Sigmund (1856-1939) Influential Viennese neurologist and founder of PSYCHOANALYSIS. After training as a doctor, he became interested in mental health and investigated the subconscious mind through hypnosis, dream analysis, childhood memories and FREE ASSOCIATION. According to Freudian theories of psychoanalysis, human beings are driven by the LIBIDO – a mixture of their sex drive and survival instinct. Freud said that the human personality has three parts: the primitive, unconscious ID, the rational EGO and the SUPEREGO, or conscience. He also proposed an elaborate theory of human sexual development. Newborn infants go through an 'oral phase', in which they gain physical gratification as well as nutrition from their mouths. As toddlers, they enter the 'anal phase', in which they derive pleasure from controlling their bowel movements. Next comes a period of latent or hidden sexuality, which later gives way to the 'phallic phase' – the discovery of, and preoccupation with, the genitals. The final 'genital' stage should bring mature, loving relationships with other people. Freud's theories, especially his view that all men wrestle with the OEDIPUS COMPLEX – a combination of sexual desire for their mothers and jealousy of their fathers – were revolutionary. A Jew, Freud fled the Nazis in 1938 and settled in London. Although many of his theories are now questioned, he remains one of the most influential figures of the 20th century.

♪A 'Freudian slip' is a verbal mistake or memory lapse which reveals an unconscious thought or emotion. For example, calling one's boss 'darling' or forgetting a dentist's appointment could signify emotional frustration or fear of the dentist.

future shock Sense of insecurity and disorientation felt by people whose societies are undergoing rapid change. The term comes from the title of a book by American author Alvin Toffler, describing the devastating effects of social and technological change in Western industrialised society, which he likened to the 'culture shock' sometimes felt by travellers.

gay rights Movement that campaigns for social acceptance and equal rights for homosexual, or 'gay', men and lesbians. In Britain, there are many affiliated groups, including Pride Trust, which organises an annual 'gay pride' march in London, and Stonewall, a pressure group which lobbies parliament and the media on issues such as legal equality for lesbians and gay men and their representation in the media.

♪In many ways, gay rights campaigners have copied the styles and organisation of the earlier women's liberation movement.

GCSE (General Certificate of Secondary Education) Examination for 16-year-olds introduced in 1988 in England, Wales and Northern Ireland. It replaced the General Certificate of Education (GCE) O level and Certificate of Secondary Education (CSE) examinations. GCSEs are offered in a wide range of subjects and are marked by 'continuous assessment' of class work as well as by formal tests. Scottish pupils take Standard Grade SCEs.

geisha In Japan, a traditional female companion or entertainer highly trained in the arts of music, dance and conversation. A few also have sexual relations with their clients. Few true geishas exist today, but some still work in restaurants, where they may be hired by women as well as men.

gender roles Social, behavioural and cultural aspects of masculinity and femininity, as opposed to biological differences. Gender roles are continually reinforced by many aspects of social life and expectations of how each sex should behave. In many cultures, men are expected to be independent, active, ambitious and able to control their emotions; women to be dependent, sensitive, more emotional and supportive.

These attitudes may have had their origins in early man's HUNTER-GATHERER lifestyle, in which males, supposedly, led an active, hunting life while females were occupied with the demands of child rearing.

♪Gender roles are blurring: FEMINISM has helped women to be independent, while today's 'new man' is encouraged to show his emotions, take an active part in child rearing, cook and do housework.

genocide Extermination of an entire national, racial or ethnic group, as attempted by the Nazi ▷HOLOCAUST. The Australian ABORIGINALS and the Bushmen of southern Africa were nearly wiped out when European settlers arrived, partly as a result of deliberate persecution, and partly because white men unwittingly carried diseases to which the natives had no resistance. The Ache Indians of Paraguay, the islanders of East Timor, the Kurds and the Tibetans have all suffered from genocidal oppression in recent decades.

♪In the 1990s, Iraqi persecution of marsh-dwelling Arabs amounted to genocide: as well as taking military action against them, the authorities drained the marshes and so destroyed their habitat, forcing them to abandon their way of life and move to the towns. The warring parties in the former Yugoslavia – especially the Bosnian Serbs – were also accused of genocide following the discovery of mass graves.

GOOD COMPANY *This Japanese woman's dress, white make-up and hairstyle proclaim her to be a geisha, or professional companion.*

gestalt (German for 'form') Approach in psychology which studies responses to whole events, instead of breaking them down into constituent parts. Just as the effect of music lies in melody, tempo and orchestration rather than in the individual notes, gestalt ▷PSYCHOTHERAPY considers the patient's overall health and analyses immediate problems, as opposed to the Freudian approach of delving into dreams and childhood memories.

ghetto Densely populated and often run-down area inhabited by poorer minority groups. Ghettos originated in the Middle Ages, when Jews were compelled, often by statute, to live in prescribed areas of cities such as Warsaw and Lodz. In effect, Jewish quarters also became ghettos in other cities, such as Vienna, Amsterdam and Munich. The practice of confining Jews to a specific area was revived by the Nazis in the 1930s as a prelude to mass murder.

♪The term is thought to derive from Venice's *Ghetto* – an iron-founding area where many Jews lived.

global village Term coined by the Canadian sociologist Marshall McLuhan (1911-80) to express his view that the progress and increased speed of modern communications had effectively reduced the whole world to the dimensions of a village.

'great man theory' View that human progress takes place because of the efforts of outstanding individuals – such as Mozart, Leonardo da Vinci, Napoleon and Jesus Christ. Thomas Carlyle, the 19th-century historian and the theory's creator, argued that 'The history of the world is but the biography of great men'. By contrast, the ZEITGEIST theory emphasises the spirit of the time rather than any one person's abilities. Most historians and social scientists believe that the truth lies somewhere in between the two theories.

group therapy Form of PSYCHOTHERAPY conducted in small groups, usually supervised by a trained therapist. By sharing experiences, group members develop insight into their emotional and interpersonal problems and realise that other people have similar problems to their own.

♪Many self-help groups, such as Alcoholics Anonymous, use group therapy techniques.

guilt and shame cultures Distinction made in anthropology, based on the way societies regulate members' behaviour. Guilt cultures have a clear moral code, usually based on religion and personal

Gypsies

conscience. In shame cultures, right and wrong are less important than fear of public disgrace, or losing face. In practice, most cultures are a mixture of both. Catholicism and Judaism are often said to be 'guilt' cultures. Japan, with its elaborate code of honour, is a 'shame' culture, where people still commit HARA-KIRI to avoid humiliation.

Gypsies Nomadic people found all over the world but especially in southern Europe. Their origins are a mystery, but their language, Romany, is related to Hindi and suggests an Indian background. Traditionally, they travel in painted horse-drawn carriages and earn money by selling flowers and lace and telling fortunes; now, most Gypsies have motorised transport and also deal in goods and livestock. In Scotland and Ireland, they are sometimes called tinkers.

The name 'Gypsy' comes from the word 'Egyptian', from a discredited theory about their origins. Gypsies usually refer to themselves as Rom or Roma (from the Romany language) or simply as 'travellers'.

hara-kiri Japanese ritual suicide by disembowelling, practised to avoid humiliation or loss of face. Many Japanese soldiers committed hara-kiri rather than surrender during World War II.

In Puccini's opera *Madame Butterfly*, the main character commits hara-kiri after being betrayed by her husband and having to give up her child.

hippies Nonconformists drawn together in the 1960s by their rejection of standard political and social values and by their vague ideals of peace, freedom and love. The trend began in the United States, fuelled by opposition to the Vietnam war, but rapidly caught on in Europe. Eastern religions such as Zen Buddhism, unkempt appearance, 'ethnic' dressing, communal living, free love and taking drugs all played a part in hippie culture, as did outdoor rock concerts such as Woodstock (1969), 'love-ins' and the declared aims of peace and 'flower power'. Hippies faded in the 1970s, but some of their ideals live on in Green parties and NEW AGE movements.

homosexuality According to some research, sexual and emotional attraction for a partner of the same sex may be a genetic trait, although social factors and upbringing are also thought to play a role. Homosexuality is not a medical or psychiatric disorder, but it is still regarded as immoral or abnormal by many.

The GAY RIGHTS movement demands equal treatment for lesbians and gay men.

HONOURS AND TITLES

People who make exceptional contributions to British public life can be rewarded by elevation to the House of Lords or by admission to one of the ancient chivalric orders, which entitle members to add initials after their names. Within most orders there are several ranks. The best-known civil honours, in order of precedence, include:

KG Knight of the Order of the Garter
KT Knight of the Order of the Thistle
GCB Knight Grand Cross of the Order of the Bath
OM Order of Merit
CH Companion of Honour
KCMG Knight Commander of the Order of St Michael and St George
KBE Knight Commander of the Order of the British Empire
DBE Dame Commander of the Order of the British Empire
CMG Companion of the Order of St Michael and St George
CBE Commander of the Order of the British Empire
OBE Officer of the Order of the British Empire
MBE Member of the Order of the British Empire

GEORGE CROSS
The highest award for civilian bravery is given for acts of heroism or courage in dangerous circumstances.

There are six main tiers to Britain's peerage: royal duke; duke; marquess; earl; viscount; baron or baroness. Since 1958, non-hereditary life peers have also been created. All peers are entitled to sit in the House of Lords, providing they are over 21, have British nationality and are not felons, bankrupts or lunatics. Archbishops rank between royal dukes and dukes, and bishops rank between viscounts and barons.

VICTORIA CROSS
The highest award for military bravery was given to Group Captain Leonard Cheshire (near left) for death-defying bombing sorties, and to Wing Commander Guy Gibson, leader of the Dambuster raids in World War II.

---

honours list In Britain, awards proposed by the prime minister but approved and granted by the sovereign at the New Year, on the sovereign's official birthday and on other special occasions. Recipients are often civil servants, industrialists, scientists, entertainers and other people deemed to have rendered outstanding public service. Military personnel are proposed by the Secretary of State for Defence. (See also 'Honours and Titles' box.)

A scandal broke in 1922 when it emerged that David Lloyd George had sold honours in return for political donations. The system is still criticised as being open to abuse, although fewer honours are given automatically and the public now plays a greater role in nominating people for them.

humours Fluids in the human body whose balance, according to an ancient theory, determine a person's character and health. The four humours were seen as blood, phlegm, choler (or yellow bile) and melancholy (or black bile). The theory represented an early attempt to classify personality types.

The theory of humours is reflected to this day in words describing moods, such as 'phlegmatic' (calm), 'choleric' (irascible) and 'melancholic' (gloomy, from Greek *melas*, black, and *khole*, bile).

hunter-gatherer Term used to describe human societies living on game and food foraged from the wild. Until about 12 000 years ago, all humans are believed to have

2 million Native Americans in the north, living in about 200 different tribes and speaking nearly as many languages. While North America was dominated by warrior tribes such as the Iroquois, Apache and Sioux, the great ▷MAYA, ▷AZTEC and ▷INCA civilisations flourished in Central and South America. European settlement brought bloody land wars and the collapse of Native American cultures, apart from a few remote tribes such as the Amazonian Indians of Brazil. In the 19th century, Native Americans in Canada and the United States were driven into restricted areas or reservations. Since the 1960s, they have campaigned to establish their land rights and increase their civil rights.

🕯The traditional image of the Native American, with headdress and bow and arrow, is based on the Plains Indian tribes such as the Sioux, Cheyenne and Crow.

nature-nurture debate Long-standing controversy about whether genetic or environmental factors have a greater influence on personality and abilities. It has led to violent disagreements over sensitive issues: for example, some might argue that criminals are born delinquent, while others believe that a bad environment or upbringing is largely to blame.

Negroid One of the major ethnic divisions of mankind, encompassing most of the indigenous African peoples south of the Sahara and their descendants now living in many other parts of the world.

🕯There are large Negroid populations in the United States, Brazil and the West Indies, brought over from Africa by slave traders to work on plantations during the 16th to 19th centuries.

New Age Term for a wide range of activities and ideas united by a common aim to replace modern materialism with new spiritual values. The New Age 'movement' is a loose alliance of groups interested in subjects such as Eastern religion, environmental issues, the psychology of Carl JUNG, astrology, alternative medicine and the occult. Some New Agers reject conventional religion in favour of ancient pagan beliefs. The name 'New Age' comes from the astrological theory that the Earth is now entering the 'Age of Aquarius' – supposedly heralding a period of world harmony and heightened spiritual consciousness.

🕯So-called 'New Age travellers' lead a nomadic HIPPIE life touring the British countryside in battered vans and buses, occasionally converging for festivals, such as Glastonbury in Somerset.

TRADITIONAL DRESS *Men of the Montana-based Crow tribe of Native Americans wearing their familiar feathered headdresses and beads.*

nimby Acronym of 'Not In My Back Yard', summarising the attitude of those who campaign against the building of institutions – which may be for the good of society as a whole, such as prisons, mental hospitals or new housing – near their own homes. The term became common in Britain after 1988, when Nicholas Ridley, the cabinet minister responsible for the environment and an advocate of rural housing developments, was found to have objected to a proposal to build houses near his home in Gloucestershire.

nuclear family Family group comprising a mother, father and children living together, as opposed to the larger extended family which would include grandparents, cousins, uncles and aunts as well. Today many believe that the nuclear family, supposedly standard in Western societies, is endangered by a high divorce rate and a growing number of one-parent families.

Oedipus complex According to Freudian theory, the unconscious desire of every young boy to have sexual intercourse with his mother and destroy his father – the rival for her love. Sigmund FREUD said that the complex (which appears in girls as the 'Electra complex' – sexual desire for the father and rivalry with the mother) develops between the ages of three and five, but is repressed, only to be resolved in an adult relationship with someone who 're-awakens' the doomed love for the unattainable parent. Freud claimed that these Oedipal feelings were at the root of many

neuroses, but modern psychoanalysis regards them as one factor among many, and some practitioners ignore them.

🕯The complex is named after the mythical Greek king ▷OEDIPUS, who unwittingly killed his father and married his mother.

one-parent family In 1991 there were about 1.3 million families in Britain in which one adult was raising a child alone. Various reasons have been put forward to explain the rising numbers of lone parents, including high divorce rates, an increase in teenage pregnancies and a decline in the social stigma of single parenthood.

oral tradition Aspects of culture passed on by word of mouth. In literate societies it is generally associated with folklore, but in cultures without writing it occupies a much more prominent position as the only way of recording history, myth and literature. Australian Aboriginals, for example, have an outstanding oral tradition.

🕯Homer's epics the ▷ILIAD and the ▷ODYSSEY were part of ancient Greek oral tradition for hundreds of years before they were written down.

ostracism Banishment or isolation from society or from a particular group, used as a form of punishment. In its most extreme form, the person is treated as if dead, as in strict Jewish families, where parents may actually hold a funeral for a child who marries outside the faith.

🕯The word comes from the Greek *ostraka* – fragments of broken pottery on which ancient Athenians wrote the names of those they wished to have exiled from the city.

Oxbridge Generic name for ▷OXFORD and ▷CAMBRIDGE, the oldest universities in Britain, founded in the Middle Ages. Each university is made up of many independent colleges, and both have a reputation for academic excellence. Former alumni include past prime ministers such as Harold ▷MACMILLAN, Harold ▷WILSON and Margaret ▷THATCHER, the newspaper magnate Rupert ▷MURDOCH and the poets T.S. ▷ELIOT and John ▷BETJEMAN. Although, in the past, Oxbridge was said to favour students from ▷PUBLIC SCHOOLS, both universities now have an equal number of undergraduates from state and independent schools.

🕯Women were first admitted to Oxbridge in 1869, when Girton College was founded in Cambridge. They were strictly segregated from men in separate women's colleges until as recently as 1977. Now nearly all the colleges are open to both sexes.

paternalism Fatherly style of management or rule where those in authority provide for people's needs but without allowing them to have full rights or responsibilities. It is the basis of political systems such as colonialism and ▷TOTALI-TARIANISM, and is sometimes an aspect of a company's staff policy: works outings and corporate private health schemes are paternalistic in character.

patriarchy Society in which men wield most of the power. This may mean simply that political decisions and public discussions are dominated by males, or that men hold absolute power over women and children in both public and domestic arenas. Some feminists argue that patriarchy is deeply rooted in religion, language and social structures, and is continually reinforced by popular culture.

permissive society Term popularly used to describe the relative sexual and moral freedom that has prevailed in Western societies since the 1960s.

Piaget, Jean (1896-1980) Swiss psychologist known for his work on mental development in childhood. By careful observation, he concluded that intellectual development took place in set stages that could not be artificially altered or speeded up: for example, he argued that until the age of about seven children cannot think logically or fully accept that other people have opinions. Piaget's work has influenced primary school teaching methods.

political correctness Policy of avoiding anything that may be offensive to certain people or groups, such as racist or sexist language and imagery. Political correctness (PC) has been an issue in the United States since the 1970s, but only took root in Britain during the 1980s. Many people equally opposed to prejudice have become disturbed by the emergence of a monolithic 'correct' set of attitudes which are often imposed in a humourless and inflexible way. The most controversial aspect of political correctness is its attempt to change people's vocabulary, replacing allegedly pejorative words such as 'mentally retarded' or 'short' with the more acceptable 'learning disabled' and 'vertically challenged'.

population Assessing the increase, composition and distribution of the world's people is an important task at both national and international levels. The rapid growth of world population this century, from 2.5 billion people in 1925 to nearly 5.66 billion

PRIVILEGED PUPILS *Boys at Eton College, one of England's major public schools, at ease in 1947. Pupils no longer wear top hats, but the white tie and tails remain official school uniform.*

in 1994, has caused great concern; it is forecast that it will be 8.3 billion by the year 2025. This trend defied the prediction of the British economist Thomas Malthus in 1801 that population growth would inevitably be checked by war, famine, disease or natural disaster. According to some estimates, there are more people alive today than have died since mankind evolved.

psychoanalysis Form of PSYCHOTHER-APY developed by Sigmund FREUD, based on the theory that mental and emotional problems are rooted deep in the UNCON-SCIOUS mind. Psychoanalysis uses skilful questioning, dream analysis, FREE ASSO-CIATION and other methods to help to discover the causes of personal difficulties, which are often traced back to early childhood traumas. Insight into these can take several years to achieve, but once attained, it is claimed that it can resolve mental disorders completely.
🔊All psychoanalysts have to undergo a period of analysis themselves before being allowed to set up in practice.

psychology Study of human and animal behaviour and all its processes. Psychologists study emotions, perception, memory, development, intelligence, behaviour, personality, mental illness and the relationship between mind and body. Psychology encompasses dozens of schools and divisions, but the lack of a unified approach, and difficulty in definitely proving anything, means that psychology is not always considered a mainstream science.
🔊Unlike ▷PSYCHIATRY, which is concerned with curing mental disorders, psychology is not a branch of medicine.

psychotherapy Generic term for all forms of non-medical treatment for mental, emotional or behavioural problems. It includes counselling, PSYCHOANALYSIS and GROUP THERAPY, and aims at helping people to achieve personal insight and self-development.
🔊In Britain, anyone may practise as a psychotherapist, but exponents of specific approaches such as Freudian psychoanalysis set their own standards for practitioners.

public schools In Britain (except Scotland), fee-paying independent schools to which the upper classes have traditionally sent their children. Most pupils who attend public schools are boarders, and they receive an all-round education designed to build 'character' as well as to enable them to pass exams. Among the best-known public schools are Eton, Harrow, Winchester, Charterhouse and Rugby.

🔖 Thomas Hughes's novel *Tom Brown's Schooldays* (1857) contains a vivid depiction of life at Rugby in the 19th century, complete with beatings and the now defunct custom of 'fagging' – under which younger boys performed menial tasks for older ones.

🔖 Public school educated people are often said to benefit from the 'old boy network' or 'old school tie', by which former pupils of their own schools supposedly give them preferential treatment.

purdah Tradition in some Hindu and Muslim cultures of barring women from public life and male society. Today it is rarely practised by Hindus, but it remains part of Muslim tradition.

🔖 The word purdah is derived from the Hindi *parda* – the screen or veil used to section off the women's quarter from the men's quarter in the home.

Pygmies Small-built people of central Africa, most of whom are under 5ft (1.5m) tall. A few groups still follow a traditional HUNTER-GATHERER way of life in the forests of the Congo basin.

race Classification of human beings based on superficial differences such as skin colour, hair type and facial features. The view that these traits indicate biologically distinct races is rejected by modern genetics, which has demonstrated the intrinsic similarity between different peoples. In British law, the term 'race' is now used to cover national and ethnic groups and does not contain any suggestion of intrinsic physical differences or ranking.

racism In Britain, racial discrimination is outlawed by the 1976 Race Relations Act, and reported abuses can be investigated by the Commission for Racial Equality. Racist principles underpinned the slave trade, the genocide of indigenous peoples, the persecution of Jews and other minorities, and the ▷APARTHEID system of South Africa.

refugees There are an estimated 45 million displaced people in the world today. They include nearly 5 million who fled conflict in the former Yugoslavia. The number of refugees has grown steadily since 1945. The Afghanistan war of the 1980s displaced 6 million people, and a similar number (including 1.7 million Mozambiquans, and 1.5 million Rwandans who fled the violence that flared after President Habyarimana was killed in 1994) have suffered as a result of wars and persecution in Africa. The most enduring refugee problem since 1945, that of Palestinians who fled Israel after its foundation in 1948, may now be resolved following Israel's peace accord with the ▷PLO in 1993 and with ▷JORDAN in 1994.

rites of passage Ceremonies that mark important transitions in a person's life, such as birth, puberty, marriage, having children, and death. Rites of passage usually involve rituals designed to single out certain individuals, mark their transition or INITIATION, and then reincorporate them back into society.

Semitic peoples Ancient CAUCASOID peoples of the Middle East, including the Babylonians, Phoenicians, Assyrians and Egyptians. The term is now used to refer to the JEWS and ARABS, who are supposedly descended from Shem, the son of Noah.

🔖 Hebrew, Arabic and other Semitic languages have a distinctive system of writing whose characters represent consonants only. Vowels are indicated by marks above and below the text, or simply left to the reader to infer.

serial killer Multiple murderer whose crimes take place over a period of time. One of the first serial killers was ▷JACK THE RIPPER, who murdered at least five London prostitutes in the 1880s. More recently in Britain, Frederick West was charged in 1994 with the murders of 12 females at and around his Gloucester homes; his wife Rosemary was charged with nine. Peter Sutcliffe (1946-), the 'Yorkshire Ripper', killed 13 women between 1975 and 1981, and Dennis Nilsen (1945-) confessed to strangling 15 men. In the USA, Jeffrey Dahmer (1960-) killed 17 people before being arrested, and Ted Bundy (1946-89) killed 23 women in a six-year spree of rape and murder.

sexism Sexual prejudice is underpinned by long-standing assumptions about what constitutes 'natural' or 'normal' behaviour for both men and women. Some argue that the sexes behave differently for cultural, rather than biological, reasons, and that given equal opportunities, men and women can achieve equal distinction in almost every field. Others believe that physical differences – especially women's ability to give birth – create fundamental dissimilarities which should be recognised.

Skinner, B.F (1904-90) American psychologist who concluded that most behaviour, both human and animal, is learnt in a process of trial and error. Skinner's theory of 'operant CONDI-

BOAT PEOPLE *Vietnamese refugees sail into Hong Kong harbour in search of freedom. They may not get a warm welcome: most boats are ordered to turn round and go back.*

TIONING' argued that people and animals repeated actions that brought rewards – 'positive reinforcement' – and avoided actions which brought punishment – 'negative reinforcement'. Skinner suggested that these methods could be used to modify behaviour and, controversially, to solve social and political problems.

Slavs Central and east European peoples with a shared cultural and linguistic background. They include the Russians, Ukrainians, Byelorussians, Poles, Slovaks,

Czechs, Serbians, Bulgarians and Croats. In the 3rd or 2nd millenium BC, Slavs migrated from Asia to remote parts of Russia, from where they spread in the 5th century, eventually becoming Christian by contact with the ▷BYZANTINE EMPIRE.

The Slavs have a long history of persecution at the hands of other Europeans. During World War II, many millions died at the hands of the Nazis, who condemned them as sub-human *Untermenschen*, fit only for slave labour and slaughter.

The word 'slave' is derived from 'slav'.

NEW EDWARDIAN *The long box jackets and narrow trousers of the Teddy boys mimicked the flamboyant costume of Edward VII's reign. The 'teds' were the first of many teenage tribes.*

sociology Study of human society, often with the aim of identifying the causes of social change. The term was coined by the 19th-century French philosopher Auguste COMTE, who suggested that human behaviour and institutions could be studied using scientific methods. There are many different areas of study, from social interaction in a family to the sociology of entire countries. Approaches to the subject range from the individualism of Max WEBER, which considers society as the sum of its members' actions, to Emile DURKHEIM's view that phenomena such as mob violence and mass hysteria show that society has a separate existence of its own.

Spock, Benjamin (1903-) American doctor whose best-selling *Common Sense Book of Baby and Child Care* (1946) revolutionised parental attitudes in the 1950s and 1960s by recommending flexibility and

tolerance rather than strict discipline. Some of his ideas remain controversial, and critics have blamed his permissive approach to child-rearing for a number of social ills, including juvenile delinquency.

structuralism Study of the structures and systems behind observable social and cultural phenomena. It developed out of the work of the Swiss linguist Ferdinand de Saussure (1857-1913), who saw language as a superficial system of signs cloaking deep underlying principles. The French anthropologist Claude LÉVI-STRAUSS took a similar approach to anthropology, and proposed, among other things, that the regulations of KINSHIP are based on universal rules of communication and exchange, and that myths reflect the structure or workings of the unconscious mind.

superego In Freudian psychology, the conscience, or part of the mind that acts as a rational, inner check on behaviour. As such, it is often in conflict with the ID.

taboo Symbolic or ritual ban on a person, object, action or word. The concept has now been extended to anything regarded with dread. Every culture has a taboo against INCEST. For Jews and Muslims, eating pork is taboo.

The word 'taboo' comes from *tabu*, a Polynesian word for 'sacred,' applied to objects reserved for religious use only.

Teddy boys Youths of the 1950s who dressed in pseudo-Edwardian (hence 'Teddy') style, with long jackets (called 'drapes'), velvet collars, thin 'drainpipe' trousers, shoelace ties, and swept-back Brylcreemed hairstyles.

unconscious Part of the mind whose thoughts and processes are hidden from the conscious mind. In the psychology of Sigmund FREUD, the unconscious contains the deep primitive impulses of the ID, together with repressed memories and desires. These can only be retrieved by PSYCHO-ANALYSIS, but can express themselves in dreams and imagination. Carl JUNG believed that as well as the personal unconscious there was a deeper COLLECTIVE UNCONSCIOUS, containing ancestral memories common to all people.

Weber, Max (1864-1920) German sociologist who is especially known for his work on political leadership, bureaucracy and capitalism. Weber said that political change was often attributable to exceptional leaders such as Charlemagne

and Napoleon who had 'charisma' – a term, meaning 'divine gift', that he borrowed from Christian theology. Weber also linked ▷PROTESTANTISM with the rise of ▷CAPITALISM: he believed that Protestant ideals of hard work, frugal living and self-control were responsible for capital being available for investment.

Weber's phrase 'Protestant work ethic' is sometimes used to mean diligent application to one's work.

white-collar Colloquial description of non-manual workers such as office and shop staff, who are expected to dress more formally than BLUE-COLLAR, or manual, labourers. Although they generally receive monthly salaries rather than weekly wages, many are members of trade unions; some still consider themselves working class.

Xhosa (KORZ-uh) Group of BANTU-speaking peoples who dominated the eastern Cape regions of South Africa from the mid 17th century. Their current population is about 3 million, making Xhosa one of the most widely spoken African languages in South Africa.

Many of South Africa's black leaders, including Nelson ▷MANDELA, are Xhosas.

yuppie Journalistic nickname, and in part an acronym, for 'Young Urban (or Upwardly mobile) Professional', meaning a career-orientated, hard-headed young adult who flaunts his or her prosperity. Yuppies appeared during the 1980s, but in the slump of the 1990s many lost fortunes made in the money markets and property.

Among other nicknames popular in the 1980s were 'dinkys' (Double Income, No Kids) and 'orchids' (One Recent Child, Heavily In Debt).

Zeitgeist German word meaning 'spirit of the time', embodying the view that human achievements reflect or develop from the essential character of an era. The opposite point of view, that history is made by the actions of a few exceptional individuals, is known as the GREAT MAN THEORY.

Zulu Powerful warrior tribe of South African BANTU-speaking peoples led by Chief Gatsha Buthelezi (1928-). They were welded into a kingdom by the early 19th-century chief Shaka, under whose military genius they conquered and occupied almost the whole of the province of Natal. They later inflicted heavy losses on British troops in the Zulu Wars before being defeated and assigned an area of Natal known as Zululand (later KwaZulu).

BRITISH HISTORY

In early times successive waves of invaders moulded Britain's
national identity, and through the centuries rulers, reformers and
rebels have shaped our political and religious institutions.
The roll call of great Britons who have left their mark on our
island story includes kings and queens, churchmen and
politicians, soldiers and seamen, explorers and empire builders.

GENERAL
KITCHENER

LILLIE LANGTRY

HENRY VIII

MARCHING FOR JOBS, 1936

EDWARD AND MRS SIMPSON *The former king with his bride, pictured at their wedding in 1937, and the document in which he announced his decision that he was giving up the throne for love.*

abdication crisis Events leading up to the abdication of EDWARD VIII in 1936. He gave up the throne in favour of his brother, George VI, in order to marry Mrs Wallis Simpson, an American divorcee who, according to the conventions of the time, was an unsuitable partner for the king.
🖋Edward announced his abdication in an emotional radio broadcast to his subjects with the famous words: 'I have found it impossible . . . to discharge my duties as king as I would wish to do without the help and support of the woman I love.'

Agincourt, Battle of (1415) Victory for HENRY V during the ▷HUNDRED YEARS' WAR, when the English longbowmen played the key role in defeating a much larger French army.

agricultural revolution Transformation of farming methods during the 18th century. The enclosure of common land, crop rotation, the introduction of the turnip, selective breeding and tools, such as Jethro TULL's seed drill, produced dramatic increases in food production, leading to radical social and economic change.

Alamein, Battles of (1942) Turning points in the campaign in North Africa during World War II. In the first battle (June-July) the Axis forces' advance towards the Nile was halted by Allied troops commanded by General Claude Auchinleck; at Alam Halfa (Aug-Sept) and in the second Alamein battle (Oct-Nov), the British Eighth Army, commanded by General Bernard MONTGOMERY, inflicted a heavy defeat on Field Marshal Erwin ▷ROMMEL's forces, forcing him to retreat and clearing the way for a rapid Allied advance out of Egypt towards Libya.

Albert, Prince (1819-61) German prince of Saxe-Coburg and Gotha who married Queen VICTORIA and became prince consort. A tireless worker, he was a patron of the arts, industry and science, and organised the GREAT EXHIBITION of 1851. After his death from typhoid fever at the age of 42, Victoria went into mourning and wore black for the rest of her life.
🖋London's Victoria & Albert Museum, Royal Albert Hall and Albert Memorial are among the many buildings erected in honour of the prince consort's memory.

Alcock (John) and Brown (Arthur Whitten) The first men to fly nonstop across the Atlantic, on June 14-15, 1919. It took Alcock, an English naval captain, and Brown his navigator, flying a Vickers Vimy biplane, 16 hours 27 minutes to complete the 1900 mile (3060 km) crossing from Newfoundland to Clifden, Ireland.

Alfred the Great (849-99) King of the Saxon kingdom of Wessex, in southern England, who defeated and made a short truce with the Danes. He established a navy to help to defend his territory against their later attacks. Alfred encouraged the arts and learning, and drew up a legal code.
🖋One winter when the Danes occupied much of Wessex it is said that Alfred fled to Athelney, in Somerset. He took shelter in a hut where a housewife, not knowing who he was, asked him to watch her loaves as they baked. Alfred allowed them to burn and was scolded by the furious woman.
🖋The gold and enamel 'Alfred Jewel' is an exquisite piece of Anglo-Saxon workmanship dug up in Athelney in 1693.

Anglo-Saxons Germanic peoples, from what is now southern Denmark and northern Germany, who settled in Britain in the 4th-6th centuries AD. The Angles, Saxons and Jutes, members of three different tribes, divided England into seven kingdoms, known as the 'Heptarchy': Essex, Wessex, Sussex, Kent, East Anglia, Mercia and Northumbria.
🖋The term 'Anglo-Saxon' is used to describe people of pure English descent, or objects with simple English qualities.

Anne (1665-1714) Queen who came to the throne in 1702, succeeding William and Mary. In her reign, England and Scotland were united by the Acts of UNION and the Union Jack or Union Flag was adopted as the flag of Great Britain. Britain also became embroiled in the War of ▷SPANISH SUCCESSION. Despite having 18 pregnancies, Anne failed to bear an heir and she was therefore the last of the STUART monarchs. (See also ▷QUEEN ANNE STYLE in 'Architecture and Engineering.')

appeasement Making concessions to a warlike nation in the hope of keeping the peace. The term specifically refers to the policy of Stanley BALDWIN and Neville CHAMBERLAIN in the face of Adolf Hitler's aggression during the 1930s. British appeasement reached its height in the 1938 ▷MUNICH AGREEMENT, when Chamberlain and other premiers allowed Germany to annex part of Czechoslovakia.

Armada, Spanish Fleet of 130 ships sent by Philip II of Spain to attempt the conquest of England in 1588. The 'Invincible Armada' was destroyed by a combination of bad weather and the English fleet under the command of Lord Howard of Effingham; Sir Francis DRAKE was his vice-admiral.

Asquith, Herbert Henry (1852-1928) Liberal prime minister from 1908 to 1916. His government introduced old age pensions, unemployment insurance and salaries for MPs, and reduced the HOUSE OF LORDS' power to veto legislation. Asquith, whose nickname was Squiffy, was ousted from power by David LLOYD GEORGE, his secretary of state for war.

Astor, Viscountess (Nancy) (1879-1964) First woman to sit in the House of Commons; she was elected as the MP for Plymouth in 1919.

Attlee, Clement (1883-1967) Labour prime minister from 1945 to 1951. His government introduced the National Health Service, nationalised the ▷BANK OF ENGLAND, the railways, coal and other industries. He granted independence to several British territories, including India and Pakistan.

Augustine of Canterbury, St (died AD *c.***605)** Italian Benedictine missionary who brought Christianity to southern England. He arrived in England in 597, and after converting King Ethelbert of Kent to Christianity he was made the first Archbishop of Canterbury.

Bacon, Francis (1561-1626) One of the leading figures of the English ▷RENAISSANCE. Bacon served as lord chancellor to JAMES I and wrote many books; some scholars believe that he was the true author of some of Shakespeare's plays. He also made important contributions to science. ⚘Bacon died of a chill caught stuffing a dead chicken with snow to see if the meat would be preserved for longer than normal.

Baden-Powell, Robert (1857-1941) Army general, and hero of the BOER WAR, who founded the Scout movement in 1907. Baden-Powell laid down the Scouts' principles of doing duty to God, country and others, and gave them their motto 'Be Prepared'. In 1910, together with his sister, he founded the Girl Guides.

Baldwin, Stanley (1867-1947) Conservative prime minister from 1923 to 1929 and from 1935 to 1937. His first government broke the GENERAL STRIKE. His reluctance to re-arm in the face of a German arms build-up during his second term of office was in line with his policy of APPEASEMENT and is seen as a serious error of judgment. Baldwin opposed the king's wishes in the ABDICATION CRISIS.

Balfour, Arthur James (1848-1930) Conservative prime minister from 1902 to 1905. He earned the nickname 'Bloody Balfour' after two Irish rioters were killed at a demonstration against his stern policy as Irish secretary (1887-91). As foreign secretary, he drew up the 'Balfour Declaration' (1917), which promised British support for a Jewish homeland in Palestine.

Bannockburn, Battle of (1314) Victory for Robert BRUCE over EDWARD II, in which the English army was all but destroyed, winning Scotland its independence from English rule.

Bayeux Tapestry Embroidery depicting the Battle of HASTINGS (1066) and the political events surrounding it. The tapestry, which is 224 ft (68 m) long, is probably contemporary and remains an important

GORY BATTLE *The Bayeux Tapestry shows the moment of King Harold's death, while below, the dead are being stripped of their armour.*

MURDER IN THE CATHEDRAL *Four knights hear what they think is an order to kill Thomas Becket (top) before slaughtering the archbishop (bottom left). Later, pilgrims pray at Canterbury (right).*

source for military, social and art historians. It is thought to have been commissioned by Odo, Bishop of Bayeux in northern France, where it can still be seen. It was almost certainly made by English nuns.

🔖 The tapestry contains a remarkable illustration of ▷HALLEY'S COMET.

🔖 The popular theory that King Harold died at the Battle of Hastings with an arrow in his eye originates in the tapestry's depiction of a soldier, struck in the eye by an archer, underneath the caption *Harold rex interfectus est* 'King Harold is killed'. Some scholars now hold that the next image, showing a man falling beneath the sword of a mounted knight, also depicts the king.

Beaverbrook, Lord (1879-1964)
Canadian-born British publisher, politician and financier who controlled the *Daily Express*, *Sunday Express* and London *Evening Standard* for many years. He was responsible for aircraft and arms production in Winston Churchill's war cabinet.

Becket, Thomas (1118-70) Diplomat, politician and close friend of HENRY II, who appointed him Archbishop of Canterbury, expecting him to turn a blind eye to royal interference in Church affairs. However, Becket became a staunch defender of the Church and resisted the king's proposed reforms. When he excommunicated several royal servants Henry is reported to have bellowed angrily 'Who will rid me of this turbulent priest?' Four knights mistakenly took these words as an order to execute the archbishop, and murdered him near the altar of Canterbury Cathedral. Henry deeply regretted his erstwhile companion's death and even had himself flogged; Becket was made a Catholic martyr and saint.

🔖 The killing of Becket is dramatised in plays by T.S. ▷ELIOT (*Murder in the Cathedral*) and Jean Anouilh (*Becket*).

🔖 Becket's tomb made Canterbury England's principal pilgrimage site. It is also the goal of the story-telling pilgrims in Chaucer's ▷CANTERBURY TALES.

Bede, The Venerable (c.673-735) Anglo-Saxon monk, theologian and historian from Jarrow, in Northumbria. His *Ecclesiastical History of the English People* was the first history of England. The Venerable Bede was also the first historian to date events from the birth of Christ.

Belgrano, General Argentinian cruiser sunk by the British submarine HMS *Conqueror* during the FALKLANDS WAR, killing 368 Argentinian sailors. The *General Belgrano* was outside the British-imposed exclusion zone when it was fired on, but Britain claimed that it still posed a danger to British ships in the area.

Besant, Annie (1847-1933) Socialist reformer, mainly remembered as a champion of women's rights. In the 1870s, her children were taken away from her after she published a pamphlet on contraception. She was an active trade unionist and organised a historic strike of matchgirls in 1888. Besant was later converted to the mystical creed of the ▷THEOSOPHICAL SOCIETY, and campaigned for home rule for India.

Bevan, Aneurin ('Nye') (1897-1960) Labour politician who, as health minister, set up the National Health Service in 1948. He was an ex-miner and trade unionist, and was one of the most influential politicians and most effective orators of his day. He resigned as a minister in 1951 over proposals to charge for some NHS services.

Beveridge Report *Social Security and Allied Services*, a 1942 document in which the economist Sir William Beveridge set out the principles of the ▷WELFARE STATE including the National Health Service. The report's promise of social security 'from the cradle to the grave' remained an important part of postwar government policy.

Bevin, Ernest (1881-1951) Trade unionist and Labour politician. An influential dockers' leader of the 1920s and 30s, he founded the Transport and General Workers Union. He was the minister of labour in Winston CHURCHILL's war cabinet and foreign secretary under Clement ATTLEE from 1945 to 1951.

🔖 The name 'Bevin Boys' was given during World War II to conscripts who had been diverted from the armed forces to work in Britain's coal mines.

Bill of Rights (1689) Parliamentary statute which made permanent the terms accepted by WILLIAM AND MARY as the price for their accession to the British throne in the GLORIOUS REVOLUTION. The bill barred Roman Catholics from the throne, guaranteed the Protestant succession, and established the supremacy of parliament over the monarchy.

Birmingham pub bombings (1974)

One of the worst IRA attacks on the British mainland. Twenty-one people were killed and 182 injured when two pubs in central Birmingham were bombed. The incident, part of a sustained terrorist campaign, prompted legislation (the Prevention of Terrorism Act) to help to combat the IRA. Six people were convicted for their part in the bombings, but they were freed in 1991 after evidence emerged that police notes on interviews with the 'Birmingham Six' may have been tampered with.

Black and Tans

British auxiliary police force sent to quell nationalist unrest in Ireland in 1920. Their brutality caused an international outcry and helped to precipitate the foundation of the IRISH FREE STATE in 1921. The nickname 'Black and Tan' (in fact, a breed of dog) arose from the black and khaki uniform they wore.

Black Hole of Calcutta

A cramped detention cell into which Indian troops drove British prisoners after capturing a British fort in 1756. A survivor claimed that 146 prisoners were locked in the dungeon, all but 23 of whom had died of suffocation by the next morning, but these figures have since been disputed.
🕯 Cramped, stuffy, dark places are still compared to the Black Hole of Calcutta.

Black Prince (Edward, Prince of Wales) (1330-76)

Eldest son of EDWARD III who was a brilliant commander, and won many victories in the ▷HUNDRED YEARS' WAR. Edward was not called the 'Black Prince' until long after his death; the name came from his black armour.

Blake, George (1922-)

Government official who was convicted of spying in 1961 and sentenced to 42 years in jail. He passed details of British secret service activities to the Russians for nine years before being caught. In 1966 two pacifists, Pat Pottle and Michael Randle, sprung him from jail. He later settled in the Soviet Union.

Blitz (1940-1)

Period during which British cities and towns were subjected to night-time bombings by the Luftwaffe. The raids claimed many lives, caused great destruction and forced people to take refuge underground, often in tube stations or in Anderson shelters. London took the brunt of the bombing, but Belfast, Birmingham, Liverpool, Manchester and Coventry also suffered badly. The centre of Coventry was razed to the ground in a ferocious attack in November 1940.
🕯 People affected by the bombings showed the 'spirit of the Blitz': a neighbourly concern for others combined with an unbending good-humoured defiance of the enemy. Bombed-out shops, for example, might bear a sign saying 'More open than usual'.

Bloody Assizes (1685)

Trials held following the MONMOUTH REBELLION, in which Judge Jeffreys, known as the 'Hanging Judge', dispensed brutal justice. About 300 people were hanged, 847 were transported to Barbados and hundreds faced corporal punishment and imprisonment.

Boer War (1899-1902)

Campaign in which Britain asserted its power over the independent Dutch (Boer) republics of the Transvaal and the Orange Free State, in ▷SOUTH AFRICA. The ▷BOERS wanted to defend the independence they had won in the ▷GREAT TREK, but after some early successes they were defeated by British forces under Lord KITCHENER.

Boleyn, Anne (1507-36)

Second wife of HENRY VIII, whom she married in 1533, and mother of ELIZABETH I. After Anne failed to bear Henry a male heir, he had her tried and executed on charges of adultery and incest.

Bonnie Prince Charlie (1720-88)

Charles Edward Stuart, 'The Young Pretender', son of the OLD PRETENDER and grandson of JAMES II. In 1745, he led a JACOBITE army through Scotland and northern England to assert his father's claim to the throne of George II. This episode, known as the FORTY-FIVE, ended in his defeat at CULLODEN (1746). During his flight from the British, he escaped to the Isle of ▷SKYE by disguising himself as Flora MACDONALD's maid. He spent most of the rest of his life in exile.
🕯 Charles's daring attempt to reclaim the throne for the Stuarts has inspired countless legends, poems and ballads, including the 'Skye Boat Song'.

Booth, William (1829-1912)

Founder of the ▷SALVATION ARMY, the missionary and temperance society run along strict military lines. His children, notably his daughters Kate (1859-1955) and Evangeline (1865-1950), carried on his work.

ROYAL WRECKAGE *The Blitz affected everyone, regardless of wealth and status. King George VI and his wife Queen Elizabeth survey a ruined section of Buckingham Palace, bombed in May 1940.*

Bosworth Field, Battle of (1485) Final battle of the Wars of the ROSES, in which Henry Tudor's rebels defeated Richard III's army. Richard was killed in the fighting, and Henry succeeded to the throne as HENRY VII.

Boudicca or Boadicea. Queen of the Iceni, a British tribe that lived in what is now Norfolk and Suffolk in the 1st century AD. In AD 61, Boudicca led a massive revolt against the Romans and won a series of victories, capturing Colchester, London and St Albans. After eventually being defeated, she committed suicide.

Boyne, Battle of the (1690) Victory for William III over the army of the former King JAMES II, who fled to France after his crushing defeat. The battle, fought near Drogheda on the River Boyne in Ireland, sealed Protestant King William's conquest of Catholic Ireland.
🔊 Loyalist ORANGEMEN in Northern Ireland still celebrate the anniversary of the Battle of the Boyne with parades and parties each July – the month of William's victory.

Britain, Battle of (August-October 1940) Series of air battles in ▷WORLD WAR II between the Luftwaffe under Hermann ▷GÖRING and the Royal Air Force. The Germans, poised to invade Britain after the fall of France, sought to gain control of the air by a campaign of bombing RAF airfields. Stubborn British resistance was aided by 'Chain Home' – the first radar early warning system in the world – and excellent fighter aircraft such as the Spitfire and the Hurricane. The Luftwaffe called off the campaign after suffering severe losses, and launched the BLITZ instead.
🔊 The pilots of RAF Fighter Command won great admiration for their bravery. Winston Churchill said of them: 'Never in the field of human conflict was so much owed by so many to so few.'

Brown, George (1914-85) Colourful Labour politician who served under Harold ▷WILSON as secretary of state for economic affairs (1964-6) and as foreign secretary (1966-8). Brown, created Baron George-Brown in 1970, is especially remembered for the prices and incomes policy he devised in the mid-1960s to curb inflation.

Bruce, Robert (1274-1329) Scottish hero who reneged on his oath of loyalty to Edward I and crowned himself King Robert I of Scotland in 1306. He freed Scotland from English rule after defeating Edward II at BANNOCKBURN.

READY FOR ACTION *Young fighter pilots at RAF Hawkinge, Kent, enjoy the sunshine between sorties during the Battle of Britain. In the background is one of their aircraft, a Hawker Hurricane.*

🔊 Bruce is said to have sat despairing of victory, watching a spider trying to anchor its web on the ceiling. Swinging desperately, the spider failed six times; on the seventh attempt it succeeded. Its persistence inspired Bruce to fight on.

Buckingham, George Villiers, 1st Duke of (1592-1628) Court favourite of JAMES I and CHARLES I. He used his intimate friendship with James to win immense power and wealth. Charles dissolved parliament in 1625 when it tried to impeach Buckingham for leading a series of disastrous expeditions against Spain. Buckingham was assassinated by a naval officer.

Burgess, Guy (1910-63) Communist spy who passed secrets to the Soviet Union while working for MI5 and the foreign office. He disappeared with Donald MACLEAN in 1951, and reappeared in Moscow five years later.

Burke, Edmund (1729-97) WHIG politician and writer mainly remembered for his influential book *Reflections on the Revolution in France*, which attacked the French Revolution as a threat to British traditions. By contrast, he was sympathetic to the aims of the American War of Independence. He also investigated corruption in the EAST INDIA COMPANY and led the impeachment of Warren HASTINGS.

cabal Five politicians who from 1667 to 1673 served as ministers to CHARLES II. The initial letters of their names – Clifford, Ashley, Buckingham, Arlington and Lauderdale – spell out 'CABAL', which has come to mean a secret group of plotters.

canals Principal means of transport during the INDUSTRIAL REVOLUTION. Britain's 'canal age' started in 1761 with the opening of the Bridgewater Canal to move coal between Worsley and Manchester. From this grew a canal network linking industrial centres and markets cheaply, safely and reliably. After the 1830s RAILWAYS made canals obsolescent. (See also ▷CANALS in 'Architecture and Engineering'.)

Canning, George (1770-1827) Tory politician who served two terms as foreign secretary, and was prime minister for six months before he died. He took Britain into the ▷PENINSULAR WAR and encouraged Spain's colonies in South America to fight for their independence. At home, he supported CATHOLIC EMANCIPATION. Canning was wounded in the thigh by his political rival Viscount CASTLEREAGH in the only duel between two serving British cabinet ministers.
🔊 Speaking of his support for South American colonies revolting against their Spanish overlords, Canning said: 'I have called the New World into existence to redress the balance of the Old.'

Canute or Cnut (*c*.995-1035). King of England, Norway and Denmark. A Dane by birth, he won the English throne in 1016 after four years of military campaigning. He married Emma, the widow of Ethelred the Unready, and ruled the English according to their own customs and laws.
🔊 Canute is said to have silenced fawning courtiers who exalted his power by commanding, in vain, the incoming tide to turn back, thus demonstrating to them man's impotence before the might of God.

Caractacus or Caradoc. British tribal chieftain of the 1st century AD who led a spirited resistance to the Roman invasion of Wales until he was defeated in AD 51.
🔸Caractacus was the son of Cymbeline (also known as Cunobelin) who inspired Shakespeare's play of the same name. His kingdom was centred on Colchester.

Caroline of Brunswick (1768-1821) Queen of GEORGE IV. Their marriage was arranged, and George never liked Caroline, who was said to be ugly, foul-mouthed and ill-washed. They separated in 1796, a year after their wedding. In 1814 Caroline went into exile, but returned to claim her place as queen in 1820, when George succeeded to the throne. She won short-lived popularity as a woman wronged by an unpopular king. Caroline was humiliated by being publicly refused admission to George's coronation, and died shortly afterwards.
🔸Caroline's coffin bore a plaque saying she was the 'injured Queen of England'.

Casement, Roger (1864-1916) Irish-born British diplomat who in 1903 issued a celebrated report detailing atrocities in the Belgian Congo. He later became a prominent member of ▷SINN FEIN, and spent much of World War I in Germany, enlisting aid in the struggle for Irish independence. Casement was arrested when a German submarine put him ashore on the Irish coast shortly before the EASTER RISING. He was later hanged for treason.

Castlereagh, Viscount (1769-1822) Foreign secretary who played a key role in forging the 'Grand Alliance' of Britain and other countries which waged war against ▷NAPOLEON from 1805 to 1807. After Napoleon's defeat, Castlereagh was one of the delegates at the Congress of ▷VIENNA (1814-15) which brought peace to Europe. Despite his remarkable foreign policy achievements, Castlereagh was disliked at home. He committed suicide, and his funeral procession was greeted with cheers.

Catherine of Aragon (1485-1536) HENRY VIII's Spanish-born first wife. She bore him five children, but only one, MARY, survived. Henry's action to divorce her precipitated the English REFORMATION.

Catholic Emancipation Early 19th-century movement to abolish discrimination in Britain against Roman Catholics. Since the REFORMATION Catholics had been unable to hold public office or sit as MPs. In 1829, new legislation restored these rights, but stopped short of full equality.

IN THE DOCK *Roger Casement was found guilty of treason after he had encouraged an Irish revolt when Britain was at war.*

Cato Street conspiracy (1820) Radical plot to assassinate members of Lord Liverpool's cabinet and then declare a republic. The plot was discovered and the conspirators, led by Arthur Thistlewood, an estate agent, were arrested at their meeting place in Cato Street, off Edgware Road in west London. Five of the plotters were subsequently hanged.

Caxton, William (c.1421-91) First English printer and publisher. He learned printing in Germany, and printed the first book in English, *The Recuyell of the Historyes*

FIRST PUBLISHER *From 1487, William Caxton put his mark on the books he printed in his shop near Westminster Abbey. Between his initials are a stylised '4' and '7', perhaps a reference to 1474, when he started printing. To the right, a page from a Book of Hours printed by Caxton on vellum in c.1477 and then illuminated by a scribe.*

of Troye (1475), in Bruges. The first book printed in England was *Dictes or Sayengis of the Philosophres* (1477), produced by Caxton from his press in Westminster. He published about 100 books in all, which included romances, poetry and an edition of Chaucer's *Canterbury Tales*.

Celts Germanic people who settled in the British Isles in the 7th to 6th centuries BC and built hill forts and burial mounds. (See also ▷CELTS in 'World History'.)
🔸In parts of Britain, clusters of ancient Celtic crosses can be found, often carved with intricate patterns or Biblical scenes.

Chamberlain, Austen (1863-1937) Conservative statesman. As foreign secretary he won the Nobel prize for peace for negotiating the 1925 Locarno Pact, which settled Germany's disputed western borders and then aimed to guarantee Europe's existing national frontiers.

Chamberlain, Joseph (1836-1914) Liberal politician who in the 1880s pressed, unsuccessfully, for radical reforms, including free education and compulsory redistribution of land to provide 'three acres and a cow' for all. He resigned from Gladstone's government in 1886 over Irish HOME RULE. As colonial secretary under Salisbury and Balfour from 1895 to 1903, Chamberlain is sometimes blamed for the outbreak of the BOER WAR.
🔸Joseph Chamberlain was the father of both Austen and Neville Chamberlain.

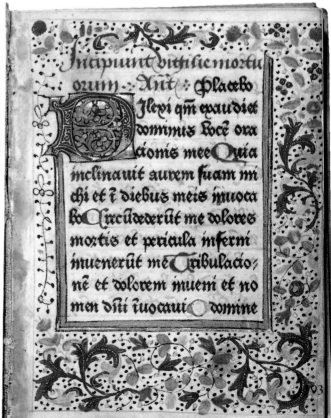

Chamberlain, Neville (1869-1940)

Conservative prime minister between 1937 and 1940. He was associated with the policy of APPEASEMENT, and tried to avoid war with Germany by negotiating the 1938 ▷MUNICH AGREEMENT with Adolf Hitler, but World War II broke out less than a year later. Chamberlain was forced to resign after British forces were defeated in the German invasion of Norway. He was succeeded by Winston CHURCHILL.

Referring to the dispute caused by the German occupation of Czechoslovakia, Chamberlain described the conflict as 'a quarrel in a faraway country between people of whom we know nothing'.

Charge of the Light Brigade (1854)

Bungled attack in the Battle of Balaclava during the ▷CRIMEAN WAR in which the British Light Brigade of cavalry, led by Lord Cardigan, charged the main Russian artillery. Of the 673 cavalrymen engaged, 247 were killed or wounded and 500 horses were lost. Unclear orders issued by Lord Raglan, the commander-in-chief, are usually blamed for the incident.

A French general, watching the Light Brigade's gallant but foolhardy advance into heavy fire, commented: '*C'est magnifique, mais ce n'est pas la guerre*' 'It is magnificent, but it is not war'.

The battle inspired Alfred, Lord Tennyson to write the famous lines 'Some one had blunder'd . . . /Into the valley of Death/ Rode the six hundred' in his poem ▷CHARGE OF THE LIGHT BRIGADE.

Charles I (1600-49)

King of Great Britain and Ireland who succeeded his father, JAMES I, in 1625. His reign was dominated by a struggle with parliament that eventually led to the CIVIL WAR and his own execution. He dissolved three parliaments because they opposed him over taxation, and then reigned for eleven years without parliament, asserting the ▷DIVINE RIGHT OF KINGS. His arbitrary rule, his claim to be able to raise taxes without parliament's consent and his pro-Catholic leanings made him immensely unpopular in England. His attempt to impose the Anglican ▷BOOK OF COMMON PRAYER in Presbyterian Scotland brought outright rebellion. Lack of funds eventually forced him to recall parliament in 1640, but his attempt to arrest five MPs for treason in 1642 led to the outbreak of civil war which lasted, with one brief interval, until 1648, when Charles's forces were defeated. Parliament tried him and found him guilty of treason; he was beheaded outside the Banqueting House in London's Whitehall.

ON TRIAL *Charles I sits accused by parliament of waging 'unnatural, cruel and bloody wars'. His death warrant (right) was signed by 59 republicans, including Oliver Cromwell.*

At his execution, which took place outside on a cold January day, Charles wore two shirts so he would not shiver and give the crowd the impression he was afraid.

Charles was a great lover of the arts. His court was a centre of artistic patronage, and he collected many paintings and sculptures by Titian, Mantegna, Raphael and others. He commissioned ▷VAN DYCK to paint his portrait and Rubens to decorate the ceiling of the Banqueting House, designed by the architect Inigo Jones.

Charles II (1630-85)

King of Great Britain and Ireland, whose RESTORATION to the throne in 1660 came after 11 years of Oliver CROMWELL's republican rule. Faced with a puritanical parliament and popular anti-Catholic sentiment (including the POPISH PLOT), Charles introduced the TEST ACT and other anti-Catholic measures – despite his preference for religious toleration and his secret alliance with Catholic France. He refused, however, to allow parliament to exclude his Catholic brother James from the succession. Charles's reign saw the reintroduction of pastimes such as bear-baiting and theatre-going, banned during the Commonwealth. His own enthusiastic pursuit of pleasure earned him the nickname 'the merry monarch'. Nell GWYN was one of his many mistresses. His marriage was childless, but he fathered at least 14 illegitimate offspring.

After his defeat at Worcester in the civil war, Charles took refuge from Cromwell's

Roundheads at Boscobel House in Shropshire, hiding by day in a hollow oak tree in the grounds. The 'Royal Oak' which can be seen there today is said to have grown from an acorn of that tree.

♟ Charles II's dying words were reportedly 'Let not poor Nelly [Nell Gwyn] starve.'

Chartism

Working-class radical movement which campaigned for six parliamentary reforms embodied in its 'charter' of 1838: universal male suffrage, annual general elections, equal electoral districts, votes by secret ballot, payment of MPs, and abolition of property qualifications for MPs. The movement, which coincided with a period of deep economic depression, spawned urban riots in 1839, but dissolved after 1848 as conditions improved.

Churchill, Winston (1874-1965)

Statesman and prime minister who led Britain through ▷WORLD WAR II. Churchill started his long parliamentary career as a Conservative in 1900, having worked as a war correspondent in the Boer War. As First Lord of the Admiralty in the Liberal government, he was in charge of the Royal Navy at the beginning of World War I. A Conservative once again, he was chancellor of the exchequer from 1924 to 1929, and played a key role in breaking the GENERAL STRIKE. His later opposition to various government policies, notably APPEASEMENT, kept him out of office until the beginning of World War II. When Neville CHAMBERLAIN resigned in 1940, Churchill took the helm of a new coalition government as prime minister and minister for defence. His stirring rhetoric and resolute leadership of the British war effort soon came to symbolise Britain's fierce resistance to Hitler. His grasp of strategy was equalled by his skill in negotiating with other Allied war leaders such as ▷STALIN, ▷DE GAULLE and ▷ROOSEVELT. He lost the 1945 general election to Clement ATTLEE, but returned as prime minister between 1951 and 1955.

♟ Churchill's oratory is still much quoted. On taking office, he told the Commons: 'I have nothing to offer but blood, toil, tears and sweat'; and as the Germans overran Europe he defiantly declared: 'We shall fight on the beaches, we shall fight on the landing grounds, we shall fight in the fields and in the streets, we shall fight in the hills; we shall never surrender.' As an author, he is especially remembered for two histories, *A History of the English-Speaking Peoples* and *The Second World War*. Churchill won the Nobel prize for literature in 1953.

♟ Churchill's trademarks included a large cigar, his 'V for victory' sign and witty but brutal ripostes. When Bessie Braddock, a formidable and outspoken Labour MP, came across Churchill in a House of Commons corridor, she rebuked him, saying, 'Winston, you're drunk!' His gruff reply was, 'Bessie, you are ugly, and tomorrow I shall be sober'. He also playfully described his political rival Clement Attlee as a 'sheep in sheep's clothing'.

Cinque Ports

Group of ports which supplied ships and men for coastal defence in exchange for special privileges from the Crown. They were important from the 13th to the 17th centuries. Sandwich, Dover, Hythe, Romney and Hastings were the original Cinque Ports. Rye, Winchelsea and others were added later.

Civil War (1642-8)

Conflict in which parliamentary forces or 'Roundheads', led by Oliver CROMWELL, defeated the 'Cavaliers' of CHARLES I. Catholics, high churchmen and most of the aristocracy supported the king, whose heartland lay in northern and western England; parliament had the support of the PURITANS, mainly in southern and eastern England, Scotland and London. The war went well for the king until the Scots joined with Cromwell's crack regiment, the 'Ironsides', to defeat royal troops at Marston Moor in 1644.

EMPIRE BUILDER *While surveying the Pacific, Yorkshire-born Captain James Cook claimed Australia and New Zealand for Britain.*

Parliament's NEW MODEL ARMY finally broke royalist resistance at NASEBY (1645); a year later, Charles surrendered and was placed under house arrest. In captivity, the king exploited divisions between parliament and army, English and Scots, Presbyterians and religious 'Independents'. A second bout of war erupted, ending in victory for Cromwell at Preston in 1648. Charles was tried and executed the following year.

Clive of India (1725-74)

Robert Clive, soldier and statesman who established British domination of India by driving out Dutch and French interests and defeating the Indian rulers of Bengal in the 1750s. Suffering from depression, he committed suicide after allegations of corruption were investigated by parliament.

Cobbett, William (1763-1835)

Writer and reformer who published his ambitious ideas in the radical journal *Weekly Political Register*. In *Rural Rides* (1830) he deplored the impact of the INDUSTRIAL REVOLUTION on the English countryside.

Cook, Captain James (1728-79)

Explorer who made three voyages in the Pacific, searching for a new continent rumoured to lie between Australia and the Antarctic. Cook charted the coasts of Australia and New Zealand, skirted the Antarctic ice field and discovered many of the Pacific islands. He was eventually killed in a skirmish with Hawaiian islanders.

cooperative movement Nineteenth-century movement which aimed to create self-sufficient agricultural and industrial communities in which people worked in partnership instead of competition. In 1844 the Rochdale Pioneers – unemployed mill workers – opened a shop selling essential goods and shared the profits among their regular customers or members, inspiring many similar ventures.

Corn Laws Legislation to protect British farmers by keeping the price of imported grain high. The Corn Law of 1815, which was wrongly blamed for rising food prices, inspired a Manchester-based protest movement – the Anti-Corn Law League, led by Richard Cobden and John Bright. The repeal of the Corn Laws in 1846 was a triumph for the movement.

Cranmer, Thomas (1489-1556) Official who worked with HENRY VIII as architect of the ▷CHURCH OF ENGLAND's break with Rome. As Archbishop of Canterbury, he organised Henry's divorces and compiled the ▷BOOK OF COMMON PRAYER. He was burned at the stake when Queen MARY, a Catholic, came to the throne.

Crécy, Battle of (1346) English triumph in the ▷HUNDRED YEARS' WAR, when foot soldiers and longbowmen led by EDWARD III defeated a larger French army of mounted knights, proving that archers could beat cavalry. The English army fired cannon, probably in order to frighten the enemy's horses, in one of the earliest recorded instances of artillery use in Europe.

WARTS AND ALL *Oliver Cromwell who despised vanity told the miniaturist Samuel Cooper to paint his craggy features with all their flaws.*

Cromwell, Oliver (1599-1658) General who led parliamentary forces to victory over CHARLES I in the CIVIL WAR. Early in the war, he formed the regiment called 'Ironsides', and he later created the NEW MODEL ARMY which finally defeated the royalists. After signing the king's death warrant in 1649, Cromwell took the reins of power himself, as leader of the Commonwealth and Protectorate (1649-60), in which the monarchy and the House of Lords were replaced by a council of state. At first he ruled with parliament, but from 1653, with the title Lord Protector, his supreme rule was backed only by the army. He was offered the crown, but refused it. Cromwell ruled as a dictator, suppressing uprisings in Wales, Scotland and Ireland with great military skill. Despite his strong puritanism Cromwell supported religious toleration. After his death he was succeeded as Lord Protector by his son Richard, whose inept rule led directly to the RESTORATION of the monarchy.

Cromwell, Thomas (c.1485-1540) Adviser to HENRY VIII who played a major role in the English REFORMATION. He implemented the DISSOLUTION OF THE MONASTERIES, but fell from favour and was executed after he had arranged Henry's unsuccessful marriage to Anne of Cleves.

Culloden, Battle of (1746) Battle at which the FORTY-FIVE REBELLION, aiming to depose King George II and restore the House of STUART, was finally crushed. It was the last battle fought on British soil.

Dambuster raid (1943) Air raid of World War II, in which a squadron of Lancaster bombers breached the Möhne and Eder dams in Germany, causing widespread flooding. Aircraft of the RAF's 617 Squadron, commanded by Wing-Commander Guy Gibson, flew very low – and at great risk – over the dams to drop 'bouncing bombs' that had been specially designed by Barnes Wallis.

Danelaw Area between the Thames and Tees rivers, colonised by Danish Vikings in the 9th century AD. The Danelaw was conquered by the kings of Wessex in the 10th century, but local place names ending in -*by*, meaning village, and -*thorpe*, meaning hamlet, bear witness to the language that was once influential in this area.

Desert Rats Nickname of the British 7th Armoured Division, which adopted the badge of the jerboa (a small, leaping rodent) while campaigning in Libya in World War II. Part of Bernard MONTGOMERY's Eighth Army, they fought with distinction at Alamein in North Africa and Italy.

Disraeli, Benjamin (1804-81) Conservative politician and 1st Earl of Beaconsfield, who was prime minister in 1868, and again from 1874 to 1880. He pursued a vigorous foreign policy of imperialism, buying Britain a major share in the Suez Canal and proclaiming Queen Victoria Empress of India. He became a close friend of Victoria, and showed great diplomatic skill in his conduct of the Congress of ▷BERLIN, at which he made peace between Turkey and Russia after war in the Balkans. ♪Disraeli was also a well-known author of political novels, including *Sybil*, *The Two Nations* and *Coningsby*. He was often known by his nickname of 'Dizzy'.

RACE FOR EMPIRE *Disraeli is urged on by Queen Victoria and her ancestors in this 1876 cartoon illustrating the perils of imperial expansion. Germany's Kaiser Wilhelm I is in the other boat.*

DANGEROUS WATERS.

ORDERLY QUEUE *Lines of British and French soldiers wait patiently on the beach at Dunkirk for boats to take them across the Channel.*

Dissolution of the Monasteries (1535-41) Closure of Britain's abbeys, monasteries and nunneries during the English REFORMATION by royal commissioners working under Thomas CROMWELL. Goods, including countless art treasures, were plundered and any land was usually sold for HENRY VIII's coffers.

Domesday Book Census compiled on the orders of WILLIAM THE CONQUEROR in 1085-6. It contains the results of a detailed survey covering most of England, and lists property holdings with their values and populations, county by county.

Drake, Sir Francis (c.1545-96) Seaman and navigator who started his career as a pirate, raiding Spanish treasure ships in the Caribbean. Supported by Elizabeth I, Drake crossed the Pacific in the *Golden Hind*, resulting in the first round-the-world voyage by an Englishman (1577-80). He also played a leading part in the defeat of the Spanish ARMADA in 1588. Drake's exploits marked the beginning of Britain's years as the world's greatest sea power.
🔱 It is said that Drake was told of the Armada's approach while playing bowls on Plymouth Hoe. He calmly ordered his ships to prepare for sailing, then went on to finish his game.
🔱 According to legend, Drake will return, to the sound of Drake's drum, if Britain faces another serious threat from abroad.

Dunkirk Scene of a remarkable retreat by the British army in ▷WORLD WAR II. Dunkirk is the anglicised spelling of Dunkerque, on the northern coast of France, which was the last precarious refuge of the British Expeditionary Force when France fell to the Germans in 1940. In less than a week, 860 naval and civilian vessels – the 'little ships' – took 338 226 men, 130 000 of whom were French, to England, saving them to fight another day.

Easter Rising (April 1916) Rebellion in which a secret organisation, the Irish Republican Brotherhood, attempted to win Irish independence from Britain. After a week of fighting on the streets of Dublin, the rebels surrendered. The harsh reprisals of the British authorities, including the execution of 14 rebel leaders, helped to strengthen demands for Irish HOME RULE, which came about in 1921.
🔱 Eamon ▷DE VALERA, a future Irish prime minister and president, was sentenced to life imprisonment for his part in the rising, but was subsequently released as part of a general amnesty in 1917.

East India Company, British Company set up in 1600 to trade in Asian spices. It won political power in India as the ▷MOGUL empire declined. By 1765, thanks to CLIVE OF INDIA, it had become the strongest single power in the country, and from 1784 the British government supervised the running of the company. In 1858, following the INDIAN MUTINY, the government took direct control of India, and in 1873 it dissolved the East India Company.
🔱 In 1843 Sir Charles Napier conquered the province of Sindh, in what is now Pakistan, for the East India Company. He is said to have reported his victory to his superiors with the punning despatch *Peccavi* – Latin for 'I have sinned'.

Eden, Sir Anthony (1895-1977) Conservative prime minister from 1955 to 1957; he resigned through ill health after he ordered an unsuccessful military intervention in the ▷SUEZ CRISIS of 1956. Earlier in his career, he served as foreign secretary to Neville Chamberlain – a post he left in 1938 because he disagreed with the policy of APPEASEMENT. He served as foreign secretary again in Winston Churchill's war cabinet between 1940 and 1945.

Edward 'The Confessor' (c.1003-66) Anglo-Saxon king of England who came to the throne in 1042. He is thought to have promised William, Duke of Normandy (WILLIAM THE CONQUEROR) the English throne in 1051. When Edward died childless, having nominated Harold II as his successor, William pursued his claim to the throne and began the NORMAN CONQUEST of England.
🔱 Edward's nickname refers to his great piety. He rebuilt ▷WESTMINSTER ABBEY and was canonised in 1161.

Edward I (1239-1307) King of England who came to the throne in 1272, succeeding his father HENRY III. He annexed Wales, but fought unsuccessfully to win control over Scotland. Edward was a vigorous law reformer, introducing compulsory trial by jury for criminal cases and limiting the power of courts run by the Church.

Edward II (1284-1327) King of England who came to the throne in 1307, succeeding his father EDWARD I. His attachment to favourites such as Piers Gaveston brought violent opposition from the barons. He lost control of Scotland when Robert BRUCE defeated his army at Bannockburn in 1314. Edward's queen, Isabella of France, together with her lover, Roger Mortimer, staged a rebellion which overthrew the king in 1326. In 1327, they forced Edward to renounce the throne in favour of his son, EDWARD III; he was then tortured and brutally murdered in Berkeley Castle.

♠ Edward was made Prince of Wales in 1301 – the first heir to the English throne to be given the title.

Edward III (1312-77) King of England who came to the throne in 1327, after his father EDWARD II was forced to abdicate. During his reign England became entangled in the ▷HUNDRED YEARS' WAR with France, and the British Isles were ravaged by the ▷BLACK DEATH.

♠ In 1348, Edward founded the Order of the GARTER – the emblem of ▷CHIVALRY which flourished at his court.

Edward IV (1442-83) King of England from 1461 to 1470, and from 1471 to 1483. Edward, the Yorkist candidate for the throne, succeeded the Lancastrian HENRY VI after defeating him at Towton in 1461, during the Wars of the ROSES. However, his reign was dominated by the continuing struggle between the houses of York and Lancaster, and in 1470 he was briefly deposed by Henry VI.

Edward V (1470-83) One of the PRINCES IN THE TOWER. He was king of England for less than three months, and was travelling to London for his coronation when he was seized by his uncle Richard, Duke of Gloucester. Edward was only 12 years old when he died in the Tower of London.

Edward VI (1537-53) King of England who succeeded his father HENRY VIII in 1547. A sickly youngster, Edward left the conduct of policy to a council of regents, but his devout Protestantism helped to advance the English REFORMATION. As he was dying of tuberculosis, he nominated Lady Jane GREY as his successor.

Edward VII (1841-1910) King of the United Kingdom who succeeded his mother, Queen VICTORIA, in 1901. During his long tenure as Prince of Wales, he was deeply frustrated by his exclusion from matters of state. He passed the time in pursuit of pleasure. A keen card-player and horse-owner, Edward was involved in a number of scandals. Lillie LANGTRY was the best known of his many mistresses. As king, he established better relations with France, laying the groundwork for the informal agreement of friendship between Britain and France known as the ENTENTE CORDIALE (1904).

Edward VIII (1894-1972) Uncrowned king of the United Kingdom who reigned from January to December 1936. The eldest son of GEORGE V, Edward was a debonair figure who enjoyed the high society of the 1920s, but he also cared deeply about the nation. He gave up the throne because of his love for Mrs Wallis Simpson, an American divorcee whom he married in 1937, prompting the ABDICATION CRISIS. He lived the rest of his life in exile with the honorary title 'Duke of Windsor'.

♠ Edward VIII is remembered for promising that 'something must be done' for the unemployed in the depressed valleys of South Wales. The fine cloth known as 'Prince of Wales check' is named after him.

Edwardian period The first decade of the 20th century, so called after EDWARD VII, the reigning monarch of the time. It was a time of reaction against the puritanical values of the VICTORIAN PERIOD, marked by elegance, luxury and relaxed morals among the wealthy and privileged. The Edwardian spirit lingered until the outbreak of World War I in 1914.

Elizabeth I (1533-1603) Daughter of HENRY VIII and Anne BOLEYN who became queen of England and Ireland in 1558. Her reign provided a period of stability and prosperity in which the nation flourished politically, militarily and culturally. A shrewd ruler, Elizabeth restored ▷PROTESTANTISM after the reign of the Catholic queen MARY I and ordered the execution of MARY QUEEN OF SCOTS (1587). Elizabeth also encouraged English exploration and colonisation of the ▷NEW WORLD. In 1588, Philip II of Spain, who had been Mary I's husband, sent out the ARMADA, partly to defend Catholicism and take revenge for English raids on Spanish shipping, but mainly to eject Elizabeth from her throne.

♠ The plays of William Shakespeare, the poetry of Edmund Spenser and the miniatures of Nicholas Hilliard are among the artistic highlights of the Elizabethan era. Spenser's *The Faerie Queen* is a well-known allegorical poem about Elizabeth.

♠ Elizabeth never married, and is often called the 'Virgin Queen'. By creating a cult of personality around herself she strengthened her personal rule. The nickname 'Good Queen Bess' is a reflection of her popularity with her subjects and the wealth which England enjoyed under her rule.

Empire, British Group of overseas dominions and colonial possessions which were ruled by Britain between the 17th and 20th centuries. The earliest outposts of the empire were trading settlements in the Caribbean, North America and the Indian subcontinent. The 18th and 19th centuries saw India conquered, large-scale white settlement in Australasia, Canada and southern Africa, and the development of a vast network of dependent states in every corner of the globe. The Royal Navy was the key to controlling the empire, while Britain's vast merchant fleet ensured the vigorous trade which 'glued' the empire together and brought huge industrial wealth at home. The empire reached its peak in 1919, when it embraced nearly a quarter of the world's population and covered more than a quarter of the earth's territory. Maintaining British rule over such a large area proved increasingly difficult as ▷NATIONALISM increased across the world. In 1931, the empire was officially replaced by the British ▷COMMONWEALTH of Nations, providing a looser framework for colonial ties with London. Almost all of Britain's former possessions are now fully independent, although some retain the British monarch as head of state.

'England expects that every man will do his duty' Signal sent by Horatio NELSON to the English fleet from his flagship, HMS *Victory*, before the naval Battle of TRAFALGAR.

♠ Nelson actually wanted to say 'England *confides* that every man . . .', but the signals officer substituted the word 'expects' because it could be represented by a single flag; 'confides' would have had to be spelt out letter by letter.

Falklands War (1982) Armed conflict following the invasion of the British-ruled Falkland Islands by Argentina, which had long claimed the islands – which they call *Las Malvinas* – as its own. On April 2, Argentinian forces easily overwhelmed the islands' small garrison, taking the governor of the Falklands, Rex Hunt, prisoner. Britain declared an exclusion zone around the islands and despatched a large naval task force to retake them. The war ended when Argentina surrendered on June 14. It cost the lives of 255 Britons and 643 Argentinians.

PLOTTERS *Guy Fawkes (third from right) and other conspirators shown scheming to blow up King James I. Fawkes's lantern (left), found in the cellars of parliament when he was arrested on November 5, 1605, would have detonated the hidden gunpowder.*

Fawkes, Guy (1570-1606) Leading conspirator in the GUNPOWDER PLOT to blow up parliament. He was a Catholic convert who had served in the Spanish army before becoming involved in the plot.
♣Although Guy Fawkes was hanged, not burned at the stake, Britons burn his effigy or 'guy' on Bonfire Night on November 5, the anniversary of the Gunpowder Plot.

Festival of Britain (1951) Exhibition of arts, sciences and technology held to mark the centenary of the GREAT EXHIBITION. Its main site was in London, on the south bank of the Thames. For many, the festival was a gesture of hope for the future during the years of austerity after World War II.
♣London's Festival Hall is the only building on the south bank constructed for the festival which survives.

'Fifteen' Rebellion (1715-16) Scottish attempt to remove the House of HANOVER from the British throne and restore the STUART line in the person of James Edward Stuart, the OLD PRETENDER. The rising was defeated at the battles of Preston and Sheriffmuir; the subsequent 'FORTY-FIVE' REBELLION was also unsuccessful.

Flodden, Battle of (1513) Battle in which Thomas Howard, Earl of Surrey, halted a Scottish invasion of England. Some 10 000 Scotsmen, including King James IV, were killed and stripped naked by the smaller but victorious English army.

'Forty-five' Rebellion (1745-6) Scottish rising which aimed to replace King George II with Charles Edward STUART – BONNIE PRINCE CHARLIE. The JACOBITE rebels – led by Prince Charles himself – got as far south as Derby, but when neither the expected French invasion nor any English pro-Jacobite rising took place, the rebels had to retreat and were defeated at the Battle of CULLODEN.

Fox, Charles James (1749-1806) WHIG statesman who championed parliamentary reform and the abolition of slavery. Fox was a bitter critic of GEORGE III and a steadfast opponent of William PITT the Younger. He supported the French Revolution, Irish independence and the American War of Independence. Fox and his rival, Lord North, formed a coalition government in 1783, known as the 'Unholy Alliance'.

CELEBRATION OF DESIGN *Poster artist Abram Games created this jaunty star as an uplifting symbol of the Festival of Britain.*

franchise Constitutional right to vote. Today all British citizens aged 18 or over (except peers, prisoners and certified lunatics) have the right to vote, but before 1832 both the right to vote and parliamentary constituencies were unevenly distributed. New industrial towns, such as Manchester and Birmingham, had no MPs, while Old Sarum, an uninhabited mound near Salisbury, returned two. Another 45 parliamentary seats were effectively controlled by only six peers. A series of REFORM ACTS followed, the first of which (1832) created fairer constituencies and extended the franchise to middle-class property owners; in 1867, working-class men in the boroughs won the right to vote, and in 1884 they were joined by their rural counterparts. To prevent intimidation and bribery, the secret ballot was introduced in 1872. The 1918 Reform Act gave the vote to men over 21 and – after years of campaigning by the SUFFRAGETTES – to women over 30, subject to certain economic and educational qualifications. In 1928 all women over 21 won the vote, and in 1969 the voting age was lowered to 18.

Frobisher, Sir Martin (c.1535-94) Seaman who in the 1570s led three voyages to Canada, during his search for a north-west passage to China. He later joined Francis Drake's expedition to the West Indies and played an important role in the defeat of the Spanish ARMADA.

Fry, Elizabeth (1780-1845) Prison reformer and philanthropist, remembered for improving the conditions for female prisoners and their children jailed at Newgate prison in London. She also did much charitable work for the homeless.

Gaitskell, Hugh (1906-63) Politician who led the Labour Party from 1955 to 1963. His moderate policies won support among the middle classes, but his opposition to unilateral nuclear disarmament divided the party.
♣In 1960, during a row with the unilateralists, Gaitskell made a pledge to 'fight and fight and fight again to bring back sanity and honesty to the party we love'.

Garter, Order of the Order of chivalry founded by EDWARD III in 1348 to honour nobles who fought alongside him in France. The king, it is said, picked up a garter dropped by the Countess of Salisbury and wore it himself, saying '*Honi soit qui mal y pense*' 'Shame on him who thinks evil of it'. Companions of the Order of the Garter wear a blue garter bearing the same slogan.

EVERYBODY OUT
Volunteer drivers, often with police protection, kept buses running. With no regular newspapers appearing both government and unions produced their own.

General Strike (1926) National strike to express solidarity with coal miners campaigning against wage cuts. Servicemen and volunteers kept essential services running, and the strike crumbled after ten days.

George I (1660-1727) Elector of HAN-OVER, in Germany, who became the first Hanoverian king of Great Britain and Ireland, succeeding Queen ANNE in 1714. George, a great-grandson of JAMES I, was Anne's closest Protestant heir; he had to put down several JACOBITE rebellions which sought to restore the exiled STUARTS.
♣ George I was an unpopular king. He spoke no English, and spent as much time as possible in Hanover, but his reign was a period of relative prosperity and stability.

George II (1683-1760) King of Great Britain and Ireland who succeeded his father George I in 1727. He took a greater interest in Britain than his predecessor, although he, too, preferred Hanover to England. George was the last British king to lead his army into battle – against the French at Dettingen, in 1743. He also suppressed the 'FORTY-FIVE' REBELLION.

George III (1738-1820) King of Great Britain and Ireland, and elector of HANOVER, who succeeded his father George II in 1760. His reign saw the beginning of the Industrial Revolution and the loss of the American colonies in the ▷AMERICAN WAR OF INDEPENDENCE. At first, he wielded considerable personal influence over the government, but William PITT the Younger, appointed prime minister in 1783, steadily brought policy back under the control of politicians. George suffered from porphyria, a metabolic disorder producing periodic bouts of insanity; these became permanent, and in 1811 his son George, later George IV, was appointed Prince Regent.
♣ George III was the first Hanoverian monarch to take a serious interest in the British Isles. 'Born and educated in this country, I glory in the name of Briton,' he told his first parliament. He was known as 'Farmer George' because of his great interest in farming and agriculture.

George IV (1762-1830) King of the United Kingdom, who succeeded his father George III in 1820. For nine years before this he had ruled as Prince Regent in place of his mentally ill father. In 1785, George secretly married Maria Fitzherbert, but this illegal union with a Catholic widow was later dissolved. His second marriage to CAROLINE OF BRUNSWICK was not successful. As Prince of Wales, he was a generous patron of the arts and leader of fashion, but he led a scandalous lifestyle which made him a target for popular ridicule. As king, he opposed both parliamentary reform and CATHOLIC EMANCIPATION.
♣ George IV was the figurehead of the REGENCY age (1811-30), a time of bold innovations in art, design and fashion.

George V (1865-1936) King of the United Kingdom, who succeeded his father Edward VII in 1910. In his reign, Ireland won its independence and Britain fought World War I, during which he changed the royal family name from the German Saxe-Coburg and Gotha to Windsor.
♣ George V was an avid stamp collector.

George VI (1895-1952) King of the United Kingdom, who succeeded his brother Edward VIII following the ABDICATION CRISIS of 1936. He overcame his reserved nature and boosted British morale during World War II, visiting troops on the Continent and defiantly remaining in London throughout the German bombing campaigns. His daughter is Queen ▷ELIZABETH II.

Gladstone, William Ewart (1809-98) Liberal politician who was prime minister four times between 1868 and 1894. He introduced the secret ballot and reformed the army, the Church and education, but failed to achieve HOME RULE for Ireland.
♣ Gladstone, nicknamed the 'Grand Old Man' of British politics, used to carry a small case with a hinged lid and two compartments, known as a 'Gladstone bag'.

Glencoe, Massacre of (1692) Incident in which the Scottish Campbell clan killed 38 members of the rival MacDonald clan. William III had ordered all the Highland clans – many of which remained loyal to JAMES II, the exiled STUART king – to swear an oath of allegiance. The deadline expired before the chief of the MacDonalds was able to take the oath, and William's administrators ordered the massacre to deter any other rebellious Scots.

Glorious Revolution (1688-9) Period in which JAMES II was deposed, WILLIAM AND MARY were crowned and the supremacy of parliament over the monarchy was firmly established. The country's hostility to James's Catholicism, deepened by the birth of a Catholic heir, prompted the offer of the crown to the Protestant prince William of Orange, James's cousin.

Gordon, Charles (1833-85) General and administrator who crushed a rebellion in China in 1860, winning the nickname 'Chinese Gordon'. Sent to the Sudan, in 1884 he disobeyed orders to evacuate troops from Khartoum and tried to hold the city against Sudanese rebels. After holding out for ten months, Gordon was killed two days before relief arrived. GLADSTONE's government, accused of delay in coming to Gordon's aid, fell soon afterwards.

Gordon Riots (1780) Anti-Catholic riots which started when Lord George Gordon led a rally to the House of Commons demanding the repeal of legislation easing restrictions on Catholics' ownership of land. During the week of violence that followed, there were some 300 deaths.

SHOWCASE FOR BRITAIN *Queen Victoria and Prince Albert perform the opening ceremony for the Great Exhibition, at which manufacturing skills were proudly displayed in the Crystal Palace.*

Great Exhibition (1851) Display organised by Prince ALBERT as an exhibition of human progress in science and technology. It was held in an enormous glass-and-iron structure, nicknamed the ▷CRYSTAL PALACE, in London's Hyde Park. Six million people visited the exhibition, which was open for six months.

⚭The palace was dismantled after the show and erected in Sydenham, south London; the area, and its football team, soon took on its name. It burned down in 1936.

Great Fire of London (1666) Fire which largely destroyed the City of London. It started in a baker's shop in Pudding Lane and blazed for six days, destroying 89 churches and 13 200 houses. More than 100 000 people were made homeless, and nine died. Sir Christopher ▷WREN directed the rebuilding of the city.

⚭Samuel ▷PEPYS gave a vivid eyewitness account of the fire in his diary.

Great Plague (1665) Serious outbreak of ▷BUBONIC PLAGUE in London, which killed more than 70 000 people. It was the last of many outbreaks of plague in Britain between the 14th and 17th centuries.

⚭The nursery rhyme ▷RING A RING O'ROSES may have its origins in the red rash and quick death of the plague's victims.

Grey, Earl (Charles Grey) (1764-1845) WHIG prime minister from 1830 to 1834. Grey secured the passage of the first of the REFORM ACTS, and abolished slavery throughout the British Empire.

⚭Earl Grey is a type of tea named after the earl. It is made of Darjeeling and China teas flavoured with oil extracted from bergamot, a perfumed citrus fruit.

Grey, Lady Jane (1537-54) Protestant great-niece of HENRY VIII who was queen of England for a mere nine days in 1553. Jane's father-in-law, the duke of Northumberland and a leading courtier, persuaded the sickly Edward VI to name her as his heir, but the choice was unpopular and most people favoured the late king's Catholic sister MARY. Jane was thrown into the Tower of London when Mary ascended to the throne, and she was executed after her father joined a Protestant rebellion against the new queen.

Gunpowder Plot Catholic conspiracy to blow up JAMES I, together with the Houses of Parliament, on November 5, 1605. Suspicions were aroused when a Catholic peer was warned not to attend parliament. The cellars under the House of Lords were searched and one of the conspirators, Guy FAWKES, was arrested there with a pile of explosives. The plotters, led by Robert Catesby, were either killed or executed.

Gwyn, Nell (*c.*1650-87) The best-known of CHARLES II's many mistresses. Nell Gwyn sold oranges to the audience at the Theatre Royal in London's Drury Lane before becoming an actress at the same theatre, where she attracted the attention of the king. 'Pretty, witty Nell', as she was known, bore Charles two children.

Hanover, House of German family, and electors, or rulers, of Hanover, descended from JAMES I's daughter Elizabeth. They received the British crown when the last STUART monarch, Queen ANNE, died heirless. The first Hanoverian kings, GEORGE I and GEORGE II, took little interest in their new country; George I never even learned English. GEORGE III, GEORGE IV and WILLIAM IV were the later Hanoverian kings. VICTORIA used her husband ALBERT's family name of Saxe-Coburg and Gotha instead.

⚭The Hanoverian period (1714-1837) saw great industrial growth, but the monarchy's power steadily dwindled.

Hardie, Kier (1865-1915) Miner and journalist who became Britain's first Labour MP in 1892. He chaired the Independent Labour Party (the precursor of today's Labour Party) and was the first leader of the Parliamentary Labour Party. His championship of the Boers during the BOER WAR and pacifism during World War I made him a controversial figure.

⚭Hardie demonstrated his loyalty to his working-class origins by wearing a working man's flat cap in the House of Commons, at a time when most MPs wore top hats.

Hastings, Battle of (1066) Battle fought near ▷HASTINGS, in East Sussex, at the start of the NORMAN CONQUEST of England. WILLIAM THE CONQUEROR led invaders from Normandy, in France, to victory over English forces under King Harold. William then declared himself king.

Hastings, Warren (1732-1818) Official of the EAST INDIA COMPANY who, as governor of Bengal, carried out a programme of vigorous reform. He improved the legal and fiscal systems of British India and stopped employees of the company trading privately. This greatly increased British power in India, but made him many enemies. Edmund BURKE and Charles James FOX led his impeachment (1787) for alleged mismanagement and extortion. He was acquitted of all charges in 1795 after a celebrated trial that lasted seven years.

Henry I (1068-1135) King of England from 1100. He succeeded to the throne after his brother WILLIAM II died in a hunting accident. Henry won Normandy from his brother Robert in 1106, and was a good administrator, setting up a well-organised treasury – the exchequer. His reign was marred by the death of William, his only son and heir, when his ship hit a rock off the French coast in 1120.

Henry II (1133-89) King of England from 1154, and the first of the PLAN-TAGENET line. An energetic and capable ruler, Henry controlled nearly half of France but based his empire in England. He soon restored order after the anarchy of STEPHEN's reign, creating an efficient civil service and introducing many legal reforms, heralding the effective beginning of ▷COMMON LAW. His struggle to bring the Church under royal control culminated in the murder of Thomas BECKET in 1170. Henry II's later years were dogged by vicious family arguments as his sons, including RICHARD I and JOHN, squabbled over their inheritance.

Henry III (1207-72) King of England who succeeded his father John in 1216, when he was just nine years old. His personal rule, which started in 1232, was marked by clashes with the nobility, whom he upset by his inefficiency, favouritism towards foreigners and assertion of royal rights. Simon de Montfort, the barons' leader, forced the king to transfer power to a commission of nobles in 1258 after an expensive and unsuccessful attempt to conquer Sicily. Civil war broke out between the king and the barons when Henry tried to claw back his authority. The king's forces won, but only after the barons had met in England's first full PARLIAMENT of Lords and Commons in 1265.

Henry IV (1366-1413) First Lancastrian king of England. His reign began in 1399 when he deposed RICHARD II, who had seized the estates of his father, JOHN OF GAUNT. Henry IV was plagued by rebellions and a shortage of money.

Henry V (1387-1422) King of England who succeeded his father Henry IV in 1413. A capable soldier and administrator, Henry devoted most of his energy to the armed pursuit of the French crown which he claimed through heredity. His victory at AGINCOURT in 1415 opened the way for him to be formally recognised as heir to the French throne. He died of dysentery on a later campaign in France.

♣Although William Shakespeare's history plays ▷HENRY IV, PARTS 1 AND 2 and ▷HENRY V are not accurate portrayals, they made Henry V an emblem of national pride and military prowess.

Henry VI (1421-71) King of England who came to the throne in 1422, aged 8½ months, after the death of his father, Henry V. Until 1442, when he took personal power, England was ruled by regents.

By 1453, when he was defeated in the ▷HUNDRED YEARS' WAR, Henry had lost most of the French lands formerly held by England. His subsequent mental break-down led to the appointment of Richard, Duke of York, as lord protector. The two men's struggle for power developed into the Wars of the ROSES, and in 1461 Henry was deposed by Richard's son EDWARD IV. He was briefly restored to the throne in 1470-1, but Edward defeated him in battle, imprisoned him and authorised his assassination soon afterwards.

♣Henry VI founded Eton College and King's College, Cambridge. The chapel at King's College was built to his own design.

Henry VII (1457-1509) The first TUDOR king, who wrested the English throne from Richard III at the Battle of BOSWORTH FIELD in 1485. His claim rested on his descent from JOHN OF GAUNT. A Lancastrian, Henry ended the feud at the

heart of the Wars of the ROSES by marrying the Yorkist heiress Elizabeth. His sound administration helped to mend the damage done by 30 years of civil war and his reign is often seen as the start of modern history.

♣Henry VII's heraldic device was a sprig of hawthorn because Richard III's crown was found under a hawthorn bush after the Battle of Bosworth Field. He also devised the 'Tudor Rose', with red and white petals symbolising the union of the red rose of Lancaster and the white rose of York.

Henry VIII (1491-1547) King of England who succeeded his father Henry VII in 1509. During his youth, Henry was an accomplished musician, sportsman and scholar – the perfect ▷RENAISSANCE prince. Under the influence of his ambitious chancellor, Cardinal Thomas WOLSEY, the first part of Henry's reign saw war against France. When the pope refused to dissolve Henry's marriage to Catherine of Aragon after her failure to give him a male heir, he broke all links with Rome and made himself head of the new ▷CHURCH OF ENGLAND in 1534, ushering in the English REFORMATION and the DIS-SOLUTION OF THE MONAS-TERIES. Henry executed his second wife, Anne BOLEYN; his third wife, Jane Seymour, died after giving birth to the future EDWARD VI. His fourth marriage, to Anne of Cleves, was a diplomatic union; Henry disliked her – calling her the 'Flanders mare' – and quickly divorced her in order to marry Catherine Howard (1540), executed two years later on a charge of adultery. In his final years Henry, now contentedly married to Catherine Parr, renewed war with France and Scotland, and ruled as a tyrant at home.

♣As a youth, Henry was well-loved, earning the nick-name 'Bluff King Hal'. However, this affection turned to fear as he became obese and bad-tempered, suffering from painful leg ulcers.

TWO HENRYS *King Henry VIII swaggers at the fore of this 1536-7 cartoon by the German painter Hans Holbein; his father, Henry VII, stands behind him.*

Hereward the Wake Anglo-Saxon nobleman from Lincolnshire who led a determined rebellion against William I during the NORMAN CONQUEST. He became a symbol of English resistance.

Home Rule Movement demanding self-government for Ireland. Championed by Daniel O'CONNELL and Charles PARNELL, Home Rule was a major political issue from the early 19th century until the outbreak of World War I. William GLADSTONE introduced two unsuccessful Home Rule bills. British rule in southern Ireland effectively collapsed after the EASTER RISING in 1916; the Irish Republican Army (▷IRA) was created soon after, and in 1922 southern Ireland gained independence as the IRISH FREE STATE, a dominion within the British Commonwealth. ▷NORTHERN IRELAND gained its own parliament at Stormont, which was dissolved in 1972.

House of Commons Elected body of PARLIAMENT that was officially separated from the HOUSE OF LORDS in the 16th century. Commoners first sat in parliament alongside barons and clergy in 1254, when HENRY III summoned knights of the shires to Westminster. In 1265, Simon de Montfort summoned merchants as well. During the ▷HUNDRED YEARS' WAR the Commons established the right to approve royal demands for taxation – a stepping-stone towards allowing the Commons to debate the general conduct of the monarch's policies. A clash with CHARLES I led to the CIVIL WAR, an ideological struggle in which the principle of the sovereignty of the people, championed by the Commons, triumphed over Charles's attempt to assert the ▷DIVINE RIGHT OF KINGS and rule without parliament. The GLORIOUS REVOLUTION (1688) finally settled the argument, making the king and his advisers subject to the will of the Commons. The 19th-century REFORM ACTS extended the FRANCHISE, making the Commons more representative of the people. The Parliament Act (1911) increased the power of the Commons and weakened that of the Lords, who were deprived of the right to amend finance bills or to permanently veto other bills passed by the Commons. At the same time, MPs were given salaries, making it possible for people without private incomes to sit in the Commons. The 20th century has seen the influence of the Lords continue to diminish, although some observers claim that the Commons' ability to sway the government has also been weakened. (See also ▷HOUSE OF COMMONS in 'Politics, Government and the Law'.)

House of Lords Unelected upper house of PARLIAMENT. The House of Lords had its origins in the Anglo-Saxon *witan* or *witenagemot*, a panel of noble advisers to the king, and in the 'great councils' of the 13th century, at which the king met barons and bishops to discuss policy. By the 15th century, an established group of prelates and hereditary peers was assembling on a regular basis. For centuries, the Lords had similar powers to the HOUSE OF COMMONS, but in 1911 they were stripped of their power to permanently veto bills passed by the lower house. Today, the Lords can only review and occasionally delay legislation approved by the Commons, but not reject it. (See also ▷HOUSE OF LORDS in 'Politics, Government and the Law'.)

Indian Mutiny (1857-8) Uprising against British rule over India which started when the rumour spread that Indian soldiers serving in the British army had been issued with a new type of cartridge greased with pork and beef fat, offending both Muslim and Hindu religious taboos. Other grievances came to the surface, and rebels claimed several towns and army garrisons. One of the worst incidents was the massacre of 200 Britons at Cawnpore. After British forces quashed the rebellion, the Crown took over the task of governing India from the EAST INDIA COMPANY .

Industrial Revolution Rapid industrialisation of Britain that began in the late 18th century. Inventions such as Arkwright's 'water frame', James Hargreaves's 'spinning jenny' and Watt's ▷STEAM ENGINE were at the heart of the revolution, which spread from the textile industry to all areas of manufacturing. CANALS and RAILWAYS were developed to move goods efficiently round the country, while cities such as Birmingham and Manchester grew rapidly, creating a demand for cheap manufactured goods – so fuelling industrialisation still further. However, the boom was accompanied by social problems of child labour, unhealthy hours and conditions of work, poor sanitation and squalid housing. By the 1860s Britain had become the richest industrialised nation – the so-called 'workshop of the world' – and other advanced nations were eager to follow the example.

Irish Free State Name used by the Republic of Ireland between 1922 and 1937, when it was a dominion within the British Commonwealth. In 1932 it was renamed Eire, and in 1949 it was proclaimed a republic and at the same time withdrew from the Commonwealth.

Jack the Ripper Nickname given to a criminal who murdered five London prostitutes in frenzied knife attacks in 1888. He mutilated his victims, removing organs from their corpses. His identity, remains

INDIA RISES UP *Gun cartridges rumoured to be greased with pork and beef fat sparked off the Indian Mutiny. The painting shows the cavalry of the Queen's Bays charging valiantly to the rescue of British citizens who were trapped by Indian rebels in the governor's residence at Lucknow.*

a mystery. Different theories have linked the killings with William Gull, Queen Victoria's personal physician; her grandson, the Duke of Clarence; the painter Walter Sickert; and James Maybrick, a Liverpool cotton broker.

Jacobites Supporters of the deposed STUART royal line after the GLORIOUS REVOLUTION. The Jacobites mounted two serious rebellions – the 'FIFTEEN' in 1715 and the 'FORTY-FIVE' in 1745 – backing the claim of the OLD PRETENDER and his son BONNIE PRINCE CHARLIE to rule instead of the Protestant Hanoverians.
⚫ The word 'Jacobite' is derived from the Latin word for James – *Jacobus*.

James I (1566-1625) The first STUART king of England, who succeeded Elizabeth I in 1603. The only child of MARY, QUEEN OF SCOTS, he had been king of Scotland (as James VI) since 1567. He was an intelligent and widely read man, and his shrewd reign in Scotland brought stability and peace. As king of England, however, he was less diligent and successful, earning the unflattering epithet of 'the wisest fool in Christendom'. James's strident assertion of the ▷DIVINE RIGHT OF KINGS and his reliance on favourites, especially the Duke of BUCKINGHAM, whom he showered with honours and privileges, brought him into conflict with parliament.
⚫ The arts, which had flourished during Elizabeth I's reign, especially drama and literature, continued to do so under James I.

He commissioned the Authorised Version, or ▷KING JAMES BIBLE (1611), which remains one of the greatest achievements of English literature.
⚫ James is remembered for writing *A Counterblast to Tobacco*, a condemnation of the new habit of smoking – introduced to Europe by Sir Walter Raleigh – as 'loathsome to the eye, hateful to the nose, harmful to the brain (and) dangerous to the lungs'.

James II (1633-1701) King of England and Scotland, who succeeded his brother Charles II in 1685. Several attempts were made to exclude him from the succession because he was a Catholic, especially following the alleged POPISH PLOT to murder King Charles. James's pro-Catholic policies aroused intense opposition, and when he produced a Catholic heir (James Edward STUART, the OLD PRETENDER) open revolt broke out. He was deposed in 1688 and the GLORIOUS REVOLUTION put his Protestant son-in-law and daughter, WILLIAM AND MARY, on the throne. James's attempt to regain the throne was thwarted at the Battle of the BOYNE, and he spent the rest of his life in exile in France.

Jameson Raid (1895-6) An attempt to overthrow the ▷BOER government in Transvaal, South Africa. Dr Leander Starr Jameson led a small armed force from Mafeking towards Johannesburg, but was easily defeated.

Jarrow March (1936) Protest march made by 200 unemployed shipbuilders from Jarrow, near Newcastle upon Tyne, to London. They carried a petition against the closure of their shipyard and against government policies which left seven out of ten workers in Jarrow out of work. The march helped to bring home the problems of the depressed north of England to the more prosperous Midlands and south-east.

John (1167-1216) King of England from 1199, the younger son of Henry II and successor to his brother Richard I. John fought against Philip II of France, Pope Innocent III and his own barons, who made him agree to the MAGNA CARTA in 1215.
⚫ John's nickname, 'Bad King John', was probably undeserved. His evil reputation is based on the work of contemporary chroniclers who bore grudges against him.

John of Gaunt (1340-99) Duke of Lancaster and fourth son of EDWARD III. He was, in effect, ruler of England in the last part of his father's reign, and he remained influential in the reign of Richard II, crushing the PEASANTS' REVOLT in 1381. The TUDOR kings based their claim to the throne on their descent from him. 'Gaunt' derives from Ghent, his birthplace.

Johnson, Amy (1903-41) Aviation pioneer who in 1930 became the first person to fly solo from London to Australia – a journey of 19 days. She made many other pioneering flights, but died in an accident delivering aircraft for the Royal Air Force.

Jutland, Battle of (1916) The only time when the two main fleets clashed in World War I. The outnumbered German fleet inflicted heavy casualties on the Royal Navy before escaping in North Sea fog. However, the German fleet returned to port for the rest of the war.

MARCHING FOR JOBS *As they pass through Lavendon, near Bedford, on their way to London, the Jarrow marchers play harmonicas. They started their 'crusade for jobs' when Palmer's shipyard closed, throwing many of the town's workers out of work.*

CALL TO ARMS *General Kitchener's eyes and finger seem to aim straight at the viewer in this classic World War I recruiting poster.*

Kitchener, Lord (1850-1916) Herbert, Earl Kitchener of Khartoum, was the soldier and administrator under whose leadership British forces recaptured Sudan and won the BOER WAR. As war secretary at the start of World War I, he organised a massive army recruitment drive.

Knox, John (*c.*1513-72) Leader of the Scottish REFORMATION and the founder of the Church of Scotland. His vehement opposition to the reintroduction of Catholicism helped to secure the abdication of the Catholic MARY, QUEEN OF SCOTS.
♟The oft-quoted title of Knox's pamphlet *The First Blast of the Trumpet Against the Monstrous Regiment of Women* is prone to misinterpretation. The word 'regiment' is used in its original meaning of 'regimen' or 'rule', not in its modern military sense.

Lancaster, House of Branch of the PLANTAGENET family which produced kings HENRY IV, HENRY V and HENRY VI. The dynasty, descendants of Edward III's son JOHN OF GAUNT, Duke of Lancaster, grew rapidly in wealth and power. The Lancastrian challenge to the House of YORK resulted in the Wars of the ROSES. In 1471, after the murder of Henry VI, the Lancastrian leadership passed to Henry Tudor, who went on to found his own dynasty as HENRY VII.

Langtry, Lillie (1853-1929) Actress and celebrated beauty, remembered for being EDWARD VII's favourite mistress.
♟Born in Jersey, Lillie Langtry was known as the 'Jersey Lily'. Oscar Wilde wrote the play *Lady Windermere's Fan* for her.

Latimer, Hugh (*c.*1485-1555) Protestant preacher and leader of the English REFORMATION. When MARY I tried to re-establish Catholicism in England, Latimer and his fellow preacher Nicholas Ridley were burned at the stake for heresy.
♟At the stake, Latimer encouraged Ridley with the words: 'We shall this day light such a candle by God's grace in England, as I trust shall never be put out.'

Laud, William (1573-1645) Archbishop of Canterbury who worked closely with CHARLES I to strengthen the ▷CHURCH OF ENGLAND and purge it of Puritanism. His rigid ecclesiastical policies contributed to the outbreak of the CIVIL WAR. Laud was eventually beheaded for treason.

Lawrence of Arabia (T.E. Lawrence) (1888-1935) Soldier and author known for leading a rebellion of Arabs against the Turks in World War I, described in his book *The Seven Pillars of Wisdom*. He argued unsuccessfully for Arab independence prior to the Treaty of Versailles. (See also ▷LAWRENCE OF ARABIA in 'Films, Entertainment and the Media'.)

Levellers Radical agitators, during the Civil War and ensuing Commonwealth and Protectorate. They called for religious freedom, a wider franchise and the abolition of the monarchy and aristocracy. Cromwell suppressed them when they began to infiltrate his NEW MODEL ARMY.

JERSEY LILY *Lillie Langtry, well-bred daughter of the dean of Jersey, caused a stir when she took to the stage – not a suitable place for a lady.*

LIGHTNING SKETCH *Augustus John captured T.E. Lawrence's likeness in just two minutes. Portrayed here in traditional Arab headdress, Lawrence championed many Arab causes.*

Liberal Party Successor to the WHIG Party; the name 'Liberal' started to replace 'Whig' in the 1830s. Under GLADSTONE in the 19th century and LLOYD GEORGE, the last Liberal prime minister, in the early 20th century, it formed the main opposition to the ▷CONSERVATIVE PARTY until internal divisions and the rise of the ▷LABOUR PARTY pushed it into third place during the 1920s. In 1988, the Liberals merged with the ▷SDP (Social Democratic Party) to form a party now called the ▷LIBERAL DEMOCRATIC PARTY.

Lib-Lab pact Parliamentary alliance in which the Liberal Party, led by David Steel, enabled the minority Labour administration of James CALLAGHAN to form a government from 1977 to 1979.

Livingstone, David (1813-73) Scottish missionary, anti-slavery campaigner and explorer who discovered the Victoria Falls, explored Lake Nyasa and mapped the Zambezi River in Africa. His disappearance in 1865 caused widespread concern. He was tracked down near Lake Tanganyika six years later by the journalist Henry Morton Stanley, who greeted him with the reserved and oft-quoted phrase: 'Doctor Livingstone, I presume?'

Lloyd George, David (1863-1945) Liberal prime minister from 1916 to 1922, at the head of a coalition government. As ASQUITH's chancellor of the exchequer (1908-15), he triggered a constitutional crisis when the House of Lords rejected his 'People's Budget' of 1909, which introduced new taxes on the income and

property of the wealthy to pay for welfare measures. Consequently, the Lords were later stripped of their power to veto money bills. Lloyd George took over as prime minister halfway through World War I. When the war ended, he conducted negotiations for Britain at the conference leading to the treaty of ▷VERSAILLES. He gave Ireland HOME RULE in 1921. When he died he had been an MP for 55 years, and his energy and eloquence made a lasting impact on British political life.
🔖 Lloyd George, an eloquent Welshman, was nicknamed 'the Welsh wizard'.

Lollards Followers of the medieval theologian John WYCLIFFE. The word 'Lollard' is derived from the old Dutch for 'mumbler', referring to the sect's quiet muttering of prayers. Lollardism attacked many established practices of the Roman Catholic Church, and it was suppressed by the Church authorities. The movement was a precursor of the REFORMATION.

Londonderry, Siege of (1689) Part of JAMES II's failed attempt to wrest power back from WILLIAM AND MARY. The Protestant city of Londonderry, in Northern Ireland, resisted an assault by James's army and was besieged for 105 days.
🔖 At one point, worn down by the siege, the citizens flung open the gates of Londonderry and prepared to surrender. A group of apprentices immediately shut them again as a sign of defiance. In Ulster, loyalists commemorate this event in the annual apprentice boys' march.

Lord Haw Haw Nickname of William Joyce (1906-46), an Irish American who broadcast Nazi propaganda from Germany throughout World War II. His nickname, which was inherited from a previous broadcaster, derived from his mocking aristocratic drawl. He was captured and hanged for treason after the war.
🔖 Joyce's broadcasts – which began 'Jairmany calling, Jairmany calling' – included bizarre commentaries on the news which caused more mirth than fear.

Luddites Textile workers who destroyed new machinery in 1811 and 1816, fearing it would put them out of work. Luddite riots began in Nottingham, and spread to Yorkshire, Lancashire, Derbyshire and Leicestershire. The workers claimed to be followers of a legendary 'Captain Ludd' or 'King Lud', and were severely punished.
🔖 Present-day opponents of technological change, especially in industry, are still sometimes referred to as Luddites.

MacDonald, Flora (1722-90) Jacobite heroine who helped BONNIE PRINCE CHARLIE to escape from Scotland to the Isle of Skye after his defeat at CULLODEN in 1746.

MacDonald, Ramsay (1866-1937) Britain's first Labour prime minister, who held office for nine months in 1924 with support from the Liberals. He returned to power in 1929 – again with Liberal support – but the Depression frustrated his plans for social reform. In 1931, impending national bankruptcy forced him to form a coalition National government with the Liberals and the Conservatives. MacDonald was expelled from the Labour Party, which was routed at the next general election, but he formed a second, mainly Conservative, National government which he led until his resignation in 1935.

Maclean, Donald (1913-83) British diplomat who acted as a Soviet spy from 1944 until 1951, when he fled to the USSR with Guy BURGESS. He was part of a spy ring with Burgess, PHILBY and Blunt.

TRAITOR *Lord Haw Haw was born in the USA, but his British passport, acquired under false pretences, made him subject to British law.*

Macmillan, Harold (1894-1986) Conservative prime minister from 1957 to 1963. Taking over from Anthony Eden, he restored national confidence after the ▷SUEZ CRISIS and for a time enjoyed considerable popularity. In 1960 his ▷'WIND OF CHANGE' speech accepted the need for decolonisation and called for an end to ▷APARTHEID. His popularity dwindled, however, when he failed to negotiate Britain's entry to the Common Market and mishandled the PROFUMO AFFAIR.
🔖 Macmillan – nicknamed 'Supermac' – is remembered for his proud boast that 'most of our people have never had it so good'.

Magna Carta (1215) List of rights and privileges – also known as the Great Charter of Liberties – sealed by King JOHN under pressure from his barons, who wanted to stop his arbitrary rule and heavy taxes. It insisted that the king should seek the barons' permission before levying taxes. One phrase of the charter – 'to no one will we sell, deny or delay right or justice' – established principles which are still the basis of ▷NATURAL JUSTICE in England and many other countries.

Marlborough, 1st Duke of (1650-1722) John Churchill, distinguished soldier and diplomat who helped James II to quell the MONMOUTH REBELLION, but deserted him during the GLORIOUS REVOLUTION. Marlborough went on to command the British army in the War of ▷SPANISH SUCCESSION. His wife, Sarah, was Queen Anne's closest friend and helped to advance his career. When she was replaced in the Queen's affections, he also fell from favour – but soon became a close confidant of GEORGE I.
🔖 The duke was given ▷BLENHEIM PALACE by the nation for his victory over France at the Battle of ▷BLENHEIM.

Mary I (1516-58) Queen of England and Ireland, who came to the throne by ousting Lady Jane GREY in 1553. She was the daughter of Henry VIII by his first wife, Catherine of Aragon. A Roman Catholic, she ruthlessly persecuted Protestants, sending about 300 dissenters to be burned at the stake. Her marriage to Philip II of Spain provoked a rebellion and dragged England into Spain's war with France; the result was the loss of Calais, England's last foothold on the Continent. Mary said that when she died, the word 'Calais' would be found engraved on her heart.
🔖 Known as 'Bloody Mary', Mary I was undoubtedly one of the most unpopular queens in British history.

TRAGIC QUEEN *A contemporary artist shows the axe about to fall on Mary, Queen of Scots in the Great Hall of Fotheringhay Castle as workmen (far left) start to burn her possessions.*

Mary, Queen of Scots (1542-87)

Queen who succeeded to the Scottish throne and staked her claim to the English throne in 1561. Her husband, Henry, Lord Darnley, murdered Mary's secretary David Riccio and was then killed himself in mysterious circumstances. In 1567, when Mary married the chief suspect, the Earl of Bothwell, the Scottish nobles forced her to abdicate in favour of her son James VI of Scotland – later JAMES I of England. Mary was imprisoned by ELIZABETH I for 20 years, but she still became the focus of Catholic plots against the English Crown. Eventually she was executed for treason.

Melbourne, Viscount (1779-1848)

Whig prime minister for five months in 1834, and from 1835 to 1841. He reformed local government and the POOR LAW, but is mainly remembered for his close friendship with the young Queen Victoria.
♟ Melbourne's wife, Lady Caroline Lamb, had a notorious affair with the dissolute poet Lord ▷BYRON.

Monmouth rebellion (1685)

Attempt to dethrone JAMES II, led by James Scott, Duke of Monmouth and illegitimate son of Charles II. Monmouth, the focus of Protestant opposition to the pro-Catholic king, landed at Lyme Regis but failed to gather enough support and was defeated at Sedgemoor. He was beheaded and his followers were punished in the BLOODY ASSIZES.

Montgomery, Bernard (Viscount Montgomery of Alamein) (1887-1976)

Commander of the British army in North Africa and Europe during World War II. His first major victory, at the head of the Eighth Army, was to defeat ▷ROMMEL at El ALAMEIN; he later commanded Allied ground forces during ▷D-DAY and the subsequent invasion of Normandy.

♟ 'Monty' is remembered as an outspoken and inspiring, if conceited, general, who won great affection from his troops. His trademark beret bore two cap badges: one denoting his rank of general, the other his regiment – the Royal Tank Regiment.

More, Thomas (1478-1535)

Statesman and scholar who served HENRY VIII until the break with Rome. A loyal Catholic, he was beheaded for refusing to recognise Henry as head of the English Church. He wrote *Utopia* (Greek for 'no place'), in which he outlined his vision of an ideal society. More was made a Catholic saint in 1935.
♟ Robert Bolt wrote a powerful play about Thomas More, *A Man For All Seasons*.

Mosley, Sir Oswald (1896-1980)

Leader of the British Union of Fascists, an extreme right-wing party which flourished in the 1930s. His party, also known as the ▷BLACK SHIRTS, is remembered for staging violent anti-Semitic marches in London's East End. An admirer of Hitler and some elements of ▷NAZISM, Mosley was interned during World War II along with his wife, Diana – one of the Mitford sisters.

BRITISH BLACK SHIRT *Oswald Mosley gives the Fascist salute – an outstretched arm – to his devotees as he marches through London.*

BORN LEADER
Cousin of the queen and the Duke of Edinburgh's uncle, Louis Mountbatten was the last viceroy of India.

Mountbatten, Lord Louis (1900-79)

Earl Mountbatten of Burma, who commanded the defence of India and campaign to expel the Japanese from Burma during World War II. In 1947, as viceroy of India, Mountbatten supervised India's transition to independence. He was assassinated by the ▷IRA while fishing with members of his family off the Irish coast.

Naseby, Battle of (1645)

Decisive defeat for the royalist army in the CIVIL WAR. Cromwell's NEW MODEL ARMY killed or captured nearly half Charles I's troops.

'nation of shopkeepers'

Napoleon's alleged description of England, showing his contempt for the country that was to defeat him at TRAFALGAR and ▷WATERLOO.

Neave, Airey (1916-79)

Politician and wartime intelligence officer who was a committed supporter of Margaret Thatcher. She appointed Neave head of her private office, and shadow secretary of state for Northern Ireland. On March 30, 1979, he was killed by an Irish terrorist bomb that exploded under his car as he left the House of Commons' car park.

Nelson, Horatio (1758-1805)

Admiral who defeated Napoleon's navy at the Battle of TRAFALGAR in 1805. Nelson's first great victory was at the Battle of the Nile in 1798, when he destroyed France's Mediterranean fleet. In 1801 he annihilated the Danish fleet at the Battle of Copenhagen. He was mortally wounded at Trafalgar and died on board his flagship, HMS *Victory*.

🔱 Lord Nelson had a long scandalous relationship with Emma, Lady Hamilton.

🔱 Nelson's appearance was distinctive, with a missing arm and a black eyepatch covering his blind right eye. When ordered to retreat during the fighting at Copenhagen, he raised his telescope to his blind eye and said that he did not see any signal. Nelson is also remembered for his message to the fleet at Trafalgar: 'ENGLAND EXPECTS THAT EVERY MAN WILL DO HIS DUTY.'

New Model Army

Parliamentary army, created in 1645 from several private armies. Thomas Fairfax was the first commander of what became an extremely well-disciplined and effective fighting force. Its next leader, Oliver CROMWELL, turned it into a powerful political force which played a vital part in his victory over CHARLES I in the CIVIL WAR and his subsequent rise to power.

Nightingale, Florence (1820-1910)

Nurse who established a battlefield hospital for British soldiers wounded in the ▷CRIMEAN WAR. She introduced strict standards of hygiene and ensured the wounded were properly fed and nursed.

🔱 Florence Nightingale was dubbed 'the lady with the lamp' for the tireless service she gave to the sick and wounded, even tending them after dark. In 1907, she became the first woman to be awarded the British Order of Merit.

Norman Conquest

Replacement of old English laws and practices by Norman institutions. The process began in 1066, when WILLIAM THE CONQUEROR won the Battle of HASTINGS and was crowned king of England. The Norman Conquest saw Anglo-Saxon noblemen replaced by barons from the Continent, who brought their form of ▷FEUDALISM with them.

Oates, Captain Lawrence (1880-1912)

Explorer who reached the South Pole with Robert SCOTT. On the return journey, suffering from severe frostbite, he decided his companions would have a better chance of survival without him. As he walked out of their tent to die in the Antarctic blizzard, he told them calmly 'I may be some time'.

O'Connell, Daniel (1775-1847)

Campaigner for CATHOLIC EMANCIPATION in Ireland. His election as MP for County Clare in 1828 forced the British government to lift restrictions on Catholics holding office. O'Connell went on to lead agitation for an independent Ireland, earning himself the nickname 'the Liberator'.

Old Pretender

James Edward STUART (1688-1766), James II's son, who became the focus of the 'FIFTEEN' and other unsuccessful attempts to restore the Stuart line after James was deposed and William and Mary came to the throne. (See also GLORIOUS REVOLUTION and JACOBITES.)

Orangemen

Members of the Orange Order, a club formed in 1795 to maintain Protestant rule in Ireland. The society is named after William of Orange, the Protestant king who replaced James II in 1689. Orangemen are staunch defenders of ▷NORTHERN IRELAND's separation from the Republic of Ireland.

Owen, Robert (1771-1858)

Welsh industrialist and visionary social reformer who made his model mill community at New Lanark, Scotland, a showcase of

DEATH OF A HERO *Triumph at Trafalgar was made bitter-sweet when Nelson was killed by a musket ball. The painting shows him in the cockpit of HMS* Victory *attended by Captain Thomas Hardy (standing, right), who brought him news of victory. 'Kiss me, Hardy' was the admiral's dying request.*

THE TIMES
For 7th NOVEMBER. 1805
BATTLE OF
TRAFALGAR
CAPTURE OF
FRENCH AND
SPANISH FLEETS
DEATH OF NELSON
List of Killed and Wounded

progressive methods in management, education and employee welfare. In later life he led over-ambitious schemes to establish nationwide trade unions and abortive efforts to found other utopian settlements. His views were influential in founding the COOPERATIVE MOVEMENT in Britain.

Palmerston, Viscount (1784-1865)

Liberal prime minister from 1855 to 1858 and from 1859 to 1865. In office, he continued the staunch defence of British interests abroad for which he was renowned as foreign secretary in the 1830s and 40s. He vigorously prosecuted the ▷CRIMEAN WAR and put down the INDIAN MUTINY.

🔧 'Pam', as he was known, is remembered above all for his aggressive foreign policy. He felt that all British subjects deserved full protection from their government, no matter where they might be. For example, in 1850 he sent warships to blockade Greece when Don Pacifico, a Portuguese moneylender who was a British citizen only by virtue of his birth in Gibraltar, was attacked by a mob in Athens.

parliament

Governmental and judicial institution which has evolved gradually from medieval meetings of king, barons and senior churchmen. During the reign of HENRY III, these traditional advisers were joined for the first time by the 'commons' – knights of the shires and representatives of important towns. EDWARD I was the first king to call regular parliaments. In the 14th century parliament wrested control of taxes from the king, and the lords and the commons, meeting separately in different chambers or 'houses', were starting to present the king with 'bills' – petitions suggesting ways to solve current problems. If these bills won royal assent, they became statute laws or 'acts of parliament'. Parliament and the monarchy now embarked on a power struggle, culminating in CHARLES I's attempt to rule alone and the CIVIL WAR. Parliament abolished the monarchy, only to demand its RESTORATION in 1660. In 1688, parliament won ascendancy over the Crown with the GLORIOUS REVOLUTION, after which its power continued to grow – as the monarchy's declined. (See also ▷PARLIAMENT in 'Politics, Government and the Law'.)

Parnell, Charles Stewart (1846-91)

Irish nationalist leader who brought HOME RULE to the centre of British politics. He converted William GLADSTONE, the Liberal leader, to his cause, but his political career was finished in 1890 when he was cited as co-respondent in a divorce case.

Peasants' Revolt (1381)

Popular uprising against RICHARD II, mostly in southeast England. The revolt was fuelled by a harsh POLL TAX, reversals in the ▷HUNDRED YEARS' WAR, poor wages and a series of bad harvests. It reached its climax when peasants from Essex and Kent, led by Wat Tyler and Jack Straw, entered London and killed government officials. Tyler met Richard II at Smithfield, after which most protesters were placated and dispersed. However, Tyler had an angry scuffle with the Lord Mayor of London, who had him beheaded.

🔧 The rebels were inspired by a couplet used as the text of a sermon by an excommunicated priest, John Ball, which asked: 'When Adam delved, and Eve span, who was then a gentleman?'

Peel, Robert (1788-1850)

Conservative prime minister from 1841 to 1846. As home secretary, he presided over CATHOLIC EMANCIPATION, belying his early reputation as 'Orange Peel' – a staunch Protestant who took stern measures against Catholic agitation. He also founded the Metropolitan Police, whose members were named 'peelers' or 'bobbies' after him. As prime minister, he moved towards free trade by reducing import tariffs and repealing the CORN LAWS. He died of injuries sustained when he was thrown from his horse.

🔧 Peel effectively founded the modern ▷CONSERVATIVE PARTY in 1834, when he made an election speech (the 'Tamworth Manifesto') which urged the party to embrace reform rather than resist it.

penny post

Postage system, invented by a former teacher, Rowland Hill, based on a uniform rate of one old penny for a letter to any point in the United Kingdom. Previously, the cost of postage had varied according to the number of sheets sent and the distance covered. The penny post was introduced in 1840, and featured the use of a prepaid postage stamp – the 'Penny Black' – for the first time.

THE FIRST STAMP *Only three out of every hundred of the 68 million Penny Blacks issued have survived. Unused examples in good condition can be worth thousands of pounds. The monarch's head is still used to identify British postal stamps.*

Perceval, Spencer (1762-1812)

Tory prime minister who came to office in 1809. He was assassinated in the House of Commons by John Bellingham, a mad bankrupt.

Peterloo Massacre (1819)

Forcible break-up of a political reform meeting at St Peter's Fields, Manchester. When members of the crowd prevented troops from arresting the speaker, the cavalry charged at them and caused a panic in which 11 people were killed and about 400 injured. The name 'Peterloo' was an ironic reference to the recent British victory at Waterloo.

PEASANT PROTEST *This medieval illustration shows London's mayor, William Walworth, about to strike Wat Tyler, leader of the Peasants' Revolt. At right, Richard II soothes the angry crowd.*

THE THIRD MAN *Kim Philby appearing before a press conference in 1955 at which he denied being a spy. Eight years later he fled to Moscow, just before it was revealed that he was a Soviet agent.*

Philby, Kim (1912-88) Pro-Soviet spy who was supposedly working for British intelligence. He passed valuable information to the Soviet Union before it was revealed that he was part of the BURGESS, MACLEAN and Blunt spy ring.

Phoenix Park Murders (1882) Murder of two British officials by members of an Irish terrorist group, the 'Invincibles'. Lord Frederick Cavendish, the new chief secretary for Ireland, and his deputy, Thomas Burke, were hacked to death with knives by 'Irish Invincibles' as they strolled in a Dublin park. The incident hardened English attitudes against the prospect of HOME RULE and William GLADSTONE's government, which had agreed a programme for Irish independence with Charles Stewart PARNELL, introduced strict measures to curb terrorism.

Picts Ancient inhabitants of Scotland, called *picti*, 'painted people', by the Romans because they painted or tattooed their bodies. They had their own language and culture which involved the unusual custom of inheriting titles and land through the female line. The Picts invaded ROMAN BRITAIN several times, but by the 10th century they had largely dispersed and been absorbed by other tribes.

Piltdown Man Skull found at Piltdown, Sussex, in 1912, which many scholars believed was the missing link which proved that humans had evolved from apes. However, in 1953, it was shown to be an elaborate hoax, made by attaching an orang-utan's jaw to a human skull.

Pitt, William, the Elder (1st Earl of Chatham) (1708-78) Statesman who, as secretary of state during the ▷SEVEN YEARS' WAR, stripped France of most of its colonial possessions and won Canada and India for Britain. He was appointed prime minister in 1766, but ill health forced him out of office two years later. His son, Pitt the Younger, also served as prime minister.
🔌 Pitt was an inspiring orator. After the war with France started badly for England, he declared arrogantly: 'I am sure I can save this country, and nobody else can.' A much-loved ruler, he was often referred to as the 'Great Commoner'.

Pitt, William, the Younger (1759-1806) Son of Pitt the Elder, who became Britain's youngest ever prime minister in 1783, at the age of 24. He reorganised the country's finances but could not push through his proposals for parliamentary reform or CATHOLIC EMANCIPATION. When war broke out with France in 1793,

Pitt introduced repressive measures to curb radicalism at home, and brought in the first income tax, with a top rate of 10 per cent, to pay for the ▷NAPOLEONIC WARS. He also passed the Act of UNION (1800), establishing formal links between England and Ireland. In his second term (1804-6) he organised an alliance with Russia and Austria to fight the Napoleonic Wars.

Plantagenets Family of English kings reigning from 1154 to 1485. Its name comes from the broom plant (in French, *plante genêt*) which Henry II's father, Geoffrey of Anjou, is said to have planted on his estates and worn in his cap. The first Plantagenets were the Angevin kings HENRY II, RICHARD I, JOHN, HENRY III, EDWARD I, II and III and RICHARD II. With Richard II's deposition in 1399, the dynasty split into the House of LANCASTER, comprising HENRY IV, V and VI and the House of YORK, comprising EDWARD IV and V and RICHARD III. The Plantagenets were succeeded by the TUDORS.

poll tax Tax levied on each 'poll' (head), payable by every adult. British governments have twice attempted to impose a poll tax based on a fixed sum per head. The first time was in 1380, and sparked off the PEASANTS' REVOLT; the second attempt was the 'community charge', a local government tax introduced in 1989-90, which provoked riots and a non-payment campaign. It was replaced in 1993 because of its widespread unpopularity.

poor law System of social welfare, introduced in 1601, which made each parish responsible for looking after its own poor and needy. The poor law was thoroughly reformed in 1834 and replaced by the now-defunct WORKHOUSE system, which aimed to put all able-bodied paupers to work in exchange for food and housing.

Popish Plot (1678) Alleged conspiracy by Catholics to murder CHARLES II and replace him with his Catholic brother James (later JAMES II). The 'plot' was later exposed as the invention of a defrocked Anglican parson called Titus Oates. The discovery that one of the Catholic 'plotters' he named had indeed been in treasonable correspondence with France, and the murder of a magistrate to whom Oates had sworn his statement, sparked off a wave of anti-Catholic hysteria and violence. Thirty-five Catholics were executed and parliament attempted to exclude James from the succession before Oates was eventually discredited and imprisoned for perjury.

potato famine Widespread starvation caused by a severe outbreak of potato blight, a fungal disease, in Ireland in 1845, 1846 and 1848. The crop failed and, as the potato was the staple diet, thousands starved to death and about a million succumbed to diseases such as cholera and dysentery because of their weakened condition. The effects of the crop failures were felt for many years afterwards.

⚓ Two million Irish people emigrated to escape the famine, and many of them settled in North America or Australia.

STARVING TO DEATH *About 4 million Irish people lived on potatoes alone. When the crop failed, famine and disease swept the country.*

pounds, shillings and pence British currency before decimalisation in 1971. 'Pound' referred originally to the Roman pound (0.327 kg) of sterling silver, from which Offa, an Anglo-Saxon king, was the first to mint 240 'pennies'. For hundreds of years they were the only unit of coinage, although they were often grouped into twelves for accounting purposes. The shilling coin, of 12 pennies, was introduced in the 16th century.

⚓ The £ symbol is a stylised 'L' for the Latin *libra*, meaning 'pound'. The shilling was denoted by the letter 's' for *solidus*, an ancient Roman coin, and the penny by 'd', short for the Latin *denarius* or 'penny'.

Pride's Purge (1648) Incident during the English CIVIL WAR in which troops under Colonel Thomas Pride arrested 45 moderate MPs and turned away a further 69 as they arrived at parliament, to prevent them seeking an agreement with CHARLES I. The remaining members of the so-called 'Rump Parliament' ordered Charles's trial on charges of treason and murder.

Princes in the Tower EDWARD V, aged 12, and Prince Richard, aged 10, the sons of EDWARD IV, who were imprisoned in the Tower of London by their uncle Richard of Gloucester (later RICHARD III) because they blocked his claim to the throne. They then disappeared, and it is widely believed they were murdered on their uncle's orders.

Profumo affair (1963) Sex scandal in which John Profumo, Harold MAC-MILLAN's secretary of state for war, was accused of putting national security at risk by his affair with Christine Keeler, who was also having a relationship with Soviet naval attaché Eugene Ivanov. Profumo was forced to resign because he admitted misleading the Commons when questioned about his friendship with Keeler.

Puritans Radical ▷PROTESTANTS who emerged in the late 16th century and became a major force in the 17th century. 'Puritans' is a term covering many religious sects, such as the ▷PRESBYTERIANS, which wanted to 'purify' the Church of England by eliminating traces of its Catholic origins, including all images of Christ, and imposing strict adherence to the Bible. The Puritans banned the traditional English maypole and forbade Christmas celebrations as part of their strict moral code. In several respects, Oliver CROMWELL's government was a Puritan regime.

⚓ Puritans insisted on teetotalism, and condemned playing sports on Sundays and theatre-going on any day as immoral. They also banned bear-baiting – not, according to at least one well-known historian, because of the pain inflicted on the bear, but the pleasure it gave to the spectators. The words *puritan* and *puritanical* have come to suggest a zeal for preventing people from enjoying themselves.

radicals General term applied to agitators for political and social reform. It was first used in the late 18th and early 19th centuries to describe those who urged Britain to follow the ▷FRENCH REVOLUTION. Radicalism brought about the first REFORM ACT and contributed to CHARTISM, eventually evolving into liberalism and the social reforms introduced by LLOYD GEORGE.

DISGRACE *At a party thrown by osteopath Stephen Ward, John Profumo (right) met Christine Keeler (above, right). Mandy Rice-Davies (above, left) was Keeler's flatmate. When Lord Astor, who lent his home for the party, denied sleeping with Mandy, she said: 'He would, wouldn't he?'*

⚓ The radical tradition has been carried on by the Labour Party, although many of Margaret ▷THATCHER's reforms have also been described as 'radical'.

railways Steam locomotion was invented for industrial use by Thomas Newcomen in 1698 and improved by James Watt in 1769 and Richard Trevithick in 1803. The first public steam railway was operated by George ▷STEPHENSON between Stockton and Darlington in 1825. The 1840s saw a speculative railway investment boom funded largely by individual entrepreneurs. By 1930 Britain had more than 19 000 miles (30 000 km) of track operated by four networks: the Great Western; the London and North Eastern; the London, Midland and Scottish; and the Southern. Britain's rail network was nationalised in 1948 and has steadily contracted. In 1963 Richard Beeching, the chairman of the British Railways Board, controversially decided to close many branch lines, wielding what came to be called the 'Beeching Axe'. There remain some 10 000 miles (16 000 km) of track, serving about 2 500 stations.

Raleigh, Sir Walter (1552-1618)

Explorer known for his expeditions to the Americas, and for allegedly bringing tobacco and the potato from the New World to the British Isles. A favourite of ELIZABETH I, he fell from favour under JAMES I and spent 13 years in the Tower of London, writing a history of the world, before being executed for treason.

🔖 Raleigh is often considered a near-ideal English gentleman of the Renaissance. A well-known legend holds that on one occasion he spread his cloak over a muddy puddle so that Queen Elizabeth would not have to soil her feet by walking through it.

from Catherine of Aragon. The DISSOLUTION OF THE MONASTERIES and the Book of Common Prayer were part of the English Reformation. In Scotland, John KNOX established PRESBYTERIANISM – which remains the national religion – for purely theological reasons. (See also ▷REFORMATION in 'World History'.)

ELIZABETHAN SEADOG *The miniature portrait by Nicholas Hilliard reveals Sir Walter Raleigh's determined character. Below, he takes prisoners during the capture of Trinidad from Spain in 1595.*

Reform Acts

Series of statutes which enlarged the parliamentary FRANCHISE and changed the structure of PARLIAMENT. The first, passed in 1832, redistributed constituencies to reflect the growth of industrial towns and replaced unequal voting qualifications, which had varied from town to town, with a uniform franchise. Three more Reform Acts were passed in the 19th century, giving the vote to working-class men and standardising the size of constituencies.

Reformation

Replacement of Catholicism as the official national religion by ▷PROTESTANTISM. In 1534, HENRY VIII created himself head of an autonomous ▷CHURCH OF ENGLAND when the pope refused to grant his request for a divorce

Regency (1811-20)

Period in which George, the flamboyant and dissolute Prince of Wales (later GEORGE IV), was regent for his father, George III, who suffered from mental instability.

🔖 The ▷REGENCY style of decorative architecture patronised by the prince regent took its name from this period.

Restoration

Return of the monarchy in 1660 following the death of CROMWELL. CHARLES II returned from exile to preside over a divided nation as it suffered the turmoils of the Great Plague, the Great Fire of London and the Dutch Wars. His reign also saw the founding of the Royal Society and a revival of the theatre. (See also ▷RESTORATION in 'Art and Design'.)

Rhodes, Cecil (1853-1902)

Statesman and entrepreneur who pioneered British expansion in southern Africa, particularly in Rhodesia (now Zimbabwe and Zambia), which was named after him.

🔖 Rhodes endowed a number of 'Rhodes scholarships' for colonial, American and German students at Oxford University.

Richard I 'The Lionheart' (1157-99)

King of England who succeeded his father Henry II in 1189. He spent most of the first half of his reign on crusades in the Middle East, and was a hostage of the German emperor for two years. The rest of his reign was spent fighting in France, where he died.

🔖 In the legend of ▷ROBIN HOOD, Robin and his men are loyal to the absent King Richard rather than to his brother JOHN.

Richard II (1367-1400)

King of England who succeeded his grandfather Edward III in 1377, at the age of ten; he was the BLACK PRINCE's son. He dealt courageously with the PEASANTS' REVOLT but was deposed in 1399 by Henry Bolingbroke (Henry IV).

Richard III (1452-85)

King of England who usurped the throne from the young Edward V in 1483. His reputation as a cruel tyrant, gained because he imprisoned and possibly murdered Edward V and his brother, the PRINCES IN THE TOWER, may be undeserved. He gave generously to schools, colleges and the Church. He was killed by Henry Tudor (later Henry VII) at the Battle of BOSWORTH FIELD after two years on the throne.

🔖 Although Richard III is often portrayed as a hunchback, there is no contemporary evidence for this. If he did have a deformity, it was not very noticeable.

🔖 Shakespeare's first real success was his historical play ▷RICHARD III.

Rob Roy (1671-1734)

Scottish outlaw who led his clan in a series of exploits similar to those of the legendary Englishman Robin Hood. He was captured and imprisoned by the English government, but was later pardoned and set free. His real name was Robert MacGregor.

🔖 Rob Roy is remembered today largely thanks to Sir Walter ▷SCOTT's novel *Rob Roy*, a glamorised account of his life.

Roman Britain

Period of Roman rule that started in AD 43, when troops of the Emperor ▷CLAUDIUS landed in Kent. ▷JULIUS CAESAR had previously made two brief exploratory missions to the British Isles, in 55 and 54 BC. In the next 40 years, the Romans conquered England and Wales in the face of opposition from tribal leaders such as BOUDICCA. The Romans introduced Christianity to the British Isles following the conversion of ▷CONSTANTINE in 313. They also undertook massive construction projects such as ▷HADRIAN'S WALL and established a network of roads which still underlie many of Britain's present-day routes. In 410, however, the imperial government in Rome decided it could no longer defend Britain against barbarian attacks, and relinquished control of its far-flung possession. Bath (in Latin, *Aquae Sulis*), Colchester (*Camulodunum*), St Albans (*Verulamium*) and London (*Londinium*) all became important towns during Roman times.

Roses, Wars of the (1455-85)
Series of wars fought by two rival branches of the PLANTAGENET dynasty for control of the English throne. Each family had a rose as its emblem – white for the YORK family, red for the House of LANCASTER. The struggle started when Richard of York claimed the throne from the weak Lancastrian king, HENRY VI. In 1460 Richard captured Henry, and was made heir to the throne; but he was killed in the same year and the Yorkist claim passed on to Edward, Duke of York – crowned EDWARD IV in 1461. In 1470, however, Henry VI was briefly restored to the throne by his cousin the Earl of WARWICK. On Edward's death, his brother RICHARD III usurped the throne, but alienated Yorkists helped the only remaining Lancastrian claimant, Henry Tudor (later Henry VII), to defeat Richard at the Battle of BOSWORTH FIELD (1485). He was crowned HENRY VII and married Edward IV's daughter, Elizabeth of York, to put an end to the family rivalry.

Russell, Lord John (1792-1878)
Liberal prime minister in 1846-51 and 1865-6. Driven by his belief that reform was the 'safety-valve of society', he won great popularity as postmaster-general for propelling the 1832 REFORM ACT through the Commons. In 1846, as leader of the opposition, he ensured that the CORN LAWS were repealed. In office, his main problems were the Irish POTATO FAMINE and dealing with the demands made by CHARTISM.

Salisbury, Marquess of (1830-1903)
Conservative prime minister in 1885-6, 1886-92 and 1895-1902. As DISRAELI's foreign secretary, he played a key role at the Congress of ▷BERLIN. As premier, he introduced free public education, steered Britain through the ▷BOER WAR and oversaw Britain's policy of SPLENDID ISOLATION.

Scone, Stone of
Block of sandstone on which ancient Scottish and Irish monarchs were crowned. It is said to have been used as a pillow by Jacob in the book of ▷GENESIS, and appeared in Ireland in the 6th century AD. Irish immigrants brought it with them to Scotland and in 1296, Edward I took it from Scone to Westminster Abbey where it was incorporated into the English coronation throne. Every English monarch since Edward II has been crowned on it.

In 1950, Scottish nationalists stole the stone as a gesture of protest against English domination. It was recovered at Arbroath Abbey four months later.

FATEFUL END *Scott (standing, centre) and his team pose at the South Pole. The last page of his expedition diary, recovered later, ends with the scrawled plea: 'For God's sake look after our people.' The entire team perished.*

Scott, Robert Falcon (1868-1912)
Naval officer who led two expeditions in Antarctica. The first (1900-4) explored the Ross Sea, on the west side of the continent, and made the first long journeys into the interior; the second, which started in 1910, was a bid to be the first to reach the South Pole. Scott unwisely chose to use ponies for haulage instead of dogs, and his team arrived at the pole after more than two months of immense hardship only to find that their Norwegian rival Roald ▷AMUNDSEN had reached it a month earlier. On the way back, the British group, including Captain Lawrence OATES, all perished in severe blizzards and temperatures as low as −44° C (−47° F). They were just 11 miles (18 km) from a supply base and safety.

Sidney, Sir Philip (1554-86)
Poet, scholar, patriot and soldier whose poems, including *Arcadia*, *The Defence of Poesie* and the sonnet series *Astrophel and Stella*, were written for the enjoyment of his friends and fellow courtiers. They were not published until after his death. He is especially remembered for his magnanimity in death, which completes the popular image of Sidney as the perfect Elizabethan Renaissance gentleman. Wounded at the Battle of Zutphen, in the Netherlands, he passed the water he was offered to a wounded footsoldier with the words: 'Thy necessity is yet greater than mine.'

Simnel, Lambert (c.1475-c.1534)
Joiner's son who tried to depose HENRY VII by pretending to be the son, brother or nephew of EDWARD IV. In 1487, after being crowned Edward VI in Dublin by his Yorkist supporters, Simnel mounted a coup attempt. With a force of German mercenaries, he crossed to England but was defeated by Henry at the Battle of Stoke. As a final humiliation, Henry employed Simnel to do menial tasks in the royal kitchens.

TRAGIC BRAVERY *British troops wait in the muddy trenches of the Somme. Sent straight towards the German guns by their misguided leaders, more than 19 000 died in the first day of the offensive.*

Somme, Battle of the (1916) British and French offensive against the Germans during ▷WORLD WAR I. The Allied infantry braved a nightmare of shells, machine gun fire, barbed wire and mud, but in 20 weeks of fighting they advanced no more than 5 miles (8 km). More than a million soldiers were killed – 420 000 Britons, 195 000 Frenchmen and at least 420 000 Germans, but German resistance remained strong. The Battle of the Somme, one of the bloodiest in history, was the first in which tanks were used.

South Sea Bubble (1720) Speculative boom which plunged Britain into a financial crisis, bringing ruin to many investors. Shares in the South Sea Company, ostensibly a trading company with interests in South America, rocketed tenfold when it took over most of the national debt. The directors used many unorthodox financial manoeuvres and even bribed government ministers to help force up the price of shares, but eventually the 'bubble' burst and the stock became worthless.
🕯Robert WALPOLE increased his political power by formulating a clever rescue scheme for the economy after the share price of the South Sea Company collapsed.

splendid isolation Foreign policy adopted by Britain in the 1870s of standing aloof from political alliances with any other powers. It was based on the unassailable strength of Britain's empire and navy, and lasted until the beginning of the 20th century. A build-up in the German navy brought Britain into the loose alliance with France known as the ▷ENTENTE CORDIALE (1904). The policy of splendid isolation is especially associated with the premiership of Lord SALISBURY, although the phrase was actually invented by a Canadian politician, Sir George Foster, in 1896.

Star Chamber Royal court that sat in closed session on cases involving the security of the state. The Star Chamber was set up in the late 14th century. Under JAMES I and CHARLES I the Star Chamber gained a reputation for tyrannical judgments, and in 1641 it was abolished. The court got its name from its original courtroom in the Palace of Westminster, which had a ceiling decorated with gilded stars.
🕯The term 'Star Chamber' is used to describe any group of people that makes arbitrary or undemocratic judgments, abuses its power or is unduly secretive.

Stephen (c.1097-1154) King of England who succeeded his uncle Henry I in 1135; he was a grandson of William the Conqueror. Backed by a majority of the English barons, Stephen seized the throne from Matilda, Henry's daughter and designated successor, breaking his earlier oath of loyalty to her. Matilda waged a long war against Stephen, and for a while held him prisoner. In 1153 the warring parties agreed a compromise; Stephen was to remain on the throne, but Matilda's son was to succeed him as HENRY II.

Stopes, Marie (1880-1958) Pioneer of birth control and women's rights, whose controversial books *Married Love* and *Wise Parenthood* (1918) were the first to popularise modern methods of ▷CONTRACEPTION. She also opened the first birth control clinic in Britain in 1921. Her frankness and plain speaking about sex shocked many people.

Strafford, Thomas Wentworth, Earl of (1593-1641) Statesman who was originally an opponent of CHARLES I but became a royalist in 1628, and was the king's chief adviser in the prelude to the CIVIL WAR. Together with Archbishop LAUD, he introduced severely authoritarian policies during Charles's personal rule (1629-40). Strafford, feared as 'Black Tom Tyrant' as lord deputy of Ireland, symbolised royal misrule and was eventually impeached and sentenced to death by parliament; he was beheaded on Tower Hill.

Stuart, House of Dynasty that ruled Scotland from 1371 to 1603 and Britain from 1603 (JAMES I) to 1714 (ANNE), except

FAMILY PLANNER *Dr Marie Stopes sits with her nurses in attendance. She attracted press ridicule by preaching contraception for all.*

for the 11 years of the Commonwealth and Protectorate. They were descended from HENRY VII's daughter Margaret Tudor, who married the Scottish king James IV. When Anne died without heirs, the crown passed to the House of HANOVER, although the Stuart OLD PRETENDER and his son BONNIE PRINCE CHARLIE continued to try to claim the throne.

suffragettes Women who campaigned for their right to vote in the late 19th and early 20th centuries. Led by Emmeline Pankhurst and her daughters Christabel and Sylvia, the suffragettes chained themselves to railings and smashed windows to win publicity and achieve their ends. When imprisoned, they went on hunger strike. Women over 30 won the vote in 1918, but equal franchise had to wait until 1928.
⚓Emily Davison, who was fatally injured when she dashed into the path of the king's horse at the Epsom Derby in 1913, was one of the movement's martyrs.

swinging sixties Nickname for the 1960s, seen in Britain as a time when moral, social and economic restraints all relaxed. The first period of real prosperity since the war coincided with a spirit of intellectual and artistic rebellion and a sexual freedom made possible by the ▷PILL.
⚓Fashion models and designers, including Jean Shrimpton, Twiggy and Mary ▷QUANT, pop musicians – especially the ▷BEATLES and the ▷ROLLING STONES – and photographers such as David ▷BAILEY were idolised by the young.

Test Act (1673) Law which excluded non-Protestants from public office. Parliament, anxious to restrict Catholic influence at the court of CHARLES II, demanded that all candidates for government and military posts declare their allegiance to the Church of England and deny the Catholic doctrine of transubstantiation. The Test Act was not repealed until 1828.

three-day week Short working week imposed by Edward ▷HEATH's government in December 1973, to conserve energy supplies during a strike by miners, railwaymen and electricity workers. At the same time, petrol rationing seemed likely in the aftermath of the ▷YOM KIPPUR WAR. The normal five-day working week was restored in March 1974, after Heath had lost a general election to Harold ▷WILSON.

Titanic Supposedly unsinkable luxury liner which sank on its maiden voyage in 1912, after running into an iceberg in the

HARD STRUGGLE *Emmeline Pankhurst is arrested outside Buckingham Palace in 1914, during a suffragette protest against the government's continued refusal to grant votes to women.*

North Atlantic. More than 1500 of the 2340 passengers and crew drowned, mainly because there were not enough lifeboats.

tithe One-tenth of an individual's annual income or produce, traditionally given to the Church to support the clergy, maintain buildings and help the poor. The custom became compulsory in England in the 10th century and proved a source of conflict between Church and people. The PURITANS and ▷QUAKERS tried to abolish tithes in the 17th century; they survived in England until the Tithe Commutation Act of 1836 and in Scotland until 1925.

Tolpuddle martyrs Six farm labourers from Tolpuddle in Dorset, who formed a trade union in 1833. They were found guilty of taking illegal oaths and deported to Australia for seven years, but protests forced the government to pardon them in 1836. They all returned to England.

Tories Political party which started in 1679-80 as a group defending the right of the Catholic James, Duke of York (later JAMES II), to succeed CHARLES II as king. They were opposed by WHIGS who endorsed the GLORIOUS REVOLUTION and

Protestant succession of William and Mary. In the 1840s the Tories became known as the ▷CONSERVATIVE PARTY.
⚓'Tory' was originally a term of abuse for dispossessed Catholic outlaws who attacked English settlers in Ireland.

Trafalgar, Battle of (1805) Naval battle fought off southwest Spain, in which a Royal Navy fleet under Horatio NELSON defeated the Franco-Spanish fleet and ended Napoleon's hopes of invading Britain. During the battle, Nelson was killed on board his flagship, HMS *Victory*.

Tudor, House of Dynasty that ruled England from 1485 to 1603, founded at the end of the Wars of the ROSES, when the Lancastrian king HENRY VII married Elizabeth of York. Henry, the grandson of Owen Tudor (*c*.1400-61) and Henry V's widow Catherine de Valois, claimed the throne as a descendant of JOHN OF GAUNT. ELIZABETH I was the last Tudor monarch.

Tull, Jethro (1674-1741) Farmer who in 1701 invented the seed drill, a device for sowing seeds in straight lines. Previously,

GIANTS COLLIDE *The* Titanic's *16 special watertight compartments were no match for the iceberg which holed it below the waterline. The 46 328 ton ship sank in slightly over 2½ hours.*

| St George England | St Andrew Scotland | First Union Jack 1606 | St Patrick Ireland | Present Union Jack 1801 |

SYMBOL OF UNION *After James I brought Scotland and England under a single crown, Britain's flag linked the crosses of their patron saints. The Irish cross was added after the second Act of Union.*

crops had been sown by wastefully scattering seeds. Tull's invention was symptomatic of a more scientific and experimental approach to farming which led to the AGRICULTURAL REVOLUTION.

turnpike trusts Bodies empowered by parliament to raise capital to build roads and levy tolls on the traffic. The 18th century, heyday of the turnpike trusts, saw many roads improved and built. Toll gates still survive on some roads and bridges, although most are no longer in use. Tolls for using some roads, however, may return.

Union, Acts of Two Acts uniting England and Wales with Scotland and Ireland. The 1707 Act dissolved the separate English and Scottish parliaments, creating a new parliament of Great Britain at Westminster. It imposed a uniform system of weights, measures and currency, but left the Scottish legal system in place. The 1800 Act transferred Irish MPs and peers to Westminster, taking effect on January 1, 1801. Both Acts of Union met resistance outside England.
♣ The term 'Great Britain' was used for England, Wales and Scotland after 1707. The 'United Kingdom' was created in 1801, when Ireland joined Great Britain.
♣ Britain's flag, the Union Flag or Union Jack, combines three crosses in a single design: St George's cross for England, St Andrew's cross for Scotland and St Patrick's cross for Ireland.

Victoria (1819-1901) Queen of the United Kingdom and its dominions, who succeeded her uncle William IV in 1837. Three years later she married Prince ALBERT of Saxe-Coburg and Gotha. After his death in 1861, she spent the rest of her life in mourning. Victoria took a keen interest in politics, especially in foreign policy – partly because of the growing British empire, and partly because her nine children married into many of the royal families of Europe. Unfortunately, many of them passed on the genetic blood disorder ▷HAEMOPHILIA, which killed one of her sons. Relations with her eldest son Edward, later EDWARD VII, were strained: he did not

meet her strict standards of morality. In 1876, she took the title Empress of India. By the 1880s Queen Victoria had become a symbol of the empire, and her golden and diamond jubilees (in 1887 and 1897) were celebrated around the globe.
♣ Victoria's comment of 'We are not amused' and her scowling, black-clad image bear out her reputation as a humourless, forbidding person. In fact her strong sense of duty masked a keen wit and sense of fun.
♣ In her later years she came to depend on John Brown, a Scottish servant who brusquely called her 'wumman'.

Victorian period The period from 1837 to 1901, when VICTORIA reigned. Britain became the most powerful industrial and military nation in the world. Social inequalities became more apparent, with a wealthy, privileged upper class in sharp contrast to poverty and hardship in the urban working

classes. And for the first time a substantial middle class emerged, partly because of the availability of cheap manufactured goods.
♣ The term 'Victorian values' implies a strong sense of public morality and an emphasis on the importance of family life – but often with an element of hypocrisy.

Vikings Warriors from Scandinavia who mounted raids on the British Isles from the 8th to 11th centuries. The first major attack on British soil was made by Norwegians on Lindisfarne in AD 793. It was Danish Vikings, however, who posed the greatest threat to Anglo-Saxon England. During the 9th century they conquered most of England except Wessex, whose king, ALFRED THE GREAT, eventually defeated them at the Battle of Edington in 878. The Vikings became Christians and in the large area of England in which they settled, known as the DANELAW, they became well integrated with the local inhabitants. (See also ▷VIKINGS in 'World History'.)

Wallace, Sir William (*c.*1274-1305) Scottish hero who led resistance to EDWARD I. He defeated the English army at Stirling Bridge in 1297 and raided northern England, but was defeated at Falkirk in 1298. He was captured by the English in 1305 and executed for treason.

ROYAL TEAM *Victoria and Albert, photographed in 1854, shared a keen sense of national duty, and enjoyed working together. After Albert's death at the age of 42, Victoria wore only black.*

IRON DUKE *Wellington, here caricatured as one of his boots, held the opinion that victory in battle was a tragedy second only to defeat.*

Walpole, Sir Robert (1676-1745)

Statesman who is generally regarded as establishing the office of prime minister, although he never officially bore the title. His rescue of the economy after the SOUTH SEA BUBBLE disaster led to his appointment as both chancellor of the exchequer and first lord of the treasury in 1721, posts he held until 1742. Walpole's services were especially valued by George I and II, and he relied on their staunch support to build a position of immense power. Walpole, a WHIG, focused on strengthening national finances while reducing taxation.

🔖 Walpole was a capable politician, but he built up power by using government patronage to buy support in parliament. 'All men have their price,' he once remarked.

Warbeck, Perkin (c.1474-99)

Flemish pretender to the English throne, who impersonated Richard, the younger of the two PRINCES IN THE TOWER, in an attempt to depose HENRY VII. He won some support in Scotland and on the Continent before landing in Cornwall in 1497, but was captured by the king's forces. Warbeck was executed two years later, after he became the focus of further plots and attempted to escape from the Tower of London.

Warwick, Earl of (1428-71)

Richard Neville, a powerful baron whose key role in the Wars of the ROSES earned him the name 'kingmaker'. He first backed the Yorkist cause, proclaiming his cousin to be King EDWARD IV and defeating the Lancastrian army in 1461. When Edward turned against him, Warwick switched sides and reinstated the Lancastrian HENRY VI in 1470. King Edward's forces defeated and killed Warwick at the Battle of Barnet in 1471.

Wellington, Duke of (1769-1852)

Arthur Wellesley, soldier and statesman who won fame, admiration and a dukedom for his campaigning in Spain during the ▷PENINSULAR WAR. He was a tough general and an outspoken one – once describing his troops as the 'scum of the earth'. Wellington was a staunch Tory, and after his great victory over Napoleon at ▷WATERLOO (1815), he pursued his political career. As prime minister (1828-30), he introduced CATHOLIC EMANCIPATION to avoid revolution in Ireland, but lost power because he opposed parliamentary reform. He remained active in politics until 1846, while continuing his military career as the army's commander-in-chief for life. He was known as the 'Iron Duke'.

🔖 The Duke of Wellington is probably the only person to have a tree, a capital city, an item of footwear and a recipe named after him. *Wellingtonia* is the Californian redwood tree or giant sequoia; Wellington is the capital of New Zealand, founded in 1840; the Wellington boot is a waterproof boot based on the style worn by the duke; and beef Wellington is a fillet of beef baked with *pâté de foie gras* in a pastry case.

Whigs

Political party formed in the late 1670s as a group seeking to exclude the Catholic JAMES II from the succession. The deposition of James during the GLORIOUS REVOLUTION was celebrated by the Whigs, aristocratic landowners who in contrast to the TORIES believed in a limited monarchy subject to the will of parliament. Under Charles James FOX, in the 1780s, the Whigs became the party of reform, religious toleration and commerce. In the 19th century the LIBERAL PARTY absorbed the Whigs.

🔖 'Whig' is believed to stem from 'whiggamore', slang for Presbyterian extremists.

Whittington, Dick (c.1358-1423)

Cloth merchant who was lord mayor of London three times. At 13 he left home to become a clothier's apprentice. He set up his own business and made a fortune. He lent money to Richard II, Henry IV and Henry V, and gave generously to charity.

🔖 An old ballad portrayed Whittington as a poor boy who came to London in search of 'streets paved with gold' but failed to find them and started for home. He heard Bow Bells ringing, seeming to say 'Turn again Whittington'; he returned to discover his cat had been sold for a fortune, and stayed – fulfilling the bells' prophecy that he would be 'thrice mayor of London'.

Wilberforce, William (1759-1833)

Evangelist, reformer and MP who campaigned against slavery for 19 years before the slave trade was abolished in British territories in 1807. Slavery itself was abolished in 1833 – days after he died.

Wilkes, John (1727-97)

Journalist and politician who became a hero of free expression. In 1763, an article in his journal *North Briton* accused ministers of putting lies into the mouth of GEORGE III. Wilkes was charged with libel, but his status as an MP protected him from prosecution. Expelled from parliament for publishing an obscene book (*Essay on Woman*) he went into exile. On his return to England in 1768 he was three times elected MP, but barred from taking his seat and imprisoned for seditious libel. 'Wilkes and liberty' became a rallying cry, and in 1774 he was re-admitted to parliament.

William I 'The Conqueror' (c.1027-87)

Duke of Normandy who took the English crown in 1066. His cousin,

CONQUERING KING *This medieval manuscript accurately portrays William I as a stern ruler and a great supporter of the Church.*

EDWARD THE CONFESSOR, had informally promised to make William his heir, but when Edward died, Harold, an Anglo-Saxon nobleman, took the throne. William defeated and killed Harold at the Battle of HASTINGS. After overcoming resistance from HEREWARD THE WAKE and others, William ruled capably, creating a ruling class of Norman knights and reorganising the land-holding system. In 1085 he commissioned the DOMESDAY BOOK, a detailed economic survey of England.

William II 'Rufus' (c.1056-1100) King of England who succeeded his father William I in 1087. His nickname is the Latin for 'red' – referring to his red hair and ruddy complexion. William was a tyrannical and unpopular king, and he extorted money from the Church. In 1096, he won a long struggle to gain control of the Duchy of Normandy from his brother Robert. William was killed while hunting in the New Forest, hit – apparently accidentally – by an arrow fired by a courtier, Walter Tirel. Some historians believe that William may have been killed deliberately on the orders of his brother HENRY I.

William III See WILLIAM AND MARY.

William IV (1765-1837) King of Great Britain and Ireland, who succeeded his brother George IV in 1830. A Lord High Admiral in the Royal Navy, he was known as 'the sailor king' as well as 'Silly Billy'.

William and Mary King and Queen of Great Britain, crowned jointly after James II fled the country in 1688 during the GLORIOUS REVOLUTION. Both William III (1650-1702) and Mary II (1662-94) were grandchildren of Charles I. Mary, daughter of James II, was heir to the throne until the birth of James's son in 1688. William, also known as William of Orange after the Dutch province he ruled, was invited to England by leading WHIGS to help to defend Protestantism and 'the liberty of England' from James, the Catholic king. He landed at Torbay with an army, and quickly won so much support that James went into exile. As king, William defeated James at the Battle of the BOYNE (1690) and brought Britain into a Dutch war against France.

Windsor, House of The current British royal family. George V, Queen Elizabeth II's grandfather, adopted the name as a patriotic gesture during World War I. He felt that his name of Saxe-Coburg and Gotha, which he inherited from Prince ALBERT, sounded too Germanic.

winter of discontent The winter of 1978-9, when Britain was paralysed by widespread strike action in protest at James ▷CALLAGHAN's attempt to limit wage rises to five per cent. The problems of rubbish piling up in the streets and the dead being left unburied contributed to Callaghan's defeat in the 1979 general election.

witan or witenagemot. Council of advisors to Britain's Anglo-Saxon kings – the word means 'council of wise men' in Old English. It was an informal assembly of lords and bishops. Although kings consulted the witan only occasionally, and it had limited powers, it established the important constitutional principle that the monarch should take account of the views of his subjects. The witan evolved into the medieval 'great council', which in turn formed the basis for modern PARLIAMENT.

Wolfe, James (1727-59) Military hero celebrated for capturing Quebec, in Canada, from France in 1759. The victory was the turning point in the ▷SEVEN YEARS' WAR between Britain and France and established Canada as British territory. Wolfe's men used a hidden path to take the French army by surprise on the Plains of Abraham. Fatally wounded in the battle, he lived long enough to hear that his troops had won.

Wolsey, Cardinal Thomas (c.1475-1530) Chief minister of HENRY VIII from 1515 to 1529. Although Wolsey increased

FALLEN CHIEF *After 14 years of great power, Cardinal Wolsey escaped being tried for treason only because he died on the way to his trial.*

the king's power at home and in Europe, Henry believed that the cardinal was acting too slowly in arranging his divorce from CATHERINE OF ARAGON. He was duly deprived of his offices of state, banished from the court and eventually arrested for treason in York. He died while being taken back to London to face almost certain death. ♟Wolsey, son of an Ipswich butcher, was the last great Catholic prelate to wield influence in Britain. The immense wealth he accumulated in office enabled him to build a grammar school in Ipswich, a college in Oxford (Cardinal College, now Christ Church) and an ostentatious palace at Hampton Court, near London.

workhouses Buildings where the able-bodied poor were housed and fed in return for labour. The first workhouses were built by groups of parishes in the 18th century. After the POOR LAW Amendment Act of 1834 had made workhouses the main agency for social welfare, they came in for widespread criticism because of the harsh conditions suffered by their inmates. In the 20th century they were replaced by the social security system.

Wycliffe, John (c.1329-84) Religious reformer whose attack on corruption in the English Church won him many followers, known as LOLLARDS. Supported by JOHN OF GAUNT, he also produced the first English translation of the Bible. When he challenged the hierarchical structure of the Church and denied the doctrine of ▷TRANSUBSTANTIATION, a synod condemned him and forced him to retire.

York, House of Branch of the PLANTAGENET family which fought the House of LANCASTER in the Wars of the ROSES. EDWARD IV, EDWARD V and RICHARD III were all members of the House of York. The dynasty takes its name from EDWARD III's son Edmund of Langley, the first Duke of York. The York dynasty was succeeded by the TUDORS.

Young Pretender Another name for BONNIE PRINCE CHARLIE, Charles STUART.

Zinoviev letter Letter discovered in 1924, purportedly written by Grigori Zinoviev, a member of the Soviet Politburo, but almost certainly a forgery, urging the British Communist Party to foment revolution. The letter received widespread publicity during the 1924 general election, and produced an anti-leftist reaction which contributed to the defeat of Ramsay MACDONALD's Labour government.

WORLD HISTORY

The world we live in is shaped by events from the past.
Empires and civilisations have risen, flourished and then withered
away. Wars have many times redrawn the global map, and
revolutions have brought about democracies – or dictatorships.
People as diverse as Julius Caesar and Joan of Arc,
Mahatma Gandhi and Mao Zedong have single-handedly
changed the course of history; their influence is still felt today.

TUTANKHAMUN

THE AMERICAN
CIVIL WAR

HITLER AT
NUREMBERG, 1935

Abbassids Family who ruled the Arab world from AD 749 to 1258. Descendants of ▷MUHAMMAD's uncle al-Abbas, they replaced the OMMAYADS. The Abbassids expanded the Muslim empire into Asia Minor, moving their capital to Baghdad.

Actium, Battle of (31 BC) Naval battle fought off the Greek coast, in which Julius Caesar's great-nephew Octavian beat the allied forces of his rival Mark Antony and the Egyptian queen CLEOPATRA. Octavian then took the name of AUGUSTUS and became the first Roman emperor.

Adams, John (1735-1826) Second president of the United States (1797-1801). He was one of America's 'founding fathers' – a signatory to the American DECLARATION OF INDEPENDENCE. Adams was the first American envoy to London and vice-president to George WASHINGTON. As president, he was appalled by the aftermath of the French Revolution, but he successfully used his diplomatic skills to avoid a threatened war with France.
🕭 Adams's son, John Quincy Adams, also served as US president from 1825 to 1829.

Albigensian Crusade Crusade proclaimed in 1208 by Pope Innocent III against heretical ▷DUALIST sects which had won the support of aristocrats in the region of Albi, in southern France. It took the barons of northern France, led by Simon de Montfort, five years of bloody fighting to subdue the heretics.

Alexander the Great (356-323 BC) Macedonian king and general who conquered Egypt and defeated Persia, extending the civilisation of Greece east to India. Alexander, a pupil of the philosopher ▷ARISTOTLE, is said to have wept because there were no worlds left to conquer. His empire was short-lived, however. Within 13 years of his death, the countries he had united were separate kingdoms again.
🕭 According to legend, before Alexander began his conquests, he succeeded in ▷CUTTING THE GORDIAN KNOT with his sword. He went on to fulfil the prophecy that the person who loosed the knot would rule a vast territory in Asia.
🕭 Alexander founded the city of ▷ALEXANDRIA, at the mouth of the Nile in Egypt, naming it after himself.

Allies Victorious allied nations of WORLD WAR I and WORLD WAR II. In World War I, the Allies included Britain and its empire, France, Italy, Russia and the USA. In World War II, the Allies – who opposed the AXIS powers – included Britain, France, the Soviet Union and the USA.

American Civil War (1861-5) War fought in the USA between 23 northern (Union) and 11 southern (Confederate) states, in which the Confederacy sought to establish itself as a separate nation. The war grew out of deep differences between the north and the south, notably over slavery – opposed by President LINCOLN, but an important part of the economy of the south. The Confederates opened the war by attacking Fort Sumter in South Carolina; most of the battles took place in the south, but the crucial battle of GETTYSBURG was fought in the north. The Confederate leader, Robert E. Lee, finally surrendered to the Unionist commander in chief, Ulysses S. GRANT at Appomattox, Virginia. The war cost more than 600 000 lives.
🕭 The novel and film ▷GONE WITH THE WIND are set during the period of the American Civil War.

American War of Independence (1775-83) War in which the 13 British colonies in North America threw off colonial rule and formed the United States of America. The fighting came at the end of a long period of tension, mainly over the British government's insistence on taxing colonists without consulting them. 'No Taxation without Representation' was the slogan of the colonists. The STAMP ACT (1765) and the BOSTON TEA PARTY (1773) led to the Battles of Lexington and Concord (1775) and the DECLARATION OF INDEPENDENCE. The American cause was greatly aided by their alliance with France, which provided ships and troops. The loss of the colonies was inevitable after the British defeat at the Battle of Yorktown (1781). Britain recognised American independence in the Treaty of Paris (1783).
🕭 The War of Independence is known in the United States as the Revolutionary War or the American Revolution.
🕭 The original 13 colonies of the United States were Connecticut, Delaware, Georgia, Maryland, Massachusetts, New Hampshire, New Jersey, New York, North Carolina, Pennsylvania, Rhode Island, South Carolina and Virginia.

LINCOLN'S WARRIORS *General Ulysses S. Grant, without hat and facing to the right, is surrounded by his generals in this 1865 painting celebrating the Union victory in the American Civil War.*

Adenauer, Konrad (1867-1976) Chancellor of the Federal Republic of Germany from 1949 to 1963, who oversaw the recovery and reconstruction of West Germany after the ravages of Nazism and defeat in World War II. Under Adenauer, West Germany regained full sovereignty and became a member of NATO and the European Economic Community.

Allende, Salvador (aa-YEN-day) (1908-73) President of Chile from 1970 to 1973. Elected as Chile's first socialist president, he faced determined opposition from the military, big business and the American Central Intelligence Agency (CIA). He was killed, or may have committed suicide, when the right-wing general Augusto Pinochet dislodged him in a military coup.

Amin, Idi (c.1925-) President of Uganda from 1971 to 1979. He came to power after he led a military coup against Milton

AWESOME POWER *The enormous mushroom cloud caused by an atomic blast, as seen during an American test explosion. The devastation of Hiroshima in 1945 (left) killed at least a quarter of a million people, either in the blast itself or by the radiation sickness that swept the city in the aftermath.*

Atatürk, Kemal (Mustapha Kemal) (1881-1938) The founder of modern Turkey, and its first president. Atatürk drove out both the occupying Greeks and the Ottoman sultan before proclaiming the republic of Turkey in 1923. He used dictatorial methods to carry out an ambitious Westernisation programme, converting his country from an Islamic to a secular state. He adopted the name 'Atatürk', which means 'father of Turkey', in 1934.
🎤Among Atatürk's reforms were the emancipation of women and the adoption of the Western instead of the Arabic alphabet. He also encouraged Turkish men to abandon their traditional fez hats.

Athens Leading city-state of ancient Greece, famous for its learning, culture and democratic institutions. Its intellectual and artistic achievements are symbolised by the ▷PARTHENON, which was built in the 5th century BC – the city's golden age. Solon, ▷SOPHOCLES and Pericles were some of its great figures. The political power of Athens, the first European ▷DEMOCRACY, was limited after its defeat by Sparta in the PELOPONNESIAN WARS.
🎤Athens had declined to the size of a village when it was chosen as the capital of newly independent Greece in 1834.

atom bomb Atom bombs have been used only twice in warfare, when the US plane *Enola Gay* dropped 'Little Boy' on Hiroshima and *Bock's Car* dropped 'Fat Man' on Nagasaki in August 1945, at the end of World War II. Possession of the atom bomb by the USA and the USSR contributed to the COLD WAR. (See also ▷NUCLEAR WEAPON in 'Technology and Invention'.)

Attila the Hun (*c*.405-53) Leader of the HUNS, a barbarian people who conquered large areas of central and eastern Europe and ravaged Italy in the declining years of the Roman Empire. His armies were notorious for their cruelty and wholesale destruction, and Attila himself was known as the 'scourge of God'.

Augustus Caesar (63 BC-AD 14) The first emperor of Rome, who was an adopted son of JULIUS CAESAR. His given name was Octavian, but he took the name Augustus in 27 BC, when he became emperor after defeating his rival Mark Antony in the battle of ACTIUM. During his reign, Rome conquered Egypt.
🎤The month of August is named after Augustus, and the era when the arts of a nation are at their height, as they were in his reign, is still called an 'Augustan age'.

Obote, and was a brutal ruler who ordered mass arrests, massacres and other atrocities. He also expelled most of Uganda's Asian population. Idi Amin was deposed in 1979 by a Tanzanian-backed coup, and went to live in exile in Saudi Arabia.

Amundsen, Roald (1872-1928) Norwegian explorer who in December 1911 became the first man to reach the South Pole, a month ahead of the Englishman Robert ▷SCOTT. Later he crossed the Arctic in an airship, and became the first man to visit both the North and South Poles.

ancien régime Political and social order that prevailed in France before the FRENCH REVOLUTION, built on a belief in ▷ABSOLUTE MONARCHY, the ▷DIVINE RIGHT OF KINGS, and a rigidly stratified society based on birth, not ability. The ostentatious wealth and privileges enjoyed by the aristocracy under LOUIS XIV and LOUIS XVI inspired bitter resentment which eventually flared up as violent revolution.

Anschluss Union of Germany and Austria, forbidden by the terms of the 1919 Treaty of VERSAILLES but orchestrated by Adolf Hitler. In 1938, after several years of Nazi disruption, Austria's pro-Nazi minister of security, Arthur Seyss-Inquart, invited Germany to invade on the eve of a poll on the issue. Austrians would probably have voted against Anschluss.

Armstrong, Neil (1930-) Commander of the Apollo 11 space mission in 1969, and the first man to walk on the Moon.
🎤When he took his first step onto the Moon's surface, Armstrong radioed back to Earth: 'That's one small step for a man, one giant leap for mankind.'

Assyria Warlike civilisation that flourished from the 13th century BC until it was conquered by neighbouring peoples in 609 BC. From the 9th to the 7th centuries BC, the Assyrians created an empire that covered much of the Middle East from their base in present-day Iraq and Turkey.

FINAL JOURNEY *Jews peer out nervously from the cattle trucks in which they are being taken to Auschwitz, whose gates bear the cruelly misleading slogan 'work makes free'. In fact, the vast majority were worked to death, or killed in the gas chambers.*

Auschwitz (OWSH-vits) Infamous CONCENTRATION CAMP complex set up by the Nazis at Oswiecim, in Poland. Up to 4 million people, mostly Jews transported from all over Europe, were murdered in the gas chambers or died of starvation, exhaustion and disease there between 1940 and 1945, during the HOLOCAUST.

Austerlitz, Battle of (1805) Brilliant victory of NAPOLEON's army over a larger Austrian and Russian force, fought in what is now the Czech Republic. The Austrians made peace with France after the battle.
🔖 On hearing the news of Napoleon's triumph, the British prime minister, William ▷PITT THE YOUNGER, said: 'Roll up that map (of Europe); it will not be wanted these ten years.'

Austria-Hungary Union of the two HABSBURG kingdoms of Austria and Hungary under a single monarch. Between 1867 and 1918, the two states shared military, foreign and financial policy, but maintained separate parliaments and administrations. The Austro-Hungarian monarchy and empire were dissolved at the end of World War I.

Austrian Succession, War of the (1740-8) War fought over who should succeed the Austrian king and Holy Roman Emperor Charles VI and so take over the HABSBURG inheritance. When the emperor died in 1740, he named his daughter Maria Theresa as his heir, but FREDERICK THE GREAT of Prussia invaded and annexed the Habsburg property of Silesia. Philip V of Spain and two German princes emerged as claimants to the Habsburg domains, and made an anti-Austrian alliance with France. Britain sided with Austria and attacked French and Spanish colonies overseas. After various campaigns – in the course of which Maria Theresa's husband, Francis, acceded to the Austrian and imperial throne – the war was ended with the restoration of all conquered lands except Silesia, which was retained by Prussia.

🔖 The War of Austrian Succession failed to calm the rivalry between European powers, and unresolved disputes eventually sparked off the SEVEN YEARS' WAR in 1756.

Avignon papacy (AVV-een-yon) Period during which popes lived in Avignon, in southern France. Clement V, a Frenchman, moved there in 1309 to avoid civil unrest and political intrigues in Rome. Several other popes followed his example and lived there until 1377, when it was judged safe to return to Rome. However, a rival line of popes, called antipopes, continued in Avignon until 1417.

Axis Coalition of countries formed by Germany and Italy in 1936; Japan joined them in 1940. The Axis powers opposed the ALLIES during WORLD WAR II.

Aztecs Native American people who ruled Mexico and neighbouring areas from the 12th to the 16th centuries, when the Spaniards led by Hernán CORTÉS conquered the region, searching for gold. The last Aztec ruler was MONTEZUMA II . The Aztecs were skilled farmers, and built up an advanced civilisation with written documents and sophisticated calendars, but their religion was based on human sacrifice.

HUMAN SACRIFICE *The Aztecs believed that divine wrath could be quenched with human blood. This 16th-century Aztec illustration shows a priest ripping the heart from a victim.*

Baader-Meinhof Revolutionary left-wing group responsible for a series of terrorist attacks and assassinations in Germany during the early 1970s. Its correct name was *Rote Armee Faktion* (Red Army Faction), but it was popularly known by the names of two of its leaders, Andreas Baader and Ulrike Meinhof. The gang helped a number of other terrorist organisations throughout the world. Baader and Meinhof were eventually arrested in 1972. They committed suicide in jail in 1976.

Babylon City in ancient MESOPOTAMIA, famed for its hanging gardens (one of the SEVEN WONDERS OF THE WORLD). Situated 55 miles (88 km) south of modern Baghdad, on the River Euphrates, it was the capital city of HAMMURABI and is thought to have been the site of the Tower of Babel. Babylon fell to the Persians in 539 BC.
🔖 The Bible tells how the Israelites were deported to Babylon and held in captivity there by NEBUCHADNEZZAR II. The phrase 'Babylonian captivity' refers to a period of involuntary extradition in a hostile land.

Balboa, Vasco Nuñez de (1475-1519) Spanish explorer who became the first European to see the Pacific Ocean. He founded a settlement at Darien, on the east coast of Panama, in 1501, and in 1513 he led an expedition across to the Pacific side of the Darien isthmus.

Balkan Wars (1912-13) Two conflicts which are widely seen as precursors to WORLD WAR I. In 1912, Serbia, Greece, Bulgaria and Montenegro attacked the OTTOMAN EMPIRE and won most of its European territories. A year later, Bulgaria and Serbia fought each other over the spoils, and others joined in. As a result of the wars, Albania was created and Serbia and Montenegro were enlarged at the expense of Macedonia. The resulting instability in the region provided the background to the assassination of the Austrian Archduke FRANZ FERDINAND by a Serbian nationalist, following which Austria declared war on Serbia. Through a combination of alliances, mobilisation plans and mutual distrust, the hostilities escalated as other nations became involved.
🔖 The term 'Balkanisation' was coined at the time to describe splitting territories into small, mutually hostile states.
🔖 After World War II, communist regimes kept peace in the area by imposing ▷TOTALITARIANISM. When communist power in the former ▷YUGOSLAVIA crumbled at the end of the 1980s, sectarian and nationalist tensions erupted again.

barbarians Term used to describe the GOTHS, VANDALS, HUNS and other peoples who attacked ancient Greece and the ROMAN EMPIRE. 'Barbarian' has since come to mean brutal or uncivilised.
🔖 The original Greek word *barbaroi* referred to the supposedly uncouth 'bar-bar' sound made by the invaders.

Bastille Prison in Paris, built in the 14th century, where political and other offenders were held, often without trial, and sometimes tortured. During the FRENCH REVOLUTION, revolutionaries demolished the building as a symbol of the destruction of absolute royal power.
🔖 The anniversary of the attack, on July 14, is called 'Bastille Day' – the most important national holiday in France.

Bay of Pigs Site of a failed attempt in 1961 by about 1500 Cuban exiles to invade Cuba and overthrow its president, Fidel ▷CASTRO. The invaders were trained and equipped by the US ▷CIA (Central Intelligence Agency), and the complete failure of the operation is regarded as the most humiliating episode in the presidency of John F. KENNEDY.

Begin, Menachem (BAY-gin) (1913-1992) Israeli prime minister from 1977 to 1983. He became the first Israeli statesman to make peace with an Arab country, when he signed the 1978 Camp David agreement with Egypt's President SADAT.

Ben Bella, Ahmed (1918-) Algerian revolutionary who led a guerrilla campaign from 1949 to 1956 to secure independence from France. The campaign ended when he was imprisoned by the French authorities. He became Algeria's first president when it became independent in 1962.

Ben-Gurion, David (1886-1973) Israeli statesman who was the driving force in the campaign for an independent Jewish nation. When Israel was created in 1948 he became the country's first prime minister.

Berlin airlift (1948-9) Operation to carry food and other goods into West Berlin, a Western enclave deep within communist-ruled territory. Since 1945, this part of the city had been jointly governed by France, Britain and the USA, while East Berlin and the surrounding territory were controlled by the Soviet Union. In 1948, the Russians tried to force the Western powers out of West Berlin by closing transport links and cutting electricity and other fuel supplies. After ten months, when the land blockade was lifted, a total of 275 000 flights had carried 2.3 million tons of cargo into West Berlin.

Berlin, Congress of (1878) Meeting convened by BISMARCK to negotiate a new ▷BALANCE OF POWER in southeastern Europe following the Russo-Turkish war of 1877-8. The Congress divided the Balkan states and also propped up the crumbling OTTOMAN EMPIRE to prevent Russian domination of the Balkans, where the Ottomans had lost much territory.

Berlin Wall Barrier which separated West Berlin from East Berlin and the rest of East Germany, which surrounded it. It

CRUEL BARRIER *East German workers build the Berlin Wall in 1961 (left), and vast crowds celebrate its demolition in 1989 (below).*

was built by the communist East German government in the summer of 1961 to stop emigration to the more prosperous West. Anyone who tried to cross it illegally risked being shot by border guards, and more than 500 people were killed trying to escape between 1961 and 1989. The wall lost much of its purpose in the summer of 1989, when Hungary and Czechoslovakia opened their borders, enabling East Germans to reach the West by making a simple detour. In November 1989 the East German government reopened the wall. It was soon demolished, and the two halves of Germany were formally reunified in October 1990.

♫ The Berlin Wall was one of the most visible signs of the COLD WAR, and was a symbol of the 'Iron Curtain'.

Bernard of Clairvaux, St (1090-1153)
French religious reformer who founded more than 70 monasteries in Europe. He was a great influence on European leaders, and his preaching inspired France to join the Second CRUSADE in 1147.

Bhopal
City in central India which was the scene of an environmental disaster in 1984. Poisonous methyl isocyanate gas leaked from a chemical plant run by the American-owned Union Carbide company, killing more than 2000 people and seriously damaging the health of a further 500 000.

Bhutto, Zulfikar Ali (1928-79)
Pakistani statesman who became his country's president following the secession of ▷BANGLADESH in 1971. He supervised the introduction of a parliamentary constitution, and became prime minister in 1973. His ambitious reform programme upset many powerful people, and he was overthrown by General Zia ul-Haq in a military coup in 1977. A court found him guilty of conspiracy to murder, and sentenced him to death; he was later executed. His daughter Benazir ▷BHUTTO has twice been elected prime minister of Pakistan.

Biafra
Oil-rich southeastern province of Nigeria, inhabited by the Ibo people, which sought independence in 1967, starting a civil war. Many died of famine before the federal government defeated the rebels.

Bill of Rights (1791)
The first ten amendments to the constitution of the United States. The 'First Amendment', which guarantees freedom of speech, religion, assembly and the press, and the 'Fifth Amendment', which sets out the rights of people accused of crimes, are the ones which are most frequently invoked.

Bismarck, Prince Otto von (1815-98)
Statesman who in 1871 created a unified German empire from around 40 smaller states. As prime minister of PRUSSIA, he made war against Denmark (1864), Austria (1866) and France (1870-1), enlarging his popularity and Prussia's sphere of influence each time. After the FRANCO-PRUSSIAN WAR, he persuaded the German states to unite under Kaiser 'emperor' WILHELM II and became the first chancellor of the German Empire. He introduced universal male suffrage and made many social and economic reforms before the Kaiser forced him to resign over policy differences in 1890.

♫ A Punch cartoon on the subject of Bismarck's resignation, entitled 'Dropping the pilot', shows him leaving a ship, with the Kaiser leaning over the side.

♫ Bismarck's stern, aggressive policies won him the nickname of 'Iron Chancellor'. He summed up his methods as 'blood and iron'.

Black Death
Type of ▷BUBONIC PLAGUE which killed about 25 million people in western Europe – about one in three of the population – in the 14th century. The first outbreak of the disease, which was carried to Europe from Asia by rats, occurred between 1347 and 1351. So many people died that the consequent shortage of labour created social and economic unrest throughout Europe, including the ▷PEASANTS' REVOLT in England and the Jacquerie in France. There were several further outbreaks of the disease throughout the Middle Ages.

Black Shirts
Nickname given to supporters of Benito MUSSOLINI's Fascist party in Italy, who wore distinctive black shirts in the 1920s. The name was also associated with Oswald ▷MOSLEY's British Union of Fascists and Adolf Hitler's SS, which both adopted a similar uniform in the 1930s.

Blenheim, Battle of (1704)
Major victory for the Anglo-Austrian army, commanded by the Duke of ▷MARLBOROUGH, over a Franco-Bavarian force, in the War of SPANISH SUCCESSION.

blitzkrieg
Form of warfare used by German forces in World War II, in which troops in tanks and armoured vehicles made fast-moving surprise attacks with close support from the air force. Strong enemy positions were encircled rather than attacked head-on. These tactics, which resulted in the swift German conquest of Poland and France, were later copied by Allied commanders.

♫ Blitzkrieg is German for 'lightning war'.

Boers
Dutch settlers in South Africa, also known as ▷AFRIKANERS, who arrived in the Cape of Good Hope in 1652. Boer is Dutch for 'farmer'. The British annexed the Cape area in 1815, and in 1835 the Boers embarked on the GREAT TREK, seeking to escape British rule and to found their own independent colonies inland. British attempts to dominate them culminated in the ▷BOER WAR (1899-1902) in which the Boers were eventually defeated.

Bolívar, Simón (1783-1830)
Venezuelan revolutionary leader who won independence from Spain for Colombia, Venezuela, Ecuador, Peru and Bolivia, which was named in his honour. He is known in South America as 'the Liberator'.

Bolsheviks
Radical Marxist group who seized power in the RUSSIAN REVOLUTION of October 1917. Led by LENIN, they acted as professional revolutionaries at the helm of a dictatorship of the proletariat. The Bolsheviks defeated their opponents, the more moderate Mensheviks, who wanted to set up a government to pave the way for a gradual transfer of power to the workers. The Bolshevik Party evolved into the Communist Party, which ruled Russia and the ▷USSR from 1918 to 1991.

♫ The word bolshevik, which means 'majority', is sometimes used loosely to describe any radical left-winger.

♫ The word menshevik means 'minority'.

Borgias (BOR-jyers)
Family which achieved great power in 15th and 16th-century Rome. Rodrigo Borgia (1431-1503) was elected Pope Alexander VI in 1492. His illegitimate son Cesare Borgia (1476-1507) was a ruthless general who conquered large areas of central Italy before being captured by his enemies, although he later escaped and was killed in battle. Cesare's sister Lucrezia (1480-1519) was a patron of the arts and a sponsor of the Italian ▷RENAISSANCE, but is mainly remembered, perhaps unfairly, as a cruel, treacherous and wanton ruler. The Borgias became notorious for killing their enemies by inviting them to a banquet and then poisoning their food and wine.

♫ Cesare Borgia is thought to be the model of the unscrupulous ruler described in ▷MACHIAVELLI's The Prince.

Bormann, Martin (1900-c.45)
Nazi leader who was appointed Adolf Hitler's deputy in 1942. Bormann disappeared in the final days of World War II, and was sentenced to death in his absence at the NUREMBERG TRIALS. For many years his

fate was a mystery, and he was thought to be hiding in South America, but remains believed to be his have been found in Berlin. It is probable that he was killed by snipers while trying to escape to freedom.

Boston Tea Party (1773) Demonstration of defiance by American colonists towards the British government, and a key incident leading to the AMERICAN WAR OF INDEPENDENCE. The government had given the ▷EAST INDIA COMPANY the right to sell tea directly to the colonies, thereby undercutting American merchants. It had also imposed a stiff tax on tea imports to Britain. In protest, a group of colonists dressed as American Indians boarded British tea ships in Boston harbour and threw their cargoes overboard.

Bourbons Royal family of France from 1582 to 1793, when LOUIS XVI was executed during the FRENCH REVOLUTION. They were briefly restored from 1814 to 1830. The Bourbons were rivals of the HABSBURG dynasty of Spain until Philip V, a Bourbon, ascended to the Spanish throne in 1700.

Boxer Rebellion (1900) Uprising of Chinese peasants aiming to expel all foreigners from China. The Boxers acquired their nickname because they practised ritual boxing, which they believed would protect them from foreign weapons. They occupied the capital, Beijing, besieging foreign legations and missions for 55 days and massacring 231 foreigners before a joint European, American and Japanese force overcame them.

Brandt, Willy (1913-92) West German statesman who was elected mayor of West Berlin from 1957 to 1966 and chancellor of West Germany in 1969. He was awarded the Nobel prize for peace in 1971. In 1974 he resigned the chancellorship after one of his staff was exposed as a communist spy. He went on to chair a commission on the world economy which in 1980 published 'the Brandt Report', recommending that the developed nations increase their level of aid to the developing world.

Braun, Eva (1910-45) Mistress of Adolf HITLER from the early 1930s. She played no role in his public career, and Hitler kept their relationship a secret. Braun eventually married him in his bunker in Berlin, one day before their joint suicide.

Bretton Woods conference (1944) Conference held at Bretton Woods, New Hampshire, USA, to consider how to organise world finance and trade after World War II. The conference, attended by 44 nations, set up the ▷WORLD BANK and the ▷INTERNATIONAL MONETARY FUND (IMF) and led to MARSHALL AID.

Brezhnev, Leonid (1906-82) Statesman who seized the leadership of the Soviet Communist Party from Nikita KHRUSCHEV in 1964, and remained the ▷USSR's head of state until his death. While Brezhnev was in office, the Soviet Union gave heavy military support to North Vietnam in the VIETNAM WAR and to Arab nations in the ▷ARAB-ISRAELI CONFLICT. He sent the Soviet army into Czechoslovakia in 1968 to depose the government of Alexander DUBČEK, and into Afghanistan in 1979 to keep its pro-Soviet puppet government in power. Brezhnev persecuted religious and political dissidents in the Soviet Union, but reached various agreements with the USA on reducing the two nations' stocks of nuclear weapons. His belief in the USSR's right to intervene in the internal affairs of WARSAW PACT countries – where there was a perceived threat to the communist bloc as a whole – became known as the 'Brezhnev doctrine'.
⚓Brezhnev is remembered for his craggy face and bushy eyebrows, and his apparent senility towards the end of his presidency.

Brian Boru (c.926-1014) Irish king who united Ireland under his rule in 1002. He drove the VIKINGS from Ireland at the Battle of Clontarf (1014), at which he was killed, aged about 88.
⚓Many Irish legends tell of Boru's magnificent palace at Kincora, in County Clare.

Briand, Aristide (1862-1932) French statesman who was prime minister 11 times between 1909 and 1929. He also served as foreign minister from 1925 to 1932. Briand was a passionate supporter of the LEAGUE OF NATIONS and of a united Europe, and helped to formulate the Kellogg-Briand pact of 1928, which aimed to outlaw war as a method of solving international disputes. Briand was awarded the Nobel prize for peace in 1926.

Bronze Age Period when copper and bronze were first used to make tools and weapons. In the Near East, this stage of human development lasted from about 4000 to 1200 BC – after the STONE AGE and before the IRON AGE.

Brown Shirts Nickname of Adolf HITLER's early militant followers the *Sturmabteilung* (SA, or stormtroopers), derived from their uniform of brown shirts. The Brown Shirts were crushed in the 'Night of the Long Knives' in 1934, and their place as the Nazi elite was taken by the SS, or BLACK SHIRTS.

Buffalo Bill Nickname of William F. Cody (1846-1917), an American frontier settler, soldier and showman. He won his name after killing buffaloes to provide meat for workers on the Kansas Pacific Railway. Cody founded a celebrated 'Wild West Show' in 1883 which featured displays of marksmanship, mock battles and demonstrations of cowboy skills and horsemanship. The show conveyed a popular image of romantic and exciting cowboy life which still endures.

Bulge, Battle of the (1944-5) Last major German counteroffensive of WORLD WAR II, mounted against the Allies in the Ardennes area of Belgium. In a surprise attack, German Panzer tanks drove a 'bulge' some 50 miles (80 km) deep into Allied lines. They were eventually repelled after heavy fighting and 200 000 casualties.

Bunker Hill, Battle of (1775) First major battle of the AMERICAN WAR OF INDEPENDENCE. British troops drove the Americans from their fort at Breed's Hill to Bunker Hill, near Boston, but only after the Americans had run out of gunpowder. Before retreating, the Americans killed and wounded so many British troops that the British were unable to follow up their victory. The battle encouraged American determination to fight for independence.

Byzantine Empire Empire that began as the eastern portion of the ROMAN EMPIRE, centred on Constantinople (previously called Byzantium, and now Istanbul). It was founded by the emperor CONSTANTINE THE GREAT in AD 330, and included parts of Europe and western Asia. As the western Roman Empire declined, Byzantium grew in importance, reaching its peak in the 6th century under JUSTINIAN. The Byzantine emperor's rule was backed by the Christian Church in the region, which later became the independent Greek ▷ORTHODOX CHURCH. Byzantium survived many barbarian attacks before it was finally conquered by the OTTOMAN EMPIRE in 1453.
⚓The word 'Byzantine' is often applied either to intricate and rigidly applied regulations or traditions, or to a complex bureaucracy – both were aspects of the Byzantine Empire. Rigid rules also imbued the rich mosaics of ▷BYZANTINE art with their ornate symbolism.

Cabot, John and Sebastian Genoese-born explorers who sailed from England to map much of the Americas. John Cabot (1450-98) explored Nova Scotia and Newfoundland in 1497 while searching for a new route to India for ▷HENRY VII. His son Sebastian (c.1476-1557) made a voyage to Brazil in 1526 for Charles V of Spain. In 1553 he set out to find a northeast passage to China for ▷HENRY VIII, but opened up a new route to Russia instead.

Caesar Family name of JULIUS CAESAR, later adopted by the first Roman emperor Augustus and his ten successors.
🔹 The emperors of Germany and Russia in modern times adapted the word *caesar* into titles for themselves – 'kaiser' and 'tsar'.

Caligula (AD 12-41) Cruel and probably insane Roman emperor who reigned for four years, from AD 37 until he was assassinated by his own guards. His bizarre excesses included appointing his horse to the Roman senate and declaring himself to be a manifestation of all the gods.
🔹 The nickname Caligula 'little boots' was given to the future emperor as a child by the troops of the imperial bodyguard. His full name was in fact Gaius Caesar Augustus Germanicus.

caliphs Rulers of the Muslim world who, after the death of ▷MUHAMMAD, combined their secular role with spiritual leadership. At first they were elected, but from AD 680, under the OMAYYADS, the position of caliph became hereditary. The ABBASSIDS seized power in 750, moving the seat of the caliphate from Damascus to Baghdad. In 1258 the Mongols conquered Baghdad and the Abbassid caliphate came to an end.

Calvin, John (1509-64) French theologian whose writings and actions played a major role in the REFORMATION. Calvin became a convert to ▷PROTESTANTISM in 1533, subsequently fleeing to Switzerland to escape religious persecution in France. His summary of Protestant beliefs, *Institutes of the Christian Religion* (1535), became the foundation of ▷CALVINISM. Calvin spent the rest of his career trying to run the city of Geneva along strict Puritan lines, imposing a dress code and banning all public entertainments.

Camp David accords Peace agreement signed by Israel and Egypt in 1978 at Camp David, the US president's official retreat in Maryland. The accords were followed in 1979 by a formal peace treaty – the first made between Israel and an Arab country.

The deal was signed by Menachem BEGIN and Anwar SADAT, under the auspices of President Jimmy ▷CARTER.

Cannae, Battle of (216 BC) Victory for CARTHAGE over ancient Rome. The Carthaginians, led by HANNIBAL, virtually destroyed the Roman army in battle near Barletta in southeastern Italy, with very little loss to themselves.

Capetians (k'PEE-sh'ns) Ruling family of France from AD 987 to 1328. Named after Hugh Capet (987-96), the founder of the dynasty, they greatly expanded their kingdom from a small area around Paris to cover most of central France.

Carolingians Dynasty founded by CHARLES MARTEL which ruled the FRANKS, succeeding the Merovingians in AD 751. The Carolingians ruled France until 987, fostering a cultural revival – the 'Carolingian renaissance'. Charles Martel's grandson was CHARLEMAGNE.

carpetbaggers Derisive nickname for politicians from the northern USA who went south in the aftermath of the AMERICAN CIVIL WAR, when former supporters of the breakaway CONFEDERATE STATES OF AMERICA were not allowed to hold public office. Some northerners are said to have arrived carrying only one carpetbag, symbolising their lack of permanent interest in the place they pretended to serve.
🔹 'Carpetbagger' is still a general term for opportunistic non-resident politicians.

OPPORTUNIST *This contemporary American caricature depicts a carpetbagger on his way south in search of office after the Civil War.*

Carthage Ancient city in north Africa that was a rival of the ROMAN EMPIRE for much of the 3rd and 2nd centuries BC. Carthage fought the PUNIC WARS against Rome, but lost in 146 BC, when the Romans destroyed the city, ploughed over its site and threw salt into the furrows so that the land would remain infertile for ever.
🔹 ▷DIDO, the lover of Aeneas in the ▷AENEID, was a queen of Carthage.

Catherine the Great (1729-96) Empress of Russia from 1762, when she oversaw the deposition and murder of her husband, Peter III. Catherine encouraged the development of western European cultural influences in Russia, strengthened the power of her nobles over the serfs and extended Russian territory towards the Black Sea and into Poland.
🔹 Catherine is remembered for taking many lovers during her reign.

Cato (234-149 BC) Roman soldier and politician who became CONSUL in 195 BC. He was a noted orator, and campaigned for higher moral standards in Rome. After visiting CARTHAGE during the PUNIC WARS, he ended all his speeches to the Roman senate with the words '*Carthago delenda est*' 'Carthage must be destroyed'.

Cavour, Count Camillo Bensi di (1810-61) Chief architect of the RISORGIMENTO, the unification of Italy, which had previously comprised many small states. He became prime minister of Piedmont-Sardinia in 1852, and by 1860 he had unified much of northern Italy. Cavour then made an agreement with GARIBALDI, resulting in southern and central Italy joining the north. For four months before he died, Cavour was the first prime minister of Italy.

Ceaușescu, Nicolae (chow-SHESS-koo) (1918-89) President of Romania from 1967 until his execution at the hands of rebels who overthrew his government in 1989. Ceaușescu ran a ruthless communist regime which violently repressed all dissent, but his refusal to allow the Soviet Union to interfere in Romania's domestic policy won him valuable support from the West and China. His megalomaniac policies included destroying ancient rural communities and moving their inhabitants to city high-rise blocks, and demolishing much of the historic centre of ▷BUCHAREST in order to build a huge palace for himself. Eventually, this provoked an army-backed popular rebellion which even the *Securitate*, his loyal secret police force, was unable to suppress.

TAIWAN'S FUTURE LEADER *Chiang Kai-shek inspects his troops for the last time on mainland China before fleeing to Taiwan in 1949.*

Celts People, originally from France, Austria and southern Germany, who expanded across Europe and into Asia Minor and Egypt between the 7th and 1st centuries BC. They were powerful fighters and good farmers, with a sophisticated religion and culture. Although they were conquered by the Romans in the 1st and 2nd centuries AD, Celtic traditions lived on in Ireland and Britain into the Middle Ages. (See also CELTS in 'British History'.)
⚓The Celts are well known for their art, which survives in many fine metal and stone items and in the Book of Kells (*c.*800), a superb illuminated manuscript of the Gospels, now in Dublin.

Chappaquiddick incident (1969) Accident in which Mary Jo Kopechne, a member of US Senator Edward Kennedy's staff, was drowned in a car allegedly driven by Kennedy when it fell off a bridge at Chappaquiddick Island, off the Massachusetts coast. Kennedy never provided a full explanation of the incident. Rumours that he was drunk, and that he delayed telling police in order to try to cover up the incident, put an end to his plans to run for the US presidency.

Charlemagne (SHAR-ler-main) (*c.*742-814) First emperor of the HOLY ROMAN EMPIRE. Charlemagne, whose name means 'Charles the Great', was made king of the FRANKS in AD 768, and expanded his territory to build an empire that stretched from Italy to Germany and from France to Hungary. The pope crowned him Holy Roman Emperor in 800, anointing him successor to the ancient Roman emperors. Charlemagne is especially remembered for his love of culture and encouragement of learning, literature and the arts.
⚓Throughout the Middle Ages, Charlemagne was widely considered to be a model for all Christian rulers.

Charles Martel (*c.*688-741) Military leader of the FRANKS who halted Muslim expansion from Spain into western Europe at the Battle of Poitiers in AD 732. He went on to found the CAROLINGIAN dynasty. His son, Pepin the Short, was the first Carolingian king and father to CHARLEMAGNE.

Chernobyl City in the Ukraine, north of Kiev, where a reactor caught fire in 1986 at a nuclear power station, causing a huge release of radiation. It was the world's worst recorded civil nuclear disaster.

Chiang Kai-shek (1887-1975) Chinese general and statesman who succeeded Sun Yat-Sen as leader of the Kuomintang (Chinese Nationalist Party) in 1925. He set up a government at Nanking, and waged a series of campaigns against the rival communist group based at Beijing. In World War II, however, he joined the communists and the Allies to fight the invading Japanese. The nationalists were overthrown in 1949 by communist forces under MAO ZEDONG, who established the People's Republic of China. Chiang fled to Taiwan, where he set up a nationalist regime which he ruled as a dictator.
⚓Chiang Kai-shek's relations with the Allies in World War II were slightly soured by his irritation at being code-named 'Peanut' in Allied communiqués.

chivalry Code of conduct for knights of the Middle Ages, especially during the 12th and 13th centuries. The word 'chivalry' is derived from the old French *chevalier*, 'knight'. The chivalric ideal emphasised bravery, military skill, generosity in victory, religious piety and ▷COURTLY LOVE.
⚓Medieval ▷ROMANCES, such as the tales of King ▷ARTHUR, are steeped in the traditions of chivalry.

Cid, El (*c.*1043-99) Nickname (meaning 'the lord') of Rodrigo Díaz de Vivar, a Spanish warrior who fought on behalf of the kingdom of Castile in a series of local wars. When the king of Castile exiled him in 1081, he fought for various Muslim leaders. He later established himself as the independent ruler of Valencia.
⚓The facts of El Cid's life have been overshadowed by many legends told about him, including the anonymous 12th-century epic *Poema del Cid*. One story says that after his death his corpse was strapped onto his horse so that he could lead his men in a final victory against the fleeing Moors.
⚓The story of El Cid was told in a colourful 1961 film starring Charlton Heston.

SWORD AND PEN *Charlemagne established his empire by force, but his court was a centre of learning. A new handwriting script, which had round 'minuscule' letters, was created there; previously, all writing had been in capitals.*

civil rights movement Drive by American black people and their supporters, especially during the 1950s and 1960s, to eliminate racial segregation and gain the same rights as white people. Segregation in housing, public services and employment opportunities was then common in the USA, particularly in the southern states. The first major event in the movement occurred in 1955, when the refusal of a black woman, Rosa Parks, to give up her bus seat to a white person sparked off a boycott of buses in Montgomery, Alabama. Martin Luther KING, Jr, emerged as the leader of the ▷BLACK CONSCIOUSNESS movement, giving his stirring 'I HAVE A DREAM' speech at a mass rally in Washington in 1963. A few years later, the US government introduced laws intended to stop racial discrimination and remove obstacles to blacks registering to vote. The movement then focused on education and changing the attitudes of white people. After the assassination of Martin Luther King in 1968, it became more militant, giving rise to the Black Power movement. Many black people around the world feel that they have still not attained racial equality and their struggle must continue.

Classical antiquity Era of European history dominated by ancient Greece and Rome, from about 500 BC to AD 500.

Claudius (10 BC-AD 54) Roman nobleman who became emperor after his nephew CALIGULA was assassinated in AD 41. Claudius himself had escaped political assassination only because his physical disabilities, including a stutter, made people think he was an imbecile with no real chance of taking power. In fact he proved one of Rome's ablest emperors, presiding over a programme of public works and important administrative reforms. He also added Britain and other territories to the ROMAN EMPIRE. Claudius was eventually poisoned by his fourth wife, Agrippina, so that her son NERO could take the throne.
🕯 The story of Claudius was told by Robert Graves in the best-selling biographical novels *I, Claudius* and *Claudius the God*, both of which were published in 1934.

CONQUEROR *Claudius, an able and unusually learned Roman emperor, ordered the conquest of Britain in AD 43 and visited it during the successful campaign.*

ELITE PRISON *Guards outnumbered inmates at Colditz Castle, the World War II prisoner-of-war camp perched on a cliff over the Mulde river in Saxony. It was the scene of many daring escapes.*

Clemenceau, Georges (KLEM-on-soh) (1849-1929) French journalist and statesman who was prime minister from 1906 to 1909 and from 1917 to 1920. After World War I he presided at the peace conference which produced the Treaty of VERSAILLES (1919). Clemenceau, nicknamed 'the Tiger', pressed for a tough peace treaty that would punish Germany for having started the war and compensate France for its economic losses.

Cleopatra (69-30 BC) Egyptian queen celebrated for her beauty, charm and luxurious living. JULIUS CAESAR fell in love with her when she was deposed after a coup, and restored her to power. For several years after Caesar had been assassinated, she lived in Egypt with the Roman politician Mark Antony. When Mark Antony committed suicide after being defeated in battle by the future emperor AUGUSTUS, Cleopatra also killed herself by allowing an asp, a poisonous snake, to bite her.
🕯 The story of Cleopatra's relations with Caesar and Antony inspired plays by Shakespeare and George Bernard Shaw.

Colditz Prisoner-of-war camp in eastern Germany where Allied officers regarded as determined escapers were imprisoned during World War II. Despite German pride in its security, 60 officers escaped from it, devising cunning disguises and fake documents to walk to freedom.

cold war Feud between the United States and the Soviet Union that dominated international politics from 1945 to the reformist era of Soviet president Mikhail ▷GORBACHEV in the late 1980s. The phrase 'cold war' refers to a state of constant hostility, espionage and counter-espionage which never erupted into a 'hot' or shooting war. The BERLIN AIRLIFT, BERLIN WALL, Iron Curtain and CUBAN MISSILE CRISIS reflected the sharp polarisation of the globe into Western and communist-influenced blocs which coloured other international disputes, including the ▷ARAB-ISRAELI CONFLICT and the VIETNAM WAR, and led to a nuclear arms race. Following years of negotiation, Gorbachev and US president Ronald ▷REAGAN signed a disarmament treaty in 1989 designed to end the arms

race. The international cooperation demonstrated in the 1991 GULF WAR was evidence that the cold war was truly over.
🔖 The atmosphere of the cold war is captured in many thrillers, especially in the spy novels by John ▷LE CARRÉ featuring the character George Smiley.

Columbus, Christopher (1451-1506)
Genoese explorer credited with being the first European to reach America in modern times. The Viking Leif ERICSSON was there before him, and there were Norse settlements in eastern Canada in the 11th century, but in the eyes of most Europeans America was just an implausible myth before the voyage of Columbus. He reached the West Indies in 1492, having sailed across the Atlantic for FERDINAND AND ISABELLA of Spain in search of a westerly passage to China. The exact place where he first landed is unknown, but likely candidates include San Salvador and Samana Cay, in the Bahamas. In the course of four separate journeys to the Americas, Columbus explored Cuba, Hispaniola, Puerto Rico, Jamaica, Trinidad, Venezuela and the Panama isthmus.
🔖 Columbus sighted land on October 12. 'Columbus Day' is a national holiday, celebrated on the second Monday in October, in many South American countries as well as in the USA.

Communist Manifesto, The
Pamphlet published in 1848, in which Karl ▷MARX and Friedrich ▷ENGELS set out the principles of ▷COMMUNISM. It closes with the words 'The workers have nothing to lose but their chains. They have a world to win. Workers of the world, unite!'

concentration camp
The first concentration camps in modern times were established by the British during the ▷BOER WAR in order to 'concentrate' enemy civilians where they could be guarded. However, concentration camps are usually associated with the rule of the NAZIS in Europe from 1933 until 1945, when they were used to confine and murder millions of Jews, homosexuals, gypsies, political dissidents and others. Some camps, such as Belsen and Treblinka, were purely extermination centres for the HOLOCAUST. The camp at AUSCHWITZ, where many prisoners were executed in gas chambers, is the most notorious Nazi camp. Concentration camps were also a feature of the Soviet Union under Joseph STALIN and ▷POL POT's Cambodia. In the 1990s, the warring parties in former Yugoslavia were also accused of setting up concentration camps.

Confederate States of America
Government formed in 1861 by the southern states who proclaimed their split from the United States and precipitated the AMERICAN CIVIL WAR. The confederate states – Alabama, Arkansas, Florida, Georgia, Louisiana, North Carolina, Mississippi, South Carolina, Tennessee, Texas and Virginia – appointed Jefferson Davis as their president. The confederacy was dissolved after the Civil War.

conquistadores
Spanish soldiers who established Spanish rule in the NEW WORLD by overthrowing the INCAS, the AZTECS and other native American peoples. They wanted to find the mythical golden land of ▷ELDORADO and to convert the heathens to Christianity. Hernán CORTÉS and Francisco PIZARRO were among the most powerful conquistadores.

Constantine the Great (c.AD 285-337)
The first Christian Roman emperor, said to have adopted Christianity after seeing a vision of the cross at the Battle of Milvian Bridge, near Rome, which won him the western half of the empire in 312. He put an end to the official persecution of Christians. Constantine became ruler of the whole empire in 324, and moved its capital from Rome to Constantinople (modern Istanbul), which became the capital of the BYZANTINE EMPIRE.

consul
The highest-ranking official in ancient Rome. In the Roman Republic, from 510 BC to 27 BC, two consuls were elected every year, and they had executive powers similar to those of a modern presidency. In the ROMAN EMPIRE, which was formed in 27 BC and collapsed in AD 476, the emperors often took the position of consul themselves, or ensured control of it by conferring it on their relatives.
🔖 Today, governments appoint 'consuls' at their embassies abroad to handle visas and to help look after their own nationals.

Coral Sea, Battle of (1942)
Crucial battle in the southwest Pacific during World War II. American naval forces repelled a Japanese attempt to invade New Guinea. Although there were heavy US losses, it was the first time that Japanese advances in the Pacific were checked.

Cortés, Hernán (1485-1547)
Spanish explorer and CONQUISTADOR. He overthrew the AZTEC rulers of Mexico and established Spanish rule over the country. When Cortés first landed in Mexico, the Aztecs welcomed him as a god.

🔖 The poet Keats wrote of the wonderment felt by 'stout Cortez when with eagle eyes/He star'd at the Pacific . . . /Silent, upon a peak in Darien'. In fact it was Vasco de BALBOA, not Cortés, who was the first European to see the Pacific.

Cossacks
People of southern Russia who first settled there in the 15th century as runaway serfs from Moscow, Lithuania and Poland. They became skilled warriors, and were particularly renowned for their horsemanship during the 16th and 17th centuries. In place of paying taxes, they supplied the Russian TSARS with scouts and mounted soldiers. After World War II, during which the Cossacks sided with the Germans, Stalin deported thousands of them to Siberia. The name *Cossack* means 'adventurer' in Russian.
🔖 Cossacks are known for their distinctive dress of tunics, high boots and sheepskin hats, and for their dances, which feature fast music and athletic leaps.

Counter Reformation
Reform movement in the Roman Catholic Church started in the 16th century in response to the Protestant REFORMATION.

Crimean War (1854-6)
War fought in the Crimean peninsula by Britain, France and Turkey against Russia, whose expansion into the OTTOMAN EMPIRE sparked off the conflict. Among the Anglo-French victories was the battle of Balaclava, where a 'thin red line' of red-coated Scottish infantrymen repelled the Russians, eventually forcing them to retreat. In the same battle, the British army sustained heavy losses in the ▷CHARGE OF THE LIGHT BRIGADE. At Inkerman, British and French troops withstood a Russian assault and inflicted heavy casualties. The Russians were defeated after a long siege forced them out of the port of Sebastopol. The campaign was marked by incompetent leadership on all sides and by disease, which claimed more lives than the fighting.
🔖 Florence ▷NIGHTINGALE cared for sick and wounded British soldiers in the Crimea, using innovative techniques that remain at the heart of modern nursing.

Crockett, Davy (1786-1836)
American frontier settler and politician. He became an American hero for his bravery in fighting against the Creek Indians in 1812, and went on to serve in the US Congress. He was killed by Mexican troops at the Alamo.
🔖 His distinctive headgear, a cap made out of raccoon (or coon) fur, earned him the title of the 'coonskin congressman'.

BRUTAL SLAUGHTER *Richard I of England watches a mass beheading of Saracens during the Third Crusade. As corpses pile up beneath the scaffold, more white-gowned prisoners are led to execution.*

Crusades Series of campaigns mounted by European powers between 1096 and 1272 to wrest the Holy Land (▷PALESTINE) from Muslim control. The official aim of the Crusades was to recapture the land where Jesus lived for the Christian world, but the expeditions were also motivated by greed for booty and new territories. The Crusaders conquered Jerusalem in 1099, but failed to secure the Holy Land and were driven out by the Muslims in 1291. However, the Crusades exposed Europeans to the culture and ideas of the Middle East.

The best-known warriors in the Crusades included ▷RICHARD THE LIONHEART, FREDERICK I BARBAROSSA and SALADIN.

The Children's Crusade (1212), in which some 50 000 children left Germany and France for Palestine only to be sold into slavery or prostitution, may have inspired the tale of the ▷PIED PIPER OF HAMELIN.

Cuban missile crisis (1962) Confrontation between the United States and the Soviet Union which brought the world to the brink of a third world war. Following the Cuban Revolution in 1959, Cuba came under the influence of the Soviet Union. The Soviet leader, Nikita Khruschev, installed nuclear missiles on the island, only 140 miles (225 km) from the US mainland. US President John F. Kennedy responded by blockading Cuba, insisting that the missiles be removed. After seven tense days Khruschev agreed to remove the missiles.

Cuban Revolution (1959) Overthrow of Cuba's American-backed president Fulgencio Batista by Fidel ▷CASTRO's guerrilla forces. Castro set up a socialist government, but it quickly became communist.

Cultural Revolution (1966-76) Movement led by MAO ZEDONG to reinforce communist ideals of equality in China. Mao dismantled the complex governmental structure that had developed after the Chinese revolution of 1949, and humiliated intellectuals and government officials by sending them out to work in the fields.

Danton, Georges (1759-94) Prominent figure in the FRENCH REVOLUTION who pressed for the execution of the king and other enemies of the Revolution. Although Danton called for 'boldness, more boldness and always boldness' in fighting enemies of the Revolution, his views were still deemed to be too moderate for extreme revolutionaries such as ROBESPIERRE, who eventually gave orders for him to be executed.

LIBERATORS' LANDING *A few days after D-Day, when 5000 ships and 150 000 men assaulted Hitler's 'Fortress Europe', American soldiers wade ashore from their landing craft, waist-deep through the cold sea. The landings took place on five beaches: 'Utah' and 'Omaha' were captured by US forces, while Canadians tackled 'Juno' and British troops overran 'Gold' and 'Sword'. The fighting was fierce, and it took weeks to secure the key German strongholds of Caen and Cherbourg.*

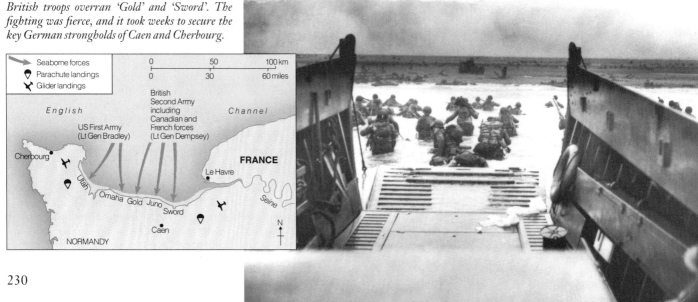

Seaborne forces
Parachute landings
Glider landings

English Channel

US First Army (Lt Gen Bradley)

British Second Army including Canadian and French forces (Lt Gen Dempsey)

FRANCE

Cherbourg
Utah
Omaha Gold Juno
Sword
Caen
Le Havre
Seine
NORMANDY

0   50   100 km
0   30   60 miles

Dark Ages
Name formerly used to describe the early Middle Ages in Europe, from about AD 500 to 900. The term refers partly to the dearth of information about the period, and partly to the political, social and economic disorder in Europe following the FALL OF ROME. For a long time it was regarded as a period of cultural decline compared with the glories of classical antiquity, but it is now recognised that the Dark Ages produced many important artistic and literary achievements.

D-Day (June 6, 1944)
Allied invasion of German-occupied France during World War II. Some 5000 ships and 9000 aircraft took part in the operation, codenamed 'Overlord', which landed 150 000 troops between Caen and Cherbourg on the Normandy coast. This marked the start of the major Allied counteroffensive in Europe.
The D-Day invasion was re-enacted in the well-known film *The Longest Day* (1962).

Declaration of Independence (1776)
Document issued by Britain's 13 American colonies, rejecting British rule and establishing the ▷UNITED STATES as a nation. It was largely written by Thomas Jefferson, and declares that 'all men are created equal' and have the right to 'life, liberty, and the pursuit of happiness'. It also justified the AMERICAN WAR OF INDEPENDENCE.

de Gaulle, Charles (1890-1970)
French general and statesman who, from his British headquarters, led the 'Free French' opposition to the Nazis and to France's collaborationist VICHY GOVERNMENT in World War II. De Gaulle served briefly as president of France after the war in 1945. He became president again in 1958 when he was called back from retirement to solve the crisis in the French colony of Algeria, where French military leaders had seized power in protest against the French government's decision to negotiate with Algerian nationalist leaders; de Gaulle eventually granted Algeria its independence in 1962. In France he introduced a new constitution (the 'Fifth Republic') which gave him sweeping powers. He increased France's international standing, acquired nuclear weapons and reconciled France with Germany, but blocked Britain's entry into the Common Market in 1967. In 1969, after the French people voted against his plans for further constitutional reform, he resigned.
De Gaulle is remembered for his high-handed manner. He once said: 'De Gaulle is not left, de Gaulle is not right, de Gaulle is not in the centre, de Gaulle is above.'

SUPREME PATRIOT *Charles de Gaulle combined an unshakeable loyalty to France with an unflinching belief in his own destiny to lead.*

Demosthenes (de-MOSS-then-eez) (c.384-322 BC)
Politician renowned as ancient Greece's greatest orator. Demosthenes is said to have overcome a childhood stutter by making himself speak with pebbles in his mouth. He is remembered for his *Philippics* – speeches in which he attacked King Philip of Macedon.

Depression, The
Worldwide economic slump, also known as the 'Great Depression', that followed the 1929 WALL STREET CRASH. Millions were thrown out of work and many companies went into liquidation. In America, President Franklin D. Roosevelt introduced the NEW DEAL in an attempt to counter the worst effects of the slump. In Europe, the harsh economic conditions experienced by many people helped to fuel the rise of ▷FASCISM.

de Valera, Eamonn (1882-1975)
Irish statesman who was prime minister of Eire three times (1932-48, 1951-4 and 1957-9) and president from 1959 to 1973. He played a key role in the ▷EASTER RISING in 1916, for which he was sentenced to life imprisonment, but was released under a general amnesty in 1917. He was also at the heart of Ireland's subsequent struggle for independence from British rule. He kept Ireland neutral during World War II.

Dias, Bartolomeu (c.1450-1500)
Portuguese navigator who in 1488 became the first European to discover the ▷CAPE OF GOOD HOPE. He rounded it unawares, driven by storms, in 1487, but sighted it on his return journey to West Africa. His discovery enabled Vasco da Gama to open up the sea route from Europe to India.

Diderot, Denis (DEED-er-oh) (1713-1784)
French philosopher and writer who edited the *Encyclopédie*, a series of books which were a major expression of the ▷ENLIGHTENMENT. Diderot's belief in the supremacy of reason over religious faith often brought him into conflict with the church. Contributors to the *Encyclopédie* included philosophers and thinkers such as ▷ROUSSEAU and ▷VOLTAIRE.

DEMAND FOR FREEDOM *Thomas Jefferson, with Benjamin Franklin to his left, lays the newly drafted Declaration of Independence before colonial representatives in Pennsylvania.*

Dien Bien Phu

Dien Bien Phu Village in French Indo-china (now Vietnam) where Vietnamese communist forces under General Giap inflicted a decisive defeat on French troops in 1954. The defeat led to the French withdrawal from Vietnam.

divine right of kings Doctrine that monarchs have a God-given right to rule, and that rebellion against them is a sin. The belief is particularly associated with the French king LOUIS XIV and ▷CHARLES I of England, who justified their ▷ABSOLUTE MONARCHY by asserting divine right.

Dreyfus affair Scandal in France involving a Jewish army officer, Alfred Dreyfus, who in 1894 was convicted of offering to betray his country's military secrets and duly imprisoned on Devil's Island – a French penal colony off French Guiana. The campaign to prove his innocence was joined by Émile ▷ZOLA and Georges CLEMENCEAU, and the issue divided French society. Antisemitism was at the root of much opposition to Dreyfus. In 1898, another officer was acquitted of treason despite evidence that he had carried out the crime for which Dreyfus had been imprisoned. Zola published an open letter, *'J'accuse'* 'I accuse', which swayed public opinion in favour of Dreyfus. After another army officer, Major Esterhazy, confessed to forging the evidence, Dreyfus was pardoned. He was exonerated of all charges in 1906.

Dubček, Alexander (1921-92) Czechoslovak premier who in 1968 introduced liberal reforms to the communist state, resulting in a period of relative freedom known as the PRAGUE SPRING. This was crushed by a Soviet-led invasion which removed Dubček from the premiership. In 1989, after the collapse of the communist government, he became chairman of the Czechoslovak parliament.

Earhart, Amelia (1898-1937) US aviator who in 1932 became the first woman to fly solo across the Atlantic. In the next few years she undertook other long-distance solo ventures, all the while advocating women's rights. The pinnacle of her career was to be a round-the-world flight which departed from California on May 20, 1937. All went well until July 2, when she vanished over the Pacific.

Eastern Question International instability resulting from the disintegration of the OTTOMAN EMPIRE in the 19th and early 20th centuries. European powers, including Britain, France, Russia, Austria and Prussia, clashed repeatedly over conflicting claims to parts of the empire. The Eastern Question gave rise to the CRIMEAN WAR, and was at the root of the Balkan problems which erupted into WORLD WAR I.

Egypt, ancient Civilisation that flourished in the ▷NILE valley from *c.*5000 BC. In *c.*3100 BC the two Egyptian kingdoms – the Upper, covering the Nile delta, and the Lower, stretched out along the valley – were united. Egyptians developed a sophisticated system of writing in ▷HIEROGLYPHS and began the tradition of burying mummified bodies in tombs. The subsequent history of ancient Egypt is usually divided into three main periods. In the 'Old Kingdom' (*c.*2700-*c.*2200 BC), a series of strong rulers or PHARAOHS developed an elaborate sun-worshipping religion and built the renowned ▷PYRAMIDS and ▷SPHINX at Giza. The 'Middle Kingdom' (*c.*2100-1786 BC) was marked by the conquest of Nubia and Libya, and ended when Egypt was invaded by a people called the Hyksos. The 'New Kingdom' (*c.*1570-*c.*1100 BC) is generally considered the peak of ancient Egyptian civilisation, when Palestine and Syria were added to its territory. Magnificent temples were built and the pharaohs were buried in the 'Valley of the Kings', where TUTANKHAMUN's almost intact grave was found in 1922. After 1100 BC Egypt's power went into decline, and in 332 BC it was conquered by ALEXANDER THE GREAT.
♣ The Old Testament stories of Joseph and Moses, the Jews' captivity in Egypt and their subsequent return to Palestine are set in the period of Egypt's New Kingdom.

Eichmann, Adolf (1906-62) Nazi official who organised the transportation of Jews to the CONCENTRATION CAMPS during the HOLOCAUST. He escaped after World War II but was captured in Argentina by Israeli agents in 1960 and smuggled back to Israel, where he was tried and hanged for crimes against humanity.

Eisenhower, Dwight D. (1890-1969) Supreme commander of Allied forces in Europe during World War II, and US president from 1953 to 1961. He commanded the Allied forces in Italy in 1943 and later directed the D-DAY landings in Normandy and the defeat of Nazi Germany. As president, Eisenhower conducted the COLD WAR and negotiated the end of the KOREAN WAR. He was a fierce opponent of communism, both at home and abroad.
♣ Eisenhower's nickname was 'Ike', and his campaigning slogan was 'I like Ike'.

Enigma Ingenious military cipher used by Germany in WORLD WAR II. The Germans used a complex programmable machine to encode messages which they believed could never be deciphered. However, after years of work on the 'Ultra' programme, by Polish and British mathematicians based at ▷BLETCHLEY PARK, Alan Turing made the crucial breakthrough, giving the Allies vital information for the rest of the war.

Entente Cordiale (on-TONT kord-YALL) Name – French for 'cordial understanding' – given to the agreement signed by Britain and France in 1904 which ended the two nations' competition for colonies in Africa and Asia by allocating spheres of influence. For example, Britain agreed to allow France a free hand in Morocco, while France recognised British interests in Egypt. The agreement was seen as a diplomatic triumph for ▷EDWARD VII.
♣ The phrase is often used to mean any friendly agreement struck after a period of mutual distrust: 'The rival companies have reached an entente cordiale on pricing.'

Ericsson, Leif (c.970-c.1030) Norwegian explorer reputed to have sailed to North America in *c.*1000 AD and landed at a place called Vinland. Locations suggested for Vinland include Newfoundland in Canada and New England in the USA. In 1004, Vikings settled in Newfoundland, but after two years they abandoned their attempt to colonise America. Though he was possibly the first European to discover America, Ericsson's travels are not as well documented as those of COLUMBUS.
♣ Like his father, ERIC THE RED, Leif Ericsson is the subject of an Icelandic saga.

Eric the Red Norwegian explorer who discovered Greenland and established a Viking colony there in AD 985.

Etruscans Most powerful culture of ancient Italy immediately preceding the Romans. At the height of their power in the 6th century BC, they were a strong cultural and religious influence on early Rome. It was trade with Greece as well as their own industry, in metalware for example, that made the Etruscans so wealthy and powerful. Their navy was one of the strongest in the Mediterranean.

Falange Spanish fascist party founded in 1933. From 1937, led by Francisco FRANCO, it was one of the principal factions in the SPANISH CIVIL WAR. After the nationalist victory in the war it provided the framework for the ruling party of Spain.

Fall of Rome Collapse of the ROMAN EMPIRE in the 5th century AD, caused by a combination of thoroughly inefficient and corrupt government and mounting pressure from invading BARBARIAN tribes from eastern Europe. The empire finally collapsed in 476, when invading VANDALS sacked the city of Rome and deposed the last emperor, Romulus Augustulus.
🔖 Edward Gibbon's 18th-century study, *The History of the Decline and Fall of the Roman Empire*, is one of the great classics of historical writing.

February Revolution (1917) First phase of the RUSSIAN REVOLUTION, sparked off by bread riots in Petrograd (now called St Petersburg), which forced Tsar NICHOLAS II from the throne.

Ferdinand and Isabella Joint rulers of the Spanish kingdoms of Castile and Aragon from 1474 until Isabella's death in 1504. Ferdinand continued to rule alone until his death in 1516. Together they united Spain and laid the foundations of its imperial greatness. They introduced the Spanish INQUISITION, expelled Jews from their country and sponsored Christopher COLUMBUS to explore the New World.

fertile crescent Region of the Middle East, stretching from the Nile Valley to the River Euphrates, generally regarded as one of the main 'cradles of civilisation'. As early as *c*.10 000 BC, people settled in the fertile crescent and became farmers, growing cereals and keeping sheep and goats.

TRAGIC CHILD *A page from Anne Frank's diary from October 1942: 'This is a photo of me as I wish I looked all the time . . . But nowadays, I'm afraid, I usually look quite different.'*

feudalism Name given in the 19th century to the system of obligations between lord and subject, or VASSAL, that provided the political, social and economic framework of medieval Europe. The king owned most or all of the land, parcels of which he gave to his leading nobles as 'fiefs'. In return, they gave him 'homage' – their loyalty and military service whenever it was needed. The nobles had a similar relationship with knights and lesser nobles, and so on. Feudalism made it possible to raise an army and decentralise administration, but it also dictated that everyone's position in society was determined by birth.

Field of the Cloth of Gold (1520) Meeting between ▷HENRY VIII of England and Francis I of France near Calais, France. They discussed forming a military alliance, but could not reach an agreement. The name refers to the lavish tents erected by the French for the meeting and the ostentatious display of wealth made by both kings.

Final Solution Nazi euphemism for the HOLOCAUST, or attempted genocide of European Jews during World War II.

Franco, Francisco (1892-1975) Spanish general who led the nationalist army to victory in the SPANISH CIVIL WAR (1936-9). Franco set up a fascist dictatorship, but he resisted approaches to join the AXIS powers and kept Spain out of World War II. His authoritarian regime continued until his death, whereupon democracy and the monarchy were reinstated.

Franco-Prussian War (1870-1) Conflict in which France was crushingly defeated by an alliance of German states led by PRUSSIA. The war was provoked by the Prussian chancellor Otto von BISMARCK's unsuccessful attempt to put a German prince on the Spanish throne. The Germans besieged Paris for five months before it surrendered in January 1871. Prussia's victory unified the German states under the Prussian king as Kaiser 'emperor' and forced France to give up Alsace and part of Lorraine, making Prussia the leading power in continental Europe.

Frank, Anne (1929-45) German Jewish girl who spent her early teenage years, from 1942 to 1944, hiding with her family from the Nazis in a secret apartment in Amsterdam. They were eventually betrayed, and Anne was deported to Belsen concentration camp, where she died of typhus. Her diary, published after the war, provides a moving account of suffering under NAZISM.

Franklin, Benjamin (1706-90) American statesman, author and scientist, who played a leading role in the USA's struggle for independence, and helped Thomas Jefferson to draft the DECLARATION OF INDEPENDENCE. Among Franklin's many inventions were bifocal spectacles and the lightning conductor – the latter was devised after he flew a kite in a thunderstorm to demonstrate that lightning would be able to flow down the wet string.

Franks Germanic people who ruled much of Europe between the 5th and 9th centuries. Frankish power was at its height under two dynasties, the Merovingians and the CAROLINGIANS.

Franz Ferdinand, Archduke (1863-1914) Nephew of FRANZ JOSEF and heir to the throne of AUSTRIA-HUNGARY. His assassination by Gavrilo Princip, a Serbian nationalist, in Sarajevo in 1914, sparked off the events that led to World War I.

Franz Josef (1830-1916) Austro-Hungarian emperor, much of whose reign was spent struggling with the forces of nationalism. In 1866 he was defeated by Prussia, and in 1867 he formed the 'Dual Monarchy' of Austria and Hungary, conceding autonomy to the Hungarians. His attack on Serb nationalism in the Balkans triggered World War I, which broke out after his nephew, Archduke FRANZ FERDINAND, was assassinated in 1914.

Frederick I Barbarossa (*c*.1123-90) Holy Roman Emperor from 1155, whose reign was dominated by struggles with the German nobility and the papacy. He mounted a series of campaigns in Italy to capture lands from the pope, and succeeded in capturing Rome in 1167. While he was leading the Third Crusade he drowned while swimming in a river.
🔖 According to legend, Barbarossa is not dead but merely sleeping, and will one day wake up to save Germany from disaster.
🔖 Barbarossa means 'red beard'.

Frederick II (1194-1250) Holy Roman Emperor from 1220, whose partial success in uniting Germany and Italy led to a long conflict with the papacy. He inherited the thrones of Germany and Sicily, and in 1229, while on Crusade, he crowned himself 'King of Jerusalem'. Frederick was a cultured ruler, encouraging artists at his court in Palermo. He was known as *stupor mundi* 'amazement of the world' because he seemingly combined extraordinary military, academic and political ability.

GUILLOTINE VICTIM *A contemporary French painting shows the crowd eagerly watching the public execution of a nobleman shortly after the beginning of the French Revolution.*

Frederick the Great (1712-86) King of
PRUSSIA from 1740, who transformed his country from a small state in northern Germany to a major power. Frederick was a brilliant soldier, and doubled the area of Prussian territory in a series of campaigns, including the invasion of Bohemia in 1744-5 and the capture of Silesia during the SEVEN YEARS' WAR. At home, he made many economic and social reforms and was a generous patron of the arts.

French Revolution (1789-99) Rebel-
lion which deposed the BOURBON kings of France and overturned the old order of French society known as the ANCIEN RÉGIME. The revolution began in 1789, when the Estates General, or French parliament, refused to grant taxes to LOUIS XVI and his extravagant queen MARIE ANTOINETTE, and the commoners declared themselves the National Assembly – the true legislature of France. A mob destroyed the BASTILLE, the state prison which had become a symbol of the king's ▷ABSOLUTE MONARCHY and despotism, and the National Assembly abolished the privileges of the nobility, confiscating church estates and issuing a Declaration of the Rights of Man. Louis and Marie Antoinette were arrested, and France was declared a republic. The king and queen were tried for treason, and executed on the guillotine in 1793. Control of the government passed to the extremist JACOBINS, led by Maximilien de ROBESPIERRE, who executed thousands of aristocrats and other 'enemies of the Revolution' during the Reign of Terror (1793-4). In a reaction against these excesses, Robespierre himself was executed and a new regime, run by a committee called the *Directoire*, came to power. Its incompetence and corruption allowed NAPOLEON BONAPARTE, a general in the revolutionary army, to seize power in 1799 and bring the revolution to an end.

France's revolutionaries were so keen to sever links with the royalist past that they invented a new calendar and a new system of measurement – the ▷METRIC SYSTEM.

Gagarin, Yuri (1934-68) Soviet cosmo-
naut who in 1961 became the first man in space, when he completed one orbit of the Earth in the spaceship *Vostok*. It was reported that he was killed in an air accident while training for the *Soyuz 3* mission.

Gallipoli (1915-16) Disastrous World
War I campaign by Allied troops to clear the Dardanelles and force a sea route through to Russia. It was Winston ▷CHURCHILL's initiative and the costly defeats between February 1915 and January 1916 around the Gallipoli peninsula in European Turkey lost him his post as First Lord of the Admiralty. But Gallipoli established the bravery not just of the British, but also of the newly formed Australian and New Zealand Army Corps (ANZAC) who formed a large part of the Allied force and suffered heavy losses. A public holiday in both countries on April 25 marks their first landing in 1915.

Gama, Vasco da (*c.*1460-1524) Portu-
guese explorer who in 1497-9 led the first expedition to sail from Europe to India via the ▷CAPE OF GOOD HOPE, on the southern tip of Africa. Bartolomeu Dias had discovered the Cape in 1488.

Gandhi, Indira (1917-84) Prime minis-
ter of India from 1966 to 1977 and from 1980 to 1984, when she was assassinated by Sikh extremists. Her father was India's first prime minister, Jawaharlal NEHRU; she was not related to Mahatma Gandhi. Although she achieved a reputation as a leader of developing nations, Gandhi's record as premier was marred by repeated accusations of corruption and her failure to control the sectarian violence which eventually led to her murder. Her son Rajiv succeeded her until he, too, was assassinated in 1991.

HUMBLE STRENGTH *Mahatma Gandhi poses outside No 10 Downing Street, where he was taking part in a conference in 1931.*

Gandhi, Mahatma (1869-1948) Indian statesman who led his country's drive for independence from Britain. After training as a lawyer in London and spending 20 years in South Africa fighting laws which discriminated against Indians, Gandhi returned to India in 1914, and won international recognition for leading a campaign of non-violent resistance and disobedience to secure Indian independence. His methods included boycotts, hunger strikes and marches to collect salt in defiance of the government monopoly. Gandhi also campaigned against India's restrictive caste system. He was imprisoned several times for his protests. In 1947 India became independent amid strife between Hindus and Muslims, and in the next year Gandhi was assassinated by a Hindu fanatic, Nathuram Godse, who believed that Gandhi was encouraging Islam in India.
🕯Gandhi was often pictured wearing a home-spun loincloth and blanket, and spinning his own thread, symbolising his dream of Indian self-sufficiency: for many years, India had imported cloth from Britain.
🕯Gandhi's first name was Mohandas. The title of Mahatma means 'great soul'.
🕯In Richard Attenborough's epic film *Gandhi* (1982) Ben Kingsley portrayed Gandhi in all his saintliness.

Garibaldi, Giuseppe (1807-82) Italian soldier and patriot who led Italy's 19th-century RISORGIMENTO or 'rebirth'. A member of Giuseppe Mazzini's 'Young Italy' movement, Garibaldi headed a revolutionary government in Rome in 1849. In 1860 he led 1000 red-shirted volunteers to expel the king of Naples, paving the way for the unification of Italy under King Victor Emmanuel II of Piedmont.
🕯To mark Garibaldi's visit to London in 1861, a British biscuit manufacturer created the Garibaldi – a flat, currant biscuit.

Genghis Khan (GENG-giss-KAAN) (c.1162-1227) Mongolian general and emperor who united his people and turned them into a formidable fighting force. His armies invaded vast areas of China, Persia and Russia, and he was notorious for his cruelty to the people he conquered. He died at the helm of one of the largest empires the world has ever known, stretching from Korea to the Black Sea.

Gestapo Secret police force in Nazi Germany. The name is an abbreviation of *Geheime Staatspolizei* 'secret state police'. The Gestapo, founded by Hermann GÖRING and headed after 1934 by Heinrich HIMMLER, often resorted to blackmail and

torture to deal with suspected opponents of Nazism. It also helped the SS to round up Jews during the HOLOCAUST.
🕯Intimidation by officialdom is sometimes called 'Gestapo tactics'.

Gettysburg Address (1863) Speech delivered by Abraham LINCOLN during the AMERICAN CIVIL WAR, dedicating a war cemetery at Gettysburg, Pennsylvania. It contains the celebrated definition of democracy as 'government of the people, by the people, and for the people'.

Gettysburg, Battle of (1863) Crucial battle in the AMERICAN CIVIL WAR, fought in Pennsylvania. It ended in victory for the Union (northern) states, and is usually considered the turning point of the war.

Goebbels, Joseph (GUR-b'lz) (1897-1945) Propaganda minister of the German Nazi regime. He said that if a lie is repeated often enough, it will eventually be believed, and that a big lie is more believable than a small one. Goebbels mastered the new media of radio and film, and devised impressive events such as the NUREMBERG RALLIES. Although he was a short, clubfooted man he had great charm and was a notorious womaniser. He poisoned his family and himself when Germany was defeated at the end of World War II.
🕯Goebbels, a superb orator, stirred Germany to wage what he called 'total war' – one which harnesses the entire resources of a country. It was he, and not (as is often thought) Winston Churchill, who

first visualised post-war Europe as being divided by an 'iron curtain' between the Soviet Union and the West.

gold rush The first major gold rush in modern times occurred in the 16th century, when Spaniards flocked to South America in search of ▷ELDORADO. The term is more usually applied to the California gold rush (1848-9), the Victoria gold rush in Australia (1851), the Witwaterstrand gold rush in South Africa (1886) and the Klondike gold rush in Canada (1896).

Göring, Hermann (GURR-ing) (1893-1946) German military pilot and air hero of World War I who became one of Adolf Hitler's closest associates and a key member of the Nazi government. He led the Luftwaffe (the German air force) and founded the GESTAPO; Hitler gave him the special rank of *Reichsmarshall*. However, Göring's pilots lost the Battle of ▷BRITAIN and failed to supply German forces besieged at Stalingrad, causing his fall from favour. He was condemned to death at the NUREMBERG TRIALS, but poisoned himself the night before he was due to be hanged.
🕯Göring, a morphine addict, wore special uniforms, make-up and a vast array of medals and jewellery, and built up a huge collection of looted art treasures.

Goths General term for Germanic tribes who invaded the Roman Empire from the Ukraine and the Balkans in the 4th and 5th centuries AD. They sacked Rome in 410.
🕯The term 'Gothic' was widely used by

STRIKING IT RICH *Prospectors pan for gold by a stream in the 1870s Dakota gold rush. Gold diggers spent backbreaking hours sifting gravel, trying to extract tiny flakes of the precious metal.*

Renaissance artists to describe medieval art and ornamentation in general. Like Gothic art, the 18th-century Gothic novel and 19th-century neo-Gothic architecture have no real connection with the Goths.

'Go west, young man' Saying originated by Horace Greeley, a 19th-century American journalist. He was referring to the many opportunities on the expanding western frontier of the USA.

Grant, Ulysses S. (1822-85) American general who led the army of the Union (northern) states to victory in the AMERICAN CIVIL WAR. He went on to serve as president (1869-77), but his period in office was marred by rampant corruption among those he appointed.
♣ Grant, a great whisky-lover, was much criticised for drinking too heavily. However, President Lincoln defended Grant's record, saying: 'If I knew what brand he drinks, I would send a barrel or two to some of my other generals.'

Great Trek Migration during the mid 1830s of several thousand BOERS from the Cape area of South Africa to the interior, where they hoped to escape British rule and the British ban on slavery. After making the trek, the Boers set up their own states in Natal and the Transvaal, and came to dominate the interior of South Africa.

Greece, ancient Greek history began when powerful 'city-states' such as SPARTA, Corinth and ATHENS emerged from the prehistoric MYCENAEAN and Minoan cultures in the 9th century BC. Traders soon extended Greek influence over most of the Mediterranean. At the beginning of the 6th century BC, Athens became the world's first ▷DEMOCRACY, and it defeated the Persians at the Battle of MARATHON (490 BC). There then began a 'golden age' of Athenian culture which has been a major influence on Western civilisation. It produced the dramas of ▷ARISTOPHANES, ▷AESCHYLUS, ▷EURIPIDES and ▷SOPHOCLES, the philosophy of ▷SOCRATES, ▷ARISTOTLE and ▷PLATO and the scientific discoveries of ▷EUCLID, ▷ARCHIMEDES, Pythagoras and ▷HIPPOCRATES. Rivalry between Sparta and Athens culminated in the PELOPONNESIAN WARS (431-404 BC), in which Athens was eventually defeated. The years of battle, however, had weakened the Greek states so much that Philip of Macedon (382-336 BC) was able to conquer and unite them into a single country. His son ALEXANDER THE GREAT extended Greek rule deep into Asia and Africa,

founding the Macedonian Empire much of which was eventually conquered by Rome in 148 BC. But Greek culture and ideas continued to flourish, and its customs permeated the ROMAN EMPIRE − a process summed up by the poet ▷HORACE as 'captive Greece made captive her rude conqueror'.
♣ The ▷VENUS DE MILO and the ▷PARTHENON are among the masterpieces of ancient Greek art and architecture.
♣ The Western alphabet evolved from the Greek alphabet, and Greek words have been incorporated into many other languages. For example, *microphone*, *nostalgia* and *hymn* are all derived from Greek words.
♣ The ▷OLYMPIC GAMES of modern times were inspired by the original Greek athletics tournament, which took place on the plains of Olympia every four years.

Gregory the Great (*c.*540-604 AD) Pope from 590 to 604. He made peace with BARBARIAN invaders in order to save Rome from pillage, and sent St ▷AUGUSTINE OF CANTERBURY to England in order to convert the Anglo-Saxons.
♣ Gregory the Great also wrote down the plainsong intoned by monks, which is known as ▷GREGORIAN CHANT.

Guernica Basque town in northeast Spain, bombed by the German *Luftwaffe* on behalf of General Franco during the SPANISH CIVIL WAR. ▷PICASSO vividly portrayed the incident in *Guernica* (1937).

Guevara, Che (g'VAAR-er, CHAY) (1928-67) Leader, together with Fidel ▷CASTRO, of the CUBAN REVOLUTION in

REBEL FIGHTER *Che Guevara's idealised face, captured in this classic 1960s poster, stared out from students' walls all over the world.*

1959. Born in Argentina, he went on to foment communist uprisings throughout Latin America. He was killed while fighting a guerrilla war in Bolivia.
♣ After his death, many young people idolised Guevara as a freedom fighter.

guilds Organisations of self-employed artisans or merchants in the Middle Ages that sought to regulate the price and quality of products such as cloth and ironwork. The guilds were at their peak from the 12th to the 14th centuries. With the rise of ▷MERCANTILISM and ▷CAPITALISM in the 17th and 18th centuries the power of the guilds declined. However, some of their functions passed to the ▷TRADES UNIONS, organised to support the growing number of company employees. Today's livery companies of the City of London, such as the fishmongers and the haberdashers, are descended from the medieval guilds.

Gulf War (1991) Battle between Iraqi forces and a United States-led coalition, following Iraq's occupation of Kuwait during a dispute over oil rights in 1990. After diplomatic negotiations failed to restore Kuwait's sovereignty, 29 countries, including the USA, Britain, France and Saudi Arabia, set out to enforce a United Nations resolution demanding an end to the occupation. The first stage was a sustained aerial bombing attack; Iraq's leader ▷SADDAM HUSSEIN responded by launching missiles at targets in Israel in a vain attempt to exploit the ▷ARAB-ISRAELI CONFLICT and disrupt the coalition by drawing Israel into the war. In February 1991, allied ground forces drove deep into Kuwait and Iraq − Iraqi troops offered little resistance before abandoning Kuwait in disarray. The war ended with the re-establishment of the former regime in Kuwait, but with Saddam Hussein still in power in Iraq.

Gutenberg, Johann (*c.*1400-68) German printer credited with introducing the modern technique of ▷PRINTING with 'movable type' − that is, with each letter on a separate block, so that it could be reused after a page was printed. Similar printing methods already existed in the Far East, but were little known in Europe. The Gutenberg Bible of *c.*1455 was the first Western book printed from movable type.

Habsburg, House of Major European royal dynasty from the Middle Ages to modern times. The Habsburgs came to power in Austria in 1278, and ruled the HOLY ROMAN EMPIRE from 1493. They reached the peak of their power in the 16th

century under Charles V of Spain, who ruled an empire that stretched from Prussia to South America. The dynasty's power ended after World War I, with the dissolution of the Austro-Hungarian empire.
♣ The Habsburg family had a hereditary deformity of the mouth and jaw which produced a protruding lower lip, known as the 'Habsburg lip' or 'Habsburg jaw'.

Haile Selassie (HYE-lee si-LASS-ee) (1891-1975)
Emperor of Ethiopia from 1930. He fled to England in 1936, following the Italian conquest of his country, but was restored to the throne in 1941. Haile Selassie played a major role as an African statesman, especially in the founding of the Organisation of African Unity in 1963. Although he was respected abroad, he did little to alleviate the poverty and hunger at home. He was deposed by the military

DESERT STORM *America's General Schwarzkopf (left) and Britain's General de la Billière helped to free Kuwait, but they were unable to stop Iraqi troops setting fire to its vast oil fields.*

in 1974, after a succession of poor harvests.
♣ Members of the West Indian ▷RASTAFARIAN sect believe that Haile Selassie was the Messiah, and that Ethiopia is the Biblical promised land. The name of their religion is derived from Ras Tafari, Selassie's name before he came to the throne.

Hammurabi
King of ancient MESOPOTAMIA who reigned from *c*.1792 to 1750 BC. He is remembered for being the first ruler to put a code of laws – the 'Code of Hammurabi' – into writing.

Hannibal (247-*c*.182 BC)
General of the ancient North African city of CARTHAGE. During the PUNIC WARS, Hannibal took a massive army from Spain through southern France to Italy in an attempt to conquer Rome. This involved taking a train of elephants across the Alps in 15 days, a feat still regarded as one of the greatest operations in military history. Although he won several victories, Hannibal did not achieve his ultimate aim of capturing Rome.

Hanseatic League
Powerful federation of prosperous cities in northern Germany which dominated trade in the Baltic and the North Sea from the 13th to the 17th centuries. Its main ports included Hamburg, Lübeck and Bremen.

Herodotus (*c*.484-*c*.423 BC)
Widely travelled ancient Greek historian, often called the 'father of history'. His account of the wars between Greece and Persia was the first narrative history, and the beginning of Western historical writing.

Hess, Rudolf (1894-1987)
Nazi politician who was Adolf Hitler's deputy until 1941, when he flew to Scotland, apparently on his own initiative, to try to negotiate a peace treaty between Britain and Germany. He was disowned by Hitler and imprisoned until the end of World War II. At the NUREMBERG TRIALS in 1946, he was sentenced to life imprisonment and spent the rest of his life in Spandau prison, Berlin; for many years he was its only prisoner.
♣ Suggestions that Hess committed suicide or was murdered, or even that the prisoner in Spandau was in fact his double, have never been substantiated.

Himmler, Heinrich (1900-45)
German Nazi leader with special responsibility for internal security and racial policy. As head of the SS from 1929, and of the GESTAPO from 1934, he directed both the repression of dissidents and the elimination of Jews and other 'undesirables' during the

HOLOCAUST. He committed suicide after being captured by British troops in the last few days of World War II.

Hindenburg, Paul von (1847-1934)
General who commanded German forces in World War I and became president of the WEIMAR REPUBLIC in 1925. In 1933, the aged Hindenburg appointed Adolf HITLER chancellor; his prestige did much to make Hitler acceptable to the Germans.
♣ The *Hindenburg*, an enormous German hydrogen-filled airship named after the general, operated as a luxury transatlantic carrier before it exploded dramatically over New Jersey in 1937.

Hirohito (1901-89)
Emperor of Japan from 1926 until his death. Essentially a pacifist, he presided over a period of militarism that culminated with Japan waging war on the Allies during World War II. After the war, he gave up the emperor's traditional claim to semi-divine status.
♣ Hirohito was widely criticised for not doing more to keep Japan out of the war.

Hitler, Adolf (1889-1945)
German dictator whose expansionist policies led to WORLD WAR II. Hitler outlined his plans for Germany in his book MEIN KAMPF, which he wrote in prison after staging the failed 'Beer Hall Putsch' in Munich in 1923 against the WEIMAR REPUBLIC. His dream was to see a blond, blue-eyed 'master race' dominate 'inferior' races, such as the Slavs and the Jews. Hitler, who was born in Austria, fought in the German army as a corporal in World War I. He took over the German Workers' Party in 1921, and renamed it the National Socialist or NAZI Party. Its blend of ▷NATIONALISM and ▷ANTI-SEMITISM won support during the economic depression of the 1920s, and in 1933 Hitler became Germany's chancellor. He banned all other parties, took the title of *Führer* 'leader' and directed a secret arms build-up, flouting the ban on German rearmament imposed by the 1919 Treaty of VERSAILLES. Germany occupied the Rhineland (1936), Austria (1938) and Czechoslovakia (1938-9) before marching into Poland on September 1, 1939 – the act which provoked Britain and France into declaring war. Hitler's blind confidence in German military superiority as well as in his own skills as commander eventually led to defeat. He escaped assassination in a bomb plot in July 1944, but committed suicide together with his wife Eva BRAUN in his bunker in the ruins of Berlin in 1945.
♣ Hitler's appearance was distinctive, with piercing blue eyes, toothbrush moustache,

severe haircut and military uniform incorporating the Nazi swastika. He was a theatrical speaker, delivering ranting speeches accompanied by vigorous arm movements and emphatic blows with his fist.

Ho Chi Minh (HOH CHEE min) (1892-1969) Vietnamese revolutionary leader, and president of North Vietnam from 1954. He led the communists of Vietnam in their efforts to drive out the forces of Japan in the 1940s, France in the 1950s and the USA during the VIETNAM WAR in the 1960s. Saigon, the former capital of South Vietnam, was renamed Ho Chi Minh City after the communists finally won the war in 1975.

Holocaust Murder of some 6 million Jews by the NAZIS during World War II. Heinrich HIMMLER and Adolf EICHMANN were among those who fulfilled Adolf HITLER's desire to exterminate the Jews. Gypsies, homosexuals, political opponents and many prominent Christian leaders were also killed in CONCENTRATION CAMPS.

Holy Roman Empire Major political institution in Europe from the 9th to the 16th centuries. Intended by its founder CHARLEMAGNE to be the Christian successor to ancient Rome, it was based in Germany, and included large areas of central and western Europe. At its height, it extended from Denmark to northern Italy. After the REFORMATION, the power of the Holy Roman Empire declined, and the position of Holy Roman Emperor eventually became a meaningless title of the HABSBURG family. This provoked the 18th-century French author Voltaire to write that the Holy Roman Empire was neither holy, nor Roman, nor an empire.

Hoover, Herbert (1874-1964) President of the USA from 1929 to 1933. Soon after he took office, the WALL STREET CRASH threw the US into the DEPRESSION. Hoover, a Republican, was reluctant to intervene and believed that private enterprise would turn the economy around. However, the economy failed to recover and he was replaced by the interventionist Democrat Franklin D. Roosevelt.

Huguenots (HEW-ger-nohz) French Protestants who were persecuted by their government as well as the Roman Catholic Church during the 16th and 17th centuries. In 1572, thousands of Huguenots died in the ST BARTHOLOMEW'S DAY MASSACRE. Although they were given freedom to practise their religion in the Edict of NANTES

(1598), they were still not accepted. When the edict was revoked by Louis XIV in 1685, many Huguenots went to live in exile in Britain and the Netherlands.

Hundred Years' War (1337-1453) Conflict between France and England which started when ▷EDWARD III claimed the French throne for himself. English armies mounted a series of campaigns in France, winning battles at ▷CRECY, ▷AGINCOURT and elsewhere, capturing much of northern France. The tide turned in 1429, when JOAN OF ARC inspired a strong French counterattack. By the end of the war, England had lost all its continental possessions except Calais.

Hungarian Uprising (1956) National revolt in Hungary against Soviet domination, led by students. The protesters – who destroyed statues of Stalin and called for free elections and political independence – toppled the Hungarian government. When the new liberal government, led by Imre Nagy, announced plans to leave the WARSAW PACT, Soviet forces invaded the country, seized Nagy and hastily restored communist rule.

INCA KNIFE *The jewelled hilt of this gold ceremonial blade, made in Peru in the 12th century, shows the intricate craftsmanship beloved by the Incas.*

Huns Asiatic people who invaded Russia in the 4th century AD and, under the leadership of ATTILA during the 5th century, conquered much of central and eastern Europe. The Huns were known for their terrible cruelty and destructiveness.
♣ The British often referred to German

soldiers as 'Huns' during World War I and World War II, as a way of emphasising their supposed brutality.

Huss, John (c.1370-1415) Church reformer from Bohemia, in the present-day Czech Republic. Huss was influenced by the English theologian John ▷WYCLIFFE, and campaigned for reforms to the Roman Catholic Church. He was burnt at the stake for heresy, provoking a revolt by his followers, the Hussites, against German rule over Bohemia. Huss later became a symbol of Bohemia's struggle for independence.

'I have a dream' Phrase from a celebrated speech given by Martin Luther KING at a rally for supporters of the CIVIL RIGHTS MOVEMENT in Washington, DC in 1963. King outlined his vision of an America free from racial prejudice, saying: 'I have a dream that my four little children will one day live in a nation where they will not be judged by the colour of their skin but by the content of their character.'

Incas South American people who built a vast empire, covering modern Peru, Ecuador, Bolivia and parts of Chile. Their civilisation reached its peak during the 15th and 16th centuries. The Inca emperor, who was believed to be a descendant of the sun god, ruled over a structured and disciplined society. In 1530, the Spanish CONQUISTADOR Francisco Pizarro conquered the Incas and plundered their gold.
♣ The Incas were skilled engineers and builders. Their roads, cities and temples can still be seen in Peru, at ▷MACHU PICCHU high in the Peruvian Andes, and elsewhere in South America.

Inquisition Court set up by the Roman Catholic Church in the 13th century to try cases of heresy and other offences against the Church. The Inquisition was conducted by Dominican monks who could force heretics to recant or do penance, or hand them over to the civil authorities for punishment. It sometimes used torture to extract confessions; the most severe penalty was burning at the stake. The Spanish Inquisition, set up in the 15th century, was particularly well known for its harshness.
♣ The Inquisition upheld the Church view that the Earth was fixed at the centre of the Universe and forced the astronomer ▷GALILEO Galilei to withdraw his contention that the Earth moved round the Sun.

Iran-Contra affair American scandal of the 1980s, in which US government officials supplied arms to Iran during the

IRAN-IRAQ WAR and used the profits to fund 'Contra' rebels fighting Nicaragua's left-wing government. Both operations were illegal, but the arms sales helped to secure the release of American hostages held by pro-Iranian factions in Beirut. President ▷REAGAN and his vice-president George ▷BUSH denied all knowledge of the affair.

Iran-Iraq War (1980-8) War which developed from a dispute between Iran and Iraq over control of the SHATT AL ARAB waterway, which runs between the two countries. Iraq's leader, ▷SADDAM HUSSEIN, also accused Iran of fomenting revolt in Iraq. After initial Iraqi successes, the conflict became a stalemate, with enormous loss of life on both sides. Western navies kept Gulf shipping lanes open but tension mounted – especially after an American cruiser shot down an Iranian airliner in 1988, killing all 290 passengers and crew. A ceasefire was agreed in 1988, and in 1990 Iraq dropped all claims to the Shatt al Arab. Iraq's use of poison gas during the conflict, especially on the Kurdish inhabitants of Halabja, caused an international outcry.

Iron Age Period of history when iron came into general use for making weapons and tools. Organised production of iron objects developed in southwestern Asia in about 1600 BC, spreading gradually westwards, reaching Egypt by about 700 BC.

Ivan III 'the Great' (1440-1505) Grand prince of Moscow from 1462. Ivan won independence from the Tatars and expanded Russia's territory northwards and eastwards by his conquests which included Novgorod and part of Lithuania.
🔊Ivan the Great rebuilt the ▷KREMLIN in Moscow using Italian architects who gave it the form it still has today.

Ivan IV 'the Terrible' (1530-84) Russia's first TSAR, who assumed the title in 1547 when he took personal power. He had been Moscow's grand duke since the age of three, but Russia had been governed by regents drawn from the boyars, or nobles. Ivan expanded his territory into the former Tatar lands of Kazan and Astrakhan, and made administrative reforms. In 1565 he started to rule by terror, introducing a secret police force and brutal methods to attack the boyars, for whom he conceived a paranoid mistrust. After killing his son in a fit of rage in 1580, he is said to have repented for more than 3000 murders.
🔊Ivan IV's Russian nickname *Groznyi*, loosely translated as 'the Terrible', more correctly means 'awe-inspiring'.

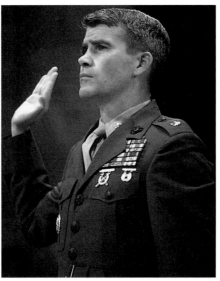

FIXER *Oliver North, a colonel in the US Marines, organised the illegal 'Iran-Contra' operation for the American government.*

Jacobins Extreme radical political group that arose during the FRENCH REVOLUTION. The Jacobins, led by ROBESPIERRE, carried out the 'Reign of Terror', in which thousands of aristocrats and other people deemed to be enemies of the Revolution were executed without trial.

Jefferson, Thomas (1743-1826) Third president of the United States, from 1801 to 1809. Jefferson was the principal author of the DECLARATION OF INDEPENDENCE. As president, he negotiated the purchase from France of 800,000 square miles (2 million km²) of territory west of the Mississippi. This 'Louisiana Purchase' effectively doubled the size of the USA.

Jenkins' Ear, War of (1739) Conflict between Britain and Spain over Spain's attempts to stop British ships trading with Spanish colonies in the Caribbean. It was prompted by the English captain Robert Jenkins, who in 1738 provoked outrage when he showed parliament his pickled ear – cut off seven years previously by Spaniards. The ensuing struggle merged into the War of the AUSTRIAN SUCCESSION.
🔊If someone likens a situation to the War of Jenkins' Ear, he is making the point that it is a foolish and costly over-reaction to a relatively minor provocation.

Jinnah, Mohammed Ali (1876-1948) Pakistan's first governor-general. A Muslim, he strived to ensure that India's Muslims and Hindus worked together in their demands for independence from Britain.

However, the 1930s saw a split between Mahatma GANDHI's Indian National Congress and the Muslim League, and Jinnah negotiated for part of India to become a separate Muslim state (Pakistan) when independence was won in 1947.

Joan of Arc (*c.*1412-31) French national heroine, nicknamed the 'Maid of Orléans', who inspired her fellow countrymen's victory over England in the HUNDRED YEARS' WAR. Claiming that she had been summoned by divine voices to drive out the English, she inspired French troops to raise the English siege of Orléans in 1429, enabling the French dauphin to be crowned as Charles VII. She was captured in 1430 and sold to the English, who put her on trial for heresy and sorcery. She was found guilty and burned at the stake.
🔊Joan of Arc was made a saint of the Roman Catholic Church in 1920.
🔊Her story has inspired many books, films and plays, most notably George Bernard Shaw's *Saint Joan*.

Johnson, Lyndon B. (1908-73) President of the United States from 1963 to 1969. He was elected vice-president in 1960, and became president after John F. Kennedy was assassinated. Johnson continued Kennedy's programme and introduced his own initiative for social reforms and civil rights to create the 'Great Society'. He also increased US involvement in the VIETNAM WAR. However, because of mounting opposition to the war, he did not stand for a second full term and retired in 1969.
🔊Johnson was called by his initials: 'LBJ'.

Josephine (1763-1814) Marie Josèphe Rose Tascher de la Pagerie, the wife of NAPOLEON. She was France's empress from 1804 to 1809, when Napoleon divorced her because she had borne him no children.
🔊Josephine is remembered for supposedly having her amorous advances rejected by Napoleon with the phrase: 'Not tonight, Josephine.' The story is apocryphal: the phrase comes from a music-hall song made popular by Florrie Forde in 1915.

Julius Caesar (*c.*100-44 BC) Roman general and statesman who came to power in 60 BC as part of a 'triumvirate', or three-man ruling council. From 58 to 49 BC, he mounted a series of military campaigns in Gaul (modern France) and Britain which brought him much prestige. The Roman senate, fearing Caesar's power, ordered him to disband his army, but he refused, ▷CROSSING THE RUBICON, the river which formed the boundary of his province, and marching on Rome. He won a civil war against Pompey, his former colleague in the triumvirate, and made himself dictator in 46 BC. Two years later, on March 15 – 'the Ides of March' – he was assassinated by a group of conspirators which included his old friend Brutus. As he lay dying of stab wounds, he allegedly said *'Et tu, Brute?'* 'Even you, Brutus?'.

🔔 Caesar summed up one of his campaigns with the celebrated message *'Veni, vidi, vici'* 'I came, I saw, I conquered'.

Justinian (*c.*AD 482-565) Emperor of the BYZANTINE EMPIRE from AD 527. He reconquered North Africa and parts of Spain and Italy from the BARBARIANS, and carried out a codification of Roman law which became the basis of many European legal systems. He also built the magnificent church of ▷HAGIA SOFIA in Istanbul.

kamikaze (KAM-ee-KAA-zee) Japanese fighter pilots of World War II who were trained to carry out suicide missions, deliberately crashing their aircraft packed with explosives onto enemy ships.

🔔 *Kamikaze* means 'divine wind' – a reference to typhoons that wrecked Mongol attempts to invade Japan in 1274 and 1281.

Katyn massacre (1940) Mass murder of 4443 Polish prisoners captured by Soviet forces early in World War II. The bodies were discovered in the Katyn forest near Smolensk, Russia, by German invaders in 1943, but the Soviets denied responsibility and blamed the Germans. In 1990, however, they admitted that Stalin's secret police had carried out the massacre.

Kennedy, John F. (1917-63) President of the United States from 1961 to 1963. A Democrat, he was the youngest ever president to win office. Kennedy was criticised for a bungled attempt to invade Cuba (the BAY OF PIGS episode) in 1961, but praised for his handling of the CUBAN MISSILE CRISIS. He was a campaigner for social reform, backing the CIVIL RIGHTS MOVEMENT, and a strong supporter of the American space programme; his goal of landing a man on the Moon within the decade was achieved in 1969. Kennedy's presidency ended with his assassination, apparently by Lee Harvey OSWALD, as he toured Dallas, Texas, in an open-top car.

🔔 Unanswered questions and inconsistent evidence about Kennedy's murder have led to speculation that Oswald may have been 'framed', or was not the sole killer.

🔔 Kennedy's appeal, based on his eloquence, youthful good looks and style, was

MUSLIM REVOLUTIONARY *The Ayatollah Khomeini, who swept to power in Iran on a great wave of popular acclaim, enforced Islamic law through teams of zealous young followers.*

helped by his elegant wife Jacqueline, who later married the wealthy Greek shipping magnate Aristotle ▷ONASSIS.

🔔 Kennedy was a compulsive womaniser and had many affairs – including, it is believed, a liaison with Marilyn Monroe.

Kennedy, Robert (1925-68) Brother of President John F. KENNEDY and, as attorney-general, a key member of his administration. He ran for the Democratic nomination for president in 1968, but was assassinated by Sirhan Sirhan, a Palestinian who opposed Kennedy's pro-Israeli stance.

Kenyatta, Jomo (*c.*1893-1978) First president of Kenya, from 1964 until his death. From 1952 to 1961 he was jailed for leading the MAU MAU terrorist campaign, which sought to remove British rule. He led his country to independence in 1963.

Khomeini, Ayatollah Ruhollah (1900-89) Political and religious leader of Iran from 1979 to 1989. Khomeini, a staunch opponent of Iran's pro-Western policies under Shah Muhammed Reza Pahlavi, went into exile in 1964. He returned to Iran in 1979, following the overthrow of the shah, and set up a theocracy, or religious government, which enforced strict observance of Islam.

🔔 Ayatollah is a title which literally means 'miraculous sign of God'.

Khruschev, Nikita (KROOS-chof) (1894-1971) Leader of the ▷USSR from 1953 until 1964. He caused a great sensation by denouncing his predecessor, Joseph STALIN, in 1956. Although Khruschev urged peaceful coexistence between his country and the West and relaxed the COLD WAR, the U-2 spy-plane incident in 1960 and the 1962 CUBAN MISSILE CRISIS were moments of acute international tension. Khruschev sent Soviet troops into Poland and Hungary to uphold communist rule. In 1964 he was unseated by fellow politburo members, who were led by his successor Leonid BREZHNEV.

INSTANT OF DEATH *Kennedy's assassination so shocked the world that a whole generation can remember exactly what they were doing on November 22, 1963, when they heard the news.*

Khruschev is remembered for his volatile and peppery style of leadership. He once engaged American vice-president Richard Nixon in a lively, impromptu 'kitchen debate' at a trade fair. During a United Nations debate in 1960, he became so angry that he took off his shoe and banged it on the table for emphasis.

King, Martin Luther (1929-68)
Black minister who led the CIVIL RIGHTS MOVEMENT in the United States. He became famous in the 1950s for leading a series of non-violent protests, such as sit-ins and boycotts, against racial segregation. In 1963 he led a civil rights march to Washington, DC, ending in a rally at which he delivered his 'I HAVE A DREAM' speech. King was awarded the Nobel peace prize in 1964. He was assassinated by James Earl Ray in Memphis, Tennessee, in 1968.

Americans remember King's achievements and celebrate his life on Martin Luther King Day, on or around his birthday – January 15th – every year.

knight
Warrior who fought on horseback in medieval Europe. The knight was a key part of the social hierarchy of FEUDALISM, in between the nobles and the peasants. As well as being soldiers, knights were supposed to follow the ideals of CHIVALRY, loyalty, honour and religious devotion.

Knighthood remains a mark of social distinction and public honour in Britain. Only men can be knighted, whereupon they take the title of 'Sir'.

Knossos (K'NOSS-oss)
Site in Crete of the capital of the Bronze Age Minoan civilisation, a precursor of ancient GREECE. The heyday of Knossos was from c.2000-1400 BC. The city was excavated at the end of the 19th century.

The frescoes and sculptures of Knossos, depicting ceremonies in which bulls were made to leap, wrestling, fishermen and many other themes, are notable for their lively and stylish execution.

The legend of Theseus overcoming the ▷MINOTAUR was set in Knossos.

Korean War (1950-3)
War between South Korea and communist North Korea, which started when North Korean troops invaded the south. Other nations soon became involved in the conflict. The United Nations sent a mainly American force under Douglas MACARTHUR to support South Korea, while Chinese troops backed North Korea. The war became a stalemate, and the combatants eventually signed a truce at Panmunjon in 1953.

AMERICAN HERO *Dr Martin Luther King was a tireless campaigner against racial discrimination. Popular fury at his assassination triggered urban riots across America.*

Kruger, Paul (1825-1904)
Statesman who was one of the leaders of the South African BOERS' struggle for independence against British rule. In 1883, he became the first president of the South African Republic, based in the Transvaal, and in 1899, he led the Afrikaners into the ▷BOER WAR. His followers gave him the affectionate nickname 'Oom (Uncle) Paul'.

South African gold coins weighing one troy ounce (31 g) are called krugerrands – after Paul Kruger.

Kublai Khan (KOOB-lye KAAN) (1215-94)
Mongol emperor from 1260, and grandson of GENGHIS KHAN. Kublai Khan completed the conquest of China, and made Beijing the capital of an empire that stretched as far west as the Black Sea, but he twice failed to conquer Japan. As China's first Mongol emperor, Kublai took the title of Shib-Tsu in 1279. He made Buddhism the official state religion and was a patron of learning and the arts.

The splendours of Kublai Khan's court were described by the Italian explorer Marco POLO, who spent 17 years there. They also inspired ▷KUBLA KHAN, a poem written by Samuel Taylor Coleridge.

Kuomintang
Chinese Nationalist Party founded by Sun Yat-sen which came to power in 1912, overthrowing the last Chinese emperor. Later, under the leadership of CHIANG KAI-SHEK, it was driven out of China by MAO ZEDONG's communists.

League of Nations
International organisation established in 1919 by the Treaty of VERSAILLES. The League brought about international cooperation on health, labour problems, refugees and other matters, but it was too weak to prevent the outbreak of World War II in 1939. After the war, it was replaced by a stronger and broader-based organisation, the ▷UNITED NATIONS.

Lenin, Vladimir Ilyich (1870-1924)
Adopted name of Vladimir Ilyich Ulyanov, the first leader of the ▷USSR which he founded in 1922. As the leader of the BOLSHEVIKS, he played a central role in the RUSSIAN REVOLUTION of 1917, eventually emerging as Russia's leader. He took Russia out of World War I, oversaw the victory of the Red Army during the RUSSIAN CIVIL WAR, concentrated state power in the hands of the Communist Party and introduced radical economic reforms to abolish capitalism. Lenin suffered a series of strokes before dying. Against his wishes he was succeeded by Joseph STALIN.

Lenin's body was embalmed and put on display in a specially built mausoleum in Moscow's Red Square. He was the great national hero of the Soviet Union, and his image featured on coins, stamps and official art. From 1924 to 1991, St Petersburg was called Leningrad in his honour.

PREACHING COMMUNISM *Lenin harangues a crowd during the Russian Civil War. On his left stands Leon Trotsky, the Red Army leader.*

WORLD HISTORY

241

HONEST ABE *President Lincoln was admired for his political moderation and progressive beliefs. His portrait appears on the American five-dollar bill as well as the one-cent coin.*

Lincoln, Abraham (1809-65) US president from 1861 to 1865. Lincoln, a Republican, prevented his country from splitting into two nations by leading the Union (northern) states to victory over the Confederates in the AMERICAN CIVIL WAR. He is also remembered for delivering the GETTYSBURG ADDRESS in 1863, and for decreeing that all slaves in the United States were free, the same year. While watching a play – *Our American Cousin* – in Washington, Lincoln was assassinated by John Wilkes Booth, a fanatical supporter of the Confederate cause.
♣ The Lincoln Memorial, in Washington, DC, contains a 19 ft (6 m) statue of the former president.

Lindbergh, Charles A. (1902-74) American aviator who in 1927 made the first solo non-stop flight across the Atlantic. He took off from New York and landed in Paris 33½ hours later, flying in a Ryan monoplane called *Spirit of St Louis*. He was later heavily criticised for urging the USA to stay out of World War II.
♣ The kidnapping and murder of Lindbergh's 20-month-old son in 1932 gained public attention around the world.

Long March March across China made by MAO ZEDONG and about 100 000 communist troops to escape the forces of CHIANG KAI-SHEK which had been closing in on them in southern and eastern China. It took Mao's troops a year to cover about 6000 miles (9600 km), starting in October 1934. Only some 10 000 of the original marchers actually completed the journey.

Louis XIV (1638-1715) King of France from 1643, known as the 'Sun King' for his power and splendour. He believed in strong personal government and ▷ABSOLUTE MONARCHY, boasting '*L'état, c'est moi*' 'I am the state'. He asserted French power overseas in a series of wars, including the War of the SPANISH SUCCESSION.
♣ Louis ordered the lavish rebuilding of the royal palace of ▷VERSAILLES, and filled it with treasures reflecting his greatness.

Louis XVI (1754-93) Last king of France before the FRENCH REVOLUTION. His failure to support reforming ministers, his expensive intervention on the rebels' side in the AMERICAN WAR OF INDEPENDENCE and the extravagance of his queen, MARIE ANTOINETTE, all helped to precipitate the revolution. Louis and Antoinette tried to flee the country, but were brought back as prisoners and beheaded for treason.

Louis Philippe (1773-1850) King of France from 1830 to 1848, known as the 'Citizen King' because of his informal manner and his support for the French Revolution. He fled France in 1793, when revolutionary leaders tried to arrest him, but returned when the monarchy was restored in 1817. Elected after his predecessor, Charles X, tried to bring back ▷ABSOLUTE MONARCHY, Louis Philippe was popular at first, but he became corrupt and was overthrown.

MacArthur, Douglas (1880-1964) American general who commanded Allied forces in the Far East and southwest Pacific during World War II. After some initial setbacks, he oversaw the defeat of Japan and supervised its occupation and the drafting of a new democratic constitution. In 1950 MacArthur was appointed to lead UN forces in the KOREAN WAR, but his threat to bomb China brought his dismissal by President TRUMAN in 1951.
♣ When Japan conquered the Philippines MacArthur was forced to leave, but he vowed 'I shall return'. He did so two years later, and drove out the Japanese.

Magellan, Ferdinand (c.1480-1521) Portuguese explorer who rounded the tip of South America in 1520 to reach the Pacific Ocean, which he named after its peaceful

SHINING KING *Louis XIV of France carefully nurtured his image of 'Sun King', and even appeared in a ballet wearing this spectacular costume.*

waters. He was killed in the Philippines, but his crew continued the journey, returning to Spain in 1522 and completing the first round-the-world voyage in history.
♣ The Strait of Magellan, between mainland South America and Tierra del Fuego, and the ▷MAGELLANIC CLOUDS, small galaxies in the southern night sky first observed and recorded by Magellan, are named after the explorer.

Maginot Line (MAJ-i-noh) Supposedly impregnable chain of fortifications built by France on its eastern border in the 1920s and 1930s to stop any future invasion from the east. During World War II the Germans simply went round it to the north.

Malcolm X (Malcolm Little) (1925-1965) American radical leader who opposed racial integration and preached in favour of black separatism. He encouraged black Americans to reject Christianity and embrace Islam. However, he was eventually assassinated by members of the Black Muslim group after he left their organisation and became an orthodox Muslim.

Manhattan Project Code-name for the US secret programme to develop the ATOM BOMB during World War II. The project,

led by Robert Oppenheimer, started in 1942, and successfully tested its first bomb near Alamogordo, New Mexico, in July 1945. Soon afterwards, US planes dropped atom bombs on the Japanese cities of Hiroshima and Nagasaki.

Mao Zedong (1893-1976) Chinese communist revolutionary leader who came to prominence when he led an army of workers and peasants on the LONG MARCH in 1934-5. He went on to use guerrilla tactics against both Japanese invaders and the forces of the Chinese nationalist government under CHIANG KAI-SHEK. In 1949, Mao took power and established the communist People's Republic of China. Mao believed that revolution must continually take place if it is not to degenerate into elitism. In the mid-1960s, he launched the CULTURAL REVOLUTION, an attempt to purge China of all traces of capitalism and elitism and to encourage agriculture.

🦂 In the 1960s, all Chinese people had to carry a copy of the *Quotations of Chairman Mao* – known as the 'Little Red Book'. Up to 800 million copies were published.

🦂 After Mao's death, his wife Jiang Qing and senior advisers, known as the Gang of Four, were jailed on charges of allegedly sabotaging communism in China.

Marathon, Battle of (490 BC) Decisive victory for the armies of ATHENS which ended the PERSIAN EMPIRE's most determined attempt to conquer Greece.

🦂 A messenger ran from the battlefield at Marathon to Athens with news of the Persian defeat, but then collapsed and died. His sacrifice inspired the modern ▷MARATHON race of just over 26 miles (42 km) – slightly longer than the original distance. The extra was added in the 1908 London Olympics, when the race was run from Windsor Castle to White City.

Marie Antoinette (1755-93) Wife of LOUIS XVI of France and daughter of Maria Theresa of Austria. Her expensive, frivolous tastes and her resistance to reform made her deeply unpopular. Eventually, both she and Louis were overthrown and executed on the guillotine during the FRENCH REVOLUTION.

🦂 Marie Antoinette was said to be so unconcerned by the problems faced by her subjects that when she was told that the people had no bread to eat, she replied thoughtlessly: 'Let them eat cake.'

Marshall Aid Popular name for the European Recovery Program, under which the United States gave large sums of money

FULLY BOOKED *In 1967, Mao Zedong (seated, centre), chairman of the Chinese Communist Party, smiles as Red Guards wave their 'Little Red Books'. Prime minister Zhou En-lai sits on his left.*

to European countries to help them to rebuild their devastated economies after World War II. General George C. Marshall, the American secretary of state, proposed the plan in 1947, and it was wound up in 1951. A total of $14 000 million was distributed under the scheme.

Mata Hari (1876-1917) Stage name – Malay for 'eye of the day' – of Margarete Gertrude Zelle, a Dutch-born dancer based in Paris during World War I. She is thought to have spied for both France and Germany, gathering information from the many senior military and government officials she took as lovers. The French executed her for espionage.

🦂 The description of 'Mata Hari' is applied to any seductive but untrustworthy woman.

Mau Mau Kenyan secret society which led an armed revolt against British rule in 1952. The society used grisly oath-taking rituals to command allegiance to its terrorist aims. About a hundred Britons and some 12 000 Africans were killed in vicious attacks before the authorities managed to quash the rebellion in 1956.

Maya (MYE-er) Native American people who lived in the region of present-day Mexico, Guatemala and Honduras. They flourished from the 3rd to 10th centuries AD. The Mayas were sophisticated astronomers who made accurate calendars, built pyramids and wrote in ▷HIEROGLYPHS.

Mayflower Square-rigged sailing ship – 90 ft (27 m) long – that carried the Pilgrim Fathers from Plymouth, England, to Plymouth, Massachusetts, in September 1620. Problems with a second vessel delayed their departure; the consequent overcrowding and bad weather prompted one death and severe discomfort for the 102 passengers – many of them fleeing religious persecution. After 66 days, rough seas forced a landing in New England, where they formed the first permanent colony.

Medici (med-EECH-ee) Ruling family of Florence from the 14th to the 16th centuries. Their immense wealth came from banking, and they patronised many

DOOMED SPY *Mata Hari's revealing dance costumes cloaked her true role as a double-dealing secret agent for both sides in World War I.*

▷RENAISSANCE artists, including ▷DONA-TELLO, ▷MICHELANGELO and ▷LEO-NARDO DA VINCI. Several members of the Medici family were popes, and Catherine and Marie were queens of France.

Mein Kampf (My Struggle) Autobiography and political testament of Adolf HITLER, which he wrote in 1925, while serving a jail sentence for attempting to overthrow the Bavarian government. In it, Hitler outlines his plan to revive Germany after World War I, blaming its problems on communists, capitalists and Jews.

Meir, Golda (may-EER) (1898-1978) Prime minister of Israel from 1969 to 1974. Her attempts to resolve the ▷ARAB-ISRAELI CONFLICT by diplomacy collapsed when the YOM KIPPUR WAR broke out in 1973.

Mesopotamia Region in modern-day ▷IRAQ, known as the 'cradle of civilisation'. It was in Mesopotamia in about 3500 BC that the first form of writing developed; this was the ▷CUNEIFORM script, inscribed on clay tablets. Agricultural organisation also began in Mesopotamia, along with detailed work in bronze and iron. Rulers such as HAMMURABI introduced a sophisticated system of codified laws.
⚲The name Mesopotamia is Greek for 'between rivers', the area being bordered by the Tigris and Euphrates rivers.

Metternich, Prince Clemens von (1773-1859) Chancellor of Austria from 1821 until he was overthrown by a revolution in 1848. Through his leadership, particularly at the Congress of VIENNA, Metternich succeeded in restoring order in Europe after the fall of NAPOLEON I. He did so, however, to the advantage of many European monarchs and at the expense of liberalism and nationalism.
⚲In the 19th century, Metternich's name became a byword for conservatism.

Middle Ages Period of European history between the fall of the Roman Empire and the Renaissance, spanning the 5th to 15th centuries AD. The Middle Ages was an era of CHIVALRY, FEUDALISM and above all, Christian spirituality. Key events in the period include the Battle of ▷HASTINGS, the CRUSADES, the BLACK DEATH and the building of many cathedrals.

Moguls (MOH-g'lz) Islamic dynasty, descended from the Mongols, which ruled India from 1526. The greatest of the Mogul emperors was Akbar, who reigned from 1556 to 1605. He expanded Mogul control over northern India and encouraged the arts and literature. The empire started to decline in the 18th century, and the last emperor was deposed by the British in 1857, following the ▷INDIAN MUTINY.
⚲The ▷TAJ MAHAL is the best-known masterpiece of Mogul architecture.

Mohammed Reza Pahlavi (1919-80) Iran's last shah, who succeeded to the throne in 1941. Helped by aid from the USA, he did much to modernise Iran. However, he also steered Iran towards authoritarian rule and allowed corruption to flourish and the economy to decline. His programme of 'Westernisation' upset religious fundamentalists, who forced him to flee in 1979 and recalled Ayatollah KHOMEINI from exile to restore strict Islamic rule.

Molotov, Vyacheslav (1890-1986) Soviet statesman who, as foreign minister, negotiated the NAZI-SOVIET PACT of 1939. He was a close ally of Stalin, and his uncompromising hostility towards the West contributed to the COLD WAR. Molotov said *niet* 'no' to so many proposals for détente that he was nicknamed 'Mister Niet' in the West. He was demoted by Khruschev following the death of Stalin in 1953. Four years later Andrei Gromyko succeeded Molotov, serving as foreign secretary for nearly 40 years.
⚲The ironic nickname of 'Molotov cocktail' was given by Finnish troops to the improvised grenades they devised, petrol-filled bottles stuffed with rags, with which they fought the Russian invaders in 1939.

Mongol Empire Massive empire created in the 13th century by GENGHIS KHAN, who united the tribes of central Asia in 1206 and conquered an area stretching from modern Korea to Turkey and from Siberia to parts of China. The next Mongol emperor, his grandson KUBLAI KHAN, expanded the empire deep into China, where he moved the Mongol capital in 1264. After 1360, under Tamerlane, the Mongols advanced into India, where their descendants established the MOGUL dynasty.

Monroe Doctrine Statement of American foreign policy issued by President James Monroe in 1823. The United States asserted its right to oppose European attempts to colonise the American continent, but also confirmed that it would not intervene in European disputes.

Montezuma II (1466-1520) Last emperor of the AZTECS, killed by a mob during the conquest of his kingdom by the Spanish conquistador Hernán CORTÉS.
⚲The upset stomach and diarrhoea which affects tourists in Mexico is sometimes humorously called 'Montezuma's revenge'.

Moors North African Muslim people who captured Spain from the GOTHS in the 8th century AD. They went on to invade France, but were halted at Poitiers in 732. Christian rulers gradually reconquered Spain from the Moors, completing the process in 1492. Moorish Spain had a vibrant culture and a freedom of ideas and religion not permitted in Christian Europe.
⚲The ▷ALHAMBRA at Granada and the Great Mosque of Córdoba, where the Moorish CALIPHS had their capital, are among the most striking architectural reminders of Muslim Spain.

Munich Agreement (1938) Pact between Britain, France, Italy and Germany, allowing Adolf Hitler to extend German territory into the Sudetenland, a frontier region of Czechoslovakia inhabited by a German-speaking minority. Neville ▷CHAMBERLAIN, the British prime minister, claimed he had won 'peace for our time', but Germany occupied the rest of Czechoslovakia and invaded Poland less than a year later. The pact is now seen as the high point of ▷APPEASEMENT.

Mussolini, Benito (1883-1945) Fascist ruler of Italy from 1922 to 1943. Mussolini had formed a dictatorship by 1928, and embarked on an ambitious public works programme, which included building motorways and upgrading the railways, to revive the Italian economy. He invaded Abyssinia (now Ethiopia), intervened to help General Franco in the SPANISH CIVIL WAR and annexed Albania in the 1930s. In 1940 he made an alliance with Germany as one of the AXIS powers of World War II. In 1943, after a string of military defeats, he resigned and was put under house arrest, but was freed in an audacious raid by German commandos led by Otto Skorzeny. Hitler helped to set up a puppet republic for Mussolini based at Salò, on Lake Garda, in German-occupied northern Italy. At the end of the war, Mussolini was captured and executed together with his mistress Clara Retacci by Italian partisans.
⚲Mussolini was nicknamed *il Duce* 'the leader' by his followers and the 'bullfrog of the Pontine marshes' by Winston Churchill. He was known for his proud, strutting manner and his dreams of restoring Rome's imperial greatness. It is said of him – by some disparagingly, and others admiringly – that he made the trains run on time in Italy.

Mycenae (mye-SEEN-ee) Civilisation which flourished in Greece during the BRONZE AGE, especially after 1600 BC. Led by strong warrior-kings who built magnificent cities and palaces, the Mycenaeans soon became the dominant influence in the Mediterranean. Their long military expedition to conquer ▷TROY was recounted by Homer in the ▷ILIAD. By 1100 BC Mycenae was no longer powerful, probably because of natural disasters, barbarian invasions and internal strife.

Nantes, Edict of (1598) Law passed by Henry IV of France giving religious freedom to the Protestant HUGUENOTS. The edict stopped the religious wars between Roman Catholics and Protestants, but it was revoked by LOUIS XIV in 1685, prompting mass Huguenot emigration.

Napoleon I (Napoleon Bonaparte) (1769-1821) Emperor of France from 1804 to 1814. A brilliant general, he led French campaigns in Italy, Malta and Egypt in the mid 1790s before staging a coup and seizing power from the Directory – a committee of revolutionary leaders – in 1799. He set up a dictatorship and embarked on a series of legal and administrative reforms – the *Code Napoleon* remains the basis of French civil law. After crowning himself emperor of the French in 1804, Napoleon conquered much of Europe in the NAPOLEONIC WARS. However, a disastrous invasion of Russia in 1812 ended in

INTO EXILE *Napoleon stares out to sea as HMS* Bellerophon *takes him towards the island of St Helena. The defeated emperor's charm is said to have impressed the entire crew of the British ship.*

the loss of two-thirds of his army. He was then defeated by the Allied armies at Leipzig, and France was invaded. In 1814 Napoleon was forced to abdicate and was exiled to the Italian island of Elba. Within a year he escaped and briefly regained power, only to be defeated at WATERLOO in 1815. The British victors banished him to ▷ST HELENA, where he died.

⚓At 5 ft 5 in (165 cm) tall, Napoleon was often nicknamed 'the Little Corporal'. Ambitious or assertive short men are sometimes said to have a 'Napoleon complex'.

⚓Napoleon is remembered for tucking his right hand into his coat and for describing the British as a 'nation of shopkeepers'.

Napoleonic Wars (1800-15) Campaigns fought by NAPOLEON Bonaparte to extend French power in Europe. Early in the wars, his army defeated Austria (at the Battle of AUSTERLITZ), Russia and Prussia. He went on to invade Portugal and Spain, precipitating the PENINSULAR WAR. In 1812, Napoleon invaded Russia and reached Moscow before being forced to retreat. He then lost two-thirds of his army due largely to the bitter winter and the Russian 'scorched earth' strategy of destroying everything as they retreated.

Nasser, Gamal Abdel (1918-70) Egyptian statesman who overthrew King Farouk of Egypt in 1952 and became prime minister two years later. He urged Arab nations to unite against Israel and to drive Western influence out of the Middle East. Elected president in 1956, he took control of the Suez Canal, provoking the SUEZ CRISIS. He made many reforms in Egypt and built the ▷ASWAN HIGH DAM. In 1967, he lost the SIX-DAY WAR against Israel.

Nazism Political creed of Adolf HITLER and his fascist National Socialist (abbreviated to Nazi) Party. The Nazis won support in the WEIMAR REPUBLIC during

EVIL GLORY *The powerful imagery and symbolism of Nazism is epitomised by this prewar Nuremberg rally, where Hitler ascends a triumphal staircase through ranks of loyal Brown Shirts.*

the 1920s and early 1930s by promising the people jobs and financial security after years of economic depression and inflation. They also promised that Germany, humiliated by defeat in World War I, would become powerful again. The Nazis came to government in 1933, banned all other political parties (declaring that their party and the German state were one) and embarked on a military build-up which led eventually to WORLD WAR II. The aim was to establish the 'Third Reich', in which the 'master race' of blond, blue-eyed 'Aryan' peoples would rule the world. Nazi racial policy led to the attempted genocide of the HOLOCAUST. Following Germany's defeat in the war, 22 Nazi leaders were convicted of war crimes at the NUREMBERG TRIALS.

The Nazis are associated with powerful symbolism and imagery, including the swastika, the stiff-armed salute, the chant 'Sieg heil' 'hail victory' and the greeting 'heil Hitler', the NUREMBERG RALLIES and the exterminations carried out at concentration camps such as AUSCHWITZ, Dachau and Belsen. They relied on the SS and the GESTAPO to retain power, and are today seen as representing an extreme form of fascism, inhumanity and violence.

Nazi-Soviet Pact (1939) Non-aggression treaty between Nazi Germany and the Soviet Union, clearing the way for both countries to invade Poland a week later – an act which precipitated WORLD WAR II. The pact was broken when Germany invaded Russia in 1941.

Nebuchadnezzar II (NEB-bew-kerd-NEZZ-er) (c.630-562 BC) King of BABYLON from c.605 BC. He created a large and powerful empire, and put down a revolt in Jerusalem in 586 BC, sending the Jews into exile – the 'Babylonian captivity'. According to the Old Testament, Nebuchadnezzar suffered spells of madness in which he believed he was an ox and went out into the fields to graze.

Nebuchadnezzar created the Hanging Gardens of Babylon, one of the SEVEN WONDERS OF THE WORLD.

A Nebuchadnezzar is a very large wine bottle – equivalent to 20 normal bottles.

Nehru, Jawaharlal (1889-1964) First prime minister of India, in power from 1947 until his death. Educated at Harrow and Cambridge, Nehru worked with Mahatma GANDHI during India's struggle to gain independence from Britain. He pursued industrialisation at home and non-alignment abroad. His daughter Indira GANDHI continued the political dynasty.

Nero (AD 37-68) Roman emperor from AD 54, notorious for his vanity and cruelty. He had his wife and mother murdered, and kicked his pregnant mistress to death. Nero also persecuted Christians, blaming them for a fire which destroyed much of Rome in AD 64. According to tradition, he sentenced the apostles ▷PETER and ▷PAUL to death. Nero committed suicide after the army had forced him from power.

According to legend, Nero caused the great fire of Rome himself, and played a lyre as he watched it. The expression 'to fiddle while Rome burns' means to take no action even though a catastrophe is occurring.

New Deal Phrase used by US president Franklin D. ROOSEVELT for his interventionist policies designed to improve conditions in America during the DEPRESSION of the early 1930s. They ranged from massive public works, such as the building of the Hoover Dam, to state-sponsored work for artists and writers. The New Deal also brought about reforms in agriculture, finance, banking and welfare.

New World The Americas, especially during the time of their first exploration and colonisation by Europeans.

Nicholas II (1868-1918) Last TSAR of Russia, who came to the throne in 1894. His refusal to support liberal movements in his country, and the excessive influence wielded at his court by RASPUTIN, made him unpopular. Nicholas was forced to abdicate during the RUSSIAN REVOLUTION. The following year he and his family were shot by revolutionary militiamen.

Nixon, Richard (1913-94) Republican president of the USA from 1969 to 1974. In 1973 the ▷WATERGATE scandal implicated Nixon in the cover-up of a burglary and bugging operation, and in 1974 he became the first US president to resign. As president, he visited China and the USSR and took US forces out of the Vietnam War.

Nkrumah, Kwame (N'KROOM-er) (1909-72) Ghanaian statesman who led his country to independence, became its first prime minister in 1957, and did much to further Pan-African awareness. He lived in exile after being overthrown in a military coup in 1966.

Nuremberg rallies Enormous open air meetings held by the Nazi Party from 1933 to 1938 in the Bavarian city of Nuremberg. Designed by Josef GOEBBELS for propaganda purposes, and staged by architect

Albert Speer, the rallies were spectacular events extolling the virtues and power of NAZISM, and included a keynote speech.

Nuremberg trials (1945-6) Trials of Nazi leaders held by the Allies after World War II. A special court tried 22 former officials, including Hermann GÖRING, Rudolf HESS and Martin BORMANN – the latter in his absence – for crimes against humanity, crimes against peace, and war crimes. Several of the accused offered the defence, rejected by the judges, that they were only obeying orders. Twelve of the Nazi leaders were sentenced to death; Göring killed himself to avoid execution.

Omayyads Ruling dynasty of the Islamic world from AD 661 to 750. Based in Damascus, the Omayyad CALIPHS presided over the expansion of their empire into Spain. Their reign also saw the division of Islam into ▷SUNNI and ▷SHI'A sects.

The Dome of the Rock, a well-known mosque in Jerusalem, was completed during the Omayyad period.

Opium Wars (1839-42, 1856-60) Trading wars provoked by a Chinese ban on British merchants importing the narcotic drug opium from India into China. The British won both wars, gaining Hong Kong, setting up trading and missionary posts in China and forcing the Chinese to legalise the opium trade.

Oswald, Lee Harvey (1939-63) The presumed assassin of US president John F. KENNEDY. Oswald, a former marine and

THE HUNTER AND THE HUNTED *Jack Ruby shoots Lee Harvey Oswald dead at point-blank range. Ruby died in custody in 1967, suffering from cancer and paranoid schizophrenia.*

a communist sympathiser, allegedly shot Kennedy from a high window as Kennedy's motorcade passed through Dallas, Texas. When captured by police he insisted he was innocent. Oswald was himself assassinated two days later by Jack Ruby, a local night-club owner. A government commission decided that Oswald acted alone in the killing, but the evidence has been repeatedly re-examined amid rumours that Oswald and Ruby had links with Cuban exiles, the Mafia and the American secret services. In 1979 a fresh inquiry held by the US Senate confirmed that a shot fired by Oswald's rifle killed Kennedy, but it also acknowledged that there may have been a conspiracy to assassinate the president.

Ottoman Empire Muslim empire founded by the Turks in about 1300. The Ottomans conquered Constantinople in 1453. At its peak, in the 16th century under SULEIMAN THE MAGNIFICENT, the empire included large parts of the Middle East and southeastern Europe. However, by the 19th century it was disintegrating, and became known as 'the sick man of Europe'. The Ottoman Empire sided with Germany in World War I, and was dismembered following its defeat. It was finally abolished by Kemal ATATÜRK in 1922.

Paris Commune Revolutionary workers' council set up in Paris for 11 weeks in 1871, after France's defeat in the FRANCO-PRUSSIAN WAR. The Communards made radical reforms, but were ejected from power by government troops. About 20 000 insurgents were killed and executed by the government during 'Bloody Week' after the fall of the Commune.

Patton, George (1885-1945) American general known for his expertise in tank warfare during World War II. He led operations in North Africa, Sicily and in the Allied invasion of Europe – notably during the bloody Battle of the BULGE. Only a few months after the end of the war Patton was fatally injured in a car crash.
🔔 Patton's stern and demanding, some-times bullying, leadership won him the nickname of 'Old Blood and Guts'. A showman who wore pearl-handled pistols, he was portrayed by George C. Scott in the Oscar-winning film *Patton*.

Pearl Harbor United States naval base in Hawaii that was attacked without warning by the Japanese air force on Sunday, December 7, 1941. President Franklin D. Roosevelt said it was 'a date that will live in infamy'. Nearly 2500 people were killed and many battleships were lost in the attack. Britain and the USA declared war on Japan the following day.

Peloponnesian Wars Series of campaigns fought by the rival Greek city-states of ATHENS and SPARTA between 431 and 404 BC. Sparta won the wars, and the Athenian Empire was destroyed. The wars weakened Greek civilisation as a whole, paving the way for the conquests of ALEXANDER THE GREAT.

Peninsular War (1808-14) Campaign fought against Napoleon's forces by the Duke of ▷WELLINGTON in Spain and Portugal. The war started as a Spanish revolt against Napoleon's brother Joseph, and developed into a long struggle to expel the French army from the Iberian peninsula. Wellington drove the French back across the Pyrenees in 1813.

Penn, William (1644-1718) English ▷QUAKER who was given lands in America in lieu of money owed to him by the British government. He used the land to set up the colony (now state) of Pennsylvania, devoted to religious toleration. Many Quaker and other religious dissidents emigrated there.

Perón, Juan (1895-1974) President of Argentina from 1946 to 1955. An ardent nationalist, his reforms upset the church and the army, who deposed and exiled him. He returned to power in 1973, but died in office. His wife Eva (1919-52), a former actress, who also held considerable power, became a popular heroine.
🔔 The musical *Evita*, by Andrew ▷LLOYD-WEBBER and Tim Rice, is loosely based on the life of Eva Perón.

Persian Empire Ancient empire in western Asia which, under Darius and XERXES, attempted to conquer Greece several times during the 5th century BC. The Persians were repeatedly defeated, most notably at the Battle of MARATHON.

Pétain, Philippe (1856-1951) French general and statesman who became a national hero during World War I. When France fell to the Germans during World War II, he became head of the VICHY GOVERNMENT. After the war Pétain, who was already in his nineties, was sentenced to death for collaborating with the Nazis; the sentence was later commuted to life imprisonment. Historians still debate whether he was a patriot or a traitor.

Peter the Great (1672-1725) Russian TSAR from 1682 to 1721, when he took the title of Emperor. Peter tried to transform Russia from a backward nation to a progressive one by introducing customs and ideas from Western European countries. He

DAY OF INFAMY *American battleships blaze after the surprise Japanese attack on Pearl Harbor – the most devastating of a wave of simultaneous assaults on Allied targets throughout the Pacific.*

BURIED CITY *A thick layer of volcanic ash swamped Pompeii, but protected it from decay. The crust of hardened ash was scraped away nearly 1700 years later to reveal houses – complete with superb frescoes and mosaics – preserved intact except for their roofs, which had given way under the weight of ash.*

even made his nobles cut off their long beards and adopt Western fashions. His methods were often extremely brutal and unpopular. He waged war against the Ottoman Empire and Sweden, and built ▷ST PETERSBURG as his capital.

pharaohs Name given to the rulers of ancient EGYPT from about 1500 BC. The pharaohs were believed to turn into gods after their death, and were buried in tombs within imposing ▷PYRAMIDS.

The best-known pharaohs are TUTANK-HAMUN, whose treasure-filled tomb was discovered in 1922, and Rameses II, who features in the Biblical account of the Jews' exodus from Egypt and built a vast monument at Abu Simbel.

Philip II (1527-98) King of Spain from 1556, king of Portugal from 1580, and consort to ▷MARY I of England between 1554 and 1558. He also inherited territories in the Netherlands and Italy, and his reign saw Spain reach the height of its power and influence. A HABSBURG and devout Catholic, Philip spearheaded the COUNTER REFORMATION, trying to crush Protestantism throughout his territories by force of arms. He fought a series of costly wars, including a notoriously unsuccessful one in 1588, when he launched the great

▷ARMADA against Elizabeth I of England. Philip II built the Escorial, a magnificent palace and monastery near Madrid.

Phoenicia (fer-NEESH-er) Ancient seafaring nation situated in what is now Israel and Lebanon. The Phoenicians flourished from the 12th to the 9th centuries BC, becoming great traders and establishing Mediterranean colonies such as CARTHAGE. The Phoenicians also developed the first alphabet that used marks to represent individual sounds rather than whole words or syllables. It was adapted by the Greeks and Romans, and eventually became the modern English alphabet.

Pizarro, Francisco (c.1478-1541) Spanish CONQUISTADOR who overthrew the INCAS and founded Peru.

Polo, Marco (1254-1324) Italian explorer reputed to be one of the first Europeans to cross Asia. He visited the court of the Mongol emperor KUBLAI KHAN in 1275, and became a government official in China. His account of his travels was widely read after his return to Italy in 1295.

Pompadour, Madame de (1721-64) Mistress of Louis XV of France, who exercised enormous influence over the king

and his policies. She was a generous patron of learning and the arts, and founded the well-known porcelain factory at Sèvres.

Both Madame de Pompadour and Louis XV are said to have remarked '*Après nous, le déluge*' 'After us, the deluge' when the French army was defeated in 1757, during the SEVEN YEARS' WAR. It implies: 'We don't care what happens after we die.'

Pompeii Ancient Roman city, near modern Naples, which was preserved when it was completely covered in ash by an eruption of the nearby volcano, Mount ▷VESUVIUS, in AD 79. Its rediscovery in 1748 yielded important information about Roman civilisation, and contributed to the emergence of ▷NEO-CLASSICISM – a revival of Classical art and architecture.

Potsdam Conference (1945) Final conference of the Allied war leaders, held near Berlin towards the end of World War II. It was attended by Stalin, Churchill (who was later replaced by Clement Attlee) and the recently-elected Harry S Truman. They fixed Poland's western frontier along the rivers Oder and Neisse and formally recognised Soviet influence in eastern Europe. They also divided Germany into zones of occupation and gave orders for the NUREMBERG TRIALS to take place.

Prague Spring Six-month period in 1968 when Alexander DUBČEK made a series of liberal reforms in communist Czechoslovakia. Freedom of the press and the arts were encouraged and criticism of the government was permitted – very unusual for a satellite state of the Soviet Union. However, Leonid Brezhnev, the Soviet leader, sent in his army to crush the new freedoms and restore the old regime.

Prohibition Outlawing of all alcoholic drinks in the USA, between 1920 and 1933. Prohibition did not stop people drinking, but merely drove them underground into 'speakeasies' where they drank illegal 'bootleg' beers, wines and spirits. The trade in alcohol was often controlled by the Mafia or gangsters such as Al Capone.

Prussia Northeastern German state which flourished in the 18th and 19th centuries, especially under FREDERICK THE GREAT. Under Otto von BISMARCK, Prussia led the unification of Germany in 1871. Its capital, Berlin, became Germany's capital.
🔥 Prussia's strong tradition of militarism almost certainly contributed to German aggression in the first half of the 20th century, and is sometimes blamed for the outbreak of both world wars.

Punic Wars (PEW-nik) Three wars fought between CARTHAGE and ancient Rome for control of the Mediterranean, between 264 and 146 BC. HANNIBAL led the Carthaginian forces in the second Punic War with some initial success, but he was eventually defeated. After the third Punic War, Carthage was finally destroyed and its citizens were sold into slavery.

Quisling, Vidkun (1887-1945) Norwegian politician who collaborated with the Germans in their conquest of Norway during World War II. The Germans rewarded him by making him leader of a puppet government which ruled the country on their behalf. After the war, he was tried and executed for treason.
🔥 The term 'quisling' is sometimes used to describe people who betray their country by cooperating with an enemy.

Rasputin, Grigory (c.1871-1916) Russian mystic and monk who gained great influence on tsar NICHOLAS II. A member of a heretical sect of flagellants, Rasputin, whose name means 'debauched' in Russian, argued that one has to sin in order to be forgiven. He was an alcoholic, and seduced many women, persuading them that they had to exhaust their sexual desires in order

DRYING UP *An officer enforcing Prohibition inspects a hollow wooden leg used to hide liquor, while others destroy thousands of dollars' worth of drink. In the end, the alcohol ban proved unenforceable.*

to achieve holiness. His apparent ability to use hypnosis to control the ▷HAEMOPHILIA suffered by Alexei, the heir to the throne, enabled him to gain a hold over the tsar's family until he was virtually able to dictate the country's affairs. Russian noblemen murdered him in 1916, but resentment of Rasputin's influence still helped to precipitate the RUSSIAN REVOLUTION.
🔥 Rasputin survived being fed cakes laced with potassium cyanide and being shot through the heart: his assassins had to shoot him four more times to kill him.

Reformation Church reform movement of the 16th century that also produced widespread political changes. ▷LUTHER, ▷CALVIN and others were instrumental in founding ▷PROTESTANTISM in Europe. (See also ▷REFORMATION in 'British History' and 'Ideas, Beliefs and Religion'.)
🔥 The start of the Reformation is often dated from 1517, when Martin Luther set out his beliefs by nailing his '95 theses' to the church door at Wittenberg.

Resistance Any underground group fighting a foreign occupier or despotic government. The term is usually applied to the European patriotic movements which attempted to undermine the Germans during World War II. By spying and carrying out acts of sabotage, they contributed towards the successful Allied liberation of the Continent in 1944-5.
🔥 The French Resistance was known as the '*Maquis*', Corsican for the dense scrubland in which bandits often hid.

Revere, Paul (1735-1818) Hero of the AMERICAN WAR OF INDEPENDENCE. On the night before the Battle of Lexington and Concord, Revere rode some 100 miles (160 km) from Boston to Lexington to warn colonists that British troops were preparing to seize military supplies and arrest revolutionaries. He also took part in the BOSTON TEA PARTY.
🔥 Revere's heroic mission inspired Henry ▷LONGFELLOW to write his well-known poem *The Midnight Ride of Paul Revere*.

Revolutions of 1848 Series of rebellions that broke out in several European nations, including France, Germany, Austria and Italy. The uprisings were unconnected events, but they were inspired either by the desire for national independence from foreign domination, as in Italy, or by demands for political and social rights for the middle and lower classes, as in Germany. In France, LOUIS PHILIPPE abdicated and the Second Republic adopted socialist policies, while in Germany the Frankfurt Assembly debated national unification.

Richelieu, Cardinal (REESH-l'yer) (1585-1642) French prelate and statesman who served as chief minister of Louis XIII. He established a powerful ▷ABSOLUTE MONARCHY in France, broke the power of the French nobility and the Protestant HUGUENOTS, and waged war against the HABSBURGS. Richelieu's efficient, sometimes ruthless, administration helped to build France into a major European power.

Richthofen, Manfred von (RIHKT-hoh-f'n) (1882-1918) German air ace of World War I, nicknamed 'the Red Baron'. He led a crack team of airmen called 'Richthofen's Flying Circus', and shot down a record 80 Allied aircraft in battle. He died when he was eventually shot down himself towards the end of the war.

Risorgimento (ri-SOR-ji-MEN-toh) Italian movement for national unification, which gained momentum in the 19th century under the leadership of GARIBALDI, CAVOUR and others. In the early 19th century, Italy was divided into small states dominated by foreign powers, but by 1870 most of Italy was united under King Victor Emmanuel II of Piedmont.
🐾 *Risorgimento* is Italian for 'resurrection'.

Robespierre, Maximilien de (1758-1794) Leader of the JACOBINS during the FRENCH REVOLUTION. He was responsible for initiating the 'Reign of Terror', when thousands of people were ruthlessly executed. Public opposition to his policies grew, and he was himself eventually guillotined after a hasty trial.

Roman Empire Greatest empire in ancient Europe, centred on Rome. According to legend, Rome was founded by Romulus in 753 BC. At first, the Romans were ruled by ETRUSCAN kings, but in 509 BC they set up a republic with two annually elected CONSULS at its head, guided by a senate. The Roman Republic grew rapidly from its origins as a small city-state, and by the 2nd century BC it was the dominant force in the Mediterranean. In 27 BC, soon after JULIUS CAESAR was murdered, Octavian brought the republic to an end and appointed himself Rome's first emperor, adopting the name AUGUSTUS. Over the next few centuries, most of Europe and parts of Africa and Asia became subject to Rome, which set up a strong colonial government and funded massive public works such as the building of ▷AQUEDUCTS and a vast network of ▷ROMAN ROADS. But as the empire grew it became increasingly unwieldy. The Rhine-Danube frontier was exposed to remorseless BARBARIAN pressure, requiring constant and expensive campaigning. The Emperor CONSTANTINE moved the capital to Byzantium and adopted Christianity early in the 4th century AD. In 395 the empire was split into two, with one emperor based in Constantinople and another in Rome. Internal weaknesses, combined with barbarian invasions from the east, led to the eventual collapse of the Roman Empire in the west in 476. In the east, however, the empire survived for another thousand years – Constantinople finally fell to the Turks in 1453.
🐾 The culture and achievements of ancient Rome exercised a strong influence on subsequent civilisations. The HOLY ROMAN EMPIRE and the ▷RENAISSANCE were respectively political and artistic attempts to bring back the 'grandeur that was Rome'.
🐾 Roman citizens spoke Latin, wore togas and bathed regularly in communal bath-houses. For all their civilised trappings, their society relied heavily on slaves.

Romanovs Ruling dynasty of Russia from the 17th century to the RUSSIAN REVOLUTION of 1917. The Romanovs, who included CATHERINE THE GREAT, PETER THE GREAT and NICHOLAS II, all believed in ▷ABSOLUTE MONARCHY.

Rome, Treaty of Treaty which established the European Economic Community – now called the ▷EUROPEAN UNION – in 1957. The six original signatories (France, West Germany, Italy, the Netherlands, Belgium and Luxembourg) agreed to set up a 'common market' and share economic growth.

Rommel, Erwin (1891-1944) German field-marshal of World War II. He led campaigns in Poland, France, Italy and North Africa, where his skilled use of BLITZKRIEG tactics won him the nickname of 'Desert Fox'. He was eventually defeated by ▷MONTGOMERY at ▷ALAMEIN. Rommel was then put in command of all German forces along the English Channel, but after being implicated in the 'July plot' to kill Adolf Hitler in 1944, he took poison rather than face almost certain execution. As a great German hero, he was given a state funeral and the circumstances of his death were kept secret.

Roosevelt, Franklin D. (ROH-zer-velt) (1882-1945) President of the United States four times, from 1933 to 1945 – longer than any other president. A Democrat, Roosevelt took office during the DE-PRESSION and quickly introduced the NEW DEAL to ease its effects. Before the bombing of PEARL HARBOR, which brought the USA into World War II, he favoured the Allies by introducing the 'Lend-Lease' system to supply them with arms. Together with Winston Churchill and Joseph Stalin he led the Allies' war effort but died a few weeks before Germany surrendered.
🐾 Roosevelt carried out his strenuous duties from a wheelchair after being crippled by polio in 1921. He was the first US president to use radio, especially in his much-loved 'fireside chats' to the American people.

Roosevelt, Theodore (1858-1919) Republican President of the United States from 1901 to 1909. As a colonel in the US Army, he led the 'Rough Riders' – a volunteer cavalry unit in the 1898 Spanish-American War. Roosevelt broke up some of America's large monopolies and brought in strict regulations on food hygiene and child labour. During his presidency, work started on the Panama Canal. Roosevelt won a Nobel peace prize for mediating in the RUSSO-JAPANESE WAR of 1904-5.
🐾 Roosevelt, popularly known as 'Teddy', was a great lover of the outdoors, and he particularly enjoyed hunting bears. The toy 'teddy bear', which became popular during his presidency, takes its name from him.
🐾 Roosevelt once summed up his approach to conducting foreign policy, saying 'speak softly and carry a big stick'.
🐾 Theodore Roosevelt and F.D. Roosevelt were distant cousins.

Rosetta Stone Slab found in Egypt in 1799, inscribed with ancient Egyptian ▷HIEROGLYPHS and demotic script, and a translation in Greek. It provided the key to understanding Egyptian inscriptions and is now in the British Museum.

Russian Civil War (1918-20) War fought between the BOLSHEVIK Red Army, led by Leon TROTSKY, and the 'White' army, which with foreign support opposed the RUSSIAN REVOLUTION. Many parts of the Russian Empire joined the battle, hoping to win independence from Moscow. At the end of the war, Poland, Finland and the Baltic states broke free from Soviet domination, but the Bolsheviks defeated the counter-revolutionary armies of Georgia, the Ukraine and other states. LENIN, their political leader, declared the Union of Soviet Socialist Republics in 1922.

Russian Revolution (1917) Two uprisings in Russia which replaced the TSARS with a communist government. In February 1917, following a series of defeats in World War I, workers and soldiers rose up, forcing Tsar NICHOLAS II to abdicate. A provisional government led by Alexander Kerensky was installed. But in the October Revolution, LENIN and the BOLSHEVIK party led another uprising which toppled Kerensky and established rule by *soviets*, or people's councils. The Revolution was followed by the RUSSIAN CIVIL WAR.
The Bolsheviks shot dead the tsar and his family at Ekaterinburg in July 1918. Anastasia, the tsar's youngest daughter, may have escaped execution. Her remains do not seem to have been among the exhumed bones proved in 1993 to be those of the murdered royal family.

Russo-Japanese War (1904-5) War which was fought between Russia and Japan over their rival claims to Korea and Manchuria. Japan won the war, becoming the first Asian country in modern times to inflict defeat on a western power.

Sadat, Anwar (1918-81) Egyptian president who succeeded Gamal Abdel NASSER in 1970. He won a Nobel prize for peace for his bold attempt to defuse the ▷ARAB-ISRAELI CONFLICT, making a peace treaty with Israel in 1978. He was assassinated by Muslim fundamentalists.

St Bartholomew's Day Massacre (1572) Slaughter of French Protestant HUGUENOTS by a Catholic mob in Paris. Catherine de MEDICI feared that her son, Charles IX of France, was being persuaded by Admiral Gaspard de Coligny, a leading Huguenot, to support the Dutch Protestants' rebellion against their Spanish overlords. After Catherine secretly backed a failed attempt on Coligny's life, she and Charles decided to kill Coligny and his companions. The murders by royal henchmen on August 24 sparked off mob violence in which about 3000 Protestants were killed.

St Valentine's Day Massacre (1929) Incident in Chicago on February 14 when Al Capone's gang of bootleggers murdered seven members of 'Bugs' Moran's rival gang, in an attempt to gain control of the illegal liquor traffic during PROHIBITION.

Sakharov, Andrei (1921-89) Russian nuclear physicist who became an outspoken critic of the COLD WAR, the arms race and the USSR's record on human rights. In 1975, Sakharov won the Nobel prize for peace, but in 1980 the Soviet authorities exiled him to Gorky. President Gorbachev allowed him to return to Moscow in 1986.

Saladin (1137-93) Muslim sultan who was the main enemy of European knights during the CRUSADES. In 1187 he defeated the Crusaders in battle and drove them out of Palestine. He defended his conquests successfully during the Third Crusade, which was mounted to try to dislodge him, but he was forced to a truce by ▷RICHARD THE LIONHEART in 1191.
Saladin's chivalrous conduct in battle earned him respect from his enemies.

Salamis, Battle of (480 BC) Victory for a small Greek fleet over the much larger navy of King XERXES of Persia, whose forces already occupied much of Greece. The Greeks destroyed nearly half the Persian fleet and scattered the rest, forcing Xerxes himself to withdraw to Asia Minor and winning time for the Greeks to regroup and eventually repel the Persian invaders remaining in northern Greece.

Salazar, Antonio de Oliviera (1889-1970) Dictator of Portugal from 1933 to 1968, when he suffered a stroke. He sought to preserve his country's colonial empire and strengthened Portugal's economy, but he did little to help the poor and the ill-educated. The first free elections were held six years after his death.

Savonarola, Girolamo (1452-98) Italian priest who crusaded against corruption in Church and state. Under his influence, the rulers of Florence instituted a stern puritanical regime. Personal ornaments, gambling equipment and pictures were burned on a 'bonfire of the vanities'. Savonarola's political enemies, including the MEDICI family, conspired with the pope, whom he had insulted, to secure his excommunication. He was convicted of heresy and duly executed.

serf Under FEUDALISM, a peasant bound to his lord's land, receiving his protection in exchange for labour. Serfdom continued in Russia until 1861.

Seven Wonders of the World Notable monuments built in ancient times, of which only the Egyptian ▷PYRAMIDS at Giza remain standing. The other six were the Hanging Gardens of BABYLON, huge stepped pyramids planted with trees and lush vegetation; the Pharos of ▷ALEXANDRIA, a magnificent lighthouse; the temple of ▷ARTEMIS at Ephesus; the tomb of King Mausolus – the origin of the word 'mausoleum' – at Halicarnassus in Asia Minor; the gold and ivory statue of ▷ZEUS at Olympia, Greece; and the Colossus of ▷RHODES, a

STILL STANDING *The sun rises behind the pyramids at Giza. Built more than 4000 years ago, they are the oldest of the ancient world's Seven Wonders, and the only ones which remain largely intact.*

huge bronze statue that straddled the entrance to the harbour of the Greek island.
🔱 There are also sometimes said to be seven wonders of the modern world. Candidates for this honour include the ▷TAJ MAHAL, the ▷GREAT WALL OF CHINA, the statues on ▷EASTER ISLAND, the ▷EIFFEL TOWER, Chartres Cathedral, the ▷EMPIRE STATE BUILDING and the ▷PANAMA CANAL.

Seven Years' War (1756-63) War between PRUSSIA, supported by Britain and Portugal, and an alliance that included Austria, France and Russia. Britain and France were fighting for control of North America and India, while FREDERICK THE GREAT of Prussia wanted to enlarge his kingdom at Austria's expense. After Prussia and Britain won, the French ceded Canada to Britain, which also consolidated its rule over much of India, while Prussia established itself as the dominant power in continental Europe.

shoguns Japanese caste of military leaders who governed the country from the 12th century until 1867. The emperors during this period were powerless figureheads.

Six-Day War (1967) War between Israel and the forces of Egypt, Syria and Jordan. Believing that Arab armies were poised to invade, the Israelis launched a pre-emptive strike and took over the ▷GOLAN HEIGHTS in southwest Syria, the Jordanian-held portion of Jerusalem, the West Bank of the River Jordan and the Sinai peninsula. Israel returned the Sinai to Egypt in 1982 and parts of the West Bank in 1994 but it has kept its other gains.

slave trade Buying and selling people for forced labour, first practised in ancient Africa. The slave trade, and slavery itself, became a vital element in the economies of Egypt, Babylon, Greece and Rome. During the Middle Ages, slavery became less common in western Europe but remained important in the Arab world. In the 15th century the slave trade was revived on a large scale by European powers, who shipped black slaves from West Africa to work in their colonies in the New World. At least 12 million slaves are believed to have been brutally exported from Africa. The efforts of William ▷WILBERFORCE helped to outlaw the slave trade in the British Empire in 1807; in 1833, slavery itself was banned. In the United States, slaves were finally emancipated by President LINCOLN in 1865. Nevertheless, 200 million people worldwide are still thought to be living and working in conditions of near slavery.

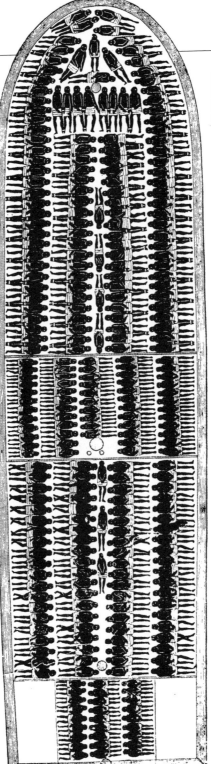

SLAVE SHIP *One in five of those sold into slavery in Africa died on board the ships which took them to America, packed inhumanly together and chained down to prevent mutiny.*

Smuts, Jan (1870-1950) Prime minister of South Africa 1919-24 and 1939-48. Smuts was an early advocate of the British ▷COMMONWEALTH and a prime mover in the formation of the LEAGUE OF NATIONS. He supported South Africa's entry into World War II on the side of the Allies.

Spanish Civil War (1936-9) War between Spaniards loyal to the socialist 'Republican' government and the rebel supporters of fascism, led by General Francisco FRANCO. Volunteers from abroad joined the fighting on both sides, seeing the war as a symbolic struggle between reform and reaction. The Soviet Union helped the Republicans, while Adolf Hitler and Benito Mussolini sent aid to Franco. Among the many horrific events of the war was the notorious bombing by the Luftwaffe of the town of GUERNICA in 1937. Eventually, the fascists won the war and set up Franco's long dictatorial rule of Spain, which lasted until his death in 1975.
🔱 George ▷ORWELL's book *Homage to Catalonia* is a vivid account of his experiences as a British volunteer for the Republicans.

FATAL MOMENT *War photographer Robert Capa took this famous picture of a Republican soldier falling during the Spanish Civil War.*

Spanish Succession, War of the (1701-14) Struggle for control of Spain after the last HABSBURG king died without an heir. England, Holland, most German states and Portugal, anxious to curb the power of France, formed a loose coalition to expel Philip, grandson of King LOUIS XIV of France, from the throne. The Duke of ▷MARLBOROUGH led the coalition armies to a series of victories. The war ended when Britain agreed to recognise Philip's rule in Spain in exchange for France handing over extensive lands in Canada.

Sparta Ancient Greek city-state founded in *c*.1000 BC which was the great rival of ATHENS. Sparta was renowned for its rigid military discipline and lack of culture. It defeated Athens in the PELOPONNESIAN WARS, but was itself beaten by a coalition of other states soon afterwards.
🔱 The term 'spartan' is still used to describe rigorous or uncomfortable conditions designed to instil a sense of discipline.
🔱 Spartans, or 'Laconians' as they were known in ancient times, had a reputation

for terseness. When one invader warned 'If I enter Laconia, I shall destroy the city of Sparta', the Spartans returned the laconic one-word message: 'If.'

Spartacus (?-71 BC) Gladiator in Rome who raised an army of his fellow slaves in a revolt against Roman rule in 73 BC. They defeated several Roman armies before they were finally crushed. Spartacus was captured and executed by crucifixion.
♟ The story of Spartacus was the subject of Stanley ▷KUBRICK's 1960 film *Spartacus*, which starred Kirk Douglas.

SS Elite corps of Nazi troops originally formed as Adolf HITLER's bodyguard, and led from 1929 by Heinrich HIMMLER. After the 'Night of the Long Knives' in 1934, when the leaders of the rival SA or BROWN SHIRTS were arrested and executed, the powers of the SS included the suppression of political opponents in Germany and the persecution of Jews and any other 'undesirables'. The SS supervised the concentration camps during the HOLOCAUST. During World War II, several SS units also fought as crack troops called the *Waffen* 'armed' SS.
♟ SS stands for the German *Schutzstaffel*, meaning 'protection squad'. Its members wore a distinctive black uniform.

Stalin, Joseph Adopted name of Joseph Vissarionovich Djugashvili (1879-1953), the Georgian dictator of the ▷USSR from 1927 until his death. Stalin was notorious for his ruthless repression of all dissent. When LENIN died in 1924, Stalin outmanoeuvred his rival Leon TROTSKY to grasp power. He later sent Trotsky into exile, and eventually ordered his assassination. Stalin's five-year plans and policies of collectivisation, which abolished private ownership, were followed by political purges in which officials and army officers were put through 'show trials' on trumped-up charges of treason before being executed. In total, his actions are believed to have resulted in the deaths of more than 50 million people. Stalin signed the NAZI-SOVIET PACT in 1939 and became Hitler's early ally in World War II, but after the German invasion of Russia in 1941 he fought with the Allies. Despite the enormous economic cost of the war and the deaths of 20 million Russians, Stalin's military and diplomatic skills expanded the Soviet Union and its sphere of influence deep into eastern Europe. He then presided over the beginnings of the COLD WAR. In 1956, Stalin's successor Nikita Khrushchev denounced him and his 'cult of personality'.

♟ *Stalin* is Russian for 'man of steel'. He gave his name to the city of Stalingrad (previously Tsaritfin, and now called Volgograd) and to ▷STALINISM. In the West, he was nicknamed 'Uncle Joe'.

Stamp Act (1765) British law that imposed a direct tax on American colonists for the first time. It required official documents and newspapers to bear a stamp to prove that the duty had been paid. Resentment against the tax fuelled the grievances that led to the AMERICAN WAR OF INDEPENDENCE.

Stone Age Period from the beginning of human history until the first smelting of metals, so called because people used stone tools and weapons. The first stone tools are believed to be more than 2 million years old. Archaeologists divide the period into the Old Stone Age, when humans lived as hunter-gatherers, and the New Stone Age (from about 10 000 BC), when the first agricultural settlements developed. In most parts of the world the Stone Age was followed by the BRONZE AGE.

Suez crisis (1956) Unsuccessful attempt by Britain, France and Israel to secure control of the Suez Canal – the vital shipping channel that links the Mediterranean and the Red Sea. It began when Egypt's President NASSER nationalised the canal, prompting fears that he might close it, cutting off oil supplies to Europe from the Persian Gulf. Three months later, Israel (later revealed to be acting as part of a previously agreed plan) invaded Egypt while British and French forces moved into the area, ostensibly to enforce a UN ceasefire. Their true aim was to regain control of the canal, but international pressure – particularly from the United States – forced them to withdraw. The incident enhanced Nasser's prestige in the Arab world and led to the downfall of Anthony ▷EDEN, the British prime minister.

Suleiman the Magnificent (1494-1566) Sultan of the OTTOMAN EMPIRE from 1520. He expanded the empire as far as Hungary, Iraq and Libya, and his navy dominated the Mediterranean. At home, he was a generous patron of the arts and introduced a series of reforms which earned him the alternative title of 'the Lawgiver'.

Sumeria One of the world's earliest civilisations, based in southern MESOPOTAMIA. The Sumerians built the first cities, such as Ur, before 3000 BC and probably invented writing with the ▷CUNEIFORM script.

Sun King Nickname for LOUIS XIV of France, capturing the splendour of his court and palace at ▷VERSAILLES. Louis himself adopted the Sun as his emblem.

Tereshkova, Valentina (1937-) Russian cosmonaut who became the first woman in space. She orbited the Earth for three days on board *Vostok 6* in 1963.

Thirty Years' War (1618-48) Struggle between France, Spain, Sweden, Denmark, Austria and numerous German states. The causes of the war were rooted in French expansionism, national rivalries, conflict between Roman Catholics and Protestants and the desire of King Gustavus Adolphus to win Swedish control of the Baltic. The war started after the Defenestration of Prague, when two Catholic members of Bohemia's ruling council were thrown out of a window by their Protestant colleagues. It ended with the Treaty of Westphalia, which limited the power of the HABSBURGS and enhanced that of France.

Thucydides **(thew-SIDD-i-deez) (c.460-c.400 BC)** Ancient Greek general and historian who wrote a detailed and influential, but unfinished, eight-volume history of the PELOPONNESIAN WAR.

POWERFUL SULTAN *Under Suleiman the Magnificent, Ottoman influence reached its height: his armies even threatened Vienna.*

LONE PROTESTER *A Chinese student defies tanks sent in against fellow rebels and their 'Goddess of Democracy and Freedom' in Tiananmen Square. He was tried and shot a few days later.*

Tiananmen Square Massacre (1989)
Incident in which Chinese troops opened fire on students staging a pro-democracy rally in the main square of China's capital, Beijing. Some 2000 demonstrators died.

Tito (1892-1980) Adopted name of Josip Broz, leader of ▷YUGOSLAVIA from 1945 until his death. Tito led communist partisan resistance to the German invasion of Yugoslavia during World War II. His men pinned down 30 German divisions and liberated their country without the need for an Allied invasion. After the war, he imposed communist rule in his country, but in 1948 Tito broke with the Soviet Union and steered an independent course. Tito's skill in ruling Yugoslavia was underlined by its collapse into bitter civil war in 1991.
🔖 The name Tito means 'this that'. He was always ordering people to 'do this . . . do that', and the nickname stuck.

Trajan (*c.*53-117) Roman emperor from AD 98, who added much territory to the ROMAN EMPIRE. He conquered Dacia (modern Romania), Mesopotamia and Armenia, as well as carrying out important reforms in agriculture and in education.
🔖 Trajan's Column, a pillar decorated with a spiral relief of battle scenes, built by the emperor to commemorate his Dacian campaign of AD 101-6, still stands in Rome.

Trent, Council of (1545-63) Roman Catholic Church Council summoned to meet the challenges resulting from the REFORMATION. It reformed many aspects of the Church and redefined its dogma, initiating the movement known as the COUNTER REFORMATION.

Trotsky, Leon (1879-1940) Russian leader who rose to power alongside LENIN after the Russian Revolution. In 1918 he founded the Red Army, which was victorious in the RUSSIAN CIVIL WAR. In favouring world communist revolution, Trotsky found himself opposed by Lenin and Stalin, both of whom insisted that communism must first develop fully within the Soviet Union. Stalin deported Trotsky in 1929, but Trotsky continued to criticise him. Eventually Stalin gave orders for a Soviet agent to assassinate Trotsky in Mexico City; the murder weapon was an ice pick.

Truman, Harry S (1884-1972) American president from 1945 to 1953. As leader in the last months of World War II, Truman ordered ATOM BOMBS to be dropped on Japan. After the war, he put forward MARSHALL AID to promote European recovery, and formulated the 'Truman doctrine' under which the USA pledged to 'contain' communism. Truman eventually sent troops to fight against communist forces in the KOREAN WAR, but vetoed proposals to use atom bombs in Korea.
🔖 Truman is remembered for his spirited leadership. He often said: 'If you can't stand the heat, get out of the kitchen', and a sign on his desk read: 'The buck stops here.'
🔖 The initial 'S' did not stand for anything. Truman had no middle name, but thought a middle initial added authority.

tsars Rulers or emperors of Russia. The first ruler to call himself 'tsar' was IVAN IV 'THE TERRIBLE' in 1547, and the last tsar was NICHOLAS II, who was deposed in the RUSSIAN REVOLUTION in 1917. In the early 20th century the ▷ABSOLUTE MONARCHY of the tsars was tempered by the formation of a parliament, the Duma.
🔖 The name 'tsar' is derived from CAESAR.

Tutankhamun (*c.*1340-*c.*1322 BC) Pharaoh of ancient Egypt who reigned for just six years before he died aged about 18. His reign was undistinguished, but the

GOLDEN KING *Tutankhamun's gold funeral mask is inlaid with semiprecious stones and glass beads. The vulture, cobra and his braided beard are symbols of protecting deities and kingship.*

discovery of his virtually untouched tomb by Howard Carter and Lord Carnarvon in 1922 is among the greatest archaeological finds of all time.

⚓ Tutankhamun is popularly known as 'King Tut'. Many people believe in the 'curse of Tutankhamun', which is said to harm or kill those who interfere with the dead pharaoh's remains or treasures. The story originated when Lord Carnarvon died during the excavations. At the moment of his death there was a power cut in Cairo – and his dog in England also died. However, Carter and most of the rest of the team lived well into old age.

U-2 American high-altitude spy plane which was shot down by a Russian missile over the Soviet Union in 1960. The pilot, Gary Powers, parachuted to safety but was arrested and found guilty by a Soviet court of spying. The U-2 incident helped to fuel the COLD WAR. Powers was released in 1962.

Valois, House of (VAL-wa) Ruling dynasty of France from 1328 to 1589. The Valois kings won the HUNDRED YEARS' WAR, but eventually their greed and ostentatious wealth made them unpopular. They were succeeded by the BOURBONS.

Vandals Baltic people who invaded the Roman Empire in the 5th century AD, conquering North Africa and eventually plundering Rome itself in AD 455.

⚓ The Vandals' pillaging of Rome made 'vandalism' a byword for wilful destruction.

vassal Under FEUDALISM, a person who placed himself in service to a lord in return for the lord's protection. The lowest and most common form of vassal was a serf.

V-E Day (May 8, 1945) Day on which the German armies formally surrendered at the end of World War II. It was marked by jubilant celebrations in Allied countries. V-E stands for 'Victory in Europe'.

Versailles, Treaty of (1919) Treaty that officially ended World War I, signed in the Hall of Mirrors at ▷VERSAILLES, France. The leading Allied figures at the negotiations were Georges Clemenceau of France, David Lloyd George of Britain and President Woodrow Wilson of the United States. The treaty assigned total responsibility for the outbreak and consequences of the war to Germany, which was made to give up land, reduce its military strength, and pay extensive reparations to the Allies. It also set up the LEAGUE OF NATIONS.

⚓ Adolf Hitler later used German dissatis-

faction with the stringent terms of the Treaty of Versailles to bolster his popularity in Germany during his climb to power. Many historians believe that the punitive character of the treaty sowed the seeds of World War II.

Verwoerd, Hendrik (fer-VOERT) (1901-66) Prime minister of South Africa from 1958 to 1966. Formerly, as minister of native affairs, Verwoerd is remembered as the architect of ▷APARTHEID – South Africa's system of racial discrimination. As prime minister, he led his country out of the British Commonwealth. Verwoerd was assassinated in Cape Town by a discontented parliamentary messenger.

Vespucci, Amerigo (ves-POOCH-ee) (1454-1512) Italian explorer who made several voyages to the NEW WORLD soon after Christopher Columbus. His account of his travels won such a wide audience that America was named after him.

Vichy government Administration of unoccupied southern France after the German invasion in 1940, during World War II. Led by Marshal PÉTAIN, it got its name because its seat was near the spa town of Vichy. Although ostensibly independent, Vichy France was essentially under German control. The Vichy regime continued to function after Germany occupied all of France in 1942, but in name only.

Vienna, Congress of (1815) Conference of European nations held after the defeat of NAPOLEON Bonaparte. It redrew the boundaries of Europe in an attempt to restore the ▷BALANCE OF POWER and lay the foundations for peace. Under the influence of Austria's Prince METTERNICH, many European territories were given to the monarchs who had held them before the French Revolution. However, the Congress largely ignored the mounting pressures of nationalism and the trend towards greater democracy in Europe.

NO MORE WAR *Winston Churchill flourishes his trademark V sign to acknowledge the cheers of the V-E Day crowd in London's Whitehall. However, Japan held out for four months more.*

INNOCENT SUFFERING *Vietnamese children flee their blazing village, bombarded with napalm by US aircraft. Phan Tim Kim (centre), her clothes burned away, runs screaming with pain and shock.*

Vietnam War (1960-75) War fought between North and South Vietnam, the two parts of what was formerly the French colony of Indochina. Following the withdrawal of French troops in 1954, the communist north, under HO CHI MINH, attempted to take over the non-communist south. This war of 'liberation' was waged by the North Vietnamese army, assisted by the powerful Vietcong guerrillas. The United States became involved partly because of the domino theory – that if one vulnerable nation were to come under communist domination, neighbouring countries would naturally follow. At first it sent advisers to the South Vietnamese government and then, from 1961, troops in ever larger numbers. At the peak of America's involvement in the war in 1969, more than half a million US soldiers were fighting in Vietnam. These were withdrawn in 1973, and South Vietnam was completely taken over by communist forces in 1975, to form the present-day nation of Vietnam.
🔱Throughout the world there were mass demonstrations against American involvement in the war, and the use of a conscript army was especially controversial. Many young Americans tried to 'dodge the draft' – avoid conscription.

Vikings Scandinavian race who plundered much of coastal Europe from the 8th to the 10th centuries AD. Brutal and destructive raiders, they were the greatest seamen of their day, travelling in longboats with high bows and sterns, ideally suited to ocean journeys. They also traded widely, and colonised Iceland, Greenland, France, Russia, Britain and Ireland. The Viking explorer Leif ERICSSON even travelled to North America, and settlers followed in his wake, but they did not stay long. (See also ▷VIKINGS in 'British History'.)
🔱The Normans were of Viking descent.

V-J Day (August 15, 1945) Day on which Japan surrendered to the ALLIES, marking the end of World War II. V-J stands for 'Victory over Japan'.

Waitangi, Treaty of (1840) Agreement by which Britain annexed New Zealand. Under the treaty, native Maori chiefs accepted British rule and protection in return for a guarantee that they would keep their land and that their people would be given the same rights as British people.
🔱The treaty, signed in two versions, one in English, another in Maori, has been subjected to much legal argument. In 1877 a judge denied that the treaty had any significance, but in 1987 the New Zealand Court of Appeal confirmed its validity.

Wall Street Crash (1929) Dramatic fall in stock prices on the New York Stock Exchange, starting on October 24, 1929, which marked the beginning of the worldwide DEPRESSION. Many investors lost vast sums in the Crash; stocks continued to fall until, by late 1932, most were worth only 20 per cent of their 1929 value.

Warsaw Pact Military alliance of communist nations in eastern Europe, organised in 1955 in response to the Western ▷NATO grouping. The Warsaw Pact countries, also known as the 'eastern bloc', included Bulgaria, Czechoslovakia, East Germany, Hungary, Poland, Romania and the Soviet Union. The alliance disintegrated in 1991, following the collapse of European communism.

Washington, George (1732-99) First president of the United States, in power from 1789 to 1797. He commanded the colonial army during the AMERICAN WAR OF INDEPENDENCE before being elected president. Washington was known as 'Father of the Nation', and was praised after his death as 'first in war, first in peace, and first in the hearts of his countrymen'.
🔱The capital city and the north-westernmost state of the USA are both named after Washington. His portrait appears on the American one-dollar bill and twenty-five-cent coin.

Watergate Scandal that forced American president Richard NIXON out of office in 1974. During the 1972 presidential election campaign, burglars in the pay of Nixon's Republican re-election committee were caught bugging the Democratic Party headquarters in the Watergate building in Washington, DC. Nixon's officials tried to obstruct several investigations into the break-in, but the president was eventually incriminated by tape recordings he himself had made in the White House. To avoid impeachment, Nixon resigned.
🔱The Watergate scandal was uncovered by Bob Woodward and Carl Bernstein, two investigative journalists who worked for the *Washington Post*. Their story is told in the film *All the President's Men*.

TRICKY DICKY *As the Watergate scandal unravelled, President Nixon was forced to admit his involvement in a cover-up.*

Waterloo, Battle of (1815) Battle fought on Belgian soil in which British, German, Dutch and Belgian troops inflicted the final defeat on NAPOLEON Bonaparte, who had escaped from his exile on Elba after the NAPOLEONIC WARS. The allies, led by the Duke of ▷WELLINGTON, received crucial reinforcements from Prussia late in the battle, turning Napoleon's defeat into a rout.

🔔Waterloo has become a general term to describe a decisive defeat. To meet your Waterloo is to be thoroughly beaten.

Weimar Republic (VYE-maar) Name given to Germany between the end of World War I in 1918 and the rise of Adolf Hitler in 1933. Weimar was the city in which a new democratic constitution was drawn up replacing the old German Empire with a republic. The Weimar government was unpopular in Germany, because it accepted the harsh provisions of the Treaty of VERSAILLES and presided over a period of economic chaos and political instability. Hitler abolished the republic soon after coming to power.

🔔Weimar Germany was a place of political freedom and considerable artistic creativity, producing the ▷BAUHAUS school of design, the artists George Grosz and Otto ▷DIX, the playwright Bertolt ▷BRECHT and many others.

🔔In the Weimar Republic ▷INFLATION made the German mark almost worthless. In November 1923 a loaf of bread cost 201 000 million marks – a wheelbarrow-load of banknotes.

Wilhelm II (1859-1941) Last kaiser (emperor) of Germany, reigning from 1888 to 1918. He was a grandson of Britain's Queen Victoria. After dismissing Chancellor BISMARCK in 1890, Wilhelm's aggressive foreign policy culminated in World War I. He led Germany through the war, and abdicated after his country's defeat. He lived the rest of his life as a country gentleman in the Netherlands.

🔔In Britain, especially during the war, Wilhelm II was known as 'Kaiser Bill'.

Wilson, Woodrow (1856-1924) President of the United States from 1913 to 1921. He is mainly remembered for introducing PROHIBITION, and for his role in World War I and the Treaty of VERSAILLES. Wilson preserved America's neutrality until 1917, when, faced with the threat of unrestricted German submarine warfare, he declared war, saying 'The world must be made safe for democracy'. He set out 'Fourteen Points', or goals for peace,

including the establishment of the LEAGUE OF NATIONS; after the war, Wilson was disappointed when the US Senate refused to allow the United States to join the League. Wilson suffered a nervous breakdown and a stroke in 1919, and his last years in office were marred by ill health.

'wind of change' Phrase first used by British statesman Harold ▷MACMILLAN during an address to the South African parliament in 1960. Macmillan described the growth of African nationalism as a 'wind of change . . . blowing through this continent'. His words were widely perceived to be a critical reference to South Africa's practice of ▷APARTHEID.

World War I (1914-18) War fought between the Allies (Britain, France, Russia, Italy and the United States) and the Central Powers (Germany, Austria-Hungary and the Ottoman Empire). The underlying causes of the war were rivalry between Austria and Russia for influence in the unstable Balkan region, and the mutual hostility of France and Germany. The assassination in Sarajevo of the Austrian heir, Archduke Franz Ferdinand, triggered the war. Britain entered the war when Germany invaded Belgium. Germany's westward advance was halted by the Allies at the River Marne, and the two sides formed a more or less static line, locked in trench warfare. The Central Powers were more successful to the east, where they defeated Russia at Tannenberg and invaded Poland and Lithuania. In 1915, Turkey inflicted a terrible defeat on British and Commonwealth forces at GALLIPOLI. In 1916 the bloody battle of the ▷SOMME and an inconclusive naval battle at ▷JUTLAND brought Allied morale to a new low. German submarine attacks in the Atlantic pushed America into the war in 1917, and in the same year tanks were used effectively for the first time, at Cambrai. By this time, the use of aircraft in battle by 'aces' such as Manfred von RICHTHOFEN was also well established. Russia's heavy losses on the eastern front helped to precipitate the RUSSIAN REVOLUTION in 1917, after which Russia withdrew from the fighting. In 1918 Germany lost 750 000 men in a failed offensive in the west, and American reinforcements began playing a vital role in delivering final victory to the Allies, when Germany agreed to an armistice. The Treaty of VERSAILLES was intended to set the seal on what was believed to be 'the war to end all wars', but the punitive measures it took against Germany were partly responsible for the rise of Adolf

Hitler and the outbreak of World War II 20 years later. Some 8 million soldiers died in World War I, most young conscripts who became known as the 'lost generation', and 16 million men were injured.

🔔The tragedy of the war inspired many writers, including Robert ▷GRAVES and Ernest ▷HEMINGWAY, and the British war poets such as Wilfred ▷OWEN and Siegfried ▷SASSOON.

🔔Remembrance Sunday – the Sunday nearest to Armistice Day (November 11) – is the occasion for remembering the dead of both the World Wars, and other conflicts. A two-minute silence is observed at 11 o'clock on the 11th day of the 11th month, the time when the armistice came into force. Wreaths of poppies, recalling the flowers that grew in the Flanders battlefields during World War I, are laid at war memorials throughout the world.

🔔The tomb of the Unknown Warrior, in Westminster Abbey, contains the remains of an unidentified British soldier who died in Flanders.

World War II (1939-45) War fought between the AXIS powers (mainly Germany, Italy and Japan) and the ALLIES (including France and Britain, and later the Soviet Union and the United States). The roots of World War II lie in the humiliating terms imposed on Germany by the Treaty of VERSAILLES and the economic collapse of the WEIMAR REPUBLIC, which fuelled the fascist extremism of NAZISM. HITLER demanded *lebensraum* – more living space for the German people. His ANSCHLUSS (union) with Austria and German demands for the Sudetenland region of Czechoslovakia were appeased by Britain and France, a policy which culminated in the MUNICH AGREEMENT. The war began when Germany invaded Poland; Britain had pledged to guarantee Poland's borders and declared war soon afterwards. For several months there was a so-called 'phoney war' with very little fighting. Germany launched a major offensive in spring 1940, conquering Norway, Denmark, the Netherlands, Luxembourg, Belgium and France by BLITZKRIEG tactics, forcing a desperate British withdrawal from ▷DUNKIRK. Hitler called off his planned invasion of Britain after the Battle of ▷BRITAIN, but he then ordered the ▷BLITZ, in which the Luftwaffe bombed British cities and industrial targets. Hitler's decision to invade the Soviet Union in 1941 was a strategic mistake, breaking the NAZI-SOVIET PACT and forcing the Russians to join the Allies. Germany was now fighting a war on two fronts, while Italy's involvement brought hostilities to the Mediterranean and North Africa. The United States was drawn into the war when the Japanese attacked the American naval base at PEARL HARBOR. Early in 1942, Japan made extensive conquests in the Pacific and invaded Burma and China, but was checked by American victories at the naval battle of Midway and elsewhere. German expansion eastwards was halted at Stalingrad and Kursk, and General ▷MONTGOMERY's ▷DESERT RATS ended ROMMEL's advance in North Africa. Allied troops forced Italy to surrender and switch sides in 1943, while RAF and US Army Air Force bombers stepped up the strategic bombing of Germany. Hitler responded to the Allied invasion of Europe (D-DAY) in June 1944 by launching pilotless V-bombs at Britain. The Allies pushed towards Germany from both east and west, uncovering the horror of the Nazi HOLOCAUST and the CONCENTRATION CAMPS. The end of the war in Europe came on V-E DAY in May 1945. Meanwhile, US forces fought a tough island-hopping campaign across the central Pacific, while American and Australian troops pushed across New Guinea towards the Philippines. The war in the Pacific ended in August 1945, after the United States dropped ATOM BOMBS on the Japanese cities of Hiroshima and Nagasaki. About 24 million soldiers – more than half of them Soviet troops – were killed in battle, and approximately 12.5 million were wounded. In contrast with World War I, there were substantial civilian casualties: an estimated 40 million civilians died as a result of the hostilities, about 20 million of whom were Chinese.

🔥The war strengthened ties between the USA and Britain. But American airmen and soldiers stationed in Britain before D-Day, armed with nylons, cigarettes, chocolate and chewing gum, earned GIs the reputation of being 'overpaid, oversexed and over here'.

🔥Codebreaking was a vital part of the Allied victory. The German ENIGMA and Japanese 'Purple' codes were deciphered with the help of the first electronic computers.

Worms, Diet of (1521) Meeting called by the Holy Roman Emperor Charles V at Worms, Germany, to interrogate the Protestant reformer Martin ▷LUTHER and encourage him to withdraw his views. Luther, who had already been excom-municated by the pope, refused to retract, saying: 'Here I stand. I can do no other. God help me.' The Diet banned his works.

Xerxes (ZERK-seez) (c.519-465 BC) King of Persia from 486 to 465 BC. Xerxes continued his predecessors' attempts to conquer Greece, bridging the Hellespont – the Dardanelles strait – in order to march into Greece at the head of a vast army. He defeated the much smaller Spartan army at Thermopylae in 480 BC, but was forced to withdraw after being defeated by the Greeks at the naval battle of SALAMIS.

Yalta Conference (1945) Meeting between Churchill, Stalin and Roosevelt, the Allied leaders, towards the end of World War II. At Yalta, a resort in the Crimea, they laid plans to disarm Germany and set up the ▷UNITED NATIONS.

Yom Kippur War (1973) War triggered by a surprise attack on Israel by Syria and Egypt on ▷YOM KIPPUR, the holiest day in the Jewish calendar. The Arabs made some initial gains, but were repelled by the Israelis after three weeks. It was the last of five wars in the ▷ARAB-ISRAELI CONFLICT.

Ypres, Battles of Three battles of World War I, fought near the town of Ypres in western Belgium. In the first battle (1914), British forces halted a German move to outflank them, but ended up in a vulnerable salient. The second battle (1915) began with an attack by the Germans, in which poison gas was used for the first time. The third battle (1917), also known as Passchen-daele after the village at its centre, was a failed Allied attempt to break out to the coast – it cost the lives of about 300 000 British soldiers and as many Germans.

🔥The correct pronunciation of Ypres is 'EE-pruh', but British troops commonly referred to it as 'wipers'.

Zhou dynasty (JOH) Chinese dynasty ruling from c.1111 BC to c.256 BC. Under the Zhou emperors, the Chinese became a great civilisation and made important advances in agriculture, technology and trade. FEUDALISM was established, and art and literature flourished. The philosopher Confucius wrote in the Zhou period giving rise to ▷CONFUCIANISM.

Zhou Enlai (JOH-en-LYE) (1898-1976) Chinese statesman who was a close ally of MAO ZEDONG and China's premier from 1949 until his death. He helped to establish closer relations between his country and Western nations in the 1970s.

THE BIG THREE *At Yalta, Churchill and Stalin flank a gaunt President Roosevelt, who died two months later. For eight days, the Allied leaders had thrashed out how to defeat and divide Germany.*

POLITICS, GOVERNMENT AND THE LAW

A host of political systems determine how nations are governed, imposing their own pattern on society. Different frameworks of law are used to discipline the complex web of human relationships. Institutions, charismatic individuals and popular opinion play as big a role as political principles in shaping our rights, freedoms and responsibilities.

NELSON MANDELA

THE HOUSE OF COMMONS

YASSER ARAFAT

absolute monarchy Form of monarchy in which the ruler is subject to no constitutional controls. The high points of absolute monarchy were marked in the 17th century by ▷LOUIS XIV and in the 18th by ▷CATHERINE THE GREAT and ▷FREDERICK THE GREAT, who used their powers to bring about important administrative and social reforms. From the 19th century absolute monarchy declined with the spread of LIBERALISM and, later, DEMOCRACY. The few remaining absolute monarchies include the Gulf states of Oman and Qatar.
⚓In England, Charles I's claim to rule by divine right as an absolute monarch was challenged and led to civil war in 1642.

Act of Parliament Legislative proposal, or BILL, which has passed through both Houses of Parliament and been given royal assent to become part of British statute law. Until 1973, when Britain joined what became the EUROPEAN UNION (EU), an Act of Parliament was the highest law of the land. Acts must now comply with EU law and, in cases of conflict, EU law has precedence.

affidavit Written statement of evidence used in a civil legal action. The author of an affidavit – the word is Latin for 'he has pledged' – swears that what is written is true and signs it before an independent witness, such as a magistrate or a court official.

Amnesty International Organisation formed in 1961 to protect HUMAN RIGHTS, gain the release of prisoners of conscience and campaign against torture and the death penalty. It works independently of all governments, and is known both for its successful lobbying campaigns and for its worldwide research into the treatment of prisoners. Its headquarters are in London.

anarchism Doctrine that all forms of authority are evil because they are based on coercion, and that societies should be organised on the basis of voluntary association. Anarchists come in many ideological colours, from left-wing communalists, who believe in self-governing local communities, to right-wing libertarians, who believe that individual freedom takes precedence over a state's right to impose taxes.

ANC (African National Congress) Organisation formed in 1912 (as the African Native Congress) to bring about majority rule in South Africa. The ANC was banned, together with all other black political parties, in 1960. It turned to a policy of armed resistance, and its leaders Nelson MANDELA and Walter Sisulu were jailed.

The South African government's policy of APARTHEID generated mass resistance and international condemnation. In 1989-90 ANC leaders were released, the ban on ANC activity was lifted, and the organisation joined in talks to prepare for democratic elections. In 1994 it won the country's first multiracial general election with a sizable majority.
⚓The ANC's claim to speak for the whole black population of South Africa has been challenged by the Zulu Inkatha movement. This led to violence between supporters of the rival organisations before the 1994 general election, when Inkatha won 43 of the 400 seats and gained three cabinet places.

Anglo-Irish Agreement (1985) Document signed by the prime ministers of Britain and Ireland, Margaret Thatcher and Garret Fitzgerald, providing for regular conferences between their two governments. As it gave the Irish Republic a say in the affairs of Northern Ireland, the agreement was opposed by ULSTER UNIONISTS. It was followed in 1993 by another Anglo-Irish accord, the Downing Street Declaration, which implied that a cessation of violence could lead to the inclusion of SINN FÉIN in official talks on Northern Ireland, but stressed that any constitutional change affecting the province depended upon the consent of a majority of its people. The IRA's pledge to cease military operations from August 31, 1994, was followed by a Loyalist ceasefire six weeks later.

apartheid Policy of racial segregation formally adopted in South Africa in 1948. Apartheid – 'separateness' in Afrikaans – discriminated between different groups on the basis of skin colour. White, black, Asian and 'coloured' (mixed descent) people were given different status in a system supposedly designed to ensure equal but separate development for each group. In reality, apartheid perpetuated the supremacy of the white minority. The role of non-whites in the political system was limited, and the 'pass laws' curtailed black people's freedom of movement. Inter-racial marriages and sexual relationships were banned. The system incurred worldwide condemnation and turned South Africa into a semi-police state which was increasingly the subject of economic, political and sporting sanctions. President DE KLERK officially abandoned apartheid in 1992 and opened constitutional discussions with the ANC.
⚓Apartheid was based on the establishment of Bantustans ('homelands') – self-ruling political units for black Africans under the umbrella of 'white' South Africa. The status of these homelands was recognised only by South Africa.

appeal courts Superior courts whose role is to hear challenges to the decisions of lower courts. The main appeal court in England and Wales is the Court of Appeal, whose rulings can themselves be challenged in the HOUSE OF LORDS. The Court of Appeal is divided into a Civil Division,

COLOUR BAR *On the buses and on the beaches, in hospitals and in homes, apartheid in South Africa grouped black, Asian and coloured people under the negative label of 'non-white' and segregated them from white people. For 36 years, mixed marriages were a criminal offence.*

presided over by the Master of the Rolls, and a Criminal Division, presided over by the Lord Chief Justice. In Scotland civil appeals are heard by the COURT OF SESSION and, ultimately, by the House of Lords in London. Scotland's highest court of appeal for criminal cases is the HIGH COURT OF JUSTICIARY. It is also possible to appeal beyond the British courts, for example to the EUROPEAN COURT OF JUSTICE.

The final court of appeal for certain Commonwealth countries and British dependencies is the judicial committee of the PRIVY COUNCIL.

Arab-Israeli conflict Political and military struggle between Israel and the Arab world that has resulted in five wars. The first was immediately after Israel's foundation in 1948, and war broke out again in 1956, 1967 (the ▷SIX-DAY WAR) and 1973. Each time Israel won and more Palestinian Arabs became refugees. Israel made peace with Egypt in 1978, but its invasion of southern Lebanon in 1982 increased tension in the region again. In 1987 Palestinians in the Israeli-occupied West Bank and Gaza Strip began an *intifada*, or uprising, against Israeli rule. In 1993 Israel and the PLO signed a peace accord giving the Palestinians limited self-rule in Gaza and the West Bank town of Jericho, and Israeli troops withdrew from these areas in 1994. In July 1994 Israel and Jordan signed an agreement ending the state of war that had existed between them since 1948.

Arab League Regional political grouping founded in 1945 by seven Arab countries. There are now 22 members of the League, stretching from Morocco to Iraq, and including the PLO. Its purpose is to ensure cooperation among its member states and protect their independence and interests. The League has had little success in resolving disputes between its members and it was badly divided by the 1990-1 ▷GULF WAR. Its headquarters is in Cairo.

Arafat, Yasser (1929-) Palestinian leader and chairman of the PLO since 1969 who has played a major role in the ARAB-ISRAELI CONFLICT. Arafat came to prominence after the 1967 ▷SIX-DAY WAR, when Israel made huge gains of territory. In the 1960s and 1970s he led a guerrilla campaign which aimed to destroy Israel, but in 1982 he started to cultivate diplomatic links with world leaders in order to influence opinion in favour of the Palestinians. In 1988 Arafat recognised Israel's right to coexist with an independent state of Palestine, in the hope of gaining a PLO platform in Middle East

VOICE OF THE ARABS *Yasser Arafat moved the struggle for a Palestinian Arab state from guerrilla war to the world conference table.*

peace talks. In 1993 he signed a peace agreement with Israel's premier, Yitzhak Rabin, which secured limited self-rule for Palestinians in Gaza and Jericho.

arms control Process of limiting the build-up of armaments and military forces by international agreement. In contrast with DISARMAMENT, whose goal is the elimination of certain weapons, arms control aims to achieve a balance of military power between potential aggressors in order to create stability and make war less likely. A key factor in arms control talks is the extent to which each side can verify the promises of the other.

During the 1970s, the USA and the USSR negotiated agreements to limit strategic nuclear weapons (SALT I and II), but this did not stop the ARMS RACE.

arms race Struggle for superiority in military systems and hardware. During the ▷COLD WAR between the USA and the USSR (1945-90), increasingly large sums of money were spent to ensure that any weapons initiative by one superpower was matched or surpassed by the other.

Assad, Hafez al- (1930-) President of Syria who seized power in 1970 in a bloodless coup. Under Assad, Syria became a major power in the Middle East. His relations with the West were damaged by alleged Syrian involvement in international terrorism, but from the late 1980s he was active in securing the release of Western hostages in Lebanon.

Attorney General Chief law officer in England, Wales and Northern Ireland, whose Scottish equivalent is the LORD

ADVOCATE. The Attorney General is usually an MP of the ruling party who advises the government on legal issues and answers questions on such issues in the House of Commons. He is also the head of the English bar and his consent is required for the bringing of certain legal actions, such as those involving offences against state security. The Attorney General's deputy is the Solicitor General.

authoritarianism Administrative system characterised by strong rule which favours absolute obedience to authority. Authoritarian rulers impose their policies irrespective of the wishes of those they govern, suppressing dissent and legitimising their behaviour by claiming special qualities. Hitler and Mussolini, for example, posed as national saviours. However, the degree of social control exerted by an authoritarian regime is less extreme than that associated with TOTALITARIANISM.

backbencher British MP of any party who is neither a minister nor a shadow minister, and therefore sits on the rear benches of the House of Commons. Backbenchers are expected to obey the voting instructions of their party WHIP. They may introduce PRIVATE MEMBERS' BILLS or put forward motions for the adjournment debates held at the end of each day's parliamentary sitting. They can challenge ministers directly during QUESTION TIME.

The powerful Conservative backbench association – which includes all the party's backbenchers – is known as the 1922 Committee. Its name marks the year in which Conservative MPs ended the parliamentary coalition formed after World War I.

bail Release of an arrested person on condition that he or she turns up at court on an appointed date to stand trial. Failure to appear on the specified date results in the person granted bail (or his guarantor) forfeiting a sum of money fixed by the court. Bail may be granted by a MAGISTRATE'S COURT, a CROWN COURT or the police.

The availability of bail without the payment of excessive sums is seen as an important civil liberty. It is enshrined in the English ▷BILL OF RIGHTS of 1689 and in the American constitution, where the eighth amendment stipulates that 'excessive bail shall not be required'.

The procedure is not always successful, as people may 'jump' bail before trial. In 1993 the Turkish Cypriot businessman Asil Nadir, who had been arrested on fraud charges, jumped bail which had been set by a British court at £3.5 million.

balance of power Situation in which rival nations or alliances perceive one another as roughly equal in power, and are therefore unlikely to gain much by waging war. Countries that wish to maintain the peace try to ensure that no single country or coalition becomes more powerful than any other in a given area.

The balance of power between the USA and the USSR after World War II, maintained by a nuclear arms race, was sometimes called the 'balance of terror'.

barrister Member of the senior branch of the legal profession in England, Wales and Northern Ireland, the junior branch being composed of SOLICITORS. Barristers give specialist opinion on complex issues and can plead cases in any court. They must be briefed by a solicitor, and cannot be approached directly by would-be clients. Members of the profession, known collectively as the bar, are either Queen's Counsel (QC) or junior barristers. They usually wear wigs and gowns in court. The bar is regulated by the INNS OF COURT and by the Bar Council, which acts as the representative body for barristers. Members of the Scottish bar are known as advocates.

To become a barrister it is necessary, after passing law exams, to join one of the Inns of Court and be 'called to the bar' in a traditional process that includes eating a number of dinners with other barristers.

bench Office or position of a judge. The term derives from the seat or bench reserved for judges in a courtroom.

The judges and senior barristers who govern each of the INNS OF COURT are known as benchers.

Benn, Tony (1925-) British Labour politician whose independence of mind and radical policies have elicited respect and condemnation in similar measure. Anthony Wedgwood Benn became an MP in 1950, but was forced to leave the House of Commons in 1960, when he inherited his father's viscountcy and seat in the House of Lords. He re-entered the Commons in 1963 having secured a change in the law that allowed him to renounce his title. Benn was a minister in the governments of Harold Wilson and James Callaghan. After Labour's general election defeat in 1979, he became a prominent spokesman for the party's left wing. He stood unsuccessfully against Denis Healey for the deputy leadership in 1981 and against Neil Kinnock for the leadership in 1988. In 1993, Benn was voted off Labour's National Executive Committee after 34 years as a member.

Bhutto, Benazir (1953-) Pakistani politician who served as prime minister from 1988 to 1990 and was re-elected in 1993. Benazir Bhutto is the daughter of Pakistan's former prime minister, Zulfikar Ali Bhutto, who was executed in 1979, leaving her as the focus of opposition to the authoritarian rule of Zia ul-Haq. After a period of house arrest in Pakistan she spent two years in Britain (1984-6) as joint leader in exile of the opposition Pakistan's People's Party. When she became prime minister in 1988 she led Pakistan back into the Commonwealth, but was dismissed in 1990 on corruption charges. After the general election of 1993 had resulted in a hung parliament, Bhutto was restored as prime minister by the National Assembly.

bill Draft of a proposed law presented for approval to a parliament. In Britain bills can be either public or private. Public bills deal with matters of public policy and are introduced either by a government or in the form of a PRIVATE MEMBER'S BILL. Private bills are introduced by an individual or a body such as a local authority wishing to gain some special power. Bills must pass through a number of stages in both the House of Commons and the House of Lords before receiving ROYAL ASSENT and becoming law as an ACT OF PARLIAMENT. These stages are: a first reading (a purely formal process when the title is read); a second reading (when the bill's principles are debated); a committee stage (when the bill is examined in detail clause by clause by a standing committee); a report stage (when the amended bill is put before the House); and a third reading (when the bill as a whole is debated). The House of Lords cannot veto a bill but has the power to delay it for up to one year.

Not all bills have to be approved by both Houses of Parliament. As a consequence of the Parliament Act of 1911, if the Speaker certifies that a bill is a money bill (one that deals only with taxation, for example) the Lords is granted one month to pass it – after which it can be sent for royal assent without the approval of the Lords.

Black Rod Officer of the House of Lords who acts as the official messenger between the Lords and the Commons. At the STATE OPENING OF PARLIAMENT, Black Rod goes to summon the Commons to hear the Queen's Speech, but the door of the Commons' chamber is ceremonially slammed in his face. He must then knock three times with his rod before he is allowed to enter. This ritual is supposed to be an assertion by the Commons of its independence of the

FIRST LADY *Benazir Bhutto of Pakistan became the first woman leader of a Muslim country, and bore a child while in office.*

monarch and her representative. As well as these ceremonial duties, Black Rod is responsible for many aspects of the day-to-day running of the Houses of Parliament.

Bundestag Lower house of the German parliament, consisting of 662 deputies elected by proportional representation for four-year terms. Together with the upper house of parliament, the Bundesrat, the Bundestag passes legislation, elects the federal chancellor and president and oversees the activities of the federal ministries.

Bush, George (1924-) Republican president of the USA between 1989 and 1993. Bush was a former director of the CIA and served as vice-president to Ronald Reagan from 1981 to 1989. During Bush's term of office, US troops invaded Panama and deposed its president, Manuel Noriega. Bush was the leading figure behind the international force that waged the ▷GULF WAR in 1991 against Iraq. His presidency was dogged by accusations that he was involved in the ▷IRAN-CONTRA affair and that his concentration on foreign policy led to the neglect of economic and social problems at home. He was succeeded as president by the Democrat Bill Clinton.

Bush is remembered for saying during his 1988 election campaign: 'Read my lips: no new taxes' – a promise he failed to keep.

bylaw Rule made by an authority that is subordinate to parliament. The most common bylaws are those made by local councils on issues relating to the government of their areas, such as environmental health. They may be used, for example, to curb litter or enforce parking restrictions. Bylaws must be confirmed by a government minister to take effect, but they are not subject to any parliamentary control.

cabinet government Form of government based on the British model in which a group of senior ministers has collective responsibility for policy-making. Any minister who is unable to give public support to a collective policy is expected to resign. Although in theory there is equality between members of the cabinet, in practice some are more powerful than others. The position of supreme authority is held by the PRIME MINISTER, who appoints all the other members and can dismiss them. The next most important posts are CHANCELLOR OF THE EXCHEQUER, foreign secretary and home secretary.

🔔The term 'kitchen cabinet' was used in the 1960s to describe Harold WILSON's practice of reaching important political decisions with the help of a small inner circle of advisers.

cabinet secretary Official head of the British CIVIL SERVICE who is a member of the cabinet and directs the cabinet secretariat. The secretariat's responsibilities – circulating information, preparing papers for meetings, setting agendas and advising on procedure – allow it to shape cabinet debate and therefore influence policy.

🔔In 1987, cabinet secretary Sir Robert Armstrong caused a stir by admitting that he had been 'economical with the truth'. The admission came while he was giving evidence in the 'Spycatcher' case, about the publication of government secrets.

Callaghan, James (Lord Callaghan)
(1912-) British Labour prime minister from 1976 to 1979. He was a key member of Harold Wilson's governments in the 1960s

CHANGE OF JOB *The death penalty 'achieved nothing except revenge' wrote Britain's best-known hangman, the dog-loving Albert Pierrepoint, after retiring to run a pub in Lancashire.*

and 1970s, serving as chancellor of the exchequer, home secretary and foreign secretary. As prime minister he entered into a short-lived alliance with the Liberal Party known as the ▷LIB-LAB PACT. His administration was dogged by high unemployment, spiralling wage claims and industrial action, culminating in the 1978-9 ▷WINTER OF DISCONTENT.

🔔In January 1979, on his return to strike-torn Britain from the Caribbean, Callaghan allegedly said: 'Crisis, what crisis?' In fact, the question was invented by the *Sun* as the headline for an interview in which he disputed that there was 'mounting chaos'.

🔔Callaghan's nickname was Sunny Jim.

capital punishment The death penalty has been phased out in most European countries but has been retained in parts of the USA, where more than 210 people have been executed since 1973. In Britain capital punishment for murder was abolished in 1965, but it still exists as the penalty for treason and for piracy at sea or in the air involving murder or attempted murder.

Carter, Jimmy (James) (1924-) US
Democratic politician and 39th president of the USA from 1977 to 1981. Carter, a peanut farmer from Georgia, where he was governor (1970-4), narrowly defeated the Republican Gerald Ford in the 1976 presidential election. He brought Egypt and Israel together to sign the ▷CAMP DAVID ACCORDS in 1978. He also kept US athletes out of the Moscow Olympics in 1980 as a protest against the Soviet invasion of Afghanistan the previous year. Carter lost popularity when Iranian revolutionaries took dozens of Americans hostage in Tehran and a bid to rescue them failed.

Castro, Fidel (1927-) Prime minister
of Cuba from 1959, and president from 1976. Castro came to power after a three-year guerrilla war in which, with the support of Che ▷GUEVARA, he overthrew the US-backed dictator Fulgencia Batista. Castro presided over his country's transformation into a communist state, building close links with the USSR. Worsening relations with the USA led to the ▷BAY OF PIGS invasion in 1961 and the ▷CUBAN MISSILE CRISIS in 1962. The collapse of communism in the USSR and eastern Europe left Castro isolated, and Cuba's mounting economic problems forced him to seek new income from tourism.

chancellor of the exchequer Chief minister in Britain responsible for financial and economic policy. As effective head of

GUNS AND ROSES *'A revolution is not a bed of roses', said Fidel Castro after seizing power in Cuba. It was one of his terser statements; his marathon harangues sometimes lasted as long as nine hours.*

the TREASURY, the chancellor has a position in the cabinet second only to the prime minister's. Each autumn he presents the Budget and the government's public expenditure estimates to the Commons. The chancellor is helped by two other ministers; the financial secretary to the treasury and the chief secretary to the treasury.

Chiltern Hundreds A formal office traditionally applied for by MPs if they wish to leave the House of Commons. MPs cannot resign, but appointment to the stewardship of the Chiltern Hundreds – a job that originally involved catching robbers in the Chiltern Hills and which technically remains an 'office of profit' under the Crown – disqualifies them from staying in the House of Commons.
🖊 The other nominal stewardship for which MPs who wish to give up their seats in the Commons can apply is that of the Manor of Northstead, in Yorkshire.

Christian democracy Set of political doctrines, shaped by 20th-century Roman Catholic ideas about social justice, which has become influential in many European countries and in Latin America. Although there are distinctions between Christian democratic parties in different countries, common themes include a strong commitment to Roman Catholic family values, hostility to communism and broad support for enlightened welfare policies.
🖊 Among those countries with strong Christian democratic parties are Germany, Italy, Chile, Venezuela and El Salvador.

BUDGET DAY *The red-leather budget box first used by Gladstone survived to be wielded by Kenneth Clarke as chancellor of the exchequer.*

CIA (Central Intelligence Agency) US national security organisation founded in 1947 to gather foreign intelligence information and to undertake secret political operations abroad. It was placed under the direction of the president and the National Security Council and now also reports to a number of congressional committees. The CIA is by far the biggest organisation of its kind in the world, employing some 3000 field officials and perhaps 9000 administrators. The agency's involvement in a series of unsuccessful assassination attempts – for example, on Fidel CASTRO – as well as other subversive activities, both inside and outside the USA, damaged its reputation. The CIA's less well-publicised successes have included 'Operation Gold' in 1955 – when a tunnel was dug into East Berlin to intercept underground Soviet telephone lines, which remained undiscovered for more than a year – and its anticipation of the Soviet missile build-up in Cuba in 1962.

circuit judge Full-time judge who tries civil cases in a COUNTY COURT and criminal cases in a CROWN COURT. Circuit judges have traditionally been recruited from the ranks of experienced barristers, but since 1992 they have also been recruited from among RECORDERS, who can be either barristers or solicitors.

CIS (Commonwealth of Independent States) Loose confederation of 12 of the 15 former republics of the USSR, excluding the Baltic states, that was created in 1991. The CIS has no common citizenship, parliament or president. Its sole declared purpose is to deal centrally with certain international laws and policies that apply to its members, through regular meetings of delegates from each republic.

civil court Court dealing with cases arising from CIVIL LAW, such as those involving divorce or libel, as distinct from a criminal court. In England and Wales civil cases are first heard in a COUNTY COURT or in the HIGH COURT OF JUSTICE. In Scotland civil cases are dealt with by a SHERIFF COURT or by the COURT OF SESSION.

civil disobedience Refusal to obey laws that are regarded as unjust, often by use of peaceful demonstrations, sit-ins and marches. The technique was made famous by Mahatma Gandhi in the 1920s and 1930s while he was leading the movement for independence in India, and in the USA by the ▷CIVIL RIGHTS MOVEMENT and opponents of the Vietnam War.

civil law Body of law dealing with the rights and obligations of private citizens, as distinct from CRIMINAL LAW. It includes such major fields as family law, contract law and TORT, which covers wrongful acts, often involving negligence, for which DAMAGES can be obtained. The term also refers to any system of law that has its origins in Roman law, in contrast to COMMON LAW.

Civil List Annual provision of funds for the royal household made by the British parliament in exchange for income from royal estates. The Civil List dates from 1697. The payments are tax-exempt.
🖊 In 1992 the number of people on the Civil List was reduced to three – the Queen, the Duke of Edinburgh and the Queen Mother – cutting the annual payment by £890 000 to £8 900 000, of which the Queen receives £7 900 000. The Prince of Wales, who is also Duke of Cornwall, is financed by income from the duchy of Cornwall; he receives no funds from the Civil List.

civil rights Freedoms given to a citizen by the state which are guaranteed either by CONVENTION or by a written CONSTITUTION. There are many such rights, among them classic freedoms, such as those of speech and religion, as well as the right to vote. Modern civil rights include protection against discrimination on grounds of race, gender or sexual orientation.

civil service People employed by the state to implement laws and policies and to carry out all duties of public administration that are not legislative, judicial or military in nature. In contrast to politicians, who must submit themselves to the electorate, civil servants in Britain are appointed in the same way as any other employed people, forming a permanent organ of administration. Although civil servants are expected to be impartial, in practice they have substantial political power because governments are often dependent on their advice. The British civil service in its present form dates from the 19th century, although it has been periodically reorganised.
🖊 All public sector workers, such as teachers, nurses and post office employees, are technically part of the civil service.

Clarke, Kenneth (1940-) British Conservative politician who was health secretary (1988-90), education secretary (1990-2) and, briefly, home secretary, before succeeding Norman Lamont as chancellor of the exchequer in 1993. He raised taxes in an attempt to reduce Britain's £50 billion budget deficit.

STARS AND STRIPES *The smiling image that wooed America with promises of economic recovery and domestic reform: Bill Clinton, the 42nd president of the United States, and his wife Hillary.*

🎙Clarke's direct, no-nonsense approach to difficult issues won him a reputation as a political 'bruiser'. He has a love of jazz, cigars and comfortable suede shoes.

Clinton, Bill (William) (1946-) US

Democratic politician and 42nd president of the USA. Clinton, a former governor of Arkansas, defeated Republican George Bush in the 1992 presidential election on the promise that he would lead the American economy out of recession, reduce the huge budget deficit and improve health, education and welfare programmes. After the election, he put his wife Hillary in charge of implementing health reforms, and appointed several other women to leading positions in the government. Clinton came under increasing criticism for a lack of decisiveness in foreign policy, and faced accusations of financial and sexual misconduct.

CND (Campaign for Nuclear Disarmament) Organisation founded in

1958 to work for the abolition of nuclear weapons in Britain. Its tactics, which included mass marches to the Atomic Weapons Research Establishment at ▷ALDERMASTON in Berkshire, achieved much publicity and attracted considerable support from intellectuals, politicians and Church leaders. Although opposed by most Labour Party leaders, CND acquired strong backing from the left wing of the party, but its influence declined after 1983, following the massive electoral defeat of Labour, which had campaigned for unilateral nuclear disarmament. From 1987 to 1990, CND was chaired by the former Catholic priest, Bruce Kent.

common law System of laws originated

and developed in England and based on previous court decisions, or PRECEDENT,

and on customs and usages, rather than on STATUTE LAW. It is fundamental to the legal systems of England and Wales, many Commonwealth countries and the USA.

Commonwealth Organisation made up

of 51 former territories of the British Empire, most of which are now independent sovereign states. The Commonwealth, which acknowledges the British monarch as its head, is a forum for international debate and technical cooperation. It is administered by a secretariat, whose secretary-general wields considerable influence on the world stage.

🎙The Commonwealth Games, an athletics contest open to all citizens of the Commonwealth, is held every four years.

communism Political doctrine aimed at

establishing – if necessary by revolution – a classless society in which goods and the means of production, such as factories and machinery, are commonly owned. The doctrine was originally associated with the writings of Karl ▷MARX and the interpretation put on Marx's ideas by ▷LENIN and his followers. During the rule of ▷STALIN (1924-53) in the USSR, communism developed into a worldwide network of parties subordinate to the political line laid down by the Communist Party of the Soviet Union. Since Stalin's death, however, many self-styled communist countries have demonstrated wide divergences from Marxist-Leninist theory. In particular, the Chinese Communist Party developed along distinct ideological lines under the influence of ▷MAO ZEDONG and advocated outright confrontation between communism and capitalism, condemning Soviet negotiations with the West as 'revisionism'. Marx believed that communism was ultimately inevitable – he saw it as a natural progression from SOCIALISM that would be achieved when the coercive organs of the state had 'withered away'. Modern communist countries have been characterised by a strong state apparatus and a powerful role for the party, but only a few survived beyond the 1980s. (See also ▷COMMUNISM in 'Business and Economics'.)

🎙The principles of communism were set out in 1848 by Marx and ▷ENGELS in *The Communist Manifesto*, a pamphlet that ends

'BAN THE BOMB' *The first CND marchers endured four days of rain and icy winds before their mile-long column of 9000 reached Aldermaston from Trafalgar Square at Easter in 1958.*

MARCH FROM
LONDON
TO
ALDERMASTON

with the words 'The workers have nothing to lose but their chains. They have a world to win. Workers of the world, unite!'

Congress National legislative body of certain countries. The US Congress is divided into the HOUSE OF REPRESENTATIVES and the SENATE. Congress can block a president's legislative programme, or override a presidential veto by a two-thirds majority in each house. It can also remove officials from office by IMPEACHMENT.

Conservative Party British political party which dates from at least the early 19th century: the word conservative was first applied to a political party in 1834, when Sir Robert Peel, the leader of the ▷TORIES, renamed his followers 'conservatives' in his Tamworth Manifesto. Although the party's policies and principles have changed over the years, it has generally been associated with the defence of property and support for private enterprise, lower taxes, the free market and the established constitutional order and opposes the nationalisation of industry. Although traditionally in favour of preserving the status quo, the Conservative Party adopted a more radical stance in the 1980s.
⚓During Margaret Thatcher's period as prime minister (1979-90), Conservatives who wholeheartedly supported her policies were known as 'drys' – in contrast to those, labelled 'wets', who showed doubts in the face of tough policy decisions or were perceived as 'soft' on social issues.

constitution Body of rules and laws governing a political system. Constitutions are usually in written form, as in the USA, but a few countries, notably Britain and Israel, have unwritten constitutions. This means that the rules governing their political systems are derived from a variety of sources, including CONVENTION.

constitutional monarchy Government by a king or queen whose powers are limited by constitutional rules to ensure that he or she governs in accordance with a democratic system, in contrast with ABSOLUTE MONARCHY. The term can also be applied to a country governed in this way.

contempt of court Offence that undermines the administration of justice. Criminal contempt is behaviour likely to obstruct the administration of justice – for example, unruly behaviour in court or comment on court proceedings that might prejudice the outcome of a case. Civil contempt is the refusal to obey the orders of a court.

convention Rules governing political conduct without having legal force. They are usually unwritten and are applied in a particular case because they have applied to similar cases in the past. The British constitution relies heavily on convention.

Council of Europe Organisation of European countries created in 1949 to deal with issues of European society. In 1950 it established the EUROPEAN CONVENTION ON HUMAN RIGHTS and the EUROPEAN COURT OF JUSTICE. Among its concerns are civil rights, environmental protection and relations between Europe and the developing world. The council includes all the members of the EUROPEAN UNION and the European Free Trade Association (EFTA), as well as Turkey, Cyprus and Malta. Its headquarters are in Strasbourg.

Council of Ministers Body of the EUROPEAN UNION (EU) responsible for political decision-making. It comprises one representative of the government of each of the 12 EU countries, but the particular minister sent to council meetings varies according to the topic under discussion. The council is the scene of some of the fiercest battles in the EU between ministers pressing for their own countries' interests.

county court In England and Wales, a court in which most civil cases are heard by a CIRCUIT JUDGE. For example, disputes between a landlord and a tenant, claims against manufacturers for faulty goods or claims for damages arising out of accidents are all heard in a county court. The court cannot award more than £5000, so larger claims are heard in the HIGH COURT OF JUSTICE. The nearest Scottish equivalent to a county court is a SHERIFF COURT.

court martial Court which exercises discipline within the armed forces. Each of the British armed services has its own disciplinary code and procedure. Although the outcome of a trial by court martial will usually be decided by serving officers, there is provision for appeal to a Courts-Martial Appeal Court, which consists of the LORD CHIEF JUSTICE and other civilian judges.

Court of Session Supreme Scottish CIVIL COURT which can conduct the initial hearing of cases and also act as an appeal court. Appeals may be made from the Court of Session to the HOUSE OF LORDS.

criminal court Court which administers criminal law and can fine people or send them to jail – as distinct from a CIVIL

COURT, in which the normal remedy is the award of DAMAGES. All criminal cases in England and Wales must be initiated in a MAGISTRATE'S COURT. Those charged with more serious offences are then committed for trial to a CROWN COURT. Appeals are heard by the Criminal Division of the Court of Appeal and by the House of Lords. In Scotland there are three criminal courts: the DISTRICT COURT, the SHERIFF COURT and the HIGH COURT OF JUSTICIARY.

criminal law Body of law dealing with offences which may result in the imposition of a punishment, such as a fine or imprisonment. The main object of criminal law is to punish the wrongdoer and to deter others from committing similar crimes. By contrast, CIVIL LAW aims to redress wrongs by compelling the wrongdoer to make compensation for what he or she has done.
⚓Courts have wide discretionary powers of sentencing in all crimes except murder and treason. Murder carries a life sentence, but judges may use their discretion: in practice, murder sentences range from an average of 12½ years for a 'domestic' crime to a minimum of 20 years for a terrorist killing.

Crown The monarch, or monarchy, in whose office supreme power in Britain is vested. The term is also used to refer collectively to government ministers and their departments. The monarch retains some powers under the ROYAL PREROGATIVE, but these must be exercised in accordance with ministerial advice.
⚓'Crown privilege' grants ministers the right to withhold documentary evidence from legal proceedings if its disclosure may be detrimental to the public interest.

Crown Court In England and Wales, a criminal court where cases are heard by a CIRCUIT JUDGE or a RECORDER. In 1971 a system of Crown Courts replaced the assizes and quarter sessions. An appeal from a Crown Court is addressed to the Criminal Division of the Court of Appeal.
⚓The best-known Crown Court in Britain is London's Central Criminal Court situated in the Old Bailey.

Crown Prosecution Service (CPS) Agency created in 1985 to decide whether or not it is in the public interest to start criminal proceedings against accused people. The CPS conducts most criminal prosecutions. Its head is the Director of Public Prosecutions. Before the CPS was formed, most prosecutions were brought by the police. Prosecutions can also be brought by private individuals.

damages Financial compensation that is awarded by a court to a successful plaintiff in a civil case. Sometimes a court may award exemplary damages – designed to punish the defendant as well as to compensate the plaintiff – but, assuming it is possible, damages are usually calculated on the basis of the amount needed to restore the plaintiff to the position in which he or she would have been if the wrong had not been done.

De Klerk, F.W. (1936-) Leader of the South African National Party and president of South Africa from 1989 to 1994. In 1990, De Klerk lifted a 30-year ban on the ANC and freed Nelson MANDELA from prison, setting in motion a series of reforms dismantling APARTHEID and introducing 'one person one vote' elections. Despite opposition from right-wingers and conflict between the ANC and the Zulu Inkatha movement, elections were held in 1994, after which De Klerk became a deputy president to President Mandela.

Delors, Jacques (1925-) French politician and economist who was president of the EUROPEAN COMMISSION between 1985 and 1994. His plan for the monetary and political union of what was then the European Community (EC) provoked disagreements within EC countries about the desirability of moves towards European FEDERALISM. Delors was succeeded by the former Luxembourg prime minister Jacques Santer in January 1995.
⚓In the late 1980s Delors was the Frenchman the British loved to hate. His attitude to European union provoked a headline in the *Sun* newspaper: 'Up Yours, Delors!'

democracy Rule by the people. Except in very small communities, direct democracy is impossible, so that most countries aspiring to democracy rely on a system in which people make their will known through elected representatives. An elected government, however, does not by itself guarantee democracy. Other essential features include PLURALISM, CIVIL RIGHTS and the RULE OF LAW.
⚓The concept of democracy originated in Athens in the 5th century BC. At that time its central doctrine was that every free-born male citizen should participate directly in making laws and decisions, and that this function should not be delegated to others.

Democratic Party One of the two major political parties in the USA. The Democratic Party evolved between 1812 and 1836 and became the representative of the agricultural southern states. By the 1920s it was also championing the interests of urban dwellers in the north. During Franklin Roosevelt's presidency (1933-45) a radical programme of economic and social reform consolidated the Democrats' hold on the US electorate. Two Democrats, John Kennedy and Lyndon Johnson, occupied the White House for much of the 1960s, but their backing for civil rights and desegregation legislation alienated supporters in the south. After 1968 the Democrats found it hard to win the presidency, although they maintained their domination of Congress. Today the Democratic Party is linked with reform of healthcare and social services, economic intervention and support for a tax system that places a proportionately greater burden on rich individuals and large corporations. Bill Clinton, a Democrat, was elected president in 1992.
⚓A cartoonist in the 1870s gave the Democratic Party its symbol of a donkey.

Deng Xiaoping (1904-) Chinese communist politician who became the effective leader of China in 1978. Originally Deng welcomed foreign investment in China, encouraged his country to open up to the outside world and oversaw a vigorous economic revival. However, China's economic experiment began to go wrong in the mid-1980s. Growing financial hardship, coupled with demands for political reform, culminated in mass protests which led in 1989 to the ▷TIANANMEN SQUARE MASSACRE and a subsequent widespread purge of dissidents. The massacre was sanctioned by Deng – a fact which greatly damaged his international reputation.

Denning, Lord (1899-) Senior British judge whose work as MASTER OF THE ROLLS from 1962 to 1982 was highly controversial because of his willingness to depart from PRECEDENT in order to achieve what he saw as a just result. Denning was also controversial because of his age – he was 83 when he retired – and because of his evident delight in making unorthodox statements. He made several outspoken attacks on the jury system.

détente Reduction of tension between countries. The term was used especially of the period in the 1970s when the US presidents Richard Nixon and Gerald Ford tried to draw the USSR into a closer relationship with the USA. The last and most fruitful period of détente between the superpowers occurred during Mikhail Gorbachev's presidency of the USSR, which saw disarmament agreements and the end of the ▷COLD WAR.

devolution Transfer of certain legislative or executive powers from a central to a regional authority. In the late 1970s, Britain's Labour government put forward a plan to create separate assemblies for Scotland and Wales within the United Kingdom, but referendums in the two countries failed to endorse the proposals. Devolution re-emerged as an important issue at the British general election of 1992, when both the Labour Party and the Liberal Democratic Party promised in their manifestoes to introduce a Scottish parliament.
⚓Northern Ireland was governed by a devolved parliament at Stormont from 1921 to 1972, when direct rule was imposed from Westminster.

diplomacy Management of international affairs by reconciling differences between countries or by promoting the interests of a particular country. All countries maintain a specialist group of diplomats to represent their interests abroad, but international crises are increasingly influenced by the intervention of such institutions as the UN.
⚓Diplomatic personnel in a foreign country have immunity from the taxation and ordinary legal processes of that country. Some of them have cars bearing CD (*corps diplomatique*) number plates, which give the diplomats special privileges.

Director of Public Prosecutions (DPP) Legal official who, as head of the CROWN PROSECUTION SERVICE, is responsible for the handling of criminal prosecutions in England and Wales and for deciding whether to prosecute. The office was created in 1879 and is subordinate to that of ATTORNEY GENERAL.
⚓In 1991 Barbara Mills became the first woman to be appointed DPP.

disarmament Reduction or elimination of part of a country's military forces and weapons in an effort to promote peace, save money or reduce tensions. The advent of nuclear weapons caused a growth in support for unilateral disarmament in some countries, spearheaded in Britain by CND. However, the main disarmament successes were brought about by multilateral talks and the strategic arms limitation and reduction talks (SALT and START) in the 1970s and early 1990s.

dissolution Process whereby a parliament is ended and a general election called. In Britain a general election must be held at least every five years. Within this period the prime minister can choose the time of the election – or be forced into calling one by a defeat in the House of Commons. ♟Parliament need not be dissolved in wartime. The parliament elected in Britain in 1935 therefore lasted until 1945.

district court Lowest criminal court in Scotland dealing with less serious crimes, presided over by a lay justice who sits without a jury and is advised by the clerk of the court or by a legal assessor. The maximum sentences that can be imposed are 60 days' imprisonment, £1000 fine, or both.

POLL POWER
A ballot box goes to the count, in the election of 1951 that brought Winston Churchill back to power at 77. The 'bulldog' appeal had worked. In the 1960s Harold Wilson turned the tide in Labour's favour; even Jo Grimond's personal popularity won the Liberals few seats.

Elizabeth II (1926-   ) Queen of the United Kingdom since 1952, when she succeeded her father, George VI. Her reign has seen Britain loosen its trade links with the COMMONWEALTH, of which she is head, and join the European Community (now the EUROPEAN UNION). Although she occupies the office in which the nation's supreme power is vested, the Queen generally exercises the ROYAL PREROGATIVE only on the advice of ministers. She has a weekly briefing with the prime minister. Her most public constitutional role is to preside at the annual STATE OPENING OF PARLIAMENT. She must give ROYAL ASSENT

BRITISH GENERAL ELECTIONS SINCE 1945

YEAR	PARTY/PM	OVERALL MAJORITY
1945 (July)	Labour Attlee	146
1950 (Feb)	Labour Attlee	5
1951 (Oct)	Conservative Churchill	17
1955 (May)	Conservative Eden	58
1959 (Oct)	Conservative Macmillan	100
1964 (Oct)	Labour Wilson	4
1966 (Mar)	Labour Wilson	96
1970 (June)	Conservative Heath	30
1974 (Feb)	Labour Wilson	No overall majority
1974 (Oct)	Labour Wilson	3
1979 (May)	Conservative Thatcher	43
1983 (June)	Conservative Thatcher	144
1987 (June)	Conservative Thatcher	102
1992 (Apr)	Conservative Major	21

to every Act of Parliament before it can become law. In 1992, when the size of the CIVIL LIST was reduced, the Queen also agreed to pay tax on her private income.
♟The Royal House of Windsor headed by Queen Elizabeth II is a focus of tradition and ceremony. But its role and image have changed significantly in the past 25 years. The core members who include Elizabeth, the Queen Mother, the Queen's husband Philip, the Duke of Edinburgh, and their two oldest children – Charles, the Prince of Wales, and Anne, the Princess Royal – remain international ambassadors. But Charles also campaigns for his environmental and architectural interests, and Anne has championed charitable causes – notably as patron of the Save The Children Fund. Of the Queen's two younger sons, Prince Andrew, the Duke of York, has a naval career while Prince Edward favours the theatre. Both Charles and Andrew are separated from their wives, respectively Diana, the Princess of Wales, and Sarah, the Duchess of York.

emergency debate Discussion of an urgent matter which displaces the normal House of Commons agenda. In an emergency a government may propose the adjournment of parliamentary business to make room for a debate on the issue. Individual MPs can ask for an adjournment in order to debate a 'specific and important matter that should have urgent consideration', but the Speaker will agree only if convinced that the urgency is genuine.
♟When Argentina invaded the Falklands in 1982, an emergency debate was held. It was the first Saturday sitting since the Suez crisis of 1956.

emergency powers Special measures which allow a government to declare a state of emergency and suspend normal legislative procedures. A state of emergency may be caused by a threat from abroad or an internal threat, such as civil war or a strike. Democratic countries have strict constitutional controls on the use of such powers.
♟Between 1970 and 1974 Edward Heath's Conservative government declared five states of emergency to deal with industrial unrest in Britain, including the imposition of a three-day working week in 1973.

European Commission Administrative body of the EUROPEAN UNION (EU) headed by 17 commissioners appointed for renewable four-year terms. The Commission, which is serviced by a 17 500-strong bureaucracy in Brussels, acts as the EU's civil service and implements the decisions

of MEPs allocated to each member country roughly corresponds to its population. The European Parliament, which includes 87 British members, meets at Strasbourg and Luxembourg and its many committees sit at Brussels. The parliament has no right of veto over laws drawn up by the EUROPEAN COMMISSION and implemented by the COUNCIL OF MINISTERS – with the result that it has little effective power – but it can reject the EU budget as a whole.

European Union (EU) Association of 12 Western European countries which replaced the European Community (EC) in 1993. The goal of the EU is to promote closer economic and political cooperation between its members and to achieve monetary union by 1999. It has its origins in the 1950s, when France, West Germany, Belgium, the Netherlands, Italy and Luxembourg – 'the Six' – came together to form the European Coal and Steel Community (ECSC), the European Atomic Energy Community (Euratom) and the European Economic Community (EEC). The most important of these, the EEC, was founded in 1957 by the Treaty of ▷ROME with a view to eliminating tariffs and promoting trade between the six members in a 'common market'. It was fused with the ECSC and Euratom in the late 1960s to create the European Community. Britain, Ireland and Denmark joined in 1973, Greece in 1981, and Portugal and Spain in 1986. The EC developed common institutions and policies, including a ▷COMMON AGRICULTURAL POLICY. In 1992 its members signed the MAASTRICHT TREATY, which led to the creation of the European Union. Austria, Norway, Sweden and Finland are due to join the EU in 1995. The main institutions of the EU are the COUNCIL OF MINISTERS, the EUROPEAN COMMISSION, the EUROPEAN COURT OF JUSTICE and the EUROPEAN PARLIAMENT.

executive Branch of government that puts into effect a country's laws. In the USA the executive (the president) is distinct from the legislature (Congress) and the judiciary in accordance with the SEPARATION OF POWERS. The executive also includes various agencies, such as the CIA, the FBI and the Environmental Protection Agency. In Britain there is no such separation between the executive and the legislature.

extradition Formal legal proceedings for removing a person from one country to stand trial in another, provided both countries have signed extradition treaties. It does not usually apply to political offences.

WORKING DAY *Television has given Britons a new insight into the role played by the Queen in the nation's affairs. The first major royal occasion to be televised was her coronation in 1953.*

of the COUNCIL OF MINISTERS. It puts forward ideas for discussion by the council and prepares the annual EU budgets. Commissioners, one of whom serves as president, are selected by member states from among their own politicians. The presidency of Jacques DELORS (1985-94) was marked by controversy over moves towards closer European integration. Luxembourg's Jacques Santer succeeded him in 1995.

European Convention on Human Rights Statement of rights drawn up by the COUNCIL OF EUROPE in 1950 and signed by almost all European countries. It came into force in 1953 and includes a code of individual rights, among them freedom of thought and religion. The convention is administered and enforced by the European Commission on Human Rights and a EUROPEAN COURT OF HUMAN RIGHTS.

European Court of Human Rights Based in Strasbourg, the judicial body of the EUROPEAN CONVENTION ON HUMAN RIGHTS. The court is composed of 32 members and makes recommendations which signatory countries should accept, but cannot be forced to do so. Individuals may petition the court, and cases may be brought against member states.

European Court of Justice Court based in Luxembourg whose role is to ensure that the law of the EUROPEAN UNION (EU) is implemented and harmonised throughout the EU countries. Actions may be brought to the court by or against member states and it may also be asked to hear cases arising from member states' domestic courts, which must defer to its decisions. The court is made up of 13 judges appointed by the member states for renewable six-year terms. The court issues a single judgment and there is no appeal.

European Parliament Legislative body of the EUROPEAN UNION (EU), whose 567 members (MEPs) are directly elected by popular vote every five years. The number

Fabianism Socialist doctrine which advocates peaceful and gradual progress towards social reform, as opposed to revolution. The Fabian Society was founded in 1884 by a group of left-wing intellectuals, including Sidney and Beatrice Webb and George Bernard Shaw. Its ideas influenced first the Liberal Party then the Labour Party, with which it has maintained strong links. Two former Labour leaders, Clement Attlee and Hugh Gaitskell, were members of the society. Fabianism has lost some influence with the rise of SOCIAL DEMOCRACY both inside and outside the Labour Party.

CRIME BUSTER *As director of the FBI for 48 years, J. Edgar Hoover relentlessly fought crime in the USA. But his power and political involvement made him a controversial figure.*

fascism Doctrine that emphasises the authority of the leader, treats DEMOCRACY with contempt and advocates NATIONALISM, often expressed in aggressively racist terms, as a way of building national unity. It is linked with extreme right-wing militaristic views and virulent hatred of communism, but it has traditionally attracted strong working-class support. Fascism flourished between the two world wars in ▷MUSSOLINI's Italy, ▷HITLER's Germany and ▷FRANCO's Spain. In 1932 Oswald ▷MOSLEY, a former Labour government minister, created the British Union of Fascists, but he failed to win power. The characteristic fascist institution was the 'corporative state' – so called because the people elected to its governing assembly represented particular institutions and power groups rather than geographical

constituencies. After World War II fascism declined, but neo-fascism sprang up in Germany and elsewhere in the 1990s.
🦟 The most prominent fascist organisations in Britain are the National Front, active in the 1970s, and the British National Party.

FBI (Federal Bureau of Investigation) Organisation created in 1908 as the investigative branch of the US Department of Justice. The FBI, which employs more than 6000 agents, developed responsibilities for criminal investigations, especially in the fields of organised racketeering, espionage and domestic security.
🦟 J. Edgar Hoover was director of the FBI from 1924 until he died in 1972. Since Hoover's death it has been revealed that he used his power to make himself invulnerable to political control, and blackmailed presidents and other top politicians with his knowledge of their sexual indiscretions.

federalism System of government in which power is divided between a national (federal) government and various regional governments. Federalism combines the benefits of size for purposes such as defence with those of self-government at local level for functions such as education.

Fianna Fáil (FEE-anna FOIL) Irish political party founded in 1926 by Eamon ▷DE VALERA with the aim of removing all British influence from Ireland. Fianna Fáil, meaning 'Soldiers of Destiny', first came to power in 1932, and has been the governing party for most of the period since. Fianna Fáil has consistently supported the reunification of Ireland.
🦟 From 1979 to 1992 Fianna Fáil was led by Charles Haughey, who was prime minister from 1979 to 1981, in 1982 and, in coalition with the Progressive Democrats, from 1987 to 1992. He resigned after a scandal concerning the 'bugging' of journalists by members of his party and was succeeded by Albert Reynolds.

Fine Gael (FINN-a GALE) Irish political party created from the wing of SINN FÉIN which supported the treaty of 1921 providing for the partition of Ireland and the creation of an Irish Free State. The party adopted the name Fine Gael, meaning 'Gaelic Nation', in 1933. It formed the first government of the Irish Free State, but, since the 1930s, it has been mostly in opposition. It favours a federal solution to the problem of Northern Ireland.
🦟 From 1977 to 1987 Fine Gael was led by Garret Fitzgerald, who was twice prime minister (1981-2 and 1983-7), heading two

coalitions with the Irish Labour Party. In 1985 he was one of the signatories to the ANGLO-IRISH AGREEMENT, which gave the Irish Republic an official right to comment on the affairs of Northern Ireland.

first past the post Voting system in which the candidate for whom the most votes have been cast is elected, even though he or she may not have won an absolute majority over the other candidates. This system, which is used in British general elections, has been criticised for its failure to reflect support for minority parties in election results. It is opposed by the Liberal Democratic Party, which supports PROPORTIONAL REPRESENTATION.

Foot, Michael (1913-) Leader of the British Labour Party from 1980 to 1983. Foot had earlier served as James Callaghan's deputy (1976-80) and LEADER OF THE HOUSE (1976-9). A long-time supporter of CND, Foot resigned as Labour leader in 1983 after his party's heavy defeat in a general election, in which it had campaigned for unilateral nuclear disarmament.

Gaddafi, Muammar (1942-) Libyan political and military leader who in 1969 helped to overthrow the monarch in a coup d'état. Colonel Gaddafi emerged as the most important figure in the ruling military

FACE OF DEFIANCE *The rugged features of Colonel Gaddafi, Libya's leader since 1969. His persistent support for several terrorist groups during the 1980s enraged Western powers.*

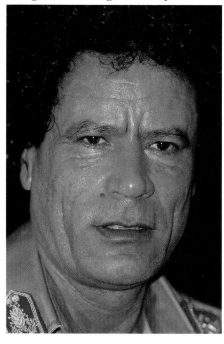

council. In 1978 he initiated the Revolutionary Committee Movement, which became a vehicle for international political intrigue and terrorism. Gaddafi's association with terrorist incidents and airline hijacking isolated him from the international community in the 1980s. In 1986 the USA retaliated against Libyan terrorism with a series of air raids and an economic blockade of the country. Although Libya has since made efforts to improve relations with the West, Gaddafi is still treated as an international pariah.

Gaullism French political movement originated by Charles de Gaulle during the 1950s. It stands for strong leadership within a highly centralised state. It also attaches great importance to French national independence, and is wary of international movements that might weaken that independence. In 1966 de Gaulle removed France from the unified military structure of NATO, and his followers maintain an ambivalent attitude to closer ties between France and the other members of the EUROPEAN UNION. Gaullism is the inspiration behind the main conservative force in France today, Rassemblement pour la République (RPR), which was founded in 1976 by Jacques Chirac.

Geneva Conventions Series of international agreements on the rules of warfare, signed between 1864 and 1949. All the conventions have tried to lay down minimum standards for the treatment of the wounded and sick, prisoners of war and, more recently, civilians in wartime conditions. The conventions have been linked from the start with the activities of the International Red Cross movement, which works to ensure that their principles are applied – as does the United Nations. The crisis in the former Yugoslavia has led to calls for a new Geneva Convention.
🔦 There are now more than 160 signatories to the Geneva Conventions. As well as sovereign states, these include such bodies as the PLO and the Pan African Congress.

gerrymandering Drawing up of electoral boundaries to deliberately give an advantage to one party. The term originated in the USA in 1812, when Eldridge Gerry, governor of Massachusetts, divided the state into new electoral districts in order to ensure that his supporters were elected. One district was so oddly shaped that it looked like a salamander and so the term 'gerrymander' was coined. Most democracies have regulations to prevent at least the most blatant forms of gerrymandering.

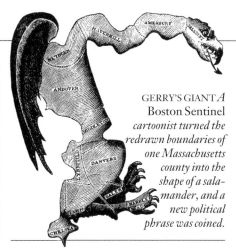

GERRY'S GIANT *A Boston Sentinel cartoonist turned the redrawn boundaries of one Massachusetts county into the shape of a salamander, and a new political phrase was coined.*

Giscard d'Estaing, Valéry (1926-) French conservative politician and president of France from 1974 to 1981. Giscard, leader of the Independent Republicans, narrowly defeated the socialist François Mitterrand in the 1974 election. Giscard's policies boosted economic growth and asserted France's international prestige. He also introduced reforms aimed at social 'reconciliation' and the creation of a 'more liberal democracy', but Mitterrand won the 1981 election. Giscard remained an influential figure in the centre-right Union for French Democracy, which he formed in 1978. He resigned from the French National Assembly in 1989 to play a greater role in the EUROPEAN PARLIAMENT, where he served as chairman of the Liberal Group.

BEFORE THE DELUGE *Openness and restructuring were the weapons with which Mikhail Gorbachev fought to reform Russia's economy. They unleashed forces that overwhelmed him.*

glasnost Policy adopted by Mikhail GORBACHEV of allowing greater intellectual freedom in Soviet society. Gorbachev, who came to power in 1985, introduced both glasnost and perestroika 'restructuring' – a wide-ranging reform strategy – with the intention of modernising Soviet society, reviving a collapsing economy and bringing the USSR closer to the West.
🔦 Examples of glasnost have included the admission of official responsibility for millions of deaths of Soviet citizens during the rule of Joseph Stalin, and the opening of state archives to journalists.

Gorbachev, Mikhail (1931-) Soviet leader who initiated the transformation of the USSR's society and economy as well as its role on the international stage. Gorbachev succeeded Konstantin Chernenko as general secretary of the Communist Party in 1985. He became executive president, with increased powers, in 1990. Gorbachev forged good diplomatic relations with the USA and brought about the end of the arms race. He encouraged greater intellectual freedom and industrial efficiency through the policies of GLASNOST and perestroika. His long-term goals were the introduction of freedom of speech and a market economy. During his leadership many former Soviet satellite countries in eastern Europe, such as Czechoslovakia and Poland, were allowed to dismantle their communist regimes and become democracies. Meanwhile the USSR experienced nationalist conflict within its own borders, resulting in its break-up in 1991 into 15 republics. Gorbachev's radical agenda generated opposition among conservatives and there was an attempted coup d'état in 1991. Although the coup failed, Gorbachev's power was broken and he was forced to hand over control to Boris YELTSIN, who had successfully defeated the coup.

governor Chief executive in each of the USA's 50 states of the USA. A governor, who serves for a two or four-year term, has extensive powers, including the right to declare a state of emergency or to call out troops to quell riots. The office of governor, especially in large states such as California, is seen as a useful preparation for the presidency. Of recent presidents, Jimmy Carter, Ronald Reagan and Bill Clinton had all been governors. The title of governor is also given to the Crown representative in a British dependency such as Hong Kong. By contrast, a governor-general is the Crown representative in certain independent territories within the COMMONWEALTH, such as Australia.

green paper British government document outlining options for proposed legislation. A green paper is more tentative than a WHITE PAPER and usually allows more time for interested parties to be consulted.

Greens Name given to political parties which are part of the environmental movement. Most of these parties were formed in the late 1970s and 1980s, when the world became increasingly conscious of the ▷GREENHOUSE EFFECT, ▷ACID RAIN and the destruction of the ▷OZONE LAYER. Green parties have found it easier to make a political impact in countries which operate a system of proportional representation. In Britain their support remains limited, but a number of 'green' issues have been taken up by the major political parties.
🕭Pressure groups such as Greenpeace and Friends of the Earth have campaigned on a wide range of issues and helped to promote the use of products such as lead-free petrol and ozone-friendly aerosols.

guillotine Procedure used in the British parliament whereby debate is terminated at a particular moment and a vote called. This is done by fixing in advance specific times for voting on successive stages of a BILL.
🕭The guillotine is an instrument of execution which was introduced in France in the 1790s by Dr Ignace Guillotin.

habeas corpus Court order, or writ, that may be used to obtain the release of a person believed to be wrongly held in a place of detention such as a prison or mental hospital. It effectively orders that the detained person be brought before a judge or court so that the court may decide whether or not his or her detention is lawful. Habeas corpus also refers to the right to demand such a hearing. Although it is still thought of as one of the most fundamental British liberties, it is now seldom invoked since in controversial situations – as, for example, when internment was in operation in Northern Ireland – the procedure for implementing it has often been suspended.
🕭The literal meaning of the Latin term *habeas corpus* is 'you shall have the body' [of the person imprisoned].

Hailsham, Lord (Quintin Hogg) (1907-) British lawyer and Conservative politician who was twice Lord Chancellor (1970-4) and (1979-87). Among several political posts, he was chairman of the Conservative Party (1957-9) and minister for science and technology (1959-64). In 1963 Hailsham disclaimed his hereditary peerage in order to make himself eligible to stand for the Conservative leadership – a bid that proved unsuccessful. He was given a life peerage in 1970.

🕭Hailsham acquired a reputation as 'the bellringer' from a stunt he staged during the closing ceremony of the 1957 Conservative conference at Brighton, when, as party chairman, he vigorously rang a handbell to rouse the party faithful.

Hansard Official report of the proceedings and debates in both the House of Commons and the House of Lords. The name derives from Luke Hansard, the House of Commons printer who began publishing the reports in 1812.

Hattersley, Roy (1932-) British Labour politician who was secretary of state for prices and consumer protection (1976-9) and became deputy leader of the Labour Party in 1983 after losing the leadership election to Neil Kinnock; both stepped down in 1992. Hattersley was a keen supporter of British membership of the European Community (now the European Union) and has represented the views of the right wing of the Labour Party.

Havel, Vaclav (1936-) Czech dramatist and politician who was elected president of Czechoslovakia after the overthrow of the Communist Party in 1989. During Czechoslovakia's period of communist rule, he had been arrested several times and was twice jailed for alleged subversive activities. Following the partition of Czechoslovakia in 1993 he remained president of the Czech Republic, adopting a conciliatory attitude towards Slovak separatists and the communists of the old regime.

head of state Person, usually a monarch or president, who acts as a country's formal or ceremonial head, in contrast with the head of government. Depending on the country's constitution, a head of state may be simply a figurehead or may, like the US president, wield executive power.

Healey, Denis (Lord Healey) (1917-) British Labour politician who was defence secretary (1964-70), chancellor of the exchequer (1974-9) and deputy leader of the Labour Party (1980-3). One of the most influential politicians of his generation, Healey's powerful intellect and combative manner made him the natural standard-bearer of the Labour Party's right wing. However, his association with the public spending cuts demanded by the International Monetary Fund (IMF) in return for a £3 billion loan in 1976 made him unpopular with the left wing and he was beaten for the Labour leadership in 1980 by Michael Foot.

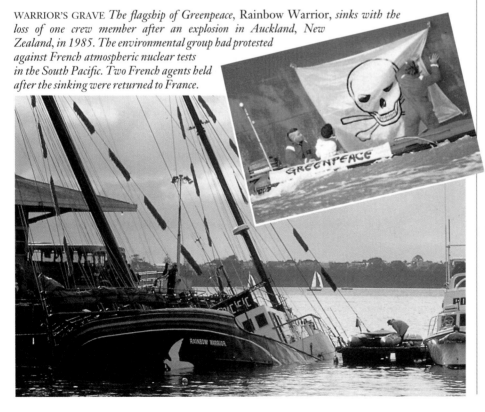

WARRIOR'S GRAVE *The flagship of Greenpeace,* Rainbow Warrior, *sinks with the loss of one crew member after an explosion in Auckland, New Zealand, in 1985. The environmental group had protested against French atmospheric nuclear tests in the South Pacific. Two French agents held after the sinking were returned to France.*

DEBATING CHAMBER *The House of Commons, rebuilt after wartime destruction, leaves one in four MPs without a seat. The party in power sits on the Speaker's right and Opposition MPs on the left.*

🎣 Healey was famed for his penetrating and dismissive comments about political opponents. In a House of Commons debate in 1978 he said that a verbal attack by Geoffrey Howe, then opposition spokesman on economic affairs, could be compared to being 'savaged by a dead sheep'.

Heath, Sir Edward (1916-) British Conservative prime minister from 1970 to 1973 who took Britain into the European Community (now the EUROPEAN UNION) in 1973. His policy of wage restraint led to a bitter struggle with the trade unions. In 1973, when energy supplies ran low – as a result of strikes by miners, power workers and railwaymen – Heath introduced a three-day working week. In a direct challenge to the unions, he ran an election campaign in February 1974 on the issue 'Who governs Britain?' No party won an overall majority, but a Labour government was formed under Harold Wilson. Heath lost another election in October of the same year. He was replaced as Conservative leader in 1975 by Margaret Thatcher. Heath returned to prominence during and after the GULF WAR, skilfully negotiating the release of many hostages including the three Britons, Michael Wainwright, Paul Ride and Simon Dunn in December 1993.
🎣 Heath's passions are music and sailing his yachts *Morning Cloud I, II and III.*

Heseltine, Michael (1933-) British Conservative politician who served as environment secretary (1979-83) and defence secretary from 1983 until his resignation in 1986 over the Westland Affair, which exposed his differences with Margaret Thatcher over policy and the management of government. In 1990 he challenged Thatcher for the leadership and, although he did not win, he attracted enough votes to precipitate her resignation. In 1990 he was again made environment secretary, in John Major's cabinet, and given the responsibility for replacing the unpopular poll tax with a council tax. Appointed trade secretary after the 1992 general election, he announced and started to implement a controversial programme of pit closures.
🎣 Heseltine's flamboyant appearance and his unorthodox behaviour in a 1976 House of Commons debate, when he seized and brandished the ceremonial mace, earned him the nickname 'Tarzan'.

High Court of Justice Part of the British SUPREME COURT OF JUDICATURE which usually deals with civil cases. It is headed by the Lord Chancellor and the Lord Chief Justice. The High Court sits at the Royal Courts of Justice in London and 26 CROWN COURTS outside London. It has three divisions. The Queen's Bench Division deals primarily with civil actions involving contract or TORT. It also hears appeals from MAGISTRATES' COURTS and certain TRIBUNALS, and has supervisory jurisdiction over all inferior courts. The Chancery Division is primarily concerned with estates and trusts. The Family Division deals with cases concerning divorce, custody of minors and probate.

High Court of Justiciary Supreme criminal court in Scotland, dealing with the most serious crimes and headed by the Lord Justice-General. There is no appeal from it to the House of Lords. The High Court is both a trial court and an appeal court. It is based in Edinburgh but when hearing trials goes on circuit to other cities and major towns. Appeals are always heard in Edinburgh. When the High Court sits as a trial court there is usually only one judge, and a jury of 15. When it sits as an appeal court it consists of at least three judges, and hears appeals from the High Court (sitting as a trial court), and from the SHERIFF COURTS and the DISTRICT COURTS.

House of Commons Lower house of the British Parliament which debates government policy and effectively makes all Britain's laws. The Commons has 651 members, each representing a single constituency and elected by a FIRST PAST THE POST system for a maximum of five years – although a prime minister can call an election within that period. The Commons, which is presided over by the Speaker, conducts its business in the form of debates on bills or motions. Most are proposed by the government, but the opposition is allocated debating time for its own motions. The time for PRIVATE MEMBERS' BILLS is severely limited, although backbenchers can use QUESTION TIME to bring pressure on a government. SELECT COMMITTEES perform an increasingly important role in the Commons. (See also ▷HOUSE OF COMMONS in 'British History'.)
🎣 Those ineligible to become MPs include peers, people under 21, civil servants, members of the police force, the regular armed forces or the clergy, people sentenced to more than one year's jail, and the insane.

House of Lords Unelected upper house of the British Parliament, composed of some 775 hereditary peers and 400 life peers, including 19 LAW LORDS and 26 bishops, which is presided over by the LORD CHANCELLOR. The chief function of the Lords is to review legislation sent to it by the Commons and amend it where it thinks necessary. Although all its decisions can ultimately be overruled by the Commons,

DAYS OF THE RAJ *At the state entry into Delhi of Britain's Viceroy, Lord Curzon, in 1903, Indian splendour combined with imperial might. These were the glory days of an empire – usually marked in red on maps – which then embraced a quarter of the world's population and land mass.*

BUY EMPIRE GOODS FROM HOME AND OVERSEAS

the Lords can delay the passing of a BILL, other than a money bill, by up to one year. The House of Lords is also the supreme APPEAL COURT in Britain. (See also ▷HOUSE OF LORDS in 'British History'.)
♪Since the late 1960s there have been several unsuccessful attempts to reform the House of Lords. In 1976 a PRIVATE MEMBER'S BILL for complete abolition, introduced by the Labour MP Dennis Skinner, was narrowly defeated.

House of Representatives Lower house of the US Congress consisting of 435 members directly elected for two-year terms. Its seats are apportioned relative to each state's population. Both the SENATE and the House of Representatives take part in virtually every aspect of US policymaking and lawmaking, but the 'House' – which has more than four times as many members as the Senate – tends to be more closely linked with local political concerns.

Howe, Geoffrey (Lord Howe) (1926-) British Conservative politician who served as chancellor of the exchequer (1979-83) and foreign secretary (1983-9). He supported Margaret Thatcher loyally until rows over foreign policy, particularly European issues, prompted his demotion to leader of the House of Commons in 1989. When he resigned from the government in 1990, Howe's speech attacking Thatcher's leadership style began the chain of events which led to her fall from power.

human rights Individual rights or freedoms thought to be fundamental to a civilised society. They include freedom of expression, movement and association, implementation of the due process of law, equality before the law, and the right not to be subjected to cruel or degrading punishment. In 1948 the UN adopted a Universal Declaration of Human Rights, and in 1950 the EUROPEAN CONVENTION ON HUMAN RIGHTS was signed. Human rights in wartime are covered by the GENEVA CONVENTIONS.

hung parliament Parliament in which no single party has an overall majority. Partly because of the FIRST PAST THE POST system used in British elections, hung parliaments are rare in Britain, but they occurred as a result of the general elections of 1924 and 1929, when minority Labour governments were formed.

Hurd, Douglas (1930-) British Conservative politician who served as Northern Ireland secretary (1984-5) and home secretary (1985-9) before becoming foreign secretary in 1989. He contested the party leadership in 1990 but ran third behind John Major and Michael Heseltine. Hurd was admired for his experience and diplomatic skills, but his rather patrician manner was thought to have counted against him.

impeachment Process of removing an official such as a president, judge or viceroy from office for serious wrongdoing. In the USA, the procedure requires the House of Representatives to submit articles of impeachment (effectively a list of complaints) which are examined by the Senate. In 1974 the House voted to impeach President Richard Nixon following the ▷WATERGATE affair, but he resigned before the case could be tried by the Senate. Several members of the US federal judiciary have been impeached. Although machinery for impeachment still exists in Britain, it has not been used since the early 19th century.

imperialism System of rule by which one country extends its authority over other territories through military force or political and economic control. One of the earliest known empires, extending from Greece to India, was created in the 4th century BC by Alexander the Great. One of the most recent was the Soviet Empire, consisting of the 15 republics of the former USSR and its satellite states in eastern Europe, which broke up in 1991.
♪Britain's imperialist heyday was in the 19th and early 20th centuries. Most former imperial territories are now independent members of the COMMONWEALTH.

industrial tribunal Panel which deals with disputes arising from employment law, particularly those concerning claims of unfair dismissal or redundancy. A tribunal usually consists of a barrister or solicitor appointed by the Lord Chancellor, and two laymen. It can declare an employer or employee in breach of contract, award compensation and order the reinstatement of a dismissed employee.

injunction Court order either obliging or preventing a particular action. An injunction may be sought to ensure that a named individual does not visit another, for example, or that a newspaper does not publish material which might impede a fair trial or which could be defamatory. In urgent cases a temporary injunction may be granted and the final outcome of the case decided at a later hearing. Anyone who fails to abide by an injunction is guilty of CONTEMPT OF COURT.

Inns of Court Four ancient legal institutions in London (Gray's Inn, Lincoln's Inn, Middle Temple and Inner Temple) to which all barristers must be admitted before they can practise law, and where most barristers have offices or 'chambers'. The inns are believed to have been set up as hostels in the 14th century for those studying common law. Prospective barristers must traditionally eat a number of dinners at the inns before they are 'called to the bar'.

International Court of Justice Chief judicial body of the UN, based at The Hague, whose main task is to arbitrate between member countries in international disputes. The court consists of 15 judges elected for nine-year terms by the UN General Assembly and Security Council. All UN members can use the court, but only those which have formally accepted its jurisdiction – wholly or in part – can be sued in it. Britain excludes all disputes involving members of the Commonwealth from the court's jurisdiction. Although the UN cannot enforce a court decision, it often succeeds in influencing public opinion.

international law Branch of law which governs relations between countries and their rights and duties with regard to one another. It deals with issues such as human rights, the recognition of states and the acquisition of territory. The bodies administering international law include the UN, the European Commission on Human Rights, the International Labour Organisation and the Inter-governmental Maritime Consultative Organisation. The usual sources of international law are conventions, treaties and international custom.

IRA (Irish Republican Army) Irish republican guerrilla force bent on securing a united Ireland. The IRA was founded in 1919, and in the run-up to the partition of Ireland in 1921 its members killed more than 700 policemen and soldiers. The organisation, which consistently refused to accept the existence of a separate Northern Ireland, was outlawed throughout Ireland when it backed Germany in World War II. It then went into decline. Following civil unrest in Northern Ireland in 1969, the IRA divided into 'Official' and 'Provisional' wings. The Official wing declared a unilateral cease-fire in 1972, but the Provisionals, or Provos, emerged as an active terrorist force. The IRA is represented in the political arena by SINN FÉIN. Since 1969 more than 3400 people have died and more than 35 000 have been injured in terrorist activities and sectarian violence involving the IRA and Northern Ireland's LOYALIST groups. On August 31, 1994, the IRA issued a cease-fire statement.

isolationism Policy of self-sufficiency by which one country deliberately avoids political, diplomatic or military commitments to other countries. When the USA declared its independence in 1776 it hoped to remain a peaceful trading nation independent of European quarrels. Since then, isolationist sentiments have intermittently dominated US foreign policy, but after its reluctant entry into World War II in 1941 the USA was obliged to assume a world role from which it did not retreat once the war was over.
🐾 Before World War I Britain took pride in its position of ▷SPLENDID ISOLATION.

Jenkins, Roy (Lord Jenkins) (1920-) British politician who served as Labour home secretary (1965-7 and 1974-6), chancellor of the exchequer (1967-70) and deputy leader of the Labour Party (1970-72). His pro-European and right-wing views were seen as being out of line with party sentiment, and in 1981, after five years as president of the EUROPEAN COMMISSION, he helped to found the SDP (Social Democratic Party) as one of the 'Gang of Four'. He was joint leader of the new party (1981-2) and served as an SDP MP (1983-7). In 1988 he became leader of the LIBERAL DEMOCRATIC PARTY in the House of Lords. He was elected chancellor of Oxford University in 1987.

Joseph, Sir Keith (1918-) British Conservative politician who served as social services secretary (1970-4), industry secretary (1979-81) and education secretary (1981-6). A disastrous speech on Conservative social policy in October 1974 – interpreted as evidence that he wished to stop the lower classes from having children – ruined his chances of standing for the party leadership. As a pioneering advocate of ▷MONETARISM, Joseph was one of Margaret Thatcher's closest political advisers. He was made a life peer in 1987.

judicial review Process whereby judges scrutinise legislation to see if it accords with the intentions of the lawmaking body or parliament. In the USA, judicial review is a crucial instrument of the SUPREME COURT, which since 1803 has had the power to strike down Acts of Congress which are incompatible with the US constitution. In Britain, the courts do not have the power to challenge Acts of Parliament and the term judicial review is used to describe the procedure of examining complaints against public bodies, such as local councils. Individuals can apply to the HIGH COURT OF JUSTICE for judicial review.

juvenile court Form of MAGISTRATE'S COURT dealing with offenders under the age of 17. Cases are heard by three lay magistrates drawn from a special panel, at least one of whom must be a woman. The court's proceedings are not open to the public. Juveniles cannot be sent to prison, but they may be sentenced to detention in a young offenders' institution, or 'borstal'.

Keating, Paul (1944-) Prime minister of Australia from 1991. He has campaigned to transform Australia from a parliamentary monarchy into a republic by the year 2000 and to replace the British monarch – who is also Queen of Australia – with an elected Australian head of state.
🐾 Keating caused a stir in 1992 by putting his arm around Queen Elizabeth II at a reception in Canberra. His action was seen as an embarrassing breach of protocol.

Kinnock, Neil (1942-) Leader of the British Labour Party from 1983 to 1992. Following Labour's defeats in the general elections of 1979 and 1983, Kinnock tackled Labour's extreme left wing and induced the party to drop its unpopular commitment to unilateral nuclear disarmament. He also made major reforms in policy and presentation, and began modernising the party structure to make it less dependent on the trade unions. Labour lost general elections in 1987 and 1992, and these results were severe personal disappointments for Kinnock, who had come under increasing attack from left-wing elements of the party. He was replaced as Labour leader in 1992 by John Smith. In 1994 he became an EU Commissioner.

Knesset Israeli parliament, whose 120 members are elected every four years by proportional representation in a single constituency. This system produces many different parties and coalition governments. Since the 1970s the religious parties, although winning only a small number of seats, have been able to exert considerable influence over Israeli governments.

Kohl, Helmut (1930-) German Christian Democratic politician who was chancellor of the Federal Republic of West Germany (1982-90) and of a united Germany from 1990. Although Kohl was seen to lack charisma and diplomatic skill, he has proved to be a shrewd political operator. He encouraged the reunification of Germany in 1990 as a long-term policy for his country, although he knew that the aftermath of integration would bring serious economic and political difficulties.

POLITICS, GOVERNMENT AND THE LAW

Labour Party British political party founded in 1900 as an alliance of trade unionists and socialist clubs. The Labour Representation Committee, as it was originally called, changed its name to the Labour Party in 1906, when it won 29 seats in the general election, under the leadership of Kier ▷HARDIE. By 1922 Labour had replaced the Liberals as the main opposition to the Conservative Party. Ramsey MacDonald formed the first Labour government in 1924, but the party did not secure an overall majority in the Commons until Clement Attlee won the general election of 1945. Attlee's government (1945-51) created the WELFARE STATE and nationalised Britain's major industries. The party formed governments in the 1960s and 1970s under Harold Wilson and James Callaghan. In 1979 increasingly left-wing policies led to a long period of opposition, and in 1981 a group of Labour right-wingers ('the gang of four') broke away to form the SDP (Social Democratic Party). In 1983 Neil KINNOCK took over the leadership from Michael Foot and sought to broaden the party's electoral appeal and abandon some of its more radical policies. After two more election defeats for Labour, Kinnock resigned and John Smith took over. Smith built on the work of Kinnock, moving the party further to the right, but died of a heart attack in 1994. He was succeeded by Tony Blair, a moderniser, also on the right wing of the party.

Law Lords Members of the House of Lords who, since 1876, have constituted the highest British APPEAL COURT. The Law Lords, formally the 'Lords of Appeal in Ordinary', comprise up to 11 former senior judges or barristers – of at least 15 years' standing – who have been given life peerages to carry out the Lords' judicial duties. They also become members of the judicial committee of the PRIVY COUNCIL.

leader of the House Member of the government responsible for the supervision of House of Commons business. Normally the leader of the House sits in the cabinet as the holder of an office, such as LORD PRESIDENT OF THE COUNCIL, which carries no departmental responsibilities. The leader of the House of Lords, also a member of the cabinet, has a similar role in the Lords.

left wing Term usually associated with individuals or parties which represent radical opposition to tradition and the established order, and which seek change in the direction of equality, SOCIALISM or MARXISM. It may also be used to distinguish a shade of opinion within a political party, as in 'the left wing of the Conservative Party'.

Leninism Doctrine associated with ▷LENIN and the BOLSHEVIK faction of the (Marxist) Social Democratic Party in Russia at the end of the 19th century. Lenin's most influential theories concerned the methods by which a Marxist revolution could be achieved and the way in which a Marxist society should be governed. He stressed the importance of a strong central party and the need to reconstruct industry and bring about a cultural revolution. After Lenin's death in 1924, his doctrines were transformed by the dictatorial rule of Stalin. In recent times Leninism has been used to justify an authoritarian party structure on the grounds that it was necessary for the achievement of a socialist revolution.

Liberal Democratic Party British political party formed in 1988 from a merger between the Liberal Party and the SDP (Social Democratic Party) with the aim of combining the best elements of LIBERALISM and SOCIAL DEMOCRACY. Although it won several by-elections under the leadership of Paddy Ashdown, the party failed to achieve similar successes at the general election of 1992.

liberalism Doctrine which champions individual freedom and progressive social reforms. Although liberals oppose dogma and too much state intervention, they believe that government should have a major role in regulating capitalism and enhancing social welfare. Elements of the liberal tradition have been crucial to the development of democracy.

lobby Group of people representing a particular interest who seek to influence legislation. In the USA, full-time lobbyists are employed to represent to the government the interests of corporate clients or pressure groups, such as a pharmaceutical company or an environmental organisation. Britain has a less well-established, more loosely structured lobby system. In Britain the term lobby is also used to refer to the political journalists who have access to cabinet ministers and senior civil servants, from whom they acquire confidential information on the understanding that they will be discreet in what they print.

local government Regional administrative bodies whose powers and functions vary from country to country, but typically include responsibility for education, housing and refuse collection. In Britain the structure of local government underwent major reforms during the 1970s. In England and Wales, county and district councils were established, as well as a third tier at parish or community level. Metropolitan counties were set up to serve large city areas. The Scottish counties were replaced in 1975 by nine regions, which have a

LORDLY LINE *A service at Westminster Abbey starts Britain's legal year in October. After it, Law Lords lead judges, barristers and officials to the House of Lords for a Lord Chancellor's Breakfast.*

REDS ON THE MAP *Senator McCarthy indicts the communist influences he claimed to have unearthed. Witnesses at an 'Un-American Activities' probe included film stars Danny Kaye, Humphrey Bogart and Lauren Bacall.*

two-tier system of local government, and three islands areas, which have a single-tier system. In Northern Ireland there is a single tier of local authorities. Councillors are usually elected for a fixed term of four years. In the 1980s Margaret Thatcher radically overhauled local government in order to curb or 'cap' the spending of allegedly profligate councils. The attempt to change the basis of local government funding from the property-based rates to the community charge, or poll tax, provoked criticism and riots and contributed to Thatcher's downfall. In 1993 the community charge was replaced by a property-based council tax.

Lord Advocate Senior law officer for Scotland and the member of the British government responsible for dealing with questions of Scottish law. He oversees criminal prosecutions in Scotland and represents the Crown in legal proceedings there.

Lord Chancellor Britain's most senior judge who is also SPEAKER of the House of Lords and head of the Chancery Division of the HIGH COURT OF JUSTICE. In contrast with the Speaker of the Commons, who is independent, the Lord Chancellor is a member of the government. He is responsible for the administration of the courts.
When he is presiding in the Lords, the Lord Chancellor (strictly, the Lord High Chancellor) sits on the 'woolsack', a square red bag stuffed with wool symbolising

national prosperity through trade. The woolsack dates from the 14th century, when England's wealth depended on wool.

Lord Chief Justice One of Britain's leading judges, second in seniority only to the LORD CHANCELLOR, and who presides over the Queen's Bench Division of the HIGH COURT OF JUSTICE.

Lord President of the Council British cabinet minister responsible for the PRIVY COUNCIL. The office is normally combined with that of leader of the House of Commons or leader of the House of Lords, but its holder cannot also be LORD PRIVY SEAL.

Lord Privy Seal Official who is keeper of the privy seal – a royal seal attached to certain documents as proof that they are issued by royal authority. The Lord Privy Seal is usually a senior cabinet minister with some other ministerial responsibility, such as leader of the House of Commons or leader of the House of Lords.

loyalist In Northern Ireland, a person loyal to the British Crown in wishing the province to remain part of the United Kingdom. Loyalists are represented in the political arena by the ULSTER UNIONISTS. The term has been devalued by its link with those who are prepared to use terrorism to achieve their ends, including illegal groups such as the Ulster Volunteer Force (UVF) and the Ulster Freedom Fighters (UFF).

Maastricht, Treaty of (1992) Agreement creating the EUROPEAN UNION (EU) signed by the 12 member states of what was formerly called the European Community. One of the principal aims of the treaty was to establish a single European currency and a European central bank by 1999. It also provided for common EU citizenship and the implementation of a common foreign and defence policy. Britain opted out of the treaty's Social Chapter on employment conditions, and secured the right to opt out of a future single currency. Ratification of Maastricht by all 12 members was completed in 1993, after referendums were held in several countries.
The movement towards monetary union suffered a setback in 1993 through the effective collapse of the European ▷EXCHANGE RATE MECHANISM.

McCarthyism Arbitrary persecution of alleged communist sympathisers for political or economic gain. The term derives from the activities of the US senator Joseph McCarthy (1909-57), who said in 1950 that he had a list of 205 communists in the STATE DEPARTMENT. Feeding on fears about the Soviet threat, McCarthy quickly gained national publicity for his campaign against subversive influences on the US government. Most of his accusations of communist links were later shown to be false and were generated by a desire for self-aggrandisement. Nevertheless, his inquiries destroyed the careers of individuals in many different walks of American life, including the diplomatic corps, the universities and Hollywood. McCarthy was censured by the Senate in 1954.

magistrate Person, also known as a justice of the peace, or JP, who is appointed by the Lord Chancellor to hear cases in a MAGISTRATE'S COURT and perform certain minor administrative duties such as issuing licences to sell alcohol. Most magistrates have no legal qualifications and receive no payment for their services. In some major cities, however, stipendiary magistrates, who are professionally qualified and salaried, are appointed to sit alone in court – rather than sitting in benches of at least two, as lay magistrates are required to do.

magistrate's court Court in which all criminal prosecutions are begun. Magistrates can hear minor offences themselves or, in the case of more serious offences and provided there is enough evidence, they can commit defendants for trial by jury at a CROWN COURT. In some cases, such as those which involve theft, a defendant may choose between trial by a magistrate's court or a Crown Court. Magistrates also have a limited jurisdiction in civil matters concerning, for example, debt, negligence and matrimonial proceedings.

Major, John (1943-) British Conservative politician who succeeded Margaret Thatcher as prime minister in 1990. Major's rise to power was swift. In 1987 he was appointed chief secretary to the treasury in Thatcher's government. He became foreign secretary in 1989 and chancellor of the exchequer a few months later. In 1992 Major led the Conservatives to a fourth successive election victory, but doubts surfaced about his effectiveness as a leader when divisions opened up in his party over the MAASTRICHT TREATY. His Citizen's Charter, an attempt to improve the quality of public services, was criticised for its lack of effectiveness. Privatisation schemes, which had proved so popular under Thatcher, ran into difficulties, and in 1994 his government was shaken by scandals and resignations over sexual and financial affairs.
🔔 In 1993 opinion polls showed that Major was the most unpopular British prime minister since such surveys began.

Mandela, Nelson (1918-) Leader of the ANC (African National Congress) who coordinated a series of actions challenging the South African government and its policy of APARTHEID. In 1964 Mandela was sentenced to life imprisonment for sabotage and treason, and he became a

HIGH FLYER *From a modest home in Brixton, John Major rose through the ranks to end up at No.10 Downing Street, with his wife Norma.*

symbol of black nationalist resistance. An international campaign helped to secure Mandela's release from Robben Island jail in 1990, after which he played a leading role in negotiations to secure majority rule in South Africa. In 1993 he and F.W. DE KLERK were jointly awarded the Nobel peace prize, and after the first multiracial general election of 1994 Mandela became the new president of South Africa.
🔔 Mandela's wife, Winnie, acted as a vociferous spokeswoman for her husband during his time in prison. However, after his release she was convicted of kidnapping and assaulting one of her followers, 15-year-old Stompie Moeketsi. The Mandelas separated soon afterwards.

Maoism Doctrines associated with the revolutionary communist leadership of ▷MAO ZEDONG in China. Maoism is characterised by a belief in the need for continuous revolution and a rejection of the Marxist assumption that socialism can only occur after a capitalist society has been established. It has particular appeal for revolutionary movements in developing countries because it argues that revolution can be achieved without an industrial working class or 'proletariat'.

martial law Rule by military authorities imposed on a population in wartime or when the civilian authority is considered to be working inadequately. Martial law is distinct from military law, which covers the rules pertaining to the discipline and administration of the armed forces.

Marxism Political and economic theories based on the writings of Karl ▷MARX (1818-83) and Friedrich ▷ENGELS (1820-1895) which are principally concerned with the establishment of a communist state. At the root of Marxism is the concept of class struggle between those who control the means of production (the 'bourgeoisie') and those who are exploited in the economic system (the 'proletariat'). Marx and Engels believed that the abolition of private property was a necessary prelude to the achievement of equality. They wrote about how the inequities of capitalism would be overcome and replaced by a 'dictatorship of the proletariat', leading to SOCIALISM and then to COMMUNISM – an idea later developed by ▷LENIN. Marxism has been interpreted and expounded by many theorists, so while the writings of Marx and Engels still constitute a core of Marxist thought, they no longer entirely define Marxism. Its practical application by governments committed to Marxism, notably the former USSR, has added further dimensions to its interpretation.
🔔 Marx believed that, in a fully developed communist state, goods would be distributed 'from each according to his ability, to each according to his needs'.

Master of the Rolls Judge who keeps the 'rolls', or register, of solicitors – admitting them to the legal profession in England and Wales. The Master of the Rolls also presides over the Civil Division of the Court of Appeal. The best-known holder of the office in modern times was Lord DENNING.

Militant Tendency Extreme left-wing faction with loosely Trotskyite principles that infiltrated the British Labour Party in

CLENCHED FIST *The stern resolve which enabled Nelson Mandela to conduct his own defence in a nine-month trial and survive 26 years in jail was still much in evidence when he was at last released.*

the late 1970s and 1980s. The faction produced its own newspaper, *Militant*, and won seats on several local councils, notably Liverpool City Council. Its leading members, including Derek Hatton, deputy leader of Liverpool's council, were expelled from the party after Neil Kinnock led a sustained campaign against them in an attempt to soften Labour's left-wing image.

minister of state Assistant to a senior minister in the British government, who is not head of a department, nor usually in the cabinet. There are normally about 30 ministers of state, each of whom is attached to a particular department, such as the Home Office or the Treasury. In the government hierarchy, such ministers are ranked below SECRETARIES OF STATE and above permanent secretaries and under-secretaries. They are directly appointed by the prime minister.

minister of the Crown Senior minister in the British government who is usually in the cabinet. Ministers of the Crown, of whom there are about 20, are chosen by the prime minister but appointed by the monarch. They include more than a dozen SECRETARIES OF STATE, who head the most important government departments.

Mitterrand, François (1916-) French socialist politician who was elected president of France in 1981, defeating Valéry Giscard d'Estaing. Mitterrand introduced a number of radical economic and political reforms, including nationalisation and decentralisation measures, but he had to modify his programme in 1983 because of worsening economic conditions. In 1986 the socialists lost their majority in the National Assembly, forcing Mitterrand to accept a period of 'cohabitation', when the left-wing president had to work with a right-wing majority in the Assembly led by Jacques Chirac. Mitterrand was re-elected president in 1988. Throughout his term of office he sought to combine support for European integration with mildly reformist social policies. From 1993 the right wing again had a majority in the Assembly, and Mitterrand had to work with the Gaullist prime minister, Edouard Balladur.

Moi, Daniel arap (1924-) President of Kenya since 1978. Moi, the successor to Jomo ▷KENYATTA, adopted an increasingly hard line towards political opposition. Domestic unrest and pressure from donors of foreign aid eventually forced Moi to hold multiparty elections in 1992, which he won against a fragmented opposition.

WILY LEADER *Riding out political and personal storms, Mitterrand has doggedly pursued a path towards European unity and socialist reform.*

Mugabe, Robert (1924-) Prime minister of Zimbabwe from 1980. He was elected the first president of his country in 1987, and the following year, after the merger of the two leading political parties, ZANU and ZAPU, Zimbabwe became a one-party state under Mugabe's leadership.

nationalism Sense of belonging to a specific nation, or a particular community, distinguished from other countries or groups by such factors as a common language, religion, historical tradition and the occupation of a clearly defined geographical region. Nationalism has its origins in the collapse of feudalism in Western Europe. However, it only adopted a coherent form during the French Revolution, spreading through Europe in the 19th century, and through Africa and Asia in the 20th, to become one of the most potent political forces of modern times. Nationalism has often been used by rulers to direct opposition towards 'foreign' threats. Although it was tarnished in the early 20th century by its links with ▷NAZISM and FASCISM, nationalism has had a revival in recent years, exemplified most dramatically in the break-up of the former USSR.

NATO (North Atlantic Treaty Organisation) International defence organisation founded in 1949 in response to the expansion of Soviet influence in eastern Europe and to the Soviet blockade of Berlin (1948-9). During the ▷COLD WAR, NATO provided the countries of Western Europe and North America with a defence umbrella against aggression from the Soviet bloc. The understanding that an

attack on any member of NATO was an attack on the whole organisation meant that the USA would come to the aid of its allies, if necessary with nuclear weapons. However, differences of opinion over nuclear strategy between the USA and the European members, and the end of the Cold War in 1990, encouraged NATO to re-examine its role in the world and consider transforming itself from a military to a political organisation devoted to the promotion of European stability.

🔧 The formation of NATO led to the Soviet bloc countries signing the ▷WARSAW PACT in 1955. In the early 1990s, after the collapse of communism in eastern Europe, some former republics of the USSR, which had previously been allied to the Warsaw Pact, applied to join NATO.

natural justice Basic rules of fair play which must be upheld if a judgment or any other decision is to be legally binding. The British version of natural justice is based on two such rules. The first states that no person should be a judge in his or her own cause – meaning that a decision made by someone with a financial or other interest in the outcome is invalid. The second concerns the right to a court hearing. It insists that a decision cannot stand unless the person affected by it was given a fair chance to state his or her case and to answer the other side's case.

natural law (or natural rights) Moral code thought to derive from an instinctive sense of right and wrong which permanently underlies all law. Natural law, sometimes called the 'higher law', may be used to challenge laws imposed by the state.

🔧 The idea of natural law originated with the ancient Greek philosophers, notably Socrates and ▷ARISTOTLE. It was championed in the 17th century by John Locke.

New Right Name given to a broad movement in the 1970s and 1980s which stressed the benefits of ▷MONETARISM and free-market solutions to economic problems. The New Right sought to promote individual freedoms and in some cases placed a strong emphasis on traditional religious and moral values. Although New Right influences permeated many parts of the developed world, the movement was particularly linked with the governments of Ronald Reagan and Margaret Thatcher. In Britain, Thatcher's government represented a sharp break with earlier traditions of conservatism. For example, it adopted a radical approach to the public sector with its vigorous policy of PRIVATISATION.

OAS (Organisation of American States) Association created in 1948 to provide mutual defence and assistance for the countries of North, Central and South America. The USA saw the OAS as a bulwark against communist threats in the Americas, while the Latin American countries were more concerned with economic and social issues. Although its international influence declined in the 1980s, the OAS, which has more than 30 members, remains a useful forum for the discussion of problems such as drug trafficking.

OAU (Organisation of African Unity) Association of African countries established in 1963 to promote African unity and solidarity, to coordinate political, economic, defence and social policies, and to eliminate colonialism in Africa. The OAU, which now has 51 members, meets annually, usually at its administrative headquarters in Addis Ababa, Ethiopia.

IN THE SWING *Robert McKenzie's television 'swingometer' in 1964 translated opinion poll forecasts into seats in the next parliament.*

Official Secrets Acts Britain's original Official Secrets Act was passed in 1911 in a mood of concern about war with Germany. It was very broadly drafted, allowing the government to prevent the disclosure of information which was inconvenient to itself even if not strictly damaging to the nation. All attempts to reform it failed until 1989. Although the new legislation eased some restrictions, it excluded a 'public interest' defence – meaning that no one charged with unauthorised disclosure of information could argue that the disclosure had been made in the public interest.
🔍 Since 1912 the British government has been able to stop publication of security-sensitive information by issuing a 'D-notice'. Although such notices are not legally binding, they have generally been complied with by the media.

oligarchy Greek word, meaning rule by the few, used to denote a small unrepresentative faction, or a country governed by such a group. The ancient Greek philosophers Plato and Aristotle used the term as a contrast to monarchy, the rule of one, and democracy, the rule of the people. Both saw oligarchy as a degenerate form of aristocracy, the rule of the best. Recent oligarchies have included the Philippines under Marcos and Romania under Ceauşescu.

ombudsman Official who acts on behalf of people who have complaints against certain public bodies. The ombudsman system, which originated in Scandinavia, was adopted by several countries from the 1960s onwards. An ombudsman was appointed in Britain in 1967. At first he had limited jurisdiction and could only accept complaints from MPs, rather than directly from the public. His jurisdiction has since been extended and other, similar officials have been appointed, including a National Health Service ombudsman who can receive complaints directly from the public.

opinion polls George Gallup first developed sampling techniques in the USA during the 1930s. They are now a staple part of any election and are often commissioned by newspapers and television as part of their coverage of current events – although they have often given rise to a number of objections. The way in which poll questions are worded, for example, can have an important effect on the responses they produce. Poll results may influence voters and they have often been inaccurate. In some countries, such as France, polls are banned in the last stages of an election.

opposition Political party or organised group opposed to the government in power. In the British parliament the term – which originated in the late 18th century – is traditionally used to refer to the second largest party in the House of Commons, whose duty is to challenge the party in power and to make preparations to form its own government should the opportunity arise. The office of leader of the opposition was officially recognised in 1937, when the holder was given an appropriate state salary.

Owen, David (Lord Owen) (1938-) British politician who served as Labour foreign secretary (1977-9) before helping to found the SDP (Social Democratic Party) in 1981. He succeeded Roy Jenkins as leader of the SDP in 1983, by which time the party had allied with the Liberal Party, but resigned in 1988 when the parties

merged. In 1992, he was made a life peer, and became one of the European Union's chief negotiators in the former Yugoslavia.

pacifism Opposition to all war, as a matter of principle. Pacifists believe that individuals should refuse to fight in national wars even if conscripted. There is a strong religious aspect to pacifism and some sects, notably the Quakers, have made it a part of their faith. In Britain the Liberal Party has always had a pacifist element, although both the Liberal and Labour parties have, more often, opposed specific wars.

Paisley, Reverend Ian (1926-) Northern Irish Protestant minister and fiery Ulster Unionist politician. Paisley, a charismatic demagogue, has been leader of the Democratic Unionists since he helped to found the party in 1972. He has resolutely opposed all initiatives to involve the government of the Irish Republic in the affairs of Northern Ireland.

parliament Assembly in which a country's laws are made. In Britain, parliament is composed of the HOUSE OF COMMONS, the HOUSE OF LORDS and the monarch. The government is responsible to parliament, which exercises a range of functions, including the passage of legislation and the scrutiny of government policy. The term parliament is also used to describe the period of time in which such an assembly is in operation. The life of a parliament is the interval between two general elections – a maximum of five years – and each parliament is divided into sessions of one year, starting in the autumn. The beginning of each session is marked by a STATE OPENING OF PARLIAMENT. (See also ▷PARLIAMENT in 'British History'.)
🔍 MPs may owe the long recess to Victorian predecessors who left the city to escape the stench of sewage in the summer heat.

parliamentary committee Group of MPs responsible for the detailed work of the House of Commons. A standing committee considers every parliamentary bill clause by clause. The membership of such a committee, which may number from 15 to 50 MPs, reflects the party balance in the Commons. By contrast, a SELECT COMMITTEE scrutinises a topic of concern in a manner less dominated by party concerns.

parliamentary privilege Special freedoms and legal immunities enjoyed by the two Houses of Parliament. Some aspects of privilege are collective – for example, the right of each House to control its own

POLITICS, GOVERNMENT AND THE LAW

WORDS AND DEEDS *The 'bobby on the beat', as seen in London's Portobello Road in 1951, is still the traditional image that most Britons associate with the police. Today, however, specially trained sections of the force are cast in a sterner role as they don riot gear to control violent demonstrations.*

procedures. Other aspects of privilege are individual – for example, an MP's immunity from libel proceedings arising from statements in the House of Commons.

Plaid Cymru Welsh nationalist party founded in 1925 to maintain Welsh cultural identity and which later became committed to gaining political independence for Wales. Plaid Cymru has won a handful of seats at each general election since 1966.

PLO (Palestine Liberation Organisation) Body founded in 1964 to act as a focus for the rights of Palestinians displaced by the creation of Israel in 1948. The PLO, dominated since the late 1960s by Yasser ARAFAT, resorted to guerrilla activity and terrorism for a time. But from the 1980s there was an increasing emphasis on diplomatic activity. Following the PLO's renunciation of violence, talks culminated in 1993 in the signing of an agreement with Israel granting limited self-rule to Palestinians in the Gaza Strip and Jericho.

pluralism Dispersal of political power among a wide variety of groups, such as trade unions, employers' associations and religious, ethnic, cultural and regional minorities, as well as political parties. Pluralists argue that public policy should emerge as a result of discussion between all interested groups. (See also ▷PLURALISM in 'Ideas, Beliefs and Religion'.)

police The British police force has its roots in the Bow Street Runners, a volunteer group set up in London in the 1740s to catch thieves. The first organised force was created in Ireland in 1814 by Sir Robert ▷PEEL, after whom its members were dubbed 'peelers'. In 1829 Peel founded London's Metropolitan Police – manned by 'bobbies'. Now known as 'the Met', it is headed by a commissioner under the ultimate control of the home secretary, with headquarters at New Scotland Yard in Westminster. The CID (Criminal Investigation Department) of the Met – which plays an important national role – was

formed in 1878 and the SPECIAL BRANCH in 1883. From the mid 19th century each county in Britain set up its own police force, some of which have since merged with a neighbouring force. Regional forces are each accountable to a police authority consisting of a committee of local councillors and magistrates. The authority appoints a chief constable, who is responsible for operational control of the force. There are about 150 000 police officers in the UK.

A country whose government exercises repressive controls over social, economic and political life, especially by means of a secret police force, is called a police state.

Pol Pot (1926-) Cambodian leader of the pro-Chinese communist Khmer Rouge movement from 1963. After becoming prime minister in 1976, Pol Pot set up a dictatorial regime which perpetrated one of the worst campaigns of mass murder in history: at least 2.5 million people – about one in three of the entire population – were killed. Many thousands of others were forced to move out of the towns to worksites in the countryside. Pol Pot was overthrown in a Vietnamese-backed coup in 1979 and resumed guerrilla warfare. The Khmer Rouge enjoyed a resurgence in the 1990s and agitated for a share in the Cambodian government.

Powell, Enoch (1912-) British Conservative politician remembered as a strong individualist and an accomplished orator. He served as minister of health from 1960 to 1963, when he resigned over the appointment of Alec Douglas Home as prime minister. In 1968 he was sacked from

Edward Heath's shadow cabinet after what became known as his 'rivers of blood' speech, which fuelled public fears about the dangers of black immigration into Britain. Powell opposed Britain's membership of what became the EUROPEAN UNION and refused to stand as a Conservative candidate in the general election of February 1974. He served as the Ulster Unionist MP for South Down from 1974 to 1987.

precedent Previous ruling by a court that influences the decision in a case where the issues are similar. The rules of precedent in the English COMMON LAW system have become increasingly strict since the 19th century and require that, with a few exceptions, courts must follow their previous decisions and those of the courts above them in the hierarchy.

prime minister Leader of the government in parliamentary systems. In theory, the British prime minister is 'first among equals' in the cabinet, but in practice the office brings with it a range of powers not shared by the rest of the cabinet. These include the powers to appoint people to the government, to set the cabinet agenda, and to request the dissolution of parliament. The prime minister is also officially First Lord of the TREASURY, although this role is in practice fulfilled by the CHANCELLOR OF THE EXCHEQUER.

prison There are several different kinds of prison in Britain: ordinary prisons for adult male and female offenders, high security prisons for the most serious offenders, open prisons for low-risk offenders, young offender institutions for those under 21, and remand centres for those aged over 21 who are being detained before trial or sentence. Prisons in England and Wales are run by the prison service, under the overall direction of the Home Office, while those in Scotland and Northern Ireland are the responsibility of the Scottish Office and the Northern Ireland Office. In the early 1990s the prison population of England and Wales – where there are about 150 penal institutions – exceeded the official capacity of 47 220, and six new private prisons were planned to alleviate overcrowding.

private member's bill Any proposed legislation concerning public policy that is introduced to the House of Commons by a BACKBENCHER. There are several ways of having such a proposal accepted for debate, but the most common is by ballot. A private member's bill usually has little chance of success unless it wins government backing, but some important pieces of legislation began life in this way, such as liberalising reforms to the laws on abortion, divorce and homosexuality.

Privy Council Group of some 400 senior British politicians, lawyers and bishops who rarely meet as a body. The Privy Council, which has its roots in the 14th century, was originally the executive through which the monarch ruled, but this role was superseded in the 18th century by the cabinet and the council's status is now largely formal. The Privy Council's remaining duties are carried out by a small inner group who, among other functions, meet to issue proclamations and orders in council. These may be made under the royal prerogative, such as an order declaring war, or to implement legislation passed by parliament. The standing committees of the Privy Council include the judicial committee, which is the supreme appeal court for some Commonwealth countries.

♣ Privy Councillors, who are appointed for life, include all cabinet ministers and the Speaker of the House of Commons. They are addressed as 'Right Honourable'.

procurator fiscal In Scotland, an officer of the SHERIFF COURT who serves as a public prosecutor and coroner. A procurator fiscal is an advocate or solicitor appointed by the Lord Advocate whose duties include initiating criminal investigations, taking statements from witnesses and conducting prosecutions, as well as inquiring into suspicious deaths. There are more than 40 such officers, each of whom is responsible for one or two sheriff court districts.

MEDIUM AS MESSAGE *A child's last crust of bread was one of the propaganda images used in Germany during the Nazis' rise to power. In America in 1942 the shadow of the swastika was invoked to aid the war effort. During the Cultural Revolution which gripped China in 1966, everyone had to carry a 'Little Red Book'.*

propaganda Information systematically produced and disseminated to influence public opinion by changing values and attitudes, with little regard to whether it distorts the truth. Interest in political propaganda grew in the period 1919-39, when the fascist movements of Italy and Germany manipulated symbols and arguments to promote their cause. Mass media such as newspapers and television can greatly enhance propaganda's influence.

proportional representation (PR) Electoral system which aims to reflect accurately all shades of political opinion in an elected assembly. One form of PR is the party list system, in which seats are given to each party in proportion to the number of votes they have won nationally. It is used by many European nations, including Germany and Italy. Under the single transferable vote system – used by, for example, the Irish Republic – voters rank candidates in order of preference. Once a candidate has enough votes to be elected, extra votes for that candidate are redistributed among other candidates according to the voters' second preferences, and so on. PR has been adopted by most democracies, but not by Britain, which favours the FIRST PAST THE POST system, which usually avoids the need to form a coalition government.

public inquiry Detailed investigation into an issue of general concern – such as the siting of a nuclear power station or the cause of a catastrophic accident – organised and paid for by the government. An inspector is appointed to conduct hearings at which any interested parties may put their arguments. The inspector then publishes a report with recommendations for action. Governments are not obliged to follow an inquiry's advice, but they often do so.

QC (Queen's Counsel) Senior barrister of at least ten years' experience who has been appointed by the Lord Chancellor to become 'one of Her Majesty's counsel learned in the law'. QCs command higher fees and form an elite from which future judges are likely to be chosen.

♣ QCs, who wear silk gowns and long wigs in court, are known informally as 'silks'. The process of being appointed a QC is described as 'taking silk'.

quango (quasi-autonomous national government organisation) Publicly funded body created by the government but operating independently of it. Quangos, which have proliferated in Britain over the past 30 years, are concerned with many areas of public life, such as health and education, industry and local government.

They perform a variety of functions; they include, for example, tourist authorities, the Health Education Authority and the Arts Council. Quangos are run by boards appointed by ministers. They have been criticised for their lack of accountability and for the extensive power of patronage which they give to governments.

Question Time A one-hour period at the beginning of each day's business in the House of Commons when members of the government are questioned on issues for which they are responsible. Although civil servants prepare answers to questions for which notice has been given, ministers can be caught off-guard by follow-up questions, known as supplementaries, for which notice is not required. The first quarter of an hour of Question Time on Tuesdays and Thursdays is traditionally allotted to questions addressed to the prime minister.

ratification Formal approval of a treaty by a parliament or another legislative body. Sometimes ratification may depend upon the outcome of a REFERENDUM. In the USA all treaties made by the president must be ratified by a two-thirds vote in favour in the Senate. In Britain treaties are ratified by parliament. The process is rarely contentious, although the ratification of the MAASTRICHT TREATY in 1993 deeply divided the Conservative Party.

Reagan, Ronald (1911-) Republican president of the USA from 1981 to 1989. He cut taxes and spent heavily on defence, which caused a rapid growth in the national debt. He sent troops into Grenada to suppress a revolution, provided aid for the Contra rebels in Nicaragua and ordered the bombing of Libya in retaliation for acts of terrorism against Americans. A leading figure of the NEW RIGHT, Reagan maintained a close relationship with the British prime minister, Margaret Thatcher. In spite of his support for the defence programme known as STAR WARS, he agreed a series of arms reductions with the Soviet president, Mikhail Gorbachev. Reagan survived an assassination attempt in 1981.

The fact that no disaster or scandal, such as the ▷IRAN-CONTRA affair, seemed to 'stick' to Reagan, or to dent his immense personal popularity, led some critics to label him 'the Teflon president'.

recorder Barrister or solicitor appointed by the Lord Chancellor as a part-time judge. Recorders usually sit in the CROWN COURT, but they may also sit in a COUNTY COURT or the HIGH COURT OF JUSTICE.

referendum Direct popular vote on an issue of public concern. Referendums have been much used in Switzerland and in the USA. In Britain they have been relatively rare. In 1975 Harold Wilson's Labour government held a referendum on Britain's continued membership of the European Community (now the EUROPEAN UNION), which then won a clear endorsement, and in 1978 referendums were held in Scotland and Wales on the government's DEVOLUTION proposals.

remand Detention of an accused person awaiting trial in a special remand centre, or in the remand section of a prison. A person who is to be remanded for more than a specified number of days – varying according to the circumstances – must normally be freed on BAIL, unless there is a special reason why bail should be refused.

Republican Party One of the two major political parties in the USA. It was established in the 1850s to oppose slavery. The party's first great leader was Abraham ▷LINCOLN, who was president from 1861 to 1865. The party dominated US government between 1860 and 1933, with prominent leaders such as Theodore Roosevelt (president 1901-9) and Herbert Hoover (1929-33). Recent Republican presidents have included Richard Nixon (1969-74) and Ronald Reagan (1981-9). Guided by a commitment to individualism and free enterprise, the Republican philosophy is RIGHT WING by comparison with that of

the rival DEMOCRATIC PARTY. Republicans generally believe that economic and political stability can best be achieved by minimal federal government intervention.

♘ The symbol of the Republican Party is an elephant. It was devised in the 1870s by the cartoonist Thomas Nast, who also invented the Democratic Party's donkey symbol. Nast based his creations on characters from Aesop's *Fables*.

Reynolds, Albert (1933-) Irish politician who succeeded Charles Haughey as leader of FIANNA FÁIL and prime minister of Ireland in 1992. In 1993 Reynolds and the British prime minister John Major signed an accord on proposals to end the conflict in Northern Ireland.

right wing Term that has no absolute definition but has come to be linked with the forces of traditional authority and with the defence of privilege and the status quo. In Western democracies, right wingers give a higher priority to economic than to social policies, seeking to cut taxes and reduce public spending, except on defence. More generally, right wingers tend to oppose social and political change unless it represents a return to what is perceived as a rosier past. In Russia, for example, the term right wing has been used to denote communists who oppose the liberalisation of society and desire a return to the certainties of the former Soviet system. Mainstream right-wing opinion in Britain is represented by the CONSERVATIVE PARTY.

STAR PERFORMER *Ronald Reagan, a former film actor, was the oldest ever US president, leaving office at 77. Wounded in an assassination bid in 1981 he told his wife Nancy: 'Honey, I forgot to duck'.*

♣The terms right wing and left wing came into use during the French Revolution, when those who supported the king took their places on the right in the French Estates-General (parliament) and their opponents sat on the left.

royal assent Approval given by the British monarch to bills that have passed through all their parliamentary stages. Although royal assent is needed for a bill to become law as an ACT OF PARLIAMENT, no monarch has refused it since 1707, when Queen Anne vetoed the Militia Bill. Assent is granted in Norman French: *La Reyne le veult* 'the Queen wishes it'.

royal prerogative Range of powers formally enjoyed by the British monarch. These powers are now normally exercised not by the monarch but by the Crown – that is, by government ministers and their departments. They include the prerogative of mercy, which can be used to pardon a criminal offence or commute a sentence, and the right to declare war. The prerogative of perfection – based on the common-law principle that 'the king can do no wrong' – gives the monarch personal immunity from all civil and criminal proceedings in Britain, although certain actions may be brought against the Crown.
♣Certain honours, such as the Order of the Garter and the Companion of Honour, remain in the personal gift of the monarch.

rule of law Belief in the supremacy of law over everyone, including officials and the government. The rule of law is thought to prevent the government from having too much power and to protect personal freedoms. The concept is particularly important in countries such as Britain that have no written constitution. In accordance with the ROYAL PREROGATIVE, the British monarch is immune from all legal proceedings.

Saddam Hussein (1937-) President of Iraq since 1979, by which time he had already established dictatorial control over the country through the Ba'ath Party. Saddam built up a network of ruthless internal security forces and used terror to wipe out dissent. In 1980 he invaded neighbouring Iran, starting an eight-year war, which ended in stalemate but devastated the economies of both countries and claimed some 367 000 lives, with more than 700 000 wounded. During the war Saddam developed chemical weapons which he used against Iraq's Kurdish population, attempted to build a 'supergun', probably to use against Israel, and started a nuclear

weapons programme. In 1990 he invaded Kuwait, triggering the ▷GULF WAR. Despite defeat in the war, Saddam stayed in power. Since 1991 he has forced many thousands of Marsh Arabs to flee the country by the systematic destruction of their homelands in southern Iraq.

sanctions Actions, often including a trade EMBARGO, taken against one country by others in reprisal for a breach of international law or act of aggression. Sanctions were applied against South Africa by opponents of APARTHEID – these were lifted in 1992. They were also imposed against white-dominated Southern Rhodesia in 1965 by countries seeking to thwart Ian Smith's Unilateral Declaration of Independence from Britain. Sanctions are not easy to enforce. They may also take a long time to produce results, or bring hardship to people whom they were not meant to hurt.

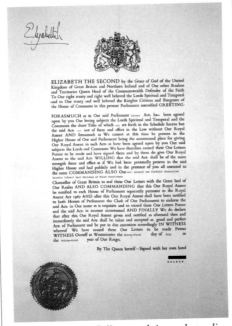

ROYAL ASSENT *Bills passed in each parliamentary session must be collectively approved by the Queen before they become laws of the land.*

SDLP (Social Democratic and Labour Party) Political party founded in Northern Ireland in 1970 by a group of independent nationalist MPs in the Stormont parliament under the leadership of Gerry Fitt. The SDLP supports the idea of a united Ireland but opposes IRA violence, believing that a settlement can be secured only by consensus. In 1993 John Hume, the leader of the SDLP since 1979, held secret peace talks with SINN FÉIN which paved the way to the IRA ceasefire statement in 1994.

SDP (Social Democratic Party) British political party founded in 1981 by the so-called 'gang of four' – Roy Jenkins, David Owen, William Rodgers and Shirley Williams – all of whom had been prominent members of the Labour Party. The new party opposed the growing power of Labour's left wing, advocating instead policies of SOCIAL DEMOCRACY. It formed an alliance with the Liberal Party and enjoyed an initial surge of support among the electorate, but this was never translated into a substantial number of seats in the House of Commons. After the 1987 election the party merged with the Liberals, forming what became the LIBERAL DEMOCRATIC PARTY, although an SDP rump continued under David Owen until 1990.

secretary of state Title given to about a dozen senior ministers in the British cabinet who are in charge of the most important government departments. These ministers include the home secretary, foreign secretary and Welsh and Scottish secretaries. In the United States, however, the secretary of state is a single senior member of the EXECUTIVE appointed by the president to take responsibility for foreign policy.

security services Government agencies whose purpose is the protection of state security and the gathering of intelligence. Their operations are often shrouded in secrecy. The main security services in Britain are MI5, MI6 and such specialist institutions as GCHQ (Government Communications Headquarters) at Cheltenham. MI5, originally named Military Intelligence section 5, was founded in 1909. It works closely with the SPECIAL BRANCH of the police force to protect internal security. MI6 – also known as the SIS, or Secret Intelligence Service – is responsible for external intelligence gathering. GCHQ is concerned with worldwide electronic surveillance. In the USA, the FBI is in charge of internal security, while the CIA takes responsibility for external operations.

select committee Group of MPs with powers to scrutinise a particular problem or set of issues and report their findings to the whole House of Commons. Since 1979 some 20 select committees have each been responsible for a particular aspect of government business, such as agriculture, foreign affairs, or transport. Membership of a committee, which numbers about 11 people, is controlled by a selection panel and reflects party strength in the Commons. Members can choose topics for inquiry and have considerable powers to mand to see relevant documents and to mmon individuals to answer questions. committee reports have sometimes been ry critical of government policy.

enate Name given to the upper house in ost two-chamber legislatures, especially federal systems such as those of the USA d Canada. A senate's method of election, rms of office and powers vary from one litical system to another. In the USA, ch of the 50 states has two senators, who rve for six years in staggered terms, e-third of the Senate being directly ected every two years. The US Senate has portant powers to confirm executive and dicial appointments, and is responsible r the ratification of treaties.

eparation of powers Principle em-died in the constitutions of some coun-ies by which the judicial, legislative and ecutive functions are separated from one other. Maintaining the independence of ch function is intended to safeguard erty by introducing checks and balances to the system. The idea of such a division iginated in the 18th century and is parti-larly associated with the writings of MONTESQUIEU. It is embodied in the US nstitution, which requires that the execu-ve (the president) be elected for a fixed rm separately from the legislature (Con-ess) and vests judicial power in the PREME COURT.

adow cabinet Leading members of the ain opposition party in the House of ommons who sit on the front bench pposite the government. In effect, the adow cabinet forms a 'government in aiting' – each member 'shadows' a vernment minister, taking charge of sues relating to that minister's depart-ent. In the Labour Party a shadow cabinet elected by Labour MPs, but in the Con-rvative Party it is chosen by the leader.

eriff In England and Wales, the chief ficer of the Crown in every county, rmally known as the high sheriff. The eriff, whose office dates from pre-orman times, retains certain legal powers, t his role is now mainly ceremonial. In otland the term denotes a judge presiding er a SHERIFF COURT. In the USA, the ief law-enforcement officer of a county d the chief executive of certain courts are so known as sheriffs.

The office of sheriff in Britain should not confused with that of lord lieutenant, ho is the British monarch's personal presentative in a particular county.

sheriff court Local Scottish court whose function resembles that of a COUNTY COURT in England and Wales, although it deals with both civil and criminal cases. A sheriff court may impose a prison sentence of up to two years, an unlimited fine, or both. If a harsher penalty is thought neces-sary, the sheriff can send the accused to the HIGH COURT OF JUSTICIARY for sentencing.

Sinn Féin (SHIN FAIN) Irish political party dedicated to the establishment of a united and independent Ireland. Sinn Féin, meaning 'We Ourselves', was founded in 1902 to lobby for ▷HOME RULE. Its first leader was Arthur Griffith, who was suc-ceeded in 1917 by Eamon de Valera. The party played a key role in winning indepen-dence for the Irish Republic, but it did not accept the Anglo-Irish treaty of 1921 because it excluded independence for the 'six counties' of Ulster. Sinn Féin is still active as the political branch of the IRA. From 1983 to 1992 its leader, Gerry Adams, was MP for West Belfast, but he never took his seat at Westminster. In 1993 the British Government offered Sinn Féin a role in discussions on Northern Ireland's future in return for an unequivocal condemnation of violence. In August the following year the IRA issued a ceasefire statement.

🔊A ban on broadcasting voices of Sinn Féin members, imposed by the British Govern-ment in 1988, was lifted in September 1994.

SNP (Scottish National Party) Politi-cal party founded in 1934 from a merger between John MacCormick's National Party of Scotland and the Scottish Party. Although the goal of the Scottish National Party is outright independence for Scot-land, it has sometimes compromised on this objective. Between 1974 and 1979 it sup-ported the DEVOLUTION proposals of the Labour government. It now argues that membership of the EUROPEAN UNION makes Scottish independence more viable. The SNP has won two or three seats in recent British general elections.

social democracy Form of SOCIALISM which rejects the goal of common owner-ship of property and nationalisation, and argues that liberal capitalism is the most efficient means of generating wealth. Social democrats believe that policies to enhance social welfare and equality should be pur-sued on the basis of expediency rather than ideology. Since 1980 most Western social-ist parties have moved towards social demo-cracy. In Britain social democratic ideas were advanced in the 1950s and 1960s by Hugh Gaitskell, Anthony Crosland and

Douglas Jay. The growing influence of the left in the 1970s caused four members of the Labour Party's right wing to split off from the rest of the party in 1981 and form the SDP (Social Democratic Party), but after 1983 Neil Kinnock moved the whole party in the direction of social democracy.

socialism Doctrine which advocates the collective ownership of the means of pro-ducing and distributing goods and the abolition of all forms of social inequality. The most influential writer on the socialist ideal was Karl Marx, who saw socialism as a transitional stage between capitalism and communism. However, many socialist movements later adopted programmes that were radically different from MARXISM and LENINISM, particularly in their rejection of the need for revolution. In Britain socialism found its main expression after 1900 in the LABOUR PARTY, which was primarily concerned with the protection and advancement of working-class interests. Socialist policies – especially on welfare and taxation – have been adopted by many Western countries, but in the 1980s most Western socialist parties accepted the broad framework of the capitalist system and moved closer to SOCIAL DEMOCRACY – concentrating on social and liberal reform rather than radical or revolutionary change.

solicitor Member of the junior branch of the British legal profession who deals directly with the public, and prepares cases for court. Since 1994 solicitors have been able to plead on behalf of their clients in the higher courts – a role that was traditionally the preserve of a BARRISTER. It is now also possible for solicitors to become judges.

Solidarity Federation of Polish trade unions formed in 1980 and based at the Gdansk shipyard. Solidarity – *Solidarność* in Polish – was independent of Poland's ruling Communist Party. After at first recognising the organisation, the Polish authorities banned it in 1981. Solidarity continued its activities in secret and was legalised in 1989, when it won power as part of a coalition government. Its leader, Lech Walesa, was elected president of Poland in 1990.

sovereignty of parliament Power of a parliament to take the final decision and to be the ultimate legal authority in a country. Britain's membership of the EUROPEAN UNION (EU) means that EU law takes pre-cedence over British law if there is a conflict – leading some people to argue that this implies that sovereignty has been trans-ferred from Westminster to Europe.

Speaker Member of the House of Commons who is elected by the other MPs to preside over debates and keep order. A Speaker must command the respect of the House as a whole and is usually a senior MP of uncontroversial views.

🖎A disruptive MP is addressed by name by the Speaker, and the House then votes on whether to suspend the offender.

Special Branch Department of the Metropolitan Police set up in 1883 to fight terrorism and protect state security. Since its creation Special Branch has been deeply involved with the affairs of Ireland, but in 1992 it handed over much of its intelligence work against the IRA to MI5, a branch of the SECURITY SERVICES.

Stalinism Doctrine derived from Joseph ▷STALIN's highly personal and autocratic adaptation of MARXISM and LENINISM in the Soviet Union. Stalin's policies in the 1920s and 1930s involved the collectivisation of agriculture, rapid industrialisation and the enforcement of ambitious 'five-year plans' for the economy. He used ruthless methods, including the suppression of all opposition and the use of terror, involving periodic purges of the party, the armed forces and society.

Star Wars Defence programme, officially known as the Strategic Defense Initiative (SDI), adopted by the USA during the presidency of Ronald Reagan. SDI centred on the development of a 'shield' in space to prevent the USA from attack by strategic nuclear weapons. After consuming a total budget of some $29 000 million, SDI was formally abandoned in 1993.

State Department Branch of the US government responsible for foreign policy, headed by the SECRETARY OF STATE. Located in an area of Washington DC known as Foggy Bottom, the State Department has frequently been viewed with suspicion by some US politicians as a source of elitist views and policies. It was a target of MCCARTHYISM.

State Opening of Parliament Official ceremony at the start of each session of the British parliament. A State Opening is held after a general election and then each autumn, usually in November. The monarch proceeds with great pomp to the House of Lords, whereupon BLACK ROD summons the Commons to join the Lords to hear the Queen's Speech, a document written by the government outlining its proposals for forthcoming legislation.

'ORDER! ORDER!' *In 1992 Labour MP Betty Boothroyd became the first woman to be elected Speaker of the House of Commons.*

statute law Body of law derived from ACTS OF PARLIAMENT rather than from the decisions of courts and judges, which make up COMMON LAW.

Steel, Sir David (1938-) British Liberal Democratic politician and leader of the former Liberal Party from 1976, when he succeeded Jeremy Thorpe. Steel's successful private member's bill of 1967 legalised abortion. He negotiated the ▷LIB-LAB PACT with the 1974-9 Labour government. He also encouraged the formation of the SDP (Social Democratic Party) in 1981 and its later alliance with the Liberals. But when the two parties merged in 1988 to form the LIBERAL DEMOCRATIC PARTY, Steel did not contest the leadership of the new party.

sub judice **(sub JUDE-issee)** Rule limiting comment on a case that is being heard in court, or is about to come before the courts, in order not to prejudice the decision. Failure to obey the rule may be interpreted as CONTEMPT OF COURT or conspiracy to pervert the course of justice – either of which could attract a prison sentence.

🖎Despite the *sub judice* rule, some cases attract wide media attention, making it difficult for juries to remain impartial.

Supreme Court Highest court in the USA, which has the power of JUDICIAL REVIEW – allowing it to strike down laws made by Congress that it regards as unconstitutional. The US Supreme Court has nine judges appointed by the president with the approval of the Senate, and exercises jurisdiction over all other courts in the nation. The court is rarely free of controversy. Different judicial philosophies dominate the bench from time to time, so that the court may be liberal in one decade and conservative in another. The court's outlawing of racial segregation in state education in 1954 and its declaration in 1973 that a right to abortion existed both generated vigorous political opposition.

Supreme Court of Judicature Superior British court created in 1873 to take over the jurisdiction of all the higher courts except the HOUSE OF LORDS. It does not sit as a single court but comprises the HIGH COURT OF JUSTICE, the Court of Appeal and the CROWN COURT.

PILLARS OF JUSTICE *Judges of the US Supreme Court hold office until they choose to retire. In 1937 President Roosevelt tried to add one younger judge for every member over 70 – but the bid failed.*

Taoiseach (TEE-shook) Official title of the prime minister of the Republic of Ireland, adopted in the 1930s. Taoiseach is an old Gaelic word for a clan leader.

Tebbit, Norman (Lord Tebbit) (1931-) British Conservative politician who served as employment secretary (1981-3) and industry secretary (1983-5). He was a leading member of the NEW RIGHT that flourished during Margaret Thatcher's leadership. Tebbit was injured, and his wife crippled, in the IRA bombing of the 1984 Conservative Party conference in Brighton, but he became the party's chairman the following year and helped to mastermind its 1987 election victory.

In 1981, in response to claims of a link between high unemployment and riots, Tebbit retorted in a typically direct and abrasive manner: 'My father did not riot. He got on his bike and looked for work.'

Thatcher, Margaret (Baroness Thatcher of Kesteven) (1925-) British Conservative prime minister from 1979 to 1990. She became Conservative leader in 1975 and led the party to three election victories, in 1979, 1983 and 1987, carrying through many radical reforms. Thatcher curbed trade union power, reduced income taxes, restricted the powers of local government, encouraged private enterprise and returned several nationalised industries to private ownership, thereby increasing the number of shareholders. Her popularity was increased by Britain's victory in the ▷FALKLANDS WAR of 1982, and by legislation allowing council house tenants to buy their homes. However, Thatcher's authoritarian style and her opposition to any loss of British sovereignty to the European Union brought her into conflict with some of her closest colleagues. These factors, combined with the unpopularity of the ▷POLL TAX, contributed to her downfall in 1990, when Geoffrey HOWE's resignation speech precipitated a party leadership challenge led by Michael Heseltine, but from which John MAJOR emerged as victor. Thatcher was Britain's first woman prime minister, and she became the longest-serving prime minister of the 20th century. She forged close links with several world leaders, in particular Ronald Reagan and Mikhail Gorbachev.

Margaret Thatcher's forthright policies and sometimes confrontational manner earned her the nickname 'the Iron Lady'.

tort Branch of British law covering wrongs, such as libel or negligence, for which one can be sued for damages in a CIVIL COURT.

totalitarianism Form of government in which the state has total control over almost all aspects of society – with the result that citizens have hardly any individual freedom. History's starkest examples of totalitarianism include the USSR in the 1930s under Joseph ▷STALIN's regime.

trade unions Associations first formed by workers in the late 18th century to protect their members from exploitation and improve their pay and working conditions. An important landmark in the development of the movement in Britain was the conviction in 1834 of the ▷TOLPUDDLE MARTYRS. In the 1850s, unions sought to control the supply of labour, and keep wages up, by imposing strict quotas on the intake of new apprentices. A central representative body, the Trades Union Congress (TUC), was founded in 1868, and in 1871 the union movement won full legal recognition. The first successful national union action was the 1889 dock strike. The union

IN AND OUT *Becoming prime minister in 1979, Margaret Thatcher showed herself to be a leader of firm principles: telling the Conservative Party conference in 1980, 'The lady's not for turning.' Her autocratic style alienated former colleagues and, after 11 years, led to a tearful farewell from Downing Street.*

movement contributed to the founding of the Labour Party in 1900, and still retains links with the party. The failure of the ▷GENERAL STRIKE in 1926 was a setback for the trade unions. Militancy grew in the 1950s and 1960s, and during the early 1970s a miners' strike helped to topple Edward Heath from power. Industrial unrest at the end of the decade culminated in the ▷WINTER OF DISCONTENT. In the 1980s Margaret Thatcher attacked union power by tough legislation. Her defeat of the miners in 1985, after a long and bitter strike, demoralised the movement as a whole. This, combined with rising unemployment, contributed to a dramatic fall in union membership, from a peak of more than 12 million in 1980 to fewer than 7.5 million in the early 1990s.

Treasury British government department responsible, in cooperation with the ▷BANK OF ENGLAND, for economic policy. The prime minister is nominally First Lord of the Treasury, but its effective head is the chancellor of the exchequer. The Treasury controls the purse strings of government, and therefore wields great power.

tribunal Public body with the power to decide the outcome of civil conflicts, especially in specialist areas of welfare policy. Tribunals were introduced in the early 20th century to provide a relatively easy way of resolving disputes about such matters as compensation for industrial injuries. They now cover a range of subject areas, including industrial disputes and social security payments. Apart from the chairman, who usually has legal qualifications, a tribunal's other members are often lay rather than professional judges.

Ulster unionist Supporter of the union of Northern Ireland and Great Britain. The Ulster Unionist Party, which for much of the 20th century has been in formal alliance with the Conservative Party, is almost exclusively Protestant. It dominated Northern Irish politics during the province's period of devolved government (1921-72). Its ties with the Conservatives were broken in 1972, when the British prime minister, Edward Heath, suspended the devolved government, imposed direct rule from Westminster and put forward plans for self-government on the basis of power-sharing between Protestants and Catholics. These changes prompted Ian PAISLEY to form a splinter group, the Democratic Unionist Party. In the 1992 general election, the Ulster Unionist Party, led by James Molyneaux, won nine of the 17 Northern Irish seats in the House of Commons; other unionist parties won four.

unilateralism Belief that countries which possess nuclear weapons should abandon them of their own accord – whether or not other countries do the same. In Britain the doctrine is associated with CND (Campaign for Nuclear Disarmament), and it became a part of official Labour Party policy for a period in the 1980s.

United Nations (UN) International organisation founded in 1945 to promote world peace and international justice and security. The UN is governed by a Security Council of 15 members, of which five – the USA, Britain, France, China and Russia – have permanent seats on the council. Permanent members have the power to veto any UN initiative they dislike – a course which is often resorted to by the USA. The UN General Assembly includes representatives from all member states, which number more than 180. The UN has committed troops to peace-keeping operations in such places as Lebanon, Korea, Cyprus, the Congo, Somalia and Bosnia. It also aims to encourage peace by improving, for example, education, health and literacy through the work of subsidiary bodies such as UNESCO (United Nations Educational, Scientific and Cultural Organisation) and WHO (World Health Organisation). Since 1992 the secretary-general of the UN has been Boutros Boutros-Ghali of Egypt.

veto Power to block legislation. In Britain the monarch theoretically has the power of veto by withholding ROYAL ASSENT, but this has not been done since 1707. In the USA the president can veto legislation sent to him from Congress. This power is

FRIEND AND FOE *Defying the anti-Gorbachev plotters, Boris Yeltsin shows his support for a president whom he would later supplant.*

frequently used, especially when the president does not have a majority in Congress. However, a presidential veto may be overturned by a two-thirds majority in each chamber of Congress.

welfare state Social and economic system in which the state takes primary responsibility for the welfare of its citizens, especially the needy. Every welfare state includes some system of social security to provide state pensions, child benefits, health care, unemployment benefit and assistance for the disabled. Britain's social security programme was established by the Labour government of Clement Attlee in 1945, three years after being proposed in the ▷BEVERIDGE REPORT. The NHS (National Health Service) was introduced in 1948 to provide free medical and dental services for everyone. Britain's welfare state is funded by taxation and ▷NATIONAL INSURANCE payments. Its soaring costs have prompted intense scrutiny by Conservative governments since 1979, leading to tighter rules about eligibility for benefits.

whip In the British parliament, a member of a political party responsible for party discipline, especially for ensuring the attendance and supervising the voting behaviour of members in important debates. The government chief whip, who lives at No. 12 Downing Street, works with the opposition chief whip to organise day-to-day parliamentary business in each House. Each week, whips, of whom there are more than 30 in total, send members of their party a schedule of forthcoming debates, underlining each item according to its importance. A 'three-line whip', when an item is underlined three times, indicates the greatest urgency, implying serious consequences for an MP failing to attend.

white paper Document issued by the British government containing proposals for legislation. Although more firmly formulated than a GREEN PAPER, its contents may still be substantially modified after public discussion.

Wilson, Harold (Lord Wilson) (1916-) Labour prime minister from 1964 to 1970 and from 1974 to 1976. During his first period in office Wilson was hampered by serious economic problems, which resulted in a devaluation of the pound and harsh exchange controls. In 1965 he was faced with a unilateral declaration of independence by Rhodesia (Zimbabwe), and in 1967 he opened tough negotiations for British entry to what became the European Union. In 1976 Wilson followed his surprise mid-term resignation with a controversial honours list, which included a peerage for his secretary, Marcia Williams (Lady Falkender). Wilson was a clever politician and a shrewd manager. He coined the phrase 'the pound in your pocket' to help to explain economic policy, acclaimed the 'white heat' of the technological revolution and once said that 'a week is a long time in politics'.

Yeltsin, Boris (1931-) President of Russia from 1990. In the late 1980s, disillusioned by the slowness of Mikhail GORBACHEV's reforms, Yeltsin campaigned for the USSR's speedy transformation into a more liberal country with a capitalist-style economy. He was elected to the newly created national legislature in 1989, and to the Russian parliament in 1990. In 1991 he was elected president of Russia after putting down a coup attempt against Gorbachev. Mounting domestic problems prompted another coup attempt in 1993, which was suppressed only after violent clashes. In December 1993 a referendum on the constitution strengthened Yeltsin's powers.

Zionism Doctrine of Jewish nationalism developed in the late 19th century. The inspiration behind the spread of Zionist ideas and the creation of a mass movement was Theodor Herzl (1860-1904). Zionists encouraged immigration to Palestine as a first step towards a Jewish state. A key turning point was the Balfour declaration of 1917, which expressed British support for a national homeland for the Jews. The massacres of the Nazi ▷HOLOCAUST increased international backing for the creation of such a homeland. In 1948 another key figure in the development of Zionism, David Ben-Gurion, became the first prime minister of an independent Israel.

BUSINESS AND ECONOMICS

For centuries, theories on market forces, inflation and exchange
rates have influenced governments' handling of the economy.
Ordinary people, as well as businesses, make economic decisions
every day when they buy something, or plan their budgets
and investments. In doing so they become increasingly familiar
with terms and practices once understood only by financiers.
Bulls, bears and white knights have lost their mystique.

ADAM SMITH'S
THE WEALTH OF
NATIONS

LLOYD'S OF LONDON

THE NEW YORK STOCK EXCHANGE

KARL MARX

accounts Set of figures, usually produced annually, which reflect a company's financial affairs. Accounts are divided into two parts – a profit and loss account and a balance sheet. They give a picture of the company's trading position, its ASSETS and LIABILITIES and the profit or loss made.

actuary Person employed by an insurance company to assess risks and set the level of premiums, or payments, by those insured. The higher the risk of a claim, the greater the premium charged.

annual general meeting (AGM) Meeting which must be held each year by every company for the shareholders to receive and approve the ANNUAL REPORT and ACCOUNTS submitted by the directors.

annual percentage rate (APR) True interest rate of a loan, calculated according to a complicated formula. The APR differs from the flat rate, which is almost always lower because the flat rate excludes management fees and interest on interest. Financial institutions, such as building societies and credit card companies, are obliged to show the APR of their loans.

annual report Document issued by companies which sets out their financial position and reviews their performance over the previous 12 months. Annual reports must contain the company's audited profit and loss accounts and BALANCE SHEET, usually accompanied by a statement from the chairman of the board of directors.

annuity Fixed regular income paid in return for the investment of a lump sum. The payments usually stop when the beneficiary dies, so the income is based on life expectancy. Men normally obtain higher annuity rates than women of the same age, because on average men do not live as long.

arbitrage Attempt to make a profit by buying and selling the same shares or commodities in different markets. For example, if shares of a company are slightly higher on the New York stock exchange than in London, speculators can make a risk-free profit by buying shares in London and immediately selling them in New York. Another form of arbitrage involves buying shares in a company likely to be the object of a TAKEOVER bid, which tends to push up its share prices.
⚓The most notorious recent arbitrageur was the disgraced American businessman Ivan Boesky who made a fortune in this way helped by INSIDER DEALING.

assembly line Line of factory workers and equipment along which a product being assembled passes from operation to operation until completed. The assembly line, together with automation, is the basis of mass production. The principle behind the production line, that manufacturing can be speeded up by being divided into simple operations, was established in the 19th century. Henry FORD developed the moving assembly line in 1913.
⚓In the classic assembly line, the product being manufactured moves on a conveyor belt past teams of workers each of whom performs a single operation. In some new versions of the assembly line system, both product and workers move together through the entire manufacturing process. This combats fatigue and boredom, and is said to produce higher standards and increase productivity.

asset Something of value which can be used to cover a LIABILITY or debt. 'Current assets' include cash or anything that can easily be sold. Buildings or land, which take longer to sell and turn into cash, are known as fixed assets. Assets may also be 'intangible', such as a trade name or GOODWILL.

asset stripping Taking over a company in order to sell off its assets at a profit rather than run it as a going concern. This usually leads to the break-up or closure of the company that has been taken over.

audit Examination by an independent accountant, or auditor, of the ANNUAL REPORT and ACCOUNTS of a company. It is a legal requirement. The auditor's certificate should state that the accounts are a 'true and fair view' of a company's financial position, or 'qualify' them by setting out any serious reservations. Auditors are legally employed by the shareholders, in whose interests they should act.

bad debt Debt which a lender is unable to recover, usually because the debtor is unable to pay. Most companies make provision for bad debts in their accounts.
⚓The biggest ever bad debts were recorded by leading banks in the late 1980s after they lent large sums of money to developing countries such as Mexico and Brazil. These countries proved unable to meet even the interest payments on the loans, let alone repay the debt itself.

balance of payments Difference between the value of what a country buys from abroad and what it sells to overseas countries. If a country exports more than it imports, it is said to have a strong balance of payments or a balance of payments surplus. If it imports more than it exports it is said to have a balance of payments deficit. There are two main elements to a country's balance of payments: 'visible' trade, in goods and raw materials, and 'invisible' trade, in services. For Britain, invisibles such as insurance and interest on foreign loans are very significant: half of all exports and 40 per cent of imports are invisibles.
⚓In 1992/3 Japan had a balance of payments surplus of US$126 billion, equivalent to about US$1000 per head of the Japanese population.

balance sheet Account showing all the ASSETS and LIABILITIES of a company which, as the term implies, must balance.

Bank of England The United Kingdom's CENTRAL BANK. It was founded as a private bank in 1694 to lend money to the government, which was fighting an expensive war against France, and it soon became the government's bank. In 1844 the bank became the only issuer of banknotes in England and Wales; commercial banks still issue notes in Scotland and Northern Ireland. In 1946, the Bank of England was nationalised and brought under closer control by the government. From its offices in Threadneedle Street in London, it acts as banker to other British banks and overall supervisor of the banking system; it also manages the country's MONEY SUPPLY and sets the MINIMUM LENDING RATE, or base rate, for the government.
⚓A sound investment, or secure place, is said to be as 'safe as the Bank of England'.

bankruptcy Formal declaration by a court of a person's inability to pay his debts. A receiver takes over all the assets of the bankrupt and sells them to pay off debts at so much in the pound. For example, if a bankrupt's assets amount to only half what he owes, his debts will be paid off at 50p in the pound. The Inland Revenue is, by law, a preferred creditor, meaning that it must be paid in advance of other creditors. Only people can be declared bankrupt; businesses are said to go into liquidation when they are unable to pay their creditors.
⚓The word 'bankrupt' is derived from *banca rupta*, Latin for 'broken bench' – the symbol of a bankrupt moneylender.

bear Investor who believes that share prices are going to fall and therefore sells in anticipation of being able to buy them back at a lower price. Bears sometimes sell shares they do not own in the hope that they will

STEALING A KISS *James Gillray's cartoon of William Pitt's desperate search for money to fight the Napoleonic Wars gave the Bank of England its nickname of 'The Old Lady of Threadneedle Street'.*

budget Forecast of future income and expenditure. Companies must set out their plans for future operations so that they can assess their cash flow and trading position. Governments, too, provide annual budgets to try to balance their estimated revenue and expenditure. In Britain, a budget is now presented by the chancellor of the exchequer in the House of Commons every autumn, not in the spring.

The chancellor takes his budget proposals to Parliament in a red box first used by William Gladstone in the 1860s.

built-in obsolescence Incorporation into products of features that will make them out of date or useless prematurely, in order to guarantee demand for replacements in the future. Manufacturers of some products, such as small electrical goods, use components which break down or wear out, necessitating the early replacement of the entire unit. New fashions can also make people feel dissatisfied with old models.

bull Investor who expects share prices to rise and therefore buys shares anticipating that he can sell them at a higher price in the future. Bulls may also contract to buy shares at current prices for future delivery, hoping that they will be able to sell them at a profit. A period when share prices generally are rising is known as a 'bull market' – the opposite of a BEAR market.

bullion Gold and silver of great purity, usually sold in bars. Zurich, in Switzerland, is the world's main bullion market.

Bullion becomes more attractive to investors in times of war and instability, because it is a tangible and a relatively inflation-proof form of wealth.

buyers' market Market in which buyers are in a position to bargain prices downwards because supply exceeds demand at current prices. For a buyers' market to emerge, the supply of a product generally has to be inflexible, or 'inelastic'. A buyers' market in baked beans, for example, will not occur because manufacturers can easily cut production to meet reduced demand. There is only a limited supply of housing, however, so a buyers' market can develop if more people wish to sell houses than buy them. (Compare SELLERS' MARKET.)

be able to buy them at a lower price before they have to deliver them to the buyer. A period when share prices are falling is known as a 'bear market'. Its opposite is a BULL market.

The term bear is short for 'bearskin jobber', alluding to their tendency to 'sell the bear's skin before catching the bear'.

big bang Changes in the London stock market introduced on October 27, 1986, by the Financial Services Act. Many traditional practices of the stock market (including dealing on the floor) were abolished overnight, making London a more competitive and responsive market for investors. The thorough nature of the reforms and their expected repercussions were likened to the ▷BIG BANG which was supposed to have given birth to the Universe.

bill of exchange Written order, similar to a cheque, which requires the holder to pay on demand, or in the future, a specified amount to another person. Bills are just a more complicated sort of IOU used to provide credit in trade. The holder of a bill can either redeem it or sell it to someone else at a discount in order to obtain the money ahead of the due payment date.

black economy Business transactions which do not appear in official figures. In order to evade tax, payments for goods or services may be made in cash and not

notified to the authorities. Because of its underground character, it is impossible to estimate the size of the black economy. In Britain, black market transactions often occur in trades where work done for cash does not appear on the company's books. Similarly, workers paid in cash may not declare their full income.

blue chip Stock of a financially sound company with a long history of profit, growth and good management. It is therefore thought to be a low-risk investment. British blue-chip companies include ICI, BP and GEC.

The term 'blue chip' originated from the top-value gambling chip used in poker, which is usually blue.

bond Financial document issued by a corporation or public body at a fixed rate of interest and usually redeemable on a fixed date. Bonds issued by companies can sometimes be converted into EQUITY, or shares, over a certain period.

Bond issues became important during the 1980s, when the JUNK BOND and the eurobond were invented.

OLD BILL *Originally introduced as a means of providing credit, particularly for foreign trade, a bill of exchange is really no more than a sophisticated type of IOU.*

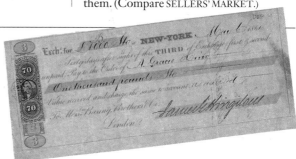

capital Material wealth, including machinery and buildings, owned by companies. The term also refers to the money needed to purchase machinery and premises, and thus any asset or resource.

capital gain Difference between the price paid for an asset such as shares or real estate and the selling price.
🔹In Britain, most capital gains are taxable after certain limits are reached. Capital gains tax applies to property, shares, works of art and other assets, however, the profit on the sale of an individual's principal residence is tax free.

capitalism Political and economic system which allows open competition between companies in a free market. Under capitalism, the means of production and distribution are held by private individuals or corporations rather than by the government on behalf of the people.

cartel Group of producers or suppliers who work together as a monopoly and set volumes and prices to enhance profits.
🔹One example of a cartel is OPEC, which attempts to increase the price of oil by restricting the exports of its members. It successfully quadrupled prices in the 1970s.

caveat emptor Latin for 'let the buyer beware'. In English law, it is the buyer's responsibility to be alert to the possibility that he may be cheated; the seller is not required to point out defects in goods for sale, although it is illegal for him to make false representations about them.

central bank Financial institution which acts as banker for a government, advises on monetary policy and is 'lender of last resort' (the source of all the money lent and borrowed by other financial institutions). Central banks oversee the banking business of a country and often supervise the printing of banknotes. They also sometimes intervene in the currency markets to manipulate exchange rates. Britain's central bank is the BANK OF ENGLAND.

commodity Product, usually in a raw or unprocessed state, such as tin, cocoa, rubber or bananas. Commodities can be traded in many ways, FUTURES and OPTIONS being particularly important. Because transactions in commodities are all on paper, the actual merchandise can be bought and sold many times without it ever moving. Tin in the ground or wheat yet to be sown can be traded in this way.

Common Agricultural Policy (CAP)

System in the ▷EUROPEAN UNION for fixing or guaranteeing the prices for major farm products such as milk, butter, meat and cereals. It has been criticised for keeping agricultural prices high and for creating enormous surpluses (such as the notorious 'butter mountains' and 'wine lakes') which were sold to non-EU countries at prices lower than those paid within the community. These have now been reduced by imposing strict quotas on the amount of any product for which farmers will be paid the agreed price. The Common Fisheries Policy is a parallel system to regulate the amount and type of fishing which can take place in coastal waters of EU countries.

communism Economic and social system in which all the means of production, distribution and exchange are nominally owned by the workers and controlled by the Communist Party and state in their name. A communist system usually has a PLANNED ECONOMY, although countries such as China are now trying to combine Communist Party control with a market economy. (See also ▷COMMUNISM in 'Politics, Government and the Law'.)

consumer credit Money borrowed to finance purchases of consumer goods. It includes credit cards, store cards, bank loans and HIRE PURCHASE. Consumer credit tends to increase when people are optimistic about their financial position, and shrink during recessions.
🔹Consumer credit is tightly regulated by the 1974 Consumer Credit Act, and interest and other charges must be expressed as ANNUAL PERCENTAGE RATES.

credit rating Assessment of an individual's ability to repay a loan. It is based on salary, existing financial commitments and debt record, as well as factors such as age.

credit squeeze Deliberate government attempt to curb purchases of consumer goods on credit in order to reduce the level of economic activity and curb inflation. The most common way of doing this is to raise INTEREST rates.

dawn raid Where a bidder for a company suddenly buys as many shares as possible, often using a third party to conceal the bidder's identity and motive, usually before mounting a full takeover bid.

deflation Fall in prices, almost always related to a decrease in economic activity and consumer spending.
🔹A long period of deflation in Britain from 1925 to 1933 saw prices fall by 20 per cent.

depression Period of drastic decline in the national economy. Business activity plummets, prices fall and the level of unemployment soars.
🔹The most severe such period was the ▷DEPRESSION of the 1930s, although many

APPLE MOUNTAIN *A French farmer throws his harvest onto a huge dump. The Common Agricultural Policy does not allow him to take his produce to market, but he is still paid a guaranteed price.*

people think that the RECESSION of the early 1990s was sufficiently deep and prolonged to be considered a depression.

devaluation Fall in the value of a nation's currency against others. This may be as a result of government policy or market pressures forcing the currency downwards.
♪ The British prime minister Harold Wilson devalued the pound sterling by 14 per cent against the dollar in 1967. The pound was effectively devalued again in 1992, when John Major took Britain out of Europe's EXCHANGE RATE MECHANISM.

developing country Any nation whose industry has grown but which has not yet developed a mature industrialised economic base.

diminishing returns Law of economics first propounded by David RICARDO. It argues that adding one unit of input (such as labour or CAPITAL) to fixed amounts of others will produce successively smaller increases in production.
♪ In common usage, the 'point of diminishing returns' is a supposed point at which additional effort or investment in a given endeavour will not yield a correspondingly improved end result.

disposable income The amount of money available for an individual or population to spend after all taxes and social insurance contributions have been taken from their gross income.

THE HUMAN COST *The Depression of the 1930s brought despair to millions of workers affected by unemployment – from the soup kitchens of America to the streets of Wigan.*

diversification Expansion of a company's products and activities into areas unconnected with its core business. Fund managers diversify their portfolios to spread risk by investing in different shares.
♪ The international company Hanson plc is an example of successful diversification. Its activities range from gold mining and cigarette-rolling, to manufacturing bricks, pans, pumps and vitamin pills.

dividend Payment made to shareholders as their share of company profits. Dividends are usually expressed as a certain number of pence per share.

Dow Jones Index Average selling price of 30 industrial stocks on the New York Stock Exchange on WALL STREET.

dumping Selling goods at a loss in order to eliminate competition or to acquire HARD CURRENCY. The term usually refers to the sale of goods by one country to another country at a large discount in order to open up new markets. The price may often be even lower than that charged in the country of origin.

economics Study of the production, distribution and consumption of goods and services. The word economics stems from a Greek word meaning 'household management'. Economics touches on many disciplines – including mathematics, sociology, psychology, accounting, geography and political theory. The attempt to build economic models is notoriously difficult because predictions of human behaviour *en masse* have proved unreliable, and many economists regard their subject as more of an art than a science.

ECU (European currency unit) Currency used by countries of the ▷EUROPEAN UNION for commercial transactions and BOND issues. It is derived from all the currencies in the EUROPEAN MONETARY SYSTEM, weighted according to the size of their economy. Because of this, it is a more stable currency than those of most member states. Currencies in the European EXCHANGE RATE MECHANISM must maintain parity with the ECU, which is planned to become the basis of a single currency for all EU member countries.

elasticity Extent to which SUPPLY AND DEMAND are affected by the response to changes in price. Demand is said to be elastic when it responds considerably to fluctuations in prices, and inelastic when it responds only slightly or not at all.
♪ Demand for luxury goods is usually more elastic than that for everyday necessities. For products which are marketed on their exclusiveness, however, demand can sometimes actually fall if prices fall.

embargo Governmental restriction on trade, aiming to put pressure on other governments by prohibiting exports to, or imports from, their countries. Embargoes are often ineffective because countries not party to the ▷SANCTIONS will step in to supply the goods, often at inflated prices. On a smaller scale, consumers can also boycott companies to bring pressure on them to change their policies or practices.
♪ An embargo was imposed on Iraq during the ▷GULF WAR of 1990-1. Iraq was unable to sell openly any of its oil abroad, it was also barred from importing any supplies.

embezzlement Theft of money that has been entrusted to one's care.

🔑 One of the worst cases of embezzlement in history was the theft of at least £400 million from the Mirror Group pension fund by the former chairman of the group, Robert ▷MAXWELL.

endowment policy Form of LIFE ASSURANCE which pays out a guaranteed sum either on death or on a fixed date, usually 10 to 30 years after the policy starts.

🔑 In Britain, endowment policies are often used to pay off MORTGAGES. The borrower pays only the interest on the loan, and uses the proceeds of the policy to pay off the principal, or actual loan, when it matures. If an endowment policy performs well, it may be worth more than the mortgage, giving the holder a tax-free lump sum after the mortgage has been paid off.

equity In stock market terminology, the shares of a company. Equity also refers to the financial value of someone's property over and above the amount owed in a MORTGAGE. For example, if a house is bought for £80,000, of which £10,000 is put down and £70,000 is borrowed, the equity in the house is £10,000. The equity will rise if property prices rise.

🔑 In the UK, a sharp fall in property prices in the early 1990s left many property-owners with 'negative equity' in their homes. The result was that many home-owners could not afford to sell their homes.

eurocurrency Money belonging to a bank, corporation or country on deposit in Europe but outside its country of origin. US dollars held by a London bank ('eurodollars') or French francs held by a German bank are both eurocurrencies. Because this money is 'stateless', it is subject to fewer regulations than domestic currencies. The eurocurrency market is an important source of international capital.

European currency unit See ECU.

European Monetary System (EMS) Financial system set up by the ▷EUROPEAN UNION in 1979 to limit fluctuations in the exchange rates of European currencies. Its main elements are the ECU, or European Currency Unit, and the EXCHANGE RATE MECHANISM (ERM).

European Monetary Union (EMU) Long-term aim of the ▷EUROPEAN UNION's financial policy, as set out in the Treaty of ▷MAASTRICHT, to replace all EU currencies with a single one – the ECU.

SMILING CROOK *After British press baron Robert Maxwell was found drowned in the Atlantic, investigators discovered he had embezzled money on a massive scale.*

exchange rate mechanism (ERM) Key element of the EUROPEAN MONETARY SYSTEM, intended to manage exchange rates within the European Union. Countries in the ERM must conduct their monetary policy to maintain the value of their currencies within certain bands compared with other European currencies and the ECU. Britain joined the ERM in 1990, but was forced to leave in 1992 after speculators put immense pressure on sterling and other currencies. To stop the ERM collapsing entirely, its bands were made much wider.

excise Duty levied on domestic goods. Alcohol, petrol and tobacco are the main sources of excise duty in Britain.

🔑 Businesses can delay paying excise by keeping goods in bonded storage. They only have to pay the duty when they take their goods out of bond.

extraordinary general meeting Special meeting of shareholders of a company. It may be called by the directors to approve a course of action, or by the shareholders to protest against decisions made by the board.

Federal Reserve System The central banking authority of the United States, commonly called 'The Fed'. It has more independence from central government than the BANK OF ENGLAND. The Federal Reserve has a seven-member board of governors appointed by the US president, and it exercises broad supervisory authority over 12 regional reserve banks, one of which (New York) is responsible for all foreign exchange dealings.

FIMBRA (Financial Intermediaries, Managers and Brokers Regulatory Association) Self-regulatory body set up

in Britain in 1986 to supervise the conduct and performance of all financial service providers. FIMBRA tries to ensure that they are solvent, honest and give the best possible advice.

financial year Any period of 12 months on which company accounts are based. The financial year should not be confused with the fiscal year, which is the accounting period used by governments for rates of tax and other matters, as set out in the annual BUDGET – although the two often cover the same dates.

🔑 In the United States, companies call their financial year a fiscal year.

fiscal policy A government's plans to control its own expenditure and taxation, which together make up the BUDGET. Another function of fiscal policy, together with monetary policy, is to regulate the level of economic activity and the BALANCE OF PAYMENTS.

Ford, Henry (1863-1947) American industrialist who revolutionised industrial mass production by introducing the first really successful moving ASSEMBLY LINE. He formed the Ford Motor Company in 1903, and in 1908 produced the Model T – the first affordable car for the mass market. 'They can have any colour as long as it's black', he said of his cheap car. By the time production ceased in 1927, more than 15 million Model Ts had been sold.

foreign exchange Global trading of currencies. Exchange rates vary according to the economic standing of the countries concerned; they are most directly affected by a change in interest rates.

franchise Licence to manufacture or market a product with an established trade name, according to an agreed format. The franchisor provides the product or raw material, sales techniques and other kinds of managerial assistance, in exchange for a fee and the loyalty of the franchisee.

🔑 The Body Shop and McDonald's are examples of franchises operating in Britain.

free enterprise Freedom of private businesses to operate competitively with the minimum of legal restrictions and government involvement. LAISSEZ-FAIRE is the principle underlying free enterprise.

Friedman, Milton (1912-) American economist who has championed FREE ENTERPRISE. His major popular work is *Capitalism & Freedom* (1962), in which he argues that welfare services discourage individual effort, and stresses the importance of keeping the money supply and inflation under tight control. He won the Nobel prize for economics in 1976.

🔔 Friedman's brand of MONETARISM was adopted with enthusiasm by Margaret Thatcher and Ronald Reagan in the 1980s.

FTSE-100 Index Listing of London STOCK EXCHANGE prices, published by the *Financial Times* newspaper. It charts movements in share prices of the stock exchange's 100 largest companies.

🔔 FTSE stands for Financial Times Stock Exchange, but in the City it is usually referred to as the 'footsie'.

futures Contract to deliver COMMODITIES or SECURITIES at a certain price on a fixed date in the future. The futures market enables companies to control their costs by HEDGING against possible price changes in the future. By buying copper futures, for example, a company knows some of the costs involved in future production because they have already been incurred – even though it may not need the copper for 18 months. Most contracts for future delivery, however, are traded by speculators who have no intention of buying the actual goods. If they expect prices to rise, they buy a futures contract in the hope of selling it on for a higher price and making a profit. If they expect prices to fall, they sell a contract to make a profit by buying back when prices fall. In this way, large supermarket chains now buy (and possibly sell) many foods before they have even been grown.

G7 Group of seven leading industrialised nations – the United States, Japan, Germany, France, Britain, Italy and Canada – which meets regularly to discuss world economic strategy.

Galbraith, John Kenneth (1908-) Canadian-born American economist who advocates strong intervention by governments to promote economic growth. In books such as *The Affluent Society* and *The New Industrial State*, Galbraith criticised American economic policies which, he argued, concentrated on individual competition and production to the alleged detriment of social services and public amenities. The result was private sector affluence amid increasing public squalor.

MOTOR MAN *Henry Ford (below) shows off one of his earliest models, made in a small workshop. His moving assembly line, devised for the Model T in 1913, was adapted and improved for the Ford Hudson (bottom) in the 1920s.*

Galbraith urged governments to intervene in the economy to counterbalance overpowerful corporations and trade unions. His views became unfashionable during the 1980s, but found more favour in the 1990s.

GATT (General Agreement on Tariffs and Trade) International body which aims to boost world trade by reducing trade barriers. GATT was set up by international treaty in 1947, and its member states, who account for more than 80 per cent of world trade, conduct tariff negotiations through a series of 'rounds'. The 'Uruguay Round' of 1986-93 became bogged down in arguments over the European Union's protectionist policies, especially the COMMON AGRICULTURAL POLICY. The participants finally agreed to implement progressive cuts in import tariffs and farm subsidies.

🔔 Frustration at the slow pace of negotiations gave GATT the nickname of 'General Agreement to Talk and Talk'.

Getty, Jean Paul (1892-1976) American oil magnate who was dubbed the 'richest man in the world'. Getty, the son of an oil millionaire, accumulated a fortune of US $4 billion in the Oklahoma oil fields. He moved to Britain in the 1940s. He was renowned for his complex marital life (he was married and divorced five times) and for his miserliness: he even installed a payphone for guests at his Surrey mansion.

🔔 Getty's great legacy is the Getty Museum in California, a vast collection of art treasures housed in a reconstruction of a Roman villa. The museum is the wealthiest buyer of art in the world.

🔔 Getty's teenage grandson, John Paul Getty III, was kidnapped by Italian bandits in 1973. He was released only after the kidnappers posted his severed ear to an Italian newspaper.

gilts Special type of SECURITIES issued by the British government in the form of interest-bearing certificates, which provide an important way for the government to borrow money. Gilts pay a guaranteed level of interest, and most must be redeemed, or cashed in, at a specified date.

🔔 Gilts got their name because the original certificates had gold borders.

gold standard Monetary system which obliged governments to be able to exchange paper currency for gold on demand. The gold standard was first adopted in the early 19th century by Britain and the USA to correct imbalances in international trade. International debts were always settled in gold, and when a country had a deficit in its BALANCE OF PAYMENTS, more gold had to be paid out for imports than it earned in exports. Gold reserves fell, forcing the authorities to lessen the MONEY SUPPLY to cover the debt. This caused prices to fall (making exports more attractive) and wages to drop (reducing demand for imports), so bringing the economy back into balance – but often at a depressed level of activity. Most currencies, led by sterling, came off the gold standard in the 1930s.

🔔 Today many countries are happy to run long-term balance of payments deficits, which they could not have done in the days of the gold standard.

goodwill Value of a business over and above that of its physical assets. It includes the company's reputation for quality and service, links with clients, suppliers and others and the value of its brand names. It is hard to calculate but can be substantial. For example, when Nestlé took over Rowntrees, the chocolate manufacturer, they appeared to pay considerably more for the goodwill than for the physical assets.

green pound Special exchange rate used to convert prices of farm products in different countries within Europe's COMMON AGRICULTURAL POLICY into sterling.

Gresham's law Principle that bad money will drive good money out of circulation, proposed by Sir Thomas Gresham, one of Queen Elizabeth I's advisers. If the British government minted gold pound coins and later began to mint the coins out of cheaper metals, the public would hoard the gold pounds (possibly for later sale at a higher price) rather than use them as a medium of exchange. Gold pounds would stop circulating, and indeed this is what happened to the gold sovereign, issued until 1931, with a face value of one pound but a market value today of at least £50.

gross domestic product (GDP) Total value of all goods and services produced in a country in a 12-month period.

gross national product (GNP) The sum of GROSS DOMESTIC PRODUCT plus the net income and interest brought in by foreign investments. GNP is an important indicator of a nation's economic health.

hard currency Any freely exchangeable currency of relatively stable value which is widely used in international trade. Where local currencies are weak or prone to fluctuation, traders may prefer to deal in US dollars or German marks. There is always more demand for a hard currency than there is supply, which means its value on the black market tends to be higher than the official exchange rate.

🔔 In weak economies, especially those with high inflation, hard currencies can virtually drive out the national currency, as in parts of the former Soviet Union.

Hearst, William Randolph (1863-1951) American newspaper publisher who built a vast and influential news empire. He was a leading exponent of 'yellow press' sensationalism, and introduced the large 'banner headline' to newspapers.

🔔 Hearst was the model for the megalomaniac newspaper proprietor Charles Foster Kane in the Orson Welles film ▷CITIZEN KANE. His granddaughter Patty Hearst was jailed in 1974 after joining the terrorists who had kidnapped her.

hedging Spreading investments over a variety of shares to cover a possible loss in some. FUTURES and OPTIONS are important methods of hedging on commodity prices, which can fluctuate sharply. A company selling to Germany in Deutsche marks may hedge its anticipated receipts by selling the Deutsche marks in a forward contract for a known value of pounds.

hire purchase Method of buying something with a loan, which is paid off in regular instalments. The repayment usually includes INTEREST on the value of the loan. Although the purchaser takes possession of the product on payment of the first instalment or deposit, he does not legally own it until the final payment is made.

🔔 Hire purchase is sometimes known as 'the never never' because the payments can sometimes seem to go on for ever.

Hughes, Howard (1905-76) American businessman who, at the age of 18, inherited most of the Hughes Tool Company, which sold a unique and highly profitable rock-drilling bit to the oil industry. Later he went into film-making and the aircraft and airline industry, where his interests included Trans World Airlines (TWA), which he sold at a vast profit in 1966. Hughes, a brilliant money-maker, violently anti-communist but at the same time anti-establishment, became increasingly eccentric, and in 1950 he went into almost total seclusion in Las Vegas, and became obsessed with personal hygiene.

🔔 Hughes is remembered for building *Spruce Goose*, an enormous wooden seaplane which flew only once, and for discovering the actress Jane Russell, whom he featured in his film *The Outlaw*.

FLYING FOLLY *Howard Hughes takes the controls of his vast wooden aircraft, the* Spruce Goose. *It flew once – and then only for a mile.*

LOADSAMONEY *In 1923 Germany experienced disastrous inflation and the mark plummeted in value. Banknotes became virtually worthless, forcing some customers to collect their cash from the bank in laundry baskets.*

income distribution Division of income among persons or households. In Britain, the total income before tax of the bottom 20 per cent of income earners is about one-seventh of that of the top 20 per cent. Governments often make the distribution of income more equal by taxing high incomes more than low ones; ▷COMMUNISM tries to achieve equal distribution.

income tax Direct tax imposed on income. A 'progressive' income tax is one in which those with higher incomes pay more tax than those with lower incomes.
⚓In Britain, income tax was first levied from 1799 to 1815 at a basic rate of three pence (1¼p) in the pound, to pay for the Napoleonic Wars. Reimposed in 1842, supposedly as a temporary measure to make up a shortfall in the government's budget, it has never been repealed.
⚓The highest rate of tax in Britain was 98 per cent on unearned income, imposed in 1974 by Harold Wilson's government.

index-linked Term describing savings or investments whose value rises or falls in line with inflation, as measured by the retail price index (RPI). It can also apply to some GILTS, wage settlements or pensions. Index-linking is valuable in times of high inflation, as it safeguards the real value of income or investment.

industrial relations Level of cooperation and communication between management and the unions or individual workers. Bad industrial relations can lead to absenteeism, high staff turnover and strikes, affecting a company's profitability.
⚓During the 1960s and 1970s the British car industry had poor industrial relations and many strikes. As a result, domestic manufacturers were unable to meet demand, and foreign competitors with good industrial relations, such as Japan, were able to take advantage and secure a large share of the domestic market.

inflation General increase in price levels, or fall in the value of money, over a period of time. If goods which cost £100 a year ago now cost £110, the rate of inflation is 10 per cent. High inflation reduces the value of people's savings and damages the economy by pushing up the price of exports which can lead to a BALANCE OF PAYMENTS crisis. Governments try to control inflation by restricting wage increases and by regulating the MONEY SUPPLY. In the wake of the 1973 oil crisis, Britain's annual inflation rate reached 26.9 per cent in 1975. Countries such as Argentina and Russia have experienced hyperinflation of 1000 per cent.
⚓In Britain, the government now uses two measures of inflation: headline inflation, which includes housing costs, and the underlying rate, which excludes them.
⚓Inflation can enter a self-sustaining spiral, when price rises fuel wage demands, which in turn bring a further increase in prices.

infrastructure Entire system of roads, railways, airports and ports, as well as energy supplies and all communications, which underpins the efficient functioning of a country and its economy.

insider dealing Use of information not available to most shareholders or the general public to make profits in share and commodity markets. Insider dealing is usually illegal, except in Japan and Germany. Defenders of the practice claim that it makes the market more active and efficient, and hurts no one. However, it can give some traders an unfair advantage. An unexplained increase in activity in a share ahead of a profits announcement, a takeover bid or a restructuring of a company is often a sign of insider trading.

insolvency Inability to pay one's debts when they become due. Insolvency occurs when a company does not have enough ASSETS or profits to cover its total LIABILITIES. Insolvent companies are banned from trading, in order to protect customers who could lose their money if the company went into liquidation.

institutional investors Groups such as insurance companies, pension funds, banks and investment or UNIT TRUSTS, which use their funds to buy shares and other securities. These investors now dominate the stock markets.

insurance Method of protecting oneself against risks by paying a premium to an insurer, who undertakes to indemnify the insured against a specified loss or course of events. The most common forms of insurance are against accidental death or ill health, or against loss, damage or destruction of property by theft, fire or accident. LLOYD'S OF LONDON is the world's most important insurance market.
⚓Almost any risk can be insured against. Dancers and athletes can insure their legs and musicians can insure their hands against damage or loss. An American radio station even took the precaution of taking out insurance against having to pay out a $1 million prize it offered to anyone finding the late Elvis Presley alive.

interest Payment made for the use of borrowed funds. There are two types of interest: simple or compound, the latter meaning that interest is calculated not only on the principal amount of the loan, but also on any outstanding interest. Interest may be paid at different intervals, so rates are quoted on a standard basis called the ANNUAL PERCENTAGE RATE.

internal market Arrangements within a large organisation intended to mimic competitive markets. Departments compete against each other and bill each other for services as if they were independent bodies. Some people believe that internal markets bring greater efficiency to organisations. Recently this idea has been introduced within the public sector in Britain – for example in the National Health Service.

International Development Association (IDA) Body set up in 1960 under the auspices of the ▷UNITED NATIONS to help developing countries by providing them with interest-free loans.

International Monetary Fund (IMF) Arm of the WORLD BANK set up in 1944 to promote international monetary co-operation and to expand world trade. It also lends money to countries with short-term BALANCE OF PAYMENTS difficulties.
🕯The IMF can attach conditions to its loans, as it did in 1976, when it insisted that the British government carry out spending cuts in return for a £1000 million loan. Its occasional insistence that countries carry out social and political reforms in return for help with debt has been controversial.

interventionism Government action to moderate the effects of the free market. Enterprise zones – districts where special grants are available to encourage business growth – and the Monopolies Commission, which can take action against the abuse of market power by large companies, are examples of government intervention. Economists, like governments, disagree on how much intervention is desirable.

investment trust Company listed on the STOCK EXCHANGE whose business is to invest in the shares of other companies. The value of investment trust shares is often below the value of the shares they own.

invisibles Imports and exports which are not physical goods. For Britain, invisibles in the form of earnings from foreign investments and from the supply of services are vital in redressing a deficit in the country's physical balance of trade.
🕯The banking and insurance services of the City of London are Britain's most important source of invisible earnings.

jobber Formerly a middleman who acted for stockbrokers buying and selling shares at the London Stock Exchange. Brokers who wished to buy shares approached a jobber, instead of going direct to another stockbroker who had shares to sell. The jobbing system was abolished during the City's BIG BANG; now investors buy directly through MARKET MAKERS.

junk bond Specialised type of BOND issued by companies in order to raise capital. They are issued in huge numbers, and give holders a very high rate of interest to compensate for the low credit rating of the issuer, which entails a high risk of total loss. Junk bonds were used to finance a number of TAKEOVER bids in the late 1980s, especially in the United States.

Keynes, John Maynard (1883-1946) British economist whose ideas dominated economic policy from the 1930s to the 1960s. His *General Theory of Employment, Interest and Money* (1936) revolutionised economic thought by suggesting that national economies need not aim to balance their budgets. KEYNESIAN ECONOMICS seeks to establish a mix of CAPITALISM and INTERVENTIONISM. It led to MONETARISM and remains influential. In 1944, Keynes played a major part in the ▷BRETTON WOODS CONFERENCE.

Keynesian economics Branch of economics associated with the theories of John Maynard KEYNES. Keynesian economists reject the theory that the free market will provide employment for everyone, and instead advocate tax cuts and government spending on public works in times of recession to fuel demand and create jobs. In order to do this, it may be necessary to run a budget deficit. When the economy booms, on the other hand, Keynesians believe that governments should raise taxes or cut spending in order to dampen down demand, and use any budget surplus to pay off their borrowings. This 'stop-start' policy has been criticised for exaggerating the cycles of economic booms and slumps.

labour Human resources used in the production process. According to the 'labour theory of value', the value of an item is determined by the amount of labour used to produce it.
🕯Mobility of labour – the ability of workers to move from one job to another in a different area or to a different occupation – is very important in a dynamic economy.

laissez-faire French phrase meaning 'allow (people) to do (as they choose)'. *Laissez-faire* economics advocates the minimum regulation or interference in the economy, so the FREE ENTERPRISE system can operate according to its own laws.

'lame duck' Company or industry which can only survive with the help of large injections of public funds.
🕯The nationalised British steel industry

was a notorious 'lame duck' in the 1970s. It has since become profitable as a private company. In the 1990s, a fall in the demand for coal led to the closure of most of Britain's collieries, because the government was unwilling to subsidise what it regarded as another 'lame duck' industry.

less developed country (LDC) Any nation with a small or non-existent industrial base. Countries with a small gross national product per capita, which usually make most of their money by selling commodities, are classified as 'less developed': they used to be called 'Third World countries'. Less developed countries often have high rates of infant mortality, short life expectancy and low levels of literacy.
🕯Many countries in sub-Saharan Africa, such as Burkina Faso and Chad, are categorised as less developed.

liability An obligation or debt. On a company's balance sheet, liabilities should be offset by ASSETS.

life assurance Insurance policy covering individuals, families and business partners against death. It is called assurance, not insurance, because the event will definitely happen sooner or later: the element of risk lies only in the timing of death. The policy provides a lump sum when it matures or when the assured person dies.
🕯Building societies usually require mortgagees to have life assurance, to guarantee payment of a loan should the mortgagee die before it has been fully repaid.

limited company Business in which each shareholder's personal liability for the company's debts is limited to the amount he has paid for his shares. Should the company go into liquidation, the shareholders lose their money but cannot be called on to meet its debts. Without the principle of limited liability, the development of the large joint stock company – the bedrock of the modern economic system – would not have been possible, because shareholders would have been exposed to excessive risks.
🕯Privately owned limited companies can add the abbreviation 'Ltd' after their name. Their publicly owned counterparts, whose shares are traded on the STOCK EXCHANGE, are known as 'Public Limited Companies', identified by the initials 'plc' after their name.

liquid asset An asset which can quickly be converted into money. Cash itself is a completely liquid asset, and finished goods are nearly as liquid – provided that a market an be found for them. Buildings, machinery and land are fixed, not liquid, assets because they could take years to sell.

liquidity The amount of cash available for the day-to-day running of a business. Liquid companies have enough money on hand to meet their financial obligations without having to sell fixed ASSETS.

Lloyd's of London World's most important INSURANCE market. Lloyd's does not transact business itself, but provides the facilities for independent underwriters, or 'names', to do so. Underwriters work in syndicates to spread the risk, but face unlimited liability in case of loss. Lloyd's evolved from informal meetings of merchants at Edward Lloyd's coffee-house in the City of London, first held in the late 17th century. There, traders who dealt in cargo would find other businessmen who would agree to pay for losses in return for a small premium.

In the 1990s, Lloyd's faced a crisis after risks had been badly underestimated. In 1994 losses declared over the previous four

OLD AND NEW *The Lloyd's building is a high-tech masterpiece, but the 18th-century Lutine Bell remains at its centre, and entries in the 'loss book' are still written with a goose quill.*

to five years were over £8 billion. Lloyd's offered a compensation package worth some £900 million to the thousands of 'names' who had suffered huge losses. The offer was rejected and Lloyd's now faces lengthy litigation.

Lloyd's produces a *Register of Shipping* which inspects ocean-going ships and classifies them according to the degree of risk they represent to insurers. A ship which is 'A1 at Lloyd's' is well maintained and run, presenting the minimum risk to insurers.

The Lutine Bell, taken from HMS *Lutine*, which sank in 1799 with a still unrecovered cargo of gold, hangs in the underwriting room at Lloyd's and used to be rung for important announcements: once for bad news, twice for good.

loss leader Product sold at or below cost price in order to entice customers into buying other items. It is common practice in supermarkets, where very competitive prices for basic foodstuffs such as milk and bread are used to attract customers.

macro-economics Study of the broad economic picture, involving the analysis of national income and expenditure, money supply, balance of payments and how they interrelate. (Compare MICRO-ECONOMICS.)

Malthus, Thomas (1766-1834) British economist who was one of the first people to warn of the dangers of over-population. Malthus's often pessimistic theories hold that populations tend to grow faster than food production, and that therefore much of the world's population will always go hungry: eventually, over-population will be checked by famine, disease or war.

market economy System in which most economic activity is controlled by individuals and private companies rather than by the government.

market maker Dealer in the London STOCK EXCHANGE who buys and sells shares on his own account in order to sell them to stockbrokers or private clients. Market makers are registered to deal in the shares of specific companies. Their bid and offer prices are displayed on dealing room screens all round the world.

market research Investigation of the needs and preferences of a particular group or market, usually by means of consumer surveys. It enables companies to estimate the strength of demand for a product before they have gone to the expense of actually producing and distributing it.

REVOLUTIONARY ECONOMIST *Karl Marx's ideas led to communist revolutions around the world, but they have yet to create the ideal and classless societies of which he dreamed.*

Marks, Simon (1888-1964) Founder of the Marks & Spencer retailing group. Marks's father Michael was a Russian immigrant who teamed up with Thomas Spencer in 1894 to run a market stall in Leeds which bore the slogan 'Don't ask the price – it's a penny'. Simon Marks worked with his brother-in-law Israel Sieff to build on these foundations. They began trading directly with manufacturers, and imposing high standards of production. They launched the St Michael trademark in 1928. Today there are around 600 Marks & Spencer stores worldwide, with an annual turnover of about £6000 million.

Marx, Karl (1818-83) German political and economic theorist whose ideas were the basis of ▷MARXISM, the theory that underlies COMMUNISM. He believed history was shaped by economic contradictions that caused economic and social systems to collapse, and that CAPITALISM was inherently flawed. According to Marx, the industrialised world was dominated by a struggle between the suppressed working class, or proletariat, and the capitalist bourgeoisie. The struggle would culminate in revolution and a temporary dictatorship of the proletariat, which would bring about an end to exploitation and create a classless, utopian society in which the state would wither away and the people would collectively own and control the means of production. Marx's theories of revolution were applied in Russia by Lenin and his successors after the 1917 Russian Revolution. Following initial success in industrial development and during World War II, the Marxist governments of Russia and eastern Europe collapsed in the 1980s. Communist systems still exist in China, North Korea, Vietnam and Cuba. (See also ▷MARX in 'Ideas, Beliefs and Religion'.)

♘Marx did much of his studying in the reading room at the British Museum. He is buried at Highgate cemetery in London.

Maxwell, Robert (1923-91) (Real name Ludwig Hoch) Czech-born media baron who, after escaping to England from German-occupied Czechoslovakia in 1940, founded the Pergamon Press. Maxwell served as Labour MP for Buckingham (1964-70). In 1984 he bought Mirror Group Newspapers, taking control of the English *Daily Mirror*, *Sunday Mirror* and *The People*, and the Scottish *Daily Record* and *Sunday Mail*. It was not until after he apparently committed suicide by jumping off his yacht that auditors uncovered debts of more than £1 billion. It emerged that Maxwell had tried to clear part of the debt by siphoning at least £400 million from his employees' pension funds.

mercantilism Economic doctrine that flourished in Europe from the 16th to the 18th centuries. Mercantilists believed that a nation's wealth and ability to conduct war depended largely on the amount of gold and silver in its treasury. Accordingly, mercantilist governments imposed extensive economic restrictions in order to ensure a surplus of exports over imports.

♘The European quest for gold-yielding colonies in Asia, Africa and America was in part a product of mercantile economics.

micro-economics Study of economics at the level of individuals and households, companies and specific industries. It mainly examines consumer and producer behaviour, including the psychology of economic decisions. Micro-economics seeks, for example, to explain why people buy expensive cars but not why exports rise and fall – an area of MACRO-ECONOMICS.

minimum lending rate Rate of INTEREST at which the Bank of England lends money to Britain's other financial institutions, it used to be called the Bank Rate. Commercial banks base their interest rates for loans on the minimum lending rate, but generally charge more because there is a risk that a loan will not be repaid, and also because they want to make a profit.

♘Changes in the minimum lending rate can have a profound effect on the economy. If the rate goes up, borrowing becomes more expensive and investment in industry suffers. If the rate goes down, foreign investors may take their money to other countries where they can get a better return on it, which affects the BALANCE OF PAYMENTS and the value of sterling.

mixed economy Most developed countries have mixed economies: economies that contain both private and state-owned businesses, and combine FREE ENTERPRISE with some degree of state control.

♘Since the 1970s, there has been a steady worldwide swing towards PRIVATISATION and away from government intervention and ownership of industry.

monetarism Doctrine which asserts that the control of the MONEY SUPPLY should be the foremost instrument by which governments regulate the economy. Monetarists such as Milton FRIEDMAN claim that inflation can be controlled by limiting growth in the money supply rather than by taxation or artificial controls on prices, incomes or the availability of credit.

♘During the 1980s many governments embraced monetarism; however, by the 1990s many of their successors opted for a more flexible policy, varying taxation and government expenditure, in addition to controlling money supply.

money laundering The process by which money obtained through criminal activity or as a result of tax evasion is converted into untraceable bank balances. Trying to trace Robert MAXWELL's missing millions through a web of foreign bank accounts was an immense task.

money supply Amount of money in circulation in a country at any given time, usually controlled by the country's CENTRAL BANK. Because the supply of money affects price levels, controlling it is an important tool in restricting INFLATION.

♘The widespread use of credit cards as an alternative to cash has made it more difficult to measure the money supply.

monopoly Exclusive control of a product or service. By restricting output, the monopolist can raise prices and profits. A firm that has a substantial market share can also influence prices. Some control over monopoly is exerted in Britain by the Monopolies and Mergers Commission, which can block mergers or acquisitions that might create over-powerful companies.

♘Several of Britain's privatised industries, including British Gas and the water companies, are NATURAL MONOPOLIES, with no prospect of any genuine competition for the foreseeable future.

mortgage Long-term loan usually used to finance the purchase of property. The lender owns the property, which acts as security for the loan, but the borrower has secure possession of it. Interest rates on mortgages are lower than on many other types of loan, because the property is usually good security against the sum borrowed.

♘There are two main types of mortgage. With an endowment mortgage, borrowers only pay off the interest on the loan, relying on an assurance policy to eventually pay off the debt. With a repayment mortgage, the borrower pays off both the interest and debt directly.

multinational Industrial or commercial enterprise which operates in several countries. Multinationals can take advantage of cheap labour or raw material costs in different countries, and can avoid import duties by producing goods in the country in which they are to be sold. It is sometimes claimed, however, that they use their international presence to bypass legal restrictions. Some multinationals are wealthier and more powerful than many nations.

♘Unilever, Royal Dutch/Shell and Nestlé are among Europe's leading multinational companies. Other well-known multinationals include Ford, Sony, Toyota and Exxon (Esso).

Murdoch, Rupert (1931-) Australian-born media tycoon whose company, News Corporation, produces magazines, newspapers, books, feature films and cable television programmes. Murdoch moved to Britain in 1969 and bought *The News of the World*. A year later he bought *The Sun*, which attracted much vilification for its right-wing stance and emphasis on sex. He went on to buy *The Times*, *The Sunday Times* and *Today* as well as several American newspapers. His television and film interests include Sky satellite television, Twentieth Century Fox film studios and six television stations in the USA which form Fox Broadcasting – one of America's major television networks.

national debt Sum owed by the government to its own citizens and to foreign creditors. Governments borrow money by selling SECURITIES, on which interest is paid, in order to cover their budget deficits – the difference between expenditure and the amount raised by taxation. England's national debt dates from 1694, when the government borrowed £1.2 million from the newly formed BANK OF ENGLAND.

national insurance System of compulsory charges on workers and employers designed to pay for Britain's ▷WELFARE STATE benefits such as the National Health Service, unemployment, sick pay and pensions. In practice, in the UK, national insurance has become part of general income taxation, as payments are now graduated according to income level.
♣At the age of 16, every British citizen is given a national insurance number which is used to record national insurance contributions and for payment of state benefits.

nationalisation Takeover by a government of a privately owned business. In Britain, many industries (such as the railways, collieries and electricity supply) were nationalised in the late 1940s. This was for ideological reasons – ▷SOCIALISM prescribes state ownership of certain industries – as well as to achieve economies of scale while preventing the formation of privately owned MONOPOLIES. It also allowed the rescue of essential industries that were close to financial collapse.
♣Nationalised industries have often been criticised for being inefficient, uncompetitive and badly managed.

national savings Government scheme to raise funds by borrowing personal savings. Most countries have some form of national savings, which pay investors interest in the same way as banks or building society accounts. In Britain, PREMIUM BONDS as well as National Savings bonds and certificates are all forms of national savings.

natural monopoly Industry or activity which lends itself automatically to being controlled by a single producer because that producer can operate at lower cost than a number of competing firms. Natural monopolies occur where very large plant is required, such as the expensive generating equipment and enormous network of cables used by electricity companies.

Nikkei Index Main share index of the Tokyo stock exchange. The Nikkei Index charts the share movements of Japan's 300 top-rated companies.

no-claims bonus Reduction in insurance premiums because no claim has been made. The system is well established in motor insurance, where premiums can be reduced by as much as 60 per cent if the driver has not made any claims for several years. It is also becoming common in insurance policies for personal possessions.

OECD (Organisation for Economic Cooperation and Development) International body comprising most of the world's advanced industrialised countries. The OECD, which was formed in 1961, aims to promote economic growth and stability for its members and to help less developed countries to expand.

Office of Fair Trading British government agency which looks at alleged unfairness in corporate and industrial practice. It enforces trading standards and investigates allegations of restrictive trade practices – agreements made between suppliers to exclude competition. The Office of Fair Trading has investigated the ice cream trade, compact disc prices, estate agencies and many other businesses.

oligopoly Any market dominated by a small number of individuals or companies. One example is the oil industry, which has sometimes operated as a CARTEL. Another is soap-powder manufacture in Britain, which is dominated by two companies: most brands of soap powder are attempts by one or other of the companies to create special niches in the market.

Onassis, Aristotle (1906-75) Greek shipping magnate who owned the largest fleet of supertankers in the world. He started his career as a switchboard operator in Buenos Aires, but by the age of 25 he had made his first million in tobacco and in trade deals between Greece and Argentina. He moved into shipping in 1932, when he purchased six vessels. At his death, his assets were estimated at US$500 million.
♣Onassis's flamboyant lifestyle included a liaison with Maria ▷CALLAS and marriage in 1968 to Jackie Kennedy, widow of US president John F. Kennedy.

OPEC (Organisation of Petroleum Exporting Countries) Group of oil-rich countries, mainly in the Middle East, which operates as a CARTEL to control oil production and to secure favourable prices for the member nations.
♣OPEC dramatically raised oil prices in 1973 partly for commercial reasons and partly in order to punish the United States and other Western nations for supporting Israel in the ▷YOM KIPPUR WAR against Egypt. The result was a severe oil shortage and global economic disruption.

option Right to buy or sell a share or a COMMODITY at a specified price at a future date. Options are a sophisticated method of HEDGING against possible price movements: instead of buying the goods, or even a FUTURES contract for delivery at a later date, traders buy a much cheaper 'call' option, to buy, or a 'put' option, to sell, the goods in the future. They will only exercise their option if the price at the time of the transaction makes it worth while.

Parkinson's law Proposition that work expands to fill the time available for its completion. It was put forward in 1955 by the British economist C. Northcote Parkinson as a partly satirical attack on civil servants: he believed that they expanded their work unnecessarily, increasing their numbers and the amount of bureaucratic paperwork at the expense of the taxpayer.

pension fund Money accumulated from the pension contributions of companies and individuals, invested to provide pensions for retired workers.
♣Pension funds invest heavily in the stock market and in property, and their managers can exert considerable influence on the money markets.

PEP (personal equity plan) British savings scheme intended to encourage the spread of share ownership. Under the scheme, small investors can invest a limited amount in the stock market, generally through a registered fund manager, and enjoy tax-free dividends and capital gains.

perfect competition Theoretical economic scenario in which there are so many producers and consumers in a market that no individual trader is large enough to affect the price. Although in reality there is no such thing as perfect competition, the market for some commodities such as wheat or tin comes close.

petrodollars US dollars earned by oil-producing countries from their exports, which are held in banks or other institutions outside those countries.
♣In the 1970s, Arab countries accumulated enormous reserves of petrodollars, which at times threatened the stability of exchange rates throughout the world as they were continually moved from country to country in search of higher interest rates.

planned economy System in which prices, wages and production levels are set by a central authority, usually the government, as part of its political programme.

The former Soviet Union and other communist countries had planned economies, but most countries have now adopted at least some degree of free enterprise.

poverty level Income below which it is deemed impossible to achieve an adequate standard of living. It fluctuates with the cost of living and with inflation.
🔸Definitions of poverty are always somewhat artificial, and may be manipulated by governments and others for political ends.

premium bond British government BOND launched in 1956, in which the interest payments, instead of being paid out directly, are used to provide prizes for a lottery in which each bond has an equal chance of winning. Cash prizes are now worth a total of £11 million a month. The largest single prize is now £1 million.

price control Government attempt to control INFLATION by stopping consumer and industrial prices rising. It is only useful as a short-term measure. Price control is often introduced as part of a general prices and incomes policy – an attempt to curb inflation by allowing incomes to rise only in line with prices.

price-earnings ratio (PE ratio) Figure relating the market value of a share to historic or prospective company profits. It is calculated by dividing the company's profit by the number of shares to give earnings per share. The current price of the share is then divided by its earnings. If a company has 1 million shares and makes a profit of £100,000, the earnings are 10p a share. If the price of the shares is £1, the PE ratio is 10; if the price is £2, the ratio is 20. Investors use PE ratios to decide whether the shares of a company are expensive or cheap compared with those of similar companies. The higher the PE ratio, the faster, generally, investors and City analysts expect profits to grow.

primary sector Section of the economy that produces and processes raw materials, fuel and foodstuffs, as opposed to manufactured goods (in the SECONDARY SECTOR) or services (in the tertiary sector).
🔸Many primary goods are produced in developing countries, and their prices fluctuate with the level of demand from the industrialised world. In recent years, prices for raw materials such as copper and iron ore and other commodities such as cocoa and cotton have been depressed, which has held back economic growth in the developing countries which produce them.

MAC'S LITTLE FLUTTER *Harold Macmillan, who introduced premium bonds, chalks up a 1960 winning number chosen by 'ERNIE' – Electronic Random Number Indicator Equipment.*

private sector Part of the economy which is not owned or controlled by the government. In the majority of developed countries, most economic activity is in private hands. The trend towards PRIVATISATION during the 1980s and 1990s has enlarged the private sector in Britain.

privatisation Sale of government-owned corporations and industries to private investors; the opposite of NATIONALISATION. In Britain in the 1980s, Margaret Thatcher's government started a massive privatisation programme, selling publicly owned companies such as British Gas, British Airways, British Telecom and Rolls Royce to the PRIVATE SECTOR.
🔸Although privatisation has made industry more efficient, its critics say that it has placed NATURAL MONOPOLIES in the hands of profiteering private managers, and that it can lead to the loss of valuable but uneconomic essential services, such as water supply to remote areas or off-peak and rural train services. It has also been argued that the profits made by these public services, or utilities, should go to the state for the benefit of all citizens, instead of being distributed among a relatively small number of investors.

profit A company's profit margin is the amount by which its sales revenue exceeds the cost of producing and distributing its goods or services. Profits can be retained, and ploughed back into the company, or, alternatively, distributed among its shareholders, and sometimes its staff.

🔸The 'profit motive' – the urge to earn money by selling goods or services – is said to drive the FREE ENTERPRISE system.

protectionism Raising the price of imports by imposing duties and QUOTAS, in order to protect domestic industries from foreign competition. Other schemes, such as the stringent imposition of safety regulations, are also sometimes used to make importing difficult. Governments can also subsidise domestic industry to make its goods cheaper than foreign imports.
🔸Europe's COMMON AGRICULTURAL POLICY is a form of protectionism, often criticised as unfair to food producers outside Europe, while the rice markets of Japan and South Korea are completely closed to foreign growers.

public expenditure Spending by the government and the public sector. Increasing public spending may create jobs and reduce unemployment, but may also fuel INFLATION by increasing demand and inflating the MONEY SUPPLY.
🔸In many Western countries, the rise in public spending since World War II has caused concern, and governments are looking at ways of curbing it.

public goods Products or services whose consumption by one person does not preclude consumption by another – for example, street lighting, the police force, or defence services. Such goods produce social benefits which are not easy to assess in terms of simple profit and loss, and are usually paid for or subsidised by governments. If matters are left to the free market, public goods may be inadequately supplied, particularly if it is difficult for private suppliers to charge consumers for them.

public sector borrowing requirement (PSBR) Amount of money a government needs to borrow in a given year. The PSBR is equivalent to the difference between the government's income and expenditure. It is mostly funded through the sale of GILTS and to a lesser degree by NATIONAL SAVINGS. The accumulated PSBRs of the past make up the NATIONAL DEBT.

quota Limit imposed by governments on imports, or by business CARTELS on production. Import quotas aim to protect home industry from foreign competition, while production quotas aim to keep prices high. To prevent over-production of foodstuffs, the European Union's COMMON AGRICULTURAL POLICY now imposes strict quotas on farmers, limiting the amount of crops they can sell for a guaranteed price.

real cost Term which can have two meanings in economics. Sometimes it is used to describe the 'opportunity cost' of something – the value of the resources used to produce a good, plus the cost of foregoing some alternative course of action. It can also mean the price of a product adjusted for INFLATION: the real cost of a chocolate bar costing 28p in 1993 was less than the same brand of bar bought in 1973 for 8p, because prices in general had risen by over 400 per cent in the meantime.

real income Income measured in terms of what it will buy. If incomes rise more quickly than prices, real incomes increase.

receiver Person appointed by a court to manage the BANKRUPTCY of an individual, or the winding-up of a company. The task of a receiver is to collect from debtors and pay off creditors.

recession Fall in economic activity characterised by declining demand, lower production and rises in unemployment. A country is said to be in recession when its GROSS DOMESTIC PRODUCT has shrunk for nine consecutive months. Deep and prolonged recessions become DEPRESSIONS.

reflation Increase in economic activity, fuelled by a general increase in demand which may be spontaneous, or brought about by government action such as cutting

taxes or investing in large-scale public works. Governments are cautious about deliberately reflating their economies, because it can lead to INFLATION.

resale price maintenance Practice by which a producer fixes the price at which retailers can sell its product. The retailer can obtain the product only if he guarantees to sell it at a certain price. Once common in Britain, resale price maintenance is now illegal except in the case of books, newspapers, magazines and pharmaceuticals. Manufacturers of other goods, however, often suggest a price for their goods – the 'recommended retail price' or RRP.

rescheduling Change in the original terms for repayment of a loan when the borrower has run into repayment difficulties. Banks may agree to accept smaller repayments spread over a longer period.
⚓ In the 1980s, banks agreed a series of debt reschedulings for various countries in Latin America and sub-Saharan Africa; devaluations of local currencies and falls in commodity prices had left them unable to pay even the interest on their debts, let alone repay the loans themselves.

reserves Currencies and gold held by a country's CENTRAL BANK in order to provide backing to national currencies and to finance international trade. Reserves are kept in stable and easily exchangeable currencies such as US dollars, Deutsche marks and yen. In a company's accounts, reserves comprise profits and other funds held back by a company for further development and not distributed as dividends.
⚓ In 1992, the Bank of England used billions of pounds from its reserves to bolster the value of the pound in a vain attempt to keep it within the fixed bands of the EXCHANGE RATE MECHANISM.

reverse takeover Process by which a large company takes over a smaller one, but in effect the smaller gains control of the larger, perhaps supplying new management. Companies can use reverse takeovers to gain a stock market quotation without having to issue shares or go through the complicated process of meeting the stock exchange's criteria for a quotation.

Ricardo, David (1772-1823) British economist who developed the theory of comparative advantage as an explanation of international trade. This held that countries which are more efficient at producing goods will still trade with those who are less efficient. Efficient countries will export

goods in which their comparative efficiency is high, and import goods where it is low. This became an important argument in support of LAISSEZ-FAIRE economics.
⚓ Ricardo's pessimistic views about overpopulation, diminishing returns and the 'iron law of wages' (that population growth will depress wages by producing an excess supply of labour), along with those of Thomas MALTHUS, led to economics being dubbed the 'dismal science'.

risk Element of chance which all investors must consider when making financial decisions. The higher the perceived risks of an investment, the higher the return is expected to be. Speculators and investors can opt for a safe, but modest return by putting their money into BLUE CHIP companies or building societies. Alternatively, they can invest in a new business venture which has the possibility of much higher returns, but a corresponding high risk of total loss. Investors spread risk by having a balanced portfolio of investments; for example by buying GILTS as well as EQUITIES in many different companies.

Rockefeller, John D. (1839-1937) American industrialist who founded the Standard Oil Company in 1870. By 1880 he controlled virtually the entire oil industry in the United States. Although he had to break up the company in 1892, following anti-monopoly legislation, he continued to dominate the oil industry until his retirement in 1911.
⚓ Rockefeller was at one time the richest man in the world, and he gave more than US$500 million to charity. He funded the Rockefeller Center in New York, and his heirs still own the building.

Rothschild Banking dynasty founded in the 18th century by Meyer Amschel Rothschild in Frankfurt, Germany. He and his sons made much of their wealth by lending money to the warring parties in the Napoleonic Wars. The Rothschilds helped to finance the growth of industry during the Industrial Revolution and continued to dominate European banking until World War II, when the Nazis confiscated many of their assets. Members of the family still own private banks in London and Paris.

RPI (retail price index) Method of measuring changes in the cost of living. Prices of the goods and services on which the vast majority of households spend their money are collected and weighted according to their importance in overall household budgets. An index is then formed

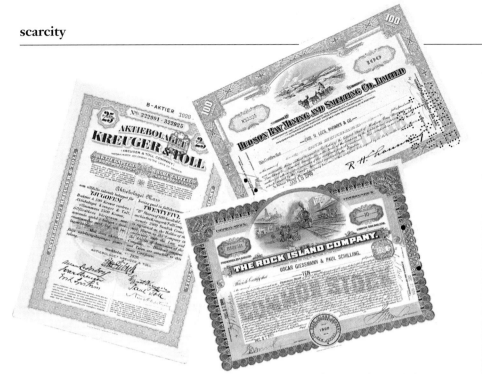

PAPER ART *In the past, shares were issued as elaborate certificates with splendid engravings romanticising industry and commerce. Today, they are often just entries in a computerised register.*

which can be used to monitor general price changes over time. The RPI is used to indicate levels of INFLATION from one month to another, and it is sometimes used in wage negotiations.

♣ Pensions and wages may be 'index-linked' so that they rise automatically in proportion to rises in the RPI, making them inflation proof.

scarcity Fundamental assumption behind all conventional economic theory. Human wants, it is said, will always exceed the resources available to fulfil them, forcing individuals to choose which of their desires will be satisfied from resources which are rationed – usually by price.

♣ John Kenneth GALBRAITH challenged this traditional assumption with his theories on the affluent society.

seasonal adjustment Modification made to economic statistics to compensate for seasonal changes in demand, supply, price or any other factors, which might otherwise obscure the long-term trend. Fruit and vegetables, for example, may become more plentiful every autumn, causing prices to fall. The RPI is provided on a seasonally adjusted basis to allow for this effect.

seasonal unemployment Periodic unemployment created by changes in the demand for different products or services at different times of the year. Holiday resorts, for example, experience seasonal unemployment outside the tourist season.

secondary sector Manufacturing and construction industries, which turn raw materials from the PRIMARY SECTOR into finished goods ready to be transferred to a SERVICE INDUSTRY in the tertiary sector for distribution, promotion and sale.

securities Documents recording ownership of assets or property which can be lodged as collateral for a loan. The term can also be used more broadly to cover all bonds, stocks, shares and equities. These are negotiable securities which can be bought and sold, and yield either interest or dividends.

Selfridge, Harry Gordon (1858-1947) American retailer who in 1909 founded Selfridge's department store in

---

CAPITALIST CLASSIC *Adam Smith's* Wealth of Nations (1776) *was the first major book on political economy. It argued strongly for untrammelled competition between businesses.*

London. He used American sales, advertising and publicity techniques to great effect. Selfridge became a British citizen in 1937.

sellers' market Market in which demand exceeds supply, allowing sellers to ask higher prices for their goods. It is the opposite of a BUYERS' MARKET.

SERPS (state earnings related pension scheme) Part of the British state pension scheme. Employees not covered by an approved company pension scheme make contributions to SERPS according to their earnings, which may entitle them to a higher pension than the basic level. Workers are now encouraged by the government to opt out of SERPS and to join private pension schemes in order to limit the social security budget.

service industry Any industry which does not make anything, but provides services to other industries or members of the public. Banking, hairdressing, transport and the theatre are all service industries and part of the tertiary sector.

♣ The service industries have grown enormously in Britain since 1945, while manufacturing industry has, relatively, declined.

shares Units of investment that represent part ownership of a company. They are also called EQUITIES. People who hold shares in a company are entitled to a portion of its net profits, paid in the form of a regular DIVIDEND. As the providers of a substantial amount of the company's CAPITAL, shareholders may also have some say in the way it is run. A company may issue any number of shares: small, privately owned companies may have as few as two shares, while British Telecom has issued more than 6 billion shares.

single European market Agreement between the members of the European Union (EU) to allow the free movement of goods, labour and capital between member states. The system aims to ensure that industries operate on equal terms in any member state, and can sell their goods freely throughout the EU. It also dictates common health and safety standards.

Smith, Adam (1723-90) Scottish economist whose book *An Inquiry into the Nature and Causes of The Wealth of Nations* (1776) argued for minimal interference in the workings of the free market. It asserted that individuals working in their own interest will somehow be guided by an 'invisible hand' which will automatically further the

interests of their community. He also proposed that wealth was mainly created by labour, and the more labour was put into a product, the higher its value would be.
♠ Adam Smith is considered the father of modern LAISSEZ-FAIRE economics.

social cost Cost seen from the perspective of society as a whole, not from an individual or corporate standpoint. For example, the cost of pollution may not be felt by the company producing it, but will affect society generally because of the decline in air and water quality. Unemployment also carries a social cost: low morale and potentially increased delinquency among the unemployed could be added to the economic cost of social security payments, lost income tax revenue and lost production. However, social costs, like the values of PUBLIC GOODS, are often difficult to measure in financial terms.

stag Stock exchange speculator who buys new share issues in the hope of selling at a quick profit when dealings begin.

stagflation Combination of low economic growth and high INFLATION, when prices and unemployment rise and investment in industry is low. The word is a blend of 'stagnation' and 'inflation'.

stamp duty Special tax payable on certain things, including share purchases and most property transactions. It is called stamp duty because an adhesive stamp was affixed to documentation during the sale as proof of payment. Now the documents are simply rubber-stamped to show the duty has been paid.

stock Type of repayable, interest-bearing debt issued by governments and companies to raise money. In Britain, stockholders are creditors of a company: unlike the shareholders, they do not own any EQUITY in the company, whereas in the US they are equivalent to shareholders.

stock exchange Place where stocks, shares, bonds and other securities are bought and sold. The world's major stock exchanges are in London, New York (WALL STREET) and Tokyo. Smaller, but nevertheless important, stock exchanges include Hong Kong, Frankfurt and Zürich.

subsistence Bare minimum needed to stay alive. In a subsistence economy, people produce almost all their necessities themselves and rarely have any left over with which to trade for other goods.

WHEELER DEALERS *At the London Stock Exchange (above), shares are traded electronically by telephone and computer. In New York (left), traders make deals face to face in the 'pit'.*

supply and demand In economic theory, the two main factors which determine price. Supply refers to the willingness of producers and others to offer goods and services for sale, while demand refers to the willingness and ability of consumers to purchase these goods. The price of the goods, and the amount sold, is the result of the interaction of these two forces. Demand is affected by such factors as income and fashion.

supply-side economics Idea that supply rather than demand is the key element in a country's economy. Supply-side economists believe that governments should concentrate on improving the quality of labour and boosting capital supply and productivity. For example, they believe that stimulating investment in industry by lowering taxes on businesses will raise production, which in turn will bring down prices and control INFLATION.

takeover Acquisition of a company by another company or, sometimes, an individual. The aim is usually to boost profits, to eliminate competition, or to achieve economies of scale. Takeover bids of publicly quoted companies, which are sometimes signalled by the bidder building up a large shareholding in the company concerned, are watched very carefully by dealers on the stock exchange. In Britain, they are monitored by a Takeover Panel.

taxation Compulsory levy imposed by central and local government. Most taxes are levied on income, expenditure or wealth. Taxes on income and capital gains are called direct taxes, while those on expenditure, such as VAT, are called indirect taxes. Taxes may be charged to individuals or to companies.

tax avoidance Minimising one's tax bill by legitimate means. Wealthy individuals and businesses sometimes avoid tax by exploiting loopholes in the tax rules. Another way is to invest or base a business in a tax haven – a country with no taxation, or very low levels of taxation, such as the Cayman Islands or Liechtenstein. The economies of such countries are often based almost entirely on the money attracted by the tax advantages they offer. Governments may also provide ways for people to minimise their tax liability. In Britain, pension contributions, TESSAS and PEPS (personal equity plans) offer a degree of tax shelter in order to encourage savings.
♠ Some wealthy people avoid tax by becoming 'tax exiles' – leaving their home countries to live where tax rates are lower. Others constantly travel between countries so that they never reside anywhere long enough to qualify as a taxpayer.
♠ Tax evasion is the illegal counterpart of tax avoidance. Taxes are commonly evaded by people not declaring their true income, or my making false claims for tax relief.

TESSA (tax exempt special savings account) Savings scheme which gives investors tax-free interest on their money, providing they leave it in the scheme for five years. There are strict limits on the amount savers can invest in TESSAs.

trade barrier Any government measure which discourages international trade. Trade barriers range from outright bans on products to import duties which make a product difficult to sell.
♣ The planned SINGLE EUROPEAN MARKET is an attempt to allow free movement of goods, labour and capital between members of the ▷ EUROPEAN UNION.
♣ Since its formation in 1947, GATT (the General Agreement on Tariffs and Trade) has sought to dismantle trade barriers throughout the world.

trade cycle Natural tendency of an economy to waver between boom periods of high production, investment and employment, and times of recession or depression.

treasury bills Specialised BILLS OF EXCHANGE used by the government as a short-term method of raising money. They are sold to the City's 'discount houses' – institutions which specialise in buying and selling bills – every week.

underwriting Process of sharing insurance risks, by which syndicates of underwriters accept liability for part of any eventual loss. Each underwriter is paid a premium for bearing his share of the risk: the more money the underwriters guarantee, or the higher risk their syndicate insures, the higher the premiums will be. By extension, INSTITUTIONAL INVESTORS underwrite new issues of shares, promising to buy surplus shares if they are not taken up by private investors.

unemployment The level of unemployment in an economy depends on the demand for labour, and is therefore an important economic indicator. Most economists now agree that full employment is almost impossible to achieve.
♣ Unemployment was high throughout the world in the 1930s, it fell in the 1950s and 1960s and rose again in the 1970s and 1980s. In Britain it peaked in July 1986, with 3 125 500 officially out of work.
♣ The relative decline of industry in Britain, including the closure of coal mines in the north of England and Wales, has resulted in severe structural unemployment: long-term joblessness as a result of fundamental changes in the economy.

unit trust Company which invites small investors to buy 'units' which are pooled to buy stocks and shares. The value of each unit is that of the total fund divided by the number of units issued, and investors can sell their units back to the fund at any time.

usury Charging excessive interest on loans. In medieval Europe, usury was common, but in most countries it is now illegal to charge more than a specified maximum interest rate.
♣ In many Muslim countries, moneylending at interest is considered to be usury and is forbidden. Instead of lending money, Islamic banks levy fees or enter leasing and profit-sharing deals with their customers.

VAT (value added tax) Sales tax levied on goods and services throughout the European Union. VAT-registered companies can generally claim back VAT they have paid on purchases, so the tax is paid only on the value they add to the goods they produce or the services they provide. Most goods and services in Britain are taxed at a standard VAT rate of 17.5 per cent. Some, such as funerals, insurance and postal services, are exempt. Others, including food, books, children's clothing and transport, are zero-rated. Zero-rating

MONEYLENDERS *Profiting from new opportunities in trade, medieval usurers take bags of coins from a strongbox for clients. The interest they charged was often phenomenally high.*

enables manufacturers or service providers to recover VAT paid to suppliers, unless the supplier is exempt. In Britain VAT is administered by HM Customs & Excise.
♣ The imposition of VAT on domestic heating fuel by the British government in 1994 caused a political furore. It was feared that the higher bills would adversely affect the poor and the elderly.

Wall Street Financial district of New York, home of the US Stock Exchange and many banks and investment companies.
♣ The financial collapse of 1929 which preceded the ▷ DEPRESSION of the 1930s is known as the ▷ WALL STREET CRASH.

white knight As the name implies, someone who rescues a business. It specifically refers to a third party who prevents a hostile takeover bid by either making a friendly bid or else acquiring a large enough shareholding to pre-empt the predator.

Woolworth, Frank Winfield (1852 - 1919) American businessman who pioneered cheap retailing with a chain of stores in the USA offering a wide variety of goods at five or ten cents each. The first Woolworth's in Britain opened in 1909, selling goods for 3d (1¼p) or 6d (2½p).
♣ The Woolworth Building, one of New York's oldest skyscrapers, was built in 1913 to house the company's head office.

World Bank International financial organisation set up after the ▷ BRETTON WOODS CONFERENCE of 1944. It is officially called the International Bank for Reconstruction and Development, and was originally concerned with providing capital for postwar reconstruction in Europe. Since the 1950s, its main priority has been to promote the economic development of its member countries. It lends money to governments and arranges finance for a wide variety of projects, especially in LESS DEVELOPED COUNTRIES. In order to join the World Bank, countries must first join the INTERNATIONAL MONETARY FUND.

yield Income derived from an investment, expressed as a percentage of its current value. Yield is important for investors in stocks and shares, who use it to calculate the likely return on their portfolio, relating the original or 'par' value of a share to its market price and its DIVIDEND by a simple formula. A 20p share paying a dividend of 2p would have a yield of 10 per cent if its market value were still 20p; if the share value had risen to 40p, however, the yield would then have fallen to 5 per cent.

FILMS, ENTERTAINMENT AND THE MEDIA

Mass entertainment is the creation of modern technology. The talent and glamour of Hollywood brought stars of the theatre to a wider cinema audience, and created new stars of its own. Today television has a mission to inform as well as to amuse. Radio remains a powerful medium, while newspapers and magazines thrive on the continuing appeal of words and pictures.

MARILYN MONROE

TREVOR McDONALD

JAMES DEAN
NATALIE WOOD
SAL MINEO

REBEL WITHOUT A CAUSE

CLINT EASTWOOD

Abbott and Costello American comedy duo of the 1940s, who moved to the cinema from vaudeville taking many of their crosstalk routines with them. Lou Costello (1906-59) was the chubby, buffoonish half, while Bud Abbott (1895-74) was the thin, bullying 'straight man'. *In Society* (1944), in which they play a pair of incompetent plumbers who wreck a mansion, is generally considered to be their funniest film.

Addams Family, The Ghoulish family created by *New Yorker* magazine cartoonist Charles Addams, and turned into a television comedy series in the 1960s. A film version was released in 1991. The characters include the parents Gomez and Morticia, their children Pugsley and Wednesday, Uncle Fester, a butler named Lurch and a disembodied hand known as Thing which scuttles busily about.

African Queen, The Romantic adventure film directed by John HUSTON in 1951, starring Katharine Hepburn and Humphrey Bogart. Based on a novel by C.S. Forester, it concerns the disreputable, gin-swigging captain of a Congo river launch, *The African Queen*, who helps a prim-and-proper missionary to escape from the hostile German forces in East Africa at the beginning of World War I.

Allen, Woody (1935-) (Real name Allen Stewart Konigsberg) Brooklyn-born comedian who has been writing, directing and acting in his own films since the late 1960s. Early movies such as *Bananas* (1971) are pure slapstick, but the romantic comedies he made with Diane Keaton, such as *Annie Hall* (1977) and *Manhattan* (1979), reveal greater depth. *Interiors* (1978) and *September* (1987) show the sobering influence of his film idol, Ingmar BERGMAN. *Manhattan Murder Mystery* (1993) marked a return to light-hearted humour.
🔱 Mia Farrow was Allen's partner and leading actress during the 1980s, when they co-starred in the marital drama *Hannah and Her Sisters* (1986). However their relationship broke up over a much-publicised child custody case in 1993.

All Quiet on the Western Front Classic anti-war film about a group of young German volunteers experiencing front line action in World War I. Their youthful patriotism turns to cynicism as one after another they are killed. Taken from Erich Maria Remarque's best-selling novel, it was made in Hollywood in 1930 by the Oscar-winning director Lewis Milestone.
🔱 An unforgettable image in the film shows the hero, played by Lew Ayres, being shot by a sniper as he reaches out for a butterfly.

Amadeus Dazzling 1984 film version of Peter Shaffer's stage play about the life and death of Mozart. Starring Tom Hulce as Mozart, with a high-pitched giggle, it highlights the feud between him and his embittered and self-professed rival, the Habsburg court composer Antonio Salieri.

American in Paris, An Highly acclaimed Hollywood musical about an ex-GI trying to succeed as a painter in Paris shortly after World War II. Directed by Vincente Minelli in 1951, it stars Gene Kelly and Leslie Caron and features music by George ▷GERSHWIN. It has a long ballet sequence – choreographed by Kelly and danced by Caron – which was considered an artistic breakthrough in the cinema.

Andrews, Julie (1935-) Wholesome British singing star who won hearts throughout the world in *Mary Poppins* (1964) and *The Sound of Music* (1965). Her less sugary roles, as in Alfred Hitchcock's spy thriller *Torn Curtain* (1966) and *That's Life* (1986), directed by her husband Blake Edwards, have generally been disappointing. On stage she was the original Eliza Doolittle in ▷MY FAIR LADY.

Apocalypse Now Spectacular Vietnam war epic co-written, produced and directed in 1979 by Francis Ford Coppola (1939-). Martin Sheen portrays an American captain sent to assassinate a renegade US Army officer, played by Marlon Brando, who is waging his own war in the hills. The most memorable scene is of a beach being strafed to the accompaniment of Wagner's *The Ride of the Valkyries*.
🔱 Plagued by Sheen's heart problems, and Brando's weight problem, the film took so long to make that show business journalists retitled it 'Apocalypse Later'.

Archers, The World's longest running radio serial – a British soap opera about country and farming folk in the fictional village of Ambridge. The first national episode was broadcast by the BBC in 1951.

Ashcroft, Dame Peggy (1907-91) British stage actress renowned for her Shakespearean roles in the 1930s. She played Desdemona to Paul Robeson's *Othello* (1930) and was an outstanding Juliet in John Gielgud's production of *Romeo and Juliet* (1932). She appeared in a handful of films, most notably Alfred Hitchcock's *The 39 Steps* (1935) and David Lean's *A Passage to India* (1984) – for which she won a Best Supporting Actress Oscar. She was made a Dame of the British Empire in 1956.

PATRIOTIC PARTNERS *Humphrey Bogart and Katharine Hepburn plan to use their dilapidated, 30 ft (9 m) steam launch,* The African Queen, *as a makeshift torpedo to sink a German gunboat.*

DEADLY ENEMIES *The forces of good and evil are epitomised by the latest screen Batman, Michael Keaton, and the most sinister of Jokers, Jack Nicholson – who received a record $6 million for the role.*

most admired sequences in cinema history: the massacre of innocent civilians on the Odessa Steps, during which a runaway pram with a baby trundles downwards.

BBC The British Broadcasting Corporation, Britain's public service radio and television station. BBC radio began in London in 1922 and the television service started in 1936: this was suspended when war broke out in 1939 and resumed in 1946. A second television channel, BBC2, followed in 1964. The corporation operates under Royal Charter and is run by a Board of Governors appointed by the monarch. It is funded by the annual TV and radio licence fee paid by those who own or rent sets.

Beatty, Warren (1937-) American 'heart-throb' actor and brother of Shirley MACLAINE. He starred in major productions such as BONNIE AND CLYDE (1967), *Shampoo* (1975) and *Heaven Can Wait* (1978). He directed and played the lead in *Reds* (1981), an account of John Reed, an American journalist who covered the Russian Revolution in 1917 and later cofounded the American Communist Party. It won Beatty a Best Director Oscar. He has since played the leads in *Dick Tracy* (1990), the comic-strip detective, and *Bugsy* (1991), the true-life story of a Hollywood gangster.

Becky Sharp First feature film made in three-colour Technicolor. Produced in Hollywood in 1935, and based on William ▷THACKERAY's novel *Vanity Fair*, it starred Miriam Hopkins in the title role.

Bergman, Ingmar (1918-) Swedish film and theatre director renowned for his haunting imagery, mystical themes and stark view of life. In 1956 he made his best-known film, *The Seventh Seal*, a parable about a knight who plays chess with Death. His other films include the comedy *Smiles of a Summer Night* (1955), *Wild Strawberries* (1957), *Through a Glass Darkly* (1961) and *Fanny and Alexander* (1982).

Bergman, Ingrid (1915-82) Swedish actress who went to Hollywood in 1938, hailed as the new Greta Garbo. Among the films that made her a star were *Intermezzo* (1939), CASABLANCA (1942), *Notorious* (1946) and *Joan of Arc* (1948). She made her last film appearance in Ingmar Bergman's *Autumn Sonata* (1978), a moving story of a bereaved woman's reunion with her daughter. She won Best Actress Oscars for her roles in *Gaslight* (1944) and *Anastasia* (1956), and a Best Supporting Actress Oscar for *Murder on the Orient Express* (1974).

Attenborough, Lord Richard (1923-) Baby-faced British character actor who made a memorable 'Pinkie', the heartless young gangster, in the 1947 film version of Graham ▷GREENE's *Brighton Rock*. He became a leading director of epics, including *Oh! What a Lovely War* (1969), *Young Winston* (1972), *Gandhi* (1982) and *Chaplin* (1992). He was knighted in 1976 and made a lord in 1993. He is the brother of the zoologist and BBC television personality Sir David Attenborough (1926-).

Avengers, The Stylish British television series of the 'Swinging Sixties' about an undercover agent called John Steed, played by Patrick MacNee. He was assisted by a string of glamorous, karate-skilled girls: Honor Blackman as Cathy Gale, Diana Rigg as Emma Peel and Linda Thorson as Tara King. In the 1970s MacNee made a comeback in *The New Avengers* with Joanna Lumley as Purdey, a former ballerina turned martial arts exponent.

Bardot, Brigitte (1934-) (Real name Camille Javal) Sultry French actress who was billed as a 'sex kitten' when she starred in her husband Roger Vadim's 1956 film *And God Created Woman*. In it she played a sexually obsessed young woman – a type she concentrated on throughout her career. She retired in 1973 and devoted herself to campaigning for animal rights.

Batman Cartoon superhero created in an American comic strip in 1939. It was turned into a children's television show in the 1960s, with Adam West as the Caped Crusader and Burt Ward as his partner Robin. They appeared in the first *Batman* film (1966). The title role was taken by Michael Keaton in two big-budget sequels: *Batman* (1989) and *Batman Returns* (1992).

Battleship Potemkin, The Highly influential Russian silent film directed by Sergei Eisenstein in 1925. It tells of a naval mutiny in Odessa in 1905 and has one of the

MELODY MAKERS *An illuminated pattern of girls with violins croon 'The Shadow Waltz' – one of the highlights of choreographer Busby Berkeley's musical hit* Gold Diggers of 1933.

Berkeley, Busby (1895-1976) American choreographer and director whose films are marked by their lavish dance routines. These were often photographed from above so that the lines of chorus girls formed fanciful, kaleidoscopic designs. His films were a tonic during the Depression years of the 1930s, and included *The Gold Diggers* series (1933-7), 42ND STREET (1933) and *Babes in Arms* (1939).

Bicycle Thieves Touching film about the plight of a long-time unemployed Italian workman when the bicycle he needs for a new job is stolen. Directed in 1948 by Vittorio DE SICA, it helped herald a new era of cinematic realism.

Birth of a Nation, The Hollywood's first and most renowned historical epic. Made in 1915, and set at the time of the American Civil War, it was hailed for its masterly use of long-shots, close-ups, fade-outs and fade-ins – techniques pioneered by the director, D.W. GRIFFITH. But it was criticised for its glorification of the Ku Klux Klan and its harsh view of black people.

Blade Runner Bleak but visually stunning 'thriller of the future', in which an ex-policeman and licensed killer, played by Harrison Ford, is commissioned to hunt down and destroy a group of homicidal, outer space robots. Made in 1982, the film had a happy ending and an obtrusive commentary. In 1992 British director Ridley Scott provided a more realistic finale and dropped the commentary.

Blind Date Popular ITV programme in which contestants pick one of three unseen potential partners for a date, through a series of questions about each other. The lucky couples have their dates in locations ranging from Tunbridge Wells to Trinidad. The show, which began in 1985, is presented by the entertainer Cilla Black.

Blue Peter Long-running BBC children's television programme that started in 1958. Among its best-known presenters were Valerie Singleton (1962-72), John Noakes (1965-79) and Peter Purves (1967-79), who were accompanied by their dogs Shep and Petra, and Jason the Siamese cat.

Bogarde, Sir Dirk (1920-) (Real name Derek Van den Bogaerde) British film actor of Dutch ancestry who rose to prominence in crime melodramas such as *The Blue Lamp* (1951) and comedies such as *Doctor in the House* (1953). His more celebrated roles include a bisexual barrister in *Victim* (1961), a sinister valet in *The Servant* (1963), a cynical Oxford don in *Accident* (1967) and a dying composer in DEATH IN VENICE (1970). He was knighted in 1992.

Bogart, Humphrey (1899-1957) Taciturn American actor who played to perfection two hard-boiled private eyes: Dashiel Hammett's Sam Spade in *The Maltese Falcon* (1941) and Raymond ▷CHANDLER's Philip Marlowe in *The Big Sleep* (1946). He appeared in four films with Lauren Bacall (1924-), including *To Have and Have Not* (1944). He married Bacall in 1945. His films – in many of which he played a gangster wearing a snap-brimmed hat and a trench coat – include *The Petrified Forest* (1936), *Angels with Dirty Faces* (1938), *The Roaring Twenties* (1939), *High Sierra* (1941), CASABLANCA (1942), The AFRICAN QUEEN (1951) for which he won a Best Actor Oscar, and *The Caine Mutiny* (1954).

Bond, James Hero of Ian ▷FLEMING's sophisticated spy novels – the film versions of which were noted for their increasingly spectacular stunts and gadgets. Bond was first portrayed by Sean Connery, who made

SUPER SPY *Dapper and dangerous, Sean Connery is ready for action as trigger-happy secret agent James Bond, also known as 007.*

ven films, from *Dr No* (1962) to *Never Say ver Again* (1983). The second Bond, rmer model George Lazenby, appeared only one film: *On Her Majesty's Secret rvice* (1969). Roger Moore became the rd Bond, starting with *Live and Let Die* 973), Timothy Dalton took over in *The ving Daylights* (1987), and was succeeded Pierce Brosnan in *Goldeneye* (1995). The ms featured exotically named villains, such Dr No and Goldfinger, and gorgeous girls.

onnie and Clyde Violent gangster film sed on the real-life exploits of two of nerica's most ruthless and daring bank bbers, who terrorised the Midwest in the rly 1930s. Starring Warren Beatty and ye Dunaway, and directed in 1967 by rthur Penn, it used a variety of stylistic cks to tell its brutal story – which began a w trend in screen savagery.

oulting, John (1913-85) and Roy 913-) Twin brothers who produced, -wrote and directed some of the funniest ritish films of the 1950s and 1960s. These cluded *Private's Progress* (1956), *Brothers Law* (1956), *Lucky Jim* (1957), *I'm All ight Jack* (1959) and *Heavens Above* (1963). hey also made suspense thrillers including righton Rock* (1947).

ranagh, Kenneth (1960-) British tor and director who launched his Ren-ssance Theatre Company in 1987 and on critical acclaim when he played *Hamlet* e following year. In 1989 he directed d took the title role in a new film version f *Henry V*. Other films he has directed d starred in include *Dead Again* (1991), eter's Friends* (1992) and *Much Ado About othing* (1993), all of which co-starred his ife Emma Thompson (1959-).

rando, Marlon (1924-) Moody merican actor trained in 'the Method' hool of acting which aims at a complete lentification – physical and mental – with e character being portrayed. His early d most notable films include *The Men* 950), *A Streetcar Named Desire* (1951), he Wild One* (1953) and *On the Waterfront* 954), for which he won a Best Actor scar. He made an impressive Mark ntony in *Julius Caesar* (1953) and his nging gambler in *Guys and Dolls* (1955) ntrasted with his menacing Mafia boss in he GODFATHER (1972). His other films clude the sexually explicit *Last Tango in aris* (1972) and APOCALYPSE NOW (1979). Brando once commented on the vast fees e commands for cameo film roles: nother day, another million dollars!'

Brideshead Revisited Sumptuous, six-part ITV adaptation of Evelyn ▷WAUGH's novel about the fortunes of an impression-able young man who becomes involved with a rich and aristocratic Roman Catholic family between the two world wars. The action switches between the stately home of Brideshead itself, Oxford, Venice and Morocco. First shown in 1981, it had a superb cast led by Jeremy Irons, Anthony Andrews, Claire Bloom and Diana Quick – with scene-stealing appearances by Laurence Olivier and John Gielgud.

Brief Encounter Heart-tugging film about the doomed love affair between a bored suburban housewife (Celia Johnson) and an unattached young doctor (Trevor Howard). Their snatched meetings take place in a dreary railway station, a local cinema and a high street tea-shop. Based on a one-act play by Noël ▷COWARD, it was directed by David LEAN in 1945 and features the romantic music of Rach-maninov's Second Piano Concerto.

Bugs Bunny Brash cartoon rabbit created by Warner Brothers in 1937. He was said to have been inspired by a scene in the comedy film *It Happened One Night* (1934), in which Clark Gable eats a carrot with gusto.

Burton, Richard (1925-84) Welsh stage and screen actor admired for his brooding presence and rich voice. Among the high-lights of his theatrical career were *Hamlet* at London's Old Vic in 1954, and King Arthur in the Broadway musical *Camelot* (1960 and 1980). He made his film debut in 1948 and his many movies include *My Cousin Rachel* (1952), *Becket* (1964), *The Night of the*

WHAT'S UP, DOC? *Bugs Bunny's catch-phrase – in a broad Brooklyn accent – marked another escapade for the brash cartoon superstar.*

Iguana (1964), *The Spy Who Came in from the Cold* (1965) and *Who's Afraid of Virginia Woolf?* (1966). He gave a fine performance as the narrator in the BBC radio production of Dylan Thomas's *Under Milk Wood*, first broadcast in 1954.

While making *Cleopatra* in 1962 Burton had a well-publicised relationship with his leading lady and future wife, Elizabeth ▷TAYLOR. In the midst of it Laurence Olivier sent him a cable asking if he wanted to be 'a great actor or a household name'. Burton's reply was: 'Both!'

Butch Cassidy and the Sundance Kid Witty, tongue-in-cheek account of two of America's most celebrated train robbers, played with great charm and style by Paul Newman as Cassidy and Robert Redford as the Kid. The film, directed by George Roy Hill in 1969, tells how the outlaws flee to Bolivia – where they come to a violent end.

Cagney, James (1899-1986) Pint-sized American actor who epitomised the screen gangster in a series of fast-paced crime dramas such as *The Public Enemy* (1931), *Angels with Dirty Faces* (1938), *The Roaring Twenties* (1939), *White Heat* (1949) and *Kiss Tomorrow Goodbye* (1950). He showed his versatility as the song-and-dance man George M. Cohan in *Yankee Doodle Dandy* (1942), for which he won an Oscar. After making the Cold War comedy *One, Two, Three* (1961), he retired to his Texas ranch. He made a dynamic comeback, at the age of 82, in *Ragtime* (1981), a story of political life in New York before World War I.

Although Cagney was best known for his tough guy roles, he began his career as a chorus boy and female impersonator.

Caine, Michael (1933-) (Real name Maurice Micklewhite) Prolific British film actor normally noted for his deadpan expression and flat, cockney accent. He played small parts for years before making an impact as an upper-class lieutenant in *Zulu* (1963). Caine found stardom as the shabby spy Harry Palmer in *The Ipcress File* (1965) and its two sequels, *Funeral in Berlin* (1966) and *Billion Dollar Brain* (1967). His best-known films include *Alfie* (1965), *Get Carter* (1971), *Sleuth* (1972), *The Eagle Has Landed* (1976), *Educating Rita* (1983), *Hannah and Her Sisters* (1986) and *Mona Lisa* (1986). He has also made two major TV films, *Jack the Ripper* (1988) and *Dr Jekyll and Mr Hyde* (1990).

Michael Caine took his professional name from that of a film starring his favourite actor: *The Caine Mutiny* (1954) with Humphrey Bogart.

Capra, Frank (1897-1991) American film director renowned for his whimsical, heart-warming comedies. They are usually about 'ordinary' people who battle bravely for their ideals, and include *Mr Deeds Goes to Town* (1936), *You Can't Take It With You* (1938), *Mr Smith Goes to Washington (1939)* and *It's a Wonderful Life* (1947).

Carry On . . . Series of bawdy British film farces which began in 1958 with *Carry On Sergeant*. Unsubtle and full of innuendo, there have been more than 30 titles so far – the most recent being *Carry on Columbus* (1992). The cast members have included Kenneth Williams, Sid James, Barbara Windsor, Bernard Bresslaw, Charles Hawtrey, Joan Sims and Hattie Jacques.

Casablanca Evocative wartime romance and adventure film directed in 1942 by Michael Curtiz, starring Humphrey Bogart, Ingrid Bergman, Paul Henreid and Claude Rains. Set largely in Rick's nightclub in Vichy-controlled Casablanca in World War II, it tells of the owner's obsession with a married woman who works for the Resistance, with whom he had an affair in prewar Paris. It builds to a tense climax at the city's fog-shrouded airport. The haunting theme tune, *As Time Goes By*, sums up the film's bittersweet quality.
One of the cinema's most misquoted catchphrases, 'Play it again, Sam', is often wrongly attributed to Humphrey Bogart. But it is Bergman who says: 'Play it, Sam.'

Cathy Come Home Powerful BBC television drama about the hardships of a homeless young family, which touched the heart of the nation in 1966. Directed by Ken Loach, and starring Carol White and Ray Brooks as the socially deprived parents, it caused a public outcry.

Chaney, Lon (1883-1930) American silent film star and master of disguise whose roles included *The Hunchback of Notre Dame* (1923) and *The Phantom of the Opera* (1925). In 1957 James Cagney starred in a biographical film about him aptly called *Man of a Thousand Faces*. His son, Lon Chaney Junior (1906-73), gave a moving performance as the dim-witted Lennie in the film *Of Mice and Men* (1939).

Channel 4 British commercial television channel launched in November 1982 to cater for minority tastes and interests. It has commissioned several critically acclaimed feature films including *My Beautiful Laundrette* (1985), *Drowning by Numbers* (1988) and *The Crying Game* (1993).

Chaplin, Sir Charles (1889-1977) British comic genius whose 'little tramp' figure – complete with baggy trousers, bowler hat, skimpy frockcoat, turned-up shoes, bamboo cane and toothbrush moustache – captivated the world. Chaplin travelled to America in 1910 as a variety performer and became a film actor, director, producer, choreographer and composer. His films include *Shoulder Arms* (1918), *The Kid* (1921), *The Gold Rush* (1925), *City Lights* (1931), *Modern Times* (1936) and *The Great Dictator* (1940), in which he spoke on screen for the first time. His last four films were *Monsieur Verdoux* (1947), *Limelight* (1951), a bitter attack on the American way of life, *A King in New York* (1957) and *A Countess from Hong Kong* (1966), with Marlon Brando, Sophia Loren and Chaplin as a seasick ship's steward. His left-wing sympathies made him a victim of the McCarthy anti-communist witch hunt of the early 1950s, and he moved from America to Switzerland – where he lived quietly with his fourth wife, Oona O'Neil, daughter of the American playwright Eugene ▷O'NEIL. He received an honorary Oscar in 1971 and was knighted in 1975.

Citizen Kane Influential film about the rise and fall of an unscrupulous American newspaper tycoon – based on William Randolph Hearst – who sacrifices personal happiness for commercial success. It is told in flashback, using a bag of brilliant technical tricks – such as mock newsreel accounts of Kane's career. Proclaimed by many critics as the best film ever made, it is the masterpiece of Orson WELLES, who in 1941, aged 26, co-wrote the script, directed and produced the film – as well as making his screen acting debut as Kane.

Clockwork Orange, A Bleak and brutal film version of Anthony ▷BURGESS's horror novel about a Britain of the future in which law and order have broken down and violence rules. Directed in 1971 by Stanley KUBRICK, it starred Malcolm McDowell as a young murderer and rapist loose in a vicious and depraved society in which gangs prowl the streets torturing and killing for pleasure, using a slangy, futuristic language against a background accompaniment of Beethoven. After being scientifically brainwashed in prison he becomes a helpless victim himself.

MAN OF MIRTH *Chaplin satirises the soulless nature of assembly-line work in* Modern Times *(1936). Starving in Alaska, he dines on shoe leather (inset) in* The Gold Rush *(1925).*

comics Two of Britain's oldest and best-loved children's comics, *The Dandy* and *The Beano*, were launched in 1937 and 1938 respectively. They featured perennial favourites such as Korky the Cat, Desperate Dan and Dennis the Menace, and were the first British comics to use American-style speech bubbles instead of captions.

Connery, Sean (1930-) Rugged Scots superstar who created the role of James BOND in the early 1960s. He successfully threw off this image in a string of international hits, including Alfred Hitchcock's *Marnie* (1964), *The Anderson Tapes* (1971), *Robin and Marian* (1976), *The Name of the Rose* (1986), *The Untouchables* (1987), for which he won an Oscar as Best Supporting Actor, and Steven Spielberg's *Indiana Jones and the Last Crusade* (1989).

Cooper, Gary (1901-61) Quietly spoken and affable star, best known for Westerns including the classic *High Noon* (1952), which won him a Best Actor Oscar. A former cowboy, he began his career as a stunt rider and, after a series of small parts in silent films, played the lead in *The Virginian* (1929). He displayed a deft talent for comedy in movies such as *Mr Deeds Goes to Town* (1936). He was equally at ease in serious dramatic roles, including a pacifist war hero in *Sergeant York* (1941), for which he won his first Oscar, and a guerrilla in Ernest Hemingway's Spanish Civil War saga, *For Whom the Bell Tolls* (1943).

Coronation Street Long-running ITV drama series which started in 1960. Set in a working-class terraced street in northwest England, it portrays the everyday lives of the residents – many of whom became national figures, including Ken Barlow (William Roache), Elsie Tanner (Pat Phoenix), Ena Sharples (Violet Carson) and Albert Tatlock (Jack Howarth).

Costner, Kevin (1955-) Intense leading man descended partly from Cherokee stock who directed and starred in *Dances With Wolves* (1990), about a US Army officer during the Civil War who becomes a Sioux brave. The movie won seven Oscars, including Best Film and Best Director. Kostner shot to stardom in 1987 in the thrillers *No Way Out* and *The Untouchables*. Among his other films are *Bull Durham* (1988), *Field of Dreams* (1989), *Robin Hood, Prince of Thieves* (1991), *JFK* (1991), *The Bodyguard* (1992) and *A Perfect World* (1993), with Clint Eastwood.

COMIC CAPERS *British boys and girls grew up with their own favourite comics, whose picture stories they followed avidly from week to week.*

Crawford, Joan (1904-77) (Real name Lucille Le Sueur) Emotional American film actress, whose staring eyes were once compared to car headlamps. She won a Best Actress Oscar for *Mildred Pierce* (1945), in which she played an ambitious waitress who succeeds in running her own restaurant. Her best-known films include *A Woman's Face* (1941), *The Story of Esther Costello* (1957) and the grotesque horror film *Whatever Happened to Baby Jane?* (1962).

Cruise, Tom (1962-) Clean-cut American film actor hailed as the world's Number One male pin-up in the early 1990s. After playing juvenile leads in the early 1980s, he graduated to adult stardom and won critical acclaim in *The Color of Money* (1986), *Rain Man* (1988), *Born on the 4th of July* (1989) and *The Firm* (1993).

Dad's Army Nostalgic comedy television series (1968-77) about the blundering exploits of a seaside Home Guard platoon during World War II. The main actors included Arthur Lowe as the pompous Captain Mainwaring, John Le Mesurier as the long-suffering Sergeant Wilson, Clive Dunn as the excitable Lance Corporal Jones, and John Laurie as the dour Scot, Private Frazer.

Dallas Glossy drama serial (1978-91) which started a Hollywood trend for television sagas about the seriously rich and powerful. It concerned the loves and rivalries affecting members of the wealthy Ewing family and their oil empire based in Dallas, Texas. Larry Hagman played the man whom audiences loved to hate, the ruthless J.R. Ewing.
🎤 'Who shot J.R?' was a much-posed question which appeared on T-shirts and mugs in 1980. The answer was a pregnant ex-lover, Kristen, played by Mary Crosby.

Davis, Bette (1908-89) Formidable American actress whose unconventional looks and powerful personality enlivened a long series of so-called 'women's pictures'. She won Oscars for her roles in *Dangerous* (1935) and *Jezebel* (1938). Among her other notable films were *The Private Lives of Elizabeth and Essex* (1939), *The Letter* (1940), *Now Voyager* (1942), *Mr Skeffington* (1944) and *All About Eve* (1950). She later won acclaim for her roles as an ageing former child star in *Whatever Happened to Baby Jane?* (1962), opposite Joan Crawford, and a deranged suspected murderess in *Hush, Hush, Sweet Charlotte* (1964). She made her last film *The Wicked Stepmother* in 1989, the year of her death.

STREET SCENE *Life in TV's* Coronation Street *is centred on the Rover's Return, one of whose gossips was Ena Sharples (inset, centre), played by Violet Carson.*

Day, Sir Robin (1923-)

Current-affairs radio and television journalist, whose flamboyant bow ties became his trademark, and whose incisive manner and blunt questions set new standards for political interviews. He presented BBC-1's *Panorama* from 1967 to 1972 and chaired the same channel's *Question Time* from 1979 to 1989, when he retired from television due to ill health. He was knighted in 1981.

YOUNG GIANT *In his final film,* Giant *(above), James Dean played an embittered young ranchhand who finds oil and achieves his dream of riches. He made his name in* Rebel Without a Cause *(top).*

Dean, James (1931-55)

Idolised American actor whose screen image of petulance and moody rebellion made him a hero with youngsters in the rock'n'roll era. His only major films, made in little more than a year, were *East of Eden* (1955), based on John ▷STEINBECK's sombre novel about an adolescent who discovers that his mother, thought to be dead, is the madam of a local brothel; *Rebel Without a Cause* (1955), a study of juvenile deliquency among the middle classes; and the Texas-set epic, *Giant* (1956). Dean died at the age of 24 when his sports car crashed in southern California in September 1955.

Death in Venice

Sumptuous and moving Italian film about the last, lonely days of a composer holidaying in a plague-threatened Venice shortly before World War I. Based on a short novel by the German author Thomas ▷MANN, it was directed in 1971 by Luchino Visconti. The film stars Dirk Bogarde and tells of the composer's doomed, idealistic love of a beautiful boy whom he sees at a distance.

De Mille, Cecil B. (1881-1959)

Autocratic American film producer-director and one of the founders of Hollywood. He went there in 1913 to make a Western, *The Squaw Man* – generally regarded as Hollywood's first feature-length film – and stayed to direct lavish Biblical epics such as *The Ten Commandments* (1923), *King of Kings* (1927) and *The Sign of the Cross* (1932). De Mille's many later films include *Samson and Delilah* (1949), the Oscar-winning circus spectacular, *The Greatest Show on Earth* (1952), and a grandiose remake of *The Ten Commandments* in 1956, lasting more than 3½ hours.

He played the tireless, all-powerful film tycoon to the hilt, telling his staff: 'You are here to please me. Nothing else matters!' During World War II there was a saying in Hollywood: 'Anyone who leaves De Mille for the armed forces is a slacker!'

Dench, Dame Judi (1934-)

Distinguished British stage and screen actress who made her debut as Ophelia in *Hamlet* (1957) at London's Old Vic theatre. Highlights from her theatrical career include playing Sally Bowles in the musical *Cabaret* (1968), and Cleopatra in Shakespeare's *Antony and Cleopatra* (1987) with Anthony Hopkins. She has appeared in television comedy series such as *A Fine Romance* (1981-5) with her husband Michael Williams. Her films include *A Room with a View* (1985) and *84 Charing Cross Road* (1986).

De Niro, Robert (1943-)

Versatile American actor whose roles have ranged from a Jesuit priest in *The Mission* (1986) to a psychopathic hoodlum in *GoodFellas* (1990). He has worked with director Martin SCORSESE on several harrowing films, playing a disturbed ex-Vietnam veteran in *Taxi Driver* (1976), a grotesque boxing champion in *Raging Bull* (1980) and a vengeful ex-convict in *Cape Fear* (1991). Among his other outstanding films are *The Godfather Part Two* (1974) for which he won an Oscar, *The Deer Hunter* (1978) and *A Bronx Tale* (1993), which he also directed.

Depardieu, Gérard (1947-)

Imposing French actor who has been acclaimed for his sensitive portrayals of eccentrics and social misfits. A school dropout at the age of 12, he later worked as an amateur boxer, lifeguard and dishwasher. His early roles were undistinguished and it was not until the 1980s that he found parts worthy of his talent – such as the husband who comes back from the dead in *The Return of Martin Guerre* (1981) and the tragic hunchback in *Jean de Florette* (1986). The doomed romantic poet *Cyrano de Bergerac* followed in 1990, as did his first Hollywood role, a wily musician in the romantic comedy *Green Card*.

Desert Island Discs

Enduring radio record programme that was created and first presented by Roy Plomley in 1942. So far more than 2000 celebrities have been asked to select the eight records and one luxury item that they would choose to have if they were cast away on a desert island. Since Plomley's death in 1985 the programme has had two presenters: Michael Parkinson and Sue Lawley.

De Sica, Vittorio (1902-74)

Italian director and character actor whose quartet of films after World War II – *Shoeshine* (1946), BICYCLE THIEVES (1948), *Miracle in Milan* (1950) and *Umberto D* (1952) – helped to set a trend in social realism. He later directed Sophia LOREN in three of her finest and most popular films: *Two Women* (1960), *Yesterday, Today and Tomorrow* (1963) and *Marriage Italian Style* (1964).

Dick Barton Fast-moving BBC radio serial about the adventures of Dick Barton, Special Agent, and his two stalwart assistants, Snowy and Jock. Broadcast each week night from 1946 to 1951, it had some 15 million regular listeners at the height of its popularity. Its hectic signature tune, *The Devil's Gallop*, became a national favourite.

Dietrich, Marlene (1901-92) (Real name Maria Magdalena von Losch) German-born American singer and actress whose ageless beauty, high cheekbones and husky voice made her a screen goddess. Dietrich's international reputation was made in 1930 with Germany's early talking picture, *The Blue Angel*, in which she played a temptress called Lola-Lola. The film was directed by Josef Von Sternberg, who made six more films with Dietrich in Hollywood.

Dirty Harry Tense and violent police thriller in which an unprincipled San Francisco policeman tracks down an insane sniper. Clint Eastwood played the detective, Harry Callahan, who is as brutal and ruthless as the killer he is out to destroy. Made in 1971 by director Don Siegel, it inspired four sequels: *Magnum Force* (1973), *The Enforcer* (1976), *Sudden Impact* (1983) and *The Dead Pool* (1988).

Disney, Walt (1901-66) American film producer and animator who created the cartoon characters Mickey and Minnie Mouse, Donald Duck, Goofy and Pluto. He began his career as a commercial artist and moved to Hollywood in the 1920s, where he made *Steamboat Willie* (1928), the first cartoon with sound and music – with Disney himself providing Mickey's voice. After *Three Little Pigs* (1933) came the world's first feature-length cartoon with sound and colour – SNOW WHITE AND THE SEVEN DWARFS (1937). He masterminded

LISTEN HERE! *In* The Ladykillers, *gangster Alec Guinness wags a warning finger at his trusting landlady, Katie Johnson.*

four more full-length children's classics: FANTASIA (1940), *Pinocchio* (1940), *Dumbo* (1941) and *Bambi* (1942). In the 1940s he combined cartoon animation and live action – a technique he later used to great effect in *Mary Poppins* (1964). Among his other cartoon films were *Lady and the Tramp* (1955), *One Hundred and One Dalmatians* (1960) and *The Jungle Book* (1967).

Doctor Who Children's BBC television series about a Time Lord, known as Doctor Who, who travels through time and space in a police telephone box called the Tardis – short for 'Time and Relative Dimensions in Space'. Actors who played the Doctor include William Hartnell (1963-6), Patrick Troughton (1966-9), Jon Pertwee (1970-4) and Tom Baker (1974-81).

Donat, Robert (1905-58) British stage and film actor renowned for his Oscar-winning performance as the schoolmaster in *Goodbye Mr Chips* (1939). Donat's good looks – and his dashing roles as *The Count of Monte Cristo* (1934) and Richard Hannay in Hitchcock's spy thriller *The 39 Steps* (1935) – made him a heart-throb. Dogged by ill health, his last film appearance was as a Chinese mandarin in *The Inn of the Sixth Happiness* (1958), with Ingrid Bergman.

Douglas, Kirk (1916-) (Real name Issur Danielovitch) Dimple-chinned Hollywood star whose many notable films include *Champion* (1949), *Ace in the Hole* (1951), *Lust for Life* (1956), in which he played the painter Vincent Van Gogh, *Gunfight at the OK Corral* (1956) and *Spartacus* (1960). His son is Michael Douglas.

Douglas, Michael (1944-) Leading actor who starred in two of the most erotic thrillers of recent times: *Fatal Attraction* (1987) and *Basic Instinct* (1992). Michael Douglas made his name in the popular TV police series *The Streets of San Francisco* (1972-5). Among his best-known films are *Romancing the Stone* (1984) and *Wall Street* (1987), for which he won a Best Actor Oscar.

Dracula films Hungarian actor Bela Lugosi was the first Hollywood star to don the Transylvanian count's cloak in *Dracula* (1931). Since then dozens of vampire films have been made, with leading actors such as Lon Chaney, Jnr, Christopher Lee, Klaus Kinski and Gary Oldman, who starred in Francis Ford Coppola's spectacular *Dracula* (1993).

🕯At his express wish, Lugosi, who died in Los Angeles in 1956, was buried in his long, silk-lined black Dracula cloak.

Ealing comedies Family of whimsical films – made at Ealing Studios in West London – which poked gentle fun at British eccentricities and values in the years following World War II. The stories were often about oppressed communities and aggrieved individuals rebelling against authority and petty bureaucracy. They included *Whisky Galore* (1949), *Passport to Pimlico* (1949), *The Lavender Hill Mob* (1951), *The Man in the White Suit* (1951), *The Titfield Thunderbolt* (1953) and *The Ladykillers* (1955).

EastEnders Down-to-earth TV serial launched in 1985 and seen as the BBC's answer to *Coronation Street*. Set in the fictitious London borough of Walford, E20, it relates the day-to-day activities of the residents of Albert Square – and of the regulars in the local pub, the Queen 'Vic'. It made household names of Leslie Grantham as 'Dirty Den', the original landlord of the Queen 'Vic', and his wife Angie, played by Anita Dobson.

Eastwood, Clint (1930-) Craggy-faced American actor-director who became an international star as The Man With No Name in the SPAGHETTI WESTERN *A Fistful of Dollars* (1964) and its two sequels: *For a Few Dollars More* (1965) and *The Good, the Bad and the Ugly* (1966). He originally made his name in TV as the cowboy Rowdy Yates in *Rawhide* (1959-66). Later he starred in

HIT MAN
Clint Eastwood played the cheroot-chewing gunman, who shot first and asked questions later, in the first batch of 'spaghetti Westerns'.

GRAND DAME *With her imperious manner, Edith Evans was ideally cast as Lady Bracknell in* The Importance of Being Earnest.

Coogan's Bluff (1968), *Where Eagles Dare,* (1969) and *The Beguiled* (1971). Then came the DIRTY HARRY sequence of thrillers and two crazy comedies, *Every Which Way But Loose* (1978) and *Any Which Way You Can* (1980). As a director he created and played the leads in the thriller *Play Misty For Me* (1971), *High Plains Drifter* (1972), *Pale Rider* (1985), *White Hunter, Black Heart* (1990), a study of an egocentric film director based upon John HUSTON, and *Unforgiven* (1992), a powerful Western which won four Oscars including Best Picture and Best Director.

Easy Rider Trend-setting film about two drop-out, drug-taking motorcyclists who travel from Los Angeles to New Orleans Mardi Gras in pursuit of 'freedom'. Their attitude and appearance, however, bring them little but abuse, hatred and scorn. Made in 1969 on a shoestring budget, the film starred Peter Fonda and Dennis Hopper, who co-wrote the script and was also the director. It made an overnight star of Jack NICHOLSON in a small but telling role as a philosophical drunk.

Eisenstein, Sergei Mikhailovich (1898-1948) Latvian film director whose films about the Russian Revolution – The BATTLESHIP POTEMKIN (1925) and *October* (1928) contain pioneering film techniques. Both were propaganda films, but include enduring images.

Emmy Prestigious award which is TV's version of the Oscar. It is presented annually by the American Academy of Television Arts and Sciences.

E.T. – The Extra-terrestrial Heart-warming fantasy film about an American boy who befriends a scared and lovable being from outer space who is stranded on Earth. With the loving help of his brother and sister, the youngster helps E.T. – a charming special effects creation, part pet and part 'human' – to return to his own planet. The film was directed by Steven SPIELBERG in 1982.

Evans, Dame Edith (1888-1976) Imposing British actress best remembered for her majestic performance as Lady Bracknell in Oscar Wilde's comedy *The Importance of Being Earnest*, which she played on the stage in 1939 and in the 1952 film version.

Fairbanks, Douglas (1883-1939) Athletic American actor known for his flamboyant performances in silent films such as *The Mark of Zorro* (1920), *The Three Musketeers* (1921), *Robin Hood* (1922), *The Thief of Bagdad* (1924) and *The Black Pirate* (1926). His career declined with the coming of sound. His son, the debonair Douglas Fairbanks Junior (1909-), played similar swashbuckling roles in films such as *The Prisoner of Zenda* (1937), *Gunga Din* (1939) and *The Corsican Brothers* (1941).

Fantasia Revolutionary Walt Disney film, made in 1940, featuring cartoon sequences set to the music of Bach, Beethoven, Schubert and Stravinsky among others, and performed by the Philadelphia Orchestra conducted by Leopold Stokowski – who has a brief conversation with Mickey Mouse. The movie's two most memorable sequences feature Mickey Mouse and many bucket-carrying broomsticks in Paul Dukas's *The Sorcerer's Apprentice*, and the ballet-dancing animals – including elephants, ostriches and hippopotamuses – in Ponchielli's *Dance of the Hours*.

Fawlty Towers Uproarious BBC television series (1975-9) about a bullying, devious and frequently panic-stricken seaside hotel proprietor. It was written by comedian John Cleese, who played Basil Fawlty, and his then wife Connie Booth, who played Polly the maid. The other main characters were Sybil Fawlty (Prunella Scales) and Manuel the waiter (Andrew Sachs). Basil Fawlty was based on a hotel owner Cleese had once met in Torquay.

Fellini, Federico (1920-93) Stylish Italian director whose films are admired for their dazzling camera work and arresting imagery. A former cartoonist, Fellini won worldwide acclaim for *La Strada* (1954), starring his wife Guiletta Masina, *La Dolce Vita* (1960) and *8½* (1963).

film noir Term borrowed from the French, literally meaning 'dark film' and used to describe the murky, doom-ridden Hollywood crime thrillers of the 1940s. Classic examples include Billy WILDER's

FLIGHTS OF FANCY *In Fellini's autobiographical 8½, a renowned film director suffering from a creative block attempts to break through it by recalling dreams and fantastic scenes from his past.*

Double Indemnity (1944), *The Killers* (1946), starring Burt Lancaster and Ava Gardner, and *Crossfire* (1947), with Robert Mitchum, Robert Ryan and Gloria Grahame.

Flynn, Errol (1909-59) Dashing, Tasmanian-born film star who became a Hollywood legend – as much for his hard drinking, fist fights and womanising as his acting. Even so, his good looks, charm and infectious sense of humour gained him fans throughout the world in *The Charge of the Light Brigade* (1936), *The Adventures of Robin Hood* (1938), *The Sea Hawk* (1940), *They Died With Their Boots On* (1941) and *Gentleman Jim* (1942).

Fonda, Henry (1905-82) Dignified American stage and screen actor. He worked with director John FORD on films such as *The Young Mr Lincoln* (1939), *The Grapes of Wrath* (1940); the Western *My Darling Clementine* (1946), in which he played the sheriff Wyatt Earp; and the comedy *Mister Roberts* (1955), in the title role of an officer aboard a US cargo ship in World War II who longs for action. Other notable films include: *Twelve Angry Men* (1956), *Fail Safe* (1964) and *Once Upon a Time in the West* (1968), in which he appeared as a sinister villain. He eventually won an Oscar for his part in *On Golden Pond* (1981), opposite Katharine Hepburn and daughter Jane Fonda. He was the father of actor-director Peter Fonda (1939-   ).

Fonda, Jane (1937-   ) American actress who shot to international fame in the title role of *Barbarella* (1967), a film based on an adult science-fiction comic strip, in which she played a voluptuous 'sex symbol' in an array of revealing costumes. She moved on to more serious and rewarding roles in *They Shoot Horses, Don't They?* (1969), and two films for which she won Oscars: *Klute* (1971) and *Coming Home* (1978). Her later films include *The China Syndrome* (1979), *On Golden Pond* (1981), *The Morning After* (1986) and *Old Gringo* (1989). She has also created extremely successful health and fitness books and videos. She is the daughter of Henry FONDA.

Ford, Harrison (1942-   ) American actor who found success with his sympathetic portrayal of two mercenary heroes: the pilot Han Solo in the STAR WARS trilogy (1977-83), and the archaeologist Indiana Jones in *Raiders of the Lost Ark* (1981). His other films include: *Blade Runner* (1982), *Indiana Jones and the Temple of Doom* (1984), *Witness* (1985), *Indiana Jones and the Last Crusade* (1989) and *The Fugitive* (1993).

Ford, John (1895-1973) (Real name Sean Aloysius O'Feeney) Irish-American director of more than 100 feature films, including many Westerns. These include classics such as *Stagecoach* (1939), starring John Wayne, *My Darling Clementine* (1946), *Fort Apache* (1948), *She Wore a Yellow Ribbon* (1949), *The Searchers* (1956) and *The Man Who Shot Liberty Valance* (1962), with James Stewart. Ford's Oscar-winning films were *The Informer* (1935), *The Grapes of Wrath* (1940), *How Green Was My Valley* (1941) and *The Quiet Man* (1952). He also made patriotic documentary films in World War II.

Formby, George (1904-61) Ukelele-playing Lancashire comedian who was one of Britain's biggest stars during World War II. He portrayed an innocent abroad in a flock of cheaply made and cheerful films. These include: *Let George Do It* (1940), *Spare a Copper* (1941), *Bell-Bottom George* (1943), *Get Cracking* (1943), *I Didn't Do It* (1945) and *George in Civvy Street* (1946).

SINGING CLOWN *Bearing his gormless grin, George Formby puts over a song in the comedy* Turned Out Nice Again *(1941)*.

42nd Street Backstage musical comedy film in which the leading lady of a Broadway show falls ill, and a girl from the chorus takes over. 'You're going out there a youngster,' the director tells her. 'But you've got to come back a star!' Made in Hollywood in 1933, it has some spectacular song-and-dance numbers devised by choreographer Busby BERKELEY.

Foster, Jodie (1962-   ) Former American child actress who won Best Actress Oscars for her performances as a rape victim in *The Accused* (1988) and as an FBI agent in *The Silence of the Lambs* (1991) opposite Anthony Hopkins. Her earlier films include *Alice Doesn't Live Here Any*

More (1974), *The Little Girl Who Lives Down the Lane* (1976) and Martin Scorsese's *Taxi Driver* (1976), in which she portrayed a teenage prostitute. She made her debut as a director with *Little Man Tate* (1991), the emotional story of a seven-year-old boy genius in which she also starred.

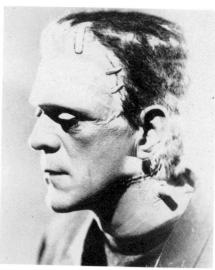
MONSTER MAN *As Frankenstein's monster, Boris Karloff spent five hours a day having his double-domed skull and make-up applied.*

Frankenstein films Series of monster movies based upon Mary Shelley's 19th-century Gothic novel. The most influential of these, *Frankenstein* (1931), was made in Hollywood with British-born Boris Karloff as Baron Frankenstein's man-made monster. It was followed by *The Bride of Frankenstein* (1935) and *Son of Frankenstein* (1939). In 1957 the original Hollywood film was remade in England by Hammer Films as *The Curse of Frankenstein*, with Peter Cushing as the scientist and Christopher Lee as the monster. (See also FRANKENSTEIN in 'English Literature'.)

Gable, Clark (1901-60) Robust American actor known as the 'King of Hollywood'. He made his greatest hit as the dashing Rhett Butler in GONE WITH THE WIND (1939). His other films include the romantic comedy *It Happened One Night* (1934), for which he won an Oscar, *Mutiny on the Bounty* (1935), *San Francisco* (1936), *Adventure* (1945), *Run Silent, Run Deep* (1958) and the posthumously released *The Misfits*, in which he plays an ageing modern cowboy opposite Marilyn Monroe.

♣ Gable's ears were so large and protruding that they had to be taped back for his film roles. He also confessed that, 'I haven't a single tooth of my own in my head!'

LONELY GODDESS *With her chiselled beauty and air of mystery, Greta Garbo played remote and ethereal heroines. She afterwards became the world's best-known – and most photographed – recluse.*

Garbo, Greta (1905-90) Aloof, Swedish actress who went to America in 1925 and became one of Hollywood's first 'legends'. Starting with *The Torrent* (1926), she made a quick succession of silent films which displayed her as an alluring vamp. These include *Flesh and the Devil*, *Love* and *A Woman of Affairs*. In 1930 came her first talking picture, *Anna Christie*, in which her opening words were, 'Gimme visky, ginger ale on the side. And don't be stingy, baby!' She followed this with romantic roles in *Grand Hotel* (1932) – in which she cried, 'I vant to be let alone!' – *Queen Christina*

(1933), *Anna Karenina* (1935) and *Camille* (1937). Her first comedy, *Ninotchka* (1939), was billed as the film in which 'Garbo laughs!' She played another comic role in *Two-Faced Woman* (1941), which was savaged by the critics, prompting her abrupt retirement from the screen.

Garland, Judy (1922-69) (Real name Frances Gumm) Vivacious American actress and entertainer who made her greatest film impact as Dorothy, the little girl who sings 'Over the Rainbow' in The WIZARD OF OZ (1939). She teamed up with Mickey Rooney for several brash and energetic 'youth' musicals including *Babes in Arms* (1939), *Strike Up the Band* (1940) and *Babes on Broadway* (1941). She then starred in *For Me and My Gal* (1942), with Gene Kelly, *Meet Me in St Louis* (1944), in which she sang the celebrated 'Trolley Song', and *Easter Parade* (1948), with Fred Astaire. However, the pressures of stardom, weight problems, alcohol and drugs played havoc with her life. Her studio contract was cancelled, but she made a powerful comeback in *A Star is Born* (1954), opposite James Mason. Her daughter is the singer and actress, Liza Minnelli (1946-).

Genevieve Delightful British comedy about the rivalry between two couples competing in the annual veteran car run from London to Brighton. Made in 1953, it starred Kenneth More, Kay Kendall, John Gregson, Dinah Sheridan – and a superb line-up of vintage vehicles.

Gere, Richard (1949-) Muscular American actor and sex-symbol who rocketed to stardom as a male escort in the film *American Gigolo* (1980). He consolidated his reputation as an actor and pin-up as a naval recruit in *An Officer and a Gentleman* (1982). After several commercial flops, Gere re-established himself as a corrupt cop in *Internal Affairs* (1989), a love-struck millionaire in the romantic comedy *Pretty Woman* (1990), and a supposedly long-lost husband in *Sommersby* (1993), an American remake of the Gérard Depardieu film *The Return of Martin Guerre*.

Gibson, Mel (1956-) American-born film actor who became an international star in the title role of the *Mad Max* trilogy (1979-1985). Made in Australia, the films dealt with a vengeful policeman in a lawless, gang-ridden society of the future. In America Gibson starred as a violent and ruthless detective in *Lethal Weapon* (1987), *Lethal Weapon 2* (1989) and *Lethal Weapon 3* (1992). In contrast, he was a convincing Prince of Denmark in Franco Zeffirelli's film version of *Hamlet* (1990).

Gielgud, Sir John (1904-) Veteran British actor and director hailed as one of the greatest Hamlets of the century – a role he has played more than 500 times. His many films date from the 1920s and the more recent ones include *Julius Caesar* (1953), as the 'lean and hungry' Cassius, *The Charge of the Light Brigade* (1968), *Murder on the Orient Express* (1974), *Arthur* (1981) for which he won an Oscar as Best Supporting Actor, and *Prospero's Books*

(1991), a fanciful version of Shakespeare's *The Tempest*. He also appeared in the TV serial BRIDESHEAD REVISITED (1981). He was knighted in 1953.

Godfather, The First of a trilogy of violent Mafia films about the corrupt Corleone family, directed in 1971 by Francis Ford Coppola and based on a best-selling novel by Mario Puzo. It starred Marlon Brando in the title role and Al Pacino as his son and heir. It won three Oscars, including Best Picture and Best Actor (Brando). *The Godfather, Part Two* (1974) won six Oscars, including best director (Coppola) and best supporting actor (Robert De Niro). *The Godfather, Part Three* (1990) again starred Pacino, but collected no honours.

Goldwyn, Samuel (1882-1974) (Real name Samuel Goldfisch) Polish-born American producer of mainly family films who set up his own company – Goldwyn Pictures – in 1917. After he left the company it merged with Louis B. Mayer Productions and Metro Pictures in 1924 to form Metro-Goldwyn-Mayer. From then on Goldwyn worked as an independent producer. His most notable films include *Wuthering Heights* (1939), *The Westerner* (1940), *The Best Years of Our Lives* (1946), *Hans Christian Andersen* (1952), *Guys and Dolls* (1955) and *Porgy and Bess* (1959).
🎤Among the so-called 'Goldwynisms' attributed to the producer are: 'Anyone who goes to a psychiatrist should have his head examined!' 'Include me out!' 'In two words: im-possible!' and, 'A verbal contract isn't worth the paper it's written on!'

Gone with the Wind Hollywood's most ambitious prewar talking film, based on the best-selling novel by Margaret Mitchell (1900-49). Made in 1939, it recounts the romantic adventures of a Southern belle named Scarlett O'Hara at the time of the American Civil War. For three years before filming began, producer David O. Selznick (1902-65) bombarded the American people with publicity about the forthcoming epic. He held a nationwide competition to find the 'ideal' Scarlett O'Hara, finally settling for the relatively unknown English actress Vivien Leigh. He fought the censors to allow Clark Gable, who played Rhett Butler, to use a mild swear word in the line, 'Frankly, my dear, I don't give a damn!'

Goon Show, The (1952-60) Eccentric British radio comedy show that was the brainchild of Spike Milligan. It involved a cast of freakish characters such as Eccles, Bluebottle and Neddy Seagoon. The show

FILM EPIC *In 1939* Gone with the Wind *was the longest, most expensive film ever released. It lasted over 3½ hours and cost $4.25 million.*

began in 1951 as *Crazy People* with Milligan, Peter Sellers, Harry Secombe and Michael Bentine. It was renamed *The Goon Show* in 1952; Bentine left shortly afterwards.

Grable, Betty (1916-73) Blonde American song-and-dance star whose legs – which she insured for $1 million – made her the leading Allied pin-up of World War II. Among her many colourful musicals were *Tin Pan Alley* (1940), *Coney Island* (1943), *Mother Wore Tights* (1947) and *Three for the Show* (1955).
🎤She said of her career that: 'There are two reasons why I'm in the movies – and I'm standing on both of them!'

Grant, Cary (1904-86) (Real name Archibald Leach) Witty and elegant British-born actor with an accent all of his own, noted for his polished romantic performances. He went to America in 1920 with a troupe of acrobats working in circuses and in vaudeville. He entered films in 1932 and had his first leading roles opposite Marlene Dietrich in *Blonde Venus* (1932) and Mae West in *She Done Him Wrong* (1933). Later comedies include *Bringing Up Baby* (1938), *Arsenic and Old Lace* (1943) and *Mr Blandings Builds His Dream House* (1948). Alfred HITCHCOCK chose him to co-star with some of Hollywood's most glamorous leading ladies in films such as: *Suspicion* (1941), with Joan Fontaine; *Notorious* (1946), with Ingrid Bergman; *To Catch a Thief* (1954), with Grace Kelly; and *North*

by Northwest (1959), with Eva Marie Saint. His later films include: *That Touch of Mink* (1962), with Doris Day; *Charade* (1963), with Audrey Hepburn; and *Father Goose* (1964), with Leslie Caron.
🎤A journalist once wired Grant's agent, asking: 'How old Cary Grant?' Grant replied to this himself, saying: 'Old Cary Grant fine. How old you?'

Great Train Robbery, The Cinema's first Western, made in New Jersey, USA, in 1903 – it lasted for 11 minutes. Writer and director Edwin S. Porter used new techniques such as panning – moving the camera to follow the action. Audiences jumped in their seats as a bandit raised his gun and – in realistic close-up – fired it straight into their faces.

Griffith, D.W. (1875-1948) Pioneer American film director who brought artistic recognition to Hollywood. In his two major films – The BIRTH OF A NATION (1915) and *Intolerance* (1916), a study of oppression throughout the ages – he developed techniques such as flashbacks and close-ups which were to influence the entire movie industry. He made only two 'talkies' – *Abraham Lincoln* (1930) and *The Struggle* (1931), a sombre study of an alcoholic – before going out of fashion.

Guinness, Sir Alec (1914-) Versatile British stage, screen and television actor. He was a notable Shylock in *The Merchant of Venice* (1937) at London's Old Vic theatre – and, after war service, was an unforgettable Fagin in David Lean's film version of *Oliver Twist* (1948). He scored a triumph in the macabre comedy *Kind Hearts and Coronets* (1949) and starred in four more EALING COMEDIES: *The Lavender Hill Mob* (1951), *The Man in the White Suit* (1951), *The Ladykillers* (1955) and *Barnacle Bill* (1957). He won an Oscar as a fanatical army officer in *The Bridge on the River Kwai* (1957). He also starred in two major BBC television series: *Tinker, Tailor, Soldier, Spy* (1979) and *Smiley's People* (1981). He was knighted in 1959.

Hancock, Tony (1924-68) British comedian who starred in the BBC radio series *Hancock's Half-Hour* (1954-59) as the doleful social misfit, Anthony Aloysius St John Hancock. The show moved to television in 1956, with Sid James (1913-76) again playing Hancock's long-suffering best friend. Hancock starred in two whimsical comedy films: *The Rebel* (1961) and *The Punch and Judy Man* (1963). Insecurity and alcoholism finally drove him to suicide.

Hepburn, Audrey (1929-93) (Real
name Edda van Heemstra Hepburn-Ruston) Beguiling, Belgian-born actress who played the cockney flower-girl Eliza Doolittle in the film version of ▷MY FAIR LADY (1964). After playing small parts in British films, including *Laughter in Paradise* (1951) and *The Lavender Hill Mob* (1951), she moved to America and made her Oscar-winning Hollywood debut as an 'off-duty' princess in *Roman Holiday* (1953), with Gregory Peck. She had leading roles in films such as *Sabrina* (1954), *War and Peace* (1956), *The Nun's Story* (1958), *Breakfast at Tiffany's* (1961) and *Charade* (1963). She retired from the screen in 1968, and made a come-back in *Robin and Marian* (1976), with Sean Connery. Her last screen appearance was as an angel in Steven Spielberg's film fantasy *Always* (1989).

Hepburn, Katharine (1907-   ) American star whose portrayals of spirited, free-thinking women have won her an unsurpassed four Best Actress Oscars from a record 12 nominations. Her winning roles were in the films *Morning Glory* (1933), *Guess Who's Coming to Dinner* (1967), *The Lion in Winter* (1968) and *On Golden Pond* (1981). Hepburn had a long relationship, both on and off screen, with Spencer TRACY – with whom she made several 'war-of-the-sexes' comedies, including *Woman of the Year* (1941), *Adam's Rib* (1949), *Pat and Mike* (1952) and *The Desk Set* (1957). Among her other notable films are *Bringing Up Baby* (1938), *The Philadelphia Story* (1940), The AFRICAN QUEEN (1951) and *Suddenly Last Summer* (1959).

Heston, Charlton (1924-) Rugged American star mostly cast in historical, adventure and science fiction epics. Among his films are: *The Greatest Show on Earth* (1952); *The Ten Commandments* (1956), as Moses; *The Agony and the Ecstasy* (1965), as Michelangelo; *Khartoum* (1966), as General Gordon; and *Planet of the Apes* (1967).

BIRDMAN OF HOLLYWOOD *Director Alfred Hitchcock makes friends with Corvis the seagull and Buddy the raven – two of the attackers that terrorise a small Californian town in* The Birds.

Hitchcock, Sir Alfred (1899-1980)
British film director renowned for the dazzling 'shock' effects in his films – and for the brief and witty appearances he made in many of his classic thrillers. He directed the first British 'talkie', *Blackmail* (1929), and among his other early thrillers were *The 39 Steps* (1935), *Secret Agent* (1936), *Sabotage* (1936) and *The Lady Vanishes* (1939). He then went to Hollywood where he made a host of critical and box office successes. These include: *Rebecca* (1940); *Shadow of a Doubt* (1943); *Spellbound* (1945), with its remarkable dream sequence designed by Salvador ▷DALI; *Notorious* (1946); *Strangers on a Train* (1951); *Rear Window* (1954); *North by Northwest* (1959); PSYCHO (1960); *The Birds* (1963); and *Marnie* (1964). The films of his final period – *Torn Curtain* (1966), *Topaz* (1969), *Frenzy* (1972) and *Family Plot* (1976) – had their quota of excitement, humour and suspense. His portly figure, double chin and funereal voice became well known to television viewers through *Alfred Hitchcock Presents* (1955-61), a series of short dramas which he introduced and occasionally directed. He was knighted in 1980.

Hoffman, Dustin (1937-) Adroit, short-statured American screen and stage actor who sprang to prominence as a sexually naive former student in the film *The Graduate* (1967). He then appeared as a tubercular cripple in *Midnight Cowboy* (1969), an 121-year-old soldier-of-fortune in *Little Big Man* (1970) and a doting single parent in *Kramer vs Kramer* (1979), for which he won a Best Actor Oscar. He

RIVALRY IN THE ARENA *The chariot race between Charlton Heston (centre) and a ruthless Roman tribune is the highlight of* Ben Hur, *which tells of the persecution of the Jews at the time of Christ.*

showed his gift for comedy in *Tootsie* (1982), as an unemployed actor who disguises himself as a woman in order to get work. He won his second Oscar for his performance as an autistic innocent in *Rain Man* (1988). He also played the title role in Steven Spielberg's *Hook* (1991).

Hollywood Capital of the film world since 1913, when Cecil B. DE MILLE made *The Squaw Man* in what was then a lawless desert area which had recently become part of Los Angeles. Early film-makers were lured by the promise of 350 days of sunshine a year and terrain that could be used to film anything from Foreign Legion epics to Wild West dramas. By the early 1930s, when sound had revolutionised the cinema, Hollywood was a thriving, self-contained community. Known as 'Tinsel Town', it was renowned for its opulent lifestyle, parties and scandals. The 'Golden Age' lasted until the early 1960s, when the majority of the studios – or 'dream factories' – were making films for television.
🎭 Marilyn Monroe once said of Hollywood: 'It's a place where they pay you $50 000 for a kiss – and 50 cents for your soul!'

Hope, Bob (1903-) British-born film comedian famed for his 'ski-slope' nose, immaculate sense of timing and skill in playing the complete screen coward. He went to America with his family in 1907. After a spell as a vaudeville dancer, and a fast-talking radio comic, he appeared in several Broadway musicals. He made his feature film debut in *The Big Broadcast of 1938* and consolidated his reputation as a funny man in *Thanks for the Memory* (1938), *The Cat and The Canary* (1939) and *The Ghost Breakers* (1940). He then teamed up with Bing ▷CROSBY and Dorothy Lamour (1914-) in the hugely popular ROAD films, starting with *The Road to Singapore* (1940). He also made a series of 'solo' comedies including: *My Favourite Blonde* (1942), *My Favourite Brunette* (1947), *The Paleface* (1948) and *Fancy Pants* (1950).

Hopkins, Sir Anthony (1937-) Welsh stage, screen and TV actor who became an international star in Hollywood, winning a Best Actor Oscar for his chilling portrayal of a serial killer, Dr Hannibal Lecter, in *The Silence of the Lambs* (1991). His early films included *The Lion in Winter* (1968), *Young Winston* (1972) and two supernatural thrillers made in America: *Audrey Rose* (1977) and *Magic* (1978), directed by Richard ATTENBOROUGH. Intense and stockily built, he played leading roles in *Howards End* (1992), *Chaplin* (1992),

Dracula (1993) and *The Remains of the Day* (1993). Highlights of his British stage career include *King Lear* (1986) and *Antony and Cleopatra* (1987).

Huston, John (1906-87) Colourful American director, screenwriter and actor who was the son of veteran character actor Walter Huston (1884-1950) and the father of actress Anjelica Huston (1952-). He directed the first of his own scripts with *The Maltese Falcon* (1941), a hard-boiled detective story starring Humphrey Bogart. He followed this with two classic gangster films: *Key Largo* (1948), with Bogart and Edward G. Robinson; and *The Asphalt Jungle* (1950), in which Marilyn Monroe

JUNGLE TROUBLE *Bob Hope (right), Dorothy Lamour and Bing Crosby face danger in their 1941 safari comedy* The Road to Zanzibar.

has a small but eye-catching part. *The Treasure of the Sierra Madre* (1948) won Huston Oscars for Best Director and Best Screenplay, while Walter Huston got the Best Supporting Actor award. John Huston won more acclaim for The AFRICAN QUEEN (1951), in which Bogart won an Oscar. Huston's other films include the quirky *Beat the Devil* (1954), again with Bogart, *The Night of the Iguana* (1964) and *Prizzi's Honor* (1985), in which Anjelica Huston won an Oscar as Best Supporting Actress.

It's That Man Again British comedy radio show – popularly known as ITMA – that made the nation laugh and boosted morale during World War II. Starring the Liverpool comedian Tommy Handley

(1896-1949), the show – a quickfire mixture of parody, satire, puns, songs and nonsense – began in July 1939. The last weekly episode was in January 1949 – three days before Handley's untimely death of a stroke. Among the characters' much-quoted catchphrases were those of the cockney charlady Mrs Mopp, 'Can I do you now, sir?'; the hard-drinking Colonel Chinstrap, 'I don't mind if I do!'; the mournful Mona Lott, 'It's being so cheerful as keeps me going!'; and the German master-spy, 'This is Funf speaking!'

ITV Commercial television began transmission in Britain in September 1955 under the title Independent Television, or ITV. The first commercial showed a tube of Gibbs toothpaste encased in a block of ice.

Jaws Nail-biting suspense film about the devastating effect a killer shark has on a crowded New England beach resort. Directed in 1975 by Steven SPIELBERG, the film cleverly builds up tension and is two-thirds under way before the shark is fully seen – after it has claimed its first victims. The movie's success led to three sequels: *Jaws II* (1978), *Jaws III* (1983) and *Jaws – The Revenge* (1987), none of which was directed by Spielberg, and none of which captured the terror of the original.

Jazz Singer, The World's first 'talking' feature film, made in America in 1927, starring the singer Al ▷JOLSON (1886-1950), whose opening lines were: 'Wait a minute, wait a minute. You ain't heard nothin' yet! You wanna hear 'Toot, Toot, Tootsie'? All right, hold on . . . ' The film was a box-office sensation with its sentimental story about the son of a cantor who becomes a popular entertainer – which reflected Jolson's own life. Audiences wept when Jolson, in black-face, knelt on one knee and serenaded his 'Mammy'. The film – with its synchronised music and snatches of dialogue – changed the course of the cinema, and many silent film actors with bad voices were put out of work.

Jurassic Park Monster movie, released in 1993 and noted for its thrilling special effects. Directed by Steven Spielberg, it tells how a fanatical millionaire, played by Richard Attenborough, creates a theme park inhabited by genetically reproduced dinosaurs which go on the rampage.

Kaye, Danny (1913-87) (Real name David Daniel Kaminsky) Exuberant American film comedian and stage and television entertainer, noted for his mimicry and tongue-twisting musical numbers. He shot to stardom with his first film, *Up in Arms* (1944). Then came a host of hits, including *Wonder Man* (1945), *The Kid from Brooklyn* (1946), *The Secret Life of Walter Mitty* (1947), *Hans Christian Andersen* (1952) and *The Court Jester* (1956). He is also remembered for his high-spirited one-man shows at the London Palladium in the 1950s.

Keaton, Buster (1895-1966) Poker-faced Hollywood clown who wrote and directed many of his own silent comedy films. These include *The Boat* (1921), *Our Hospitality* (1923), *The Navigator* (1924) and *The General* (1926), commonly regarded as his masterpiece.

Kelly, Grace (1929-82) American cinema actress and former society beauty whose cool charm brought her stardom. Her films include the classic Western *High Noon* (1952); three Hitchcock thrillers, *Dial M for Murder* (1954), *Rear Window* (1954) and *To Catch a Thief* (1955); and the melodramatic *The Country Girl* (1954), for which she won an Oscar. In 1956 she gave up her film career to marry Prince Rainier III of Monaco. She was killed when her car plunged off a mountain road on the Riviera.

KING OF THE CITY *An outsize and rampant King Kong, grasping the girl he has kidnapped, is superimposed against the New York skyline.*

HIGH LIFE *In 1956 Grace Kelly starred in the Cole Porter musical*, High Society. *She played an aloof socialite nicknamed 'Miss Frigidaire'.*

Kendall, Kay (1926-59) Sophisticated, red-headed British film actress, best remembered for her exhilarating trumpet-blowing scene in the comedy GENEVIEVE (1953). She made her movie debut in *Fiddlers Three* (1944), starring the music-hall comedian Tommy Trinder. Her other films include *Simon and Laura* (1955) and *The Reluctant Debutante* (1958).

Keystone Cops, The Frenzied troupe of comics formed in 1912 by Hollywood's 'comedy king', producer Mack Sennett (1880-1960). Their silent shorts were famed for their car chases, stunts and custard-pie battles. They disbanded in 1920.

Kind Hearts and Coronets Cynical black comedy starring Dennis Price as a distant heir to the Dukedom of Chalfont. To succeed to the title he cold-bloodedly murders six members of the aristocratic d'Ascoyne family – each played by Alec Guinness – who stand in his way. Directed by Robert Hamer in 1949, it has a wit and style reminiscent of Oscar Wilde.

King Kong Classic monster film, made in 1933, about a giant ape known by his captors as King Kong. Shipped from a remote Pacific island to New York, Kong is put on show in a circus – from which he escapes. He goes berserk, wrecking cars, terrorising the city and abducting a scantily clad blonde played by Fay Wray (1907-   ). Girl in hand, he makes his last desperate stand on top of the Empire State Building, where he tries to fight off the planes sent to shoot him down.

Appearing to stand some 50 ft (15 m) high on screen, Kong was actually a 16 in (40 cm) animated model.

Kubrick, Stanley (1928-   ) American director, writer and producer who caused a public outcry with his disturbing film A CLOCKWORK ORANGE (1971). His other movies – all of which have caused controversy – include the black comedy *Dr Strangelove: Or How I Learned to Stop Worrying and Love the Bomb* (1963), the spectacular science fiction epic *2001: A Space Odyssey* (1968), the horror film *The Shining* (1980), in which Jack Nicholson played a deranged writer intent on murdering his wife and son, and the harrowing Vietnam drama *Full Metal Jacket* (1987).

Lancaster, Burt (1913-94) Brawny American film star who began his show business career as a circus acrobat. He sang and danced in US Army shows during World War II and made a compelling film debut in *The Killers* (1946). Other leading roles followed in *Brute Force* (1947); *Criss Cross* (1949); *Trapeze* (1956), in which he played an acrobat; *Gunfight at the OK Corral* (1957); *Sweet Smell of Success* (1957); *Elmer Gantry* (1960), for which he won an Oscar for his portrayal of a hypocritical evangelist; and *The Birdman of Alcatraz* (1962). He later played an ageing gangster in *Atlantic City* (1980), a Texas oil magnate in the British-made *Local Hero* (1983), and a train robber in *Tough Guys* (1986), which also starred Kirk Douglas.

Laurel and Hardy Bowler-hatted comedy duo whose screen antics kept audiences laughing for more than a quarter of a century. The thin, nervous one – Stan

BUDDIES *Stan Laurel (left) smiles innocently, while Ollie Hardy seems about to scold: 'Here's another nice mess you've gotten me into!'*

Laurel (1890-1965) – was born Arthur Stanley Jefferson in England. The fat, bullying one – Oliver Hardy (1892-1957) – was born Norvell Hardy Junior in America. They teamed up in 1927 and made scores of films including *The Music Box* (1932), which won a Best Short Film Oscar, *Bonnie Scotland* (1935), *Way Out West* (1937) and *A Chump at Oxford* (1940). They toured Britain after World War II as a music-hall act, delighting their old admirers and winning many new ones.

Lawrence of Arabia Sweeping adventure film about the enigmatic British soldier-scholar T.E. Lawrence, dashingly played

by Peter O'Toole, who fought as an Arab guerrilla leader in the Middle East in World War I. Directed in 1962 by David Lean, the 3½ hour picture combined breathtaking desert scenes with high action – such as the blowing up of a railway train. Its superb cast included Jack Hawkins as General Allenby, Alec Guinness as Prince Feisal, and Anthony Quinn as an arrogant Arab chief. It won a Best Film Oscar. (See also ▷LAWRENCE OF ARABIA in 'British History'.)

Lean, Sir David (1908-91) Illustrious British director whose masterpiece, LAWRENCE OF ARABIA, set a new standard in screen epics, gaining him a Best Director Oscar. His early, small-scale films include: *This Happy Breed* (1944); *Blithe Spirit* (1945); two magnificent Dickens adaptations – *Great Expectations* (1946) and *Oliver Twist* (1948); *Hobson's Choice* (1953); and *Summer Madness* (1955), a touching romance set in Venice with Katharine Hepburn and Rossano Brazzi. He won his first Oscar for *The Bridge on the River Kwai* (1957), with Alec Guinness. His next two epics, *Dr Zhivago* (1965) and *Ryan's Daughter* (1970), were slated by many of the critics – although the public flocked to see them. Disheartened, he did not make another film until *A Passage to India* (1984), from E.M. Forster's novel about the clash of eastern and western cultures in British-ruled India. He was knighted in 1984.

Leigh, Vivien (1913-67) Radiant English stage and screen actress who played the vivacious Southern belle, Scarlett O'Hara, in GONE WITH THE WIND (1939) – for which she won an Oscar. She made her film debut in the British comedy *Things Are Looking Up* (1934) and played opposite Laurence Olivier in *Fire Over England* (1937). The couple married in 1940 after starring together in *Romeo and Juliet* in New York. They continued their partnership in the wartime morale-raiser *That Hamilton Woman* (1941), in which she played Emma Hamilton to Olivier's Lord Nelson. Her later films include: *Caesar and Cleopatra* (1945); *Anna Karenina* (1948); *A Streetcar Named Desire* (1951), in which her performance as another Southern belle, the neurotic Blanche Dubois, gained her a second Oscar; *The Deep Blue Sea* (1955); *The Roman Spring of Mrs Stone* (1961); and *Ship of Fools* (1965). Her career and marriage were blighted by mental illness.

Lemmon, Jack (1925-) American comic actor who made his name playing highly strung misfits before turning to

more serious roles. He worked with Billy WILDER in a string of comic hits including *Some Like It Hot* (1959), *The Apartment* (1960) and *The Fortune Cookie* (1966), with Walter Matthau (1920-). He also appeared with Matthau in the film version of Neil Simon's *The Odd Couple* (1967) and in *The Front Page* (1974), again directed by Wilder. Lemmon showed his dramatic talents as an alcoholic in *Days of Wine and Roses* (1962), a garment manufacturer fighting middle age in *Save the Tiger* (1973), for which he won a Best Actor Oscar, and a bereaved father in *Missing* (1981).

Lloyd, Harold (1893-1971) Bespectacled silent film comedian whose stunts made audiences laugh with fear and delight. They included a skyscraper-climbing contest in *Safety Last* (1923), in which he apparently clung for his life from the hands of a clock. He made dozens of comedies including *Girl Shy* (1924), *The Freshman* (1925), *The Kid Brother* (1927) and *Speedy* (1928). His few talking pictures – such as *The Sin of Harold Diddlebock* (1947) – were box-office flops. But he found new and appreciative audiences with two collections of highlights from his silent movies: *Harold Lloyd's World of Comedy* (1962) and *Harold Lloyd's Funny Side of Life* (1963).

GOOD FRIENDS *Insurance clerk Jack Lemmon woos elevator girl Shirley MacLaine in the cynical comedy of office life* The Apartment.

Lockwood, Margaret (1916-90) Britain's most popular female film star of the 1940s. Her best-known – and most infamous – movie was *The Wicked Lady* (1945), in which she shocked audiences as an aristocratic 17th-century highwaywoman in a revealingly low-cut dress. Her other films included Hitchcock's *The Lady Vanishes* (1938), *The Man in Grey* (1943), *Jassy* (1947) and *Cast a Dark Shadow* (1955).

LOVE MATCH Sophia Loren showed her comic flair in The Millionairess *(1960), about a romance between the world's richest woman and a poor Indian doctor, played by Peter Sellers.*

Loren, Sophia (1934-) (Real name Sofia Villani Scicolone) Voluptuous Italian actress and former beauty queen who became an international star and sex symbol in Hollywood productions in the 1950s. They included *The Pride and the Passion* (1957) and *Desire Under the Elms* (1958). She blossomed as a serious actress in Vittorio DE SICA's war drama *Two Women* (1960), for which she won a Best Actress Oscar, and starred in major epics such as *El Cid* (1961), *The Fall of the Roman Empire* (1964) and *Operation Crossbow* (1965). She also made two hit comedies with actor Marcello Mastroianni (1923-), *Yesterday, Today and Tomorrow* (1963) and *Marriage Italian Style* (1964). In the 1980s she turned to television work, including a remake of *Two Women* (1989).

Modest about her figure, Loren was quoted as saying, 'Everything you see, I owe to spaghetti!'

Losey, Joseph (1909-84) American film director who was driven out of the USA during the communist witchhunt of the 1950s. He moved to Britain, where he made some of the best films of the 1960s, including *The Servant* (1963), *King and Country* (1964) and *Accident* (1967) – all of which starred Dirk BOGARDE. He also directed *The Go-Between* (1971) and a sumptuous version of Mozart's *Don Giovanni* (1979).

Loy, Myrna (1905-93) Elegant American film actress who was hailed as the 'Queen of Hollywood' in the late 1930s. She first worked in silent films including

Ben Hur (1925) and moved smoothly into talking pictures, in which her charm was much in demand. In 1934 she co-starred with William Powell (1892-1984) as the husband-and-wife detective team, Nick and Nora Charles, in the first of *The Thin Man* series of films. She later appeared in the comedies *Mr Blandings Builds His Dream House* (1948) and *Cheaper by the Dozen* (1950).

Lumière brothers French pioneer film-makers – Auguste (1862-1954) and Louis (1864-1948) – who in December 1895 presented the first-ever moving pictures to a paying audience. The venue was a cafe in Paris and the short films – one of which showed workers leaving the brothers' photographic plate factory in Lyons – were shown by means of a combined motion-picture camera and projector which the brothers had invented.

MacLaine, Shirley (1934-) Ebullient American actress, singer and dancer who began her career as a Broadway chorus girl. She made her film debut in Alfred Hitchcock's black comedy *The Trouble With Harry* (1955) and starred in a string of comedies and musicals, including *The Apartment* (1960) and *Sweet Charity* (1968). She won an Oscar for her performance opposite Jack Nicholson in the marital drama *Terms of Endearment* (1983).

McQueen, Steve (1930-80) Poker-faced American film actor – and former reform-school inmate – who specialised in rugged, he-man roles. He starred in action films such as *The Magnificent Seven* (1960); *The Great Escape* (1963); *Bullitt* (1968), which featured a roller-coaster car chase over the hills of San Francisco; *The Getaway* (1972); *Papillon* (1973); and *The Towering*

MAGAZINES TO INFORM AND ENTERTAIN

Sales figures are one measure of a magazine's success and popularity. But some of the smaller circulation journals have an influence that has made them household names – and some that are no longer published live on in the memory of the reading public.

The Economist Weekly international news and business journal, with comment on politics, economics and finance. Founded in 1843. Circulation (UK) 103 268.

Good Housekeeping Monthly women's magazine with a practical focus on family life and the home, fashion, beauty, health and consumer news. Founded in 1922. Circulation (UK) 501 654.

Hello! Glossy weekly packed with flattering photographs and gossipy articles on royalty and other celebrities. Founded in 1988. Circulation (UK) 441 656.

National Geographic Magazine International glossy monthly on travel, wildlife, environment and anthropology, noted for its photography. Founded in 1888. Circulation (UK) 354 429.

Picture Post (1938-57) Weekly display case for leading photographers and an important social document. Still remembered for its forceful photojournalism.

Private Eye Fortnightly mix of cartoons, satire and investigative journalism. Often sued by those it has attacked. Founded in 1961. Circulation (UK) 179 523.

Punch (1841-1992) Satirical humorous weekly with cartoons about the British way of life. It was a familiar feature of doctors' and dentists' waiting-rooms.

Radio Times Weekly with comprehensive radio and television programme listings, and related profiles and articles. Founded in 1923. Circulation (UK) 1 441 280.

Reader's Digest General interest monthly with accessible, accurate writing on almost any subject. The world's most widely read magazine. Founded in the USA in 1922 and in Britain in 1938. Circulation (worldwide) 28 million; (UK) 1 784 733.

The Spectator Right-of-centre political weekly with arts reviews, columns and cartoons. Founded in 1828, it is the oldest continuously published English-language magazine. Circulation (UK) 48 672.

Time International news and general interest weekly, noted for its brisk writing style and strong pictures. Founded in the USA in 1923 and in Europe in 1946. Circulation (UK) 107 000.

Vogue Influential fashion, trends and lifestyle monthly. The British edition was founded in 1916, when war prevented the import of glossy American magazines. Circulation (UK) 183 439.

Woman's Own Women's weekly with emphasis on health, looks and lifestyle, and articles on celebrities. Founded in 1932. Circulation (UK) 757 569.

Circulation figures: Jan-June 1994. Source: ABC.

Inferno (1974). He extended his acting range in a film version of Ibsen's *An Enemy of the People* (1977). Despite suffering from terminal cancer, he gave a typical, tight-lipped performance in the Western *Tom Horn* (1980), and as a modern-day bounty hunter in *The Hunter* (1980).

Magic Roundabout, The Children's television puppet show first screened by the BBC in 1965. It was originally narrated by Eric Thompson and the characters included Dougal the dog, Brian the snail, Dylan the rabbit, a girl called Florence, and a character called Zebedee, who bounced up and down on a spring, and ended every programme with the words, 'Time for bed'.

March of Time, The Extremely influential film-documentary series founded in America by *Time* magazine in 1935 and shown as part of cinema programmes. Each month the 20-minute films explored subjects such as the growth of Nazi Germany and the rise to power of the dictators Mussolini and Stalin. The series ran until the late 1940s, when it gradually gave way to current affairs programmes on television, including *CBS Report* in the USA and *Panorama* and *World in Action* in Britain.

Marx Brothers Family of American film comedians who were at their anarchistic peak in the early 1930s. Best known were the piano-playing Chico (real name Leonard, 1886-1961), who chased women and assumed a ludicrous Italian accent; the silent Harpo (real name Adolph, 1888-1964), who played the harp and communicated by means of a bicycle horn; and the wise-cracking, woman-chasing Groucho (real name Julius, 1890-1977), who loped around with a painted-on moustache and outsize cigar. The straight man Zeppo (real name Herbert, 1901-79), appeared in their first five films and then became a show-business agent. The lesser-known Gummo (real name Milton, 1893-1977), left the act before the first Marx Brothers film was made and became their business manager. Their films include *Animal Crackers* (1930), *Monkey Business* (1931), *Horse Feathers* (1932), *Duck Soup* (1933), *A Night at the Opera* (1935), *A Day at the Races* (1937) and *A Night in Casablanca* (1946). Groucho later appeared in a handful of films such as *A Girl in Every Port* (1952) and hosted the popular American quiz show *You Bet Your Life* on radio (1947-58) and also on television (1956-61).

Groucho Marx was known for his witty quips, such as: 'I never forget a face, but in your case I'll be glad to make an exception.'

M*A*S*H Highly popular American television series (1972-82), inspired by the hilarious 1969 Hollywood film of the same name. The initials stand for 'Mobile Army Surgical Hospital'. The series starred Alan Alda as Captain 'Hawkeye' Pierce, chief surgeon of an eccentric medical unit in the Korean War. Awash with blood, guts, sex and cynical black humour, *M*A*S*H* reflected some uncomfortable truths about the horrors of modern warfare.

Mason, James (1909-84) Suave and sinister villain of British-made costume dramas including *The Man in Grey* (1943), *Fanny by Gaslight* (1944) and *The Wicked Lady* (1945), which entertained audiences during World War II. He made his film debut in *Late Extra* (1935) and was constantly in work on both sides of the Atlantic for the rest of his long career. Among his most memorable films were: *The Seventh Veil* (1945); *Odd Man Out* (1947); *The Desert Fox* (1951), in which he played Field Marshal Rommel; *Julius Caesar* (1953), as Brutus; *A Star is Born* (1954); *Lolita* (1961); *Georgy Girl* (1966); *The Verdict* (1982); and *The Shooting Party* (1984).

Mastermind Quiz programme launched by BBC-1 in 1972 and revived every year since then. Contenders seated in a black leather chair face two minutes of questions on a subject of their choice, and a further two minutes of general knowledge questions. The words 'I've started so I'll finish' – used by interrogator Magnus Magnusson whenever the time-buzzer interrupts a question – is a catchphrase of the programme.

Merchant-Ivory Independent British film company headed by American director James Ivory (1928-) and Indian producer Ismail Merchant (1936-). The company is renowned for its stylish period films, especially its adaptations of novels by E.M. ▷FORSTER, such as *A Room With a View* (1985) and *Howards End* (1992), which won an Oscar for Emma Thompson. Their adaptation of the novel by Kazuo Ishiguro, *The Remains of the Day* (1993), with Emma Thompson and Anthony Hopkins, also won critical acclaim.

Metropolis Visually dazzling German film depicting a future society in which workers toil in a soulless underground city ruled by a privileged elite. Directed in 1926 by Fritz Lang (1890-1976), it tells how a deranged scientist invents a female robot who incites the workers to rebel. The success of the film, with its spectacular, geometric sets, started a school of science fiction films about mad inventors and their schemes.

FREEDOM RIDER *Steve McQueen did his own stunt motorcycle riding as an Allied prisoner of war who daringly attempts to break out of a German detention camp in* The Great Escape *(1962).*

Milligan, Spike (1918-) Eccentric Irish comedian who was the creative genius behind the bizarre humour of the GOON SHOW. His off-beat comedy series for BBC Television, *Q*, began in 1965 with *Q5* and ended in 1980 with *Q9*. Among his films are: *The Bed Sitting Room* (1969), a surreal post-nuclear war comedy adapted from a play by Milligan; *Monty Python's Life of Brian* (1979), a religious satire; and *Yellowbeard* (1983), a farcical pirate tale.

Mills, Sir John (1908-) Upright British film actor who went from playing a plucky able seaman in *In Which We Serve* (1942) to a stiff-upper-lip Army officer in *Tunes of Glory* (1960). He began his career in the 1930s as a chorus boy in musical comedies. Among his best-known movies are *Scott of the Antarctic* (1948), *The History of Mr Polly* (1949), *Hobson's Choice* (1953), *Ice Cold in Alex* (1958), and David Lean's Irish melodrama, *Ryan's Daughter* (1970), for which he won an Oscar for his portrayal of a village simpleton. He is the father of actresses Juliet Mills (1941-) and Hayley Mills (1946-), who made her screen debut opposite him in the thriller *Tiger Bay* (1959). He was knighted in 1977.

Minder Endearing ITV series starring George Cole as Arthur Daley, a shady London businessman with an eye for a quick deal and a shrewd bargain, and Dennis Waterman as Terry McCann, an ex-boxer who looks after his boss's person and interests. The series started in 1979, and in 1991 the job of Arthur's minder was taken over by his nephew, Ray, played by Gary Webster. *Minder* ended in 1994.

Mitchum, Robert (1917-) Strapping, droopy-eyed American star of gangster classics such as *Crossfire* (1947), *Out of the Past* (1947) and *Where Danger Lives* (1950). In 1943, his first year in Hollywood, he appeared in some 18 films, starting as an extra in *Hoppy Serves a Writ* and ending with a supporting role in *Gung Ho*. He made his mark in *The Story of G.I. Joe* (1945) and played the lead in a host of major productions including *Night of the Hunter* (1955), *The Sundowners* (1960), *Cape Fear* (1961), *Ryan's Daughter* (1970), *The Friends of Eddie Coyle* (1973) and two private eye films: *Farewell My Lovely* (1975) and *The Big Sleep* (1978). On TV, he starred in the miniseries *The Winds of War* (1983) and its sequel *War and Remembrance* (1989).

Monroe, Marilyn (1926-1962) (Real name Norma Jean Baker) Sultry American actress who became an international sex symbol of the 1950s. After working as a photographic model – and posing in the nude for a pin-up calendar – she went to Hollywood and got small but telling parts as the mistress of a crooked lawyer in *The Asphalt Jungle* (1950) and a would-be actress in *All About Eve* (1950). She sparkled in films such as *Gentlemen Prefer Blondes* (1953), *How to Marry a Millionaire* (1953), *The Seven Year Itch* (1955) and Billy Wilder's classic gangster spoof, *Some Like It Hot* (1959). Her last finished film was *The Misfits* (1961), written by her third husband, playwright Arthur ▷MILLER. Unpunctual and unreliable, she was fired from *Something's Got to Give* in 1962. Shortly afterwards she died of a drug overdose in mysterious circumstances.

🔑 She was renowned for her pert exchanges with the Press. These included: 'What do you wear in bed?' Answer: 'Chanel No. 5!' 'You had nothing else on?' Answer: 'Sure – I had the radio on!'

Monty Python's Flying Circus BBC television comedy series (1969-74) noted for the lunatic humour of its sketches such as 'The Dead Parrot' and 'The Ministry of Silly Walks'. It was written and performed by a team of former university humorists, including John Cleese, Graham Chapman, Eric Idle and Michael Palin. The imaginative and witty graphics were the work of American animator Terry Gilliam. The team's feature films include *Monty Python and the Holy Grail* (1974) and *Monty Python's Life of Brian* (1979).

More, Kenneth (1914-82) Jaunty British film actor who started his career as a revue artist at London's Windmill Theatre in the mid 1930s. He was perfectly cast as the perennial medical student in *Doctor in the House* (1954), and the rootless ex-RAF officer in *The Deep Blue Sea* (1955), co-starring Vivien Leigh. His many other films included *Reach for the Sky* (1956), as the legless, RAF war hero Douglas Bader, *Sink the Bismark* (1960) and *The Comedy Man* (1963), in which he played a middle-aged actor whose career was going downhill.

Morecambe and Wise Much-loved British comedy double act in the tradition of ABBOTT AND COSTELLO and LAUREL AND HARDY. Bespectacled comic Eric Morecambe (1926-84) and straight man Ernie Wise (1925-) teamed up in music halls in the early 1940s. The first *Morecambe and Wise Show* was shown in 1961 by ITV.

LEG SHOW *Comedian Tom Ewell admires Marilyn Monroe's legs as she straddles a New York air grating in* The Seven Year Itch *(1955). Barriers held back crowds who gathered to watch the scene.*

They made three feature films: *The Intelligence Men* (1965), *That Riviera Touch* (1966) and *The Magnificent Two* (1967).

Mostel, Zero (1915-77) Outsize American film and stage actor who was equally effective as a cowardly villain or a frenzied confidence trickster. He gave hilarious performances as Pseudolus, a scheming Roman slave in *A Funny Thing Happened on the Way to the Forum* (1966), and as an impoverished and unscrupulous Broadway producer in *The Producers* (1968), written and directed by Mel Brooks (1926-).

Newman, Paul (1925-) Blue-eyed American actor and sex symbol who became one of Hollywood's leading film stars from the mid 1950s onwards. His numerous films include *Somebody Up There Likes Me* (1956), *Cat on a Hot Tin Roof* (1958), *The Hustler* (1961), *Hud* (1962), *Cool Hand Luke* (1967); and two enormously popular films with Robert Redford: BUTCH CASSIDY AND THE SUNDANCE KID (1969) and *The Sting* (1973). These were followed by *The Towering Inferno* (1974), *Absence of Malice* (1981), *The Verdict* (1982), *The Color of Money* (1986), which won him an Oscar, *Blaze* (1989) and *Mr and Mrs Bridge* (1990). He directed his wife Joanne Woodward (1930-) in *Rachel, Rachel* (1968).

Newton, Robert (1905-56) Menacing, wild-eyed British actor who was ideally cast as Long John Silver in the film version of Robert Louis Stevenson's *Treasure Island* (1950). He was equally effective playing a deranged artist in *Odd Man Out* (1947), the murderous Bill Sikes in *Oliver Twist* (1948), and Dr Arnold, the autocratic headmaster of Rugby School, in *Tom Brown's Schooldays* (1951).

New Wave Name given to a group of young French film directors in the late 1950s and early 1960s who used outdoor locations, hand-held cameras and who oversaw each aspect of film-making, from script to editing, claiming to be the sole 'authors' of the finished works. Their films included François TRUFFAUT's *The Four Hundred Blows* (1959), Alain Resnais's *Hiroshima Mon Amour* (1959) and Jean-Luc Godard's *Breathless* (1960).

Nicholson, Jack (1937-) Charismatic American film star who specialises in portraying bizarre characters, such as an axe-wielding maniac in *The Shining* (1980), a sex-obsessed satan in *The Witches of Eastwick* (1987) and the malign Joker in *Batman* (1989). He scored his first major success in EASY RIDER (1969). His other outstanding films include: *Five Easy Pieces* (1970); *The Last Detail* (1973); *Chinatown* (1974); *One Flew Over the Cuckoo's Nest* (1975), for which he won an Oscar; *Terms of Endearment* (1983), which won him another Oscar; *Prizzi's Honor* (1985); *Ironweed* (1987); *The Two Jakes* (1990), which he also directed; and *Wolf* (1994).

Niven, David (1910-83) Sophisticated British actor who worked as a Hollywood extra before being signed as a typical English gentleman. He appeared in *The Charge of the Light Brigade* (1936) and *Bachelor Mother* (1939). Commissioned in the British army in World War II, he was released to make two stirring propaganda films: *The First of the Few* (1942), about the birth of the Spitfire, and *The Way Ahead* (1944). His many other films include: *A Matter of Life and Death* (1946); *Around the World in Eighty Days* (1956); *Separate Tables* (1958), for which he won an Oscar; *The Guns of Navarone* (1961); and *The Pink Panther* (1963). He wrote two witty, best-selling autobiographies: *The Moon's a Balloon* (1971) and *Bring on the Empty Horses* (1975).

THE MEN AND WOMEN WHO READ THE NEWS

Newscasters on British television and radio have become stars in their own right, with their own followings of fans and admirers. The key quality is their ability to deliver the day's events with clarity and conviction, though each has his or her distinctive style. Some are informal and relaxed, ending each bulletin with a quip – as did Sir Alastair Burnet and Reginald Bosanquet of Independent Television News (ITN). Others, such as Anna

Ford, mix glamour with authority. Moira Stuart of the BBC is more earnest. Trevor McDonald of ITN, Britain's first black newscaster, who went on to be the 'News at Ten' anchorman, also has a candid no-nonsense style.

Trevor McDonald

Reginald Bosanquet · Alastair Burnet

Alvar Liddell · Kenneth Kendall · Robert Dougall · Angela Rippon

Richard Baker

Anna Ford

Peter Sissons · Moira Stuart

BRITAIN'S NATIONAL DAILY NEWSPAPERS

Newspaper	Circulation / Owner	Description
THE ⬛⬛⬛ TIMES 1788	484 776 News International plc	Nicknamed 'The Thunderer' in 1831 from an article on the Reform Bill urging people to 'thunder for reform'.
THE SCOTSMAN 1817	83 553 Thomson Corporation	Influential Scottish morning newspaper, founded as a weekly and published daily since 1855.
The Guardian 1821	402 748 Guardian Newspapers Ltd	Founded as *The Manchester Guardian*, it changed its title in 1959 for national status and moved to London in 1964.
The Daily Telegraph 1855	1 007 711 Telegraph Newspaper Trust	Claimed to have the world's largest newspaper circulation in 1877. Its first crossword puzzle dates from 1925.
FINANCIAL TIMES 1888	297 463 Pearson Longman	Printed on pink paper to distinguish itself from rivals. Became known as 'the stockbroker's Bible'.
Daily Record 1895	736 674 Mirror Group	Scottish tabloid which has incorporated the *Daily Mirror* since 1986. Mixes popular appeal with left-wing politics.
Daily Mail 1896	1 793 922 Associated Newspapers	Britain's first popular daily newspaper, renowned for its Femail pages for women and its financial news.
Daily Express 1900	1 367 394 Express Newspapers	Last newspaper to leave Fleet Street in 1989. Known for promoting British interests and products.
Daily Mirror 1903	2 492 891 Mirror Group	Coronation Day issue sold 7 161 704 copies – a record for a British daily. Began life as a ladies' newspaper.
The Sun 1969	4 071 083 News International plc	First topless Page Three girl appeared in 1970. Most memorable headline: 'Freddie Starr ate my hamster.'
Daily Star 1978	747 347 United Newspapers	First national newspaper to introduce Bingo in 1981, as a circulation stunt. Sister paper of the *Daily Express*.
THE INDEPENDENT 1986	280 824 Newspaper Publishing plc	Daily press newcomer that set out aiming to be editorially, financially and politically independent.
TODAY 1986	587 213 News International plc	Launched by Eddie Shah as Britain's first colour daily paper. Sold to Rupert Murdoch's News International in 1987.

Ownership and circulation, Jan–June 1994. Source: ABC.

Olivier, Lord Laurence (1907-89) Outstanding British actor and director who brought Shakespeare to the cinema-going public with his film versions of *Henry V* (1944), *Hamlet* (1948), for which he won a Best Actor Oscar, and *Richard III* (1955). He came to prominence in *Fire Over England* (1936) and went to Hollywood for *Wuthering Heights* (1939), *Rebecca* (1940), *Pride and Prejudice* (1940) and the morale-boosting *That Hamilton Woman* (1941), in which he played the British naval hero Lord Nelson, opposite the Emma Hamilton of his second wife, Vivien Leigh. He portrayed the seedy music-hall comedian Archie Rice in the stage and film versions of John Osborne's *The Entertainer* (1957 and 1960). He later co-starred with Michael Caine in the thriller *Sleuth* (1972). Among his many theatrical highlights were his 1964 portrayal of Othello at London's National Theatre, of which he was the first Director (1963-73). On television he gave virtuoso performances in *Brideshead Revisited* (1981), *A Voyage Round My Father* (1982) and in the title role of Shakespeare's *King Lear* (1983). Olivier and Vivien Leigh were divorced in 1960; in 1961 he married the British actress Joan Plowright. He was knighted in 1947, and in 1970 became the first actor ever to be made a peer.

Oscar Popular name for the American Academy Award, a gold-plated statuette given since 1929 by the Academy of Motion Picture Arts and Sciences to each of the winners of its annual trophies.
The statuette is said to have been 'christened' by a Hollywood secretary, who said it reminded her of her Uncle Oscar.

O'Toole, Peter (1932-   ) Volatile Irish stage and screen actor who became an international star in David Lean's LAWRENCE OF ARABIA (1962). He appeared in a quick succession of major productions, including *Becket* (1964), *Lord Jim* (1965) and *The Lion in Winter* (1968). His later films include *The Stunt Man* (1980) and *The Last Emperor* (1987). On stage, he is best remembered for his title roles in *Hamlet* (1963) and *Jeffrey Bernard is Unwell* (1989).

Pacino, Al (1940-   ) Dynamic American actor of Sicilian descent who was ideally cast as the urbane Mafia don Michael Corleone in the GODFATHER films of 1972, 1974 and 1990. He also starred in crime films such as *Serpico* (1973), *Dog Day Afternoon* (1975), *Sea of Love* (1989) and the comic-strip *Dick Tracy* (1990). He won an Oscar for his role as a blind ex-military officer in *Scent of a Woman* (1992).

Peck, Gregory (1916-   ) Dignified American star in films for 20 years before winning an Oscar as a lawyer who defends a Negro on a rape charge in *To Kill a Mocking Bird* (1962). He found stardom in his first film, *Days of Glory* (1943), and brought distinction to *Gentlemen's Agreement* (1947) and *Twelve O'Clock High* (1949), as well as Westerns such as *The Big Country* (1958). His later films include the occult thriller *The Omen* (1976).

Pink Panther, The Riotous comedy film starring Peter SELLERS as the accident-prone Inspector Clouseau on the trail of a master criminal called The Phantom who has stolen a priceless jewel known as the Pink Panther. Made in 1963 by the American director Blake Edwards (1922-   ), the film's success inspired seven sequels and a highly popular cartoon series.

Planet of the Apes Chilling science fiction film starring Charlton Heston in which astronauts trapped in a time warp land on an alien planet ruled by a race of intelligent but often brutal apes. The film, made in 1967, has a surprise ending which punches home its moral message. It led to five sequels and a television series.

Poitier, Sidney (1924-) Black American film star whose screen success played a significant part in promoting racial equality in the 1950s and 1960s. Several of his films dealt with racial issues and prejudice. They

Price, Vincent (1911-93) Sepulchral-voiced American actor who was the undisputed 'King of the Horror Film'. After a distinguished Hollywood career, he made the chilling *House of Wax* (1953), in which he played a homicidal sculptor who exhibits his embalmed victims in an eerie wax museum. This was followed by *The House of Usher* (1960), *The Masque of the Red Death* (1964), *The Abominable Dr Phibes* (1971) and *Theatre of Blood* (1973).
🕯A notable art collector, Vincent Price was reputed to be the highest-paid lecturer on painting in the United States.

Puttnam, David (1941-) London-born producer hailed as the 'saviour' of the ailing British film industry in the 1980s. His movies include the Oscar-winning *Chariots of Fire* (1981), *Local Hero* (1983), *The Killing Fields* (1984) and *The Mission* (1986).

Redford, Robert (1937-) American actor and director who rose to superstar status opposite Paul Newman in the Western *Butch Cassidy and the Sundance Kid* (1969) and the crime caper *The Sting* (1973). His later films include *The Great Gatsby* (1974), *All the President's Men* (1976), *Out of Africa* (1985), *Havana* (1990) and *Indecent Proposal* (1993). He directed the domestic drama *Ordinary People* (1980) which won Best Film and Best Director Oscars, and *A River Runs Through It* (1992).

Redgrave, Vanessa (1937-) English stage, film and TV actress and left-wing political activist. She starred in the film *Morgan - A Suitable Case for Treatment* (1966), a satirical portrait of London in the 'Swinging Sixties'. Among her other films are *Blow Up* (1966), *Isadora* (1968), *Julia* (1977) and *Steaming* (1985). Highlights of her theatrical career include Henrik Ibsen's *The Lady from the Sea* (1976) and Tennessee Williams' *Orpheus Descending* (1988). She won an Emmy for her performance in Arthur Miller's harrowing TV drama about Auschwitz, *Playing for Time* (1980). She is the daughter of the distinguished actor Sir Michael Redgrave (1908-85), and the sister of actress Lynn Redgrave (1943-) and actor Corin Redgrave (1939-). She was once married to the Oscar-winning film-maker Tony Richardson (1928-91), director of *Tom Jones* (1963).

DESERT FIGHTER *Peter O'Toole, as Lawrence of Arabia, urges on his devoted Bedouin troops during their uprising in World War I against their hated overlords – and Germany's allies – the Turks.*

included *No Way Out* (1950), *The Defiant Ones* (1958), *Lilies of the Field* (1963), for which he won an Oscar, *To Sir with Love* (1967), *In the Heat of the Night* (1967) and *Guess Who's Coming to Dinner* (1967).

Polanski, Roman (1933-) Controversial Polish director whose films often portray people in the throes of sexual and mental torment. They include *Knife in the Water* (1962, Poland) and a crop of movies made in Britain, America and France, such as *Repulsion* (1965), *Rosemary's Baby* (1968), *Macbeth* (1971), *Chinatown* (1974), *Frantic* (1988) and *Bitter Moon* (1992).

Potter, Dennis (1935-94) English dramatist, best known for his controversial television plays which include *Pennies from Heaven* (1978), *The Singing Detective* (1986) and *Lipstick on Your Collar* (1993).

Prisoner, The Imaginative British television series that achieved cult status in the late 1960s, and again when it was reshown in 1976 and in the mid 1980s. Starring an enigmatic Patrick McGoohan, it related the efforts of a former secret agent to escape from an inhospitable village in which he was unaccountably trapped. The series was filmed in the Welsh tourist resort of ▷PORTMEIRION.

Psycho Director Alfred HITCHCOCK's masterpiece of horror, dark humour and suspense. Made in 1960, the film stars Janet Leigh as a thief on the run and Anthony Perkins (1932-92) as a mother-obsessed young proprietor of a remote motel in which the fugitive spends the night. The heroine is then slashed to death in the shower by a maniac wielding a knife. It started a trend for so-called 'slasher' films.

Reed, Sir Carol (1906-76) British film director who made three highly acclaimed post-war movies: *Odd Man Out* (1947), *The Fallen Idol* (1948) and *The Third Man* (1949). Among his later films were *Outcast of the Islands* (1951), *Trapeze* (1956), *Our Man in Havana* (1959) and *Oliver!* (1968), which won Oscars for Best Picture and Best Director. Reed was knighted in 1952, the first British film director to be so honoured.

Richardson, Sir Ralph (1902-83) Highly regarded British stage and screen actor with a rich voice and theatrical manner. Among his many films were *The Fallen Idol* (1948), *Outcast of the Islands* (1951) and *Dr Zhivago* (1965). Highlights of his stage career include *Flowering Cherry* (1958), *What the Butler Saw* (1969), *Home* (1970) and Harold Pinter's *No Man's Land* (1975). He was knighted in 1947.

'Road' films Series of crazy comedies starring Bing Crosby, Bob Hope and Dorothy Lamour (1914-). Starting with *Road to Singapore* (1940) and ending with *Road to Hong Kong* (1962), the films were a lively hotchpotch of song-and-dance, quips and puns, asides to the audience, romantic rivalries and, in *Road to Morocco* (1942), talking camels.

Robinson, Edward G. (1893-1973) (Real name Emanuel Goldenberg) Romanian-born American film actor specialising in 'tough guy' and gangster roles. He shot to stardom in *Little Caesar* (1930), a thinly disguised portrait of the Prohibition racketeer Al Capone. His other crime films included *Bullets or Ballots* (1936), *Double Indemnity* (1944), in which he gave a memorable performance as a tenacious insurance investigator, and *Key Largo* (1948).

Room at the Top Pioneering English film which, in 1959, dealt with sex in an adult and open way. Based on John Braine's best-selling novel, it starred Laurence Harvey as a brash young Yorkshireman on the make – socially and financially – and Simone Signoret in an Oscar-winning performance as the worldly wise married woman with whom he has a passionate affair. Director Jack Clayton faithfully captured the look and feel of life in the industrial North.

Rossellini, Roberto (1906-77) Highly influential Italian film director. His trilogy of newsreel-like films – *Open City* (1945), *Paisa* (1946) and *Germany, Year Zero* (1947) – used amateur actors and real-life settings to bring everyday realism to the European postwar cinema. His later films included *Stromboli* (1949) which starred Ingrid BERGMAN, whom he married the following year. He is the father of actress Isabella Rossellini (1952-).

Rossiter, Leonard (1926-84) Foxy-faced British comic actor who starred in the television comedy classics *Rising Damp* (1974-8) and *The Fall and Rise of Reginald Perrin* (1976-80). He played supporting roles in films such as *Billy Liar* (1963), *Oliver!* (1968), *Barry Lyndon* (1975), *Brittannia Hospital* (1982) and *Trail of the Pink Panther* (1982). He died while performing in a West End production of Joe Orton's black comedy *Loot*.

Rumpole of the Bailey Engaging ITV comedy series about a scruffy, ageing, wine-imbibing lawyer named Horace Rumpole – played by the Australian character

DEFECTIVE DETECTIVE *The hapless Inspector Clouseau, played by Peter Sellers, is on the track of a jewel thief in* The Pink Panther *(1963).*

actor Leo McKern (1920-). Created in the 1970s by playwright and lawyer John Mortimer, Rumpole is the scourge of London's Old Bailey – the Central Criminal Court – and is cowed only by his indomitable wife, 'She who must be obeyed!'

Russell, Ken (1927-) Provocative British film and TV director who caused an outcry with his bold film adaptation of D.H. Lawrence's *Women in Love* (1969). He followed this with a bizarre version of Tchaikovsky's life and loves in *The Music Lovers* (1970), the sacrilegious *The Devils* (1971) and the raucous rock opera *Tommy* (1975). Later films include *Crimes of Passion* (1984) and *Whore* (1991). In 1993 he directed an explicit TV version of D.H. Lawrence's novel *Lady Chatterley's Lover*.

Rutherford, Dame Margaret (1892-1972) Eccentric British character actress who made her name playing 'dotty old ladies'. These included Agatha Christie's spinster detective Miss ▷MARPLE in the film *Murder She Said* (1961) and its sequels, the irrepressible medium Madame Arcati in Noël Coward's *Blithe Spirit* both on stage and screen (1941 and 1945), and the upright Miss Prism in Oscar Wilde's *The Importance of Being Earnest* – on stage in 1939 and on screen in 1952. She won an Oscar for her supporting role as the scatter-brained Duchess of Brighton in Terence Rattigan's *The V.I.Ps* (1963). She was made a Dame of the British Empire in 1967.

Schwarzenegger, Arnold (1947-) Austrian bodybuilder and former Mr Universe whose appearance in an American film documentary called *Pumping Iron*

(1977) led to a Hollywood career. Among his best-known films are *Conan, the Barbarian* (1981), *The Terminator* (1984), *Predator* (1987), *Total Recall* (1990) and the comedy *Kindergarten Cop* (1990).

Scofield, Paul (1922-) Eminent British actor renowned for his portrayal of Sir Thomas More in Robert Bolt's *A Man for All Seasons*, which he played on stage in 1960 and in the film of 1966, for which he won an Oscar. His other films include *The Train* (1964), *Scorpio* (1972) and *When the Whales Came* (1989). Highlights of his theatrical career include *Hamlet* (1956), *The Family Reunion* (1957), *King Lear* (1962), *Staircase* (1966), *Uncle Vanya* (1970), *Amadeus* (1979) and *Othello* (1980).

Scorsese, Martin (1942-) Virtuoso American director who has worked with actor Robert DE NIRO on several violent and harrowing films such as *Mean Streets* (1973), *Taxi Driver* (1976), *Raging Bull* (1980), *GoodFellas* (1990) and *Cape Fear* (1991). He also made *The Color of Money* (1986), the controversial *The Last Temptation of Christ* (1988) and the romantic *The Age of Innocence* (1993), with Daniel Day-Lewis and Michelle Pfeiffer. In 1987 he directed the Michael Jackson video *Bad*.

Sellers, Peter (1925-80) Versatile British comic actor who became an international star in two films directed by Stanley Kubrick: *Lolita* (1962) and *Dr Strangelove: Or How I Learned to Stop Worrying and Love the Bomb* (1964). Sellers started out as a comedian and impressionist and was a member of the GOON SHOW radio team (1952-60). He then enjoyed great success as the bumbling French detective Inspector Clouseau in the PINK PANTHER movies of the 1960s and 1970s. Among his other film comedies were *The Ladykillers* (1955), *I'm All Right, Jack* (1959), *Only Two Can Play* (1962), *The Party* (1968), *There's a Girl in My Soup* (1970) and *Being There* (1979).
🎤'If you asked me to play myself,' Sellers once stated, 'I wouldn't know what to do. I don't know who I am or what I am!'

Smith, Dame Maggie (1934-) Flamboyant British actress and comedienne who in 1969 won an Oscar for her performance as the unorthodox Scottish schoolteacher in Muriel ▷SPARK's *The Prime of Miss Jean Brodie*. Her other films include *Travels With My Aunt* (1972), *A Room With a View* (1985), *The Lonely Passion of Judith Hearne* (1987) and *The Secret Garden* (1993). Highlights from her distinguished stage career include Desdemona in *Othello* (1964),

Lettice and Lovage (1987) and Lady Brack-nell in Oscar Wilde's *The Importance of Being Earnest* (1993). She was made a Dame of the British Empire in 1990.

Snow White and the Seven Dwarfs

Walt DISNEY's full-length cartoon master-piece, it was completed in 1937 after two years' production work and at a cost of some $1½ million. Taken from a story in Grimms' *Fairy Tales*, it featured a beautiful maiden, a handsome prince, an evil and terrifying stepmother and the seven lovable dwarfs, each with his own distinctive personality: Doc, Bashful, Dopey, Grumpy, Happy, Sleepy and Sneezy.

Spaghetti Westerns

Name given to a batch of bloodthirsty cowboy films made in Italy and Spain in the 1960s. Italian director Sergio Leone (1921-89) began the trend with *A Fistful of Dollars* (1964) and its sequels *For a Few Dollars More* (1965) and *The Good, the Bad and the Ugly* (1966).

Spielberg, Steven (1947-)

Phenomenally successful American film director and producer responsible for a string of financially record-breaking movies. They include JAWS (1975), *Close Encounters of the Third Kind* (1977), *Raiders of the Lost Ark* (1981), E.T. (1982), *Indiana Jones and the Temple of Doom* (1984), *Indiana Jones and the Last Crusade* (1989), *Hook* (1991), JURASSIC PARK (1993) and *Schindler's List* (1994) – a moving account of how one man saved a group of Jews from the Holocaust, which won Oscars for best film and best director.

CLOSE ENCOUNTER *Steven Spielberg gets together with E.T., the stranded alien who loves people, but who longs to return to his own planet.*

STAR-TREKKERS *The starship* Enterprise *was crewed by (standing) the black communications officer, Lieutenant Uhura, Dr 'Bones' McCoy, and (sitting) pointed-eared Mr Spock and the ship's commander, Captain Kirk.*

Spielberg began as one of television's youngest ever directors, and was only 23 when he made *Duel* (1971), a gripping story about a motorist who is pursued by the unseen driver of a mammoth and menacing petrol tanker.

Stallone, Sylvester (1946-)

Robust American film actor who shot to fame in *Rocky* (1976), a boxing drama which he wrote himself and which won a Best Picture Oscar. It inspired four sequels all written by Stallone, three of which – *Rocky II* (1979), *Rocky III* (1982) and *Rocky IV* (1985) – he directed. Stallone's 'Rambo' film series, about a violent Vietnam veteran, have also proved popular. He has described Rocky and Rambo as 'money-making machines that can't be switched off'.

Star Trek

American science fiction television series set aboard the starship USS *Enterprise* in the 23rd century. Commanded by Captain James T. Kirk (played by William Shatner), and with the pointed-eared half-alien Mr Spock (Leonard Nimoy) as the first officer, the *Enterprise* and its crew met danger and hostility wherever they ventured. The series ran from 1966-9 and was followed by *Star Trek: the Motion Picture* (1979) and five film sequels.

Star Wars

Spectacular space-age adventure film with stunning special effects. Directed by George Lucas in 1977, it told of a fight between the forces of good and evil. It made a star of Harrison Ford as space pilot Han Solo and gave Alec Guinness his most unusual – and best-paid – role as the space knight Obi-Wan Kenobi. Its international success led to two equally exciting sequels: *The Empire Strikes Back* (1980) and *The Return of the Jedi* (1983).

Stewart, James (1908-)

Lanky, slow-speaking American actor who came to prominence in two classic comedies directed by Frank CAPRA: *You Can't Take It With You* (1938) and *Mr Smith Goes to Washington* (1939). He later appeared as a cynical reporter in *The Philadelphia Story* (1940), for which he won an Oscar, and a would-be suicide in Capra's small-town fantasy *It's a Wonderful Life* (1947). He starred in several Westerns, including the classic *Destry Rides Again* (1939), with Marlene Dietrich. He also played the lead in three HITCHCOCK thrillers: *Rear Window* (1954), *The Man Who Knew Too Much* (1955) and *Vertigo* (1958). His other notable films include *Harvey* (1950), in which he played the intoxicated friend of an invisible rabbit, *Anatomy of a Murder* (1959), *The Flight of the Phoenix* (1965) and the Civil War drama *Shenandoah* (1965).

ILL-FATED *Elizabeth Taylor as the Queen of Egypt, and Richard Burton as the Roman general Mark Antony, mix politics and passion in* Cleopatra *(1963), the story of their doomed romance.*

Streep, Meryl (1951-) American film star able to assume a variety of accents. She gave outstanding supporting performances in *The Deer Hunter* (1978) and *Manhattan* (1979) before graduating to leading roles. These include: a vindictive ex-wife in *Kramer vs Kramer* (1979), for which she won a Best Actress Oscar; a fallen English-woman in *The French Lieutenant's Woman* (1981); a Polish ex-concentration camp inmate in *Sophie's Choice* (1982), which won her a second Oscar; a Danish aristocrat in *Out of Africa* (1986); and an Australian murder suspect in *Cry in the Dark* (1989).

Sunset Boulevard Bitter but brilliant Billy WILDER film, made in 1950, about a former silent star desperate to stage a comeback and a frustrated screenwriter

hired to write a script that will make her 'big' again. The leads were played by Gloria Swanson (1897-1983), herself a former silent screen goddess, and William Holden (1918-81). Among the supporting cast were silent comedian Buster Keaton, silent director Eric Von Stroheim and director Cecil B. De Mille, who played himself.

Tarzan More than 80 feature films, as well as a TV series, have been made about the athletic English nobleman, Lord Grey-stoke, who is abandoned in the African jungle as an infant and is brought up by apes. Based on a character created by the American novelist Edgar Rice Burroughs (1875-1950), the first Tarzan film, *Tarzan of the Apes*, was made in 1918 and the most recent, *Greystoke*, in 1984. Among the

best-known Tarzans have been the former Olympic swimmer and gold medallist Johnny Weissmuller (1904-84), Lex Barker (1919-73) and Gordon Scott (1927-).

Taylor, Elizabeth (1932-) British-born actress who became a child star in Hollywood at the age of ten after being evacuated to California during World War II. She went from playing wholesome young girls in films such as *Lassie Come Home* (1943) and *National Velvet* (1944), to sensual women in *Cat on a Hot Tin Roof* (1958) and *Butterfield 8* (1960), for which she won an Oscar. Among her other films are *Father of the Bride* (1950), *Suddenly, Last Summer* (1959), *A Little Night Music* (1977) and *The Mirror Crack'd* (1980).

🔔Miss Taylor has been married eight times – twice to Richard BURTON (1964-74 and 1975-6), whom she met when they were filming *Cleopatra* (1963). They later co-starred in several films including *Who's Afraid of Virginia Woolf?* (1966), for which she gained her second Oscar.

Temple, Shirley (1928-) Holly-wood's most popular child star of the 1930s. Her cheerful personality, sunny smile and bubble curls provided welcome relief from the gloom of the Great Depression, in films such as *Little Miss Marker* (1934), *Curly Top* (1935), *Dimples* (1936), *Rebecca of Sunny-brook Farm* (1938) and *The Little Princess* (1939). As a teenager her appeal waned, although she continued making films until the late 1940s.

🔔In the 1960s she began a successful politi-cal career in the Republican Party as Mrs Shirley Temple Black, serving as the US representative to the United Nations (1969-70), ambassador to Ghana (1974-6), chief of protocol at the White House (1976-7) and ambassador to Czechoslo-vakia (1989-92).

That Was The Week That Was Hard-hitting BBC television satirical show of 1962-3, known in short as *TW3*. Led by David Frost, a team of comics, writers, singers and commentators analysed the events of the week – ridiculing the ineffi-ciency and hypocrisy of politicians and public figures. Thought by the BBC to be politically subversive, the show was drop-ped before the general election of 1964.

Tom and Jerry Cartoon series about the running battle between a belligerent cat named Tom and his harassed opponent, Jerry the mouse, who always comes out on top. Created in Hollywood in 1937 by animators William Hanna and Joe Barbera,

LAST RESPECTS *US cavalrymen, led by veteran captain John Wayne, give a military funeral to a trooper and former Confederate general killed by Indians in* She Wore a Yellow Ribbon *(1949).*

the series has been criticised for its emphasis on violence. Even so, its highly imaginative animation helped it to win Best Cartoon Oscars for seven of the shorts, including *Mouse Trouble* (1944) and *The Two Mouseketeers* (1951).

Tracy, Spencer (1900-67) Sturdy American film actor noted for his natural and realistic performances. He became a major star in 1937 when he won an Oscar for *Captains Courageous*, in which he played a Portuguese fisherman. He gained a second Oscar portraying the real-life Father Flanagan, head of a community for juvenile delinquents, in *Boys' Town* (1938). He later teamed up with Katharine HEPBURN – with whom he had a long personal relationship – in a series of witty, war-of-the-sexes comedies. Hepburn also co-starred in his last film, *Guess Who's Coming To Dinner* (1967). His other notable movies included *Bad Day at Black Rock* (1955) and *Inherit the Wind* (1960).

Truffaut, François (1932-84) French film director whose key movie is the auto-biographical *The Four Hundred Blows* (1959), telling how a boy, played by Jean-Pierre Leaud, escapes from a brutal reform school and roams the streets of Paris. It ends abruptly with a static close-up of the boy's face – a device much imitated by other directors. He also made a series of films about the amatory adventures of a sensitive young man – again portrayed by Leaud. These include *Stolen Kisses* (1968), *Bed and Board* (1970) and *Love on the Run* (1979).

Ustinov, Sir Peter (1921-) All-round British show business personality known for his portrayal of Agatha Christie's detective Hercule ▷POIROT in *Death on the Nile* (1978) and *Evil Under the Sun* (1982). Ustinov directed and starred in a film version of his Cold War stage comedy *Romanoff and Juliet* (1961), and won Best Supporting Actor Oscars for his roles in *Spartacus* (1960) and in *Topkapi* (1964). He was knighted in 1990.

RADIO REALISM *Orson Welles' radio version of* The War of the Worlds *(1938) was so realistic that many Americans panicked, fearing that Martians had landed in New Jersey. The story was also filmed, in 1952.*

Valentino, Rudolph (1895-1926) Italian-American silent film star whose so-called 'animal magnetism' gained him the title of 'The Great Lover'. His sensuous mouth, flaring nostrils and staring eyes – used to good effect in *The Four Horsemen of the Apocalypse* (1921), *The Sheik* (1921) and *Blood and Sand* (1922) – captivated women around the world and started a vogue for dark-haired, dark-eyed Latins.

🕯Valentino's death from peritonitis caused several of his female fans to commit suicide, and 80 000 hysterical mourners attended his lying-in-state in New York. He was commemorated in a popular song of the time: 'A New Star in Heaven Tonight'.

Wayne, John (1907-79) (Real name Marion Michael Morrison) Robust American film actor known for his rolling walk and drawling speech. He graduated from singing-cowboy parts to an Oscar-winning performance as the hard-drinking, over-weight, one-eyed lawman Rooster Cogburn in the Western *True Grit* (1969). Nicknamed 'Duke' after a dog he had as a boy, he was chosen by director John Ford to play the Ringo Kid in *Stagecoach* (1939). He then starred in scores of Western, war and action films including *Red River* (1948), *Sands of Iwo Jima* (1949), *The Quiet Man* (1952), *The High and the Mighty* (1954), *The Searchers* (1956) and *Rio Bravo* (1958). He gave a moving performance in his last film, *The Shootist* (1976), a portrait of an ageing gunfighter dying of cancer at the start of the century.

🕯As an actor-director Wayne made the patriotic *The Alamo* (1960) and the *The Green Berets* (1968), in which he expressed his support for American military involvement in Vietnam.

Welles, Orson (1915-85) 'Boy genius' of Hollywood who, at the age of 26, directed, produced, co-wrote and starred in the trail-blazing CITIZEN KANE (1941). His

333

SEX SYMBOL *Fur-clad Mae West symbolises feminine allure in* Goin' to Town *(1935), as an oil heiress who breaks into high society.*

second film, *The Magnificent Ambersons* (1942), a sombre family saga, was also hailed as a masterpiece. Although he lost some of his early brilliance, he directed and starred in some stylish thrillers such as *The Stranger* (1946), *The Lady from Shanghai* (1948) and *Touch of Evil* (1958). He also made three highly personal Shakespeare films: *Macbeth* (1948), *Othello* (1952) and *Chimes at Midnight* (1966), in which he was a swaggering Falstaff. Among his other notable roles were the crooked Harry Lime in *The Third Man* (1949), a fanatical preacher in *Moby Dick* (1956) and a melodramatic courtroom lawyer in *Compulsion* (1959).

West, Mae (1892-1980) American stage and screen actress renowned for her buxom figure – after which an inflatable life-jacket was named in World War II – and for the sexual innuendo of her dialogue. The most famous instance of this is the often mis-quoted 'Why don't you come up sometime and see me?' from the film *She Done Him Wrong* (1933).

♪ Among Mae West's sayings were: 'It's not the men in my life, it's the life in my men that counts'; and 'When I'm good I'm very good, but when I'm bad I'm better'.

Widmark, Richard (1914-) Blond American actor with a chilling, high-pitched giggle who specialised in portraying cold-blooded killers. He made a memorable film debut in *Kiss of Death* (1947) as a psychopathic murderer seeking vengeance on a stool-pigeon. He followed this with *Road House* (1948) and *Night and the City* (1950), an atmospheric thriller set in the postwar London underworld. He scored another major hit with *Madigan* (1968), in which he played a dedicated New York cop. He also starred in a 1970s television series based on the character.

Wilder, Billy (1906-) Austrian-born director and writer who has made some of Hollywood's most sparkling and cynical sex comedies. These include: *The Seven Year Itch* (1955), with Marilyn Monroe; *Some Like It Hot* (1959), with Monroe, Jack Lemmon and Tony Curtis; and the Oscar-winning *The Apartment* (1960), with Lemmon and Shirley MacLaine. Among his other notable films are: *Double Indemnity* (1944); *The Lost Weekend* (1945), a grim study of an alcoholic, with Ray Milland, which won Best Director, Best Screenplay and Best Actor Oscars; SUNSET BOULEVARD (1950); and two lurid newspaper stories, *Ace in the Hole* (1951), with Kirk Douglas, and *The Front Page* (1974), with Jack Lemmon and Walter Matthau.

Williams, Kenneth (1926-88) Outrageous British comedian who, with his saucy voice, haughty demeanour and shocked expression, was one of the mainstays of the CARRY ON film series. He made his name in long-running radio shows such as *Round the Horne* and *Hancock's Half Hour*, on which he coined the catchphrase, 'Ere, stop messin' about!'

Wisdom, Norman (1915-) Diminutive comedian and singer who was Britain's biggest box-office draw in the 1950s. Dressed in an ill-fitting suit and flat cap, he played a shy, accident-prone clown in most of his films from *Trouble in Store* (1953) onwards. As a serious actor, he won praise as a terminally ill cancer patient in a BBC television play, *Going Gently* (1981), with Judi Dench.

Wizard of Oz, The Enchanting musical fantasy film which, in 1939, made a star of the young Judy GARLAND. In it she plays Dorothy, a little girl from Kansas whose farm is hit by a tornado, which transports her and her dog Toto from their dull, sepia world to the Technicolor land of Oz, ruled by the Wizard in the Emerald City. Despite

sharing some wonderful adventures with three new friends, the Scarecrow (played by Ray Bolger), the Tin Man (Jack Haley) and the Lion (Bert Lahr), Dorothy finally realises that there is no place like home. Her song, 'Over the Rainbow', won an Oscar. Directed by Victor Fleming, the film was based on the classic children's book *The Wonderful Wizard of Oz* (1900) by Frank L. Baum.

X-certificate Introduced by the British Board of Film Censors in 1951, films with an X-certificate could be shown in the cinema only to adults aged 21 or over. It was replaced in 1982 by the 18-certificate.

Yes, Minister Satirical BBC television series of the early 1980s about life behind the scenes in Whitehall. It starred Paul Eddington as Jim Hacker, an ambitious but weak-minded government minister, and Nigel Hawthorne as his devious Civil Service aide, Sir Humphrey. It was followed in 1986 by *Yes, Prime Minister*, in which Hacker moved into No. 10 Downing Street with Sir Humphrey still in attendance.

Z Cars Gritty BBC television police series (1960-78) which set a new standard in 'cops-and-robbers' realism. Set in the north of England, it starred Stratford Johns as Inspector Barlow and Frank Windsor as Inspector Watt. It inspired the equally popular crime series *Softly, Softly*, which ran from 1966 to 1976.

Zeffirelli, Franco (1923-) Italian stage and film director whose lively, fast-moving Shakespeare films are aimed squarely at the youth market. He began with a rumbustious version of *The Taming of the Shrew* (1966) with Richard Burton and Elizabeth Taylor, and followed this with *Romeo and Juliet* (1968) starring the young Leonard Whiting and Olivia Hussey. He chose the American-born actor Mel Gibson to play the title role in *Hamlet* (1990). Zeffirelli also directed the internationally successful television series *Jesus of Nazareth* (1977), with Robert Powell as Christ.

Zinnemann, Fred (1907-) Veteran Austrian-born director whose films include the classic Western *High Noon* (1952), *From Here to Eternity* (1953), for which he won a Best Director Oscar, *The Nun's Story* (1958) and the historical drama *A Man For All Seasons* (1966), which gained him another Oscar. In the 1970s he turned to political subjects, making the thriller *The Day of the Jackal* (1973) and *Julia* (1977), set in Nazi Germany in the 1930s.

MUSIC, SONG AND DANCE

The appeal of music is ageless and universal: it makes us want to sing and dance, and stirs the human soul. From Beethoven to the Beatles, and Bach to the blues, melody, rhythm and harmony have been interpreted by great singers, instrumentalists and conductors to excite, to sadden and to haunt our memories long after the last note has been played.

BILLIE HOLIDAY

VERDI'S DON CARLOS

ELVIS PRESLEY

MOZART

Abba Swedish pop group of the 1970s who became the most successful group since the Beatles. Formed in 1973, it consisted of two married couples who invented the name Abba using the initial letters of their first names – Anni-Frid Lyngstad-Fredriksson and Benny Andersson, and Bjorn Ulvaeus and Agnetha Fältskog. In 1974 they won the Eurovision Song Contest with the song 'Waterloo'. The many hit records that followed made them one of Sweden's most lucrative exports. The group split up in 1983 as the couples divorced.

Albinoni, Tomaso Giovanni (1671-1750) Italian violinist and prolific composer of vocal and instrumental works. He wrote more than 50 operas, and was one of the first composers to write concertos for the solo violin. The anguished Adagio in G Minor, an anachronistic movement for organ and strings, was in fact constructed by Remo Giazotto from a small fragment of melody by Albinoni.

alto Lowest range of the female singing voice – also called contralto – or the highest adult male voice apart from COUNTER-TENOR. The word is Italian for 'high'.

aria Song for a solo voice in an opera, oratorio or cantata, such as 'Nessun Dorma' from Puccini's opera *Turandot*. The word is Italian for 'air' or 'tune'.

Armstrong, Louis (c.1900-71) New Orleans jazz trumpeter and singer, considered to be one of the greatest jazz musicians of all time. His nickname was 'Satchmo' or 'Satchelmouth'. He rose to fame in the 1920s and was renowned for his inspiring improvisations and gravelly voice. Armstrong brought jazz to a global audience and is credited with the invention of scat singing – a jazz vocal style in which improvised sounds are used rather than actual words. He appeared in more than 50 films, including *High Society* (1956) and *Hello, Dolly!* (1969). Armstrong's recording of the song 'What a Wonderful World' was a No.1 hit in Britain in 1968.

Ashkenázy, Vladimir (1937-) Russian born pianist and conductor who took Icelandic nationality in 1972. Ashkenázy is noted for his interpretations of Chopin, Schumann and Beethoven. In 1987 he became the music director of London's Royal Philharmonic Orchestra.

Ashton, Sir Frederick (1904-88) Distinguished British dancer, choreographer and ballet director, who helped to make

PERFECT PARTNERSHIP *Fred Astaire's imaginative routines looked easy, but they took weeks to perfect. In the background, he and Ginger Rogers go through their paces in a scene from the film* Top Hat *(1935), one of their many classics of the musical screen.*

ballet popular and build the career of Margot FONTEYN. Ashton was director of the Royal Ballet from 1963 to 1970, and was a prolific choreographer of ballets in widely varied styles. They include such works as *Façade* (1931), *Les Patineurs* (1937), *Symphonic Variations* (1946), *La Fille mal Gardée* (1960), *Enigma Variations* (1965) and the ballet film *Tales of Beatrix Potter* (1971).

Astaire, Fred (1899-1987) (Frederick Austerlitz) American entertainer who revolutionised the film musical with his innovative tap-dance routines. He was admired for his charm, grace and seemingly effortless dancing. From 1916 to 1932 Astaire was partnered by his sister Adele, who

appeared in Broadway shows with him until she married and retired from the stage. Astaire then turned his attention to Hollywood and met newcomer Ginger Rogers in 1933. They made ten musical films together including *Flying Down to Rio* (1933), *Top Hat* (1935) and *Follow the Fleet* (1936).

In 1932, Fred Astaire's appraisal for his Hollywood screen-test was: 'Can't act. Can't sing. Can dance a little.'

Bach, Johann Sebastian (1685-1750) German organist and choirmaster, generally considered to be the greatest composer of the BAROQUE era. A staunch Protestant, his religious faith colours his work, notably in the Mass in B Minor and the St John and St Matthew Passions. He also wrote more than 200 church and secular cantatas and many works for organ, including the dramatic *Toccata and Fugue in D minor*. Bach's enormous output also includes the six *Brandenburg Concertos* and four orchestral suites: *Suite No.3 in D* includes the popular *Air on the G String* melody. Bach fused intense feeling with supreme musical logic: he was a master of the FUGUE, with its subtle interweaving of two or more melodies into a satisfying whole. After his death, his music was largely forgotten until Mendelssohn launched the Bach revival with a performance of the St Matthew Passion in 1829.

🔊 Bach was a member of the most remarkable family in musical history, consisting of 40 professional musicians spanning seven generations. Twice married, Bach had 20 children. Two of his sons, Carl Philipp Emanuel (1714-88) and Johann Christian (1735-82), played an important part in the development of the early symphony.

Bacharach, Burt (1928-) American popular composer who teamed up with lyricist Hal David to write classic hits such as 'Walk On By' and 'Always Something There to Remind Me'. In the film world Bacharach won an Oscar for 'Raindrops Keep Fallin' on My Head' from *Butch Cassidy and the Sundance Kid* (1969).

Balanchine, George (1904-83) (Georgi Balanchivadze) Russian-born American ballet dancer, and one of the greatest

---

TIMELESS GENIUS *In his lifetime, Bach was better known as an organist than a composer. His composing fame came after his death.*

BALLET TERMS

à terre Various floor steps which do not entail any jumps.

batterie, battu Jump during which a dancer beats the calves sharply together.

corps de ballet Group of dancers who support the principal dancers.

divertissement Separate dance within a ballet, designed as entertainment or to show off a dancer's technique.

élevation Any high jump in ballet.

entrechat Vertical jump during which the dancer beats the calves together, landing on one or both feet.

fouetté Spectacular pirouette in which the dancer whips the raised leg out to the front and side in order to achieve momentum for another turn.

jeté Jump from one leg to the other.

pas Basic ballet step in which the weight is transferred from one leg to another. The term is also used in combination to indicate the number of performers in a dance; a *pas seul* is a solo and a *pas de deux* for two.

pirouette Complete turn on one leg, which is performed on the ball of the foot by men, or on the toes by women.

plié Bending the legs from a standing position; *demi-plié* involves bending the knees as far as possible while keeping the heels on the ground.

relevé To rise, with a slight spring, off the heel and onto the ball of one or both feet.

soutenu A prolonged movement, executed at a slower tempo than usual.

---

choreographers in the history of ballet. He became chief choreographer of Sergei DIAGHILEV's Ballets Russes in 1925 and formed a lifelong friendship with the composer STRAVINSKY; their collaboration began in 1928 with the ballet *Apollon Musagète*. In 1933, Balanchine went to America where, as artistic director, he raised the New York City Ballet to a company of international standing.

ballet Artistic dance form which originated in the formal dances of French court entertainments, notably under Louis XIV (1638-1715). Dancing on the tips of the toes was introduced early in the 19th century, and modern ballet developed in the early 20th century, influenced by Russian dancer and choreographer Mikhail Fokine (1880-1942) and Russian impresario Sergei DIAGHILEV.

baritone Middle range of the male singing voice, higher than BASS and lower than TENOR. The word is from the Greek *bari* meaning 'deep' and *tone* meaning 'sound'.

baroque In music, the term applied to the elaborate, much ornamented music of composers between 1600 and 1750. Baroque composers include MONTEVERDI, PURCELL, VIVALDI, BACH and HANDEL.

Bartók, Béla (1881-1945) Hungarian composer and pianist, who collected eastern European folk songs and adapted them to produce a discordant, primitive style of music. His works include six string

quartets, the opera *Duke Bluebeard's Castle* (1911), three piano concertos and *Music for Strings, Percussion and Celesta* (1936). In 1940 Bartók moved to America, where he lived on the verge of starvation until he was commissioned by the conductor of the Boston Symphony Orchestra Serge Koussevitzky to write the *Concerto for Orchestra* (1943), his most popular and tuneful work. He died just as his work was beginning to receive recognition.

Basie, Count (1904-84) (William Basie) American jazz pianist and band leader who developed the big-band sound. He formed his first orchestra in 1936 and led a band until his death. The Count Basie Orchestra was one of the most important and successful SWING bands: a style of jazz that was popular in the 1930s and 1940s.

bass Lowest range of the male singing voice. Also an abbreviation for the lowest-stringed instrument, the double bass. The word is Italian for 'low'.

Beach Boys, The (Brian Wilson, Dennis Wilson, Carl Wilson, Mike Love, Al Jardine, Bruce Johnston) The most commercially successful American pop group of the 1960s, whose melodic pop songs idealised the sun-and-surf Californian lifestyle. Brian Wilson was one of the first producers to use electronic music effectively; he gave the band their sophisticated and highly technical sound, notably on the album *Pet Sounds* (1966) and the classic pop song 'Good Vibrations' (1966).

FAB GEAR *By the end of 1963, the Beatles were the most influential group in Europe, setting fashions in hairstyles and clothing with their clean-cut image of 'mop tops' and collarless jackets.*

Beatles, The British pop group, the leading exponents of the Liverpool sound or 'Mersey beat' which emerged in the 1960s. The Beatles grew out of a skiffle group formed by John Lennon in 1956, with Paul McCartney and George Harrison joining in 1957 and Ringo Starr in 1962. Two original members, Stuart Sutcliffe and Pete Best, left before the Beatles found fame. Lennon and McCartney proved to be one of the most successful song-writing teams in history. Their first single, 'Love Me Do', was released in 1962; in 1965 the Beatles were awarded MBEs and by 1966 they had become the most successful and wholesome pop group in the world. However, influenced by drugs and 'flower power' their music took a new direction with the album *Sgt Pepper's Lonely Hearts Club Band* (1967), an experimental adventure in music and technology that captured the psychedelic spirit of the time. The demise of the 'Fab Four' began in 1968 when McCartney became disillusioned with Lennon's relationship with girlfriend Yoko Ono, and the group split up in 1970. Fans hoped for a reunion until Lennon was shot dead outside his New York apartment in December 1980. In 1994 there was talk of the three remaining Beatles getting back together and recording some new songs 'for old times' sake'.
🎤 John Lennon (1940-80) was a figurehead of the peace movement of the 1960s. He married Yoko Ono in 1969 and settled in New York. His solo hits include 'Give Peace a Chance' (1969) and 'Imagine' (1971). When his son Sean was born in 1975, Lennon became a reclusive 'house-husband' until the release of his comeback album *Double Fantasy* (1980). A track called 'Starting Over' topped the charts after Lennon was killed.
🎤 McCartney (1942-) formed the band Wings in 1971 with his wife Linda on keyboards. Wings had a series of successful albums and the song 'Mull of Kintyre' (1977) became the first single to sell more than two million copies in Britain.

bebop Style of jazz developed by black musicians in the 1940s. With its fast, driving rhythms, complex harmonies and sophisticated improvisations, bebop, or bop, evolved into the modern jazz of the 1950s and 1960s. Dizzy GILLESPIE and Charlie PARKER were prominent exponents.

Beecham, Sir Thomas (1879-1961) English conductor and renowned interpreter of the composer DELIUS. Beecham founded the London Philharmonic Orchestra in 1932 and later became artistic director of Covent Garden's Royal Opera House. He went on to found the Royal Philharmonic Orchestra in 1946.

Beethoven, Ludwig van (1770-1827) German composer and pianist who led music from the Classical into the Romantic era and strongly influenced its later development. Building on the foundations laid by Haydn and Mozart, he enlarged the scope of all the major musical forms. At the age of 30 Beethoven began to lose his hearing, and by 1824 he had become totally deaf. He was often said to shout and curse as he composed; but the wild emotion in Beethoven's music was tempered by his respect for musical discipline and logic. Beethoven's works include nine symphonies, 16 string quartets, five piano concertos and 32 piano sonatas. His most popular works include the Third or *Eroica* Symphony (1803-4), the Sixth or *Pastoral* Symphony (1807-8), the Ninth or *Choral* Symphony (1817-23), the *Moonlight Sonata* (1800-1), the opera *Fidelio* (1805-14) and the Mass in D or *Missa Solemnis* (1819-22).
🎤 The opening bars of Beethoven's Fifth Symphony (1804-8) contain the best-known sequence of four notes in classical music. They have been described as 'The sound of Fate knocking at the door'.

CULT COMPOSER *A drawing of Beethoven made in 1818. In the Romantic era that followed, he was hailed as a musical demigod.*

Berlin, Irving (1888-1989) Russian-born American composer and lyricist. He wrote the unofficial American anthem 'God Bless America' (1918, revised 1938) and 'White Christmas' (1942), one of the largest-selling songs in history. Berlin also wrote Broadway musicals such as *Annie Get Your Gun* (1946) and the songs for Hollywood films such as *Top Hat* (1935).

Berlioz, Hector (1803-69) French composer, music critic and leading exponent of the Romantic movement. His originality and imaginative orchestration were first displayed in his bizarre *Symphonie fantastique* (1830), which is notable for its freedom from classical form and expansive scoring for a very large orchestra. Berlioz was attracted by the sublime and wrote a monumental Requiem Mass known as *Grande messe des morts* (1837); but he could also produce delicate work, as in the oratorio *The Childhood of Christ* (1854). His masterpiece is generally considered to be the two-part opera *The Trojans* (1863).
🎵A *Missa Solemnis* composed by Berlioz in 1824 was discovered in an organ loft in Antwerp in 1991. It received its British premiere in Westminster Abbey in 1993.

Bernstein, Leonard (1918-90) American conductor and composer, who worked in both the classical and popular fields of music. He wrote a number of serious choral and symphonic works, but is best remembered for his musicals *On the Town* (1944, filmed in 1949) and *West Side Story* (1957, filmed in 1961). He wrote the music for several Hollywood films including *On the Waterfront* (1954), and was conductor of the New York Philharmonic (1958-70).
🎵In 1984 in New York, Leonard Bernstein conducted a new recording of *West Side Story* featuring the opera stars José CARRERAS and Kiri TE KANAWA.

Berry, Chuck (1926-) American singer, songwriter and guitarist, renowned for his sharp, witty lyrics. A key figure in the evolution of popular music, Berry pioneered ROCK'N'ROLL with songs such as 'Roll Over Beethoven' and 'Johnny B. Goode' (1958). Both the Beatles and the Rolling Stones helped to turn Berry into a cult hero by recording many of his songs.

Bizet, Georges (1838-75) French composer whose reputation rests chiefly on the opera *Carmen* (1873-4). He wrote several other operas and an early symphony (1855) which lay undiscovered for 80 years. His orchestral suites from *Carmen* and from Alphonse Daudet's play *L'Arlésienne* are his most famous concert works.

blues Style of American folk music that evolved from the folk songs of black southern Americans, especially 'work songs' sung by Negroes about their oppression. The blues song form has often been used in jazz, rhythm and blues, and rock. Bessie Smith (1894-1937) was the outstanding blues singer of her generation.

Bolshoi Ballet Moscow-based ballet company formed in 1776, renowned for an athletic and vigorous style of dancing. The Bolshoi's most celebrated productions include modern versions of *Spartacus* (1968) and *Ivan the Terrible* (1975).

Bowie, David (1947-) British singer, composer and actor, renowned for his constantly changing image and sound. Bowie had his first hit single with 'Space Oddity' in 1969 and went on to become one of the leading figures of rock in the 1970s. His most bizarre creation was the image of an androgynous alien for the album *The Rise and Fall of Ziggy Stardust and the Spiders from Mars* (1972). His feature films include *The Man Who Fell To Earth* (1976) and *Merry Christmas Mr Lawrence* (1983).

Brahms, Johannes (1833-97) German composer who was born in Hamburg and made his career in Vienna. As a young man he wrote expansive and passionate music, but as he grew older his works became more concentrated. From the 1860s he was hailed as the saviour of classicism by opponents of WAGNER's so-called modernism. His works include four symphonies, two monumental piano concertos and a lyrical violin concerto, quantities of chamber music and songs, and choral works including his massive *A German Requiem*.

BROADWAY MAESTRO *A vibrant scene from the musical* West Side Story *conveys the energy of Leonard Bernstein's forceful score.*

Bream, Julian (1933-) British guitarist and lute player who won international popularity and acclaim in the 1950s. He has made a major contribution to the revival of interest in Renaissance music.

Britten, Benjamin (1913-76) British composer who made his name in 1945 with his tragic opera *Peter Grimes*. He was a child prodigy – by the age of ten he had written string quartets and piano sonatas. Among his works are the operas *The Turn of the Screw* (1954) and *Death in Venice* (1973); the orchestral composition *The Young Person's Guide to the Orchestra* (1946); and the choral *War Requiem* (1962). The male leading roles in Britten's operas and song cycles were written for his lifelong companion and muse, the tenor Sir Peter Pears (1910-86). Britten was awarded a life peerage in 1976.
🎵In 1948, Britten founded the annual summer music festival held at ALDEBURGH in his native Suffolk.

Broadway Principal theatre district of New York City, centred on part of the street called Broadway, in Manhattan.

Brown, James (1928-) American singer known as the 'Godfather of SOUL'. Brown has played a key role in the development of soul music since the 1960s. Political songs such as 'Say it Loud, I'm Black and I'm Proud' (1968) also made him a figurehead of the black rights movement. His electrifying dance routines inspired many people including Michael Jackson. Brown also inspired the RAP movement of the 1980s. Hit records include 'I Feel Good' (1965) and 'Sex Machine' (1970).

Brubeck, Dave (1920-) American pianist and composer who did much to popularise jazz with the white middle classes during the 1950s and 1960s. He is best known for the hit record 'Take Five', in 5/4 time, which was in fact composed by Paul Desmond, the alto-saxophonist in the Dave Brubeck jazz quartet.

Bruckner, Anton (1824-96) Austrian composer and organist. He was a friend and pupil of WAGNER, whom he met in 1865. Bruckner did not write a major work until he was in his forties, and it was not until his sixties that he gained recognition. His most important compositions are his nine symphonies and large choral works, especially the three masses and the *Te Deum*.

DYNAMIC DIVA *Maria Callas was a compelling singer and actress, but she also had a reputation for being temperamental and unreliable.*

Cage, John (1912-92) American composer of avant-garde music, and pupil of SCHOENBERG. Cage experimented with both electronic and traditional instruments. He invented the 'prepared piano' by inserting objects such as rubberbands and screws between the strings to create new sound effects. Cage treated all sounds as a musical experience, even silence: his *4 minutes 33 seconds* (1952) is a silent work in which the only sounds are those made by the audience. His *Imaginary Landscape No.4* (1951) uses 12 randomly tuned radios.

Cahn, Sammy (1913-92) Witty American lyricist and performer of his own material with his one-man stage and TV show, *Words and Music*. He was renowned for providing material for Frank Sinatra, with songs such as 'All the Way', 'Love and Marriage' and 'My Kind of Town'. Cahn won Oscars for his lyrics for several films, including *Three Coins in the Fountain* (1954), and *A Hole in the Head* (1959).

Callas, Maria (1923-77) (Maria Kalogeropoulou) American-born Greek soprano who became one of the most celebrated and controversial performers of the 20th century. She was renowned for her dramatic interpretations of Italian Romantic composers. Though her vocal technique was considered far from perfect, Callas gave some of the most passionate and memorable performances of all time, especially in the title role of Puccini's *Tosca*.
🎤Callas's personal life was as colourful as her career. At the height of her fame she became the mistress of the Greek shipping millionaire Aristotle Onassis, but after ten years together Onassis suddenly abandoned her to marry Jackie Kennedy, widow of the assassinated American president. Three years later Callas died alone in her Paris flat from a heart attack.

Calloway, Cab (1907-) Leading American band leader, composer and singer, renowned for his eccentric showmanship and big band jazz sound. In the 1930s he worked at the celebrated Cotton Club in Harlem, New York.
🎤The critics called Calloway 'The King of Hi-De Ho' because of his bizarre style of scat singing: a jazz vocal style using meaningless sounds and syllables.

cantata Musical composition for voice and instruments: normally a small-scale oratorio for solo singers accompanied by a small chorus and orchestra.
🎤The master of this form was BACH, who composed more than 200 cantatas.

Carpenters, The Pop duo, consisting of Richard Carpenter (1946-) and his sister Karen (1950-83). They sold more than 50 million records during the 1970s and were renowned for their close harmonies and middle-of-the-road appeal. Their hit records include '(They Long to Be) Close to You' (1970), 'Yesterday Once More' (1973) and 'Top Of The World' (1973). Karen Carpenter died of heart failure brought on by anorexia nervosa.

Carreras, José (1946-) Spanish tenor who, with PAVAROTTI and DOMINGO, became one of the leading tenors of the 1980s and 1990s. The onset of leukaemia interrupted his career in 1987 but he made a triumphant return to the stage in 1990.

Caruso, Enrico (1873-1921) Italian tenor, generally considered to be the finest of all time. He made his debut in 1894 and sang most of the great tenor roles in French and Italian opera. Among the most popular were Cavaradossi in *Tosca*, Canio in *Pagliacci* and Rodolpho in *La Bohème*.
🎤In 1902, sales of 'Vesti la Giubba' from the opera *Pagliacci* made him the earliest recording artist to sell more than a million copies of a record.
🎤The Italian tenor Beniamino Gigli (1890-1957) was regarded as Caruso's successor.

Casals, Pablo (1876-1973) Spanish cellist and conductor. He raised the status of the cello as a major instrument with his performances of concertos, chamber music and the unaccompanied cello suites of Bach, which he rescued from near-oblivion.

Cash, Johnny (1932-) American singer, songwriter and guitarist, of part Cherokee Indian descent, renowned for his gravelly baritone voice. Cash was one of the first stars of COUNTRY AND WESTERN music: in America he has had a grand total of 129 country and 50 pop hits. A champion of American Indian rights, Cash recorded an album of Indian protest songs in 1964 called *Bitter Tears*. In the 1970s he embraced Christianity and moved into gospel music. Hit records include 'Ring of Fire' (1963) and 'A Boy Named Sue' (1969).
🎤Cash is nicknamed 'The Man In Black', and in 1971 he had a hit of that name.

Charles, Ray (1930-) American singer, songwriter and pianist, blind from the age of seven. An outstanding RHYTHM AND BLUES singer, he also performed jazz, soul, country and pop music. His biggest hits include 'Georgia on my Mind' (1960) and 'I Can't Stop Loving You' (1962).

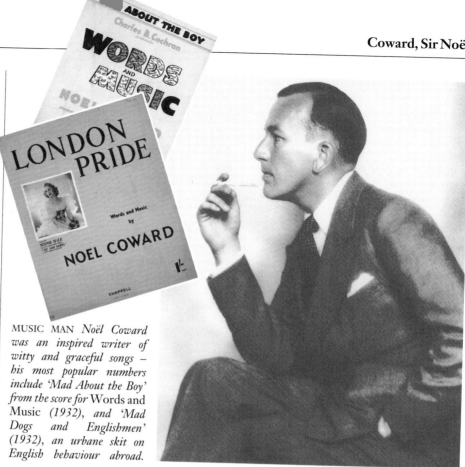

MUSIC MAN *Noël Coward was an inspired writer of witty and graceful songs – his most popular numbers include 'Mad About the Boy' from the score for* Words and Music *(1932), and 'Mad Dogs and Englishmen' (1932), an urbane skit on English behaviour abroad.*

Charleston Popular dance, characterised by frantic arm movements and sidekicks. It was originally popular with black people from the southern states of America and is named after the city of Charleston in South Carolina. The dance featured in the black revues of the 1920s in New York, and turned into a world-wide craze following a musical called *Runnin' Wild* (1923).

Chevalier, Maurice (1888-1972) French singer, revue artiste and actor who, with his debonair charm and roguish chuckle, came to epitomise the romantic Frenchman. He is best remembered for the film *Gigi* (1958), in which he sang 'Thank Heaven For Little Girls'.

Chopin, Frédéric (1810-49) Polish composer, almost exclusively of piano music, including 24 *Preludes* and two sets of *Études*. In Paris, Chopin became a celebrated figure of the Romantic era. His friends and admirers included Berlioz, Liszt and Mendelssohn, and he had a long romance with the novelist George ▷SAND. Chopin suffered from poor health and died of tuberculosis.
🔔 Chopin was fiercely patriotic – it was only the Russian occupation of his homeland that forced him to spend much of his life in Paris – and he carried a silver urn full of Polish earth wherever he went.

Clapton, Eric (1945-) British guitarist and a leading figure in RHYTHM AND BLUES. Clapton first had success with the rock band Cream (1966-8), whose music paved the way for bands such as Led Zeppelin and later generations of heavy metal groups. As Derek and the Dominoes, Clapton had a big hit with 'Layla' in 1972. Having overcome heroin addiction, Clapton re-launched his career with a recording of Bob Marley's 'I Shot the Sheriff' (1974). Later hits included 'Lay Down Sally' and 'Wonderful Tonight' (both 1978).

classical Term which, strictly speaking, applies to European music written between approximately 1750 and 1825. Classical composers include HAYDN, MOZART and BEETHOVEN. However, the term is often used to describe any European or American music written in a scholarly tradition.

Cochran, Eddie (1938-60) American guitarist, one of the great singers and songwriters of ROCK'N'ROLL. He is best remembered for the songs 'Summertime Blues' (1958) and 'C'mon Everybody' (1959). Cochran died in a car accident.

Cole, Nat King (1917-65) American singer and pianist. Although he began his career as a jazz pianist, Cole made his name as a popular balladeer with his smooth and romantic style, epitomised in songs such as 'Mona Lisa' (1950), 'Unforgettable' (1951) and 'When I Fall In Love' (1957).

contralto Lowest range of the female singing voice.

Copland, Aaron (1900-90) American pianist, conductor and composer, whose use of folk song has established a style of modern American concert music known as the 'Americana' style. He produced his most popular work in the late 1930s and 1940s: two cowboy ballets called *Billy the Kid* (1938) and *Rodeo* (1942), his masterpiece *Appalachian Spring* (1944), and the highly acclaimed *Third Symphony* (1946). He also wrote music for films.
🔔 One of Copland's most impressive compositions, *Fanfare for the Common Man* (1942), was used for the television coverage of the 1968 Mexico Olympics.

Cotton, Billy (1899-1969) British band leader who started his musical career as a drummer in the army, and formed his first band in 1923. He presented a variety show called *The Billy Cotton Band Show* on radio (1949-57) and television (1957-68), which became a national institution. Cotton introduced his shows with the rousing catchphrase: 'Wakey, WAY-key!'

countertenor Highest naturally produced adult male voice, with a range above that of TENOR. Countertenors today sing roles previously given to the artificially induced castrato male voice.

country and western Commercial form of American folk music. Jimmie Rodgers (1897-1933) is credited as the first artist to merge rural hillbilly music with American popular song: he inspired the trend for 'singing cowboys' such as Roy Rogers. Well-known country and western artists include Hank Williams, Tammy WYNETTE and Dolly Parton.

Coward, Sir Noël (1899-1973) British playwright, composer, actor and director, renowned for his foppish sophistication and quintessential Englishness. He wrote the music and words for the operetta *Bitter Sweet* (1929) and the revue *Words and Music* (1932). His wittiest songs are the satirical numbers he wrote in the 1930s including 'Don't Put Your Daughter on the Stage Mrs Worthington' and 'Mad Dogs and Englishmen'. He was noted for his one-man cabaret performances in London and Las Vegas in the 1950s.

Crosby, Bing (1904-77) (Harry Lillis Crosby) One of the most successful American recording artists of the 20th century, with sales of more than 400 million records. Crosby called himself 'The Groaner' and he popularised a new, relaxed style of singing. In the late 1920s the microphone was a recent invention, and Crosby was the first solo singer to use it to good effect – influencing crooners such as Tony Bennett and Frank Sinatra. Crosby's greatest hits include 'White Christmas' (1942), 'Silent Night' (1942) and 'Swinging on a Star' (1944). Crosby is also renowned for the series of ▷ROAD FILMS he made with Bob Hope.

🎵 Crosby was nicknamed 'Bing' because of his childhood obsession with an American comic-strip character called 'Bingo' that appeared in a local newspaper.

JAZZ GIANT *Miles Davis took up the trumpet at the age of 13 and developed a pensive style that made him a leading figure in modern jazz.*

Davis, Miles (1926-91) American jazz trumpeter and composer, one of the most influential musicians in jazz. He launched the 'cool jazz' movement (a lighter style with less impassioned improvisation) with his recordings of 1948-9, which were reissued under the title *The Birth of the Cool.* Davis later experimented with electronic instruments and fused jazz with rock.

🎵 Other pioneers of cool jazz include Dave Brubeck, Stan Getz and Chet Baker.

Debussy, Claude (1862-1918) Influential French composer, a musical revolutionary who set out to free music from the 'barren traditions' which he felt were stifling it. His intoxicating use of harmonies created a sensual musical dream world, and had a profound influence on modern Western music. Debussy lived a bohemian life in Paris, where he was idolised by young students and artists. The critics described him as a musical impressionist – a label which Debussy hated. He had his first success with the delicate orchestral piece *Prélude à l'après-midi d'un Faune* (1892-4), and his only completed opera, *Pelléas et Mélisande* (1892-1902), won him international acclaim. Debussy's best-known orchestral works include *Nocturnes* (1897-9) and *La Mer* (1903-5).

Delius, Frederick (1862-1934) British composer of German parentage who made his home in France in 1889. Influenced by Debussy and Grieg, his works were impressionistic in style. Delius made his mark in England after 1907 where he was championed by Sir Thomas BEECHAM, who called him 'the last great apostle of romance, emotion and beauty in music'. His output included the choral works *Appalachia* (1902) and *Sea Drift* (1903), and the orchestral works *Brigg Fair* (1907) and *On Hearing the First Cuckoo in Spring* (1913).

de Valois, Dame Ninette (1898-) Irish-born British ballet dancer and choreographer. After dancing with DIAGHILEV's Ballets Russes (1923-6), de Valois opened a ballet school in London. In 1931 she founded the Vic-Wells Ballet – the company that became the ROYAL BALLET at Covent Garden in 1956. Her ballets include *The Rake's Progress* (1935) and *The Prospect Before Us* (1940).

Diaghilev, Sergei (Dee-AH-gi-lev) (1872-1929) Russian impresario who, as the founder of the Ballets Russes, was the greatest single influence on ballet in the 20th century. Diaghilev introduced Russian ballet to the West in 1909 with a historic season in Paris. For the next 20 years his Ballets Russes dominated the world of ballet. Diaghilev's unique position resulted from his insistence on using only outstanding talents among dancers (Pavlova, Nijinsky and Markova), composers (Debussy, Satie, Ravel, Stravinsky and Prokofiev) and artists (Bakst, Matisse, Picasso and Cocteau). Diaghilev's most notable productions include *The Firebird* (1910), *Petrushka* (1911) and the sensational *The Rite of Spring* (1913), all by STRAVINSKY.

diva Italian word for 'goddess', usually reserved for great operatic sopranos such as Maria Callas, Kiri Te Kanawa and Jessye Norman. The term can also be applied to mezzo-sopranos and contraltos.

Domingo, Placido (1941-) Spanish operatic tenor renowned for his fine acting and musical versatility. He has sung more than 75 different roles, from the works of Puccini to Wagner, and recorded many solo albums of popular songs. Domingo was only 21 years old when he was made lead tenor with the Tel Aviv opera company, and by the 1970s he had become one of the biggest international opera stars.

Domino, Fats (1928-) (Antoine Domino) American singer, pianist and songwriter, who pioneered the New Orleans style of RHYTHM AND BLUES in the 1950s. His boogie-woogie piano playing style, with its repeated rhythmic and melodic pattern in the bass, influenced rock-'n'roll music; his best-known songs include 'Ain't That a Shame' (1955), 'Blueberry Hill' (1956) and 'Blue Monday' (1957).

Donegan, Lonnie (1931-) Glasgow-born singer and guitarist who was one of Britain's first pop idols. His hit record 'Rock Island Line' established the British SKIFFLE craze in the mid 1950s – when small bands with guitars and washboards played American FOLK and BLUES songs.

🎵 It was Donegan who inspired John Lennon to form a skiffle group, which evolved into the Beatles.

Doors, The (Jim Morrison, John Densmore, Robbie Krieger, Ray Manzarek) American rock band formed in 1965, whose controversial songs were inspired by the drug culture of the time. The band's focus, Jim Morrison (1943-71), was noted for his bizarre personality and lurid poetry. Despite commercial and critical success with songs such as 'Light My Fire' (1967), the use of drugs and alcohol made Morrison's behaviour increasingly erratic. He died of a suspected overdose.

Duncan, Isadora (1877-1927) American dancer whose 'natural' style proved the starting point of the modern dance tradition. Inspired by Classical Greek dancing, she championed an expressive style of movement, dancing in bare feet and flowing draperies. Duncan made her Chicago debut in 1896, toured all over Europe and opened schools in Russia. She was strangled by her own scarf when it caught in the rear wheel of a moving car.

du Pré, Jaqueline (1945-87) British cellist who mesmerised audiences with her passionate interpretations, particularly of the Elgar Cello Concerto. She married the Israeli pianist and conductor Daniel Barenboim in 1967. Stricken by multiple sclerosis in 1973, she taught until her death.

Dvořák, Antonín (VORR-jhack) (1841-1904) Czech composer who used the folk songs of his Bohemian peasant background to inject colour and gaiety into his music. He loved the countryside, and his orchestration often reflects pastoral elements. His Czech nationalism is particularly evident in the *Slavonic Dances* (1878; 1887) and *Slavonic Rhapsodies* (1878). When Dvořák went to New York as head of the National Conservatory (1892-5) he was inspired by American Indian chants and Negro spiritual melodies to write his ninth symphony, *From the New World* (1893).

Dylan, Bob (1941-) (Robert Zimmerman) American folk singer and songwriter who became a spokesman for millions of disaffected young people of his generation – while his artistry was a major influence on his musical peers. A strong supporter of the civil rights and anti-war movements, Dylan wrote protest songs such as 'Blowin' in the Wind' (1963) and 'The Times they are a-Changin'' (1964). In 1988 he joined George Harrison, Roy Orbison and Tom Petty to record an album called *The Traveling Wilburys*.

FOLK HERO *In the 1960s Bob Dylan became pop music's leading poet and composer. He named himself after the poet Dylan Thomas.*

POMP AND GLORY *Elgar's stirring symphonies and orchestral works epitomised the self-confidence of Edwardian England's golden age. His later works, however, were more soulful and melancholic.*

Elgar, Sir Edward (1857-1934) The most outstanding British composer since PURCELL. Self-taught, Elgar enjoyed only modest success with his early choral works, but made a great impact with his orchestral work *Enigma Variations* (1899). The oratorio *The Dream of Gerontius* (1900) was initially unpopular, but later confirmed his stature. Other works include the five *Pomp and Circumstance* marches (1901-30), the first of which provided the tune for 'Land of Hope and Glory'.

Ellington, Duke (1899-1974) American jazz composer, songwriter and band leader. He began his career as a jazz pianist, and formed his own band in 1924. In the 1930s his orchestra became renowned for its residency at the Cotton Club in Harlem, New York. The band travelled the world recording, broadcasting and playing concerts until his death. Ellington was a prolific composer, writing jazz pieces, standard ballads and full-scale suites. Some of his most popular songs include: 'Mood Indigo', 'Sophisticated Lady' and 'Don't Get Around Much Anymore'. He wrote several film scores including the dramatic music for *Anatomy of a Murder* (1959).

English National Opera Opera company at London's Coliseum Theatre. It was set up in 1974 by the former Sadler's Wells Opera. Its productions are sung in English.

Evans, Sir Geraint (1922-92) Welsh baritone, one of the most distinctive British opera singers. He made his Covent Garden debut in 1948 and was renowned for his comic opera roles, such as Beckmesser in Wagner's *Die Meistersinger* and the title role in Verdi's *Falstaff*.

Fauré, Gabriel (1845-1924) French composer and organist, noted particularly for his *Requiem* (1887-1900). He wrote many lyrical songs and piano pieces: his best-known compositions include the song cycle *La Bonne Chanson* (1892-4), the opera *Pénélope* (1913) and incidental music to *Pelléas and Mélisande* (1898).

Ferrier, Kathleen (1912-53) British contralto, one of the most loved singers of her time. She worked closely with Benjamin BRITTEN, who wrote the title role in *The Rape of Lucretia* (1946) for her. She died of cancer at the height of her career.

Fields, Gracie (1898-1979) British singer, comedienne and actress. Her Lancashire humour and flair for singing comic songs such as 'I Took My Harp to a Party' and 'The Biggest Aspidistra in the World' won her great popularity in the 1930s. Fields toured the world during World War II to entertain the Allied troops. Her theme song 'Sally' inspired the title of her first film, *Sally in Our Alley* (1931).

Fitzgerald, Ella (1918-) American jazz singer, known for the clarity of her voice and scat singing style – which uses meaningless syllables instead of words. She built up a reputation as the finest female jazz vocalist since Billie Holiday with songs such as 'A-Tisket a-Tasket' and 'Ev'ry Time We Say Goodbye'.

folk music Simple form of popular music that originated with ordinary people of a region singing about their experiences. Because the songs were never written down, and the authors were forgotten, true folk music is described as timeless. Modern folk revivalists include Woody Guthrie, Joan Baez, Bob Dylan and Ewan MacColl.
♪ Composers such as Dvořák, Grieg, Bartok and Vaughan Williams made use of folk tunes and rhythms in their compositions.

Fonteyn, Dame Margot (1919-91) (Margaret Hookham) British ballerina renowned for her perfect technique and seemingly effortless dancing. She established an unequalled reputation in such classic roles as Aurora in *The Sleeping Beauty* (1939), and in the many ballets created for her by Frederick ASHTON. Her legendary partnership with Rudolph NUREYEV was formed in 1962 when they first danced together in *Giselle*; Fonteyn was almost twice his age. In 1964 Fonteyn's husband, the Panamanian diplomat Roberto Arias, was the victim of an assassination attempt which left him paralysed. Because Fonteyn had to help nurse and support him, she was in financial difficulty when he died in 1989, and a special benefit gala was held for her at Covent Garden the following year.

fugue Instrumental or vocal composition in which individual tunes, or 'voices', are harmoniously interwoven. A fugue begins with a short tune which is sung or played alone: this tune is called the 'subject' and recurs throughout as the main theme. As the first voice finishes the subject, a second voice picks it up in a different pitch, and this second entry of the subject is called the 'answer'. While the second voice goes through the answer, the first voice continues with a new theme that combines with the answer. If third and fourth voices enter, they repeat the process, eventually creating a four-part texture. The fugue continues in a similar manner. The greatest exponent of the fugue was BACH.

Genesis English rock group formed in 1967 by Anthony Phillips, Mike Rutherford, Tony Banks and Peter Gabriel. In 1970 Phillips was replaced by Steve Hackett, and Phil Collins joined as drummer. Genesis began as an experimental 'art-rock' band and Gabriel made a charismatic front man with his theatrical performances and outrageous costumes. He left in 1975 to be replaced by Collins as lead vocalist, and the band began to develop a more mainstream style. They became one of the top acts of the 1980s with albums such as *Duke* (1980) and *Invisible Touch* (1986).

Gershwin, George (1898-1937) American pianist and composer who bridged the gap between popular and classical music. Gershwin often worked with his brother Ira (1896-1983), who was a gifted lyricist. Together they wrote the musical comedies *Lady, Be Good* (1924) and *Funny Face* (1927). Ira also worked with Gershwin on the ground-breaking folk opera *Porgy and Bess* (1935). George Gershwin sprang to prominence in his own right with the symphonic work *Rhapsody in Blue* (1924), followed by the concert piece *An American in Paris* (1928) which inspired the film of the same title in 1951.

Gilbert and Sullivan Sir William Schwenk Gilbert (1836-1911) and Sir Arthur Seymour Sullivan (1842-1900), librettist and composer respectively, were the English authors of a series of popular comic operettas. They first worked together on a play in 1871 and, encouraged by the theatrical agent Richard D'Oyly Carte, continued their partnership with the operetta *Trial by Jury* in 1875. Carte built the Savoy Theatre in 1881 to stage their works, and the three of them began a series of operettas, known as the Savoy Operas. Notable works include *The Pirates of Penzance* (1879) and *The Mikado* (1885).

Gillespie, Dizzy (1917-92) American jazz trumpeter, band leader and composer. Gillespie played a major part in establishing the trends of modern jazz; he was a leading exponent of BEBOP. Gillespie played with a number of different bands in the 1930s and early 1940s before forming his own band in 1944. His compositions include 'Night in Tunisia' (1942) and 'Groovin' High' (1944). He continued to play and record into the 1980s.
♪ Gillespie was nicknamed Dizzy because of his penchant for clowning. He originated the jazz 'uniform' of dark glasses and beret.

Glyndebourne Small opera house in Sussex, home of the annual Glyndebourne Festival. The festival was founded in 1934 and is noted for its high standard of production, particularly of the works of Mozart.
♪ The original opera house was rebuilt in 1994. Opera-goers traditionally eat a picnic in the grounds during the long interval.

ORIENTAL UPDATE The Mikado *(1885) is one of the most popular Gilbert and Sullivan operettas. Shown below is a scene from a production by the English National Opera, which is set in the 1920s.*

AGE OF AQUARIUS *The two heads on the original poster for* Hair *form the figure* ∞, *which is the mystical symbol for infinity.*

hardships of the Depression, and travelled throughout America as a street singer. One of his best known songs, 'This Land Is Your Land', is regarded by many Americans as an alternative national anthem.

Hair Ground-breaking American musical, concerned with the Vietnam war and hippie lifestyle of the 1960s, with score by Galt MacDermot and lyrics by Gerome Ragni and James Rado. *Hair* opened in London in 1968 on the night the censorship laws were relaxed: it was the first time that nudity had been allowed on a West End stage, and the first attempt to bring rock music to the theatre. A film version was made in 1979 and the show had a brief revival at London's Old Vic in 1993. Memorable songs include 'Aquarius', 'Let the Sunshine In' and 'Good Morning Starshine'.

SHAKE, RATTLE AND ROLL *Bill Haley, top centre, and his Comets became immensely successful in the early years of rock'n'roll.*

GRAND SCALE *Handel represented music at its most majestic and sublime. His* Messiah *brought him unrivalled wealth and fame.*

Goodman, Benny (1909-86) American band leader, composer and clarinet player who was known as the 'King of Swing' – a style of jazz played by big bands in the 1930s and 1940s. In New York in 1935 he formed the Benny Goodman trio with Gene Krupa and Teddy Wilson; a year later Lionel Hampton made it a quartet. For 30 years Goodman maintained his reputation as one of the finest jazz musicians.

gospel music Joyful, jazz-inspired religious music, associated with the Protestant revivalism of the late 19th century, when black slaves of America evolved a repertoire of gospel and SPIRITUAL songs. In 1928 a club pianist called Thomas A. Dorsey began to write popular gospel songs: he founded the National Convention of Gospel Singers and came to be known as the 'Father of Gospel Music'. He discovered and toured with Mahalia Jackson, who was nicknamed the 'Gospel Queen'.

Gregorian chant Unaccompanied choral chant, sung in unison, derived from the earliest Christian PLAINSONG and codified by Pope Gregory the Great (AD 590-604) into a repertoire of Roman Catholic melodies.

Grieg, Edvard (1843-1907) Norwegian composer whose music reflects the influence of folk song. He is best known for two orchestral pieces originally written to accompany Ibsen's play *Peer Gynt* (1875), and his Piano Concerto in A minor (1868).

Guthrie, Woody (1912-67) American songwriter and folk singer who flourished in the 1930s. A champion of the poor, he wrote songs about social injustice and the

Haley, Bill (1925-81) American singer and guitarist. Haley was known as the 'Father of Rock'n'Roll', for though he did not invent the style, he was the first artist to bring it to the masses. In 1953 he formed the band Bill Haley and his Comets, and their recording of 'Rock Around The Clock' was used in the film *The Blackboard Jungle* (1955). Haley's sound was so revolutionary that it led to cinema riots, with young people dancing in the aisles and ripping up seats. The record sold 22 million copies worldwide and re-entered the charts in 1968 and 1974. Haley's plump 'nice guy' image made him an unlikely hero. Although he was mobbed when he visited Britain in 1957, he soon lost his crown to the new king of rock'n'roll, Elvis Presley.

Hammerstein II, Oscar (1895-1960) American songwriter, renowned for his poetic and sentimental lyrics. He collaborated with Richard RODGERS on a series of big-scale musicals such as *Oklahoma!* (1943) and *Carousel* (1945). He also worked with a number of other composers, including Jerome KERN with whom he wrote *Show Boat* (1927), the first American musical to be based upon a serious work of fiction.

Handel, George Frideric (1685-1759) German-born composer of the baroque era, who became a naturalised British subject in 1726. Handel wrote 46 operas, including the occasionally revived *Julius Caesar* (1724), but he is best known for his *Water Music* suite (1717) and his magnificent *Messiah* oratorio (1742). Beethoven admired Handel above all other composers, saying 'To him only I bow the knee'.
♪ It is traditional for the audience to stand during the 'Hallelujah Chorus' of Handel's *Messiah*. This tradition began at the oratorio's first London performance in 1743 before George II, when the king was so moved by the exultant chorus, he rose to his feet, followed by the rest of the audience.

Haydn, Joseph (1732-1809) Austrian composer who was prominent in the development of the string quartet and the

LADY SINGS THE BLUES *Billie Holiday was renowned for her searching and intense interpretations of torch songs, but personal insecurity and the pressures of club life led to her career's tragic decline.*

Hendrix, Jimi (1942-70) American electric guitarist of the 1960s. His experimental guitar style, using special effects such as feedback and distortion, revolutionised the use of the instrument in rock music and helped to inspire HEAVY METAL music. Hendrix was one of the first black rock stars, but his audience was mainly white. In 1966 he went to London and formed a group called the Jimi Hendrix Experience: the next year they had three hits with 'Hey Joe', 'Purple Haze' and 'The Wind Cries Mary'. Hendrix was a flamboyant showman; as part of his stage act he would play the guitar with his teeth. He died at the height of his fame after taking drugs.

Holiday, Billie (1915-59) (Eleanora Fagan) American singer and leading jazz vocalist of her day. Although Holiday was not a true BLUES singer, everything she sang had a blues 'feel'. She was a gifted interpreter of lyrics and her voice had a unique, coarse timbre. She had her first recording session with the Benny Goodman band in 1933 and her first solo concert in 1946, in New York, but Holiday cut a tragic figure in the music world, and her career was blighted by drugs and alcohol. By the 1950s her voice and her health began to fail, and she died of a drugs-related illness.

Holly, Buddy (1936-59) American singer, guitarist and composer, one of the great pioneers of ROCK'N'ROLL. Holly produced some of the most innovative pop songs of the 1950s, experimenting with production techniques and developing his 'hiccupping' vocal style. In 1957 he had four hits with his band The Crickets, including 'That'll Be The Day' and 'Oh Boy'. His first solo hit record was 'Peggy Sue' (1957); he died in a plane crash two years later.

Holst, Gustav (1874-1934) English composer of partly Swedish descent, with a somewhat mystical musical style. He is best known for his orchestral suite *The Planets* (1918), the choral *Hymn of Jesus* (1920) and the opera *The Perfect Fool* (1923).
♪ The central melody from 'Jupiter' (No.4 of *The Planets*) is the music for Holst's hymn 'I Vow to Thee my Country'.

Iglesias, Julio (1943-) Spanish crooner whose multilingual records and romantic image made him an international superstar. By the end of the 1980s his albums had sold more than 100 million copies in seven languages. His first big English-language hit, 'Begin the Beguine', topped the British charts in 1981.

symphony: his 107 symphonies and 68 string quartets revealed the rich possibilities of both forms. He also wrote operas, concertos, masses and oratorios. *The Creation* (1799) and *The Seasons* (1801) were prompted by hearing oratorios by Handel during visits to England. Haydn's genial nature earned him the nickname 'Papa'.

heavy metal Style of guitar-based rock music characterised by loud, fast and intense playing. It developed in the 1960s with blues-based groups such as Cream (whose guitarist was Eric CLAPTON) and rock guitarist Jimi HENDRIX, who used heavily amplified music. The term 'heavy metal' was inspired by the song 'Born To Be Wild', a rebellious anthem recorded by a

hard-rock band called Steppenwolf in 1968 and adopted by motorcycle gangs. The song contains the phrase 'heavy metal thunder' from the William Burroughs novel *Naked Lunch*. The band Black Sabbath helped to pioneer heavy metal in Britain with the record *Paranoid* (1970).

Helpmann, Sir Robert (1909-86) Australian ballet dancer, choreographer and actor, renowned for his dramatic style. He moved to England in 1933 and became one of the first stars of the Sadler's Wells Ballet, partnering Margot Fonteyn. In 1965 Helpmann became artistic director of the Australian Ballet. He appeared in the ballet films *The Red Shoes* (1948) and Rudolph Nureyev's *Don Quixote* (1973).

Jackson, Michael (1958-19)

American pop singer who began singing with his brothers in the Jackson Five when he was only five years old, and proved to be a natural showman. Jackson released his first hit solo album *Off The Wall* (1979) and had instant success with the single 'Don't Stop Till You Get Enough'. In 1982 his *Thriller* album became the most successful album of all time, with sales of over 40 million. Seven of the tracks became Top 10 hits including 'Billie Jean' and 'Beat It'. In 1993 Jackson gave a rare television interview in which he denied some bizarre rumours – including the allegation that he had taken drugs to make his skin turn white. Later that year he faced fresh allegations – this time of child abuse; he denied them but made a substantial out-of-court settlement. In 1994 he married Lisa-Marie Presley, Elvis Presley's daughter, in a secret ceremony in the Dominican Republic.

LIVING LEGEND *Much speculation has grown up around Michael Jackson because of his reclusive personality. The media often portray him as a lonely victim of his fame and success.*

Janáček, Leoš (YAN-a-check) (1854-1928)

Czech composer who derived inspiration from folk song and the rhythms and inflections of the Czech language. His work includes the operas *The Cunning Little Vixen* (1923) and *The Makropoulos Affair* (1925), the orchestral piece *Sinfonietta* (1926) and the *Glagolitic Mass* (1926).

jazz

Musical style created by black Americans in New Orleans at the start of the 20th century. Jazz has its roots in black folk songs, SPIRITUALS, BLUES and RAGTIME. It evolved via the big band jazz of the SWING era in the 1930s with band leaders such as Duke Ellington, Count Basie, Cab Calloway and Benny Goodman, through the experimental BEBOP jazz of the 1940s developed by musicians such as Dizzy GILLESPIE and Charlie PARKER, to the lighter 'cool jazz' movement of the late 1940s launched by Miles DAVIS.
🎤 The American jazz pianist Jelly Roll Morton (1889-1941) made the bold claim that he 'created' jazz in 1902, when he began playing the piano in a New Orleans brothel at the beginning of his career.

John, Elton (1947-)

(Reginald Dwight) English rock singer, pianist and songwriter who is one of the most successful rock pianists in the world. He teamed up with lyricist Bernie Taupin in 1969 and enjoyed success with his first album *Elton John* and the hit single 'Your Song' (1971). To cloak his shyness and lack of confidence, John adopted a flamboyant image with outrageous costumes and spectacles. His many hit singles include 'Goodbye Yellow Brick Road' (1973), his tribute to Marilyn Monroe, 'Candle In The Wind' (1974), his first No.1, with Kiki Dee, 'Don't Go Breaking My Heart' (1976), 'I'm Still Standing' (1983) and 'Sacrifice' (1990).
🎤 Elton John was the chairman of Watford Football Club from 1973 to 1990.

Jolson, Al (1886-1950)

(Asa Yoelson) American singer and actor, renowned for his dynamic stage presence and black make-up. Jolson joined a minstrel show in 1909 and became the star attraction. He began recording and touring: some of his best-known songs included 'Mammy', 'Swanee' and 'Sonny Boy'. In 1927 Jolson became a big box office attraction when he made the first full-length talking picture The ▷JAZZ SINGER. A fresh wave of popularity began when Jolson entertained American troops during World War II. Two films were made about Jolson's life: *The Jolson Story* (1946) and *Jolson Sings Again* (1949).

Jones, Tom (1940-)

Welsh pop singer renowned for his powerful voice and his masculine image. Jones started singing in working-men's clubs (billed as 'Tiger Tom') and had hit singles with songs such as 'It's Not Unusual' (1965) and 'Delilah' (1968). In the 1970s Jones became a cabaret star in Las Vegas. In 1988 he revitalised his image with the hit record 'Kiss'.

Joplin, Janice (1943-70)

American singer known for her rebellious spirit and expressive, searing voice on records such as 'Ball and Chain' and 'Piece of My Heart' (both 1968). The single 'Me and Bobby McGee' reached No.1 in America after she died of a heroin overdose.

Joplin, Scott (1868-1917)

American composer and pianist, who in the 1890s helped to evolve RAGTIME, a musical style that swept the world until it was displaced by jazz towards the end of World War I. Joplin wrote two operas and even planned a ragtime symphony. One of his best-known works is 'Maple Leaf Rag' (1899). Joplin's work enjoyed a revival after his piano composition 'The Entertainer' was used in the film *The Sting* in 1973.

Karajan, Herbert von (1908-89)

Austrian conductor and opera impresario, known for his precision and faithfulness to the composer's intentions. In 1955 he became conductor of the Berlin Philharmonic Orchestra, resigning only three months before his death. In 1956 he was appointed artistic director of the Salzburg Festival of Music and Opera.
🎤 Karajan was a controversial figure because of his membership of the Nazi Party: he stayed in Berlin during the war and gave special performances for Hitler.

GIVING VOICE *Al Jolson made screen history when he starred in the first talking feature-length movie,* The Jazz Singer *(1927).*

Kelly, Gene

UPBEAT DOWNPOUR *Gene Kelly happily weathers a Hollywood storm, in the unforgettable scene from* Singin' in the Rain.

Kelly, Gene (1912-) Versatile American musical star and director, renowned for his athletic dancing, inventive choreography and winning smile. Kelly made his film debut in *Me and My Girl* (1942) and won a reputation as a dancer and choreographer in *Cover Girl* (1944). Some of his most memorable films include *Anchors Aweigh* (1945) in which he danced with Jerry the cartoon mouse, *On the Town* (1949), *An American in Paris* (1951) and *Singin' in the Rain* (1952). He directed the film musical *Hello, Dolly!* in 1969.

Kennedy, Nigel (1956-) British virtuoso violinist, renowned for his impassioned performances and informal, almost punk appearance. He made his London concert debut in 1977 and has appeared with all the major British orchestras. His recording of Vivaldi's *The Four Seasons* (1986) achieved unprecedented sales for a classical recording. In 1993 Kennedy declared that he was tired of playing 'dead' concertos, and wanted to concentrate on jazz.

Kern, Jerome (1885-1945) Celebrated American songwriter who was a founding figure of the 20th-century American musical. His early musical comedy successes such as *Oh Boy!* (1917) and *Sally* (1920) were surpassed by his musical masterpiece *Show Boat* (1927), which he wrote with Oscar Hammerstein II. After 1939 Kern devoted himself to film music and later the concert platform. Some of Kern's best-known songs include 'The Way You Look Tonight', 'A Fine Romance', 'Ol' Man River' and 'Smoke Gets in Your Eyes'.

Kirov Ballet Russian ballet company based at the Kirov State Theatre of Opera and Ballet in St Petersburg. The company succeeded the Imperial Russian Ballet and inherited its elegant style of dancing. Three of its most notable dancers – Natalia Makarova, Rudolf Nureyev and Mikhail Baryshnikov – defected to the West and gained international reputations. Although the emphasis of Soviet ballet shifted to Moscow after 1945, the company still enjoys worldwide acclaim.

Klemperer, Otto (1885-1973) German conductor and composer, celebrated for his highly individual interpretations of Beethoven, Mahler and Richard Strauss. Klemperer's outstanding career began in 1907 in Prague, where he became conductor of the German Opera on the recommendation of Mahler. As a Jew he was forced out of Nazi Germany in 1933 and went to America. Klemperer went on to conduct many major orchestras all over the world. He was prominent in London as principal conductor of the Philharmonia Orchestra from 1955 until his death.

Last, James (1929-) (Hans Last) Popular German conductor and composer who has sold more than 50 million albums worldwide with his big band arrangements of classic pop hits. He formed his own orchestra in 1964 and achieved international popularity with his 'Non-Stop Dancing' albums: these provided a party atmosphere by incorporating sounds of clapping and laughter between the tracks.

Led Zeppelin (Robert Plant, Jimmy Page, John Paul Jones, John Bonham) British heavy-rock band formed in 1968, renowned for the sheer volume of their sound. They grew out of the British blues scene and became one of the biggest acts of the 1970s, especially in America. Led Zeppelin are now regarded as one of the most influential bands of the rock era. Robert Plant's passionate vocals and Jimmy Page's screeching virtuoso guitar inspired later generations of HEAVY METAL groups. Their best-known song, 'Stairway To Heaven' (1971), is considered by many to be the definitive heavy-rock song. The group disbanded in 1980 after the death of drummer John Bonham from alcohol poisoning. Led Zeppelin reunited for the global Live Aid charity concert in 1985 with Phil Collins on drums, and for a record company anniversary concert in 1988 with Bonham's son, Jason, on drums.

Lee, Peggy (1920-) (Norma Egstrom) American popular singer, songwriter and actress. Her clear yet husky voice suited many forms of music including jazz, Latin American and folk. She was discovered by band leader Benny Goodman in Chicago in 1941 and worked with him for a few years until she went solo. In the 1950s, Lee appeared in films and was nominated for an Oscar for her performance as a fading singer in *Pete Kelly's Blues* (1955). Her greatest hit single was 'Fever' (1958).
♪ Peggy Lee's voice featured in the Walt Disney cartoon film *The Lady and the Tramp* (1956), in which she sang her own composition 'He's a Tramp', and provided the voice for the Siamese cats.

Lehár, Franz (1870-1948) Austro-Hungarian composer of operetta and light music. After Johann Strauss, Lehár was the greatest figure in Viennese operetta. His most popular work, *The Merry Widow* (1905), brought him international fame. Before the theatre came to dominate his life, Lehár wrote many songs and orchestral pieces, including the well-known 'Gold and Silver' concert-waltz (1902).
♪ The Austrian tenor Richard Tauber (1891-1948) was renowned for his interpretations of Lehár's works and became his principal singer. Tauber is particularly associated with the song 'You Are My Heart's Delight' from Lehár's operetta *The Land of Smiles* (1929).

Les Misérables Operatic musical based on the novel by Victor Hugo, with score by Claude-Michel Schönberg, libretto by Alain Boublil and lyrics by Herbert Kretzmer. Set in the midst of the French Revolution, it follows the lives of an ex-convict named Jean Valjean, and Javert the police chief who is his sworn enemy. The musical was first produced in Paris in 1980, and opened in London in 1985.
♪ Schönberg and Boublil have since written the highly successful musical *Miss Saigon* (1989), which is based on the story of *Madam Butterfly*.

Liberace (1919-87) (Wladziu Valentino Liberace) American pianist and entertainer, renowned for his flamboyant presentation with glass pianos, ornate candelabras and sequinned costumes. A child prodigy of Polish-Italian stock, Liberace was a talented classical musician. His natural showmanship, and spirited and extravagant interpretations of the popular classics, made him one of the most commercially successful pianists of the 1950s, and he was still filling concert halls in the 1980s.

♣ Liberace's lavish and eye-catching wardrobe was the inspiration for artists such as Gary Glitter and Elton John.

libretto Text of an opera, oratorio or musical comedy: the book of words that are sung and spoken. The word is the Italian for 'small book'.

Liszt, Franz (1811-86) Hungarian virtuoso pianist, composer and teacher, generally regarded to have been the greatest performer of his time. Liszt was a flamboyant showman, renowned for his often fiery style of composition and performance. He popularised the 'symphonic poem' – an orchestral piece influenced by literature, art or emotions. Examples of such works include *Les Préludes* (1854). Hungarian gypsy tunes provided Liszt with the inspiration for his popular piano works the *Hungarian Rhapsodies*, some of which he later re-wrote for full orchestra. His later works became progressively more sombre.

♣ Liszt championed the composer Wagner, who married Liszt's daughter Cosima.

Lloyd, Marie (1870-1922) (Matilda Wood) British comedienne and music-hall singer who made her debut at the age of 15. Her cockney humour won her great popularity and she was famous for her risqué interpretations of such numbers as 'A Little of What You Fancy Does You Good' and 'Oh, Mr Porter'.

Lloyd Webber, Andrew (1948-) British composer of some of the longest-running musicals in the history of British theatre. In 1968 Lloyd Webber and lyric writer Tim Rice wrote the rock musical *Joseph and the Amazing Technicolor Dreamcoat*; it was staged in the West End in 1973 and revived in 1992. In 1969 Lloyd Webber and Rice wrote another biblical rock opera, the controversial *Jesus Christ Superstar*. Next came *Evita*, based on the life of Eva Perón, wife of the Argentinian president; the show was staged in London (1978) and contained the memorable song 'Don't Cry For Me, Argentina'. Lloyd Webber parted company with Rice to work on *Cats* (1981), a feline fantasy based on T.S. Eliot's poems from *Old Possum's Book of Practical Cats*, containing the hit song 'Memory'. More successful shows followed with *Starlight Express* (1984), *Phantom of the Opera* (1986) and *Aspects of Love* (1989). A stage production of Billy Wilder's classic Hollywood film *Sunset Boulevard* had its premiere in

MORALE BOOSTER *In World War II, Vera Lynn was every soldier's favourite singer, and a nostalgic link with home for troops abroad.*

London in 1993. In the same year Lloyd Webber was knighted for his services to the arts, and was given a star on the Hollywood Walk of Fame.

♣ In September 1991 Lloyd Webber made theatre history by becoming the first person to have six shows running simultaneously in London's West End.

Lynn, Dame Vera (1917-) British singer who became known as 'The Forces' Sweetheart' of World War II with sentimental songs such as 'We'll Meet Again' and 'White Cliffs of Dover'. In the 1940s she entertained the troops in war zones and made her first film, also called *We'll Meet Again*. In the 1950s Lynn had her own radio series for servicemen called *Sincerely Yours* and she topped the British charts with 'My Son, My Son'. She has continued to make regular appearances at soldiers' reunions and commemorations.

McCormack, Count John (1884-1945) Enormously popular Irish tenor famed for the purity of his voice and his fine technique. After conquering the operatic world he concentrated on recitals, performing Irish folk songs and sentimental ballads. He became an American citizen in 1917 and was made a papal count in 1928.

MacMillan, Sir Kenneth (1929-92) Scottish ballet dancer and choreographer. He directed the Royal Ballet from 1970 to 1977, after which he became its principal choreographer. MacMillan's ballets express intense emotion and include *Romeo and Juliet* (1965), *Anastasia* (1971), *Manon* (1974), *Mayerling* (1978) and *Isadora* (1981).

THREE OF THE BEST *Among Andrew Lloyd Webber's many successful shows are* Jesus Christ Superstar *and* Cats. *Below, actor Michael Crawford who was renowned for his sinister yet sensitive portrayal of* The Phantom of the Opera.

BLONDE BOMBSHELL *Madonna sports her trend-setting 'bullet-bra' on her 1990 world tour. It was designed by Jean Paul Gaultier.*

Madonna (1958-) (Madonna Louise Ciccone) American pop star who was one of the most successful female singers and songwriters of the 1980s. Madonna rose to fame with the catchy pop song 'Holiday' in 1984. She was adopted as a symbol of sexual liberation by millions of young female fans, known as 'wannabes'. Her many other hits include 'Like a Virgin' (1984) and 'Vogue' (1990). Madonna's overtly sexual image and expert manipulation of the media was highlighted in 1992 by her book *Sex*, in which she appeared nude. Her film career – in which she sought to become a modern day Marilyn Monroe – has been less successful.

Mahler, Gustav (1860-1911) Austrian composer and conductor who wrote long, intensely emotional works for large orchestras. Mahler earned his living as an operatic conductor, and only composed during summer breaks. His works include nine symphonies (and an unfinished tenth), the song-symphony *Das Lied von der Erde* (The Song of the Earth) (1909), and the haunting song-cycle *Kindertotenlieder* (Songs on the Death of Children) (1904).

Mancini, Henry (1924-94) American composer and conductor who wrote the scores for more than 100 films. In 1961 he won an Oscar for his music to *Breakfast at Tiffany's* which includes the ever-popular song 'Moon River'. Mancini also wrote the theme for *The Pink Panther*, in 1964.

Manilow, Barry (1946-) American singer and songwriter who is one of the world's most popular solo performers. In the 1960s Manilow started writing advertising jingles, then worked as arranger for the singer Bette Midler, before achieving solo success. His hit singles include 'Mandy' (1975), 'Could It Be Magic?' (1978) and 'I Made it Through the Rain' (1981).

Mantovani, Annunzio Paolo (1905-1980) Italian-born British composer, conductor and arranger. He created an ethereal sound with his orchestra, known as the 'cascading strings', which made him one of the most successful album sellers in the history of popular music. He led his first orchestra in 1925. His arrangement of an old song called 'Charmaine' became the first of several million-selling singles in 1951, and was followed by a series of hit albums in the 1950s and 1960s.

Marley, Bob (1945-81) Jamaican singer and songwriter who became the first international REGGAE superstar with his group Bob Marley and the Wailers, formed in 1964. The group had their first hit in Britain with 'No Woman No Cry' (1975), followed by songs such as 'Jamming' (1977) and 'One Love' (1984). Marley died of cancer while touring America, and received a state funeral in Jamaica.

Mass Roman Catholic service of Communion. 'High Mass' ('Missa Solemnis') has been the principal form of religious music since the Middle Ages, and has inspired composers to write some of their finest work, such as Bach's great Mass in B Minor. The 'Proper' of the Mass contains parts which vary with the Church seasons and are sung to traditional plainsong, an unaccompanied vocal melody which is free in rhythm, like speech. The 'Ordinary' of the Mass contains five unvarying sections, which have been set to music in many different ways. They are: *Kyrie* ('Lord have mercy . . .'), *Gloria* ('Glory be to God . . .'), *Credo* ('I believe . . .'), *Sanctus* ('Holy, holy, holy . . .') and *Agnus Dei* ('Lamb of God . . .'). (Compare REQUIEM Mass.)

Melba, Dame Nellie (1861-1931) Australian soprano whose voice was known for its flexibility and purity. Her best-loved roles included Mimi in Puccini's *La Bohème*, Gilda in Verdi's *Rigoletto* and the title role in Donizetti's *Lucia di Lammermoor*.
🌶 Peach Melba ice cream and Melba toast were both named after Dame Nellie.

THE LANGUAGE OF MUSIC

adagio Slow and leisurely.

allegretto Briskly, but more slowly than allegro.

allegro Quick, lively.

amoroso Lovingly.

andante Moving gently, flowing.

animato Animatedly.

cadenza Unaccompanied, sometimes improvised, passage by a soloist in a concerto.

chord Group of two or more notes played together.

coda Short additional passage at the end of a movement or composition.

counterpoint Set of two or more melody lines played together and in harmony.

crescendo Rising volume and intensity.

forte Loudly.

fortissimo Very loudly.

grave Solemnly.

largo Slowly, stately.

legato Smoothly and evenly.

leitmotif Musical phrase associated with a particular character or situation.

pianissimo Very softly.

piano Softly.

pizzicato Played by plucking rather than bowing the strings of an instrument, such as a violin or cello.

presto Fast.

rallentando Gradual slowing down.

recitative Sung narrative in opera or oratorio, in the rhythm of ordinary speech.

reprise Repetition of a phrase, or return to an earlier theme.

staccato Crisply, sharply.

syncopation Accentuation of a beat in each bar that is normally unaccentuated.

tempo Pace at which a work is performed.

tutti All together.

vibrato Slight wavering of pitch, used in singing and on some instruments, usually to add emotion.

vivace Lively.

Mendelssohn, Jacob Felix (1809-47)

German Romantic composer. An enthusiastic traveller, his overture *The Hebrides* (1830) and *Italian* and *Scottish* symphonies (1833, 1842) were inspired by extended tours. Mendelssohn was a great favourite of Queen Victoria, and during her lifetime his oratorio *Elijah* (1846) rivalled Handel's *Messiah* in popularity. His buoyant violin concerto of 1844 is much loved.

Menuhin, Sir Yehudi (1916-)

American-born violinist of Russian parentage, who took British nationality in 1985. He made his professional debut at eight and made a famous recording of Elgar's Violin Concerto (with the composer himself conducting) when he was 16. Bartók's sonata for solo violin (1945) was one of various works written specially for him.

Michael, George (1963-)

British singer and songwriter who formed Wham! with Andrew Ridgely in 1981. After many hits, including 'Careless Whisper' (1984), Michael went solo. His first solo album *Faith* reached No.1 in Britain and America and sold 12 million copies.
🎵In 1994 Michael lost a legal battle with Sony over his contract.

Miller, Glenn (1904-44)

American band leader, trombone player and composer. His orchestra, formed in 1938, was noted for its smooth, sophisticated performances of dance numbers such as 'Moonlight Serenade' and 'In The Mood'. Miller joined the army during World War II and entertained the Allied forces. In 1944 his plane disappeared and is presumed to have crashed into the English Channel.

Monteverdi, Claudio (1567-1643)

Italian composer, usually considered to have written the first major operas. In 1613 he became musical director at St Mark's, Venice, where he remained until his death. His greatest works include the operas *Orfeo* (1607), *The Return of Ulysses* (1640), as well as the religious pieces *Selva morale e spirituale* (1641) and *Vespers* (1610).

Motown

Black independent record company formed by songwriter Berry Gordy in 1959, which influenced the sound of the 1960s by blending pop music with RHYTHM AND BLUES and GOSPEL. The Detroit-based label became a mini music industry, discovering new talent and using its own songwriters and producers. A golden era followed with acts such as the Four Tops, Marvin Gaye, the Jackson Five, Smokey Robinson, Diana Ross and the Supremes, the Temptations and Stevie Wonder. Gordy sold the label to MCA in 1988.
🎵Motown was named after 'Motortown', the nickname for the city of Detroit, the centre of the American car industry.

Mozart, Wolfgang Amadeus (1756-1791)

Austrian composer and one of the great geniuses of Western music. As a small

CHILD PRODIGY *Mozart (inset) was four when he began giving concerts. Among his many works was* Eine Kleine Nachtmusik (above).

IN THE MOOD *Glenn Miller joined the army in 1942 and formed a service band whose nostalgic sound still conjures up wartime memories.*

boy he toured the courts of Europe, dazzling kings and courtiers with his brilliant keyboard playing. In 1781, after an unhappy period of musical employment in the service of the Archbishop of Salzburg, Mozart settled in Vienna as a freelance composer, and became the toast of the city, despite attempts by the head of the Vienna Opera, Antonio Salieri, to obstruct his young rival's career by planting people to boo and hiss at his concerts. Mozart wrote more than 600 compositions, including over 60 symphonies, 27 piano concertos, 23 string quartets, and several operas. Especially well loved are the short work for strings *Eine Kleine Nachtmusik* (*A Little Night Music*) (1787), and the operas *the Marriage of Figaro* (1786), *Don Giovanni* (1787) and *The Magic Flute* (1791). The obvious charm and technical brilliance of his music are deceptive; though Mozart was often crude and full of boyish spirits, his letters reveal an understanding of human nature in all its complexity.
🎵It is a common myth that Mozart died a neglected and impoverished genius. In reality, while Mozart's freelance income was unpredictable, he often indulged his love of high living and his memorial service in Prague was attended by thousands.
🎵Mozart's works were identified by their Köchel (K) number, after the German scholar who catalogued them.

Mussorgsky, Modest Petrovich (1839-81) Russian composer of great originality, who wanted his music 'to portray the soul of man in all its profundity'. His works include the opera *Boris Godunov* (1868-72), the orchestral work *Night on the Bare Mountain* (1867) and the piano suite *Pictures at an Exhibition* (1874), made famous by Ravel's orchestration of 1922.

My Fair Lady Musical based on George Bernard ▷SHAW's comedy *Pygmalion*, about a cockney flower girl who is transformed into a 'lady'. With music by Frederic Loewe, and book and lyrics by Alan Jay Lerner, it opened on Broadway in 1956 with Julie Andrews as the flower girl, Eliza Doolittle, Stanley Holloway as her dustman father, and Rex Harrison as the phonetics expert who teaches Eliza how to talk and behave in polite society. A film version was made in Hollywood in 1964.

Nijinsky, Vaslav (c.1889-1950) Russian ballet dancer and choreographer whose superb technique and exceptional dramatic gifts made him the greatest male dancer of his time. As leading dancer with DIAGHILEV's Ballets Russes in Paris, he excelled in such contrasting ballets as *Schéhérazade* (1910) and *Petrushka* (1911). As a choreographer, his radically original style caused a scandal when the *Rite of Spring* was first produced in Paris in 1913 to music by STRAVINSKY. Nijinsky retired in 1919, suffering from schizophrenia.

Norman, Jessye (1945-) American soprano who has been one of opera's greatest stars since the 1980s. She combines power with exquisite control and is renowned for her interpretations of Berlioz, Wagner, Mahler and Richard Strauss.

Novello, Ivor (1893-1951) Welsh composer, playwright and actor, who wrote one of the most popular tunes of World War I, the patriotic 'Keep The Home Fires Burning'. With his matinée idol good looks, he starred in films in the 1920s and 1930s including Hitchcock's silent thriller, *The Lodger* (1926). Novello's romantic musicals include *The Dancing Years* (1939) and *Perchance to Dream* (1945).

Nureyev, Rudolf (1938-93) Russian dancer and choreographer who trained with the KIROV BALLET and defected to the West in 1961. Through his energy and versatility he quickly established himself as one of the outstanding male dancers of the post-war era. He joined the Royal Ballet in 1962 and formed a memorable partnership with Margot FONTEYN. Despite ill health and advancing years, Nureyev never wanted to retire from dancing: he gave his last performance in Berlin in 1992.

Offenbach, Jacques (1819-80) Composer, born in Germany, whose highly successful French operettas include *Orpheus in the Underworld* (1858) and *La Belle Hélène* (1864). In 1876 he began a more serious work, *Tales of Hoffman* (1881), but died during rehearsals of the production.

Oliver! Musical by the British composer Lionel Bart, based on Dickens' ▷OLIVER TWIST. It opened in London's West End in 1960 with Ron Moody as Fagin. *Oliver!* was made into an Oscar-winning film in 1968, and has often been revived on stage. Memorable songs include 'Food, Glorious Food' and 'Consider Yourself'.

operetta Comic or light-hearted opera, with a good deal of spoken dialogue, such as GILBERT AND SULLIVAN's *The Mikado* (1885) and Franz Lehár's *The Merry Widow* (1905).

GRACE AND POISE *Rudolf Nureyev dances Romeo to Dame Margot Fonteyn's Juliet in Vienna in 1967. Their artistry transcended their age gap – Fonteyn was almost 20 years older than Nureyev.*

COURT DRAMA *A scene from Verdi's* Don Carlos *(1867) sumptuously produced at Milan's renowned opera house, La Scala.*

STORIES OF BEST-LOVED OPERAS

The Marriage of Figaro (1786) Mozart's greatest comic opera centres on the intrigues surrounding the approaching marriage of Figaro (Count Almaviva's servant) and Susanna (Countess Almaviva's maid). The Count tries to seduce Susanna before she marries, but Figaro manages to outwit his master. On hearing *Figaro* for the first time, the Austrian emperor Joseph II told Mozart that it had 'too many notes'.

La Traviata (1853) Romantic opera by Verdi. Violetta Valéry, a Parisian courtesan suffering from consumption, is so moved by the devotion of a young man called Alfredo Germont, that she leaves town to set up home with him. Germont's father persuades her to renounce his son, who in turn denounces her as faithless. In the final deathbed scene, the two lovers are reconciled, only for Violetta to collapse and die in Alfredo's arms.

Der Ring des Nibelungen (1869–76) Four separate operas: *Das Rheingold*, *Die Walküre*, *Siegfried* and *Götterdämmerung*, make up this massive 15-hour cycle, which took Richard Wagner 25 years to complete. The story revolves around a ring that gives its wearer supreme power. In *Das Rheingold*, Wotan, the ruler of the gods, forces a dwarf called Alberich, the forger of the ring, to surrender it to him. The curse that the vengeful dwarf lays on all the wearers of the ring is the subject of the next three operas. Eventually the curse is lifted by the self-sacrifice of Wotan's favourite daughter Brünnhilde.

Aïda (1871) Verdi's grand opera about the love of the Egyptian warrior Radames and the slave Aïda – who is in fact the daughter of the ruler of Ethiopia. As they plan to run away together, Radames accidentally betrays his country by revealing some military secrets. He is overheard and condemned to be buried alive. Aïda smuggles herself into his tomb to die with him.

Carmen (1875) Now one of the world's most popular operas; *Carmen* was a flop when it was first performed in Paris in 1875 (the audience was shocked by its daring realism), and its disappointed composer, Georges Bizet, died soon afterwards. It tells the story of the beautiful gypsy Carmen who bewitches a corporal called Don José. He deserts his regiment for her, but Carmen soon tires of him and takes up with the bullfighter Escamillo. The rejected José stabs Carmen to death.

La Bohème (1896) Puccini's first international triumph, which has some of the best-known arias ever written. Set in Paris, a Bohemian poet called Rodolfo falls in love with a consumptive seamstress called Mimi. They later quarrel and part – as do Rodolfo's friend, the artist Marcello, and his mistress Musetta, with whom he has just been reunited. Both men are pining for their former loves when Musetta returns, closely followed by Mimi, who has collapsed and is dying. The opera ends tragically with Rodolfo embracing her lifeless corpse.

Tosca (1900) Set in Rome in Napoleonic times, Puccini's tragic epic tells the story of Tosca, a great opera singer who is in love with Cavaradossi, a painter. He helps a revolutionary to escape and is arrested by Scarpia, the sadistic chief of police who himself desires Tosca. The singer agrees to let Scarpia have his way with her, if he will spare Cavaradossi's life. Tosca manages to stab Scarpia, but the dead villain has the last laugh. Though he assured Tosca that he would fake Cavaradossi's execution, he ordered the firing squad to use real bullets. The betrayed Tosca kills herself as Scarpia's minions arrive to arrest her.

Madam Butterfly (1904) Puccini's tear-jerking masterpiece tells the story of the doomed relationship between Cio-Cio-San, a young Japanese geisha girl, and Pinkerton, a lieutenant in the US navy. Pinkerton sees his Japanese-style marriage to Butterfly as a temporary arrangement, while she considers the ceremony to be binding, and bears him a child. When Pinkerton returns to Japan with his new American bride to reclaim his son, Butterfly commits suicide.

Turandot (1926) Puccini's last opera features the aria 'Nessun Dorma' and is set in ancient Peking. Calaf, the disguised son of an exiled ruler, wins the hand of the cruel and haughty Princess Turandot by answering three riddles correctly; the penalty for failure is death. Calaf then goes on to win her love with a passionate kiss.

OPEN-AIR OPERA *Italian tenor Luciano Pavarotti's 1990 concert in Hyde Park was one of his most successful – bringing opera to the masses.*

Orbison, Roy (1936-88) American singer and composer of country-influenced ROCK'N'ROLL, a kind of music also known as 'rockabilly'. His mournful falsetto voice made him one of the most distinctive singers of the 1960s. Orbison set out to be a songwriter but decided to record 'Only the Lonely' (1960) when it was rejected by Elvis Presley. His most popular songs include 'Oh, Pretty Woman' and the ballads 'Crying' and 'It's Over'. Shortly before his death Orbison enjoyed renewed success as a member of the Traveling Wilburys, a 'supergroup' formed with leading musicians Bob Dylan, George Harrison and the guitarist Tom Petty.

Paderewski, Ignace Jan (1860-1941) Polish concert pianist, composer, patriot and politician, renowned for his interpretations of Chopin. During the occupation of Poland he refused to play until the country was liberated. In 1919 he became liberated Poland's first prime minister.

Paganini, Nicolò (1782-1840) Italian violinist and composer who raised violin playing to new heights of virtuosity and showmanship. Because Paganini so astonished audiences with his techniques, he was rumoured to be in league with the devil. His works include six violin concertos and 24 caprices (compositions that do not follow any strict form). His Caprice No.2 in A Minor became the basis for compositions by Brahms, Rachmaninov and Andrew Lloyd Webber, among others.

Parker, Charlie (1920-55) American jazz saxophonist and composer, also known as 'Bird', renowned for his technical agility and adventurous improvisation. In the early 1940s, along with Dizzy GILLESPIE, Parker developed a modern jazz form known as BEBOP with fast, driving rhythms, complex harmonies and sophisticated improvisations. From 1945 Parker led his own groups in New York and Hollywood, but an addiction to heroin and alcohol contributed to his early death.

Pavarotti, Luciano (1935-) Ebullient Italian tenor whose powerful voice and outgoing personality made him an international star soon after his operatic debut in 1961. In 1990 Pavarotti had a hit record with the aria 'Nessun Dorma' from Puccini's oriental opera *Turandot*, which was used by the BBC as the theme song for soccer's 1990 World Cup. That same year, his concert in London's Hyde Park attracted an enthusiastic audience of 150 000.

Pavlova, Anna (1881-1931) Russian ballerina who was the most celebrated dancer of her day. She danced all the major roles with the Imperial Russian Ballet, appeared with DIAGHILEV's Ballets Russes and formed her own company in 1913. She toured the world, mesmerising audiences with her poignant solo 'The Dying Swan'.

Piaf, Edith (1915-63) French cabaret singer of the 1950s renowned for her waif-like appearance, strong voice and emotional delivery. Born into poverty, Piaf was singing on the streets of Paris when she was 15. She was discovered by a cabaret owner who nicknamed her *La môme piaf* 'little sparrow'. She is best remembered for her songs 'La Vie En Rose', 'M'lord' and the defiant 'Non, Je Ne Regrette Rien'.

REBEL ROCK *With his sultry blues voice, sullen curled lip and gyrating hips, Elvis Presley became the greatest exponent of rock'n'roll. His image was reproduced everywhere – even on American stamps.*

Pink Floyd (Original members: Roger Waters, David Gilmour, Nick Mason, Rick Wright and Syd Barrett) British rock band formed in 1966 specialising in concerts with fantastic light shows. Their *Dark Side Of The Moon* (1973) sold more than 25 million copies. In 1979 they had their first No.1 hit single with 'Another Brick in the Wall', from their album *The Wall*.

plainsong Unharmonised early Christian chanting in free rhythm based on the words of prayers and psalms.

Porter, Cole (1891-1964) American songwriter noted for his witty, sophisticated lyrics. He established his reputation with musicals such as *The Gay Divorcee* (1932) and *Anything Goes* (1934). As the result of a riding accident, he was a semi-invalid for the last 27 years of his life. During this time, however, he produced his masterpiece *Kiss Me Kate* (1948) and the film score for *High Society* (1956). Among Porter's best-known songs are 'Night and Day' and 'I Get a Kick Out of You'.

Presley, Elvis (1935-77) American singer and guitarist, widely regarded as the embodiment of ROCK'N'ROLL. Presley was renowned for his remarkable vocal range and ability to sing the BLUES. His music was a unique mixture of RHYTHM AND BLUES, GOSPEL and COUNTRY AND WESTERN. In 1956, when Presley had hits with 'Heartbreak Hotel' and 'Hound Dog', his rebellious image made him the archetypal pop idol. After being drafted into the US Army from 1958 to 1960, Presley re-emerged as a clean-cut crooner with ballads like 'Are You Lonesome Tonight?' His popularity suffered when, seduced by Hollywood, he made a stream of lightweight musical films, but he revived his career in the late 1960s with songs such as 'In The Ghetto' and 'Suspicious Minds'. Presley spent his last years as a cabaret artist in Las Vegas. Dependent on drugs, his bloated body attired in vulgar costumes, he seemed to have become a symbol of decadence. It is a testament to his enduring fame, however, that 20 million of his records were sold in the 24 hours after his death. He remains the biggest-selling solo artist of the 20th century.
🎤 Presley's provocative hip-swivelling routine was deemed too suggestive for television in the 1950s, and he was shown only from the waist up. He was nicknamed 'Elvis the Pelvis' and later 'The King'.

Prince (1960-) (Prince Rogers Nelson) American singer, songwriter and actor who is one of the most inventive pop artists of

RULE BRITANNIA *British conductor Sir Malcolm Sargent presides over the jingoistic last night of the Proms in 1966. He was chief conductor of the concerts from 1948 until his death on 1967.*

modern times. Renowned for his sexual lyrics and outrageous image, Prince is now known by a symbol based on the combined male and female sex signs. By mixing soul, funk, disco and rock he has had many hits since his first major album and film *Purple Rain* (1984) including 'The Most Beautiful Girl in the World' (1994).

Prokofiev, Sergei (1891-1953) Russian composer and pianist whose work was both classical and experimental. He won international renown with his first symphonic work, the *Classical Symphony* of 1917. Prokofiev lived abroad from 1918 and was associated with DIAGHILEV's Ballets Russes. He returned to Russia in 1934. His works include the fantasy opera *The Love for Three Oranges* (1919), the ballet *Romeo and Juliet* (1935) and the musical fable for children *Peter and the Wolf* (1936).

Proms, the Abbreviation for London's annual summer series of Promenade Concerts. Begun by the conductor Sir Henry Wood in 1895, the Proms were held in the Queen's Hall until it was destroyed in an air raid in 1941, since when their venue has been the Royal Albert Hall.

Puccini, Giacomo (1858-1924) Italian opera composer, whose music is notable for its romantic melody and strong sense of drama. Puccini achieved overnight success with the opera *Manon Lescaut* in 1893. He went on to write three of the world's most popular operas: *La Bohème* (1896), *Tosca*

(1900) and *Madam Butterfly* (1904). His final masterpiece *Turandot* was completed by Franco Alfano from Puccini's notes after the composer's death, and staged in 1926.

punk rock Subversive musical movement, launched as a reaction to rock bands who 'took themselves too seriously'. The name 'punk' comes from the American slang for something rotten and worthless. The music was renowned for its aggressive, anti-establishment lyrics. Punk rock was launched in Britain by the Sex Pistols in 1976 and had burnt itself out by 1980.
🎤 Punk fashions featured outlandish spiked hair, ghoulish make-up and ripped clothes held together with safety pins.

Purcell, Henry (1659-95) Organist and one of the greatest of all English composers. He was the only significant English composer of the BAROQUE period, composing operas, church and chamber music, and ceremonial music for state occasions. His best-known work is Britain's earliest opera *Dido and Aeneas* (1689), specially written for a girls' school in Chelsea.

Queen (Original members: Freddie Mercury, John Deacon, Brian May, Roger Taylor) British rock band, renowned for their lead singer Freddie Mercury's flamboyant showmanship. Formed in 1970, Queen had a major success with 'Bohemian Rhapsody' (1975), which was accompanied by one of the first ever pop videos. The band split up after Freddie Mercury died in 1991.

Rachmaninov, Sergei (1873-1943)
Russian composer and virtuoso pianist who excelled at the interpretation of the late Romantic composers, and dazzled audiences with his own concertos and solo pieces. He settled in America after the Russian Revolution of 1917.

ragtime Style of jazz written largely for the piano from the 1890s until about 1919 and popularised by such composers as Scott JOPLIN. Ragtime, or 'ragged' music, features syncopation – in which strong beats become weak, and vice versa.

Rambert, Dame Marie (1888-1982)
Polish-born dancer and teacher, one of the great pioneers of modern British ballet. In 1913 she began to work for DIAGHILEV's Ballets Russes. She became a British citizen in 1918 and founded a ballet school in 1926. From 1935 her company was known as the Ballet Rambert.

rap music Style of music which originated in black New York street culture as 'performance' poetry, with themes of social comment and satire. Rap became a musical form when an instrumental backing was added. One of the first examples was 'Rapper's Delight' (1979) by the Sugar Hill Gang.

Rattle, Simon (1955-) British conductor who made his London debut when he was 20. He became the youngest conductor to appear at the PROMS, and greatly enhanced the status of the City of Birmingham Symphony Orchestra when he was appointed principal conductor in 1980. Rattle was knighted in 1994.

Ravel, Maurice (1875-1937) French 'impressionist' composer who is often paired with Debussy, though Ravel's compositions are more classical in style. He wrote piano music of great technical difficulty, two small-scale operas and the ballet *Daphnis and Chloé* (1912). Ravel wrote his ballet score *Boléro* in 1928.

Redding, Otis (1941-67) American singer and songwriter of the 1960s, regarded as one of the greatest male SOUL singers because of his emotional vocal style. His best-known hit single is the pensive '(Sittin' On The) Dock of the Bay' (1968).

Reeves, Jim (1923-64) American singer renowned for his smooth, velvety voice. Known as 'Gentleman Jim', his style of music appealed to both country and pop fans. His hits include 'He'll Have to Go' (1960) and 'Distant Drums' (1966).

reggae Popular music of Jamaican origin, characterised by a strong offbeat rhythm. Reggae is used by black movements and sects such as the ▷RASTAFARIANS to express social issues. It became popular with white audiences in the late 1960s and was promoted throughout the world by Bob MARLEY during the 1970s.

Reinhardt, Django (1910-53) Belgian gypsy jazz guitarist who was the first European to have a strong influence on American jazz. He began working in Paris in 1922. His left hand was mutilated in a fire in 1928 but he devised a fingering technique to overcome the disability.

requiem A MASS with biblical passages and prayers for the admission of the dead to heaven. It contains no *Gloria* or *Credo* sections, but has four parts that are not in the ordinary mass: *Requiem aeternam* ('Rest eternal'), *Dies irae* ('Day of wrath'), *Lux aeterna* ('Light eternal') and *Libera me* ('Deliver me'). Celebrated requiems have been written by Berlioz, Fauré, Mozart and Verdi. An outstanding modern example is Benjamin Britten's *War Requiem*.

rhythm and blues Style of black popular music, also known as R&B, which originated in America in the 1940s. A fusion of BLUES and JAZZ using drums, electric guitars and saxophones, R&B was the first black music to become widely popular with white audiences. Attracted by its powerful rhythms, white musicians used R&B as an important element of ROCK'N'ROLL. In the early 1960s an R&B movement developed in London, influencing rock groups such as the Rolling Stones. Early pioneers of R&B include Muddy WATERS, B.B. King, Bo Diddley and Ray CHARLES.

Richard, Cliff (1940-) (Harry Webb) Singer who began his career as Britain's answer to Elvis Presley. In 1958 he formed a group called the Drifters, who evolved into the Shadows, and had a No.2 hit with a rock'n'roll number called 'Move It', soon followed by the first of many No.1s, 'Living Doll' (1959). Richard went on to cultivate a middle-of-the-road image in the 1960s, with a string of family film musicals such as *The Young Ones* (1962) and *Summer Holiday* (1963). He converted to Christianity in 1966 and is known for his special gospel tours. In 1968 Richard was runner-up in the Eurovision Song Contest with 'Congratulations'. Having survived the ever-changing musical trends of four decades, Richard has established himself as Britain's most durable pop artiste.

🎤 The Shadows featured guitarist Hank Marvin and was the most influential instrumental rock'n'roll group in Britain during the late 1950s and early 1960s.

Rimsky-Korsakov, Nicolai (1844-1908) Russian composer noted for his vivid orchestration and oriental subject-matter, as exemplified in the symphonic suite *Scheherazade* (1888) and the opera *The Legend of Tsar Sultan* (1900). The latter contains the famous orchestral interlude, 'The Flight of the Bumble Bee'.

Robeson, Paul (1898-1976) American singer and actor of the stage and screen, one of the most important black performers of his time. He made his mark as Joe in the musical *Show Boat* in 1928, and became associated with the song 'Ol' Man River'. Robeson promoted GOSPEL music, recorded a great many SPIRITUALS, and was an active campaigner for black civil rights.

rock'n'roll Music craze of the late 1950s which combined elements of white American COUNTRY AND WESTERN with black RHYTHM AND BLUES and boogie woogie – a style of jazz piano-playing with a characteristic rolling bass line played eight beats to the bar. Bill HALEY and the Comets launched the era with the song 'Rock Around the Clock' in 1955, and a year later Elvis PRESLEY emerged as 'the King' of the genre. Other important artists include Chuck BERRY, Eddie COCHRAN, Fats DOMINO and Buddy HOLLY.

🎤 Britain's first rock'n'roll star was Tommy Steele with a song called 'Rock with the Cavemen' (1956).

Rodgers, Richard (1902-79) American popular composer. He collaborated with the librettist Lorenz Hart (1895-1943) on *Pal Joey* (1940) and other musicals, but is especially remembered for those he produced with Oscar HAMMERSTEIN II, including *Oklahoma!* (1943), *Carousel* (1945), *South Pacific* (1949), *The King and I* (1951) and *The Sound of Music* (1959), which were all turned into successful films after they had appeared on the stage.

🎤 The song 'You'll Never Walk Alone' from *Carousel* became an anthem for Liverpool football club.

Rolling Stones, The British group often hailed as the greatest rock'n'roll group in the world. Mick Jagger and Keith Richard (later Richards) formed the band in 1962, and became one of the most successful songwriting teams of all time. They were joined by Brian Jones on guitar, Bill

Wyman on bass and Charlie Watts on drums. Their music was inspired by RHYTHM AND BLUES artists such as Bo Diddley and Muddy Waters, and by their rock'n'roll hero Chuck Berry. The Stones had early No.1 hits with 'Little Red Rooster' (1964), '(I Can't Get No) Satisfaction' (1965), and 'Get Off of My Cloud' (1965). While their rivals, the Beatles, were considered to be clean-cut and fairly conventional at the time, the Stones had long hair and an anti-establishment image. Brian Jones left the band in 1969 with a drug problem, and was found dead in his swimming pool shortly afterwards. He was replaced by Mick Taylor until 1974, and then by Ron Wood. The band made two of their finest albums in the 1970s: *Sticky Fingers* (1971) and *Exile on Main Street* (1972). During the 1980s the group remained among the biggest live attractions in rock, and successfully toured internationally in the 1990s.

Romantic In music, the period between 1825 and 1900, an era of emotional expressiveness when European composers used their music to explore human feelings. The era was influenced by the much earlier work of composers such as Haydn and Mozart. Romantic composers include Berlioz, Brahms, Chopin, Liszt, Mahler, Schubert, Schumann, Tchaikovsky, Verdi and Wagner. (See also ▷ROMANTICISM in 'Art and Design' and 'World Literature'.)

Ross, Diana (1944-) American soul singer who started out as a member of the most successful 'girl group' of all time, the Supremes, and who became the greatest black female artist of the rock era. The Supremes' hits include 'Stop! In The Name of Love' (1965). In 1970 Ross went solo and soon had an American No.1 with 'Ain't No Mountain High Enough'. She had a British No.1 with 'Chain Reaction' in 1986.

Rossini, Gioacchino (1792-1868) Italian opera composer, known throughout Europe for his vivacious melodies and sparkling comic writing. He wrote 38 operas, both comic and serious, within 19 years, and was only 24 when he wrote his masterpiece *The Barber of Seville* (1816). After writing *William Tell* (mainly known for its overture) in 1829, Rossini composed no more operas.

Royal Ballet National ballet company of Britain. Founded in 1931 by Dame Ninette DE VALOIS as the Vic-Wells Ballet. The company later became known as the Sadler's Wells Ballet before being granted its present name by Royal Charter in 1956. Its most memorable dancers have included Robert HELPMANN, Margot FONTEYN and Rudolph NUREYEV.

Saint-Saëns, Camille (1835-1921) French composer noted for his constant experimentation, which prevented him from developing a recognisable personal style. Some critics claimed that his beautiful harmonies and elegant musical forms were superficial, but they are the reasons why his music has remained popular. His works include the opera *Samson and Delilah* (1877), the descriptive suite *The Carnival of the Animals* (1886), and his Symphony No.3, called the 'Organ' Symphony (1886).

Satie, Erik (1866-1925) French pianist and composer, chiefly of piano works and ballets. An eccentric but truly original composer, he led a bohemian life in Paris, participating in many avant-garde projects. Satie's music used simplicity of technique to achieve novel and surreal effects: his ballet *Parade* (1917) for DIAGHILEV's Ballets Russes included parts for typewriters and steamboat whistles and caused an outcry at its premiere. In the 1920s he became something of a cult figure among young French composers who were influenced by his uncluttered music.

Schoenberg, Arnold (1874-1951) Austrian composer who abandoned harmony in favour of a harsh, dissonant style based on a 12-tone scale rather than the traditional musical key. Through it he attempted to express the strange world of the mind and emotions, but its lack of melody provoked public hostility. His works include *Five Pieces for Orchestra* (1909), the vast choral work *Gurrelieder* (1900-11) and *Pierrot Lunaire* (1912).

🎵A disapproving critic coined the term 'atonal' for Schoenberg's later music: that is, music that is not in any fixed key. Although Schoenberg hated the term, it has remained in use to this day.

Schubert, Franz (1797-1828) Austrian composer renowned for his melodic genius. A short, shy and pudgy man, Schubert lived an unconventional life in Vienna, supported by a circle of devoted friends who called themselves 'Schubertians'. He was

OLD-TIMERS *The Rolling Stones made their debut in 1962 and are seen here, still touring, 30 years later. They have probably enjoyed the longest and most consistent success of any rock group.*

amazingly prolific; in his brief lifetime he wrote more than 600 songs, nine symphonies and 25 major chamber works, as well as piano music, operas and choral music. His Symphony No.8, called 'The Unfinished' (1822), is one of the most popular orchestral works ever written.

Schumann, Robert (1810-56) German Romantic composer with a genius for harmony. His gentle, poetic music is most clearly represented by his songs and piano pieces which reflect his love for his wife, the pianist Clara Wieck. A period of great creativity before and after Schumann's marriage in 1840 was succeeded by mental illness, and in 1854 he attempted suicide and was confined to an asylum. He is best known for his four symphonies, the song cycle *Dichterliebe* (1840), and his piano works, especially *Carnaval* (1835) and the Piano Concerto in A Minor (1846).

Schwarzkopf, Elisabeth (1915-) German operatic soprano, renowned for her acting and interpretations of Mozart and Richard Strauss. She made her first appearance at Covent Garden in 1947.
♪When Schwarzkopf was a guest on BBC radio's *Desert Island Discs*, all the records she chose were her own.

Shostakovich, Dmitri (1906-75) Russian composer – one of the most prolific and widely acclaimed of the 20th century. His 15 symphonies and 15 string quartets represent the last link with the great classical tradition. Shostakovich wrote his First Symphony (1926) when he was only a student, making him world famous at the age of 20. Because he was influenced by Western avant-garde music, his compositions sometimes clashed with Soviet musical policy, and Shostakovich was forced to appease the establishment by confessing to 'unworthy stylistic tendencies'.

Sibelius, Jean (1865-1957) Finland's leading composer. Born at a time when his country was under Russian domination, he was inspired by ancient Finnish legends to write stirring patriotic works such as *Finlandia* (1899). His greatest achievements are his seven symphonies (1899-1924) which evoke the lakes and pine forests of Finland, and his violin concerto (1903). He once said, 'It pleases me to be called an artist of nature, for nature has truly been the book of books for me'.

Simon and Garfunkel American vocal duo of the 1960s and early 1970s. With Paul Simon's thoughtful folk-rock songs

and Art Garfunkel's angelic voice, they became one of the most popular duos in the history of rock. In 1970 their album *Bridge Over Troubled Water* became one of the best-selling albums of all time, but the duo split up at the peak of their career. They reunited in 1982 to give a concert in New York's Central Park.

Sinatra, Frank (1915-) American singer and actor, widely regarded as the greatest lyric interpreter of his time. He rose to fame during World War II and became the first popular singer to induce hysteria among his teenage fans. Sinatra's first stage appearance in New York in 1942 caused a sensation and led to film roles in musicals such as *On the Town* (1949). His popularity waned in the early 1950s, but he revived his film career with a dramatic role in *From Here to Eternity* (1953), for which he won an Oscar. Sinatra also made a comeback as a singer; his voice and style had mellowed on albums such as *Songs For Swingin' Lovers* (1956). More film musicals followed including *High Society* (1956) and *Pal Joey* (1957). Among his memorable hits are 'My Way' (1969) and 'New York, New York' (1980). Since he announced his retirement in 1971, 'Ol Blue Eyes' has given many 'farewell' performances.

skiffle Type of jazz music popular with youngsters in the mid 1950s. Skiffle groups used improvised instruments such as washboards and bottles to render folk songs and simple melodies to a fast, rhythmic beat.

Solti, Sir Georg (1912-) Hungarian-born British conductor. He was musical director of the Royal Opera at Covent Garden (1961-71) and the Chicago Symphony Orchestra (1969-91).

Sondheim, Stephen (1930-) American composer and lyricist, widely regarded as one of the most influential popular music composers of modern times. He wrote the lyrics for Bernstein's *West Side Story* (1957), and had his first success as both lyricist and composer with *A Funny Thing Happened on the Way to the Forum* (1962). His many shows include *A Little Night Music* (1973) featuring the song 'Send in the Clowns'.

soprano Highest range of the female singing voice: from the Italian *sopra*, meaning 'above'. Famous sopranos include Maria Callas, Jessye Norman, Joan Sutherland and Kiri Te Kanawa.
♪Mezzo-soprano is the middle range of the female voice, lower than soprano and higher than ALTO.

BALLROOM FAVOURITE *The waltz is a flowing dance in rapid triple time, dating from the 18th century. With the help of composer Johann Strauss II (inset), the dance became universally popular in the 19th century.*

soul music Style of black American popular music combining elements of GOSPEL and RHYTHM AND BLUES, which had its golden age in the 1960s. Sam Cooke was the first gospel singer to turn pop star: his No.1 record 'You Send Me' (1957) marked the beginning of the soul era, and Cooke became a model for the soul stars who followed. Early exponents include James BROWN, Aretha Franklin, Marvin Gaye, Ben E. King, Wilson Pickett, Otis REDDING and Percy Sledge.

spiritual Type of religious song originated by black Americans in the early 19th century. Many of the songs allude to the days of slavery and are concerned with biblical themes of deliverance. Several spirituals such as 'Nobody Knows the Trouble I've Seen' and 'Swing Low, Sweet Chariot' have become standard pieces of music for concert singers. Negro spirituals gained widespread popularity when they were promoted by a group called the Fisk Jubilee Singers in the 1870s, and by the American singer and actor Paul ROBESON in the late 1920s.

Springsteen, Bruce (1949-) American rock singer and songwriter, known as 'The Boss'. In 1974 an American critic called Jon Landau (who later became Springsteen's manager) wrote the now-famous words, 'I have seen the future of rock'n'roll – it's called Bruce Springsteen'. Springsteen lived up to this prediction with energetic performances and thoughtful songs about the state of America. His most successful albums were *Born To Run* (1975) and *Born In The USA* (1984) which has sold more than 12 million copies.

Stewart, Rod (1945-) British rock singer of Scottish descent, renowned for his hoarse vocals and jet-set lifestyle. He enjoyed two successful careers in the 1970s, as a solo artist and front man for a band called the Faces. His many No.1 hit singles include 'Maggie May' (1971), 'Sailing' (1975) and 'Do Ya Think I'm Sexy?' (1978).

Stockhausen, Karlheinz (1928-) German avant-garde composer who abandoned conventional music to become one of the leading exponents of electronic music. His *Gesang der Jünglinge* (1955-6) was the first and one of the greatest masterpieces of electronic music: it combines electronic sounds with the voice of a boy soprano and has a mystical streak which often runs through Stockhausen's music. In recent years he has concentrated on experimenting with dramatic music and on opera.

RARE FIDDLE
This Stradivarius violin came from the workshop of instrument maker Antonio Stradivari. His surviving violins are now regarded as virtually beyond price because of their incomparable tone and projection.

Stradivarius Any stringed instrument made by Antonio Stradivari (1644-1737), who was born in Cremona, Italy. Stradivari is generally considered to be the greatest violin maker of all time. He also made superb violas and cellos.

Strauss II, Johann (1825-99) Austrian composer, also known as Johann Strauss the Younger. He was the son of Johann Strauss I (1804-49), a famous composer of light music known as 'The Father of the Waltz'. Strauss II was hailed as 'The Waltz King' when his dance music became fashionable all over Europe. He wrote 400 waltzes including 'The Blue Danube' (1867), and many polkas, mazurkas and marches. He also composed the music for the popular operetta *Die Fledermaus* (1874).

Strauss, Richard (1864-1949) German composer and conductor. He is best known for *Der Rosenkavalier* (1911), one of the most popular operas written in the 20th century, and for *Thus Spake Zarathustra* (1896), a piece for orchestra that was later used to great effect in the science-fiction film *2001: A Space Odyssey* 1968).

Stravinsky, Igor (1882-1971) Russian-born American composer who was one of the greatest musical innovators of the 20th century. He founded his international reputation on his music for DIAGHILEV's Ballets Russes, beginning with the ballet *The Firebird* (1910), but his work was not readily accepted. The harsh and discordant score for *The Rite of Spring* (1913) caused a riot when it was first performed in Paris. Later pioneering works include the oratorio *Oedipus Rex* (1927), the *Symphony of Psalms* (1930) for chorus and orchestra, and the opera *The Rake's Progress* (1951).

Streisand, Barbra (1942-) American singer and actress, one of the world's most successful female performers. She sprang to fame in the Broadway musical *Funny Girl* (1964) in which she played the role of entertainer Fanny Brice. She repeated the role in the film of 1968, which won her an Oscar. Among her later hits were songs such as 'The Way We Were' (1974) and 'Evergreen' (1977). During the 1980s Streisand took complete control of her career, producing, directing, writing and starring in the film *Yentl* (1983).

Sutherland, Dame Joan (1926-) Australian operatic soprano, renowned for her vocal range. After Maria CALLAS retired from the stage, Sutherland became the world's most highly regarded soprano. She was coached by her husband, the conductor Richard Bonynge, and the couple helped to popularise the operatic masterpieces of the Italian composers Bellini and Donizetti. Sutherland retired in 1990.
🕭 Sutherland was a *coloratura* soprano: that is, her voice was suited to a style of vocal music that demanded great agility.

swing Style of jazz popular in the 1930s and 1940s, characterised by a lively rhythm suitable for dancing. Swing was played in an organised fashion by big bands, as opposed to the improvised jazz played by smaller groups. The 'Swing Era' had its heyday between 1935 and 1944 and featured the bands of Count BASIE, Duke ELLINGTON, Benny GOODMAN and Glenn MILLER.

Tchaikovsky, Peter Ilyich (1840-93) Russian composer whose Romantic music expressed the emotional extremes he felt within himself, from brooding melancholy to a magical sense of elation. He wrote six symphonies, three piano concertos, a violin concerto and ten operas, including *Eugene Onegin* (1878). His ballets *Swan Lake* (1875), *Sleeping Beauty* (1888) and *The Nutcracker* (1892) are among the foundation works of classical dance. Tchaikovsky also wrote the rousing *1812 Overture* (1880) which incorporates the 'Marseillaise' and the tsarist Russian national anthem.
🕭 Tchaikovsky died of cholera after drinking infected water. It is thought he did this deliberately after suffering from guilt as a result of his homosexual leanings.

Te Kanawa, Dame Kiri (1944-) New Zealand singer, one of the leading operatic sopranos of modern times. She arrived in England in 1965 and joined the Royal Opera three years later. Her first major success was as the Countess in

Mozart's *Marriage of Figaro* in 1971. Te Kanawa sang in BERNSTEIN's 1985 recording of *West Side Story*, and topped the pop charts with the Rugby World Cup theme song 'World in Union' in 1991.

tenor Highest normal range of the male voice, apart from ALTO. Famous tenors include Enrico Caruso, Luciano Pavarotti and Placido Domingo.

Tippett, Sir Michael (1905-) British composer who together with Benjamin BRITTEN led the revival in British music after World War II. Tippett was greatly influenced by jazz music and the composers Purcell and Stravinsky. He won international success with the poignant oratorio *A Child of Our Time* (1941). His other works include five operas, four symphonies and several concertos.

Toscanini, Arturo (1867-1957) Italian conductor, renowned for his fiery interpretations of Beethoven, Verdi and Wagner. Because he was extremely shortsighted, he committed all scores to his phenomenal musical memory. Toscanini was artistic director of La Scala (Milan's opera house) at various times between 1898 and 1929, the Metropolitan Opera (1908-15) and he conducted the New York Philharmonic Orchestra (1928-36). In the 1920s he was noted for his opposition to Mussolini and the rise of facism in Italy.

Turner, Tina (1938-) American rock and soul singer. She was discovered by guitarist Ike Turner in 1956, when she joined his rhythm-and-blues band, and later became his wife and co-star, recording hits such as 'River Deep, Mountain High' (1966). Their stormy marriage broke up in 1976, and Tina Turner went solo. She became one of the biggest stars of the 1980s with her album *Private Dancer* (1984).

Vaughan Williams, Ralph (1872-1958) English composer who became one of the leaders of the 20th-century revival of English music. Vaughan Williams was greatly influenced by folk tunes as well as by Tudor music, as can be heard in his *Fantasia on a Theme of Thomas Tallis*, for strings (1910). His works include nine symphonies, the *Fantasia on Greensleeves* (1934) and the operas *Riders to the Sea* (1932) and *The Pilgrim's Progress* (1951).

Verdi, Giuseppe (1813-1901) Italian composer and one of the masters of Italian opera. After being rejected as a student by the Milan Conservatory in 1832 for being insufficiently talented, he studied privately. His first opera *Oberto* (1839) was only a moderate success, but fame came three years later with *Nabucco*. With his gifts for melody, drama and orchestral colour, Verdi wrote a series of popular operas including *Rigoletto* (1851), *La Traviata* (1853) and *Aida* (1871). By 1882 Verdi had retired to work on his beloved farm, but he was tempted back to composition by two Shakespeare adaptations – *Otello* (1887) and *Falstaff* (1893) – which are widely regarded as his masterpieces. The patriotic fervour of his early operas linked him closely with the movement for Italian unification; he became a symbol for Italian liberty and died a national hero.

Vivaldi, Antonio (1678-1741) Italian composer and virtuoso violinist. In 1703, Vivaldi became musical director of an orphanage and musical conservatory for girls in Venice; he also took holy orders and entered the priesthood. The public nicknamed him the 'Red Priest' because of his flaming red hair. Energetic and prolific, Vivaldi wrote 447 concertos, 46 operas and many works for the church. By the time he had written his best-known work, a set of four violin concertos entitled *The Four Seasons* (1725), he was recognised and admired throughout Europe. By 1730, however, Vivaldi's music had fallen out of favour with the Italian public. In 1741 he left Venice for Vienna, where he died and was buried in a pauper's grave.

Wagner, Richard (1813-83) (VAHG-ner) German composer who revolutionised opera with his richly expressive music. Wagner dreamed of merging words, drama and music into a total work of art, with a series of vast, highly dramatic works which he called 'music dramas'. He wrote his own texts, and used the orchestra to help tell the story by writing a score of continuous music (rather than the traditional division into arias and recitatives) and by developing a device called the *leitmotif* – a recurring musical theme identified with a particular person, emotion, event or idea. His ideal of 'music drama' inspired generations of composers including Debussy and Richard Strauss. Wagner's best-known composition is his monumental cycle of four operas, *The Ring of the Nibelung*, an epic based on German mythology, which lasts about 15 hours and took 25 years to complete. *The Ring* was first performed at Wagner's own opera house at Bayreuth in 1876. His other works include *The Flying Dutchman* (1843), *Tristan and Isolde* (1865) and *The Mastersingers of Nuremberg* (1868).

Waller, Fats (1904-43) American jazz composer, pianist and entertainer, remembered for his exuberant performances. He was a prolific composer of shows and hit songs such as 'Ain't Misbehavin' (1929).

Waters, Muddy (1915-83) American blues singer, guitarist and composer. In the 1940s he established himself as 'King of the Chicago Blues' with his unique moaning and shouting style. He had a great influence on the British RHYTHM AND BLUES boom of the 1960s, inspiring white enthusiasts such as The Rolling Stones. His songs include 'Hoochie Coochie Man' (1954) and 'Got My Mojo Working' (1957).

Who, The (Original members: Pete Townshend, Roger Daltrey, John Entwistle and Keith Moon) British rock group who formed in 1964. Pete Townshend was renowned for his guitar-smashing antics and youth anthems such as 'My Generation' (1965). Drummer Keith Moon died of a drugs overdose in 1978, and the reformed band split up five years later. They reunited in 1985 for the Live Aid concert.
♩In 1969 Townshend wrote the spectacular rock opera *Tommy*. It was made into a film by Ken Russell in 1975, and turned into a successful Broadway musical in 1993.

Williams, John (1941-) Australian guitarist, based in Britain from 1952. He and fellow guitarist Julian BREAM helped to re-establish the classical guitar as a solo and ensemble instrument.

Wonder, Stevie (1950-) American singer, songwriter and multi-instrumentalist who has been the most successful black recording artist of the rock era. Blind from birth, Wonder was a child prodigy and joined MOTOWN Records in 1962 as 'Little Stevie Wonder', when he had an American No.1 hit single with 'Fingertips (Part 2)'. In the late 1960s Wonder began to co-write his own material and to experiment with electronic technology, pioneering the use of the synthesiser in black music in songs such as 'Superstition' (1972). In 1983 he wrote one of his most popular songs, 'I Just Called To Say I Love You' for the film *The Woman in Red*.

Wynette, Tammy (1942-) Country singer who has been hailed as 'The First Lady of Country Music'. She is renowned for her impassioned songs about loneliness, which she sang from the bitter experience of a string of broken marriages. She is best known for the songs 'D.I.V.O.R.C.E.' and 'Stand By Your Man' (both 1968).

SPORT AND LEISURE

Ever since the ancient Greeks held the first Olympic Games, individuals and teams have enjoyed pitting their strengths and skills against each other in competitive sports. Every age has produced its sporting personalities and national champions. Ardent fans urge them on to set new standards of excellence, sharing the drama and the emotion of great sporting moments.

STANLEY MATTHEWS

STEFFI GRAF

MUHAMMAD ALI
V. JOE FRAZIER, 1974

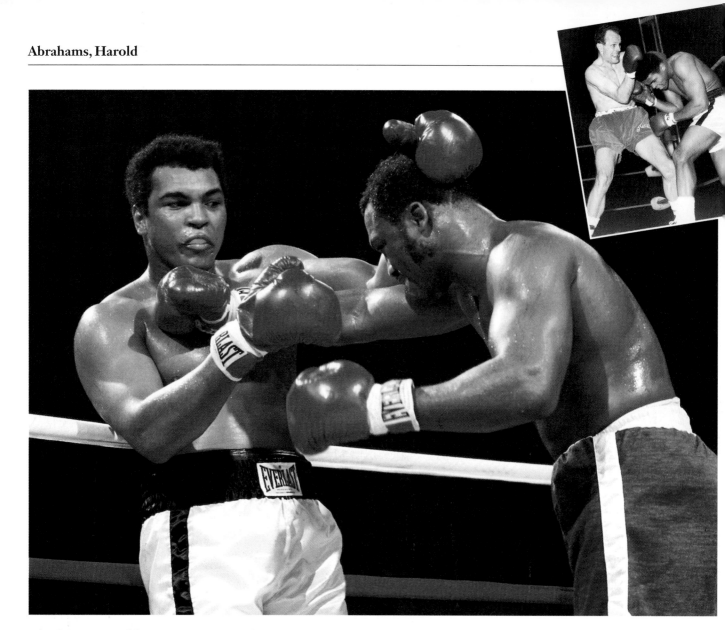

Abrahams, Harold (1899-1978) British athlete who won the 100 m gold medal at the 1924 Olympics in Paris. As a Jew, he also won a battle against the anti-Semitism then rampant in British sport. Afterwards he became a leading athletics broadcaster.
In 1981 Abrahams was the subject, together with the Scottish runner and rugby international Eric Liddell (1902-45), of the Oscar-winning film *Chariots of Fire*.

Agassi, Andre (1970-) US tennis player who won the Wimbledon singles title in 1992 and the US Open singles championship in 1994. Agassi built up a cult following among young people attracted by his appearance and style – long hair, flashy tennis clothing and aggressive play. He is known for his charm and general good manners on court.

Ali, Muhammad (1942-) American heavyweight boxer who proclaimed himself 'the Greatest' and proved it by dominating

the world championship scene between 1964 and 1979. Sensationally, he first won the title at the age of 22 by defeating Sonny Liston. Born Cassius Marcellus Clay in Louisville, Kentucky, he was known as the 'Louisville Lip' for his repartee and boasts of being able to 'float like a butterfly and sting like a bee'. During a colourful and controversial career he adopted the militant Black Muslim religion and changed his name accordingly. In 1967 Ali became a rallying point for opposition to the Vietnam War when he refused to serve in the US Army – for which he was deprived of his world title. He returned to the ring in 1970 and regained the title four years later. Ali made his last winning comeback in 1978, when he beat Leon Spinks. He has suffered for some years from Parkinson's disease.

American football National sport of the USA, played by two teams of 11 whose aim is to pass or run the oval ball over their opponents' goal line, for a touchdown,

DOUBLE VICTORY *Muhammad Ali beat Joe Frazier in 1974 on his way to regaining the world title. As Cassius Clay he defeated Britain's Henry Cooper (inset) in 1963, despite being floored in the fifth round.*

worth six points. A kick through the goal, or touchdown conversion, earns one point, and a field goal – kicked like a penalty in rugby union, but taken as an option by the attacking side – earns three points. Professional teams have a squad of 45 players to choose from, with different teams for offence and defence, and specialist kickers. The season reaches a climax each January with the SUPER BOWL.

America's Cup International yachting contest held every three or four years culminating in the best of seven races between two ocean-going yachts, the defender and the challenger. The yachts have a crew of 11 and are about 65 ft (20 m)

long. Countries wishing to challenge the cup-holders take part in a series of elimination races. The contest is named after the schooner *America*, which beat Britain's best in a race round the Isle of Wight in 1851. The cup, donated by the Royal Yacht Squadron, stayed in US hands for the next 132 years. Then, in 1983, the Australian yacht *Australia II* beat the US defender *Liberty*. However, the USA won back the trophy in 1987 with *Stars and Stripes* and retained it in 1992 with *America III*.
⚓In 1990, after a controversial legal battle, the New York appeals court ruled that although *Stars and Stripes* was a catamaran it had not violated the original race rules – which stated that the competing yachts should be monohulls.

angling Fishing with rod and line which takes three main forms. In game fishing, or fly fishing – mainly for salmon or trout – fish are attracted to the hook with lures or flies. Flies are known as 'wet', 'dry' or 'nymphs'. Nymphs and wet flies are fished under water and resemble tiny water creatures. Dry flies are fished on the surface of the water and are meant to look like insects alighting momentarily. In coarse fishing – for freshwater fish other than those of the salmon family – the hook is baited with food (for example, maggots, worms or bread) and is held on the bottom with a weight or suspended just below the surface by a float. Teams compete in coarse-fishing contests for the total weight of fish caught. Sea fishing from a beach, pier or boat generally uses the same techniques as coarse fishing. It may yield anything from bass weighing less than a kilogram to a shark weighing half a ton.

Arkle One of the greatest steeplechasers of all time and the pride of Ireland in the 1960s. A gelding, he won all but eight of his 35 races, including three Cheltenham Gold Cups. His career ended in December 1966, when he broke a bone in a foot.

Ascot, Royal Four-day race meeting held each June and traditionally attended by the British monarch. It ranks with Wimbledon and Henley as a major occasion in the English sporting and social calendar. Its showpiece is the 2½ mile (4 km) Ascot Gold Cup for horses of four years and above. The racecourse was founded by Queen Anne in 1711.
⚓Royal Ascot is noted for its extravagant fashions – especially the display of outrageous hats on Ladies' Day, when many female racegoers vie to catch the eye of newspaper and television cameras.

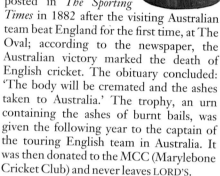

Ashes, The Cricket contest between England and Australia, usually consisting of a series of five Test matches. Its name derives from a mock obituary notice posted in *The Sporting Times* in 1882 after the visiting Australian team beat England for the first time, at The Oval; according to the newspaper, the Australian victory marked the death of English cricket. The obituary concluded: 'The body will be cremated and the ashes taken to Australia.' The trophy, an urn containing the ashes of burnt bails, was given the following year to the captain of the touring English team in Australia. It was then donated to the MCC (Marylebone Cricket Club) and never leaves LORD'S.

athletics Sports encompassing track and field events, cross-country and road running, and walking, which are widely regarded as the leading events of the OLYMPIC GAMES. Track and field events also have their own world championships. Road events include the MARATHON.
⚓Egypt provides the first known evidence of organised running, *c.*3800 BC, and athletic prowess was highly valued at the ancient Olympic Games in Greece. Modern athletics contests date from 1812, when the Royal Military College at Sandhurst in Berkshire founded its annual sports day. Five years afterwards the world's first athletics club, the Necton Guild, was established in Norfolk.

backgammon Board game for two players in which counters are moved according to the throw of two dice. The board is divided into two identical sides, one for each player, consisting of 12 elongated triangles, called points, divided by a central strip, the bar. Players aim to manoeuvre their own set of 15 counters from one triangle to another around the board, without being sent back to the start or being blocked by their opponent, and so be the first to take them off. When gambling, a doubling dice can be used by each player alternately to double the stakes.

badminton Court game, played as singles or doubles, in which players volley a shuttlecock over a high net with light, strung rackets. Points may be scored only by the

server, who forfeits the serve when he or she loses a rally. A game runs to 15 points or, in women's singles, 11. A match is decided over three games.
⚓The game originated in the 1870s at Badminton – seat of the dukes of Beaufort.

Badminton Horse Trials Britain's foremost three-day event, held each spring at Badminton House, in Gloucestershire. The most successful British contestants at Badminton include Lucinda Green, who won the event six times between 1973 and 1984, and Virginia Elliott (née Leng), who won in 1985, 1989 and 1993.

Ballesteros, Severiano (1957-) Spanish golfer who first won the Open Championship in 1979 and became the leading European player in the early 1980s. 'Seve' played a major part in Europe's Ryder Cup successes against the USA. He won the US Masters in 1980 and 1983, as well as two more Open Championships, in 1984 and 1988.

Bannister, Sir Roger (1929-) British athlete who was the first man to run a mile in under four minutes. He did so on May 6, 1954, at Oxford, clocking 3 min 59.4 sec for the distance. A medical student at the time,

RECORD MILER *Roger Bannister hits the tape at the end of his record-setting sub four-minute mile at the Oxford University track in 1954.*

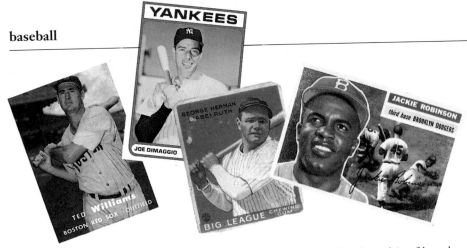

HARD-HITTING HEROES *Baseball fans in America have been thrilled by the exploits of legendary batters such as (left to right): Ted Williams, Joe DiMaggio, Babe Ruth and Jackie Robinson.*

REACHING HIGH *American basketball star Earvin 'Magic' Johnson (centre) was one of the sport's dominating players, standing at 6 ft 9 in (2.06 m). He retired in 1992.*

Bannister believed that there was no physical reason to prevent man from running faster in order to break the psychological barrier of the four-minute mile.

baseball US sport, developed in the mid-19th century from the old English game of rounders. It is played nine-a-side on a 90 ft (27.4 m) square 'diamond' infield with a large outfield. The batter stands in front of the 'home plate', one point of the diamond, with 'bases' at the three other points. At the middle of the diamond is a small mound from which the pitcher throws the ball. The batter's aim is to hit the ball and run round the bases – right back to the home plate, if possible, to score a home run. Alternatively, he may stop at any base, and complete his run when another batter hits the ball. There are a number of ways in which the fielding side can get a batter out, and when three batters are out that innings ends. Each side has nine innings. American professional baseball is played in two leagues, and the season culminates in a feverishly followed world series between the respective champions.

basketball Five-a-side court game in which opposing teams hand-pass or dribble, by bouncing, a ball and attempt to throw it through the opposing team's basket. A 'basket' earns from one to three points depending on how it is made. A game can be divided into two periods of 20 minutes or four 12-minute quarters, and a team may have up to seven substitutes. The baskets are fixed at a height of 10 ft (3 m) to a backboard at each end of the court. The world's most renowned basketball team, the Harlem Globetrotters of New York, was founded in 1927 to play exhibition games.

Becker, Boris (1967-) German tennis star who became the youngest Wimbledon men's singles champion when he won the

title in 1985 at the age of 17. He retained the title in 1986 and won it again in 1989. A powerful serve-and-volley player, he led Germany to their first ever Davis Cup triumph in 1988.

Best, George (1946-) Northern Irish footballer who became the first British 'pop idol' of soccer in the 1960s as one of Manchester United's star players. Before his decline in the early 1970s, when tales of his riotous private life filled the gossip columns, Best was probably the most talented player in Europe. A goal-scoring winger, he won two League championship medals with United and a European Cup medal in 1968, when he was European Footballer of the Year. He scored 137 goals in 361 League games for United, and won 37 caps for Northern Ireland.
🍷Known for his love of wine, women and night-life, Best, with typical cheek, called his 1991 autobiography *The Good, the Bad and the Bubbly.*

billiards Game played with one red and two white balls on a baize-covered table measuring 12 ft by 6 ft (3.7 m by 1.8 m), with six pockets. Players strike a cue ball (white or spot white) and score points by potting another ball, going 'in-off' (sending the cue ball into a pocket off another ball) or making a 'cannon' (hitting both the other balls with the cue ball). A player continues to build up 'breaks' until he or she fails to score, when it becomes the other player's turn. Games are usually played up to a certain number of points.
🍷Famous players of the game have included Mozart, who composed music while relaxing at billiards, and Mary, Queen of Scots, who was heartbroken when parted from her billiards table during her life imprisonment.

blackjack Casino card game based on pontoon, or *vingt-et-un* (twenty-one), in which the 'bank' (dealer) deals out cards – each of which has a value in points – to players round the table. The object is to get nearer to a total of 21 points, without exceeding it, than the dealer.

bobsleighing Winter sport in which a two or four-man crew sit in a sleigh and shoot down a twisting track of solid ice with steeply banked bends at speeds of more than 90 mph (145 km/h). The driver steers the bob by moving the front runners by means of ropes or a type of steering wheel. The brakeman, at the back, uses the brakes only to stop the bob at the end of a run or to correct skids. In a four-man bob, the two middle men help to steer by shifting their weight at bends. The first run was built at St Moritz, Switzerland – home of the Cresta Run – in 1904.

Bobsleighing acquired its name from the way in which members of early teams 'bobbed' their bodies back and forth in order to increase the speed of their sleighs at the start of a run.

Border, Allan (1955-) Australian all-round cricketer who captained his country in 93 of his 156 Tests, scoring a world record 11 174 runs at an average of 50.56. Known for his courage and tenacity at the crease, he was also a reliable slow left-arm bowler, taking 39 Test wickets – including 7-46 against the West Indies in 1989. Border retired from Test cricket in May 1994.

Borg, Bjorn (1956-) Swedish tennis player who set a modern record by winning five successive Wimbledon men's singles titles between 1976 and 1980. In a period dominated by serve-and-volley champions, Borg reigned supreme on grass with a counter-attacking baseline game based on topspin, demonstrating an ice-cool temperament. He excelled on European clay, and won the first of his six French Opens in 1974 at the age of 18. In 1975 he led Sweden to their first Davis Cup success.

Botham, Ian (1955-) English cricketer who made his Test debut in 1977 and broke many all-round records with his big hitting and penetrating swing bowling. He became the first player to score a century and take more than ten wickets in a Test, hitting 114 and taking 6-58 and 7-48 against India in Bombay in 1980. A controversial and colourful character, known as 'Beefy' for his strapping physique, Botham was often in the news for his flamboyant off-field behaviour. He is well remembered for his role in the 1981 Ashes, when his batting and bowling feats almost single-handedly snatched victory from Australia.

bowls Game played with biased bowls (large balls) sometimes called woods which take a curved path when rolled. Flat-green bowls is played on a flat lawn, while crown-green bowls – popular in the north of England – is played on a green with an irregular surface rising to between 8 in (20 cm) and 18 in (46 cm) at its centre. A bowls game ranges from singles to four-a-side. In singles, each player has four bowls; in fours, each has two. A small white ball known as a jack is the target. A point is scored for each bowl nearer the jack than the nearest of an opponent's.

boxing Fighting with gloved fists inside a raised ring. Boxers fight in weight divisions, ranging from strawweight (7 st 5 lb/ 47.627 kg) to heavyweight (over 12 st 7 lb/81 kg). In amateur boxing, a major Olympic sport, competitors fight three three-minute rounds. Lengths of professional fights vary, with a maximum of 12 three-minute rounds for title bouts. A fight may be won by a knock-out, when a floored boxer is unable to get to his feet during a count of 10 seconds, on points after it has 'gone the distance' – that is, the maximum time has elapsed – or by the intervention of the referee.

Boxing gave birth to the phrase 'the real McCoy', or genuine article. It was coined in the USA by Charles 'Kid' McCoy, the world welterweight champion in 1896, who used it to distinguish himself from another fighter named Al McCoy.

Boycott, Geoffrey (1940-) Prolific opening batsman for Yorkshire and England. His single-minded approach to run-making provoked criticism that he put himself before the team. As county captain in the 1970s, Boycott caused friction by his determination to be both player and administrator. This, and Yorkshire's lack of cricketing success, led to his losing the captaincy in 1978. He is the only batsman to average more than 100 in two English seasons, in 1971 and 1979.

ENTER THE DON *Renowned for his quick eye and nimble footwork, Don Bradman's record of 974 runs in a Test series, made against England in 1930, still stands.*

Bradman, Sir Donald (1908-) Australian cricketer, known as 'the Don', regarded by some as the greatest batsman of all time. In a career lasting from 1927 to 1948, he scored 28 067 runs at an average of 95.14, and in Tests he made 6996 runs at an average of 99.96. His highest score was 452 not out for New South Wales against Queensland in the 1929-30 season; his highest in Tests was 334 against England in 1930 – both world records at the time. He captained Australia in five Test series.

British Lions Name used by the rugby union side made up of players from the 'home' countries of the British Isles, including the Irish Republic, when they tour overseas. The first tour took place in 1888, to Australia and New Zealand, although the side was not called the 'Lions' until the 1924 tour of South Africa.

Bruno, Frank (1961-) British heavyweight boxer who became a celebrity without actually winning anything of note – not even the British title. The youngest ever ABA (Amateur Boxing Association) heavyweight champion, in 1980, he beat Anders Ekland for the European championship in 1985. He almost floored world champion Mike Tyson in their 1989 fight.

In television interviews with the BBC sports broadcaster Harry Carpenter, Bruno often finished his sentences by saying, 'Know what I mean, 'arry?' – which became a national catchphrase.

Budd, Zola (1966-) South African long distance runner known for competing in her bare feet. In 1984 she took up British citizenship and was a finalist in the 3000 m at the Los Angeles Olympics, in which she accidently tripped the American runner Mary Slaney who fell; Budd came 7th. She won the world cross-country titles in 1985 and 1986. She returned to South Africa in 1988, married, and as Zola Pieterse was 4th in the 1993 world cross-country race.

Busby, Sir Matt (1910-94) Football manager who created three superb teams for Manchester United – the last of which, in 1968, became the first English club to win the European Cup. As a wing-half, Busby played for Manchester City, Liverpool and Scotland before World War II. He managed United from 1946 to 1969. His so-called 'Busby Babes' team was involved in a catastrophic air crash in Munich in February 1958. Eight of its star players died in or shortly after the crash, but Busby survived his severe injuries and went on to rebuild the team.

FINAL RUN *Donald Campbell was killed on Coniston Water in the Lake District in 1967, when his speedboat* Bluebird *somersaulted and broke up at almost 330 mph (530 km/h).*

Campbell, Sir Malcolm (1885-1948) and Donald (1921-67) British father and son racing-car and speedboat drivers. Malcolm was the first person to hold both the world land and water speed records at the same time, and Donald was the second. Malcolm called his boats *Bluebird* and his son used the same name for his boats and cars. Malcolm broke the land speed record nine times between 1924 and 1935, and was the first to smash the 300 mph (482 km/h) barrier. He broke the water speed record three times between 1937 and 1939. Donald broke the water speed record seven times between 1955 and 1957 and the land speed record once, when he broke the 400 mph (643 km/h) barrier, on the Lake Eyre salt flats, South Australia, in 1964.

Campese, David (1962-) Flamboyant Australian rugby union player who has scored a record 54 tries in international games as wing-threequarter. He made his Test debut against New Zealand in 1982 aged 19, and went on to play 87 times for Australia up to the beginning of October

1994. He inspired Australia to their 1991 World Cup victory, when he was joint leading scorer in the tournament with six tries.

casino games Gambling in casinos was legalised in Britain in 1960, since when the country has become one of the world's major gambling centres, with some 120 casinos. Popular games include BLACKJACK, or 21, ROULETTE and baccarat.

Charlton, Bobby (1937-) English footballer who played a major role in England's 1966 World Cup triumph. Charlton was one of the 'Busby Babes' who survived the Munich air crash in 1958. He scored 199 goals in 606 League appearances for Manchester United, helping the team to win the European Cup (1968), the FA Cup (1963) and the Football League three times, in 1957, 1965 and 1967. A forward famed for his runs through the middle of the field and devastating shot with either foot, Charlton scored a record 49 goals for England in 106 internationals. Charlton was knighted in 1994.

Charlton, Jack (1935-) English footballer and manager, who is the elder brother of Bobby. He won 35 caps for England and also helped England to their World Cup success in 1966. A tall centre-

HIGH CARDS *Sums large and small change hands in card games in Britain's casinos.*

half, nicknamed 'the Giraffe', Charlton scored 70 goals in a record 629 League appearances for Leeds United. In 1986 he became the manager of the Republic of Ireland team and took the side to the World Cup finals in 1990 and 1994.

Cheltenham Gold Cup Blue riband of National Hunt racing – a non-handicap steeplechase event for five-year-olds and upwards, held over 3 miles 2 furlongs (5.3 km). First run in 1924, the Gold Cup forms part of the National Hunt Festival at Cheltenham, Gloucestershire, each March.

Christie, Linford (1960-) British sprinter who won the 100 m gold medal in the 1992 Olympics in Barcelona. At 32, he was the oldest man ever to win this event. In 1993 he won the gold medal at the world championships in Stuttgart – coming within a hundredth of a second of the world record – to complete the 'full set' of Olympic, World, European and Commonwealth titles. He successfully defended the last two titles in 1994.

Classics Five English horse races held annually for three-year-olds: the 2000 Guineas, the Derby, the St Leger and, for fillies only, the 1000 Guineas and the Oaks. The 2000 and 1000 Guineas are run over 1 mile (1.6 km) at Newmarket, the Derby and Oaks over 1 mile 4 furlongs (2.4 km) at Epsom, and the St Leger over 1 mile 6 furlongs 127 yd (2.9 km) at Doncaster.

Clough, Brian (1935-) English football manager known for his outspoken views and abrasive personality. As a player, Clough was capped twice by England, but his career as a goal-scoring centre-forward was cut short by injury. As manager of Nottingham Forest, he twice helped the club to win the European Cup.

Coe, Sebastian (1956-) British middle-distance runner who was the first athlete to win the Olympic 1500 m twice, in

1980 and 1984. Coe set an unrivalled nine world records between 1979 and 1981, including records for the 800 m, 1500 m and the mile. His world records for the 800 m and 1000 m still stand. In 1992, he became a Conservative MP.

Comaneci, Nadia (1961-) Romanian gymnast who, at the age of 14, became the first person to attain a perfect 10 score at the Olympic Games in Montreal in 1976.

Compton, Denis (1918-) English international at both cricket and football. A graceful, if unorthodox, batsman, Compton played in 78 Test matches, forming a celebrated partnership with his Middlesex county colleague Bill Edrich. In 1947 he scored 3816 runs and hit 18 centuries in the English first-class season – records that still stand. In 1948, he made the fastest ever triple century – 300 for MCC (Marylebone Cricket Club) against North Eastern Transvaal – in 181 minutes. He played football as a left-winger for England during World War II and later won League championship and FA Cup medals with Arsenal.
 ♪ Dark and handsome, Compton advertised a popular brand of haircream in the 1950s and was dubbed the 'Brylcreem boy'.

Connolly, Maureen (1934-69) Diminutive US tennis player known as 'Little Mo'. She won the US Open singles title in 1951 at the age of 16, and two years later became the first woman player to achieve the grand slam. She won the Wimbledon singles championship three times (1952-4) and retired a short while later after crushing a leg in a riding accident.

Cooper, Henry (1934-) Enormously popular British heavyweight boxing champion of the late 1950s and 1960s who held the British and Empire titles for a record ten years. He twice won the European heavyweight crown. In 1963, at London's Wembley stadium, he floored the future world champion Cassius Clay (Muhammad

Ali) with his devastating left hook, known as 'Enry's 'ammer. Only the bell and the fact that his glove had split saved Clay. A badly cut eye in the next round, however, forced Cooper to retire from the fight. Three years later a similar eye injury ended his attempt to wrest the world title from Ali.

Cram, Steve (1960-) One of Britain's great middle-distance runners of the 1980s, rivalling Sebastian Coe and Steve Ovett. In 1985 he set new world records for the 1500 m, the 2000 m and the mile in the course of 19 days. His mile record of 3 min 46.32 sec was not broken until 1993.

GOING FOR GOLD *Britain's Linford Christie – the personification of grace and power – beat all-comers to take the gold medal in the 100 m at the Olympic Games held in Barcelona in 1992.*

cricket Eleven-a-side game in which a hard leather ball is bowled from a crease, or line, at one end of the 22 yd (20 m) long pitch to a batsman defending the wicket at the other, who then attempts to score runs. The object is to score more runs than the opposing team. Six balls bowled in succession constitute an 'over'. If the ball dislodges at least one of the two bails set on the three stumps of the wicket, the batsman is bowled out. Other ways of dismissal include being caught and lbw (leg before wicket), when a ball that, in the umpire's opinion, would have hit the stumps hits a batsman. A batsman can also be 'stumped' if he plays at the ball, misses, and is out of his crease when the wicket-keeper strikes the stumps with the ball in his hand, or by throwing the ball. Batsmen score four runs by hitting the ball past the boundary, and six runs if it clears the boundary without bouncing first. County matches last up to four days and Test matches up to five. Famous English grounds include Headingley, in Leeds, Old Trafford, in Manchester, and The Oval and LORD's, in London.

croquet Game played on a lawn, or court, in which players use long-handled mallets to drive coloured balls through a series of hoops, then on to a wooden peg. The first player or doubles team to hit the peg wins.

curling Team game in which players slide disc-like granite stones, known as curling stones, across a long, narrow ice-rink towards a target called a tee. Competitors carry special brooms with which they vigorously 'soop', or sweep, the ice in front of the moving stones to try to correct their speed and direction. As the game progresses, players and spectators give loud cries of 'Soop! Soop!' Since 1969 curling has had its own world championships, contested by teams from countries such as Scotland, the USA, Canada, Sweden and Norway.

cycle racing Bicycle sport that takes place on road or track. Road events include stage races, long-distance races on circuits on the open road, shorter races on closed circuits, and time trials, in which competitors set off at intervals. Races held on specially banked tracks include sprints, pursuit and time trials. In sprints, the two competing riders jockey for position, sometimes almost coming to a standstill as they try to manoeuvre into the best position just above and behind the other rider, for the sudden, final dash. In pursuit, riders, or teams of riders, start at opposite sides of the track and chase each other over several laps. Cycle racing is also held off-road. In cyclo-cross, road racing machines are used on short but difficult circuits where riders often have to carry their cycles. Mountain bike events are held on larger circuits.

The British cyclist Chris Boardman won the 1992 Olympic Pursuit title, broke the World Hour Record in 1993, and won the World Pursuit Championship in 1994. The Spanish cyclist Miguel Induráin, who has won the TOUR DE FRANCE on four occasions, set a new World Hour Record at a distance of 32.96 miles (53.04 km) in 1994.

Dalglish, Kenny (1951-) Scottish footballer whose achievements at club level as both player and manager are

PEDAL POWER *Competitors in the Tour de France turn on the power at the Perpignan stage of the race. Miguel Induráin of Spain (inset) has won the race four years in succession, 1991-4.*

unsurpassed. Equally accomplished as a striker and in midfield, Dalglish played for Celtic (1970-7) and Liverpool (1977-89), scoring more than 100 League goals for each club. He helped Celtic to win nine major titles, and at Liverpool he was a member of the team that won three European Cups, four League Cups, the FA Cup in 1986 and the Football League six times. He made a record 102 appearances for Scotland. In 1986, his first season as player-manager of Liverpool, Dalglish guided the club to the League and Cup double. He repeated the League championship success in 1988 and 1990. He resigned from Liverpool in 1991 but returned to the game later that year as manager of Blackburn Rovers.

darts Pub game that has become a worldwide international sport through the influence of television. Players take turns to throw three darts at a circular board divided into scoring sectors numbered 1 to 20. Darts that land in the 'bull's-eye' in the centre of the board score 50, and 25 for an outer bull. Normally, scores are deducted from a starting number, usually 501 or 301, and the game is won by the first player to throw a 'double' that brings his or her score exactly to zero.

Davis, Joe (1901-78) English snooker player who reigned supreme in the game from 1927 until his retirement from championship play in 1947. He won the world title 15 times and was the first player to make snooker's maximum 147 break in competitive play, in 1955. He also won the world billiards championship four times.
♘Joe Davis' brother Fred (1913-) won the world snooker title three times.

Davis, Steve (1957-) English snooker player (no relation to Joe Davis) who won his first world title in 1981 at the age of 23, and went on to dominate the game in the 1980s. Davis won his sixth world title in 1989 with an 18-3 victory over John Parrott – the greatest margin of victory in a modern world final. He was overtaken as world No.1 in the early 1990s by Stephen Hendry but continued to be rated among the world's top five.
♘Although some critics regarded Davis as a 'boring' player, his sportsmanship and good humour made him a fine ambassador for snooker in an era when the game became a major television sport.

Davis Cup International tennis team event for men, held annually since it was established in 1900 by the US player

MASTER POTTER *Cool, calm and collected, Steve Davis prepares to take another shot. His skills have made him the 'players' player'.*

Dwight Davis. Teams must qualify for inclusion in a world group comprising the top 16 tennis-playing nations, which take part in a yearly knock-out tournament. Each round of the tournament consists of five matches, two pairs of singles and one doubles, played over a three-day period and not necessarily involving the same players in each match.

decathlon Athletics competition in which men take part in ten track and field events over two days. The events, in the order in which they are contested, are: 100 m, long jump, shot, high jump, 400 m, 110 m hurdles, discus, pole vault, javelin and 1500 m. Points are awarded, according to scoring tables, for each performance.
♘Tests of all-round sporting ability have their origins in the ancient Greek Olympics. The decathlon was revived in the USA in the 1880s.

Derby England's chief CLASSIC horse-race for three-year-olds, run annually over 1 mile 4 furlongs (2.4 km) at Epsom since 1780. The Derby has given its name to great races all over the world, including the famous Kentucky Derby in the USA.
♘The name of the race was determined by the toss of a coin between Lord Derby and Sir Charles Bunbury in 1779.

Desert Orchid Spectacular British steeplechaser who captured the public imagination with his bold front-running and flamboyant jumping. A grey – almost snowy white – 'Dessie' recorded the first of his four King George VI Chase wins at Kempton Park in 1986. Four times Horse of the Year, Dessie achieved a dramatic

Cheltenham Gold Cup win in 1989 when, after looking beaten with two fences to go, he went on to beat Yahoo in a storming finish. In the 1990 Irish Grand National, giving the best of his rivals 26 lb, he won with ease despite a serious blunder at the last fence.

DiMaggio, Joe (1914-) US baseball star who led the New York Yankees to ten World Series titles between 1936 and 1951. He is best known for two things: his unrivalled streak of safe hitting (securing at least one base hit) in 56 consecutive games in 1941 and his brief and highly publicised marriage in 1954 to the Hollywood superstar Marilyn Monroe.
♘DiMaggio's grace and style as a player, as well as his outstanding ability, made him the idol of a generation. Paul Simon's popular song 'Mrs Robinson', written in 1967 for the Dustin Hoffman film *The Graduate*, included the words: 'Where have you gone, Joe DiMaggio? A nation turns its lonely eyes to you.'

diving Sport in which competitors dive into the water from high springboards and platforms, performing graceful acrobatics as they descend. Judges award points for take-off, technique, grace and entry into the water. The points are then multiplied by a factor reflecting the degree of difficulty of each dive to arrive at the diver's score.
♘Between 1982 and 1988 Greg Louganis of the USA won four Olympic gold medals and five world titles, making him the most successful diver of all time.

dressage Equestrian sport in which horses perform a series of disciplined movements at the walk, trot and canter. Judges mark horses and riders, both of which must be well groomed as well as proficient. Dressage is an event in its own right as well as being the first phase in a three-day event.

Elliott, Herb (1938-) Australian middle-distance runner who enjoyed a brief period of world supremacy before retiring in 1961 at the age of 23. From 1954 Elliott was unbeaten in mile and 1500 m races. In 1958 he chopped 2.7 sec off the world mile record with a time of 3 min 54.5 sec, and he broke the 1500 m record for the second time when winning gold at the 1960 Rome Olympics. Elliott brought a new dimension to miling, habitually starting his surge for the tape with about a third of a mile to go. Despite the shortness of his career, Elliott is still regarded by some as the greatest ever middle-distance athlete of all time.

FA Cup (Football Association Challenge Cup)

Annual knock-out competition in which more than 500 senior clubs linked to the Football Association take part. Five qualifying rounds are held before the first round proper, when clubs from the lower divisions of the Football League enter the competition. Clubs from the FA Premier League and the First Division of the Football League enter in the third round proper in early January. The final, held at London's Wembley stadium in May, is watched by millions on television in many different countries. The Scottish FA Cup is contested under the auspices of the Scottish Football Association.
♣ The first FA Cup final took place in 1872 at the Kennington Oval, in London. A crowd of 2000 was present.

Faldo, Nick (1957-)

British golfer ranked No.1 in the world in the early 1990s. He turned professional in 1978 and won his first 'major', the Open Championship, in 1987. In 1990, he became the first player for 24 years successfully to defend the US Masters and was the first non-American to win the PGA of America Player of the Year award. He won the Open Championship again in 1990 and 1992, but was forced into second place in 1993 by the Australian Greg Norman. From 1977 to 1993 Faldo played in nine Ryder Cups. He was awarded the MBE in 1988.

Fangio, Juan Manuel (1911-)

Argentinian racing driver, regarded by many as the greatest of all time. His record five world drivers' championships (in 1951, 1954, 1955, 1956 and 1957) still stands. Fangio won his first title in an Alfa-Romeo

SPEED CHAMP *Former garage mechanic Juan Fangio at the wheel of his Maserati, in which he won his last World Championship in 1957.*

CUP FEVER
Since it was first held in 1872, the FA Cup final has fired the imagination of the soccer-going public. Programmes of the games have become much sought after collectors' items.

and also triumphed in a Maserati, a Mercedes and a Ferrari, winning a total of 24 major grands prix.

fencing Sport developed from duelling in which there are three classes, each named after the type of sword used: foil, épée and sabre. Fencers wear white padded uniforms and faceguards. The object in a bout – which usually lasts for a specified period – is to make a 'hit' on your opponent by touching a particular target area of the body with the sword. In foil and épée, only the point may be used; in sabre, the blade edge may also score hits. Target areas are the trunk for foil, the whole person for épée, and the body, arms and head for sabre.

field sport Sporting activity that takes place in the country, especially hunting, shooting or fishing (see ANGLING). In Britain, hunting involves the pursuit of foxes, hares or deer with a pack of dogs during a season that runs from November to March. In foxhunting and the less common staghunting, hunters ride horses; while in beagling, the most popular way of hunting hares, the hunters follow on foot.
♣ The hunting of otters was outlawed in 1981, and growing public opposition in Britain to all forms of hunting has prompted several local councils to ban such activities from their land.

Fischer, Bobby (1943-) US chess player who in 1972 became the first – and, so far, only – American to win the world championship, beating Boris Spassky of the former USSR. In 1975 he was stripped of the title after refusing to defend it against Anatoly Karpov of the USSR, and became a recluse. An eccentric genius, Fischer won his first US championship at 14, and at 15 became the youngest ever international grandmaster. Hungarian Peter Leko, aged 14, has since become the youngest grandmaster. In 1992 Fischer beat Spassky in a rematch by ten games to five.

fishing See ANGLING.

football Team game in which a ball is kicked, carried or sometimes thrown. The term is most commonly used to refer to association football, or soccer, the world's most popular sport, which is played in over 190 countries. Association football is an 11-a-side game that originated in its present form in late 19th-century England. The WORLD CUP is held every four years.
♣ The word soccer derives from Oxford student slang for 'association'.

Football Association (FA) Governing body of association football in England, where it is responsible for the organisation of all football, including the Premier League and the Football League, with its three divisions. Founded in 1863, the Football Association was the first body of its kind and has been the model for similar bodies worldwide.

Formula One The major class of grand prix motor racing. The Fédération Internationale de l'Automobile (FIA) lays down conditions and standards – 'formulae' – of engine, fuel, design, and so on, for various classes of single-seater racing cars. The standards for Formula One are changed regularly, a prime concern being to keep speeds within safety limits.

Fosbury flop Revolutionary style of high-jumping invented by US athlete Dick Fosbury, who used it to win the high-jumping event in the 1968 Olympics in Mexico City. Competitors approach the bar from an angle in a wide arc, turning as they reach the bar, clearing it head first and face up and landing on their backs. All leading high-jumpers now use the 'flop'.

BITTER TEARS *Paul Gascoigne breaks down after a booking in England's World Cup semi-final defeat by West Germany in 1990. Even had England won, he was out of the final, which West Germany went on to win.*

Gascoigne, Paul (1967-) English footballer whose explosive midfield skills helped England to reach the semi-finals of the 1990 World Cup finals in Italy. Gascoigne made his debut for England in 1988, joining Tottenham Hotspur in the same year for a British record fee of £2 million. Growing media interest in his footballing skills and riotous private life induced 'Gazza' mania, which heightened when injury forced the delay of his transfer from Spurs to the Italian club Lazio. After some much-publicised surgery, Gascoigne finally joined Lazio in 1992, for a fee of £5.5 million, although his return to international football had many setbacks – largely due to injury and lack of fitness. Even so, he is the player around whom the England side for the 1998 World Cup could be built.

gliding Sport in which light aircraft are kept aloft and guided by skilful use of rising air currents called thermals. Most gliders are launched by tow from an aeroplane and operate without engines, but motor-gliders – in which an engine is used to launch or land the craft or to sustain it in flight – are becoming more popular. Gliding world championships are held, with competitions for distance and speed of flight.

golf Game played on grass courses which, full-size, consist of 18 holes, each set in a smoothly mown green and, normally, approached by a roughly mown fairway 100-600 yd (90-550 m) long. The object is to hit a golf ball from the tee (a plastic peg set in the ground by the golfer) along the fairway to the green and finally into the hole, in as few strokes as possible. A target number of strokes is set for each hole, according to its distance from the tee. This is called the par for the hole. A score of 1 over par for a hole is known as a bogey; 1 under par is a birdie; 2 under par is an eagle; 3 under par is an albatross or double eagle. Clubs with varying degrees of loft are used for the various types of shot, such as driving off the tee, chipping out of a bunker or putting on the green. The accepted international authority on the rules of the game is the Royal and Ancient Golf Club at ▷ST ANDREWS, which organises the OPEN CHAMPIONSHIP. Other leading international competitions include the US Open and the RYDER CUP.

🦯 Club golfers earn a 'handicap' based on their performances in competition. This is the number of strokes a player may subtract from his or her score, and enables players to compete in amateur golf on equal terms.

Gonzales, Pancho (1928-) Flamboyant American tennis star, hailed as the world's finest-ever player, who was the top tennis professional in the 1950s. Coming from a poor, Mexican-American family in Los Angeles, the young Gonzales could not afford tennis lessons, and taught himself. He was ranked number one in the world in 1948 before turning professional in 1949, and was said to have been the best player never to have won the Wimbledon men's singles title. After tennis went 'open', he is remembered for his epic 22-24, 1-6, 16-14, 6-3, 11-9 win over young American Charlie Pasarell at Wimbledon in 1969.

Gooch, Graham (1953-) English cricketer who played as opening batsman for Essex and England and served as captain of both sides, leading Essex to three county championships between 1986 and 1992. He captained England twice in 1988 and returned to the job in 1990. In 107 Tests Gooch hit 8293 runs, achieving a batting average of 43.87, and in the early 1990s he was ranked the world's No.1 batsman. He was the first to score a triple-hundred and a century in the same first-class match, 333 and 123 against India at Lord's in 1990. But Gooch was not regarded as a successful England captain and resigned in 1993, which was the same year in which he became the leading English runscorer in Test cricket.

🦯 In 1982 Gooch captained an English 'rebel' tour to South Africa, for which he suffered a three-year ban from taking part in international cricket.

Gower, David (1957-) Graceful left-handed batsman who was regarded as the 'golden boy' of English cricket in the 1980s, captaining his country 32 times. From 1991, when he lost first the England captaincy and then his place in the team – following an escapade in Australia, when he 'buzzed' a hired Tiger Moth plane low over the ground while the England team were batting – Gower became the focal point of a protracted controversy. A vigorous campaign to have him reinstated to the side in 1992 was unsuccessful and he retired from top-class cricket the following year. He was England's leading Test runscorer, with a record 8231 runs in 117 Tests (an average of 44.25) until 1993, when he was overtaken by Graham Gooch.

Grace, W.G. (William Gilbert) (1848-1915) Most influential English cricketer of the 19th century. A larger than life character, 'W.G.' dominated the cricket field and the game itself, becoming a national figure. He played in 22 Tests, all against Australia, and led England in 13. A forceful batsman and medium pace bowler, he scored 54 211 runs, including 124 centuries, and took 2809 wickets in a career lasting nearly 44 seasons. He did not retire from first-class cricket until he was 60.

CRICKETING DOCTOR *With his bushy beard, W.G. Grace was one of the best-known people in Victorian England. Although he was a doctor of medicine, cricket was his passion in life.*

Graf, Steffi (1969-) German tennis player who in 1987, at the age of 17, became the youngest woman ever to win the French Open. In 1988 Graf was only the third woman ever to achieve the grand slam, breaking Martina Navratilova's six-year dominance of Wimbledon. However, at Wimbledon in 1994 Graf became the first top-seeded woman to be defeated by an unseeded player – American Lori McNeil – in an opening round match. She won the singles title in 1989, 1991, 1992 and 1993.

Grand National World's most famous steeplechase, held annually at Aintree, near Liverpool, since 1839, and the most severe test of jumping and stamina in British horse racing. Each of the 16 fences is jumped twice over a distance of 4 miles 4 furlongs (7.25 km), except the Chair and the water jump which are jumped once.

grand slam Term used in several sports to indicate victory in all the major events in one year or season. The grand slam in tennis means winning a Wimbledon singles title and the US, French and Australian Open championships; in golf, it means winning the (British) Open, the US Masters, PGA and OPEN CHAMPIONSHIPS.

Greaves, Jimmy (1940-) English footballer who was a prolific goalscorer for Chelsea, Tottenham Hotspur and England.

TRIPLE WINNER *Steeplechaser Red Rum is the only horse to have won the Grand National three times – in 1973, 1974 and 1977.*

BORN WINNER *Renowned for her power play, guts and determination, Steffi Graf has been thrilling tennis spectators in her native Germany and abroad since she was in her teens.*

An inside-forward, he set a post-war record of 41 goals in a season and scored 44 in 57 games for England. After an unhappy spell in Italy with AC Milan, he joined Spurs and by 1969 had topped the First Division scorers for the sixth time. His greatest disappointment was the injury which prevented him from playing for the victorious England team for the closing stages of the 1966 World Cup.

greyhound racing Primarily a gambling sport in which six specially bred greyhounds race round an oval track over distances ranging from 210 m to 1100 m in pursuit of an 'electric hare'. This device travels on a rail at the side of the track and causes the starting stalls to spring open automatically. Top greyhounds reach speeds in excess of 40 mph (64 km/h).

Gunnell, Sally (1966-) British hurdles champion whose major triumphs began when she switched from the 100 m to the 400 m event in 1988. She achieved a unique grand slam by winning the 1992 Olympic 400 m title in Barcelona, the 1993 World title in a world record time of 52.74 sec, and the European and Commonwealth titles in 1994, when she also captained the British women's athletics team.

gymnastics Competitive gymnastics is at least 2500 years old but its modern revival dates from 1811 when the first open-air gymnasium was inaugurated in Germany. Several gymnastics events were included in the first modern Olympics in 1896. Since World War II the sport has been dominated by competitors from Japan, China, eastern Europe, the former USSR, and more recently, the USA.

Hadlee, Sir Richard (1951-) New Zealand all-round cricketer who played in 86 Tests between 1973 and 1990. As a right-arm fast bowler, Hadlee took 431 Test wickets – a world record that stood until 1994, when it was overtaken by India's Kapil Dev. An aggressive left-handed batsman, he scored 3124 Test runs, averaging 27.16. He played ten seasons in England for Nottinghamshire.

Hendry, Stephen (1969-) Scottish snooker player who in 1990 became – at the age of 21 – the youngest player ever to win the world championship. Hendry has triumphed in many other major tournaments, overtaking Steve Davis as the world's top player. He won his fourth world title in 1994, when he beat England's Jimmy White 18-17 in the final, adding to his prize money of more than £6 million.

Henley Royal Regatta Oldest rowing regatta in the world, held annually in early July on the river Thames at Henley, Oxfordshire. World class oarsmen compete for such prizes as the Diamond Sculls (single), Steward's Cup (coxless fours) and the Grand Challenge Cup (eights).

Higgins, Alex (1949-) Northern Irish snooker player whose swashbuckling style of play in the 1970s earned him the nickname 'Hurricane' Higgins. He won the 1972 world title at the age of 23, becoming the youngest ever champion. Beset by personal problems, however, he did not win the world title again until 1982, when he beat Ray Reardon 18-15 in an emotional final. Higgins' other major tournament successes included the Irish cham-

pionships of 1983 and 1989. He also helped Ireland to win snooker's World Cup in 1985, 1986 and 1987.

Hill, Graham (1929-75) and Damon (1960-) British father and son motor-racing drivers. Graham was world champion in 1962 and 1968 and runner-up three times in between. His other victories included the Indianapolis 500 in 1966 and the Le Mans 24-hour race in 1972. He was killed in a plane crash in 1975. In 1993 Damon won three grands prix in a row, in Hungary, Belgium and Italy; in pursuit of the 1994 world title, he won at Silverstone – something his father never achieved.

Hobbs, Sir Jack (1882-1963) English cricketer whose world runscoring record of 61 760 remains unsurpassed. Hobbs played for Surrey and England between 1905 and 1934. He made 199 centuries of which 98 were scored after he had reached the age of 40. He averaged 56.94 in his 61 Tests. He was knighted in 1953, the first professional cricketer to be so honoured.

hockey Fast 11-a-side team game played with curved wooden sticks in which the object is to hit a hard leather ball through the opposing team's 12 ft (3.6 m) wide goal. A hockey stick has one flat side, which must be used to hit the ball. Fouls include raising

the stick above the shoulder when striking the ball and using the stick in any way that might obstruct or endanger an opponent.

horse racing Equestrian sport embracing both flat racing and National Hunt racing in which only thoroughbreds take part. Horses begin to race 'on the flat' as two-year-olds, over distances of between 5 furlongs (1000 m) and 1 mile 2 furlongs (2000 m). Older horses race mainly over distances of between 5 furlongs and 2 miles (3200 m) or more. A race may be a handicap, in which the weight a horse must carry is calculated according to its past form, or a non-handicap, in which the weight carried is based simply on the horse's age and sex.

Hunt, James (1947-93) Flamboyant British motor-racing driver who made his grand prix debut at Monaco in 1973 and, from the number of crashes he had, was known as 'Hunt the Shunt'. In 1975 he won the Dutch Grand Prix and the following year captured the world drivers' championship with six grand prix wins in a McLaren, beating Niki Lauda by a single point. He died in 1993 from a heart attack.

Hutton, Sir Len (1916-90) Cricketer who was opening batsman for Yorkshire and England from 1934 to 1955 and England's first 20th-century professional captain

ELEGANCE AFLOAT AND ASHORE *Crowds line the riverbanks at Henley-on-Thames in 1908 to watch the regatta. It has become a popular event in the English social calendar since it began in 1839.*

in 1951, leading his country in 23 Tests. Hutton scored 364 against Australia at The Oval in 1938, a Test record that stood for 20 years. Under him, England regained the Ashes in 1953 and retained them in Australia in the 1954-5 series. In 79 Tests he scored 6971 runs, averaging 56.67.

ice hockey Fast six-a-side team game played on a 67 yd by 33 yd (61 m by 30 m) ice rink with a goal at each end. The puck – a small hard rubber disc – travels at speeds of up to 100 mph (160 km/h), and players may reach up to 28 mph (45 km/h) on their skates. During a game there are three 20-minute periods of playing time. With regular substitution, players are seldom on the ice for more than two or three minutes at a time, except for the heavily padded and protected goalkeeper.

⚜ A feature of ice hockey is the 'sin bin', a glass pen in which over-aggressive players who have been awarded time penalties are obliged to sit before rejoining the game.

Indianapolis 500 Best-known motor race in the USA, first run in 1911. The 500-mile (805 km) race – one of 16 races in the Indy car series – is held in May at the Indianapolis Motor Speedway, Indiana – a track known as 'the Brickyard' as it was paved in 1909 with 3.2 million bricks. Indy cars are about 50 per cent heavier than Formula 1 cars as they have to sustain average speeds of more than 200 mph (320 km/h).

Jacklin, Tony (1944-   ) British golfer who in 1969 became the first Briton for 18 years to win the Open Championship. In 1970 he took the US Open by seven strokes – the widest winning margin for nearly 50 years. Jacklin gained fresh honours as the non-playing captain of Europe's Ryder Cup team from 1983 to 1989, leading the squad to victory over the USA in 1985 and 1987 – the first on US soil. Again under Jacklin's captaincy, Europe retained the Cup in 1989 after a 14-14 tie.

John, Barry (1945-   ) Brilliant Welsh rugby union fly-half who, in partnership with scrum-half Gareth Edwards, inspired Cardiff, Wales and the British Lions to a series of triumphs in the late 1960s and early 1970s. In 1971 John scored a record 180 points in 16 games with the British Lions in New Zealand, where he earned his nickname, 'the King'.

judo Sport developed from the Japanese martial art of ju-jitsu – the idea of which is to turn an opponent's strength to one's own advantage. Judo means the 'gentle way',

and the aim is to win by throwing an opponent on his or her back or by forcing a submission – or failing that to win on points. Players are graded according to skill by a system of coloured belts, progressing to a series of advanced 'dan' grades, marked by the wearing of black belts.

karate Japanese form of unarmed combat – karate means 'empty hand' – which is also practised as a sport. There are two kinds of competitive karate. 'Kumite' are carefully controlled sparring matches, divided into different weight categories, in which judges award points for attacking moves. In 'kata' events, contestants do not fight each other but are marked for their individual routines, which include kicks, punches and strikes. The first world karate championships were held in Tokyo in 1962.

Khan, Imran (1952-   ) Pakistani all-round cricketer who captained his country 48 times between 1982 and 1992. In 88 Tests he scored 3807 runs and took 362 wickets. His career reached a climax in 1992, when he led Pakistan to victory over England in the World Cup limited-overs tournament. He also played county cricket for Worcestershire (1971-6) and for Sussex (1977-88).

King, Billie Jean (1943-   ) US tennis player who won a record 20 Wimbledon titles between 1961 and 1979 and was a pioneer of the movement to gain more recognition for women's tennis. King developed an aggressive serve-and-volley game which, allied to an unquenchable spirit, brought her 39 grand slam victories, including 12 singles titles, and a world number one ranking five times between 1966 and 1974. In 1970 King became one of the founders of the women's professional tennis tour.

Korbut, Olga (1955-   ) Soviet gymnast who caught the imagination of millions of television viewers around the world with her performances at the 1972 Munich Olympics, when she was 17. She won individual gold medals on the beam and in the floor exercises. Time and again her sparkling routines brought the house down. She was the first gymnast to perform a back somersault on the beam.

lacrosse Team sport in which players catch, carry and pass a ball in a net on the end of a stick called a 'crosse'. Rules for the men's game (10-a-side) and the women's (12-a-side) differ, although the object is the same – to score goals.

⚜ The sport developed in North America in

the 18th century from an Indian game, 'baggataway'. To French travellers, the stick reminded them of a bishop's staff – 'la crosse'.

Laker, Jim (1922-86) English off-spin bowler best known for an achievement unique in first-class cricket: in 1956, he took 19 wickets for England against Australia at Old Trafford. His 9-37 in the first innings was the best Test bowling analysis for 60 years; his 10-53 in their second was the best ever. The same season, while playing for Surrey, Laker had taken all ten wickets in an innings against the Australian tourists. He helped Surrey to win the county championship every year from 1952 to 1958, and later played for Essex (1962-4).

land speed record Fastest speed achieved on land by a manned vehicle. The contest for the land speed record began in 1898, with two drivers outdoing each other until one of them, Camille Jenatzy, a Belgian, reached 65.8 mph (106 km/h) in an electric car. Steam and petrol provided the power for later records, but rocket or jet engines are now used. Over the past 70 years, the record has been fought out

LAUDING THE LION *A forceful batsman and penetrating fast bowler, Imran Khan – known as 'The Lion of Pakistan' – was a pin-up with the ladies, who admired his good looks.*

SMALL WONDER *Olga Korbut, the darling of the 1972 Munich Olympics, began as a gymnast at the age of 11. She retired after winning a team gold medal in the 1976 Olympics.*

between British and American contenders. In October 1983 the British driver Richard Noble roared across the Black Rock Desert in Nevada, USA, to set a new record of 633 mph (1019 km/h) in *Thrust 2*, powered by a Rolls-Royce jet engine.

Lara, Brian (1969-) Trinidadian batsman who set a world individual scoring record in first-class cricket with his 501 not out for Warwickshire against Durham in June 1994 – on his way to another world record of seven centuries in eight innings. In April 1994 the little left-hander had made the highest score in Test history with 375 for the West Indies against England in Antigua.

Lauda, Niki (1949-) Austrian racing driver who won his first world drivers' championship in 1975. A horrifying crash in the 1976 German Grand Prix at the Nurburgring circuit left him trapped in his blazing Ferrari. Lauda suffered severe facial burns, but six weeks after receiving the last rites he was back on the track – and won two more world titles, in 1977 and 1984.

Laver, Rod (1938-) Australian left-handed tennis player who is the only person to have won the grand slam twice. He won his first Wimbledon singles title in 1961, and completed the grand slam in 1962 before turning professional, which excluded him from major tournaments. When the rules of tennis were changed in 1968 to allow amateurs and professionals to compete, he won Wimbledon that year and completed his second grand slam in 1969.

Le Mans Twenty-four-hour race for sports cars held annually at Le Mans in north-west France. Created in 1923 as a test of endurance for standard four-seaters, Le Mans is now dominated by two-seater sports cars, the most powerful of which are faster on the straight than Formula One cars. Each car has two or three drivers who take turns at the wheel as the race progresses through the day and night. The most successful drivers have been Jacky Ickx of Belgium, who won the race six times, and Derek Bell of Britain, who won it five times.

Lenglen, Suzanne (1899-1938) French tennis star regarded by some as the finest lady player ever. Lenglen had a magnetic personality and thrilled the crowds as she leapt about the court like a ballerina. In the seven years from 1919 to 1926 she lost only one singles match, when illness forced her to withdraw. She won 15 Wimbledon titles, including six singles, and the Olympic singles and mixed doubles in 1920.

Lewis, Carl (1961-) US sprinter and long-jumper who has won eight Olympic gold medals – making him one of the most successful athletes of all time. Lewis won four golds at the Los Angeles Olympics in 1984, for the 100 m, 200 m, 4 × 100 m relay and long jump. At Seoul in 1988 he won the 100 m (after Canadian Ben Johnson had been disqualified for using drugs) and the long jump. In the 1991 world championships in Tokyo, he set a world record in the 100 m with 9.86 sec but suffered his first long-jump defeat for more than a decade at the hands of team-mate Mike Powell. Lewis got his revenge at Barcelona in 1992, winning his third long-jump gold, and then his eighth Olympic gold, helping the US 4 × 100 m relay team to a new world record.

Lillee, Dennis (1949-) Australian cricketer widely acknowledged as the finest fast bowler of his generation. Between 1971 and 1984 he took 355 wickets in Test cricket, including 167 against England – the most by any bowler against one country. Lillee was briefly suspended after a Test against Pakistan in 1981 for aggressive behaviour towards the Pakistani captain Javed Miandad.

Lineker, Gary (1960-) English footballer respected as much for his clean conduct and sportsmanship as his supreme ability to score goals. He enjoyed an exemplary career as a striker with Leicester, Everton, Barcelona and Tottenham Hotspur. He won 80 caps for England, 18 as captain, scoring 48 goals – one short of Bobby Charlton's England record. Lineker gave up international football in 1992 to play soccer in Japan, finally retiring in 1994.

SETTING THE STYLE *Suzanne Lenglen shocked people in the 1920s with her daringly short calf-length skirts and fiery temperament. She was also known for the bandanna holding back her hair.*

long jump Track-and-field event performed with a running start about 100 ft (30 m) from the take-off board. If the athlete starts his jump beyond the board then it is disallowed. The men's record for the long jump is held by Mike Powell of America, who jumped 29 ft 4½ in (8.95 m) in Tokyo in August 1991. The long jump was first held in the Greek Olympic Games in 708 BC and was introduced into the modern Olympics in 1896.

Lord's Cricket ground in northwest London which is the headquarters of the ruling bodies of cricket – the MCC (Marylebone Cricket Club), the TCCB (Test and County Cricket Board) and ICC (International Cricket Council) – and also the main home ground of the Middlesex county side. Both the major domestic finals, the Benson and Hedges Cup and the Nat-West Trophy, and one of the annual Test matches between England and a foreign

touring team are played at Lord's – as well as Oxford versus Cambridge and Eton versus Harrow. The ground was opened in 1814 by the entrepreneur Thomas Lord.

Louis, Joe (1914-81) Idolised American boxer who was world heavyweight champion from 1937 to 1949. He held the title for longer than anyone else and was a wonderful ambassador of the sport. The 'Brown Bomber', as Louis was known, became champion at the age of 23, and retired undefeated after defending his title against 25 challengers. He returned to the ring in 1950 at the age of 36, but failed to regain the title.

McEnroe, John (1959-) US tennis star who was one of the most talented and exciting players of modern times. A fast left-hander, McEnroe was particularly admired for his deft and delicate touch play and his extraordinary range and imagin-

ation on court. He reached the Wimbledon semi-finals in 1977, at the age of 18. He won the US title in 1979 and ended Bjorn Borg's Wimbledon supremacy in 1981 to become world No.1, a position he held until 1984. McEnroe won four US Opens and three Wimbledon singles titles, and led the US to four triumphs in the Davis Cup.
McEnroe was notorious for his on-court tantrums. His outbursts included the remarks – directed at linesmen and referee respectively – 'You guys are the pits of the world!' and 'You *cannot* be serious!'

Mansell, Nigel (1953-) British racing driver who finally won the world drivers' championship in 1992, at the age of 38. Mansell began his Formula 1 grand prix career in 1980, driving for Lotus, then Williams and Ferrari. He was championship runner-up in 1986 and 1987, and again in 1991, having rejoined Williams. He made no mistake in 1992, winning a

JUMPING FOR GLORY *US athlete Mike Powell (below) set a new world record with a long jump of 29 ft 4½ in (8.95 m) in Tokyo in 1991. He broke one of the longest-standing athletics records of 29 ft 2½ in (8.90 m) set by fellow American Bob Beamon (left), in Mexico City in 1968.*

YES, I DID CHEAT

DIVINE HELP *Diego Maradona handles the ball past Peter Shilton to put England out of the 1986 World Cup. Maradona later said the goal had been scored by the 'Hand of God'.*

record nine grands prix, including the first five, in his Williams-Renault. In 1993 Mansell came third in his debut in the INDIANAPOLIS 500, and became the first 'rookie', or newcomer, to win the Indy car championship in his first year of participation. In 1994, however, he competed in the French Grand Prix, paving his return to Formula 1 racing.
⚲ For a period in 1993 and 1994, Mansell was the only racing driver in history to hold both the Formula 1 and the Indy car championship titles simultaneously.

Maradona, Diego (1960-) Argentinian footballer who led his country to victory in the 1986 World Cup and was widely acknowledged as the world's most gifted player of the 1980s. A midfielder, Maradona could wriggle through the tightest of defences. He joined Napoli in 1984 for a then world record fee of £6.9 million. In 1991 he was twice arrested for possession of cocaine and suspended from football for 15 months. He made a comeback in 1993 with the Spanish club Sevilla. However, in 1994, while playing for Argentina in the World

Cup, Maradona was barred from the game for another 15 months after testing positive for the banned drug ephedrine.

marathon Longest Olympic running event, contested over a distance of 26 miles 385 yd (42.195 km). Marathons are also held annually in several major cities, including Boston, London and New York. These events have sometimes attracted more than 25 000 runners of all standards, including many who run for charity. The world best times for the marathon for men and women are held by Belayneh Dinsamo of Ethiopia (2 hr 6 min 50 sec) and Ingrid Kristiansen of Norway (2 hr 21 min 6 sec).
⚲ A marathon was introduced in the first modern Olympics in 1896 to commemorate the legendary run of Pheidippides, who brought the news to Athens of the Greek victory over the Persians at Marathon in 490 BC – and then died.

Marciano, Rocky (1923-69) US boxer who was world heavyweight champion from 1952 to 1956. Known for his outstanding stamina and relentless two-fisted slugging, he beat Jersey Joe Walcott for the title in his 43rd fight, and successfully defended it six times. Marciano retired undefeated and died in a plane crash on the day before his 46th birthday.

WINGED WONDER *Stanley Matthews was famed for his ability to leave defenders standing as he dribbled his way past them.*

martial arts Physical skills derived from Asian techniques of armed or unarmed combat. Some martial arts are linked with religious beliefs; others are practised for self-defence or sport. They include JUDO and KARATE, from Japan, and kung fu, from China. Kick boxing and SUMO WRESTLING, often grouped as martial arts, are primarily competitive sports.

Matthews, Sir Stanley (1915-) English footballer who played on the right wing for Stoke and Blackpool and did not retire from top-class football until the age of 50. Nicknamed 'the Wizard of Dribble', Matthews demonstrated superb ball control, speed off the mark and bewildering powers of deception. In a career that spanned four decades (1932-65), he played 54 full internationals for England, rarely scoring, but setting up many goals for others with his perfect crosses.
⚲ Stanley Matthews is particularly remembered for the so-called 'Matthews final' at Wembley in 1953, when he inspired Blackpool to a dramatic winning comeback against Bolton Wanderers to gain his one and only FA Cup winners' medal.

MCC (Marylebone Cricket Club) Governing body of cricket from 1787 to 1969, which, as a private club, remains responsible for the laws of the game. The MCC's headquarters is LORD'S cricket ground in London.

mile Classic middle-distance running race, the Blue Riband of the track, which has survived metrification. A four-lap test of stamina, speed and tactics, the mile race has retained the prestige it acquired after World War II, when breaking the four-minute barrier became the holy grail of athletics. Long after Roger Bannister's historic run in 1954, the four-minute mile was a measure of excellence. New Zealander John Walker was the first to break 3 min 50 sec in 1975, and by the early 1990s the women's world record had been reduced to nearly 4 min 15 sec. The mile is neither an Olympic nor a world championship event.
⚲ The current mile record holder is Nour-redine Morceli, of Algeria, with a time of 3 min 44.39 sec.

modern pentathlon Four-day competition involving five sports: showjumping, épée fencing, pistol shooting, swimming (300 m freestyle) and cross-country running (4 km). Points are awarded for each discipline. The contest – based on the skills needed by a battlefield messenger – was devised for the 1912 Olympics.

WHEELER-DEALERS *According to psychologists, dealing in property when playing Monopoly appeals to the tycoon hidden in everyone.*

Monopoly World's most popular board game in which property is bought and sold, with some players becoming 'rich' and others going 'bankrupt'. It was invented in America in 1932 by Charles Farrow, an unemployed heating equipment salesman. Some 2 million sets are sold each year throughout the world.

Moore, Bobby (1941-93) English footballer who captained England in their 1966 World Cup triumph. A central defender with a great ability to read the game, he was always a move ahead of the opposition. For most of his career he played for West Ham, leading them to victory in the 1964 FA Cup and the 1965 European Cup Winners' Cup. Moore won his first England cap in 1962, and became their youngest ever captain in 1963. In all he won 108 international caps – a record at the time.

Moss, Stirling (1929-) British racing driver whose name became synonymous with the sport even though he never won the world championship title. A dynamic personality and a brilliant driver, Moss won his first grand prix, the British, in a Mercedes, in 1955. He won 16 grands prix in all, finishing second in the world championship four times and third three times. He retired after a serious crash at Goodwood in 1962.

motorcycle racing Chiefly, grand prix racing on motorbikes, but also encompassing motocross, speedway, drag racing and trials. Classes of motorcycle have varied from 50 cc to 1000 cc or above. There are world championships for 125 cc to 500 cc and also for motorcycles with sidecars.

Although no longer a grand prix event, the Isle of Man TT (Tourist Trophy) retains a special place in the sport, and thousands of enthusiasts make the pilgrimage to the island each year to watch or compete in the racing.

National Hunt racing Branch of British professional horse racing for jumpers that takes the form of either steeplechasing or hurdling. Steeplechase fences are formidable barriers, 4½ ft (1.3 m) or more in height, and some have ditches on the take-off side. There are also water-jumps. Hurdles are up to 3 ft 6 in (1.07 m) high and may be knocked over. Horses must be at least three years old to compete over hurdles, and four years old for steeplechasing, and race distances range from 2 miles to 4½ miles (3.2 km to 7.2 km).

Navratilova, Martina (1956-) Czech-born, left-handed tennis player who dominated the women's game for most of the 1980s and won the Wimbledon singles title a record nine times. Navratilova defected to the USA in 1975, won the Wimbledon title in 1978 and 1979, and became a US citizen in 1981. She was ranked No.2 behind Chris Evert for a couple of years, but remoulded her playing style and came back even more strongly. Her all-round game kept her at the top of the rankings for five years, between 1982 and 1986. By 1993 she had won a record 164 singles titles as well as 162 doubles titles. She retired after losing the 1994 Wimbledon final to Conchita Martinez of Spain.

netball Seven-a-side game played mainly by women, indoors or outdoors, on a hard court. The object is to score goals by throwing a large ball through a hoop set 10 ft (3 m) from the ground at each end of the court. The ball is passed by throwing with one or both hands. Players may not take a step while holding the ball, but can pivot on one foot before passing it.

Nicklaus, Jack (1940-) US golfer hailed as the greatest ever player of the game. He won the US Amateur title in 1959 and 1961 before turning professional. In his first pro tournament he beat Arnold Palmer in a play-off for the 1962 US Open. He won a record 18 grand slam tournaments – three Open Championships, six US Masters, five US PGAs and four US Opens.

Nurmi, Paavo (1897-1973) Finnish athlete who dominated middle-distance running in the 1920s, setting 35 world records. The 'Flying Finn', who ran with a stopwatch in his hand, won nine gold medals in three Olympics, over distances ranging from 1500 m to 10 000 m.

OUT OF THE BUNKER *Known as the 'Golden Bear', Jack Nicklaus combined the ability to play his way out of trouble, together with tremendous power off the tee and an unquenchable will to win.*

Olympic Games Held every four years, the modern games were inaugurated in Athens in 1896, at the instigation of Baron Pierre de Coubertin, a French scholar who was inspired by the excavation of the ancient Olympic site – where the games were first held in about 776 BC. In the 1896 games, 311 male contestants from 13 countries took part in nine sports. Almost a century later, in 1992 at Barcelona, nearly 10 000 competitors from 169 nations took part in 257 events. In 1996 the Olympic Games will be held in Atlanta, USA, and in 2000 in Sydney, Australia. The WINTER OLYMPICS are also staged every four years.

♟ The Paralympic Games, international games for the disabled, are now held immediately after the Olympics, usually at the same venue. Men and women – who may be, for example, partially sighted or wheelchair-bound – compete in 18 different sports, including basketball, judo and sailing, against people with disabilities similar to their own. Winners are awarded medals equivalent to those presented at the Olympic Games.

Open Championship One of the world's four grand slam golf championships. Inaugurated at Prestwick on the west coast of Scotland in 1860, when eight players took part, the Open is also the world's oldest such championship. It is played annually at different British seaside courses, over four 18-hole rounds.

orienteering Running sport in which competitors must find the quickest route through woods and rough country. Starting a minute apart, runners armed with a special compass and map have to check in at all the control points marked. There are always several possible routes to the next checkpoint, none of which runs in a straight line. Competitors need good judgment and map-reading skills, as well as the stamina to cover as much as 12½ miles (20 km). The sport originated in Sweden in 1918, and now has its own world championships.

Ovett, Steve (1955-) British athlete who, with Sebastian Coe, enabled Britain to dominate middle-distance running in the late 1970s and early 1980s. He beat Coe at his strongest event, the 800 m, in the 1980 Moscow Olympics, but Coe got his revenge in the 1500 m. In 1980-1 Ovett set world records in the 1500 m and the mile.

GREEK RACE *Athletic events were part of the ancient Greeks' Olympics.*

GREEK GRACE *Throwing the discus was an event in the pentathlon of the Greek Olympics. It was mentioned by the epic poet Homer.*

FAST START *Jesse Owens gets away in the 200 m race in the 'Hitler Olympics' of 1936. He won in the Olympic record time of 20.7 sec.*

Owens, Jesse (1913-80) US athlete whose record-breaking feats at Ann Arbor, Michigan, on May 25, 1935, are unparalleled in the world of sport. In 45 minutes he set five world records and equalled another. First he equalled the 100 yd record of 9.4 sec. He then set a long-jump record that stood for 25 years, with a leap of 26 ft 8¼ in (8.13 m). His last four records were made in two races, the 220 yd sprint and the 220 yd hurdles – his times of 20.3 sec and 22.6 sec also counted as records for the 200 m sprint and 200 m hurdles.

♟ In 1936, at the Berlin Olympics, Owens won four gold medals – for the 100 m and 200 m sprints, the sprint relay and the long jump. At the same time, as a black, he refuted the Nazi theory of Aryan supremacy. As a result, the German chancellor, Adolf Hitler, who attended the Games, allegedly refused to acknowledge him, and left the stadium in a rage.

Palmer, Arnold (1929-) US golfer whose flair and style attracted a massive following, dubbed 'Arnie's army', and who helped make golf one of the fastest growing sports of the 1960s. He won 80 tournaments, including four US Masters, two Open Championships and one US Open. By 1968 Palmer had become the first player to amass earnings of $1 million from golf. He continued to play at the highest level until the late 1980s.

Pelé (1940-) (Real name Edson Arantes do Nascimento) Brazilian footballer who is regarded as the greatest and most popular player of all time. From his explosion onto the world scene as a 17-year-old in the 1958 World Cup in Sweden to his thrilling performances 12 years later in Mexico, Pelé played what he called 'his beautiful game' with infectious joy. In his 18-year career Pelé scored 1281 goals in 1363 games and scored 77 goals in 92 internationals – helping Brazil to win three World Cups.

♟ A plaque in Rio de Janeiro's Maracana stadium commemorates 'the most beautiful goal ever seen'. It was scored by Pelé for his club Santos in March 1961, when he beat every man in the Fluminense team before putting the ball in the net.

pelota Fastest ball game in the world, in which players hit a ball with a scoop-shaped wicker racket, known as a chistera, against any of three walls of a court – at speeds in excess of 187 mph (300 km/h). A version of the game known as jai-alai (pronounced hie-a-lie) is popular in Latin America and the USA.

penalty shoot-out Exciting but ultimately unsatisfactory way of determining the results of soccer matches in competitions where a match is still tied after extra time has been played and there are no provisions for a replay. Five players from each side take alternate penalty kicks at the opposing goalkeeper. If the number of successful kicks is equal, the other players continue taking kicks, one from each side, until one scores and the opponent does not.

Perry, Fred

TITLE BOUND *Fred Perry returns a low shot from Australian Jack Crawford, whom he beat in the Wimbledon final in 1936. Perry started as a table tennis player, and was world champion in 1929.*

Perry, Fred (1909-) British tennis player who won the Wimbledon singles title in three successive years (1934-6), when he was also ranked No.1 in the world. Perry was also the mainstay of Britain's successful DAVIS CUP team from 1933 to 1936, when he turned professional. Among his other triumphs were three US singles titles. After his retirement from play, Perry became a successful tennis commentator.

🎾 Perry was the first, and last, Briton to win the Wimbledon men's singles title since 1909, when A.W. Gore won.

Piggott, Lester (1935-) Doyen of British jockeys who rode his first winner at the age of 12 and was still galloping home ahead of the field 47 years later. Although partial deafness and a speech impediment made him shun publicity, Piggott became popular with the public. He was champion jockey 11 times, first in 1960, and last in 1982. He was nicknamed 'Long Fellow' on account of his being considerably taller than the average jockey, at 5 ft 8 in (1.73 m), and his upright, bottom-in-the-air riding style. Piggott is a master tactician and a shrewd judge of horses. He won a record 29 CLASSICS, including a record nine Derbies, before retiring in 1985 to train horses with his wife Susan. However, he was convicted in 1987 of tax offences and jailed for three years, of which he served one. Piggott returned to the saddle in 1990 and two years later won his 30th classic, the 2000 Guineas, on Rodrigo de Triano.

polo Game played on horseback between teams of four. Riders use long wooden mallets to strike a small white ball into goals at either end of a grass field measuring 300 yd by 200 yd (274 m by 183 m). Of Indian origin, the game gets its name from the Tibetan word for ball, 'pulu'. A full game consists of as many as eight seven-minute periods called 'chukkers'. Special horses called 'polo ponies' are trained for the game. Riders usually change onto fresh ponies between chukkers. Polo is popular in South and North America. In Britain it has traditionally been regarded as a fashionable

PUNTER'S PRIDE *Lester Piggott was first choice when the ladies fancied a flutter. 'I'll back whatever Lester's riding,' they said – earning him the title of the 'housewives' favourite'.*

upper-class occupation. The Prince of Wales remains a keen fan of polo, despite a number of injuries as a player.

pool Any of several games played on a six-pocket billiards table measuring 7 ft by 4 ft (2.1 m by 1.2 m). There are 15 'object' balls – two sets of seven balls, differentiated by colour or numbers, and one black – and a white cue ball that must be struck by the cue. Two players compete, and the first to pocket one set of coloured balls, followed by the black, wins.

professional foul Euphemism commonly used in association football to denote an offence committed deliberately in order to gain an advantage. When a player uses a professional foul to prevent an attempt at goal, he can be sent off.

Prost, Alain (1955-) French racing driver who has triumphed in a record number of grands prix. A shrewd tactician behind the wheel, Prost – known as 'the Professor' – was world drivers' champion in 1985, 1986, 1989 and 1993. By the summer of 1993, he had won 51 grands prix, mostly in a McLaren. After a patchy spell with Ferrari in the early 1990s, he switched to the Williams team in 1993.

Queensberry rules Set of regulations formulated in England in the mid 1860s that transformed prize fighting into the modern sport of boxing. The rules were drawn up by the Amateur Athletic Club and published under the name of the 8th Marquess of Queensberry, a patron of the sport. They banned throwing and wrestling, limited rounds to three minutes, and allowed a fighter ten seconds to get to his feet after being knocked down.

rally Motor race contested in stages on public and closed roads, much of it over rough terrain. Standard road vehicles are strengthened and modified for rally conditions and fitted with a range of special equipment, such as extra lights and light-weight driving seats. Drivers must complete each stage in a set time or lose points. A navigator uses a route map to warn the driver of corners, bumps or inclines. Some rallies last several days, the most famous being the Monte Carlo Rally, first held in 1911. Other major rallies include the Lombard-RAC Rally, in Britain, and the longest annual event, the Safari Rally, in Kenya, which has covered as much as 3874 miles (6234 km). There are world rally championships based on performances in a number of specified events.

Ramsey, Sir Alf (1920-) English footballer and manager who guided England to World Cup triumph in 1966. Ramsey won 32 caps as right-back for England before retiring in 1955, when he became manager of Ipswich Town and helped the side to win the Second and First Division titles in successive years (1961-2). Between 1963 and 1974 Ramsey proved himself the most successful England manager ever, losing just 17 out of 110 matches.

Richards, Sir Gordon (1904-86) British jockey whose many records on the British turf are unlikely ever to be surpassed. He was champion jockey 26 times in a 29-year period (1925-54) and rode 4870 winners in the course of his career. He exceeded an annual total of 200 winners 12 times, including a record 269 in 1947. In 1933 he rode a record 12 consecutive winners. An immensely popular figure, Richards was knighted in 1953. He celebrated by riding Pinza to victory in the Derby – the only big race to have eluded him – before retiring to become a trainer.

Richards, Vivian (1952-) West Indian cricketer who was an exciting batsman and an inspiring captain of his country. He played in 121 Tests, accumulating 8540 runs, with an average of 50.23, to beat Gary Sobers' West Indian record. His best season was against England in 1976, when he scored 829 in only four Tests. During that year he made a world record 1710 Test runs. In England, Richards played for Somerset (1974-86) and later Glamorgan (1990-3). He made his highest score – 322 for Somerset against Warwickshire in 1985 – in just under five hours, becoming the first West Indian to score 300 in a day. 'Viv', holds the record for the highest innings in a one-day game – 189 not out against England at Old Trafford in 1989. From 1980 to 1991 he captained the West Indies to 27 victories in 50 Tests.

Robinson, Sugar Ray (1920-89) US boxer who was possibly the greatest of all time. An all-round fighter, with a devastating punch and brilliant ringcraft, he was world welterweight champion from 1946 until 1950, before moving up to middleweight. He established a record by winning the world middleweight crown on five separate occasions, once after retiring for more than two years. In 1961, at the age of 41, he almost won it for a sixth time, but was held to a draw by Gene Fullmer.
♪ Robinson is particularly remembered in Britain for his two fights against Randolph Turpin in 1951. Two months after their fight in London, which he lost on points, Robinson took on Turpin again in New York, stopping him with a dramatic knockout after looking well beaten.

rodeo Traditional North American sport that developed out of ranching skills in the late 19th century. Rodeo shows include the riding of broncos – wild or half-tamed horses – steer wrestling and bull riding.

roulette Gambling game in which a small metal ball is spun in a horizontal wheel before settling into a section numbered 1-36 (alternately red and black) plus a green zero (there are two zeros in the US game). Players make their bets by placing chips, or counters, on the betting layout, which is a table top marked into numbered sections corresponding to those on the wheel. Odds vary according to the type of bet, of which there are many. For example, long odds (35-1) are given on any one single number, known as 'en plein'; short odds (even money) are given on black or red, on high numbers (19-36), known as 'passe', or low numbers (1-18), known as 'manque'.

rounders English ball game played, with a rounded bat, between two teams, usually of nine players. Members of the batting side successively attempt to hit the ball and reach 'home' by running round all four bases, or posts, without stopping before the ball is retrieved – so scoring a rounder. In contrast to BASEBALL, a game which derived from rounders, a player cannot score by running home on another player's hit.

rowing Each oarsman or woman in a boat, or 'racing shell', rows with one oar or, in the case of sculling, two oars. Competitive events involve coxed boats, in which a lightweight cox steers and controls the pace, or coxless boats, which are steered by a member of the crew operating a rudder with his feet. The number of oarsmen in a boat can be one, in sculling only (singles), two (pairs, or double sculls), four (fours, or quadruple sculls) or eight (eights). Championship races are usually contested over a distance of 2000 m for both men and women. Rowing has been an Olympic sport since 1900, and there are also world championships. Britain's Steve Redgrave has won three Olympic gold medals for rowing; the last two for coxless pairs with Andy Holmes and Matthew Pinsent.
♪ The Oxford and Cambridge Boat Race and HENLEY ROYAL REGATTA are held on the ▷THAMES every year.

rugby league Game created in 1895 when a group of rugby football clubs in the north of England broke away from the amateur world of RUGBY UNION. Among several changes to the rules, the number of players in a team was reduced in 1906 from

SPORT AND LEISURE

DRIVING AMBITION *Finnish rally star Markku Alen and co-driver Ilkka Kivimaki forge through the night in the 1992 Lombard-RAC Rally. Winners in 1988, this time the pair came fourth.*

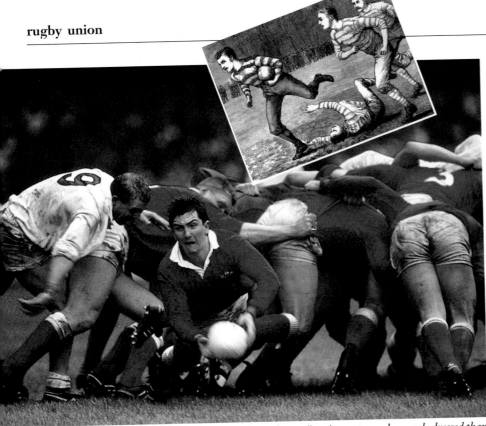

NEW STYLE, OLD STYLE *In Victorian times, rugby players (inset) were more decorously dressed than they are today, but the rough and tumble was just as much a part of the game as it is now.*

15 to 13. A unique feature of rugby league is the play-the-ball rule, which comes into force when a player is tackled while in possession. The tackled player keeps the ball, puts it on the ground and heels it to a team-mate who is positioned behind him. Each side retains the ball for a period of six tackles. If the side in possession has not scored or kicked away the ball when the sixth tackle is made, the opposition restart the game with a play-the-ball at the site of the sixth tackle. A scrum is called when the ball is kicked out of play, or when there has been a 'knock-on'. That is, when the ball has been hit, dropped, or otherwise played with hand or arm, in the direction of the opposition's goal-line. A try is worth four points, a conversion and a penalty goal two each and a drop goal one point.

rugby union Amateur 15-a-side rugby football game. The oval ball may be handled and passed as well as kicked – but it may not be thrown or knocked forwards. A try, when the ball is touched down over the opposing team's goal line, scores five points. A try may be 'converted' for an extra two points if the kick at goal that follows is successful. Three points are given for a penalty goal or drop goal. One of the features of the game is the set scrum, in which the two sets of forwards interlock together against each other, the ball is

thrown in and the opposing 'hookers' try to kick the ball backwards out to their own team. If the ball goes over the touchline, the game is restarted with a 'line-out', when the opposing forwards group themselves into two parallel lines and try to gain possession of the ball when it is thrown back into play. Among the highlights of the rugby union calendar is the annual Five Nations tournament between England, Wales, Scotland, Ireland and France. Teams representing the four 'home' countries – England, Wales, Scotland and Ireland – known as the BRITISH LIONS, play series against Australia, New Zealand and South Africa. The growing popularity of the sport around the world was reflected by the launch of a World Cup series in 1987.

🔊 Rugby union is said to have originated in the early 19th century at Rugby public school in Warwickshire, where during a football match in 1823, a boy named William Webb Ellis picked up the ball and ran with it. It was not until 1871 that the Rugby Football Union was founded, after the FOOTBALL ASSOCIATION had banned the handling of the ball.

Ruth, Babe (George Herman) (1895-1948) US baseball star whose big hitting made him the greatest American sporting hero of the 1920s. Babe Ruth began his baseball career as a highly successful pitcher

in 1914 for the Boston Red Sox, but his hitting steadily improved, and in 1919 he set a major-league home-run record of 29. He signed for the New York Yankees the following year and slugged a stupendous 54 home runs. A left-hander and a fine outfielder, Ruth set record after record with the Yankees. He led the American league in home runs 12 times, achieving his milestone record 60 in 1927, and hit a record 714 'homers' in a 22-year league career.

Ryder Cup Team tournament played every two years between male golfers from Europe and the USA. The trophy was presented in 1927 by British businessman Samuel Ryder for a competition between the professional golfers of Britain and the USA, but in 1979 the British team was expanded to include players from the rest of Europe. The scoring is based on holes won, rather than on strokes taken, with a total of 28 pairs and singles matches played over three days. The US post-war dominance of the Ryder Cup ended in 1985, when Europe won the competition under the captaincy of Tony JACKLIN.

Scrabble Popular board game in which 2-4 players vie to score points by forming interlocking words with lettered tiles on a 225-square board. Invented in 1931 as Criss Cross, it was redesigned and renamed Scrabble in 1948 and marketed in the USA. It came to Britain in 1954.

Seles, Monica (1973-) Serbian-born tennis player who in 1992 briefly overtook Steffi Graf as the world's No.1. A left-hander with double-handed forehand and backhand, she won the French Open in 1990 at 16, becoming the youngest winner of a grand slam tournament. Between 1991 and 1993 she achieved six more grand slam victories, taking her career earnings to nearly $7 million. Seles attributed her defeat by Steffi Graf in the 1992 Wimbledon final to her efforts to curb her habitual on-court 'grunt'. She has not, so far, won the Wimbledon title.

🔊 Seles has not competed since she withdrew from the game when she was stabbed in the back by a male spectator – a fanatical supporter of Steffi Graf – while on court in a tournament in Hamburg in April 1993.

Senna, Ayrton (1960-94) Brazilian racing driver who triumphed in the world drivers' championship in 1988, 1990 and 1991. He was killed in May 1994 when his Williams-Renault crashed at more than 190 mph (305 km/h) at the Imola track in Italy during the San Marino Grand Prix.

Shankly, Bill (1913-81) Liverpool football manager who was idolised by the club's supporters, and led the team to the longest period of supremacy ever enjoyed in the English game. After a distinguished playing career as a half-back with Preston and Scotland, Shankly became manager of Liverpool in 1959 – turning a rather ordinary Second Division team into League champions within five years. He guided the club to two more League championships, two FA Cups and the 1973 UEFA Cup before retiring in 1974.

🎣 'Football's not a matter of life and death.' Shankly once said. 'It's more important than that!'

Shilton, Peter (1949-   ) English footballer who proved himself one of the world's finest goalkeepers. Shilton was apprenticed in 1966 to Leicester City, where he was coached by Gordon Banks, goalkeeper in England's victorious World Cup team. Shilton succeeded Banks at Leicester and later played for Stoke City, Nottingham Forest (where he won League and European Cup medals), Southampton and Derby County. He won his first England cap in 1970, going on to achieve a world record 125 caps before retiring from international football in 1990. Two years later he was appointed player-manager of Plymouth Argyle.

shooting Gun sport that falls into four broad categories – pistol, airgun, rifle and clay-pigeon shooting – involving a variety of weapons and targets. In clay-pigeon shooting, contestants fire at saucer-shaped 'birds' made of a mixture of pitch and chalk. They are released from a spring catapult, called a trap, which varies the angle of flight so that the shooter has to sight the target before firing. The main rifle shooting contest in Britain takes place each July at Bisley Camp, in Surrey, the headquarters of the National Rifle Association.

show jumping Equestrian sport in which competitors jump a number of fences over a set course. Mistakes are penalised by faults, which in some competitions may also be incurred by taking longer than a specified time limit to complete the course. If a horse knocks down any part of a fence or puts a foot in a water jump, it incurs four faults. Refusal to jump a fence incurs three faults, while fall of horse or rider is worth eight. If two or more riders are tied at the end of a round with no faults or the same number of faults, there may be a jump-off to decide the winner, usually over a shortened course and against the clock. The most successful

British riders in the past 30 years have included Pat Smythe, David Broome, Harvey Smith, Nick Skelton and John and Michael Whitaker.

ski jumping Snow sport in which skiers jump from huge ramps and soar through the air before landing, often more than 330 ft (100 m) away. Judges award points for style through the air and on landing, as well as for the distance jumped. Ski poles are not used, and only men take part.

🎣 At the 1988 Winter Olympics at Calgary, Canada, Britain's only ski jumper Eddie 'the Eagle' Edwards achieved a personal best of 255 ft (78 m) – more than 66 ft (20 m) shorter than his rivals. For safety reasons, the International Ski Federation have since introduced strict qualification standards for World Cup and Olympic competitions, which bar inexperienced competitors from top-class events.

ski racing Sport classified as either Alpine or Nordic. Alpine ski racing, first included at the Olympic Games in 1936, embraces slalom and downhill events. Competitors start at intervals and races are decided purely on time. In slalom, skiers speed down a steep mountainside, twisting and turning in and out of as many as 75 gates – pairs of poles bearing coloured pennants. In the downhill competitions, skiers take the

fastest route to the finish. Nordic skiing – which includes SKI JUMPING and langlaufing, formed part of the first Winter Olympics, at Chamonix, France, in 1924. In langlaufing, skiers race across country on long, lightweight skis over distances ranging from 3 to 31 miles (5 to 50 km).

🎣 Freestyle is a form of competitive skiing popularised in the early 1970s which includes 'aerials' (spectacular jumps from special ramps), ballet performed to music (like figure skating on skis) and acrobatics, or 'hot-dogging', on bumpy slopes (moguls).

🎣 The Ski Club of Great Britain was the first Alpine skiing club in the world. It was founded in 1903.

snooker Game played on a standard billiards table with one white cue ball, 15 red balls and six balls of different colours. Players try to strike the white cue ball in such a way that it hits a coloured ball into any of the six pockets. The different coloured balls must be potted alternately with the reds (worth one point). Once potted, red balls remain in the pockets but other colours are returned to their starting spots on the table, until all 15 reds have been potted. Then the colours are potted in sequence: yellow (two points), green (three), brown (four), blue (five), pink (six) and black (seven). A sequence of successful shots is called a break. The highest possible

SNOW GIANT *Italian ski racer Alberto Tomba – nicknamed 'La Bomba' – won the World Cup at slalom and giant slalom in 1988 and 1992, the giant slalom in 1991 and the slalom in 1994.*

score (without a previous foul by an opponent) – for potting all the balls in one break – is 147. The 'frame', or game, ends when all the balls have been potted or one of the players concedes. A 'snooker' is a position in the game in which the cue ball comes to rest in a place where a player cannot hit the coloured object ball or balls directly.

♣ Snooker was devised in 1875 by British Army officers in India, who were tired of playing billiards. The name is thought to have come from 'Snookers', or first-year cadets at London's Royal Military Academy.

Sobers, Sir Gary (Garfield) (1936-) West Indian cricketer who was possibly the best all-rounder in the history of the game. An elegant left-handed batsman, he scored 8032 runs in his 93 Tests – a record at the time – at an average of 57.78. His 365 not-out against Pakistan in 1958 beat Len Hutton's Test record by one run. In turn, this was beaten by the West Indian batsman Brian LARA, with 375 against England in 1994. Sobers was the first player to hit six sixes in an over – for Nottinghamshire against Glamorgan in 1968. He was also a fine left-arm medium-fast bowler, taking 235 Test wickets. He captained the West Indies between 1965 and 1972.

Spitz, Mark (1950-) US swimmer who won an unprecedented seven gold medals at the 1972 Olympics in Munich. His victor-ies, in individual and relay events, were all in world-record times. He had previously won two golds, a silver and a bronze at the 1968 Olympics in Mexico City.

squash Racket game played with a soft rubber ball on an indoor court with four walls. The rackets have smaller heads but longer handles than those used in tennis. The ball is served from special boxes marked on the floor, and only the server can score points. If he or she loses a rally, service goes to the opponent. Players take alternate shots and the ball must hit the front wall before it touches the floor. However, it can hit any of the other walls before or after the front wall. The ball may be played on the volley, but must not be allowed to bounce on the floor more than once. The first player to score nine points wins the game. However, if the score reaches eight-all the receiver of the serve can extend the game to ten points. Matches are played over the best of five games.

Stein, Jock (1922-85) Football manager of Glasgow Celtic and Scotland. He became Celtic manager in 1965, and in 13 seasons guided them to ten Scottish League titles, eight Scottish FA Cups and six League Cups. In 1967 Celtic became the first British club ever to win the European Cup. Stein was manager of Scotland from 1978 to 1985.

Stewart, Jackie (1939-) Scottish racing driver who won 27 grands prix and three world drivers' championships. A former British champion at clay-pigeon shooting, Stewart transferred his interests to the racing circuit in 1960, and after successes in a BRM won his first world championship in a Matra in 1969. He won two more world titles, in 1971 and 1973.

sumo wrestling Traditional Japanese form of wrestling in which two huge contestants grapple together, with the aim of being the first to throw, push, pull, twist or slap the other onto the floor or out of the small ring. Bouts rarely last for more than a few seconds. Professional Japanese wrestlers belong to 'stables', where they train for big tournaments which last 15 days and are held six times a year in Japan.

Super Bowl Contest in AMERICAN FOOTBALL between the champions of the two national leagues: the American Football Conference (AFC) and the National Football Conference (NFC). It was first held in January 1967 in the Los Angeles Coliseum.

FAR-REACHING FINAL *Each January, fans of American football watch the Super Bowl championship live on television across the world.*

RIDING THE WAVE *Blown by the wind, a vast wave threatens to engulf a board surfer who must judge to the split second when to 'cut-out', or leave the wave before it crashes down on top of him.*

surfing Water sport in which participants stand or lie on special boards, using them to 'catch' and 'ride' big waves while performing graceful moves, stunts and other routines. The best surfing beaches are in the Pacific, and the sport is widely practised on the coasts of Australia, California and Hawaii. World championships are held annually. Body surfing, without boards, is particularly popular in Australia.

Surtees, John (1934-) English sportsman who has the unique distinction of having won both the motorcycling and the

SPORT AND LEISURE

motor-racing world championships. Surtees won his first motorcycling title in 1956 at the age of 22, riding in the 500 cc class for MV Agusta. He went on to triumph in both the 350 cc and 500 cc championships in three successive years (1958-60) before retiring from the sport in 1960 to take up motor racing. In 1964 he won the world drivers' title in a Ferrari.

swimming Major Olympic sport, involving a variety of strokes and distances. In freestyle events, swimmers may officially swim any stroke, but in practice they choose the fastest – front crawl. Backstroke, breaststroke and butterfly are the other strokes. All four are used in medley events. Freestyle distances range from 50 m to 1500 m and distances for other strokes from 50 m to 200 m. Swimmers must touch the end of the pool at each turn, and rules govern how a turn should be made. Races are timed to one-thousandth of a second.
⚓In synchronised swimming, the swimmers perform graceful, ballet-like routines

in the pool. There are solo, duet and team competitions, in which synchronisation plays a vital part. Points are awarded according to the degree of difficulty and quality of manoeuvres.

table tennis Game played with small wooden bats and a light celluloid ball on a wooden table measuring 9 ft (2.7 m) by 5 ft (1.5 m) with a 6 in (15 cm) high net across the middle. The aim is to score points by hitting the ball across the net so that an opponent cannot hit it back. Each player has five serves in succession, and the first player to reach 21 points (with a lead of two points) wins a game. In doubles, players must hit the ball alternately. Top-ranking players can retrieve smashes from as far as 20 ft (6 m) behind the table.

tennis World's leading racket sport, played on courts with standard dimensions – 78 ft (23.77 m) long by 27 ft (8.23 m) wide – but on a variety of surfaces, including grass, cement, clay, tarmac and rubber-

MAN MOUNTAIN *The world's heaviest sumo wrestler, 41 st (263 kg) Konishiki – known as the 'Dump Truck' – prepares to take on an opponent. He owes his weight to eating vast quantities of a special high-protein stew.*

ised carpet on most indoor courts. The original surface used for tennis was grass, and the sport is still sometimes called lawn tennis. At the start of each point, the ball is served from behind the baseline into a service court on the other side of the net. The rally then continues until one player fails to return the ball into their opponent's side of the court. On fast surfaces such as grass, the powerful serve-and-volley game is dominant: as soon as a player has served a ball, he or she moves up towards the net to try to volley the return. On slower surfaces, the 'baseline' game, marked by long rallies of groundstrokes, prevails. Matches are divided into sets and games. A set is won by the first player to be two games ahead and win six games. If a set reaches six-all, then a

MAKING A SPLASH *Maltese-born Virginia Elliott (née Leng) – seen taking 'Murphy Himself' through a tricky water-jump at Badminton in 1988 – is one of Britain's greatest three-day eventers.*

tie break is played, unless it is the deciding set, in which case play sometimes continues until one player wins by being two games ahead. A match is usually the best of three sets – although in major events, such as Wimbledon and other grand slam tournaments, men play the best of five.

🔔The tie break operates when the score reaches six games all in any set except, on occasions, the final set of a three or five-set match. The first player to win seven points takes the game and set providing he or she leads by two points. If the score reaches six points all, the game is extended until this margin is achieved.

🔔Real tennis is played on an indoor court and the ball can be played off the roof.

tenpin bowling Indoor game in which players roll a heavy ball down a wooden alley and try to knock over ten upright wooden clubs known as 'pins'. Players have ten frames, or turns, in a game and are allowed two attempts at each frame. If all ten pins fall on the first ball, it is called a 'strike'. If it takes two deliveries to knock down all ten pins, it is called a 'spare'.

🔔Tenpin bowling started in the USA in the 1800s to beat a law banning ninepins, which had become dominated by gamblers.

Thompson, Daley (1958-) British athlete who won the DECATHLON gold medals at the 1980 and 1984 Olympics, and broke the world points record for the event four times. He won the decathlon in the first world athletics championships in 1983, as well as three Commonwealth and two European titles. Plagued by injury later in his career, he retired in 1992 and took up commentating on athletics.

Thorpe, Jim (1888-1953) US athlete, baseball and football star who was one of the greatest ever all-round sportsmen. Part American Indian, part French and Irish, Thorpe won both the DECATHLON and the pentathlon in the 1912 Olympics in Sweden by huge margins. But his record was later expunged and his medals withdrawn for having received a few dollars for playing baseball during a college vacation, thus infringing his amateur status. He played major-league baseball (1913-19) and American football in the 1920s, when he was one of the game's star players.

🔔Thorpe, who died in poverty in 1953, was portrayed by Burt Lancaster in the film *Man of Bronze*. In 1982 his medals were returned to his family and his name was restored to the Olympic champions' roll.

three-day event Demanding equestrian challenge for both horse and rider. Points are awarded in three separate disciplines – DRESSAGE, speed and endurance, and SHOW JUMPING – each contested on separate days. The second stage, called speed and endurance, is divided into four phases: roads and tracks, steeplechase, another round of roads and tracks, and cross-country. It is an Olympic sport and has its own world championships.

Torvill, Jayne (1957-) and Christopher Dean (1958-) British ice dancing pair whose innovation, artistry and perfect harmony on the rink raised the profile of the sport and caught the imagination of a worldwide audience. Torvill and Dean reigned supreme in ice dancing in the early 1980s before turning professional. They won four world championship titles as well as the 1984 Olympic gold medal. In 1994, after the rules had been changed to allow professionals to take part in top-class competitions, Torvill and Dean made a comeback, winning the European championships. Controversially, they only won bronze at the Winter Olympics in Norway.

Tour de France World's best-known cycling race, staged annually over three weeks in summer and covering some 2500 miles (4000 km) of France and parts of neighbouring countries. Every stage is a race in itself, but riders' times for each stage are added together to determine the overall winner. Sponsored riders compete in teams of 12. Team members help each other, especially their top rider or riders. Some, called 'domestiques', carry drinks and help with punctures, as well as acting as pacesetters – they even give up their own bikes to team mates if necessary. The race leader traditionally wears a yellow jersey.

Trueman, Fred (1931-) English fast bowler for Yorkshire and England who, in 1963, became the first man to take 300 wickets in Test cricket. Known as 'Fiery Fred' for his volatile temperament, he made an impact in his first Test season, as a 21-year-old in 1952, taking 29 wickets in four Tests against India, including 8-31 at Old Trafford. At first he relied on sheer pace, but as he matured he cultivated a devastating outswinger (a ball that swings away from the batsman after bouncing). He was also a useful tail-end batsman and once scored 104 for Yorkshire.

Tyson, Mike (1965-) US boxer who, at 20, was the youngest ever man to win a world heavyweight title. He took the heavyweight division by storm and became undisputed world champion in 1987. Tyson – whose neck measurement is a massive 19½ in (49.5 cm) – looked set to be champion for years to come. But his career was affected by the collapse of his marriage to an actress, followed by late-night brawls and arrests. After winning ten world heavyweight title fights, he lost his title in 1990 to the little-known American James 'Buster' Douglas in Tokyo.

In 1992, following a sensational trial, Tyson was sentenced to six years' imprisonment for the rape of an 18-year-old student.

Venables, Terry (1943-) Coach of the England soccer team, who replaced Graham Taylor in January 1994. As a player, he represented England at youth, amateur, under-23 and senior levels. He became manager of Crystal Palace in 1976. In 1984 he was appointed manager of the Spanish club Barcelona, taking them to the final of the 1986 European Cup. Barcelona lost, but Venables' next club, Tottenham Hostpur, won the FA Cup in 1991 under his guidance. England's chances of success in the 1996 European Championship rest on his shoulders.

volleyball Outdoor or indoor team game invented in 1895 to improve the health of out-of-condition US businessmen. Volleyball became an Olympic sport in 1964 and is now played by men and women at all levels. Two six-member teams compete to score points by hitting a large inflated ball over a net into the opposing team's court, so that they cannot return it or are forced to play the ball out of court. After a ball has been served, each team is allowed to hit it three times in the air with their hands or arms before sending it over the net. The first team to reach 15 points wins the set, but they must have a two-point lead or play on until one is established.

Wade, Virginia (1945-) The last British tennis player to win a Wimbledon singles title. Wade took the US singles in 1968 with a 6-4:6-2 victory over Billie-Jean King in the final, and beat Evonne Goolagong (later Evonne Cawley) to win the Australian title in 1972. But it was not until 1977, in the championships' centenary year, that she finally triumphed at Wimbledon beating the Dutch finalist Betty Stove in three sets.

water polo Seven-a-side team game played in a special pool measuring from 65 ft to 100 ft (20 m to 30 m) long and 26 ft to 65 ft (8 m to 20 m) wide, with water at least 3 ft 3 in (1 m) deep. Team members can swim with the ball and pass it to each other with the aim of throwing it into their opponents' goal. Except for the goalkeeper, they may not touch the ball with both hands or punch it, and only the goalkeeper may stand to play the ball.

weightlifting Sport in which participants compete in many different categories according to their bodyweight. There are two main recognised lifts: the snatch, a lift from floor to overhead in one continuous movement; and the clean and jerk, a lift in two stages – first to the shoulders (the clean) and then overhead (the jerk). A contestant may have three attempts. Once the weight on the bar has been increased, no one can attempt a lighter lift.

In 1988 Leonid Taranenko of the former USSR set a clean and jerk record of 586¼ lb (266 kilos).

Wimbledon Tennis club in southwest London that has become synonymous with the All-England Lawn Tennis Championships – the world's most prestigious tennis event. The first championships were held at Wimbledon in 1877. All the singles finals have been played on the centre court, which holds 14 000 spectators. There are 18 grass courts at Wimbledon, and some 20 other courts. The championships are held annually in the last week of June and the first week of July. As well as men's and women's singles, doubles, and mixed doubles, the fortnight includes tournaments for juniors and veterans.

windsurfing Water sport, also known as boardsailing, in which participants stand on a board in the water and steer by tilting a sail. The sail is attached to a small mast, which is connected to the board by a universal joint. There are freestyle windsurfing competitions, in which contestants perform tricks, balances and other

HOT ICE *Jayne Torvill and Christopher Dean put passion into ice dancing with their torrid rendition of Ravel's* Bolero, *which drew record-breaking maximum marks from championship judges.*

manoeuvres. Windsurf racing was introduced into the Olympics in 1984.

🎣 The windsurfing sailboard was invented in 1958 by a 12-year-old English schoolboy, Peter Chilvers.

Winter Olympics International games held separately from the Olympic Games since their inauguration in 1924. Before that, ice skating and ICE HOCKEY had sometimes been included in the summer games. Since 1994 the winter games have been held in the middle of the four-year cycle of the summer games – rather than the winter and summer games being staged in the same year. Major events include SKI JUMPING, figure-skating, speed skating, cross-country skiing and BOBSLEIGHING.

World Cup International association football tournament, first held in 1930, when it was contested by 13 countries and won by the hosts, Uruguay. More than 140 countries now take part in qualifying stages, of which 24 reach the finals. The first round of the finals is played in six groups of four teams, and all the teams within a group play each other. The top two from each group, together with the best four of the others, make up the last 16, and thereafter it becomes a knock-out competition. The first World Cup was the Jules Rimet Trophy, named after the Frenchman who pioneered the tournament. Brazil won the trophy outright in 1970, when they became the first country to win three World Cups. Italy and Germany later achieved the same

feat, and in 1994 Brazil achieved a record fourth World Cup victory. The present trophy is the FIFA World Cup.

🎣 In 1966, when England hosted and won the World Cup, the trophy was stolen and later found in a garden by a dog called Pickles.

world drivers' championship International competition for grand prix racing drivers. The championship was inaugurated in 1950, and the first race was the British Grand Prix at Silverstone. Points are awarded for placings in each of the season's major grands prix: ten for a win, six for second place, four for third, and three, two and one for the minor positions. Juan Manuel Fangio of Argentina won the championship a record five times between 1951 and 1957. Recent winners include Alain Prost of France, Ayrton Senna of Brazil and Nigel Mansell of Britain.

wrestling Group of sports in which two contestants attempt to throw or immobilise each other. Wrestling formed part of the ancient Greek Olympics, and it was one of the original sports in the modern Games. The two Olympic styles are freestyle and Greco-Roman. The main differences between them is that use of the legs and holds below the waist are not allowed in Greco-Roman. There are ten weight categories for each style. Many cultures practise their own form of wrestling, including SUMO in Japan; 'glima' (Iceland), in which wrestlers grasp each other by means of a hip harness; 'yagli' (Turkey), in

which the wrestlers are covered in oil; and 'Cumberland and Westmorland' (northern England), in which each wrestler joins his own hands behind the other's back, and the two contestants try to wrestle each other to the ground from a chest-to-chest clinch. In professional all-in wrestling there are almost no restrictions on the holds.

yacht racing Water sport comprising both 'one-design' events – in which strict rules govern the yachts' shape and sail area – and handicap races for various classes of vessel. Race distances cover anything from a couple of miles in a one-man dinghy to the four-yearly Whitbread Round the World race over a course of some 32 000 nautical miles that takes some six months. Crews, which range from one to a dozen, depending on the size of vessel, work to make the best use of the wind. Yachting has been an Olympic sport since 1900. The first women-only class was introduced in 1988. One of the world's best-known yachting competitions is the AMERICA'S CUP. The Admiral's Cup, an international team event culminating in the Fastnet Race, is held every two years to coincide with the Cowes Week yachting festival in the Isle of Wight.

Zaharias (née Didrikson), Mildred 'Babe' (1911-56) US sportswoman who was possibly the greatest ever all-rounder. In 1932, at the US Women's National Athletics Championships, she alone represented the Employers Casualty Company and won five of the eight events she entered, tying for first in another. This gave her 30 points – enough to win the team championship and beat the 22-woman Illinois team into second place. That year she won the Olympic hurdles and javelin gold medals and was placed second for the high jump. She was also a fine baseball and basketball player. She took up golf in 1934 and reached the top as an amateur and then as a professional.

Zatopek, Emil (1922-　) Czech athlete who was one of the greatest long-distance runners of all time. Between May 1948 and July 1954, he ran 38 races at 10 000 m and won them all, including two Olympic finals. In 1952 he won three Olympic golds: the 5000 m, the 10 000 m and the marathon – a unique treble. Despite an ungainly style on the track, he set 18 world records at distances ranging from 5000 m to 30 000 m. He ran with his arms flailing and head rolling, and a look of agony on his face – as if he might collapse at any moment. However, he was a master tactician who built up his stamina by arduous training.

WORLD-BEATERS *Jubilant English soccer captain Bobby Moore brandishes the World Cup as he is chaired from the field after England's 4-2 victory over West Germany at Wembley Stadium in 1966.*

FOOD AND DRINK

Mealtimes are milestones in the day: they divide it into smaller, manageable periods, and offer a break in routine and a chance to relax. The human race has turned nourishment into an elaborate social ritual and a sensual indulgence. Never before has such a range of foods and drinks from across the world been so widely available. Baklavas, blinis and sushi, tequila, cassis and schnapps are no longer foreign to us.

DETAIL OF A STILL LIFE BY JACOB VAN FOPPENS (c. 1596-1666)

al dente (al DEN-tay) Italian term meaning 'to the tooth'. It is used to describe pasta which is cooked through but remains firm enough to bite. Slightly crisp vegetables may also be described as al dente.

Angostura bitters Reddish-brown spicy tonic mostly used to flavour drinks – for example, pink gins.
🍴 The tonic was originally used as a medicinal cure for fever and was named after the Venezuelan town of Angostura (now Ciudad Bolívar) in which it was invented.

anise Aromatic plant whose liquorice-flavoured seeds, called aniseeds, are used to flavour food as well as drinks such as pastis and OUZO. Its leaves can be used in salads and fish soups. The Asian star anise is an eight-pointed, star-shaped fruit.

antipasto Italian term, meaning 'before the meal', used to describe appetisers.

aquavit Scandinavian clear, alcoholic spirit, served chilled. It is usually made from grain and flavoured with cumin and aniseed or fennel.

Armagnac Dry, golden-brown brandy distilled in Gers, southwest France. It gets its colour from the casks of local oak in which it is matured, sometimes for as long as 40 years. Its process of manufacture is similar to that of COGNAC.
🍴 The age of the spirit is marked on the bottle as three-star or ★★★ (three years old), VO (five to ten years old), or VSOP (up to 15 years); *Hors d'Age* (beyond age) has been aged for at least 25 years.

artichoke The heart and fleshy parts of the leaves of globe artichokes, shaped like large thistle heads, are usually eaten steamed or boiled, with a vinaigrette sauce. Jerusalem artichokes – knobbly tubers with a nutty-flavoured flesh – are often used in soups. Chinese artichokes are similar to Jerusalem artichokes.
🍴 In Japan, red artichoke tubers – which have a purgative effect – are traditionally served to an unwanted guest.

au gratin Dishes served 'au gratin' are usually sprinkled with a mixture of grated cheese and breadcrumbs and are browned under a grill or in the oven until crusty.

bagel Ring-shaped traditional Jewish roll which is boiled for a few seconds before being baked, giving it a slightly chewy texture. Bagels are often filled with smoked salmon and cream cheese.

COLD COLLATION DISHES.

VICTORIAN STANDARDS *Mrs Beeton's* Book of Household Management *was the housewife's bible. Beeton wrote it because she felt that 'there is no more fruitful source of family discontent than a housewife's badly cooked dinners and untidy ways'.*

baklava Greek or Turkish triangular sweet made of alternate layers of thin *filo* pastry, chopped pistachio nuts and almonds mixed with sugar and spices. A boiling syrup of honey, sugar, rose water and lemon juice is poured over after cooking.

béarnaise Creamy sauce made from egg yolks, white wine vinegar and butter, and flavoured with shallots, chervil, tarragon and peppercorns. It is typically served with steak, poached salmon or fresh asparagus.

béchamel White sauce made with butter, flour and milk infused with bay, onion, peppercorns and nutmeg.

Beeton, Mrs (Isabella) (1836-1865) British cookery writer who, during her short life (she died after the birth of her fourth child) wrote the definitive Victorian book on cookery and housekeeping, the *Book of Household Management* (1860).

bhaji Indian savoury dish made from vegetables, herbs – usually including coriander – and spices. Onion bhajis are rolled into balls, covered in flour and deep-fried.

biltong South African strips of dried beef, buffalo, venison, antelope or ostrich.

bisque Thick soup usually made from shellfish, enriched with cream, wine, egg yolks and brandy. The classic bisque is made with lobster.

blanquette White stew made of veal, lamb or chicken in a cream sauce containing onions and, usually, mushrooms.

blini Small leavened pancake made with buckwheat flour and often served with soured cream and CAVIAR.

Bombay duck Small fish found off the west coast of India which are dried on racks in the sun and flavoured with the pungent and garlicky herb asafetida.

borscht Beetroot soup served with soured cream which originated in eastern Europe and is still popular in Russia and Poland.

boudin blanc Delicately spiced French sausage made from finely minced white meat bound with fat and breadcrumbs,

cereal or flour, eggs, cream, milk and spices.
♪ Boudin noir is the French equivalent of a British black pudding.

bouillabaisse (BOO-ya-bess) French soup or stew made with fish stock, fish fillets, vegetables and herbs. This is separated into two courses: as a broth poured over slices of dry, stale bread, and then as a dish of fish and vegetables. Black bouillabaisse contains cuttlefish and its ink.

bourguignon (bor-gin-NY-on) Method of cooking food in red wine, mushrooms, onion, bacon pieces and herbs.

bresaola (brezz-OW-la) Cured reddish-brown beef tenderloin from Italy. It is dried for two months before being sliced very thinly and served with olive oil, lemon juice, black pepper and parsley. A similar dish is carpaccio – thin slices of raw beef.

brochette French equivalent of a KEBAB in which vegetables or meat are threaded on a skewer (a brochette) and then grilled, barbecued or fried.

bulgur Nutty-flavoured 'cracked' wheat – boiled and coarsely dried – which is often used as the basis for TABBOULEH.

calzone Italian savoury, rather like a pasty, made with pizza dough which is folded over a variety of fillings and sealed before being baked.

carob Bean with a sweet pulp which is often used as a chocolate substitute because it has a lower fat content and contains no caffeine.

cassis Sweet blackcurrant liqueur. A small amount of cassis – one part in 20 – mixed with white wine makes Kir; with Champagne it is called Kir Royale.

cassoulet French casserole made with haricot beans and goose, pork or duck.

caviar Ripe eggs of sturgeon. It is typically served from a dish which sits on a bed of crushed ice, and eaten with soured cream on BLINIS or fresh white toast. There are many substitutes, the most common being lumpfish roe which are dyed red or black and are only a fraction of the price.
♪ The most expensive food in the world is beluga caviar from sturgeons, which live mainly in the Caspian and Black seas.

chapatti Unleavened Indian bread made from coarse wholemeal flour, salt and water, and brushed with GHEE.

chicory or endive. White and crisp salad vegetable which has a slightly bitter taste, especially if it is old. Curly endive or *frisée* looks more like a lacy, pale green lettuce. Radicchio is a purple and white chicory.

chocolate Mixture made from roasted and ground cocoa (cacao) seeds and sugar, often with added milk, fruit or nuts.
♪ The percentage of cocoa in chocolate varies from 2 per cent in white chocolate to 70 per cent in dark chocolate.

chorizo Dry Spanish sausage made from cured pork or beef, seasoned with garlic and red pepper. It can be eaten raw, fried, or added to a white bean stew called *fabada*.

chowder Thick soup or stew, usually made with clams, shellfish or fish.

ciabatta (cha-BA-ta) Unleavened Italian white bread, popular for its thick, soft centre, made with olive oil and flour.

cognac Brandy made from the double distillation of white wine. The alcohol from the first distillation is distilled again. It is matured in seasoned oak casks, where it may stay for up to 60 years. Only brandy produced in the area round the town of Cognac, in the Charente region of western France, can be called cognac.
♪ Three-star cognac is aged for between three and five years, VSOP cognac for between five and 15 years and Napoléon for a minimum of 30 years.
♪ Fine champagne is a type of cognac made from grapes from the Champagne region in southwest France.

confit (con-FEE) Meat preserve made by slowly cooking a piece of meat – typically duck – in its own fat. The meat is then covered in the same fat and stored in a sealed pot or jar.

consommé Clear, thin soup made from clarified stock, and served hot or cold.

POPULAR EUROPEAN CHEESES

Brie	France, cow's milk	Flat round, with a white, downy rind and mild-flavoured centre which should be soft, almost runny, when ripe.
Camembert	France, cow's milk	Small, flat round with a soft, white rind. The centre has an earthy flavour, and should be soft but firm when eaten.
Cheddar	England, cow's milk	Hard and golden. It has a smooth taste and should be matured for at least 12 to 18 months.
Chèvre	France, goat's milk	White and crumbly with a white, downy rind and a mild salty and creamy taste. Usually made in small rolls.
Edam	Netherlands, cow's milk	Mild, yellow and firm, made in large ball shape with a red wax rind. A similar cheese, without the rind, is Gouda.
Feta	Greece, goat's, cow's or sheep's milk	Snow-white, crumbly and slightly salty. Very moist, ripened in a mixture of its own whey and brine.
Gorgonzola	Italy, cow's milk	Blue, pale veins with a crinkly, tan rind. It is moist and buttery with a strong and pungent aroma.
Gruyère	Switzerland, cow's milk	Waxy, mild cheese with small holes. Emmenthal – a similar cheese – has much larger holes.
Jarlsberg	Norway, cow's milk	Semi-hard with large holes and a dry rind. It has a nutty, sweet flavour.
Mozzarella	Italy, water-buffalo's or cow's milk	Hand-made fresh cheese, shaped into balls and kept in salted whey or brine. It is soft and white, with a bland milky flavour, and provides the 'stringy' topping for pizzas.
Parmesan	Italy, cow's milk	Rock-hard salty cheese. To enjoy the full, almost spicy flavour of *Parmigiano Reggiano* – Parmesan matured for at least three years – it must be freshly grated.
Ricotta	Italy, cow's or sheep's milk	White and crumbly whey which is low in fat – similar to cottage cheese.
Roquefort	France, sheep's milk	Semi-hard blue cheese which is matured in the damp, cool Combalou caves. It is widely regarded as one of the world's finest cheeses.
Stilton	England, cow's milk	A firm cheese, which can be either white or blue. When ripe, it has a sharp, tangy flavour.

cordon bleu Term used for an outstanding cook or a very high standard of cooking. The term means 'blue ribbon' and was originally the highest order of knighthood in France, the members of which wore a blue sash. The term probably became used in cooking because French cooks often wore an apron with blue ribbons.

coulis Purée of fruit or vegetables which is thin enough to pour.

couscous (cooss-cooss) Type of semolina made from coarsely ground hard wheat rolled into pellets. When soaked or steamed, it swells like rice. It is a staple food in North Africa.

crème fraîche Slightly sharp or sour-tasting thick cream made from cow's milk.

creole The cuisine of the West Indies. Savoury creole dishes of shellfish, salt cod, chicken and pork are typically cooked in a spicy tomato, pepper and onion sauce and served with rice. Sweet creole dishes often use banana or pineapple with rum.

croissant French pastry, made by layering butter with enriched yeast dough. Croissants were first made in Budapest in 1686. Bakers working at night heard Turkish assailants digging underground and gave the alarm. The city was saved and the bakers created the pastry to mark the victory, choosing the crescent shape after the emblem on the Ottoman flag.

crudités Hors d'oeuvre of raw vegetables – for example carrots, cucumber, celery and peppers – sliced or cut into sticks and eaten with dips such as TZATZIKI or HUMMOUS.

Daiquiri Cocktail made with four parts white rum to one part lime juice, a dash of sugar syrup and crushed ice.

dauphinoise (doe-fin-WAHZ) French method of oven-baking thinly sliced potatoes covered with milk or cream. Gratin dauphinoise is made by adding beaten egg and grated cheese to the dish.

dhal Indian word for various kinds of split lentils, beans or other pulses, and the term used to describe their cooked state. Dhal is served seasoned with garlic and spices such as cumin and coriander, and may be puréed.

dolmades (dol-MARD-ez) Minced lamb and rice rolled in vine leaves and cooked in stock, olive oil and lemon juice. It originates from Turkey and Greece.

Dry Martini Cocktail with two parts gin to one of dry vermouth, and a green olive or twist of lemon. The drier the martini, the smaller the proportion of vermouth.

enchilada (EN-chill-ARD-a) Spicy Mexican corn pancake, or TORTILLA, filled with meat, beans or chicken and topped with chilli sauce and cheese.

en croûte A dish cooked in a pastry case. It is a French term, meaning 'in a crust'.

en papillote (on pap-ee-YOT) Method of cooking and serving food in oiled or buttered paper or foil. This seals the food and keeps in all the juices and flavours.

entremets (on-tra-MAY) French term meaning 'between dishes' which is used for dishes served between courses, such as a sorbet or a small salad.

Escoffier, Auguste (1847-1935) French chef who began his career aged 13 in his uncle's restaurant in Nice. He went on to work in Paris and opened the Savoy Hotel in London in 1890, before moving to the Carlton Hotel in 1898. Escoffier invented many recipes, including PEACH MELBA, and wrote several influential books, including *Ma Cuisine* (1934). France awarded him both the Legion and the Officer of Honour in recognition of his work. Escoffier is known as 'the king of chefs and the chef of kings'.

felafel (fell-AFF-ul) A Middle Eastern dish of deep-fried patties made from spiced, crushed beans or chickpeas. Felafel is often served in pitta bread with salad and TAHINI or chilli sauce.

florentine Any dish made, served or garnished with spinach and coated in a Mornay sauce; the name comes from the Florence region, formerly a spinach-growing area. A florentine is also a round, flat biscuit made with dried fruit and nuts, coated on one side with chocolate.

focaccia (fo-CATCH-ee-a) Savoury, soft Italian flat bread made with olive oil and usually topped with garlic and rosemary.

foie gras (FWA-GRA) Goose or duck liver, usually gently poached or braised. Goose foie gras is a creamy white or light pink, while duck foie gras tends to be darker and has a slightly stronger flavour. Both have a very high fat content as birds are force-fed to enlarge the liver artificially. Foie gras is normally served as an hors d'oeuvre.

fondue Swiss speciality prepared at the table. Cheese (usually Gruyère), white wine, kirsch and seasonings are melted in a dish over a spirit lamp. Diners dip cubes of bread into the fondue sauce. In a fondue bourguignonne, cubes of raw meat are cooked in hot oil in the fondue dish and then dipped into sauces such as mustard, horseradish or mayonnaise. Raclette is another melted cheese dish from the Valois canton in Switzerland. Local cheese is grilled until it melts and is then eaten with potatoes, gherkins and pickles.

fricassée (fri-cass-AY) Stew of chicken, veal, lamb or fish in a white sauce containing small onions and mushrooms.

fromage frais Fresh soft cheese made with fermented skimmed milk, which sets like yoghurt. It can be used as a slightly lighter and sharper substitute for cream.

gazpacho Chilled or iced Spanish soup of tomato, cucumber, red peppers, onions, garlic, olive oil and bread.

ghee Clarified butter made from buffalo's or cow's milk and used in Indian cooking. It has a sweet, slightly nutty flavour.

gnocchi (NYOCK-ee) Italian dumplings made from potatoes, semolina or flour, eggs and cheese, served in a tomato sauce.

goulash Rich meat, tomato and onion stew seasoned with paprika. The term derives from the Hungarian *gulyás hus*, meaning 'herdsman's meat'.

grappa Italian clear spirit which is made by distilling what remains of grapes (such as skins, pulp and stalks) after pressing to extract the juice for wine.

gravad lax Scandinavian dish of thinly sliced raw, marinated salmon, traditionally served with a sweet mustard and dill sauce.

guacamole (gwacka-MO-lay) Mexican dish of mashed avocado, tomato and seasoning served with crisp TORTILLAS or as an accompaniment to meat.

gumbo Thick soup from Louisiana made with OKRA and a variety of other ingredients such as ham or fish.

haggis Scottish speciality of sheep's stomach stuffed with oatmeal, onions, fat and spiced sheep's offal. Haggis is boiled and served with mashed turnip or 'neeps' on Burns' Night, January 25.

halva Middle Eastern sweetmeat made from roasted, ground sesame seeds mixed with boiled sugar. It is often flavoured with pistachio nuts, honey or vanilla.

Harvey Wallbanger Cocktail made with one measure of vodka to two measures of fresh orange juice, a dash of Galliano liqueur and crushed ice.

hollandaise Rich sauce of butter, egg yolk and lemon juice served hot or cold with fish, vegetable or egg dishes.

HERBS AND SPICES *Many herbs, used for garnishing dishes as well as for adding flavour, are also valued for their medicinal properties. Almost all recipes call for spices – some as exotic as saffron, others as common as salt and pepper.*

hummous (**WHO-muss**) Middle Eastern purée of chickpeas, TAHINI, garlic, lemon juice and olive oil. It is usually served with PITTA bread or as a dip with crudités.

julienne Fine matchstick strips of vegetables, used as a garnish, sautéed in butter, or served as a salad.

kebab Chunks of meat and sometimes vegetables threaded on a skewer and roasted, grilled or barbecued.
⚘ A doner kebab consists of slices of spit-roasted lamb served in pitta bread with raw onions, chilli sauce and salad.

kedgeree Traditional breakfast dish of flaked fish – usually smoked haddock – rice, hard-boiled eggs and onions.
⚘ The term derives from the Indian rice and

lentil dish called *khichri*. Anglo-Indian chefs adapted this in the 19th century, using fish and eggs instead of lentils.

lamb's lettuce or mâche. Dark green salad leaf with a mild flavour which is often served whole with the root.

macrobiotic Term given to diets for healthy living which consist mainly of grains and vegetables, and sometimes fish. Meat, fruit and alcohol are forbidden.
⚘ This system derives from the Zen Buddhist principle of balancing the feminine (yin) and the masculine (yang).

Margarita Cocktail made with four parts TEQUILA to two parts lemon or lime juice. Traditionally, it should be served chilled with salt around the rim of the glass.

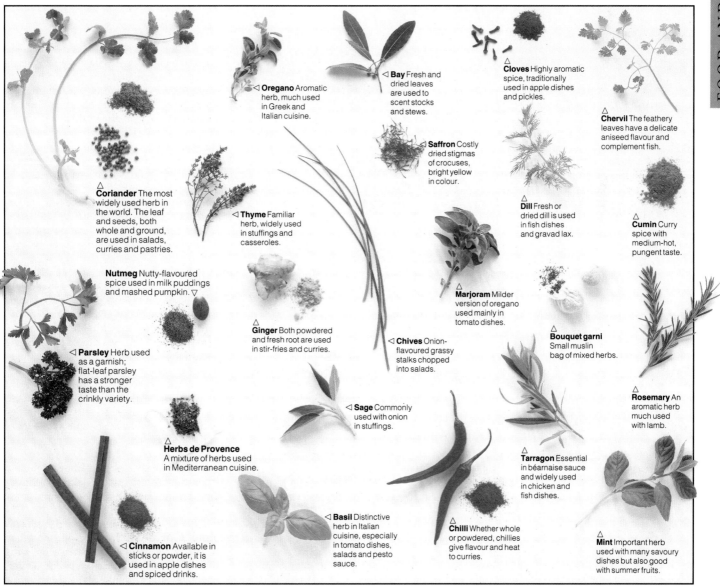

Oregano Aromatic herb, much used in Greek and Italian cuisine.

Bay Fresh and dried leaves are used to scent stocks and stews.

Saffron Costly dried stigmas of crocuses, bright yellow in colour.

Cloves Highly aromatic spice, traditionally used in apple dishes and pickles.

Chervil The feathery leaves have a delicate aniseed flavour and complement fish.

Coriander The most widely used herb in the world. The leaf and seeds, both whole and ground, are used in salads, curries and pastries.

Thyme Familiar herb, widely used in stuffings and casseroles.

Dill Fresh or dried dill is used in fish dishes and gravad lax.

Cumin Curry spice with medium-hot, pungent taste.

Nutmeg Nutty-flavoured spice used in milk puddings and mashed pumpkin.

Ginger Both powdered and fresh root are used in stir-fries and curries.

Marjoram Milder version of oregano used mainly in tomato dishes.

Chives Onion-flavoured grassy stalks chopped into salads.

Bouquet garni Small muslin bag of mixed herbs.

Parsley Herb used as a garnish; flat-leaf parsley has a stronger taste than the crinkly variety.

Sage Commonly used with onion in stuffings.

Rosemary An aromatic herb much used with lamb.

Herbs de Provence A mixture of herbs used in Mediterranean cuisine.

Tarragon Essential in béarnaise sauce and widely used in chicken and fish dishes.

Cinnamon Available in sticks or powder, it is used in apple dishes and spiced drinks.

Basil Distinctive herb in Italian cuisine, especially in tomato dishes, salads and pesto sauce.

Chilli Whether whole or powdered, chillies give flavour and heat to curries.

Mint Important herb used with many savoury dishes but also good with summer fruits.

meze or mezze (**mezz-AY**) Selection of spiced hors d'oeuvre traditionally served with OUZO or raki in Greece or Turkey. Meze often include DOLMADES, olives and dried meats.
♣Meze is Turkish for a 'small bite'.

mushrooms Apart from familiar flat and button mushrooms, other cultivated varieties include shiitake, an oriental mushroom used in stir-fries, and oyster mushrooms, which have a slight shellfish flavour. Wild mushrooms and fungi are generally more expensive and highly flavoured. They include: perfumed, golden trumpet-shaped chanterelles; spongy, meaty ceps; sweet, strong morels; and expensive, intensely earthy walnut-sized TRUFFLES.

nan Leavened Indian flatbread cooked in a charcoal or *tandoori* oven. Nan is traditionally teardrop-shaped and served with curry.

niçoise Dishes from Nice or the surrounding region in southeast France and typically made with tomatoes, olives, anchovies, garlic and green beans.

noisette French word, meaning 'little nut', used to describe small, boned lamb steaks, usually tied with string.

okra or ladies' fingers. Green vegetable resembling a small, ridged chilli pepper in appearance, but with a soft, seeded centre and bland flavour.

osso bucco Italian stew made from unboned knuckle of veal, tomatoes and onions. It is usually served with pasta or rice and *gremolata* – a mixture of citrus peel, garlic, parsley and spices.

ouzo Greek aniseed-flavoured clear spirit which becomes milky when water is added to it. It is traditionally served with MEZE.

paella Spanish dish of rice, shellfish, chicken and vegetables flavoured with saffron and cooked in a flat pan or *paellara*. Ingredients vary according to the region.

panettone (pan-eh-TOE-nee) Traditional Italian Christmas sweet bread, shaped like a rounded pyramid with the top sliced off. It has a very light texture, and contains egg yolks and mixed fruit.

pastrami Highly seasoned smoked beef which is traditionally thinly sliced and eaten on rye bread. The word comes from the Yiddish word *pastra*, meaning 'preserve'.

peach melba Dessert invented by the French chef ESCOFFIER which is made with poached peach halves and vanilla ice cream, covered with sweetened raspberry purée, sometimes sprinkled with sliced almonds.
♣The dish was named after Dame Nellie Melba, the celebrated Australian soprano.

pesto Italian sauce made from basil, garlic, pine nuts, Parmesan cheese and olive oil, which is served with pasta. A French version called *pistou* can be added to soups.

pilaf or pilau. Eastern method of cooking rice. The rice is browned with spices before stock and vegetables are added. The rice is covered and cooked slowly without stirring until it has absorbed all the liquid.

Pina Colada A sweet creamy cocktail usually made with three parts white rum, four parts pineapple juice and two parts coconut milk, with a dash of sugar syrup.

VERSATILE PASTA *The best pasta is made from durum wheat and water, sometimes with added egg, spinach or other colourings and flavourings. It is available fresh or dried, in a wide variety of shapes.*

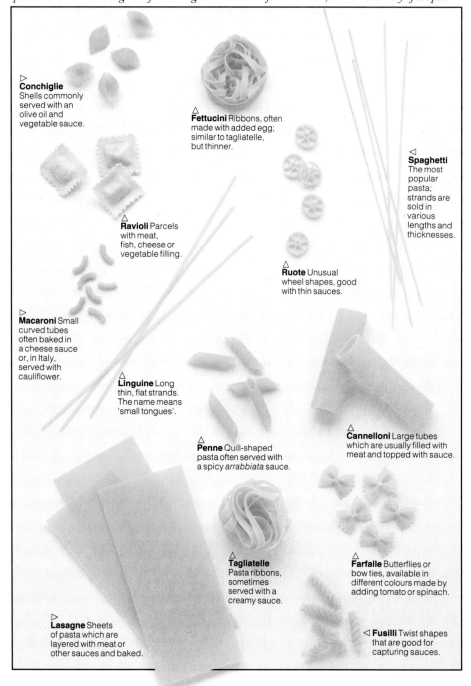

Conchiglie Shells commonly served with an olive oil and vegetable sauce.

Fettucini Ribbons, often made with added egg; similar to tagliatelle, but thinner.

Spaghetti The most popular pasta; strands are sold in various lengths and thicknesses.

Ravioli Parcels with meat, fish, cheese or vegetable filling.

Ruote Unusual wheel shapes, good with thin sauces.

Macaroni Small curved tubes often baked in a cheese sauce or, in Italy, served with cauliflower.

Linguine Long thin, flat strands. The name means 'small tongues'.

Penne Quill-shaped pasta often served with a spicy *arrabbiata* sauce.

Cannelloni Large tubes which are usually filled with meat and topped with sauce.

Tagliatelle Pasta ribbons, sometimes served with a creamy sauce.

Farfalle Butterflies or bow ties, available in different colours made by adding tomato or spinach.

Lasagne Sheets of pasta which are layered with meat or other sauces and baked.

Fusilli Twist shapes that are good for capturing sauces.

pitta Flat, slightly leavened bread which originated in the Middle East. It is chewy and faintly sweet, and can be slit open after heating to take a variety of fillings.

polenta Italian cornmeal which can be boiled and served soft, like semolina, or baked into a firm cake which can be served plain or topped with a sauce.

pot-au-feu Traditional French stew flavoured with aromatic herbs which can be served in two parts: as a soup (the broth) and then as a main dish (the meat).

pretzel Dry, crusty traditional German bread, typically hard-baked in the shape of knots, salted and served as a snack.

prosciutto (**pro-SHOOT-oh**) Italian cured ham which is matured for eight months to two years. The most famous is Parma ham, often sliced very thinly and served with fresh melon or green figs.

quenelle Dumpling made with spiced meat or fish bound with egg whites and cream, beaten egg or butter and flour. This mixture is then shaped and poached in water. Quenelles are often served AU GRATIN, with sauces or in soups.

rillettes (**ree-YET**) Coarse pâté made from cooked fish, meat or poultry. It is usually served as an hors d'oeuvre.

risotto Italian dish made by gently frying onions and *arborio* or 'risotto' rice in butter and gradually stirring in stock and any other ingredients until the rice is cooked and can absorb no more liquid.

rocket or arugula. Green salad leaves shaped rather like those of the dandelion and having a clean, peppery flavour.

samosa Indian savoury of deep-fried triangular filo pastry pockets filled with a mixture of spiced beans or chickpeas, potato or meat, herbs and vegetables.

sashimi Japanese dish of thinly sliced raw fish, often served with pickles, soy sauce and horseradish paste. (Compare SUSHI.)

satay Malaysian or Indonesian dish of grilled spiced meat skewered on wooden sticks, usually served with a peanut sauce.

sauerkraut German dish of shredded cabbage preserved by being layered with salt and allowed to ferment. It is often served hot with potatoes and meats.

schnapps Strong German spirit similar to AQUAVIT. It is made from a wide variety of fruit and should be served ice-cold.
In Germany, schnapps refers to almost any strong spirit. It means 'snatch' or 'gasp' – which evokes the manner in which it should be drunk and the subsequent effect.

Screwdriver Cocktail of two parts gin or vodka and one part orange juice. If gin is used, a dash of sugar should be added.

Singapore Sling Cocktail made with three parts gin to one part cherry brandy, the juice of a lemon or lime, water, sugar, fresh mint and a slice of orange.

smorgasbord Scandinavian savoury selection of hot or cold dishes served either as an hors d'oeuvre or a full buffet meal.

squash Group of vegetables of the gourd family which includes the courgette, vegetable marrow, pumpkin and butternut. They can be sautéed, boiled, stuffed, steamed, puréed or used in soups.

sushi Japanese savoury delicacy which usually consists of seaweed rounds filled with seasoned rice and raw fish or shellfish, served with pickled ginger and a type of horseradish paste.

sweetbreads Culinary term for the thymus gland and the pancreas of pigs, lambs or calves. These are typically blanched and then fried in butter.

tabbouleh Middle Eastern cold dish of steamed BULGUR wheat mixed with mint, parsley, tomatoes, onions and lemon.

taco Mexican dish of fried TORTILLAS filled with meat or beans with GUACAMOLE, black-bean or chilli sauce.

tahini or tahina. Thick sesame seed paste used in Greek and Lebanese cooking, and an important ingredient in HUMMOUS.

tapas Spanish selection of savoury hors d'oeuvre, which might typically include potato omelette, smoked sausage, spinach with pine nuts, garlic, chickpeas, olives, grilled prawns and fried calamares (squid).

tapenade Salty purée of black olives, anchovies, capers, lemon juice and garlic often used in pasta sauces.

taramasalata Greek speciality; a pale pink purée made from smoked cod's roe, blended with olive oil and lemon juice.

tequila Mexican spirit made from the pulp of the tequila plant. It is often used in cocktails, but is also served as a 'short' which is traditionally knocked back in one gulp after sucking a slice of lime or lemon and putting a pinch of salt on the tongue.

teriyaki Japanese style of cooking. Fish or meat is marinated in soya sauce and rice wine and then grilled over charcoal.

terrine Any food cooked in a terrine – a deep earthenware dish with a tight-fitting lid. Terrines are most commonly used to make pâté. They are usually placed in a *bain-marie*, or large pan of hot water, in the oven, which gently cooks the contents.

tiramisu Layered Italian dessert consisting of sponge flavoured with coffee and Marsala wine, or rum and brandy and creamy, soft mascarpone cheese.

tofu or bean curd. White purée of soya beans which is set solid. It has little taste but absorbs other flavours and can be used in creamy puddings or stir-fries. Tofu is high in protein and is eaten by many vegetarians, as well as being a staple food in Japan and other east Asian countries.

tortilla (**tor-TEE-yah**) Thin cornmeal pancake used in South America to make TACOS, tostadas (deep-fried flavoured crisps), and ENCHILADAS.

truffles Walnut-sized and highly valued fungi with an unmistakable scent which grow underground on the roots of some trees. There are three types of edible truffle in Europe: the White Winter, the Black Winter (or Perigord) and the Black Summer. White truffles, the best of which come from Alba in northwest Italy, are the most expensive.
Truffles are located by pigs or trained dogs which sniff them out.

tzatziki Greek dip made with thick yoghurt, cucumber, garlic and herbs and served with pitta bread or crudités.

vichyssoise (**vee-shee-SWARZ**) French soup made with leeks, potatoes, chicken stock and cream, usually served chilled.

vinegar Oxidised beer (malt vinegar), wine or cider which is used as a condiment, in salad dressings (vinaigrettes) and in sauces. It is often flavoured with herbs, garlic, fruit or chilli. The most expensive is the rich and dark balsamic vinegar, which should be matured for at least ten years.

vitello tonnato Classic Italian dish consisting of cold poached veal with a caper, tuna fish and anchovy sauce.

whisky Spirit made by distilling fermented grain, such as barley and wheat. It is the main spirit produced in Scotland and in Ireland, where it is spelt 'whiskey'. A single malt is the product of a single distillate; most brands are blended. Popular American whiskeys include Rye (distilled from rye) and Bourbon, which has to have at least 51 per cent maize, and which gets its dark colour from the oak barrels in which it is aged.
🔑 The word whisky comes from the Gaelic *uisge beatha*, meaning 'water of life'.

wild rice Long purplish-black grain of a North American aquatic grass, often served as an accompaniment or in salads.

wok Large Chinese steel frying pan with a rounded bottom and a domed lid, used for stir-frying, deep-frying and steaming.

zabaglione (za-bah-lee-OWN-eh) A light, Italian dessert made by whisking together egg yolks, sugar and Marsala wine in a bowl resting over a pan of simmering water.

zucchini Another word for courgette.

THE LANGUAGE OF WINE

Appellation Contrôlée or Appellation d'Origine Contrôlée, often shortened to AC or AOC. Term on the label of French wines indicating that the wine comes from a specific area and only uses permissible grape varieties. The equivalent initials in other countries are DOC and DOCG in Italy; DO in Spain; and DTW, QbA and QmP in Germany.

Bordeaux Red Bordeaux, made from a blend of the Cabernet Sauvignon, Cabernet Franc and Merlot grape varieties, fall into four main types: Médoc, Pomerol, St Émilion and Graves – which can also be white. Most white Bordeaux, such as Sauternes, are made chiefly from Sauvignon and Sémillon grapes. In Britain, red Bordeaux is called claret.

Burgundy French wine-producing area where red Burgundies are made from the Pinot Noir grape, except for Beaujolais which is made from Gamay. Chardonnay grapes are used for white Burgundies. The six areas of Burgundy are Chablis, Côtes de Nuits, Côtes de Beaune, Côte Chalonnaise, Mâconnais and Beaujolais.

Cabernet Sauvignon Black grape of the best Bordeaux and New World red wines, with a blackcurrant and cedarwood aroma.

PRINCIPAL WINE REGIONS OF FRANCE *The distinct flavours of French wine-producing areas have inspired many great New World wines.*

Champagne Making Champagne in the vineyards around Rheims and Épernay by the traditional méthode champenoise involves a second fermentation in the bottle, the daily turning of the bottles with the neck downwards, and the freezing and expelling of wine in the neck, where the sediment has collected. The clear wine is then topped up with wine and sugar before the bottle is corked. The amount of sugar determines the wine's sweetness: Doux is the sweetest, followed by Demi Sec, Sec, Extra and Brut – the driest. Champagne bottles are named according to the number of normal-sized bottles they contain: a magnum (two); a jeroboam (four); a methuselah (eight); a balthazar (16); and a nebuchadnezzar (20).

Chardonnay White grape used for Burgundy, Champagne and many of the New World's white wines – which are often aged in oak to give them a distinctive bouquet.

corked A wine obviously tainted by a loose or decaying cork.

cru French for 'growth' or crop, used in wine classification. Best are premier cru wines, followed by cru classé and cru bourgeois.

cuvée French term for a batch of unblended wine produced at the same time, or with grapes from the same vineyard.

Eiswein Sweet German 'ice wine' made with grapes picked and pressed after the frost has frozen them on the vine, thereby reducing their water content.

en primeur French term for a very young wine, synonymous with the Beaujolais description 'nouveau'.

Gewürztraminer German grape with an aroma of elderflowers or lychees.

Hock English name for white wines from the German Rhine.

Merlot Important grape variety used in red Bordeaux wines as well as Italian, east European and New World wines.

Muscat White grape variety mainly of Alsace and the Languedoc region of France, where it is used to make dry or sweet fruity wines with an intense grapey aroma. In Italy, Muscat is used to make Asti Spumante.

New World Wine from Australia, New Zealand, the Americas and South Africa.

noble rot Fungus which, when introduced during fermentation, produces the honeyed sweetness of several sweet white wines such as Sauternes and Auslese.

non-vintage Wine with no mention of the year of production on its label, often because it is a blend of different vintages.

pétillant French term for wine that is slightly sparkling, due to induced or accidental second fermentation in the bottle.

Pinot Noir Black Burgundy grape, now grown worldwide. Pinot Blanc is the white version of the grape.

Riesling Classic white grape used in German and some European white wines.

rosé Pink wine, usually made from the white juice of red grapes which gets its colour from 'sitting' on the dark skins for a while. Americans often refer to rosé as blush.

Sauvignon Blanc White grape with an aroma of grass or gooseberries, used mainly in dry white wines.

Sémillon Grape used in sweet white wines, or blended with Chardonnay for drier wines.

spumante Italian for 'sparkling', as in Asti Spumante or Martini Spumante.

Syrah Red grape with a peppery aroma, used to make Côtes du Rhône. In the New World it is called Shiraz.

ullage Gap in a bottle between the wine and cork. An ullaged bottle may have an ill-fitting cork, unless it is very old.

Zinfandel Californian grape used in full, heavy reds, as well as in white and rosé wines.

PLACES AND LANDSCAPES
OF BRITAIN

No country in the world is richer than Britain in its patchwork of natural beauty. No country of a similar size can offer a richer heritage of landscapes and buildings where history has been made and left its enduring mark. Hills, moors and river valleys shaped over millions of years are dotted with towns and villages, castles and stately homes, each with a story to tell of human endeavour over the centuries.

CHATSWORTH, DERBYSHIRE

Aberdeen Third largest city in Scotland, lying on the east coast at the mouth of the River Dee. It is known as the 'Granite City' as the local stone is used in many of its buildings. In the early 14th century Robert ▷BRUCE fought rivals there for the Scottish throne. Aberdeen is Scotland's largest fishing port, and since the North Sea oil boom began in the 1970s it has been the main supply centre for the industry.

Aberfan Village on the River Taff in Mid Glamorgan, South Wales. In 1966, mining waste from a giant tip which overlooked the village engulfed part of Aberfan – 144 people, including 116 schoolchildren, died.

Abergavenny Welsh market town on the River Usk in Gwent. It has a labyrinth of narrow streets containing Tudor buildings. Abergavenny is a base for exploring the BRECON BEACONS which lie to its west.

Aberystwyth Welsh seaside resort, on Dyfed's west coast. The first college of the University of Wales was founded there in 1872. The town is also home to the National Library of Wales. Among the library's 3 million volumes is the 12th-century *Black Book of Carmarthen*, the oldest known Welsh manuscript.

Aldeburgh (ALD-bruh) Suffolk resort and yachting centre. The composer Benjamin ▷BRITTEN was one of the founders of the Aldeburgh Festival of Music, which has taken place at the nearby Snape Maltings Concert Hall every June since 1948. Britten's opera *Peter Grimes* is set in the town.

Aldermaston Village in Berkshire and the site of the Atomic Weapons Establishment where research was carried out for Britain's H-bomb. The first H-bomb was tested in 1957 and protest marches between London and Aldermaston, led by the Campaign for Nuclear Disarmament, were organised between 1958 and 1963.

Alnwick (AN-ick) Northumberland town on the River Aln, that was once a vital stronghold against the Scots. The Percy family, first earls, then dukes of Northumberland, ruled much of northern England throughout the Middle Ages from 11th-century Alnwick Castle. In the 19th century the Percy family restored the castle's interior in Renaissance style.

Althorp Ancestral home of the Princess of Wales, in Northamptonshire. The house has belonged to the Spencer family since it was built in 1508.

Alton Towers Britain's best-known leisure park, with a 'white-knuckle' corkscrew rollercoaster and more than 100 other amusements. It is situated in Staffordshire, on the former estate of the earls of Shrewsbury, and includes landscaped gardens and a house which, when completed in the 19th century, was the largest private house in Europe. Most of the house is now a ruin but parts of it have been restored and are open to the public.

Anglesey Low-lying island off the northwestern coast of Wales, linked to the mainland by two imposing bridges over the Menai Strait. Anglesey has been a centre of Celtic culture since ancient times. In the 1st century AD the island was the site of a fierce stand by the druids against Roman invaders. A handsome 13th-century castle built by Edward I still stands in the resort of BEAUMARIS. A causeway links Holy Island to the west coast of Anglesey.

Arbroath Scottish holiday resort and east-coast fishing port in Tayside known for its 'smokies' – haddock smoked over wood-chip fires. The red sandstone ruins of Arbroath Abbey date from 1178. In the abbey the Declaration of Arbroath, asserting Scotland's independence from England, was made in 1320.

Arran Scottish island in the Firth of Clyde, with rugged mountains rising to 2866 ft (873 m) at Goat Fell. It is often called 'Scotland in miniature' for its variety of rocks, hills, glens and lochs. The island covers 200 sq miles (518 km^2) and attracts many tourists, walkers and geologists.
🔔Arran is well known for its knitwear, made of thick creamy-coloured wool in complex cable and patterned designs.

Arthur's Seat Extinct volcano and public park in EDINBURGH. A dramatic landmark, it stands 823 ft (251 m) high and offers a panoramic view of the city.
🔔The name has no connection with King Arthur, but may be connected with the 6th-century Prince Arthur of Strathclyde.

Ashbourne Derbyshire market town in the PEAK DISTRICT. Annually, at Shrovetide, the inhabitants play football across the town, between goals 3 miles (5 km) apart. Ashbourne is also known for its gingerbread and for its mineral water.

Avebury Stone Circle Biggest prehistoric stone circle in the world, ringing a Wiltshire village of thatch and brick. The sandstone blocks, brought from the nearby Marlborough Downs, were raised in about 2400 BC. The circle originally consisted of some 180 stones set in an outer ring and two inner rings and surrounded by a bank and ditch. Only 49 stones survive above ground today. The function of the monument is a mystery, but fertility rites or cult ceremonies may have taken place there.

SILENT SENTINELS *Avebury may have been a ritual centre for local farmers 4000 years ago. In the Middle Ages many of its stones were broken up by villagers, who feared their pagan associations.*

🔔About 1 mile (1.6 km) south of Avebury is Silbury Hill, a huge man-made mound 130 ft (40 m) high. It is at least 2700 years old, but its purpose is unknown.

Aviemore Scottish winter sports resort in the Highland Region, between the Monadhliath and Cairngorm Mountains. Recreations include skiing, ice-skating, curling, golf and water sports. Aviemore is also a base for walks in the Spey Valley.

Avon County in southwest England, created in 1974 and named after its principal river. It borders the River Severn estuary and incorporates the cities of BATH and BRISTOL. Avonmouth is a major port and WESTON-SUPER-MARE a seaside resort.

Avon, River Name of several English rivers – *avon* is Celtic for 'river'. The longest is the Avon that rises near Naseby, Northamptonshire, and flows for 96 miles (154 km) via Stratford-upon-Avon to join the River Severn near Tewkesbury in Gloucestershire. Another Avon rises near Tetbury in Gloucestershire to flow for 75 miles (120 km) through Bath and Bristol to the Severn estuary at Avonmouth.

Axminster Small market town on the River Axe in Devon, where the high-quality, hand-tufted carpets originated in 1755.
🔔Bells in Axminster's church used to be rung to signal that a carpet was finished.

Ayr Scottish port in Strathclyde Region, overlooking the Firth of Clyde. The town is closely associated with Scotland's national poet, Robert ▷BURNS, who was born 3 miles (5 km) away at Alloway. Burns mementos are displayed in the Tam O'Shanter Museum. Ayr has several miles of sandy beaches, and is a popular holiday resort.

Badminton Village of the southern Cotswolds, in Avon. Badminton House – home of the dukes of Beaufort since 1682 – is where the game of ▷BADMINTON is said to have originated in the 1870s. Three-day event horse trials are held each May.

Baker Street London street and home of Sir Arthur Conan Doyle's 19th-century fictional private detective Sherlock Holmes. His address, No. 221B, was fictitious, and the supposed site is now occupied by the Abbey National building society.

Bakewell Market town in Derbyshire, on the River Wye at the heart of the Peak District. Bakewell tarts, known locally as Bakewell puddings, were first made there by a cook at the Rutland Arms who mistakenly spread egg mixture, intended for pastry, on top of a strawberry tart.

Balmoral Scottish country home of the royal family, situated in the Grampian Region. It lies among wooded hills by the River Dee and has formal and landscaped gardens. Prince Albert paid £31 000 for the castle in 1852. Using grey granite quarried on the estate, he had it rebuilt in the grand Scottish Baronial style, with distinctive pepperpot turrets. Crathie Church, where the royal family worships, faces the bridge leading to the castle's main entrance.

original market cross was destroyed in 1602, and the present one is Victorian.
🔔Banbury cakes – spiced dried fruit in flaky pastry – date from the 16th century.

Bangor University and cathedral city in Gwynedd, on the northwest coast of Wales. A Celtic monastery was founded there in AD 525, 70 years before St Augustine brought Christianity to Canterbury. Bangor Cathedral dates from the 13th century.
🔔The Bishop's Garden, near the cathedral, includes a Biblical Garden that contained every plant mentioned in the Bible that can survive in the Welsh climate.

ROYAL DEESIDE *The colourful splash of Balmoral's formal gardens contrasts with the brooding mountain backdrop of the castle where Queen Victoria said 'all seemed to breathe freedom and peace'.*

Bamburgh (BAM-bruh) Northumberland village which is dominated by a 12th-century castle on a crag 150 ft (45 m) above the North Sea. Roman ▷POLANSKI directed his film of *Macbeth* there in 1972.
🔔In 1838, Grace Darling became a national heroine when she rowed out with her father, keeper of the lighthouse on nearby Longstone Island, to rescue nine men from the wrecked steamship *Forfarshire*.

Banbury North Oxfordshire market town made famous by the nursery rhyme 'Ride a cock horse, to Banbury Cross'. The

Barrow-in-Furness Cumbrian town on a peninsula jutting into Morecambe Bay. The town grew up around 12th-century Furness Abbey, whose red sandstone ruins still stand. Barrow prospered as an industrial centre in the Victorian age, and by 1870 it had the world's largest steelworks. Many of Britain's nuclear submarines were built in the dockyards, and shipbuilding and engineering remain important industries.

Bass Rock Scottish islet in the mouth of the Firth of Forth, in Lothian Region. It is the core of a former volcano, and its sheer sides rise 350 ft (106 m) above the water. Bass Rock is noted for its colonies of sea birds including gannets, puffins, fulmars, guillemots and kittiwakes.

Bath City in Avon renowned for its Roman Baths and Georgian architecture. The baths still receive hot spring water through Roman plumbing which visitors can sample in the Pump Room. The city, built within a loop of the River Avon, became fashionable when the dandy Richard 'Beau' Nash (1674-1762), as master of ceremonies, brought members of London's high society to enjoy the baths, balls and concerts. The 18th-century architects John Wood the Elder and his son John Wood the Younger made the city a showpiece of Georgian architecture: the Royal Crescent was the world's first crescent, and one house has been restored and furnished to re-create its 18th-century appearance. Bath Abbey, begun in 1499, is a fine example of the ▷PERPENDICULAR style; its tower is 162 ft (50 m) high, and carved angels climb ladders to heaven on the west front.
🥄 Bath buns, invented in the city, are sweet, sticky buns containing currants and spices. The Sally Lunn, also made in Bath, is a muffin-like tea cake.
🥄 Bath Oliver biscuits were invented by Dr William Oliver (1695-1764), who also founded the Royal Mineral Water Hospital in Bath and specialised in treating gout.

Beachy Head Dramatic chalk headland in East Sussex, which at 534 ft (163 m) above sea level is one of the south coast's highest cliffs. Beachy Head is a noted vantage point, and its vertical drop makes it a popular site for hang-gliding. It has also been the scene of many suicides.
🥄 The name of Beachy Head derives from the French *Beau Chef*, 'beautiful headland'.

Beaulieu (BEW-ly) Hampshire village at the head of the River Beaulieu. At Palace House, Lord Montagu's National Motor Museum houses a collection of more than 200 historic vehicles. The nearby village of Bucklers Hard was a busy naval shipyard in the 18th century, and the Bucklers Hard Maritime Museum re-creates its past with life-size effigies in vivid tableaux.

Beaumaris Resort and sailing centre on the coast of Anglesey. Its imposing, moated 13th-century castle is the last of eight castles built by Edward I in north Wales.

Bedford County town of Bedfordshire on the Great Ouse river. John Bunyan (1628-88) wrote *The Pilgrim's Progress* while imprisoned in Bedford County Jail for his Nonconformist religious beliefs.

Benbecula Tiny island between North and South Uist in the Outer HEBRIDES. In 1746, Bonnie Prince Charlie escaped from the English by rowing a boat from Benbecula to the Isle of SKYE, disguised as Flora MacDonald's maid. The island is used by the army as a site for testing missiles.

Ben Macdui Scottish mountain which at 4300 ft (1310 m) is the highest in the CAIRNGORMS. Ben is the Scottish term for mountain, from the Gaelic, *beann*, 'peak'.
🥄 Having been told that Ben Macdui was the highest mountain in Britain, Queen Victoria rode a donkey to its summit in 1847. It was later shown that Ben Nevis was higher: the queen was not amused.

REFLECTED GLORY *In 500 million years, the weather has flattened the peak of Ben Nevis. However, it remains Britain's highest summit.*

Ben Nevis Britain's highest mountain, rising to 4406 ft (1343 m) in the Lochaber district of Scotland's Highland Region. A 5 mile (8 km) footpath, starting near Fort William, leads to the summit.
🥄 The annual, gruelling, Ben Nevis race in early August dates from 1895 when a local hairdresser ran from Fort William to the top of the ben and back.

Berkeley, Vale of Valley between the Cotswold Hills and the River Severn, in Avon and Gloucestershire. Berkeley Castle contains the cell where Edward II was murdered in 1327. The Slimbridge Wildfowl and Wetlands Trust, founded by Sir Peter Scott in 1946, is also in the valley.

Berkshire Agricultural county in southern England, often known as Royal Berkshire because it includes WINDSOR, with its royal castle. Other towns include Reading, the county town, and Slough.
🥄 Sir John ▷BETJEMAN wrote the poem *Slough*, deriding the ugliness of the town.

Berwick-upon-Tweed Historic border town at the mouth of the River Tweed, which has changed hands between England and Scotland 13 times. Elizabethan walls

SPA FOR ALL CENTURIES *A majestic sweep of 30 houses, fronted by graceful Ionic columns, makes Bath's 18th-century Royal Crescent one of the most elegant streets in Britain. The Classical style recalls Bath's heyday under the Romans, into whose Great Bath (left) hot spring water still bubbles through the original Roman plumbing.*

still encircle the town, which has elegant Georgian streets and squares. Three bridges span the River Tweed: the early 17th-century Berwick Bridge, with its 15 arches, Robert Stephenson's Royal Border Bridge built to carry the railway in 1850, and the Royal Tweed road bridge of 1928.

Betws-y-Coed Welsh town and holiday resort, in Snowdonia, Gwynedd. The vale of the River Conwy, the Fairy Glen, the Conwy Falls and the Swallow Falls are noted local beauty spots. Betws-y-Coed means 'house of prayer in the wood'.

Beverley Market town in Humberside known for its spectacular 13th-century minster, which is larger than many cathedrals and one of the finest Gothic buildings in Europe. A 14th-century church stands at the other end of the main street.

Biggin Hill Kent village, southeast of London, known for its ▷BATTLE OF BRITAIN airfield. A chapel records the 453 pilots stationed there who died in the war.

Billingsgate Site on the north bank of the Thames by London Bridge, well known as a fish market from the 16th century. Billingsgate porters carried fish boxes on their leather hats, and were notorious for their coarse language. The market was moved to West India Dock in 1982.

Birmingham Second largest city in Britain, situated in the West Midlands, in the heart of England. In the 19th century, its factories and many thriving small businesses made Birmingham 'the workshop of the world', producing everything from pennibs to steam engines. The National Exhibition Centre (NEC) was opened in 1976, and the International Convention Centre (ICC), which opened in 1991, houses Symphony Hall – home to the City of Birmingham Symphony Orchestra (CBSO). In 1990 the Sadler's Wells Royal Ballet moved to Birmingham and is now known as the Birmingham Royal Ballet. The city has two universities.

Black Country Industrial area of the West Midlands, extending north of Birmingham; Wolverhampton is sometimes called its 'capital'. The name derives from the soot and grime produced by numerous mines and factories in the 19th century.

Blackheath Residential area of southeastern Greater London which surrounds an open common – the remnant of a once-extensive heathland where the rebel

Wat Tyler rallied his peasant army in 1381. The heath afterwards became notorious as the haunt of highwaymen.

Black Mountains Mountain range in Powys, south Wales which rises to 2660 ft (811 m) at Waun Fach. The Black Mountains lie mainly at the eastern end of the Brecon Beacons National Park, almost on the border with England. From a distance they appear black and lacking in vegetation.
🔱 Black Mountain is the name for a separate range of peaks at the western end of the Brecon Beacons.

Blackpool Seaside resort in Lancashire, whose 7 mile (11 km) promenade is dominated by the 518 ft (158 m) high Blackpool Tower – modelled on the Eiffel Tower in Paris. The town has three piers and is noted for its Pleasure Beach and the autumn illuminations which line a stretch of the promenade known as the Golden Mile.

Blenheim Palace Country seat of the dukes of Marlborough, outside Woodstock in Oxfordshire. Queen Anne had the palace built for John Churchill, the first Duke of Marlborough, in gratitude for his victory over the French at the Battle of Blenheim in 1704. The baroque palace was designed by Sir John ▷VANBRUGH and completed in 1722. In 1764 'Capability' ▷BROWN dammed the River Glyme to create a lake in the landscaped park.
🔱 In 1874, Blenheim Palace was the birthplace of Winston Churchill, a descendant of the 1st Duke of Marlborough.

Bletchley Park Country house in Buckinghamshire, and the site of the top-secret Government Code and Cypher School (GC&CS), predecessor to GCHQ at Cheltenham, during World War II. It was there that cipher experts cracked the secrets of the 'Enigma' coding machine, used by the Germans for sending messages to and from commanders in the field. Some 10 000 people worked at the centre in conditions of strict security. Their activities, which produced intelligence code-named 'Ultra', were not made public until 1974.

Bodmin Moor Granite upland in Cornwall, rising to 1375 ft (419 m) at Brown Willy. Tors and prehistoric remains scatter the moorland. Jamaica Inn at Bolventor was the setting for the novel of the same name by Daphne du Maurier.
🔱 At Dozmary Pool, near Bolventor, ▷KING ARTHUR is said to have received his magical sword Excalibur from the Lady of the Lake, who was Merlin's mistress.

Bognor Regis Seaside resort in West Sussex where George V went to convalesce after a serious illness in 1929, and granted the town its title of 'Regis' (Royal).
🔱 George V's dying words, to a courtier who suggested he might one day be well enough to return to Bognor Regis, were reputed to be 'Bugger Bognor'. However, the king's official last words were reported as 'How is the Empire?'

Bournemouth Seaside resort on Poole Bay, Dorset, noted for its mild climate, sandy beach and cliff ravines, or chines. There are fine coastal views.
🔱 In many of his Wessex novels, Thomas Hardy referred to Bournemouth as Sandbourne, 'a Mediterranean lounging place on the English Channel'.

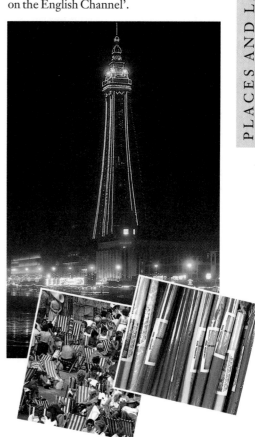

SEEING THE SIGHTS *A lift whisks Blackpool visitors to a bird's eye view of the town and its closely packed seaside amusements and delights.*

Bournville Suburb of Birmingham in the West Midlands, and the headquarters of the Cadbury chocolate and cocoa firm since 1879. Bournville model factory and village were created by a Quaker businessman, George Cadbury, the company's owner. The design was an early example of a garden city and influenced later town planning.

Braemar Scottish village in the Grampian Region, known for the Royal Highland Gathering held on the first Saturday of September and usually attended by members of the royal family. Traditional events include athletics, piping and caber tossing.

Brecon Beacons Mountains in south Wales, rising to 2907 ft (886 m) at Pen y Fan in Powys. The Brecon Beacons National Park covers 519 sq miles (1344 km²) and is popular with walkers.

Brighton Seaside resort in East Sussex. The popularity of sea bathing and the patronage of the Prince Regent, later George IV, from 1793 transformed the fishing village of Brighthelmstone into the fashionable resort nicknamed London-by-the-Sea. The prince commissioned the Royal Pavilion, an extravagant oriental style building designed by John ▷NASH, who also built Brighton's elegant Regency terraces lining the seafront. Today, narrow streets known as 'The Lanes' are lined with antique shops. Brighton has a yachting marina, a long promenade and two piers, although one is now derelict.
⚓ Brighton's Grand Hotel was bombed by the IRA during the Conservative Party's 1984 annual conference. The bomb, meant to murder Margaret Thatcher and her cabinet, killed three people, including Sir Anthony Berry MP and the wife of John Wakeham, the government's chief whip.

Bristol City and administrative centre of Avon, on the River Avon 7 miles (11 km) from its mouth on the Bristol Channel. From Norman times Bristol was one of Britain's major ports; in the 18th and 19th centuries it prospered through trade with America, including traffic in slaves. The city has art galleries and museums, a 12th century cathedral and the Theatre Royal – home of the Bristol Old Vic. Much of the former dock area has been redeveloped for housing and leisure, and there are nuclear and aeronautical engineering works. The docks house the SS *Great Britain*, built by Isambard Kingdom ▷BRUNEL in 1843. Brunel's Clifton Suspension Bridge crosses the Avon Gorge in a 702 ft (214 m) span; it was completed in 1864.
⚓ Bristol's docks have an extreme tidal range. Sailing ships moored there had to tidy away spars and rigging to stop damage occurring as the tide fell. Hence the phrase 'all shipshape and Bristol fashion'.
⚓ The phrase 'to pay on the nail', meaning to pay promptly, derives from bronze pillars or 'nails' on which transactions were made outside the Bristol Corn Exchange.

BY THE SEA *Brighton's Victorian visitors poured onto a new Palace Pier; its domes and pinnacles were designed to echo those of the Royal Pavilion which had been completed 70 years earlier. The quest for a souvenir started the trend of sending seaside postcards.*

Broadmoor High security hospital for mentally ill patients at Crowthorne in Berkshire. Inmates have included Peter Sutcliffe, 'the Yorkshire Ripper', and Ronnie Kray, one of the gangland twins.

Broads, The Low-lying area in East Anglia, comprising more than 30 shallow lakes which spread out from the rivers Yare, Bure and Waveney; they are now known to be the result of medieval peat diggings. The area, also known as the Norfolk Broads, is a popular sailing centre and a nature reserve. The five major broads are Wroxham, Barton, Hickling, Ormesby and Filby.

Broadstairs Seaside resort in Kent where Charles Dickens wrote *David Copperfield* while staying at Bleak House – now the Dickens and Maritime Centre. An annual Dickens Festival is held in the town in June.

Buckingham Palace Official London residence of the British sovereign, and the scene of investitures, garden parties and state banquets. The original house was built in 1702-5 by the Duke of Buckingham, bought by George III in 1762 for £28 000 and later remodelled by John Nash as a palace for George IV.
⚓ The state rooms of the palace were opened to the public in 1993, to raise funds for repairs to Windsor Castle after it was badly damaged by fire in 1992.

DUSK OVER CALM WATERS *The reed-fringed Norfolk Broads are linked with slow-moving rivers to form some 200 miles (320 km) of waterways, a paradise for the small-boat sailor and the naturalist.*

Burghley House Country mansion in Cambridgeshire, and one of the grandest surviving Elizabethan houses in Britain. It was built between 1553 and 1588 by Sir William Cecil, Elizabeth I's chief minister, who later became Lord Burghley. The house is noted for its carved woodwork, painted ceilings, furniture and paintings.
⚓The ground plan of Burghley House is in the form of an 'E', a tribute to Elizabeth I.

Bury St Edmunds Market town in Suffolk which owes its name to the Saxon king St Edmund, whose remains were brought there after he was martyred by the Danes in AD 869. Ruins of an abbey built around St Edmund's shrine 200 years later include a Norman tower and 14th-century gate.

Buxton Derbyshire spa town and resort overlooking the River Wye in the Peak District. Its warm mineral waters, popular in Roman times, prompted the 5th Duke of Devonshire to develop the town as a spa in the 18th century. Buxton mineral water is still sold today. The town has a small but attractive opera house which hosts an annual classical music festival.

Cairngorms Scottish mountain range spanning Highland and Grampian regions and including AVIEMORE, the winter sports resort. Its highest point is BEN MACDUI.

Cambridge University city on the River Cam, and the administrative centre of Cambridgeshire. The first university college was Peterhouse, founded in 1284 by the Bishop of Ely; the most recent, Robinson, opened in 1979. King's College has a magnificent chapel, completed in 1515 in ▷PERPENDICULAR style. Lawns known as The Backs slope down to the river.

Canterbury City in Kent, on the River Stour. Its cathedral – the seat of the archbishop and primate of the Anglican Church – was begun in the 11th century, although its central tower, known as 'Bell Harry', was not completed until 1505.
⚓Thomas ▷BECKET was murdered in the cathedral in 1170, and his shrine became one of Christendom's principal centres of pilgrimage. He was canonised in 1173.

Cardiff Seaport at the mouth of the River Taff in South Glamorgan, which has been the capital of Wales since 1955. The Normans built a fort there, and parts of Cardiff Castle date from that period. Cardiff was a modest market town until the coal and iron industry developed in the 19th century – by 1900 it produced more coal than any other

city in the world. The Civic Centre built in the early 1900s contains some of Europe's finest neo-Classical buildings. The coal industry has declined, but the city's docks still handle general cargo.
⚓The national stadium, Cardiff Arms Park, is home to the Welsh rugby team.

Castle Combe One of the prettiest villages in England, near Chippenham in Wiltshire, where former weavers' cottages of Cotswold stone line the main street. The village was transformed to look like a port for the film of *Dr Dolittle*. A motor racing circuit lies at the edge of the village.

Castle Howard Palatial mansion in North Yorkshire. It was begun in 1699 in baroque style to the design of Sir John ▷VANBRUGH. A 70 ft (21 m) dome crowns the central block. The house stands in parklands which include formal gardens, lakes, a mausoleum and a temple.
⚓Castle Howard was used as a set for the television series ▷BRIDESHEAD REVISITED.

Cerne Abbas Small village in Dorset renowned for the chalk figure known as the Cerne Abbas Giant cut into a nearby hillside. The 180 ft (55 m) high figure depicts a naked man holding a club, and is thought to be a 5th-century pagan fertility symbol.

Chartwell Country house near Westerham in Kent which was Sir Winston Churchill's country home from 1924 until his death in 1965. The house contains items associated with his life and career.

Chatsworth One of England's grandest stately homes, situated in Derbyshire and the seat of the dukes of Devonshire. Begun in 1687, it has been much altered over the centuries. The gardens are noted for the dramatic 17th-century Cascade – a staircase of water flowing down a hillside.

Cheddar Gorge Scenic pass through the Mendip Hills in Somerset. The limestone cliffs rising to 450 ft (137 m) above the road were probably cut by a stream which now

ACROSS THE BRIDGE *When 'Capability' Brown landscaped the 1000-acre (450 ha) grounds of Chatsworth he diverted the River Derwent to pass within view of the Duke of Devonshire's home.*

runs underground. Caves filled with stalactites and stalagmites are a tourist attraction, and the area is a centre for pot-holing.
⚓ Cheddar cheese was first produced in the village of Cheddar in the 17th century.

Chelsea Residential district on the north bank of the River Thames, southwest London, centred on King's Road. The area has long been associated with literary and artistic circles as well as with fashion. The Chelsea Royal Hospital, built by Sir Christopher Wren, is home to about 420 retired soldiers, known as Chelsea Pensioners, who wear distinctive uniforms of scarlet in summer and navy blue in winter.
⚓ The Chelsea Flower Show is held in the grounds of the Royal Hospital every May.

Cheltenham Elegant spa town on the River Chelt in Gloucestershire. The springs that made it fashionable in the early 18th century still flow at the Pittville Pump Room. The town is best known for its Ladies' College, its annual music and literature festivals, and its racecourse, where the Cheltenham Gold Cup has taken place every March since 1924, except in the years 1943 and 1944 during World War II.

Chequers Mansion in Buckinghamshire, built in the 16th century. Given to the nation by Lord Lee of Fareham in 1917, it has been the official country home of the British prime minister since Lloyd George took up residence in 1921.

Chester City on the River Dee, and county town of Cheshire. It was founded by the Romans as Deva in the 1st century AD. By medieval times it had become a walled city; the walls survive and can be walked. Two-storey shopping galleries, known as The Rows, date from medieval times.
⚓ The Chester cycle of religious mystery plays, dating from Middle Ages, is still performed every five years; the next performance will be in 1997.

Cheviot Hills Range of chalk and clay hills in Northumberland, which extends along the England-Scotland border and rises to 2677 ft (816 m) at The Cheviot.

Chichester County town of West Sussex. Its layout follows the original Roman plan: four straight streets cut the city into quarters and meet at the 16th-century market cross. The town has a Norman cathedral, and parts of the medieval city walls survive. The Festival Theatre holds an annual summer season of drama. To the west lies FISHBOURNE ROMAN PALACE.

Chilterns Range of chalk hills in southern England, running northeast from the River Thames at Goring Gap in Berkshire to the Bedfordshire-Hertfordshire border. Much of the Chilterns are covered with beech woods, and the highest point is Coombe Hill at 852 ft (260 m).
⚓ A British MP who wishes to resign from the House of Commons may by tradition apply for the stewardship of the ▷CHILTERN HUNDREDS.

City of London Commercial and financial centre of the capital, lying on the north bank of the River Thames. The area – known as the Square Mile – is bounded by the Roman wall which once enclosed Londinium. The Bank of England, founded in 1694, is sited there, together with the Stock Exchange and the headquarters of many banks, stockbroking companies and other financial institutions. Mansion House, the official residence of the lord mayor of London, is also in the City. St Paul's Cathedral and the Tower of London are two of the City's outstanding landmarks.
⚓ Medieval street names recall the six Roman gates which led into the City: Cripplegate, Ludgate, Newgate, Aldgate, Aldersgate and Bishopsgate.

Cliveden Country house in Buckinghamshire, overlooking a wooded stretch of the River Thames known as Cliveden Reach. The Italianate mansion was built in the 1850s by Sir Charles Barry for the 2nd Duke of Sutherland, who later sold it to the millionaire Astor family.
⚓ In the early 1960s Cliveden was associated with the ▷PROFUMO AFFAIR.

Clwyd County in northeast Wales, bordered by England to the east. Dairy farming is an activity in the valleys of the rivers Clwyd and Dee. Much of the terrain is rugged sheep pastureland, the hills rising to 2265 ft (690 m) at Foel Wen. Castles at Chirk, Ewloe, Rhuddlan and Denbigh recall the turbulent medieval period when the borderlands were fiercely contested between the Welsh and the English. The county town is Mold.

Colchester Town on the River Colne in Essex which claims to be the oldest in England. In the 1st century BC it was the capital of the ancient British ruler Cunobelinus – the inspiration for Shakespeare's Cymbeline, and also said to be the 'Old King Cole' of the nursery rhyme. The later Roman town Camulodunum was burned down by ▷BOUDICCA in AD 60; relics are displayed in the Norman Colchester

Castle. Oysters have been cultivated here for centuries, and there is an annual Oyster Feast in October.

Conwy Welsh market town, on the estuary of the River Conwy in Gwynedd. Conwy is an outstanding medieval walled town, overlooked by a 13th-century castle. There are fine Elizabethan and Georgian buildings, and a quayside cottage only 6 ft (1.8 m) wide, said to be the smallest house in Britain. Thomas Telford's suspension bridge, completed in 1826, and Robert Stephenson's tubular railway bridge of 1848, both cross the river at Conwy.

Cornwall County noted for its warm climate and dramatic coastline, which ends at the granite cliffs of Land's End – the southwestern tip of the British mainland. East of the rugged BODMIN MOOR, the River Tamar forms the border between Cornwall and Devon. Truro is the county town, and PENZANCE is a popular resort.
⚓ Cornish pasties – semicircular sealed pies containing meat, potato, swede and onion – were first made for tin miners in the 18th century. The miners held them by the edge to prevent any poisons from the tin getting onto the main part of the pasties.
⚓ The sovereign's eldest son inherits the Duchy of Cornwall, consisting of lands mostly in Cornwall, Devon and Somerset.

Cotswold Hills Range of rolling limestone hills which cuts across Gloucestershire. Cotswold stone gives local buildings their attractive warm, golden hue.

Covent Garden Area in central London surrounding a large piazza which for more than 300 years housed the capital's main fruit, vegetable and flower market. The original piazza was designed by Inigo ▷JONES in the 1630s. In 1974 the market moved south of the Thames and shops, cafés and restaurants now occupy the central market buildings.
⚓ The nearby Royal Opera House is referred to as 'Covent Garden'.

Coventry Industrial city in the West Midlands which was devastated by German bombs in World War II. The new cathedral, consecrated in 1962, houses Graham ▷SUTHERLAND's immense *Christ in Glory* tapestry, and a cross made from charred roof beams of the bombed 14th-century cathedral. Local industries include car and motorcycle manufacturing.
⚓ The expression 'sent to Coventry', meaning that a person is ostracised, dates from the English Civil War when Royalist

prisoners were sent to be held in Coventry.
♣According to legend, Lady ▷GODIVA
rode naked through Coventry on a white
horse to secure a promise from her husband
that he would cut taxes for the local people.

Cowes Resort on the Isle of Wight, at
the mouth of the River Medina. A yachting club was founded there in 1815, and
an international regatta, Cowes Week, is
held annually in August.

Darlington Market town in County
Durham, northeast England. Britain's first
stretch of railway, from Stockton-on-Tees
to Darlington, opened in 1825, and the
steam train which made the 10 mile (16 km)
trip – George Stephenson's *Locomotion* – is
in the town's Railway Museum.

Dartmoor Moorland and National Park
in Devon, where ponies roam. Dartmoor
prison opened in 1809 at Princetown.
♣Yellowmead Down on Dartmoor was the
setting for Sir Arthur Conan Doyle's *The
Hound of the Baskervilles*.

Dartmouth Port and holiday resort on
the estuary of the River Dart, Devon. A
15th-century castle overlooks the harbour
mouth. North of the town is the Britannia
Royal Naval College, which since 1905 has
trained naval cadets including George V,
George VI and Prince Charles. Dartmouth
Museum recalls the area's maritime history.

Dee, River Name of several British rivers
– *dee* is an Old English word meaning
'river'. The longest River Dee runs through
the Grampian Region of Scotland.

Derbyshire County in north central
England which encompasses the PEAK DIS-
TRICT National Park. Porcelain known as
Derbyware or Crown Derby has been
manufactured in the city of Derby since the
18th century. The county town is Derby.

Devil's Dyke Deep V-shaped hollow on
the downs above Brighton, East Sussex.
According to legend, the Devil dug the
dyke in an attempt to flood the Weald with
the English Channel and drown all its
churches. However, the Devil fled when he
mistook an old lady's candle for sunrise.

Devon County in southwest England
which incorporates DARTMOOR and parts
of EXMOOR. Devon's scenic beauty and
mild climate attract many tourists; Torquay
is the main holiday resort and EXETER the
county town. Devon is well known for its
dairy products, especially clotted cream.

MOORLAND GIANT *Each of the 170 grey granite outcrops on Dartmoor, such as Combestone Tor
near Dartmeet, has its own distinctive shape, sculpted by the weather over thousands of years.*

Docklands Business and leisure centre in
London, on the River Thames east of the
City. It was developed in the 1980s after
London's extensive Victorian docks had
fallen into disuse. The Docklands Light
Railway links the City with the Isle of Dogs,
and the extension of London Transport's
Jubilee Line is intended to bring more
business to the area.

CITY GIANT *The 800 ft (240 m) high No.1,
Canada Square, at Canary Wharf in London's
Docklands, is Britain's highest building.*

Dorset Chiefly agricultural county in
southwest England. The county town is
Dorchester, and BOURNEMOUTH, Swanage
and Weymouth are popular coastal resorts.
♣Many Dorset places appear in the novels
of Thomas ▷HARDY, including Dorchester
which he referred to as 'Casterbridge'.

Dover Seaport in Kent, and the main port
for passengers travelling by sea to and from
the Continent. Its harbour is dominated by
the celebrated white cliffs.
♣Channel swimmers traditionally swim
from Shakespeare Beach, Dover, to Cap
Gris-Nez. Captain Webb was the first to
make the 21 mile (34 km) crossing in 1875.

Dundee City on the north side of the
Firth of TAY, and administrative centre of
Tayside Region, east Scotland. Dundee is
linked to the south side of the firth by rail
over the Tay Bridge, rebuilt in 1888, and by
a road bridge opened in 1966. Engineering,
shipbuilding and servicing the North Sea
oil rigs are important local industries. Traditional Dundee products include 'jam, jute
and journalism'. In the 19th century
Dundee was the centre for manufacturing
jute goods, marmalade has been made there
since 1797, and the city was the birthplace
of much-loved children's comics such as
Beano and *Dandy*. Dundee cake is a rich fruit
cake decorated with almonds.

Dunvegan Castle Stronghold on the Isle of Skye, and the seat of the chiefs of Clan MacLeod since the 13th century. Castle treasures include a drinking horn holding the equivalent of two bottles of wine, which a 12th-century chief is said to have drained at a draught. The Castle's Fairy Flag reputedly has powers to protect the MacLeods if waved at times of danger.

Durham City on the River Wear, and administrative centre of County Durham in northeast England. Its magnificent Norman cathedral stands on a rock peninsula 70 ft (21 m) above the river. Durham Castle was founded on the same neck of land by William the Conqueror in 1072. It is now part of Durham University.

East Anglia Region of eastern England including Norfolk, Suffolk and parts of Cambridgeshire and Essex. Once an Anglo-Saxon kingdom, the area prospered in the Middle Ages through the wool trade. It includes large parts of the fertile FENS.

East End Area of east London centred on London's docks and thought of as the historic working-class heart of the capital. The DOCKLANDS development has begun to breathe new life into the area's disused docks. Well-known areas of the East End include Stepney, Whitechapel, Limehouse, Bethnal Green, Bow and the Isle of Dogs.
🔥True Eastenders must be born within hearing distance of the bells of St Mary-le-Bow on Cheapside, whose bell in the Middle Ages warned citizens that the City's gates were closing for the night. They are called cockneys and have their own dialect. (See box on ▷RHYMING SLANG.)

Edinburgh Capital of Scotland and administrative centre of Lothian Region, on the Firth of Forth. The backbone of Edinburgh's Old Town is the ROYAL MILE, which runs from Edinburgh Castle to the Palace of HOLYROODHOUSE. Some medieval buildings survive in the Old Town, while the Georgian New Town is noted for its fine neo-Classical architecture. The castle dates from the 12th century and overlooks PRINCES STREET, the New Town's principal thoroughfare. The annual Edinburgh International Festival of Music and Drama, which started in 1947, is held in late August and early September.
🔥Edinburgh used to be called 'Auld Reekie' because of the smoke that hung over it during the Industrial Revolution. The city's real name is derived from Edwin, King of Northumbria in the 7th century.

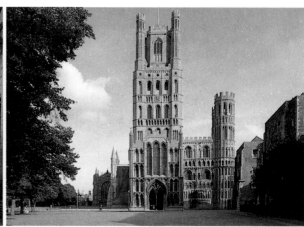

CATHEDRAL IN THE FENS *Ely Cathedral's majestic Norman nave rises to a wooden ceiling painted with Biblical scenes. At the foot of the western tower are the carved arches of the Galilee Porch.*

Ely City in Cambridgeshire, on the River OUSE. Ely was formerly known as the Isle of Ely, because it stood on slightly higher ground above a landscape of low-lying fens. The fens were drained in the 17th and 18th centuries, but Ely still appears isolated. The surrounding marshes were the scene of Hereward the Wake's last stand against William the Conqueror in 1070.

Epsom Town in Surrey known for its racecourse on the Epsom Downs, where the Derby has been held on the first Wednesday of June since 1780.
🔥In the 17th and early 18th centuries Epsom was known for its medicinal spring, from which Epsom salts – powdered crystals used as a purgative – were distilled.

Essex County between Greater London and the North Sea coast. It is mainly low-lying, with many dormitory towns serving the capital. SOUTHEND-ON-SEA and Clacton are popular coastal resorts; the county town is Chelmsford.

🔥The satirical term 'Essex man', coined in the 1980s, refers to materialistic, upwardly mobile men, who have working-class roots but capitalist right-wing views.

Eton Small town in Berkshire, opposite Windsor on the River Thames. Eton College, the world-renowned boys' public school, was founded in 1440.
🔥The broad white 'Eton collar' takes its name from the school's uniform, as does the waist-length Eton jacket and the Eton crop, a short haircut for women.

Exeter County town of Devon, on the River Exe. Exeter was heavily bombed in World War II, but its beautiful Gothic cathedral and its close survived. Exeter also has a university, and a maritime museum on one of Britain's oldest canals.

Exmoor National Park, covering 265 sq miles (686 km²) of Devon and Somerset. The moor's bleak landscape was the setting for R.D. Blackmore's novel *Lorna Doone*.

CASTLE ON A CRAG *Edinburgh's great castle crowns a granite hilltop in the centre of the city, like a fortified acropolis of ancient Greece. Classical monuments on Calton Hill strengthen the city's claim to the title of the 'Athens of the North'.*

Fair Isle Southernmost island of the SHETLAND group, known for its patterned knitwear and bird sanctuary. Fair Isle has a population of about 180 and is Britain's most remote inhabited island – 21 miles (34 km) from its nearest neighbour.

Fens, The Low-lying area of East Anglia extending across areas of Cambridgeshire, Lincolnshire, Norfolk and Suffolk. The Fens were originally marshland, and parts have been drained since Roman times. It is one of the most fertile agricultural areas of England, now drained by diesel and electric pumps. Wicken Fen in Cambridgeshire is the last sizable expanse of undrained fenland, and is maintained as a nature reserve.

Fingal's Cave One of Britain's scenic wonders, on the tiny Scottish island of Staffa just west of Mull in the Inner Hebrides. The cave is 66 ft (20 m) high and 227 ft (69 m) deep, and its six-sided, black basalt formations create a spectacular forest of columns, some 36 ft (11 m) tall. The cave is named after Finn MacCool, a hero of Celtic folklore who is also supposed to have built the Giant's Causeway – a collection of some 40 000 basalt columns on the northeast coast of Antrim, in Ireland, which was once joined to Fingal's Cave.
♪ Fingal's Cave inspired Felix Mendelssohn to compose his overture *The Hebrides*.

Firth of Forth Estuary of the River Forth and an inlet of the North Sea. Edinburgh's main port, Leith, and Rosyth naval base are among the ports on its banks. It is crossed by the ▷FORTH RAIL BRIDGE, opened in 1890, and the 1964 Forth Road Bridge.

Fishbourne Roman Palace Largest surviving Roman building in Britain, between Chichester and Bosham in West Sussex. Discovered in 1960, it dates from about AD 75 and originally had four wings and about 100 rooms paved with elaborate mosaics, some of which survive.

Fishguard Welsh port in Dyfed and a terminal for passenger ferries to Ireland. Lower Fishguard's beautiful harbour was used as the setting for the 1971 film version of Dylan Thomas's ▷UNDER MILK WOOD.
♪ The last landing by a foreign army on mainland Britain occurred at nearby Carregwastad Point in 1797, during the Napoleonic Wars.

Flamborough Head Headland in north Humberside, jutting into the North Sea. The 150 ft (45 m) high chalk cliffs, eroded by sea and wind, have many caves.

Flatford Mill Watermill on the River Stour near Ipswich in Suffolk. The stream, surrounding meadows and buildings have hardly changed since John ▷CONSTABLE painted them in the 19th century.

Fleet Street Road in the City of London which runs from Ludgate Circus to Temple Bar. Already well known for its taverns, Fleet Street became the heart of the British newspaper industry in the 18th century. The last remaining national newspaper offices moved to other sites in the 1980s.
♪ Fleet Street was named after the River Fleet, which now runs underground.

Folkestone English Channel port in Kent. It is a terminus for hydrofoil crossings to Boulogne, and just north of Folkestone, at Cheriton, is the British terminus of the ▷CHANNEL TUNNEL.

Forest of Dean Ancient area of woodland and open country in Gloucestershire, once a royal hunting forest. Since Roman times, the local people have mined iron ore and coal in the forest, and some privately owned coal mines are still in operation. There are dramatic views of the River Wye from Symonds Yat Rock.

Fountains Abbey Britain's largest and finest monastic ruin, near Ripon in North Yorkshire. The Cistercian abbey, founded in 1132, lies next to the 18th-century landscaped gardens of Studley Royal.

Glamis (Glarms) Scottish village near Kirriemuir in Tayside Region. Its magnificent pink-grey castle dates mainly from the late 17th century, when it was renovated by Patrick Lyon, 1st Earl of Strathmore. Turrets were added in the style later called Scottish Baronial. The Queen Mother – daughter of the 14th Earl – spent much of her childhood there, and the castle was the birthplace of Princess Margaret.
♪ Glamis is said to be the most haunted house in Scotland. One legend tells of a hideously deformed heir who was imprisoned for life in a secret room.
♪ In Shakespeare's play, Macbeth was the Thane, or ruler, of Glamis and supposedly lived in an earlier, 11th-century fortress on the same site.

Glasgow Scotland's largest city, and administrative centre of the Strathclyde Region, on the River Clyde. The city prospered after Scotland's union with England in 1707, especially through trade in New World tobacco and sugar. It continued to expand following the Industrial Revolution, but by the end of the 19th century its fortunes declined and areas such as the Gorbals became notorious for their slums. Sauchiehall Street in the heart of the city became renowned for its music halls at the beginning of the 20th century. The Glasgow School of Art is one of several buildings in the city designed by the architect Charles Rennie ▷MACKINTOSH. Manufacturing now accounts for fewer

CAVE OF THE GIANT *Slim basalt columns support the arched roof of Fingal's Cave, and natural stepping stones lead into the cavern that early travellers thought had been shaped by a Celtic giant.*

than one job in five, although two shipyards remain in operation and distilling is still an important local industry.

♠ On the outskirts of Glasgow, Pollok Country Park houses the Burrell Collection, a wealthy shipowner's eclectic art collection with 8000 objects from many cultures, including ancient civilizations.

♠ Celtic and Rangers are the two leading Glasgow football clubs: together they are known as the Old Firm. The Roman Catholic supporters of Celtic and the Protestant fans of Rangers have often clashed.

Glen Coe Scottish glen in Highland Region, between Loch Leven and Rannoch Moor. It has been known as the 'Glen of Weeping' since 1692 when 38 members of the Macdonald clan were massacred by the pro-English Campbells.

Gloucester County town of Gloucestershire. It was the Roman fortified town and river-port Glevum, and then became the Anglo-Saxon capital of Mercia. The town commanded the lowest crossing of the River Severn between England and Wales. Its cathedral has some of Britain's finest ▷PERPENDICULAR architecture.

Grampian Mountains Range of mountains extending across central Scotland, bounded to the north by the Great Glen and to the south by the central Lowlands. BEN NEVIS – Britain's highest peak – lies at

FORTIFIED FRONTIER *Dipping and climbing to follow the natural contours of the land, the snaking coast-to-coast course of Hadrian's Wall separated Roman Britain from the wild northern tribes.*

the western end of the Great Glen. The mountains give their name to the Grampian Region of northeast Scotland, whose administrative centre is ABERDEEN.

Grantchester Village beside the River Cam in Cambridgeshire. It has attracted writers such as Chaucer, Milton and Byron and was immortalised by Rupert ▷BROOKE in his poem 'The Old Vicarage, Grantchester'. Brooke lived at the Old Vicarage, and it is now the home of Lord Archer (the politician and novelist Jeffrey Archer).

Grantham Town in Lincolnshire which was once an important staging post on the Great North Road (A1). Many old coaching inns still survive. Sir Isaac ▷NEWTON carved his name at the local school, and the former premier Margaret ▷THATCHER (née Roberts) was born above her father's grocery shop in the town.

WINDOWS ON THE STARS *Two onion-shaped domes at Greenwich house telescopes which made astronomical history. The museum to which they now belong also includes an hour glass (left), a Nautical Almanac and a nocturnal, used for measuring time by observation of the stars.*

Grasmere Village in the Lake District noted as the home of the poet William ▷WORDSWORTH who lived at Dove Cottage, now a museum. Grasmere Sports, held every August, include fell-racing, hound-trailing and Cumbrian wrestling.

Great Malvern Spa town on the east side of the Malvern Hills in Hereford and Worcester, known for its spring water sold there since the 18th century. It stages an annual drama and music festival founded in 1929 by Sir Edward ▷ELGAR, who lived in the town, and George Bernard Shaw.

Greenwich London borough on the River Thames south bank. It is the site of the Old Royal Observatory, Royal Naval College, National Maritime Museum and the Queen's House – England's first Palladian-style building, built by Inigo ▷JONES in 1635. The tea clipper *Cutty Sark* and *Gipsy Moth IV*, in which Sir Francis Chichester became the first man to sail solo around the world, stand in dry dock.

♠ The Greenwich meridian (0° longitude) on which Greenwich Mean Time (GMT) is based, passes through the Observatory.

Gretna Green Scottish village in Dumfries and Galloway Region. Just over 1 mile (1.6 km) from the border with England, it was long known as a place where eloping English lovers could marry without the consent of their parents, because of differences in Scottish law. The ceremony was usually performed by the local blacksmith. Such marriages became illegal in 1940.

Hadrian's Wall Roman wall built between AD 122 and 136 by Emperor Hadrian to defend the northern boundary of Roman Britain. It extends for 73 miles (117 km) from the River Tyne to the head of the Solway Firth. Sections of the wall survive, and several forts, camps and milecastles have been excavated; they include Housesteads – a garrison fort – and Vindolanda, possibly Hadrian's headquarters during the construction of the wall.

Hampstead District in north London which was a popular spa village in the 18th century, and has long attracted writers, artists and musicians. Hampstead Heath is the highest point in London, at 436 ft (133 m) above sea level; its 800 acres (324 ha) of woodland and hills are a popular place of recreation. Outdoor concerts are held every summer at Kenwood House.
♣ London Underground's deepest tunnels run 250 ft (76 m) under Hampstead.

Hampton Court Palace Tudor palace on the River Thames, on the western outskirts of London. It was built by Cardinal ▷WOLSEY but handed over to Henry VIII after its completion in 1514. There are fine pieces of furniture, tapestries and paintings, and the gardens have a noted maze. Part of the palace was damaged by fire in 1986, but it was restored and reopened in 1992.

Harrogate Resort town in North Yorkshire which has been a spa since Tudor times. There is still an old sulphur well in the Royal Pump Room Museum.
♣ In 1926, the crime novelist Agatha Christie was found in a hotel in Harrogate, apparently suffering from amnesia, ten days after the discovery in Surrey of her abandoned car had caused a nationwide sensation.

Harrow Borough in northwest London. Harrow School, one of Britain's best-known public schools, was founded in 1572; former pupils include Lord Byron, Lord Palmerston and Sir Winston Churchill.

Hastings Coastal resort in East Sussex. The Battle of ▷HASTINGS (1066) was fought nearby on the outskirts of the town of Battle. Hastings was one of the five original ▷CINQUE PORTS. Hastings Old Town, which lies between two hills, is noted for its tall huts for drying fishing nets.

Hatfield House Red-brick Jacobean mansion in Hertfordshire, built by Robert Cecil, 1st Earl of Salisbury, between 1608 and 1611. Its splendours include the black and white marble hall, the carved oak grand staircase, and the 180 ft (55 m) Long Gallery. The house stands close to the site of the Old Palace of Elizabeth I, one wing of which survives. The then Princess Elizabeth was sitting under a nearby oak when she heard of her accession to the throne.

Haworth West Yorkshire moorland village noted for its parsonage where the writers Charlotte, Emily and Anne ▷BRONTË lived. The house is a museum.

Hay-on-Wye Welsh town in Powys, overlooking the River Wye. It has many secondhand bookshops, and is a base for walking in the BLACK MOUNTAINS.

Heathrow World's busiest international airport, situated on the western outskirts of London. Opened in 1946, it has four terminals used by 90 airlines flying to 220 destinations in 85 countries. Some 48 million passengers use Heathrow every year.
♣ At peak times, a plane takes off or touches down at Heathrow every 90 seconds.

Hebrides Group of 500 islands off the west and northwest coast of Scotland, 20 of which are inhabited. They are also known as the Western Isles, and divided into the Outer Hebrides, of which Lewis and Harris is the largest island, and the Inner Hebrides, where SKYE is the largest island.

Henley-on-Thames Riverside town in Oxfordshire – the venue every July since 1839 of the world famous rowing regatta. Traditionally, spectators picnic on the banks; men wear colourful blazers and straw boaters and women wear elaborate hats.

Hereford City on the River Wye in Hereford and Worcester. Its cathedral was begun in the 11th century and contains the *Mappa Mundi* 'Map of the World' – one of the world's oldest maps, dating from 1290 – and a chained library of some 1500 books, some dating from the 9th century.

Highlands, Scottish Area north of a 'line' between the Firth of Clyde on the west coast and the town of Stonehaven on the east coast. The Highlands include an administrative area known as the Highland Region. They have a turbulent history of clan feuds and fierce battles; the ▷CULLODEN battlefield and the scene of the massacre at GLEN COE can be visited. A rift valley, the Great Glen, bisects Scotland between Inverness and Fort William; the Caledonian Canal runs its length, linking a series of lochs, including LOCH NESS.

Holy Island (or Lindisfarne) Island 1 mile (1.6 km) off the Northumbrian coast, linked to the mainland by a causeway at low tide. St Aidan built a monastery there in AD 635. There are ruins of an 11th-century priory, and a 16th-century castle – rebuilt by Sir Edwin Lutyens in 1902.
♣ The Lindisfarne Gospels, an ornate illuminated manuscript that is a masterpiece of English Celtic art, was made on the island in the 7th century.

HOLY RELICS *A priory on Holy Island, founded in 1093, was dissolved in 1537 and used for a time as a military storehouse. Its ruins now lie open to the winds and the sea birds which shelter there.*

Holyroodhouse, Palace of Official Scottish residence of the sovereign, at one end of the ROYAL MILE in Edinburgh. For six years the 16th-century palace was the home of Mary, Queen of Scots and in 1566 her Italian secretary David Rizzio was murdered in her private apartments.

Home Counties English counties which lie nearest to London. Originally, the term was only applied to Kent, Surrey, Middlesex and Essex, but now it is often used to include Buckinghamshire, Berkshire, Hertfordshire and East Sussex.

Hull (or Kingston upon Hull) City and port in Humberside, on the north shore of the Humber estuary and linked to the river's south bank by the ▷HUMBER BRIDGE. The city was devastated by bombing in World War II, but one building that survived is Wilberforce House, the home of the anti-slavery campaigner William Wilberforce, who was born in Hull in 1759.
🐚 The British poet Philip ▷LARKIN was librarian at Hull University.
🐚 Hull is the only city in Britain to have its own private telephone system. It has been in operation since 1904.

Hyde Park Central London park which incorporates Rotten Row, a broad riding track fashionable since the 18th century, and Speakers' Corner, where aspiring orators have expounded since Victorian times. The Serpentine lake runs through the centre of the park.
🐚 Hyde Park's 344 acres (139 ha) and the 275 acres (111 ha) of Kensington Gardens form one of the largest open spaces in the heart of any of the world's major cities.

Ilkley Moor Expanse of moorland between Airedale and Wharfedale, West Yorkshire, rising to 1321 ft (403 m). The title of the folk song *On Ilkla Moor baht 'at*, means 'on Ilkley Moor without a hat'.

Inverewe Subtropical garden on a headland in northwest Scotland. Although it lies on almost the same latitude as St Petersburg, Russia, the ▷GULF STREAM helps to promote mild, humid weather in which exotic plants, trees and bamboos can flourish. The 64 acre (26 ha) garden was created by Osgood MacKenzie in 1865.

Inverness Northernmost major city of Britain, often referred to as the 'capital' of the Highlands. The city stands at the head of the Moray Firth and at the entrance to the man-made Caledonian Canal, which connects Scotland's east and west coasts.

BLOSSOM TIME *Spring flowers at Kew Gardens frame a temple named after Aeolus, the Greek god of the winds.*

Iona Scottish island in the Inner HEBRIDES which was an ancient druidical shrine, and became a cradle of Christianity when St Columba founded a monastery there in AD 563. It is the burial place of 60 kings of Scotland, Ireland and Norway. The Labour leader John Smith was buried there in 1994.

Ironbridge Gorge Birthplace of the ▷INDUSTRIAL REVOLUTION, on the River Severn in Shropshire. At Coalbrookdale in 1709 Abraham Darby revolutionised ironmaking by smelting iron ore with coke. In 1779 the world's first cast-iron bridge was built across the gorge. The Ironbridge Gorge Museum includes a reconstructed 19th-century industrial town.

John O'Groats Tiny Scottish village in Highland Region which is the most northerly inhabited place on mainland Britain. John O'Groats lies 876 miles (1410 km) by road from LAND'S END.
🐚 The northernmost point on the British mainland is Dunnet Head, 12 miles (19 km) west of John O'Groats. Unst – part of Shetland – is the northernmost island.
🐚 John O'Groats is named after a Dutchman – Jan de Groot – who settled there in 1496.

Kendal Cumbrian town on the River Kent, in the Lake District, known as the 'auld grey town' because of its numerous limestone buildings. Kendal mint cake, a sugar and peppermint block favoured by mountaineers and explorers, has been made in the town since 1869.

Kensington Area of west central London noted for its many museums, which include the Victoria and Albert Museum, the Science Museum and the Natural History Museum. The grounds of Kensington Palace form Kensington Gardens, a large public park just north of the Albert Hall.

Kew Area of west London, known for its Royal Botanic Gardens, founded in 1759. The gardens, which cover 300 acres (121 ha), contain almost 40 000 varieties of plants and have a fine 18th-century pagoda, an orangery and the Palm House – a Victorian curved-glass conservatory.
🐚 Visitors can walk through ten different computer-controlled 'climates' in the futuristic Princess of Wales Conservatory, which opened in 1987.

Kielder Forest Britain's largest manmade forest, which lies in Northumberland and encompasses 125 000 acres (50 600 ha) of conifers. Kielder Water is the largest reservoir in Europe, covering 2684 acres (1086 ha); it was created by damming the North Tyne River.

Knole One of the largest houses in Britain, near Sevenoaks in Kent. It was begun in 1456 by Thomas Bourchier, Archbishop of Canterbury, and acquired by Henry VIII in 1538 simply by saying he liked it. It was completed during the reign of Elizabeth I, who gave Knole to the Sackville family.
🐚 Knole is curiously linked to the calendar; originally having 365 rooms, seven courtyards, 52 staircases and 12 entrances.
🐚 Drop-end Knole sofas date from the 17th century and were named after an example found at the house.

Lacock Picturesque village near Chippenham in Wiltshire. In Lacock Abbey Henry Fox Talbot made his pioneering photographic experiments in the 1830s.
🐚 Much of the village is owned by the National Trust, which ensures that incongruous additions are kept out of sight; residents share a communal television aerial on a nearby hillside.

Lake District Area of scenic grandeur comprising 16 major lakes, including Windermere, Ullswater, Coniston Water, Grasmere and Derwent Water, set among the Cumbrian mountains in northwestern England. Scafell Pike is the highest peak in England, rising to 3210 ft (978 m). The area has been a National Park since 1951.
🐚 The Lake District's attractions were popularised by the so-called Lake Poets; Wordsworth, Coleridge and Southey.

HOME FOR A SAINT *In AD 685 an early Christian saint, Herbert, chose Derwent Water as the site of his hermitage; visitors have sought out the seclusion of the Lake District's widest lake ever since.*

Land's End Headland of granite cliffs at the tip of Cornwall which is the westernmost point of England, 876 miles (1410 km) from JOHN O'GROATS.

Leeds City in West Yorkshire, on the River Aire, which prospered through the wool trade from medieval times and is still a major centre of clothing manufacture. City Varieties, one of Britain's last original music halls, was the setting for the television music hall show *The Good Old Days.*

Leeds Castle Fairytale castle in Kent, standing on two islands in a lake fed by the River Len. Named after a Saxon called Leed, or Ledian, who built a wooden fortification on the site, the present castle was begun in 1119 by the Normans, enlarged by Edward I in the 13th century, altered by Henry VIII and largely rebuilt in 1822.

Lincoln County town of Lincolnshire, on a hill above the River Witham. Lincoln Castle was begun in 1068 and beside it is a fine cathedral built between the 11th and 15th centuries. Lincoln green, a cloth of yellowish green made in the city, is said to have been worn by Robin Hood and his band of merry men. Much of the surrounding fenland has been drained for agriculture, and to the northeast are rolling hills known as the Wolds.

Liverpool City and port on the River Mersey. By the middle of the 18th century it was one of the biggest and most prosperous ports in the world. Today the Victorian Albert Dock, which closed in 1972, has been renovated as a complex of museums and galleries and a centre for water sports: it houses the Granada Television Studios, the extension of the London Tate Gallery, and the Merseyside Maritime Museum. The story of the Beatles, who brought Liverpool worldwide fame in the 1960s, is told in a walk-through exhibition. Liverpool has two imposing 20th-century cathedrals; the Gothic-style Anglican cathedral, built between 1904 and 1978, is the largest in Britain. The Royal Liver Building has twin towers topped by statues of the mythical Liver Birds from which the city is said to have taken its name.

🛦 Liverpool Football Club has been England's most successful in recent times – winning three European Cup Championships in the late 1970s and early 1980s. 'You'll never walk alone' – the title of a song in the musical *Carousel* – is written above the gates of the club's home ground, Anfield, and is a popular football anthem.

Lizard Point Southernmost point on the British mainland, at the tip of the Lizard peninsula in Cornwall. The headland is noted for its dramatic cliffs and for a greenish local rock called serpentine.

Llanfair PG Commonly used shortened form of the name of a Welsh village on Anglesey in Gwynedd. Its full name, Llanfairpwllgwyngyllgogerychwyrndrobwllllantysiliogogogoch means 'The church of St Mary in the hollow of the white aspen near the rapid whirlpool of St Tysillio's church close to the red cave'.

🛦 Even Llanfair PG's full name is exceeded in length by that of a station on the Fairbourne Railway in Gwynedd, called Gorsafawddacha'idraigodanheddogleddollônpenrhynareurdraethceredigion.

FIT FOR A QUEEN *Edward I gave Leeds Castle in Kent to Eleanor of Aquitaine, and English queens owned it for the next 200 years. In later years, private owners have added to its magnificence.*

Llŷn Peninsula Welsh peninsula in Gwynedd, jutting into the Irish Sea. It was one of the earliest inhabited parts of Wales, and has ancient hut circles known as the Town of Giants on the easternmost peak of Yr Eifl. Pwllheli is the main resort.
In the beach at Porth Oer is renowned for its 'whistling sands' – the fine sand whistles when it is compressed underfoot.

Loch Lomond Britain's largest lake – 23 miles (37 km) long and up to 5 miles (8 km) wide. It has 30 islets and extends along the border between the Central and Strathclyde regions of Scotland.

Loch Ness Scottish loch in the Great Glen, in Highland Region, and the home of the legendary ▷LOCH NESS MONSTER. The 12th-century Urquhart Castle stands on a tongue of land jutting into the loch.

London Capital city of the United Kingdom, on the River Thames. It is one of the world's largest and most cosmopolitan cities, with 6.9 million inhabitants. London originated from the Roman settlement Londinium, an area now occupied by the CITY OF LONDON. The Great Plague struck London in 1664-5, and in 1666 its medieval buildings were largely destroyed by the Great Fire. Among the buildings that replaced them was Sir Christopher Wren's St Paul's Cathedral. The City of London is today one of the world's leading banking and insurance centres. Other notable areas of London include the City of WESTMINSTER, the West End, KENSINGTON, CHELSEA and the EAST END.
In 2000 years London has grown from a Roman city of 1 sq mile (2.6 km²) to the 616 sq miles (1595 km²) of the present Greater London, from Barnet in the north to Croydon in the south, and Uxbridge in the west to Dagenham in the east.

Longleat Fine Elizabethan mansion near Warminster in Wiltshire, and the country home of the Marquess of Bath. The sumptuous interior includes the vast Red Library and the bedroom in which the Marquess (then Viscount Weymouth) painted scenes from the ▷KAMASUTRA. The park and woodlands were landscaped by 'Capability' Brown and now include a safari park.

Ludlow Historic Shropshire market town on the River Teme, noted for its black and white half-timbered buildings, dating from Tudor times. Ludlow Castle, dating from 1085, and the 14th-century St Laurence's Church, a building of red sandstone, dominate one of Britain's finest townscapes.

MONARCHS OF MAN *Norse kings ruled the Isle of Man from the 12th-century Castle Rushen, whose limestone towers still dominate Castletown Bay. Since 1907 motorcycle champions have ruled over the island's roads during the annual Tourist Trophy races.*

Lundy Island in the Bristol Channel, off the north coast of Devon, owned by the National Trust and leased to the Landmark Trust, which administers and maintains the island. Puffins breed on the narrow cliff ledges and at least 250 other species of bird have been recorded.
In The island's name originates from *Lunde* – an Old Norse word for 'puffin'.

Maiden Castle England's most dramatic earthwork fortification, southwest of Dorchester, in Dorset. A hilltop 2 miles (3.2 km) round is protected by three ditches with ramparts 90 ft (27 m) high. From around 300 BC the earthwork housed an entire town, which was stormed by the Romans in AD 43.

Man, Isle of Island midway between England and Ireland which, although it belongs to the British Crown, is self-governing. Its parliament, the Tynwald, is one of the world's oldest legislative assemblies, having met regularly for more than 1000 years. The island is 32½ miles (52 km) long and 13 miles (21 km) across; Snaefell is the highest peak on the island at 2036 ft (620.5 m). The capital and main port is Douglas. The Manx cat, a tailless breed, is unique to the island.
In The island's coat of arms – a three-legged symbol – dates back to the 13th century and represents the island's motto: 'Whichever way you throw me I will stand'.

Manchester Industrial city on the River Irwell and administrative centre of the metropolitan county of Greater Manchester. In Roman times it was called Mancunium, and residents are still known as Mancunians. Manchester was at the centre of Britain's cotton manufacturing during the Industrial Revolution. The city benefited from a network of railways and canals: the Liverpool and Manchester railway opened in 1830, and the Manchester Ship Canal, completed in 1894, linked

Manchester to the estuary of the River Mersey and brought ocean-going ships to the thriving textile factories. The city is the home of the Old Trafford cricket ground, the Hallé Orchestra, and many libraries, including Chetham's – the oldest free public library in England.

🕯The *Manchester Guardian*, now known simply as *The Guardian*, was founded by Manchester Liberals in 1821.

Marble Arch Triumphal marble arch designed by John ▷NASH and erected in 1827; it was meant as the royal entrance to Buckingham Palace. In 1851 it was moved to its present position at the northeastern corner of Hyde Park in London.

Marlborough Market town on the River Kennet in Wiltshire which has one of Britain's widest high streets, lined with Georgian buildings and colonnaded shops.

🕯Marlborough College lies on the edge of the town. In 1968 it became the first boys' public school in Britain to admit girls to the upper school and, in 1986 it became the first to become completely co-educational.

Mayfair Exclusive area of central London, bordered by Oxford Street, Regent Street, Piccadilly and Park Lane. Its 18th-century and early 19th-century streets and squares include Bond Street, Savile Row, Berkeley Square and Grosvenor Square.

🕯The name of Mayfair derives from an annual fair which was held every May until the 18th century. It was stopped because it was considered too noisy by residents.

Mendips Range of limestone hills in Somerset which runs northwest from the Frome Valley, reaching 1068 ft (325 m) at Blackdown. The hills include CHEDDAR GORGE and WOOKEY HOLE.

Mersey, River Formed by the confluence of the rivers Tame and Goyt in northeast England, the Mersey flows for 70 miles (113 km) from Stockport to the Irish Sea. Two road tunnels and one rail tunnel run under the Mersey, and the city of Liverpool stands on the north bank of its estuary.

Milton Keynes New town in Buckinghamshire, built in 1967. Since 1971 it has been the home of the Open University.

🕯Milton Keynes' concrete cows and many roundabouts have been the butt of jibes directed at supposedly soulless new towns.

Morecambe Coastal resort on Morecambe Bay in Lancashire. Its attractions include the Central Pier and a 4 mile (6.4 km) promenade, known for its autumn illuminations. Low tides at Morecambe Bay reveal 80 sq miles (200 km²) of dry sand, where the tide is said to come in at the speed of a galloping horse.

Mousehole (MOW-zull) Fishing village in Cornwall which was once the centre of the Cornish pilchard-fishing industry.

🕯The traditional local dish, stargazy pie, gets its name from the whole fish heads, left to stare out through the crust.

🕯In 1981, eight lifeboatmen and four shipwrecked sailors died when Mousehole's lifeboat was lost amid 60 ft (18 m) waves.

Mull Island of the Inner HEBRIDES, off the west coast of Scotland. Its mountains rise to 3169 ft (966 m) at Ben More. The main town is Tobermory. Off Mull lies the much smaller island of Staffa, noted for its huge cavern FINGAL'S CAVE.

Mumbles, The Welsh seaside resort on the Gower peninsula in West Glamorgan, which commands magnificent views of Swansea Bay from Mumbles Head.

Newcastle upon Tyne County town and port of Tyne and Wear, on the north bank of the River Tyne. The city lies in Tyneside, an industrial region which was once one of the world's largest shipbuilding centres. It has also been at the centre of the English coal trade since the 13th century. The city was the home of the engineers George and Robert Stephenson.

🕯A person from Tyneside is known as a 'Geordie' – probably a corruption of George, a common local name.

🕯Newcastle's importance as a coal-shipping centre gave rise to the expression 'coals to Newcastle', which means taking anything to a place where there is already an abundance of it.

New Forest Area of heath and woodland covering 90 000 acres (36 500 ha) in Hampshire. It was made a royal hunting preserve by William the Conqueror in 1079.

🕯While hunting in the New Forest, William II was killed by an arrow, probably shot by a supporter of his brother Henry.

Newmarket Market town in Suffolk regarded as the centre of British horse racing. Racing began at Newmarket during the reign of James I (1603-25) and the town is the home of the Jockey Club, founded in 1750, and the National Stud, established in 1916. The four main races held annually at Newmarket are the One Thousand Guineas, the Two Thousand Guineas, the Cambridgeshire, and the Cesarewitch.

Norfolk Flat and largely agricultural county in East Anglia, bordering on the North Sea. The shallow lakes of the

SPANS ACROSS THE TYNE *The soaring arch of the Tyne Bridge, opened in 1928, carries the main road into the heart of Newcastle. Five other city bridges cross the river with a filigree of steel.*

CITY OF SPIRES *Domes and spires fret the Oxford skyline, and Hertford College's Bridge of Sighs brings a touch of Venice to the city.*

BROADS lie between the coast and the county town, Norwich, while low-lying FENS provide some of the most fertile farmland in the country. Great Yarmouth is the largest holiday resort on the coast.
⚓ The Norfolk jacket – a single-breasted jacket with a belt and large side pockets – was formerly worn by hunters when duck shooting in Norfolk.

North Downs Ridge of chalk hills in southeastern England which runs from Guildford in Surrey to Dover in Kent. The North Downs lie roughly parallel to the SOUTH DOWNS, with an area known as the Weald lying in between.
⚓ The word 'downs' comes from the Anglo-Saxon word for dunes, which the hills' gentle undulations resemble.

Northumberland England's northernmost county, bordered by Scotland and the North Sea. The PENNINES in the west and the CHEVIOT HILLS to the north both descend to a coastal plain. There are no major cities, and sheep farming is the major industry. Tourist attractions include HADRIAN'S WALL, as well as fine castles such as BAMBURGH and Warkworth. NEWCASTLE UPON TYNE, once the county town, now

falls within Tyne and Wear, but remains the administrative centre. Morpeth is the present-day county town.

Norwich County town of Norfolk on the River Wensum. Norwich has a magnificent Norman cathedral with superb 15th-century fan vaulting and a spire which rises to 315 ft (96 m) - making it the second highest in England, after Salisbury. The city's narrow streets date from medieval times when Norwich was a centre of the wool trade. In the city centre, 30 medieval churches are dominated by a Norman castle which houses the city's museum and art gallery. The University of East Anglia lies northwest of the city.
⚓ Norwich City football club are known as the Canaries after the Norwich Canary – a distinct breed reared in the city.

Nottingham City on the River Trent and county town of Nottinghamshire, known for its traditional lace-making industry. Nottingham and the nearby Sherwood Forest are associated with the legendary outlaw ▷ROBIN HOOD.

Offa's Dyke Ancient earthwork rampart which ran for some 170 miles (273 km) from Prestatyn on the north Wales coast to Chepstow in the south. It was built by Offa, an 8th-century Anglo-Saxon king of Mercia, to mark the boundary between Wales and his kingdom and formed the first border between England and Wales. Some 80 miles (130 km) of ditch and embankment survive along part of the long-distance Offa's Dyke Path.

Old Bailey Popular name for the Central Criminal Court, the Crown Court for the CITY OF LONDON and Greater London, which stands in a street of the same name. The green-domed building, with its bronze figure of Justice holding her scales, was built in 1907 on the site of Newgate Prison.

Old Man of Hoy Britain's tallest sea-stack, or rock pillar, situated off Hoy in the ORKNEY Islands. It rises 450 ft (137 m) above the sea and can be seen from the Scottish mainland 16 miles (26 km) away. It was first climbed in 1966.

Orkney Group of 70 Scottish islands, separated from the mainland's north coast – 6 miles (10 km) away – by the Pentland Firth. The islands have been occupied for 6000 years and 18 of them are still inhabited. As well as cattle farming and fishing, the islands also serve the North Sea oil industry. The Orkney's chief islands are

Hoy, Sanday and Mainland, which is home to many prehistoric monuments and the capital, Kirkwall. Scapa Flow was used as a naval base during both world wars.
⚓ The Orkney islands belonged to Norway for 300 years before they were acquired by Scotland in 1472, and many of the people are of Scandinavian descent.

Ouse, River Name of several English rivers. The longest is the Great Ouse, which rises in Northamptonshire and flows for 160 miles (260 km) to meet the Wash near King's Lynn. Yorkshire's Ouse, formed by the rivers Swale and Ure, flows for 60 miles (100 km) and joins the River Trent at the Humber estuary. The Sussex Ouse flows for 30 miles (50 km) into the English Channel at Newhaven.

Oxford County town of Oxfordshire and historic university city, lying at the junction of the River Thames and the River Cherwell. Oxford is Britain's oldest university: the first college, University College, was founded in 1249 and there are now 36 colleges and more than 25 000 students. Christ Church, founded in 1546, has a chapel which serves as the city's cathedral, and the university's Bodleian Library, founded in 1602, is one of the world's most important libraries.
⚓ Oxford blue, a dark blue, gets its name from the colour of the ribbon given to those who represent the university at sport. A Cambridge blue – given for the same honour – is a light blue.

Paisley Scottish town in Strathclyde, on the western outskirts of Glasgow, which is one of the world's largest producers of cotton thread. It has given its name to a fabric pattern originating in Kashmir, which was copied in Paisley in 1770 from material sent home by Scottish troops.

Peak District Upland area of limestone dales and peat moors in central England, forming the southern end of the PENNINES. Lying mostly in Derbyshire, the Peak District was Britain's first National Park.

Pennines Range of hills in northern England which forms the 'spine' of the country. Starting north of the River Trent in Derbyshire the Pennines extend northwards to the Cheviot Hills on the Scottish border. All the major rivers of northern England rise in the Pennines, which reach 2930 ft (893 m) at Cross Fell.
⚓ The Pennine Way, a 250 mile (400 km) path from Edale in Derbyshire to Kirk Yetholm over the border in Scotland, is

Britain's most challenging long-distance walk, but the number of walkers has caused problems of erosion in some places.

Penzance Cornish seaside resort on Mount's Bay, and the most westerly town in England. It is known for its mild climate, and subtropical plants in the Morrab Gardens near the seafront. ST MICHAEL'S MOUNT lies 3 miles (4.8 km) offshore.

Perth Scottish city on the River Tay in Tayside. The Scottish parliament met there on occasions, and it was the home of many Scottish kings. John ▷KNOX launched the Scottish Reformation from the pulpit of St John's Kirk, Perth, in 1559.

Petticoat Lane Large Sunday market selling a wide range of clothes, leather goods and bric-a-brac, situated in and around Middlesex Street (originally Petticoat Lane) in east London.

Petworth House Mansion in West Sussex, set in 2000 acres (810 ha) of parkland landscaped by 'Capability' ▷BROWN. The house is a mixture of styles; dating from the 14th century, it was largely rebuilt in the late 17th century for the 6th Duke of Somerset. The Carved Room displays fine woodcarving by Grinling ▷GIBBONS. The Turner Room is devoted to the works of the artist J.M.W ▷TURNER (1775-1851), who was a frequent visitor and had a studio in the house. Petworth was given to the National Trust in 1947.

Piccadilly Street in central London running from Piccadilly Circus to Hyde Park Corner. Burlington House, home of the Royal Academy of Arts, and the Ritz Hotel are among its fine buildings. Piccadilly Circus is the heart of London's theatreland and is known for its night-time illuminations and its statue popularly supposed to be of Eros, but actually representing the Angel of Christian Charity.
🔔 The area takes its name from 'piccadils' – stiff collars made by an Elizabethan tailor who lived in the district.

Plymouth City and naval base in Devon, between the Tamar and Plym estuaries on Plymouth Sound. In 1588, Sir Francis Drake is said to have nonchalantly finished a game of bowls on Plymouth Hoe before sailing to meet the challenge of the Spanish Armada. The Pilgrim Fathers left Plymouth for America on the *Mayflower* in 1620. The city is linked to Saltash in Cornwall by Isambard Kingdom ▷BRUNEL's Tamar Bridge.

LITTLE ITALY *Clough Williams-Ellis, who created the Mediterranean-style village of Portmeirion on a wooded Welsh headland, chose pastel colours for the buildings to reinforce their Italianate charm.*

Polperro Fishing village and tourist resort on the south coast of Cornwall. It is noted for its small harbour – Polperro means St Peter's Pool – its colour-washed cottages and its ban on cars.

Poole Coastal resort in Dorset, with a large natural harbour used since the 13th century. Its sheltered waters are popular with wind-surfers, and commercial boats have largely been replaced by leisure craft.
🔔 Brownsea Island in the middle of the harbour became the birthplace of the Boy Scout movement when Lord Baden-Powell held his first camp there in 1907. The island now has a large nature reserve.

Portland, Isle of Peninsula in Dorset linked to the mainland by Chesil Beach. The pale Portland limestone from its quar-ries has been used in the construction of many buildings, including Buckingham Palace and St Paul's Cathedral. A castle on the northern shore was built by Henry VIII. On the southern tip of the isle, known as Portland Bill, a lighthouse overlooks waters with dangerous tidal currents.

Portmeirion Privately owned fanciful Welsh coastal village in Gwynedd, on a sandy estuary between Porthmadog and Harlech. Its colourful, cosmopolitan structures were pieced together from 1925 by the Welsh architect Clough Williams-Ellis (1883-1978). Inspired by the Italian village of Portofino, he set the romantic buildings amid terraced gardens, flights of steps and exotic plants.
🔔 The cult television series *The Prisoner* was filmed in Portmeirion in the late 1960s.

Portobello Road Thoroughfare in west London known for its all-day Saturday market, where miscellaneous items from Victoriana to secondhand clothes are sold.

Portsmouth City in Hampshire and site of Britain's principal naval base. Nelson's flagship HMS *Victory* and the hull of Henry VIII's flagship *Mary Rose*, which sank on her maiden voyage in 1545 and was raised from the bottom of the Solent in 1982, are among the ships preserved in Portsmouth.
🐚 Portsmouth ferries run to France, Spain, the Isle of Wight and the Channel Islands.

Potteries Cluster of towns around Stoke-on-Trent in Staffordshire which were at the heart of the pottery industry from the 17th century. The Potteries, also known as the Five Towns, were Burslem, Hanley, Longton, Tunstall and Stoke. In 1910 they amalgamated with a sixth town, Fenton, to form Stoke-on-Trent.
🐚 The author Arnold ▷BENNETT was born in Hanley and set many novels in the Five Towns – renaming them Bursley, Hanbridge, Longshaw, Turnhill and Knype.

Princes Street Thoroughfare in the centre of Edinburgh. It is lined with shops and hotels on the north side, while on the south side there is a superb view across Princes Street Gardens to the Old Town and Edinburgh Castle.
🐚 The 'princes' were the sons of George III (1738-1820), who changed the name from St Giles' Street because at the time this was the name of an unsavoury area of London.

Quantock Hills Ridge of red sandstone hills in Somerset which rise to 1261 ft (384 m), overlooking the Bristol Channel.
🐚 Samuel Taylor Coleridge wrote his poems 'The Ancient Mariner' and 'Kubla Khan' while living at Nether Stowey, in the Quantocks, from 1797 to 1800.

Regent's Park One of London's largest parks, laid out by John ▷NASH for the Prince Regent in the early 19th century. Nash designed the boating lake, and also the imposing terraces which border the park on three sides. The park has a rose garden and an open air theatre, and is also home to London Zoo. The zoo, founded in 1828, houses more than 8000 animals, including 200 species of birds in the walk-through Snowdon Aviary but its future is threatened by shortage of funds.

Regent Street Major shopping street in central London, designed by John ▷NASH in the early 19th century. It was originally

SPANNING THE CENTURIES *The hilltop ruins of Richmond's 11th-century castle tower above the bridge built in 1789, after the tumultuous River Swale had swept away several predecessors.*

built to join Carlton House, the home of the Prince Regent, to Regent's Park. The street has been partly rebuilt, but retains its original curved sweep into Piccadilly Circus. Among its shops are Liberty's department store and Hamley's toy shop.

Rhondda Valley Area of Mid Glamorgan in south Wales. Once a coal-mining region, it has seen its traditional industries decline in recent decades. The last pit was closed in 1990, and massive land reclamation schemes have transformed the area.
🐚 The tradition of the Welsh male voice choir originated in the Rhondda Valley. Choirs grew up there during the Industrial Revolution, formed by chapel-going workers and farm labourers.

Richmond Market town at the eastern entrance to Swaledale, North Yorkshire. The ruins of a Norman castle, including a

CITY LIGHTS *The glittering tracery of Christmas illuminations stretch above shoppers crowding the broad curve of London's Regent Street.*

keep 100 ft (30 m) tall, sit high on a crag above the River Swale, dominating the town's large cobbled marketplace. The Georgian Theatre Royal, built in 1788 and restored in 1962, is the second oldest in England after Bristol's Theatre Royal.

Richmond upon Thames Borough of Greater London, on the southwestern outskirts of the capital. The borough includes KEW Gardens, HAMPTON COURT PALACE and Richmond Park – 2470 acres (1007 ha) of heath and planted woodland, with large herds of fallow and red deer.

Ripon Cathedral city in North Yorkshire. The cathedral, built between the 13th and 16th centuries, includes a Saxon crypt. The spectacular remains of the Cistercian FOUNTAINS ABBEY, founded in 1132 and dissolved by Henry VIII in 1539, lie to the southwest of the city.
🐚 At nine o'clock every evening an official called the Ripon Hornblower blows his horn in an 1100-year-old ceremony known as 'Setting the Watch'. In medieval times the sound of the horn announced that the city was in the care of a wakeman, or watchman, for the night.

Rochdale Industrial town in Greater Manchester. The cooperative movement began there in 1844 when a group of working men formed the Rochdale Society of Equitable Pioneers, and opened a shop selling goods on a profit-sharing basis. The shop is now a museum.
🐚 Rochdale was the birthplace of the singer and comedienne Gracie Fields, and a theatre in the town is named after her.

Rochester Cathedral city and port on the estuary of the River Medway in Kent, which is closely associated with Charles Dickens. The author spent much of his childhood there and frequently referred to Rochester in his writings. The 16th-century Eastgate House contains the Charles Dickens Centre.

Rockall The most remote British islet, in the Atlantic Ocean, 191 miles (307 km) west of the Hebrides. Rockall is 70 ft (21 m) high and only 83 ft (25 m) across.
🌑Britain's claims to the islet and to oil and fishing rights in the surrounding area were reinforced when a Briton, Tom McClean, camped on the rock for 39 days in 1985.

Romney Marsh Large expanse of land reclaimed from the sea, extending along the English Channel coast between Hythe in Kent and Winchelsea in East Sussex. Long-wool sheep graze flat pastures intersected by dykes, many of which lie below sea level. Several of the remote villages have particularly fine churches.
🌑Romney Marsh used to be a haven for smugglers, known as 'owlers' because of their night time activities.

Romsey Market town on the River Test in Hampshire which is a trout and salmon-fishing centre. Its abbey, founded in 907 and enlarged in the 12th century, is one of Europe's finest Norman buildings.
🌑Broadlands, at Romsey, was the home of Lord Mountbatten, last Viceroy of India, and houses an exhibition of his career.

Ross-on-Wye Market town built on sandstone cliffs above the River Wye in Hereford and Worcester. The town's narrow, steep streets are lined with black and white buildings, a 17th-century arcaded market hall and a 14th-century church. Ross-on-Wye is one of the main tourist centres for the Wye Valley.

Royal Mile, The Thoroughfare in the centre of EDINBURGH which extends for almost 1 mile (1.6 km), from Edinburgh Castle to the Palace of HOLYROODHOUSE.

Rugby Industrial town in Warwickshire, known for its public school. The game of rugby football is said to have originated at the school in 1823 when a pupil, William Webb Ellis, carried the ball instead of kicking it in a football match.
🌑The Victorian school and its headmaster, Dr Thomas Arnold, are graphically described in *Tom Brown's Schooldays*, a novel written by ex-pupil Thomas Hughes.

Runnymede Meadow on the banks of the River Thames near Egham in Surrey where, in 1215, King John put his seal on the ▷MAGNA CARTA.

Rye Market town in East Sussex, on the Channel coast. It was once one of the ▷CINQUE PORTS but now lies 2 miles (3 km) inland, due to the silting up of the estuary of the River Rother. The many old buildings on its steep cobbled streets include the Mermaid Inn, which dates from Tudor times and was a haunt of smugglers.

Saffron Walden Market town in Essex, with a superb 15th-century church. The town has the remains of a Norman castle, and many fine half-timbered buildings decorated with pargeting – ornamental plasterwork common in East Anglia.
🌑The name 'Walden' comes from the Saxon *weale-denu* meaning 'wooded valley'. 'Saffron' was added in Tudor times when the town was an important centre of the trade in saffron, a yellow dye made from the locally grown autumn-flowering crocus.

St Albans Cathedral city on the River Ver in Hertfordshire, which was founded nearly 2000 years ago as the Roman city Verulamium. The city gets its name from Alban, a Roman soldier who became Britain's first saint. An 11th-century cathedral, which has the longest nave in England, now stands on the hill where Alban was beheaded in AD 209 for harbouring a Christian priest. The remains of the Roman city, including its theatre and city wall, lie on the opposite bank of the River Ver.

St Andrews Scottish town in Fife, on the North Sea coast. The town is the birthplace of modern golf and home of the Old Course – the world's earliest golf course, dating from 1754. St Andrews University, founded in 1410, is the oldest in Scotland.
🌑St Andrews is named after the patron saint of Scotland, whose bones are said to have been taken there in AD 345 and whose crucifixion on a X-shaped cross is symbolised in the Scottish national flag.

St Ives Attractive Cornish harbour town with steep cobbled streets. Former inhabitants include the potter Bernard ▷LEACH, the artist Ben ▷NICHOLSON and the sculptor Barbara ▷HEPWORTH. The St Ives Tate, an extension of the Tate Gallery in London, was opened in 1993.

St Michael's Mount Small island linked by a causeway at low tide to the village of Marazion on the Cornish mainland. Its fairytale castle, which was once a 14th-century priory, has been the home of the St Aubyn family since 1647.

OLD STONES *St Andrews Cathedral, built in the 12th century, was once Scotland's largest. The Royal and Ancient Golf Club (left), founded at St Andrews in 1754, is the ruling authority on the game.*

SOARING ELEGANCE *Salisbury Cathedral's slender spire rises higher than any other in England, and a tracery of fan-vaulting tops the stained glass of its octagonal Chapter House.*

Salisbury Cathedral city in Wiltshire at the confluence of the River Avon and the River Wylye. ▷SALISBURY CATHEDRAL, built between 1220 and 1258 in Early English style, soars above the town with a spire 404 ft (123 m) tall. The cathedral replaced an earlier one north of the town, at a hilltop site now known as Old Sarum.
🌿Salisbury Cathedral and its surrounding water meadows are the subject of many paintings by the artist John ▷CONSTABLE.

Salisbury Plain Chalk upland in Wiltshire, which was a centre of settlement in prehistoric times. It has many archaeological remains including STONEHENGE.

Saltaire Victorian 'factory' village created beside the River Aire, West Yorkshire by the industrialist Sir Titus Salt (1803-76). In 1853, Salt opened a six-storey, 545 ft (166 m) long mill, housed its 3000 workers in streets named after members of his large family, and provided a school and a church. The buildings remain virtually unchanged.

Sandhurst Village in Berkshire which is the site of the Royal Military Academy, where army officers are trained. The Academy is the successor to the Royal Military College, which was founded at Great Marlow but moved to Sandhurst in 1812.

Sandringham Norfolk village and site of a country residence of the royal family, Sandringham House, which was converted in 1870 to a mock-Jacobean style. It is set in 20 000 acres (8100 ha) of heathland, forest and park, some of which is open to the public at certain times of the year.

Sandwich Town on the River Stour in Kent. In the Middle Ages it was a port but it is now 2 miles (3 km) inland, due to the silting up of the River Stour. Sandwich has three championship golf links.
🌿The sandwich was named after a local nobleman, the 4th Earl of Sandwich, in the 18th century. Unwilling to leave the gaming table for a meal, he made do with a slice of beef between two pieces of bread.

Savernake Forest Expanse of oak and beech covering 200 acres (80 ha) in Wiltshire. It is a remnant of one of England's oldest forests and the only English forest still privately owned. The Grand Avenue, a 4 mile (6 km) beech drive, was designed in the 18th century by 'Capability' ▷BROWN.

Scarborough Seaside resort and port in North Yorkshire. Its twin sandy bays are separated by a promontory crowned by the ruins of a 12th-century castle.
🌿It was at Scarborough that sea bathing first became popular in 1660 – a century before Brighton became fashionable.
🌿In 1993, Holbeck Hall Hotel slid into the sea, with part of Scarborough's coastline.

Scilly, Isles of Group of islands some 25 miles (40 km) southwest of Land's End. Five of the islands are inhabited by a population of about 2000. The largest is St Mary's, followed by St Martin's and Tresco. Warmed by the waters of the Gulf Stream, the Isles of Scilly are noted for their early potatoes and spring flowers.
🌿According to legend, the Isles of Scilly are King Arthur's lost kingdom of Lyonesse.

ON PARADE *'Serve to lead' is the motto of the Royal Military Academy at Sandhurst, whose former pupils include Winston Churchill.*

Scone Palace (Scoon) Scottish pink stone castellated mansion in Tayside which was built in 1803, on the site of several earlier ancient palaces. The nearby Moot Hill was the coronation site of the Scottish kings, where from 836 they were crowned seated on the Stone of ▷SCONE.

Sellafield Nuclear reprocessing plant and power station on the Cumbrian coast. The site was known as Windscale when the reprocessing plant opened in 1951, but the name was changed in 1957 when the establishment was expanded to include the nearby Calder Hall nuclear power station. There is an exhibition centre.
🌿Since a fire at Windscale in 1957, the site has been dogged by controversy over the possibility of radiation dangers.

TASTE OF THE TROPICS *Around the abbey ruins on Tresco in the Isles of Scilly, exotic subtropical plants flourish in the mild climate.*

Severn, River Britain's longest river, which rises in Wales and meanders for 220 miles (354 km) through the Vale of Powys, Shrewsbury, Worcester and Gloucester, and into the Bristol Channel.
🌿At flood-tide, incoming tidal water from the Bristol Channel fills the narrowing Severn estuary and sweeps upstream in a wall of water – as high as 9 ft (3 m) – known as the Severn Bore. The bore can reach Gloucester – 10 miles (16 km) upstream.
🌿The Severn Road Bridge, a toll bridge linking Wales and England, was opened in 1966. A little way downstream an even longer bridge – spanning nearly 3½ miles (5.6 km) – is due to be completed by 1996.

Sheffield Fourth largest city in England, on the River Don in South Yorkshire. It has a 15th-century cathedral, a university founded in 1905 and several art galleries. The City Museum is largely devoted to Sheffield's 400-year-old tradition of steel production and its Sheffield plate cutlery.

Sherwood Forest Ancient oak forest covering 450 acres (182 ha) in Nottinghamshire. The forest once covered the whole of the western part of the county.
🔥 The area is associated with ▷ROBIN HOOD and his outlaws; their meeting-place is said to have been an ancient hollow tree, the Major Oak, which is 30 ft (9 m) in circumference and possibly 500 years old.

Shetland Archipelago of almost 100 islands 125 miles (200 km) off the north coast of Scotland. About 23 000 inhabitants live on 19 of the islands – most of them on the largest island, Mainland, which includes Lerwick, the chief town. There are Bronze Age remains at Jarlshof, on Mainland, and on Mousa, an uninhabited island. The islands have bred the Shetland sheepdog and pony, and are rich in bird life. They still service the North Sea oil industry.

Shrewsbury County town of Shropshire which is almost an island in a wide loop of the River Severn. Historically its position on the England-Wales border gave the town great strategic importance, and the town's narrow approach is guarded by a medieval castle. Its streets still contain many half-timbered Tudor buildings.

Shropshire English county which borders Wales. The Industrial Revolution began at IRONBRIDGE on the River Severn, but Shropshire is now largely agricultural.
🔥A.E. ▷HOUSEMAN immortalised the county's rolling landscape in his collection of poems entitled *A Shropshire Lad*.

Sissinghurst Castle Garden One of the finest gardens in Britain, designed around the ruins of a Tudor mansion in Kent. It was created in the 1930s by the diplomat Harold Nicolson and his wife, the novelist and poet Vita Sackville-West. The garden is a series of 'outdoor rooms' which are all completely different in layout and colour; the White Garden is planted entirely with white or silver plants.

Skye, Isle of Largest and most spectacular of the islands of the Inner HEBRIDES, five minutes by ferry from Kyle of Lochalsh on the Scottish mainland. It is dominated by the jagged Cuillin Hills, which rise to more than 3000 ft (900 m) and provide some of the most strenuous mountaineering country in Britain. The capital, Portree, is on the east coast.
🔥Flora Macdonald brought Bonnie Prince Charlie to Skye, disguised as her maid, as he fled the English in 1746. The episode is told in the 'Skye Boat Song'.

HEIGHTS AND DEPTHS *A rising winter sun lights up the great horseshoe of peaks that make up the Snowdon range, and the still waters of Llynnau Mymbyr pick up their snow-capped reflection.*

Smithfield London's central meat market, built in 1868 on the site of a cattle market dating back to the 12th century. The nearby Norman church of St Bartholomew the Great was founded in 1123, as was St Bartholomew's Hospital. For centuries Smithfield was a site of executions, including the burning of Protestant martyrs by Queen Mary in the 1550s.

Snowdon Highest mountain in England and Wales, which rises to 3560 ft (1085 m) in Gwynedd. On a clear day, the view from the summit takes in Ireland's Wicklow Mountains to the west and the Lake District peaks to the northeast. The steep Snowdon Mountain Railway runs from Llanberis almost to the top. Snowdonia, the area surrounding Snowdon, became a National Park in 1951. It includes 30 miles (48 km) of the north Wales coast as well as spectacular hills, forests and lakes.

Soho Area of central London traditionally thought of as the capital's 'red-light' district but now equally well known for its cafés, bars and restaurants. Soho Square and the narrow streets round it were laid out in 1681, and many fine buildings remain. Chinatown, Shaftesbury Avenue and Berwick Street fruit and vegetable market add to Soho's bustling atmosphere.
🔥The district's name is said to derive from the hunting cry used by Charles I in the parkland that once covered the area.

Solent Wide sea channel that separates the Isle of Wight from the coast of Hampshire, and leads into Southampton Water.
🔥The Solent's double tide, caused by the funnelling of tides round the Isle of Wight, allows twice as many daily departures from Southampton as from other British ports.

Somerset Mainly agricultural county of southwest England, bordering the Bristol Channel. The area includes the QUANTOCK HILLS and the MENDIPS, cut by gorges and riddled with caves such as WOOKEY HOLE. The orchards around the county town of Taunton produce cider – known locally as 'scrumpy', from *scrump*, a local word meaning 'small apple'.

Southampton Hampshire's largest city and port, at the head of Southampton Water. The Pilgrim Fathers originally set sail for America from Southampton, aboard the *Mayflower* in 1620, but were forced to dock at Plymouth. Southampton was the departure point for the *Queen Mary* and the ill-fated *Titanic*; it is still used by the *QE 2*.

South Downs Ridge of chalk hills which run roughly parallel to the NORTH DOWNS for 80 miles (130 km) from Winchester in Hampshire to BEACHY HEAD in East Sussex.

Southend-on-Sea Resort on the north bank of the River Thames estuary in Essex. It became a popular 'day-out' destination

HOME FOR THE GODS *The pantheon is one of the Classical-style buildings which provide focal points in the landscaped gardens at Stourhead.*

for many holidaymakers from London's East End after the development of the railways in the mid 19th century. It has many parks and the world's longest pleasure pier – 1⅓ miles (2.1 km) long.

Spalding Market town in the heart of Lincolnshire's bulb-growing region. In spring the flat fenland around the town is covered with a carpet of colourful tulips. The banks of the River Welland are lined by elegant Georgian houses.

Spey, River Fast-flowing river in the highlands of northeastern Scotland. It rises in the Mondhliath Mountains and flows northeast through AVIEMORE, reaching the North Sea at Spey Bay. It is known for its salmon fishing and flows through the area that produces Scotland's finest whisky.

Staffordshire County in central England, renowned for its pottery industry. The 30 000 acres (12 140 ha) of conifer forests and moorland known as Cannock Chase separate Wolverhampton from the POTTERIES, which now lie within Stoke-on-Trent. The county town is Stafford.

Stansted London's third largest airport, east of Bishop's Stortford in Essex. Its new terminal which opened in 1991 was designed by Sir Norman ▷FOSTER.

Stirling University town overlooking the River Forth. Its castle, once a residence of Scottish kings, stands on an outcrop 250 ft (76 m) above the town. The Scots won victories over the English at Stirling Bridge (1297) and ▷BANNOCKBURN (1314).

Stockton-on-Tees Market town in Cleveland, linked to DARLINGTON by the first stretch of railway in 1825.

Stoke-on-Trent Town in Staffordshire, formed in 1910 when the cluster of towns known as the POTTERIES amalgamated. The area has been the centre of the pottery industry since the 17th century: Wedgwood, Minton, Spode and Doulton all have their factories there.

Stonehenge Prehistoric stone circle built near Amesbury in Wiltshire. The giant upright stones, or sarcens, which rise to 20 ft (6.1 m) above Salisbury Plain, were

HOME FOR THE GODS *The pantheon is one of the Classical-style buildings which provide focal points in the landscaped gardens at Stourhead.*

erected in *c*.1560 BC – nearly 1200 years after Stonehenge was started. (See also ▷STONEHENGE in 'Myths and Legends'.)

Stourhead Palladian house in Wiltshire surrounded by one of the earliest and best examples of English landscape gardening. The gardens were designed by Henry Hoare, a London banker, in the 1740s – ten years before 'Capability' Brown rose to prominence. Hoare dammed the River Stour to create a large lake, which he surrounded with Classical temples and follies.

Stowe Fine 17th-century mansion, in Buckinghamshire. Its grounds – dotted with lakes and temples – were designed by 'Capability' ▷BROWN and William Kent. Stowe became a school in 1923.

Stratford-upon-Avon Small Warwickshire town where William Shakespeare (1564-1616) was born and buried. The

town's wide streets are lined with Tudor half-timbered houses and many 18th-century buildings. The riverside Royal Shakespeare Theatre is the home of the Royal Shakespeare Company. In the nearby village of Shottery is the 16th-century cottage where Shakespeare's wife, Anne Hathaway, was born.

Suffolk Mainly agricultural county in East Anglia. It has a wealth of fine old towns, including Woodbridge, Bury St Edmunds, Lavenham and the horse-racing town of NEWMARKET. The peaceful valley of the River Stour inspired artists such as John Constable and Thomas Gainsborough, as well as the composer Benjamin Britten, who started the annual Aldeburgh Music Festival in 1948. The fishing port of Lowestoft lies on the easternmost point of the British mainland. Ipswich is the county town.
🔔 The county's name derives from its Saxon label, the land of 'south folk'.

Swansea Second largest city in Wales and the administrative centre of West Glamorgan, situated at the mouth of the River Tawe on Swansea Bay. Copper smelting began in Swansea in the late 18th century, and in the 19th century it expanded into a major industrial centre and coal-exporting port, though its prosperity declined greatly after World War II. The docks have now been largely redeveloped for housing and are the home of the Maritime and Industrial Museum which opened in 1977.
🔔 Swansea was the birthplace of Dylan ▷THOMAS (1914-53), and many of his short stories recall his life in the city.

Swindon Wiltshire town which became important after the 19th-century railway boom, when Isambard Kingdom ▷BRUNEL made it the headquarters of his Great Western Railway. Swindon grew again between 1960 and 1980 when many companies moved there to take advantage of its good road and rail communications.

Syon House Stately home on the outskirts of west London. It was originally a nunnery, and was turned into a castellated mansion in Tudor times. In the 1760s its interior was sumptuously renovated by Robert ▷ADAM and its grounds landscaped by 'Capability' Brown.

Tay, River Longest river in Scotland, renowned for its salmon fishing. Rising in the Grampians, it flows for 118 miles (190 km) through lochs Dochart and Tay, and into the North Sea through the Firth of Tay. Before entering Loch Dochart

SYON'S GLORY *A bronze of the* Dying Gaul *and statues of Gaul's Roman conquerors adorn Robert Adam's Great Hall at Syon House.*

it is known as the Fillan, and from there to Loch Tay as the Dochart.
🔔 In December 1879 the firth was the scene of the Tay Bridge disaster, when a train plunged from the bridge into the water, with the loss of 100 lives.

Tees, River Rising in the Pennines, in northeastern England, the River Tees flows eastwards, eventually reaching the North Sea at the port of Middlesbrough. Its wild upper reaches are known as Teesdale.

Telford New Town near IRONBRIDGE in Shropshire. It was created in 1965, and takes its name from Thomas ▷TELFORD, the Scottish 19th-century civil engineer who designed many of Britain's canals, roads, bridges, tunnels and docks.

Tewkesbury Town on the River Avon in Gloucestershire. Its magnificent abbey church has fine medieval stained glass, an impressive Norman nave and a 148 ft (45 m) high central tower – the largest remaining Norman tower in England.

Thames, River Rising in the Cotswolds, the Thames flows east for 210 miles (338 km) through Oxford (where it is also known as the Isis), Reading and central London, southeast of which it joins the North Sea in a wide, tidal estuary. The Thames flows past so many celebrated historic sites that it has been aptly described as 'liquid history'.
🔔 The gated Thames Barrier at Woolwich, east London, was completed in 1982 and protects the capital against flooding.
🔔 The annual boat race between Oxford and Cambridge universities, starts at Putney Bridge and ends at Mortlake.

Tintagel Village on the northern coast of Cornwall, near Camelford, with a ruined 12th-century clifftop castle said to be the birthplace of King Arthur. Stained-glass windows in a nearby hall tell the story of the Knights of the Round Table.

Tintern Abbey Ruined abbey beside the River Wye near Chepstow in Gwent, which was founded by Cistercian monks in the 12th century and greatly enlarged over the next two centuries.
🔔 The abbey inspired paintings by J.M.W. Turner and the reflective poem ▷TINTERN ABBEY by William Wordsworth.

TRANQUIL TINTERN *White-robed Cistercian monks once worked and prayed in Tintern Abbey, whose great walls still rear heavenward among the woods that flank the River Wye in Gwent.*

Torbay Name for the combined seaside resorts of Torquay, Paignton and Brixham in Devon. It is also known as the 'English Riviera' because of its palm trees, subtropical gardens and beaches, which have attracted visitors since the 18th century.

Tower Bridge London's best-known bridge, spanning the River Thames next to the Tower of London. The two halves of its centre span, each weighing 1000 tons, can be raised hydraulically in order to allow large ships to pass through.

Tower of London Norman fortress on the north bank of the River Thames in the City of London, and one of the country's principal tourist attractions. The Keep, or White Tower, was built in the 11th century, as the original tower of London. The outer fortifications were added in the 12th and 13th centuries. In the Middle Ages the tower was used as a prison and place of execution. Prisoners were brought by river to Traitor's Gate, and executed either on Tower Green within the castle grounds or publicly at nearby Tower Hill. The Tower houses the Crown Jewels.

🕯The 'Princes in the Tower', the sons of Edward IV, are said to have been murdered in the Bloody Tower in 1493 on the orders of their uncle, Richard III. Anne Boleyn and Catherine Howard, wives of Henry VIII, were beheaded in its grounds.

🕯Ravens have been kept at the Tower since the time of Charles II, who was told that the Tower would crumble and the monarchy fall if the ravens left.

🕯Yeoman warders, also known as 'beefeaters', have guarded the Tower of London since 1326. On state occasions they wear a gold, red and black uniform which dates from Tudor times.

Trafalgar Square Grand London square designed by John ▷NASH in the early 19th century and named after Lord Nelson's great naval victory of 1805. Nelson's Column soars 162 ft (48 m) above four enormous bronze lions designed by Sir Edwin ▷LANDSEER. The National Gallery is situated on the square's north side.

Tunbridge Wells Spa town in Kent which became a fashionable centre for taking the waters, gambling and socialising after a spring of iron-bearing water was discovered in 1606. The Pantiles, a 17th-century promenade, leads to the spring.

🕯The town was given a 'Royal' prefix by Edward VII when he visited in 1909.

🕯Tunbridge Ware, small wooden objects decorated with coloured mosaic, were produced in the town from the end of the 17th century until the 1920s.

Tyne and Wear Industrial coastal county of northeast England named after the two rivers which cross it. It includes NEWCASTLE UPON TYNE and the resorts of Tynemouth and Whitley Bay.

CITY TREASURES *At the eastern approach to the capital, the Tower of London begun by William the Conqueror stands by the mighty Tower Bridge completed in 1894. Just upstream, HMS Belfast – a World War II cruiser – is moored and is open to the public.*

POET'S PROSPECT *Sir Walter Scott thought this view of Warwick Castle seen from across the River Avon was unsurpassed in England.*

Warwick County town of Warwickshire on the River Avon. The river curves around Warwick's 14th-century castle, one of the best preserved in Britain. Parts of Warwick's medieval town wall also survive.

Wash, The Large sea inlet which separates Lincolnshire from Norfolk. It is fed by the Ouse, the Welland and other rivers, and is bounded by marshland, sand and shingle.

Wells Small city in Somerset with a superb medieval cathedral. Its 13th-century west front comprises a gallery of medieval sculpture arranged in six tiers; more than 300 of the original 400 figures survive. Inside, the cathedral has scissor-shaped arches built in 1338 to support the tower when the cathedral began to collapse. The nearby Bishop's Palace is surrounded by a freshwater moat, fed by the wells that give the city its name.

Westminster, City of London's administrative centre, and the site of the Houses of Parliament, the government ministry buildings of Whitehall, the medieval Westminster Abbey (from which the area takes its name), and Buckingham Palace.

Weston-super-Mare Coastal resort on the Bristol Channel in Avon. At low tide its sandy beach stretches for more than 1 mile (1.6 km) out to sea. It was a fishing village until 1841, when the railway made it accessible to holidaymakers.

Westward Ho! Small seaside resort in north Devon, named after an adventure story written by Charles Kingsley in 1855 but set in the time of the Armada. It is the only place name in the United Kingdom with an exclamation mark.

West Yorkshire County in north central England which incorporates the clothing centre of Leeds together with Bradford, Halifax, Huddersfield and Wakefield.
The town of HAWORTH was the home and inspiration of the Brontë sisters.

Whitehall Main thoroughfare in Westminster, central London, which runs between Trafalgar Square and Parliament Square. It is lined with government ministry buildings, including the Home Office, the Foreign Office and the Treasury. Whitehall also includes the Cenotaph – a monument to the dead of both world wars – and half-way along its western side is Downing Street, site of the official residence of the prime minister (No.10) and the chancellor of the exchequer (No.11).

White Horse Hill Stretch of downland near Wantage, Oxfordshire, bearing the chalk-cut figure of a horse. Tradition says that the 347 ft (106 m) long horse marked King Alfred's victory over the Danes at the Battle of Ashdown in AD 871, but archaeologists believe it may be as much as 2000

years old. Uffington Castle, an Iron Age fort, crowns White Horse Hill.
Nearby is the flat-topped Dragon Hill where, according to legend, St George killed the dragon. There are patches where grass will not grow – said to be the places where the dragon's blood was spilled.

Wight, Isle of Island county covering 147 sq miles (381 km²) off the Hampshire coast, and separated from the mainland by the Solent and Spithead channels. In the 19th century the poet Lord Tennyson lived on the island, and Osborne House was Queen Victoria's favourite summer residence. Newport is the county town.
Every August the island stages a yachting regatta during Cowes Week.

Wilton Small town in Wiltshire, known for carpet-making since the 17th century. Wilton House, the stately home of the Earl of Pembroke, was begun in Elizabethan times; its later Palladian-style south front was damaged by fire in 1647 soon after its completion, and restored by Inigo Jones. A noted 'double cube' room is 60 ft (18 m) long and 30 ft (9 m) in width and height. The formal gardens contain an elegant Palladian-style bridge, dating from 1751.

Wiltshire Agricultural county of southern England which runs from the Marlborough Downs and the Cotswolds in the

HORSE ON THE HILL *Bold slashes in the chalk set the White Horse in vigorous motion across the downs above Uffington. The figure, which may be 2000 years old, is only clearly visible from the air.*

north to Salisbury Plain in the south. It includes SALISBURY and the prehistoric sites of STONEHENGE and AVEBURY. Trowbridge is the county town.

Wimbledon Suburb of southwest London known throughout the world as the home of the All England Lawn Tennis Club, where international championships have been held annually in June or July since 1877. There is a museum devoted to the history of tennis.
🔖 Wimbledon Common was the setting for Elizabeth Beresford's book *The Wombles*.

Winchester County town of Hampshire, on the River Itchen. In Anglo-Saxon times Winchester was the royal capital of Wessex and of England until the late 12th century. Its austere Norman cathedral was begun in 1079, and at 556 ft (170 m) long it is Europe's longest medieval church. Winchester College was founded in 1382 by the churchman William of Wykeham – its pupils are known as Wykehamists. It is the oldest boys' public school in England and was the model for Eton and other schools.
🔖 The belief that if it rains on St Swithin's Day (July 15) it will rain for 40 days is connected to a story about a 9th-century bishop of Winchester, St Swithin: in 971, against his wishes, his remains were transferred from churchyard to cathedral and rain fell for 40 days and nights.

Windsor Town on the south bank of the River Thames in Berkshire which is dominated by Windsor Castle, home of English monarchs for the last 900 years, and the largest inhabited castle in England. The castle was built in stages by successive medieval kings, and is a vast complex of towers and apartments. The most elaborate building is St George's Chapel which was begun in 1475. A fire in 1992 caused extensive damage to the state apartments.
🔖 During World War I the British royal family changed their German name, Saxe-Coburg Gotha, to Windsor.

Woburn Abbey Country mansion set in a 3000 acre (1200 ha) landscaped park near Dunstable in Bedfordshire. It is the ancestral home of the dukes of Bedford and houses many important works of art. Woburn is also known for its Wild Animal Kingdom, where elephants, lions, giraffes and other species roam free.

Wookey Hole Series of caves in the MENDIPS in Somerset, cut by the River Axe. The caves are an eerie but beautiful domain of stalactites, stalagmites and watercourses. Mineral seams give the walls a dramatic range of colours.

Woolwich Borough on the River Thames in southeast London. Woolwich Dockyard, founded in Tudor times and closed in 1869,

built many of the navy's 'wooden wall' ships. The Royal Artillery moved to the barracks there in 1776, and Woolwich Arsenal remained a major armaments-producing centre throughout World War II.
🔖 Arsenal football club was founded in 1886 by workers in the Woolwich Arsenal, hence its popular name, the Gunners.

Worcester City on the River Severn in Hereford and Worcester. Its striking cathedral, built between the 11th and 14th centuries, contains the tomb of King John. The Royal Worcester Porcelain Works have produced fine bone china and porcelain in the city since 1751.
🔖 Worcestershire sauce – a piquant mixture of soy sauce, vinegar and spices – was first made in the city in the 1820s.

Wye, River Rising on the slopes of Plynlimon in central Wales, the Wye winds southeast for 130 miles (210 km) past Hereford, Monmouth and Tintern Abbey, entering the Severn estuary near Chepstow. Symond's Yat Rock, northeast of Monmouth, rises 400 ft (122 m) above the River Wye providing superb views of a 5 mile (8 km) horseshoe bend in the river. The Wye Valley is widely regarded as one of the most beautiful river valleys in Britain.

York Historic city on the River Ouse in North Yorkshire. The city, which was known as Eboracum to the Romans and Jorvik to the Vikings, is surrounded by a 3 mile (4.8 km) long medieval wall and the city centre still has a medieval street layout, overhung by half-timbered houses. York Minster is England's largest medieval cathedral. The building of the cathedral – the fourth on the site – began in *c*.1220 and continued for more than 250 years. Its magnificent 14th-century stained glass windows survived a fire in 1984 which badly damaged the roof. The city has a university and has been the home of the National Railway Museum since 1975.
🔖 At the Jorvik Viking Centre, opened in 1984, visitors can travel in time cars around a reconstruction of life in York when it was a Viking settlement.
🔖 The suffix '-*gate*' on York street names does not refer to any kind of barrier – it is simply the Viking word for 'street'.

Yorkshire Dales Valleys eroded by rivers which wind down the eastern slopes of the Pennines. The main dales are Swaledale, Wensleydale, Nidderdale, Wharfedale and Airedale. Renowned for their harsh, unspoilt beauty, the Dales lie within the Yorkshire Dales National Park.

PATTERNS IN THE SNOW *Dry-stone walls criss-cross the white blanket on Kisdon Hill in Swaledale, where an isolated farmhouse and its outbuildings ride out the rigours of the North Yorkshire winter.*

NATIONS AND PLACES
OF THE WORLD

Our world has grown smaller. Remote corners of the Earth can be
reached in only a few hours. Scenes of distant wars, droughts
and disasters appear daily on television, compelling immediate
interest. Holiday resorts and places rich in culture, architecture or
history lure us abroad, while deserts, mountains, exotic isles
or icy wastes astound us with their natural beauty.

FLOATING MARKET, THAILAND

GOLDEN GATE BRIDGE

LEANING TOWER OF PISA

Acapulco Resort on Mexico's south coast, renowned for its cliff-divers who plunge from more than 120 ft (37 m) into a rocky shallow cove. To avoid hitting the rocks, divers take off as a large wave comes in.

Aden Port in Yemen, and the chief trading centre of southern Arabia. Aden was under British rule from 1839 until 1967.

Aegean Sea Arm of the Mediterranean Sea between Greece, Turkey and Crete. The Aegean is studded with islands in three groups: the Cyclades, the Sporades and the Dodecanese, one of which is RHODES.

Afghanistan Country in southwest Asia, divided by the Hindu Kush mountain range. Its capital is the ancient city of KABUL. Afghanistan is one of the world's least developed countries, and many of its people are semi-nomadic livestock herders. Nearly all Afghans are Muslims.
Troops of the former USSR occupied Afghanistan from 1979 to 1989.

Alaska Largest of the states of the USA in area but the second smallest in population, after Wyoming, with just over 550 000 people. Alaska was bought from Russia in 1867 for US$7.2 million. Huge oil reserves along the Arctic coast are its chief source of wealth. The biggest city is Anchorage but the state capital is Juneau, which is accessible only by sea and air.
North America's highest mountain, the 20 320 ft (6194 m) Mount McKinley, is in the south of Alaska.
In 1989 the *Exxon Valdez* oil tanker spilled more than 11 million gallons (50 million litres) of crude oil in Prince William Sound, off Alaska's southern coastline.

Albania Poorest European nation, with more than half its population working on the land. The capital is Tiranë. Hard-line communists controlled Albania from 1944 to 1990, since when economic, political and social reforms have been introduced. However, Albania remains the least accessible country in Europe to foreigners.

Aleutian Islands Chain of 14 large and 55 small islands extending westwards from Alaska. These rainy, mountainous, treeless islands are the home of some 1000 ▷ALEUTS whose main industry is fishing.

Alexandria Port on the Nile delta and second largest city of Egypt, founded by Alexander the Great in 332 BC. The Pharos, or Lighthouse, of Alexandria was one of the Seven Wonders of the World.

In ancient times the Library at Alexandria held more than 400 000 scrolls; all had been destroyed in sieges and wars by 300 AD.

Algeria North African country – the continent's second largest after Sudan – which gained independence from France in 1962 after a long war. More than 85 per cent of the country is in the SAHARA desert, where there are huge deposits of natural gas and petroleum. Berbers established a kingdom in about 2400 BC, and Arabs arrived from the 7th century bringing Islam, now the faith of most Algerians.
The French Foreign Legion's battles against the Berbers were immortalised in P.C. Wren's novel *Beau Geste*.

Alice Springs Nearest town to AYERS ROCK in Australia's Northern Territory.
Nevil Shute's 1950 novel *A Town Like Alice* made Alice Springs world famous.

Amazon World's longest river, flowing for some 4195 miles (6751 km) across Peru and northern Brazil. It is now considered to be longer than the Nile if measured from its true source, discovered in 1971 in the snow-covered Andes of southern Peru, to the Pará Estuary – its farthest mouth. Seven of the Amazon's tributaries are more than 1000 miles (1600 km) long, and it ends in a delta so vast that two channels are separated by an island which is about the size of Switzerland.
The Amazon rain forest covers an area 24 times the size of the United Kingdom.

Amritsar Indian city whose Golden Temple is the most sacred shrine of SIKHISM. In the Amritsar Massacre of 1919, troops under the British General Dyer killed about 400 Indians. In 1984 Indian troops stormed the Golden Temple, which had been occupied by Sikh extremists.

HOT CONTINENT *Harsh deserts cover one-third of Africa, and hot and humid rain forests lie along the Equator. Only six per cent of the land is arable, yet two out of three people work on the land.*

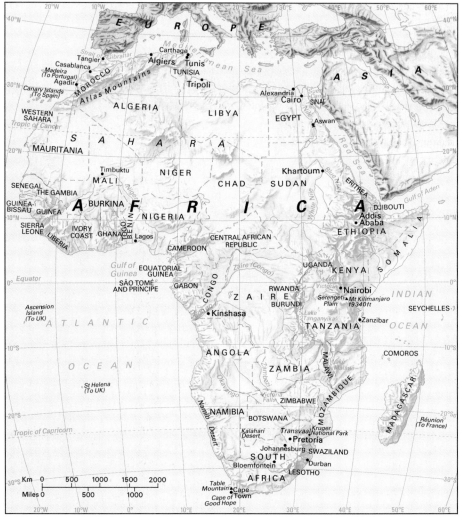

NIGHT SCENE *Lights outline the gables on houses in Amsterdam and one of the city's 1000 bridges that cross more than 100 canals.*

Amsterdam Capital and largest city of the Netherlands. The old city of canals and gabled houses dates mainly from 1650-1720. Amsterdam was the home of ▷REMBRANDT and, during World War II, the Jewish girl ▷ANNE FRANK. It has been a diamond-cutting centre since the 1570s.

Andes World's longest mountain range, running along South America's Pacific coast for 5000 miles (8000 km). The highest point is Aconcagua, 22 834 ft (6960 m). The ▷INCA Empire embraced much of the northern Andes, and the ruins of MACHU PICCHU, one of their cities, stand 7480 ft (2280 m) up in the mountains.

Andorra Tiny principality in the Pyrenees between Spain and France, known for its ski resorts and duty-free goods.

Angel Falls World's highest waterfall, with a drop of 3212 ft (979 m), on a tributary of the River Carrao in Venezuela.
♨ The falls are named after Jimmy Angel, an American pilot who, in 1935, was the first white man to see them.

Angola Country in southwestern Africa with vast but largely unexploited mineral resources. Luanda is the capital and largest city. The country's independence from Portugal in 1975 was followed by civil war between the Marxist government and the pro-Western opposition group UNITA, one of the longest running wars in Africa.

Antarctica Barren continent almost twice the size of Australia surrounding the South Pole. Even in the summer, ice and snow cover 98 per cent of Antarctica, and in places the ice is more than 2½ miles (4 km) deep. The 1959 Antarctic Treaty has resulted in international cooperation in the interests of scientific research, and scientists are Antarctica's only inhabitants.
♨ A Norwegian team led by Roald ▷AMUNDSEN was the first to reach the South Pole in 1911, a month before the British team led by Captain ▷SCOTT.

Aral Sea Inland sea in central Asia. Water has been diverted from rivers that feed the sea to irrigate crops, and in 1990 the area of the sea had shrunk so much that it was only just over half the size it was in 1970.

Ararat Highest mountain in Turkey, rising to nearly 16 945 ft (5165 m) not far from Turkey's eastern border. Ararat was the Biblical landing place of Noah's Ark.

Arctic Area extending from the North Pole to the Arctic Circle at latitude 66° 32″, the southernmost latitude at which the Sun does not set at the northern midsummer, and remains below the horizon all day at midwinter. Much of the Arctic Ocean, which surrounds the North Pole, is permanently covered by pack ice, 7-10 ft (2-3 m) thick. Polar bears live in the Arctic.
♨ Robert Peary, an American naval officer and explorer, led the first party to reach the North Pole, on April 6, 1909.

Argentina Second largest country in South America, after Brazil. The Andes stretch along its western border, and BUENOS AIRES is the capital and largest city. The vast majority of the Spanish-speaking people live in towns and cities, but much of the country's wealth comes from its fertile plains, including the almost treeless pampas, where cattle are reared in huge numbers. In southern Argentina is the barren highland of PATAGONIA.
♨ The ▷FALKLANDS WAR was prompted by Argentina's invasion of the Falkland Islands in April 1982.
♨ Argentina's best-known couple were Juan ▷PERÓN who was president from 1946 to 1955 and from 1973 to 1974 and his popular wife Eva on whose life the long-running musical *Evita* was based.

Arizona Arid southwestern state of the USA, noted for its magnificent canyon scenery, including the GRAND CANYON.

ICE AND FIRE *A plume of smoke rising above Antarctica's McMurdo Sound marks Mount Erebus, a 12 447 ft (3794 m) volcano named after a ship of Sir James Ross's Antarctic expedition of 1841.*

Ascension Island Tiny volcanic island in the South Atlantic Ocean, only 34 sq miles (88 km²) in area. It is 700 miles (1130 km) from the nearest land – the island of ST HELENA, which is only slightly larger – and some 950 miles (1530 km) from Africa. ♣ Ascension Island was an important air-sea staging post during World War II and the 1982 Falklands War.

Aswan High Dam Massive dam on the Nile in Egypt, completed in 1971 and built to keep the river level constant throughout the year to control flooding. The dam has brought drawbacks as well as advantages; previously the annual floods deposited fertilising silt on the land, but now farmers must use expensive chemical fertilisers. Lake Nasser formed behind the dam.

♣ The USA and Britain, concerned about Egypt's purchase of arms from communist sources, withdrew their pledges of financial aid for the dam in 1956. President Nasser then nationalised the Suez Canal which was followed by the ▷SUEZ CRISIS.

Athens Historic and busy capital of Greece. It is built around the rocky hill of the Acropolis, where the ▷PARTHENON, built in the 5th century BC, survives from the golden age of ancient Greece.

Atlanta Capital of the US state of Georgia. During the American Civil War the city was burned by Union troops led by General Sherman. In the 1960s Atlanta was the centre of the Civil Rights Movement. In 1996 it will host the Olympic Games.

Atlantic Ocean World's second largest ocean, almost three times the size of Africa. The Atlantic stretches from the North Pole to the South Pole, and from Europe and Africa on one side to the Americas on the other. The Atlantic Ocean grows about 1 in (25 mm) wider each year as two of the Earth's tectonic plates move apart. Molten rock which wells up to fill the space has slowly formed a huge ridge that runs down the length of the ocean. Iceland and Ascension Island are peaks on the ridge.

LARGEST CONTINENT *Asia makes up a third of the Earth's land area, and is home to three-fifths of the world's population. It contains both the planet's highest and lowest points on land – Mount Everest and the shores of the Dead Sea.*

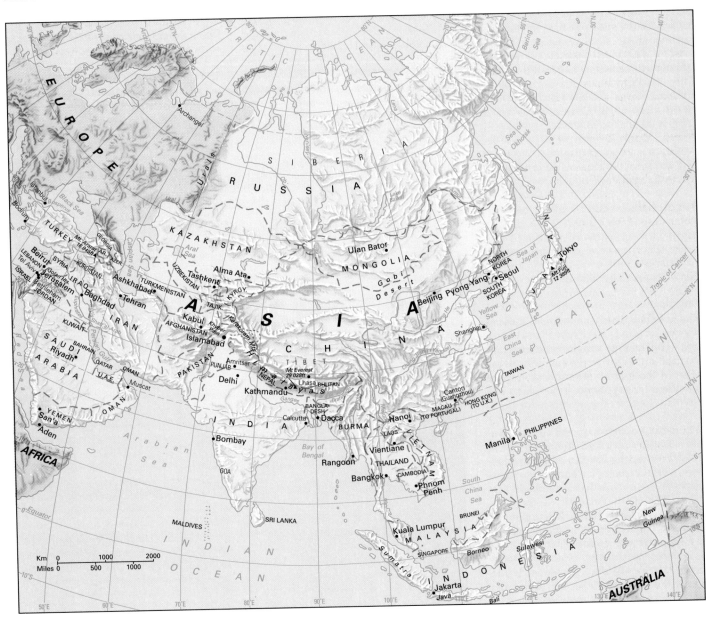

Australia World's sixth largest country in area but with a population of only 17.8 million, most of whom are concentrated in towns and cities around the coast. Few people live in its vast arid interior of deserts, scrub and huge sheep and cattle stations. CANBERRA is the nation's capital, but its largest cities are SYDNEY and Melbourne. ▷ABORIGINALS have lived in Australia for at least 50 000-60 000 years but they now make up only 1 in 65 of the population. The first British settlers – half of whom were convicts – landed in 1788. Since the mid 1960s immigrants have arrived from countries such as Hong Kong, China and Vietnam, as well as Europe.
🦘Australia's national rugby team, the Wallabies, is named after native animals which look like small kangaroos.

Austria Small, mountainous and politically neutral country in central Europe. Austria was once the centre of a vast empire, ruled by the ▷HABSBURG dynasty from the 13th century until the end of World War I. The capital city is VIENNA.
🎵Austria has produced many great composers, including Haydn and Mozart.

Ayers Rock Giant rock near Alice Springs in central Australia, rising 1142 ft (348 m) from the plains. It is a sacred place to the Aboriginals, who call it Uluru.

Azerbaijan Country, formerly part of the USSR, west of the Caspian Sea. Baku, the capital, is the centre of oil production, Azerbaijan's main industry. Conflict over the Armenian-dominated territory of Nagorno-Karabakh, in the west of the country, has resulted in many deaths.

Baghdad Capital of Iraq, on the banks of the Tigris. The city centre has modern hotels, international banks and department stores; farther out are narrow, dusty alleys lined with colourful bazaars. Baghdad was bombed during the 1991 ▷GULF WAR.

Bahamas Caribbean state made up of some 700 islands. Most Bahamians live on New Providence, where the capital Nassau is located, and Grand Bahama. The main industry is tourism.

Bahrain Small and largely barren Persian Gulf emirate, made up of Bahrain Island and 32 smaller islands. In 1931 Bahrain became the first Arab country to strike oil.

Baikal, Lake World's deepest lake, in southern Siberia. It holds as much water as all five American Great Lakes combined.

FLOATING MARKET *Shopping, like many other daily activities, takes place on the water in the canal-webbed centre of old Bangkok.*

Bali Indonesian island off Java's east coast. The hot climate, long beaches, ancient Hindu monuments, and traditional art, music and dancing attract many tourists.

Balkans Mountainous area of southeast Europe, encompassing Albania, Bulgaria, Greece, Romania, the former Yugoslavia and European Turkey. Turks occupied parts of the Balkans from the 15th century until the ▷BALKAN WARS of 1912-13; Austria-Hungary also ruled territory there. Sectarian tensions erupted after the fall of communism at the end of the 1980s.

Bangkok Capital of Thailand whose old city is known for its *klongs* or canals, and for its temples. The streets are clogged with traffic, including *tuk-tuks* – three-wheeled mopeds with a rear passenger seat. There is also a seedier side to Bangkok, which has been called the 'Sex Capital of the World'.

Bangladesh One of the world's poorest and most crowded countries, straddling the Ganges-Brahmaputra delta and subject to floods and to cyclones that sweep in from the Bay of Bengal. The country's 123 million people are mostly rural Muslims. Bangladesh was formerly East Pakistan and became independent in 1971 after a war that cost more than 1 million lives.

Barcelona Spain's second-largest city and a major port, known for its nightlife and for the flamboyant Art Nouveau buildings of the Spanish architect Antonio ▷GAUDI. Barcelona staged the 1992 Olympic Games.

FAR APART *Distances are vast in Australia: it measures 2700 miles (4350 km) from east to west, and at least 900 miles (1450 km) of ocean separate Australia from its 'neighbour' New Zealand.*

BAVARIAN FANTASY *The fairy-tale Neuschwanstein Castle was the work of Ludwig II, king of Bavaria from 1864 to 1886. Inside, paintings of scenes from Wagner's operas decorate the rooms.*

Bavaria Large south German state, whose lakes, mountains, forests and picturesque towns and villages draw many tourists. Germany's highest peak, the 9721 ft (2963 m) Zugspitze, is in the Bavarian Alps. Industry is centred on the state capital MUNICH, and Nuremberg, where Nazi war criminals were tried after World War II.
🐾 BMW stands for *Bayerische Motoren Werke* – Bavarian Motor Works. The company was founded in 1929.

Bay of Bengal Arm of the Indian Ocean that is subject to dramatic tropical cyclones. In 1970 a cyclone and tidal wave in the bay killed at least 300 000 people in the coastal region of Bangladesh.

Beijing (formerly Peking) Capital of China and its second largest city after Shanghai, with a population of more than 10.87 million. The Mongol leader Kublai Khan made the city the capital of his empire in 1267, and it was renamed Beijing, 'Northern Capital', in 1403. Today, the wide streets throng with pedestrians, cyclists and buses; private cars are rare. In the city centre are Tiananmen Square, one of the world's biggest public squares and the site of Mao Zedong's mausoleum, and the Forbidden City, the private domain of China's emperors from 1421 to 1911,

from which commoners were excluded on pain of death. The palace buildings, which together have 9999 rooms, are surrounded by a 35 ft (11 m) high wall.

Beirut Capital of Lebanon, on the Mediterranean Sea. The city was founded by the Phoenicians in the 14th century BC and later became an important Greek and Roman trading centre. Before 1975 Beirut was the trade and financial centre of the Middle East. In the late 1970s and 1980s parts of the city were badly damaged during civil wars and an Israeli invasion. During the reconstruction work that followed, archaeologists investigated remains of the city's ancient civilisations.

Belfast Capital of Northern Ireland on the River Lagan, with Black Mountain rising in the background and fine public buildings that recall its prosperous past. The linen industry flourished in Belfast in the 17th century, and the Industrial Revolution brought prosperity, with engineering and shipbuilding among the main industries; the city's Harland and Wolff shipyard was founded in 1862. There has been sectarian conflict in Belfast since 1969; the Falls Road is a predominantly Catholic (Nationalist) area and the Shankill Road a predominantly Protestant (Unionist) area.

Belgium Small European kingdom which has two distinct regions – the Flemish-speaking north and the French-speaking south. The dividing line runs roughly east-west through the capital, BRUSSELS. The Battle of Waterloo was fought just south of Brussels. During World War I Allied troops fought the Germans from muddy trenches across this low-lying country; Ypres and Passchendaele, both the scenes of heavy fighting, are in Flanders in the northwest of the country. Belgium was again a battlefield during World War II, when Allied troops fought the Germans in the Battle of the Bulge in the Ardennes region. Nevertheless historic towns including Antwerp, Bruges and Ghent have largely survived the many wars.
🐾 Belgium is known for its fine chocolate.

Belgrade Capital of Serbia and of the former Yugoslavia, its oldest part built on hills overlooking the confluence of the Danube and Sava rivers. Its important strategic position has led to various occupations throughout its history. In 1941 the city was devastated by the Germans during World War II, and it suffered more damage when it was liberated by Soviet and Yugoslav forces in 1944.

Belize Warm, humid Central American country whose Caribbean coast has miles of sandy beaches protected by coral reefs. The beaches, and the spectacular ruins of Maya temples, now attract tourists. Belize was formerly British Honduras, and achieved independence in 1981.
🐾 The coast is subject to hurricanes, and in 1961 Belize City was so badly damaged that the capital was moved from there to Belmopan in the mountainous and jungle-covered interior.

Bering Strait Channel connecting the Bering Sea and the Arctic Ocean, named after the Danish explorer Vitus Bering, who in 1728 established that North America and Asia were two separate continents.
🐾 During the Ice Ages, people crossed from Asia to colonise North America; sea levels were lower and a land bridge existed between the two continents.

Berlin Germany's capital city before 1949 and since 1991. In the interim years it was divided by the ▷BERLIN WALL. East Berlin was the capital of the German Democratic Republic, and is not as prosperous or as busy as the Western half of the city. At the centre of the reunited city stands the Brandenburg Gate, the ceremonial entrance to the Unter den Linden – a wide boulevard named after its lime trees and lined with stately public buildings. A 1100 ft (335 m) television tower dominates the city's skyline of modern buildings, the result of rebuilding after massive wartime damage. A string of lakes surrounded by pine woods brings tranquillity to the city's outskirts.

Bermuda British colony made up of 150 western Atlantic islands, 20 of which are inhabited, lying 875 miles (1400 km) east of Charleston in the US state of South Carolina. The capital, Hamilton, is on Great Bermuda, the largest island. Bermuda's economy depends almost entirely on year-round tourism. But lenient tax laws have also attracted wealthy people and financial institutions to the islands.
⚓ Ships and aeroplanes are reputed to have disappeared mysteriously in the ▷BERMUDA TRIANGLE, an area of the Atlantic between Bermuda, Puerto Rico and Florida.

Berne Capital of Switzerland, with many well-preserved 18th-century buildings. Bears – Berne's heraldic symbol – are kept in a large pit by the River Aare.

Bethlehem Birthplace of Jesus, 5 miles (8 km) south of Jerusalem, and an important goal of Christian pilgrimage. A grotto beneath Bethlehem's Church of the Nativity is reputedly the site of the manger in which Jesus lay.

Bhutan Small Himalayan kingdom which admits few tourists. Bhutan was ruled by monks until 1907, and villages grew up around fortified Buddhist monasteries or *dzongs*. Nearly all the Bhutanese are farmers, although less than one-tenth of the land is cultivated; almost three-quarters of Bhutan is covered with forest.

Black Forest Pine-clad mountain range in southwest Germany. Its distinctive houses, with eaves stretching almost to the ground, and spa towns such as Baden-Baden, make it popular with tourists. The River Danube rises in the Black Forest.
⚓ The cherries that grow in some Black Forest valleys led to the creation of the Black Forest gâteau – a chocolate cake filled with cream and cherries and flavoured with kirsch, a cherry liqueur.

Black Sea Tideless sea connected to the Mediterranean by the BOSPORUS, the Sea of Marmara and the Dardanelles. The CRIMEA peninsula extends into the Black Sea.
⚓ The Romans called the Black Sea 'Pontus Euxinus' – 'friendly sea'. However, fog and severe storms make it dangerous in winter.

Blue Mountains Range of mountains, with sheer-sided valleys, that lie inland from Sydney, Australia, and rise to 3609 ft (1100 m). The mountains are named after the blue haze of oil droplets, given off by eucalyptus trees, which is visible for miles.
⚓ Some of the finest coffee in the world is grown on the lower slopes of another range called the Blue Mountains, in Jamaica.

Bodrum Market town and holiday resort on Turkey's Aegean coast, built on the site of the ancient city of Halicarnassus. It was the birthplace of Herodotus, the 5th-century BC Greek historian.
⚓ The Mausoleum of Halicarnassus, built in the 4th century BC, was one of the Seven Wonders of the World. It was probably destroyed by an earthquake between the 11th and 15th centuries.

Bogotá Capital of Colombia, built on a plateau 9200 ft (2800 m) up in the Andes. It was founded in the 16th century by a Spanish conquistador seeking the mythical land of ▷ELDORADO. Bogotá's Gold Museum houses many artefacts of the Chibcha Indians who lived on the plateau before the Spaniards arrived.

Bolivia Landlocked South American country that was part of the powerful Inca Empire conquered by the Spanish in the 16th century. Half of Bolivia's population lives on a windswept, treeless plateau 12 000 ft (3700 m) up in the Andes. Many people are farmers, growing maize and potatoes. The main cash crop, however, is coca whose leaves are the source of cocaine; Bolivia is one of the major suppliers of the drug. La Paz, the world's highest capital city – 11 850 ft (3610 m) above sea level – lies southeast of Lake TITICACA.
⚓ Bolivia is named after Simón Bolívar, who helped to win independence from Spain for several South American countries, including Bolivia.

Bologna North Italian city in the foothills of the Apennines, with two 12th-century leaning towers. It is an important publishing centre and hosts an international children's book fair every spring.
⚓ Bologna is famous for pasta – its nickname is 'La Grassa' or 'the Fat City' – and gives its name to 'bolognese' sauce.

Bombay Hot, humid and cosmopolitan city on India's west coast that is the country's financial and commercial centre, and also the centre of India's film industry. Its main growth took place after the Suez Canal opened in 1869, when the city became known as the 'Gateway to India'. Many Victorian public buildings bear witness to the days of British rule.

Bonn Historic German city on the Rhine, founded as a Roman fort. It was heavily bombed during World War II, and in 1949 was transformed from a dignified university town into the West German capital. In 1991 it was decided that Berlin should once again be the capital and seat of government, although the Bundestag, or parliament, and federal ministries will remain in Bonn until the end of the decade.
⚓ Beethoven was born in Bonn in 1770.

Bordeaux French port on the Gironde estuary and the heart of the Bordeaux, or claret, wine-growing region.

Borneo Densely forested and mountainous southeast Asian island in the west Pacific. The northern part of the island comprises the sultanate of BRUNEI and the Malaysian states of Sarawak and Sabah; the south is part of INDONESIA.

Bosnia-Herzegovina Country that was part of the former YUGOSLAVIA, and declared its independence in 1991. From 1482 to 1878 the mainly mountainous land was controlled by Turks who had an enormous influence; Bosnia-Herzegovina was noted for its superb Islamic art and architecture, including mosques, covered bazaars, baths, fountains and bridges. At the outbreak of civil war in 1992 some 40 per cent of the people were Muslims, 32 per cent were Serbs and 18 per cent Croats. The capital, SARAJEVO, was badly damaged during the civil war.

Bosporus Narrow strait, 18 miles (29 km) long and nowhere more than 2½ miles (4 km) wide that forms part of the link between the Black Sea and the Mediterranean Sea. The city of ISTANBUL is at the southern end of the strait.

Boston Port and capital of Massachusetts in the northeast USA. It was founded in 1630 by English Puritans who named it after Boston in Lincolnshire, where many of them had come from, and has some elegant 18th-century buildings. In Cambridge, across the Charles River from Boston, are Harvard – America's oldest university founded in 1636 – and the Massachusetts Institute of Technology.
⚓ In 1773 angry citizens boarded a ship and threw overboard a cargo of tea, a gesture of resistance to British taxes that became known as the ▷BOSTON TEA PARTY.

Botany Bay Shallow inlet in the southern suburbs of Sydney, Australia, where Captain Cook landed in 1770. It was planned to establish a convict colony there, but the site proved to be unsuitable and the first settlement of 1788 was established instead on the nearby harbour of Port Jackson, now spanned by the Sydney Harbour Bridge.
🔖 The name of Botany Bay comes from the rich variety of new plants found there by Sir Joseph Banks, the botanist who travelled with Captain Cook.

Botswana Sparsely populated country in southern Africa, with only 1.3 million people in an area two and a half times the size of the United Kingdom. The south and west of Botswana are part of the KALAHARI desert, and in the north a huge inland river delta, the OKAVANGO, teems with wildlife.
🔖 Botswana's first president was Sir Seretse Khama – in office from 1966 when the British protectorate of Bechuanaland won independence until his death in 1980.

Brasília Purpose-built capital of Brazil, founded in 1960. It is laid out on an open plateau in the heart of Brazil in the form of an aeroplane. Residential areas form the 'wings', and an avenue of public and government buildings the 'fuselage'. The cathedral is built as a stylised crown of thorns.

Brazil Huge country occupying almost half of South America. The capital is BRASÍLIA, but the biggest cities are SÃO PAULO and RIO DE JANEIRO. Brazil's population, a melting pot of different races, is largely Portuguese-speaking. In 1494 the Treaty of Tordesillas, signed by the Spanish and Portuguese kings, granted to Spain all newly found land west of a fixed line of longitude. Land to the east of the line, which included Brazil, went to Portugal. One-third of the country is covered by the Amazon basin's humid ▷RAIN FOREST, which is known as the *inferno verde*, or green hell. The clearance of areas of rain forest has caused concern to conservationists. Elsewhere, there are arid scrublands, fertile savannahs, remote highlands and prairie grasslands where gauchos, or cowboys, herd cattle on vast ranches. The IGUAZÚ FALLS are on the border of Brazil and Argentina. Brazil produces more than a quarter of the world's coffee, and pioneered the production of fuel from sugar.
🔖 Brazil has produced the great Formula One motor racing drivers Emerson Fittipaldi, Nelson Piquet, and Ayrton Senna, and footballers such as Pelé, Jaïrzinho, and Sócrates. Brazil's soccer stadiums have a total capacity of 4 million people.

Brittany Peninsula of northwest France. Celts fled there from the Anglo-Saxons in Britain in the 5th and 6th centuries AD, taking their culture with them: Breton, a language related to Welsh and Cornish, is still spoken in the west. Brittany has many prehistoric standing stones, and at Carnac, on the south coast, some 3000 stones dating from 2500 to 200 BC form avenues and circles extending over 2½ miles (4 km).

Brunei Oil-producing state on the north coast of Borneo, ruled by a sultan who is said to be one of the world's richest people. In many villages on the swampy coastal plains, the houses are raised on stilts.

Brussels Capital of Belgium, and headquarters of the European Union and NATO. Many of the buildings in the old part of the city date back to the 15th century, including the city hall with its 315 ft (96 m) high spire which dominates the central square. All signs in the city are in both Flemish and French, reflecting Belgium's two nationalities.
🔖 Brussels sprouts, first grown in the 13th century, are named after the city.

Bucharest Capital of Romania, with tree-lined boulevards, shady parks and handsome houses and public buildings. In the 1980s, President ▷CEAUSESCU cleared 2½ sq miles (6 km²) of the older part of the city centre to make way for a new civic centre whose main boulevard leads to a massive parliament building.
🔖 Bucharest used to be described as the 'Paris of Eastern Europe'.

Budapest Capital of Hungary with two distinct parts – Buda on the west side of the Danube, and Pest on the east side. They are linked by several bridges, the oldest of which is the Chain Bridge (1839-49). Much of old Buda was devastated during World War II, but its medieval churches, town houses and royal palace have been beautifully restored. Pest has wide avenues, large open squares and bustling street cafés. Its river frontage is dominated by the vast domed parliament building.

TWIN CITY *Budapest straddles the Danube: the fairy-tale turrets of the Fisherman's Bastion on the Buda shore, or west bank, frame parliament's floodlit dome on the Pest side, east of the river.*

Buenos Aires Lively river port capital of Argentina on the River Plate, founded by Spanish settlers in 1536. It has been nicknamed the 'Paris of Latin America' because its traditional architecture resembles that of late 19th-century France.
🔖 The name Buenos Aires is a shortened form of the city's full name: Ciudad de la Santísima Trinidad y Puerto de Nuestra Señora la Virgen María de los buenos aires (City of the Most Holy Trinity, and Port of Our Lady the Virgin Mary of good winds).

Bulgaria Country in southeast Europe, under Turkish rule from 1396 until the last links were severed in 1912, and under communist rule from 1946 to 1989. The capital is Sofia. Tobacco and wine are major products, and Bulgaria's Black Sea coast attracts many tourists.

🕯Bulgaria produces nearly three-quarters of the world's rose oil, used for making perfume. The petals are picked before dawn so that they keep their fragrance.

Burgundy Region of hills and valleys in east-central France whose vineyards produce some of the world's finest and most popular wines, including Côte de Beaune, Chablis and Beaujolais.

Burma Buddhist country in southeast Asia, known locally as Myanmar. The capital, Yangon (Rangoon), is at the swampy mouth of the Irrawaddy river. Trees cover two-thirds of the country, providing teak and rubber. In the east, where the borders of Burma, Thailand and Laos meet, opium poppies are grown in the 'Golden Triangle', although the authorities have had some success in the fight against the drug trade.

🕯Mandalay, immortalised in Rudyard Kipling's ballad, is Burma's second city and the country's cultural heart.

Cairo Cosmopolitan capital of Egypt and largest city in Africa, on the river Nile. The bazaars and mosques of the crowded older areas contrast with the wide streets and modern office blocks of the newer parts.

🕯The Great ▷PYRAMID and the ▷SPHINX are in the Cairo suburb of El Giza.

🕯Cairo's Al-Azhar University is one of the world's oldest, founded in about AD 970.

Calcutta India's largest city, with a population of 11 million people, and the capital of the state of West Bengal. Calcutta was founded in 1690 by the East India Company, and the prosperous trading centre was India's capital city until 1911 when New Delhi was proclaimed capital.

🕯In 1979, the Roman Catholic nun Mother Teresa received a Nobel prize for her work with Calcutta's poor.

🕯In 1756, European prisoners were held in the ▷BLACK HOLE OF CALCUTTA.

California Prosperous western state, the most populous and third largest in the USA. It is subject to earthquakes, especially along the San Andreas fault on which SAN FRANCISCO lies. The SIERRA NEVADA mountain range rises in the east of the state. California's sunny climate attracts tourists and is ideal for growing fruit and vegetables.

Wine is produced in the Sonoma and Napa valleys. LOS ANGELES is the biggest city, and the state capital is Sacramento.

🕯Gold that drew early settlers gave California its nickname of 'The Golden State'.

🕯Hollywood, Disneyland and 'SILICON VALLEY' are all in California.

Camargue Flat region of marshes, lagoons and farmland in the Rhône delta in southern France. It is known for the black bulls and small white horses that live there.

Cambodia (formerly Kampuchea) Rural, rice-growing Southeast Asian country. The 1970s were a particularly bloody decade for the country. It was drawn into the ▷VIETNAM WAR, and then ruled by the brutal regime of ▷POL POT and the Khmer Rouge, who evacuated entire towns including the capital, Phnom Penh.

🕯At ▷ANGKOR, deep in the jungle of northwest Cambodia, are the magnificent ruins of the Khmer civilisation that dominated the area from the 9th to the 15th centuries. There are more than 600 elaborately carved Hindu temples, some as big as cathedrals, and extensive irrigation canals.

Canada World's second largest country after Russia. Canada extends over six time zones, and it takes four and a half days to cross from coast to coast by train. Much of the country is virtually uninhabited; more than half is covered by forests broken by thousands of lakes; the Rocky Mountains tower to more than 10 000 ft (3000 m) in the west; and the far north, including the huge Baffin Island, is a frozen treeless wilderness. Wheat and other grains are grown on the prairies in the south of the interior. Most Canadians live in the far south, especially around Vancouver in the west and in the eastern urban area near the Great Lakes and the St Lawrence Seaway which includes OTTAWA, Canada's capital city, TORONTO and MONTREAL. The official languages are English and French, reflecting the origins of early European settlers. The ▷SEVEN YEARS' WAR that ended in 1763 resulted in France surrendering its colonies to Britain, and as a Commonwealth country Canada retains its ties with Britain. However, many French speakers in QUEBEC favour independence for their province. Inuits and Native Americans now make up only two per cent of the population.

🕯The Mounties – Royal Canadian Mounted Police – nowadays travel in motor vehicles. Horses, and the traditional wide-brimmed hats and scarlet tunics, are used only on ceremonial occasions.

🕯In 1896, gold was discovered at Bonanza Creek, a tributary of the Klondike River in Yukon Territory, in the far northwest of Canada. Thousands of prospectors joined the ▷GOLD RUSH.

Canary Islands Group of seven islands and several islets off Africa's northwest coast which all belong to Spain. They include Tenerife, Gran Canaria, Fuerteventura and Lanzarote. The warm climate all year round attracts many tourists.

🕯Tenerife is dominated by the 12 198 ft (3718 m) volcano Pico de Teide, the highest point in Spanish territory.

🕯The Canary Islands are named after the fierce dogs that lived there – the name comes from *canis*, the Latin word for dog.

Canberra Australia's capital city, laid out on a formal plan with many parks. Canberra is primarily a seat of government, rather than a business or commercial centre, and with a population of about 300 000 is much smaller than Sydney or Melbourne.

Canton (Guangzhou) Vibrant, cosmopolitan city in south China. Between 1759 and 1842 Canton was the only Chinese port open to Europeans, except the Portuguese who traded from Macau. Europeans exported silk, porcelain, tea and other goods, but the Chinese showed little interest in imports. Britain's attempts to expand trade by importing opium, and China's attempts to stop them, led to the ▷OPIUM WARS of the mid 19th century.

TEEMING STREETS *Traders pack the narrow streets of Calcutta, a densely populated and cosmopolitan centre of commerce.*

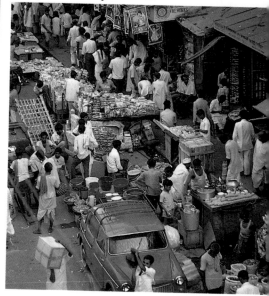

FANTASY LAND *The improbably sculpted domes and towers of southwest China's Guilin Hills rise above precisely patterned paddy fields. Caves beneath the hills are rich in stalagmites and stalactites.*

Cape of Good Hope Tip of South Africa's Cape Peninsula, which was a landmark for navigators. It got its name from the Portuguese explorer Bartolomeu Dias 'for the promise it gave of finding India'.

Cape Town South Africa's oldest city, founded by the Dutch in 1652, and capital of Western Cape province. The country's parliament sits in Cape Town, although the government's administration is in Pretoria. The city is overlooked by the flat-topped Table Mountain, which is sometimes swathed by its 'tablecloth' – a layer of cloud that rolls over the top when a southeast wind blows.

Caspian Sea World's largest inland body of water, bigger than Germany, and famed for its sturgeon, the source of caviar.

Central African Republic Impoverished country of bush and rolling grassland in the heart of Africa. In 1977, the country's leader Jean-Bedel Bokassa crowned himself emperor in a wildly extravagant ceremony. Bokassa was overthrown in 1979.
♟ Bokassa's gift of diamonds to Giscard d'Estaing – then the French finance minister – caused a scandal in 1973.

Central Park Large park in the centre of New York, covering an area one and a third times the size of London's Hyde Park and Kensington Gardens combined. Central Park contains a zoo, and also Cleopatra's Needle, one of a pair of Egyptian obelisks that are 3500 years old; the other is on London's Victoria Embankment. The park has a reputation for being unsafe after dark, because of frequent muggings.

Challenger Deep Deepest known spot in the oceans, in the Marianas Trench east of the Philippines. The greatest recorded depth is 36 197 ft (11 033 m).
♟ In 1960, a Swiss-American team made a record descent of 35 810 ft (10 915 m) into the Marianas Trench in a bathyscaph.

Chang Jiang (Yangtze) World's third longest river, after the Amazon and the Nile, flowing for 3915 miles (6300 km) down narrow valleys, across farmland and through impressive gorges before it enters the East China Sea near Shanghai.

Channel Islands Group of islands in the English Channel, consisting of Jersey, Guernsey, Alderney, Sark and several smaller islands and islets. Jersey, the largest island, is little more than 12 miles (20 km) from the French coast. The islands are dependencies of the British Crown, and have their own legislative assemblies and legal systems. The mild climate attracts many tourists, and the islands produce spring flowers and vegetables, especially tomatoes. The islands were occupied by Germany during World War II.

Chicago Third largest city in the USA after New York and Los Angeles. Sited at the southern end of Lake Michigan, it is known for its innovative architecture, including that of Frank Lloyd ▷WRIGHT in the city's suburbs, and has the world's tallest office building, the ▷SEARS TOWER.

CITY SLICKERS *Ice skating is just one of many facilities in New York's Central Park, which also has an open-air theatre, sports facilities, gardens, woods and boating lakes within its varied landscape.*

⚑During the years of Prohibition, gangsters including Al Capone controlled the illegal sale of alcohol in Chicago.

Chile Long, narrow South American country sandwiched between the Andes and the Pacific Ocean. The capital is Santiago. In between the barren Atacama desert in the north and the cold and windswept forests and glaciers of the south is the fertile area that produces Chile's wine. In 1973 military leaders under General Augusto Pinochet overthrew the Marxist government of President Salvador ▷ALLENDE.
⚑EASTER ISLAND, 2350 miles (3780 km) away in the Pacific Ocean, is part of Chile.

China World's third largest country in area, but by far the most populous with more than 1160 million inhabitants – one in five of the world's population. The majority of people are Han, or Chinese, but there are also 55 other ethnic groups. Most of the fertile land and the largest cities, including SHANGHAI and the capital BEI-JING, are in densely populated eastern China. Western China has bleak plateaus, high mountains including the Himalayas, and barren deserts. China has one of the world's oldest civilisations – one dynasty of rulers succeeded another from about 1766 BC until 1911. After a power struggle between communists and nationalists led by ▷CHIANG KAI-SHEK, China became a communist state in 1949 under the leadership of ▷MAO ZEDONG, who introduced the ▷CULTURAL REVOLUTION in 1966. Since the early 1980s China has encouraged free enterprise but has avoided any far-reaching political reform. In 1989 the army crushed demonstrations in Beijing's ▷TIANANMEN SQUARE MASSACRE. Agriculture employs about 60 per cent of China's workers.
⚑Early Chinese inventions include the compass, paper, porcelain, gunpowder, silk and printing from movable type.

Cologne City on the Rhine in Germany, founded by the Romans; the city takes its name from *colonia*, the Latin word for colony. Cologne cathedral, one of Europe's most splendid Gothic buildings, survived World War II bombing.

Colombia South American country with the fertile valleys and snow-covered peaks of the Andes in the west, and hot grassy plains and tropical jungles in the east. The capital is BOGOTÁ. Coffee, grown mostly on small farms, is the leading export.
⚑Colombia's production of cocaine and other illegal drugs, based around Medellin, grew dramatically in the 1980s.

ISLAND FORTRESS *Huddled behind its massive walls at the southern tip of Corsica, the town of Bonifacio perches on a white limestone cliff, offering spectacular views over the sea to Sardinia.*

Copenhagen Capital of Denmark, with many buildings dating from the 16th and 17th centuries. The Tivoli Gardens amusement park is in the city centre; a statue of the Little Mermaid of Hans Christian Andersen's story is on the waterfront. Royal Copenhagen porcelain has been made in the city since 1775.

Corfu Fertile Greek island, popular with tourists. Corfu is the most northerly of the Ionian Islands off Greece's Adriatic coast, and the northern part of the island is less than 5 miles (8 km) from the coast of Albania. Corfu Town (Kérkira) has 16th-century Venetian fortifications, and a cricket ground – the island was ruled by Britain between 1815 and 1864.

Corsica Mountainous Mediterranean island, north of Sardinia, that is part of France. Much of the interior is covered with aromatic shrubs and cork oaks, with forests higher up. The capital is Ajaccio.
⚑Corsica was the birthplace, in 1769, of the French emperor Napoleon I.

Costa Rica Mountainous and heavily forested country in Central America. Coffee and bananas are the main exports. Costa Rica abolished its army in 1948 to stop military coups and its governments have been unusually stable for the region.

Côte d'Azur Mediterranean coastal strip which includes Monte Carlo and the French resorts of Nice and Cannes, the site of an international film festival each spring.

Crete Largest of the Greek islands, lying south of the mainland. The main town is Heraklion. The Minoan civilisation with its palace at ▷KNOSSOS flourished there between 3000 and 1100 BC.
⚑In Greek mythology, the ▷MINOTAUR was born to a queen of Crete.

Crimea Peninsula of Ukraine extending into the Black Sea. One of its resorts is Yalta, scene of the World War II conference. The ▷CHARGE OF THE LIGHT BRIGADE took place in Crimea in 1854.

Croatia South European country that was one of the more prosperous parts of the former YUGOSLAVIA. Many tourists used to visit the sunny beaches along its Dalmatian coast. The country was under Hungarian, and later Habsburg control from 1102 until 1918. In 1991 Croatia declared its independence from Yugoslavia. The capital is Zagreb.

Cuba West Indian country and the largest island in the Caribbean. The capital is Havana. A communist government led by Fidel ▷CASTRO came to power in 1959. In 1961, Cuban exiles landed at the island's ▷BAY OF PIGS in an unsuccessful attempt to overthrow Castro's regime, and the following year the world was brought to the brink of war by the ▷CUBAN MISSILE CRISIS. The economy was weakened in the early 1990s by the collapse of communism in the former USSR and the subsequent loss of aid.
⚑Havana cigars, rolled by hand, are made from tobacco grown in northwest Cuba.

Cyprus Dry, sunny island in the eastern Mediterranean Sea, whose beaches and mountains attract many tourists. The capital is Nicosia. Greeks make up 80 per cent of the population and Turks 19 per cent. Greek Cypriots' campaigns in the 1950s for union with Greece were spearheaded by the EOKA movement, and by Archbishop Makarios, who was the island's first president after its independence from Britain in 1960. Turkish forces invaded northern Cyprus in 1974, and in 1983 the Turks declared the occupied area to be the 'Turkish Republic of Northern Cyprus', which is recognised only by Turkey.
♨ The Greek name of the island, *Kypros*, means copper, which has been extensively mined since prehistoric times.

Czech Republic Central European country born on January 1, 1993 when the former republic of Czechoslovakia split into the Czech Republic and SLOVAKIA. The capital is PRAGUE. The republic is known for crystal made in Bohemia, the western part of the country, and for its beer, especially pilsner lager which originated in the western city of Plzeň in 1842. Spa towns include Karlovy Vary (Carlsbad) and Mariánské Lázně (Marienbad).
♨ Wenceslas I – the 'Good King' of the popular Christmas carol – ruled Bohemia in the early 10th century.

Dallas One of the largest cities in the USA, on the Texas plains. It is a centre of the American oil and electronics industries, and also a major cotton market. It also inspired the television soap opera *Dallas*.
♨ President John F. Kennedy was assassinated in Dallas in 1963.

Damascus Capital of Syria and one of the world's oldest cities, important since the third millennium BC. The old walled city has a mosque built in AD 708; in the modern part of Damascus there are high-rise hotels and office blocks.
♨ Damask cloth, a fabric with a complex patterned weave, has been made in Damascus since the Middle Ages.

Danube Europe's second longest river after the Volga and a major transport route, flowing from southern Germany to its delta in the Black Sea. Cities on its banks include Vienna, Budapest and Belgrade.

Dead Sea One of the world's saltiest lakes, lying between Israel and Jordan. Its shores, 1299 ft (396 m) below sea level, are the lowest point on the world's land surface. The Dead Sea is rich in minerals which are said to provide those who bathe in it with therapeutic effects, especially for arthritis and respiratory problems. The sea's black mud is claimed to be beneficial for the skin.

PILLARS OF SALT *Dotting the mineral-rich waters of the Dead Sea are tiny islands – the tips of columns of salt that form as the water evaporates in summer temperatures as high as 50°C (122°F).*

Death Valley Huge depression that includes North America's hottest, driest and lowest place, 282 ft (86 m) below sea level in California. Temperatures in the summer can reach more than 52°C (125°F).

Delhi Capital of India, with two distinct parts. Old Delhi is a crowded maze of narrow streets centred on the 17th-century Red Fort built by the emperor Shah Jahan, who also built the Taj Mahal. New Delhi, designed by Sir Edwin ▷LUTYENS, was laid out between 1912 and 1931 as a new capital city, with broad tree-lined avenues, government buildings and gardens.

Denmark Small, densely populated kingdom in northern Europe, consisting of the Jutland peninsula and more than 400 islands. The capital, COPENHAGEN, stands on Zealand, the largest island. Denmark is prosperous with a well-organised farming industry, known for its butter and bacon.

Dresden Historic city in eastern Germany. It was once one of the most beautiful cities in Europe, with many baroque buildings, but Allied bombing raids in February 1945 destroyed more than half the city. Most of Dresden's best-known buildings have been restored.
♨ Dresden china, a delicate porcelain, is made in nearby Meissen. The industry moved from Dresden to Meissen in 1710.

Dublin Capital of the Republic of Ireland, at the mouth of the River Liffey. Its many fine Georgian buildings include Leinster House, where the Dáil, or Parliament, sits. Trinity College library houses the Book of Kells, an illuminated Celtic manuscript of around AD 800. The General Post Office in O'Connell Street was the headquarters of the rebel Irish Volunteers during the ▷EASTER RISING of 1916. Dublin's Phoenix Park is one of the biggest urban parks in Europe, and includes a zoo, a racecourse and the President's residence. Guinness stout has been brewed in Dublin since 1759.
♨ Dublin was the birthplace of the writers Jonathan Swift, Oscar Wilde, George Bernard Shaw and James Joyce.

Easter Island Tiny, remote Pacific island 2350 miles (3780 km) west of the coast of Chile, to which it belongs. The island is known for the 1000 or so giant stone statues carved between AD 1000 and 1500; the largest statues are 70 ft (21 m) high.

East Timor Indonesian province that gained independence from Portugal in 1975, only to be invaded by Indonesia nine

ACROSS EUROPE Rich in culture and cities, Europe stretches from the Atlantic to the Ural Mountains. Russia spans Europe and Asia.

days later. Since then more than 200 000 Timorese have been killed, and Indonesian forces still remain despite ten UN resolutions calling for their withdrawal.

Ecuador South American country straddling the Equator; the country's name means 'Equator' in Spanish. The capital is Quito. The Andes run down the centre of the country, and contain several snow-capped volcanoes. To the west is a large plain, and to the east are dense tropical forests and savannahs where oil is exploited. The Galápagos Islands lie 680 miles (1100 km) west of Ecuador, to which they belong. Their distinctive wildlife helped to inspire ▷DARWIN's theory of evolution.

Egypt Arab country in North Africa, whose capital is CAIRO. Desert makes up 96 per cent of the land. Nearly all Egyptians live in the densely populated valley and delta of the NILE or along the ▷SUEZ CANAL where the green irrigated land contrasts with the desert beyond. Rural dwellers of the valley and delta are known as *fellahin*. The ▷PYRAMIDS, the Sphinx and the temples at Luxor are among the many remains of the civilisation of ▷ANCIENT EGYPT. The port of ALEXANDRIA was a major city in ancient times. ▷CLEOPATRA ruled Egypt in the 1st century BC.

El Salvador Small but densely populated Central American country, with rugged highlands and volcanoes. The capital is San Salvador. From 1979 to 1992 the country was torn by civil war between left-wing guerrillas (FMLN) and the US-backed, right-wing government. The conflict was ended by both sides compromising. Two out of every five people work on the land, and coffee is the most valuable crop.

Ethiopia Mountainous northeast African country, formerly known as Abyssinia. Ethiopia has existed for 2000 years, and during the 19th century was one of the few parts of Africa that was not a European colony, although the Italians controlled it from 1936 to 1941. Emperor ▷HAILE SEL-ASSIE was overthrown in 1974, and the monarchy replaced by a Marxist military republic which was itself overthrown in 1991. In the 1970s and 1980s the country suffered from civil war, drought and severe famine. The capital is Addis Ababa.

Euphrates River rising in Turkey and flowing through Syria and Iraq into the Persian Gulf. The Mesopotamian cities of Babylon and Ur were on the Euphrates.

Finland North European country where forests and 55 000 lakes make up the vast majority of the surface area. Forestry and the production of paper and other wood products are central to the economy. Finland's scenery and legends inspired the composer ▷SIBELIUS. About 1700 Lapps live in Lappland in the far north. In 1939-40, Finnish troops led by Marshal Mannerheim put up a heroic resistance to Russian forces. The capital is Helsinki.
🎙 The sauna originated in Finland.

Florence Beautiful city in north central Italy whose churches, Renaissance palaces and works of art attract many tourists. Leonardo da Vinci, Michelangelo and Raphael were all ▷FLORENTINE artists. The wealthy Medici family were rulers of the city and patrons of the arts from the 15th to the 18th centuries.

Florida 'Sunshine State' in the southeast USA. The swamps and mangrove forests of the Everglades, in southern Florida, are rich in wildlife. The Florida Keys, a string of coral islands, stretch southwest from MIAMI to Key West. The city of Orlando, in central Florida, is a base for visiting the John F. Kennedy Space Center, the Epcot Center and Walt Disney World.

France Western Europe's largest country, noted for its culture, food and wine. PARIS, the romantic capital; the châteaux of the LOIRE valley; the scenery of the Alps and

Pyrenees; and the sunshine of the CÔTE D'AZUR all attract many tourists. Gaul, roughly equivalent to modern France and Belgium, was conquered by the Romans by 50 BC. In the late 5th and early 6th centuries the land was invaded by the Franks, from whom the name 'France' comes, and whose king ▷CHARLEMAGNE built up the first great French empire. In 1066 the Duke of Normandy, in northern France, conquered England and became King William I. During the next four centuries England and France fought many battles, most notably during the ▷HUNDRED YEARS' WAR (1337-1453). Over the next 200 years France became increasingly powerful, reaching its height during the reign of ▷LOUIS XIV. The absolute rule of the French kings came to an end with the ▷FRENCH REVOLUTION (1789-1799), after which ▷NAPOLEON I ruled France, and much of western Europe, until his defeat at Waterloo in 1815. Later in the 19th century, France acquired huge tracts of northwest Africa and colonies in Southeast Asia.

OLD BRIDGE *Florence's shop-lined Ponte Vecchio has spanned the River Arno since 1345. The cathedral dome (inset) dates from 1461.*

After World War II, a *rapprochement* with Germany led to the creation of the European Economic Community, now the European Union, in which France plays a leading role. The crisis over Algeria's independence (1958-62) led to Charles ▷DE GAULLE's re-emergence as his country's leader. In the 1960s France became a leading industrial nation. France is divided into 22 regions and 96 *départements*, two of which make up CORSICA.
🎙 France produces nearly 400 cheeses, and some of the world's finest wines, such as those from BURGUNDY and Champagne.

Ganges River that rises in the Himalayas and flows through northern India to end in the world's biggest delta. To Hindus, the Ganges is the holiest river; people are cremated on its banks and their ashes scattered in the water, in the belief that their souls will go straight to heaven.

Gaza Strip Land on the eastern Mediterranean coast occupied by Israel in 1967. The Palestinians were given limited self-government in 1994.

Geneva Swiss city on the shores of Lake Geneva (Lac Léman), where a 476 ft (145 m) fountain rises into the air. The Red Cross has its headquarters in Geneva.

Germany West European country that is one of the world's leading industrial economies, and the dominant economic force in the European Union. The capital is BERLIN, although the Bundestag, or parliament, and the federal ministries are in BONN. Frankfurt is the financial centre, MUNICH is the largest city of south Germany, and Hamburg is the biggest port. Before 1871, Germany consisted of many small states, the strongest of which were ▷PRUSSIA and BAVARIA. When the German states united and Prussia's prime minister, Otto von ▷BISMARCK, became chancellor, the Prussian king became Germany's Kaiser Wilhelm I. His grandson Kaiser Wilhelm II took Germany into World War I. In the 1920s Germany experienced massive inflation, and also the rise of ▷NAZISM under Adolf ▷HITLER. In 1933 Hitler was appointed chancellor by Hindenburg, the German president; Hitler's invasion of Poland in 1939 led to World War II. In 1949 the country was divided into the communist German Democratic Republic (East Germany), and the Federal Republic of Germany (West Germany) whose chancellor, Konrad ▷ADENAUER, oversaw his country's recovery. The two parts of Germany were reunited on October 3,

NATURE'S HANDIWORK *The Colorado River cut through many layers of rock to produce the Grand Canyon, 1 mile (1.6 km) deep in places.*

1990. The west's Chancellor ▷KOHL became leader of the united country, and the east's leader, Erich Honecker, went to Chile. He died in exile on May 29, 1994.

Ghana West African country with tropical forests in the south and arid plains in the north. The capital is Accra. Ghana was the first black African country to achieve independence from European colonial rule; before 1957 it was the British colony of the Gold Coast. Ghana's first prime minister, Kwame ▷NKRUMAH, encouraged all Africans to throw off colonial rule.

Gibraltar Peninsula of southern Spain that is only 3 miles (5 km) long, but rises to 1394 ft (425 m) at the Rock of Gibraltar. It has been a British colony since 1713. Barbary apes live on the Rock.

Golan Heights High, bare hills in southwest Syria, occupied by Israel since 1967.

Grand Canyon Spectacular gorge in Arizona, in the southwest USA. The canyon is 280 miles (450 km) long – almost the distance from London to Dumfries.

Great Barrier Reef World's longest coral reef system, 1250 miles (2000 km) long, off the northeast coast of Australia. Colourful fish live in huge numbers among the 350 species of coral. Tourism is carefully controlled, for the delicately balanced ecosystem is easily harmed by human activity.

Great Lakes Freshwater, North American lakes that cover the same area as the United Kingdom. Lakes Superior, Huron, Erie and Ontario straddle the border between Canada and the USA. Lake Michigan lies within the USA. Niagara Falls is between lakes Erie and Ontario.

Greece South European country that was the cultural centre of the Mediterranean world 2500 years ago. The capital and by far the largest city is ATHENS. Greece consists of a largely mountainous mainland and about 1400 islands, including the Ionian Islands to the west of the mainland,

the Sporades, Cyclades and Dodecanese to the east, and Crete to the south. After World War II, communist guerrillas and nationalist troops fought a civil war. A military coup took place in 1967. A quarter of the people work on the land, growing olives, grain and vines on small farms.

Haiti Poor agricultural country making up the western third of the West Indian island of Hispaniola; the rest of the island is the Dominican Republic. The capital is Port-au-Prince. From 1957 to 1986 Haiti was oppressively ruled by the Duvalier family – first by Dr François 'Papa Doc' and his special police, the *Tontons Macoutes*, and then by his son Jean-Claude 'Baby Doc'. A military coup in 1991 ousted the democratically elected president Jean-Bertrand Aristide. In 1994 US forces intervened to restore democracy. ▷VOODOO is still practised in Haiti.

Hawaii Group of volcanic north Pacific islands that became the 50th US state in 1959. Hawaii is also the name of the largest island. The capital, Honolulu, and ▷PEARL HARBOR are both on the island of Oahu.

439

CROWDED COLONY *Hong Kong, with its innumerable skyscrapers, is one of the most densely populated places in the world. More than half the population lives on or above the tenth floor.*

Himalayas World's highest mountain range, curving across southern Asia for some 1500 miles (2400 km) and containing the world's highest peak, MOUNT EVEREST 29 028 ft (8848 m). Of the Earth's 109 peaks that rise to more than 24 000 ft (7300 m), 96 are in the Himalayas.

Hong Kong Densely populated, prosperous British territory on China's south coast. Hong Kong Island, its waterfront lined with high-rise banks and offices, is connected by road and rail tunnels to Kowloon and the New Territories. Hong Kong Island and part of Kowloon peninsula were acquired by Britain between 1841 and 1860. In 1898 the New Territories comprising north Kowloon and many islands were leased from China for 99 years. In 1997 the governor is due to return Hong Kong to China on behalf of Britain.

Huang He China's second longest river, after the Chang Jiang (Yangtze). The name means Yellow River, and refers to the huge amount of silt that colours the water.

Hungary Landlocked country in central Europe, with vast, intensively farmed plains. The capital is BUDAPEST and the people are Magyars, whose language is related to Finnish. Austrian Habsburgs controlled Hungary from 1699 until 1867,

when the Austro-Hungarian dual monarchy was established. From the late 1940s until 1989 Hungary was a communist country. In 1956 troops of the former USSR crushed the ▷HUNGARIAN UPRISING.

Iceland European island country in the North Atlantic Ocean. The country's economy is based on fishing. One-ninth of the island is permanently covered by snow and ice, but there are also volcanoes and hot springs. The capital is Reykjavík.

Iguazú (Iguaçu) Falls Spectacular waterfall on the border of Brazil and Argentina, made up of some 275 cascades which plunge over a crescent of cliffs.

India Second most populous country in the world after China, with a population of 903 million – one in six of the world's people. Hindus make up nearly 83 per cent of the population; ▷HINDUISM probably developed from beliefs brought by invaders from the northwest after about 2000 BC. Islam, followed by 11 per cent of Indians, was introduced in the 12th century, and in the 16th century most of India came under the control of the Muslim Mogul Empire. The Moguls brought new art and architecture, which reached its peak with the ▷TAJ MAHAL. There are also 18 million Christians and 17 million Sikhs, as well as

Buddhists, Jains and others. There are 14 official languages and more than 1000 minor languages and dialects; Hindi is the most widely spoken language, and English, for example, is used in commerce. The British East India Company, a trading company, was established in 1600. British influence increased as the power of the Mogul Empire declined and in 1857, after the ▷INDIAN MUTINY, the British government assumed direct responsibility for India. The drive for independence from Britain, achieved in 1947, was led by Mahatma ▷GANDHI. The capital is DELHI, but the largest cities are BOMBAY and CALCUTTA. Three-quarters of the people live in rural villages. The Himalayas are in the far north of India, and the GANGES flows down from the mountains and across a vast plain. India has a summer monsoon season when most of the rain falls.

Indian Ocean World's third largest ocean, after the Pacific and Atlantic; it lies between Asia, Antarctica, Africa and Australia. Indian Ocean islands include the Seychelles, the Maldives and Mauritius.

Indonesia Southeast Asian country, consisting of more than 13 600 islands, most of them forested and mountainous. The capital, Jakarta, is on Java, where three-fifths of Indonesians live. The country also includes Sumatra, Sulawesi, and parts of BORNEO and New Guinea. Indonesia's 300 ethnic groups speak 250 different languages, but most people follow Islam, brought by Muslim traders in the 14th century. With a population of more than 185 million, Indonesia is the world's largest Muslim nation. European spice traders arrived in the 16th century, and the Dutch East India Company made Jakarta (then Batavia) the centre of their trading empire. Dutch rule lasted until 1949. Oil, natural gas and rubber are major exports; tourism is also important – especially for the island of BALI.
🜨 Krakatoa, the volcanic island which was blown apart in a huge eruption in 1883, lay between the islands of Java and Sumatra.

Iran Islamic republic in western Asia where the ancient ▷PERSIAN EMPIRE was founded. The country's interior is a huge desert. Iran's wealth comes mainly from oil and natural gas, and in the 1960s and 1970s the Shah of Iran used oil revenue to finance the country's modernisation. A revolution against his rule led, in 1979, to the establishment of an Islamic republic led by Ayatollah ▷KHOMEINI. From 1980 to 1988 Iran fought its neighbour in the ▷IRAN-IRAQ WAR. The capital is Tehran.

Iraq West Asian country crossed by the EUPHRATES and TIGRIS rivers. Much of Iraq was formerly the ancient region of ▷MESOPOTAMIA. Oil dominates the country's economy. In 1979 ▷SADDAM HUSSEIN became president; he took his country into the ▷IRAN-IRAQ WAR of 1980-8, and his invasion of Kuwait caused the ▷GULF WAR in 1991. The capital of Iraq is BAGHDAD.

The early Mesopotamian civilisations of ▷SUMERIA and ▷ASSYRIA, and the city of ▷BABYLON, were all in present-day Iraq.

Ireland, Republic of Country making up about five-sixths of the island of Ireland. A mild, humid climate is responsible for the landscape's countless shades of green which earn Ireland the popular name of 'Emerald Isle'. The River Shannon, which meets the Atlantic Ocean at Limerick, is the longest river in the British Isles. The capital is DUBLIN, and the official languages are Irish, spoken in the Kerry and Connemara regions of the west, and English. English rule of the whole island began in the 16th century with the Tudors, who wanted to establish Protestantism in place of Roman Catholicism. In 1800, the Irish Parliament was abolished and Ireland was united with Britain. A growing campaign for Home Rule entered a new violent phase with the 1916 ▷EASTER RISING. The Irish Free State came into being in 1922, but without six counties in the north where Protestant descendants of 16th and 17th-century English and Scottish settlers wanted to retain ties with Britain. The last constitutional ties with Britain were severed in 1949 when Ireland became a republic. Formal direct links were re-established in 1985 with the signing of the ▷ANGLO-IRISH AGREEMENT. Ireland has experienced massive emigration, starting in the 1840s during the ▷POTATO FAMINE caused by crop failure and continuing this century. Before the famine the population was 8 million; now it is 3½ million.

Israel Country at the eastern end of the Mediterranean Sea. The DEAD SEA and the Sea of Galilee are both on Israel's border, and water from the Sea of Galilee is channelled southwards to irrigate the arid Negev region. Kibbutzim (communal settlements) produce 35 per cent of Israel's crops; many have factories as well. Israel was born in 1948 as a homeland for the Jews, who now make up over 80 per cent of the population. The remainder are mostly Arabs. The ▷ARAB-ISRAELI CONFLICT has led to five wars. The capital is JERUSALEM; the second largest city is TEL AVIV-JAFFA. (See also ▷ARAB-ISRAELI CONFLICT in 'Politics, Government and the Law'.)

Istanbul Turkey's largest city, on the BOSPORUS. The oldest part of this ancient city is built beside an inlet known as the Golden Horn. The Blue Mosque, named for the blue tiles decorating its interior, is one of nearly 500 mosques whose domes and minarets rise above the city; the ▷HAGIA SOFIA has been in turn a cathedral, mosque and museum. The city was called Byzantium until AD 330, when the Roman emperor Constantine moved his capital there and renamed it Constantinople. It was then the capital of the ▷BYZANTINE EMPIRE until 1453, and of the ▷OTTOMAN EMPIRE until 1922. Constantinople was renamed Istanbul in 1930.

Italy Country consisting of a boot-shaped peninsula extending into the Mediterranean, and the islands of SICILY, just off the boot's toe, and SARDINIA, to the west of its ankle. Italy is rich in art and architectural treasures – frescoes and bronze sculptures left by the ▷ETRUSCANS, impressive ruins that recall the glories of the ▷ROMAN EMPIRE, and churches and museums packed with Renaissance art. After the fall of Rome, the peninsula was politically fragmented for 15 centuries until the mid 19th-century ▷RISORGIMENTO – the movement for unification, whose leading figures were Garibaldi and Cavour. Unification took place in 1870. From 1922 to 1943 the Fascist dictator Benito ▷MUSSOLINI ruled Italy. Among Italy's many splendid cities are FLORENCE, VENICE, and the capital ROME. Now the country is a major industrial power, although industry and commerce tend to be concentrated in the north; the south is less prosperous.

Jamaica West Indian island country with palm-fringed beaches that attract many tourists. Sugar is an important crop, and so is the coffee grown in the Blue Mountains. Jamaica became independent from Britain in 1962; the capital is Kingston.

Jamaica is the home of ▷REGGAE music.

Japan Country in the north Pacific Ocean made up of four main islands: Honshu, Hokkaido, Kyushu and Shikoku. Much of the land is mountainous, and most people are crowded into towns and cities around the coast, especially in and around TOKYO, the capital. Earthquakes, volcanic eruptions and tsunamis are a constant threat, and the stately Mount Fuji, Japan's highest mountain at 12 389 ft (3776 m), is a volcano that last erupted in 1707. From the 12th century until 1867 shoguns ruled the country and samurai made up a warrior caste. Japan was virtually closed to foreigners from the 1630s until the 1850s, when an American fleet under Commodore Perry forced Japan to open its ports. The Japanese occupied Korea in 1910 and Manchuria in the 1930s, and embarked on a war against China in 1937. In 1941 they bombed the American

WHITE NOISE *The seething white maelstrom and soaring spray of the Iguazú Falls are formed as the Iguazú river drops into a narrow gorge with a roar that can be heard 15 miles (24 km) away.*

military base of ▷PEARL HARBOR, and by mid 1942 had conquered much of Southeast Asia. After atomic bombs were dropped on Hiroshima and Nagasaki in World War II and Japan's surrender, Emperor ▷HIROHITO renounced his divine status and assumed the role of a constitutional monarch. Japan's economy made a dramatic recovery and the country is now one of the world's major industrial powers. Japan owes much of its success to its disciplined, loyal and well-educated work force.

Jerusalem Capital of Israel, and a holy city for Jews, Christians and Muslims. Jerusalem's walled Old City is divided into Armenian, Christian, Jewish and Muslim quarters. It has many historic religious sites, including the western wall, or Wailing Wall, the only remnant of the Jewish temple destroyed by the Romans in AD 70; the Church of the Holy Sepulchre, built where Jesus was buried; and the Dome of the Rock, an octagonal mosque built on the site of the temple and over the spot where the prophet Muhammad ascended into heaven. The Knesset, the Israeli parliament, is in the newer part of the city.

PEDAL POWER *Bicycle rickshaws are one of the best ways to travel around the markets and narrow streets in the old part of Kathmandu.*

Johannesburg South African city and the country's business centre. It started as a gold-mining settlement and is now the hub of a sprawling metropolis called the Witwatersrand, where about half the world's gold is mined. The black township of Soweto (an abbreviation of South-Western Townships) is on the edge of 'Jo'burg'.

Jordan Arab kingdom in southwest Asia, four-fifths of which is desert. The capital, Amman, is a major financial centre for the region. Since World War II, Jordan has

received many refugees as a result of the ▷ARAB-ISRAELI CONFLICT. In 1967, Jordan lost the WEST BANK – territory west of the River Jordan and Dead Sea – to Israel. In 1988, King Hussein, Jordan's monarch since 1952, renounced administrative responsibility for the West Bank. In 1994 Jordan and Israel signed an agreement ending 46 years of war.

⚓ The ruins of PETRA are in south Jordan.

Kabul Capital of Afghanistan, standing in a valley flanked by steep hills. The city is more than 3000 years old, and during the 16th century was the capital of the Mogul Empire.

Kalahari Sandy semi-desert in Botswana, Namibia and South Africa with abundant wildlife that includes lions, buffaloes, gemsboks and springboks.

⚓ Laurens Van der Post described his search for Bushmen (Basarwa) in his 1958 book *The Lost World of the Kalahari.*

Karakoram Mountain range in the disputed border area of India, Pakistan and China. Eighteen of the craggy peaks are more than 25 000 ft (7600 m) high. The highest peak in the Karakoram, and second highest in the world, is the 28 250 ft (8611 m) K2, given that name because it was the second Karakoram peak to be measured. It is also known as Godwin Austen, after Colonel H.H. Godwin Austen who first surveyed it.

Kathmandu Capital of Nepal, lying 4344 ft (1324 m) above sea level in a fertile valley in the Himalayas. The old part of Kathmandu is a maze of narrow streets lined with buildings with carved wooden balconies; elsewhere there are European-style buildings. During the 1960s many hippies were attracted to Kathmandu by the easy availability of drugs there.

Kazakhstan Huge central Asian country, formerly part of the USSR, that is almost the same size as India but has only 17 million people. Much of Kazakhstan is rather dry, the flat or rolling land is used as pasture for sheep and goats. The Muslim Kazakhs are the country's biggest ethnic group, closely followed by Russians. The capital, Alma-Ata, has twice been rebuilt after earthquakes.

Kenya East African country whose capital is Nairobi. Tea and coffee are grown in the fertile southwest of the country, but much of the rest of Kenya is scrub and desert. In the 1950s the ▷MAU MAU conducted a

violent campaign against British rule; Jomo Kenyatta, once jailed as the leader of the Mau Mau, became Kenya's first president after independence in 1963. Many tourists visit Kenya on safari, to see wildlife that includes elephants, cheetahs and giraffes. Some of the oldest fossil remains of modern man's ancestors – 2 million years old – have been found in northern Kenya near Lake Turkana. Mombasa, Kenya's second largest city, was occupied by Arab traders in the Middle Ages.

Khartoum Capital of Sudan, at the junction of the Blue Nile and White Nile. In 1884–5 an Egyptian garrison and Britain's General Charles ▷GORDON were besieged in Khartoum by Sudanese followers of a local religious leader, the Mahdi; Gordon was killed before relief arrived. The city, one of the world's hottest capitals, was later rebuilt by Lord Kitchener, and the streets laid out in the design of the Union Jack.

Khyber Pass Main pass in the mountains between Afghanistan and Pakistan. It has been a major trading and invasion route.

Kiev Capital of Ukraine, dating from the 6th century AD. In the 9th century, Kiev was the capital of the original Russian state; its grand prince converted to Christianity and made it the state religion in 988. The modern city, a major centre of industry, suffered severe damage in World War II, and was rebuilt with tree-lined boulevards.

Kilimanjaro Africa's highest mountain and an extinct volcano, rising to 19 340 ft (5895 m) in Tanzania. It is snow-capped all year, even though it is little more than 200 miles (320 km) from the Equator.

Kurdistan Region around north Iraq and the neighbouring parts of Turkey, Iran and Syria, inhabited by Muslim Kurds. The Kurds have often been victims of suppression; in 1991, after the Gulf War, many Kurds fled from Iraqi forces after rising against the regime of ▷SADDAM HUSSEIN.

Kuwait Small emirate at the head of the Persian Gulf, with immense reserves of oil which have been used to develop the economy. The capital is also called Kuwait. Iraq's invasion of Kuwait in 1990 led to the ▷GULF WAR in 1991. Nearly all the land is desert, and sea-water distillation plants supply most of the country's water.

Laos Mountainous, forested and poor communist country in Southeast Asia. Laos lies to the west of Vietnam, and during the

CASTLE COUNTRY *Chambord, with 440 rooms and 50 staircases, is the largest of the many châteaux that add grace and grandeur to the Loire valley. In spite of its size, the castle was never completed.*

Vietnam War (1960-75) it suffered from bombing raids and troops moving through the country. The capital is Vientiane.

Las Vegas City in Nevada, USA, known for its neon lights and gambling casinos which attract more than 20 million people from all over the world every year.

Lebanon Small country at the eastern end of the Mediterranean Sea, with spectacular mountains separating the coastal plain from the fertile Beqa'a valley. The capital, BEIRUT, is on the coast. Complex religious and political differences caused civil war between 1975 and 1990 and seriously damaged the economy of this once-prosperous country. Lebanon is still unstable.
The Lebanese coast was the homeland of the ▷PHOENICIANS, who founded the coastal trading cities of Tyre and Sidon.
Cedars of Lebanon, the country's national symbol, were used to build Solomon's Temple in Jerusalem, and were imported by the ancient Egyptians. Only a few cedar forests remain.

Leipzig City in eastern Germany, and a centre of trade and culture for many centuries. Leipzig's international trade fair was first held in 1165. Martin Luther, who launched the Protestant Reformation, was active there; the composers J.S. Bach and Mendelssohn worked in the city and Wagner was born there; and the writer

Goethe studied at Leipzig University. Some historic buildings destroyed during World War II have been restored.

Lhasa Remote capital of the Xizang Autonomous Region of China (formerly Tibet), standing 12 140 ft (3700 m) above sea level. The city has many Buddhist monasteries and temples. Lhasa Potala Palace was the former home of the ▷DALAI LAMA.

Liberia Small West African country founded in 1847 by freed slaves from the USA. Liberia is the only African country that has never been ruled by a foreign power. Civil war erupted in 1990. The capital is Monrovia.
Ships of many nationalities register in Liberia because of the tax advantages the 'flag of convenience' offers.

Libya Large north African country, nearly all of which lies in the Sahara desert. Most people are concentrated near the Mediterranean coast around the capital, Tripoli, and the city of Benghazi. Oil dominates the economy. Since 1969 Libya has been ruled by Colonel ▷GADDAFI. On the coast east of Tripoli are the ruins of Leptis Magna, an ancient city inhabited successively by the Phoenicians, Carthaginians and Romans.

Liechtenstein Tiny principality between Austria and Switzerland, that is less than half the size of the Isle of Wight and has just

under 30 000 people. The capital is Vaduz. Liechtenstein's lenient tax laws have encouraged many firms to register there.

Lisbon Capital of Portugal spreading over seven hills beside the estuary of the Tagus river. In the 15th century Lisbon's trade links with newly discovered lands in Africa brought wealth and great splendour. An earthquake in 1755 destroyed much of the city but some fine old buildings remain.
Vasco da Gama left Lisbon in 1497 on the voyage in which he rounded the Cape of Good Hope and found a sea route to India.

Loire Longest river in France, rising in the Massif Central and flowing north and west to the Atlantic Ocean, downstream from Nantes. The Loire valley is lined by many imposing châteaux, and wines such as Muscadet, Sancerre and Vouvray are produced along its banks.

Los Angeles Sprawling American city in southern California. Most people drive to work on the multi-lane freeways, and the city suffers from traffic jams and air pollution caused by exhaust fumes. One of its districts is Hollywood, renowned as the centre of the American film and television industries. Beverly Hills, home of many celebrities and wealthy people, is also a district of Los Angeles. Disneyland is in Anaheim, south of the city.

Louisiana Mostly low-lying state of the southern USA, which includes the Mississippi delta. The capital is Baton Rouge and the largest city is NEW ORLEANS.
Louisiana was named after Louis XIV of France – French settlers began arriving there in 1699. The French sold their territory, extending from the Mississippi to the Rockies and from the Gulf of Mexico to Canada, to the USA in 1803 for US$11.25 million. This so-called Louisiana Purchase doubled the area of the USA.

Lourdes French town in the foothills of the Pyrenees where in 1858 a peasant girl, Marie-Bernarde Soubirous, known as Bernadette, said that she had seen the Virgin Mary. A healing shrine now attracts some 5 million pilgrims every year, for some of whom miraculous cures have been claimed.

Luxembourg Small, prosperous grand duchy the size of Oxfordshire, lying between Belgium, Germany and France. It is the seat of the European Court of Justice. The capital is also called Luxembourg. The people speak Luxembourgish, but French and German are also official languages.

Macau Tiny Portuguese territory, only 6 sq miles (16 km²) in area, in south China. Portuguese merchants used it as a trading post from the 1520s, but its importance declined as Hong Kong, 40 miles (64 km) to the east, flourished. However, it is still a major trade centre and its casinos attract many tourists. Macau is due to be returned to China in 1999.

Machu Picchu Magnificently sited ruins of an ▷INCA city 7480 ft (2280 m) up in the Peruvian Andes. They were brought to the world's attention in 1911 by Hiram Bingham, an American archaeologist.

Madagascar Country and the world's fourth largest island, off Africa's east coast. Despite its location, the Malagasy people are primarily of Indonesian descent. The capital of this poor country is Antananarivo.
🐾 Madagascar has many plants and animals found only on the island, including lemurs.

Madeira Mountainous island in the Atlantic Ocean, with subtropical vegetation, 440 miles (710 km) west of Morocco. Madeira and its neighbouring islands are part of Portugal; the capital is Funchal.
🐾 Madeira wine, a fortified wine similar to sweet sherry, makes a good accompaniment to Madeira sponge cake.

Madrid Capital and largest city of Spain, situated on dry plains in the centre of the country. Madrid is the home of one of the world's major art galleries, the Prado, which contains works by leading Spanish artists including ▷GOYA, ▷EL GRECO and ▷VELÁSQUEZ.

Malawi Long, narrow country in southeast Africa, bordering Lake Malawi. It has great natural beauty, but poverty is widespread. Dr Hastings Banda became president in 1964 when Malawi gained independence from Britain. His 30-year dictatorship ended with the country's first multiparty elections in May 1994 when Bakili Muluzi was elected president.

Malaysia Kingdom in Southeast Asia, consisting of a peninsula of the mainland, and the more rural states of Sabah and Sarawak which are in the northern part of the island of Borneo. Much of the land is mountainous and covered with luxuriant forest. Malays, who are mostly Muslims, make up 60 per cent of the population and dominate politics; the Chinese, who make up 30 per cent, dominate business. The capital is Kuala Lumpur. Malaysia is one of the world's leading rubber producers.

AWESOME MOUNTAIN *The Matterhorn was first conquered in 1865 by a team led by Edward Whymper, an English wood engraver.*

Maldives Country of about 1300 low-lying coral islands in the Indian Ocean, 400 miles (640 km) southwest of Sri Lanka. Sandy beaches, palm trees and lagoons attract many tourists; fishing is the other main source of income. The capital is Malé.

Malta Mediterranean island country, 50 miles (80 km) east of Tunisia, made up of Malta, the smaller island of Gozo and tiny Comino. The capital, Valletta, is on Malta. Many foreign powers have dominated the islands, including the Knights of St John from 1530 to 1798, and the British, who had a naval dockyard that closed in 1979. Malta achieved full independence from Britain in 1964; Dom Mintoff was prime minister from 1955 to 1958 and from 1971 to 1984.
🐾 Malta was awarded the George Cross after withstanding German and Italian bombardment during World War II.

Marshall Islands Pacific Island country of some 1250 coral islands, more than 2500 miles (4000 km) east of the Philippines. In the late 1940s and 1950s the USA exploded 64 nuclear weapons on Bikini and Enewetak atolls.
🐾 The bikini bathing garment was named after Bikini atoll, because of the 'atomic' impact it had on onlookers.

Massachusetts Northeast coast state of the USA. The Pilgrim Fathers established a settlement there at Plymouth on Cape Cod Bay in 1620, after sailing from England on the *Mayflower*. The city of Salem was founded in 1626, and in 1692 witchcraft trials held there led to the execution of 20 townsfolk, most of them women. The state capital is BOSTON.

Matterhorn Magnificent, pyramid-like mountain 14 688 ft (4477 m) high, in the Alps on the Swiss-Italian border.

Mediterranean Sea Almost tideless sea connected to the Atlantic Ocean by the Strait of Gibraltar. Several ancient civilisations – Egyptian, Minoan, Mycenaean, Phoenician, Greek and Roman – arose around the Mediterranean. Concern in the early 1970s about water pollution led to many Mediterranean countries taking steps to improve the water quality.

Memphis City and major cotton market on the Mississippi river in the US state of Tennessee. The singer Elvis ▷PRESLEY spent much of his life there and was buried at his mansion, Graceland, now a museum.
🐾 The civil rights leader Martin Luther King was assassinated in Memphis in 1968.

Mexico Predominantly mountainous Central American country that has both harsh deserts and tropical forests. The south is sometimes hit by earthquakes, and has active volcanoes. Magnificent ruins of early civilisations include those of the ▷MAYA, who lived in the low-lying Yucatán peninsula, and the ▷AZTECS, who were conquered by the Spaniards between 1519 and 1521. Mexico has oil fields and silver mines. The capital is MEXICO CITY.

Mexico City World's largest city, with about 16 million people. The city stands 7350 ft (2240 m) above sea level, and has Aztec ruins, palaces built in Spanish colonial times, and many modern buildings. New buildings are constructed to withstand earthquakes; a strong quake in 1985 killed more than 7000 people. The city hosted the Olympic Games in 1968.

Miami Large city on Florida's Atlantic coast, where many Cuban exiles have settled. Miami's Art Deco District has impressive architecture, but the crime rate is high and many drugs from South America enter the USA there. The warm temperatures all year round draw holidaymakers to the resort of Miami Beach.

Milan Italy's second largest city and the country's centre of finance, industry, fashion and publishing. Older buildings include the Gothic cathedral, and the convent of the late 15th-century church of Santa Maria delle Grazie, where Leonardo da Vinci painted his fresco The ▷LAST SUPPER. The Galleria, a huge 19th-century glass-roofed building, now a shopping arcade, is near La Scala, the opera house.

Mississippi Major river in the USA, flowing 2350 miles (3780 km) from northwest Minnesota to its delta in the Gulf of Mexico. At St Louis it is joined by the Missouri, and the 3740 miles (6020 km) Mississippi-Missouri is the world's fourth longest river system. The muddy waters of 'Old Man River' carry vast amounts of freight. A system of levees and side channels usually helps to prevent flooding but in 1993 two months of heavy rain brought floods to an area bigger than Scotland.
🦎Mark ▷TWAIN set his novels *The Adventures of Tom Sawyer* and *The Adventures of Huckleberry Finn* around the Mississippi.

Monaco Tiny, rich principality on the French Riviera, stretching along the coast for just over 2 miles (3.2 km). The palace of the ruling Grimaldi family is on the rocky headland of Monaco town, and further along the coast is the resort area of Monte Carlo, with its ornate casino.
🦎The present head of state, Prince Rainier III, came to the throne in 1949. He married the film star Grace ▷KELLY in 1956.
🦎The Monaco Grand Prix takes place in the town's winding streets every May.

Mongolia High, arid country between Russia and China, much of it covered with grassland or the wastes of the Gobi desert. The capital is Ulan Bator. Mongolia was a communist country from 1924 to 1990.
🦎Some of Mongolia's nomadic herdsmen live in circular, dome-topped tents called *gers* in Mongolian, or *yurts* in Russian.

Mont Blanc Western Europe's tallest peak, 15 770ft (4807 m) high, in the Alps on the French-Italian border.

Montreal Canadian city, in Quebec province, built around a wooded hill called Mount Royal from which it takes its name. Montreal has tall modern buildings, picturesque cobbled streets and underground shops and restaurants that give protection from both the bitterly cold, snowy winters and the hot summers.
🦎Montreal claims to be the world's second largest French-speaking city, after Paris.

Morocco Kingdom in northwest Africa. The rugged Atlas Mountains rise to more than 13 000ft (4000 m) behind the fertile coastal lands; further inland is the harshness of the ▷SAHARA. The capital is Rabat, but the largest city is Casablanca, scene of a World War II meeting between Allied leaders and the inspiration of the film starring Humphrey Bogart and Ingrid Bergman. Marrakech, the former capital at the foot of the Atlas Mountains, is a bustling and colourful city whose *souks* – markets and bazaars – attract many tourists.

Moscow Capital of Russia and formerly of the USSR. The ▷KREMLIN, in the heart of Moscow, is a fortress with government buildings, palaces and cathedrals within its walls. Just outside the walls are Red Square, the site of military parades during the Soviet era; the 16th-century St Basil's Cathedral, with its magnificent colourful domes; and the department store GUM. The city was besieged by Napoleon I in 1812. Moscow is also known for its palatial underground railway stations.

Mount Everest World's highest mountain, at 29 028 ft (8848 m), in the Himalayas on the border of China and Nepal. It was named after Sir George Everest, a British Surveyor General of India. Edmund Hillary, a New Zealander, and Tenzing Norgay, a Sherpa, were the first people to reach the summit, in 1953.

Mount Rushmore Mountain in the Black Hills of South Dakota, USA, where the faces of four US presidents – George Washington, Thomas Jefferson, Abraham Lincoln and Theodore Roosevelt – were carved in a granite cliff between 1927 and 1941. The heads are 60 ft (18 m) high, with mouths about 18 ft (5.5 m) wide.

Mount St Helens Large ▷VOLCANO in Washington state, USA, that erupted violently in 1980. Ash rose 15 miles (24 km) into the air, and trees were flattened over an area of about 230 sq miles (600 km²).

Mozambique Poor agricultural country in southeast Africa that was plagued by civil strife from the late 1970s to the early 1990s. Mozambique's problems were aggravated by drought in the 1980s. The country was a Portuguese colony until 1975, and then a Marxist state until 1990. The capital, Maputo, is a major port; it was formerly called Lourenço Marques.

Munich Germany's third largest city, and capital of the state of Bavaria. It has impressive public buildings and churches, and many museums, art galleries, theatres and concert halls.
🦎Munich is known for its beer gardens, and also for the *Oktoberfest*, a beer festival held in late September and early October which attracts more than 6 million people. Between them they drink some 5 million litres (9 million pints) of beer.
🦎During the 1972 Munich Olympics, Arab guerrillas of the Black September organisation held Israeli athletes hostage and demanded the release of 200 Palestinians held in Israeli jails. Eleven athletes, five terrorists and a policeman were killed.
🦎Hitler's rise to power began in Munich.

ROOM WITH A VIEW *A wintry Moscow sun, seen through the wrought iron of a hotel balcony, outlines the impressive snow-touched turrets of the Kremlin on the far side of Red Square.*

Namibia Arid, sparsely populated country in southwest Africa, ruled by South Africa from the end of World War I until 1990. From the mid 1960s SWAPO, the South-West Africa People's Organisation, conducted a guerrilla war against South African rule. Inland is the Namib Desert – a strip of harsh wilderness where frequent fogs often supply the only moisture. In the north, off the Skeleton Coast, treacherous currents, strong winds and fog have caused many shipwrecks. Namibia is a major diamond producer. The capital is Windhoek.

Naples Beautifully sited Italian city built around the Bay of Naples, with VESUVIUS in the background. It has fine churches and museums that contain many works of art, as well as narrow streets and densely populated alleys lined with decaying buildings.

Nepal Kingdom which runs along the southern slopes of the HIMALAYAS. Its southern border with India is only just above sea level, but 100 miles (160 km) to the north are MOUNT EVEREST and other mighty peaks that lie on the northern border with China. Sherpas, a group of people from northeast Nepal, sometimes act as guides and porters to mountain expeditions. The capital is KATHMANDU.
⚲ The British East India Company enlisted Gurkha hillmen to serve in their armies in the early 19th century. About 4500 Gurkhas still serve in the British army, and carry the traditional curved knife, the kukri.

Netherlands Prosperous and densely populated kingdom where one-sixth of the land has been reclaimed from the sea. Agriculture employs a tiny proportion of the workforce but is intensive and scientific, with dairy farms, huge areas of glasshouses, and fields of tulips and other flowers. The Netherlands was a major sea power in the 17th century. The Dutch East India Company's trade in spices led to Dutch rule in what is now Indonesia, and the company also established a garrison in what is now Cape Town. The Dutch settlement of New Amsterdam grew to be New York. Trade brought prosperity to AMSTERDAM, which is the capital, though The Hague is the seat of government. Rotterdam is one of the world's biggest ports.
⚲ The Netherlands has produced many great painters, including ▷VAN EYCK, Frans ▷HALS, ▷REMBRANDT, ▷VERMEER and ▷VAN GOGH.

New Orleans City on the Mississippi delta in the southern USA. Annual Mardi Gras parades with colourful floats last for about two weeks and end on Shrove Tuesday. The city's French Quarter has buildings in French and Spanish colonial styles, with iron trellis balconies.
⚲ ▷JAZZ originated in New Orleans.

New York Cosmopolitan, vibrant city and the biggest in the USA, with more than 7 million people. The heart of New York, the borough of Manhattan, contains the city's major business and cultural institutions. These include the financial sector of Wall Street; the twin-towered World Trade Center; Times Square, named after the building formerly occupied by *The New York Times*; Greenwich Village, the haunt of students and artists; the theatres of Broadway; and a multitude of museums. Central Manhattan is laid out as a grid of numbered streets. The smartest shops and the ▷EMPIRE STATE BUILDING are on Fifth Avenue, and CENTRAL PARK lies between 59th Street and 110th Street. The residential area of Harlem lies to the north of Central Park. New York's other four boroughs are Brooklyn and Queens, both on Long Island, and the Bronx and Staten Island. The Brooklyn Bridge, the world's longest suspension bridge when it opened in 1883, spans the East River and connects Brooklyn to Manhattan. The Statue of Liberty stands in New York Harbor.
⚲ Europeans arrived at the site of New York in 1609, and in 1624 the Dutch bought Manhattan island from local people. The settlement, called New Amsterdam, was taken over by the English in 1664 and renamed New York.

DESERT LIFE *Flamingos gather in a saltpan beneath towering sand dunes in Namibia's long, narrow Namib Desert. Sometimes rising to 1000 ft (300 m) high, the dunes are among the Earth's highest.*

New York's nickname, 'The Big Apple', which was both a dance and a Harlem night club, was probably coined by jazz musicians in the 1930s. It was adopted in the 1970s as a slogan to promote the city.

New Zealand Country slightly larger than the United Kingdom, but with only 3.5 million people. Three-quarters of New Zealanders live on North Island, the slightly smaller of the two main islands where the largest city, Auckland, and the capital, Wellington, are located. North Island has hot springs and geysers at Rotorua, and active volcanoes. South Island is dominated by the Southern Alps where 14 peaks exceed 10 000 ft (3000 m). The first New Zealanders were Polynesians who arrived about 1000 years ago; they adopted the name ▷MAORI, meaning normal, to distinguish themselves from Europeans, who arrived in large numbers from the 1830s. Sheep outnumber people by 16 to 1. Kiwis – nocturnal, flightless birds with long bills – are native to New Zealand and are the country's national symbol.

Niagara Falls Majestic waterfalls, with a drop of about 175 ft (53 m) on the Niagara River, which form part of the border between Canada and the USA. The American Falls and Bridal Veil Falls are on the US side of the border and the Horseshoe Falls are on the Canadian side.

Nicaragua Central American country whose agricultural economy has been undermined by civil war. In the 1970s, Sandinista guerrillas opposed the government of President Somoza, which was overthrown by the guerrillas in 1979. Civil war broke out in the 1980s between the Sandinista government and the US-backed Contras. The capital, Managua, was badly damaged by earthquakes in 1931 and 1972.

Nigeria Most populous African country. Nigeria has oil fields around the Niger river delta, and oil and gas dominate the economy, although more than half of the people work on the land. The capital moved from Lagos to Abuja, a new city on a politically neutral site in central Nigeria, in 1991.

Nile World's second longest river, flowing 4145 miles (6670 km) from its most distant headstream, in the African state of Burundi, to its delta in the Mediterranean. The Nile flows out of Lake Victoria and on through lakes and swamps to Khartoum, where it is joined by the Blue Nile, which rises in the Ethiopian highlands. The Nile's annual floods brought fertility to its valley and

allowed the civilisation of ancient Egypt to flourish. The ASWAN HIGH DAM, completed in 1971, now regulates the river's flow.

Northern Ireland Province of the United Kingdom, made up of six counties: Antrim, Armagh, Down, Fermanagh, Londonderry and Tyrone. All except Fermanagh lie around Lough Neagh, the largest lake in the UK. The magnificent coastal scenery includes the Giant's Causeway, composed of thousands of hexagonal basalt columns packed together. Deep-rooted hostility between Northern Ireland's Catholics and Protestants erupted in violence in 1969. The capital of Northern Ireland is BELFAST and the second-largest city in the province is Londonderry.

North Korea Communist country in the northern half of the Korean peninsula in east Asia. The state was formed in 1948, and

fought the ▷KOREAN WAR against South Korea between 1950 and 1953. Kim Il-sung was the country's leader from 1948 until his death in 1994, when his son Kim Jong Il took over. North Korea lost a major ally with the collapse of communism in the USSR. Tensions between North and South Korea persist, and the North's nuclear potential has attracted world concern. The capital is Pyongyang.

Norway Prosperous Scandinavian kingdom with impressive mountain scenery. About a third of Norway lies north of the Arctic Circle, but the coast, deeply indented with fjords, is kept almost entirely ice-free by the northward extension of the Gulf Stream. Its seafaring tradition dates back to ▷VIKING times, and fishing is an important industry. North Sea oil is a major source of revenue. King Harald V succeeded Olav V in 1991. The capital is OSLO.

VAST LANDS *The two huge countries that make up North America – Canada and the United States of America – cover an area nearly as large as that encompassed by all 43 countries in Europe.*

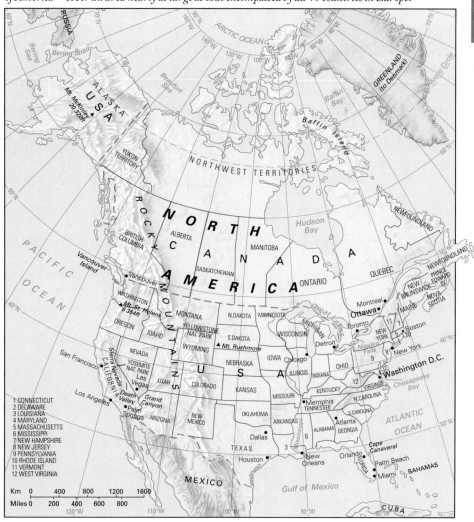

Oberammergau Small town in the far south of Germany. A Passion play was performed there in 1634 to celebrate deliverance from the plague, and has been staged by the townspeople every ten years since then – apart from a few exceptions during wars. The next performance of the play will be in 2000.

Okavango African river rising in Angola and ending in an inland delta in northern Botswana. The delta's marshes and swamps, which expand with the winter rains and contract in summer, are a haven for wildlife in the parched heart of Africa.

Oklahoma Southwestern state of the USA, forming part of the Great Plains. Drought struck in the 1930s and dust storms blew away the dry, over-cultivated top soil. The barren land of northwestern Oklahoma, and of neighbouring states, became known as the Dust Bowl.
♣The migration of 'Okies' to seek their living elsewhere was the subject of John ▷STEINBECK's novel *The Grapes of Wrath*.

♣The musical *Oklahoma!* was set in an Oklahoma farming community in the early years of the 20th century.

Oman Sultanate on the southeast coast of the Arabian Peninsula, most of whose income comes from oil. Rugged mountains in the north and south flank a vast desert plain. A small region of Oman is isolated from the rest of the country by part of the United Arab Emirates, and overlooks the Strait of Hormuz. The capital, Muscat, was a major trade centre in the 5th century BC.

Ontario Province in central Canada. Most people live in the southeast corner which includes OTTAWA, Canada's capital, and TORONTO, the state capital, and also the NIAGARA FALLS. Few people live in the heavily forested north of the province.

Oporto/Porto Portugal's second city, at the mouth of the River Douro. The city gave its name to port wine, which can only be made from grapes which are grown in the Douro basin and shipped from Oporto.

Oslo Capital and main port of Norway, spreading over a large area at the head of the vast Oslofjord. The city has also been known as Christiania, after Christian IV, king of both Norway and Denmark, who had the city rebuilt after a disastrous fire in 1624. Maritime exhibits on the waterfront include reconstructed Viking ships; the ship *Fram* in which Roald ▷AMUNDSEN travelled to the Antarctic for his 1911 polar expedition; and the raft used by Thor Heyerdahl in his Kon-Tiki expedition.
♣A collection of work by the Norwegian artist ▷MUNCH can be seen in Oslo.

Ottawa Spacious, leafy capital of Canada in the province of Ontario. In 1857, when Ottawa was a lumber town, Queen Victoria proclaimed it Canada's capital and dashed the hopes of Montreal, Toronto and other contenders for the position.

OASIS *Antelopes move across an island in the swampy Okavango delta, which is also the home of hippos, lions and huge flocks of birds.*

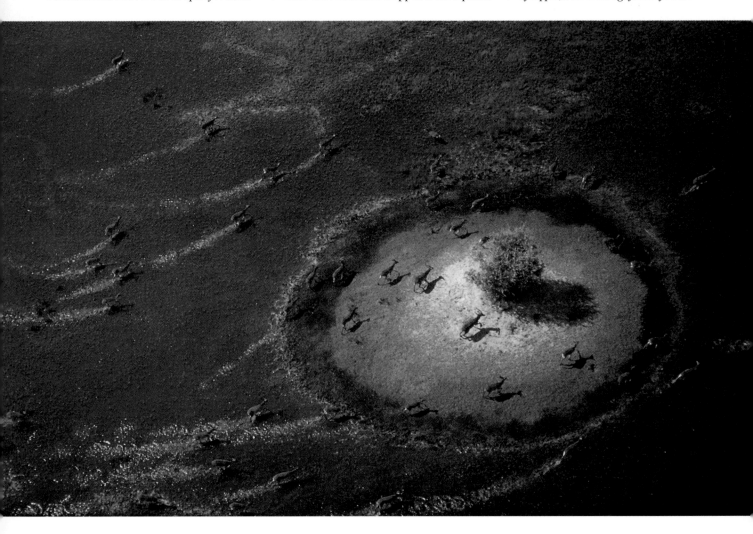

Pacific Ocean World's largest ocean, covering one-third of the Earth's surface; its area of 64 million sq miles (166 million km²) is greater than that of all the planet's land surface combined. The Pacific stretches from the Arctic to the Antarctic, and is bounded by Asia, Australia and the Americas. The ocean floor has vast underwater mountain ranges and trenches, including CHALLENGER DEEP – the deepest known spot in any ocean. There are three main groups of volcanic and coral islands: Melanesia, Micronesia and POLYNESIA.
⚓The Portuguese explorer Ferdinand ▷MAGELLAN, leader of the expedition which circumnavigated the world in 1519-22, gave the ocean its name because it was relatively free from violent storms.

Pakistan Largely rural country in southern Asia. Part of Pakistan is a dry plain crossed by the River Indus, but the north has some of the world's highest mountains. When India gained independence from Britain in 1947, Pakistan was created for its Muslim minority and then consisted of West Pakistan and East Pakistan, 1000 miles (1600 km) apart. In 1971, East Pakistan became the separate state of ▷BANGLADESH. Soon afterwards Zulfikar Ali ▷BHUTTO became the first president of the new Pakistan. His daughter Benazir ▷BHUTTO has twice been elected prime minister. The capital is Islamabad.
⚓A major early civilisation flourished at Mohenjo Daro in the Indus valley.

Palestine Land at the eastern end of the Mediterranean Sea. In Biblical times Palestine was the homeland of the Jews, and has since been ruled by many powers, including the Romans, Arabs and Turks. After World War I Palestine was administered by Britain under a League of Nations mandate, until the state of Israel was born in 1948. During the war that followed, almost 600 000 Palestinian Arabs fled from their homes. The ▷PLO has campaigned for the rights of Palestinians.

Palm Beach Resort on the Atlantic coast of Florida, USA, where many affluent Americans spend the winter.

Palm Springs Relaxed resort and home of many show business people in the desert of southern California, USA.

Panama Small, narrow Central American country cut into two by the ▷PANAMA CANAL. In 1989, US troops invaded the country, to overthrow the regime of General Noriega. The capital is Panama City.

⚓Panama became famous for exporting hand-woven hats, made in Ecuador, from the leaves of the palm-like jipijapa plant that grows in South and Central America.

Papua New Guinea Pacific country northeast of Australia, made up of the mountainous mainland – the eastern half of New Guinea – and many islands. The country's rain forests are home to a vast range of animals, including birds of paradise and giant butterflies. The capital, Port Moresby, is on the mainland.

Paraguay Landlocked South American country. Nearly all Paraguayans live in the east of the country, especially around the capital, Asunción; very few people live in the west, amid the dry forest and thorny scrubland of the Gran Chaco. In 1954, General Stroessner seized power and ran a fascist dictatorship until he was finally ousted by a coup in 1989. The country's first free elections were held in 1993.
⚓Josef Mengele – the Nazi 'Angel of Death' who conducted grotesque medical experiments at the Auschwitz concentration camp – lived in hiding in Paraguay until his death in 1978.

Paris Elegant capital of France on the River Seine. One of the world's major tourist centres, its attractions include the ▷EIFFEL TOWER; the Arc de Triomphe and Champs-Elysées; the Gothic ▷NOTRE-DAME Cathedral, begun in 1163; the white-domed Sacré-Coeur on top of the artists' hill, Montmartre; the ▷POMPIDOU CENTRE, the Louvre museum, which houses the *Mona Lisa*, and its pavement cafés. Many of the city's boulevards and parks date from the 1850s and 1860s and are the work of Baron Georges Haussmann. Paris has attracted artists, musicians and writers for centuries, and is still the centre of the fashion industry. At the start of the ▷FRENCH REVOLUTION, rebels stormed the city's Bastille fortress on July 14, 1789. In World War II German forces occupied Paris unchallenged: in a bid to prevent destruction, the French government had declared it an open city. It was liberated by the Allies in August 1944. In 1968, huge student riots in the city led to the resignation of President De Gaulle.

Patagonia Barren plateau, three times the size of the United Kingdom, in southern Argentina and Chile. Some of its people are descendants of Welsh settlers who began arriving in the 1860s. The Chilean city of Punta Arenas, in the far south of Patagonia, is the world's southernmost city.

Pennsylvania State in the eastern USA named after its founder, William ▷PENN. The capital is Harrisburg, but the largest city is Philadelphia, where the Thirteen Colonies' ▷DECLARATION OF INDEPENDENCE from Britain was signed in 1776.

Persian Gulf (also called the Arabian Gulf, or simply The Gulf) Arm of the Indian Ocean, surrounded by oil-producing countries. The Persian Gulf is linked to the Gulf of Oman by the Strait of Hormuz, and is an important shipping lane. The ▷GULF WAR took place in 1991.

Perth Sunny capital of Western Australia. Perth was named after the Scottish county of Perth, birthplace of Sir George Murray, Britain's Secretary of State for the Colonies when the city was founded in 1829.
⚓Perth is the world's most isolated major city; even Sydney is a four-hour flight away.

Peru South American country with high peaks in the Andes, and hot, wet, forested lowlands. The capital is Lima. Peru was the home of the ▷INCAS before their empire fell to the Spanish conquistadores in the 1530s. Half of all Peruvians are Indians, some of whom live at high altitudes, herding alpacas for their wool and using llamas as beasts of burden. The Maoist Shining Path organisation conducted a violent terrorist campaign in Peru in the 1970s and 1980s; the group's leader, Abimael Guzmán, was imprisoned in 1992.

Petra Ruined city in Jordan with buildings cut into sheer sandstone cliffs. An Arab people, the Nabataeans, made it their capital in the 4th century BC. The city was a flourishing centre of the spice trade but was deserted after an earthquake in AD 551.
⚓In his poem *Petra*, the Reverend John Burgon described Petra as 'A rose-red city half as old as Time' because of the effect of sunrise and sunset on its pinkish-red rock.

Philippines Southeast Asian country made up of more than 7000 islands which are subject to earthquakes, volcanic eruptions and typhoons. About half of all Filipinos work on the land. The country is named after King Philip II of Spain, and was ruled by Spain for more than three centuries. Ferdinand Marcos ruled the Philippines for two decades, aided by his wife Imelda who was known for her large collection of shoes. An election in 1986 swept Corazon (Cory) Aquino to power. The capital is Manila.
⚓The paper used to make Manila envelopes was originally made from the fibre of a plant grown in the Philippines.

LEANING TOWER *The remarkable 179 ft (55 m) high bell tower of Pisa's cathedral started to lean even before it was finished, in 1174.*

Pisa Italian city on the River Arno in Tuscany, whose ▷LEANING TOWER is a major tourist attraction. ▷GALILEO, the astronomer and mathematician, was born in Pisa in 1564. In Roman times Pisa was a port, but silting of the river has left it 6 miles (10 km) inland.

Poland Central European country whose borders have moved many times. At the end of the 18th century Poland was divided between Russia, Prussia and Austria, and it only regained sovereignty in 1918. Its invasion by Germany in 1939 sparked World War II during which six million Poles, half of them Jews, were killed. Many of them died in ▷AUSCHWITZ concentration camp; others died in the ▷KATYN MASSACRE. The capital, WARSAW, and the historic city of Cracow are both on the Vistula – Poland's longest river. In 1980 strikes in the shipbuilding city of Gdansk led to the formation of ▷SOLIDARITY, headed by Lech Walesa. Multiparty elections were held in 1989, ending more than 40 years of communist rule.
⚓In 1978 Cardinal Wojtyla of Cracow became Pope John Paul II, the first non-Italian pope since 1523.
⚓Notable Poles include the astronomer ▷COPERNICUS; Marie ▷CURIE, who discovered radium; and ▷CHOPIN.

Polynesia Largest of three groups of islands in the Pacific Ocean; the others are Melanesia and Micronesia. The Polynesian islands are scattered between New Zealand,

Easter Island and the Hawaiian Islands, and include TAHITI, TONGA and WESTERN SAMOA. New Zealand's Maoris are Polynesians. Melanesia means 'black islands' and refers to the peoples' dark skins; the people of the Solomon Islands, New Guinea and Fiji are predominantly Melanesians. The MARSHALL ISLANDS and Kiribati (formerly the Gilbert Islands) are part of Micronesia.

Portugal Country on the Iberian Peninsula's Atlantic coast. Around the coast, fishermen catch sardines, tuna and anchovies, and fish canning is an important industry. The warm climate and sandy beaches of the Algarve, in the far south, attract holidaymakers. In the 15th century Prince Henry the Navigator (1394-1460) encouraged early explorers; Vasco da ▷GAMA and Bartolomeu ▷DIAS made notable voyages, and the Portuguese were the first Europeans to reach China and Japan by sea. In 1500 the Portuguese reached Brazil, which they governed until 1822. This century Portugal was under dictatorship rule for almost 50 years until a coup in 1974. The capital is LISBON.
⚓Portuguese wines include vinho verde, from the northern Minho province, Dão, and port, named after the city of OPORTO.

Potsdam Historic German city, home to Prussian kings and German emperors. Potsdam's Sans Souci Palace and Park were built by Prussia's ▷FREDERICK THE GREAT. The city hosted the 1945 Potsdam Conference, in which the Allied leaders decided the future administration of Germany.

Prague Capital of the Czech Republic. The 14th-century Charles Bridge, lined with statues, crosses the Vltava River. On one side of the river, the castle, cathedral and royal palace crown Hradčany hill. On the other side are the Town Hall, with its 15th-century astronomical clock, and Wenceslas Square, a broad boulevard with a statue of St Wenceslas on horseback. Since the downfall of communism in 1989 Prague has attracted many tourists.

Pretoria Administrative capital of South Africa, decorated in spring by the mauve flowers of thousands of jacaranda trees.

Provence Mediterranean region in southeast France. The quality of light and spectacular scenery inspired Impressionist painters, including ▷CÉZANNE and ▷RENOIR.

Puerto Rico Fertile, mountainous Caribbean island to the east of Hispaniola. Puerto Rico's predominantly Spanish-

speaking people are US citizens. The mountains and beaches attract tourists, and tax laws encourage US businesses to set up factories there. The capital is San Juan.

Punjab, India Prosperous Indian state where most of the country's Sikhs live. The city of AMRITSAR contains the holiest of Sikh shrines, the Golden Temple.

Punjab, Pakistan Predominantly flat province, crossed by several great rivers that supply water for irrigation. It was part of the pre-independence Indian province of ▷PUNJAB, which in 1947 was divided between Pakistan and India. Nearly all the people are Muslims.

Pyrenees Mountain range lying between France and Spain, and rising to 11 169 ft (3404 m) at Pico de Aneto. The tiny Catalan-speaking state of ANDORRA is in the eastern Pyrenees; the Basque people live in the west in both Spain and France.

Quebec Canada's largest province. The far north is a treeless frozen waste; much of the remainder is covered with forest broken by lakes. Most people live in the south, along the St Lawrence river. More than 80 per cent of Quebec's people are French-speaking, and many are pressing for self-government. The largest city is MONTREAL, and the state capital is Quebec city, founded in 1608 by French settlers.

Queensland Northeastern state of Australia, with the GREAT BARRIER REEF just off the coast. A coastal plain, where sugar cane is a major crop, is separated from the arid interior by the Great Dividing Range. The capital is Brisbane, and the tourist resort of Cairns is in northern Queensland.

Red Sea Long, narrow arm of the Indian Ocean and a major trade route, linked to the Mediterranean Sea by the Suez Canal.
⚓The Red Sea's name comes from occasional blooms of algae which turn the sea a reddish-brown colour.

Reykjavík Capital of Iceland, said to have been founded by Viking settlers in AD 874. Buildings in Reykjavík are heated by hot water piped from nearby volcanic springs, which also give the city its name, which means 'smoking bay'.

Rhine European river flowing north from Switzerland to the North Sea. Barges carry freight – mainly iron ore, coal and oil – along the Rhine. The river was once heavily polluted, but water quality has improved since the mid 1970s. As it flows towards Bonn, the Rhine passes through a gorge with vineyards and castles on its slopes. Basle and Cologne are also on the Rhine. The Lorelei rock rises above the Rhine gorge. In German legend, the rock was the home of a nymph whose singing lured boatmen to their deaths.

Rhodes Largest of the Greek Dodecanese islands, off Turkey's southwest coast. The Colossus of Rhodes – a 110 ft (33 m) statue of the sun god Helios – was one of the Seven Wonders of the World. From the 13th to the 16th centuries, Rhodes was the headquarters of the Knights of St John, a Christian order established to care for pilgrims and the sick which took on a military role during the ▷CRUSADES. The island attracts many tourists.

Rhône European river flowing south from Switzerland to its delta in the Mediterranean Sea, via Lake Geneva (Lac Léman) and Lyons. The CAMARGUE is within the Rhône delta. Vineyards on the Rhône's hilly banks south of Lyons are the source of Côtes-du-Rhône wines.

Rio de Janeiro Spectacularly sited Brazilian city, overlooked by the Sugar Loaf mountain and Corcovado, crowned with a statue of Christ with outstretched arms. Huge numbers of tourists visit the wide sandy beaches of Copacabana and Ipanema, and also the colourful Carnival which takes place just before Lent every year. Shanty towns climb the city's steep slopes. Rio was Brazil's capital city until 1960, when the new city of BRASÍLIA became the capital.

Rocky Mountains Mountain range, with magnificent scenery and vast forests, that stretches for 3000 miles (4800 km) along the western side of North America, from Mexico to Alaska. The highest point, at 14 433 ft (4399 m), is Mount Elbert in the US state of Colorado. Areas of particular beauty that are protected from development include Yellowstone National Park in the USA, and Banff National Park in Canada. Bighorn sheep, mountain lions and grizzly bears live in the Rockies.

Romania Former communist country in Eastern Europe. The forested Carpathian Mountains sweep in an arc around Transylvania, the setting for the story of ▷DRACULA. Moldavia, the northeast region of Romania, has monasteries with exterior wall paintings that date from the 16th century. The Danube reaches the Black Sea in Romania, and its delta has abundant wildlife. Many tourists visit the Black Sea coast. Romania's ruthless dictator, President ▷CEAUSESCU, was shot with his wife Elena on Christmas Day 1989 after a short revolution that started in Timisoara, in western Romania. BUCHAREST, the capital, is on a plain in the south.

Rome Italy's capital on the River Tiber. Modern Rome spreads well beyond the seven hills on which the ancient city was built after it was founded in the 8th century BC, supposedly by ▷ROMULUS AND REMUS. Surviving relics of the time when the so-called Eternal City was the capital of the Roman Empire include the Colosseum, where gladiators fought and Christians were thrown to the lions; the Forum, which

was the centre of government; and the ▷PANTHEON, a temple dedicated to all the gods. Many of Rome's palaces and churches date from the 16th and 17th centuries. ▷ST PETER'S BASILICA is part of the VATICAN, a walled state within the city.

Russia World's largest country, nearly as big as Canada and the USA combined and stretching almost halfway round the globe. Russia is home to some 75 different races, although Russians make up more than 80 per cent of the population. The Russian language is written in the Cyrillic alphabet. The second biggest group of people are the Tatars, who are Muslims. MOSCOW, the capital, ST PETERSBURG and almost all the other major cities lie west of the Ural Mountains. Few people live east of the Urals, in SIBERIA. The far north of Russia is a frozen, treeless wilderness dotted with lakes and bogs, and much of the remainder of the country is covered with vast tracts of forest. Almost all of Russia has intensely cold winters, and in the centre of the country January temperatures regularly fall below −40°C (−40°F). Moscow rose to prominence in the 14th and 15th centuries, when its grand prince effectively became Russia's leader. Grand Prince Ivan, known as ▷IVAN THE GREAT, greatly strengthened Moscow's position, and it was his grandson, ▷IVAN THE TERRIBLE (1533-84), who first took the title of tsar. In the following years, nobles were given land and the services of peasants in return for obedience to the tsar, and serfdom was established in 1649. ▷PETER THE GREAT (1682-1725) introduced Western ways and built the capital of St Petersburg. His reforms were continued by ▷CATHERINE THE GREAT (1762-96). Serfdom was abolished in 1861, but a huge gulf remained between the peasants, who made up the vast majority, and the elite. A revolution in 1905 resulted in the introduction of the Duma, or parliament, but continued unrest and the rigours of World War I led in 1917 to the abdication of Tsar ▷NICHOLAS II and the ▷RUSSIAN REVOLUTION. Russia then became by far the largest republic of the USSR, which was set up in 1922 and ceased to exist in December 1991. The first president of the new state of Russia was Boris ▷YELTSIN.

Rwanda Central African country that gained independence from Belgium in 1962. However, hostility between the peasant Hutus (85 per cent of the population) and their former Tutsi overlords exploded in a wave of violence in April 1994 after the death of President Habyarimana in an unexplained aircrash. About 500 000

CITY GUARDIAN *Since 1931 the 98¹⁄₂ ft (30 m) statue of Christ the Redeemer has kept watch over Rio de Janeiro from the 2330 ft (710 m) summit of Corcovado, known locally as the 'Hunchback'.*

Rwandans, mostly Tutsi, were slaughtered by Hutu death squads. Fearing reprisals, some 2 million Hutu refugees had fled the country by the end of July.

Sahara Desert in north Africa that is the world's biggest desert: it is almost as large as the USA. Sand dunes cover only about 15 per cent of the Sahara, and much of the rest is bare rock or gravel. The highest mountains, the Tibesti, rise to more than 11 000 ft (3350 m); the lowest point is in Egypt's Qattara Depression, 436 ft (133 m) below sea level. In summer, ground temperatures can reach 70°C (158°F), and most places receive less than 5 in (12.5 cm) of rain a year. Saharan peoples include the Tuareg and Berbers. The desert has huge deposits of oil and other minerals.
⚜ Deep in the Sahara, on the Tassili N'Ajjer plateau, rock paintings more than 6000 years old show elephants and cattle, indicating that the land was once fertile.

St Helena Remote, mountainous island, only 47 sq miles (122 km²) in area, in the South Atlantic Ocean, 1200 miles (1930 km) west of Africa's southwest coast. It is a British colony whose dependencies include ASCENSION ISLAND and TRISTAN DA CUNHA. St Helena has no airport, and a Royal Mail ship calls only once a year.
⚜ Napoleon I was exiled to St Helena from 1815 until his death in 1821. Boer prisoners were held there during the Boer War.

St Moritz Swiss skiing resort and spa. The first organised bobsleigh competition was held on the St Moritz Cresta Run in 1898, and the resort hosted the Winter Olympic Games in 1928 and 1948.

St Petersburg Grand Russian city with wide avenues, many canals and bridges, and neo-Classical baroque buildings. St Peters-

ROAD WAYS *Lights outline San Francisco's 4200 ft (1280 m) long Golden Gate Bridge, and cable cars (inset) climb the steep streets.*

burg was founded in 1703 by Tsar ▷PETER THE GREAT who wanted to open a 'Window on the West' and bring European culture to Russia, and was built on marshy islands in the River Neva delta, using huge gangs of forced labour. It was Russia's capital from 1712 to 1918, and was known as Petrograd from 1914 to 1924 and then Leningrad until 1991, when its name reverted to St Petersburg. In the city centre are the Peter and Paul fortress, once a political prison; the Hermitage Museum, housed in the Winter Palace of the tsars; and Nevsky Prospekt, the main shopping street. The Russian Revolution began in St Petersburg in 1917, and during World War II more than a million people died there during a siege by German and Finnish forces.
⚜ The composer ▷TCHAIKOVSKY, the goldsmith ▷FABERGÉ and the ballerina ▷PAVLOVA all worked in St Petersburg. The ▷KIROV BALLET is based in the city.

Salzburg Austrian city whose castle, the 11th-century Hohensalzburg, crowns a craggy hill and overlooks the towers and domes of the city's many churches.
⚜ ▷MOZART was born in Salzburg in 1756, and the city's music academy is called the Mozarteum. The town's world-renowned music festival is held every summer.
⚜ The musical and film *The Sound of Music* was based on the story of Maria Von Trapp, who was a postulant in the Nonnberg Abbey, which is situated near the castle.

San Francisco Hilly and sometimes foggy city in California, standing on the tip of a peninsula between the Pacific Ocean and San Francisco Bay. The ▷GOLDEN GATE BRIDGE spans the bay's entrance, and the San Francisco-Oakland Bay Bridge connects San Francisco with the cities of Oakland and Berkeley to the east. San Francisco lies on the San Andreas Fault and was almost destroyed by an earthquake in 1906. A severe earthquake in 1989 caused less damage, partly because newer buildings had been constructed to withstand earthquakes. In the late 1960s and early 1970s the city was adopted by hippies as the centre for 'flower power'. Tourists flock to San Francisco to ride on the cable cars that climb the steep streets, to visit the seafood restaurants, and to wander around its Chinatown.
⚜ Alcatraz, a rocky island in San Francisco Bay, was a prison from 1861 to 1963; the gangster Al Capone was one of its inmates. Now it is open to the public.

San Marino Tiny country, only 24 sq miles (62 km²) in area, surrounded by Italy. The population is 23 000. The capital, also called San Marino, is a walled town with towers and ramparts built on a steep hill. Much of the country's revenue comes from the sale of stamps and duty-free goods.

São Paulo Brazilian city, the largest in South America and one of the largest in the world, with more than 10 million people. São Paulo has attracted people from a number of countries, and there are many Paulistas, as the citizens are called, of German, Japanese and Italian descent. Its prosperous centre has impressive skyscrapers, but there are also extensive slums.

Sarajevo Capital of Bosnia-Herzegovina, which was formerly part of Yugoslavia. Archduke Franz Ferdinand, heir to the Austro-Hungarian throne, was assassinated in the city in 1914, sparking off World War I. The city was heavily shelled during fighting in the civil war of the early 1990s.
⚜ Sarajevo hosted the Winter Olympic Games in 1984.

Sardinia Sparsely populated, mountainous Italian island, 130 miles (210 km) from the mainland. Sardinia has about 7000 *nuraghi* – squat, cone-shaped structures built out of huge blocks of stone between 2000 and 250 BC. Cork is taken from evergreen cork oaks. The capital is Cagliari.

Sargasso Sea Relatively calm area of the Atlantic Ocean, south of Bermuda, named after its patches of floating sargassum weed.

In nautical legend, ships caught in the weed were doomed to circle the sea for ever, crewed by the ghosts of dead sailors.

Saudi Arabia Desert kingdom with vast reserves of oil, whose capital is Riyadh. The prophet ▷MUHAMMAD was born in the western city of ▷MECCA, and Saudi Arabia's legal system is based on Islamic law. Alcohol is forbidden, for non-Muslims as well as Muslims, and theft and adultery are severely punished. Turks ruled the land from the early 16th century, and in 1902 Ibn Saud started a campaign to free the land from Turkish rule and unite the tribes of Arabia. In 1932 he became king of the new state of Saudi Arabia. During World War I, ▷LAWRENCE OF ARABIA helped the campaign against the Turks. Nearly all the country is harsh desert; the Rub al-Khali, or Empty Quarter, in the south of the country is particularly forbidding.

Seoul Capital of South Korea. The city has risen from the ashes of the 1950-3 Korean War when it was largely destroyed and its population shrank to 50 000. Now Seoul is a bustling modern high-rise metropolis with thriving industry and appalling traffic congestion, and a population of nearly 10 million. Seoul hosted the Olympic Games in 1988.

Serbia Formerly the largest and most populous state of Yugoslavia, with two autonomous regions: Vojvodina, which was once part of Hungary, and predominantly Albanian Kosovo. The capital of this mountainous land is BELGRADE, on the Danube. Serbia was the dominant state in the Balkans during the Middle Ages, and was then ruled by Ottoman Turks until it became completely independent in 1878. After the breakup of Yugoslavia in 1991-2, Serbia and Montenegro claimed to form a successor state to Yugoslavia. Serbia then pursued aggressively expansionist plans in BOSNIA and CROATIA.

Serengeti Plain Vast area of northern Tanzania. Huge herds of wildebeests, zebras and gazelles live in the Serengeti and migrate as they follow the rains to new grazing grounds. Part of the plain is a national park the size of Northern Ireland.

Seville Main city of Andalucía on the Guadalquivir River in southern Spain. Muslim Moors lived there from the 8th to the 13th centuries, and Moorish architecture survives in the narrow twisting streets of the old town, and in the Alcázar fortress and palace begun in 1181. Seville's 15th-century cathedral, where Christopher Columbus is said to be buried, is built on the site of a mosque. The adjacent Giralda bell tower was one of the mosque's minarets.

Seychelles Scattered group of 115 islands with palm-fringed beaches in the Indian Ocean. Most people live on Mahé, which is more than 1100 miles (1800 km) east of Mombasa on the Kenyan coast. The isolated islands have several unique species of plants and animals such as giant tortoises that live on the outlying coral atoll of Aldabra.

Shanghai China's largest city and main port, with a population of more than 12 million. In 1842 Shanghai was one of the first Chinese ports opened to foreign trade. People from Britain, France, America and Japan made it a major trade and finance centre and built impressive European-style banks, hotels and business premises. In the 1930s Shanghai was noted for both its wealth and its decadence. Today it is an important manufacturing centre.

Shanghai's Yu Yuan Garden of Happiness is the model for the design on 'willow pattern' chinaware.

Shatt al-Arab Tidal river, formed by the union of the TIGRIS and the EUPHRATES rivers, which flows into the Persian Gulf. The waterway's lower reaches form the disputed Iran-Iraq border, and disagreements over navigation rights were a cause of the ▷IRAN-IRAQ WAR (1980-8).

Siberia Huge, inhospitable region of tundra, swamps and forests in eastern Russia. Siberian winters are exceptionally severe: in the Yakut region of eastern Siberia, January temperatures average −43°C (−46°F), and have fallen to a Northern Hemisphere record of −70°C (−94°F). Yet in summer the temperature rises to 19°C (66°F). The region's enormous mineral wealth includes coal, oil and gas, and also diamonds, iron ore and gold. Siberia has been a place of exile for political prisoners and criminals, especially during the Stalin era; the dissident writer Alexander ▷SOLZHENITSYN was interned there during the 1940s and 1950s, and graphically described his experiences in his novel *One Day in the Life of Ivan Denisovich*.

Sicily Largest of the Mediterranean islands, at the tip of the Italian 'boot'. Mount Etna, Europe's largest and most active volcano, is at the eastern end of the island; repeated eruptions – most recently in 1991-2 – vary its height of around 10 900 ft (3320 m). The capital is Palermo. The ▷MAFIA originated in Sicily.

Siena Beautiful medieval city in Tuscany, central Italy. Siena's central square, the Piazza del Campo, is surrounded by historic buildings that include a massive 13th-century palace, the Palazzo Pubblico. The Palio horse race takes place in the city streets each summer, with the riders and their mounts decked in medieval regalia.

MODERN HERITAGE *The ornate buildings round Seville's Plaza de España belie appearances. They do not date from the city's distant past but were built for the Spanish-American Fair of 1929.*

Sierra Nevada Range of magnificent mountains in the western USA, mainly in east California. The Sierra Nevada's highest point, the 14 494 ft (4418 m) Mount Whitney, rises above the Sequoia National Park, where the world's most massive tree – named after General Sherman – is 275 ft (83.8 m) high and measures 103 ft (31.4 m) round the base. YOSEMITE NATIONAL PARK is also in the Sierra Nevada. Gold was discovered in the mountains in 1848, and attracted thousands of prospectors.

'Silicon Valley' Area of western California, USA, between Palo Alto and San Jose. It is named after the silicon chips used in the electronics and computing industries, of which it is a major centre.

Sinai Desert peninsula of Egypt, between the two northern arms of the Red Sea. The Bible describes how Moses was leading the Israelites out of Egypt when he received the Ten Commandments at Mount Sinai, thought to be the 7500 ft (2285 m) Jebel Mūsā. After the formation of Israel in 1948, Sinai became a region of conflict between Arabs and Jews; it was occupied by Israel in 1967, and returned to Egypt in 1982.

Singapore Hot, clean, prosperous island country, its area less than half that of London, off the tip of Malaysia's mainland peninsula. Densely populated Singapore is a major international port and business centre and the capital, Singapore city, has many gleaming glass and concrete skyscrapers. The country was founded as a trading post by Sir Stamford Raffles of the British East India Company in 1819, and quickly attracted traders from many countries. Chinese people now make up 75 per cent of the population, Malays 14 per cent and Indians 7 per cent.
♨ Singapore's Raffles Hotel was visited by the writers Rudyard Kipling and Somerset Maugham. The Singapore Sling cocktail was invented there.

Slovakia Central European country that came into being on January 1, 1993, after Czechoslovakia split into the ▷CZECH REPUBLIC and Slovakia. The capital, Bratislava, is on the Danube. The High Tatras, in the north of the country, rise to 8710 ft (2655 m) and attract many tourists.

Slovenia Small central European country, formerly the most prosperous republic of Yugoslavia, that became an independent country in 1992 with Ljubljana as the capital. Tourists visit Slovenia's mountains, and Lake Bled in the Julian Alps.

Somalia Very poor country extending round the easternmost tip of Africa. The country's poverty is aggravated by drought and, since 1988, civil war. The capital is Mogadishu. In 1991 the north of Somalia broke away and declared itself the Somaliland Republic, but its independence has not yet been recognised.

South Africa Country occupying the southern tip of the African continent. Parliament sits in CAPE TOWN between January and July, but the administration is based in PRETORIA and the highest court is in Bloemfontein. The largest city is JOHANNESBURG. South Africa is the continent's most developed country, and much of its wealth comes from gold, diamonds and other minerals. Nearly three-quarters of South Africans are black. The biggest group are ▷ZULUS, most of whom live in the east. Whites make up 16 per cent of the population. Slightly more than half of them are ▷AFRIKANERS, the Afrikaans-speaking descendants of early Dutch settlers who arrived in Cape Town from 1652. Britain first took control of the Cape in 1795. Many ▷BOERS, as the settlers of Dutch descent were then called, resented British rule and anti-slavery legislation, and in the

CIVILISATIONS *Before Europeans arrived in Central and South America the Maya flourished in Mexico, Guatemala and Honduras; the later Aztecs in Mexico; and the Incas in the northern Andes.*

1830s Boer Voortrekkers moved northwards in a migration known as the ▷GREAT TREK. Boers and British clashed again in the ▷BOER WAR of 1899-1902. In 1948 an Afrikaner-dominated Nationalist government was elected, which implemented a policy of ▷APARTHEID for more than 40 years. The ▷ANC and other black political parties were banned in 1960, and the ANC leader Nelson ▷MANDELA was imprisoned in 1962, a year after South Africa left the Commonwealth. The ban on ANC activity was lifted on February 2, 1990, and Mandela was released after 28 years of imprisonment. The apartheid system was officially abandoned in 1992. Other countries then eased trade, cultural and sports sanctions imposed since 1977. Conflict arose between supporters of the ANC and those of the Zulu-dominated Inkatha Freedom Party, led by Chief Buthelezi. The first non-racial elections were held in 1994, 342 years after the arrival of the first whites in the Cape. On May 2, 1994, Nelson Mandela was elected president, and the following month South Africa rejoined the Commonwealth. Spectacular South African scenery includes the Garden Route – a stretch of the southern coast backed by trees and flowering plants – and the Drakensberg Mountains in the east. The country is rich in wildlife.

🔥South Africa's first wine was made in 1659, from vines planted by Dutch settlers soon after their arrival seven years earlier.

South Korea East Asian country that since the early 1960s has changed from an agricultural society into a major industrial power. The ▷KOREAN WAR (1950-3) left the country exhausted, but now textiles, cars, electronic goods and ships are produced efficiently and cheaply. Industry is concentrated in the densely populated northwest – centred on the capital SEOUL – and in the south; few people live in the forested mountains of the east.

Spain Large country with many distinctive regions, occupying most of the Iberian Peninsula and separated from France by the PYRENEES. The sunny coast makes Spain the most popular holiday destination in Europe, with more than 40 million tourists arriving every year. Away from the busy coastline is a mostly dry, often mountainous country, cut through by valleys and gorges. Muslim Moors conquered most of Spain in the 8th century. Christians started to reconquer it in the 11th century, and the Moors were finally driven out in 1492, the year in which the Italian-born Christopher ▷COLUMBUS sailed under a Spanish flag to

North America. Spanish conquistadores and explorers followed him, and by the 1560s Spain's New World empire extended from Argentina to California. Spain's power began to decline after England defeated the Spanish ▷ARMADA in 1588. The ▷SPANISH CIVIL WAR of 1936-9 was followed by the dictatorship of General ▷FRANCO, which ended with his death in 1975. Democracy was restored, with King Juan Carlos on the throne. Spain's capital MADRID is in Castile, the heart of the country. Its second city, BARCELONA, is in hilly Catalonia, part of whose coast is the Costa Brava. Farther south are Valencia and the resort of Benidorm. The southern part of Spain is Andalucía, the land of flamenco dancers, bullfights, Moorish architecture and the Costa del Sol; its biggest city is SEVILLE. Basques live in the western Pyrenees. Many Basques want their own state; ETA, the Basque separatist militant wing, has sometimes campaigned violently. La Rioja, south of the Basque country, produces Spain's best table wines. Galicia and Asturias, in the northwest, are green, fertile areas.

🔥The CANARY ISLANDS, and the Balearic Islands – Majorca, Minorca, Ibiza, Formentera and Cabrera – are part of Spain.

🔥Paella, one of Spain's best-loved dishes, is made from rice, shellfish, chicken and vegetables, and flavoured with saffron.

Sri Lanka Island country shaped like a teardrop off the southern tip of India. Tea, rubber and coconut are among Sri Lanka's main exports. Colombo, the capital, has European-style buildings that date from the time of British rule, when the country was called Ceylon. The Sinhalese, who make up 75 per cent of the population, are mostly Buddhists; Tamils – 18 per cent of Sri Lankans – are mostly Hindus and live mainly in the north. Tension between Sinhalese and Tamils has led to violence.

🔥Sri Lanka had the world's first woman prime minister, Sirimavo Bandaranaike (1960-5 and 1970-7).

🔥One of Sri Lanka's former names is Serendip, from which the word serendipity – the making of happy discoveries by accident – was coined by the English writer Horace Walpole.

Stockholm Clean, graceful and beautifully sited capital of Sweden, spanning several islands. In the Old Town are 16th and 17th-century buildings, the Royal Palace and the Parliament building, which stands on its own island. The City Hall has a massive square tower, and a Golden Hall whose walls are clad in gilded mosaic tiles.

🔥Nobel prizes, founded by the Swedish chemist Alfred ▷NOBEL (1833-96), are awarded in Stockholm, except for the peace prize which is awarded in Oslo.

Strasbourg Historic French city only 2½ miles (4 km) from the border with Germany. Strasbourg is the headquarters of the Council of Europe; sessions of the European Parliament are also held there.

Sudan Africa's largest country, crossed by the Nile. Muslim Arabs live in the north, and black Africans speaking many different languages live in the south. Sudan has major problems with drought, famine and civil war, and has also had a huge influx of refugees fleeing famine in Ethiopia, Eritrea and Chad. The capital is KHARTOUM.

Sweden North European kingdom with many forests, lakes, waterfalls and rivers. The forests provide the raw material for factories producing all kinds of wood products. Sweden is also known for the clean design of its furniture, glass and cutlery. The arctic north has heavy snow for eight months of the year and the temperature there can fall to −40°C (−40°F). Most people live in the south, especially around the capital, STOCKHOLM. The standard of living is generally very high, but so are taxes. Sweden last fought a war in 1814.

🔥Smörgåsbord is a Swedish buffet meal that includes fish (especially herring), meat, salads and cheese.

Switzerland Mountainous country in the Alps. Switzerland's many magnificent peaks include the Eiger, the Jungfrau and the Matterhorn on the Italian border, all of which are more than 13 000 ft (3960 m) high. The capital of this prosperous and efficient country is BERNE, but the biggest cities are Zürich, Basle and GENEVA. Switzerland is made up of 26 cantons. Four languages are spoken: 73 per cent of the people speak German, 20 per cent French, 4 per cent Italian, and less than 1 per cent Romansch, a dialect spoken in eastern Switzerland and also in northern Italy. The country is a major financial centre – its code of banking secrecy encourages enormous foreign investment – and is also known for watchmaking and chocolate, and for Gruyère and Emmenthal cheese. Switzerland is not a member of the United Nations, NATO or the European Union, but despite its political neutrality every man is liable for military service.

🔥Swiss women were only granted the vote in 1971. The Swiss hold many more referendums than other countries.

IDYLLIC ISLAND *Tahiti, the original South Sea paradise, rises from a ring of coral atolls in the Pacific. Traditional lifestyles (inset) are being eroded by tourism and the motor car.*

Sydney Australia's biggest city and oldest settlement, and the state capital of New South Wales. The striking ▷SYDNEY OPERA HOUSE, its roof shaped like white sails, stands on the harbour near the broad ▷SYDNEY HARBOUR BRIDGE. British settlers, some of them convicts, arrived in 1788 in BOTANY BAY, now in the city's suburbs, and made their first settlement very close to the spot where the Opera House now stands. The cosmopolitan city has many beaches, including Bondi Beach which is popular with tourists.
🗝The Olympic Games will be held in Sydney in the year 2000.

Syria Oil-exporting country in the Middle East, extending inland eastwards from the Mediterranean Sea. Away from the coast and the coastal mountains, much of the land is arid grassland that turns green after the sparse rain. Nearly all Syrians are Muslims. The capital, DAMASCUS, is one of the world's oldest cities, and Phoenician traders sailed from what is now Syria's coast from about 1200 BC. Crusaders intent on recovering Christian holy places from Muslim control built castles that include the magnificent Krak des Chevaliers, in the coastal mountains. Syria has been involved in the conflict between Arab countries and Israel, and in 1967 Israel occupied the Golan Heights in the mountainous south-west of Syria. Archaeological sites include the ruins of Palmyra, an oasis city destroyed by the Romans in AD 273.

Tahiti South Pacific island of great beauty, lying nearly 2500 miles (4000 km) northeast of New Zealand's North Island. Tahiti is the largest island of French Polynesia, and the capital is Papeete.
🗝Tahiti's idyllic beauty was captured by the French painter Paul ▷GAUGUIN, who lived there from 1895 to 1901.

Taiwan Island off China's southeast coast. In the late 1940s, 2 million Chinese supporters of ▷CHIANG KAI-SHEK's Nationalist Party fled to Taiwan from ▷MAO ZEDONG's communist forces on the mainland. Now the mainlanders and their descendants make up 15 per cent of the population. Since the 1960s Taiwan has grown rapidly to become a major economic power, exporting electronic goods, clothes, shoes

and many other products. Taiwan has luxuriant vegetation and mountains rising to more than 13 000 ft (4000 m). Portuguese travellers in the 16th century called the island *Ilha Formosa* 'Beautiful Island' and Taiwan was once known as Formosa. The capital is T'ai-pei.

Tanzania East African country that came into being in 1964 when Tanganyika united with the hot, humid island of Zanzibar. Africa's highest mountain, the snow-capped KILIMANJARO, rises in northern Tanzania, and lakes Victoria, Tanganyika and Malawi lie round the country's borders. Much of the interior is dry grassland. Tanzania has abundant wildlife, and there are vast national parks and game reserves such as the 11 mile (18 km) wide crater of the extinct Ngorongoro volcano, and the SERENGETI National Park. Tanzania's first president was Julius Nyerere, who ruled the country until he resigned in 1985. In the early 1970s, huge numbers of people were moved to new villages that were intended to supply everything necessary for communal agriculture. People later drifted back to their original homes. Dodoma, in the centre of Tanzania, has replaced Dar es Salaam as capital.
🗝A scheme to grow groundnuts (peanuts) in Tanganyika in the late 1940s proved to be a costly failure, because of inadequate rainfall and difficulties with cultivation.

Tasmania Island off Australia's southeast coast, and one of the country's six states. The Dutch explorer Abel Tasman landed a party there in 1642, and named it Van Diemen's Land after the governor general of the Dutch East Indies who had sent him on the voyage. In 1788 the island was annexed to Britain as part of New South Wales; the penal settlement of Port Arthur was established in 1830 and received 12 000 convicts during the 40 years it lasted. The state capital is Hobart.

Tel Aviv-Jaffa Israeli city on the Mediterranean Sea, and the country's centre of business and culture. Tel Aviv was founded in the early 20th century by Jewish settlers from the ancient and crowded port of Jaffa – the Biblical port of Joppa – and the two settlements have now merged.

Texas Big southern state of the USA, more than three times the size of Britain. Oil has generated wealth in Texas since 1901. As well as extensive flat plains with cattle ranches, there are cotton fields, dense forests and craggy mountains. The state capital is Austin, but the biggest cities are

DALLAS, San Antonio and Houston, the headquarters of NASA, the National Aeronautics and Space Administration. Texas was part of Mexico until 1836 when it broke away after a revolution, and was then an independent republic until it became part of the USA in 1845.

♦ In 1836, 187 Texans – including the folk hero Davy ▷CROCKETT – were besieged by the Mexican army in the Alamo, a Spanish mission in San Antonio. All were killed.

Thailand Buddhist kingdom in Southeast Asia, and the only country in the region that was never a European colony. Thailand was called Siam until 1939. King Bhumibol, who has reigned since 1946, is treated with great reverence. The centre of Thailand is a vast expanse of paddy fields. In the north are forested mountains rich in teak, where elephants are used to handle heavy logs in the more difficult country. Many tourists visit the capital BANGKOK – which the Thais call Krung Thep – and resorts such as Ko Samui and the island of Phuket.

♦ During World War II, Thailand was occupied by the Japanese whose prisoners of war and slave labourers built a railway bridge over the River Kwai, in the west of the country. An estimated 65 000 people died while building the bridge and the railway line: the story was told in the 1957 film *The Bridge on the River Kwai*.

Tibet High, remote part of China, making up the Xizang Autonomous Region to the north of the Himalayas. Mount Everest is on the border of Tibet and Nepal. Tibet is often referred to as the roof of the world and much of it is a virtually uninhabited, windy and bitterly cold plateau, about 15 000 ft (4500 m) high. Most people live round the south and east of the plateau, where the climate is milder and the land can be cultivated. Tibet has been part of China at various times in the past, and also since a Chinese invasion in 1950. Before that it was ruled from its capital, LHASA, by a Buddhist priestly aristocracy headed by their spiritual leader, the ▷DALAI LAMA. Many monasteries were destroyed during China's Cultural Revolution.

Tierra del Fuego Group of islands at the extreme south of Argentina and Chile, between which countries they are divided. The Portuguese navigator Ferdinand ▷MAGELLAN saw fires lit by the native peoples as he passed through the strait – named after him – between the main island and the mainland. He called the land Tierra de los Fuegos, meaning 'Land of Fire'; it was later changed to the Spanish Tierra del Fuego.

Tigris Major river of southwest Asia, flowing for nearly 1150 miles (1850 km) through Turkey, Syria and Iraq. It joins the Euphrates to form the Shatt al-Arab waterway. Some of the earliest civilisations grew up between the Tigris and Euphrates, in ▷MESOPOTAMIA; the Assyrian cities of Ashur and Nineveh were on its banks.

Timbuktu West African town on the edge of the Sahara, in central Mali. Timbuktu was founded in the 11th century and quickly became a major trading centre for salt carried by Saharan caravans and goods traded along the Niger river. Timbuktu's gold and salt were known in Europe in the Middle Ages. The city was also a centre of Islamic teaching. Tribal wars from the 16th century sent it into decline.

Titicaca, Lake South America's largest lake, 12 505 ft (3812 m) up in the Andes on the border of Bolivia and Peru and surrounded by ice-capped peaks. Remains of the Inca and pre-Inca civilisations survive on the lake's Islands of the Moon and the Sun, as well as at the ancient city of Tiahuanaco to the south. The Uru people live on the lake on vast floating 'islands' made out of totora reeds, which they also use to build their houses and boats.

♦ The local people have larger hearts and lungs than normal to cope with the effects of oxygen deficiency at the high altitude.

Tokyo Prosperous, crowded, expensive capital of Japan and one of the world's largest cities, with more than 11 million people. Tokyo, formerly Edo, replaced Kyoto as Japan's capital in 1868, when it was given its present name, meaning 'Eastern Capital'. The city has been rebuilt twice this century: first after an earthquake in 1923, and then after damage during World War II. Now Tokyo is one of the world's major financial centres, with high-rise office buildings constructed to withstand earthquakes. The city's neon-lit Ginza district, not far from the Imperial Palace, has restaurants, night clubs and shops.

Tonga Pacific kingdom made up of 169 coral and volcanic islands, 2000 miles (3200 km) northeast of Sydney, Australia. The temperature is around 27°C (80°F) all year. The British explorer Captain Cook visited the islands in 1773 and called them the Friendly Islands because of the welcome he received from the people.

♦ Tonga's Queen Salote, who reigned from 1918 to 1965, became popular when she braved the heavy rain to wave to the crowds at Queen Elizabeth II's coronation in 1953.

Toronto Canada's biggest city and the capital of the province of Ontario, built on the shores of Lake Ontario. Toronto has the world's tallest free-standing structure: the 1815½ ft (553.4 m) CN (Canadian National) Tower, a communications tower with a revolving restaurant 1135 ft (346 m) above the ground. Toronto is Canada's business and manufacturing centre, and a cosmopolitan city whose Italian, Chinese, Greek and Portuguese immigrants have created distinctive 'villages' within the city.

Trinidad and Tobago Hot Caribbean island country lying just off the coast of Venezuela. The capital, Port of Spain, is on lively Trinidad which is by far the larger of the two islands and the home of calypso music and steel bands. Oil has been tapped on Trinidad since 1867, and the revenue makes the islands one of the more prosperous Caribbean countries. Palm-fringed beaches sheltered by coral reefs attract many tourists – especially to the more tranquil Tobago.

♦ In the south of Trinidad is a pitch lake formed by crude oil oozing through porous rocks. It is 285 ft (87 m) deep in the middle.

Tristan da Cunha Remote, windswept Atlantic Ocean island, 38 sq miles (98 km²) in area and some 1500 miles (2400 km) west of Cape Town, in South Africa. Tristan da Cunha is part of the British dependency of ▷ST HELENA and is inhabited by 300 or so people. Most of the island is a volcano, which erupted in 1961; the people were evacuated to Britain but chose to return to the island two years later.

Tunisia North African country that has been ruled by many peoples – Phoenicians, Romans, Byzantines, Arabs and Turks. From 1881 to 1956 Tunisia was a French Protectorate. Every year more than 3.5 million tourists go to Tunisia for the sun and superb beaches, and also to visit the fine Roman remains and the site of ▷CARTHAGE, in a suburb of Tunis, the capital.

Turin Prosperous, historic north Italian city on the River Po. The city centre has fine squares, a Roman city gate and 17th and 18th-century buildings. Fiat and Lancia cars are made in Turin.

♦ The Turin Shroud, a piece of cloth 13½ by 3½ ft (4.1 by 1.1 m) and bearing the faint image of a man, is stored in Turin's cathedral. For centuries many Christians believed that this was the cloth in which Christ's body was wrapped after the Crucifixion. Tests in 1988 dated the shroud as being made between 1260 and 1390.

CHIANTI COUNTRY *Vineyards that clothe the Tuscany hillsides are the source of Chianti wine, some of which is sold in wicker-covered flasks.*

Turkey Country bridging the continents of Europe and Asia, with beautiful coasts, historic sites and fine Islamic architecture. The European part, Thrace, is separated from Anatolia, the considerably larger Asian part, by the narrow Dardanelles and Bosporus straits, and the Sea of Marmara. The interior of Anatolia is rather dry – rolling plains in the west give way to increasingly high, rugged and forested land in the east, where the winters are snowy and intensely cold. Remains of ancient civilisations include Çatal Hüyük, one of the earliest towns, and the cities of ▷TROY, Ephesus and Pergamum. During World War I Allied troops fought on the beaches of ▷GALLIPOLI, a peninsula in European Turkey overlooking the Dardanelles. After World War I, Kemal ▷ATATÜRK introduced major reforms to westernise the country. Now many tourists visit Mediterranean and Aegean coastal resorts such as BODRUM and Marmaris. The capital is Ankara, but the largest city is ISTANBUL.

Tuscany Prosperous, historic region of Italy, with many fine cities including SIENA, PISA and FLORENCE, the capital. Tuscany's terraced hillsides are planted with olive groves and vineyards. Marble is quarried at Carrara, and honey-coloured Tuscan stone is used for many buildings.

Uganda East African country which, though crossed by the Equator, has a surprisingly temperate climate, since much of the land lies at least 3000 ft (900 m) above sea level. The capital is Kampala. Lake Victoria, Africa's largest lake, lies partly in Uganda and is one of the main sources of the Nile which flows across the country. Four out of five Ugandans work on the land. Since the late 1980s Uganda's economy has started to recover from more than 20 years of political instability and civil war, and the brutal rule of Idi ▷AMIN, Uganda's leader from 1971 to 1979.
🕯In 1976, a French airliner was hijacked by Palestinian guerrillas and flown to Entebbe airport, not far from Kampala. An Israeli commando unit rescued all but three of the hostages in a dramatic raid.

Ukraine Southeast European country, formerly part of the USSR, whose capital is KIEV. The Ukrainian steppes, and especially the 'black earth' land in the west, are intensively cultivated, but Ukraine also has heavy industry, a result of rich deposits of iron ore, coal, gas and oil. In 1986 the ▷CHERNOBYL nuclear disaster took place in northern Ukraine. Ukraine's CRIMEA peninsula extends into the Black Sea and has many holiday resorts.
🕯Cossack communities lived in Ukraine from the 15th century. They were fine horsemen, and until the early days of the Soviet era were allowed a degree of self-government in return for military service.

United Arab Emirates (UAE) Rich oil-producing federation of Persian Gulf emirates, formed in 1971. The largest emirates are Abu Dhabi and Dubai, and the capital is Abu Dhabi city. The coast was once known as the Pirate Coast because Arab pirates preyed on European ships. A truce arranged by Britain in the 19th century ended piracy; the area became known as the Trucial Coast or Trucial States.

United States of America World's fourth largest country, after Russia, Canada and China. The USA is 38 times the size of the United Kingdom but has only four and a half times as many people; the most populous areas are the eastern seaboard and the California coast. The capital is WASHINGTON DC, but the biggest cities are NEW YORK, LOS ANGELES and CHICAGO. The USA has almost every type of landscape and climate: tundra in Alaska, deserts with tall cacti in Arizona, snow-capped peaks in the Rocky Mountains, and rich farmland in the Midwest states south of the GREAT LAKES. The first Americans came from Asia over a land bridge across the Bering Strait about 25 000 years ago. Spaniards explored the south and west of what is now the USA in the early 16th century. The first permanent English settlement was Jamestown, founded in Virginia in 1607. Thirteen years later the Pilgrim Fathers landed at Plymouth in Massachusetts. Settlement spread rapidly westward, driving ▷NATIVE AMERICAN Indians from their tribal territories. The immigrants who flocked to the 'land of opportunity' were mainly Europeans until

HOMES IN THE ROCK *At Üçhisar, in Cappadocia, central Turkey, soft volcanic rock has been weathered into an other-worldly landscape, which people hollowed out to make homes.*

the second half of the 20th century, when Asians, Africans and South Americans arrived in larger numbers. On July 4, 1776, the 13 British colonies adopted the ▷DECLARATION OF INDEPENDENCE from Britain which resulted in the formation of the USA. In the southern states cotton plantations were worked by African slaves, and slavery was a major issue in the ▷AMERICAN CIVIL WAR. After the Civil War, the economy grew rapidly, uninterrupted by World War I, until the ▷WALL STREET CRASH of 1929 marked the start of the Depression. After World War II the USA emerged as a superpower. A champion of capitalism, it adopted a policy of opposing communism which led to involvement in the ▷KOREAN WAR (1950-3) and the ▷VIETNAM WAR (1960-75), and also to a campaign, in which Senator Joseph McCarthy was prominent, of accusing citizens of communist sympathies. Today the USA is a republic made up of 50 states and the District of Columbia; the last states to join were ALASKA in 1867 and HAWAII in 1959. Each state represented in both ▷SENATE and ▷CONGRESS is responsible for making its own laws about, for example, drinking, divorce, gambling and the death penalty, which is retained by 36 states. The ▷DEMOCRATIC and ▷REPUBLICAN Parties dominate US politics. Democrat presidents have included Woodrow ▷WILSON, who promoted the idea of a League of Nations; Franklin D. ▷ROOSEVELT, whose 'New Deal' brought recovery from the Depression; and John F. ▷KENNEDY, who was president at the time of the 1962 ▷CUBAN MISSILE CRISIS. The first great republican president was Abraham ▷LINCOLN, who led the northern states to victory during the American Civil War. The republican President ▷EISENHOWER was supreme commander of Allied forces in World War II; and Richard ▷NIXON improved relations with the USSR and China before resigning over the Watergate scandal in 1974. Bill ▷CLINTON, a democrat, succeeded republican President ▷BUSH in 1992 and was the first democratic president for 12 years.

♣America is named after the Italian explorer Amerigo ▷VESPUCCI.

♣The US flag – the stars and stripes – has 50 stars representing the present states, and 13 stripes representing the original states.

USSR (Union of Soviet Socialist Republics)
Former country that from 1922 to 1991 covered nearly one-sixth of Earth's land surface, and had people of more than 100 different nationalities. It was established after the ▷RUSSIAN REVOLUTION nominally as a federation, but in fact

MASTERPIECE *In the Vatican City, a shaft of sunlight illuminates the sumptuous interior of St Peter's Basilica. Much of it was designed by Michelangelo, who was appointed architect in 1546.*

MOSCOW, the capital, kept control of all the USSR's constituent republics. Soviet leaders included ▷LENIN, ▷STALIN, ▷KHRUSHCHEV, ▷BREZHNEV and ▷GORBACHEV. After World War II the ▷COLD WAR developed between the USSR and the West. Gorbachev's appointment as general secretary of the Communist Party in 1985 introduced an era of *glasnost*, or political 'openness', and *perestroika*, or economic 'restructuring'. In 1991 one after another of the USSR's 15 republics broke with Moscow, and became the independent countries of Armenia, AZERBAIJAN, Belarus, Estonia, Georgia, KAZAKHSTAN, Kyrgyzstan, Latvia, Lithuania, Moldova, RUSSIA, Tajikistan, Turkmenistan, UKRAINE and UZBEKISTAN. All except Estonia, Latvia and Lithuania became members of the ▷CIS (Commonwealth of Independent States).

Utah
State in the western USA which has extraordinary rock formations, including those of Monument Valley where the 1939 film *Stagecoach*, and other Westerns, were shot. The capital, Salt Lake City, was founded in 1847 by ▷MORMONS led by Brigham Young, and is the headquarters of the Mormon Church. Nearby is the Great Salt Lake; land speed records have been set on the Bonneville Salt Flats west of the lake.

Uzbekistan
Central Asian country of deserts and plains that was formerly part of the USSR. The capital, Tashkent, was

rebuilt after an earthquake in 1966. The ancient city of Samarkand, in southern Uzbekistan, was an important place on the Silk Road between China and Europe, and in the 14th century became the capital of the Tatar warlord Tamerlane. Uzbeks, who are Muslims, make up 70 per cent of the people, and Russians are the country's biggest minority. The ARAL SEA is on the northern border of Uzbekistan.

Vatican City
Walled city within Rome, which is the home of the Pope and headquarters of the Roman Catholic Church, and also the world's smallest state, with an area of less than one-fifth of a square mile (0.5 km²). The population is fewer than 1000. Many tourists visit the Vatican City to see Michelangelo's frescoes in the Sistine Chapel, and ▷ST PETER'S BASILICA.

Venezuela
South American country with oil fields in the north around Lake Maracaibo – in fact a pear-shaped inlet of the sea. The capital is Caracas. Most Venezuelans live along the Caribbean coastline; inland lie the *llanos* – undulating plains where cowboys herd cattle. South of the Orinoco river, and making up about half the country, are the Guiana Highlands whose massive flat-topped mountains that loom above lush jungle were the inspiration for Sir Arthur Conan Doyle's novel *The Lost World*. The world's highest waterfall, ANGEL FALLS, is in the eastern highlands.

MOORING PLACE *Beyond the gondolas tied to their mooring posts is Venice's Church of Santa Maria della Salute, begun in 1631-2 and built in thanksgiving for release from the plague.*

Venice North Italian city built on 118 low islands in a lagoon, and one of the world's great architectural and cultural treasures. The islands are separated by narrow canals and linked by more than 400 bridges. The wider Grand Canal, lined with palaces, winds through the heart of Venice and is crossed by the late 16th-century Rialto Bridge. Around Venice's Piazza San Marco are St Mark's Basilica, the 324 ft (99 m) high Campanile, and the Doges' Palace, built in the 14th to 15th centuries as the official residence of the city's elected leader. The Bridge of Sighs spans the canal between the Doges' Palace and the state prison. The city was founded in the 5th century AD, and became a major trading state that reached the height of its power in the early 15th century. Venice suffered disastrous floods in 1966. At one time the city was sinking, but measures have been taken to prevent further damage.

🕭 Venice was the birthplace of the artists ▷BELLINI, ▷GIORGIONE and ▷TITIAN, and the city was immortalised in the paintings of ▷CANALETTO. Paintings and frescoes adorn many Venetian churches.

🕭 Gondolas have been painted black since 1562, when a law was passed to curb excessive decoration.

🕭 Glass has been made on Murano, an island in the lagoon, since the 13th century.

Verona City in northern Italy with fine Roman remains, including a theatre carved into the hillside and the 22 000-seat Arena where gladiators once fought. Every summer, the Arena is the setting for grand opera performed in the open with casts of hundreds. Some of Verona's churches are striped with red and white stone.

Vesuvius Volcano, 4190 ft (1277 m) high, rising behind the Italian city of Naples. Vesuvius last erupted in 1944, but its best-known eruption was in AD 79, when the city of ▷POMPEII was buried under ash and lava, and Herculaneum under mud flows. The volcanic soils are fertile, and vines are grown on the lower slopes.

Victoria Falls One of the world's most spectacular waterfalls, 354 ft (108 m) high and with a mile (1.6 km) wide rim, on the Zambezi river where it forms the Zambia-Zimbabwe border. The Kololo people who once lived near the falls called them *Mosi-oa-Tunya*, meaning 'the smoke that thunders' – a reference to the cloud of spray that rises 1600 ft (500 m) above the falls. Below the falls, the Zambezi zigzags through gorges for more than 40 miles (64 km). Dr David ▷LIVINGSTONE, the Scottish missionary and explorer, was the first European to see the falls, in 1855, and named them in honour of Queen Victoria.

Victoria, Lake Africa's largest lake, the size of the Republic of Ireland, lying between Kenya, Tanzania and Uganda. The British explorer John Speke became the first European to see the lake, in 1858, during his search for the source of the Nile. He named it in honour of Queen Victoria.

Vienna Capital of Austria, on the Danube. Before 1918 Vienna was the capital of the mighty Austro-Hungarian Empire. Many imposing buildings, such as the Opera House and the Hofburg palace, line the 2½ mile (4 km) long Ringstrasse boulevard which replaced the old city walls in the late 1850s. Hitler's march into Vienna in 1938 temporarily united Austria and Germany, and Vienna was severely damaged by Allied bombing during World War II. The Allies controlled the city from 1945 to 1955 and divided it into four sectors occupied by Britain, France, the USA and the USSR. It was against this backdrop that the writer Graham Greene set his script for the film *The Third Man*.

🕭 Vienna is known for the waltz, its pastries and also for music – especially opera, the Vienna Philharmonic Orchestra and the Vienna Boys' Choir, whose choristers have included the composers ▷HAYDN and ▷SCHUBERT. ▷MOZART, ▷BEETHOVEN, ▷BRAHMS, and Johann ▷STRAUSS the Elder and Younger also lived in Vienna.

🕭 The Spanish Riding School is housed in part of the Hofburg palace. The school's Lipizzaner horses were originally imported from Spain, giving the school its name.

Vietnam Communist country in Southeast Asia. Vietnam was a French colony from the 1880s. In 1954, after the French finally withdrew, the country was divided into communist North Vietnam and non-communist South Vietnam. The North's attempt to reunite the country under communist rule resulted in the ▷VIETNAM WAR. Despite American intervention from 1961 to 1973, South Vietnam fell to the communists in 1975 and the unified state was set up in 1976. Two million Vietnamese were killed during the war, and afterwards many thousands of 'boat people' fled by sea. The capital is Hanoi, the former capital of North Vietnam; Saigon, the former capital of South Vietnam, is now called Ho Chi Minh City.

Virginia Historic eastern seaboard state of the USA, whose capital is Richmond. The state was named after England's Queen Elizabeth I, the 'virgin queen'. English settlers arrived in 1607, and Williamsburg, the state capital from 1699 to 1780, today has renovated and reconstructed colonial buildings. In Virginia also are Mount Vernon – the home of George Washington, the first US president – and battlefields of the War of Independence and the American Civil War. The Shenandoah Valley and part of the Blue Ridge mountains are in the west of Virginia. The state of West Virginia was once part of Virginia, but broke away during the ▷AMERICAN CIVIL WAR to form a separate state.

Virgin Islands Group of about 100 Caribbean islands, most of them uninhabited, east of Puerto Rico. About a third of the islands are a British colony, and the rest are owned by the USA. Tourists enjoy the sandy beaches, tropical climate and good sailing.

Volga Europe's longest river, and a trade route between Europe and Asia since the Middle Ages. The Volga flows for 2292 miles (3688 km) through forest, steppe and semi-desert to its delta in the Caspian Sea. Dams across the river have created a string of huge lakes. The city of Volgograd – known as Stalingrad from 1925 to 1961 – was virtually destroyed in the 1942-3 Battle of Stalingrad.
♪ The Volga Boat Song tells the story of Stepan Razin, the 17th-century leader of a popular uprising who sailed along the Volga with his followers.

Warsaw Capital of Poland, on the River Vistula. During World War II Warsaw was occupied by the Germans who confined 500 000 Jews to a walled ghetto. Many of them died of disease or were transferred to death camps, and the ghetto was razed after an abortive uprising in 1943. By the end of the war more than half of the city's prewar population had been killed or deported, and only one in ten of its buildings were fit for use. After the war, part of the city's historic centre was restored, and a modern new city was created beyond it.

Washington DC Capital of the United States of America. The city's civic buildings are grouped around The Mall, a long park flanked by museums and government buildings, one of which is the Smithsonian Institution. The domed white Capitol, and the Library of Congress, stand at one end of The Mall on Capitol Hill. Near the Potomac River at the other end of The Mall is the Lincoln Memorial, which resembles a Greek temple and houses a statue of Abraham Lincoln, the 19th-century US president. The White House, the president's official residence, is set back from The Mall. DC stands for District of Columbia – the territory ceded by the states of Maryland and Virginia in 1788-9 to provide a site for the new, purpose-built capital city. The name Columbia – taken from Christopher Columbus – is the poetical name for America and was used more liberally in the 18th century. Washington DC is not part of any state, and is under federal jurisdiction. Government is the main activity.

West Bank Area of land about 80 miles (130 km) long and 30 miles (50 km) wide lying to the west of the River Jordan and the northern half of the Dead Sea. It was governed as part of Jordan from 1950 to 1967, when it was seized by Israel during the ▷SIX-DAY WAR. An Israeli military administration was set up and Jewish settlements established, leading to conflict between the Jewish settlers and the West Bank's Palestinian population. In 1988 Jordan's King Hussein renounced administrative responsibility for the West Bank. In 1993 Israel agreed to a limited form of self-rule for Palestinians in the West Bank town of Jericho, and a timetable was set for elections and further negotiations.

Western Australia Largest of Australia's six states, more than ten times the size of the United Kingdom yet with about as many people as Hampshire. In the interior there are sand dunes and salt lakes that form after rain; sheep farming is the major enterprise in less arid areas. Gold prospectors flocked to Western Australia in 1886, and gold is still mined there. Most people live in and around PERTH, the state capital.

Western Samoa Pair of mountainous islands fringed with coral reefs, lying more than 2000 miles (3200 km) northeast of Brisbane, Australia. Coconut oil is the country's main export, but tourism is becoming increasingly important. Rugby, especially seven-a-side, is very popular.
♪ The writer Robert Louis ▷STEVENSON lived in Western Samoa for several years and was buried there in 1894.
♪ Margaret ▷MEAD did much to promote the field of anthropology in 1928 with her book *Coming of Age in Samoa*.

West Indies Group of islands to the east of Central America. The main islands are CUBA, JAMAICA, Hispaniola (the states of HAITI and the Dominican Republic), PUERTO RICO and TRINIDAD. Smaller islands include Barbados, Grenada, St Vincent, St Lucia and the VIRGIN ISLANDS. Before Europeans arrived, the islands were inhabited by the Arawak, Carib and Ciboney peoples. After the voyages of Christopher Columbus, Spain, France, Britain and the Netherlands all claimed islands for themselves, and introduced West African slaves to work on sugar plantations. Several islands are still European colonies.
♪ Columbus called the islands the Indies because he thought that he had reached the Indies of east Asia. The islands were later called the West Indies, to distinguish them from the East Indies.

PROUD CENTRE *Washington's imposing white marble Capitol, home of the US Congress, was built between 1793 and the 1860s. A bronze statue, 'Freedom', stands on top of the dome.*

WINTER GUISE *Hummocks of snow form on rocks in Yosemite's Merced River, looking for all the world like buns topped with icing. The sheer face of Half Dome rises in the background.*

Yellowstone National Park World's first national park, established in 1872. Nearly all the park – more than one-third of the size of Wales – is in the US state of Wyoming. Yellowstone is known for its geysers, bubbling mud pools and rock terraces deposited by mineral-laden hot springs, but it also has canyons, waterfalls and lakes. The best-known geyser, Old Faithful, erupts about once every 1¼ hours, sending a stream of boiling water more than 100 ft (30 m) into the air.

Yemen Country created in May 1990 when the Yemen Arab Republic merged with the People's Democratic Republic of Yemen (South Yemen). The mountainous west has enough rainfall to support forests and crops, but much of the country is dry. The capital is the walled city of San'a, but part of ADEN is the commercial centre.
🔱 The ruined city of Marib, in western Yemen, was once the capital of the ancient kingdom of Sheba. The Bible describes how the Queen of Sheba visited King Solomon to test his wisdom.

Yosemite National Park (Yo-SEM-itty) Mountain area of the Sierra Nevada, in the western USA. Yosemite has many lakes, rivers and gorges, and also towering cliffs that include the side of the granite peak aptly called Half Dome, which at almost 2000 ft (610 m) is one of the world's sheerest rock faces. The 2425 ft (739 m) Yosemite Falls is the highest waterfall in North America. Black bears live in the park.

Yugoslavia South European country that was formed in 1918 and broke up amid war and bloodshed in 1991. The capital was BELGRADE, and Yugoslavia's constituent states were BOSNIA-HERZEGOVINA, CROATIA, Macedonia, Montenegro, SERBIA and SLOVENIA. Marshall ▷TITO, Yugoslavia's communist leader from 1945 to 1980, broke with the USSR and developed the country's own brand of communism. Tourists flocked to sunny islands and beaches along the Dalmatian coast, to the medieval port of Dubrovnik, and to resorts in the mountains that make up three-quarters of the country. Slovenes and Croats, whose

countries were once part of the Habsburg Empire, are predominantly Roman Catholic. Centuries of Turkish rule had enormous influence in Bosnia-Herzegovina, and many people there are Muslims. Serbs, Montenegrins and Macedonians are predominantly Orthodox Christians, and use the Cyrillic alphabet. After Tito's death, nationalism resurfaced. Slovenia, Croatia and Bosnia-Herzegovina declared their independence from Yugoslavia in 1991, with the former Yugoslav republic of Macedonia following in 1992. Serbia and Montenegro claim to be the successor to the former state of Yugoslavia, but the claim is not internationally recognised.

Zaire Large country in central Africa, one-third of which is covered with thick, luxuriant rain forest. The 2900 mile (4670 km) long Zaire River, Africa's second longest river after the Nile, rises in the south of the country and flows through the forest. From 1885 to 1908 Zaire was the personal colony of Belgium's King Leopold II; it was known as the Belgian Congo until independence in 1960. Zaire is very poor, even though it is the world's largest producer of diamonds. The capital is Kinshasa.
🔱 The brutal treatment of local people by Leopold II's agents was depicted in Joseph Conrad's novella ▷HEART OF DARKNESS.

Zambia Country in south-central Africa, whose name comes from the Zambezi river which forms part of the border with Zimbabwe. Much of Zambia is high woodland and savannah that becomes increasingly dry towards the southwest. Before independence in 1964 the country was the British colony of Northern Rhodesia. Kenneth Kaunda was the country's head of state from independence until 1991. The capital is Lusaka, and copper is the major export.

Zimbabwe Landlocked country of south-central Africa, much of which is savannah dotted with massive granite hills. Zimbabwe was the British colony of Southern Rhodesia from the end of the 19th century until 1965, when Ian Smith's white minority government made a unilateral declaration of independence, and called the country Rhodesia. After international pressure and a protracted guerrilla war, legitimate independence was secured in 1980, with black majority rule and Robert ▷MUGABE as prime minister. The capital is Harare, formerly known as Salisbury.
🔱 The country takes its name from Great Zimbabwe, the ruins of massive stone buildings that were occupied by the Shona-Karanga civilisation (c.AD 1200-1450).

THE EARTH AND
THE ENVIRONMENT

Our planet has been moulded by massive cycles of creation and destruction over 4600 million years. Human life remains at the mercy of awesome natural phenomena over which we have no control. But increased understanding of our environment has shown us the challenge we face in ensuring that human activities do not threaten the delicate balance that sustains life on Earth.

LIGHTNING BOLT

RAIN FOREST, VENEZUELA

KILAUEA VOLCANO, HAWAII

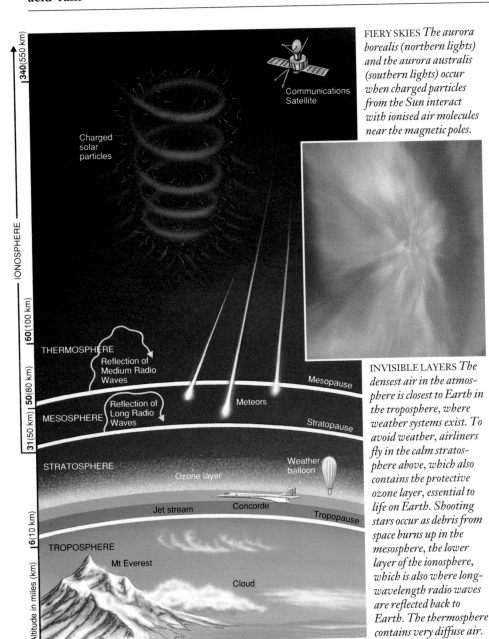

Altitude in miles (km)

340(550 km)
60(100 km)
50(80 km)
31(50 km)
6(10 km)

IONOSPHERE

Charged solar particles

Communications Satellite

THERMOSPHERE
Reflection of Medium Radio Waves

Reflection of Long Radio Waves

MESOSPHERE

Mesopause

Meteors

Stratopause

STRATOSPHERE

Ozone layer

Weather balloon

Jet stream

Concorde

Tropopause

TROPOSPHERE

Mt Everest

Cloud

FIERY SKIES The aurora borealis (northern lights) and the aurora australis (southern lights) occur when charged particles from the Sun interact with ionised air molecules near the magnetic poles.

INVISIBLE LAYERS The densest air in the atmosphere is closest to Earth in the troposphere, where weather systems exist. To avoid weather, airliners fly in the calm stratosphere above, which also contains the protective ozone layer, essential to life on Earth. Shooting stars occur as debris from space burns up in the mesosphere, the lower layer of the ionosphere, which is also where long-wavelength radio waves are reflected back to Earth. The thermosphere contains very diffuse air.

acid rain Corrosive rain which damages masonry, destroys trees, kills freshwater fish and causes loss of vegetation through increased acidity in soil. Sulphur dioxide from coal-burning power stations and nitrogen oxides from car exhausts react with oxygen in the air and dissolve in rain droplets in clouds, forming dilute but lethal solutions of sulphuric and nitric acids. Acid rain can be carried a long way from its source by the prevailing winds – from Britain to Scandinavia, for example. Active volcanoes, which release quantities of sulphur dioxide and hydrogen sulphide, also cause acid rain. Acid rain was first recognised in 1859, but its effect on vegetation was not fully realised until the 1970s.

air mass Huge body of air that is nearly uniform in temperature and humidity, and which is separated from other air masses by COLD or WARM FRONTS. An air mass can extend for hundreds of miles. There are three types: tropical (warm), polar (cold) and arctic/antarctic (moist and cool). The first two are categorised as either 'maritime' (formed over the sea, and moist) or 'continental' (formed over land, and dry). The movement of air masses, and of the fronts between them, is responsible for weather.

anticyclone Area of high pressure in the atmosphere, sometimes known as a 'high'. Winds blow outwards from the centre of an anticyclone, spiralling clockwise in the Northern Hemisphere and anticlockwise in the Southern – the opposite way to a CYCLONE. Anticyclones bring settled weather: warm and dry in summer, and cold and clear in winter.

🔑During winter, descending air in an anticyclone may create a TEMPERATURE INVERSION, trapping smog for days.

atmosphere Narrow layer of gases that surrounds the Earth, and enables life to exist. Retained by the Earth's gravitational pull, it contains about 78 per cent nitrogen, almost 21 per cent oxygen and 1 per cent argon, about 0.2 per cent water vapour and 0.03 per cent carbon dioxide, with trace amounts of other gases. The atmosphere shields the Earth from the Sun's harmful rays, the cold of outer space, and bombardment by meteoroids. Closest to Earth is the troposphere, where air density is at its greatest. Temperature decreases with height and weather systems form here. Above the troposphere's ceiling, or tropopause, temperature increases with height, preventing air from moving vertically. The IONOSPHERE, which contains electrically charged particles, extends outwards from the upper atmosphere or stratosphere. Charged particles are captured by the Earth's magnetic field and drawn towards the poles, causing MAGNETIC STORMS and auroras.

🔑A primordial atmosphere consisting of nebular gas (mainly hydrogen) left over from the formation of the solar system would have been stripped from the Earth by intense radiation from the Sun. The atmosphere replacing it, formed from volcanic gases, had little free oxygen and a hundred times more carbon dioxide than it does now. Much of the carbon dioxide has been removed by living things: over many millions of years it has been 'locked up' in the bodies of long-dead organisms and turned into sedimentary rock and fossil fuels. The atmosphere's oxygen content has increased mainly due to plants' ▷PHOTOSYNTHESIS.

atmospheric pressure Weight of air above the Earth's surface that creates pressure on it. The standard atmospheric pressure at sea level – defined as one atmosphere – is 14.7 lb per square inch, or 1013.25 millibars. As altitude increases there is less air overhead, causing atmospheric pressure to fall off at about 3.5 millibars for every 100 ft (30 m) climbed. Above 8000 ft (2400 m), air pressure and oxygen supply are low enough to cause altitude sickness. Above 180 miles (300 km), the pressure is as low as any man-made vacuum. Air pressure also varies with different meteorological conditions, and its measurement using a barometer is a principal means of WEATHER FORECASTING. Places of equal pressure are linked on weather maps by lines called isobars. Areas of high pressure – associated with settled weather – have a pressure of 1010 millibars and above. Low pressure systems, which bring unsettled weather, have a pressure of 1000 millibars or below. Rapid falls in atmospheric pressure herald storms.

atoll Ring-shaped CORAL REEF enclosing a lagoon, most common in the Pacific Ocean. Charles ▷DARWIN was the first to suggest, correctly, that they had formed around the rim of a submerged volcano, or island.

Beaufort scale Measure of wind speed that relies on observed indicators such as the height of waves. Devised by Admiral F.B. Beaufort in 1805, it ranges from force 0, calm with a wind speed of less than 1 knot (1.6 km/h), to force 12, a hurricane with wind speeds of more than 64 knots (117 km/h). Forces 13 to 17 were added by the US Weather Bureau in 1955 to describe the most severe storms. Originally based on the effects of wind on a fully rigged man-of-war, it is still used at sea. In meteorology it has been largely replaced by the direct measurement of wind speed.

biosphere Uppermost layer of the Earth's surface, and its lower atmosphere, which is inhabited by life. The term also refers to an artificially closed environment where inter-dependent plants and animals form a self-sustaining ▷ECOSYSTEM.
⚱ Between 1991 and 1993, eight volunteers spent two years isolated inside Biosphere 2 (Biosphere 1 is Earth), a sealed 3 acre (1.2 ha) glass and steel structure outside Tucson, Arizona. The experiment, the first of a series, was designed to investigate the feasibility of building a settlement on Mars.

bog Waterlogged peaty soil providing a distinctive and valuable habitat. Most of northern Europe's bogs have been lost through drainage and afforestation.
⚱ The acidic, oxygen-deficient bog environment has remarkable qualities of preservation. In 1984, the largely intact body of an Iron Age man was discovered in a bog at Lindow Moss, Cheshire, with his last meal of griddle cakes in his stomach. He had been ritually executed in about 200 BC.

cave Natural cavity or series of underground chambers and passages eroded by water. Caves are formed by underground streams, by wave erosion along coasts and by water dissolving rock, as in limestone cave systems with their distinctive STALACTITES AND STALAGMITES. Caves also form in glaciers and in solidified volcanic lava.
⚱ The world's most extensive cave system is under the Mammoth Cave National Park in Kentucky, USA. Potholers can explore over 300 miles (480 km) of charted passages.

CFCs (chlorofluorocarbons) Chemical compounds, also known as Freons, containing carbon, chlorine and fluorine, used as insulators, solvents, refrigerants and aerosol propellants. CFCs, known to be partly responsible for holes in the OZONE LAYER, are being replaced by isobutanes. However, CFCs are likely to be used in the developing world for many years to come.

climate Long-term weather conditions of a particular place, including temperature, rainfall, humidity, sunshine and wind speed. Climate is largely determined by latitude, altitude and location in relation to major landmasses and oceans: in coastal regions temperature is modified by proximity to the sea, while in the centre of a continent it will reach great extremes. The most widely used classification of climates is: tropical (hot and wet), desert (dry), warm or cool temperate, polar or mountain. Within this scheme there are specific types.

the landmasses caused by CONTINENTAL DRIFT, and changes in the Sun's temperature as well as in the composition of gases in the ATMOSPHERE. Some periods of change such as the ICE AGES, when the general climate was 10-12°C (18-22°F) colder than at present, continued for thousands of years. Within these huge cyclical changes are smaller variations, such as the 'little ice age' that lasted from the 15th to the 19th century; rivers froze regularly in the colder winters – the last Thames 'frost fair' was held in 1814. Since the 1880s, temperatures across the world have risen, prompting theories on GLOBAL WARMING. By the 1980s the Earth's temperature was rising at over 0.2°C (0.36°F) per decade.

cloud Mixture of minute water droplets and ice crystals in the atmosphere. Clouds form when warm, moist air ascends and cools, and the water vapour it contains condenses around microscopic particles of dust or smoke. Clouds typically contain one million water droplets per cubic metre (35 cu ft), and one million cloud particles are needed to form a single raindrop. Clumps of cloud form when air rises quickly, while slow-rising air forms cloud sheets. Cirrus, cirrostratus and cirrocumulus clouds, which form at 16 500-50 000 ft (5-15 km), are composed almost entirely of ice crystals.

Cirrus   Altostratus above nimbostratus   Cumulonimbus   Altocumulus

CLOUD PATTERNS *Feathery plumes of cirrus, or mares' tails, are often the first sign of bad weather. Altostratus clouds often cover the entire sky and can turn into rain clouds, such as nimbostratus. Anvil-shaped cumulonimbus herald thundery storms and altocumulus usually indicate fair weather.*

For example, Cape Town in South Africa has a warm temperate Mediterranean-type climate with a dry summer; Britain's climate, also warm temperate, is maritime type – mild and moist.

climatic change Throughout the Earth's history, major fluctuations in climate have been caused by many factors: volcanic eruptions that obscure the Sun, the impact of METEORITES, the changing positions of

White altocumulus clouds, which indicate fine weather, and grey altostratus clouds which produce rain, form at 6500-23 000 ft (2-7 km). Nimbostratus, at 3000-9000 ft (1-3 km), are also rain clouds. Dark, anvil-shaped cumulonimbus clouds rise to 32 800 ft (10 km), and herald an approaching COLD FRONT and thunderstorms. Hazy, low-level stratus clouds produce overcast skies, and low-level cumulus clouds often bring drizzle.

coal Black sedimentary rock formed from vegetation which partially decomposed in swamps, predominantly during the Carboniferous period (see GEOLOGICAL TIME SCALE). It built up into thick peat beds which compacted when other rock formed on top. Pressure and underground heat slowly transformed the peat into coal. The main types of coal are anthracite, the hardest coal, with over 90 per cent carbon; bituminous coal, used as house coal, containing over 80 per cent carbon; and lignite or brown coal, which contains around 70 per cent carbon and many impurities.

Coal fuelled Britain's ▷INDUSTRIAL REVOLUTION, and coal mining remained one of the country's most important industries until after World War II. The workforce of 1.2 million men in 1920 had shrunk to less than 27 000 by the 1990s.

cold front Leading edge of an advancing cold AIR MASS. Relatively dense cold air undercuts warmer, thinner air leading to a rapid drop in ground temperature. Showers or sometimes thunderstorms follow. The rain stops abruptly after the front passes. Cold fronts can move at up to 40 mph (64 km/h). (Compare WARM FRONT.)

continent One of seven landmasses of the Earth's crust – Asia, Africa, North America, South America, Australasia, Europe and Antarctica – which cover nearly 30 per cent of the Earth's surface. Continental features include margins or boundaries (typically undersea), chains of old and young fold mountains, a central sediment-covered platform and the shield – the oldest part. Shield areas, such as north Canada and central Africa, are remnants of former continents that broke up and recombined – part of a process explained by PLATE TECTONICS.

continental drift The first comprehensive theory of continental drift was outlined by the German meteorologist Alfred Wegener in 1912. He based his ideas partly on the fact, noted three centuries earlier, that the eastern bulge of South America fitted almost exactly into the bight of Africa's west coast, but mainly on the similarities between fossils found in the coalfields of Europe and North America. He believed that for most of the Earth's history there had been a single continent, Pangaea, surrounded by an ocean, Panthalassa. It is now believed that Pangaea became two proto-continents, separated by the Tethys Sea: Gondwanaland, comprising South America, Africa, India, Australia and Antarctica; and Laurasia, which combined North America, Europe and the rest

of Asia. Despite steadily mounting evidence, Wegener's theory was not generally accepted until it was incorporated into the theory of PLATE TECTONICS, developed in the 1950s and 1960s.

CONTINENTS ON THE MOVE *An original landmass, Pangaea, split into two proto-continents, Laurasia and Gondwanaland. The Tethys Sea became the Mediterranean. Movement continues today with North America moving away from Europe, and India pushing into the Himalayas. It has been calculated that in about 250 million years' time Australia could collide with North America's west coast.*

225 million years ago

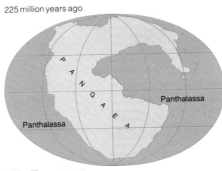

135 million years ago

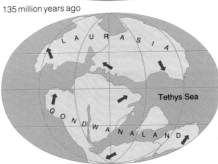

40 million years ago

250 million years from now

coral reef Undersea ridge or hillock built from the skeletons of coral, a marine animal, related to jellyfish and sea anemones, that lives in warm seas. Because coral colonies live on the skeletons of previous generations huge submarine structures, such as ATOLLS or Australia's ▷GREAT BARRIER REEF, have slowly built up.

Coriolis effect Apparent force acting on an object moving across the Earth's surface, due to the Earth's rotation. The apparent velocity of an object at rest on the Earth's surface rises from zero at the poles to a maximum at the Equator. When moving away from the Equator, an object appears to deflect to the right in the Northern Hemisphere and to the left in the Southern Hemisphere. Consequently, an object moving in a north-south direction also appears to be moving east or west. The Coriolis effect is responsible for the pattern of WINDS and OCEAN CURRENTS and is an important consideration in air travel, missile guidance and launching spacecraft.

cyclone Area of low pressure in the atmosphere, often called simply a 'low'. Winds blowing inwards to 'fill' the depression adopt a spiral pattern because of the CORIOLIS EFFECT, moving anticlockwise in the Northern Hemisphere and clockwise in the Southern – the opposite of an ANTICYCLONE. In mid to high latitudes a cyclone is referred to as a depression and is associated with unsettled weather. In tropical regions it is associated with high winds and torrential rain. (See also HURRICANE.)

DDT (Dichlorodiphenyltrichloroethane) Powerful insecticide used during World War II to kill lice, fleas and mosquitoes – greatly reducing the incidence of typhus, malaria, plague and yellow fever which these insects carry. Later, DDT was used widely as an all-purpose agricultural pesticide, but resistant strains of insect pests soon developed. It was then found that DDT was picked up by insect-eating animals and became concentrated as it passed along the food chain. In Britain, for example, the peregrine falcon was almost wiped out. In the 1960s, the use of DDT was banned in most parts of the world.

deforestation Felling and clearing of forest, usually for timber or to make way for agriculture. Over the past 5000 years the great forests that once covered the temperate zones of Europe and North America have been steadily cleared. Today, the loss of RAIN FOREST in Southeast Asia and South America is causing widespread concern.

POWER OF NATURE *The San Francisco earthquake of October 1989 registered 7.1 on the Richter scale and caused many buildings and elevated roads to collapse. Amazingly only 24 people were killed.*

desert Arid region where average rainfall is less than 10 in (25 cm) a year, usually in areas where there are persistent belts of high-pressure ANTICYCLONES, such as the Sahara, or where mountains prevent the passage of rain, such as the Gobi Desert of Mongolia and northeast China. In the Sahara, daytime temperatures can reach 51°C (124°F) but at night, they may drop to 15°C (59°F). The Gobi has a winter temperature falling to −40°C (−40°F). True deserts cover only 5 per cent of the Earth's land area, but with their associated arid and semi-arid regions, they affect around one-third of the land surface. Deserts spread largely because of over-grazing and drought, such as in the Sahel, in the southern Sahara.

The Atacama desert in northern Chile is the driest in the world. In the town of Calama there was no rain from 1570 to 1971.

Earth The only inhabited planet orbiting the Sun. It has three major parts: the ATMOSPHERE; the OCEANS; and ROCK made up of an inner and outer core, a mantle and a crust. The inner core, some 1500 miles (2400 km) across, is thought to be solid iron and nickel – reaching 4500°C (8100°F). Around it is an outer core, about 1365 miles (2200 km) thick, composed of molten iron, probably mixed with sulphur and oxygen, at a temperature of about 2200°C (4000°F). The mantle, between the core and the crust, is about 1800 miles (2900 km) thick, and is composed of hot rock – mainly iron-magnesium silicates (peridotite). The continental crust is largely granite and supports the continents. It is an average of 20 miles (32 km) thick, although it can be more than 37 miles (60 km) thick at mountain ranges. The oceanic crust is made largely of basalt and gabbro and is 4-10 miles (6-16 km) thick. Newer than continental crust, it is constantly being formed along OCEAN RIDGES. The Earth is not a perfect sphere: because of its rotation, it bulges slightly at the Equator, having an equatorial circumference of 24 902 miles (40 076 km) and a polar circumference of 24 860 miles (40 074 km). Its total surface area is 197 000 000 sq miles (510 000 000 km²). Land covers 57 000 000 sq miles (148 000 000 km²). As the Earth orbits the Sun, it tilts by about 23½ degrees – on its axis from the perpendicular – the reason for seasons outside the tropics. (See also ▷EARTH in 'Science, Space and Mathematics'.)

The human race has been in existence for less than one-thousandth of the Earth's 4600 million-year history (see GEOLOGICAL TIME SCALE).

earthquake Violent tremor in the Earth's crust caused by the sudden release of stresses at the edges of the Earth's crustal plates, a process explained by PLATE TECTONICS. Earthquakes occur most frequently around the rim of the Pacific Ocean and along the trans-Asiatic belt which extends through the Mediterranean Sea and eastward via Asia to the Pacific. The energy from these disturbances is transmitted to the surface by SEISMIC WAVES.

The magnitude, or energy, of an earthquake is measured on the RICHTER SCALE. Another scale – the Mercalli scale – grades earthquakes from 1 to 12 according to the disturbance felt by people, from tiny tremors to total destruction.

ecosystem Community of interdependent plants and animals and the physical environment they occupy. A pond or the entire world can be viewed as a single ecosystem, but usually the term refers to a single type of habitat, such as desert or fresh water. Each organism occupies a 'niche' which determines its relationship with other living things in the ecosystem – for example, its position in the food chain.

El Niño Warm OCEAN CURRENT that in some years replaces the normally cold, rich fishing waters off northern Peru in December or January, with devastating effects on the local economy. It occurs when northerly winds replace the prevailing southerlies, driving warm water shoreward and downward. The life cycle cannot be supported and great numbers of fish and sea birds die. The cause for these changes is not known, but it is linked with anomalous weather around the world. In 1992, when El Niño emerged early, there was drought in Indonesia, eastern Australia and northeast Brazil, a hurricane in Samoa, freak storms in California and months of heavy rain in Alaska and Canada.

environment Surroundings in which an organism lives, including the climate, the physical and chemical conditions of its habitat, and its relationship with other living things. Since the 1960s, 'Green' or environmental concerns, such as POLLUTION, and the need to recycle materials and reduce waste, have become major political issues. Some industrial countries now have environmental protection agencies to police the producers of pollution.

erosion Gradual breaking down of landforms and removal of the debris to another place, by ice (especially during periods of GLACIATION), rivers, waves, rain and wind. Over hundreds of years, the processes of erosion can reshape entire landscapes and play an important part in the ROCK cycle.

eutrophication Build-up on lakes, ponds and slow-moving rivers of microscopic ▷ALGAE which may block sunlight and deplete levels of oxygen in the water – killing other forms of aquatic life. The algae result from excess fertilisers and human waste.

fault Fracture in the Earth's crust where forces transmitted through the movement of tectonic plates displace the two sides relative to each other. Faults may range from a mere inch to hundreds of miles – such as the San Andreas Fault in California. Horizontal or vertical movement along a major fault line causes EARTHQUAKES.
🔱 The Highlands of Scotland are bisected by the Great Glen fault line. It separates the sedimentary Highland plateau from the metamorphic rock of the Grampians.

flood Several factors may cause flooding: excessive rain, sudden spring thaws, TSUNAMIS and storms at sea, as when a tidal surge is funnelled down the North Sea or up the Adriatic. Flash floods are caused by sudden thunderstorms in dry valleys, where the volume of rainfall overwhelms the natural or artificial drainage.
🔱 Engineers designing dams, bridges and drainage channels, calculate the magnitude of a flood in terms of how often it is likely to occur. The Thames Barrier should protect London from a flood likely to occur only once in 1000 years.
🔱 In 1993, the Mississippi river rose 32 ft (10 m), overtopping levees and flooding over two-thirds of its flood plain – an event estimated as likely to occur once every 500 years. The cost of the resulting damage was estimated at some $10 billion.

FAULT LINE *Two enormous parts of the Earth's crust slide slowly past each other at the San Andreas Fault, causing earthquakes and making a dramatic scar across California.*

fold Bending or buckling of ROCK strata under intense pressure, for example where the Earth's plates collide, forcing the land to rise, as in MOUNTAIN BUILDING. When the rocks are eroded, the effects of the folding action can be seen in the diagonal or twisted forms of the exposed strata – once the flat sedimentary floors of ancient seas.

Gaia hypothesis Theory proposed by the English scientist James Lovelock in 1969 that the Earth can be regarded as a single integrated living organism composed of a delicate web of interconnected ECOSYSTEMS. This network, named 'Gaia' after the 'Earth Mother' of Greek mythology, regulates the global environment, but pollution created by humans may be upsetting this stability – damaging the OZONE LAYER and giving rise to GLOBAL WARMING.

gemstones Crystals prized for rarity, form, iridescence and hardness. Of some 3000 minerals, no more than 100 are used as gemstones. Only the finest specimens are considered precious, including aquamarine and emerald (from the mineral beryl), alexandrite and cat's-eye (chrysoberyl), ruby and sapphire (corundum), diamond (carbon), amazonite and moonstone (feldspar), garnet, lazurite, opal, peridot (olivine), quartz, spinel, topaz, tourmaline and zircon. Others such as jade, serpentine and turquoise are popular for carving. Some organic materials – amber, jet, coral and pearl – are also considered gemstones.
🔱 Some diamonds are 3000 million years old. The British Crown Jewels contain the two biggest stones cut from the Cullinan diamond found in South Africa in 1905.

geological time scale History of the Earth as revealed by the ▷FOSSIL record and the stratification, or sequence of rock layers. By the end of the 18th century, the processes of deposition and EROSION that

AEONS OF TIME *Precambrian rock represents 85 per cent of the Earth's history, but contains few fossils. Life forms developed and proliferated during the other three eras – the Palaeozoic 'ancient life', the Mesozoic 'middle life' and the Cenozoic 'modern life'. The Cenozoic is divided into the Tertiary and Quaternary periods. The Quaternary is further divided into the Pleistocene epoch, when the Earth underwent a series of ice ages during which Homo sapiens – the ancestors of modern man – appeared; and the current Holocene epoch, which began 10 000 years ago.*

Time in millions of years

| 4600 PRECAMBRIAN | 570 PALAEOZOIC | 225 MESOZOIC | 65 CENOZOIC | 0 |

PRECAMBRIAN ERA
The Earth was formed about 4600 million years ago. The first primitive single-celled animals appeared 600 million years later.

PALAEOZOIC ERA *Creatures emerged from the sea at about the same time that flying insects evolved – approximately 500 million years ago. The first mountains and trees thrust towards the sky from the previously flat landscape.*

MESOZOIC ERA *Flowering plants, dinosaurs, mammals and birds developed during the three periods of the Mesozoic era – the Triassic (225-190 million years ago), Jurassic (190-130 million years ago) and Cretaceous (130-65 million years ago).*

CENOZOIC ERA
In the current geological era, the Himalayas and the Rockies were formed as the Earth's huge continental 'plates' collided with each other. Life on Earth took its present form with the evolution of a wide variety of mammals, including man.

produced rock strata were partly understood and it became clear that the Earth must be vastly older than the 6000 years estimated from the Bible. During the early 1800s, fossils found in sedimentary rock were organised into their chronological sequence which allowed the development of a geological time scale, divided into eras, periods and epochs. Potassium-argon dating is now used to determine the age of ROCK, even the oldest formed some 4500 million years ago.

geothermal energy Heat obtained from hot rocks lying close to the Earth's surface. It is used to heat buildings directly and to generate electricity in countries such as Italy, Japan and Iceland. Steam from hot springs, or water pumped into boreholes, which quickly turns to steam – reaching temperatures of up to 350°C (630°F) – may be used to drive turbines.

glaciation Large accumulation of ice, such as glaciers and ice sheets formed from compacted snow during ICE AGES. The term also describes the erosion caused by ice, sometimes thousands of feet thick, moving over the Earth's surface. Ice sheets, now confined to Greenland and Antarctica, are the source of ICEBERGS. Like ice sheets, glaciers move slowly under the enormous weight of ice, scouring the landscape, carving out valleys and depositing mounds of debris called moraine. Retreating ice leaves U-shaped valleys such as fjords and the firths of Scotland.
☘ The Antarctic ice cap is on average 0.75 mile (1.2 km) thick and contains more than 90 per cent of the Earth's ice.

global warming Theory that the world is warming up due to the GREENHOUSE EFFECT. Levels of carbon dioxide in the atmosphere have been rising since the Industrial Revolution took effect in the 1780s. More recently, the clearing of RAIN FOREST has added to the problem, as trees absorb carbon dioxide during ▷PHOTO-SYNTHESIS. If the emission of carbon dioxide and other 'greenhouse gases' – produced by power stations, industry and cars – continues to grow at the present rate, the average global temperature could increase by 1.8°C (3.2°F) by 2030, causing other unpredictable effects on the climate and on sea level. The governments of many countries are committed to stabilising carbon dioxide emissions by the year 2000.

greenhouse effect Gases in the atmosphere act in the same way as glass in a greenhouse, trapping the Sun's heat and

DEADLY STORM *Trees at Palm Beach, Florida, bend before 125 mph winds in 1945. Hurricanes on land are mercifully short-lived: cut off from the sea, they usually blow themselves out after one day.*

effectively keeping the planet 30°C (54°F) warmer than it would otherwise be. This maintains the surface of the Earth at temperatures where water is liquid and life is possible. However, there are fears that the steadily increasing levels of 'greenhouse gases' such as carbon dioxide and methane will cause GLOBAL WARMING.

Gulf Stream Warm OCEAN CURRENT that originates in the Gulf of Mexico and flows up the east coast of North America before travelling northeastwards across the Atlantic Ocean. Eventually the warm water reaches northwestern Europe, where it leads to a mild, moist climate.

hail Ice balls created by updrafts which carry water droplets to the tops of storm clouds, where they freeze. More water condenses and freezes around these ice particles, until they become too heavy and fall to the ground.

humidity Amount of water vapour in the atmosphere. Air at 30°C (86°F) can hold six times as much water vapour as it can at freezing point. Humidity is therefore expressed as a percentage of the maximum amount of moisture the atmosphere can carry at a given temperature, and is thus termed relative humidity.
☘ Air conditioning aims to keep humidity at 50 to 60 per cent. Humidity below 20 per cent dries the throat leaving it vulnerable to infection. In Singapore City humidity sometimes reaches 98 per cent.

hurricane Name for a tropical CYCLONE in the North Atlantic, the Caribbean and the northeast Pacific, accompanied by high winds and torrential rain. In the northwest Pacific and China seas they are called typhoons; in the Indian Ocean and southwest Pacific they are known as cyclones. They form over warm water with a surface temperature of at least 27°C (81°F) and at latitudes high enough for the CORIOLIS EFFECT to be appreciable. At their centre is the 'eye', an area of calm air around which winds blow at up to 180 mph (290 km/h). Winds of 75 mph (120 km/h) – BEAUFORT SCALE force 12 – are designated hurricanes. The hurricane in Britain in October 1987 had wind speeds of 100 mph (160 km/h).

hydrologic cycle Constant circulation of water between air, land and sea. Water evaporates from the oceans. Some falls back into the sea again, but the rest falls on land as rain, snow or hail. Some evaporates again directly, some passes back to the atmosphere through plant transpiration, some finds its way back to the oceans through streams and rivers, and some goes into the ground, where its upper limit is known as the WATER TABLE. A small but vital amount is taken up by living things and incorporated into their tissues.

ice ages Long periods of climatic change when temperatures fell and GLACIATION occurred over a wide area. There have been a number of ice ages over the past 3000 million years. During the Pleistocene epoch, the most recent period of extensive glaciation, the polar ice caps advanced and retreated at least four times to cover most of northern and central Europe – at one time covering as much as 30 per cent of the Earth. The last ice sheet retreated about 11 000 years ago, leaving debris as far south as London. With more of the Earth's water frozen in ice sheets, SEA LEVEL was as much as 430 ft (130 m) lower than it is today. The English Channel was dry and a land bridge between Alaska and Siberia allowed early Mongoloid peoples to colonise the Americas. (See also CLIMATE.)

iceberg Floating mass of freshwater ice that has calved from an ice shelf, the seaward end of a glacier, or an ice sheet. Some 12 000 icebergs are calved each year from the glaciers of west Greenland. About 375 a year drift south into the Atlantic, where some, towering up to 550 ft (170 m) above sea level, are a hazard to shipping. Most melt within two years. On average the ice in icebergs is about 5000 years old. The tip of an iceberg, visible above the water, represents only about one-ninth of its total volume. The Ross Ice Shelf, off the Antarctic coast, is about the size of France, making it the world's largest body of floating ice.
⚓The 'unsinkable' SS *Titanic* sank on her maiden voyage in 1912 after hitting an iceberg – 1500 people lost their lives.

ionosphere Region of the upper ATMOSPHERE between 35 miles (60 km) and 190 miles (300 km) above the Earth, where air molecules or atoms are charged electrically (ionised) by absorbing short-wave radiation from the Sun. Ionised layers reflect radio signals and are thus of great importance in communications, although higher frequency VHF and UHF signals pass straight through them without reflection, and can only be received in line of sight of the transmitter, or satellite. The ionosphere is affected by MAGNETIC STORMS.

irrigation Artificial distribution of water by canals, pipelines and ditches to land that would otherwise be too dry for crops to flourish. Worldwide, an area about the size of western Europe is irrigated. Some 65 per cent of it is in the rice-growing areas of China, India, Pakistan and Southeast Asia.

lava Molten ROCK or magma that flows from volcanic vents and fissures at a temperature of 1100°C (2000°F), which is high enough to melt steel. When lavas cool, they solidify to form igneous rock. Froth on the surface of a lava flow solidifies into pumice – the only rock that floats in water.

lightning Giant electric spark of up to 100 million volts produced by a variation in the electric charge of different thunder clouds (sheet lightning) or between clouds and the ground (forked lightning). It is caused by a build-up of static electricity generated by particles of snow, hail or rain buffeted about by warm, rising air currents within thunder clouds. Forked lightning begins with a faint leader stroke branching and darting from side to side, taking the route of least resistance to the ground, quickly followed by a massive luminous return stroke. The peak current of the return is around 100 000 times the current flowing through a normal light bulb. Air in the lightning's path superheats to 16 000°C (28 800°F) and expands supersonically before contracting rapidly, causing a clap of thunder.
⚓Benjamin ▷FRANKLIN invented the lightning conductor, first using it in 1752.

magnetic poles Two points on the surface of the EARTH where its magnetic lines of force meet; a compass needle is drawn to the north magnetic pole. The Earth acts as a large magnet because of a mass of iron at its core. Electric currents in the core generate most of its magnetic field, though about 10 per cent is produced by currents in the IONOSPHERE. The magnetic poles change position slowly, but remain around 1000 miles (1600 km) from the geographic poles – the Earth's axis of rotation.
⚓Simple compasses have been used in navigation at sea since the 12th century.

STROKES OF BRILLIANCE *The central core of a lightning bolt is estimated to be as much as five times hotter than the surface of the Sun.*

magnetic reversal Switch in direction of the Earth's magnetic field – the magnetic north pole becomes the magnetic south pole and vice versa. The last switch occurred about 30 000 years ago, but many more are known to have occurred during the Earth's history. The reversals are recorded by the magnetic basalt rock that forms where SEA-FLOOR SPREADING takes place. As molten basalt oozes from the sea floor and solidifies, it takes up the magnetic orientation of the Earth at that time, forming bands, or strata, magnetised first in one direction, then the other. From this the rock's geographical latitude and place of origin can be determined.
⚓During a period of magnetic reversal, cosmic-ray particles that would normally be deflected by the Earth's magnetic field reach the surface of the planet, causing genetic mutation in living things. This may explain the sudden extinction of some species or the sudden appearance of others.

magnetic storm Disturbance of the Earth's magnetic field caused by ▷SOLAR WIND – charged particles from the Sun – which is responsible for auroras in the ATMOSPHERE. Magnetic storms can disrupt computer systems, radio and satellite communications, cause failure of electrical transmission lines, and increase doses of radiation to people on transpolar flights.

meteorite Rock or metal that has fallen to Earth from meteoroids – parts of asteroids or comets. Unlike ▷METEORS – another name for shooting stars – meteorites reach the Earth's surface without completely burning up. The commonest are stone meteorites (aerolites), which may contain particles of iron. Iron meteorites (siderites) often contain nickel and other metals. The largest meteorites found intact each weighed 60 tons. One landed at Grootfontein, Namibia, the other in Kansas, USA.
⚓In 1992 a 26 lb (12 kg) meteorite was found embedded in the bonnet of a car at Peekshill, in New York State. Though such an occurrence is rare, statistically a meteorite impact large enough to kill 100 people is likely to happen every 100 years.
⚓A crater at Chicxulub, Mexico, 112 miles (180 km) wide was caused when a meteorite some 6 miles (10 km) across exploded. This impact would have released energy equivalent to 10 000 atom bombs, and its aftermath may have destroyed half the Earth's living creatures, including the dinosaurs.

monsoon Large-scale reversal of WINDS in the tropics. The word, from the Arabic for season, originally applied to the winds of the Arabian Sea, which blow for six months from the northeast and six months from the southwest. It is now used for any wind system that reverses seasonally, especially the winds of south and southeast Asia. These blow cool and dry from the north from November to April, then warm and wet from the southwest from May to September when they carry torrential rain.

mountain building Deformation of the Earth's crust by warping, faulting or folding, or by deposition of volcanic material – processes which are all explained by PLATE TECTONICS. Dome mountains occur where the crust warps upwards without fracturing. At fracture zones, FAULT-block mountains are forced upwards. FOLD mountains result from layers of sedimentary rock being forced upwards. The Earth's largest volcanic ranges are the OCEAN RIDGES, which are still being built, as are two major fold mountain systems on land which were formed during the last 50 million years. One, stretching from the Himalayas to the Alps, Pyrenees and Atlas Mountains, is caused by India colliding with the rest of Asia, and by Africa colliding with Europe, due to continuing CONTINENTAL DRIFT. The other, responsible for creating the Andes, results from Pacific crustal plates sliding under the Americas.

natural gas Fossil fuel which is a mixture of methane and other gases such as propane, butane and helium that occurs in underground reservoirs of porous rock. Natural gas is often found near oil deposits, as it is made by the same processes.

nuclear waste Items that are dangerously radioactive, most notably spent fuel rods from nuclear power stations. There is controversy over the disposal of nuclear waste, especially since the effects of widespread contamination have become known following accidents such as ▷CHERNOBYL in 1986. Some dumping has taken place at sea, for example in the Arctic and the deep Marianas Trench off the Philippines, but an international treaty now forbids this. High-level waste from the chemical reprocessing of spent fuel rods from power stations and decommissioned nuclear weapons causes huge problems as it remains radioactive for thousands of years. Nevertheless, THORP, a Thermal Oxide Reprocessing Plant for separating plutonium from nuclear waste, was opened at Sellafield, Cumbria, in 1994.

The Waste Isolation Pilot Plant in New Mexico, USA, has been designed to store contaminated material until AD 12 000.

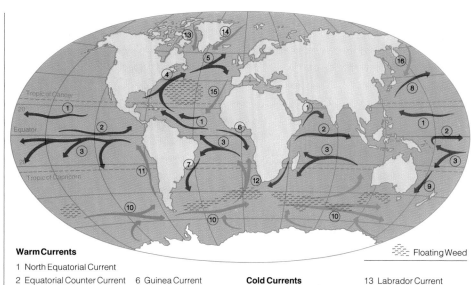

Warm Currents

1 North Equatorial Current
2 Equatorial Counter Current
3 South Equatorial Current
4 Gulf Stream
5 North Atlantic Drift

6 Guinea Current
7 Brazil Current
8 Kuroshio Current
9 East Australian Current

Cold Currents

10 West Wind Drift
11 Peru (Humboldt) Current
12 Benguela Current

13 Labrador Current
14 East Greenland Current
15 Canaries Current
16 Oyashio Current

Floating Weed

EVER-MOVING OCEANS *The oceans' surface currents carry great bodies of cold or warm water to different parts of the globe and have long been used by trading ships. Although most currents remain fairly constant, some can suddenly change course – usually during unseasonal or extreme weather.*

oasis Area in a desert surrounding a well or natural spring where there is enough water to support plant life. The water is supplied from deposits, or aquifers, in underlying sandstone; its source is sometimes more than 500 miles (800 km) away.

occluded front Region of a weather system where a WARM FRONT is overtaken by a COLD FRONT moving rapidly around a CYCLONE or depression. This pushes the warm air upwards, causing cloud and rain.

ocean Salt water oceans formed when water vapour escaped from the Earth in huge volcanic eruptions. As it fell it cooled, covering nearly 71 per cent of the Earth's surface with water. Run-off from the land dissolved minerals from the rocks, making the sea salty. The three principal oceans are the Pacific (which covers nearly 40 per cent of the globe), the Atlantic and the Indian. The ice-covered Arctic and the waters surrounding Antarctica, called the Antarctic or Southern Ocean, are much smaller.

ocean currents Surface currents are driven by prevailing WINDS and form part of huge ocean gyres – circular movements of water in each of the great ocean basins which flow clockwise in the northern seas and anticlockwise in the southern seas, due to the CORIOLIS EFFECT. A major surface current is the warm GULF STREAM which diverges to form the North Atlantic Drift;

another example is the Peru (Humboldt) Current, which in some years produces EL NIÑO. Deep ocean currents result from contrasts in the density of different water masses – for example, dense cold water is carried from the polar areas, and gradually warms to emerge at the tropics.

ocean depths The average depth of the oceans is nearly 2½ miles (4 km), with the greatest depths recorded in the Pacific Ocean trenches – 6¾ miles (10.9 km) in the Marianas Trench near the Philippines. The continental shelf regions, with an average depth of 660 ft (200 m), are of greatest economic importance, for their fishing and oil deposits. The continental slope also holds an enormous abundance of marine life – down to a depth of around 3300 ft (1000 m), below which light does not penetrate and photosynthesising plants cannot exist. But even below this depth, down to about 6600 ft (2000 m), there is a substantial animal population including giant squid and angler fish. Beyond the continental slope is the ocean floor, with depths of 20 000 ft (6000 m), characterised by the sediment-covered abyssal plain. Here scavenger fish such as the rat-tails live.

ocean ridges Series of volcanic mountains forming a 50 000 mile (80 000 km) chain along the ocean floors – the largest single feature on the Earth's crust. Sometimes the mountains rise over 10 000 ft

LETHAL POLLUTION *Effluent foams on a polluted stream near Zabrze, Poland. The city has been declared an environmental disaster area and has one of the highest infant mortality rates in Europe.*

(3000 m) to form islands such as Iceland along the Mid-Atlantic Ridge. The ridges, which form where SEA-FLOOR SPREADING takes place, help to confirm the theory of PLATE TECTONICS.

Hydrothermal vents on ocean ridges, produced by undersea volcanic activity, may have been the source of the earliest life forms on Earth. Water is driven by convective circulation and rises to temperatures above 100°C (212°F). Heat-loving microbes thrive there, providing a food source for giant plant-like tube worms.

oil Naturally occurring viscous mixture, including fossil hydrocarbons which yield combustible fuels, petrochemicals and lubricants which are extracted at different stages of ▷OIL REFINING. Crude oil consists of the partially decomposed remains of tiny sea plants and animals which have been buried under layers of rock.

Offshore oil production, which began as early as 1896 off California, now accounts for 25 per cent of total output. This will increase as offshore technology develops.

ore Rock containing minerals that yield metals or any other important elements in quantities sufficient to make mining economical. One example is bauxite, the chief ore of aluminium. Gold, silver, platinum and copper can be mined as pure metals, but most metals are found as alloys or as chemical compounds. They are deposited in veins in rocks by water containing dissolved salts. Different minerals crystallise out at different water temperatures. After ores are mined, metals are extracted by crushing, heating, electrolysis and by other chemical methods, and also by using bacteria. (See also GEMSTONES.)

ozone layer Thin concentration of ozone gas, O_3, in the upper ATMOSPHERE – 12-25 miles (20-40 km) above the Earth. Ozone is formed by the action of ▷ULTRA-VIOLET RADIATION from the Sun on atmospheric oxygen. It shields the Earth from the harmful effects of this radiation which would otherwise kill or injure most living things on the planet. Ozone can easily be destroyed by chemical reaction, especially by CFCs and nitrogen oxides from car exhausts. Satellite surveys show large 'holes' in the ozone layer around the poles, and over large urban conurbations, especially in summer. It is feared that these may be linked to an increase in skin cancers and eye cataracts, which are associated with over-exposure to ultra-violet radiation.

plate tectonics Theory that the EARTH's crust is made up of distinct plates, whose movement causes CONTINENTAL DRIFT and MOUNTAIN BUILDING. There are nine main plates, and as many as 16 smaller ones. Some plates diverge at OCEAN RIDGES, pushed apart by molten rock, or magma, forcing its way up between the plates. This process can throw up volcanic mountains above sea level. Where plates collide, or converge, one plate can sink under another, forcing the other upwards. This is called a subduction zone, and these zones circle the Pacific in a so-called 'ring of fire', where volcanoes erupt and earthquakes occur with great frequency. The plates are thought to float on denser matter beneath the Earth's crust, carried by convection currents in the

RIFTS AND COLLISIONS THAT SHAKE THE EARTH *Movement of the Earth's tectonic plates builds mountain ranges, fuels volcanoes, unleashes earthquakes and constantly renews the Earth's crust.*

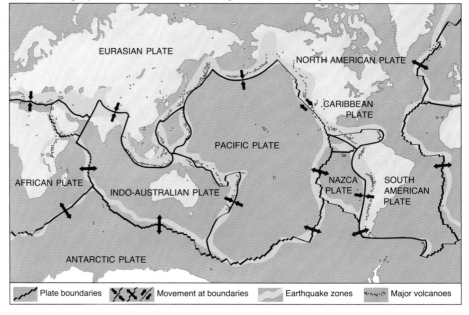

hot mantle. Over millions of years the plates have moved around the globe, reconstructing the landmasses.

🕯Hotspots occur where there are isolated magma vents within the Earth's plates; 16 of them have been identified. When a plate moves slowly over a hotspot a chain of volcanic islands forms – such as the Hawaiian Islands, where Mauna Kea rises 32 800 ft (10 000 m) from the ocean floor.

pollution Contamination by poisonous or harmful matter, as in the discharge of sewage or toxic waste, such as heavy metals, into rivers or the sea. Other forms of pollution include NUCLEAR WASTE, the emission of gases that cause ACID RAIN, GLOBAL WARMING and photochemical SMOG, and CFCs which damage the OZONE LAYER. High levels of heat, light and noise generated by industrial processes, traffic noise and amplified music are also forms of pollution. Many Western countries are introducing tougher laws to control pollution.

radiocarbon dating The age of organic material can be determined by measuring the extent of the decay of the radioactive isotope carbon-14. Radiocarbon dating is used extensively by geologists, palaeontologists and archaeologists. Carbon-14 is produced naturally in the atmosphere by the action of cosmic rays on nitrogen. During photosynthesis it is absorbed by green plants as carbon dioxide and spreads to animals through the food chain. As long as organisms continue to live, they absorb carbon-14. When they die, the absorption ceases. Carbon-14 has a radioactive ▷HALF-LIFE of 5700 years – that is, in 5700 years half the carbon-14 will have turned back into nitrogen. So by measuring how much carbon-14 remains in a sample, it is possible to work out its age. Rocks can be similarly dated using potassium-argon.

rainbow When sunlight falls on rain, spray or fog, the droplets split light into its constituent colours (red, orange, yellow, green, blue, indigo and violet), or ▷SPECTRUM, because of ▷REFRACTION. In the sky, a rainbow appears in the opposite direction to the Sun. Sometimes a double (or even triple) rainbow appears, the fainter rainbow appearing higher in the sky.

rain forest Thick forest that grows where rainfall is typically over 60 in (152 cm) a year. Equatorial, or tropical, rain forests are wet all year round. Subtropical rain forests have a MONSOON, or a wet season, and a period of drought. Rain forests are particularly rich in plant and animal life, possibly because the habitat has remained unaltered for millions of years, allowing an enormous number of species to evolve. A typical equatorial rain forest has a many-layered tree canopy. The tallest trees tower at 165 ft (50 m), with a lower layer at about 65 ft (20 m) and a third up to 50 ft (15 m). The highest level is occupied by leaf-eating monkeys, woodpeckers and flying squirrels. Inhabiting the lower canopy are immensely varied insects, fruit-feeders such as bats and hummingbirds that rely on nectar. Epiphytes, such as orchids and bromeliads grow on tree hosts without harming them.

🕯A current annual loss (now mainly in Asia) of some 20 000 sq miles (52 000 km²) of rain forest from logging and agriculture may have damaged the Earth's ability to absorb carbon dioxide, contributing to GLOBAL WARMING. It has also caused the extinction of many plants and insects. Since most nutrients and energy are locked up in the vegetation, its destruction exposes thin, poor soils to erosion.

reforestation Replanting of forest trees in an area that has been stripped of forest cover either by felling or fire. Afforestation is the planting of trees in an area not previously forested – such as a wetland.

Richter scale Measure of magnitude of an EARTHQUAKE detected on a seismograph. Introduced by C.F. Richter in 1935, the scale begins at 0 – the smallest earthquake Richter could detect – and increases by one unit for each ten-fold increase in magnitude. For example, an earthquake measuring 6 on the Richter scale – the 1994 earthquake in Los Angeles measured 6.6 – is 1000 times more powerful than one measuring 3. One of the largest recorded quakes, measuring 8.3, hit Chile in 1960.

rift valley Steep-sided, flat-bottomed valley formed by subsidence of the Earth's crust between two FAULTs.

🕯The East African Rift Valley is part of a rift system that runs from the valley of the River Jordan and the Dead Sea, through the Gulf of Aqaba, and across eastern Africa to the coast near Beira in Mozambique – a distance of 4000 miles (6400 km).

river Originating in run-off from lakes, springs or meltwater from snow fields or glaciers, rivers shape the landscape. They play an important part in the HYDROLOGIC CYCLE and in the EROSION of land above and below ground, where cave systems are formed. The speed of water flow in rivers,

UNSEASONAL SANCTUARY *This Venezuelan rain forest is home to a vast range of wildlife, but like other rain forests, it has no seasonal rhythm – every plant has its own independent life cycle.*

ROCK OF AGES *Layers of sedimentary rock line canyons in Arizona (top left); the hexagonal columns of Antrim's Giant's Causeway are igneous basalt (left); and marble at Pilbara, Australia, is a good example of metamorphic rock (above).*

which determines the amount of sediment eroded and transported, varies greatly; maximum flow usually occurs at the centre of the channel – nearer the banks it is reduced by friction. Some rivers fan out into a delta of several channels as they reach the sea, while others flow through a single estuary. Near the sea, rivers often cross a flat area where the river slows, depositing sediments as it meanders across a flood plain. An oxbow, or crescent-shaped, lake may form after a period of flood when the river cuts through its banks, bypassing the loop of a meander. An upheaval of the landmass may raise the flood plain, whereupon the process of erosion begins again.

⚓ Rivers deposit up to 8000 million tons of sediment into the oceans every year.

rock Main material of the Earth's crust, composed chiefly of various minerals. Rock can be classified into three types: igneous, sedimentary and metamorphic, according to its origin. Igneous rock is cooled directly from magma ejected from the mantle as LAVA. Examples of igneous rock include granite, the basis of continental rock and much used in building and road construction, and basalt, generated at ocean ridges. These are made up principally of the minerals quartz, feldspar, mica and hornblende, and vary in their crystal size according to how near the Earth's surface they were formed; glass-like obsidian is a surface-cooled rock, while gabbro, a basalt that

cooled deep below the Earth's crust, is made up of ½ in (13 mm) crystals. Sedimentary rock results from layers of muds and sands being deposited at the bottom of ancient seas and compressed, leaving clearly defined strata. Sandstone, shale, limestone and coal, which is formed from organic matter, are all examples of sedimentary rock. Metamorphic rock is a result of the transformation of sedimentary or igneous rock by heat, pressure and chemical action underground. Slate, schist and marble are examples; marble is metamorphosed limestone with the same chemical composition, but much denser and harder.

⚓ In the process known as the rock cycle, igneous rock is eroded and laid down as sedimentary rock, which in turn may be transformed by the action of heat and pressure into metamorphic rock, before volcanic activity turns it back into igneous rock. An entire cycle takes millions of years.

⚓ Potassium-argon is used to date rock, in a method similar to RADIOCARBON DATING. By taking the ratio of rates of decay of potassium-40 and argon-40, one meteorite was found to be 4500 million years old.

sea-floor spreading Enlarging of the sea floor on either side of an OCEAN RIDGE. It occurs where tectonic plates are moving apart and hot magma wells up from the Earth's interior. The sea floor is spreading by as much as 6½ in (17 cm) a year at some ridges. (See also PLATE TECTONICS.)

sea level The mean surface height of the sea, measured from a fixed point on land over a period of 19 years, and used as a reference point for all other altitudes. Sea level is constantly fluctuating due to tides, atmospheric pressure, winds and currents; the density of sea water can also affect it. Satellite surveys are now used to measure changes in sea level.

⚓ Major climatic changes such as ICE AGES caused a lowering of sea level because sea water was locked up in ice caps. During the last ice age, the huge weight of ice caused much of northern Europe and North America to sink. When the ice retreated, these areas started to rise, sometimes leaving coastal features well inland. Stockholm is still rising at a rate of 16 in (40 cm) a century. Sea level has also continued to rise since the last ice age – at a rate of about ½ in (13 mm) a year this century. This may also be partly due to the melting of ice caps as a result of GLOBAL WARMING.

seismic wave Shock wave transmitted through the Earth from an EARTHQUAKE or explosion, which can cause giant waves or TSUNAMIS. The reflection and refraction of man-made seismic waves are used to locate oil, natural gas and minerals, as well as to study the Earth's inner structure.

smog Mixture of smoke and fog that hangs in a pall over large cities. There are two types: sulphurous smog, produced by coal burning, and photochemical smog, caused by the action of sunlight on hydrocarbons and nitric oxides emitted from car exhausts. The gases formed, including ozone, which is toxic at low altitudes, damage plants, irritate the eyes and cause distress to people with respiratory complaints.

soil Agriculturalists classify soils as sands, clays, or loams. Sands have large particles (0.02–2 mm) and dry out quickly in the sun. Clays have tiny particles (0.002 mm) and are heavy, sticky and easily waterlogged. Loam is a fertile mixture of sand, clay, humus (dead and rotting organic material) and living organisms. Geologists classify soils according to their origin: alluvial soils are formed by particles of eroded rock deposited by rivers; drift, or till, is left by glaciers; loess is soil that has been carried by the wind; and sedimentary soil comes directly from the breakdown or weathering of the underlying bedrock. In horticulture, soil is measured in terms of its acidity or alkalinity – its pH value. This can vary in a garden, depending on how the soil has been treated, but ranges from pH5 (acid) to pH8 (alkaline) with most plants preferring pH6.5.

stalactites and stalagmites Tapering rock formations in limestone caves which hang from the roof (stalactites) or grow from the floor (stalagmites). They form mainly from calcium carbonate, although other carbonates and sulphides are also deposited. Taking thousands of years to grow, stalactites and stalagmites do not necessarily form in pairs, but where they do, they eventually join to form a column.

temperature inversion A rise in the temperature of the atmosphere with increasing altitude – the reverse of the usual situation in which air temperature drops with altitude. Temperature inversions prevent air circulating freely in convection currents and often occur at a COLD FRONT or WARM FRONT. They can often happen over cities where air pollution prevents sunlight from reaching the ground: warm air in the upper atmosphere traps cooler, polluted air near the ground, causing SMOG. Nocturnal temperature inversions frequently lead to fog.

thunderstorm Storm caused by strong, rising air currents, accompanied by LIGHTNING. When a deep layer of moist air is forced to rise by a COLD FRONT or by heating from warm ground, the water vapour in it condenses, releasing heat and accelerating the updraft. Higher still the water droplets freeze, releasing yet more heat. The clouds rise until they reach the tropopause in the ATMOSPHERE, where hot air can rise no further, giving them their flat-topped anvil shape. This generates a down-current, leading to heavy rain or hail.
🔥Although thunder and lightning occur at the same time, light from a stroke travels nearly 700 times faster than sound so that the thunder is heard later – about 5 seconds for every 1 mile (1.6 km) away.
🔥Thunderstorms are rare in polar regions where the ground produces little heat, but in Java they occur on up to 320 days a year.

tidal wave Common but incorrect name for a TSUNAMI – a large incoming wave.

tide Regular rise and fall of sea level caused by differences in the gravitational pull on different points on the Earth's surface. Because it is nearer to the Earth, the Moon's effect is more than twice that of the Sun, while other planets produce much slighter effects. Where the Moon's pull is dominant, tides occur 50 minutes later each day, because of the Moon's motion. Where the Sun is dominant, as at Tahiti, tides occur at the same time each day. When the Sun and Moon are both in the same

direction, at a new or full Moon, their effects reinforce one another, producing a particularly high or spring tide. At first and last quarters of the Moon, the Sun and Moon pull in opposite directions, producing a low or neap tide. The shape and size of the oceans moderate the effects of the Moon's gravitational force. Tides range from 54½ ft (16.6 m) at the Bay of Fundy, Nova Scotia, to 2 ft (60 cm) around the shores of the Mediterranean.
🔥A tidal range of 10 ft (3 m) or more can be harnessed to generate electricity. Tidal power stations operate at the Bay of Fundy and on Brittany's River Rance. The Severn Estuary is Britain's most suitable site.
🔥Tidal friction has slowed the Earth's rotation. Daily growth lines on fossilised corals from the Devonian period 400 million years ago show that within one year, which lasted about the same length of time as now, there were more than 400 days.

tornado Narrow, rapidly spinning funnel of air that descends from a thundercloud – an extreme example of spiralling air in a CYCLONE. Tornadoes, also known as twisters, are stronger than HURRICANES, blowing at speeds of up to 500 mph (800 km/h), with a violent updraft that lifts lorries and even entire buildings.
🔥Tornadoes occur commonly in 'Tornado Alley' which runs northeastwards across Oklahoma and Kansas, USA. Warm, moist air from the Gulf of Mexico meets cold, dry air from the Rockies on the Great Plains, giving rise to daily storms in late spring.

tsunami Japanese word for a giant wave caused by an earthquake. At sea the wave may be hundreds of miles long and travel at speeds of up to 400 mph (650 km/h). In deep water it is relatively harmless, but in shallow water its speed and length diminish rapidly causing it to rear up as high as 270 ft (82 m) as the waters surge inland.

volcano Vent in the Earth's crust from which molten rock, or magma, in the form of LAVA, is ejected, together with gases and ash. Active volcanoes usually lie along plate boundaries and their existence is explained by PLATE TECTONICS. The shape of the volcano depends on the composition of its lava. In Hawaii eruptions occur slowly with fluid, low silica lava flowing over large areas. Stromboli, off north Sicily, and also Mount Fuji, Japan, erupt more strongly,

VOLATILE VOLCANO *The Hawaiian volcano Kilauea spewing volcanic ash 1000 ft (300 m) high into the air. Kilauea erupts about every three weeks, for just a few hours or for days at a time.*

expelling ash and rivers of more viscous, high silica lava, resulting in a steeper sided, cone-shaped volcano. Some eruptions such as Mount St Helens in California, which blew in 1980, and Mount Pinatubo in the Philippines, which erupted in 1991, made huge explosions, throwing out rock, ash and clouds of gas into the atmosphere, probably causing GLOBAL WARMING, by stopping heat from the Earth escaping, and other long-term changes to the weather. The most violent explosions blow out the interior of the volcano forming a crater, called a caldera if it is more than ½ mile (1 km) wide. Lava domes occur where the lava is so viscous that it simply piles up over the vent. Fissure vents are narrow cracks emitting lava which can be several miles long.
♒ In 1883, the eruption of Krakatoa – a volcanic Indonesian island – had 26 times the power of the greatest H-bomb test.

warm front Leading edge of an advancing warm AIR MASS. Cold air is relatively dense and warmer air tends to override it, producing a wide band of cloud and gentle persistent rain and, sometimes, widespread fog. Warm fronts tend to travel slowly and can easily be caught up by fast-moving COLD FRONTS to form OCCLUDED FRONTS.

waterspout TORNADO that occurs at sea. The vortex can suck water vapour thousands of feet into the air. Most waterspouts occur in the tropics but they can also occur in higher latitudes in summer. Waterspouts more than 100 ft (35 m) in diameter can overturn boats and cause damaging winds.
♒ In a few cases, showers of fish have been known to fall on land after a waterspout has sucked them into the sky.

water table Upper level of ground water in subterranean rock. If a layer of rock that holds water, such as sandstone, is underlaid by a layer of impermeable rock, it forms an aquifer, or underground reservoir from which water can be extracted via bore holes. If the rock surfaces, or outcrops, the water will emerge as a spring. Where water pressure in an aquifer is high enough to force the water above the water table, an artesian well can be sunk to extract water without the need for pumping.
♒ Overuse of water or drought may cause a fall in the water table from which it may take years to recover. In some arid regions resources of 'fossil' water, that existed for thousands of years in underground reservoirs, cannot be renewed. In the Middle East, scarcity of ground water, as well as diversion of water from rivers upstream, is a cause of conflict as populations swell.

weather forecasting Scientific weather forecasting began in the 17th century with the development of barometers to measure ATMOSPHERIC PRESSURE. This only became of practical significance in the 1830s when the telegraph allowed the rapid transmission of data. First attempts at shipping forecasts were made in the 19th century. Forecasters today use charts produced by computers from data collected from weather balloons (radiosondes), high-flying aircraft and satellites. The rate of approaching weather or wind speed is measured with an anemometer; at sea it is given according to the BEAUFORT SCALE.

westerlies Dominant wind system that normally blows from the 'horse' latitudes – 30° North or South – towards the poles. The wind is from the southwest in the Northern Hemisphere (hence 'southwesterlies') and from the northwest in the Southern Hemisphere. The westerlies are associated with changeable weather.

whirlpool Strong, swirling eddy or maelstrom where two tidal currents meet. Notable whirlpools occur in the Naruto Strait between Japan's Inland Sea and the Pacific; in the Strait of Messina between Sicily and mainland Italy; and off Sicily's north coast – the Charybdis whirlpool.

wind Movement of air from areas of high ATMOSPHERIC PRESSURE to areas of low pressure. Differences in atmospheric pressure are largely due to the Sun warming the atmosphere and the Earth unequally. Winds do not blow directly from a place with high pressure to places with low

pressure, their path is curved due to the CORIOLIS EFFECT. There are three main belts of prevailing wind either side of the Equator: the trade winds, the WESTERLIES and the polar easterlies, which strongly influence OCEAN CURRENTS. Along the Equator there is a region of low wind, known as the Doldrums, where the northeast and southeast trade winds meet. Sailors were dependent on the trade winds for their voyages west, hence their name. In some areas seasonal reversal of the wind results in a MONSOON. As well as the seasons, the Earth's physical features affect winds, especially local winds such as the cool summer mistral, which blows along the Rhône Valley, and the hot spring sirocco from the Sahara. In coastal areas winds often reverse daily. Strong winds may combine with high tides causing storm surges and flooding.
♒ Wind turbines are increasingly being used to produce electricity. They have the benefit of causing no air pollution, but where they are large and numerous they can be quite noisy and obtrusive.

wind-chill Index devised by the US army to assist in the design of cold-weather clothing. The stronger a cold wind blows, the quicker a body cools. It is easier to survive low temperatures in calm air than considerably higher temperatures in a strong wind. Wind-chill is incorporated into weather forecasts in cold climates by giving the equivalent temperature in calm air. At freezing point, 0°C (32°F), a 25 mph (40 km/h) wind gives a wind-chill equivalent of −16°C (3°F). At −40°C (−40°F), the same 25 mph wind gives a wind-chill equivalent of −75.5°C (−104°F).

THE WAY THE WINDS BLOW *Wind systems often start near the Equator where warm air – heated by the land and sea – rises, leaving an area of low pressure beneath it which 'sucks in' surrounding air.*

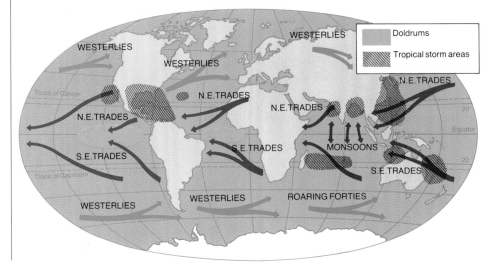

THE LIVING WORLD

Since the first living cells appeared on Earth some 4000 million years ago, evolution has produced more than 1.5 million species of living organisms. Wild plants, from tiny algae to huge trees, and wild animals from lowly insects to proud lions, have been supplemented by forms domesticated for human uses. Uniting the natural world is the discovery that one type of molecule, DNA, controls all forms of life.

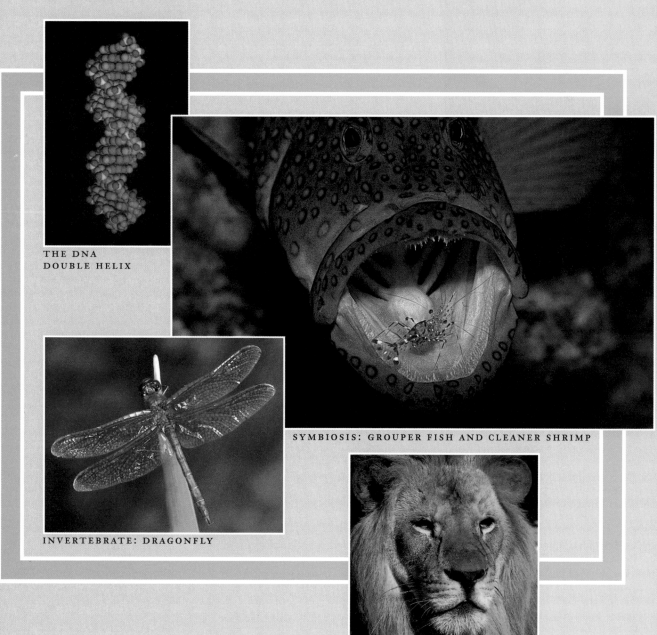

THE DNA
DOUBLE HELIX

SYMBIOSIS: GROUPER FISH AND CLEANER SHRIMP

INVERTEBRATE: DRAGONFLY

VERTEBRATE: LION

FLYING FIGHTERS *A resident male mute swan surges across the water in a show of fierce aggression to threaten an intruder. When his territorial rival fails to retreat, he strikes out with wings so forceful they can kill an opponent.*

acquired characteristics Features that an organism acquires during its lifetime. The muscles developed by a body builder are one example. In the early 19th century, the French biologist Jean Baptiste Lamarck (1744–1829) suggested that parents might pass on such acquired characteristics to their offspring, and so bring about evolutionary change. Lamarck believed, for example, that giraffes 'stretched' their necks by browsing on tall trees, and that each generation 'inherited' slightly longer necks from their parents. However, his theories were superseded by those of British naturalist Charles DARWIN.

adaptation Any feature or special ability that improves an organism's chances of survival in its environment. Adaptations can be anatomical, physiological or behavioural. The fins of fishes and whales are adaptations to water; the wings of bats and birds are adaptations to air; and hibernation is an adaptation to cold winters. Such adaptations are usually the result of natural selection over many generations. Adaptations of individuals during their own lifetime – for example, the development of greater lung capacity by people who move to mountain areas where there is less oxygen – are not passed on to their offspring, and they are more properly called ACQUIRED CHARACTERISTICS.

aestivation Dormancy in reponse to heat or drought; the summer counterpart of HIBERNATION. Breathing almost ceases, and the animal stops eating. Aestivators are usually cold-blooded. For example, some African lungfish species spend the summer buried in dried swamp mud, becoming active again when the autumn rains come.

aggression Animals use aggression to attack, to defend and to threaten opponents, usually of the same species. Aggression is used to establish and defend a territory, as well as during courtship, when rival males compete fiercely for females. It is also used to establish and maintain a position within a social hierarchy. Between members of the same species, aggression generally takes the form of ritualised fighting where injury is unlikely to occur. However, fighting between members of different species, over food, for example, often results in injury or even death.

algae Simple plant-like organisms which live mainly in water, although some species are found in damp conditions on land. There are more than 25 000 species of algae ranging from microscopic single cells to seaweeds up to 200 ft (60 m) in length. Algae belong to the kingdom Protista.

alternation of generations Phenomenon among all plants and some animals of alternating between asexual and sexual REPRODUCTION from one generation to the next. Among plants, mosses and ferns show alternation of generations most clearly. The green moss plant reproduces sexually to produce a spore-producing capsule. This reproduces asexually, releasing spores that grow into a new sexually reproducing stage. Animals showing alternation of generations include greenfly, which during the summer reproduce asexually, producing large numbers of offspring; in the autumn, they reproduce sexually, ensuring variation in their young.

amino acids Building blocks of PROTEINS, which are found in all living things. All amino acids are made up of combinations of carbon, hydrogen, nitrogen and oxygen; some also contain sulphur. Plants and some microorganisms can make all the amino acids they require through PHOTOSYNTHESIS. Animals can make only some of the amino acids they need; the remainder have to be supplied by their diet.

amoeba Single-celled protozoan that can be up to 1 mm in length. Most species of amoeba live in water, mud or soil; some are parasitic, and one species is responsible for human amoebic dysentery. Amoebas move by sending out projections called pseudopodia ('false feet'). They feed on other tiny organisms and bacteria by surrounding and engulfing them. Amoebas, which belong to the kingdom Protista, reproduce asexually, simply by splitting in two.

amphibians Cold-blooded vertebrates such as frogs, toads, newts and salamanders that typically spend part of their lives on land and part in water. Most amphibians begin life as water-dwelling LARVAE before changing, by METAMORPHOSIS, into air-breathing adults. They have moist, soft skin, with poison glands, but without scales, which would inhibit respiration. Amphibians evolved from fish 370 million years ago and were the first vertebrates to emerge from the sea – where life began – and to walk on land.
🔖The term amphibian derives from the Greek *amphibios*, 'living a double life'.

angiosperms Flowering plants belonging to the phylum Angiospermophyta and comprising by far the largest group of plants, ranging from the oak tree to the daisy. All angiosperms (literally 'cased seeds') produce seeds within a mature ovary, or fruit, unlike the other seed-bearing plants, or GYMNOSPERMS.

animal Unlike plants, animals cannot manufacture their own food. They obtain it by eating either plants, animals or both. With some exceptions, such as coral, most animals are also able to move from one location to another. They usually have specialised senses and respond quickly to stimuli. They range in complexity from simple sponges to humans, but they all belong to the kingdom Animalia. (See box.)

annelids Soft-bodied, segmented worms belonging to the phylum Annelida. Annelids have a simple circulatory and nervous system. Some 9000 species are found in sea and fresh water as well as most habitats on land; these include earthworms, ragworms and leeches. The largest, a South African earthworm, grows up to 22 ft (7 m) long.

annual Flowering plant which completes its life cycle within one year. (Compare BIENNIAL and PERENNIAL.)

antennae Pair of long thin sensory organs which project from the heads of ARTHROPODS. The antennae can be moved around and are normally used to touch, smell and judge air and water currents. Some crustaceans also use them for swimming.

arachnids Class of ARTHROPODS, mostly land-living, characteristically having four pairs of legs, simple eyes and no antennae.

They include spiders, scorpions, ticks and mites. Spiders have poisonous fangs, while scorpions have claws and a poisonous sting; both are carnivores, or flesh-eaters. Most mites and ticks are parasites.

arthropod Organism belonging to the phylum Arthropoda, a group of invertebrates which have a hard external segmented skeleton, supporting and protecting the body. Its antennae, mouthparts and jointed legs are all arranged in pairs. Arthropods make up about 85 per cent of all animal species. The main arthropod groups are INSECTS, ARACHNIDS, CRUSTACEANS, centipedes and millipedes.

autotroph Organism that can make all the complex organic molecules necessary for it to survive from simple inorganic molecules. The most familiar autotrophs are green plants, which make food and materials for growth and repair using sunlight energy, water and carbon dioxide by PHOTOSYNTHESIS. Other autotrophs include ALGAE and some BACTERIA. All other organisms are HETEROTROPHS.

bacteria (singular: bacterium) Microscopic, mostly single-celled organisms that are among the simplest living creatures and lack the nucleus found in more complex cells. They make up the kingdom Monera. Simple bacteria were the first forms of life to appear on Earth 4 billion years ago. Some types of bacteria are HETEROTROPHS, living as parasites, or as SAPROTROPHS which play a vital role in breaking down dead matter and recycling it into the soil. Other types are AUTOTROPHS, using light or chemicals as their source of energy. Many parasitic bacteria cause diseases, such as tetanus in humans, and crown gall in plants. The genetic manipulation of bacteria for commercial purposes – for example, the mass production of human insulin – is an important aspect of biotechnology.

biennial Flowering plant which requires two growing seasons to complete its life-cycle. Food reserves built up in the first season are used to produce flowers and seeds in the second. Biennials include caraway, hemlock and the evening primrose. (Compare ANNUAL and PERENNIAL.)

THE ANIMAL KINGDOM

The animal kingdom's wide embrace includes birds, fish, insects and human beings. Invertebrates evolved from single-celled organisms more than 600 million years ago; vertebrates evolved from invertebrates some 100 million years later. Animals may be as different as leeches and lions but the vast majority share typical characteristics, such as the power of locomotion, fixed structure and limited growth. They are grouped into around 35 phyla and then into classes such as mammals and birds, as this simplified chart shows.

ANIMALS
Kingdom Animalia   (* = number of species)

INVERTEBRATES   **VERTEBRATES**

SPONGES *Phylum Porifera* * 9000

ROUNDWORMS *Phylum Nematoda* * 12 000 e.g. eelworm

MOLLUSCS *Phylum Mollusca* * 100 000 e.g. snail, octopus

ECHINODERMS *Phylum Echinodermata* * 7000 e.g. starfish, sea urchin

CHORDATES *Phylum Chordata*

COELENTERATES *Phylum Coelenterata* * 9000 e.g. jellyfish, coral

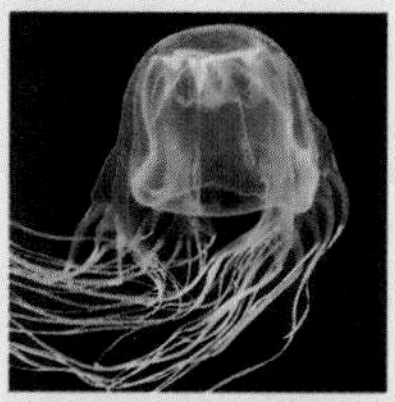

FLATWORMS *Phylum Platyhelminthes* * 20 000 e.g. tapeworm

TRUE WORMS *Phylum Annelida* * 15 000 e.g. earthworm, leech

CARTILAGINOUS FISH *Class Chondrichthyes* * 620 e.g. shark, ray

REPTILES *Class Reptilia* * 6000 e.g. snake, crocodile

BIRDS *Class Aves* * 9000

ARTHROPODS *Phylum Arthropoda*

BONY FISH *Class Osteichthyes* * 25 000+ e.g. cod, plaice

MAMMALS *Class Mammalia* * 4000 e.g. lion, monkey

INSECTS *Class Insecta* * 800 000+

MILLIPEDES *Class Myriapoda* * 7500

SPIDERS/SCORPIONS *Class Arachnida* * 70 000

AMPHIBIANS *Class Amphibia* * 4000 e.g. frog, salamander

CENTIPEDES *Class Chilopoda* * 2500

CRUSTACEANS *Class Crustacea* * 32 000 e.g. crab, lobster

bioluminescence Production of light by certain living organisms. Some animals use the light to attract a mate, others to attract a meal. Glow worms, fireflies as well as some algae and deep sea fish are bioluminescent.

birds There are more than 9000 species of birds. They range in size from the bee hummingbird which weighs just 0.05 oz (1.6 g) to the flightless North African ostrich which may weigh as much as 275 lb (125 kg) and stand 8 ft tall. Birds can be found in almost all the Earth's habitats. Scientists now believe they evolved from flesh-eating dinosaurs around 220 million years ago. They became adapted to flight by evolving feathers, hollow bones for lightness, and feet modified as claws. Feathers not only permit flight, they also insulate the body, enabling birds to maintain their constant high body temperature of up to 40.5° C (105° F) which allows them to be so active. Most birds incubate their eggs in nests, sometimes in huge colonies, and care for their young, which, in many species, are born naked and helpless. Many birds migrate in autumn to warmer feeding grounds, returning in spring to breed. Birds are warm-blooded vertebrates and belong to the class Aves. (See also MIGRATION.)

bivalve Mollusc with a shell made of two parts or valves connected by an elastic hinge. Bivalves, which include mussels, oysters and clams, live in sea and fresh water; some attach themselves to rock, while others bury themselves in sand or mud. Most feed on small particles extracted from water. Some bivalves are hermaphrodites with male organs developing first.

bulb Short underground stem wrapped in fleshy leaves which enclose a young shoot. In spring, the shoot grows upwards, using food from the fleshy leaves. After flowering, the plant dies back, storing food in the bulb during the winter ready to grow again next spring. Tulips, irises and onions all grow from bulbs. (Compare CORM.)

camouflage Most animals use camouflage to escape their predators, but avoiding detection can also be useful for animals waiting to ambush prey. Leopards, for example, are difficult to see in dappled sunlight. Countershading – a dark back and a light stomach – is used by many fish, such as sharks and barracudas. Seen from above, the fish blends into the dark water, while from below, the light belly disappears into the sunlit surface. Chameleons change colour to blend with their surroundings by using pigment cells that can produce different patterns as well as colours.

carbohydrates Group of organic compounds which are the main source of energy for living things. Energy is derived by breaking down carbohydrates in RESPIRATION. The simplest carbohydrates are sugars, such as glucose and sucrose. But they are stored in complex forms – as glycogen in animals and as starch in plants.

cell Basic unit of life and the smallest part of a living organism that can lead an independent existence. Some simple organisms, such as BACTERIA, consist only of single cells, but all higher animals and plants are composed of large numbers of cells, organised into specialised tissues and organs; the human body contains 50 million million cells. All cells are enclosed within a thin membrane, which controls the passage of water, chemicals and waste products in and out of the cell. Within the membrane is the protoplasm which, in almost all cells, is divided into a nucleus and the watery cytoplasm. The nucleus is the control centre of the cell. It is here that the genetic material DNA, which contains the coded instructions for the growth and maintenance of the cell, is stored. The manufacturing centre of the cell is the cytoplasm, which is scattered with a number of structures called organelles. Among these are the mitochondria, where the reactions involved in RESPIRATION, the universal source of energy for the cell, take place, and the RIBOSOMES, where instructions from the DNA are used to assemble ENZYMES and other proteins. Plant cells differ from animal cells in having a tough outer wall of cellulose, which helps support the plant, and a central vacuole filled with sap, which keeps the cell rigid. Green plant cells also contain lens-shaped organelles, called chloroplasts; these are filled with the pigment chlorophyll, which captures the Sun's energy during PHOTOSYNTHESIS.

cell division The process that enables living things to grow, maintain themselves and reproduce. When a cell divides, it passes on a copy of its paired CHROMOSOMES, which contain the genetic material DNA, to each of its two offspring. In ordinary cell division, known as mitosis, each 'daughter' cell receives an exact copy of the parent cell's chromosomes. Mitosis is the form of cell division that takes place when a single fertilised cell develops into a complex multi-cellular organism such as a human being. The mechanism by which cells differentiate during growth to become, for example, nerve, muscle or bone, is still one of the great mysteries of biology. A different form of cell division, called meiosis, is used to produce sex cells, such as sperm or eggs: the daughter cells receive only half the full complement of chromo-

CLEVER COLOURING *The horned toad adopts a convincing camouflage to avoid detection by predators and merges into the leafy background of its natural habitat in the rain forests of Malaysia.*

ANIMAL AND PLANT CELLS

The cell is the microcosm of life. It builds up and breaks down molecules, stores energy and releases it, sends and receives messages and reproduces. Its nucleus, containing DNA, floats in cytoplasm enclosed in a membrane. Although their structure is different, both animal and plant cells grow and develop by replicating their cells and dividing them.

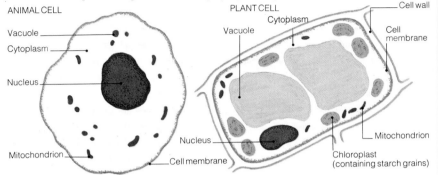

ANIMAL CELL
Vacuole
Cytoplasm
Nucleus
Mitochondrion
Cell membrane

PLANT CELL
Cytoplasm
Vacuole
Nucleus
Cell wall
Cell membrane
Mitochondrion
Chloroplast (containing starch grains)

CELL TYPES *There are marked differences in the shape, structure and components of an animal cell (left) and a plant cell (right) which has chloroplasts for photosynthesis and is enclosed by a rigid wall.*

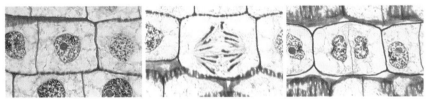

DIVISION *Images of an onion root cell during mitosis – cell division. First it duplicates its chromosomes. The duplicated chromosomes are pulled apart, each set is encircled by a separate nuclear membrane, and two new nuclei are formed. The cell is then ready to divide into two identical cells.*

somes, so that when the egg is fertilised by a sperm, the full complement is restored. In meiosis, the initial duplication of chromosomes is followed by mingling of genetic material between the two strands of each chromosome pair; the cell then divides to give two daughter cells, both of which divide once again with no further duplication of chromosomes to give a total of four daughter cells, each containing only a single strand of each chromosome pair.

cellulose Major component of plant cell walls which helps to support plants. Cellulose is a complex CARBOHYDRATE.
🐾Animals lack the enzymes to break down cellulose, so those with a diet high in cellulose – such as rabbits, cattle, horses, sheep and termites – use the services of specialised bacteria in their digestive systems. Without these bacteria, such animals would die.

cephalopod Class of marine mollusc, including squid, cuttlefish and octopus. They are distinguished by the mobile 'arms' around their heads used for catching and holding their prey, as well as by their excellent eyesight and their beaks. All

cephalopods are predators and excellent swimmers. They swim by squirting out water in a form of jet propulsion.

cetaceans Group of aquatic mammals that includes whales, porpoises and dolphins. Unlike fish, cetaceans breathe air; they do not have scales, they are warm-blooded, they give birth to their young live and they suckle their babies. Cetaceans breathe through a blowhole in the top of the head, and some whales can hold their breath for several hours.

chlorophyll See PHOTOSYNTHESIS.

chromosomes Coiled structures in the nucleus of cells which carry the GENES that determine the characteristics of every organism. Chromosomes always come in pairs, except in sex cells, and all members of a species have the same number. Humans have 23 pairs. Chromosomes only become visible under a microscope when the DNA molecules from which they are formed become shorter and thicker just before the cell splits in two, during CELL DIVISION. Mammals, which reproduce sexually, have a pair of sex chromosomes that are identi-

fied as X and Y; females have two Xs and males have an X and a Y.
🐾Sometimes during meiosis – the process of cell division that produces sex cells – chromosomes fail to separate, leaving the offspring with an extra chromosome in each cell. In humans, an extra chromosome in pair 21 causes Down's syndrome.

circadian rhythm A 24-hour cycle of behaviour, as for example in sleep patterns and in the movement of flowers' petals. It is usually determined by the presence or absence of light. Normal patterns of behaviour continue for a few days if a subject is deprived of the normal cycle of light and dark, but then a new circadian rhythm emerges. (See also ▷BIORHYTHMS.)

classification System of arranging organisms into groups according to physiological, anatomical, or other characteristics. Organisms are divided into five kingdoms; animals, plants, fungi, protists (single-celled organisms and seaweeds), and monerans (bacteria and blue-green algae). Each kingdom is divided into phyla (singular: phylum), each phylum is divided into classes, each class into orders, each order into families, and each family into genera (singular: genus). Each genus contains one or more species; species are organisms that are very similar and that can interbreed to produce fertile offspring. Humans (*Homo sapiens*), for example, belong to the genus *Homo*, the family Hominoidea (together with gorillas and chimpanzees), the order Primates (with apes, monkeys and lemurs), the class Mammalia (all mammals), the phylum Chordata (with birds, reptiles, amphibians and fishes) and the kingdom Animalia (all animals).
🐾The modern system of classification and naming of species was devised by the Swedish botanist Carolus Linnaeus (1707-78).

climax community Final stage of succession in a stable ▷ECOSYSTEM. Barring human intervention or natural disaster, a climax community should stay the same almost indefinitely. The most common examples are forests, such as the Brazilian rain forest, but others include areas of the African savannah or the prairies of the American west, where there are large herds of grazing animals.

clone Organism that is genetically identical to its parent because it has been produced by asexual REPRODUCTION. Some plants, such as strawberries and blackberries, clone themselves by means of vegetative propagation, sending out horizontal shoots, or runners, that root themselves, and produce new plants. Single-celled organisms which reproduce by budding, or splitting in two, such as yeast or amoebas, are also cloning. Some invertebrates, such as aphids, reproduce rapidly by cloning.

The possibility of cloning humans or extinct organisms, such as dinosaurs, is a favourite theme of science fiction writers. While such a process is possible in theory, many biologists doubt whether it will ever be achieved in practice.

cocoon Protective covering of eggs or larvae produced by some invertebrates. Many insect larvae spin a cocoon around themselves in preparation for turning into pupa, during their METAMORPHOSIS.

Most commercial silk is obtained from the cocoon of the Chinese silk moth.

coelenterate Animals that belong to the phylum Coelenterata are mostly sea-dwelling, and include jellyfish, anemones and corals. They have a central digestive cavity with a single opening that takes in food and expels waste. The opening is surrounded by tentacles with stinging cells which inject poison into prey.

cold-blooded or exothermic. Term which describes an animal whose body temperature is largely dependent on its environment. In fact, the blood of a cold-blooded animal may be very warm. All animals,

apart from birds and mammals, are cold-blooded. As their temperature increases, the more active cold-blooded creatures become. Lizards, for example, bask on warm rocks until they are warm and active enough to go in search of food.

conifers Most conifers have needle-like leaves and are EVERGREEN, although some, such as larches, drop their needles once a year. The group includes shrubs and cone-bearing trees such as cedars, pines and firs. The oldest trees are conifers, the 5000-year-old bristlecone pines. A sequoia known as 'General Sherman' in California is the most massive single living thing; it has a girth of 80 ft (24 m) and stands 267 ft (81 m) high. The tallest living tree is a Californian redwood – 371 ft (113 m) high. Most conifers are GYMNOSPERMS and belong to the phylum Coniferophyta.

corm Swollen stem at the base of a plant which forms an underground food store during dormant periods. In spring, the corm provides energy for the growth of leaves and flowers. Crocuses and gladioli grow from corms. (Compare BULB.)

cotyledons First seed leaves of a plant, which form part of the embryo plant and provide the food for it to grow into a seedling. Flowering plants are classified either as MONOCOTYLEDONS, which have one cotyledon in their seeds, or as DICOTYLEDONS which usually have two.

courtship Pattern of behaviour which an animal adopts to show it is ready to mate with one of its own species. The distinctive pattern is designed to attract a mate and also to counter the potential partner's natural fear or aggression. Animals such as peacocks give elaborate displays, while some male frogs and toads puff up their throats and croak. Courtship displays are also an important part of sexual selection.

crustacean Group of mainly aquatic arthropods, which includes crabs, shrimps and barnacles; woodlice are terrestrial crustaceans. Crustaceans typically have a hard outer skeleton, jointed limbs used for movement and capturing food, a body divided into an abdomen and a head with compound eyes and a thorax covered by a shield-like carapace.

The world's largest crustacean is the Japanese spider crab, which measures 18 in (46 cm) across its body and up to 10 ft (3 m) from the tip of one leg to the tip of the leg

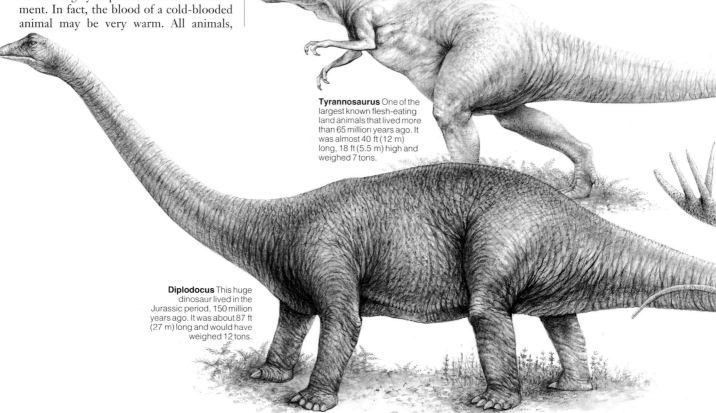

Tyrannosaurus One of the largest known flesh-eating land animals that lived more than 65 million years ago. It was almost 40 ft (12 m) long, 18 ft (5.5 m) high and weighed 7 tons.

Diplodocus This huge dinosaur lived in the Jurassic period, 150 million years ago. It was about 87 ft (27 m) long and would have weighed 12 tons.

opposite. Lobsters are more commonly measured by weight, and some giants weigh more than 40 lb (18 kg).

cultivar Cultivated variety of plant developed as a result of agricultural or horticultural intervention. Strains of many plants, such as wheat, have been bred to be resistant to pests and bad weather conditions, while still producing a high yield.

Darwin, Charles Robert (1809-82) British naturalist whose concept of natural selection formed the basis for his theory of EVOLUTION. Darwin began to develop his ideas in the 1830s during an expedition to South America and the Galápagos Islands on HMS *Beagle*. In 1859, he published *On The Origin of Species by Means of Natural Selection*, in which he set out his theory that species evolve because nature selects those characteristics that help an individual to survive and breed. This, and his later *The Descent of Man* (1871), suggesting that humans and apes shared a common ancestor, provoked violent opposition from the Church, since it challenged the Biblical account of the Creation and implied that humans had not been created in God's

EVOLUTIONIST *Charles Darwin who conceived the once provocative theory that humans and apes share a common ancestry.*

image. However, most scientists adopted Darwin's theories. They have since been modified and extended in the light of advances in genetics, and are today readily accepted by all but the most conservative of religious fundamentalists.

deciduous Term describing plants that, unlike EVERGREENS, shed their leaves at the end of each growing season – in autumn in temperate regions, or at the start of the dry season in the tropics. Leaf fall helps prevent water loss when water is scarce, either because the soil is frozen or dry. The term may also describe antlers, or children's milk teeth, that are shed at a specific stage.

dicotyledons or dicots. Most abundant of the two groups of flowering plants, with some 170 000 species. Dicotyledons have two or more COTYLEDONS in their seeds, net-veined leaves, and flower parts arranged in multiples of four or five. They include the majority of deciduous trees, cactuses and roses. (Compare MONOCOTYLEDONS.)

Stegosaurus This slow-moving Jurassic dinosaur, a herbivore which lived 150 million years ago, grew up to 30 ft (9 m) long, weighed around 2 tons and had a brain about the size of a satsuma.

dinosaurs Group of REPTILES, now extinct, which were the dominant land animals on Earth from around 230 million to 65 million years ago. Dinosaurs – the name comes from the Greek for 'terrible lizard' – lived on every continent and at least 1000 species have been recorded, ranging from fiercesomely equipped predators such as *Tyrannosaurus rex* and the savage *Velociraptor* to giant browsing herbivores, or plant-eaters, like the huge, long-necked *Brachiosaurus* and the armour-plated *Stegosaurus*. Some dinosaurs were probably endothermic (warm-blooded), unlike modern-day reptiles. They laid eggs and some showed parental care. The two main divisions of the dinosaurs were the Saurischia, or lizard-hipped dinosaurs, which included the flesh-eaters, as well as huge plant-eaters such as *Apatosaurus*; and the Ornithischia, or bird-hipped dinosaurs, which included herbivores such as iguanodons and duck-billed hadrosaurs. The reason for the extinction of the dinosaurs remains a mystery. The fact that many other species became extinct at around the same time – including such groups as the giant flying pterosaurs and the marine plesiosaurs – suggests that some cataclysmic event, such as a collision with an asteroid resulting in a sudden change in climate, might have been responsible.

In his film *Jurassic Park* (1993), Steven Spielberg invented a new 'type' of the *Velociraptor* family because none of the species then known about

Brachiosaurus This Jurassic herbivore measured up to 82 ft (25 m) long, 52 ft (16 m) high and weighed about 70 tons.

were large enough for the film's dramatic purpose. After the film was made, fossils were discovered of a dinosaur that matched his invention in almost every detail. It was named *Utahraptor* after the North American state in which it was found.

DNA (deoxyribonucleic acid) Molecule found in the cells of all living things, which contains the genetic information that makes individuals different from each other but similar to their parents and others of the same species. In all except the most primitive cells, DNA is found in the CHROMO-SOMES in the cell nucleus. It consists of two long chains of organic compounds, called nucleotides, joined together in a double helix structure – like a twisted rope-ladder. Before CELL DIVISION, the DNA molecule 'unzips' down the middle and each half acts as the template for the creation of the missing half; in this way, two molecules are created where there was one before. There are only four kinds of nucleotides, and many thousand are required to make up one gene. Each gene controls the manufacture of a single protein, for example an ENZYME, using a closely related 'messenger' molecule called RNA to carry the genetic message from the nucleus to the cytoplasm, where it ensures that AMINO ACIDS are linked in the correct order to produce a specific protein. The arrangement of nucleotides copied from DNA onto RNA determines which amino acids are used: this is the genetic code. The combined effect of many different genes can determine eye or hair colour, or whether the organism will become a flower or a human being.

The unravelling of DNA's structure in 1953 won Nobel prizes for James Watson, Francis Crick and Maurice Wilkins, and led to, among other discoveries, genetic engineering, DNA 'fingerprinting' and the attempt to map the entire human DNA.

dodo Extinct bird which lived on Mauritius, with several related species on other islands in the Indian Ocean. Its numbers dwindled after the arrival of man; flightless and ponderous, it was an easy target for hunters. The last dodo was sighted in 1681.

dormancy Period in the life cycle of a plant or animal during which normal functions are slowed down or suspended.

echolocation Method used by bats, dolphins and some other animals to detect objects using hearing rather than sight. They emit sounds, usually as high-pitched clicks or pulses, and form a picture of their surroundings from the returning echoes.

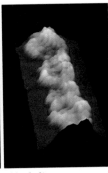

COIL OF LIFE *The double helix structure of DNA, modelled by computer (left) and seen through an electron microscope (right), contains the inherited genetic code that controls all life.*

egg Reproductive cell of the female animal; after fertilisation, it contains the developing EMBRYO and its food supply. Birds and most reptiles deposit the egg externally, in a protective shell, and normally incubate their eggs until hatching. Mammals and a few other animals nurture the embryo within the body and give birth to live young – a process called viviparity.

embryo Developing plant or animal, from the time the fertilised egg or ZYGOTE begins to divide until germination, birth or hatching. In mammals, the embryo is called a foetus once organs start developing; this occurs after eight weeks in humans.

enzyme Protein molecule that acts as a biological catalyst. Enzymes speed up virtually every chemical reaction that takes place in living things; without them, the processes of life would grind to a halt. They work by a type of 'lock and key' mechanism, in which only certain molecules will attach to a particular enzyme. The reaction – combining, changing, or breaking down of molecules – then takes place. Some enzymes only operate in the presence of

TAME FOOL *Dodos were named after the Portuguese word for idiot,* doudo. *The large, ungainly birds became extinct because they were so trusting and could easily be caught and killed.*

other factors known as coenzymes. In mammals and some other animals these are frequently derived from vitamins.

ephemeral Plant that completes its life cycle in the space of a few days or weeks. Many garden weeds, such as groundsel and willow-herb, are ephemeral, as are plants that bloom in the desert after rain.

epidermis Outermost layer of cells covering a plant or the body of an animal and providing a waterproof, protective cover.

epiphyte Plant that grows on another plant without harming or helping it, as many mosses and orchids do. Epiphytes are common in rain forests where airborne moisture is plentiful and minerals can be obtained from the surface of the plants they are growing on. (Compare PARASITE.)

evergreen Term describing trees and shrubs that apparently keep their leaves all year round; in fact, their leaves are lost and replaced, but not all at the same time. In hot countries most trees are evergreen. In temperate or cold climates most evergreens are CONIFERS or GYMNOSPERMS.

evolution Process by which living things change and diversify over time to produce new forms of life. Scientific theories of evolution emerged during the 19th century, as geologists and biologists began to question the Biblical account of Creation. An early and now discredited proposal, by the Frenchman Jean Baptiste LAMARCK, was that species had evolved through the inheritance of ACQUIRED CHARACTERIS-TICS. The modern theory of evolution, however, derives from the concept of natural selection put forward by Charles DARWIN (and at about the same time by the zoologist A.E. Wallace) in 1859. Darwin noted that organisms always produce more offspring than are needed to maintain the population, and that there are differences between individuals within a species. He argued that, in the competition for food and mates, those organisms best suited to the environment would be most likely to survive and pass on their individual characteristics to their offspring: successful or advantageous characteristics would survive while unsuccessful ones would be bred out – the process of natural selection. As the environment changed, or as new individual variations arose, so new characteristics would become desirable and the species would change. Eventually, entirely new species would emerge. The rediscovery of the work of the Austrian monk and botanist

Gregor MENDEL in 1900 provided a genetic basis for natural selection, and set the seal on the acceptance of Darwin's concept.

exoskeleton Hard external covering shown most clearly by the largest group of invertebrates, the ARTHROPODS which includes INSECTS and CRUSTACEANS. It performs many of the functions of an internal skeleton – protecting and supporting the internal organs and providing attachment for the muscles. Bony exoskeletons are found in tortoises, although these animals have internal skeletons as well.

extinction Disappearance of a species from the Earth. In the past, extinction has generally been the result of failure to adapt to changing climate or habitat, or to the success of some species at the expense of others. In recent times, the extinction of most species has been caused by human interference; the disappearance of many large mammals around 10 000 years ago was probably due to hunting by prehistoric humans. Modern destruction of rain forests is estimated to account for the extinction of as many as 6000 species a year.

fats See LIPIDS.

fermentation Breakdown of glucose and other sugars that releases energy, without using oxygen. Yeast is used in the production of wine and beer to ferment sugars, producing carbon dioxide and ethanol (alcohol). (Compare RESPIRATION.)

ferns Group of non-flowering plants belonging to the phylum Filicophyta. Unlike MOSS, they have true roots, stems and complex leaves. There are about 11 000 species of fern today, the largest of which, the tree ferns, grow to 80 ft (24 m). The fern plant reproduces by ALTERNATION OF GENERATIONS, releasing spores from the undersides of certain leaves. The spores germinate and eventually produce male and female sex cells which fuse to produce a ZYGOTE, which grows into a new fern plant.

fertilisation Fusion of male and female sex cells during sexual REPRODUCTION to form a single cell or ZYGOTE. Fertilisation can take a number of forms, either inside the female's body, as with birds and mammals, or externally, as with most amphibians and fish, where the male fertilises the eggs after the female has laid them. In flowering plants, fertilisation takes place after POLLINATION. A pollen tube grows towards the ovule, and carries the male sex cell to the female sex cell.

fish Diverse group of cold-blooded aquatic vertebrates. There are more than 25 000 species of fish. They breathe by extracting oxygen from the water through GILLS. Fish are divided into three types: cartilaginous, bony and jawless. Cartilaginous fish, such as sharks and rays, have a skeletal system made out of cartilage instead of bone. By far the most numerous and successful group are the bony fish, whose skeleton is made of lightweight bone; these range from minnows to ocean sunfish which can weigh more than two tons. Jawless fish, such as the lamprey, have a funnel-shaped, sucking mouth. They have neither jaws nor paired fins. Fish usually reproduce by the female laying eggs, which the male then fertilises; most fish then abandon the eggs but some will care for them either by guarding them, incubating them, or, as in the case of the seahorse, by tucking them in a pouch. In cartilaginous fish, fertilisation takes place within the female's body, after which some species lay eggs with horny cases ('mermaid's purses'); while others give birth to live young as mammals do.

flight Only insects, birds and bats are capable of true flight, using either one or two pairs of wings. All flying animals have extremely lightweight bodies and strong muscles. Birds' wings are adapted to their lifestyles. For example, songbirds, which use flapping flight, have short, stumpy wings, whereas albatrosses, which travel long distances using gliding flight, have long, tapering wings. In order to hover, as hummingbirds and some insects do, the wings are flapped very rapidly and vertically instead of diagonally.

flower Reproductive structure of ANGIOSPERMS, or flowering plants. Most flowers have brightly coloured petals to attract the insects that pollinate them, but those pollinated by the wind are normally small and

THE ANATOMY OF A FLOWER

Flowering plants – or angiosperms – are the most abundant and varied group of plants on Earth. Whether large or small, colourful or inconspicuous, every flower has the same basic function: to produce seeds so that its genes can survive. The typical flower consists of concentric rings of sepals, petals and stamens, with one or more pistils at the centre.

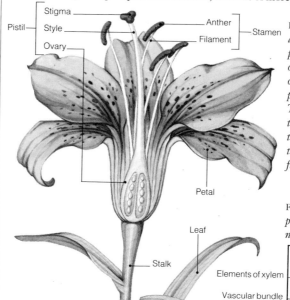

Pistil — Stigma, Style, Ovary
Stamen — Anther, Filament
Petal
Leaf
Stalk

BLOOM AND GROW *All parts of a flower are crucial. Sepals protect the bud until the flower opens. Petals attract insects and other pollinators. Filaments support pollen-producing anthers. The sticky stigma traps pollen. A tube then grows down through the style and fertilises egg cells in the ovary, which matures into a fruit that protects the seeds.*

FOOD AND WATER *Xylem and phloem cells carry water and nutrients throughout the plant.*

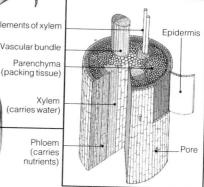

Elements of xylem
Vascular bundle
Parenchyma (packing tissue)
Xylem (carries water)
Phloem (carries nutrients)
Epidermis
Pore

inconspicuous. Most plants have male and female organs in the same flower, but some plants have separate male and female flowers. The male part, the stamen, produces pollen which contains male sex cells. The female part, the carpel, is made up of the stigma, the style and the ovary. The stigma, at the top of the style, usually has a sticky surface which receives the pollen. The style leads into the ovary within which are ovules containing the female sex cells. After FERTILISATION the ovule becomes a SEED, surrounded by the ovary which becomes the FRUIT.

fossil Remains or traces of an organism that existed in the past, preserved in rock, peat, ice, or other materials. Usually only the hard parts of the body such as the bones, shells or teeth are found as fossils in rocks; soft parts usually decay before they are fossilised. However, dinosaur footprints and prints of ferns, made in mud before it turned to rock, have been found.
♣ The oldest fossils date back some 4000 million years and provide the earliest evidence of the ORIGIN OF LIFE.

fruit Seed-bearing part of a plant; many foods that are thought of as vegetables are technically fruits. The fruit is usually formed from the ovary of the flower after fertilisation, and its biological role is to enclose and protect the seed, and help in seed dispersal. Fruit and seeds may be dispersed whole, or the fruit may open to release the seeds. Fruits are divided into two main groups: dry, such as poppy or sycamore, and succulent, such as pineapple or tomato.

fungi Like animals, fungi are unable to make their own food. Some, such as mushrooms, are SAPROTROPHS which feed on and break down dead animals and plants in the soil, others are parasites. Fungi also include moulds, rusts, toadstools, puffballs, mildews and yeasts.

gamete Sex cell, such as a sperm or an egg. One gamete joins with another – of the opposite sex – to form a ZYGOTE during FERTILISATION. Gametes are formed by a type of CELL DIVISION called meiosis.

gastropod Class of molluscs which includes snails, limpets, whelks and slugs. Typically, gastropods have a head with eyes and tentacles, a rasping tongue or radula, and a large, muscular 'foot' on which they move. Many have a spiral-shaped shell.
♣ The name gastropod derives from Latin and means 'stomach-foot' – from the way they appear to walk on their stomachs.

gene Section of DNA which forms the basic unit of inheritance. Each gene controls, on its own or with other genes, a particular characteristic. During REPRODUCTION, genes are passed on from parents to offspring. Genes occur in pairs on separate chromosomes; genes within pairs may be identical, or one gene may be dominant and the other recessive, in which case the characteristic controlled by the dominant gene will be the one shown by the organism. For example, if a human has one gene for brown eyes, and one for blue eyes, the brown eye gene dominates and that individual will have brown eyes. Each chromosome is composed of thousands of genes. Genetics, pioneered by Gregor MENDEL, is the study of how genes are inherited.

germination Beginning of a seed's growth into a seedling. Germination takes place only when conditions such as moisture and temperature are suitable.

gills Internal or external respiratory structures in aquatic animals including crustaceans, fish and amphibians. Gills are far more efficient than lungs, taking in about 80 per cent of the oxygen in the water which passes through them.

gizzard Part of the digestive tracts of some toothless animals, such as birds and many invertebrates, where food is broken down by a grinding action prior to chemical digestion. In crustaceans the gizzard's tough lining is drawn out to form 'teeth'; birds swallow stones to assist the process.

glucose Simple sugar produced by plants during PHOTOSYNTHESIS. The energy locked inside glucose is released during RESPIRATION to power all life activities.

grasses One of the commonest groups of flowering plants. They are MONOCOTYLEDONS, and their fruits are grains, many of which are cultivated as sources of food, such as wheat, maize, barley and oats.

growth Process usually achieved by CELL DIVISION and cell growth. All multicellular (many-celled) organisms begin life as a single cell which divides repeatedly. Groups of cells form different tissues, such as muscle or nervous tissues. In animals, growth takes place at different rates in almost all parts of the body. Plant growth is restricted to meristems at the tips of roots and shoots, and around the stem. However, plants continue to grow throughout their lives although, as in the case of some perennials, they may die back in winter.

gymnosperms Group of plants, including CONIFERS, that are non-flowering but produce seeds. The name gymnosperm, meaning 'naked seed', refers to the seeds not being enclosed in an ovary. (Compare ANGIOSPERM.)

heterotroph Organism that needs an external source of food to provide energy and materials for growth and repair. All animals and fungi, many bacteria and a few plants are heterotrophs. All are ultimately dependent on AUTOTROPHS, organisms that can make their own food.

hibernation Dormant state in which some creatures, including hedgehogs, insects and snails, survive winter. Their metabolism slows right down and, in warm-blooded animals, body heat drops to just above ambient temperature.

hybrid Offspring produced by crossing parents with distinct genetic differences. F1 and F2 hybrids are the first and second generation of offspring, produced by crossing different varieties of the same species. When different species are crossed, the offspring may be sterile, as when a horse and a donkey mate to produce a mule.

insects There are more than 800 000 known species of insects, and probably several million yet to be identified. Insects, which are ARTHROPODS, have three body parts: the head, the thorax and the abdomen. The head has two antennae and a pair of compound eyes. Attached to the thorax are six legs and, typically, two pairs of wings, although some insects have no wings at all. Insects breathe through holes in the thorax called spiracles. They do not have teeth, and their mouthparts vary according to the way they live. For example, grasshoppers have chewing mandibles for eating vegetation; mosquitoes have piercing mouthparts for sucking blood; and butterflies have coiled tubes, which they unroll to feed on nectar. All insects can reproduce sexually. Female insects lay eggs. After hatching, insects develop from juvenile stages to adults by METAMORPHOSIS. Different insects communicate in different ways. Cicadas, for example, use sound; fireflies use light; and many insects, including moths, use PHEROMONES.

instinct or innate behaviour. Behaviour that is inherited, not learned or modified by environmental influences. Many animals are born with responses to stimuli they will meet in their environment already incorporated in their nervous systems. It enables

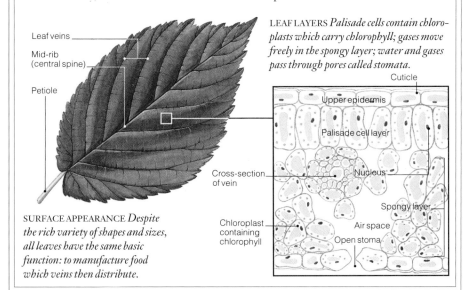

THE STRUCTURE OF A LEAF

Leaves are the most specialised and efficient food factories in a plant because they are the site of photosynthesis. When sunlight strikes a leaf, energy is absorbed by the green pigment chlorophyll. Chlorophyll acts as a catalyst to bring about chemical reactions between water and carbon dioxide – the raw materials plants use to manufacture food.

Leaf veins

Mid-rib (central spine)

Petiole

LEAF LAYERS *Palisade cells contain chloroplasts which carry chlorophyll; gases move freely in the spongy layer; water and gases pass through pores called stomata.*

Cuticle

Upper epidermis

Palisade cell layer

Cross-section of vein

Nucleus

Spongy layer

Air space

Open stoma

Chloroplast containing chlorophyll

SURFACE APPEARANCE *Despite the rich variety of shapes and sizes, all leaves have the same basic function: to manufacture food which veins then distribute.*

---

them to perform actions impossible for each generation to learn afresh. Examples of instinctive behaviour include worker bees constructing combs or newly-hatched turtles digging themselves out of the sand and making for the sea.

invertebrate Any animal without a backbone. (See Animal Kingdom box.)

larva Juvenile form of an animal that is very different from the adult, such as a frog tadpole or a fly maggot. A larva develops into an adult through METAMORPHOSIS.

leaf Food factory of most plants, where PHOTOSYNTHESIS takes place. The cells that make up the inner part of the leaves contain chloroplasts packed with chlorophyll, the green pigment that traps sunlight during photosynthesis. Above and below these cells are the upper and lower epidermis which, with the thin outer cuticle, protect the leaf and make it waterproof. Pores, or stomata, in the lower epidermis can be opened or closed by the guard cells that surround them. Carbon dioxide, one of the raw materials for photosynthesis, enters the leaf via the stomata, while oxygen, one of the products, passes out through them. Veins carry water and the products of photosynthesis to and from a leaf. In DECIDUOUS plants, flat leaves expose a large area of photosynthetic cells to sun-

light to ensure efficient food production; and in many EVERGREENS, needle-like leaves minimise water loss.

lichens Symbiotic association between FUNGI and ALGAE. The algae produce food for the fungi by PHOTOSYNTHESIS, and the fungi give protection to the algae and absorb water and minerals from their surroundings. Lichens can survive in harsh environments, such as arctic regions, where few plants can exist. (See SYMBIOSIS.)

lipids Group of compounds found in living organisms that include fats, oils and steroids, such as ▷CHOLESTEROL. Fats in animals are used for energy storage and, in mammals, for insulation. Some plants store oil in seeds to fuel their future growth. A type of lipid, called phospholipid, forms part of the structure of all cell membranes.

mammals Class of warm-blooded vertebrates which evolved more than 225 million years ago from mammal-like reptiles and is characterised by adult females that suckle their young. Today there are three types. Monotremes, which include the duckbilled platypus, are the only surviving mammals that lay leathery eggs and suckle their young from glands in the skin. The other two types of mammal, the MARSUPIALS and the placental mammals, both have mammary glands. Placental mammals, which,

during prenatal development, are nourished in the womb by a placenta, are by far the most successful of the three mammal types; they have 17 orders as opposed to the single order of marsupials. Although some mammals such as humans, elephants, seals, pigs and CETACEANS are relatively hairless, most species are covered in fur or hair which helps them to regulate their body temperature.

🔥The largest mammals are female blue whales, which can be more than 110 ft (34 m) long and weigh as much as 180 tons.

marsupials Group of mammals, found in Australasia and the Americas, which includes kangaroos, koalas and opossums. They differ from other mammals in that their young are born in a relatively undeveloped state and, guided by smell, find their way from the birth canal to an external pouch. Here the tiny marsupial remains, latched onto a teat during its early development. Later, it may leave the pouch for brief periods, returning for food and shelter until its development is complete.

Mendel, Gregor (1822-84) Austrian botanist and monk who first devised a theory of heredity in 1866. He proposed that individual characteristics were determined by 'factors' which are passed from parent to offspring. He based his ideas on experiments he conducted with pea plants. His work remained unnoticed until it was rediscovered in 1900. His theories were proved to be largely correct when scientists identified GENES.

FATHER OF GENETICS *The plant-breeding experiments of the Austrian monk and botanist, Gregor Mendel, conducted in his monastery garden, formed the basis of modern genetics.*

metamorphosis Transformation from juvenile to adult form that takes place in insects, amphibians and other animals. In complete metamorphosis, a larva changes into a pupa and on to an adult stage, or imago; insects like the beetle and the butterfly, for instance, look quite different from any of their earlier stages. In incomplete metamorphosis, as in the grasshopper, the adult looks very similar to the juvenile stage, or nymph. Metamorphosis can also occur in amphibians, such as the frog which grows from a legless, lungless tadpole into an animal that can live on land.

migration Periodic two-way movement of an animal population, commonly birds, grazing animals, seals, turtles and some fish. Animals migrate to follow a food source, to breed and to avoid cold winters. Migration is usually prompted by seasonal changes in the weather or in the hours of daylight. Frogs may move only a few hundred yards, whereas some birds migrate thousands of miles. The longest annual migrators are the Arctic terns which fly from pole to pole every year, a round trip of more than 20 000 miles (32 000 km). Migrating birds use a variety of navigational aids, including the position of the Sun and stars and the Earth's magnetic field.

mollusc Soft-bodied invertebrates, often with shells, which include GASTROPODS, such as snails, BIVALVES, such as oysters, and CEPHALOPODS, such as squid.

monocotyledons or monocots. One of two groups of flowering plants. Monocotyledons have one COTYLEDON in their seeds and their flower parts are arranged in threes or multiples of three. They include palm trees, lilies and grasses. (Compare DICOTYLEDONS.)

moss Simple land plant without true leaves, stems or roots. Mosses, which belong to the phylum Bryophyta, do not have a vascular system like other plants. Instead they absorb moisture directly through their 'leaves' and 'stems'; this explains why most live in wet habitats. Mosses show ALTERNATION OF GENERATIONS in their life cycle.

mutation Change in the genetic material (DNA) of a cell that may cause it to look or behave differently from a normal cell. Most mutations are harmful, although beneficial mutations passed down the generations may be part of natural selection and therefore contribute, as all variations may, to the process of EVOLUTION.

Caterpillar feeding on milkweed

Larva changing into a pupa

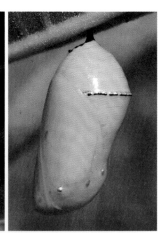
Pupa suspended from milkweed

Adult emerging from its pupa

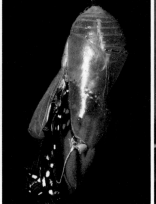
Metamorphosis is almost complete . . .

Adult monarch butterfly

LIFE'S DRAMATIC CHANGES *In the monarch butterfly, the transformation from egg to adult may take as little as two weeks. Eggs hatch into caterpillars which eat, grow and moult several times. The caterpillar, or larva, changes into a pupa from which emerges the spectacular winged adult.*

nitrogen cycle Constant recycling of nitrogen between the atmosphere and living things within an ▷ECOSYSTEM. Nitrogen is essential to all living things, as it is a basic constituent of protein. Plants make proteins using nitrates from the soil; animals obtain proteins by eating plants. Soil bacteria release nitrates from decaying organisms and the cycle begins again. Some bacteria make nitrates using nitrogen; others release nitrogen back into the air.

nymph Juvenile stage of an insect such as the grasshopper or dragonfly that resembles the adult except that its wings and reproductive organs are undeveloped.

origin of life The Earth formed around 4.6 billion years ago. The first signs of life probably appeared some 4 billion years ago as the Earth cooled and the oceans filled. The crucial step was the appearance of AMINO ACIDS – the building blocks of proteins – and the nucleic acids, molecules that can replicate themselves and control the assembly of proteins. There are several theories as to how these organic molecules were formed. One suggests that methane, ammonia and carbon dioxide in the early atmosphere reacted together during violent electrical storms; the resulting molecules dissolved in the oceans to produce a primeval 'soup' in which, over millions of years, the first living systems evolved. Alternative theories suggest that life began around hot water vents in the deep oceans, or that it arrived on meteorites from space. The first living organisms were single cells that resemble the most primitive forms of bacteria in existence today.

ovary Female reproductive organ in animals and some plants, where egg cells are produced. (See also FLOWER.)

parasite Organism which lives on or in the body of another larger organism, known as a host, on which it feeds. Parasitism differs from SYMBIOSIS in that only the parasite benefits from the association; the host generally suffers. (Compare EPIPHYTE.)

perennial Plant that continues to grow and flower each year. Herbaceous perennials die back each autumn and survive the winter underground as BULBS, CORMS or RHIZOMES. Woody perennials, such as trees and shrubs, have permanent woody stems, but may lose their leaves in winter. (Compare ANNUAL and BIENNIAL.)

pheromone Chemical released by an organism which has a specific effect on a member of the same species. Pheromones play an important role in the behaviour of many animals, in particular, insects and mammals. For example, the queen in a termite colony produces a pheromone that stops the reproductive development in the ovaries of other females.

A male emperor moth is able to detect a pheromone released by a female from 7 miles (11 km) away.

photosynthesis Process by which plants and some other organisms use sunlight to make glucose. In plants, photosynthesis takes place in the chloroplasts, which are concentrated in the cells of the LEAF. Chloroplasts are packed with chlorophyll, a green pigment, which captures the Sun's energy. This energy is then used to split hydrogen molecules from water, and combine them with carbon dioxide to form glucose. Glucose can be stored as starch or converted to other substances, such as LIPIDS and proteins, needed by the plant. The simple raw materials, water and carbon dioxide, are obtained from the soil and air respectively. In the day, when photosynthesis is occurring, oxygen is released into the air as a waste product.

Most oxygen in the atmosphere has been produced by photosynthesis.

plankton Collective term for all the minute organisms that drift with the current in seas and lakes. Plankton is an important source of food in aquatic communities; the world's largest living animal, the blue whale, feeds solely on plankton.

plant One of the five main divisions of the living world, plants are distinguished from other organisms in two ways: they can manufacture their own food, and they have no means of locomotion. Plants range in size and complexity from simple mosses to giant sequoia and redwood trees. The most successful and numerous group of plants are flowering plants or ANGIOSPERMS.

plant hormones Substances that regulate the growth and development of plants. Auxins, for example, which are produced at the growing tips of stems, roots and young leaves, encourage cells to elongate. Their effects also include growth responses, or TROPISMS, such as phototropism – growing towards light. Other plant hormones help to initiate germination of seeds; trigger fruit ripening and promote leaf fall and dormancy in seeds.

plant tissues Most multicellular green plants, except mosses, have roots, stems and leaves. These are all made up of three basic types of tissue: vascular, ground and epidermal. The transport or vascular system in plants carries two lanes of traffic. Xylem carries water and minerals from the roots and phloem carries sucrose and other nutrients from the leaves. Surrounding the vascular system is the ground tissue which, depending on its site in the plant, is used for photosynthesis, support or water absorption. The surface of the plant is covered by the epidermis – a protective outer layer.

pollen Tiny structures that contain the male sex cells of a seed-bearing plant. They are usually produced in huge numbers in pollen sacs located on the anthers of flowers and on the male cones of conifers. In order for a plant to be fertilised, POLLINATION must take place.

pollination Transfer of POLLEN from a male to a female organ of a plant, usually of a different plant of the same species. Some plants, such as conifers, grasses and some deciduous trees, are wind pollinated; pollen is blown by the wind to another plant. But most flowering plants have evolved a complex interdependent relationship with animals, especially insects, that feed on the FLOWERS and pollinate them at the same time. The bright colours and scents of flowers attract insects, which come to obtain the flower's nectar. In reaching the nectar, the insect brushes against the anthers – picking up pollen which it carries to the stigma of another flower. Other animals that pollinate plants include bats, hummingbirds and honey possums.

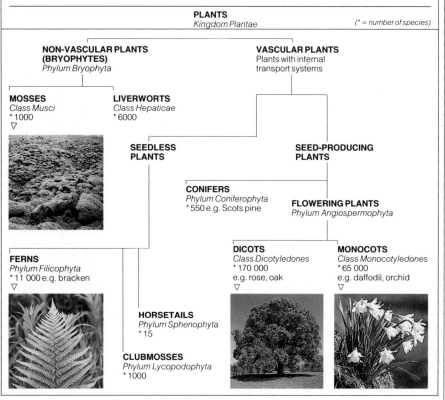

THE PLANT KINGDOM

All plants, from the smallest moss to the tallest tree, share a common feature – they make their own food by trapping energy from the sun. Plants, which evolved from green algae over 450 million years ago, make up one of the five kingdoms of living organisms. They are divided into various phyla, the largest of which contains the flowering plants.

PLANTS
Kingdom Plantae
(* = number of species)

NON-VASCULAR PLANTS (BRYOPHYTES)
Phylum Bryophyta

VASCULAR PLANTS
Plants with internal transport systems

MOSSES
Class Musci
* 1000

LIVERWORTS
Class Hepaticae
* 6000

SEEDLESS PLANTS

SEED-PRODUCING PLANTS

CONIFERS
Phylum Coniferophyta
* 550 e.g. Scots pine

FLOWERING PLANTS
Phylum Angiospermophyta

FERNS
Phylum Filicophyta
* 11 000 e.g. bracken

DICOTS
Class Dicotyledones
* 170 000
e.g. rose, oak

MONOCOTS
Class Monocotyledones
* 65 000
e.g. daffodil, orchid

HORSETAILS
Phylum Sphenophyta
* 15

CLUBMOSSES
Phylum Lycopodophyta
* 1000

predation Killing and eating of one animal (the prey) by another (the predator). Many predators' main hunting sense is vision; animals such as the dragonfly, hawk and cat, have particularly keen eyesight. Most others track their prey by scent.

primate Group of mammals that includes monkeys, apes and humans. Primates are distinguished by large brains, opposable thumbs – giving them dexterous hands – three-dimensional colour vision, a reduced snout and two mammary glands.

proteins Group of organic compounds found in all living things. Proteins are made from long chains of AMINO ACIDS, linked together in a set sequence controlled by GENES in the cell's nucleus. A particularly important group of proteins are ENZYMES, which control all the cell's chemical reactions. Proteins such as keratin and collagen give strength and elasticity to hair, feathers and scales, as well as to skin and tendons. Proteins are also an important part of muscles as well as being involved in the clotting of blood. A living organism may contain more than 10 000 different kinds of protein, each with an individual task.
🦪 Eating foods that provide a good balance of proteins is vital to people's health.

protists Microscopic organisms, most of which are single-celled, that are divided into two groups: protozoans and algae. Protozoans, such as amoeba, are described as animal-like because most eat other organisms. This group also includes the parasites that cause malaria and sleeping sickness. Algae are plant-like because they make their own food by photosynthesis. Protists belong to the kingdom Protista.
🦪 The White Cliffs of Dover are made from the remains of billions of foraminiferans – protists with microscopic shells made of calcium carbonate.

reproduction There are two types of reproduction: asexual and sexual. Asexual reproduction involves only one parent producing offspring, or CLONES identical to it. Some simple organisms, such as amoeba, reproduce asexually just by splitting in two. Many plants reproduce asexually by vegetative reproduction – sending out shoots which take root to produce independent offspring. Sexual reproduction requires the production of male and female sex cells which fuse to produce a ZYGOTE during FERTILISATION. The offspring produced by sexual reproduction receive half of each parent's GENES and so are not identical to either parent, but a 'cross' between the two.

reptiles Class of cold-blooded vertebrates, which includes turtles, lizards and snakes, crocodiles and alligators. Reptiles, which live predominantly on land, typically have scaly skins and lay leathery eggs. The largest living reptiles are the Komodo dragon, a carnivorous lizard that can grow to be more than 15 ft (4.6 m) long, and saltwater crocodiles which can weigh more than 2 tons. Reptiles' eyesight varies: some snakes can distinguish only between light and dark, whereas most lizards have keen eyesight for hunting. Crocodiles and alligators have excellent hearing when their

---

HOW SEEDS TRAVEL

Plants have evolved many strategies to send their seeds far away and ensure that young plants colonise new areas instead of crowding around them and competing for light and nutrients.

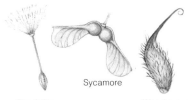

Sycamore

Dandelion   Wood avens

BLOWING IN THE WIND *Parachute and wings propel seeds through the air; hooked bur seeds cling to animals' fur.*

Poppy   Blackberry   Broom

MOVERS AND SHAKERS *Breezes shake seeds from poppy 'heads'; birds sow fruit seeds in droppings; pods burst to fling contents away.*

---

heads are out of the water; some lizards and snakes can hear only deep sounds. Both snakes and lizards use their tongues to detect odour molecules in the air. They can track prey by flicking their tongue out and transferring the molecules it has picked up into special sensory organs in the roof of the mouth. Some snakes, such as rattlesnakes, can hunt by detecting the body heat of their prey. Most reptiles lay eggs, but some give birth to live young.

respiration Process occurring in all cells which releases energy from organic compounds such as glucose. This energy is used to power all cell reactions and all activity, although some is lost as heat. Anaerobic respiration does not require oxygen but releases only small amounts of energy; it occurs during fermentation, and in muscles during exercise. Aerobic respiration requires oxygen and produces more energy.

rhizome Underground horizontal stem of some plants which acts as a food store during the winter. In spring the rhizome produces buds from which new leaves and flowers grow. Plants with rhizomes include irises, ferns and many grasses.

ribosome One of many tiny structures known as organelles found in the cytoplasm of all CELLS. Ribosomes provide the site for the assembly of proteins from their building blocks – amino acids – using 'construction plans' provided by the genetic material DNA located in the cell nucleus.

RNA or ribonucleic acid. Complex organic compound which carries and translates the genetic information contained in DNA. It implements DNA's instructions to build specific proteins, so determining all an organism's characteristics. There are three types of RNA – messenger, transfer and ribosomal. Messenger RNA transcribes the message from DNA in the nucleus, linking up with the RNA in the RIBOSOME. Transfer RNA lines up AMINO ACIDS in the correct order to construct a specific protein.

root Part of a plant which absorbs water and minerals from the soil. Basically roots divide into two types – tap roots and fibrous roots. Tap roots reach vertically down into the soil. Dandelions have large tap roots, but in carrots and parsnips they are larger still – swollen with food reserves. Fibrous roots form a dense threadlike web underground. Grasses all have fibrous roots. In some cases, roots grow directly from shoots or leaf cuttings; these are called adventitious roots and are found, for example, in strawberry plants that spread by sending out shoots, or runners, that take root.

ruminants Even-toed MAMMALS which include deer, giraffes, cattle and goats. The success of this group – Artiodactyla – is a result of its complex and efficient digestion of vegetation, which is not normally a very nourishing food source. The digestive system consists of four or more 'chambers' or stomachs. Grazed food passes to the first chamber or rumen where its cellulose is partially digested by bacteria. The partially digested food – the cud – is then returned to the mouth for further chewing before being swallowed and further digested.

saprotroph Organism that obtains its nutrition by absorbing the dead remains of other organisms in the earth surrounding it. Saprotrophs are important 'decomposers' – recycling nutrients for plants and animals to reuse. Most saprotrophs digest their food externally by secreting ENZYMES on to the food, turning it into a solution which they can then absorb. Many bacteria and fungi are saprotrophs.

seed Part of a plant that develops from the ovule after fertilisation and contains the EMBRYO capable of germinating to produce a new plant. The seed also contains the embryo's store of food, in the form of COTYLEDONS or oil, and it is enclosed by a protective seed coat. The seeds of flowering plants are protected within a fruit. Some seeds can lie dormant for several years, but when the embryo starts to grow, the seed splits open; this is called GERMINATION.

seed dispersal Plants disperse their seeds in a variety of ways to ensure they do not grow too close to the parent plant and thereby compete with it for water, light and nutrients. Seeds dispersed by the wind are either very light, such as dandelion 'parachutes' or, like sycamores, have fruits flattened as wings to help them glide. The fruit of the gorse bush dries, twists and then bursts open explosively, catapulting out its seeds. Fruits such as burs have hooks that stick to animals which distribute the seeds. Animals also eat succulent fruits such as rose hips or blackberries; the seeds pass through their intestines unharmed and are deposited as droppings. Coconuts can float for long distances in the sea until they land on a beach where their seeds germinate.

senses Their are five main senses: sight, hearing, touch, taste and smell, although not all animals have all of them. The more complex eyes of insects, higher molluscs such as the octopus, and vertebrates, focus light onto light-sensitive cells which send a message to the brain where it is interpreted as an image. The compound eyes of insects are made up of many separate 'mini-eyes' which are very good at detecting sudden movements – making it difficult to swat flies. Many animals communicate using sound; invertebrates do not have ears, although some detect sounds with their antennae. Fish use their lateral line – an ear-like organ – to detect vibrations in the water. Birds sing to attract a mate, or declare their territories. The sense of smell is crucial to most animals; it is especially useful for identifying mates and often provides the means for finding food.

social insects Termites and hymenopterans (bees, ants and wasps) live in large colonies, whose members are organised into castes. All social insects have a queen, which is the only fertile female, and workers which are sterile. Hymenoptera workers are all female; the only function of the males is to fertilise the queen, after which they die. The queen is little more than an egg-laying machine, totally dependent on the workers for food and grooming. Termites and some species of ants have a soldier caste, which attacks prey and defends the nest. If a nest gets too full, all or part of the population must move, which is why bees swarm. Control of the colony is often achieved through the production of PHEROMONES released by the queen.

species Group of organisms that share many similarities, and which breed with each other. 'Species' and below them 'sub-species' form the lowest category in the CLASSIFICATION hierarchy. Each species has a scientific name which, unlike its common name, is recognised internationally. The scientific name is made up of a generic name, giving the genus to which the organism belongs, and a specific name, which defines the species. The trout, for example, is *Salmo trutta*, while the name for its close relative, the salmon, is *Salmo salar*.

sperm Male reproductive cell. The sperm of animals and spermatozoids of simple plants consist of a head section containing CHROMOSOMES which penetrates the ovum at fertilisation, and a tail section with which they swim. Because sperm need liquid in which to swim, plants, such as ferns, can reproduce only in damp conditions.

spore Reproductive cell that can develop into a new organism. Spores are produced by bacteria, fungi and seedless plants, such as FERNS. They can be spread far and wide by wind, water and animals. Spores are minute – a single mushroom may produce billions. Some protists produce dormant spores to survive unfavourable periods of weather.

starch Complex carbohydrate consisting of glucose subunits, used as an energy store in plants. Potatoes are an example of starch being stored in tubers. Starch is also a major energy source for humans and other animals.

THE LIVING WORLD

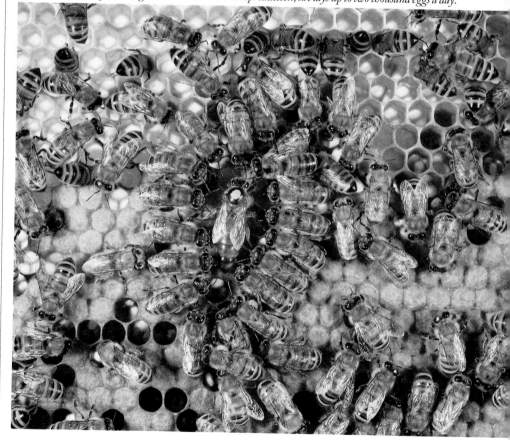

QUEEN BEE *At the centre of her colony, the queen bee is surrounded by dozens of her daughters – sterile workers who feed and groom her. Her work is reproduction; she lays up to two thousand eggs a day.*

FISHY FRIENDS *The huge mouth of the grouper fish holds no fear for the tiny cleaner shrimp which is trusted to trim off dead skin and remove parasites and fungus infestations from around its jaws.*

symbiosis Permanent or long-term association between individuals of different species, especially one that is to their mutual benefit. One example is LICHEN, a symbiotic relationship between a fungus and an alga. Where only one benefits, the relationship is commensal; if one gains, at the other's expense, it is parasitic.

The relationship between flowering plants and their pollinating insects may be regarded as symbiotic: the insect obtains food from the plant, which is in turn fertilised by the insect.

territory Many animals, especially birds, fish and mammals, establish territories for feeding or breeding. Even in densely populated bird colonies, each couple will create a small territory around the nest. Some large mammals, such as tigers, may establish territories of several square miles for hunting. Members of the same species usually maintain their personal territory by displays of AGGRESSION.

tissue Group of similar cells which perform a specific function for an organism, such as muscle tissue or nerve tissue.

transpiration Loss of water vapour to the atmosphere from plants, mainly through the stomata, or 'pores', of the LEAF. As water is lost the plant replaces it by drawing more up its stem through its roots – creating a transpiration stream. In a healthy plant with adequately moist soil this poses no problem, but plants in drier areas may suffer water loss and wilt. Plants can control transpiration by opening and closing their stomata; stomata generally close at night or when the daytime heat becomes too intense. A large tree may transpire 19 gallons (87 litres) of water each day.

tree All trees are classified as either flowering ANGIOSPERMS or non-flowering GYMNOSPERMS. Hardwood trees are angiosperms, most of which are DECIDUOUS, and all softwood trees are gymnosperms, which include most EVERGREENS. A chief characteristic of the tree is the trunk of WOOD, which grows outward as well as upward. Some CONIFERS live for up to 5000 years, but the oldest living thing is a 10 000-year-old regenerating creosote bush, found in the Mojave Desert.

tropism Ability of the root or stem of a plant to grow towards, or away from, a stimulus. Most plant shoots grow towards the light, while some, such as sunflowers, turn towards it – a process known as phototropism. Gravity's effect on plants is known as geotropism; roots grow downwards in response to it, while shoots respond negatively by growing upward.

tuber Enlarged underground stem or root which acts as a food store. Potatoes are stem tubers, while dahlias have root tubers.

vertebrate Animal that has a bony or cartilaginous backbone, such as fish, birds and mammals. (See Animal Kingdom box.)

virus Simple biological 'system' which is not really a living organism because it cannot reproduce without the assistance of living host cells. Viruses are parasites of animals, plants and some bacteria. Viruses frequently lead to disease and are responsible for the common cold, herpes, polio, rabies, ▷AIDS and many other diseases.

warm-blooded or endothermic. Term describing an animal which has a constant body temperature, independent of the external temperature. All birds and mammals are endotherms. Both have a high metabolic rate which releases heat to maintain body temperature. Heat loss is reduced by feathers in birds and by hair, and a layer of fat, in most other animals. Internal mechanisms monitor body temperature constantly, and control it by triggering automatic processes which help to lose or retain heat, such as sweating or shivering.

wood In cross-section there are four main parts to wood – bark, cambium, sapwood and heartwood. Just inside the protective bark lies the thin layer of cambium where growth takes place, leaving a new ring every year. Between the bark and the cambium lies the phloem, PLANT TISSUE that carries sucrose and other nutrients around the tree or shrub. The sapwood is xylem – tissue that carries water up from the roots, and turns into heartwood when it dies. Wood is divided into two types: hardwood, produced by flowering trees (ANGIOSPERMS), and softwood, from non-flowering trees (GYMNOSPERMS). Although some so-called hardwoods, such as balsa, are softer than softwoods, such as pine, most – like teak and mahogany – are much harder.

yeast Type of fungus that obtains its energy through FERMENTATION and reproduces asexually by budding – 'growing' another organism. Yeasts are used in brewing to ferment sugars into alcohol, and in baking to produce the carbon dioxide which causes bread to rise.

zygote Fertilised EGG that results from the joining of the nucleus of an ovum with that of a SPERM in animals, or of a female gamete with a male gamete in plants. It develops, by CELL DIVISION, into an embryo.

MEDICINE, HEALTH
AND THE HUMAN BODY

The human body is a natural machine far more complex and
subtle than any we have been able to invent for ourselves.
In more than 2000 years of observation and experiment we
have learnt to eradicate some of the diseases that
once afflicted us and to alleviate and cure many others. Yet all
the advances of medical science have only reinforced our
sense of wonder at the body's capabilities.

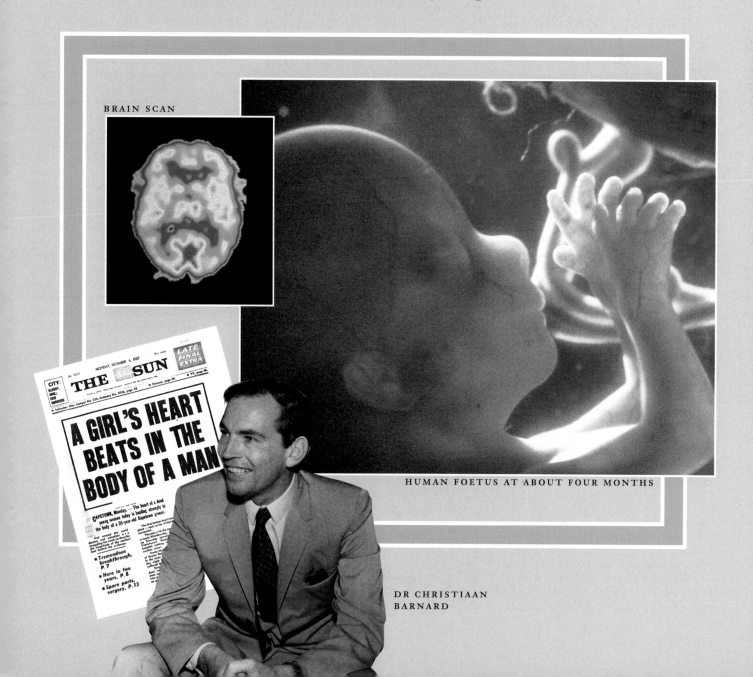

BRAIN SCAN

THE SUN

A GIRL'S HEART BEATS IN THE BODY OF A MAN

HUMAN FOETUS AT ABOUT FOUR MONTHS

DR CHRISTIAAN
BARNARD

abortion Premature ending of pregnancy either naturally, through miscarriage, or artificially, by medical termination. Although medical abortion is practised widely, it is controlled in most countries by legislation, and in some countries, such as the Republic of Ireland, it is forbidden altogether. In Britain, it is illegal to abort a foetus after 24 weeks of pregnancy, except when there is a severe foetal handicap or a risk to the mother's life or health. In developed societies, about 1 in 5 women has an abortion during her life.

Pressure groups in favour of legalised abortion are termed 'pro-choice' groups, those against call themselves 'pro-life'.

Achilles tendon Body's largest and strongest tendon which connects the calf muscles to the heel bone. It is sometimes torn during strenuous exercise.

acne Skin disorder most common during adolescence, when increased levels of sex hormones cause glands in the skin to overproduce sebum, an oily secretion. Sebum accumulates in skin pores to produce whiteheads and blackheads, especially on the face, chest, upper back and shoulders. Blocked pores may become infected with bacteria, producing reddened inflamed spots, filled with pus. Picking or scratching spots spreads infection and may cause scarring. Acne cannot be prevented but it can be controlled. Exposure to sunlight is effective, and severe cases can be treated with antibiotics. The condition also improves with age and usually clears up by the mid twenties. Acne is not caused by dirty skin and harsh cleansing may even exacerbate the condition.

acupuncture Traditional Chinese technique in which needles are inserted into the skin to cure illness or relieve pain. Practitioners claim that the needles unblock the body's invisible energy channels, known as meridians. Acupuncture has been practised for more than 3500 years in the Far East, but it has only recently gained acceptance in the West and is still not fully understood.

acute illness Sudden or short-lived condition that may, or may not, be severe. (Compare CHRONIC ILLNESS.)

adenoids Pads of tissue at the back of the nose which, with the tonsils, prevent germs from entering the respiratory system. They form part of the LYMPHATIC SYSTEM. Infected adenoids swell, and if they begin to interfere with breathing and speech they may need to be surgically removed.

adrenaline Hormone that increases heart rate, air supply to the lungs and blood supply to muscles, and promotes the release of glucose into the blood for immediate energy – preparing the body for action and helping it to cope with fear, stress or exercise. Adrenaline is released by the adrenal glands located near the top of each kidney in response to signals from the autonomic NERVOUS SYSTEM.

ageing Natural deterioration of the body, which begins during reproductive years and accelerates after middle age. Its underlying cause is the steadily decreasing ability of body cells to divide and repair themselves. Skin becomes wrinkled as it loses its elasticity, short-term memory may become impaired, CATARACTS and GLAUCOMA become a risk, and bones become increasingly brittle (see OSTEOPOROSIS).

AIDS Acquired Immune Deficiency Syndrome – a normally fatal condition in which the body's IMMUNE SYSTEM breaks down as a result of infection by the Human Immunodeficiency Virus (HIV). It is possible to carry the virus – or be HIV positive – for ten years or more without developing AIDS. The virus is carried in blood, semen and other body fluids, and is typically transmitted during unprotected sexual intercourse, by transfusion of infected

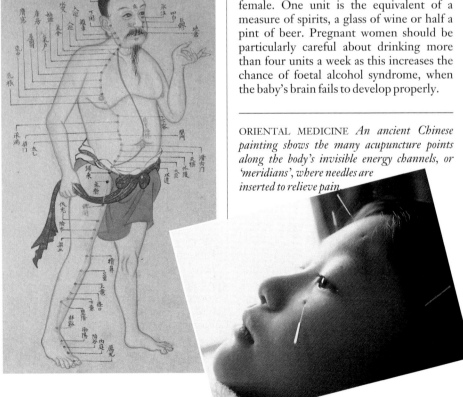

blood or through sharing an infected hypodermic needle. It is also transmitted from mother to foetus. HIV cannot be transmitted through casual physical contact. Once in the bloodstream the virus attacks cells which are part of the immune system. Sufferers eventually die of opportunistic infections – those that do not normally affect people with healthy immune systems – such as rare forms of pneumonia and skin cancer. There is no cure. The disease is most prevalent in south and central Africa, where it affects 1 in 12 people. About 8800 people in the UK had been diagnosed as having AIDS by the end of 1993, of whom 5900 had died.

alcoholism or alcohol dependence. Mental or physical addiction to alcohol produced by its heavy and long-term consumption. There are two main types of alcoholic – steady drinkers and bingers or dipsomaniacs. Severe alcoholics may experience symptoms including memory lapses and hallucinations. Sudden withdrawal can produce severe trembling and convulsions, known as delirium tremens or 'DTs'. Long-term alcohol abuse leads to CIRRHOSIS, liver failure and general physical and mental ill health. There is some evidence that alcoholism has a genetic link, but social and psychological factors are regarded as far more important. The Health Education Authority recommends a maximum alcohol consumption of 21 units a week for an adult male and 14 for an adult female. One unit is the equivalent of a measure of spirits, a glass of wine or half a pint of beer. Pregnant women should be particularly careful about drinking more than four units a week as this increases the chance of foetal alcohol syndrome, when the baby's brain fails to develop properly.

ORIENTAL MEDICINE *An ancient Chinese painting shows the many acupuncture points along the body's invisible energy channels, or 'meridians', where needles are inserted to relieve pain.*

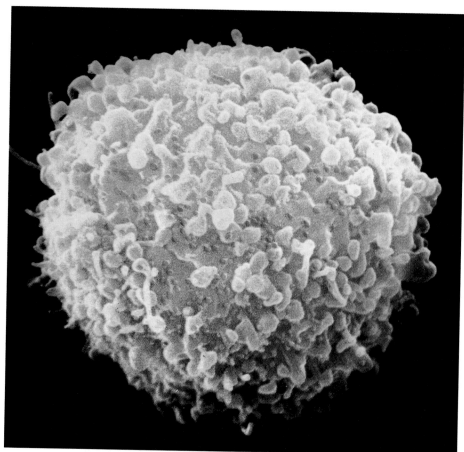

KILLER VIRUS *A false-colour image shows a T-lymphocyte cell – which is the body's basic unit of defence against infection – being 'attacked' by green particles of the HIV virus, which causes AIDS.*

♨ Alcoholics Anonymous (AA) is a self-help organisation for alcoholics who are trying to stop drinking. The first step for members is to admit they have a drinking problem. AA calls alcoholism a disease for which the only cure is total abstention.

allergy The IMMUNE SYSTEM of people with allergies misidentifies harmless substances as harmful and its subsequent defence produces an allergic reaction. Symptoms include itchy eyes, a runny nose, rashes or vomiting, brought on by the release of histamine in the body. Among the most common allergies are HAY FEVER – caused by inhaling pollen – and those caused by exposure to dust mites or eating gluten or dairy products. Allergies are usually relieved with antihistamines but severe reactions may be life-threatening and require an injection of adrenaline.

alternative medicine Any form of treatment outside the range of orthodox medicine, such as HOMEOPATHY, OSTEOPATHY, CHIROPRACTIC and ACUPUNCTURE. It is also known as complementary medicine.

Alzheimer's disease Progressive deterioration of the brain which is one of two causes of DEMENTIA. The other is multiple STROKES. Alzheimer's can occur at any age, but is more common in people over 50. It is characterised by increasing confusion, memory loss, apathy and depression. Controversial evidence that excessive aluminium in the blood contributes to Alzheimer's has led to warnings about cooking in aluminium saucepans – especially acidic foods that react with the metal.
♨ In 1992 a team at St Mary's Hospital in London made a breakthrough in the search for a cure when it identified the gene linked to the disease.

amniocentesis Test taken to detect abnormalities in an unborn child, usually between the 16th and 18th weeks of pregnancy. Some of the amniotic fluid surrounding the foetus is drawn off by inserting a hollow needle into the uterus. Foetal cells in this fluid are then checked for evidence of several conditions including DOWN'S SYNDROME. The test carries less than a 1 in 50 risk of miscarriage.

anaemia Most common disease of the blood in which not enough red cells are produced. Anaemia is usually caused by excessive bleeding, for example, heavy periods; or a form of malnutrition, such as a lack of iron, vitamin B_{12} or folic acid. Some pregnant women become anaemic because the developing foetus depletes their iron level. (See also SICKLE CELL ANAEMIA.)

anaesthetic Local anaesthetics block nerve signals to the brain from a particular part of the body and are used for minor surgery. General anaesthetics – which cause the patient to lose consciousness – are used for major, or very painful, surgery.
♨ Before the introduction of anaesthetics in 1846, it was not uncommon for patients to die of shock from the pain even if an operation was otherwise successful. The first anaesthetics were ether and chloroform; Queen Victoria used chloroform during the birth of her eighth child.

aneurysm Abnormal swelling of an artery in a region that has been weakened by injury or ATHEROSCLEROSIS, although sometimes it can be congenital. If an aneurysm bursts, it can be fatal.

angina Chest pains sometimes accompanied by a choking feeling as a result of an insufficient supply of blood to the HEART.

anorexia nervosa Psychological eating disorder known as the 'slimmer's disease', typically affecting teenage girls. No matter how emaciated she becomes the sufferer believes she is overweight and refuses to eat enough. The condition can go on for years and a normal eating pattern may never be regained; a high proportion of sufferers go on to develop BULIMIA.

antibiotic Drug used to fight bacterial infection. The first modern antibiotic to be used medically was penicillin, originally obtained from a mould by the Scottish bacteriologist Alexander FLEMING in 1928. Antibiotics can now be produced synthetically. They may dissolve the bacterium, impair its ability to take in nutrients, or prevent it from dividing.
♨ Primitive antibiotics have been used for many centuries. In ancient Egypt, a poultice of rotting material was used to treat skin problems or infected wounds.
♨ In 1994, a 'flesh-eating', gangrene-like disease called necrotising fasciitis resurfaced in England and other countries. The potentially fatal disease was caused by a bacterium called *Streptococcus* Type A, more commonly known for causing sore throats.

Scientists suggest that increased resistance to antibiotics may have allowed the bacterium to develop its frightening powers.

antibodies Proteins manufactured by certain white blood cells to fight foreign invaders in the body, such as bacteria, viruses and parasites. They play a major part in the IMMUNE SYSTEM. Each antibody combats a particular infection: for example a measles antibody would not fight a cold virus. Marker molecules called antigens, carried by the invader, enable the antibody to identify and destroy it; the invader either dissolves, or is engulfed by white blood cells. Once the body has an effective antibody it becomes immune to that disease. This is the basis of IMMUNISATION.

anticoagulant Any substance that slows down or prevents the clotting of blood. Artificial anticoagulants are used to treat blood clots (see THROMBOSIS).

appendix Closed tube, the length of the middle finger, joined to the beginning of the large intestine. It is believed to be associated with the immune system in humans, and is involved in digestion in some plant-eating animals. Appendicitis or inflammation of the appendix is fairly common and the usual cure is surgical removal. A burst appendix, which usually goes on to cause peritonitis – the inflammation of the abdominal cavity's membrane – can be fatal without swift and appropriate action.

arthritis Inflammation of the tissues in the joints resulting in stiffness and pain. The two most common forms of the disease are osteoarthritis and rheumatoid arthritis. Osteoarthritis results from wear and tear on joints – usually the knees, hips and spine. Rheumatoid arthritis, which affects three times as many women as men, is caused by the body's immune system acting abnormally and may damage tendons, ligaments and tissues as well. In extreme cases, feet and hands can become deformed.

asthma Difficulty in breathing, caused by narrowing and inflammation of the bronchial tubes. The attack may be brought on by many factors including exercise, anxiety or an allergic reaction to pollen or house dust. Sufferers can relieve attacks by breathing in a bronchodilator drug – that makes the bronchial tubes wider – from an inhaler. The incidence of childhood asthma has increased rapidly since the early 1980s; some experts believe this is due to air pollution, others blame a rise in allergies, smoking during pregnancy or a poor diet.

atherosclerosis Narrowing of the arteries caused by fat building up along the walls of the artery and solidifying into obstructive mounds containing CHOLESTEROL and other substances, resulting in reduced blood flow. This increases the risk of heart attack, stroke and aneurysms. A heart attack, caused by blood clotting on these fatty obstructions called plaque, is the commonest cause of death in people over 40 in Western countries.

atrophy Wasting away of an organ or tissue through underuse or lack of nutrients, or as a result of paralysis.

autism Behavioural disorder which affects 1 in 2000 children. The causes of autism are still unknown, but they are probably physical. It affects significantly more boys than girls. An autistic child is unable to relate socially and seems to be absorbed in its own private world. The child will often display obsessive behaviour and repeatedly copy other people. At the same time the child may have 'islets' of skill, usually in areas which involve abstract thought such as music and maths. About one-third of autistic children have average IQs. Although there is still no cure for autism, a great deal can be done to help with appropriate education and support.

WORLD APART *Stephen Wiltshire sits beside his drawing of the financial district of New York. An extraordinary ability to retain and reproduce architectural images is one of the main pleasures in this young autistic artist's private world.*

back pain Most people suffer back pain at some time in their lives, but it is seldom a sign of serious disease and usually goes away within a week. Often the cause is muscle or ligament strain, especially when the lower, lumbar, region is affected. Any pain in the lower back is classified as lumbago. Severe, persistent pain may be a symptom of a slipped disc or a disease affecting internal organs, such as gallstones.

benign Term describing a condition which is not life-threatening. It is most often used to describe tumours or growths which are not MALIGNANT or cancerous.

beta blockers Drugs used to treat heart disorders and high blood pressure. They reduce the heart's workload by blocking signals from the autonomic nervous system that would otherwise increase both heart rate and blood pressure.

bile Greeny-brown fluid produced by the liver and stored in the gall bladder. It is released into the small intestine to excrete waste and to help digest fats. (See JAUNDICE.)
🦠 A bilious attack has nothing to do with bile and is usually the result of over eating.

bilharzia or schistosomiasis. Tropical disease affecting the blood vessels of the liver, spleen, bladder and other organs which causes fever and extreme tiredness. It is caused by flukes (parasitic worms). More than 200 million people in 70 countries – mainly in Africa, South America and Asia – are affected.

biorhythms Functions of the body that vary on a regular basis. Most, like sleepiness and wakefulness, follow a 24-hour, or circadian, cycle.
🦠 When the ▷CIRCADIAN RHYTHM is disrupted – by flying long distances across several time zones – people often find it difficult to adjust their sleeping patterns, and so suffer from jet lag.

blood Fluid that acts as a transport medium around the CIRCULATORY SYSTEM, and which also helps to defend the body against infection. The average adult male has 10-12 pints (5.5-6.5 litres) of blood; an adult female usually has 8-10 pints (4.5-5.5 litres). It is made up of blood cells suspended in plasma. Plasma, the fluid part of the blood, carries food, ANTIBODIES, blood-clotting proteins, HORMONES and waste around the body. Red blood cells contain haemoglobin, a protein which picks up oxygen in the lungs – giving blood its bright red colour – and releases it in the tissues.

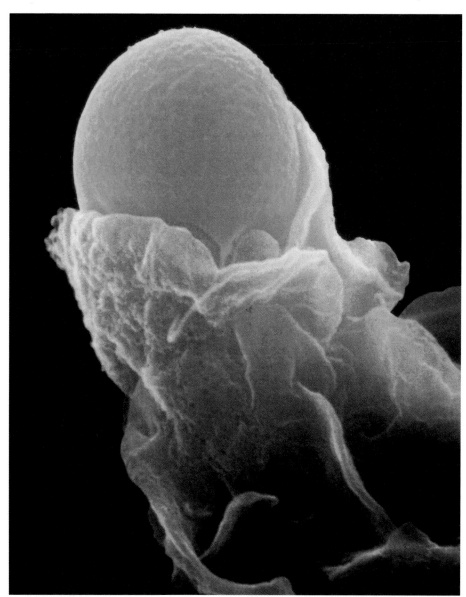

DYING BLOOD CELL *After 120 days and thousands of trips through the bloodstream, the red blood cell begins to expire. A white blood cell is seen here catching, engulfing and digesting the ageing cell.*

White blood cells fight infection. Platelets play an important role in blood clotting. Common diseases of the blood include ANAEMIA and LEUKAEMIA.

blood group There are four basic BLOOD groups – A, B, AB and O. In a blood transfusion, donor and recipient must share the same blood group, otherwise the recipient may have a serious, possibly fatal, reaction. Individuals are also classified as Rh+ (Rhesus positive) or Rh– (negative). A Rh– mother may need an injection after pregnancy to avoid antibodies killing her unborn baby's red blood cells. All blood types are determined genetically and may be used to help prove parentage.

blood pressure The pressure exerted by blood as it travels through the main arteries of the body. Blood pressure is determined by the elasticity of arteries, and the volume of blood forced into them at any time by the heart. When the heart contracts, pressure is at its highest (systolic) and when it relaxes, pressure is at its lowest (diastolic). Pressure is expressed by putting the systolic number over the diastolic. The average reading for a healthy adult is roughly 120/80, but this increases with age. Men tend to have slightly higher blood pressure than women. High blood pressure or hypertension increases the risk of heart attack and stroke. Low blood pressure, hypotension, is often the cause of fainting and dizziness.

497

blood vessels Flexible tubes through which the blood flows around the circulatory system. All arteries carry blood away from the heart under high pressure. The thick elastic muscular walls of the arteries expand when the heart forces blood into them, then contract to push blood onward round the body. The pressure wave passing along an artery with each heartbeat can be felt as the pulse. Veins carry blood towards the heart. Veins have thinner walls and carry blood at low pressure; valves prevent blood flowing backwards. The smallest and most numerous blood vessels, the capillaries, link arteries and veins.

bones See SKELETON.

brain The brain and spinal cord together form the central NERVOUS SYSTEM, linked by nerves to all parts of the body. As well as thought, memory and emotion, the brain controls the running of the body, constantly monitoring blood pressure, breathing and balance. It is divided into three main sections: the cerebellum, the brainstem and the cerebrum. The cerebellum controls balance, coordination, and posture. The brainstem controls breathing, blood pressure and digestion and links the brain to the spinal cord. The

complexity of the cerebrum is what differentiates human brains from those of other animals. Its thin outer layer is a mass of 'grey matter' called the cerebral cortex. It is here that conscious thought takes place, information from sensors, such as eyes and skin, is analysed and voluntary movements are initiated. Inside it is 'white matter' – a mass of nerve fibres that connects the cortex to the rest of the brain. The left hemisphere controls the right side of the body and communication skills such as writing and speech, mathematics and reasoning. The right hemisphere controls the left side of the body, spatial skills, artistic and musical activities, and creativity. Immediately beneath the cerebrum, the hypothalamus controls hunger, thirst, sex drive, aggression and sleep, and is directly connected to the PITUITARY GLAND. Lack of oxygen to the brain at birth, or at a later stage in life, can cause permanent brain damage. Stroke, EPILEPSY and meningitis are all brain disorders.

bronchitis Inflammation of the bronchi – the large air passages that connect the windpipe to the lungs – causing coughing, breathlessness and increased phlegm. Acute bronchitis is an infection caused by bacteria or viruses. Chronic bronchitis is a serious disease usually caused by smoking. It may lead to emphysema and heart failure.
Chronic bronchitis and emphysema are more common in the UK than anywhere else in the world, causing about 30 000 deaths every year.

bubonic plague Highly infectious, sometimes fatal bacterial disease affecting the lymphatic system. The bacteria are carried by rat-borne fleas. The lymph nodes become swollen, creating buboes or lumps, and the victim suffers a high fever, severe thirst and blood poisoning and becomes confused. Today, the disease is easily treated with antibiotics, but in the Middle Ages the so-called ▷BLACK DEATH killed millions of people across Europe.

bulimia Eating disorder characterised by binging followed by induced vomiting. The condition typically affects women in their late teens and early twenties and is often linked with ANOREXIA NERVOSA.

Caesarean section Operation to deliver a baby by cutting through the mother's abdomen. It is often necessary if the baby is in an awkward position or if the mother's pelvis is too small for the baby's head to pass through. In Britain, up to 1 in 5 babies is born by Caesarean.

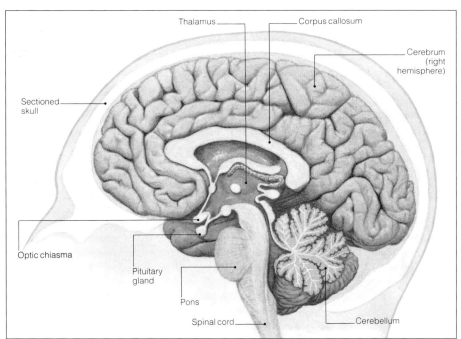

Thalamus — Corpus callosum

Cerebrum (right hemisphere)

Sectioned skull

Optic chiasma

Pituitary gland

Pons

Spinal cord

Cerebellum

BRAIN POWER *A cross-section of the brain shows its three main sections – the cerebellum, the brainstem and the cerebrum. Below, two scans, using radioactive dye, show how much glucose the brain uses to power thinking. The brain of a highly intelligent person, on the right, uses less glucose (yellow) to find the correct answers to an abstract problem than the brain of someone with average intelligence, on the left. This suggests that efficiency rather than hard work is the mark of an 'intelligent' brain.*

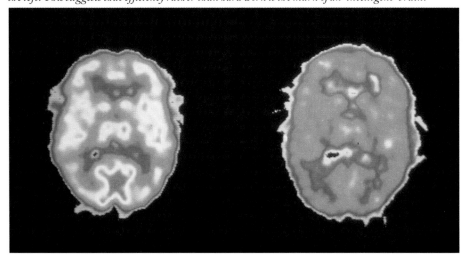

cancer Disorder caused by rogue cells multiplying unchecked in a tissue or organ and to form a MALIGNANT tumour. Cancer kills by preventing the normal functioning of organs. It may spread throughout the body. Cancer may be triggered by environmental factors such as diet, pollution, smoking, a virus, or stress; in some cases, the tendency to develop cancer is inherited. Orthodox treatment includes RADIOTHERAPY, CHEMOTHERAPY and surgery. Some cancers usually only affect people over 40 years old but some forms of LEUKAEMIA are most common in children. One in 20 British women develop breast cancer; in men lung cancer is twice as common as any other form. In the West, cancer is the second most common cause of death, after heart disease. (See also SKIN CANCER.)
🦋 A substance such as tobacco smoke that can cause the body's cells to become cancerous is known as a carcinogen.

cartilage Tough connective tissue which covers the ends of bones and enables joints to move smoothly. It also forms the shock-absorbing discs between the vertebrae. Ears, the end of the nose and the rings of the windpipe are cartilage. In unborn babies, most of the skeletal structure begins as cartilage and gradually turns to bone.

cataract Painless condition of the eye that occurs when the lens becomes opaque. Many elderly people suffer some degree of cataract. It is part of the normal ageing process, but sometimes it is the result of diabetes or injury. Symptoms include deteriorating vision and better vision in half-light than daylight. Cataracts can be treated by replacing the lens.

cellulite Fatty deposits usually found on the thighs and buttocks. It can be reduced by exercise and eating a healthy diet.

cerebral palsy Any disorder affecting muscle control which is caused by damage to a child's developing brain. The most common cause is lack of sufficient oxygen to the foetal brain, but damage may result from injury before or during birth. Effects vary from slight clumsiness to spasticity. PHYSIOTHERAPY, occupational therapy and speech therapy can help.

cervical smear A test to detect precancerous cells in the tissue of the cervix. A minute specimen of tissue is taken from the cervix for examination. The test takes only seconds and is almost always painless. Women who have been sexually active should have a test once every three years.

BLOOD ON THE MOVE *Above, an image magnified 600 times shows red blood cells packed into a tiny capillary. Below, the body's network of major arteries and veins. Arteries carry oxygenated blood (red) from the heart; veins carry deoxygenated blood (blue) back to the heart. The exceptions are the pulmonary artery and vein, which carry blood to and from the lungs.*

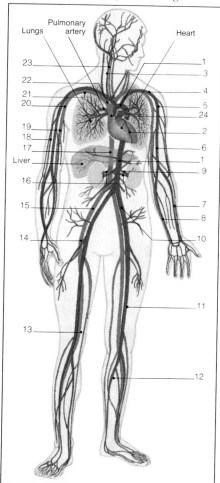

Arteries		**Veins**	
1	Aorta	13	Saphenous
2	Coronary	14	Femoral
3	Common carotid	15	Common iliac
4	Subclavian	16	Renal
5	Axillary	17	Inferior vena cava
6	Brachial	18	Cephalic
7	Radial	19	Basilic
8	Ulnar	20	Axillary
9	Renal	21	Subclavian
10	Common iliac	22	Brachiocephalic
11	Femoral	23	Internal jugular
12	Tibial	24	Superior vena cava

chemotherapy Any treatment using anti-cancer drugs which specifically attack cancer cells by interfering with their reproduction and absorption of nutrients. Chemotherapy may also disturb the activity of normal cells causing distressing side effects such as hair loss or nausea.

chickenpox Highly infectious childhood viral disease. Symptoms include a temperature and a rash on the body and, often, in the mouth and ears. These form blisters and then itchy scabs. The virus may resurface in later life to cause SHINGLES.

childbirth After nine months of pregnancy, the womb begins to contract and the cervix opens up. As contractions become longer and stronger, the baby will be forced (normally head first) down into the vagina and out into the world. After delivery, the umbilical cord is clamped and cut. About ten minutes after the baby is born, the placenta – or afterbirth – is expelled. Breech babies are born bottom or feet first. A CAESAREAN SECTION may be necessary if the baby is in this position, or if the mother's pelvis is too narrow. Lack of oxygen during birth may cause birth defects.

chiropractic Form of holistic, alternative medicine based on manipulation of the spine. It is founded on the idea that disease or pain is caused by interference with the nervous system. Compare OSTEOPATHY.

cholera Acute, sometimes fatal, bacterial infection prevalent in Africa and Asia. It is caused by swallowing contaminated water or food. Symptoms include diarrhoea, vomiting and muscle cramps. If untreated the patient may die of dehydration.

cholesterol Substance found in all body cells. It is also involved in the manufacture of hormones and vitamin D, and the transport of fats around the body. Most cholesterol is made in the liver; the rest is obtained from cholesterol-rich foods such as eggs and dairy products. High levels of cholesterol in the blood are associated with ATHEROSCLEROSIS.
🦋 Britain has one of the highest rates of heart disease in the world, largely due to a diet which contains too much saturated fat.

chronic illness Long-term condition or a recurring illness which may or may not be severe. (Compare ACUTE ILLNESS.)

circulatory system System of BLOOD VESSELS through which the blood is circulated around the body by the pumping action of the heart. It supplies all parts of the body with food and oxygen, and also removes wastes. There are two parts to the circulatory system: the pulmonary circulation connects the heart to the lungs; the systemic circulation connects the heart with the rest of the body. Dark red blood – with low levels of oxygen – enters the pulmonary circulation when it is pumped by the right side of the heart to the lungs. Here it picks up oxygen before travelling back to the left side of the heart, which pumps the bright red oxygen-rich blood into the main arteries of the systemic circulation. Blood passes along smaller and smaller vessels, finally reaching the microscopic capillaries where it gives up its nutrients and oxygen. Oxygen-poor blood flows from the capillaries into the veins that carry it back to the right side of the heart.

circumcision Removal of the foreskin of the penis. In some Western countries, such as the USA, it is performed on most male babies as a matter of course. Circumcision is only medically necessary when the foreskin is too tight. Female circumcision, a brutal and unnecessary operation, varies from removal of the tip of the clitoris to the complete removal of the outer genitalia, causing permanent damage and a possible risk to life. In some 30 countries, however, more than 100 million women have undergone the operation.

cirrhosis Chronic disease of the LIVER in which liver cells are replaced by scar tissue, which prevents the organ from functioning properly. Cirrhosis is usually caused by alcoholism or hepatitis. If discovered early, it may be arrested, but when advanced, a transplant may be the only cure.

colostomy Operation in which part of the colon is pulled through the abdomen wall and made into an artificial opening. A disposable bag is attached to the opening to hold the faeces as they are discharged. A colostomy may be necessary if the colon is cancerous or blocked.

colour blindness Inability to distinguish between colours, most commonly between red and green. This condition is hereditary, and much more common in men; it can be genetically carried by women who are not themselves colour blind. About 1 in 12 men in Britain are colour blind.

coma State of deep unconsciousness in which all response to stimuli is lost. A coma can be caused by a head injury, a disease such as meningitis or diabetes, a stroke or a drug overdose. A coma may last for hours, days and even years, or the patient may never regain consciousness.
♟The longest coma was that of a woman who died in the USA in 1978 at the age of 43. She had been in a coma for 37 years.

concussion Dizziness or a temporary loss of consciousness caused by a blow to the head or a loud explosion. Anyone suffering from concussion should be kept under observation for 24 hours in case any new symptoms develop that may indicate brain damage. Repeated concussion can lead to permanent brain damage – one of the main hazards of boxing.

congenital Term meaning 'present at birth'. It is used to describe conditions which develop before or during birth, such as cerebral palsy, Down's syndrome or a harelip. (See also HEREDITARY.)

conjunctivitis Inflammation of the conjunctiva – the transparent covering of the white of the eye and inner lining of the eyelid. The eye becomes red and itchy. It may be caused by infection or allergy, and can be treated with ointment or eyedrops.

contraception Prevention of pregnancy by mechanical, chemical or hormonal methods. The diaphragm and the condom stop the sperm and the egg from meeting. The IUD (intrauterine device) prevents implantation of the fertilised egg in the womb. Spermicides are chemicals that kill sperm. The most successful method is the PILL, which contains hormones that prevent ovulation. New methods include female condoms and hormonal implants.
♟The Roman Catholic Church forbids its members to use artificial contraception.

cornea Transparent, protective front part of the EYE which helps focus light on the retina. Tears keep the cornea moist and healthy. A damaged or diseased cornea can usually be replaced by a corneal transplant.

cot death also known as Sudden Infant Death Syndrome (SIDS). Inexplicable and sudden death of a previously healthy baby, usually between one and six months old. Breathing stops for no apparent reason. Doctors believe that risk factors include: the temperature of the room, smoking, bottle feeding, a sudden viral infection, bedding that is too soft or too warm, or the position in which the baby sleeps – it should lie on its back.

cyst Abnormal lump or swelling, formed by the growth of a small sac filled with fluid or semi-solid matter. Cysts are generally harmless although they may have to be removed if they interfere with the functioning of the tissues in which they grow.

cystic fibrosis Hereditary disease affecting 1 in 2000 babies in the West. The mucus-secreting glands of the lungs, pancreas and intestines produce large amounts of thick, sticky mucus. This causes chronic lung infection and prevents the absorption of fats and other nutrients from the small intestine. With modern treatment, most sufferers survive to adulthood. One person in 20 carries the cystic fibrosis gene; these carriers show no symptoms. The gene was identified in 1989 and cystic fibrosis may become the first disease to be treated by ▷GENETIC ENGINEERING.

cystitis Inflammation of the bladder lining, usually caused by bacteria travelling up the urethra. Its main symptoms are a

---

COLOUR CHECK *Below left, colour blind people see a number; those with normal vision see patches of colour. Below right, those with normal vision see the number 57; the colour blind see the number 35.*

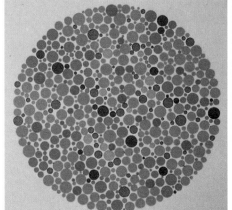
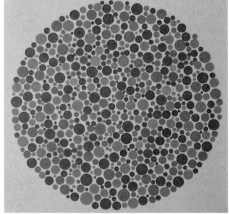

frequent urge to urinate, and a burning pain when urine is passed. It is far more common in women, because their urethras are shorter than men's and more easily infected.

dementia Any progressive loss of mental functions. The commonest causes are strokes and Alzheimer's disease. One in 5 people over 75 is affected by dementia. Memory loss and confusion are the first symptoms. Sufferers eventually become unable to care for themselves.

dentistry Stopping tooth decay, curing gum disease, repairing damaged teeth and providing false teeth are all part of dentistry. Specialised treatments include orthodontics – the straightening of teeth – oral surgery, and denture design and construction. Advances in technology have greatly improved the general condition of tooth care but better diet and oral hygiene have been equally important. (See also TEETH.)

depression There may be a reason for depression, such as redundancy or the death of a spouse and it is a normal part of the grieving process. Symptoms include insomnia and lethargy. Only when there appears to be no outside cause, when the condition appears to be chronic or when it is part of MANIC DEPRESSION, is depression regarded as a treatable mental illness.

detached retina An injury may cause the retina to become detached from the back of the EYE, but it also happens spontaneously. Fluid builds up between the retina and the outer layer of the eye. If diagnosed in time, the condition may be reversible.

diabetes Disorder caused by the body's inability to regulate the level of glucose in the blood by means of the hormone INSULIN. Symptoms include thirst, excessive urination and weight loss. If untreated, the person may go into a diabetic coma. Treatment usually involves a careful diet and may include taking tablets or injections of insulin. Long-term effects include heart and artery problems, impaired vision, kidney disease and nerve disorders.

dialysis Process of removing wastes from blood through a membrane, used in the treatment of kidney disease. In one method, haemodialysis, blood enters the dialysis machine, or artificial kidney, from the patient. Wastes, toxic substances and excess water pass through the membrane from the blood into dialysis fluid. Cleaned blood is returned to the patient, and the dialysis fluid is discarded. It takes between two and

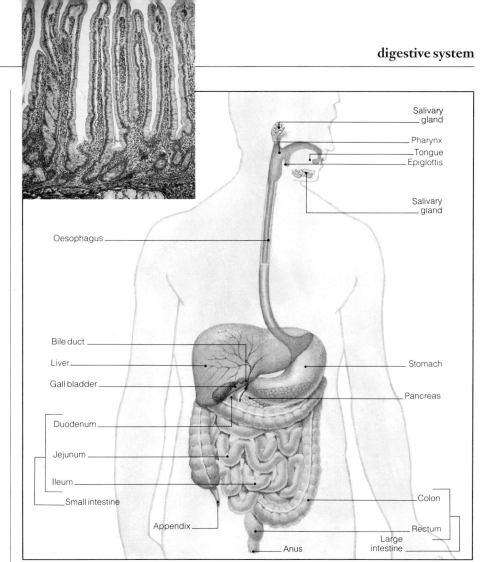

DIGESTING FOOD *The diagram shows the body's digestive system. Above is a false-colour image of a section through the small intestine. This secretes intestinal juice which contains enzymes which break down food. Nutrients from the food are then absorbed from the intestines into the blood through capillaries in tiny villi, seen here as finger-like projections in the intestinal wall.*

six hours to purify or clean an adult's blood. Dialysis normally has to be carried out two or three times a week.

diarrhoea Usually caused by infection or food poisoning, diarrhoea can also be the result of stress or excess alcohol. Those affected should drink plenty of soft drinks to rehydrate the body and replace lost sugar and mineral salts.

Dehydration caused by diarrhoea is the biggest cause of infant mortality in the developing world. About 45 million children die of it every year.

digestive system Group of organs that breaks down food into a form which can be absorbed and used by the body. A few foods, such as vitamins and minerals, can be absorbed directly into the bloodstream, but most need to be broken down by enzymes into smaller and simpler molecules. Fats become fatty acids, proteins become amino acids and carbohydrates are turned into sugars. The process begins in the mouth, where chewing pulps food which travels down the oesophagus and arrives in the stomach where it is mixed with hydrochloric acid and the enzyme pepsin which breaks down proteins. The churning action of the stomach reduces food to a soup-like liquid called chyme. The stomach stores chyme, passing small amounts at intervals to the small intestine. Here digestion is completed by enzymes secreted by the pancreas into the small intestine and by the wall of the small intestine itself. Fat digestion is assisted by the release of bile from the gall bladder. Simple food substances are then absorbed into the blood or LYMPHATIC SYSTEM. The remaining waste passes through the large intestine where water is absorbed, then moves into the rectum from which it is expelled as faeces. Food usually takes one or two days to go through the whole digestive system.

diphtheria Rare, and sometimes fatal, bacterial infection. Symptoms include a sore throat and a greyish-black film at the back of the throat from where bacterial toxins may spread, damaging the heart and nervous system. The disease can be prevented by immunisation.

Down's syndrome Congenital condition caused by the existence of an extra ▷CHROMOSOME. It leads to moderate or severe learning difficulties and is characterised by certain physical features. People with Down's syndrome have a flat facial appearance, eyes which slant upwards on the outside edge of the eye, and with an extra fold of skin on the inner edge, as in Mongolian races. This led to the condition being called mongolism, but the term is no longer used. The condition can be detected during the early stages of pregnancy by carrying out an AMNIOCENTESIS test. One in every 700 babies is born with Down's syndrome. The incidence rises with the age of the mother, especially after 35.

dreams People dream during a stage in their sleeping called rapid eye movement (REM) sleep. This occurs about five times a night, when the brain's electrical activity suddenly increases dramatically. Dreams may be a way for the brain to sort out the events and emotions of the previous day. Newborn babies appear to dream more than twice as much as adults. Some types of psychoanalysis, pioneered by Sigmund ▷FREUD, involve a detailed examination of the patient's dreams.

drug Any chemical substance which changes the functioning of the body or affects a disease. Drugs can be naturally occurring, such as caffeine in tea and coffee, or synthetic, such as paracetamol.
🔦£122 billion was spent on medicinal drugs in 1992: Europe and the USA account for two-thirds of the money spent.

drug addiction Physical or psychological dependence on a drug. Both prescribed medication and drugs such as heroin, morphine and nicotine can be addictive. Drugs such as heroin create a physical dependence. To end the dependency, the addict will either have to be weaned slowly off the drug itself and onto a less harmful substitute, or go 'cold turkey' – stop completely. Sudden withdrawal from heroin may produce symptoms including cramps, diarrhoea, vomiting and even fits. Some people seem to be far more prone to addiction than others. There may be a genetic link, but social factors are also important.

dysentery Inflammation of the intestines which causes severe abdominal pain, fever, and diarrhoea (often mixed with blood). It is usually contracted in tropical and subtropical regions following contact with faeces. Dysentery is usually bacterial or amoebic. Treatment of the condition involves the replacement of body fluids and sometimes a course of antibiotics.
🔦Dysentery is ENDEMIC in several countries, and as many as 1 in 10 people are affected by it throughout the world.

dyslexia Difficulty in recognising words, letters and sometimes numbers. A dyslexic sees characters interchanged, such as *folwer* for *flower*. Dyslexics are slow readers but this is not a reflection of their intelligence.

ear Organ of hearing and balance. The visible part of the ear, the pinna, collects sound and funnels it down a short canal to the eardrum. The eardrum is a thin membrane, like the skin of a real drum, which vibrates in response to sound. Tiny bones in the middle ear transmit vibrations from the eardrum to the fluid-filled cochlea in the inner ear. Vibrations travelling through the fluid stimulate nerve cells that send impulses along the auditory nerve to the brain where they are interpreted as sound. The inner ear also contains three fluid-filled semicircular canals concerned with balance. When the body moves, the fluid shifts, stimulating hair cells which send nerve impulses to the brain, that keep it informed about the body's posture and movement. Earaches, most common in childhood, are usually caused by an infection of the middle ear. Conductive deafness – when the bones of the middle ear are malfunctioning or the canal is blocked – can sometimes be helped by surgery. Perceptive deafness, when the inner ear or the auditory nerves are damaged, sometimes after too much exposure to loud noise, is incurable, but can usually be alleviated with the use of a hearing aid. One in 6 people in the UK has impaired hearing.
🔦Sudden changes in altitude, in an aeroplane for example, can cause the ears to 'pop'. This is caused by uneven pressure on the two sides of the eardrums equalising.

ectopic pregnancy Development of the embryo outside the uterus, usually in a Fallopian tube. About 1 in 200 pregnancies is ectopic. Because there is a considerable risk that the Fallopian tube may rupture, an operation must be performed to prevent internal bleeding.

eczema or dermatitis. Inflammation of the skin which causes redness, itching and cracking. The skin can become infected. Usual causes are allergy and stress. It is common in babies and children but most grow out of it. Treatment includes emol-

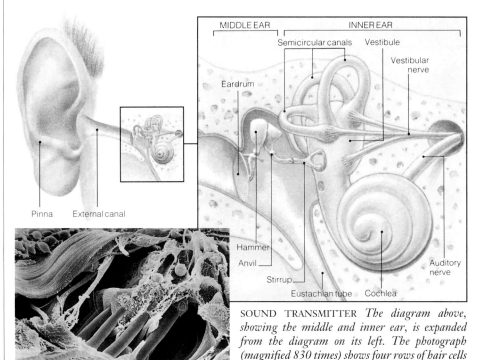

SOUND TRANSMITTER *The diagram above, showing the middle and inner ear, is expanded from the diagram on its left. The photograph (magnified 830 times) shows four rows of hair cells in the cochlea. Each cell contains about 100 hairs that turn sound waves into electrical impulses, which the brain can then interpret as sound.*

lients to keep the skin moist and steroid ointments and creams. Eczema is often coupled with asthma or hay fever.

electrocardiogram (ECG) Recording of the electrical activity of the heart detected by electrodes attached to the chest and limbs. The read-out of the heart's electrical impulses on a monitor or graph paper helps doctors to accurately assess the condition of the heart.

embolism Blockage of an artery caused by a blood clot, gas bubble or some other substance. Embolisms can sometimes cause a stroke or heart attack.

emetic Substance which induces vomiting, which may be used when a person has swallowed a poison or an irritant. Typical emetics are concentrated salt water solution or ipecac. Use of an emetic without medical supervision can be dangerous.

emphysema Disorder in which the air sacs in the lungs become damaged and lose their elasticity reducing the uptake of oxygen into the bloodstream. It is usually caused by smoking, although air pollution may make the condition worse. Symptoms include shortness of breath and frequent coughing or 'smoker's cough'. Emphysema may put a strain on the heart, increasing the likelihood of heart disease. The damage is irreversible, although the condition can sometimes be halted.

encephalitis Inflammation of the brain usually caused by a viral infection. Its most common cause in Britain is the herpes cold sore virus; it may also occur as a complication of mumps and measles. Most people recover in response to treatment. However, in rare cases, the condition can lead to brain damage or even death.

endemic Term which describes a widespread disease or condition which is constantly present in a population or region, such as dysentery in India. (Compare EPIDEMIC and PANDEMIC.)

endocrine system Glands which secrete HORMONES directly into the blood. Among other functions the endocrine system regulates growth, metabolism, sexual development and response to stress. Most endocrine glands are controlled by hormones released by the PITUITARY GLAND which is, in turn, influenced by the hypothalamus in the brain. The endocrine system includes the adrenal and THYROID glands, the ovaries, pancreas, and testes.

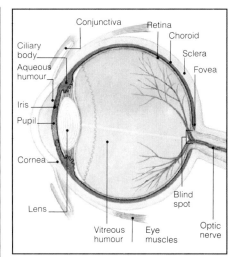

EYE MAKE-UP *A cross-section of the eyeball shows its three main layers: the tough, white, outer sclera protects the eye; the middle, choroid is dark and stops light reflecting within the eyeball; and the inner layer, or retina, contains light-sensitive cells called rods and cones.*

endorphins Natural painkillers which are produced by the body. Endorphins are released at times of stress such as trauma, and also during strenuous exercise, such as marathon running.
🔔Opium based drugs, such as morphine, have a similar chemical structure to that of endorphins. Some doctors believe these drugs cause particularly severe withdrawal symptoms because they have replaced the addict's natural endorphins.

endoscope Tube-shaped instrument, usually flexible, used for viewing the body's interior. It consists of a bundle of ▷FIBRE-OPTIC tubes, with a light at its tip and an eyepiece or camera at the viewing end. Specialised attachments can be used to take tissue samples for biopsy.

epidemic Rapid and extensive spreading of a contagious disease. Unlike ENDEMIC diseases, an epidemic usually only lasts for a few weeks or months. (Compare ENDEMIC and PANDEMIC.)

epilepsy Disorder of the brain which leads to fits or seizures and sometimes loss of consciousness. Epilepsy is the result of abnormal electrical activity in the brain. It sometimes runs in families, or can develop after brain damage. Attacks may be triggered by anxiety, fatigue or flashing lights. Epilepsy affects 1 person in every 200. The condition can usually be controlled with anti-convulsant drugs. Types of epilepsy include: *petit mal*, a momentary loss of

concentration or consciousness; and *grand mal*, a more prolonged loss of consciousness coupled with convulsions.
🔔The ancient Greeks called epilepsy the sacred disease and believed it was a punishment from the gods.

eye The mechanism of the eye is similar to that of a camera. The CORNEA and the lens focus light through the pupil onto the retina. The pupil is like a camera's aperture; tiny muscles in the coloured iris adjust its diameter, so that the right amount of light is let in. The central cavity is filled with jelly-like vitreous humour, which maintains the shape of the eye. The retina is made of sensitive nerve tissue connected to the optic nerve. It contains 130 million light receptors: rods, which deal with black-and-white vision; and cones, which deal with colour vision. Nerve impulses travel along the optic nerve to the brain where images are analysed. When the eyeball is too long the cornea and the lens cannot focus the image onto the retina properly, causing shortsightedness or myopia. Long sight or hypermetropia, is the result of an eyeball that is too short. Astigmatism – vision which distorts the image – is caused by a misshapen cornea. Total or partial blindness is due to malfunctions of the eye, optic nerves or the part of the brain that processes the image.

fainting Momentary loss of consciousness due to a reduction in oxygen supply to the brain. People faint for a variety of reasons: shock, fear, a stuffy atmosphere, pain, the sight of blood, or blowing too hard into a wind instrument. People with low blood pressure are especially prone to fainting.

fever Raised body temperature often caused by the immune system fighting infection. It is a symptom of many acute illnesses. Any temperature of 38°C (100°F), or above, is classified as a fever. High fevers may be accompanied by delirium and, especially in children, by convulsions.

Fleming, Alexander (1881-1955) British bacteriologist who, in the summer of 1928, discovered the first antibiotic, when he noticed a mould had inhibited the growth of a bacteria in a culture dish. The mould was *Penicillium notatum*; Fleming named the bacteria-killing substance it released, PENICILLIN. It was developed into a medicine by two other scientists, Howard Florey and Ernst Chain, and saved thousands of lives during World War II. In 1945, Fleming, Florey and Chain were jointly awarded the Nobel prize for medicine.

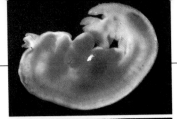

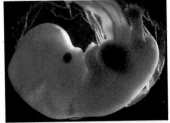

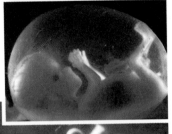

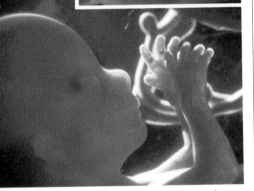

FOETAL FORMATION *The top picture shows a tiny 28-day-old human embryo. At seven weeks, it is little more than an inch (25 mm) long and has arm and leg buds. At 14 weeks, facial features and limbs are evident. At four months, the ears, nose and mouth are formed.*

foetus Term for an unborn child after the eighth week of pregnancy when it becomes recognisably human. For the first eight weeks it is called an embryo.

fontanelles Two soft areas on the top of a newborn baby's head where the bones of the skull do not fully form until the baby is about a year old.

food poisoning Illness caused by eating food contaminated with poison, a virus, or bacteria such as SALMONELLA or LISTERIA. Symptoms include abdominal pain, vomiting and diarrhoea. Botulism is a rare and usually fatal form of food poisoning caused by botulin, the most poisonous bacterial toxin known.

fracture Break or crack in a bone usually caused by injury. Fractures are called greenstick when the bone splits but does not break. Bone regenerates naturally, and in healthy people a fracture will mend perfectly if the bones are properly aligned with, for example, pins or by a plaster cast.

Galen (*c.*129-199 AD) Greek physician to five Roman emperors, who wrote a vast encyclopaedia of medicine. His ideas dominated medical practice until the Renaissance, when they were denounced by PARACELSUS. Galen made significant advances in the understanding of anatomy, notably by identifying the importance of the spinal cord in muscle control. However he also made a number of serious errors, and his theory that health was ruled by four ▷HUMOURS misdirected medical practice for the next 1400 years.

gall bladder Small pear-shaped sac attached to the underside of the liver, which stores and concentrates BILE until it is discharged via the bile duct into the small intestine when food enters from the stomach. Gallstones – hard, pebble-like chemical deposits – can build up and cause severe pain or obstruct the flow of bile if they become lodged in the bile duct. They can often be removed by keyhole surgery.

gangrene Death of body tissue due to lack of blood supply. The affected area becomes discoloured or black. Gangrene may lead to infection, in which case antibiotics may help. Amputation of a limb is sometimes necessary to stop the gangrene spreading to other parts of the body.

gastroenteritis Inflammation of the stomach and intestines. Symptoms range from mild stomachache to severe diarrhoea and vomiting as in dysentery and cholera.

German measles or rubella. Infectious viral disease, usually occurring in children, which causes a body rash and swollen neck glands. If a woman catches it in the first three months of pregnancy, her baby may be born deaf or with a damaged heart.

germs Common term for microscopic living organisms – including ▷BACTERIA and ▷VIRUSES – which cause disease. Germs were not recognised as a cause of illness until the 19th century, when the French scientist Louis Pasteur identified the bacterium which causes anthrax.

gingivitis Inflammation of the gums caused by a bacterial infection. It is often the result of inadequate brushing of the teeth. The gums tend to bleed easily and in severe cases may become ulcerated.

glands Organs or groups of cells which produce a secretion, such as enzymes or hormones. Glands are either ENDOCRINE or exocrine. Exocrine glands, which include sweat, salivary and digestive glands, release secretions directly to the body's outer and inner surfaces. Lymph nodes, an important part of the immune system, are also called glands. Lymph nodes swell noticeably in the neck, groin and armpits when the LYMPHATIC SYSTEM fights infection.

glandular fever or infectious mononucleosis. Viral infection common in young adults, sometimes transmitted by kissing. Symptoms include fever, headache, sore throat and swollen glands in the neck, armpits and groin. The victim may feel lethargic for several weeks or months before fully recovering from the illness.

glaucoma Disorder of the EYE which usually occurs after the age of 40. Vision at the edge of the visual field is gradually lost and may result in 'tunnel vision' and eventual blindness. The condition is caused by blockage in the eyes' internal drainage ducts, leading to increased pressure of the fluid in the eyeball. If diagnosed early, it can usually be controlled by eye-drops.

glue ear Common childhood complaint caused by an accumulation of fluid in the middle EAR usually following a cold or upper respiratory infection. Glue ear causes temporary slight deafness.

gout Disorder causing attacks of ARTHRITIS often in only one joint at a time, especially in the hands and feet. Crystals of uric acid collect in the joint and cause severe pain, redness and swelling. The big toe is often affected. The condition is associated with kidney stones and is caused by a high level of uric acid in the blood.
🖋Contrary to popular belief gout is not caused by drinking too much port.

haemoglobin Pigment in blood that carries oxygen. Haemoglobin gives blood its red colour: the more oxygen present, the brighter the red.

haemophilia Hereditary disorder caused by a lack of the blood-clotting agent Factor VIII which results in excessive bleeding when any blood vessel is even slightly injured. Painful bleeding into joints is common. Haemophilia is transmitted down the maternal line, but affects only male offspring. It is treated with regular infusions of Factor VIII.
🖋Queen Victoria was a carrier of haemo-

philia, and through her daughters' marriages she passed the disorder into the royal families of Germany, Spain and Russia. The Russian monk Rasputin gained enormous influence over the Russian Tsarina Alexandra through his apparent ability to control the Crown Prince's haemophilia.

haemorrhoids or piles. Condition in which VARICOSE VEINS form inside or outside the anus, leading to bleeding and pain. The most common cause is insufficient fibre in the diet, but pregnant women often suffer from haemorrhoids due to increased pressure on the large intestine.

hair Made up of dead cells composed largely of the protein keratin, hair is divided into three types: downy hair called lanugo that covers the foetus; fine vellus hair on the body; and longer terminal hair on the scalp. Terminal hair appears in the armpits, pubic area and, in men, on the face after puberty. Hair is always falling out and being replaced, but permanent hair loss leading to baldness is common in men. Hair goes grey because of lack of the pigment melanin.

halitosis or bad breath. Chronic bad breath may be a sign of some disorder, such as gingivitis, a digestive complaint or lung disease. But normally it is due simply to eating strong-smelling food.

harelip Congenital defect in which the upper lip is split down the middle, because the skin did not fully fuse as the baby developed in the womb. The condition can usually be repaired with plastic surgery, when the baby is about three months old. A harelip is often associated with a cleft palate – the roof of the mouth is divided into two halves from front to back.

Harvey, William (1578-1657) English physician and anatomist who first accurately described the circulation of the blood. He published his theory that blood was pumped around the body along the blood vessels by the heart in 1628. Until then GALEN's theory that blood ebbed and flowed like the tide had been accepted almost universally.

hay fever Allergy to pollen which usually affects sufferers in the spring and early summer. The pollen irritates the mucous membrane of the nose and throat. Symptoms include sneezing, a runny nose, watering eyes and, sometimes, conjunctivitis. Antihistamines are commonly prescribed. 🎤Children born just before the pollen season seem to be more prone to hay fever.

heart The average human heart beats 2500 million times in a 70-year life. The heart is divided down the centre by a thick, muscular wall. Each side is subdivided into two connecting chambers: the atrium above and the ventricle below. One-way valves separate each atrium from its ventricle, and each ventricle from the artery that leaves it. BLOOD is pumped by both sides of the heart working in unison to maintain even pressure. First the atria squeeze the blood they have collected into the ventricles below. The right ventricle then contracts to pump blood through the arteries to the lungs and back to the left side of the heart; the left ventricle pumps it round the rest of the body. The heart gets its own blood supply from the coronary arteries. The most common disease of the heart is an insufficient blood supply, caused by partially blocked coronary arteries. This can cause ANGINA and lead to a HEART ATTACK. Defects in the heart's structure are quite common at birth but can often be repaired with surgery. TRANSPLANT SURGERY may be necessary if any of the heart's chambers are damaged beyond repair.

heart attack Sudden loss of blood supply to an area of the heart. This is the most common cause of death in developed countries. In the UK 160 000 people die from heart attacks every year. It is usually caused by a blockage in a coronary artery narrowed by ATHEROSCLEROSIS. Symptoms include pain and pressure in the chest, which may spread to the left arm, neck and jaw, but sometimes the attack goes unnoticed. A heart attack may lead to cardiac arrest, when the heart stops completely. A heart bypass operation may be considered for someone who has ANGINA. Blood vessels are taken from another part of the body and grafted beside the blocked coronary arteries. A triple or double bypass refers to the number of arteries bypassed.

heartburn Burning feeling in the chest, produced when stomach acid flows up into the oesophagus, often after a heavy meal.

heart failure Condition in which the heart is unable to pump enough blood round the body, usually because of a HEART ATTACK, high blood pressure, anaemia, an irregular heart rhythm, or a thyroid condition. Symptoms include difficulty in breathing, especially when lying down flat, fatigue and swelling in the legs. Heart failure may also affect the functioning of other organs, such as the kidneys. Drugs can be taken to reduce the work the heart has to do and improve its performance.

hepatitis Inflammation of the liver, usually caused by a virus but sometimes induced by drugs and other chemical substances including alcohol. Severe cases can lead to permanent liver damage. Patients are advised to avoid alcohol for up to a year after the illness has passed. Symptoms include fever and JAUNDICE. The two most common viral forms are hepatitis A and B. Hepatitis A is spread through contaminated food and water and is common in tropical and subtropical countries. Hepatitis B, which is more serious, is spread through contaminated syringes, sexual intercourse and blood transfusions. IMMUNISATION against both hepatitis A and B is available.

herbal medicine Use of plants and their extracts as drug treatment. Herbalism dates back to prehistoric times, and many of today's drugs are based on plant extracts. For example, digitalis, a drug used to treat heart failure, is extracted from foxglove leaves. The first contraceptive pill was based on extracts from the Mexican yam.

hereditary Any characteristic, such as eye colour, or any condition, such as haemophilia, that can be passed on through the genes. Not all CONGENITAL conditions – those that are present at birth – are genetically transferred, but the HUMAN GENOME PROJECT is finding that many conditions have a hereditary component, such as certain forms of cancer and Alzheimer's disease. These discoveries have prompted renewed interest in the ▷NATURE-NURTURE DEBATE.

hernia Abnormal protrusion of an organ through the muscle wall containing it, usually of the intestine through the abdominal wall. The condition is only dangerous if the blood supply to the protruding region is cut off. Surgery is then urgently required. If part of the stomach protrudes through the diaphragm into the chest cavity it is called a hiatus hernia. This may lead to heartburn.

herpes Blister-like sores on the skin or mucous membranes caused by the herpes simplex virus. There are two main types of herpes that are caused by different forms of the virus: cold sores and genital herpes. Some people only have an initial attack, while others suffer repeated outbreaks. If a pregnant woman has an outbreak of genital herpes when she is about to give birth, she should be given a Caesarean section to avoid harm to the baby. The diseases CHICKENPOX and SHINGLES are caused by a virus closely related to herpes simplex.

Hippocrates (*c.*460-370 BC) Greek physician who was regarded as the founding father of Western medicine. Although the writings once ascribed to Hippocrates are now known to have been written by more than one person, his contribution to the study of disease and the understanding of the doctor's role were nonetheless quite considerable. Unlike his predecessors, who were magicians as much as physicians, Hippocrates was convinced that diseases had natural causes. He was the first to keep case notes – the systematic chronicling of a patient's disease which doctors still use today. He also established the ground rules for the doctor/patient relationship, which are still the root of all modern codes of medical ethics. An extract from the Hippocratic oath is as follows: 'Whatsoever house I enter, there will I go for the benefit of the sick, refraining from all wrongdoing. Whatsoever things I see or hear in my attendance on the sick which ought not to be voiced abroad, I will keep silence thereon.' The writings of Hippocrates are full of aphorisms, some of which have become household phrases, such as 'Desperate diseases require desperate remedies'.

MEDICINE MAN *While his Greek contemporaries believed sickness was an affliction sent by the gods, Hippocrates was the first physician to recognise that disease had a natural cause.*

histamine Chemical in the body which can cause inflammation, narrow the airways into the lungs, and stimulate the stomach's production of acid during ALLERGIC reactions which may be countered by the use of antihistamine drugs.

HIV See AIDS.

hives also known as nettle rash or urticaria. The condition is marked by the sudden appearance of large, itchy, red or white bumps on the skin. These may be caused by an allergic reaction to a particular food or drug, or exposure to heat, cold or sunlight.

Hodgkin's disease Cancer of the lymph tissues. The lymph nodes, liver and spleen become enlarged. Its cause is unknown, but it is most common in men between the ages of 20 and 30. If the disease is identified in its early stages, the prognosis is good.

holistic medicine Branch of ALTERNATIVE MEDICINE that aims to treat the whole person – mind and body together – instead of treating a problem in isolation.

homeopathy Branch of ALTERNATIVE MEDICINE based on the premise that like cures like. Practitioners prescribe a minute amount of the same substances which given in large doses to a healthy person would produce the symptoms of the disease.

hormones Chemical messengers produced by the ENDOCRINE SYSTEM and by other organs including the kidneys, intestines, brain and the placenta, which secretes hormones during pregnancy. Some hormones maintain a constant environment inside the body – INSULIN, for example, regulates the amount of glucose in the blood. Other hormones – such as OESTROGEN, TESTOSTERONE and growth hormones – effect long-term changes including a child's growth and sexual maturation. ADRENALINE triggers swift responses in the body when danger, injury or illness occur. Hormone replacement therapy (HRT) is used when production of female sex hormones falls off: women are given oestrogen and progestogen to relieve the symptoms of their menopause.

Human Genome Project Worldwide programme to identify all human genes. The project is coordinated from Washington DC, but scientists from all over the world are participating. There are about 70 000 human genes: by 1994 more than 2 500 had been identified, including the genes for Alzheimer's disease, breast cancer and cystic fibrosis.

hyperactivity Constant overactivity, usually in pre-pubescent children. They are unable to concentrate and sleep for only a few hours a night. Hyperactivity has only recently been recognised as a real disorder, so little is known about causes or cures. Paradoxically, stimulants have been found to have a calming effect in some cases.

hyperventilation Rapid breathing pattern, usually caused by anxiety, which leads to too much carbon dioxide being taken from the blood. This results in a rapid heart beat, dizziness and tingling of the lips, fingers and toes. Sometimes the person faints. Sufferers should breathe slowly in and out of a paper bag for a few minutes to build up carbon dioxide in the blood.

hypnosis Waking state of extreme relaxation in which the person enters a trance, loses touch with their environment and becomes extremely susceptible to suggestion. Hypnotism was used as a form of therapy, mainly for 'hysteria', in the 19th century and is still used today to help people to abandon habits such as smoking and get over phobias.

hypothermia Abnormally low body temperature which can lead to unconsciousness and death. It is most common in infants and the elderly living in poorly heated accommodation, but it can affect anyone exposed to cold for a long period of time. Hypothermia is diagnosed when body temperature falls below 35°C (95°F).

hysterectomy Surgical removal of the whole of the uterus or the body of the uterus because of cancer or menstrual abnormalities. If the operation is to stop the spread of cancer, Fallopian tubes and ovaries may also be removed. It is one of the most frequently performed operations. After hysterectomy, menstruation ceases and the woman can no longer bear children.

immune system Body's defence system against infection and cancer. The system is usually highly efficient. Foreign organisms and cancers are detected and killed without any noticeable effect on the person. Only during prolonged battles will the victim develop fever, inflammation, or swollen lymph glands. The first line of defence consists of physical barriers, such as skin, liquids such as mucus that trap micro-organisms, and white blood cells called phagocytes that 'eat' foreign invaders that get into blood or tissues. The second line of defence is the immune system proper, which targets specific invaders. The immune system has two types of response to intruders: humoral and cellular, both controlled by cells called lymphocytes. In a humoral response, B-lymphocytes are stimulated by the presence of the invader to release specific killer chemicals called ANTI-BODIES. These lock onto the invader and immobilise it, allowing phagocytes to move in and engulf it. The cellular response involves two types of T-lymphocytes. T-helper lymphocytes recognise abnormalities within body cells, such as cancer or the presence of a virus. These then stimulate T-killer lymphocytes to destroy the abnormal body cell. The B and T lymphocytes that survive a battle are the memory of the immune system. They will act immediately if the same threat appears, sometimes providing immunity to the disease for good. Transplants are usually rejected as foreign bodies by the immune system unless its activity is suppressed by drugs. The AIDS virus attacks the T-helper cell directly, so wrecking the immune system.

immunisation Introduction of a mild dose of an infection into the body, which stimulates resistance to it. The germs used have usually been killed or weakened. Young children are immunised against diseases including diphtheria, polio and tetanus. Edward JENNER pioneered the process in 1796. (See also VACCINATION.)
The World Health Organisation successfully eradicated SMALLPOX in 1979 through a global immunisation programme. It was the first disease to be totally eradicated by human effort.

incubation period The time between infection and the appearance of symptoms. This may be a few hours, as with some food poisoning, or many years as with AIDS.

infertility treatment In men, infertility is usually caused by a failure to produce enough healthy sperm. In women, it may be a failure to ovulate. Sometimes fertility treatment is simply a matter of a change in diet, and relaxation exercises. In women, and occasionally in men, there may be a hormonal imbalance for which hormone treatment may be the solution. If the problem is not hormonal, there are several options available. With artificial insemination, sperm can be injected into the cervix with a syringe. Microsurgery may be used to repair the Fallopian tubes if they are blocked. Another possible option is *in vitro* fertilisation, when the egg is fertilised by sperm in the laboratory and then placed in the womb; babies conceived this way are often called test-tube babies.

influenza An acute, infectious disease caused by any of a large number of related viruses. Symptoms of 'flu' include fever, muscle pain, headache, loss of appetite, coughing and a sore throat. Vaccines are available against some strains, but owing to the rapid mutation of the virus, they may only be effective for short periods.
In the flu pandemic of 1918-19, some 15 million people died worldwide. The only countries unaffected were New Guinea, St Helena and a few Pacific islands. In the UK, 150 000 people died. It was the worst global plague since the 14th-century Black Death.

insulin Hormone secreted by the pancreas that enables the body to use glucose and so control glucose levels in the blood. People with DIABETES have difficulties producing insulin and may need regular injections.

intravenous Term meaning literally 'within a vein'. An intravenous drip can be used to supply drugs, fluids or nutrients directly into a vein.

irritable bowel syndrome Both constipation and diarrhoea can be caused by this condition, in which the bowel muscle functions spasmodically. The lower abdomen may also become distended and painful. It is thought that it is often caused by stress and is particularly common among women aged between 20 and 40.

jaundice Yellowing of the skin and eyes, caused by an excess of BILE pigment in the blood. It is a symptom of liver disease, blockage in the bile duct or the excessive destruction of red blood cells. Newborn babies often develop jaundice before their livers have started to work efficiently.

Jenner, Edward (1749-1823) British physician and pioneer of immunisation. In 1796 he proved that the body could resist infection if it could build up immunity to a disease when given it in a less potent form. Jenner found that inoculation with cowpox made people immune to smallpox.

kidneys Pair of organs that filter waste from the blood and excrete it, together with excess water, as urine. They also maintain the body's chemical balance and produce a hormone that stimulates production of red blood cells. Humans can survive perfectly well with only one kidney. People with kidney disorders may need to have regular DIALYSIS to filter out the waste artificially. Inflammation of the kidneys is called nephritis. Kidney stones are small lumps of calcium salts that form in the kidneys. Stones cause pain as they pass through the urinary tract and larger ones may obstruct the kidney or ureter, causing severe pain and back pressure on the kidney. They can usually be surgically removed or destroyed by ultrasound.

laryngitis Strained or inflamed vocal cords which give the sufferer a hoarse, whispery voice. The condition is caused by overuse or infection. Singers may develop benign nodes on their vocal cords. The nodes may have to be surgically removed.

larynx or voice box. Framework of cartilage, muscles and ligaments which contains the vocal cords. The entrance is guarded by the epiglottis which prevents food from going down the trachea. Sound is produced when air passes between the vibrating vocal cords. The pitch of the note varies as the controlling muscles contract and relax. The Adam's apple is the front of the larynx. When boys reach puberty the larynx grows, causing the voice to deepen.

legionnaires' disease Form of pneumonia, sometimes fatal, caused by bacteria that live in the water and air-conditioning systems of buildings. The bacteria grow best in temperatures of 20-50°C (68-122°F), so hotels and large institutions should keep main water tanks and air-conditioning plants below the minimum temperature. The disease was first identified in 1976 when 29 members of the American Legion died after staying at a hotel in Pennsylvania.

lentigo Flat discoloured areas of skin which usually appear after the age of 50. They are harmless, but unlike freckles, they are not stimulated by exposure to the sun.

leprosy Bacterial infection that causes damage to the nerves and sometimes disfigurement. Large hard patches appear on the skin. Because of loss of feeling, some sufferers (the term 'leper' is no longer considered appropriate) injure themselves and become repeatedly infected. Eventually this may lead to the loss of extremities. Leprosy has a long incubation period of about three to five years and by the time there are any symptoms – loss of feeling in the hands and feet, muscle weakness, or paralysis of parts of the body – the disease is well established. Antibacterial drugs will kill the bacteria, but any disfigurement is irreversible. About 20 million people in the world, mainly in India and Brazil, have leprosy.

♟ Contrary to popular belief leprosy is not very contagious. It can be caught only through intimate contact with someone in the early stages of the disease.

leukaemia Cancer of the white BLOOD cells. Abnormal white blood cells multiply at the expense of red blood cells and platelets, causing anaemia, bruising and bleeding. In severe cases, white blood cells may take over the bone marrow entirely, stopping any other blood cells from being produced. Leukaemias can be acute or chronic; the form of leukaemia also depends on the type of white blood cell involved. People who have been exposed to radiation are more likely to suffer from it. Chemotherapy and radiotherapy may cure certain forms of leukaemia. In children, treatment can now provide a complete cure for more than half of those affected.

lice Parasitic insects which feed on blood and live on the surface of the skin. Their bites cause severe itching and the skin irritation which results is called pediculosis. Three species of lice infest human beings: head lice, body lice and pubic lice, or crabs. Body lice are pin-head sized and lay their eggs in clothing. Head and pubic lice are smaller. All three can be got rid of with medicated shampoos or ointments. Head lice lay grey eggs, or nits, in the hair and commonly infest schoolchildren whose heads often come into close contact.

ligament Tough band of fibrous, flexible tissue that connects bones to one another and supports some internal organs. Ligaments ensure that joints only move in the right direction – preventing the knee from twisting, for example. If a ligament is torn it can take several weeks or months to heal.

Lister, Joseph (1827-1912) British surgeon who revolutionised surgery in 1865 with the introduction of antiseptics. Lister used carbolic acid to demonstrate that antiseptics kill germs and so reduced the incidence of wounds becoming infected. He was inspired by the contemporary work of the French bacteriologist PASTEUR who discovered that germs cause disease. Lister published his first results in 1867, and although he encountered some jealousy and opposition, the facts were too clear and dramatic to be denied. The antiseptic method rapidly came into universal use.

STERILE SURGERY *Joseph Lister, seated centre, with staff in King's College Hospital, London, 1891. By persuading other surgeons to use antiseptics he almost certainly saved thousands of lives.*

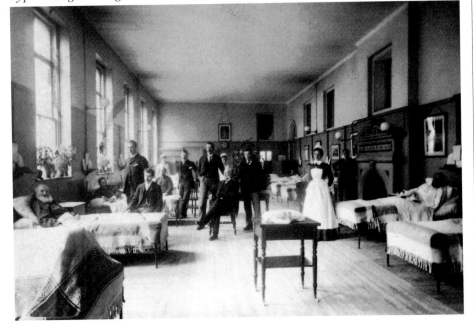

listeria Bacteria found in dairy products, especially soft cheeses and milk, that cause a type of food poisoning. The symptoms are diarrhoea, a sore throat and a headache. In a healthy adult, listeria is fairly harmless, but it can be life-threatening to unborn or young children and the elderly.

liver The body's chemical factory and largest organ. The liver performs at least 22 major functions. Humans can survive with just a quarter of their liver, and the tissue can regenerate if part of the liver is damaged. Blood flows into the liver through the hepatic artery from the aorta, and through the portal vein directly from the intestines. The liver stores glucose and vitamins A, D, and B_{12}. It converts excess amino acids – the building blocks of proteins – into urea which is excreted in the urine. It removes poisons, drugs and alcohol from the blood and renders them harmless. It also manufactures important proteins and breaks down old red blood cells. Liver disorders include HEPATITIS and CIRRHOSIS. Cancers from elsewhere in the body commonly spread to the liver.

lungs Pair of spongy, air-filled organs that form the main part of the RESPIRATORY SYSTEM. The lungs are made up of millions of minute air sacs called alveoli. Oxygen from the air taken into the lungs passes through the thin membranes of the alveoli into the blood; carbon dioxide passes in the opposite direction into the air which is breathed out. The lungs are extremely delicate, and long-term irritation such as smoking or pollution damages them permanently, and may cause EMPHYSEMA, BRONCHITIS or CANCER.

♟ Lung disease was a common occupational hazard. For example, miners often got black lung from coal dust; brown lung, caused by cotton fibres, affected workers in cotton mills and farmer's lung was a reaction to mouldy hay. Although such conditions still occur most are now fairly rare.

lymphatic system Network of small vessels through which lymph, derived from excess tissue fluid, is carried from the body's tissues back to the bloodstream. Lymph is a clear yellowish fluid made up of proteins, fats and white blood cells – mainly lymphocytes that play an important part in the IMMUNE SYSTEM. Lymph nodes or glands, situated along lymphatic vessels, act as a barrier to infection by filtering out harmful bacteria. The nodes are small and soft but become swollen when fighting infection. The lymphatic system also transports fats from the small intestine.

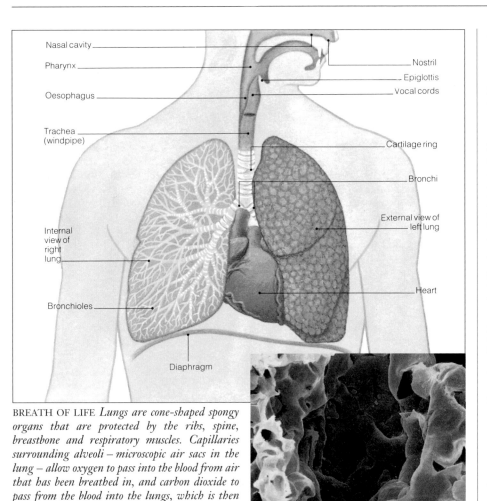

BREATH OF LIFE *Lungs are cone-shaped spongy organs that are protected by the ribs, spine, breastbone and respiratory muscles. Capillaries surrounding alveoli – microscopic air sacs in the lung – allow oxygen to pass into the blood from air that has been breathed in, and carbon dioxide to pass from the blood into the lungs, which is then exhaled. Each lung has about 300 million alveoli, one of which is magnified 1050 times, on the right.*

mad cow disease Common name for bovine spongiform encephalitis (BSE), a fatal disease of cattle. Brain tissue is destroyed and becomes full of microscopic holes. Victims become weak and uncoordinated. The condition has an incubation period of up to ten years and as yet the cause is unclear, however the disease has been linked to cattle feed infected with scrapie – a similar disease in sheep. In 1988, BSE had reached epidemic proportions in British cattle. Diseases similar to BSE have since been identified in several other mammals, particularly the domestic cat, and there have been fears that humans might contract the disease by eating contaminated beef.
🦠Several people who have been injected with growth hormones – extracted from corpses' pituitary glands – have contracted Creutzfeld-Jakob disease which affects the human brain in a similar way to BSE.

malaria Tropical disease caused by parasites carried by mosquitoes and injected into the bloodstream when the mosquito bites. About 300 million people a year contract malaria, and it is the greatest medical hazard facing travellers to the tropics. Once in the bloodstream, the parasites travel to the liver where they reproduce. Malaria is characterised by a particular type of recurring fever; this starts with chills, after which the temperature soars, then the patient is drenched with sweat as the body tries to cool down.

malignant Term for conditions which may be life-threatening as opposed to those that are BENIGN. It is usually used to describe harmful cancers, or any illness that is fast-developing and dangerous.

malnutrition Lack of adequate nutrients – typically proteins and carbohydrates – due to a poor diet or diseases which impede the body's ability to digest food. Malnutrition retards growth, leaves the body susceptible to infection, causes anaemia and hampers the normal function and regeneration of cells, leading to muscle wastage and damage to the organs and bones. At least 1.5 billion people in the world – more than 1 in 4 – suffer from malnutrition.

mammogram Breast X-ray used to check for tumours. Women aged between 50 and 64 should have one every three years.

manic depression Mental disorder characterised by abnormal mood swings, from euphoria to deep DEPRESSION. In a manic period, a sufferer may be hyperactive, speak rapidly, have delusions, and be elated and then irritable. The drug lithium whose benefits were first reported in 1949, has been used to counteract the mood swings, with a success rate of nearly 80 per cent.
🦠Artists and writers are apparently six times more likely to suffer mood swings than the rest of the population.

mastectomy Surgical removal of all or part of a breast, usually performed to treat breast cancer. Radical mastectomy may also include taking out the muscles and lymph nodes in the armpit.
🦠Despite advances in diagnosis, Britain has the highest death rate from breast cancer in the world.

mastitis Bacterial infection which causes a breast to become red, swollen and tender. Mastitis usually occurs when a mother is breastfeeding her baby.

ME Myalgic encephalomyelitis or post-viral fatigue syndrome – also nicknamed 'yuppie flu'. A condition characterised by extreme fatigue. There may also be dizzy spells, headaches, muscle pains, depression and anxiety; but these last two symptoms may be due to the difficulty of diagnosis and the long duration of the disease. ME also tends to get worse the more the victim exercises; active people seem to be more prone to the syndrome. It can last from two months to more than two years and, since there is no definitive test, diagnosis is by a process of elimination. ME usually develops after a viral infection, but the exact cause of the disease is still unknown. It was first identified in 1934 in the USA and its diagnosis increased rapidly in the 1980s.

measles Acute contagious disease, caused by a virus. Symptoms include a fever, sore eyes, cough and a rash of red spots on the limbs, face, chest and back. Measles can lead to pneumonia, ear infections and, rarely, inflammation of the brain. It is a major cause of infant mortality in the developing world. Immunisation is possible when a child is about 15 months old.

melanin Dark brown pigment in the skin and hair which determines the tone of the complexion. Melanin is produced by cells in the skin that are sensitive to sunlight. The pigment absorbs the sun's harmful ultraviolet rays and protects the body from burning and developing SKIN CANCERS. A sun tan is the result of stimulated melanin production. People with white hair and pink eyes who have no melanin and therefore no colouring are known as 'albinos'.

Red hair is caused by a special red pigment, which competes with melanin. People with very red hair produce very little melanin in their skin, which is why they burn easily in the sun.

memory Little is known about how memory works, but its main seat is believed to be the hippocampus in the centre of the forebrain, although long-term memory is believed to be stored throughout the brain. Memory works in three phases. First a piece of information or an impression such as a sound, or image, is registered and goes into short-term memory for between a few seconds and a few hours. Then, if it has made a deep impression, or it crops up repeatedly – like a friend's phone number – it is stored in the long-term memory. The majority of people can hold about six to eight pieces of information in their short-term memory. When asked to remember more than that, the more recent facts tend to push out those that were stored earlier. The final phase, retrieval, may be stimulated by a smell or an emotion, for example, or it may be done at will. Gradual loss of memory is associated with the onset of DEMENTIA.

meningitis Inflammation of the meninges – the membranes surrounding the brain and spinal cord. The disease is usually due to infection by a virus or bacterium. Symptoms include severe headaches, a stiff neck or back, high fever, vomiting, sensitivity to light and a dark, blotchy rash. Viral meningitis is usually mild, but bacterial meningitis can, without early diagnosis and treatment with large doses of antibiotics, result in brain damage or even death.

menopause Cessation of menstruation, marking the natural end of a woman's fertile years, and the physical changes associated with it caused by the reduction in levels of the hormone OESTROGEN. Periods may stop abruptly, gradually get farther and farther apart, or become progressively lighter. Many women have hot flushes and night sweats, which may continue for two to five years. Other women find menopause passes them by almost unnoticed. Hormone replacement therapy, (HRT) using oestrogen patches or tablets, is usually an effective remedy. During and after menopause, the bones become more brittle (see OSTEOPOROSIS) and fat levels increase in the blood, which can lead to atherosclerosis. The average age for menopause is between 45 and 55.

menstruation or periods. Monthly discharge of the blood-enriched lining of the womb via the vagina, which normally lasts from three to seven days. This marks the beginning of a menstrual cycle – changes which prepare the uterus for pregnancy. The monthly cycle lasts for about 28 days and is controlled by the hormones oestrogen and progesterone secreted by the ovaries. About two weeks after menstruation, the womb lining has built up again, and one of the ovaries releases an egg. If fertilised the egg implants in the womb lining, and pregnancy begins. Otherwise, the cycle continues.

metabolism Chemical processes occurring in the body's cells. When complex substances are broken down to provide the body with energy, it is called catabolism. When they are built up, during protein synthesis, for example, it is called anabolism. The metabolic rate is the amount of energy the body uses. Naturally thin people often have a high metabolic rate.

microsurgery Surgery in which the surgeon views the operation through a binocular microscope. It has dramatically improved the success rate for operations on cataracts, lazy eyes and some disorders of the ear. Microsurgery makes it possible to sew severed limbs back onto the body, because each minute blood vessel and nerve ending can be individually reconnected.

migraine Severe headache, often accompanied by nausea or vomiting, It may be preceded by sparks of light in the field of vision. Light and noise increase the pain. Some people may have one migraine in a lifetime, others are afflicted often. It can be quite disabling, lasting for as long as two days.

THE MAIN BRANCHES OF MEDICINE

Cardiology	Area of medicine that deals with the heart.
Chiropractic	Branch of medicine that relieves pressure on the nerves by manipulation of the spine and joints and so removes the source of pain or discomfort.
Endocrinology	Study and treatment of the body's hormone-producing glands, such as the pituitary, thyroid and pancreas.
Epidemiology	Study of disease in communities, including control of epidemics.
Gynaecology	Branch of medicine that deals with the female reproductive system.
Haematology	Study of the blood and treatment of blood diseases, such as leukaemia.
Immunology	Study of the body's immune response to disease.
Neurology	Medicine of the human nervous system, including the brain, spinal cord and nerves. It deals with conditions such as epilepsy and Parkinson's disease.
Obstetrics	Care of a woman during pregnancy and childbirth. Modern technology, such as ultrasound scanning, helps to ensure a safer birth and a healthy baby.
Oncology	Treatment of cancer by means of surgery, radiotherapy or drugs.
Ophthalmology	Medical and surgical treatment of disorders of the eye, including injuries, cataracts and glaucoma and the prevention of blindness.
Orthopaedics	Branch of surgery concerned with treatment of bones, muscles, ligaments and tendons. It also includes manipulation, exercise and the fitting of braces.
Osteopathy	Practice of therapy based on manipulation of bones and muscles.
Paediatrics	Branch of medicine dedicated to the physical and emotional health of children and young people. It deals with childhood diseases, growth and development.
Pathology	Study of disease, including post-mortem examinations.
Psychiatry	Medicine of abnormal behaviour and disorders of the mind.
Rheumatology	Area of medicine that deals with joints, muscles and connective tissues and seeks to treat diseases such as arthritis and gout.
Urology	Study of the urinary tract, which includes the kidneys and bladder.

motor neuron disease (MND) Progressive form of paralysis which usually occurs in those aged over 50. The cause is unknown. Nerves that control the body's muscle action degenerate, leading to muscle wastage. Eventually the muscles controlling speech, swallowing and breathing may become impaired. In the most severe cases, the victim dies within a few years, but in others the advance of the disease may be very slow or, in some instances, may even stop altogether.

♟In 1963, the physicist Stephen Hawking was diagnosed as having MND at the age of 21. However, he continues to write and research, despite being severely disabled and having a computer-generated voice.

mucous membrane Thin lining of the passages and cavities of the body such as the mouth, respiratory system and the digestive tract. The lining secretes mucus – a slippery, sticky fluid which lubricates and protects the membrane.

multiple pregnancy In Britain about 1 in 80 pregnancies lead to the birth of twins. There are two types of twin pregnancy. Either two eggs are released from the ovary at once, or the egg divides at an early stage in the pregnancy: the latter results in 'identical' twins. The presence of more than two foetuses in the womb is rare and usually due to fertility treatment.

multiple sclerosis (MS) Progressive disease of the nervous system which typically affects adults aged between 20 and 40 living in a temperate climate. In Britain, 1 in every 1000 people suffers from MS. Nerves in the brain and spinal cord lose their protective covering, becoming unable to function. This may lead to problems with vision, sensation and muscle control. MS occurs with different degrees of severity and speed. In severe cases it can lead to crippling paralysis: however, the condition is usually interspersed with periods of remission and improvement.

mumps Acute viral disease, usually contracted during childhood. Symptoms include a fever and swollen salivary glands. If the disease occurs in teenage or adult males, it may cause inflammation of the testes, sometimes resulting in sterility. A vaccine is available for children more than a year old.

muscles Body tissues, made up of bundles of muscle fibres, that are capable of contraction – or getting shorter – usually when they are stimulated by a nerve impulse. The human body has three types of muscle. The

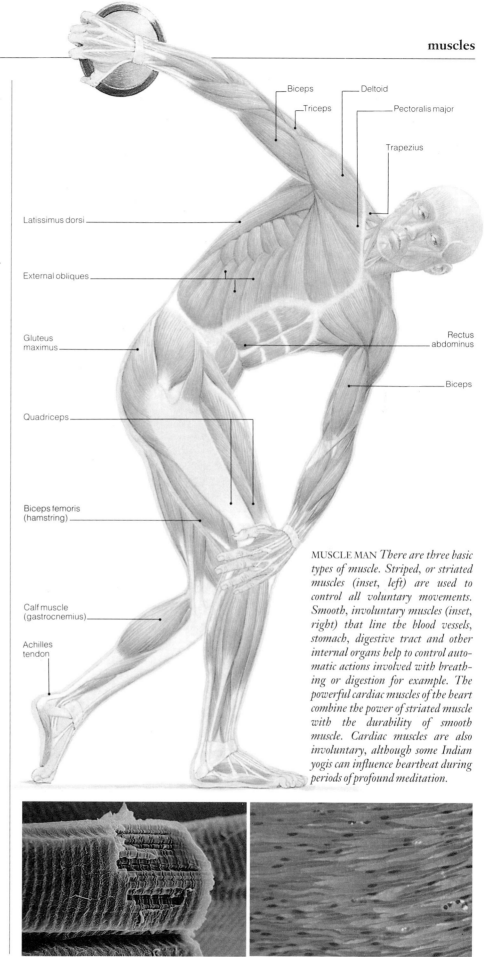

Biceps — Deltoid
Triceps — Pectoralis major
Trapezius
Latissimus dorsi
External obliques
Gluteus maximus
Rectus abdominus
Biceps
Quadriceps
Biceps femoris (hamstring)
Calf muscle (gastrocnemius)
Achilles tendon

MUSCLE MAN *There are three basic types of muscle. Striped, or striated muscles (inset, left) are used to control all voluntary movements. Smooth, involuntary muscles (inset, right) that line the blood vessels, stomach, digestive tract and other internal organs help to control automatic actions involved with breathing or digestion for example. The powerful cardiac muscles of the heart combine the power of striated muscle with the durability of smooth muscle. Cardiac muscles are also involuntary, although some Indian yogis can influence heartbeat during periods of profound meditation.*

most widely distributed is skeletal or striped muscle. There are about 650 skeletal muscles in the body, most attached to bones; they produce voluntary movements such as walking or nodding the head. The largest skeletal muscle is the gluteus maximus in the buttocks; the smallest is the stapedius in the ear. Smooth or involuntary muscle is found inside organs. It works under automatic control, in a process called peristalsis for example, food is gradually pushed along the intestine. Cardiac muscle is found only in the heart. It beats automatically, nonstop throughout a person's

life – an average of 2500 million beats in a 70-year lifetime. Nerve impulses from the autonomic NERVOUS SYSTEM speed up or slow down contractions according to the body's needs.

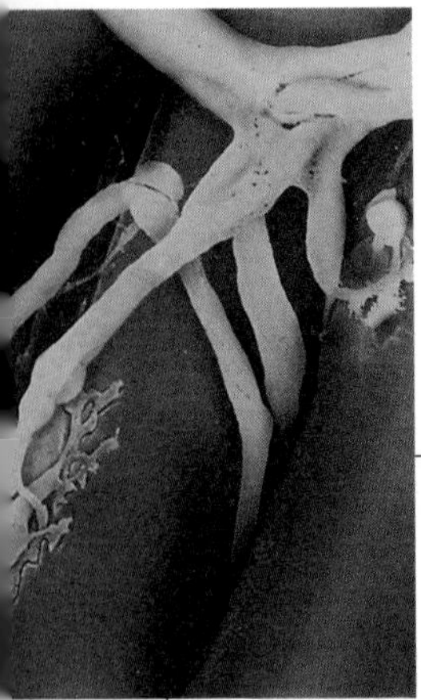

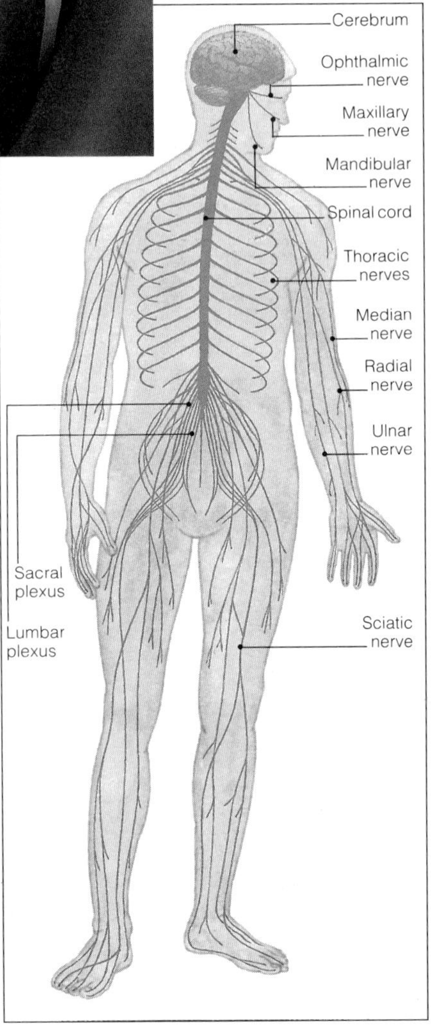

muscular dystrophy (MD) Hereditary disease in which the muscles are enlarged but weak. Children with some forms of MD may survive into late middle age, although they are likely to be disabled. But children with the most common form of MD, which affects only boys, rarely survive into their 20s. Adults who contract MD have quite a good chance of never suffering severe disability.

nervous system Network that controls and coordinates all the body's activities. At its core are the BRAIN and SPINAL CORD, forming the central nervous system (CNS). The CNS consists of billions of interconnected nerve cells that receive information from sense organs – eyes, ears, nose, tongue and skin. The brain processes and stores information before sending out appropriate instructions to muscles and body organs. Simple reflexes are controlled by the spinal cord. The autonomic nervous system automatically regulates involuntary functions such as heart rate and breathing rate. Linking the CNS to the rest of the body is the peripheral nervous system (PNS). This consists of a network of nerves, composed of bundles of neurons up to $3\frac{1}{4}$ ft (1 m) long. Impulses are relayed electrically and chemically along neurons at more than 330 ft (100 m) per second. Impulses pass from one neuron to the next across a SYNAPSE. Disorders of the nervous system include MOTOR NEURON DISEASE, POLIO, MULTIPLE SCLEROSIS, DEMENTIA, and some kinds of deafness or blindness. Trapped nerves – causing NEURALGIA – are extremely painful; SCIATICA which occurs in the spinal cord, is a common example.

neuralgia Spasmodic and severe pain, caused by the irritation or compression of a nerve. Neuralgia sometimes occurs after an attack of shingles.

neurosis Mental disorder which has no physical basis. Victims still have a grip on reality, and are usually aware of their own abnormal feelings. Phobias, OBSESSIVE-COMPULSIVE DISORDERS and eating disorders are all neuroses.

obesity An obese person is someone who weighs more than 20 per cent above the maximum recommended weight for their sex and height. Reasons may be dietary, genetic, hormonal or stem from a mental

disorder. Obesity carries with it an increased risk of conditions such as high blood pressure and heart disease.
In Britain, 1 person in 20 is obese.

obsessive-compulsive disorder Neurosis, or mental illness, characterised by repetitive, ritualised behaviour. This may, for example, manifest itself as an obsession with germs. Sufferers may wash themselves, their house or their car over and over again, no matter how clean things are and even if they are aware that their behaviour is bizarre. Other sufferers may dress or undress in a ritualised sequence or repeatedly check that a door is locked or a cooker has been turned off.

oestrogens Group of hormones mainly secreted by the ovaries, but also by the adrenal glands and, during pregnancy, by the placenta. Oestrogen hormones help to control MENSTRUATION and the smooth running of the female REPRODUCTIVE SYSTEM, and also stimulate development of secondary sexual characteristics at puberty. Synthetic oestrogen is used in the PILL, and in drugs that treat menstrual disorders, as well as some cancers.

osteopathy Branch of alternative medicine that involves manipulation of the body to restore normal usage. Osteopathy differs from CHIROPRACTIC which aims to treat many conditions mainly by manipulation of the spine.

osteoporosis Condition in which bones become brittle and susceptible to fracture. Osteoporosis is most common among women after they have been through the menopause. This is because their ovaries stop producing oestrogen which, among its other functions, helps to maintain bone density. Without this hormone, bones lose calcium and become weaker.

ovaries Pair of female sex glands located on either side of the pelvis. These are a vital part of the female REPRODUCTIVE SYSTEM because they secrete the sex hormones OESTROGEN and progesterone and produce eggs. Every woman is born with about 700 000 immature egg cells in her ovaries, about 450 of which will ripen during her lifetime. At ovulation an egg is released into the Fallopian tube about 14 days before the next period of MENSTRUATION. This is the most likely time for becoming pregnant. Ovarian cysts, which are common in women between the ages of 25 and 60, can usually be removed easily. If the cyst is large the whole ovary may need to be removed,

NERVOUS SYSTEM *The diagram shows the brain, spinal cord and the body's network of nerves. Signals, or electrical impulses, are carried from one end of a nerve cell to the other. Signals are passed on, chemically, to the next nerve at a synapse (inset).*

- Cerebrum
- Ophthalmic nerve
- Maxillary nerve
- Mandibular nerve
- Spinal cord
- Thoracic nerves
- Median nerve
- Radial nerve
- Ulnar nerve
- Sacral plexus
- Lumbar plexus
- Sciatic nerve

although the woman's fertility is usually maintained by her remaining ovary. Most ovarian cysts are benign.

pacemaker Electronic device that regulates the heart rate, first introduced in the USA in 1952. In a healthy heart, a node at the top of the right ventricle sends out electrical impulses which control the contractions of the heart. If this fails an artificial pacemaker can be implanted. Some 'demand' pacemakers function only when the heart is not producing its own electrical impulses at the correct intervals. It is sensitive enough to detect these delays and by filling in the gaps, maintains a normal rhythm. Some models include a radio transmitter and receiver, which means a doctor can adjust the rate of the pacemaker from outside the patient's body.

pancreas Large gland, located behind the stomach, which plays a dual role. As part of the ENDOCRINE SYSTEM, the pancreas secretes INSULIN directly into the bloodstream to control the blood glucose level. As part of the DIGESTIVE SYSTEM, it produces pancreatic juice, an enzyme-laden fluid, which breaks down fats, carbohydrates and proteins in the small intestine. The pancreas also produces sodium bicarbonate which neutralises stomach acid when it reaches the small intestine.

pandemic Infectious disease that spreads quickly among the population of a large area, such as a continent. The INFLUENZA pandemic of 1918-19 affected the whole world. (Compare EPIDEMIC and ENDEMIC.)

Paracelsus (1493-1541) Swiss physician who challenged the teachings of GALEN and contemporary doctors. He said that doctors' existing medical practices only resulted in 'killing and laming'. Paracelsus travelled widely in Europe and the Middle East and revived the teachings of HIPPOCRATES. Perhaps his greatest contribution to medicine was his holistic approach: he believed that diet, environment and the patient's relationship with the doctor were all vital parts of a cure.

paralysis Loss of voluntary movement due to the nervous system being damaged – somewhere between the brain and the nerves controlling the muscles of the affected area. Paralysis can be caused by a condition such as MOTOR NEURON DISEASE, PARKINSON'S DISEASE, MUSCULAR DYSTROPHY or a STROKE. It is classified according to which parts of the body are affected. Paraplegia is the paralysis of both legs and sometimes part of the trunk; hemiplegia affects one side of the body; and quadriplegia affects all four limbs.

paranoia Feeling of persecution or belief that all events are connected to, and conspiring against, oneself. Paranoiacs often belief that they have a mission, or that they are superior to the rest of the world. Schizophrenia, brain damage, alcoholism and manic depression may all lead to the development of paranoia.
⚜ Peter Sutcliffe, the 'Yorkshire Ripper' who murdered 14 women, was paranoiac. He believed he heard God's voice telling him to get rid of prostitutes.

Parkinson's disease Chronic disease of the nervous system that usually occurs in late middle age; it affects 1 in 1000 of the general population in Britain and 1 in 100 people aged over 65. Symptoms include shaking, partial paralysis of the face and stiffening of the muscles, causing a shuffling gait. It appears to be caused by a deficiency of dopamine – a chemical that transmits nerve impulses – in part of the brain that controls normal muscle contraction. Symptoms of the disease can be minimised by administering the drug L-dopa, a precursor of dopamine. Transplant of healthy brain tissue may be a future option.

⚜ After an epidemic of encephalitis lethargica in 1917-27 in the USA, several patients developed Parkinson's disease and fell into coma-like states which lasted until 1970 when Dr Oliver Sacks administered the drug L-dopa and the patients awoke. However, most patients were unable to cope with their 'awakening' and they fell back into their 'comas'.

Pasteur, Louis (1822-95) French scientist who discovered that GERMS cause disease. Pasteur's most important contribution to science was his discovery of microorganisms, which he first identified when studying the spoilage of wine during its fermentation. He discovered that by gently heating the wine he killed the bacteria that were turning it into vinegar; this process became known as pasteurisation. Pasteur also perfected immunisation, pioneered by the English doctor JENNER. He found that if he allowed bacteria or viruses to die before using them in a vaccine, it was just as effective and posed no danger. Pasteur discovered vaccines for anthrax as well as for rabies.
⚜ Today, the Pasteur Institute, founded by Pasteur himself, remains one of the most important research institutes in the world. Researchers there were among the first to identify the HIV virus that causes AIDS.

PASTEURISATION *Louis Pasteur, acknowledged as France's greatest scientist, proved infections were caused by living organisms, and his discoveries led to the development of antiseptics. Among the many tributes paid to him, the engraving (inset), dated 1895, hails Pasteur as a benefactor of humanity.*

513

WONDER DRUG *Alexander Fleming discovered penicillin in 1928, after a fungus spore settled on a bacteria specimen in his laboratory. He noticed that the bacteria died wherever the fungus grew.*

penicillin First ANTIBIOTIC – discovered by Alexander FLEMING in 1928. Penicillin, derived from a common mould that grows on fruit, is effective against a host of different bacteria including some of those that cause tonsillitis, bronchitis and syphilis.

🔦Although Fleming discovered penicillin, it was the pathologist Howard Florey and biochemist Ernst Chain who realised its importance in fighting infection. They managed to isolate and produce the active ingredient in the mould early in World War II and consequently thousands of lives were saved.

physiotherapy Treatment of disorders through physical means, such as massage, manipulation, ultrasound, heat treatment and breathing exercises. Physiotherapy is often necessary after an injury, a major operation, or for arthritis. Children with learning disabilities have also been found to respond to activities which teach balance and coordination.

pill, the Oral contraceptive. The most common type works by regulating a woman's production of OESTROGEN and progesterone, so that she fails to ovulate. Adverse side-effects continue to be a subject of debate. It appears, for instance, that women using certain types of the pill may have a slightly higher risk of developing breast cancers or a thrombosis. The first oral contraceptive was developed in 1956.

pituitary gland Master gland of the EN-DOCRINE SYSTEM, which regulates the functioning of many other glands in the system. The pituitary is directly connected to, and controlled by, part of the brain called the hypothalamus. Pituitary hormones influence growth, production of skin pigment, production of milk and contraction of the womb during labour, as well as many other bodily activities.

placebo Substance, with no medicinal powers, used in place of a drug. In drug trials, some of the subjects are given placebos while the others are given the real drug. This is to combat the 'placebo effect', when people believe they are being cured just because they are taking a pill. Placebos may be prescribed if doctors think patients need reassurance rather than medication.

placenta Fleshy disc-shaped organ that develops in the womb and is attached to the womb lining during pregnancy. The baby is attached to the placenta by the umbilical cord. The placenta contains a dense network of blood vessels and passes oxygen and nutrients from the mother's blood to that of the baby, carrying waste back the other way. After the baby is born, the placenta separates from the uterus wall and is expelled by the muscular contraction of the womb as the afterbirth. Some diseases, such as rubella, and some drugs, such as nicotine, can pass across the placenta.

plaque Thin layer of bacteria and mucus which forms on teeth even when they are brushed regularly. Bacteria in plaque break down sugary food releasing acids that erode the teeth and cause decay. Plaque also refers to a fatty deposit on an artery wall – a symptom of ATHEROSCLEROSIS.

pneumonia Inflammation of the lungs caused by bacteria or viruses. Symptoms include fever, pains in the chest and coughing. Most forms can be treated with antibiotics, but pneumonia can become severe and the patient may require hospital treatment. It can be a complication of several other illnesses such as bronchitis, chickenpox or measles. LEGIONNAIRES' DISEASE is a form of pneumonia.

polio or poliomyelitis. Acute viral infection which can cause inflammation of the central nervous system. Polio may be mild, with symptoms amounting to no more than a fever and headache, or severe, leading to paralysis or death. The first vaccine against polio was prepared by a Pittsburgh physician, Jonas E. Salk, in the early 1950s and used in 1954. It contained polio virus that had been killed with formalin. Three years later a Cincinnati virologist, Albert Bruce Sabin, began immunisation with his weakened live polio virus. Vaccination has reduced the incidence of polio in Britain from more than 6000 a year in 1956 to less than ten a year.

🔦The World Health Organisation hopes to eradicate polio by the year 2000.

post-natal depression State of despair that can affect a woman in the first year after having a baby. She may have to be treated for depression. This reaction is not only associated with a first child; equally, a mother who has suffered from post-natal depression with her first baby might have no adverse reaction after subsequent births.

post-traumatic stress syndrome Anxiety that comes on after a particularly violent event, such as war, rape, torture, a natural disaster or a crash. Sufferers may suffer flashbacks, recurring nightmares, depression and feelings of alienation or guilt.

pregnancy At conception a woman's egg is fertilised by a sperm and implants in the womb, where it develops into an embryo, and then a foetus. Pregnancy usually lasts about 280 days. With today's medical knowledge, babies that are born two and even three months premature often survive. If the foetus starts to grow outside the womb – usually in one of the Fallopian tubes – it is called an ECTOPIC PREGNANCY. The foetus is most vulnerable to infection, poisoning and miscarriage during the first three months of pregnancy.

premenstrual syndrome (PMS) also known as premenstrual tension (PMT). Irritability, fatigue, clumsiness and depression brought on by hormonal changes after ovulation and before menstruation. For most sufferers PMS may last a few days before and during a period, but some women suffer for two weeks every month. Taking evening primrose oil or vitamin B_6 seems to help some sufferers; progesterone tablets or suppositories, prescribed by a doctor, may help others.
♣ Premenstrual syndrome has been successfully used as a defence in murder trials.

prostate gland Chestnut-sized gland in the male reproductive system which secretes part of the fluid in semen. It is located at the base of the bladder. In elderly men it may become enlarged, and impede urination – a condition known as benign prostate hypertrophy. After lung cancer, prostate cancer is the most common cancer that affects Western men.

psoriasis Skin disease in which skin cells are produced too quickly, causing patches of scaly, itchy skin. Psoriasis is sometimes coupled with painful swelling of the joints. Sufferers tend to have their first attack between the ages of 10 and 30, and recurrent attacks for the rest of their lives. Psoriasis is not infectious.

psychiatry The study and treatment of mental illness. Psychiatrists may prescribe drugs, counselling or ▷PSYCHOTHERAPY. Until the middle of the 19th century, no distinction was made between mental illness and mental handicap. Now many psychiatric diseases, for example MANIC DEPRESSION and SCHIZOPHRENIA, can be treated with some success by medication.

psychosis Serious mental diseases such as SCHIZOPHRENIA and MANIC DEPRESSION in which the sufferer's mood changes or thoughts become disordered. The disorders are often traceable to physical or chemical abnormalities in the brain. Some psychoses run in families, and responsible genes may soon be identified. (See also HUMAN GENOME PROJECT.)

psychosomatic disorder Condition with physical symptoms caused by psychological factors, such as some ulcers, eczema or IRRITABLE BOWEL SYNDROME.

puberty Physical and psychological changes in adolescence. Boys grow pubic and facial hair, their voices break, their genitalia grow and they start producing sperm. Girls grow pubic hair, begin to menstruate and develop breasts. The development of these secondary sexual characteristics is caused by changes in HORMONE levels. Puberty normally starts between the ages of 10 and 15, but is usually later in boys than in girls.

rabies or hydrophobia. An acute viral disease endemic among wild animals throughout most of the world, especially dogs, foxes and, in South America, bats. Rabies has been kept out of Britain through a strict programme of quarantine. The virus is carried in the animal's saliva and transmitted to humans through bites or the licking of an open wound. The virus attacks the nervous system and causes paralysis, muscle spasms, foaming at the mouth, fear of water, and hallucinations. The victim must be treated before symptoms appear, otherwise death is almost inevitable. The first vaccine was developed by PASTEUR.
♣ About 10 000 people die of rabies every year in India.

radiation sickness Illness following exposure to ▷RADIATION. Effects depend on the amount of radiation and the length of exposure. A victim may start vomiting and have diarrhoea and be dead in hours, days or weeks. But symptoms may not appear for about two weeks, when the immune system has broken down and the body begins to succumb to infection. In this case, a bone marrow transplant may save the victim's life. Long term exposure to low doses of radiation may cause CANCER.

radiotherapy Treatment of a disease, usually cancer, with X-rays and other forms of ▷RADIATION, which attacks abnormally multiplying cells. The treatment is based on the fact that abnormal, rapidly growing cancer cells are more susceptible to low levels of radioactivity than most normal more stable cells. Nevertheless, radiotherapy may have unpleasant side effects such as hair loss, vomiting and nausea.

reflex Automatic, predictable reaction to a stimulus, for example shivering in response to cold. Simple reflexes such as this are often controlled by the autonomic nervous system. They are an important survival mechanism. Babies are born with complex primitive reflexes such as sucking at the nipple and gripping with their hands. They grow out of these after a few months.

repetitive strain injury or RSI. Specific symptoms which affect people such as supermarket checkout staff and keyboard operators, whose work involves the constant repetition of certain movements, Symptoms include aching neck, shoulders and back, tingling fingers and, in advanced cases, inability to move the fingers and hand without severe pain. Doctors are still unsure why some people are more susceptible than others. The condition can be controversial when there are no physical signs, although some sufferers develop swollen and inflamed tendons.

reproductive system Organs and glands involved in the production of male and female sex cells, fertilisation, pregnancy and birth. In human males, sperm are made in the testes; they travel past the seminal vesicles and through the prostate gland which secrete fluids that mix with the sperm to produce semen. During sexual intercourse, when semen is ejaculated through the penis into the female vagina, sperm can survive inside the female for up to five days. In females, the ovaries release a ripe egg, or in some cases of MULTIPLE PREGNANCY, several eggs. As the egg travels down the Fallopian tubes it is fertilised by a sperm to form a zygote, which implants in the womb and grows into a FOETUS. Hormones, TESTOSTERONE in males, and OESTROGEN and progesterone in females, play a vital role in the production of sex cells and the maintenance of the reproductive system. Those unable to conceive may try INFERTILITY TREATMENT.

respiratory system Organs involved in breathing and gas exchange. When the diaphragm flattens, and the ribs move upwards and outwards, air is sucked into the body through the nose and mouth. Air travels down the trachea, into the bronchi – the two main channels branching from the trachea into each LUNG. Then it flows along the bronchioles – the airways that branch out from the bronchi – and into the millions of tiny air sacs called alveoli. Here gas exchange takes place in the capillaries which surround each alveolus. Oxygen passes into the blood and carbon dioxide passes into the air which is forced out of the lungs when the diaphragm moves up.

rheumatic fever Disease which causes inflammation of the joints and can dangerously weaken heart valves. It is uncommon in the West, but is still a major cause of child mortality in the developing world. The disease, preceded by a streptococcal throat infection, is treated with penicillin.

rheumatism Blanket term for pain of the joints and muscles, most common among the elderly. The term includes many disorders, chiefly ARTHRITIS.

rickets Children's disease in which bones soften, bend and deform. Rickets is caused by vitamin D deficiency, due to poor diet or lack of sunlight. Vitamin D is vital for the absorption of calcium, a major component of bones. In victims of rickets the chest, pelvis and spine may become deformed, long bones bend and certain joints become enlarged. Early treatment with mineral and vitamin supplements can be successful.

ringworm Group of highly contagious fungal skin conditions, characterised by a ring appearing on the skin's surface. This happens because the fungus grows evenly outward while the skin at the centre of the ring recovers. Ringworm is usually treated with antifungal agents.

rubella see GERMAN MEASLES.

salivary glands Glands in the mouth that secrete saliva in response to, or anticipation of, food. The largest are the parotid glands, which swell during MUMPS.

salmonella Bacteria that are a common cause of FOOD POISONING, often through infection of poultry products. The bacteria release a toxin into the intestines causing diarrhoea, nausea and fever. Adults usually recover from salmonella poisoning in about two to five days, but small children and the aged may be more seriously affected. Many strains are resistant to antibiotics. A rarer form of salmonella causes TYPHOID.
🦠 Salmonella takes its name from Dr Salmon, (1850-1914) a US veterinary surgeon who identified the bacteria.

scans Painless techniques of viewing the inside of the body. The oldest type of scan is the ▷X-RAY. Computerised Axial Tomography (CT or CAT) scans create a three-dimensional image by taking X-rays from all around the body. Ultrasound, which produces a three-dimensional image by bouncing sound waves off organs, is commonly used to look at babies in the womb. Magnetic Resonance Imaging (MRI) scanners can distinguish between different tissues of the body by comparing their magnetic properties. MRI scans are used to detect diseases such as strokes, cancer and prolapsed discs.

scarlet fever Acute bacterial infection that causes a fever, sore throat, chills and a red rash. Once a common cause of death, it can now be treated with penicillin. It may lead to RHEUMATIC FEVER.

schizophrenia One of the most common psychotic disorders. In Britain, about 1 person in every 120 is schizophrenic. Treatment with drugs can often be effective. Schizophrenics have a fragmented view of reality, their understanding of the world being as distorted as a view in a broken mirror. The most common symptoms, unique to schizophrenia, are hearing voices and feeling as if thoughts have been inserted into the mind from somewhere else. Many schizophrenics also suffer from PARANOIA or that they are someone else. The cause is unknown, but there is a strong hereditary element.

sciatica Pain caused by pressure on the sciatic nerve, which runs from the lower spine to the feet. It is usually caused by a prolapsed disc in the spine and results in pain in the buttock and thigh.

scurvy The first disease found to have been caused by vitamin deficiency; in the mid 18th century, it was linked to a lack of vitamin C. With scurvy, wounds fail to heal, teeth become loose and fall out and bones become weak.
🦠 When the cause of scurvy was identified,

SKELETAL SYSTEM *There are 206 bones in the human body, and they are all interconnected by joints. The shape and mobility of joints vary greatly to suit their functions. For example, joints in the adult skull are fused together to protect the brain. In the limbs, where mobility is required, the bones are linked by hinge or ball and socket joints. Bone is made from concentric bundles of sheets called lamellae (above), shown here at 600 times their actual size.*

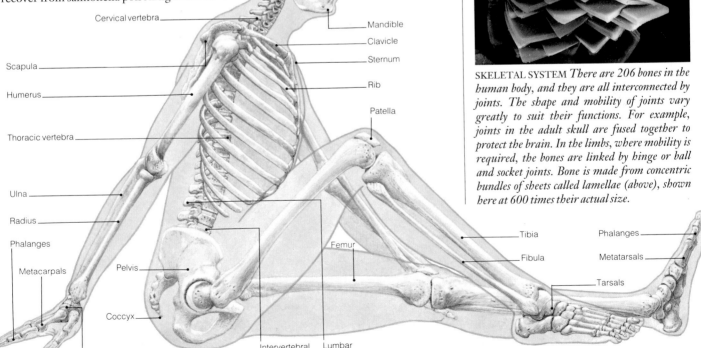

Skull
Mandible
Clavicle
Sternum
Rib
Patella
Cervical vertebra
Scapula
Humerus
Thoracic vertebra
Ulna
Radius
Phalanges
Metacarpals
Pelvis
Coccyx
Carpals
Intervertebral disc
Lumbar vertebra
Femur
Tibia
Fibula
Phalanges
Metatarsals
Tarsals

the British navy began issuing sailors with limes to suck in order to stave off the disease – hence the term Limey, often used in American slang for a Briton.

seasonal affective disorder (SAD) Chronic DEPRESSION in the dark months of winter, which appears to be related to increased production of the hormone melatonin in the brain. Sufferers improve if they are exposed to artificial, full-spectrum daylight for as little as half an hour every day. About 1 in 100 of the British population is estimated to suffer from the disorder in its true form. It is more common in Scandinavia where there is very little sunlight in winter.

shingles Re-emergence of the virus that causes chickenpox which may have lain dormant for years. The virus attacks nerve endings, producing a painful rash. This normally disappears after two to three weeks but the pain may persist for months.

shock Sudden, severe drop in blood pressure which can cause coma or death if untreated. Circulation slows dramatically, extremities may go grey or blue, body temperature plummets and pupils dilate. Shock is brought on by injury, but may also be caused by an acute illness or allergy.

sick building syndrome Set of flu-like symptoms apparently caused by working in modern office buildings. Itchy eyes, headache, fatigue and aching muscles are the commonest complaints. The cause has not been identified, but lack of both fresh air and daylight seem to be factors.

sickle cell anaemia Hereditary blood disease mainly affecting people of West African origin. It causes deformed crescent-shaped red blood cells to block capillaries, preventing tissues from getting enough oxygen to function efficiently.

skeleton The body's frame is made of bone and CARTILAGE. Humans have 206 bones, which consist of flexible collagen fibres reinforced with the minerals calcium and phosphorus. A typical long bone, such as the thigh bone, has a compact outer layer surrounding a honeycomb of lighter spongy bone. The central core is occupied by marrow. The red marrow of certain bones produces the body's blood cells.

skin Body's largest organ which acts as a waterproof covering, keeps out micro-organisms and protects the body from the sun's damaging ultra-violet rays. The skin has two layers, which cover subcutaneous fat. The lower layer – the dermis – contains nerve endings which respond to temperature, touch and pain. The dermis also contains SWEAT GLANDS which help to control the body's temperature, and sebaceous glands which produce the oily sebum to prevent the skin from drying out. The thin outer layer – the epidermis – is tough because its cells contain keratin, which is also the main constituent of hair and nails. The epidermis is constantly shedding dead cells and growing new ones. Skin also contains the pigment MELANIN which causes suntan, freckles and moles.

skin cancer Common form of cancer in the UK which occurs most frequently in older people who have been exposed to strong sunlight for long periods. There are three main types. Basal cell carcinoma, or rodent ulcer, usually appears as a small lump on the face which grows slowly and which should be removed surgically. This form of cancer rarely spreads to other parts of the body. Squamous cell carcinoma often appears as a slowly spreading ulcer on the hand, lip or ear. Malignant melanoma, the most serious type of skin cancer, often grows from a mole which enlarges, becomes lumpy and starts to bleed. Both of these forms, especially melanoma, can spread to other parts of the body and may prove fatal if not treated promptly by surgical removal of the cancer. Some scientists blame holes in the ozone layer for the rise in the incidence of skin cancer.

sleep Sleep is divided into two types. Most sleep is 'orthodox' – when brain waves and metabolism slow down. This is normally interrupted for a period of about 20 minutes, five times a night, by rapid eye movement (REM) sleep, in which the eyes move back and forth as if watching a high-speed tennis match. During REM sleep the brain is very active and DREAMS occur. Young adults may need eight hours sleep a night but less as they get older. Babies or invalids may sleep for up to 18 hours.

sleeping sickness or trypanosomiasis. Parasitic disease endemic in tropical Africa. It is spread by the tsetse fly and affects humans and wild animals. Early treatment with drugs is required; in advanced cases, victims become totally lethargic and eventually may fall into a coma and die.

slipped disc Painful condition caused by displaced cartilage between the vertebrae of the spine causing pressure on the adjoining nerves of the SPINAL CORD.

smallpox Highly contagious viral infection eradicated in 1979 by global VACCINATION. It used to be a major cause of death; those who survived it were left disfigured by pockmarked skin.
🗝 Today the smallpox virus exists in only two laboratories: one in Atlanta, Georgia, and one in Moscow.

smell The only sense that is linked directly to the memory – often prompting a distant recollection. Olfactory receptors located in the roof of the nasal cavity detect odours, and send impulses to the brain which are interpreted as smells. The sense of smell contributes to TASTE.
🗝 The average person can differentiate between 10 000 odours.

snoring People who snore may be overweight or sleep on their backs, but snoring may be caused by excess alcohol or a cold. Snorers may also stop breathing for brief moments during sleep, which is why they then take big, gulping breaths through the mouth; known as sleep apnoea, this can signal a serious blockage of the airways.

spina bifida CONGENITAL defect in which a portion of the spine has not developed, leaving part of the spinal cord exposed. Surgery in the first few days of life may cure the problem, but spina bifida can lead to serious disability.

spinal cord Thick string of nerve tissue that runs down the centre of the spine which acts as the main highway for nerve impulses to and from the brain. Together with the brain it makes up the central NERVOUS SYSTEM. The spinal cord also controls some REFLEX responses without recourse to the brain.

spleen Organ to the left of the stomach which destroys worn-out red blood cells and is a site of white blood cell production. In the foetus, the spleen produces red blood cells. It is possible to live without a spleen, but rupture of the spleen can be fatal – usually through loss of blood.

steroid Group of chemicals derived from CHOLESTEROL, some of which help to build proteins: sex hormones and vitamin D are both steroids. Synthetic steroids are used extensively in medical treatment, for example to reduce inflammation.
🗝 Synthetic protein-building steroids, usually called anabolic steroids, have been used illegally by some athletes to build up muscle strength, despite dangerous side-effects, such as weakening the heart muscle.

stress Tension or distress caused by an emotional or mental state, such as anxiety, or a physical factor, such as injury. Stress can disrupt the body's normal functioning and contribute to certain illnesses such as heart disease. Many complaints, such as eczema, migraine and ulcers, may be directly related to mental stress.

stroke Damage to part of the brain caused by the interruption of its blood supply due to the blockage of a blood vessel or bleeding in the brain. Strokes are a major cause of death in the developed world. High blood pressure, often associated with ATHERO-SCLEROSIS, increases the risk of a stroke. The effects of a stroke can range from temporary paralysis and slurred speech to permanent brain damage or death. Middle-aged or elderly people are most likely to suffer a stroke.

sweat glands Tiny glands in the skin that release sweat (water, salt and minerals) onto the skin's surface to cool the body – by ▷EVAPORATION – when it is too hot. Sweating is also caused by fear and anxiety.

synapse Gap between the endings of two nerve cells, or neurons, which forms a connection between them. An impulse travels along a nerve cell electrically. At the synapse it stimulates the release of a chemical called a neurotransmitter which passes across the synapse to the next neuron causing it to send an impulse along its length.
♣Amphetamines and narcotics work by acting on the synapses, increasing or limiting the amount of neurotransmitters.

syphilis Disease transmitted by sexual contact or by a mother to her foetus. Symptoms include painful sores, called chancres, usually around the genitalia, followed by a rash and more widespread sores. The disease may then lie dormant for as long as 30 years before erupting in its final phase which can damage the heart, brain and skin. Some victims go insane, experiencing total personality changes and delusions of grandeur. The disease can usually be cured quite easily with antibiotics if it is diagnosed and treated early on.
♣One year after Columbus brought syphilis back from the New World, the French army experienced the first mass outbreak of the disease. It then spread rapidly. Famous people who contracted syphilis include Henry VIII and Schubert.

tapeworm Parasitic worm, up to 30 ft (9 m) long, that lives in the human intestine where it absorbs food and produces eggs which are expelled in the faeces. Tapeworms are acquired by eating infected meat or fish that has not been properly cooked.

taste Without the sense of SMELL, taste would be crude, able to distinguish only between sweet, salt, sour and bitter. Each of these is detected by tastebuds on a different area of the tongue – sweet at the tip, salt and sour at the sides and bitter at the back. What the brain perceives as flavour is a combination of taste and smell.

teeth The crown of a tooth (the part outside the gums) is made mainly of dentine covered with a thin coat of enamel – the hardest substance in the body. The root of the tooth is embedded deeply in the jaw-bone and held there by a cement-like substance. At the centre of the tooth is the pulp, containing blood vessels and nerves. An adult's full set of 32 teeth gradually replaces the 20 milk teeth from the age of about six. There are eight incisors, used for cutting, four canines for tearing, eight premolars for shearing, and 12 molars for grinding. The hindmost molars, or wisdom teeth, are the last to appear. Tooth decay, or caries, is still widespread in the West because of the high levels of sugar in the diet. Fluoride helps to protect against caries, but plans to fluoridise local water supplies have often met considerable public opposition. Inflammation of the gums, or GINGIVITIS, is a common complaint.
♣The gums recede naturally with age, leaving more of the tooth exposed – hence the term 'long in the tooth'.

temperature, body The optimal temperature for efficient body functioning is around 37°C (98.6°F), but temperatures vary slightly between individuals, as well as fluctuating during the day. The body uses several techniques to maintain a constant temperature. These include sweating and expansion of the blood vessels in the skin to lose heat, and shivering and contraction of blood vessels in the skin to conserve heat. A high temperature often indicates that the body is fighting an infection, as in a fever. Babies with temperatures over 40°C (104°F), require immediate medical attention to cool them down. Similarly, temperatures below 35°C (95°F), which indicate a person is suffering from HYPOTHERMIA, are potentially dangerous.

tendon Tough band of tissue that connects muscle to bone. Unlike LIGAMENTS, tendons are not elastic. Rheumatoid arthritis and age may weaken the tendons. They can also become inflamed if subjected to repeated strain, as in tennis elbow and REPETITIVE STRAIN INJURY.

testosterone Male sex hormone, produced in the testes, that controls the development of male sexual characteristics. After PUBERTY it promotes normal sperm production. Some sportswomen have misused artificial testosterone to build up strength.

tetanus or lockjaw. Acute infectious disease in which the body's voluntary muscles, including those in the jaw, seize up and lock 4-25 days after infection. It is caused by bacteria that live in the soil entering the body through a wound, a burn or an animal bite, and releasing a toxin which attacks the central nervous system. Due to mass immunisation, the condition is now rare in the West. A routine booster is recommended every ten years.

thalidomide Drug developed in the late 1950s and prescribed as a sedative and sleeping pill. It was withdrawn in 1961 when it was identified as the cause of serious congenital deformities in more than 5000 babies.

thrombosis A blood clot. If it occurs in the blood vessels supplying the brain it causes a stroke. Thrombosis in arteries supplying the heart (coronary thrombosis) is the cause of heart attacks. Thrombosis often occurs in blood vessels narrowed by ATHEROSCLEROSIS.

thrush or candidiasis. Fungal infection commonly affecting the vagina and sometimes the mouth. Normally, the fungus is kept in check by bacteria. When these are weakened, for example by antibiotics, the fungus can multiply rapidly. Symptoms include a thick, itchy white vaginal discharge. The condition can usually be easily treated with antifungal drugs.

thymus Organ in the chest, in front of the heart, which is associated with the LYM-PHATIC SYSTEM and plays an important role in building up the body's IMMUNE SYSTEM. The thymus is most active between birth and puberty while the body is building up its immune response.

thyroid gland Important ENDOCRINE gland located in the throat, which secretes hormones that control the body's rate of METABOLISM and growth. Iodine is essential for the formation of the hormones, and deficiency may cause goitre, in which the thyroid gland swells. Underactivity of the

HIGH HOPES *Dr Christiaan Barnard, who performed the first heart transplant, gave patient Louis Washkansky, a 55-year-old South African grocer (inset), an 80 per cent chance of survival. After his operation Washkansky said he had never felt better, but 18 days later he died of pneumonia.*

thyroid gland – hypothyroidism – is associated with obesity, lethargy and dry skin and hair. Overactivity of the thyroid – hyperthyroidism – leads to rapid pulse, overactivity, weight loss and bulging eyes.

tinnitus Ringing, buzzing, whistling or hissing in the ears with no external cause. It is usually a symptom of inflammation or injury, or it may accompany loss of hearing in the higher frequency range in old age. There is often no effective treatment.

tonsils Two pads of lymph tissue at the back of the throat. Like the ADENOIDS, they form part of the LYMPHATIC SYSTEM. Tonsillitis – inflammation of the tonsils due to infection by bacteria or viruses – is a common complaint among children. Today, tonsils are only removed if there are serious and repeated complications.

touch Sense that detects temperature, texture and pain. The different types of receptors, in the form of specialised nerve endings, are found throughout the skin, as well as in some of the MUCOUS MEMBRANES. They are particularly concentrated in the face and hands.

toxins Poisonous substances produced from living things. They include animal products such as snake venom, secretions from the skin of some frogs and toads, and alkaloids manufactured by plants. Fungal toxins that kill bacteria are used as antibiotics. Human diseases, such as TETANUS, are caused by the toxins produced by bacteria rather than by the bacteria themselves.

transplant surgery Replacement of a damaged or diseased organ or tissue with a healthy one. Blood is the most frequently transplanted tissue, and corneas have also been transplanted since the 1930s. Kidney, heart and liver transplants are now common.

trauma Injury to mind or body. In the short term it is often followed by SHOCK; in the longer term, it may lead to POST-TRAUMATIC STRESS SYNDROME.

tuberculosis (TB) Infectious bacterial disease that leads to the formation of small nodules, or tubercles, which destroy tissue. It is spread by coughing and sneezing and normally affects the lungs, although it can affect the whole body. Victims may cough up blood, and suffer from chest pains, weight loss and fever. The disease can be cured using drugs, and vaccination can be given to those at risk. In the 19th century TB, then known as consumption, was responsible for about a quarter of all deaths. TB still causes some 3 million deaths a year in poorer parts of the world, and despite widespread inoculation programmes, is on the increase in pockets of urban deprivation in cities such as London and New York.

tumour Abnormal tissue growth which may be BENIGN (harmless) or MALIGNANT (cancerous). Malignant tumours may spread to other sites throughout the body (metastases or secondary tumours) and can be fatal if untreated.

typhoid Highly infectious and potentially fatal bacterial disease that spreads through contaminated water supplies. It attacks the intestines, causing abdominal pain and bleeding, as well as high fever, headaches and a state of confusion. Typhoid can be treated with drugs, but immunisation is always recommended when travelling anywhere with poor sanitation.

typhus Group of serious infectious diseases caused by bacteria-like organisms called rickettsiae. They are transmitted by fleas, lice, ticks and mites, often in conditions of poverty and overcrowding.

ulcer Inflamed open sore on the skin or on a mucous membrane such as the inside of the mouth, or stomach lining. Ulcers may be the result of poor blood supply, inadequate tissue drainage, injury, tumour, infection or general tiredness. Mouth ulcers are the most common, and usually heal without treatment. Gastric and duodenal ulcers are sometimes caused by excessive acidity, often aggravated by smoking, stress or alcohol. These ulcers can usually be treated with drugs and alkalis, which counteract the acidity, and sometimes by antibiotics. However, in some instances ulcers may require surgery.

urine Fluid made up of water, urea – the end product of protein breakdown – and other chemicals surplus to the body's requirements. It is produced in the kidneys by filtering the blood, and passes down two thin tubes called ureters to the bladder.

VITAMINS: SOURCES AND USES

Vitamin	Sources	Uses
A (retinol and carotene)	Liver, fish, egg yolk, carrot, greens, dairy products.	Bone growth; skin repair; vision; immune system.
D (calciferol)	Sunlight on human skin; yeast, egg, margarine.	Calcium and phosphorus for healthy bones and teeth.
E (tocopherol)	Vegetable oil, egg, nuts, margarine, wholegrain, greens.	Protection of cell membrane, and of vitamins A and C.
B_1 (thiamin)	Cereals, white flour, soya flour, yeast, meat, nuts.	Breaks down carbohydrates; healthy nervous system.
B_2 (riboflavin)	Yeast, dairy products, egg, cereal, greens.	Processing of energy; forming enzymes; body tissue.
B_3 (niacin)	Meat, fish, potato, bread, cereal, wheatgerm, peanuts.	Cell energy; circulation; cholesterol; skin, nervous system.
B_5 (pantothenic acid)	Offal, beans, egg, wholegrain, wheatgerm, peanuts.	Cell energy; skin and hair; nervous and immune systems.
B_6 (pyridoxine)	Yeast, wholegrain, fish, nuts, egg, potato, meat, greens.	Processing of protein; nervous system; haemoglobin.
B_{12} (cobalamin)	Lean meat, liver, kidney, milk, fish, shellfish, egg.	Red blood cells; nervous system; DNA and RNA.
C (ascorbic acid)	Citrus fruit, tomato, capsicum, berries, potato, greens.	Connective tissues; hormones; general chemical and physical processes; protects vitamin E.
Folic acid	Liver, kidney, raw or lightly cooked greens, brewer's yeast/ yeast extract, nuts, citrus fruit.	Production of red blood cells; maintenance of nervous system, formation of DNA and RNA.

Here it is temporarily stored until it is excreted through the urethra. In men, the urethra is also the passage through which semen is ejaculated during intercourse. Infections of the urinary tract are common and some are sexually transmitted. A burning sensation during urination is usually the result of inflammation of the urethra. Urine tests are often used to aid diagnosis of disease, as well as testing for the presence of alcohol or drugs. Pregnancy tests check urine for hormones from the placenta.

uterus or womb. Hollow, strongly muscled organ in which the foetus is protected and nourished during pregnancy and which contracts to expel the baby during CHILDBIRTH. The uterus is located behind the bladder in the lower abdomen. During fertile years, the womb lining is expelled once a month during MENSTRUATION.

vaccination Method of IMMUNISATION pioneered by JENNER. The term comes from the Latin *vacca* meaning cow because the vaccine he used to prevent SMALLPOX was derived from the milder cowpox.

varicose veins Swelling of the veins due to valve malfunctioning. They most often affect the legs. Pregnant women, obese people and those who stand for long periods are likely sufferers. Varicose veins around the anus are known as HAEMORRHOIDS. The veins can usually be shrunk and closed with injections, otherwise they can be removed by surgery.

vasectomy Cutting and tying of the tubes in the male reproductive system which carry sperm from the testes to the urethra. It is used as a form of CONTRACEPTION. The operation may be reversible and does not cause impotence.

venereal diseases Infections transmitted during sexual contact or intercourse. The best known are SYPHILIS, gonorrhoea, nonspecific urethritis and, more recently, AIDS and HERPES. Doctors now generally refer to them as sexually transmitted diseases.

vertigo Unpleasant sensation of giddiness, usually due to disorder of the organs of balance in the inner EAR. It can also be brought on by HYPERVENTILATION, high blood pressure or intoxication.

viral infections Group of common and sometimes serious diseases, including the common cold, herpes, influenza, rabies, chickenpox and AIDS. Viruses operate by taking over the functioning of a cell with its own DNA, and then using it to manufacture more viruses. Healthy cells produce a protein called interferon which prevents many viral infections from spreading. Unlike bacteria, viruses are not affected by antibiotics; however, drugs inhibit some, such as the herpes virus. The main defence is VACCINATION, but for some viruses, such as AIDS, no vaccine has yet been discovered, despite a great deal of research.

vitamins Substances that are essential for normal metabolism and growth, and which the body is unable to manufacture for itself. Vitamins are therefore an essential component of the diet, and their absence leads to a variety of deficiency diseases. Each of the main vitamins has a specific role. (See vitamins box.)

wart Small solid growth on the skin, also known as a verruca if it occurs on the sole of the foot. They are caused by a virus and are generally harmless. Hands and feet are the usual sites, but other parts of the body can be affected. Genital warts, transmitted through sexual contact can be treated with ointments. Medical treatments include freezing or burning them off; they can also be removed by laser.

whooping cough also known as pertussis. Sometimes severe infectious childhood disease caused by bacterial infection of the air passages. It is marked by violent fits of coughing, followed by a 'whoop' as air is gulped back into the lungs. There may also be fever, loss of appetite and vomiting. In its early stages whooping cough can be treated with antibiotics but they are not always effective. In Britain, the incidence of the disease has been reduced by routine vaccination of babies. Although immunisation may cause brain damage in a very small number of cases, the risk is still considerably less than the danger of catching whooping cough itself.

yellow fever Infectious disease prevalent in tropical areas of West Africa and South and Central America. It is caused by a virus carried by mosquitoes. Symptoms include fever and yellowing of the skin, which gives the disease its name. In severe cases, the victim may go into a coma and die. Before the discovery of the means of transmission, and the development of an effective vaccine, yellow fever was one of the great plague diseases, spreading from European settlers in affected areas. Many thousands of labourers died from it during the construction of the Panama Canal.

SCIENCE, SPACE
AND MATHEMATICS

From the tiniest atomic particles to the planets that whirl in space,
our Universe functions according to basic laws of physics
and chemistry. Scientists armed with the language of mathematics
have discovered much about the nature of matter and energy,
space and time; but their studies have revealed new
mysteries in quarks and quanta, big bangs and black holes.

ALBERT EINSTEIN

THE STRUCTURE
OF THE ATOM

SUBATOMIC COLLISION

VOLCANOES
ON MARS

AERODYNAMIC DESIGN *The body shapes of modern cars are the product of extensive aerodynamic testing for stability and fuel efficiency.*

absolute zero The lowest possible temperature. It is defined as 0 on the KELVIN scale (0K) and corresponds to $-273.15°C$. Absolute zero cannot be achieved, but scientists studying the properties of materials at very low temperatures (see CRYOGENICS) have reached within a few millionths of a degree of it. At absolute zero, there would be no heat energy left in a body.

acceleration Rate at which the VELOCITY of an object is changing. It is usually measured in metres per second per second (m/s^2). An object that maintains the same speed but changes its direction is also being accelerated. Acceleration is sometimes expressed in terms of the acceleration of a falling body due to the Earth's gravity, g (approximately equal to $9.81 m/s^2$). Prolonged accelerations above $4g$ are harmful to the human body. (See NEWTON'S LAWS OF MOTION.)

acid Corrosive substance which has a pH below 7 and turns LITMUS PAPER red. When dissolved in water, acids react with metals, alkalis and other BASES to form salts. Technically, acids are compounds capable of producing positive hydrogen IONS in solution. Some acids, such as sulphuric acid (H_2SO_4) and hydrochloric acid (HCl), give up hydrogen ions easily and are highly reactive. Others, such as sulphurous acid (H_2SO_3), give them up less easily and are less reactive. Organic acids, including vinegar (acetic acid) and lemon juice (citric acid), occur widely in nature.

aerodynamics Study of the flow and turbulence of gases, and of the interaction between moving objects and the atmosphere. It is particularly concerned with the principles of flight and with the design of more efficient shapes for aeroplanes and motor vehicles. Wind tunnels are used to test the 'drag' of new cars.

alcohol Naturally occurring compound formed by the fermentation of sugars. There are many different types of alcohol, all distinguished by having a hydroxyl group (OH) attached to a HYDROCARBON chain. Ethyl alcohol, or ethanol, the intoxicating component of beers, wines and spirits, has the formula C_2H_5OH. Wood alcohol (methyl alcohol or methanol) has the formula CH_3OH. Alcohols are used in the manufacture of many drugs, solvents, cleaning agents and explosives.

algebra Branch of mathematics in which numbers and numerical relationships are represented by letters and other symbols. It is used to express mathematical relationships in general terms, so that they can be applied to a whole set of numbers. Thus PYTHAGORAS'S THEOREM is expressed algebraically as $a^2 + b^2 = c^2$, which holds good for any right-angled triangle, whereas $3^2 + 4^2 = 5^2$ is true only for a triangle with these precise measurements. Algebra can also be applied to problems in logic (see BOOLEAN ALGEBRA).

alkali Compound, usually a metal hydroxide, which forms a strong BASE when dissolved in water – for example, caustic soda (sodium hydroxide, NaOH). Some minerals, such as potash (potassium carbonate, K_2CO_3), are also referred to as alkalis. Alkali solutions feel soapy, and are used in the manufacture of soaps.

alloy Mixture of two or more metals, or of a metal and another material. Very few metals are now used in their pure state. Examples of alloys include brass, containing copper and zinc, and the many types of steel, made from iron with small amounts of carbon and a variety of other elements. A modern car may contain more than 100 different alloys. The development of lightweight aluminium alloys made the construction of commercial airliners possible.

alternating current (AC) Electric current whose flow alternates rapidly in direction (at 50 cycles per second in the UK). AC, unlike DIRECT CURRENT (DC), can be easily stepped up to very high voltages (400 000 volts or more) for long-distance transmission and then stepped down to a safer domestic voltage (240 volts in the UK) using transformers. Mains current is always AC. (See also ELECTRICITY.)

amp, ampere Unit of electric current or the rate of charge flowing through an electric circuit. It is named after André-Marie Ampère (1775-1836), the French mathematician, physicist and philosopher remembered for his important work on electricity and electromagnetism. The intensity of electric shocks depends on amperage. (See also OHM.)

amplitude Height of a crest, or the depth of a trough, of a WAVE, measured from the midpoint of the cycle. Amplitude modulation, or AM, involves altering the amplitude of a wave, usually a radio wave, in such a way that it carries information to the receiver. (See also FREQUENCY.)

anode Positively charged electrode in a battery or in the process of ELECTROLYSIS. (Compare CATHODE.)

antimatter Matter composed of SUBATOMIC PARTICLES in which certain properties of a normal particle, such as electric charge, are reversed. The antiparticle corresponding to an ELECTRON is a positron, which has the same mass as an electron but a positive instead of a negative charge. An antiproton has the same mass as a PROTON but a negative instead of a positive charge. Contact between antimatter and matter results in the annihilation of both, with the release of large quantities of energy. Particles of antimatter are sometimes produced naturally by COSMIC RAYS but they can also be created in PARTICLE ACCELERATORS.
Very little antimatter has been found in our part of the Universe, but it is theoretically possible that other parts of the Universe are composed entirely of antimatter.

Arabic numerals The numbers 1, 2, 3, 4, 5, 6, 7, 8, 9 and 0. This system of notation originated in India and was brought to Europe in the 14th century by the Arabs. Unlike the more cumbersome ROMAN NUMERALS, which they replaced, Arabic numerals were able to represent zero.

Archimedes (*c.*287-212 **BC**) Greek scientist, mathematician and inventor, best remembered for Archimedes' principle. This states that any body partially or totally immersed in a liquid or a gas becomes buoyed by an amount equal to the weight of fluid it displaces: a boat floats and a hot air or helium balloon rises because they weigh less than the water or air they displace.
Archimedes is said to have run naked through the streets of Syracuse shouting *Eureka!* 'I have found it!' after he realised,

INVENTION UNDER SIEGE *When Syracuse was besieged, Archimedes turned his genius to the design of fortifications and weapons – so successfully that the city held out for three years.*

while bathing, that the volume of an object can be measured by the volume of water it displaces. He used this fact to prove that a supposedly solid gold crown did not have the right DENSITY to be pure gold.

🔱 Archimedes also investigated machines, including the lever, and is supposed to have said 'Give me a place to stand and I will move the Earth' – in other words, given a long enough lever and a fulcrum near the object to be moved, it is possible for a single man to move anything, no matter how heavy. The Archimedes screw, which he invented, is still used to raise water for irrigation in Egypt.

Aristotle (384-322 BC) Greek philosopher and scientist regarded as the founder of the European scientific tradition. Aristotle emphasised the importance of the direct observation of nature and believed that all events should have causes, which brought him into conflict with his tutor, ▷PLATO. He laid the foundations for the study of anatomy and embryology and devised a 'ladder of nature' which ranked living things in terms of their complexity – the basis for the science of classification or taxonomy. He also founded the study of ▷LOGIC in which he believed that ▷SYLLOGISM should be the basis of all logical thought. (See also ▷ARISTOTLE in 'Ideas, Beliefs and Religion'.)

asteroid Small, irregularly shaped lump of frozen rock or metal orbiting the Sun. There are more than 2000 asteroids, mostly in the asteroid belt between Jupiter and Mars. Ceres, the largest, is 584 miles (940 km) in diameter. Asteroids may be fragments of a shattered planet, and are also called 'minor planets' or 'planetoids'.

atom The basic building block of matter. The atom is the smallest unit of a chemical ELEMENT that still retains the properties of the element. The concept of the atom was first put forward by the Greek philosophers Leucippus (5th century BC) and Democritus (460-370 BC), but it was not generally accepted until the early 19th century, when the English scientist John DALTON showed how it explained CHEMICAL REACTIONS and COMPOUNDS. The modern theory of the atom stems from the work of Ernest RUTHERFORD and Niels BOHR in the early 20th century. They demonstrated that the atom is not an indivisible particle of matter, as had previously been thought, but is in fact mainly composed of empty space, with negatively charged ELECTRONS orbiting in distinct 'shells' or 'energy levels' round a positively charged nucleus, which is itself composed of positively charged PROTONS and uncharged NEUTRONS. A large amount of NUCLEAR ENERGY is contained within the atomic nucleus, which is released when nuclei are split or when they fuse together. This is the basis of nuclear reactors and nuclear weapons such as the atom bomb.

🔱 Theoretical physicists dealing with the extreme conditions found in PARTICLE ACCELERATORS or the interior of stars have further divided the atomic nucleus into whole families of SUBATOMIC PARTICLES in their attempts to understand the basic

AT THE HEART OF MATTER *Four electrons circle the four protons and five neutrons, which are themselves made up of triplets of quarks, in the nucleus of a beryllium atom.*

nature of matter and energy (see QUARKS and UNIFIED FIELD THEORIES). The notion of electron shells and orbits has had to be considerably modified to take account of the UNCERTAINTY PRINCIPLE and QUANTUM MECHANICS.

atomic number The number of PROTONS in the nucleus of an atom of a particular chemical ELEMENT. The higher the atomic number, the heavier the atom. The PERIODIC TABLE represents the elements arranged in order of their atomic numbers. (Compare ATOMIC WEIGHT.)

atomic weight or, more correctly, relative atomic mass. The MASS of an atom measured on a scale in which the carbon ISOTOPE C^{12} is taken as 12. Atomic weights of the naturally occurring elements range from just over 1 for hydrogen to about 238 for uranium. Since most of the mass of an atom resides in the nucleus, the atomic weight is roughly equivalent to the number of PROTONS and NEUTRONS in the nucleus. (Compare ATOMIC NUMBER.)

average Figure that is typical or representative of a set of figures, and thus allows general conclusions to be drawn about the set as a whole. It generally refers to the mathematical average, or mean. (See MEAN, MEDIAN AND MODE.)

axiom In mathematics, a proposition which cannot itself be proved but from which other results are derived. An important axiom in Euclidean geometry (see EUCLID) is that only one line can be drawn through a point that will be parallel to another given line.

axis Straight line about which an object may be rotated (axis of rotation) or divided into symmetrical halves (axis of symmetry). In mathematics, axes are the horizontal and vertical reference lines (the x axis and y axis) used to plot points on a graph. The Earth's axis of rotation runs, by definition, through the North and South Poles.

background radiation Any form of radiation, for example light or radioactivity, that is generally present in the surroundings. It often has to be eliminated before scientific experiments can be performed, and it also interferes with such things as radio transmission. It is sometimes referred to as 'noise'. Background radiation due to radioactivity comes from cosmic rays and from naturally occurring radioactive isotopes in rocks. (See also COSMIC BACKGROUND RADIATION.)

GATEWAYS THROUGH SPACE AND TIME *Gas spirals into a black hole from a nearby star; the fate of matter in a black hole is a mystery, but it may emerge in another region of space and time.*

base Substance which, when dissolved in water, reacts with ACIDS to form SALTS. In technical terms, bases form negative IONS in solution, usually hydroxyl ions (OH⁻), and are capable of accepting a positive hydrogen ion from an acid. ALKALIS form bases when dissolved, as does ammonia (NH_3), and the oxides and hydroxides of metals are mostly bases, for example caustic soda (sodium hydroxide, NaOH) and quicklime (calcium oxide, CaO). Bases have a pH of 7 to 14 and turn LITMUS PAPER blue. In ORGANIC CHEMISTRY, bases generally contain nitrogen. The genetic codes contained in ▷DNA are stored as a sequence of organic bases.

benzene Clear liquid HYDROCARBON, the simplest of the group known as 'aromatic' compounds in ORGANIC CHEMISTRY. Benzene has the formula C_6H_6, with six carbon atoms linked in a hexagonal ring. The structure is very stable. Vast numbers of compounds, including phenols and steroids, are formed by substituting other elements or groups of elements for the hydrogen atoms, or by joining several benzene rings together.
🕯The hexagonal ring structure of benzene was first recognised in 1865 by the German chemist Friedrich August Kekulé von Stradonitz (1829-96) after he had a dream about a snake biting its own tail.

big bang theory The most widely accepted theory of the birth of the Universe. It states that all matter and energy in the Universe were created in a single colossal explosion between 15 000 and 20 000 million years ago. Thereafter, the cosmic soup of dispersed matter became 'lumpy' and began to coalesce to form stars and galaxies. There is evidence for the big bang theory in the RED SHIFT of distant galaxies, which shows that the Universe is still expanding, and in the existence of microwave COSMIC BACKGROUND RADIATION, thought to be the 'echo' of the big bang. (See also STEADY-STATE THEORY.)
🕯Scientists do not know whether the expansion of the Universe will continue for ever. The 'oscillating Universe' theory claims that the expansion will stop because of the mutual gravitational attraction of all the matter in the Universe. The Universe will then contract back into a vanishingly small space, another big bang will occur and a new universe – possibly with different laws of physics – will be born.

binary star Pair of stars which revolve around a common centre of gravity; also known as a double star. About half the stars in the sky are binary or multiple stars. Variable stars, whose brightness seems to wax and wane, are often 'eclipsing binaries', which obscure each other as they revolve.

binary system In mathematics, a system of counting based on the number 2 instead of the number 10 – the basis of the decimal system. Whereas the decimal system uses units ($10^0=1$), tens ($10^1=10$), hundreds ($10^2=100$), thousands ($10^3=1000$) and so on to represent numbers, the binary system uses units (2^0), twos (2^1), fours (2^2), eights (2^3) and so on. The advantage of the binary system is that any number can be represented by a combination of only two digits, 0 and 1. It can thus be represented by a series of 'ons' and 'offs' in an electronic circuit, and is the basis of the digital ▷COMPUTER.

black hole Object in space that exerts a gravitational pull so strong that nothing, not even light, can escape from it. It is thought that a black hole is the end product of the death of a massive star – about ten times the mass of the Sun – in a SUPERNOVA. Once the star ceases to burn, there is nothing to stop the remaining matter from collapsing inwards under the force of its own gravity. There is theoretically no end to the collapse and all that is left is what is termed a 'singularity' – which may represent a doorway to another universe. Astronomers now believe they have detected at least one black hole in our own galaxy.

Bohr, Niels (1885-1962) Danish physicist best known for his work on the structure of the atom, for which he won a Nobel prize in 1922. Bohr's work led to modern QUANTUM MECHANICS. He fled to America during World War II and, despite misgivings, helped to develop the atom bomb.

boiling point Temperature at which a liquid turns to a gas and ceases to increase in temperature. As liquid is heated, the temperature rises and the rate of evaporation increases. However, at the boiling point, all the remaining liquid evaporates with no further increase in temperature. The boiling point of water is defined as 100° on the Celsius scale.

bond, chemical Linkage between atoms that binds them into MOLECULES. Atoms form bonds because they behave as if they were seeking an ideal number of electrons in their outer 'shells'. They will give up or accept electrons from other elements, or in some cases share them, in order to achieve this number, forming bonds as they do so. Most elements are chemically stable when they have eight electrons in their outer shell; hydrogen is an exception, needing two. Thus oxygen, with six electrons in its outer shell, and hydrogen, with one, can each fill their outer shells if a single oxygen atom shares an electron with each of two hydrogen atoms, forming a molecule of water with the formula H_2O. Bonds in which electrons are shared are called 'covalent' bonds. Chlorine with seven electrons in its outer shell, and sodium with one, will bond if the sodium atom donates its electron to the chlorine atom. The sodium atom acquires a positive charge and the chlorine atom a negative one; the electrical attraction between them forms an 'ionic' bond. (See also VALENCE.)

Boolean algebra The application of mathematical techniques to ▷LOGIC. Developed by the British mathematician George Boole (1815-64), it is fundamental to the design of circuits in modern electronic computers. Boolean algebra is also the basis for SET THEORY.

Boyle's law Principle which states that, at a constant temperature, the pressure of a given mass of gas is inversely proportional to its volume. The principle is used in barometers, which monitor changes in air pressure by measuring the expansion and contraction of a fixed mass of gas. The law is named after the British scientist and philosopher Robert Boyle (1627-91), one of the founders of modern chemistry.

Brahe, Tycho (1546-1601) Danish astronomer who, over a 20-year period, catalogued the position and movements of more than 1000 stars and planets with great accuracy – a remarkable achievement in the days before telescopes. Brahe believed that the planets revolved around the Sun, but that the Sun itself revolved around a stationary Earth. Ironically, it was Brahe's own data that enabled his assistant, Johannes KEPLER, to prove that the Earth revolves around the Sun – as had been suggested by Nicolaus COPERNICUS.

bubble chamber Device used to observe the tracks of SUBATOMIC PARTICLES created by collisions in a PARTICLE ACCELERATOR. It consists of a pressurised container of liquid hydrogen kept just below its boiling point. When pressure is released, as happens in the wake of a fast-moving particle, the liquid starts to boil, forming strings of bubbles that can be photographed and analysed.

buffer A solution, usually containing a weak ACID and a BASE or SALT, which maintains a constant level of acidity or pH when further acids or bases are added. Buffers are familiar in the form of medicines designed to decrease stomach acidity.

calculus Branch of mathematics that deals with quantities that are continuously changing. Differential calculus studies rates of change at a particular moment in time, while integral calculus deals with the sum of the changes over a period of time. Differential calculus would be used to work out the acceleration of a car whose speed (or velocity) was changing, while integral calculus would be used to calculate the distance it had travelled. Calculus was developed independently in the 17th century by Isaac NEWTON in England and Gottfried ▷LEIBNIZ in Germany.

calorie The amount of heat required to raise the temperature of 1 gram of water by 1°C. Since heat is simply a form of energy, it is usually measured in JOULES rather than calories (1 calorie = 4.184 joules). Dieticians, however, still use Calories – with a capital 'C' (also called kilocalories and equal to 1000 calories with a small 'c') – to measure the energy content of foods.

capillary Tube with a very small internal diameter, such as the fine blood vessels that supply the individual cells of the body. Capillaries draw up liquids by the action of SURFACE TENSION on the walls of the vessel. Plants absorb and raise water from the soil through capillaries in their roots.

carbon Non-metallic chemical element which forms the basis of all living tissue (see ORGANIC CHEMISTRY). Pure carbon occurs naturally as diamond, graphite, charcoal and soot. It forms two stable oxides. Carbon monoxide (CO), a constituent of car exhaust, is highly poisonous. Carbon dioxide (CO_2) is produced by burning organic matter, including fossil fuels, and is a major contributor to the ▷GREENHOUSE EFFECT.

catalyst Substance that initiates, or speeds up, a chemical reaction without itself being changed. Catalysts are used throughout the chemical industry. In living things, ▷ENZYMES act as biological catalysts.

catastrophe theory The mathematical study of sudden or discontinuous change. It is used to analyse situations in which small changes bring about large, catastrophic, effects – the collapse of a bridge, for example, or panic on the stock market. It has been applied to situations as diverse as domestic arguments and epidemics.

SCIENCE, SPACE AND MATHEMATICS

DANCE OF THE PARTICLES *Showers of subatomic particles, created in the high-energy 'atom smashers' at CERN (below) and Brookhaven (right), trace out intricate arabesques inside the bubble chamber as they are born, decay and die.*

THE HAMMER AND THE FORCE *In order to keep the hammer from flying off at a tangent while he whirls it around, the hammer thrower must exert centripetal force. As soon as he lets go, and the centripetal force is removed, the hammer will hurtle in a straight line to its ultimate, and possibly medal-winning, destination.*

cathode The negatively charged electrode in a battery, or in ELECTROLYSIS, to which positive ions move. (Compare ANODE.)

Celsius Temperature scale, in which water freezes at 0° and boils at 100°, and each degree is one hundredth part of the range between the two. Originally known as centigrade, the scale was renamed Celsius in 1948, after the Swedish astronomer Anders Celsius (1701-44) who devised it. One Celsius degree is equivalent to $1\frac{4}{5}$ Fahrenheit degrees; to convert Celsius to Fahrenheit, divide the Celsius temperature by 5, multiply by 9 and add 32; 20°C is $^{20}/_5 \times 9$ (=36) plus 32, which equals 68°F.

centre of gravity The point in an object through which its entire weight (or mass) can be considered to operate. For an object to stay upright, a line drawn perpendicularly through its centre of gravity must fall within the area of its base. If it falls outside, the object will topple over.

centripetal force Force that keeps revolving objects on a circular path when they would otherwise move in a straight line. Centripetal force appears to be balanced by a corresponding centrifugal force – which is what seems to throw the passengers against the doors when a car goes round a bend. In fact there is no such thing as centrifugal force, merely inertial resistance to the centripetal force.

chaos theory Branch of mathematics dealing with systems that are inherently unstable and unpredictable. Developed with the aid of powerful computers during the 1970s and 1980s, it has considerable implications for much that happens in the real world – the weather, the economy, the flow of traffic or turbulence in liquids, and many other things. In chaotic systems, very small changes may have very large cumulative effects – as if the flapping of a butterfly's wings in Mexico were to produce a tornado off the coast of Indonesia.

chemical reaction Process in which the bonds that hold chemical compounds together are rearranged to form new compounds. Chemical reactions are represented by equations, in which the original compounds (the reagents) are shown on the left, and the products on the right. Thus the equation $C + O_2 \rightarrow CO_2$ represents the combining of a single atom of carbon with two atoms of oxygen to form a molecule of carbon dioxide. All chemical reactions either release or absorb energy, usually in the form of heat. The rate at which a reaction happens is affected by such factors as temperature, pressure, surface area and the presence or absence of a CATALYST.

chemistry Study of the composition of substances and of the ways in which they interact. Its main branches are ORGANIC CHEMISTRY, which deals with the properties of carbon compounds, inorganic chemistry, which deals with all other elements, and physical chemistry, which is concerned with such properties as temperature, pressure and volume.

chromatography Method of separating and analysing the components of a mixture of chemical compounds. Chemicals are absorbed to different degrees when passed through absorbent material – just as the dyes in an ink blot will separate when water is dripped onto blotting paper. In gas chromatography, the sample is vaporised and carried by an inert gas through a tube filled with liquid-coated particles. Analysis of the gas as it leaves the tube provides a sensitive means of identifying the components of even complex organic mixtures.

circle Closed curve that is everywhere equally distant from a fixed point, known as the centre. Any line that crosses a circle and passes through the centre is known as a diameter, and any line from the centre to the boundary of the circle is known as a radius. The distance round the outside of a circle (its circumference) divided by the diameter is equal to π or PI. The area of a circle is equal to πr^2, where r is the radius, and is greater than the area enclosed by any other figure of equal circumference.

cold fusion Fusion of hydrogen nuclei to form helium (see NUCLEAR FUSION) at moderate temperatures rather than at millions of degrees centigrade. If it could be achieved, which many scientists doubt, cold fusion would provide almost inexhaustible supplies of clean, safe and cheap power.

colloid Mixture in which fine particles of one substance are dispersed, without being dissolved, in another. Fog, paints and butter are all colloids. (See also EMULSION.)

comet Lump of dust, stones and frozen gas, often referred to as a 'dirty snowball', that follows a highly elliptical orbit round the Sun. As it approaches the Sun, the comet heats up and gives off a bright cloud of dust and gas. The tail of a comet points away from the Sun and is caused by the SOLAR WIND. The best known is HALLEY'S COMET, but the comet Shoemacher-Levy achieved celebrity in 1994 when it collided with JUPITER.

compound Substance containing two or more ELEMENTS combined in specific proportions. Compounds are the product of a chemical reaction and, unlike mixtures, they cannot be separated by physical means. Water (H_2O) is a compound of hydrogen and oxygen, while common salt (sodium chloride or NaCl) is a compound of the metal sodium and the gas chlorine.

condensation Conversion of a vapour into a liquid, the opposite of EVAPORATION. It is generally the result of cooling, and is most marked where a vapour comes into contact with a cold surface. Dew and fog are both caused by the condensation of water droplets as moisture-laden air cools down.

conduction Transfer of energy through a medium which is itself apparently unchanged. For example, wires conduct electricity, the bottom of a pan conducts heat, and optical fibres conduct light. (Compare CONVECTION; RADIATION.)

conic sections Curves formed by slicing through a cone. Depending on the angle of the slice, the curve may be an ellipse, a parabola or a hyperbola. (See also BOX.)

conservation, laws of Fundamental principles of science. They state that, in self-contained systems, various quantities always remain constant – for example, the amount of energy or matter in a set of chemical reactions, or the total momentum in a system of moving bodies.

constant Number or quantity that never varies or changes. The SPEED OF LIGHT in a vacuum, PLANCK'S CONSTANT and PI are universal constants – they remain the same at all times and in all places.

constellation Group of stars that appear close together in the sky, often represented in pictorial form as an animal or mythological figure formed by drawing lines between the stars. All objects in the sky are assigned to one of 88 constellations for naming and identification. Well-known constellations of the Northern Hemisphere include the Plough and the 12 signs of the ZODIAC.

convection Transfer of heat within a fluid (gas or liquid) by the movement of the fluid itself. As heat is applied to the fluid, the warmer areas expand, become less dense and rise; cooler fluid takes their place. The ascending fluid loses heat through mixing with cooler fluid and sinks again, causing circular convection currents to develop. Convection currents caused by uneven heating of the Earth's surface drive the circulation of air in the atmosphere, which gives rise to winds and weather. (Compare CONDUCTION; RADIATION.)

coordinates Set of numbers used to define the position of a point on a surface or in space. Map coordinates and latitude and longitude are familiar examples. Cartesian coordinates are used to define a point in relation to two axes (x and y) drawn at right angles to each other, and are used for drawing graphs.

Copernicus, Nicolaus (1473-1543) Polish astronomer who believed that the Sun, not the Earth, was at the centre of the Universe, thus challenging the established

CONIC SECTIONS

Conic sections play an important role in several branches of physics, including astronomy. They were first studied in detail by the Greek philosopher Apollonius (*c*.262-190 BC).

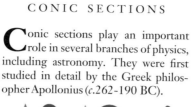

Circle   Ellipse   Parabola

CUTTING THE CONE *As a cone is sliced at increasing angles, the exposed curve changes from a circle to an ellipse and then to a parabola, whose arms can never meet. Eventually, the slice intersects both halves of a double cone, forming a double-branched hyperbola.*

Hyperbola

orthodoxy that had prevailed since the time of PTOLEMY in the 2nd century AD. However, it was another hundred years before GALILEO and KEPLER provided the theoretical and observational evidence for the theory and established what became known as the Copernican revolution.

cosmic background radiation Weak MICROWAVE radiation in space thought to represent the 'echo' of the BIG BANG. It was discovered in 1965 and appeared to be uniformly distributed throughout space. However, in 1992, the Cosmic Background Explorer satellite (COBE) found 'ripples' in the microwave background, providing evidence for the first time of how the original 'soup' of matter started to become 'lumpy' and how the first seeds of the stars and galaxies may have been formed.

cosmic rays Streams of electrons, protons and other atomic fragments, moving close to the speed of light, which continuously 'rain' down on the Earth's upper atmosphere. There, they interact with further atomic nuclei, producing showers of SUBATOMIC PARTICLES at the Earth's surface. The origin of cosmic rays is uncertain; some come from the Sun but others appear to come from SUPERNOVAS or PULSARS.

cryogenics Branch of physics dealing with the behaviour of materials at temperatures close to ABSOLUTE ZERO. It includes such phenomena as superfluidity – the ability of liquid helium to flow up the sides of its container – and SUPERCONDUCTIVITY, in which materials conduct electricity without resistance.

A number of people with incurable illnesses have had themselves deep frozen immediately after death in the hope that it will one day be possible for them to be thawed out and cured. Cryogenic preservation has also been suggested as a possible way of sending astronauts on long space journeys.

crystal Solid in which the atoms are arranged in a rigid geometrical pattern or lattice structure. The regular shapes of crystals reflect their internal structure. Most minerals, including common salt and sand, occur in crystalline form, although the crystals are often microscopically small.

Curie, Marie (1867-1934) French chemist, born Marie Sklodowska in Poland, who, with her husband Pierre, discovered the radioactive elements radium and polonium. The Curies refused to patent their work and tirelessly promoted the use of radium in the treatment of cancer. Marie Curie herself died of leukaemia caused by her heavy exposure to radioactivity.

Marie Curie remains the only person ever to win the Nobel prize in two different sciences – physics and chemistry.

MARRIAGE OF MINDS *Pioneering work on radioactivity won fame for the Curies and earned Marie two Nobel prizes.*

SCIENCE, SPACE AND MATHEMATICS

Dalton, John (1766-1844) British chemist and founder of modern atomic theory. He proposed that every ELEMENT was composed of atoms of a distinct type and weight, which combine with atoms of other elements in simple proportions to make COMPOUNDS. In 1803, he published the first table of atomic weights.

dark matter Invisible matter which may make up as much as 99 per cent of the mass of the Universe. Some dark matter consists of planets, dead stars, black holes and general stellar debris, but much of it may consist of hypothetical particles such as axions and gravitons. The fate of the Universe depends on the amount of dark matter it contains. If there is enough of it, the Universe will have sufficient mass for the force of gravity to restrain and then reverse its expansion. (See BIG BANG THEORY.)

Davy, Sir Humphry (1778-1829) English chemist and pioneer of electrochemistry, who also invented the miner's safety lamp. Davy was the first person to isolate sodium, potassium, calcium and other elements using ELECTROLYSIS.

decibel Unit of power used to measure the loudness or intensity of sound, usually abbreviated to dB. The faintest audible sound is rated at 0dB, normal speech is about 50dB and an aircraft jet engine at close range is some 120dB.

decimal system System of counting in which FRACTIONS are represented as sums of tenths, hundredths, thousandths and so on. The fractional part of a number is shown to the right of a decimal point, the whole number part to the left. Thus the number $1\frac{1}{4}$ is expressed as 1.25. Many numbers cannot be satisfactorily represented as decimals. For example, π (PI) continues for an infinite number of decimal places and even the simple fraction $\frac{1}{3}$ is 0.33333 . . . recurring.

degree In geometry, a unit of measurement of angles, equal to $\frac{1}{360}$ of a circle. A right angle is 90°, an acute angle is less than 90° and an obtuse angle is between 90° and 180°. A degree is divided into 60 minutes, each of which is further divided into 60 seconds. A degree is also a unit of temperature (see CELSIUS, FAHRENHEIT and KELVIN). Degrees in both geometry and physics are denoted by the symbol °.

density Measure of the amount of matter in a given volume of a substance, expressed as its mass per unit volume. It is usually measured in kilograms per cubic metre (kg/m³). Density is often expressed as relative density (sometimes known as specific gravity), the density of a substance relative to that of water at 4°C, the temperature at which it is most dense.

Descartes, René (1596-1650) French philosopher and mathematician, known in science for the development of analytical, or COORDINATE, geometry, a powerful mathematical tool in which algebra and geometry are combined. He also made contributions to the study of light, astronomy and biology. He believed that the material world was ruled entirely by mathematical laws and that science should be subject to the same rigorous standards of proof as mathematics itself. (See also ▷DESCARTES in 'Ideas, Beliefs and Religion'.)

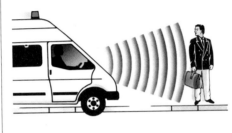

SIREN CALL *The rise and fall in the pitch of a passing ambulance siren is due to the Doppler effect; sound waves bunch up as the siren approaches, raising the pitch, and spread out as the siren recedes, lowering the pitch.*

diffraction Bending or spreading out of light, sound or other waves as they pass around an obstacle or through an aperture. It means that shadows are not sharp-edged, and waves from different parts of the obstacle or from adjoining apertures may experience INTERFERENCE. In light, this produces 'fringes' of light and dark lines or bands of colour. Diffraction gratings of many fine parallel slits exploit this phenomenon to separate light into its constituent colours. (See SPECTROSCOPY.)

diffusion Spreading of one substance through another by random movement of atoms or molecules. Odours, for example, diffuse through the air, and coloured ink will diffuse through a glass of still water.

direct current (DC) Electric current that flows in one direction only, from positive to negative (compare ALTERNATING CURRENT). Direct current is supplied by batteries, or can be produced from alternating current using a rectifier.

distillation Separation of a liquid mixture into its components by boiling it and then condensing the vapour. The different components condense at different temperatures, allowing them to be separated from each other. Distillation can be used to purify a liquid, as in distilled water, or to separate out the different components, or fractions, from a complex mixture, as in the distillation of petroleum from crude oil, or brandy from wine.

Doppler effect Apparent change in the FREQUENCY of sound, or of electromagnetic radiation such as light, as its source approaches or recedes from an observer. The RED SHIFT in the light from distant galaxies is a form of Doppler effect.

E=mc² The equation that demonstrated that mass could be converted into energy, and vice versa, and led to the development of the atom bomb and nuclear power. Formulated by Albert EINSTEIN in 1905, it states that the energy content (E) of a particle of matter is equal to its mass (m) multiplied by the square of the speed of light in a vacuum (c^2). The equation follows directly from the theory of RELATIVITY.

Earth Third planet from the Sun, and the only planet known to have an atmosphere that can support life. It moves in an elliptical orbit at an average of 92.86 million miles (149.4 million km) from the Sun, travelling at about 67 000 mph (107 000 km/h) and taking 365 days, 5 hours, 48 minutes and 46 seconds to perform a complete orbit. It rotates on its axis once every 23 hours, 56 minutes and 4.1 seconds. The Earth is the fifth largest planet in the Solar System, as well as the most dense. It has a single MOON. (See also ▷EARTH in 'The Earth and the Environment'.)

eclipse Blocking out of light from one celestial object by another. The most familiar are solar and lunar eclipses (see diagram on facing page).

Einstein, Albert (1879-1955) One of the greatest scientists of all time, born in Germany. In the space of a few years at the beginning of the 20th century, Einstein transformed human understanding of the physical universe. He is known mainly for

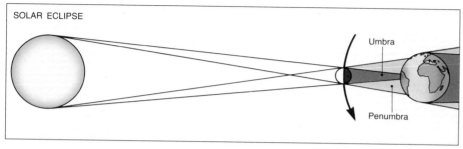

SOLAR ECLIPSE

Umbra

Penumbra

SOLAR ECLIPSE *Eclipses of the Sun are total when seen from within the umbra, allowing views of the Sun's corona or outer halo (left), but only partial when seen from within the larger area of the penumbra.*

his theory of RELATIVITY, and for his uncompleted work towards UNIFIED FIELD THEORIES. He also made major contributions to THERMODYNAMICS and to the studies of light that led to QUANTUM MECHANICS. Remarkably, he published his major discoveries while working for the Swiss patent office – having been rejected for a teaching post as a Jew. Einstein emigrated to America in 1934 after the Nazis came to power in Germany, and in 1940 he was instrumental in persuading President Roosevelt of the need for America to develop the atom bomb before Hitler (see ▷MANHATTAN PROJECT). After 1945, he campaigned against the proliferation of the very nuclear weapons which his own work had helped to create.

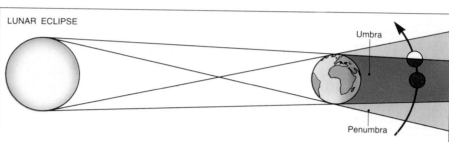

LUNAR ECLIPSE

Umbra

Penumbra

ECLIPSES OF THE MOON *Lunar eclipses can occur only when the Moon is full and when the Earth is positioned between the Sun and the Moon. They are visible across half the surface of the Earth.*

electric charge Fundamental property of matter that enables one body to exert a force on another. Two bodies with the same charge – positive or negative – repel each other; those with opposite charges attract each other. All the phenomena associated with electric charge are derived from the interactions of SUBATOMIC PARTICLES – the ELECTRON has a negative charge, the PROTON an equal positive one. An excess or deficiency of electrons gives rise to charged bodies and thus to STATIC ELECTRICITY and electric currents.

electricity Phenomena associated with an imbalance of ELECTRIC CHARGE in a system. Static charges give rise to STATIC ELECTRICITY, while moving charges, for example electrons flowing down a copper wire in an electric circuit, produce an electric current. The size of the imbalance, which drives the current, is known as the potential difference or electromotive force, and is measured in VOLTS; the magnitude of the current is measured in AMPS. Moving electric charges are associated with magnetic fields and ELECTROMAGNETIC RADIATION. Electricity is produced commercially in ▷BATTERIES and ▷ELECTRIC GENERATORS by converting chemical, nuclear or other forms of energy into electrical energy. It is also produced naturally in, for example, muscles and nerves.

electrolysis Splitting of a chemical compound, either in liquid form or in solution, by passing an electric current through it. The IONS in the solution migrate to the electrodes – positive ions to the CATHODE, negative ions to the ANODE – where they give up or receive electrons to form atoms, which are deposited on the electrode or bubble off as gas. Electrolysis is used to refine metals and in ▷ELECTROPLATING.

electromagnetic induction Production of an electric current in a circuit when placed in a changing magnetic field. It is the basis for the ▷ELECTRIC GENERATOR and for such devices as the transformer.

FATHER OF MODERN PHYSICS *The theory of relativity and other work by Albert Einstein revolutionised 20th-century science.*

electromagnetic radiation Form of energy consisting of WAVES of electrical and magnetic fields vibrating at the same frequency at right angles to each other. All electromagnetic waves travel at the speed of light, or 186 281 miles per second (299 782 km per second). But their wavelengths (the distance between peaks or troughs) range from several miles for low frequency RADIO WAVES to less than the radius of an atom for high frequency GAMMA RADIATION; in between are MICROWAVES, INFRARED RADIATION, LIGHT, ULTRAVIOLET RADIATION and X-RAYS.

electromagnetism Major branch of physics linking ELECTRICITY, MAGNETISM, and LIGHT and other forms of ELECTROMAGNETIC RADIATION in a single theoretical framework. The foundations of electromagnetism were laid by Michael FARADAY and James Clark MAXWELL in the 19th century, and during the 20th century electromagnetism was established as one of the fundamental forces in the Universe.

electron Stable SUBATOMIC PARTICLE with a negative charge and a very small mass, a constituent of all matter and the basic unit of ELECTRICITY. Electrons are normally found circling the nucleus of an ATOM, and their number and arrangement determine the chemical properties of an element (see BOND, CHEMICAL; VALENCE). Although generally thought of as particles, electrons also behave as waves, the description of which is an important aspect of QUANTUM MECHANICS.

element Chemical substance that cannot be broken down into simpler substances. Each chemical element is composed of a specific type of ATOM, and forms COMPOUNDS by combining with other elements. There are 92 naturally occurring elements, of which hydrogen is the simplest and uranium the most complex. A further 17, all radioactive and known as the transuranic elements, have been produced artificially. (See also PERIODIC TABLE.)

ellipse Curve resembling a flattened circle. An ellipse can be drawn by passing a loop of string round two pins on a board, and then tracing a curve with a pencil held taut against the string. The pins represent the two foci of the ellipse. The orbits of the planets and many comets are ellipses. A CIRCLE is an ellipse with its two foci at the same point. (See also CONIC SECTIONS.)

emulsion Type of COLLOID in which fine droplets of one liquid are dispersed in another. Salad dressing is an emulsion of oil in vinegar. Soaps and detergents contain emulsifying agents which encourage the dispersion of oil in water.
The 'emulsion' on photographic films is not a true emulsion, but consists of silver halide grains dispersed in gelatine.

energy The capacity to do WORK. Every change in the Universe, however small, involves energy. It exists in many different forms, including HEAT, ELECTRICITY, MAGNETISM, chemical energy, as well as LIGHT and other forms of ELECTROMAGNETIC RADIATION. Objects can have energy by virtue of their motion (kinetic energy), or their position (potential energy). The fact that mass can be converted into energy and energy into mass (see $E=MC^2$) is exploited in reactions that release NUCLEAR ENERGY. The standard scientific unit of both energy and work is the JOULE.

entropy Measure of the disorder of any system; the more disordered it is, the higher the entropy. The molecules in a crystal, for example, are highly ordered and the entropy is very low whereas the molecules in a gas are very disordered and the entropy is high. In any spontaneous process, and whenever work is done, entropy always increases and energy is converted into a less usable form – waste heat for example. It has been suggested that the universe will, untold billions of years from now, become so disordered that no further usable energy will be available – the so-called 'heat death of the Universe' – but not all physicists agree with this proposition.

equation Mathematical statement of equality, usually used to allow an unknown quantity to be given a value. An equation, for example $5 + x = 9$, can be solved by performing the same operation on each side of the equation (in this case, subtracting 5), to give a value for the unknown x (in this case 4). Simultaneous equations can be used to discover the values of two or more unknowns as long as there are as many equations as there are unknowns.

equilibrium Condition in which a system will remain unless disturbed. In stable equilibrium, as with a ball resting at the bottom of a funnel, the system will return to its initial state when disturbed. In unstable equilibrium, as with a ball resting on an upturned bowl, a relatively small displacement will give rise to a large movement from the original position.

equinox The moment when the Sun lies directly overhead at the Equator and when day and night are of equal length (the term means 'equal night'). In the Northern Hemisphere, the spring, or vernal, equinox takes place around March 23 and the autumn equinox around September 23. (Compare SOLSTICE.)

Euclid (*c.*300 BC) Greek mathematician whose *Elements* remains the basis for much of modern GEOMETRY. One of the basic axioms of Euclidean geometry is that given a line and a point separate from it, only one line can be drawn through the point, which is parallel to the first line. This cannot be proved and attempts to replace it with the axiom that either no lines or many lines can be drawn through the point gave rise to 'non-Euclidean' geometries during the early 19th century, which are now essential to many aspects of modern physics.

evaporation Change of a liquid into a vapour, the opposite of CONDENSATION. In any liquid, there will be some fast-moving molecules with sufficient energy to escape from the surface into the atmosphere. Because of the removal of energy, the remaining liquid cools down. The rate of evaporation increases with temperature. Evaporation of water from the oceans is a major factor in the Earth's climate.

exponential growth Rate of growth which is continuously accelerating. Populations, for example, which depend on the number of people able to breed, would increase exponentially if unchecked.

Fahrenheit Temperature scale on which water freezes at 32° and boils at 212°, devised by Gabriel Fahrenheit, a German instrument-maker, in the 18th century. For most scientific purposes, it has been superseded by the CELSIUS or centigrade scale.

Faraday, Michael (1791-1867) English physicist and chemist whose discovery of ELECTROMAGNETIC INDUCTION and

SPARK OF GENIUS *Michael Faraday, pictured in his laboratory at the Royal Institution, pioneered the study of electromagnetism and laid the foundation of the modern electricity industry.*

invention of the dynamo (see ▷ELECTRIC GENERATOR) in 1831 laid the basis for the electricity industry. He also set out Faraday's Laws of ELECTROLYSIS, and demonstrated the effect of magnetism on polarised light. The scientific unit of capacitance – the ability to store electric charge – the farad is named in his honour.

Fermat's last theorem Celebrated mathematical puzzle posed by the French mathematician Pierre de Fermat in the 17th century. It has been known since at least the time of the ancient Greeks that $3^2 + 4^2 = 5^2$, but mathematicians wondered whether a similar equation could be written with cubes, fourths or higher powers. Fermat claimed to have proved that this was impossible, but left no record of his proof. A complete proof still eludes scholars after more than 300 years although it has been shown to be true for many specific cases.

Fermi, Enrico (1901-54) Italian-born physicist who in 1942 completed the world's first ▷NUCLEAR REACTOR – underneath the stands of the football stadium at the University of Chicago – and thus ushered in the nuclear age.

Fibonacci sequence Sequence in which each number is the sum of the two preceding numbers. Named after the Italian mathematician Leonardo Fibonacci – who published it in 1202 – the sequence starts: 1, 1, 2, 3, 5, 8, 13, 21 . . . The Fibonacci sequence occurs widely in nature – for example, in the whorls of pine cones and other forms of spiral growth, and in the distances of the planets from the Sun.

fluorescence The ability of certain substances to absorb light (or other forms of ELECTROMAGNETIC RADIATION) and to emit light of a different wavelength or colour. It is similar to phosphorescence, but fluorescence ceases as soon as the incoming radiation stops, whereas phosphorescent materials (as on a television screen) continue to emit light for a short time.

force External agent – a push or a pull – that causes a change in the state of motion of a body, that is, it imparts an ACCELERATION to it. The greater the force the greater the acceleration, and the greater the MASS of the body, the lower the acceleration produced by a given force. (See NEWTON'S LAWS OF MOTION.) Force is measured in newtons. One newton is the force required to give a mass of one kilogram an acceleration of one metre per second per second.

GINGERBREAD MAN *In the fractal shape (above), known as the Mandelbrot set, lurk numerous smaller 'gingerbread men' at every level of magnification.*

formula, chemical Representation of the composition or structure of a MOLECULE using symbols for its constituent ELEMENTS. The formula for water, H_2O, shows that a molecule of water contains two hydrogen atoms and one oxygen atom. Structural formulae also show how the atoms are bonded, so that it is possible to distinguish between different ISOMERS. Thus ethyl alcohol and dimethyl ether have different structural formulae:

$$\begin{array}{cc} \text{H} & \text{H} \\ | & | \\ \text{H}-\text{C}-\text{C}-\text{OH} \\ | & | \\ \text{H} & \text{H} \end{array} \quad \text{and} \quad \begin{array}{cc} \text{H} & \text{H} \\ | & | \\ \text{H}-\text{C}-\text{O}-\text{C}-\text{H} \\ | & | \\ \text{H} & \text{H} \end{array}$$

although both can be written as C_2H_6O.

four-colour theorem Proposition that a mapmaker needs only four colours to draw any map, however complicated, so that no two adjoining countries share the same colour. The theorem remained unproved for more than 100 years until, in 1976, two American mathematicians finally demonstrated that it must be true.

fractal Shape or structure which, although it appears to be entirely irregular, nevertheless displays distinct patterns. Fractal shapes are made up of numerous smaller versions of the same shape, each of which in turn is made up of still smaller versions. Fractals occur widely in nature in such features as cloud formations, coastlines, plants and other organic structures. They are also produced on computers, using complex equations similar to those underlying CHAOS THEORY, for example to simulate growth patterns or to create special effects for the cinema.

fraction Part of a whole number. If a number is divided into eight parts, then each part may be represented as ⅛ of the whole. The number above the line is known as the numerator and the number below the line as the denominator. Fractions expressed as ratios of whole numbers are called common or vulgar fractions; those that use the decimal system are called decimal fractions.

freezing point Temperature at which a liquid changes into a solid. Under normal conditions, it is the same as the MELTING POINT. Freezing is generally accompanied by a decrease in volume and an increase in density; water is an exception – it expands, which is why ice floats.

frequency The number of complete cycles of a vibration or WAVE motion (such as SOUND or ELECTROMAGNETIC RADIATION) that take place in a given unit of time. It is usually measured in HERTZ (1Hz = 1 cycle per second), and can be calculated by dividing the velocity of a wave by its WAVELENGTH – the frequency of a wave increases as its wavelength decreases. (See also AMPLITUDE.)

friction Resistance to the relative motion of two touching surfaces. It is the force that stops a car when the brakes are applied. Friction is usually dissipated as heat, as when meteors burn up in the Earth's atmosphere. Ball-bearings reduce friction by allowing surfaces to roll rather than slide, while lubricants make sliding easier.

galaxy Vast grouping of thousands of millions of stars, together with clouds of dust and gas, held together by gravity. Galaxies rotate, tending to take up a spiral shape, with a bright central nucleus of older stars, and spiral arms of younger and newly forming stars. Eventually, the spiral closes in, leaving an elliptical galaxy, which may ultimately collapse into a BLACK HOLE. The Universe contains at least 1000 million galaxies. The Earth and the Solar System lie in a spiral arm of the MILKY WAY, which is itself part of a cluster of around 20 galaxies known as the local group.

Galileo (full name Galileo Galilei) (1564-1642) Italian astronomer and mathematician who built the first effective telescope and used it to prove that the Earth moves round the Sun. Galileo made many other scientific discoveries. A swinging lamp in Pisa cathedral is said to have made him realise that the rate at which a pendulum swings depends on its length rather than the distance through which it swings, which led to the development of pendulum clocks. He demonstrated that freely falling objects accelerate at the same rate, whatever their mass, and that projectiles follow the path of a PARABOLA. His observations proving that the Earth moves round the Sun confirmed the theory put forward by the Polish astronomer Nicolaus COPERNICUS, but conflicted with the teachings of the Church that the Earth was the centre of the Universe and the Sun revolved around the Earth. This brought him to the attention of the ▷INQUISITION and he was forced to recant, under threat of torture. He is said to have muttered, after his public recantation, *E pur si muove* 'And yet it moves'.

gamma radiation Form of ELECTROMAGNETIC RADIATION with the highest energy, shortest wavelength and highest frequency in the electromagnetic spectrum. Gamma rays are produced by the decay of radioactive nuclei (see RADIOACTIVITY) as well as by pulsars, quasars and other objects in space. They are used in ▷RADIOTHERAPY, particularly in the treatment of cancer, and to sterilise medical equipment.

gas The least dense state of matter. Gases completely fill the vessel in which they are contained. According to the kinetic theory of gases, the molecules of a gas are in constant random motion, and their collisions with the walls of the container give rise to pressure. The relationship between the temperature, pressure and volume of an 'ideal' gas (one in which the molecules have no volume and exert no forces on each other) is given by BOYLE'S LAW. However, real gases usually diverge widely from this, because of the existence of small intermolecular forces.

geometric progression Sequence of numbers in which each number is obtained by multiplying the previous one by a constant factor. For example, in the sequence 1, 2, 4, 8, 16, 32 each number is twice the preceding one. In an arithmetic progression, by contrast, each number is derived by adding a constant number to the previous one, as in 2, 4, 6, 8, 10.

geometry Branch of mathematics that deals with the properties of space and the various different ways of describing it. It is thus concerned with the measurement and relationships of points, lines, angles, surfaces and solids. Standard Euclidean geometry (see EUCLID) is concerned with two and three-dimensional space (planes and solids), while non-Euclidean geometry deals with multiple dimensions. In analytic geometry, algebraic equations are used to represent geometric figures. (See also TOPOLOGY; FRACTAL.)

Gödel's theorem One of the most important mathematical proofs of the 20th century, produced by the Austrian-born mathematician Kurt Gödel in 1931. Until then, many mathematicians (including Bertrand ▷RUSSELL) had believed that the whole of mathematics could be constructed from a few basic axioms. Gödel's theorem showed that this was impossible.

graph Visual representation of numerical relationships. It generally takes the form of a series of points, plotted against two sets of COORDINATES set at right angles to each other, and connected by a line or curve. Graphs have many uses in statistics and engineering. In some cases, data may be better presented as a set of vertical or horizontal bars rather than a curve (as in a bar graph or histogram). Another common graphical device is the pie chart, which shows the relation of the parts to the whole by illustrating them as segments of a circle.

gravitation Force of attraction between all forms of matter. It makes objects fall towards the centre of the Earth, holds the planets in orbit round the Sun, and keeps stars and galaxies together. The Law of Universal Gravitation, first laid down by Isaac NEWTON, states that the force of attraction between two bodies is proportional to their masses and inversely proportional to the square of the distance between them – in other words, doubling the mass of one of the bodies doubles the force of attraction, while doubling the distance between them reduces the force to one-quarter. Although the Newtonian system works well enough to land a man on the moon, it has been supplanted in modern physics by Einstein's general theory of RELATIVITY, which treats gravitation as a distortion of the SPACE-TIME continuum caused by the presence of large masses. Although gravity is the weakest of the fundamental forces of nature, it is effective at long range and, on a cosmic scale, it is by far the most important.

🍎A falling apple may well have inspired Newton to conceive his theory of gravitation, since he sometimes sat in the apple orchard in his garden, but there is little evidence that the apple hit him on the head.

A MATTER OF GRAVITY *Galileo (centre) demonstrated the principles of gravity some 50 years before Newton; contrary to myth, he did so using an inclined plane, not the leaning tower of Pisa.*

hydrogen

SCIENCE, SPACE AND MATHEMATICS

OMEN IN THE SKIES *Edmond Halley predicted the return of the comet that bears his name in the 17th century. It was first photographed in 1910 and later by the space probe* Giotto *in 1986.*

helix Spiral shape, resembling a spring. Helical structures occur widely in the natural world, the most famous example being the double helix of ▷DNA.

hertz (Hz) The international unit of FREQUENCY: 1 Hz is equal to one cycle (from peak to peak of a wave) per second. It is named after Heinrich Rudolph Hertz (1857-94), the German physicist who was the first to send and receive RADIO WAVES, and who also demonstrated the electromagnetic nature of light.

Hooke's law In physics, the principle that the amount an elastic body stretches out of shape is in direct proportion to the force acting on it. This is why the weight markings on the faces of kitchen scales, which work with a spring, are the same distance apart. The law is named after Robert Hooke (1635-1703), the English scientist and inventor of the modern microscope, who first stated it in 1678.

Hubble, Edwin (1889-1953) American astronomer who demonstrated the existence of galaxies beyond the Milky Way. He also discovered the RED SHIFT in the light from distant stars, which shows that galaxies are receding at a rate that increases in proportion to their distance from us – the foundation of the BIG BANG THEORY. The ratio between the distance of a galaxy and the rate at which it recedes is known as Hubble's constant, and is estimated at 15 to 30 kilometres per second per million LIGHT YEARS. This gives an age for the Universe – the time since the expansion began – of 10 to 20 thousand million years.

half-life The time taken for half the nuclei in a sample of a radioactive ISOTOPE to decay. Because the rate of decay continuously slows down, the half-life remains constant, however many of the nuclei have already decayed. Half-lives of radioactive substances can range from millionths of a second to thousands of millions of years.

Halley's comet Best known of the COMETS, seen most recently in 1986 when it was studied intensively and photographed by the space probe *Giotto*. Its 76-year orbit round the Sun takes it from a point beyond Neptune to within the orbit of Venus. It is named after Edmond Halley (1656-1742), the British Astronomer Royal who studied it in 1682 and correctly predicted that it would return in 1759.

Hawking, Stephen (1942-) British theoretical physicist and author of the best-selling *A Brief History of Time* (1988), in which he explained his theories of space, time and the origins of the Universe to a wide readership. Despite severe physical disability, he has made substantial contributions to the study of BLACK HOLES and GRAVITATION, as well as the 'theory of everything' (or UNIFIED FIELD THEORIES).

heat Form of energy that is transferred from a hotter body to a colder one. Heat is transferred in three ways; CONDUCTION, CONVECTION and RADIATION. As the colder body is heated, the atoms and molecules of which it is composed speed up. At the melting and boiling points, heat continues to be supplied without any increase

in temperature; the increase in internal energy of the body takes the form of a change in molecular structure rather than an increase in temperature (see LATENT HEAT). Different materials require different amounts of heat to achieve the same rise in temperature. Those with a low heat capacity, such as metals, require a small amount of heat; those with a high heat capacity, such as water, require a large amount. The specific heat of a substance is the amount of heat required to raise 1 kilogram of the substance through 1°C. Heat is one of the the key concepts in THERMODYNAMICS. It is measured in either CALORIES or JOULES.

heavy water (D_2O) Form of water in which hydrogen is replaced by one of its heavier ISOTOPES, deuterium or tritium. Heavy water slows the neutrons given off during NUCLEAR FISSION and is used to control the rate at which fission takes place in some types of ▷NUCLEAR REACTOR.

helium (He) Best known of the NOBLE GASES and the next lightest chemical element after HYDROGEN. It is very unreactive and will not catch fire, which makes it suitable for filling airships and balloons. It becomes a liquid at temperatures close to ABSOLUTE ZERO and when cooled still further it exhibits superfluidity – it flows with no measurable VISCOSITY.
🔦Helium is one of the most abundant elements in the Universe since it is formed by the NUCLEAR FUSION of hydrogen nuclei, the process from which the Sun and other stars derive their energy.

hydrocarbons Organic chemical compounds composed entirely of CARBON and HYDROGEN. They occur mainly in petroleum, coal and natural gas products and are of great importance as the starting point for the manufacture of an enormous variety of industrial chemicals.

hydrogen (H) Colourless and odourless gas, the lightest and simplest of the chemical elements. It provides the fuel for NUCLEAR FUSION in the stars and is the most abundant element in the Universe. Hydrogen has a single ELECTRON in orbit around a nucleus that contains a single PROTON. It is highly flammable and is sometimes used as a fuel. In combination with oxygen, it forms water. It has two 'heavy' ISOTOPES: deuterium, with a neutron as well as a proton in the nucleus, and tritium, with two neutrons. They are both important in the nuclear power industry.

533

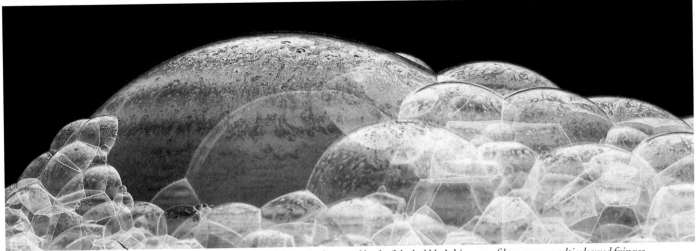

BUBBLE RAINBOW *Interference between light waves reflected from the front and back of the bubbles' thin soapy films causes multicoloured fringes.*

inertia Tendency of a body to resist any change to its state of rest or uniform motion in a straight line. The larger a body's MASS, the greater its inertia.

infrared radiation Form of ELECTRO-MAGNETIC RADIATION with wavelengths between those of visible light and microwaves. Radiant heat – from a glowing coal fire, for example – consists of infrared radiation. (See also ▷ INFRARED DEVICES.)

interference Effect produced by the interaction of two or more different wave motions, for example light, sound or the ripples on a pond. Where the crests or troughs of the waves coincide, they reinforce each other. Where crests coincide with troughs, they cancel each other out. In the case of light, this creates patterns of light and dark, or colour fringes such as those on the surface of a soap bubble; in the

PERPETUAL STORM *Jupiter's Great Red Spot, site of a continuous raging storm, is thought to owe its colour to the presence of red phosphorus.*

case of sound it creates wavering 'beats', used to tune musical instruments. Interference is also the basis of ▷ HOLOGRAPHY.

ion An ATOM, or group of atoms, that has lost or gained one or more ELECTRONS, and thus carries a positive charge (a cation) or a negative charge (an anion). Many compounds form ions in solution, and atmospheric gases are ionised by incoming solar radiation and by electrical discharges during storms.

isomers Chemical compounds whose MOLECULES are made up of the same numbers of the same atoms, but which differ in the arrangement of the atoms, for example ammonium cyanate, NH_4CNO, and urea, $CO(NH_2)_2$. Isomers are very common in organic chemistry.

isotopes Different forms of the same ELEMENT. The difference lies only in the number of NEUTRONS in the nucleus. They have identical chemical properties, but different atomic masses. Nearly all elements occur naturally as a mixture of isotopes. (See also RADIOACTIVITY.)

joule Unit of ENERGY and WORK, defined as the amount of work done by a force of 1 newton moving through 1 metre, or the amount of energy dissipated by 1 watt in 1 second. It is named after the British physicist James Prescott Joule (1818-89), who first demonstrated that heat energy and mechanical energy are interconvertible.

Jupiter Largest planet in the Solar System – with a volume 1300 times that of Earth – and the fifth farthest from the Sun. It has a 'year' of 11.86 Earth years, but a 'day' of about 9 hr 50 min. Its most prominent feature is the Great Red Spot, covering an

area twice the diameter of Earth. Jupiter is composed mainly of hydrogen and helium. The atmosphere is mostly hydrogen, methane and ammonia, which forms dense white clouds. There are at least 16 moons. ✦ The collision of the comet Shoemaker-Levy with Jupiter in July 1994 was termed 'the astronomical event of the decade' and is expected to yield valuable information about the planet.

Kelvin (K) Standard unit of temperature, based on the CELSIUS scale but with its starting point at ABSOLUTE ZERO (0K or −273.15°C) rather than the freezing point of water (273.15K or 0°C). It is named after the British physicist Lord Kelvin (1824-1907), a pioneer in the study of thermodynamics and electromagnetism.

Kepler, Johannes (1571-1630) German astronomer and mathematician whose laws of planetary motion, based on the observations of Tycho BRAHE, showed for the first time that the planets moved in elliptical orbits round the Sun. Kepler's work provided important support for Nicolaus Copernicus's Sun-centred theory of the Universe, and gave Isaac Newton the raw material for his theory of gravitation.

kilogram (kg) Standard international unit of MASS, equal to 1000 grams or 2.2046 pounds. It is defined as the mass of the International Prototype Kilogram, a platinum-iridium cylinder kept under controlled conditions at the International Bureau of Weights and Measures near Paris. (See also METRIC SYSTEM; SI UNITS.)

kinetic energy Energy possessed by a body by virtue of its motion. It is calculated as $\frac{1}{2}mv^2$, where m is the MASS of the body and v its VELOCITY. (See also ENERGY.)

latent heat The heat released or absorbed, without a change of temperature, when a substance undergoes a change of state, such as freezing, boiling, evaporating or condensing. A moistened finger held up to test the wind is colder on the side facing the wind because the moisture draws latent heat from the finger as it evaporates. In the same way, the evaporation of sweat from the skin draws excess heat from the body.

Lavoisier, Antoine (1743-94) French scientist who is regarded as the founder of modern chemistry. He demonstrated that combustion involved a reaction with a constituent of the air which he called oxygen, so finally laying the PHLOGISTON theory to rest. He also worked out the law of conservation of mass and devised the modern method of naming compounds.

lens Device for focusing light, consisting of a disc of glass or other transparent material, each face of which is curved like the surface of a sphere. Lenses may be either convex (converging) or concave (diverging). A converging lens magnifies any object placed inside the focal length. Simple lenses are used to correct people's sight defects: concave lenses correct short sight and convex lenses correct long sight. Optical instruments, such as cameras, telescopes and microscopes often contain compound lenses composed of a combination of concave and convex lenses in order to reduce optical distortion.

light Form of ELECTROMAGNETIC RADIATION that is visible to the naked eye. It has wavelengths between those of infrared and ultraviolet radiation. Light plays a unique part in science: it makes visual observation possible, and the speed of light in a vacuum is one of the fundamental physical constants of the Universe. Scientists have debated whether light is composed of particles or waves since the time of Isaac Newton, who, in 1666, was the first to split ordinary light into its ▷SPECTRUM of component colours. Newton thought of light as a stream of luminous corpuscles, with a different corpuscle for each colour. This explained many properties of light, such as REFLECTION and REFRACTION reasonably well. However it could not explain the phenomenon of INTERFERENCE, which was demonstrated by the Englishman Thomas Young in 1802, and implied that light must be a wave motion. The wave theory also accounted for DIFFRACTION. Nevertheless, neither theory was entirely satisfactory, and it was not until the beginning of the 20th century, when Max Planck proposed that

light was emitted as packets of energy called PHOTONS, that the modern view of the nature of light began to emerge. Light is now thought of as both particle and wave – referred to as complementarity – with the wave-like behaviour of photons being explained and described by QUANTUM MECHANICS.

light year Distance covered in a year by light travelling in a vacuum – 5·88 million million miles or 9·46 million million kilometres. It is used as a unit for measuring distances in astronomy, although it has largely been superseded for scientific purposes by the parsec, a unit which is equal to 3.26 light years.

liquid State of matter in which atoms or molecules are held together by mutual attraction to the extent that they cannot move as freely as in a gas, but are not rigidly fixed as in a solid. Liquids take the shape of their container and are relatively incompressible. Pressure in a liquid is transmitted equally in all directions, providing the basis for ▷HYDRAULIC machines.

litmus paper Paper impregnated with litmus, a purple vegetable dye that turns red in ACIDS and blue in ALKALIS, used to determine if a solution is acid or alkaline.

SIMPLE LENSES *Convex or converging lenses bend parallel beams of light inwards to a single point called the focus. Concave or diverging lenses bend light outwards so that it appears to come from a focus behind the lens. Most optical instruments use combinations of the two.*

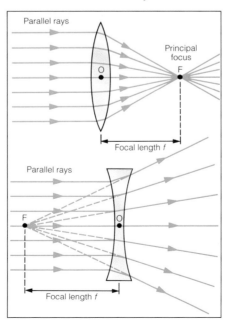

Parallel rays

Principal focus

O

F

Focal length *f*

Parallel rays

F

O

Focal length *f*

logarithms Mathematical device once used to simplify the multiplication and division of complicated numbers. If two numbers are expressed as the POWERS of the same base number (usually 10), they can be multiplied by adding the powers together and divided by subtracting them. By referring to published tables, complex calculations could be carried out.

♣Many natural phenomena are best measured using logarithmic scales, for example sound intensity (decibels), earthquake magnitude (the Richter scale) and acidity (pH). Because numbers on a logarithmic scale represent powers of 10, the number 3 is 1000 times greater than 1, rather than 3 times greater – as it would be on a simple linear scale.

machine Device that converts ENERGY or FORCE into a usable form, that is one that can do WORK. Simple machines include the lever, the pulley, the inclined plane (wedges and screws) and the wheel and axle.

Mach number Speed through the air or other gas expressed as a multiple of the speed of SOUND under the same conditions. An aircraft travelling at the speed of sound is at Mach 1; Concorde flying at more than twice the speed of sound reaches Mach 2.3. The unit is named after the Austrian physicist and philosopher Ernest Mach (1838-1916).

Magellanic clouds Two faint patches of light close to the MILKY WAY, visible in the Southern Hemisphere. They are important to astrophysicists because they offer the opportunity to study nearby stars that are not in our own galaxy. They were first recorded by Ferdinand Magellan in 1519.

magnetism Property possessed by some materials, notably iron, cobalt and nickel, to attract or repel other similar materials. Magnets may be permanent, retaining their magnetism in all circumstances, or temporary, retaining their magnetism only when in a magnetic field. Every magnet has two poles, a north pole and a south pole. Like poles repel each other, while opposite poles attract. Magnetic fields are also created by ELECTROMAGNETIC INDUCTION when a suitable material is surrounded by a fluctuating or moving electric field. Electricity and magnetism are manifestations of the same fundamental force, ELECTROMAGNETISM (See also ▷MAGNETIC POLES in 'The Earth and the Environment'.)

magnitude Measure of the brightness of a star. The scale was devised by the Greek astronomer Hipparchus in about 130 BC.

He graded stars from 1 the brightest, to 6, barely visible to the naked eye. Apparent magnitude is less useful to astronomers than 'absolute magnitude', the brightness a star would have if it were a set distance (1 parsec or 3.26 light years) away.

Mars Fourth planet from the Sun and nearest to the Earth, also known as the 'red planet' and named after the Roman god of war. Half the size of Earth, Mars has a 'year' of 687 days and two small moons, Phobos and Deimos.
The largest known volcano in the Solar System, Olympus Mons, is on Mars. With a height of 17 miles (27 km), it would collapse if Martian gravity were as strong as Earth's.

mass Intrinsic property of MATTER. Mass is a measure of the gravitational attraction between one body and another, when it is equivalent to WEIGHT. It is also a measure of a body's INERTIA, or resistance to ACCELERATION. According to the theory of RELATIVITY, a moving object's mass increases with its velocity, becoming greater as the speed of light is approached, with its weight and inertia increasing correspondingly. An observer travelling with the object would not detect any change in these properties. Because mass and energy are interconvertible (see E=MC^2), mass is often referred to as mass-energy. (See NEWTON'S LAWS OF MOTION.)

mathematics The universal language of science. The whole complex and diverse structure of mathematics is based on sets of simple AXIOMS. Pure mathematics includes the study of NUMBERS, ALGEBRA, GEOMETRY, CALCULUS and TOPOLOGY. Applied mathematics generally refers to physics (particularly MECHANICS), but mathematical techniques are used in all branches of technology, engineering, economics and the social sciences. Recent developments in mathematics include CHAOS THEORY, FRACTAL geometry and CATASTROPHE THEORY.

matter Anything that has MASS or that exists in space and time. All matter in the Universe is thought to have been formed in the BIG BANG, when the Universe was created. (See also ANTIMATTER.)

Maxwell, James Clerk (1831-79) Scottish physicist, whose work led to major advances in THERMODYNAMICS and ELECTROMAGNETISM. The four equations that bear his name laid down the fundamental principles of electromagnetic waves, demonstrated the electromagnetic nature of light, and predicted the existence of other forms of electromagnetic radiation.

mean, median and mode Three different ways of expressing an average for a set of figures. The mean is the same as the arithmetical average and is arrived at by dividing the total for the whole group by the number in the group: the average age of 100 people whose combined ages equal 5000 is 50. The median is the middle value of the group; half the individual figures fall below the median and half above. If the same group of 100 people is made up mainly of people over the mean age of 50, balanced by a smaller number of very young people, the median age will be over 50. The mode is the most commonly occurring value in the group. For example, if 52 is the commonest age in the group then 52 is the mode. (See also NORMAL DISTRIBUTION CURVE; STATISTICS.)

mechanics Branch of applied mathematics that lies at the heart of classical physics. It deals with objects in motion as a result of the forces acting on them (dynamics), and with stationary objects where the forces are in equilibrium (statics). (See NEWTON'S LAWS OF MOTION.)

melting point The temperature at which a solid turns to a liquid. Under normal conditions, it is the same as the freezing point. The heat required to melt a solid without raising its temperature is known as LATENT HEAT.

Mendeleev, Dmitri Ivanovich (1834-1907) Russian chemist who devised the modern PERIODIC TABLE, grouping the elements according to their chemical properties. He also predicted the existence of several hitherto undiscovered elements.

MARTIAN LANDSCAPE *Viking spacecraft images, enhanced by computer, reveal high volcanic peaks framing the great Valles Marineris canyon, an awesome gash over 1850 miles (3000 km) long and up to 5 miles (8 km) deep.*

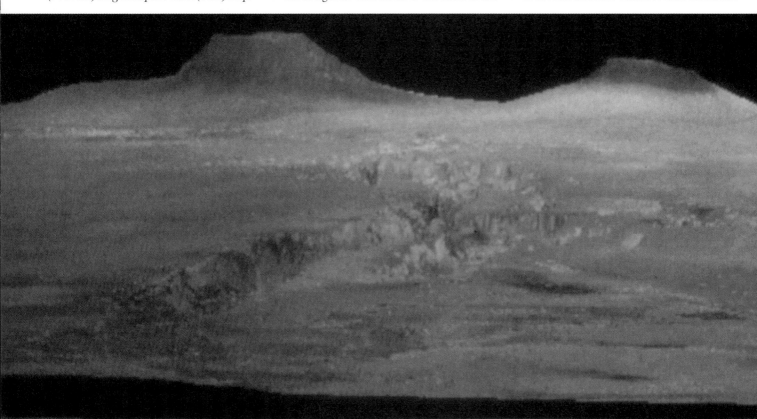

Mercury Planet closest to the Sun, named after the Roman messenger of the gods. It has little or no atmosphere and surface temperatures vary enormously from −160°C (−256°F) to more than 300°C (572°F) between day and night.

metal Element such as iron, copper or zinc that possesses most or all of the following properties: it is relatively hard, but malleable and can be formed into sheets and wires; it reflects light and has a lustre when polished; and it is a good conductor of heat and electricity. About 75 per cent of elements are metallic. (See PERIODIC TABLE.)

meteor Material from interplanetary space that enters the atmosphere and burns up in a streak of fire, forming a 'shooting star'. Meteors are thought to be particles of debris from comets and asteroids. Normally, about five shooting stars are visible each hour, but when 'meteor showers' occur there may be thousands every hour.

metre International unit of length (see SI UNITS) equal to 39.37 inches. The French Revolutionaries devised the metric system at the end of the 18th century, defining the metre as one 10 millionth of the distance from the North Pole to the Equator on the line of longitude which passes through Paris. Until 1960, the standard was set as the distance between two lines on a platinum bar kept under controlled conditions in Paris. It is now defined as the distance travelled by light in 1/299 792 458 of a second.

metric system System of weights and measures based on the principle that all units are derived from the base unit by multiplying or dividing by multiples of 10. The derived units have standard prefixes:

tera-	1 million million (10^{12})
giga-	1000 million (10^{9})
mega-	1 million (10^{6})
kilo-	1 thousand (10^{3})
hecto-	100 (10^{2})
deca-	10 (10^{1})
deci-	1 tenth (10^{-1})
centi-	1 hundredth (10^{-2})
milli-	1 thousandth (10^{-3})
micro-	1 millionth (10^{-6})
nano-	1 thousand millionth (10^{-9})
pico-	1 million millionth (10^{-12})

The metric system was the basis for the system of SI UNITS which was accepted internationally in 1960.

Michelson-Morley experiment Crucial experiment in the history of physics, named after the two American physicists who carried it out in the 1880s. It was designed to detect the presence of the 'ether', the medium through which light was thought to travel in space. It failed in its purpose but, in doing so, it showed that light does not require a medium through which to travel, and paved the way for Einstein's proposition that the speed of light is constant, whatever the speed of the observer – the fundamental assumption of the theory of RELATIVITY.

microwaves Type of ELECTROMAGNETIC RADIATION, with wavelengths lying between those of radio waves and infrared radiation. The COSMIC BACKGROUND RADIATION of the Universe is composed of microwaves. They are used in the ▷MICROWAVE OVEN and in telecommunications.

Milky Way Hazy band of light encircling the night sky. It is composed of thousands of millions of stars in the spiral arms of our own GALAXY.

molecule Group of atoms held together by chemical BONDS. It is the smallest unit that still retains the characteristic properties of a chemical COMPOUND. Molecular weight is the sum of all the ATOMIC WEIGHTS of the atoms in the molecule. It ranges from 2.016 for the lightest molecule, hydrogen (H_2), to 10 000 or more for organic molecules such as ▷PROTEINS, and into the millions for large POLYMERS.

momentum Tendency of a moving body to continue moving. For a body moving in a straight line (linear momentum) it is the product of the body's MASS and its VELOCITY; thus a light fast-moving body may have the same momentum as a heavy slow-moving one. The principle of conservation of momentum requires that the total momentum of a system remains the same: the recoil of a cannon has the same momentum as the shot it fires, though the shot moves much faster than the cannon. Rotating bodies have 'angular momentum'. Conservation of angular momentum is the basis for the ▷GYROSCOPE.

Moon Earth's only natural satellite, and the only extraterrestrial body on which man has set foot (see ▷APOLLO PROJECT). The Moon orbits the Earth about every 28 days at an average distance of 240 000 miles (386 000 km); its mass is about one-eightieth that of Earth, and its volume about one-fiftieth. It is about 2000 miles (3200 km) in diameter. It has no atmosphere, and its gravity is only one-sixth that of Earth. It owes its heavily cratered surface to the impact of ▷METEORITES as well as volcanic activity. It is thought that the Earth and the Moon formed some 4600 million years ago. Several other planets also have moons – 20 or more in the case of SATURN. (See also ECLIPSE; ▷TIDE.)

nebula Cloud of dust and gas in the sky. Some nebulae, such as the Horsehead nebula, are dark because they obscure the stars behind them and neither emit nor reflect light themselves. The Orion nebula, however, emits light because of a hot star at its centre, and the Pleiades and Andromeda nebulae shine by reflected light from

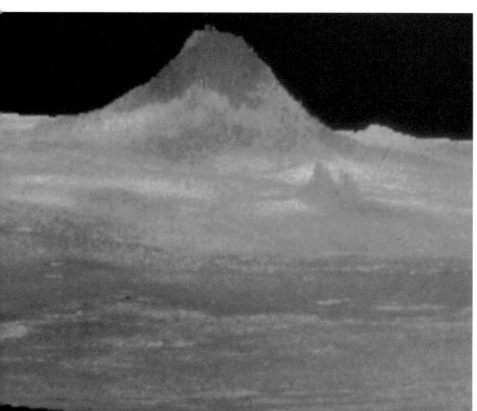

QUEST
FOR THE STARS
Isaac Newton's reflecting telescope, built with his own hands, is preserved by the Royal Society. It was only one of the many achievements of a genius whose ideas governed science for more than 200 years.

nearby stars. Nebulae may be the result of a SUPERNOVA, as in the case of the Crab nebula, whose explosion was noted by Chinese astronomers in 1054, and which has a PULSAR at its centre.

Neptune Eighth planet from the Sun, and fourth largest in the SOLAR SYSTEM. It is not visible to the naked eye. Neptune has a 'year' of around 185 Earth years. In 1989 the Voyager space probe confirmed that its atmosphere consisted mainly of methane and hydrogen.

neutrino A SUBATOMIC PARTICLE with no mass and no electric charge, but with a characteristic 'spin', produced by COSMIC RAYS and PARTICLE ACCELERATORS. It was predicted as early as 1931, but because it has virtually no effect on other types of matter, its existence was not proved experimentally for another 30 years.

neutron A SUBATOMIC PARTICLE found in the nucleus of the ATOM. It has much the same mass as a PROTON, but no electric charge. Only the hydrogen atom has no neutrons; heavier elements have more than one proton in the nucleus, which would normally repel each other because of their positive charge. The neutron acts as the 'glue' that holds the nucleus together.

neutron star Small, almost unimaginably dense star, left behind after a large star has reached the end of its life in a SUPERNOVA. The matter in the star collapses under the force of its own gravity, crushing electrons and protons together to form NEUTRONS. A teaspoonful would weigh several thousand million tons. Even larger stars are thought to carry on collapsing indefinitely, forming BLACK HOLES. PULSARS are rapidly rotating neutron stars.

Newton, Sir Isaac (1642-1727) English physicist and mathematician, one of the great figures in the history of science. His most notable achievements were NEWTON'S LAWS OF MOTION, which established the science of MECHANICS, his discovery of the law of GRAVITATION and CALCULUS, which has been an essential tool of mathematics and physics ever since. Newton made the first reflecting telescope, and was the first to use a prism to split light into the colours of the spectrum. He also studied heat, acoustics and fluids. The newton, a unit of FORCE, is named after him.
🔎Newtonian physics offered a model of the Universe, in which it seemed that everything was determined by fixed physical laws. In the 20th century, however, Albert Einstein's theories showed that Newton's laws did not work at speeds approaching that of light (see RELATIVITY), nor with particles the size of an electron (see QUANTUM MECHANICS). Nevertheless, Newton's laws are still valid for most purposes.

Newton's laws of motion Three basic laws that govern the relationships between forces and motion. They state: 1 Every body continues in a state of rest or uniform motion in a straight line unless acted upon by an external force, such as friction or gravity. 2 The acceleration produced when a force acts on a body is directly proportional to the force applied and inversely proportional to the mass of the body: the stronger the force and the lower the mass, the greater the acceleration. 3 To every action, there is an equal and opposite reaction: for example, a bullet forces a gun to recoil as strongly as the gun forces the bullet forwards. The whole of classical MECHANICS is based on these laws. (See also ACCELERATION; FORCE; INERTIA; MASS; MOMENTUM and VELOCITY.)

nitrogen Colourless, odourless gas which makes up 80 per cent of the atmosphere. Nitrogen compounds can be ACIDS (for example nitric acid HNO_3) or ALKALIS (ammonia NH_3). These compounds are of great importance in nature as essential components of proteins and DNA. Oxides of nitrogen include nitrogen dioxide (NO_2), a pollutant emitted by car exhausts, and nitrous oxide or laughing gas (N_2O). Nitrogen salts (nitrates and nitrites) are widely used in the manufacture of explosives, fertilisers and dyes.

noble gases Group of gases that make up group 0 of the PERIODIC TABLE. They are also known as the inert gases because of their lack of chemical reactivity. The most important is HELIUM; the others are neon, argon, krypton, xenon and radon. They glow in bright colours when an electric discharge is passed through them, and are used in commercial 'neon' lighting.

normal distribution curve Important concept in STATISTICS. It is also known as the 'bell' curve because of its shape. When market researchers or opinion pollsters want to know the preferences of the population as a whole, they interview a sample. The normal distribution curve shows how much the answers from the sample can be expected to differ from the answers that the whole population would give. Most results will fall close to the central mean value; a few will vary by quite a wide margin; and still fewer will be misleading freak results. The smaller the sample, the greater the margin of error and hence the wider the bell, and the larger the sample, the narrower the bell.

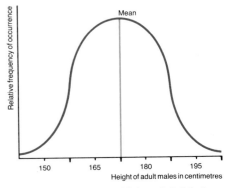

BELL-SHAPED CURVE *Adult male height is an example of a characteristic that produces a 'normal' distribution curve when plotted on a graph. Statisticians use the normal distribution curve to evaluate the results of samples and to test hypotheses about such things as the effectiveness of drugs or whether diet affects height.*

nova Star that suddenly increases in brightness by around 10 000 times, becoming visible to the naked eye; the word *nova* is Latin for 'new'. The star is not destroyed by the eruption, although it loses some of its mass. It gradually fades again over a period of years. Novas (or novae) are thought to occur when an old WHITE DWARF star pulls material from its companion in a BINARY STAR system and starts burning again. (Compare SUPERNOVA.)

nuclear energy Energy released during reactions involving the atomic nucleus. When light atomic nuclei fuse together (NUCLEAR FUSION) or when large nuclei split apart (NUCLEAR FISSION), a small proportion of the mass of the atoms concerned is converted into energy according to Einstein's mass-energy equation $E = MC^2$. Since C (the speed of light) is so great, the conversion of tiny amounts of mass produces huge quantities of energy.

nuclear fission Splitting of heavy atomic nuclei into smaller fragments. In the process, a small amount of mass is converted into a very large amount of nuclear energy. Most ▷NUCLEAR REACTORS use the fission of a uranium isotope, U235, or a plutonium isotope, P238, as their source of power. The reaction is initiated when a neutron strikes the uranium or plutonium nucleus. This splits, releasing three more neutrons, which may then go on to split further nuclei in a 'chain reaction'. Provided there is a sufficient 'critical mass' of fuel present, an uncontrolled chain reaction rapidly builds up to an awesome explosion, as in the atomic bomb. However, if some of the neutrons are absorbed, it is possible to control the reaction and to allow a steady release of energy, which can be used to produce electricity in a nuclear power station. Nuclear fission produces many highly radioactive by-products and ▷NUCLEAR WASTE disposal is a matter of concern. (Compare NUCLEAR FUSION.)

nuclear fusion The combining of light atomic nuclei to form larger ones; in practice, it usually refers to the fusion of two nuclei of deuterium or tritium (isotopes of hydrogen) to form a helium nucleus. The nuclear energy released in the transformation is even greater than that produced by fission. It is the source of the Sun's energy and is used in the hydrogen bomb. Fusion produces very little in the way of radioactive by-products and would offer a clean source of energy for millions of years to come, since deuterium is easily extracted from sea water. However, the reaction is only known to take place at temperatures approaching those in the interior of the Sun, and there is no known material that could act as a container. Nuclear physicists are experimenting with hot PLASMA sus-

pended in strong magnetic fields and have succeeded in sustaining fusion reactions, generating a few megawatts of power, for short periods. (See also COLD FUSION.)

numbers The basis of all counting and measuring. The theory of numbers is a major branch of mathematics, and there are various types of number. The most familiar are the integers or whole numbers, and their derivatives, fractions, which together make up the 'rational numbers'. There are 'irrational numbers' which cannot be expressed in terms of integers, for example π (PI) and the square root of 2 ($\sqrt{2}$). And there are 'imaginary numbers', based on the square root of -1 (or i). Imaginary numbers combined with rational or irrational numbers are called 'complex numbers': equations involving these are fundamental to CHAOS THEORY and FRACTAL geometry.

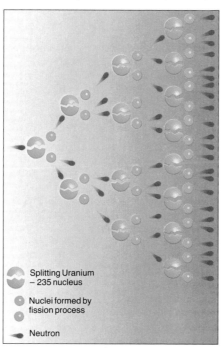

Splitting Uranium
– 235 nucleus

Nuclei formed by
fission process

Neutron

CHAIN REACTION *Once nuclear fission has begun, the reaction accelerates, unless checked, culminating in a massive nuclear explosion.*

octane Liquid HYDROCARBON (C_8H_{18}) found in petroleum. The octane rating of a fuel is a measure of its ability to prevent preignition, or 'knocking'.

ohm Measure of electrical RESISTANCE. It is named after the German physicist George Simon Ohm (1789-1854), who is remembered for Ohm's law, which states that the current passing through a conductor is proportional to the POTENTIAL DIFFERENCE across it. The law is usually

expressed as $v = ir$, where v is the potential difference in VOLTS, i is the current in AMPS and r the resistance in ohms.

orbit Path followed by a celestial object such as a planet or satellite as it revolves around another under the influence of gravity. Orbits are always elliptical. The point at which the orbit approaches closest to the parent body is the 'perigee' (or perihelion in the case of the Sun); the farthest point is the 'apogee' (or aphelion).

organic chemistry Major branch of chemistry dealing with the compounds of CARBON, which are more numerous than those of all the other elements put together. Organic compounds make up the fabric of all living things. They are subdivided into two main groups: 'aliphatic' compounds, in which the carbon atoms are joined in straight or branching chains; and 'aromatic' compounds (so called because they often have a pleasant aroma), based on BENZENE which has a ring structure.

Until the early 19th century it was thought that organic compounds could only be produced by living things. But in 1828, the German chemist Friedrich Wöhler succeeded in producing urea, an organic compound, from ammonium cyanate, which is inorganic.

osmosis Tendency of a solvent (usually water) to diffuse through a membrane until the concentrations of the solutions on either side of the membrane are equal. For this to happen, the membrane needs to be semipermeable, as it is in living tissues, particularly cell walls. Osmosis can lead to considerable differences in pressure on either side of the membrane. It is osmotic pressure that keeps plant cells rigid; the loss of it through lack of water leads to wilting.

oxidation Combining of an element with oxygen. Familiar examples are the burning of fossil fuels, in which carbon is oxidised to carbon dioxide, and rusting when iron is oxidised to ferric oxide. All living things derive their energy from oxidation reactions of one sort or another, usually by 'burning' ▷GLUCOSE inside the cell during ▷RESPIRATION. Technically, oxidation involves the removal of electrons from an atom, and is always accompanied by its opposite – a REDUCTION reaction.

oxygen Colourless odourless gas, the most abundant element on Earth. It makes up about 20 per cent of the weight of the atmosphere, about 90 per cent of the water and about 50 per cent of the Earth's crust;

FUNDAMENTAL PHYSICS *The Large Electron-Positron (LEP) collider, 100 metres below ground on the French-Swiss border north of Geneva, is Europe's largest particle accelerator or 'atom smasher'.*

uncombined, it normally forms molecules containing two atoms (O_2). However, it combines readily with most other elements to form oxides. Metallic oxides are mostly BASES in solution; nonmetallic oxides are ACIDS. Oxygen is produced by plants during ▷PHOTOSYNTHESIS and consumed by plants and animals during ▷RESPIRATION.

ozone Form of OXYGEN containing three atoms in each molecule (O_3) rather than the usual two. It has a characteristic pungent odour and is blue in concentrated form. It is formed by the action of ultraviolet light or electrical discharges (such as lightning) on ordinary oxygen and is a harmful component of photochemical ▷SMOG. In the atmosphere, the ▷OZONE LAYER filters out ultraviolet radiation from the Sun.

parabola Path traced out by any projectile, such as a golf ball, which is propelled away from the Earth and then drawn back by gravity. Dish aerials are often parabolic in cross-section, as are the mirrors used in reflecting telescopes, since they focus radiation to a point. (See CONIC SECTIONS.)

parallax Apparent shift in the position of an object when viewed from two different places. Viewing close objects first through one eye and then the other provides one example. Parallax techniques are used in astronomy to measure the distance of stars.

particle accelerator Essential tool of modern theoretical physics, also known as an 'atom smasher'. Particle accelerators are used to accelerate SUBATOMIC PARTICLES to speeds approaching that of light so that physicists can study what happens when they collide, and gain greater understanding of the nature of matter and energy. The particles are accelerated by powerful electromagnets either in linear accelerators in a straight line or, in the more common cyclotrons and synchrocyclotrons, in a circular tunnel. The principal particle accelerator in Europe, with a tunnel $16\frac{3}{4}$ miles (27 km) long, is at CERN in Geneva.

periodic table Method of arranging the chemical elements in order of their ATOMIC NUMBERS, in such a way that the members of each vertical group show markedly similar properties, and horizontal rows show regular variations in properties going from left to right. Thus the elements in group I, starting with lithium, sodium and potassium, are all METALS and highly reactive; moving to the right, the elements become less and less metallic and eventually become such typical nonmetals as carbon, sulphur and chlorine. The 'periodic' nature of the table is due to the fact that the number of electrons in the outer shell of an atom determines its chemical properties (see VALENCE); elements in each vertical group have the same number of electrons in their outer shells, while each horizontal period has one more electron shell than the previous one. Some groups of elements have the same numbers of electrons in the outer shell, but different numbers in the penultimate shell. These are the TRANSITION ELEMENTS in groups 1b to 7b and 8. There are also two groups, the lanthanide series or rare earths, and the radioactive actinide series, which are both transition series within the main transition series.

pH A measure of the strength of an ACID or BASE. It is based on the concentration of hydrogen ions in a solution; the higher the concentration, the lower the pH. Pure water has a pH of 7, acid solutions less than 7, and alkaline ones greater than 7.

phlogiston Substance once thought to be given off during combustion and which, when recombined with ash, would reconstitute the original substance. The phlogiston theory was a basic principle of 18th-century chemistry, until it was discredited by the French chemist Antoine LAVOISIER.

photoelectricity Change in the electrical properties of a material when struck by light or some other form of electromagnetic radiation. It generally refers to the photoelectric effect in which light waves release electrons where they strike the material, thus creating a current.

photon A 'particle', or quantum, of light or some other form of electromagnetic energy. (See PLANCK'S CONSTANT; QUANTUM MECHANICS.)

physics Scientific study of MATTER and ENERGY and the ways in which they interact. It has traditionally been concerned with MECHANICS, ELECTRICITY and MAGNETISM, HEAT and LIGHT. During the 20th century many of the fundamental principles of physics have been challenged. The result has been the development of new areas of study, such as SUBATOMIC PARTICLES, QUANTUM MECHANICS and RELATIVITY.

pi (π) Symbol for the ratio of the circumference of any circle to its diameter. It is an irrational number – that is, it cannot be written exactly as a fraction or decimal. It is approximately equal to 3.14 or $3\frac{1}{7}$.

Planck's constant Universal constant, of fundamental importance in QUANTUM MECHANICS. It relates the energy E of a quantum of radiation to its frequency v by the formula $E=hv$, where h is Planck's constant. It is named after the German physicist Max Planck (1858-1947) who, in 1900, provided the first satisfactory explanation for one of the puzzles of classical physics – why light sometimes behaves like a wave and sometimes like a particle.

planet Any of the nine major bodies orbiting the Sun in the SOLAR SYSTEM. The name comes from the ancient Greek word for 'wanderer'. It is probable that many other stars have planetary systems.

plasma Gas at very high temperatures or pressure in which electrons have been split from their atoms, leaving positively charged IONS and free electrons. Plasma is sometimes referred to as the fourth state of matter. Plasmas are the focus of research into controlled NUCLEAR FUSION.

Pluto Smallest planet in the SOLAR SYSTEM and usually farthest from the Sun. However, it has a highly elliptical 248-year orbit and for part of the time – between 1979 and 1999, for example – it is closer to

the Sun than Neptune. Its discovery in 1930 was predicted by theory to account for observed irregularities in Neptune's orbit.

polarised light Light in which the electrical and magnetic vibrations, which normally occur in all directions at right angles to the path of the light, have been reduced to a single plane. Much of the light around us is partially polarised by reflection; polarising sunglasses filter out this polarised light, thus reducing glare.

polymer Very large molecule made up of many repeating sub-units, or monomers. Naturally occurring polymers include ▷PROTEINS, ▷CELLULOSE and nucleic acids. Synthetic polymers include ▷PLASTICS and synthetic fibres.

potential difference Electrical 'pressure', analogous to a difference in water levels, that causes a current to flow. It is also referred to as the electromotive force (emf). It is measured in VOLTS.

power In mathematics, the indication of the number of times a number must be multiplied by itself. Thus 2^3, or two to the power of three, is $2 \times 2 \times 2$, or 8; similarly 10^6 is $10 \times 10 \times 10 \times 10 \times 10 \times 10$, or 1 million. The number representing the power is called the exponent. Any number to power 0 is, by definition, equal to 1. Different powers of the same number can be multiplied by adding their exponents together; $2^3 \times 2^3 = 2^6 = 64$. (See LOGARITHMS.)

power In physics, the rate of doing WORK, generally involving the conversion of energy into a useful form, such as movement, with a loss of heat. It is measured in JOULES per second, or WATTS.

precession Wobbling of the Earth in space, or a cyclic movement of the axis of rotation of any spinning body, such as a ▷GYROSCOPE or spinning top, when subjected to a TORQUE or turning force. The Earth's axis, for example, traces out a cone every 26 000 years because of the

TABLE OF THE ELEMENTS *The chemical elements were first organised into a periodic table by the Russian chemist Dmitri Mendeleyev in 1869. A modern version, below, shows the elements arranged in horizontal rows in sequence of atomic number and divided into vertical groups of similar elements.*

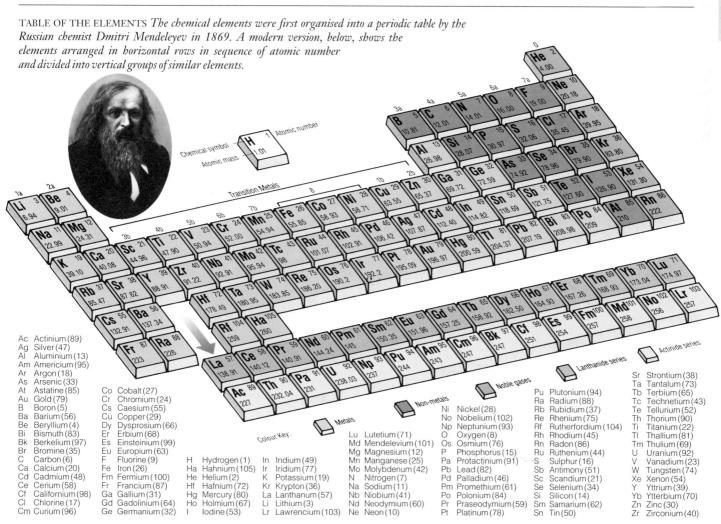

Ac Actinium(89)
Ag Silver(47)
Al Aluminium(13)
Am Americium(95)
Ar Argon(18)
As Arsenic(33)
At Astatine(85)
Au Gold(79)
B Boron(5)
Ba Barium(56)
Be Beryllium(4)
Bi Bismuth(83)
Bk Berkelium(97)
Br Bromine(35)
C Carbon(6)
Ca Calcium(20)
Cd Cadmium(48)
Ce Cerium(58)
Cf Californium(98)
Cl Chlorine(17)
Cm Curium(96)

Co Cobalt(27)
Cr Chromium(24)
Cs Caesium(55)
Cu Copper(29)
Dy Dysprosium(66)
Er Erbium(68)
Es Einsteinium(99)
Eu Europium(63)
F Fluorine(9)
Fe Iron(26)
Fm Fermium(100)
Fr Francium(87)
Ga Gallium(31)
Gd Gadolinium(64)
Ge Germanium(32)

H Hydrogen(1)
Ha Hahnium(105)
He Helium(2)
Hf Hafnium(72)
Hg Mercury(80)
Ho Holmium(67)
I Iodine(53)

In Indium(49)
Ir Iridium(77)
K Potassium(19)
Kr Krypton(36)
La Lanthanum(57)
Li Lithium(3)
Lr Lawrencium(103)

Lu Lutetium(71)
Md Mendelevium(101)
Mg Magnesium(12)
Mn Manganese(25)
Mo Molybdenum(42)
N Nitrogen(7)
Na Sodium(11)
Nb Niobium(41)
Nd Neodymium(60)
Ne Neon(10)

Ni Nickel(28)
No Nobelium(102)
Np Neptunium(93)
O Oxygen(8)
Os Osmium(76)
Pa Protactinium(91)
Pb Lead(82)
Pd Palladium(46)
Pm Promethium(61)
Po Polonium(84)
Pr Praseodymium(59)
Pt Platinum(78)

Pu Plutonium(94)
Ra Radium(88)
Rb Rubidium(37)
Re Rhenium(75)
Rf Rutherfordium(104)
Rh Rhodium(45)
Rn Radon(86)
Ru Ruthenium(44)
S Sulphur(16)
Sb Antimony(51)
Sc Scandium(21)
Se Selenium(34)
Si Silicon(14)
Sm Samarium(62)
Sn Tin(50)

Sr Strontium(38)
Ta Tantalum(73)
Tb Terbium(65)
Tc Technetium(43)
Te Tellurium(52)
Th Thorium(90)
Ti Titanium(22)
Tl Thallium(81)
Tm Thulium(69)
U Uranium(92)
V Vanadium(23)
W Tungsten(74)
Xe Xenon(54)
Y Yttrium(39)
Yb Ytterbium(70)
Zn Zinc(30)
Zr Zirconium(40)

pull of the Sun and Moon on its equatorial bulge. This causes a gradual change in the apparent positions of the stars.

pressure The FORCE per unit area acting on a surface. The standard scientific unit of pressure is the pascal, named after the French scientist and religious philosopher Blaise Pascal (1623-62). One pascal is equal to a force of 1 newton acting on a surface of 1 square metre. Others units include pounds per square inch (psi); the atmosphere (14.7 psi); and the bar (100 000 pascals). Pressure is transmitted uniformly in all directions. Thus a force applied to one part of a fluid system can be made to do WORK in another; this is the basis of ▷HYDRAULICS. In a gas, pressure is the result of molecules striking the walls of the container. For a fixed mass of gas, pressure increases with temperature and decreases with increasing volume (see BOYLE'S LAW).

prime number Number larger than 1 that cannot be divided by any whole numbers other than itself and 1. The theory that every even number above 2 is the sum of two primes has never been proved, but no exceptions have ever been found.

probability The chance that a particular event will occur, usually expressed as a number between 0 (no chance at all) and 1 (certainty) or as the ratio between the number of outcomes that give a specific result and the number of possible outcomes. The probability of throwing an even number at dice is ³⁄₆ or 0.5.

proton A SUBATOMIC PARTICLE found in the nucleus of the atom. It has equal but opposite (positive) charge to the ELECTRON, but about 1000 times the mass. The number of protons is equal to the ATOMIC NUMBER of an element.

Ptolemy (Claudius Ptolemaeus, 2nd century AD) Alexandrian astronomer and mathematician whose synthesis of Greek astronomical knowledge in the *Almagest* produced the so-called Ptolemaic system of the Universe. This system, in which the Sun and planets were held to orbit the Earth, dominated astronomy for 1500 years, until the Sun-centred system proposed by COPERNICUS gained acceptance.

pulsar Rapidly rotating NEUTRON STAR which emits a bright beam of radiation as it rotates, like a flashing lighthouse. Pulsars were discovered in 1967 and more than 600 are now known. Pulsar is short for 'pulsating radio star'; most pulsars emit at radio wavelengths although other wavelengths have been detected. The fastest pulsars emit pulses more than 500 times a second.

Pythagoras's theorem Statement that the square on the hypotenuse of a right-angled triangle is equal to the sum of the squares on the other two sides. It was first proved by the Greek mathematician Pythagoras in the 6th century BC, but had been applied earlier by Egyptian builders to ensure corners were square. The simplest example is a triangle with sides of 3, 4 and 5 units.

quantum mechanics Fundamental theory of physics which, together with the theory of RELATIVITY, forms the basis of much of 20th-century science. It states that energy can only be released or absorbed in discrete packets or quanta – the PHOTON, for example, is a quantum of light energy. An electron in orbit round an atom does not move smoothly from one energy level to another, but performs a 'quantum leap', emitting or absorbing a photon as it does so. This simple premise has far-reaching consequences. One of these is the UNCERTAINTY PRINCIPLE, which states that it is impossible to know the position and the MOMENTUM of a particle simultaneously. So the wave-like behaviour of light and electrons represents a 'graph' of the probabilities of a particle or quantum being in a particular place at a particular time. Essentially, the behaviour of matter becomes a question of probabilities. Quantum mechanics accords well with classical physics for large-scale phenomena, but at the subatomic level and at extreme temperatures, only quantum mechanics can explain such puzzles as the superfluidity of HELIUM, SUPERCONDUCTIVITY, the behaviour of ▷SEMICONDUCTORS, PHOTOELECTRICITY and the ability of an electron or photon to be in two places at the same time. The modern view of atomic structure and chemical elements is based on quantum theory.

🔊Einstein could not accept the role of chance in this marrying of quantum mechanics with the theory of relativity, saying 'God does not play dice' with the Universe.

quarks Fundamental constituents of matter from which certain heavy SUBATOMIC PARTICLES, notably PROTONS and NEUTRONS, are built. They are endowed with properties that have been given such names as colour, flavour and charm. Quarks, which have not yet been observed, were posited in 1963 by US physicist Murray Gell-Mann and named on a whim from the phrase 'three quarks for Muster Mark' in James Joyce's *Finnegans Wake*.

quasar Intensely brilliant star-like object – the name is short for quasi-stellar object. Quasars appear to be receding from us at close to the speed of light; if so, they would be the brightest and most distant objects in the Universe. Quasars are thought to be the bright centres of galaxies containing massive BLACK HOLES.

radiation Energy sent out in the form of particles or waves. The term is applied to ELECTROMAGNETIC RADIATION as well as SOUND, but it more often refers to RADIOACTIVITY, when it takes three forms: alpha radiation consists of the ejection of two protons and two neutrons – an alpha particle – from a decaying atomic nucleus; beta radiation is composed of high-energy electrons, emitted when a neutron decays into a proton and a corresponding electron; and GAMMA RADIATION is a highly energetic and penetrating form of electromagnetic radiation, which may accompany both alpha and beta radiation.

radioactivity Emission of RADIATION as a result of the spontaneous disintegration of unstable atomic nuclei. Every chemical element has at least one radioactive ISOTOPE (or radioisotope), although only around 50 occur in nature. The others have been produced artificially in PARTICLE ACCELERATORS or as the by-products of NUCLEAR FISSION in power stations and atomic bombs. Radioactivity was discovered in uranium compounds by the French physicist Henri Becquerel in 1896 – the becquerel, the unit of radioactivity, is named after him. Radioisotopes are of great value in many branches of science, industry and medicine. They can be used to 'label' chemical compounds so that their progress in chemical reactions, or their fate inside the body, can be tracked. They can also be used to kill cancerous tumours. However, radioactivity can also be extremely hazardous to human health, causing birth defects, ▷RADIATION SICKNESS as well as cancer. Because radioisotopes may have a HALF-LIFE of thousands of years, they present considerable problems of disposal.

radio waves Form of ELECTROMAGNETIC RADIATION with the longest wavelengths (between 30 cm and 100 km) and the lowest frequencies in the electromagnetic spectrum. Because they pass through the atmosphere and obstacles such as buildings, they are used for the transmission of radio and television broadcasts. Longer wavelengths are also reflected by the upper layers of the atmosphere, allowing communication around the world.

THE COLOURS OF LIGHT *The ability of a prism to split light into its spectrum by refraction was first demonstrated by Isaac Newton.*

red giant Large and luminous star which is reaching the end of its life. The Sun will begin to expand once it has exhausted the hydrogen fuel in its core – in about 5000 million years' time – becoming a red giant 100 times larger than it is now, before finally collapsing to form a WHITE DWARF.

red shift Increase in the wavelength of light reaching us from distant stars and galaxies. It is similar to the DOPPLER EFFECT: just as the pitch of a receding police siren falls, so light from a star is shifted towards the red end of the spectrum as it travels away from us. Red shift was discovered by the American astronomer Edwin HUBBLE, and demonstrated that distant galaxies are receding at rates that approach the speed of light. It provides the main evidence for the BIG BANG theory.

reduction Removal of oxygen, or a similar element, from a compound. All reduction reactions involve a corresponding OXIDATION reaction and the two are often referred to as a 'redox' reaction.

reflection Bouncing of a ray of light, or other wave, off a surface. From a smooth surface, such as a mirror, the reflected ray makes the same angle to the perpendicular as the arriving, or incident, ray. Reflected sound waves are familiar as echoes.

refraction Bending of a ray of light, or other form of energy wave, when it passes from one transparent medium to another,

for example from air to water. Refraction is responsible for the apparent bending of a straw at the point where it enters a glass of water. It is also the mechanism by which a LENS is able to form enlarged or reduced images. The amount by which the light is bent depends on its wavelength; red is refracted least and violet most. Refraction of light by a prism produces the SPECTRUM, just as raindrops split light to form a ▷RAINBOW. Light striking a surface at an angle greater than the 'critical angle' is not refracted but reflected, as in optical fibres.

relativity, theory of Fundamental theory of physics concerned with the nature of time, space and motion, put forward as the 'special theory of relativity' in 1905 by Albert EINSTEIN. It is based on the startling assumption that the speed of light is constant whatever the speed of the observer – it does not appear to travel faster even if the observer is moving rapidly towards it. Similarly, all other laws of physics will appear to be the same to all observers moving at constant relative velocities with respect to each other. The consequences of these assumptions are far reaching. The theory predicts that time will move more slowly on a fast-moving object; a moving clock, for example, will run more slowly than a stationary one. Other predictions are that a body's mass will increase with speed while its length will decrease, and that mass and energy are equivalent (see E=MC²). If a body were able to travel at the speed of light (which is impossible), it would have infinite mass, zero length and time on it would come to a standstill. These predictions have been proved over and over again, and it is now accepted that the classical physics expressed by NEWTON'S LAWS OF MOTION, while adequate to explain most earthbound events, do not apply to the Universe as a whole. In 1915, Einstein put forward the 'general theory of relativity', in which he demonstrated that GRAVITATION and ACCELERATION are equivalent – an observer standing in a lift cannot tell whether the force pressing him to the floor is due to gravity or to upward acceleration of the lift. Since a beam of light would appear to be bent as seen by an accelerating observer, so too should it be bent by gravity. This has been confirmed by observation and leads to the conclusion that space itself is curved.

resistance Property of a material that makes it impede the passage of an electric current. It is calculated as the POTENTIAL DIFFERENCE in volts across a circuit, or part of a circuit, divided by the current in AMPS. It is measured in OHMS.

resonance Reinforcement of the natural frequency of vibration of an object when a force is applied with the same frequency. Soldiers break step when crossing a bridge in case their marching rhythm corresponds with the natural frequency of the bridge, which could cause it to vibrate to the point of collapse. Singers can break wine glasses by singing loudly a note with a frequency equal to the natural frequency of the glass.

Roman numerals Numbers represented by combinations of letters, rather than by the more familiar ARABIC NUMERALS. The letter I is equivalent to 1, V to 5, X to 10, L to 50, C to 100, D to 500 and M to 1000. Intermediate numbers are derived by adding succeeding letters together, except where a smaller letter is followed by a larger one, when the smaller is subtracted from the larger. Thus 8 is written as VIII and 9 as IX. The date 1066 would be written as MLXVI, while 1999 would be MCMIC.

Rutherford, Sir Ernest (1871-1937) New Zealand-born physicist who, in 1919, was the first to split the atomic nucleus when he converted nitrogen into oxygen and hydrogen. His work at the Cavendish Laboratory, Cambridge, laid the foundations for the modern understanding of radioactivity and the structure of the atom.

SPLITTING THE ATOM *Sir Ernest Rutherford in his laboratory. He achieved the alchemists' dream of transmutation of the elements.*

salt Chemical compound formed by the reaction of an ACID and a BASE. Common salt or sodium chloride (NaCl) is formed by the reaction of hydrochloric acid (HCl) with sodium hydroxide (NaOH). Most minerals are salts.

Saturn Sixth planet from the Sun and the most distant visible to the naked eye. It is famous for its rings, which may represent material left over from its formation. It is the second largest planet in the Solar System, with a mass about 95 times greater than Earth's, but since it is largely composed of hydrogen and helium gases, it is also the least dense. It has a 'year' of 29.46 Earth years and a 'day' of just over 10 hours. It has more than 20 moons, the largest of which, Titan, is about the size of Mercury.

set theory Branch of mathematics that deals with numbers or objects as members of distinct groups or sets. Thus the pupils in a school (the 'universal' set) would contain any number of subsets, for example red-haired pupils, male pupils, female pupils and blue-eyed pupils. In some cases, the sets overlap – some red-haired pupils will also be female and have blue eyes. In other cases they will have no members in common – no female pupils will be male pupils. These relationships can be represented algebraically by BOOLEAN ALGEBRA and visually by VENN DIAGRAMS. Set theory provides the basic language and structure for most branches of modern mathematics. It is also basic to the creation of all computer programs.

silicon Second commonest element (after oxygen), known chiefly for its widespread use as a ▷SEMICONDUCTOR in the electronics industry. It occurs mainly as silica (which includes quartz, one of the chief constituents of sand and glass) and as silicates – some 95 per cent of the Earth's crust is composed of silicate minerals.
🔎 It has been suggested that alternative forms of extraterrestrial life might be built on a framework of silicon, just as life on Earth is based on carbon compounds.

SI units Abbreviation for *Système International d'Unités*, the internationally accepted standard for units of measure since 1960. Examples include the METRE (length), the KILOGRAM (mass) and the JOULE (energy).

Solar System The SUN and all the celestial objects held by its gravity. These include the nine major PLANETS, including EARTH, and their moons as well as countless ASTEROIDS, COMETS and METEORS.

solar wind Constant stream of electrically charged subatomic particles boiled off from the surface of the Sun. It is responsible for the tails of comets. Gusts of solar wind, caused by solar flares, interact with the Earth's magnetic field and with charged particles in the atmosphere, causing auroras and radio interference.

solstice Time of year when the overhead Sun is at its greatest angle to the Equator. At the summer solstice, around June 21, the Sun is directly overhead at the Tropic of Cancer at noon and the Northern Hemisphere has its longest day. At the winter solstice, around December 22, it is directly overhead at the Tropic of Capricorn, and the Northern Hemisphere has its shortest day. (Compare EQUINOX.)

sound Form of WAVE motion which can be detected by the ear. It depends on the physical displacement of a medium, for example air, for transmission and unlike light and other types of electromagnetic radiation, sound cannot travel in a vacuum. The FREQUENCY of a sound wave determines the pitch of the sound, the AMPLITUDE determines its loudness. The

speed of sound through air varies with the conditions but is about 760 mph (1220 km/h) at sea level. An aircraft flying close to this speed builds up waves of pressure in front of it, like the bow wave of a boat. When it passes through the sound barrier, the waves are released as a sonic boom.

space-time Concept arising from the theory of RELATIVITY, in which time and the three dimensions of space are treated as a single space-time continuum. It recognises that both space and time are defined by the SPEED OF LIGHT.

spectroscopy Analysis of the SPECTRUM of light or other forms of ELECTROMAGNETIC RADIATION emitted or absorbed by a substance in order to investigate its structure. Different atoms and molecules produce distinctive lines in the spectrum. Astronomers examine the light from distant stars to analyse their composition, and chemists can analyse complex compounds.

spectrum Bands of colour produced when a beam of white light is passed through a prism and split into its component wavelengths. All forms of ELECTROMAGNETIC

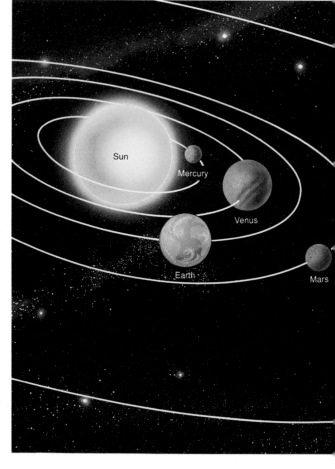

SUN AND PLANETS *The Sun dominates the Solar System, making up more than 99 per cent of its total mass. Its gravitational attraction is strong enough to keep tiny Pluto in orbit, at the extreme edge of the observable Solar System, between 2700 and 4600 million miles (4350 and 7400 million km) away. The Solar System is thought to have formed about 4700 million years ago, when a cloud of gas and dust contracted to create an extremely compact centre which was surrounded by a disc of particles, that very slowly coalesced into Earth and the other major planets.*

RADIATION can be split up into a spectrum. Examination of spectra by SPECTROSCOPY yields valuable information about the structure and composition of substances. See DIFFRACTION; LIGHT; REFRACTION.

speed Rate of change of distance with respect to time, calculated on the distance travelled divided by the time elapsed. Unlike VELOCITY, speed is independent of direction.

speed of light Universal physical constant, approximately equal to 186 000 miles (300 000 km) per second in a vacuum. (See also LIGHT; RELATIVITY.)

standard deviation In STATISTICS, a measure of how closely an average, or mean, represents the individuals in a population. If most people earn well below or well above average income, for example, the standard deviation is high; if most earn around the mean value, the standard deviation is low. (See MEAN, MEDIAN AND MODE; NORMAL DISTRIBUTION CURVE.)

star Ball of hot, luminous gases fuelled by nuclear reactions at its core. The SUN is a fairly typical medium-sized star. Stars are thought to form when clouds of interstellar dust and gases draw together and start to contract under the influence of their own gravity. Eventually, the compressed core becomes hot enough for NUCLEAR FUSION to begin. This generates sufficient energy to halt the contraction and the star continues to burn for anything from a million to many billions of years, depending on how large it is and how brightly it burns. When all its hydrogen has been converted to helium, gravity again contracts the core until it reaches the temperature at which the conversion of helium into carbon begins. This generates so much heat that the star's outer layers expand considerably. The star becomes a RED GIANT. Finally, when even the helium has gone, there is nothing to stop the star from collapsing to form a WHITE DWARF. For very massive stars, however, the process ends differently. The fusion reactions in the core can become so violent that the star explodes in a SUPERNOVA, throwing off most of its outer layers and leaving a dense NEUTRON STAR behind. Even this may not be the end for the most massive stars of all. These may continue to collapse under their own gravity, ending their lives as a BLACK HOLE.

static electricity An ELECTRIC CHARGE that has built up on an object, either because rubbing it has dislodged some of its electrons, or because a charge has been induced by an opposite static charge nearby. People sometimes pick up a static charge from the friction of their shoes against certain types of carpet. Static is also responsible for ▷LIGHTNING.

🔥 Static electricity was well known to the Greeks, who noticed that a piece of amber rubbed with a cloth would pick up small pieces of fluff. The word electricity comes from *elektron*, the Greek word for 'amber'.

statistics Branch of mathematics concerned with the collection and analysis of large quantities of data, particularly where the data are of a kind that cannot be predicted with any accuracy. It is of great importance in fundamental physics, economics, the social sciences, market research, drug testing and in the framing of many aspects of public policy. Statistics provides a way of analysing the factors that affect a situation. Many variables affect road safety, for example, but statistics may indicate which ones are most closely correlated with the accident rate and so suggest

Jupiter

Saturn

Uranus

Pluto

Neptune

the most effective preventive measures. It also provides a way of estimating the significance of a set of data, particularly one drawn from a sample, when it differs from the expected or normal result. A high incidence of a disease in a particular area might happen by chance, or there might be environmental factors involved; statistical analysis will indicate how likely it is that there is an environmental cause, and provides the tools for identifying the factors involved. (See also MEAN, MEDIAN AND MODE; NORMAL DISTRIBUTION CURVE.)

steady-state theory Proposition that the Universe has no beginning and no end, but has always looked much the same in all directions and from all points in space. The Universe is expanding, but new matter is constantly being created to fill the void. This theory, associated with Sir Fred Hoyle, Hermann Bondi and Thomas Gold, has now given way to the BIG BANG THEORY.

stress and strain Internal forces produced in a body by the application of an external force (stress) and the deformations that result (strain). There are basically four types: bending; shearing; stretching and compression; and torsion (twisting). The response of materials to stress and strain is a crucial aspect of engineering.

subatomic particles The fundamental constituents of matter. Several hundred subatomic, or elementary, particles are known, but scientists believe that they fall into three main groups. One group, known as 'gauge bosons', is responsible for transmitting the fundamental forces of nature; the PHOTON, for example, carries the electromagnetic force. The second group, the hadrons, includes the 'heavy' baryons, for example the proton and the neutron (thought to be composed of QUARKS), as well as lighter particles called mesons. The third group are the leptons, or light particles, which include various types of ELECTRONS and NEUTRINOS. A major goal of modern physics is to incorporate all elementary particles and the universal forces of nature into a single mathematical framework (see UNIFIED FIELD THEORIES).

Sun Star at the centre of the SOLAR SYSTEM. It is an average star, 865 000 miles (1 392 000 km) in diameter and with a mass about 1000 times that of the rest of the Solar System combined. Like most stars it is composed mainly of hydrogen, most of the remainder – about 30 per cent – being helium. It derives its energy from NUCLEAR FUSION reactions in the core, where the temperature reaches some 15 000 000°C (27 000 000°F), converting an estimated 600 million tons of hydrogen into helium every second. The Sun's visible surface, the photosphere, with a temperature of around 5500°C (9900°F), is a seething cauldron which sends off jets of very hot gas into the surrounding chromosphere, and where relatively dark patches, or SUNSPOTS, are seen periodically. The outer layer, the corona, is a halo of thinly spread material that has boiled off from the surface. The Sun is thought to have formed about 4700 million years ago. When it has exhausted its nuclear fuel in about 5000 million years' time, it will expand to become a RED GIANT before finally shrinking to a WHITE DWARF.

sunspot Cooler area on the surface of the Sun, which appears dark by comparison with the surroundings. Sunspots are associated with strong magnetic fields, and with solar flares which send streams of charged particles into the Earth's atmosphere. There they interact with the Earth's magnetic field, causing auroras and radio blackouts. Sunspots often appear in groups, and their numbers fluctuate in a cycle of approximately 11 years.

superconductivity Ability of some metals and other materials to conduct electricity with no resistance when cooled to very low temperatures. An electric current in such a material will continue to circulate indefinitely. Ceramic materials have recently been discovered that become superconducting at the relatively high temperature of liquid nitrogen (above −210°C (−346°F). If these can be incorporated into electrical circuits, superconductors will have an enormous impact in industry and transport.

supernova Cosmic explosion of extraordinary violence, in which a massive star (about ten times the mass of the Sun) is destroyed or throws out a substantial part of its mass. The remnant forms a NEUTRON STAR or a BLACK HOLE. For a brief period, the exploding star shines as brightly as 100 million suns and may be clearly visible to the naked eye. A supernova was observed in 1987 in the large MAGELLANIC CLOUD.

surface tension Force of attraction between molecules of a liquid, or between the liquid and its container, which makes the surface behave like a thin elastic skin. It is surface tension that causes water to form small droplets on a polished surface, that draws liquids up CAPILLARY tubes, and enables pond insects to walk on water.

thermodynamics Branch of physics concerned with the relationships between heat and other forms of energy, including mechanical work. It is important in many industrial and engineering applications, for example in determining the efficiency of vehicle engines or in the design of chemical manufacturing processes. There are three main laws of thermodynamics. The first states that energy can neither be created nor destroyed, merely converted from one form into another; the total energy of an isolated system will remain constant. The second law states that heat will not flow spontaneously from a colder body to a hotter one; the ENTROPY of a self-contained system can never decrease, only increase or remain the same. The third law states the impossibility of achieving the temperature of ABSOLUTE ZERO.

topology Sometimes referred to as 'rubber-sheet' geometry, the study of those properties of figures and shapes that are not changed by stretching and squeezing. The London Underground map is an example of a topological map. It preserves the connections between lines, and the positions of stations relative to one another, but distorts distance and actual location. Topology is used in a similar way in the design of integrated electronic circuits. In recent years it has developed into an important branch of abstract mathematics, and has played a major role in the development of FRACTAL geometry and CHAOS THEORY.

torque Turning effect of a force on a body able to rotate. It is measured by multiplying the force by its distance from the centre of rotation. In a car engine, torque is generated by the force that the pistons exert on the crankshaft.

transition elements Series of metallic elements that form a separate group within the PERIODIC TABLE. They include many of the metals that are important in industry, including iron, copper, nickel, zinc, silver and gold. They readily form alloys, and are also widely used as CATALYSTS. Their properties are very similar because they have the same number of electrons in their outer shell and differ only in the number of electrons in their inner shells.

triangle Three-sided figure whose internal angles always add up to 180°. A triangle with all its sides and all its angles equal, at 60°, is called an equilateral triangle; one with two sides, or angles, equal is an isosceles triangle; and one with all its sides and angles unequal is a scalene triangle.

trigonometry Branch of geometry that deals with the relationships between the sides and angles of right-angled triangles, and their application in such diverse fields as surveying, navigation and the study of wave forms. If an angle is regarded as being contained within a right-angled triangle, then the ratios between the three sides of the triangle can be calculated. Three main ratios are used: the sine, the cosine and the tangent (usually abbreviated to *sin*, *cos* and *tan*). The sine is particularly important since it is used to analyse such natural wave motions as light and sound.

twin paradox Apparent contradiction predicted by the theory of RELATIVITY. A twin who travels from the Earth at near the speed of light will, when he returns, be younger than his earthbound twin. The effect has been verified using very fast planes and highly accurate atomic clocks.

ultraviolet radiation Form of ELECTRO-MAGNETIC RADIATION with wavelengths between those of visible light and X-rays. It can be detected by its effect on photographic film and by the FLUORESCENCE it produces in certain materials, for example clothes that have been washed in 'whiter than white' detergents. It has powerful effects on living tissues: longer wavelengths produce tanning of the skin and the formation of vitamin D, but shorter wavelengths can be lethal to living tissue and are associated with skin cancer.
⚘ Most of the Sun's short-wavelength ultraviolet radiation is filtered out by the ▷OZONE LAYER. Without this protection, most forms of life on Earth would die.

uncertainty principle Statement that it is impossible to measure exactly both the position and the momentum of a particle of matter simultaneously, since the very act of measurement alters the situation at the moment it is being observed. First proposed by the German physicist Werner Heisenberg (1901-76), it became one of the cornerstones of modern QUANTUM MECHANICS. Although the uncertainty is only significant at the subatomic scale, some philosophers have argued that it undermines any attempt to predict the behaviour of the Universe as a whole and that all forms of DETERMINISM are therefore doomed.

unified field theories Theories that attempt to explain the four different fundamental forces of nature – the strong and weak nuclear forces, electromagnetism and gravity – as aspects of a single natural phenomenon. Current theories interpret

forces in terms of the exchange of subatomic particles, although the hypothetical particle that carries the gravitational force – the graviton – has not been found. It is likely that the other three forces can be unified in a 'grand unified theory' (GUT) by treating the particles as 'strings' or 'superstrings' rather than as simple point-like objects. GUTs are sometimes referred to as 'theories of everything', since they would provide a single theoretical framework for the whole physical universe.

uranium Radioactive metal, used as a fuel in ▷NUCLEAR REACTORS and the ▷ATOM BOMB. It occurs in the ore pitchblende and has three naturally occurring ISOTOPES. The most stable is U235, with a HALF-LIFE of 710 million years; it undergoes NUCLEAR FISSION when struck by a neutron, and can initiate a chain reaction. The same process converts U238 to plutonium, which can also be used as a nuclear fuel.

Uranus Seventh planet from the Sun, discovered by the English astronomer William Herschel in 1781; it was the first planet to be discovered by telescope. It is nearly 15 times heavier than Earth, and about four times greater in diameter. It has a 'year' of 84 Earth years, and a 'day' of around 17 hours. Uranus has an ice-coated rocky core, swathed in a thick blanket of hydrogen, helium and methane, which gives the planet a greenish tinge. It was visited by Voyager 2 in 1986 and revealed to have 15 moons, 10 more than previously thought, and 11 thin rings of rocky debris circling the equator.

vacuum Space that contains no matter. In practice, an absolute vacuum is unachievable since some molecules will always escape from the container's walls. A vacuum is therefore taken to mean a space filled with gas at very low pressure. A vacuum cannot transmit sound, or allow heat to pass by conduction. Vacuum flasks are used to keep liquids hot or cold.

valence Also called valency; the number of chemical BONDS an atom of an element can make when combining with other atoms to form a molecule. Oxygen with a valency of 2 combines with two hydrogen atoms with valencies of 1 to form water, H_2O. Valencies vary according to an element's position in the PERIODIC TABLE, ranging from 1 for the strong metals, such as sodium, and the halogens, such as chlorine, to 4 or higher for such elements as carbon and silicon. Some elements are capable of showing more than one valency; nitrogen, for example, may have valencies of 3 or 5.

vector Quantity that is defined in terms of its direction as well as its size. Velocity, acceleration and force are all vector quantities, but speed is not. Two vector quantities, for example the forces of wind and current on a sailing boat, can be combined by drawing a parallelogram whose sides represent the size and magnitude of the forces; the resultant force and its direction is then represented by the diagonal.

velocity Speed in a particular direction; velocity is a VECTOR quantity and, unlike speed, has direction as well as magnitude.

Venn diagram Visual representation of the properties and relationships of sets (see SET THEORY). Each set, for example the set of male pupils or the set of female teachers in a school, is represented by a circle. The circles will overlap when the different sets have members in common, but not if they have no members in common, as in the case of male pupils and female teachers. The circle representing blue-eyed individuals would, however, overlap with both the other circles, while the set of blue-eyed males would overlap with only one.

Venus Second planet from the Sun, sometimes visible in the east before dawn or in the west at dusk – when it is referred to as the morning or evening star. Venus is similar in size to Earth, but its atmosphere is largely composed of unbreathable carbon dioxide, and the surface is shrouded by thick clouds of corrosive sulphuric acid.

viscosity Friction or drag within a fluid – a liquid or a gas. It determines the speed at which a liquid will flow, and sets limits on the rate at which an object can move through it; a parachutist falls at a speed where the drag of the air is just equal to the force of gravity. When the speed of flow passes a certain point, turbulence sets in – the motion of the particles of gas or liquid becomes chaotic and the viscosity no longer determines the rate of flow.

volt Unit of electrical POTENTIAL DIFFERENCE or electromotive force. It is named after Alessandro Volta (1745-1827), the Italian physicist who invented the first battery. It is defined in such a way that a current of one AMP flowing under a potential difference of one volt carries a power of one WATT.

water (H_2O) Colourless, odourless and tasteless liquid, the basis for all the chemical processes of life. In the form of ice and the oceans, it covers about 74 per cent of the

Earth's surface. Water owes many of its properties to the strength of the attraction between individual molecules, known as hydrogen bonding. Because of this it is liquid at normal temperatures rather than gaseous, unlike other similar compounds, such as hydrogen sulphide (H_2S). It also reaches maximum density at 4°C (39°F) and expands when it freezes, so that ice floats on water. It is a good solvent, and conducts electricity fairly well in the presence of dissolved salts. Its capacity to absorb large amounts of heat is one of the main determinants of the Earth's climate.

watt Unit of POWER, equivalent to a rate of energy usage of one JOULE per second. A current of one AMP flowing across a potential difference of one VOLT dissipates one watt of power. One horsepower is equal to 746 watts. The unit is named after the Scottish engineer and steam-engine pioneer James ▷WATT. Power is usually measured in kilowatts (kW) – 1000 watts – and power consumption is usually measured in kilowatt hours (kWh).

wave Regular disturbance or vibration that travels through a medium or through space and transfers energy but not matter. Light, sound and the ripples on a pond all travel by means of waves. Ripples on water are an example of transverse waves, in which the vibration is at right angles to the direction of travel. A floating cork bobs up and down as a wave passes; it does not travel with the wave. Light and other forms of ELECTRO-MAGNETIC RADIATION are also transverse waves composed of electrical and magnetic vibrations at right angles to each other. They do not require a medium through which to travel. Sound is an example of a longitudinal wave, in which particles of matter, such as molecules in the air, vibrate from side to side parallel to the direction of travel, forming waves of increasing and decreasing compression. All waves have WAVELENGTH, FREQUENCY and AMPLITUDE. They also show characteristic

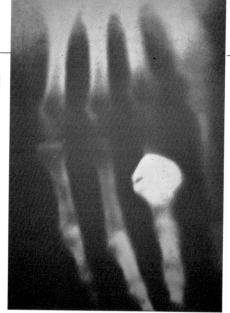

FIRST X-RAY *Wilhelm Roentgen used the new type of radiation he discovered in 1895 to photograph his wife's hand, wedding ring included.*

properties of REFLECTION, REFRACTION, INTERFERENCE and DIFFRACTION. In QUANTUM MECHANICS, the fundamental particles of matter are treated both as particles and as waves. The wave-like behaviour of the electron, for example, makes the electron ▷MICROSCOPE possible.

wavelength Distance between successive peaks or troughs of a wave. As the wavelength increases, the FREQUENCY decreases; the speed of the wave divided by its wavelength is equal to its frequency.

weight The force of gravity acting on an object. It differs from MASS, the amount of matter in a body, in that it varies according to the strength of the gravitational field. An object weighs less at high altitudes or on the Moon, than at the surface of the Earth, although its mass remains the same.

white dwarf Small, hot, dense STAR representing the final stages in the life of a medium-sized star. White dwarfs are now thought to be the contracted cores of RED GIANT stars that have thrown off their expanded outer layers. The material of a white dwarf is so compact that a thimbleful would weigh several tons. White dwarfs cool over billions of years and eventually fade into invisible cinders.

work Application of ENERGY. Like energy, it is measured in JOULES. One joule of work is done when a force of one newton acts through a distance of one metre in the direction in which the force is being applied. It is also the work done when one WATT of power is expended for one second.

X-rays Penetrating and highly energetic ELECTROMAGNETIC RADIATION with very short wavelengths. They are capable of passing through considerable thicknesses of material, but are more strongly absorbed by dense materials such as metal or bone than by skin or flesh. This makes them valuable for medical examination, as well as for testing metal structures for cracks or flaws. They are also used in X-ray crystallography, which uses the DIFFRACTION of an intense beam of X-rays to examine the structure of complex biological molecules, such as proteins and DNA.

Zeno's paradoxes A number of statements leading to absurd but apparently inescapable conclusions, which were put forward by the Greek philosopher Zeno of Elea in the 5th century BC. The best known concerns the race between Achilles and a tortoise. Achilles allows the tortoise a 100 metre start, and runs ten times as fast as the tortoise; by the time he has reached the tortoise's starting point, the tortoise has gone a further 10 metres; by the time he has covered the next 10 metres, the tortoise is still a metre ahead; and so on *ad infinitum*. In other words, Achilles can never catch or overtake the tortoise. Similar paradoxes appeared to show that an arrow flying through the air cannot be in motion and that one runner can travel twice as far as another in the same time although they are both running at the same speed. It was not until the 19th century that mathematicians resolved Zeno's paradoxes satisfactorily.

zodiac Band of 12 constellations through which the Sun appears to move during the course of the year: Aries, Taurus, Gemini, Cancer, Leo, Virgo, Libra, Scorpio, Sagittarius, Capricorn, Aquarius and Pisces. Today the constellations are no longer in the areas covered by their zodiacal signs, because the 'wobbling' of the Earth on its axis – PRECESSION – has changed the Sun's apparent path through the stars. (See also ▷ASTROLOGY in 'Myths and Legends'.)

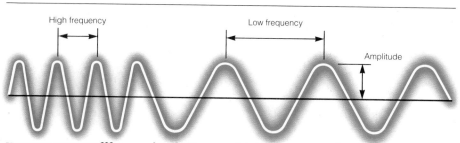

High frequency   Low frequency   Amplitude

WAVES OF ENERGY *Waves are described in terms of their frequency, wavelength and amplitude, and all transmit energy from one place to another. They can also be used to transmit information: both frequency and amplitude can be modulated to carry a coded message to a receiver such as a radio set.*

TECHNOLOGY AND INVENTION

Early humans became inventors to survive. Their successors helped to create the earliest civilisations, and new tools and technological breakthroughs have followed century by century. In the modern world, faster communications and transport have accelerated innovation worldwide, taking humans into space and increasing the range of their comfort and conveniences on Earth.

THE WONDER OF
HOLOGRAMS

STEPHENSON'S
ROCKET

THE SPACE
SHUTTLE DISCOVERY

THOMAS EDISON

MOON WALKER *American astronaut Edwin 'Buzz' Aldrin walks on the Moon where he landed with Neil Armstrong from Apollo 11. Armstrong can be seen reflected in Aldrin's space helmet visor.*

aerofoil Aeroplane wings, helicopter rotor blades and hydrofoils all have an aerofoil cross-section – curved on top, flat underneath, rounded at the front and tapering to the rear. It is this shape that provides aircraft with enough lift to fly. As the aircraft moves forward, air flows over the wings or blades, and as the air passes over the curved top surface, it speeds up. When air moves faster, its pressure drops. Thus, pressure below the wings or blades exceeds that above it, and the aircraft lifts.

aeroplane The key to aeroplane flight lies in the AEROFOIL cross-section of the wings. As the plane moves forward, the air pressure below the wings is high enough, compared with the air pressure above them, to support the plane in the air. Early planes were propelled through the air by propellers, driven by piston engines, but in most modern aircraft, the forward force, or thrust, is provided by JET ENGINES. To climb, descend or turn, the pilot manipulates hinged surfaces at the rear of the wings and tail. To be efficient, aeroplanes must be as light as possible, so they are built from

aluminium alloys and, increasingly, from carbon fibre materials. To keep air resistance (drag) to a minimum, the plane's fuselage is streamlined and the surfaces made as smooth as possible. The shape of aeroplane wings varies. Slow planes, such as the Hercules, which has a cruising speed of 350 mph (560 km/h), have wings at right angles to the fuselage. Airliners such as the Boeing 767 and the Airbus 320 travel at speeds of up to 560 mph (900 km/h) and have their wings swept back at an angle. The supersonic Anglo-French plane CON-CORDE cruises at 1350 mph (2170 km/h) and has sharply swept-back wings and a pointed nose to minimise drag. The first aeroplane flight was made by the WRIGHT BROTHERS in 1903.

aerosol can Specialised can, first developed commercially in 1941, which delivers a fine spray. Inside the can, the product – such as hair spray or fire-extinguishing foam – is held under pressure with a propellant gas. When the nozzle is depressed, a valve releases the pressure and allows a mixture of the propellant and

contents to spurt out. The propellant evaporates immediately in the air.

Chlorofluorocarbons (▷CFCs) were once common propellants, but were damaging the Earth's ▷OZONE LAYER. They have been largely replaced by isobutanes, believed to be less harmful to the environment.

amplifier Electronic device that takes a weak electric signal and converts it into a stronger one. The amplifier in a stereo system, for example, makes the signal strong enough to power the loudspeakers.

Apollo project American space programme aimed at landing a man on the Moon. The first successful landing took place on July 20, 1969, when Neil ▷ARM-STRONG and Edwin 'Buzz' Aldrin emerged from Apollo 11's lunar module, code-named *Eagle*, to spend 13 hours on the Moon. Michael Collins, the third member of the crew, remained in orbit. Five other successful landings followed, the final mission being Apollo 17 in December 1972. The last three missions took a wheeled 'lunar rover' to transport the astronauts and their equipment over greater distances than earlier missions.

The Apollo missions brought back 846 lb (383 kg) of Moon rock, yielding information about its composition and history.

aqualung Compact, portable underwater breathing apparatus which allows divers to move freely and to breathe safely at depths of up to 164 ft (50 m). Compressed air, carried in a cylinder on the diver's back, is delivered to the diver via a device which automatically matches the pressure of the air to that of the surrounding water. It was developed by Jacques Cousteau, a French naval officer and ocean explorer, and Emile Gagnan, an engineer, in 1943. The aqualung, or scuba (Self-Contained Underwater Breathing Apparatus), enables a diver breathing normally just below the surface to stay down for some 45 minutes.

artificial intelligence Branch of computer science concerned with developing ways of imitating aspects of human intelligence, such as learning by experience, solving problems, making decisions, recognising shapes and understanding language.

AWACS (Airborne Warning And Control System) RADAR equipment, carried in a disc-like structure mounted on top of an aircraft's fuselage, and used to monitor aircraft movement. AWACS planes fly at 30 000 ft (9000 m), and can detect targets up to 290 miles (460 km) away.

TELEVISION PIONEER *John Logie Baird, the Scottish engineer and television inventor, adjusting his wireless vision transmitter.*

Babbage, Charles (1791-1871) British mathematician who, in 1834, designed an 'analytical engine' that had many of the features of today's computer. His mechanical device could be programmed, using punched cards, to perform mathematical calculations. The machine was never built, although a small experimental portion was under construction at the time of Babbage's death. In 1991 the Science Museum in London built, from Babbage's original plans, a less complex calculating engine – the Difference Engine No. 2, designed between 1847 and 1849. The engine works perfectly and weighs nearly 3 tons.

Baird, John Logie (1888-1946) Scottish inventor and television pioneer. Baird's earliest success came in October 1925, when, using apparatus that included biscuit tins and darning needles, he produced an image of a ventriloquist's dummy on a television screen. Baird's system, based on mechanical scanning, was used in experimental broadcasts by the BBC from 1929, but was superseded by a superior electronic scanning system when public broadcasting began in 1936. Baird's other inventions included an infrared night-vision device (1926), colour and stereoscopic televisions, demonstrated in 1928, and video recorders, marketed in 1935.

🐝 Although television has been one of the most influential inventions, Baird made very little money from his discovery.

Bakelite First synthetic PLASTIC, invented in 1909 by Leo Baekeland, a Belgian-born chemist working in the USA. By treating phenol (derived from coal-tar) with formaldehyde, Baekland obtained a powdered resin which, when heated, could be moulded by pressure into almost any shape. Bakelite, once set, was heat resistant and a good electrical insulator; everything

from light switches to kitchenware was made from it. Bakelite's success led to the growth of the modern plastics industry.

bar code Set of vertical lines representing coded information that can be read with an optical scanner and interpreted by a computer. Most product packaging has a bar code that stores information about the item; shops with computerised checkouts use the bar codes to produce itemised receipts and to monitor stock levels.

battery Device that produces ▷ELECTRICITY as a result of chemical reactions between its components. The most common type is the zinc-carbon or dry cell battery, used for example to power torches. It has a zinc casing containing a moist paste which conducts electricity, and a central carbon rod. When the battery is connected into a circuit, ▷ELECTRONS flow from the battery's negative terminal to the appliance and back to the battery's positive terminal. Eventually the chemicals are used up, and the battery stops working. Car batteries contain lead plates, one of which is coated with lead oxide, immersed in sulphuric acid. Chemical reactions between the plates and acid produce electricity to power the starter motor and ignition system. When the engine is running, electricity from the generator keeps the battery charged. The first battery was developed in 1800 by the Italian physicist Alessandro

Volta, after whom the ▷VOLT is named. 🐝 Jars, dating from about 50 BC, with copper rods suspended from wax plugs, were found in Iraq in 1938. The jars once contained acid which, combined with metal rods, would have generated about 2 volts – enough for gold and silver plating.

Bell, Alexander Graham (1847-1922) Scottish-born emigrant to the USA who patented the first TELEPHONE in 1876. Bell experimented on a telephone system while developing his father's work on a method of teaching deaf people to speak, in which symbols represented the position of the lips and tongue. Bell's other developments included the photophone, which transmitted sounds on a beam of light, and a HYDROFOIL which in 1919 attained a speed of 70 mph (112 km/h).

🐝 The first intelligible words transmitted by telephone were: 'Mr Watson, come here, I want to see you!' spoken by Bell to his assistant, Thomas Watson.

🐝 The decibel, used for measuring the loudness or intensity of sound, is named after Alexander Graham Bell.

bicycle The first bicycle was built in 1839 by Scottish blacksmith Kirkpatrick Macmillan, and had pedals attached to rods which turned the back wheel. In 1861 the French coachbuilders Pierre and Ernest Michaux invented a bicycle which was driven by pedals attached to the front

MOVING AHEAD *The penny-farthing gave way to the safety cycle in 1885. Graeme Obree (bottom right) set a world record of 4 min 20.894 sec for 4 km in 1993. His cycle's design stems from the 1900 Raleigh (right).*

wheel. The so-called 'penny-farthing' first appeared in the 1870s; it had front wheels as big as 5 ft (1.5 m) across, to make each push of the pedals go farther. The true ancestor of the modern bicycle was John Starley's 1885 Rover safety cycle, made in Coventry. It had wheels of similar size; a chain transferred the drive from the pedals to the rear wheel. After 1888, pneumatic tyres were incorporated into the designs of bicycles by Raleigh and other manufacturers. Today's bicycles have strong but light frames made from aluminium, titanium or fibre-reinforced plastics.

In 1992, Britain's Chris Boardman won an Olympic gold medal riding a bicycle of revolutionary design developed by the car makers Lotus. It had a one-piece single moulded body made from CARBON FIBRE.

biotechnology The use of living organisms, particularly microorganisms, in industrial processes. Brewing, baking and cheese-making represent ancient forms of biotechnology, but the industry has been revolutionised in recent years by advances in genetics and GENETIC ENGINEERING. Specially designed microorganisms are now used to produce a wide range of drugs and other chemicals such as ENZYMES, to refine ores and to clear up oil slicks and other forms of pollution. Biotechnology offers a clean and highly energy-efficient alternative to normal industrial processes.

'black box' Popular name for the flight data recorder and cockpit voice recorder carried by aircraft. It records information such as speed, altitude and position, and conversations among the flight crew and between the crew and air traffic controllers. The 'black box' is carried in the rear of the aircraft and is designed to survive the impact of a crash and any resulting fire, so that the information it carries can be used to pinpoint the cause of the accident.

Black boxes are actually painted in bright, reflective colours to make them easier to spot in wreckage or at night.

blast furnace Invention that opened the way for the Industrial Revolution by making iron much easier to produce. A blast furnace consists of a steel tower, lined with bricks and up to 200 ft (60 m) tall, in which metal, usually iron, is smelted from its ore. It is so called because hot air is blasted into the furnace to make the raw materials burn more fiercely. In iron smelting, a mixture of iron ore, coke and limestone is heated to temperatures which reach 1600°C (2900°F). Molten iron and slag are tapped off at the bottom of the

furnace. Iron from a blast furnace is called pig iron; most of it is recast in other furnaces to make STEEL. Iron smelting began in what is now Turkey around 1500 BC. In Europe, furnaces capable of producing molten iron developed in the 14th century, and were fuelled by charcoal, but in 1709 Abraham Darby introduced a much more efficient coke-fired furnace. In 1856 Henry Bessemer invented a 'converter' to produce steel from molten pig iron, cheaply and on a large scale.

Braun, Wernher von (1912-77) German-born rocket engineer, and chief architect of the early American space programme. Von Braun led the team that developed the V-2 rocket – V stood for *vergeltungswaffe* 'vengeance weapon' – which bombarded London at the end of World War II. After surrendering to the Allies he went on to design the *Jupiter C* rocket which launched the first American satellite, *Explorer 1*, in 1958, and the *Saturn V* rocket which was the launch vehicle for the APOLLO PROJECT spacecraft.

breathalyser The breathalyser was first used in 1939, when the police in Indianapolis, USA, introduced the 'Drunkometer' developed by an American doctor, Rolla N. Harger. In many early breathalysers, alcohol in the breath was detected by crystals which changed colour. The latest breathalysers work electronically.

In Britain, it is an offence for a driver to have more than 35 micrograms of alcohol in 100 ml of breath, or more than 80 milligrams in 100 ml of blood.

HAPPY SNAPS *The Kodak Brownie camera, developed in 1890 by George Eastman, sold in the US for $1 and turned photography into a pastime for millions of people.*

camera The basic principle of the camera is a light-proof chamber with an opening (or aperture), a shutter and ▷LENS at one end, and at the other a piece of film with a light-sensitive coating. The shutter opens briefly to let in light through the aperture, and the lens focuses an inverted image onto the film. Processing the film completes the

chemical changes begun by the light striking it. The aperture size and the time the shutter stays open (the shutter speed) can be varied, and the lens can be moved backwards and forwards to focus on subjects at different distances. In many cameras these adjustments are automatic. Compact cameras normally have one built-in lens, and a separate viewfinder. In single-lens reflex (SLR) cameras the viewfinder allows the photographer to see through the single main lens via a mirror which flips out of the way, in a reflex action, when a picture is taken. In 1839 Louis Daguerre, a French painter, produced a permanent image – the Daguerreotype – on silver-coated copper sheets. It could only be reproduced by being rephotographed. In the same year, the English scientist Henry Fox Talbot, working at Lacock Abbey in Wiltshire, developed a negative from which multiple prints could be made. In 1888 George EASTMAN introduced flexible film to replace glass plates; modern colour film was developed by Kodak in 1936.

Polaroid cameras develop pictures instantly, using a film pack that contains film, chemicals and printing paper. They were developed by US inventor Edwin Land in 1947, after his daughter's disappointment that his photographs of her would have to be sent away to be processed.

capacitor (also condenser) Device used in electronic circuits to store electric charge. Capacitors typically consist of two metal plates separated by insulation. They are essential components of MICROCHIPS and are used in car distributors to stop electricity jumping between contact breakers.

car The pioneers of the motor car were the German engineers Gottlieb Daimler (1834-1900) and Karl Friedrich Benz (1844-1929). Daimler developed the first lightweight, petrol-powered INTERNAL-COMBUSTION ENGINE in 1883, and fitted it first to a bicycle, and then in 1886 to an open carriage. In 1885 Benz developed the first practical car powered by a petrol engine; the three-wheeled vehicle had a top speed of 8 mph (13 km/h), and was an entirely new vehicle, unlike Daimler's 'horseless carriage'. In 1908 Henry ▷FORD began mass producing the Model T, and brought car ownership to a far wider public. In the early days of development, electric cars vied with internal-combustion engine models, after improved storage batteries became available in 1881. However their popularity was short-lived because they lagged behind petrol-driven cars in performance and range. Research continues to

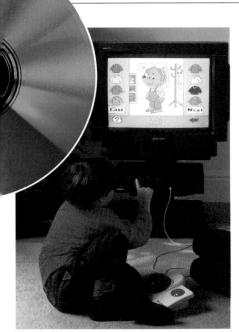

VERSATILE DISC *The coded sound on a compact disc seen at 930 times its actual size (inset). Often used for educational purposes, CD-i – interactive CD – lets the viewer control images.*

reduce cars' toxic emissions and the amount of petrol that they use. A catalytic converter fitted to the car's exhaust system changes the hydrocarbons and toxic carbon monoxide that are produced when petrol is incompletely burned into non-toxic carbon dioxide and water vapour. Lead tetraethyl, added to petrol to improve its performance, leads to lead emissions in the exhaust, and unleaded petrol is now available. To improve safety, cars are built with 'crumple zones' at the front and rear of the rigid 'passenger cell' to absorb the impact of a crash, and windscreen glass shatters to small fragments, rather than slivers.
🔹 Britain's earliest cars were subject to a speed limit of 4 mph (6 km/h) in the country, and 2 mph (3 km/h) in towns. A man with a red flag walked in front of the vehicle to warn of its approach. The limit was raised to 12 mph (19 km/h) in 1896.

carbon fibre Threads of carbon which reinforce plastic to produce a strong, light material that can withstand high temperatures. Carbon fibre is used in the construction of aircraft and sports equipment.

cat's-eye Road marking stud that reflects headlights, developed in 1934 by Percy Shaw, a Yorkshire road contractor. Glass prisms are set in a rubber pad. When the stud is depressed by the tyres of passing traffic, the prisms are pressed against the rubber, wiping them clean.

CD-ROM A COMPACT DISC incorporating a read-only memory – information on the disc can be read but not altered. Text, graphics, photographs and moving pictures can be stored on CDs in the form of a pattern of microscopic pits which are 'read' by a laser beam, as in audio CDs. CD-i – interactive CD – is a CD-ROM which is played through a television and allows the viewer to control the images. CD-i products are used for recreational and educational purposes: for example, children can 'create' their own planet, and see how animal life is affected by changes in climate.
🔹 The entire 20-volume Oxford dictionary can be stored on a single disc.

cellphone (or cellular telephone) Mobile radio telephone system in which the country is divided into areas, or cells, 3-10 miles (5-16 km) across. Each cell contains a radio transmitter connected via a switching system to the national telephone network. When the phone is switched on, it 'tells' the cellphone system where it is, so that calls made to it can be relayed from the nearest cell transmitter. Calls made from a cellphone are picked up by the nearest cell aerial and routed to the telephone network. When calls are made by people on trains or in cars, for example, the call is handed over from one transmitter to the next without breaking the conversation. About 90 per cent of the United Kingdom is covered by cells, and some British cellphones can be used in other European countries.

cinematography The principle underlying the making of films for cinema is that a cine-camera takes a series of still photographs on a roll at the rate of 24 frames (pictures) per second. The film is held stationary for a split second while each frame is exposed, then wound on one frame. The developed film is projected onto the screen at the same speed of 24 frames per second, using a cine-projector which again holds each frame still while it is projected. Persistence of vision – the ability of the human eye to retain an image for a fraction of a second – merges the advancing frames to create the illusion of continuous movement. Motion pictures were first achieved in Leeds by Augustin Le Prince, in 1888. The soundtrack is now printed along one side of the film, but in early 'talkies' the soundtrack was played on a separate disc.

clock One of the earliest ways of measuring the passage of time, used by the Egyptians around 2000 BC, was to compare shadows cast by the Sun against a marked scale. Several early civilisations developed water clocks, in which water flowed steadily into or out of a vessel marked with a scale. Mechanical clocks were developed in China in the 8th century AD, and in Europe in the late 13th century. The early European clocks were driven by a system of falling weights. Clocks driven by the energy stored in coiled springs appeared in the 15th century; the mechanism was light enough to be used for portable clocks and watches. In about 1656, the Dutch astronomer Christiaan Huygens designed the pendulum clock, exploiting ▷GALILEO's discovery in 1582 that a pendulum always takes the same time to complete a swing. Long-case, or 'grandfather', clocks became popular in the late 17th century. Clocks powered by electricity were invented in 1840 and became widely used after World War I, when mains electricity was installed in many homes. Quartz clocks were invented in 1929. Electric current from a battery stimulates constant vibrations in a quartz crystal and the vibrations are converted into one-second 'ticks'. Atomic clocks – accurate to one second in at least 1000 years – were first made in the USA in 1948. They work by counting the natural oscillations of atoms.
🔹 Atomic clocks are so accurate that time is now actually defined by them. One second is defined as the time taken for an atom of caesium to vibrate 9 192 631 770 times.

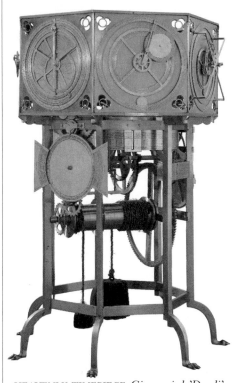

HEAVENLY TIMEPIECE *Giovanni de'Dondi's astronomical clock of 1350 stands 3 ft (0.9 m) high. This replica is based on his drawings.*

553

AIR SUPREMACY *The grace and power of Concorde impress even when it is stationary. In the air it is unsurpassed – capable of flying from London to New York in 2 hr 54 min and 30 sec.*

puter's hardware. The main systems unit includes a memory, in which programs and data are stored, and a central processing unit, which controls all computer operations. Items such as printers and MODEMS are known as peripherals. Inside the computer, MICROCHIPS carry the memory needed for processing. Permanent information is stored on removable 'floppy' disks, or 'hard' disks sealed inside the computer. The advent of the microchip in the 1970s led to personal computers (PCs) and portable battery-operated 'lap-tops'. Computers have a memory capacity measured in millions of bytes, or megabytes. A byte is a set of bits (binary digits) representing a piece of data, which can then be used by the computer.

The Internet is a worldwide network of computer networks which communicate via telephone lines. As many as 35 million people are believed to be linked to the Internet which is unregulated and unpoliced. Anyone with access to a personal computer and a modem can dial in, and, for the cost of a local call, hook up to a network. Britain is second only to the US as the world's largest user. Internet was originally set up in 1969 by Pentagon researchers as a secure communications system in the event of nuclear war.

In 1834, Charles BABBAGE designed an 'analytical engine' that had many of the features of the modern computer. The first electronic computer was completed in the USA in 1939.

computer program Set of instructions given to a computer to direct it to carry out certain operations. Programs are usually written in languages such as FORTRAN, COBOL, BASIC and C, which allow the programmer to communicate with the computer in a form of English. The computer translates these 'high level' languages into machine code – the series of ▷BINARY SYSTEM digits by which they operate.

Concorde Supersonic passenger jet developed jointly by Britain and France. Brian Trubshaw piloted its maiden flight in March 1969. Concorde cruises at a speed of up to 1460 mph (2349 km/h) – 2.2 times the speed of sound – and at a height of about 49 000 ft (almost 15 000 m).

diode Device that allows electric current to pass in one direction only. Diodes can change ▷ALTERNATING CURRENT into ▷DIRECT CURRENT, for example, in television receiver circuits. Diodes are usually made of SEMICONDUCTOR materials and are essential components in MICROCHIPS.

compact disc (CD) Small disc, 4¾ in (12 cm) across, storing data, especially music, in digital form. To record music on CD, sound signals from the microphone are converted into the 1s and 0s of the ▷BINARY SYSTEM , and stored on the surface of the disc as a pattern of microscopic pits separated by unpitted (flat) areas. The pattern of pits and flats mirrors the pattern of 1s and 0s. During playback, a laser beam 'reads' the pattern of pits and flats and produces signals which represent the signals recorded. When fed to a loudspeaker, they reproduce the original sounds faithfully. The CD was developed by Philips in 1972. By the early 1990s it was the established medium for audio recordings. High quality reproduction is possible using digital recording because the sound is stored as precise digits, not as imprecise waveforms as they are on ordinary tape or disc.

compass Device for determining geographical direction. The magnetic compass relies on a magnetised needle that is free to rotate on a pivot until aligned with the magnetic field of the Earth. The needle points towards the north ▷MAGNETIC POLE. Gyrocompasses, which work on the principle of gyroscopic inertia, are not affected by the presence of iron, or by the magnetic anomalies of the Earth's magnetic field, and are used in ships and aircraft.

computer Versatile electronic device that stores and processes information, or data, according to a COMPUTER PROGRAM – a series of instructions. The program and other operating instructions are known as the computer's software. The units that physically make up a computer, such as the keyboard, the visual display unit (VDU) and the main systems unit, are the com-

LIGHT TOUCH *Thomas Alva Edison, the prolific American inventor who patented almost 1100 inventions, is seen with two electric lamps, products of his fertile imagination. Inset are one of his lamps in its holder and pages from one of the 3500 notebooks in which he recorded his ideas.*

Dolby system Electronic circuitry which is used for suppressing background hiss in tape recordings. The system was patented in 1968 by the American electronic engineer Ray M. Dolby.

Eastman, George (1854-1932) American pioneer of 'snapshot' photography. In 1888, Eastman introduced the easy-to-use Kodak camera complete with flexible, paper-backed roll film. The film had 100 exposures and the whole camera was returned to the manufacturers for developing. In 1889, Eastman substituted celluloid for the paper in roll film, making processing simpler and cheaper.
🕭 Eastman's publicity slogan for the Kodak camera was: 'You press the button, we do the rest.'
🕭 Eastman introduced the name 'Kodak' after experimenting with different words beginning and ending with the letter K. He felt it was a 'strong, incisive sort of letter'.

Edison, Thomas Alva (1847-1931) Prolific American inventor who patented nearly 1100 inventions. Edison's favourite invention was the phonograph of 1877 – the first device that could both record and replay sound. The very same year, Edison also improved Alexander Graham Bell's

telephone transmitter and made the instrument easier to use by separating the mouthpiece and earpiece. In 1879 he produced a successful light bulb, at the same time as the physicist Joseph Swan was developing a bulb in Britain. Realising the potential of electric lighting, Edison designed the world's first large-scale power station and in 1882 supplied a district of New York with electricity.
🕭 Edison defined genius as: 'one per cent inspiration and 99 per cent perspiration'.

electric generator Machine that produces electric current, and works on the principle of ▷ELECTROMAGNETIC INDUCTION first demonstrated by the British scientist Michael Faraday in 1831. At its simplest a generator consists of a rotating shaft carrying wire coils, surrounded by a magnet. Current is induced in the coils by the rotation of the shaft. There are two basic types of generator: alternators, which produce ▷ALTERNATING CURRENT (AC), and dynamos, which produce ▷DIRECT CURRENT (DC). Power stations produce alternating current for general distribution; the rotating shaft is driven by turbines which are powered by steam (in coal, oil and nuclear power stations) and by water in hydroelectric power stations.

electric motor Machine that converts electricity into mechanical motion, widely used in factories, transport and in home appliances from washing machines to toothbrushes. The electric motor is constructed like an ELECTRIC GENERATOR, but works in the opposite way. Basically, a wire coil is positioned between the jaws of a magnet; electric current is passed through the coil, creating a magnetic field that interacts with the field of the stationary magnet and forces the coil to turn.

electroplating Process by which a material is coated with a thin layer of metal, by means of ▷ELECTROLYSIS. Electroplating, which began commercially in the 1840s, can be used to protect metals against corrosion, and to coat cheaper metals with more valuable ones, such as silver. To coat an object with copper, the object is immersed in a solution of a copper compound such as copper sulphate, along with sheets of pure copper. The object and the copper sheets are connected into an electric circuit with the copper sheets acting as positive electrodes and the object acting as a negative electrode. When the current is switched on, copper disappears from the copper sheet and reappears on the object.
🕭 Electroplated nickel silver (EPNS) is a product of electroplating. Sheffield plate was produced not by electrolysis, but by fusing silver onto copper.

ergonomics Study of how human beings interact with machines and with their work environment. Its aim is to improve design, especially of machines and the workplace, and so achieve the greatest efficiency and comfort with the minimum of stress.

escalator The first moving staircase, invented by Jesse W. Reno, was installed as a novelty ride on the pier at Coney Island, New York, in 1894. Modern escalators are inclined at about 30°, and rise at a rate of up to 120 ft (36 m) per minute. The stairs are carried by a continuous chain that runs around a wheel turned by an electric motor.
🕭 The world's longest escalator is in an underground station in St Petersburg; it has 729 steps and a vertical rise of 195 ft 9½ in (59.7 m).

fax Short for facsimile transmission. Method of sending written messages and photographs along telephone lines. In a fax machine, the document or photograph to be transmitted is scanned by a light beam. The pattern of reflected light is converted into electric signals which are fed to a MODEM, which produces signals suitable for transmission along the telephone lines. In the receiving machine, another modem reverses the process, and the signals are fed to a printer where a facsimile of the original image is formed. Colour fax machines scan the image three times, using red, blue and green filters to separate the colour components of the image. At the receiving end, the three images are printed one on top of the other, using three different colour toners. A Scottish clockmaker, Alexander Bain, developed the principle of fax transmission in 1843, and his prototype used a sheep's jawbone and springs made from heather. The first fax was a photograph wired from Paris to the *Daily Mirror* in 1907, using equipment devised five years earlier by Arthur Korn, a German physicist.

Fibreglass Trade name for the tough material made from plastic reinforced with a mesh of fine glass fibres. Fibreglass is used to make a variety of products, including boat hulls, car bodies and fishing rods. Loft insulation is made of loose mats of Fibreglass – without plastic reinforcement.

fibre optics Branch of science and engineering concerned with the transmission of light through fine glass fibres. A typical fibre is between ⅟₅₀₀₀ and ⅟₂₅₀ in (0.005 and 0.1 mm) across – less than the width of a human hair. Light introduced into one end of an optical fibre travels down the fibre by bouncing off the sides, with little light escaping. Telephone signals can be sent along optical fibres by coded pulses of LASER light. Optical fibre cables take up far less space than the older copper cables, and can carry more information at much higher speeds. In medicine, optical fibres – which can be easily twisted and bent – are used in ▷ENDOSCOPES, which enable doctors to see inside the body and perform microsurgery with tiny instruments or laser beams.

fingerprinting The pattern of ridges, whorls and loops on the skin of each person's fingertips is unique to that person, and does not change. Tiny amounts of sweat on the fingers transfer this pattern to most smooth surfaces that the fingers touch, and the pattern can be revealed by dusting the surface with fine powder. Computers can be used to match prints, but final matching is by painstaking visual inspection. William Herschel of the Indian Civil Service used fingerprints in 1877 to check that Army pensioners did not draw their pensions more than once. Herschel's technique was improved by the scientist Sir Francis Galton and by Edward Henry – who became Commissioner of the Metropolitan Police. Scotland Yard opened a fingerprint department in 1901.

firearms The first reliable revolver in which a revolving chamber moves a fresh bullet into the firing position after one has been fired was produced by the US inventor Samuel Colt in 1835. In the semi-automatic pistol, the next bullet moves into place automatically but each shot has to be triggered; automatic weapons, such as submachine guns, continue firing once the trigger is pulled. Rifles have spiral grooves, or 'rifling', running the length of the barrel to improve the accuracy of the bullet's flight. Shotguns, which fire pellets, have a smooth-bore barrel, as no great accuracy can be given to a charge of pellets. Primitive firearms date from the 14th century but large muskets were not developed until the 16th century. In 17th-century flintlocks, the charge was ignited by the spark produced when flint struck roughened steel. The gas-operated Kalashnikov AK 47 rifle, invented in 1947 by Russian designer Mikhail Kalashnikov, is capable of automatic fire at the rate of 650 rounds per minute.

gears Sets of toothed wheels that mesh together so that one wheel turns the other. Two wheels meshing together turn in opposite directions, which can be used to reverse the direction of motion in a car, for example. Gears also enable an engine to propel a car at different speeds while always working at an efficient number of revolutions (revs) per minute. When one wheel has more teeth than the other, there is a change in speed – the wheel with more teeth rotates slower. Bevel gears mesh at right angles and turn the axis of rotation through 90°. Most bicycles are fitted with derailleur gears, which have different sets of chain rings and sprockets that can be combined to give up to 24 gears.

genetic engineering Alteration of the characteristics of an organism by direct manipulation of its ▷GENES. The ▷DNA of different species can be mixed together in the hope that beneficial features of one can be transferred to the other, but increasingly scientists are now able to use the technique of gene-splitting to insert individual genes. Pigs, for example, can be genetically altered to have hearts made of human tissues, or to produce human hormones; and plants can be given resistance to disease. Genetic engineering is the basis of the flourishing BIOTECHNOLOGY industry, and it was used

SEEING IS BELIEVING *Industrial fibre optic cables (right) are used to provide a powerful point of light for precision work in a constricted area, in medicine, for example. Each cable contains 10 000 individual fibres; each fibre is about 47 microns thick. The optical fibre strands (below) have been magnified to three times their actual size.*

RECORD FLIGHT *The Russian-born American inventor Igor Sikorsky flying his VS300 helicopter in April 1941. He kept the machine airborne for a world record of 1 hr 15 min 14¹/₂ sec.*

for the first time to cure a rare hereditary deficiency disease in 1993; it has become controversial because it could in theory allow scientists to 'design' human beings.

genetic fingerprinting also known as DNA fingerprinting. Just as every person's fingerprints are different, so too are the precise sequences of genes in their ▷DNA. Techniques developed in 1984 can produce a visual record of this sequence from samples of blood or other tissues. Closely related people have similar sequences of genes, and genetic fingerprinting is used by immigration authorities and in paternity suits to establish fatherhood. It has also been used as proof against suspects in rape and murder cases.

glass The main component of glass is sand. Sand, soda and limestone are heated in a furnace to a temperature of some 1500°C (2700°F) when it turns into a molten mass which cools to form clear glass. Float glass, used for shop windows and mirrors, is made by floating molten glass from the furnace on a bath of molten tin, which ensures the glass remains flat as it cools. Special types of glass include heat-resistant glass, which contains boric oxide, and crystal glass, which contains lead and has a characteristic sparkle when cut. Safety glass is manufactured in such a way that it disintegrates into fragments rather than slivers. Laminated glass, used for car windscreens, has plastic sandwiched between two layers of glass; if the glass is shattered, it sticks to the plastic. Glass-making began in the Middle East in about 3000 BC, and in the 1st century BC the Syrians invented the blowpipe – a hollow tube which when dipped into molten glass could be used to blow it. Mass production began in the 19th century.

gyroscope Device that consists of a rapidly rotating wheel within a supporting frame. Because of its intertia, or resistance to change, the wheel, or rotor, of the gyroscope maintains its orientation in space no matter how the frame is moved. This directional property is used in such devices as the gyrocompass, found in ships and aircraft, and ship's stabilisers. A child's spinning top is an example of a gyroscope.

hacker Someone who, without permission, uses a computer, a MODEM and the telephone network to gain access to other

GHOST PICTURES *A schoolboy marvels at the three-dimensional hologram hovering in mid-air at the museum of La Villette in Paris.*

computers. Once connected, the hacker uses trial and error to find the computer's password codes that allow access to its files. Hackers have committed fraud and serious breaches of security, and many countries now have stringent laws against hacking.

helicopter The rotor blades of a helicopter have an AEROFOIL cross-section like that of an aeroplane wing, and when they rotate they develop enough lift to support the helicopter in the air. The rotor can provide propulsion in all directions as the pilot alters the pitch, or angle, of the rotating blades. The single-rotor Sea King helicopter can operate at night and in almost all weathers, and is used for search and rescue. The twin-rotor Chinook helicopter can carry 44 soldiers, and cargo both inside and underneath. Chinooks and Sea Kings were used in the 1991 Gulf War. ▷LEONARDO DA VINCI sketched an 'air gyroscope' in the 15th century; it would have risen into the air and then dropped. The first practical helicopter, the twin-rotored Fa-61 was built in Germany by Heinrich Focke in 1936. Three years later the Russian-born aeronautical engineer Igor Sikorsky constructed the first single-rotor machine, the VS-300, in the USA.

hologram Three-dimensional image of an object, made using LASER light. The light is split into two beams. One beam is directed at the object, and is reflected off it and onto a photographic plate. The other beam is shone onto the photographic plate. The two beams coincide to create an ▷INTERFERENCE pattern on the plate, which is then developed. Shining laser light through the pattern produces a realistic-looking 3-D image. Reflection holograms, used on credit cards to make them harder to forge, can be viewed in ordinary light. Holography was invented in 1947 by the Hungarian-born British physicist Denis Gabor, but did not become practical until the development of the laser in 1960.

hovercraft Vehicle that glides over land or water on a 'cushion' of high-pressure air. The air pressure is sufficient to lift the craft above the surface, reducing friction with the ground. Fans deliver the pressurised air to the cushion, which is often surrounded by a flexible 'skirt' to hold the air in. Air propellers drive the craft forward. The SRN-4 hovercraft used as cross-Channel ferries can carry 420 passengers and 60 cars at speeds up to 75 mph (120 km/h). The British electronics engineer Christopher Cockerell (1910-) launched the first full-size hovercraft in 1959.

hydraulics Branch of technology concerned with devices that transmit pressure through fluids. Car brakes work by hydraulic pressure, and consist of fluid-filled pipes connecting the brake pedal to the wheels. When the brake pedal is pressed down, it forces a piston down the master cylinder. The pressure travels through the liquid towards the brake pads, and forces smaller pistons to move and push the pads against the wheels with increased force.

hydrofoil Underwater wing fitted fore and aft to the bottom of a boat, to increase its speed. In cross-section the wing has the AEROFOIL shape of an aeroplane wing. As the boat moves forward, water pressure above the wing becomes lower than that below. This forces the foil to rise up, raising the boat's hull out of the water and greatly reducing water resistance. The Boeing Jetfoil uses water jets to propel it at speeds of up to 45 mph (72 km/h).

infrared device Piece of equipment that emits ▷INFRARED RADIATION, or detects the infrared radiation that is emitted by all warm objects. The automatic focusing mechanism on a camera works by bouncing an infrared beam off the subject and measuring the time it takes to return. Infrared detectors are used to look for bodies in smoke-filled buildings and among the debris of earthquakes. In intruder alarm systems, the heat difference between the intruder's body temperature and that of the surroundings triggers the alarm.

internal-combustion engine Type of engine in which combustion of fuel takes place inside an enclosed cylinder. Most cars use a four-stroke petrol engine: the engine produces power with four strokes, or movements, of the pistons, usually contained within four or more cylinders. On the first stroke, the piston moves down the cylinder, sucking in a mixture of petrol and air through an open inlet valve. On the second, the inlet valve closes and the piston moves back up the cylinder, compressing the mixture. When the piston reaches the top, the mixture is ignited by a spark from the spark plug; the burning mixture expands and forces the piston back down the cylinder, forming the third power stroke. On the fourth stroke, the piston moves back up the cylinder, forcing the exhaust gas out of the now open exhaust valves. The pistons turn a crankshaft linked to the car's wheels via a transmission system. The German inventor Nikolaus August Otto perfected a four-stroke engine, powered by gas, in 1876.

⚓Turbochargers increase an internal combustion engine's power by forcing more air into the engine cylinders with a turbine-driven compressor, or pump. The turbine is driven by the flow of exhaust gases.

irradiation Exposure to radiation, such as ▷GAMMA RADIATION, which in large doses can kill living organisms. Irradiation is used in some countries, including the UK, to help preserve food; the rays kill off the microorganisms that cause decay. However, there is some concern that irradiation may also destroy vitamins.

jet engine Gas-turbine engine, usually used for aircraft, that produces thrust by jet propulsion – a jet of gases shooting backwards from the rear of the engine. The simplest jet engine is the turbojet. Air is taken in and compressed. Fuel (kerosene) is sprayed into the compressed air and ignited, and the hot gases produced expand and spin the blades of a turbine – which drives the compressor – before escaping as a propulsive jet. RAF officer Frank Whittle took out his patent on a jet engine in 1930. Seven years later he tested a practical engine, first used in a plane in 1941.

⚓In Germany during World War II, the engineer Hans von Ohain developed the Messerschmitt Me-262 jet fighter. It was faster than the first British jet fighter, the Gloster Meteor, but was not produced early enough, or in sufficiently large numbers, to influence the course of the war.

laser (Light Amplification by Stimulated Emission of Radiation) Electronic device that produces a concentrated beam of very pure light. In laser light, unlike ordinary light, all the waves have the same length and are exactly in step, with their crests and troughs coinciding. Lasers can be used to drill holes in metal, send telephone signals along optical fibres, carry out delicate surgery, and play COMPACT DISCS. The first laser was built by American physicist Theodore H. Maiman in 1960.

LCD (Liquid Crystal Display) Method of displaying the numbers in electronic devices such as digital watches and calculators, first used in 1971. The display for each character is usually made up of seven segments, each with liquid crystals built into them. The application of electricity changes the structure of the liquid crystal, twisting the path of light and effectively turning the segment on or off.

LED (Light Emitting Diode) Tiny crystal of SEMICONDUCTOR material that glows when an electric current passes through it. LEDs, invented in 1962, are used in digital displays and for indicating that power is on in electronic devices.

lift The modern safety lift was invented in 1853 by the American engineer Elisha Otis. The passenger car is connected to a counterweight by a steel cable that passes over a pulley at the top of the lift shaft. The

RADIO PIONEER *The young Guglielmo Marconi, pictured soon after his arrival in England in 1896. He had left his native Italy having failed to gain financial support for his development of radio.*

A MARVEL IN MINIATURE *The intricate circuitry of a microchip, magnified × 60, with (inset) a complete chip on a fingernail × 2 which contains thousands of electronic circuits and components.*

counterweight moves down as the lift moves up, and vice versa. So only the difference between the weight of the counterweight and the car with its passengers has to be moved – minimising the load on the motor used to turn the pulley. Otis's safety device was a clamp that automatically gripped a guide rail if the hoist rope broke. His lift allowed the growth of the skyscraper, leading to dramatic changes in the skyline of many cities.

lighting Until the 19th century, oil lamps and candles were the principal means of lighting. The earliest oil lamps, made more than 40 000 years ago, were hollowed-out stones which held burning animal fat. In 1780, the Swiss chemist Ami Argand developed a much more practical oil lamp with a glass chimney and a tubular woven wick; air was drawn up through the centre of the wick, making it burn brighter than earlier lamps. Candles were first made more than 2000 years ago by dipping strands of cotton or flax into animal fat. Gas lighting – using coal gas – was introduced in the United Kingdom in 1806, but gave rather low illumination until 1885, when Carl Auer, a Viennese chemist, invented a gas mantle that gave a much brighter light. Electric-powered lamps were invented independently by two men: Joseph Swan of Newcastle upon Tyne in 1878, and Thomas EDISON in the USA in 1879. The modern light bulb, a development of their work, contains a filament of fine coiled tungsten wire. When the light is switched

on, the wire heats up to as much as 2500°C (4500°F) and glows white hot. Neon lamps were invented in 1910 when the French chemist Georges Claude passed electric current through neon gas, producing an orange-red light. Other gases produced different colours. In fluorescent lamps, introduced in 1939, gas – usually mercury vapour – gives off invisible ultraviolet light which is absorbed by a fluorescent coating on the inside of the tube, which then gives out visible light. Energy-saving bulbs are small fluorescent tubes. They consume less electricity and last much longer than ordinary (incandescent) light bulbs.

magnetic tape Plastic tape coated with fine magnetic particles – usually of iron oxide or chromium oxide – used in audio, video and data recording. During recording, light and/or sound waves are converted into electric signals which rearrange the magnetic particles into a pattern representing them. When the tape is played back, the pattern is read and used to reconstruct the original sound, pictures or other information. The magnetic recorder was invented by Valdemar Poulsen, a Dane, in 1898. Video tapes were introduced for professional use in 1956, and Philips introduced tape cassettes in 1964.

Marconi, Guglielmo (1874-1937) Italian electrical engineer who developed the 'wireless telegraph', the forerunner of the radio. Marconi carried out his first experiments in Italy in 1895, but the fol-

lowing year moved to Britain. By 1897 wireless telegraphy had a range of 12 miles (19 km), and in 1901, Marconi sent the first transatlantic radio signal from Poldhu in Cornwall to St John's in Newfoundland. GEC-Marconi Electronics Ltd was founded by Marconi in 1897 as the Wireless Telegraph and Signal Company. He shared the Nobel prize for physics in 1909.

microchip (or silicon chip) A very thin sliver of silicon or other SEMICONDUCTOR material, about ¼ in (7 mm) square, that contains thousands of electronic components and circuits. The circuits are built up in a step-by-step process, which involves 'doping' the silicon – adding impurities to alter its electrical properties – and depositing metals to form connections. The first practical integrated circuits were exhibited in 1959. Microprocessors, devised in 1969, are microchips that contain all the circuits needed to enable them to function as the main systems units of COMPUTERS.

microfilm Photographic film often used to store documents and newspapers, reduced to about ¹⁄₂₀th of their original size. The film is read in a viewer that magnifies the text to a readable size.
⚲ In the 1850s, English craftsman John Benjamin Dancer produced minute photographic slides. One of them was of Queen Victoria's family mounted in a ring, with a transparent stone as a magnifying glass.

microscope Optical device containing a system of lenses and mirrors which allows objects to be magnified by up to 2500 times (× 2500). The object is placed on a platform and illuminated; the objective lens, closest to the object, produces a magnified image of the object, and this image is then viewed and further magnified by a lens in the microscope's eyepiece. Higher magnifications can be obtained with electron microscopes, which use beams of ▷ELECTRONS to project a magnified image onto a screen. Transmission electron microscopes, in which the beam passes through the object, magnify up to a million times. Scanning electron microscopes, working by reflection, give magnifications up to × 200 000; the beam scans the surface of the object allowing three-dimensional images to be built up.
⚲ The optical microscope was probably developed in Holland in 1590 and subsequent discoveries upset many existing scientific theories. For example, it had been thought that fleas were formed from dust and dirt, but the microscope revealed that they emerged from minute eggs.

microwave oven Microwaves, a type of ▷ELECTROMAGNETIC RADIATION, cause the water molecules in food to vibrate at about 2.5 billion times a second, generating heat which allows food to be cooked in a very short time. The higher the water content of the food, the quicker the food cooks. Metal containers must not be used in microwave ovens because the radiation is reflected by metal. The first microwave oven was patented in 1953.

missile The first long-range ballistic missile was the German World War II V-2 rocket bomb, developed by Wernher von BRAUN. Intercontinental ballistic missiles (ICBMs), usually launched from silos sunk into the ground, have a range of more than 6000 miles (9700 km). Advanced missiles are fitted with a guidance system. Some are fitted with infrared homing or heat-seeking devices, which lock onto the hot engines of the target plane. RADAR and LASERS are also used in almost all guidance systems. Cruise missiles are jet-propelled throughout their flight, and navigate by means of a map stored in their memories. They are able to hit individual buildings from a range of 1550 miles (2500 km).

modem (short for modulator-demodulator) Device which enables computer data and FAX messages to be transmitted along telephone lines. When transmitting, the modem takes digital signals from the computer and converts them into sound signals suitable for transmission by telephone. When receiving, the modem turns these signals back into digital signals that the fax machine or computer can interpret.

Montgolfier brothers Joseph (1740-1810) and Étienne (1745-99), French paper-makers who built the first hot-air balloon to carry human passengers, on November 21, 1783. Ten days later, the French physicist J.A.C. Charles launched a hydrogen-filled balloon which remained airborne for two hours.

Morse, Samuel (1791-1872) American pioneer of the electric telegraph, and inventor of Morse code. (See box.)

napalm Jellified petrol used in flame-throwers and incendiary bombs, developed by US scientists during World War II at the request of the US Army. It burns intensely and sticks to its target, human or otherwise.

Nobel, Alfred Bernhard (1833-96) Swedish inventor of dynamite and gelignite. A pacifist, Nobel hoped that the

Samuel Morse

MORSE CODE

Samuel Morse invented the Morse code in 1844 to make it quicker to send long-distance messages over the electric telegraph that he developed in 1837. Used at sea until 1993, the distress call SOS is rendered · · · — — — · · ·

A ·—	J ·———	R ·—·
B —···	K —·—	S ···
C —·—·	L ·—··	T —
D —··	M ——	U ··—
E ·	N —·	V ···—
F ··—·	O ———	W ·——
G ——·	P ·——·	X —··—
H ····	Q ——·—	Y —·——
I ··		Z ——··

destructive power of his invention would deter warfare. His financial interests in explosives and in Russia's Baku oilfields brought him an immense fortune, the bulk of which he left to found the Nobel prizes. They were to be awarded to those who have 'conferred the greatest benefit on mankind' in physics, chemistry, physiology or medicine, literature and peace. Economics was added in 1969. The prizes were worth more than £500 000 each in 1994.

HAPPY LANDING *The first manned flight to land safely took place near Paris in 1783. Two volunteers flew 5 miles (8 km) in a hot-air balloon designed by the Montgolfier brothers.*

nuclear reactor Unit in which controlled ▷NUCLEAR FISSION takes place to provide energy for nuclear power stations and nuclear powered ships. The central core of a reactor contains nuclear 'fuel', such as uranium. The rate of fission is controlled by rods that can be pushed into and out of the core. In a power station, the heat produced in the core by fission is extracted by a coolant and is used to boil water into steam, which drives the station's turbines that spin the electricity generators. The whole reactor is enclosed in thick, steel-reinforced concrete. The commonest type of reactor is the pressurised water reactor (PWR), whose core is cooled with water kept under high pressure so that it does not boil, even when heated above boiling point. The water is passed through a heat exchanger, where it gives up its heat to a second, unpressurised, water circuit where the water boils and produces steam. High-level radioactive ▷NUCLEAR WASTE from power stations can be disposed of by storing it as a liquid in steel tanks encased in concrete, or fusing it into glass cylinders which are then buried deep underground. Major accidents have occurred in nuclear power stations at Three-Mile Island, USA, in 1979, and ▷CHERNOBYL, then in the USSR, in 1986.

nuclear weapon Explosive device in which energy is released by ▷NUCLEAR FISSION or ▷NUCLEAR FUSION. Atom bombs use the nuclear fission of uranium or plutonium to bring about a runaway chain reaction which is accompanied by the release of huge amounts of energy as light, heat, blast and deadly radiation. American scientists, led by Robert Oppenheimer, tested the first ▷ATOM BOMB in July 1945, at the Alamogordo Bombing Range in southern New Mexico. Three weeks later, the US Air Force dropped atom bombs on the Japanese cities of Hiroshima (August 6) and Nagasaki (August 9); more than 220,000 people died. By 1952, scientists had developed the even more powerful hydrogen bomb, in which energy was produced by nuclear fusion. Neutron bombs – small hydrogen bombs – produce high levels of radiation, with only limited heat and blast, and are designed to kill people, rather than destroy buildings.

nylon The original wholly synthetic fibre, first produced by a team led by Wallace H. Carothers in the USA in 1935. Some of its first uses were for nylon stockings, introduced in 1938, and for underwear, allowing women who had never been able to afford silk to wear silk-like clothes. Nylon fibres are made by forcing a molten polymer or plastic through tiny holes in a nozzle called a spinneret; the stream from each hole then solidifies into a thread.

oil refining The processing of crude oil (petroleum) into fuels, chemicals and other useful products. Petroleum, recovered from beneath the Earth's surface, is a mixture of hundreds of different compounds called ▷HYDROCARBONS. The first refinery process, called distillation, or fractionation, splits the crude oil into its components or fractions: crude oil is heated, and the resulting hot vapour is passed into a steel tower where the different fractions condense, and are tapped off, at different levels. The major fractions are the fuels petrol, kerosene, diesel oil and heating oil. Further refining can produce more fuels and chemical raw materials such as petrochemicals, which are used to make a range of plastics and other products.

paper Most paper is made from specially grown softwood trees, whose logs are mechanically shredded or chemically treated in order to extract the cellulose fibres and form a pulp. The pulp is then washed, mixed with dyes and other substances, and allowed to flow on a wire-mesh belt. The water drains away, and the damp web of paper is dried and rolled into a continuous sheet. The earliest true paper was made by the Chinese from around AD 105; it reached Europe in the 8th century, and gradually replaced parchment and vellum, which were made from animal skins. Linen and cotton rags were the basic raw materials of paper until 1850, when the use of wood pulp helped to meet the increasing demand. High-quality paper still contains some rag pulp.

photocopier Most photocopiers work on the principle of xerography – dry writing – developed in 1938. Light reflected from the document being copied falls on a rotating drum charged with electricity. Only the parts of the drum that did not receive light – because of writing, or some other image, reflected from the original – remain charged, and attract black 'toner' powder. A sheet of paper then passes over the drum and the toner is transferred to the paper and fixed with heat and pressure. Colour photocopiers repeat the process three times over, using filters to break down the image into its coloured components, and coloured toners to reconstruct it.

plastics Most plastics are made from petrochemicals – obtained during the refining of oil – by a process called polymerisation. It involves joining together small molecules, or monomers, to make large molecules, or ▷POLYMERS. The first synthetic plastic, BAKELITE, appeared in 1909. More plastics were developed during the next 40 years, but it was not until the 1950s that they started to flood the market. Plastics can be moulded into almost any shape quickly and cheaply and they do not corrode or conduct electricity. However, they may give off poisonous fumes when burnt, and because they do not rot, it is difficult to dispose of them.

power station Electricity is produced in power stations by turbogenerators – ELECTRIC GENERATORS spun by turbines. In most power stations, high-pressure steam spins the turbines. The steam can be produced from water heated in a boiler by burning coal or oil, or by the heat from a NUCLEAR REACTOR. In hydroelectric power stations, the turbines are spun by fast-flowing water. The electricity generated in British power stations is 25 000 volts AC (▷ALTERNATING CURRENT). At this voltage, much power would be lost during transmission by overhead wires, so the voltage is stepped up to 275 000 or 400 000 volts, using a transformer. The voltage is then reduced again to 240 volts for use in the home. Electricity is distributed by power cables called the national grid.

printing The earliest developments in printing took place in China. In AD 868, a book was printed using a wooden block with the text and illustrations raised in relief. Two centuries later, a Chinese alchemist printed from clay blocks with individual words raised in relief; the blocks could be reused in different combinations. Independently, in about 1450, Johann ▷GUTENBERG developed the same idea of reusable, or movable, type. Gutenberg's printing process consisted of small pieces of metal, each bearing a mirror image of one letter raised in relief. Ink was spread over the block of letters, and the paper pressed against them. This method, known as letterpress, has been largely superseded by offset-litho printing. In this method, the printing plate is produced in such a way that only the image areas – the type and illustrations – will accept the greasy ink. The images are transferred first to a rubber 'blanket' and then to the paper. Another printing process, called gravure, is the reverse of letterpress – the image is etched into the printing surface. Only the recesses in the printing plate retain ink, which is then transferred to paper. In the late 1960s printing and large-scale publishing began to be computerised. With a microcomputer-based or desk-top publishing system, text and graphics are combined on a computer screen. Once a page is complete, the entire image is transferred to a phototypesetting device. The phototypesetter projects the image electronically onto photographic film, which is used to prepare printing plates. Modern presses print at high speeds; in the type of press used to print this book, 10½ miles (17 km) of paper passes through the press every hour.

radar (Radio Detection and Ranging) Method of detecting objects and measuring their distance by bouncing radio waves off them. Radar is used in air traffic control systems to monitor the position of aircraft. Police use radar to gauge the speed of vehicles; the radio wave returns to the radar equipment at a different frequency from the outgoing wave, and the speed can be calculated from this difference. Astronomers use radar to investigate planets; the pattern of radar reflections mirrors the topography of a planet, such as the surface features of cloud-covered Venus. Weather forecasters also use radar – to detect rain; the radio waves are reflected from raindrops. Radar was developed in Britain in the late 1930s. By the outbreak of World War II radar stations were used to detect aircraft up to 100 miles (160 km) away.

radio Transmission of signals by the use of ▷RADIO WAVES, as in radio broadcasting. In radio transmission, signals representing sounds are combined with a radio wave that acts as a carrier. The sound signal changes, or modulates, the ▷AMPLITUDE (AM) or ▷FREQUENCY (FM) of the so-called carrier wave. The carrier wave is then broadcast. In the radio receiver, the carrier wave is demodulated and the sound signals retrieved. Guglielmo MARCONI pioneered what came to be called 'wireless telegraphy' in 1895. In 1906 Reginald Fessenden successfully transmitted speech for the first time, at a wireless station he had built in Massachusetts, USA. In Britain, the British Broadcasting Company, later the British Broadcasting Corporation (BBC), began regular radio broadcasts in 1922.

recycling The processing of waste products so that they can be used again helps to save materials, and uses less energy than would be needed to make new products from raw materials. Recycling aluminium, for example, uses much less electricity than is used in extracting the metal from bauxite. Other metals that are recycled include the steel from car bodies, which is crushed and returned to steel works, and silver, extracted from used photographic film. Broken glass, separated into different colours, is melted in the furnace with the other ingredients used to make new glass; broken glass of mixed colours can only be used to make green glass. Waste paper is pulped, cleaned and bleached to remove most of the ink and dirt before being reused. The many different types of plastic, mostly made from oil, are cheap to produce so long as oil supplies are plentiful, giving little economic incentive to recycle them.

refrigerator Cold slows down the growth of the microorganisms that cause food to decay. A refrigerator works by circulating a cooling agent, or refrigerant, through pipes inside and outside the cabinet. The cooling agent is a substance that can change from liquid to vapour (a change that absorbs heat) and back from vapour to liquid (a change that releases heat). As it passes through the pipe inside the cabinet, the refrigerant, in liquid form, goes through an expansion valve, then evaporates and absorbs heat from the cabinet, causing the temperature to drop. The refrigerant, now a gas, is pumped into a compressor, and changes back to liquid form, losing heat from pipes at the back of the refrigerator. The liquid refrigerant then passes back to the expansion valve, and the cycle starts again, keeping the temperature of the domestic refrigerator at 0-5°C (32-41°F). Freon, a ▷CFC, was the most widely used refrigerant, but alternatives are now being introduced because of the damage CFCs cause to the Earth's ozone layer. The first mechanical domestic refrigerator was developed in 1879 when the German inventor Karl von Linde modified an industrial model he designed six years earlier.

resistor Component in electronic circuits that resists the passage of electricity. Resistance is measured in ▷OHMS, named after Georg Simon Ohm, a German physicist.

robot Mechanical device, usually controlled by computer, that simulates human actions. The industrial robots used in car factories are machines with flexible mechanical arms that carry out specific tasks according to a built-in computer program. More advanced robots may be fitted with sensors, such as electric 'eyes', so that they can recognise the shape of objects they handle and perform a wider range of jobs. About 95 per cent of each vehicle's welds are performed by robots.
🐛 The word 'robot' is derived from the Czech word *robota*, meaning slavery.

FLYING EYE *The American space shuttle* Discovery *blasts off in April 1990 carrying the Hubble telescope. Once in orbit the telescope proved to be flawed, but it was repaired in December 1993.*

rocket Device or motor that is propelled by a stream of gases escaping from the rear. The gases are produced by burning fuel in oxygen; space rockets carry their own source of oxygen, and can therefore travel outside the Earth's atmosphere. The rocket's fuel and oxygen-provider (oxidiser) are called its propellants. Most rockets use liquid propellants, such as kerosene or liquid hydrogen as fuels, and liquid oxygen as oxidiser. Rockets are the only engines that can develop enough speed to overcome the Earth's gravitational pull, and are used to launch satellites and space stations. Conventional rockets can be used only once, but the SPACE SHUTTLE is partly reusable. The American physicist and engineer Robert Hutchings Goddard launched the first liquid-fuelled rocket in 1926.

satellite Between 400 and 500 working man-made moons, or satellites, orbit the Earth, many of them relaying telephone calls and television signals between ground stations around the world. Most are positioned in geostationary orbit – about 22 300 miles (35 900 km) above the Earth's Equator, the height at which they complete one orbit of the Earth in 24 hours. The satellites therefore appear stationary in the sky, and antennae of ground stations can be permanently locked onto them. *Telstar*, launched in 1962 (although not in geostationary orbit), carried the first live television pictures across the Atlantic. *Early Bird*, launched in 1965, could carry 240 simultaneous telephone conversations; the latest *Intelsat 6* communications satellites can each handle 30 000 telephone calls at a time. Weather satellites, such as the European Space Agency's *Meteosat*, give a global view of cloud patterns, supplying information about weather over the oceans. Other satellites carry remote-sensing equipment, which uses different types of ▷ELECTROMAGNETIC RADIATION to collect information about, for example, surface vegetation, rock types and pollution.
🐛 The world's first artificial satellite was the USSR's *Sputnik 1*, launched on October 4, 1957, the 40th anniversary of the Russian Revolution. The satellite measured 23 in (58 cm) in diameter.

semiconductor Material, such as silicon, that only partly conducts electricity, used to make electronic devices such as DIODES, RESISTORS and TRANSISTORS.

sewing machine First labour-saving device used widely in the home. The American inventor Elias Howe produced the forerunner of the modern sewing machine in 1846, but it was Isaac Singer, a mechanic from New York, who made the

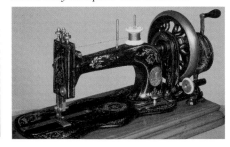

SEWING THE SEED *Many of the innovations in Isaac Singer's sewing machine of 1865 are still used in today's computer controlled units.*

first machine for domestic use in 1851. Modern domestic machines still use the stitching mechanism of early machines.

smart card Plastic card like a credit card, but incorporating a microchip. A smart card can carry details of previous transactions, the cardholder's credit balance and other financial details. The cards (used widely in France) are capable of carrying personal data, such as fingerprints, and information that needs to be updated, such as medical records.

solar cell Device that converts solar energy into electricity. Solar cells are made from layers of silicon, specially treated to develop a voltage when sunlight falls on them. They are used to power satellites and pocket calculators, but are too expensive for large-scale generation of electricity.
♨Solar panels, which are fitted on roofs facing the Sun, consist of liquid-filled pipes set in a dark material to absorb the maximum amount of heat. The heat absorbed by the liquid can then be used for domestic heating.

sonar (Sound Navigation And Ranging) Method of detection, communication and navigation used at sea, in which pulses of sound are sent out by a transmitter and reflected back as an 'echo' by any object in their path, such as wrecks or submarines. Sonar is used for locating shoals of fish, mapping the ocean floor and the examination of shipwrecks.

space probe Spacecraft designed to escape the Earth's gravitational pull and explore the solar system. Probes have taken close-up pictures of all the planets except Pluto. The first space probe was the USSR's *Luna 1*, launched in January 1959; after passing some 3000 miles (5000 km) from the Moon, it went into orbit around the Sun. The USA's *Viking* space probes explored Mars in 1976, mapping almost the entire planet; landing craft sent back close-up pictures of the red surface and tested the soil for signs of life – with no success. The US space probes *Voyager 1* and *2* were launched in 1977 and have sent back pictures of Jupiter and Saturn. *Voyager 2* visited Uranus and Neptune in 1989 after a journey of 4.4 billion miles (7 billion km).

space shuttle Space transport system, with a reusable winged space plane, or orbiter, built to carry astronauts, satellites and scientific equipment into space and back. The US space shuttle consists of the rocket-powered orbiter, which is the size of

a medium airliner, riding on a large tank carrying fuel for the orbiter's engines; there are also two rocket boosters to provide extra power at lift-off. The orbiter and rocket boosters are reusable; when the orbiter returns to Earth, it lands on a runway. The shuttle was first launched in April 1981, with the orbiter *Columbia*.
♨When the second orbiter, *Challenger*, was launched in January 1986, it exploded shortly after lift-off, killing all seven crew.

space station Large manned spacecraft with living and working space, designed to remain in orbit for an extended period. The first space station was the USSR's *Salyut 1*,

launched in 1971. The USA launched the *Skylab* space station in 1973; at 89 ft (27 m) long, it was the largest space station launched so far. In 1986 the USSR's *Mir* space station went into orbit; two Soviet cosmonauts completed a record 366-day stay in *Mir* in 1988. NASA's proposed space station *Freedom*, which was to be a joint project with Europe, Japan and Canada scheduled for launch in the mid 1990s, has been shelved because of escalating costs.

stealth technology The design of military aircraft to make them invisible to radar. An aircraft built using stealth technology is made of materials that absorb radio waves

STEALTHY *Innovative design, novel construction materials and special paints render the American B2 Stealth bomber invisible to radar. The most successful stealth plane is the Lockheed F-117, inset.*

and its shape is designed to deflect radio waves, rather than reflect them back to their source. The USA's successful stealth plane, the Lockheed F-117 or 'Black Jet', was introduced in April 1990, and saw action in the 1991 Gulf War.

steam engine The first machine that harnessed the power of expanding steam to drive a piston back and forth in a cylinder was designed by Thomas Newcomen, a Devon blacksmith, in 1712; it was used to pump water out of mines. The engine was reliable but wasted much heat. James Watt, a Scottish instrument-maker, developed the steam engine, and in 1776 began manufacturing more efficient engines that were the main driving force behind the Industrial Revolution. The steam piston engine was superseded by the INTERNAL-COMBUSTION ENGINE and ELECTRIC MOTOR.

steel Strong, stiff alloy of iron, containing carbon and traces of other metals, that is one of the world's major construction materials. Steel is made by refining pig iron

RAILWAY PIONEER *George Stephenson, who perfected the design of the railway steam engine after building the* Rocket *in 1829. He foresaw the country being criss-crossed by railways.*

A STAR IS BORN *The birth of a star, upper centre, in the Orion Nebula as seen by the American Hubble space telescope. Inset, the telescope being placed in orbit in 1990.*

from the BLAST FURNACE, often using the basic oxygen process in which a jet of pure oxygen is blasted at supersonic speed into the molten iron. The oxygen burns out impurities, including carbon, until only the required amount of carbon remains. Steel was made on a large scale only after 1856, when the inventor Henry Bessemer patented a method of blowing air through molten pig iron in a pear-shaped container known as a Bessemer converter. Stainless steel, developed in 1913, usually contains 18 per cent chromium and 8 per cent nickel and is very resistant to corrosion.

Stephenson, George (1781-1848) British-born engineer and pioneer of the passenger and freight-carrying steam TRAIN. (See also George ▷STEPHENSON in 'Architecture and Engineering'.)

submarine Underwater vessel that sinks by filling its ballast tanks with water and resurfaces by expelling the water with compressed air. Non-nuclear submarines use battery-powered electric propulsion under water and a diesel engine, which also recharges the batteries, at the surface. The forerunner of the modern submarine was built by an American, John Holland, in 1898. Germany used its first U-boat – *Unterseeboot* – to sink enemy shipping early in World War I, and inflicted heavy losses with U-boats during both world wars.
⚓Nuclear submarines can stay under water indefinitely, but are limited by the supplies they can store. In 1982-3, the British nuclear submarine HMS *Warspite* remained submerged for a record 111 days.

Superglue Fast-acting, strongly bonding adhesive based on acrylic resin. In the tube, the resin is liquid and remains so because of the presence of a chemical stabiliser. When applied to a surface, the stabiliser is neutralised by moisture which is present on almost any surface exposed to air. This allows the resin molecules to join together in long chains and set into a plastic film that bonds the surfaces together.

Teflon Trade name for the plastic polytetrafluoroethylene (PTFE). One of the most slippery substances known, PTFE also resists very high temperatures and is affected by few chemicals. It is used for nonstick coatings on pans and other cooking utensils, as well as for coating skis.
⚓One of PTFE's first uses was the heat protection of spacecraft and missiles.

telephone A telephone's mouthpiece contains a microphone whose diaphragm is vibrated by sound waves. These vibrations are converted into electrical signals that travel to the earpiece of the person being called via copper cables, optical cables, communications satellites or CELLPHONE radio links. In the earpiece, the signals pass through the coils of a small electromagnet – causing its magnetism to fluctuate. This makes a diaphragm vibrate and sets up sound waves that are replicas of those that entered the microphone in the mouthpiece. The mouthpiece and earpiece have reverse functions and in modern telephones both are incorporated in a single handset. Alexander Graham BELL patented the telephone in the USA in 1876. Now the telephone network also carries fax messages, computer data and electronic mail, and, on videophones, images.

telescope The two basic types of optical instrument used to produce magnified images of distant objects are refractors, which use lenses to gather and focus light, and reflectors, which use mirrors. The most powerful telescopes are reflectors; on Mount Semirodniki in the Caucasus, the world's biggest telescope has light-gathering mirrors 20 ft (6 m) across, so powerful that it is believed they could detect the light from a candle 15 000 miles (24 000 km) away. The Hubble space telescope, in orbit since 1990, is a reflecting telescope controlled remotely from Earth. Hans Lippershey, a Dutch spectacle-maker, built one of the first telescopes, using lenses, in 1608. A year later, the Italian scientist ▷GALILEO built an improved instrument which he used to observe the Moon, Venus and Jupiter. In 1668, Sir Isaac ▷NEWTON built the first reflecting telescope, and its mirror arrangement is still the one most used in amateur instruments today. Radio telescopes use a large metal dish to collect radio waves emitted by stars. Electronic circuits convert incoming signals into a visual image on a display screen.

television The British inventor John Logie BAIRD gave the world's first demonstration of television in 1925, and colour transmission was introduced by RCA in the USA in 1953. Inside the television camera, light is split up into its red, green and blue components, each of which is directed to a separate electron tube. Within each tube is a photoconductive layer which turns the light into tiny electric charges of varying intensity – the brighter the light, the greater the charge. A beam of electrons scans the photoconductive layer in a series of horizontal lines – 625 in Britain – and the result is electrical signals that mirror the pattern of electric charge on the photosensitive layer. The signals are combined with a RADIO carrier wave and transmitted. A TV aerial picks up the carrier wave and feeds it to a television set. The signals are separated

from the carrier wave and fed into the television's picture tube – a type of cathode-ray tube – that works like a television camera in reverse. Inside the tube, the red, green and blue picture signals are fed to three electron guns which produce electron beams of varying strength. The beams travel through a perforated mask and hit a phosphor-coated screen, making it glow. The mask ensures that the red signal beam hits phosphor that emits red light, the green signal beam hits phosphor that emits green light, and so on.

🔌 In 1993 the average Briton watched almost 26 hours of television each week.

thermostat Device to maintain a preset temperature. The thermostat in central heating systems contains a bimetallic strip – two metals, which expand at different rates when heated, joined side by side. As the temperature changes from the preset level the strip bends, and the bending and straightening causes the heating circuit to be turned on and off automatically, to maintain the required temperature.

train From about the 14th century, horse-drawn trucks ran on wooden rails in European mines. The first steam locomotive was built by Richard Trevithick, a Cornish engineer, in 1803, for the Coalbrookdale Ironworks in Shropshire. In 1825 George STEPHENSON (1781-1848), a Northumberland-born engineer, built the world's first public railway – 10 miles (16 km) of track between Stockton and Darlington – and the steam engine *Locomotion* which travelled on it. With his son Robert (1803-59), Stephenson built the *Rocket* to run on the Liverpool and Manchester Railway, which opened in 1830. By 1841, 1300 miles (2090 km) of track had been laid, and in 1851 railways carried 6 million people to London for the Great Exhibition. The steam engine reached its greatest speed in 1938 when the British locomotive *Mallard* reached 126 mph (203 km/h). An electric locomotive was first demonstrated in 1879, and it was adopted for underground railways to avoid the problem of smoke and dirt. The first electric underground railway, the six mile (10 km) City and South London Railway, was opened in 1890. Diesel locomotives first ran in Germany in 1912, and in 1928 Britain had its first diesel-electric locomotives, in which a diesel engine generates electric current which is fed to motors which turn the wheels. In 1964 Japan introduced the streamlined electric *shinkansen*, or 'bullet' train, which can travel at 160 mph (256 km/h). France's electric

TGV (*train à grande vitesse*) can cruise at 170 mph (274 km/h) and is the world's fastest passenger train. Experiments have been carried out with magnetic levitation, or maglev, in which the train 'floats' above the track, avoiding friction between wheels and track. In experiments in Germany and Japan, maglev trains have reached speeds of 310 mph (500 km/h).

🔌 Manchester engraver George Bradshaw produced railway maps from 1838 and timetables from 1839. Bradshaw's timetables were published until 1961.

🔌 British Railways was created in 1948, with the nationalisation of the four railways: the London, Midland and Scottish Railway; the London and North-Eastern Railway; the Great Western Railway; and the Southern Railway.

transistor A SEMICONDUCTOR device that can amplify or control electrical signals in electronic circuits or act as a high-speed switch. It consists of a sandwich of three semiconductor materials. By feeding current to the middle of the 'sandwich', current between the outer layers of the transistor can be amplified or switched on or off. Developed in 1948, transistors began a revolution in electronics: they were far smaller than the thermionic valves that they replaced, required much less power and were more reliable. Transistors are now a major component in the integrated circuits on MICROCHIPS.

🔌 The first transistor radios were developed in the USA in 1954, making pocket-sized radios possible for the first time.

Velcro Trade name for a plastic fastener consisting of minute hooks on one strip of material which catch loops on a facing strip. The Swiss engineer Georges de Mestral devised Velcro in 1948.

HOOKED *Magnified 20 times, the nylon hooks and loops of Velcro. The fastener was inspired by the way burs cling to fur and clothing.*

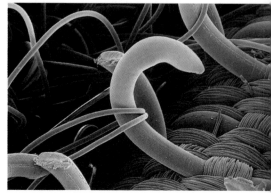

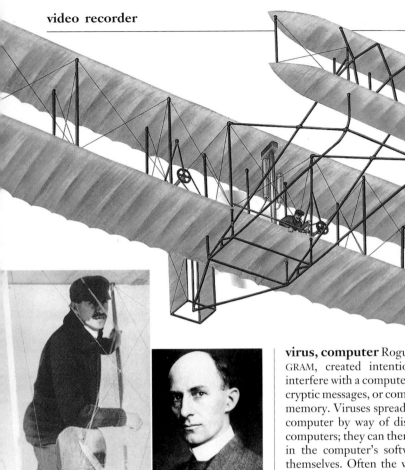

FIRST FLIGHT *Orville Wright (left) pilots the first powered flight by a heavier-than-air machine at Kitty Hawk in North Carolina in 1903. Later the same day Wilbur flew their aeroplane 825 ft in 59 seconds.*

video recorder Also called videotape recorder (VTR) and videocassette recorder (VCR). Video recorders were first produced in the USA by Ampex in 1956, but home video recorders did not appear until the mid 1970s. Picture signals are recorded on broad MAGNETIC TAPE in much the same way as sounds are recorded in a tape recorder. But in contrast to a tape recorder, where the sound signals are recorded on lengthwise tracks, the picture signals are recorded as diagonal tracks to fit in more information. Home video camcorders have their own built-in video recorder unit.

virtual reality Sophisticated simulator system, first developed in 1985, which enables the user to enter an imaginary world created by computer. The user wears special goggles and gloves, and 'moves around' the three-dimensional environment. Architects can walk around buildings which have not yet been built, and cardiac surgeons can enter a simulated heart.

virus, computer Rogue COMPUTER PROGRAM, created intentionally, which can interfere with a computer's operation, leave cryptic messages, or completely wipe out its memory. Viruses spread from computer to computer by way of disks from 'infected' computers; they can then install themselves in the computer's software and replicate themselves. Often the virus remains inactive until triggered by, for example, a name, statistic or date; a widespread virus, called Michelangelo, only becomes active on the artist's birthday, March 6.

water purification Water may be collected in reservoirs, taken from rivers, or pumped up from water-bearing rocks underground. To make it fit for use, it is first allowed to stand so that most suspended matter, such as algae and dirt, settles to the bottom; the rest is treated chemically, and removed by filtration. Chlorine is used to kill any surviving microorganisms. Additional treatment may be needed to remove metals or nitrates that have entered the water from agricultural land.

Watt, James (1736-1819) Scottish engineer who greatly improved the power and efficiency of the steam engine. In partnership with Matthew Boulton, he began manufacturing steam engines in Soho near Birmingham in 1776. They played a key role in the industrial revolution. Watt coined the term 'horsepower' and gave his name to the ▷WATT, a unit of power.

wheel One of the most important of human inventions, the wheel was being used by potters by 3500 BC, just before wheeled vehicles were first used in Sumeria and southern Poland. Spoked wheels were fitted to high-speed war chariots in Egypt and Syria by 2000 BC. Toothed gear wheels, pulleys and water wheels to turn stones for grinding corn were all used by the 1st century BC. The flywheel – a heavy wheel or disc that rotates on a shaft, storing energy – was first used in 1781 when James Watt fitted one to his steam engine. Before the mid 19th century, wheels were protected by iron tyres, which damaged roads and were noisy. Pneumatic tyres were invented in 1845 by the Scottish engineer Robert Thomson. His 'aerial wheels' ran for over 1200 miles (1900 km), but proved too expensive to be commercially successful. They were further developed by John Boyd Dunlop in 1888, and adopted for bicycles. The French rubber manufacturer Michelin fitted pneumatic tyres to a Peugeot motor car in 1895.

word processor COMPUTER system designed to manipulate text and, often, illustration. Modern word-processing software can produce sophisticated documents in a range of typefaces; it is often used for 'desk-top publishing'.

Wright brothers Wilbur (1867-1912) and Orville (1871-1948) Wright – American pioneers of flight, who made the first powered flight on December 17, 1903, at Kill Devil Hill, near Kitty Hawk, North Carolina. On its maiden voyage, their aircraft, *Flyer*, flew for 12 seconds against a strong wind and covered 120 ft (37 m).

Zeppelin, Count Ferdinand von (1838-1917) German pioneer of the rigid, metal-framed airship. In 1900 Zeppelin built his first cigar-shaped craft – 420 ft (128 m) long, with an aluminium frame covered with cotton. The craft contained huge bags of hydrogen, which is lighter than air, to provide lift. During World War I he went on to supply many 'zeppelins' for military use, some of which made bombing raids over Britain.
⚓ Travel by airship was fashionable during the 1930s, even though 48 people died when Britain's *R101* crashed in 1930. However, in 1937 the *Hindenburg*, the world's largest airship, burst into flames, signalling the end of the airship era.

Zworykin, Vladimir (1889-1982) Russian-born American physicist who in 1923 invented the iconoscope, the first electronic television camera tube. Zworykin's system soon superseded the mechanical system of John Logie BAIRD. He also made important contributions to the development of the electron MICROSCOPE.

INDEX

*Page numbers in **bold** type indicate a main entry on a subject; page numbers in roman type indicate additional references. Page numbers in italic type indicate an illustration.*

A

Aalto, Aalvar **154**
'Abandon all hope, ye who enter here' **62**
Abba **336**
Abbassids **220**, 226
abbey **154**
Abbott and Costello **308**
abbreviation **10**
abdication crisis **188**
Abercrombie, Sir Patrick **154**
Aberdeen **398**
Aberfan **398**
Abergavenny **398**
Aberystwyth **398**
Abominable Dr Phibes, The 329
Abominable Snowman **76**
Aboriginals **170**, 177, 179, 183, 429
abortion **494**
Abraham **92**, 104, 179
Abraham Lincoln 319
Abrahams, Harold **362**
Absalom, Absalom! 40
Absalom and Achitophel 39
Absence of Malice 327
absolute monarchy **260**
absolute zero **522**, 527, 534, 546
absolution **92**
abstract art **118**
Abu Dhabi 458
Abuja, Nigeria 447
Abu Simbel 248
AC *see* alternating current
Academy Award 328
Acapulco **426**
acceleration **522**, 531
accent **10**
  acute **10**
  cedilla **12**
  circumflex **12**
  diaeresis **15**
  grave **17**
  tilde **29**
  umlaut **30**
Accident 310, 324
accounts **290**
Accra **439**
Accused, The 317
Ace in the Hole 315, 334
Achebe, Chinua **32**
Achilles *68*, **76**
  and the tortoise 548

Achilles' heel **10**, 76
Achilles tendon **494**
acid **522**, 535, 540
acid rain **464**
acid test **10**
acne **494**
Aconcagua 427
acquired characteristics **478**, 484
acronym **10**
acropolis **154**
Acropolis, Athens 154
acrylic **118**
actinide series 540, *541*
actinium *see* periodic table **541**
Actium, Battle of **220**
active voice **10**
Acts of Parliament **260**, 286
  Consumer Credit (1947) 292
  Financial Services 291
  Parliament (1911) 203
  Poor Law Amendment 218
  Prevention of Terrorism 191
  Race Relations (1976) 185
  Reform 199, 201, **212**, 213
  Stamp 253
  Test **215**
  Tithe Commutation 215
  of Uniformity 95, 108
  of Union **216**
actuary **290**
acupuncture **494**
acute illness **494**
AD (*anno Domini*) **10**
adage **10**
adagio **350**
Adam, Robert **154**, 163, 421
Adam and Eve **92**, 100, 109
Adam Bede 39
Adams, Ansel **118**
Adams, Gerry 285
Adams, John **220**
Adams, John Quincy 220
Adam's apple 507
Adam's Rib 320
adaptation **478**
Addams, Charles 308
Addams Family, The **308**
addiction, alcohol 494, 495
addiction, drug **502**, 503
Addis Ababa 437
Addison, Joseph **32**
Aden **426**
Adenauer, Konrad **220**, 438
adenoids **494**
ad hoc **10**
adjective **10**
ad lib **10**
ad nauseam **10**
adobe **154**
adolescence 515
Adonais 54
Adonis **76**
Adoration of the Magi, The Leonardo da Vinci 132
adrenaline **494**, 506

adverb **10**
Ae Fond Kiss 36
Aegean Sea **426**
Aegisthus 76
Aeneas **76**
Aeneid **62**
aerobic *see* respiration
aerodynamics **522**
aerofoil **550**, 557, 558
aerolites (meteorites) 470
aeroplane 522, **550**, 563
aerosol can **550**
Aeschylus **62**, 87
Aesop **62**
Aesop's Fables **62**
aesthetes **62**
aestivation **478**
affidavit **260**
Affluent Society, The 295
Afghanistan **426**
Africa, map of *426 see also* individual countries
Africa, South **454**, 455, independence 241
  Orange Free State and 191
  sanctions against 284
African Queen, The **308**, 310, 320
African Unity, Organisation of (OAU) 237
Afrikaners **170**, 224, 454
Afro-Caribbean **170**
Aga Khan 114
Agamemnon, King **76**, 81
Agamemnon 73
Agassi, Andre **362**
ageing **494**
age of consent **170**
Age of Innocence, The 330
Age of Reason 109
aggression **478**
Agincourt, Battle of **188**, 202
Aglaia 82
Agnes Grey 35
agnosticism **92**
Agony and the Ecstasy, The 320
agreement **10**
agricultural revolution **188**
Agrippina 228
Ahura Mazda 116
Aïda **353**
AIDS **494**, *495*, 507
Airbus **550**
air conditioning 469
aircraft **550** 552, 563
Aire, River 411, 418
air mass **464**
airship(s) 566
air traffic control 561
Ajaccio, Corsica 435
Akashi-Kaikyo Bridge **154**
Akbar, Mogul emperor 244
al-Abbas 220
Alamein, Battles of **188**, 196
Alam Halfa 188
Alamo, San Antonio 457
Alamo, The 333
Alamogordo bombing range 560
alarm systems 558

Alaska **426**
Alba, Italy 395
Alban, St 417
Albania 223, 244, **426**
Albee, Edward 59
Albert, Prince **188**, *201*, *216*
Albert Dock, Liverpool 411
Albert Hall 410
Alberti, Leone Battista **154**
Albert Memorial 166, 188
Albigensian Crusade **220**
Albigensians 95
albino 510
Albinoni, Tomaso Giovanni **336**
Alcatraz 452
Alcázar 453
Alchemist, The 44
alchemy **76**
Alcock and Brown **188**
alcohol **522**
Alcoholics Anonymous (AA) 177, **495**
alcoholism 174, **494**, 513
Alcott, Louisa May **32**
Alda, Alan 325
Aldabra 453
Aldeburgh **398**
Aldeburgh Music Festival 339
al dente **390**
Aldermaston **398**
Alderney 434
Aldrin, Edwin 'Buzz' *550*
aleatory music 340
Alecto 81
Alen, Markku *381*
Aleut **170**
Aleutian Islands 170, **426**
A levels **170**
Alexander the Great 14, 93, **220**, 236, 426
Alexander VI, Pope 224
Alexandra, Tsarina 505
Alexandria 220, 251, **426**
Alexandria, Pharos at 251
Alexei, Prince 249
Alfano, Franco 355
Alfa-Romeo 370
Alfie 311
Alfred Hitchcock Presents 320
Alfred Jewel, the 188
Alfred the Great **188**, 216, 423
algae 468, **478**, 490
algebra **522**
Algeria 231, **426**, 438
Alhambra, The **154**, 244
Ali, Muhammad **362**, 367
Ali, Mohammed Pasha 163
Alice Doesn't Live Here Any More 317
Alice's Adventures in Wonderland **32**, 37
Alice Springs **426**
alienation **170**
aliphatic compounds 539
alkali **522**, 524, 535
All About Eve 313, 326
Allah **92**,103
allegory **62**
allegretto **350**

allegro **350**
Allen, Woody **308**
Allende, Salvador **220**
All England Lawn Tennis Club 424
allergy **495**
All For Love 39
Allies **220**
alligators 490
All My Sons 47
alloy **522**
All Quiet on the Western Front **62**, **308**
All the President's Men 256, 329
allusion **10**
Alma-Ata, Kazakhstan 442
Almagest (Ptolemy) 542
alma mater **10**
Aln, River 398
Alnwick 398
Alnwick Castle 398
alpha particles 542
Alpine ski racing 383
Alps 471
Alsace 233
alternating current (AC) **522**, 554, 555, 561
alternation of generations **478**, 485, 488
alternative medicine **495**
Alternative Service Book 95
Althorp 398
altitude sickness 464
alto **336**
Alton Towers 398
aluminium *see also* periodic table **541**
  alloys 522
  recycling of 561
alveoli 515
Always 320
Alzheimer's disease **495**, 501
Amadeus 53, **308**, 330
Amazon **76**, 83, **426**, 432
Amazonian Indians 183
Ambassadors, The 43
amber 545
ambiguity **10**
ambrosia **76**
America *see* America, Central; America, North; America, South; United States of America
America, Central, map of *454*
America, North 232
  Canada **443**, 447, 448
  Depression 231, 256, 459
  highest mountain in 426
  map of *447*
  Pilgrim Fathers 243
  slavery in 28
  United States of **458**
America, South, map of *454*
American Civil War **220**, 226, 229, 235, 459
American constitution 105, 261, 275, 285
American Declaration of Independence **231**, 233
American football **362**, 386
American Gigolo 318

American Indian **170**
American in Paris, An **308**, 344
Americans, Native **182**, 183
American War of Independence **220**, 225, 242, 249, 253, 256
America's Cup **362**
americium *see* periodic table **541**
Amies, Sir Hardy **118**
Amin, Idi **220**, 458
amino acids **478**, 484, 488, 490
Amis, Kingsley **32**
Amis, Martin **32**
Amish **92**
Amman **442**
ammonia **524**
Amnesty International **260**
amniocentesis **495**
amoeba **478**, 490
Amoretti **55**
amoroso **350**
amp, ampere **522**, 529
Ampère, André-Marie **522**
ampersand **10**
amphetamine **518**
amphibians **478**, *479*
amphitheatre **154**
amplifier **550**
amplitude **522**, 548
Amritsar **426**, 450
Amsterdam **427**
Amundsen, Roald **221**, 427, 448
Anabaptists **92**
anabolism **510**
anaemia **495**, 509
anaerobic *see* respiration
anaesthetic **495**
anagram **10**
Anaheim **443**
Analects **96**
analogy **10**
analytical geometry **526**, 532
anarchism **260**
Anastasia, Grand Duchess 251
Anastasia **309**, 349
Anatolia **458**
Anatomy Lesson of Dr Tulp, The 143
Anatomy of a Murder **331**, 343
ANC (African National Congress) **260**
Anchorage, Alaska **426**
Anchors Aweigh 348
ancien régime **221**
Ancient Mariner, The Rime of the **52**
Ancient of Days, The **34**
Andalucía **453**, 455
andante **350**
Andersen, Hans Christian **62**, 435
Anderson Tapes, The 313
Andes **427**, 437, 471
And God Created Woman 309
Andorra **427**, 450
Andrews, Anthony 311

Andrews, Joseph 40
Andrews, Julie **308**, 352
androgyny **170**
Aneto, Pico 450
aneurysm **495**
Anfield, Liverpool 411
Angel, Jimmy **427**
Angel Falls **427**, 459
Angelico, Fra **118**
Angels with Dirty Faces 310, 311
Angelus, The (Millet) 136
angina **495**, 505
angiosperms **478**, 485, *489*
Angkor **154**, 433
Angkor Wat *102*
Anglesey **398**
Anglican communion **92**, 99
Anglicanism **96**
angling **363**
Anglo-Catholicism 109
Anglo-Irish Agreement **260**, 270
Anglo Saxon, architecture **154**
Anglo-Saxon Attitudes 60
Anglo-Saxons 48, **188**
Angola **427**
Angostura bitters **390**
Angry Young Men **32**
anima 180
animal **478**
    cells **480**, *481*
    conditioning 174
    growth **486**
    kingdom *479*
    migration **488**
Animal Crackers 325
Animal Farm **32**, 48
Animal Liberation Front 170
animal rights **170**
animato **350**
animism **92**
animus 180
anion 534
anise **390**
aniseed **390**
Ankara 458
Anna Christie 318
Anna Karenina **62**, 318, 323
Anna of the Five Towns 33
Anne, Queen **188**, 206, 284, 401
annelids **479**
Anne of Cleves 196, 202
Anne of Green Gables **32**
Annie Get Your Gun 338
Annie Hall 308
Annigoni, Pietro **118**
annual (flower) **479**
Annual General Meeting (AGM) **290**
Annual Percentage Rates (APR) **290**
annual report **290**
annuity **290**
annunciation **92**
Annunciation, Botticelli's *92*
annus mirabilis **10**
anode **522**, 529
anonymous **10**
anorexia nervosa **495**

Anouilh, Jean 190
Anschluss **221**
Antananarivo 444
Antarctica **427**, 469, 470, 471
Antarctic Treaty (1959) 427
ante- **10**
antelopes **390**, *448*
antennae **479**
anther *485*, 489
Antony, Mark 220, 228
anthrax 504, 513
anthropology **170**, 181
anti- **10**
antibacterial drugs 508
antibiotic **495**, 514
antibodies **496**, 507
Antichrist **93**
anticoagulant **496**
anticyclone **464**, 467
Antigone **76**
Antigone **62**
antimatter **522**
antimony *see* periodic table **541**
antipasto **390**
anti-Semitism **170**, 179, 207, 232
antiseptics 508
antisocial personality **171**
antithesis **10**
Antony and Cleopatra **32**, 314, 321
antonym **10**
Antrim 447
ants 491
Antwerp 430
anxiety 514
Anything Goes 355
apartheid 255, **260**, 455
Apartment, The **323**, 324, 334
Apatosaurus 483
apes 490
aphorism **11**
Aphrodite (Venus) **76**, 83, 87, 90
apocalypse **93**
Apocalypse Now, **308**, 311
Apocrypha **93**
Apollo (god) **76**, 85,108
Apollonius 527
Apollo Project 221, 537, **550**, 551
a posteriori **93**
apostles **93**, 101
Apostles' Creed **93**
apostolic succession **93**, 110
apostrophe **11**
appeal courts **260**
appearance and reality **93**
appeasement **188**
Appellation Contrôlée (AC) **396**
appendix **496**
apple of discord **76**, 83
appliqué 148
Après-Midi d'un Faune, L' 69
a priori **93**
apropos **11**
aptitude test **171**
aqua- **11**
aqualung **550**

Aquarius *90*, 548
Aquarius, Age of 183
aquavit **390**
aqueducts **154**
Aquinas, St Thomas *93*, 108
Arabian Nights, The **62**
Arabic language 185
arabic numerals **522**
Arab League **261**
Arabs **171**
    Israel and 226, 236, 244, 245, 258, **261**
arachnids **479**
Arafat, Yasser **261**, 281
Aragon 233
Aral Sea **427**, 459
Ararat **427**
Arawak 461
arbitrage **290**
Arbroath **398**
    Declaration of 398
    'smokies' 398
Arbus, Diane **118**
Arcadia 56
Arc de Triomphe 449
arch- **11**
arch **155**
archaeology 181
archaism **11**
Archer, Lord Jeffrey **32**, 408
Archers, The **308**
archetypes 173
Archimedes **522**, *523*
Architects' Collaborative (TAC), The 161
Arctic **427**
    Ocean 427
Argand, Ami 559
Argentina 198, 247, **427**,449
    see also Falklands War
Argo 77, 83
argon *see* periodic table 538, **541**
Argonauts 77, 84
argot **11**
aria **336**
Arianism **93**
Arians 93
Arias, Roberto 344
Aries *90*, 548
Aristophanes **62**, 71
Aristotle 64, **93**, 106, **523**
arithmetic progression 532
Arius, Bishop 93
Arizona **427** *474*
Arjuna, Prince 94
Arkle **363**
Ark of the Covenant **93**
Armada, Spanish **189**, 197, 198, 199, 455
Armageddon **93**
Armagh 447
Armagnac **390**
Armani, Giorgio *118*
Armenia 459
Armistice Day 257
Arms and the Man 54
arms control **261**, 267
arms race **261**
Armstrong, Louis **336**

Armstrong, Neil **221**, *550*
Armstrong, Sir Robert 263
Arno, River *438*, 450
Arnold, Kenneth 89
Arnold, Matthew **32**
Arnold, Dr Thomas 32, 417
aromatic compounds **524**, 539
Arouet, François-Marie *see* Voltaire 74
Around the World in Eighty Days 62, *63*, 327
Arp, Hans, 123
Arran **398**
arranged marriage **171**
Arrangement in Gray and Black 152
Ars Amatoria 71
Arsenal Football Club 424
arsenic *see* periodic table **541**
Arsenic and Old Lace 319
art, modern **136**
Art Deco
    architecture **155**
    art **118**
Artemis **77**
arteries **496**, 498, *499*, 500
art for art's sake **118**
art galleries **126**
art galleries and museums of the world **126**
arthritis **496**
arthropod **479**, 480, 485
Arthur, King **77**, 84, 401, 418, 421
Arthur 318
Arthur's Seat **398**
artichoke **390**
article **11**
artificial intelligence **550**
Artiodactyla 490
Art Nouveau
    architecture **155**
    art **118**, *149*
Arts and Crafts Movement **118**, **155**
arugula (rocket) 395
Arup, Sir Ove **155**, 167
Aryans **171**
asafetida 390
Ascension Island **428**, 452
asceticism **93**
ascorbic acid 520
Ascot, Royal **363**
Ashbourne **398**
Ashcroft, Dame Peggy **308**
Ashdown, Battle of 423
Ashdown, Paddy 276
Ashes, The, *363*
Ashkenazy, Vladimir **336**
Ashley, Laura **119**
Ashton, Sir Frederick **336**
Ashur 457
Asia, map of *428*
    see also individual countries
As I Lay Dying 40
Asimov, Isaac **32**
Asphalt Jungle, The 321, 326
Asquith, Herbert Henry **189**
Assad, Hafez al- **261**
assembly line **290**

assets 290
   liquid 298
asset stripping 290
assimilation 171
Associated Newspapers 328
Assyria 221, 457
Astaire, Adele 336
Astaire, Fred 318, 336
astatine see periodic table 541
Astérix 63
asteroid 483, 523
asthma 496
astigmatism 503
As Time Goes By 312
Asti Spumante 396
Astor, Lord 211
Astor, Viscountess (Nancy) 189
Astor family 404
astral body 77
astral plane 77
astral projection 77
astrology 77, 90, 548
   see also Zodiac, and
   individual signs
Astrophel and Stella 55
Asturias 455
Asunción 449
Aswan High Dam 428
As You Like It 72
Atacama Desert 467
Atatürk, Kemal 221, 458
à terre (ballet) 337
atheism 93
Athena 77, 83-8
Athens 221, 236, 243, 247, 267, 428
atherosclerosis 496
athletics 363, 369, 379
   see also individual sports
   and athletes
Atlanta 428
Atlantic City 323
Atlantic Ocean 428
Atlantis 77
Atlas 78
Atlas Mountains 445
atmosphere 464, 467, 469, 472, 475
atmospheric pressure 464, 476
atoll 465
atom 523
   nucleus 523, 529
   smasher see particle
     accelerator
   splitting 543
   see also nuclear energy;
    nuclear fission
atom bomb 221, 242, 254, 529, 539, 560
   see also Hiroshima;
    Nagasaki
atomic mass 534
   see also atomic weight
atomic number 523
Atomic Weapons Research
   Establishment 265, 398
atomic weight 523, 537
A Town Like Alice 426
atrium 155
atrophy 496
Atropos 81

Attenborough, Sir David 309
Attenborough, Lord Richard 235, 309, 321
Attila the Hun 221
Attlee, Clement 189, 195, 270, 276, 288
Attorney General 261
Atwood, Margaret 32
Aubusson factory 148
Aubrey, John 88
Auchinleck, General Claude 188
Auckland 447
Auden, W. H. 32
audit 290
Audrey Rose 321
Auer, Carl 559
au fait 11
Augean Stables 78, 83
au gratin 390, 395
Augustan writers 33, 221
Augustine of Canterbury, St 189, 236
Augustine St 94
Augustus Caesar 33, 173, 221
Auld Lang Syne 36
'Auld Reekie' (Edinburgh) 406
Aunt Sally 11
aurora 464, 544
Aurora Leigh 35
Auschwitz 222, 229, 449, 450
Auslese wine 396
Austen, Jane 33, 39
Austerlitz, Battle of 222
Austin, Texas 456
Australia 170, 429
   Gallipoli 234
   Great Barrier Reef 466
   map of 429
Australian Ballet, The 343
Australopithecus 181
Austria 221, 429
Austria-Hungary 222
Austrian Succession, War of the 222, 239
Austro-Hungarian Empire 222, 233, 429, 460
authoritarianism 261
autism 496
auto- 11
autotroph 479
auxins 489
Avalon 78
avant-garde 11, 358
Ave Atque Vale 56
Avebury Stone Circle 398
Avengers, The 309
average (statistics) 523, 536
Aviemore 399
Avignon papacy 222
Avon 399
Avon, River 399
AWACS (airborne warning and control system) 550
Awdry, Reverend W. 57
Axe, River 399, 424
axiom 523
axis 523
Axis coalition 222
Axminster 399

ayatollah 94
Ayer, A. J. 94,
Ayers Rock 429
Ayr 399
Azerbaijan 429
Aztecs 222, 454

B

B2 stealth bomber 563
Baader, Andreas 222
Baader-Meinhof 222
Baal 94
Ba'ath Party 284
Babar the Elephant 63
Babbage, Charles 551
Babel, Tower of 223
Babes in Arms 310, 318
Babes on Broadway 318
babies
   temperature of 518
   whooping cough in 520
baby boom 171
Babylon 223, 437
Babylon, Hanging Gardens of 246, 251
Babylonian exile 223
Bacall, Lauren 277, 310
Bacchae, The 63
Bacchanalia 78
Bacchus 78
Bach, Carl Philipp Emanuel 337
Bach, Johann Christian 337
Bach, Johann Sebastian 105, 336, 337, 340
Bacharach, Burt 337
Bachelor Mother 327
backbencher 261
back-formation 11
backgammon 363
background radiation 523
back pain 497
Bacon, Francis (1561-1626) 54, 189
Bacon, Francis (1909-1992) 119, 124
bacteria 479, 480
Bad 330
bad breath 505
Bad Child's Book of Beasts, A 33
Bad Day at Black Rock 333
bad debt 290
Baden-Baden 431
Baden-Powell, Robert 189, 415
Badminton 399
Badminton Horse Trials 363
Baekeland, Leo 551
Baez, Joan 344
Baffin Island 433
bagel 390
Baghdad 429
Bahaism 94
Bahamas 429

Bahrain 429
Baikal, Lake 429
bail 261, 283
Bailey, David 119
Bain, Alexander 556
Baird, John Logie 551, 565
Bait, The 37
Bakelite 551, 561
Baker, Chet 342
Baker, Richard 327
Baker, Tom 315
Baker Street 399
Bakewell 399
   tarts 399
baklava 390
Baku 429, 560
Balaclava, Battle of 194, 229
balance of payments 290
balance of power 262
balance sheet 290
Balanchine, George 337
Balboa, Vasco Nunez de 223
Bald Prima-Donna, The 69
Baldwin, James 33
Baldwin, Stanley 189
Balearic Islands 455
Balfour, Arthur James 189
Balfour Declaration (1917) 189, 288
Bali 429, 440
Balkanisation 223
Balkans 429
Balkan Wars 223
Ball, John 209
ballad 63
Ballad of Reading Gaol, The 59
Balladur, Edouard 279
Ballantyne, R.M. 46
Ballard, J.G. 33
Ballesteros, Severiano 363, 370
ballet 337
Ballets Russes 337, 342, 348, 352, 354, 355, 357
ballet terms 337
ball lightning 78
balloon, hot-air 560
Balmoral 399
balsa 492
balsamic vinegar 395
balthazar (bottle) 396
Baltic Sea 237
Baltic states 251
Balzac, Honoré de 63,
Bambi 315
Bamburgh 399
Bananas 308
Banbury 399
Banda, Dr Hastings 444
Bandaranaike, Sirimavo 455
Banff National Park 451
Bangkok 429
Bangladesh 224, 429, 430
   tidal wave (1970) 430
Bangor 399
bank, central 292, 303
Bank, World 306
banking 294, 298
Bank of England 290, 301, 303
bank rate 300

bankruptcy 290
Banks, Gordon 383
Banks, Sir Joseph 432
Bannister, Sir Roger 363, 377
Bannockburn, Battle of 189
Banqueting House, London 62, 194
Bantu 171
Bantustans 260
baptism 94,
Baptist churches 94
bar (law) 262
Barbados 461
Barbarella 317
barbarians 223
Barbera, Joe 332
Barcelona 429, 455
Barchester Chronicles 58
Barchester Towers 58
bar code 551
Bar Council 262
Bardot, Brigitte 309
Barenboim, Daniel 343
bar graph 532
baritone 337
barium see periodic table 541
bark 492
Barker, Lex 332
bar mitzvah 94, 179
Barnacle Bill 319
Barnard, Dr Christiaan 519
Barnet, Battle of 217
barometer 476, 525
baroque architecture 155
baroque art 119
baroque music 337, 355
Barraud, Francis 29
Barretts of Wimpole Street, The 35
Barrie, Sir J.M. 33
barristers 262
Barrow-in-Furness 399
Barry, Sir Charles 155, 404
Barry Lyndon 330
Bart, Lionel 352
Bartók, Béla 337, 351
baryons 546
Baryshnikov, Mikhail 348
basal cell carcinoma 517
basalt 474
base 524, 525
baseball 364, 381
Basic Instinct 315
Basie, Count 337
basil 393
basilica 155
Basilica of Our Lady of Peace, Yamoussoukro 155
basketball 364
Basle 451, 455
Basques 450, 455
bas-relief 119
Bass Rock 399
bass voice 337
Bastille 223, 449
Bastille Day 223
bat 484, 485
Bates, Alan 32, 60
Bath 400
   Abbey 400
   Marquess of 412

Roman Baths 400
Royal Crescent 400
Bath, The (Cassat) 121
Bather, The (Ingres) *129*
Bath Oliver biscuits 400
Batista Fulgencio, President 230, 263
Batman **309**, 327
bat mitzvah 94
Baton Rouge 443
batterie (ballet) **337**
battery 529, **551**
Battle, East Sussex 409
battlements **155**
battles *see* names of individual battles
Battleship Potemkin, The **309**
battu (ballet) **337**
Baudelaire, Charles Pierre **63**
Bauhaus School
architecture **156**, 161, 163, 257
art **119**, 130
Baum, Frank L. 334
Bavaria **430**
Bavarian State Art Gallery 126
Bay Area Rapid Transit (BART) 167
Bayeux Tapestry **189**
bay leaves *393*
Bay of Bengal **430**
Bay of Fundy 475
Bay of Pigs **223**
Bayreuth opera house 360
BBC (British Broadcasting Corporation) **309**, 327, 551, 561
BC (Before Christ) **11**
BCE (Before the Common Era) 11
Beach Boys, The **337**
Beachy Head **400**
Beagle, HMS 483
beagling 370
Beamon, Bob 376
Beano, The 313
bear **290**
Beardsley, Aubrey **119**
bear market 291
béarnaise sauce **390**
Beasts and Superbeasts 52
Beatles, The **338**, 357, 411
Beaton, Sir Cecil **119**
Beat the Devil 321
Beatty, Warren **309**, 311
Beaufort, Admiral F.B. 465
Beaufort, Dukes of 399
Beaufort scale **465**, 469, 476
Beau Geste 426
Beaujolais **396**
Beaulieu **400**
Beaumarchais 66
Beaumaris 398, **400**
Beauvoir, Simone de **63**
Beaverbrook, Lord **190**
bebop **338**, 354
béchamel **390**
Becker, Boris **364**
Becket, Thomas **190**, 202, 403
Becket 190, 328

Beckett, Samuel **63**,
Becky Sharp **309**
Becquerel, Henri 542
Bed and Board 333
Bede, The Venerable 158, **190**
Bedford **400**
Dukes of 424
Bedford Park, London 166
Bedivere, Sir 77, 81
Bedouins 171
Bed Sitting Room, The 326
bee *491*
see also social insects
Beecham, Sir Thomas **338**, 342
Beeching, Richard 211
'beefeaters' 422
beer 436, 445, 485
Beerbohm, Sir Max **33**
Beethoven, Ludwig van 73, **338**, 345
Beeton, Mrs (Isabella) **390**
beetroot soup 390
Beggar's Opera, The **33**
Begin, Menachem **223**
Beguiled, The 316
behaviour
animal 184, 185
human 174, 184, 185
behaviourism **171**
Beijing 254, **430**
Being and Nothingness (Sartre) 113
Being There 330
Beirut **430**, 443
Belarus 459
Belfast **430**
see also Ireland, Northern
Belfast, HMS *422*
Belgium **430**
Rwanda and 451
Belgrade **430**, 462
Belgrano, General **190**
belief **94**
Belize **430**
Bell, Alexander Graham **551**, 555, 565
Bell, Derek 375
Bell, The 47
Bell, Vanessa 34, 60
'bell' curve 538
Bellerophon, HMS *245*
Bellerophon (mythology) 86
Bellingham, John 209
Bellini, Giovanni **119**, 133, 460
Bell Jar, The 50
Belloc, Hilaire **33**
Bellow, Saul **35**
Belmopan, Belize 430
Belsen 229, 233
Benbecula **400**
Ben Bella, Ahmed **223**
bench (law) **262**
benchers 262
Benchley, Peter **33**
Bend in the River, A 47
bene- **11**
Benedict, St **94**, 154
Benedictines 94
Bengal 433
Benghazi 443

Benguela Current *471*
Ben-Gurion, David **223**
Ben Hur **320**, 324
Benidorm 455
benign **497**
Ben Macdui **400**
Benn, Tony **262**
Bennett, Alan **33**
Bennett, Arnold **33**, 416
Bennett, Tony 342
Ben Nevis **400**
Bentham, Jeremy **94**
Bentine, Michael 319
Benz, Karl Friedrich 552
Beowulf **34**, 48
Beqa'a valley 443
Berbers 426, 452
Beresford, Elizabeth 424
Bergman, Ingmar 308, **309**
Bergman, Ingrid **309**, 312, 315, 319, 330
Bering, Vitus 430
Bering Strait **430**, 459
Berkeley, Busby **310**, 317
Berkeley, George **94**
Berkeley, San Francisco 452
Berkeley, Vale of **400**
Berkeley Castle **400**
Berkeley Square 413
berkelium *see* periodic table **541**
Berkshire **400**
Berlin 249, **430**
Berlin airlift **223**
Berlin, Congress of 213, **223**
Berlin, East 264, 430
Berlin, Irving **338**
Berlin Olympic Games (1936) 379
Berlin Philharmonic Orchestra 347
Berlin Wall **223**
Berlioz, Hector **339**, 357
Bermuda **431**
Bermuda Triangle 78, **431**
Bernard of Clairvaux, Saint **224**
Berne **431**, 455
Bernini, Giovanni Lorenzo **119**, **156**
Bernstein, Carl 256
Bernstein, Leonard **339**
Berry, Sir Anthony 402
Berry, Chuck **339**, 357
Berwick-upon-Tweed **400**
beryllium *see* periodic table **541**
Besant, Annie 115, **190**
Besier, Rudolf 35
Bessemer, Henry 552, 564
Best, George **364**
Best, Pete 338
Best Years of Our Lives, The 319
beta-blockers **497**
beta radiation 542
bête noire **11**
Bethlehem 173, **431**
Betjeman, Sir John **34**
betrothal **171**
Betws-y-Coed **401**
Bevan, Aneurin ('Nye') **190**

Beveridge, Sir William **190**
Beveridge Report **190**
Beverley, Humberside **401**
Beverley Hills 443
Bevin, Ernest **190**
'Bevin boys' 190
Beyle, Henri *see* Stendhal 73
Beyond Reasonable Doubt 32
Beyond the Fringe 33
'beyond the pale' **11**
Bhagavad Gita **94**
bhaji **390**
Bhopal disaster **224**
Bhumibol, King 457
Bhutan **431**
Bhutto, Benazir 224, **262**, 449
Bhutto, Zulfikar Ali **224**, 449
Biafra **224**
Biba **119**
Bible, The **94**, 108
biblio- **11**
bicycle **551**
Bicycle Thieves **310**, 314
Biedermeier **119**
biennial (flower) **479**
'Big Apple', The 447
big bang theory **524**, 527, 536, 543
Big Broadcast of 1938, The 321
'Big Brother is watching you' **34**
Big Country, The 328
Big Foot 76
Bigger Splash, A (Hockney) *128*
Biggin Hill **401**
Biggles **34**
Big Sleep, The 36, **310**, 326
bikini 444
Bikini atoll 444
bile **497**, 507
bilharzia **497**
bilingual **11**
bilious attack 497
bill **262**
Local Government 173
private member's **282**
billiards **364**, 383
Billière, General Peter de la *237*
Billingsgate **401**
Billion Dollar Brain 311
bill of exchange **291**, 306
Bill of Rights (English) **190**
Bill of Rights (US) **224**
Billy Budd 46
Billy Cotton Band Show, The 341
Billy Liar **34**, 330
biltong **390**
binary star **524**, 539
binary system **524**
Binet, Alfred 179
Bingham, Hiram 444
bio- **11**
bioluminescence **480**
biopsy 503
biorhythms **497**
biosphere **465**
Biosphere 2 465

biotechnology 479, **552**, 556
birds **480**, 488
Birdman of Alcatraz, The 323
Birds, The **63**, *320*
Birmingham 191, **401**
Birmingham pub bombings **191**
Birmingham Royal Ballet 401
Birmingham Symphony Orchestra, City of (CBSO) 356, 401
birth
defects 499, 500, 542
multiple 511
Birthday Party, The 50
Birth of a Nation **310**, 319
Birth of the Cool, The 342
Birth of Venus 119
Bishop's Garden, Bangor 399
Bishop's Palace, Wells 423
Bisley Camp (shooting) 383
Bismarck, Prince Otto von **224**, 233, 257, 438
bismuth *see* periodic table **541**
bisque **390**
bits (binary digits) 554
Bitter Moon 329
bivalve **480**
Bizet, Georges **339**, 353
Black, Cilla 310
Black and Tans **191**
Black Beauty **34**
blackberry **490**, 491
Black Book of Carmarthen 398
'black box' **552**
black comedy **65**
black consciousness **171**
Black Country **401**
blackcurrant liqueur (cassis) 391
Black Death **224**, 498, 507
black economy **291**
Black Forest **431**
Blackheath **401**
Black Hills, South Dakota 445
black hole **524**, **532**, 534, 542
Black Hole of Calcutta **191**, 433
blackjack **364**
Blackmail 320
Blackman, Honor 309
black market 291, 296
Blackmore, R.D. 406
Black Mountains **401**
Black Painting (Goya) 127
Black Pirate, The 316
Blackpool **401**
Black Power movement 228
Black Prince **191**
Black Prince, The 47
black pudding 391
Black Rod **262**
Black Sabbath (band) 346
Black Sea 391, **431**, 436, 451
Black September 445

Black Shirts *207*, **224**
Blade Runner **310**, 317
Blair, Tony 276
Blake, George **191**
Blake, Peter **120**,
Blake, William **34**, *36*, 58
blank verse **34**
blanquette **390**
Blarney Stone **78**
blast furnace **552**, 564
Blavatsky, Madame H.P.
   115
Blaze 327
Bleak House **34**
Bled, Lake 454
Blenheim, Battle of 206,
   224, 401
Blenheim Palace 167, 206,
   401
Blessed Damozel, The 52
Bletchley Park **401**
Blind Date **310**
blindness 503
blini **390**
Bliss, and Other Stories 46
Blithe Spirit 323, 330
Blitz **191**
blitzkrieg **224**
Blixen, Karen *63*
Bloemfontein 454
Blonde Venus 319
blood 495, **497**, 505
   cells *497*
   circulation of 505
   clotting 496, 497, 503,
     518
   typing 497
Blood and Sand 333
blood group **497**
blood poisoning 498
blood pressure **497**, 498,
   503, 505, 512, 520
blood transfusion 497
blood vessels **498**, *499*, 500
Blood Wedding 69
Bloody Assizes **191**
'Bloody Mary' *see* Mary I
Bloom, Claire 311
Bloomsbury Group **34**
Blow Up 329
Blue Angel, The 315
Bluebeard **78**
Bluebird *366*
blue blood **11**
blue chip **291**
blue-collar *172*, 186
Blue Danube, The 359
Blue Lamp, The 310
Blue Mosque, Istanbul 441
Blue Mountains, Australia
   431
Blue Mountains, Jamaica
   431, 441
Blue Peter **310**
Blue Ridge mountains 460
blues (music) **339**, 357, 360
blue-stocking **172**
blue whale 487, 489
Blunt, Anthony 206
blush (rosé wine) 396
Blyton, Enid **34**
BMW (Bayerische Motoren
   Werke) 430
boarding schools 175

Boardman, Chris 368, 552
boardsailing 387
Boat, The 322
'Boat people' *185*, 460
bobsleighing **364**, 452
Boccaccio, Giovanni **64**
bodhisattva Avalokitshvara
   97
bodhisattvas 95
Bodleian Library, Oxford
   414
Bodmin Moor **401**
Bodrum **431**, 458
Bodyguard, The 313
body language **172**
Boeing 550, 558
Boers **224**, 454-5
   Great Trek 191, 236, 455
Boer War **191**, 195, 201,
   229, 241, 455
Boethius, Anicius 95
bog 465
Bogarde, Sir Dirk **310**, 314,
   324
Bogart, Humphrey *277*,
   308, **310**, 311, 312, 321
Bognor Regis **401**
Bogotá **431**
Bohemia 238, 253, 436
bohemian **120**
Bohr, Niels 523, **524**
boiling point **524**
Bokassa, Jean-Bedel 434
Bolero 356
Boleyn, Anne **191** 202
Bolger, Ray 334
Bolívar, Simón **224**, 431
Bolivia **431**, 457
Bologna **431**
bolognese sauce 431
Bolsheviks **224**, 251
Bolshoi Ballet **339**
Bolt, Robert 46, 207, 330
Bolventor 401
Bombay **431**
Bombay duck **390**
bona fides **11**
Bonanno 162
Bonanza Creek 433
Bonaparte, Joseph 247
Bonaparte, Napoleon 208,
   215, 234, 239, **245**
bond, chemical **291**, **524**,
   547
Bond, James **310**
Bondi, Hermann 546
Bondi Beach 456
bonding **172**
bone(s) 512, *516*, 517
bone marrow transplant
   515
Bonham, John 348
Bonifacio, Corsica *435*
bon mot **11**
Bonn **431**
Bonnard, Pierre **120**, 139
Bonner, Yelena 251
Bonneville Salt Flats 459
Bonnie and Clyde **311**
Bonnie Prince Charlie
   (Charles Edward Stuart)
   191, 400, 419
Bonnie Scotland 323
bony fish *see* fish

Bonynge, Richard 359
boogie woogie 342, 356
Booker prize **34**, 41, 47, 52
Book of Changes 103
Book of Common Prayer
   95, 194, 196
Book of Hours 193
Book of Household
   Management 390
Book of Kells 227, 436
Book of Mormon 107
Book of Shadows 90
Book of the Dead **78**
Boole, George 525
Boolean algebra **525**, 544
Booth, Connie 316
Booth, Evangeline 191
Booth, John Wilkes 242
Booth, Kate 191
Booth, William *113*, **191**
Boothroyd, Betty *286*
Bordeaux **431**
   wine **396**
Border, Allan **365**
Borg, Bjorn, **365**
Borges, Jorge Luis *64*, 69
Borgia, Cesare 224
Borgia, Lucrezia 224
Borgia, Rodrigo 224
Borgias **224**
Bormann, Martin **224**
Borneo **431**
Born in the USA 359
Born on the 4th of July 313
boron *see* periodic table **541**
borscht **390**
Bosanquet, Reginald *327*
Bosch, Hieronymus *114*,
   120
Bosnia-Herzegovina **431**,
   452, 462
bosons 546
Bosporus **431**, 458
Boston **431**
Bostonians, The 43
Boston Tea Party **225**, 431
Boswell, James **34**, 43
Bosworth Field, Battle of
   192, 202
Botany Bay **432**, 456
Botham, Ian **365**
Bothwell, Earl of 207
Botswana **432**, 442, 448
Botticelli, Sandro 76, *92*,
   119, **120**
bottle sizes,396
botulism 504
Boublil, Alain 348
Boucher, François **120**, 124
Boudicca **192**, 404
boudin blanc **390**
boudin noir **391**
bouillabaisse **391**
Boulogne 407
Boulting, John and Roy
   311
bouquet garni *393*
Bourbons **225**
bourguignon **391**
Bournemouth **401**
Bournville **401**
Boutros-Ghali, Boutros 288
bovine spongiform
   encephalitis (BSE) 509

Bower, Doug 79
Bowie, David **339**
bowls 365
Bow Street Runners 281
Boxer Rebellion **225**
boxing 365, 380
Boycott, Geoffrey **365**
Boyle, Robert 525
Boyle's law **525**, 532
Boyne, Battle of the **192**
Boy Scout movement 415
Boys' Town 333
Boy Who Cried Wolf, The 62
brachiosaurus *483*
bracken 489
brackets **11**
Bradbury, Ray 32
Bradford, West Yorkshire
   423
Bradman, Sir Don **365**
Bradshaw railway
   timetables 565
Braemar **402**
Brahe, Tycho **525**
Brahma 95
Brahman **95**, 172
Brahms, Johannes **339**
brain **498**
   cross-section *598*
   damage 498, 500, 509,
     513, 518
Braine, John 330
brainwashing *172*, 174
brakes, car *558*
Branagh, Kenneth **311**
Branch Davidian sect 174
Brandenburg Gate 430
Brando, Marlon 308, **311**,
   312, 319
Brandt, Willy **225**
Braque, Georges **121**, 123
Brasília, Brazil **432**, 451
brass 522
Bratislava 454
Braun, Eva **225**
Braun, Wernher von **552**,
   560
Brave New World **35**
Brazil **432**, 452
   Amazonian Indians 183
Brazil Current 471
Brazzi, Rossano 323
bread
   bagel 390
   chapatti 391
   ciabatta 391
   croissant 392
   focaccia 392
   nan 394
   panettone 394
   pitta 395
   pretzel 395
breadline **172**
Breakfast at Tiffany's 320,
   350
Breakheart Pass 46
Bream, Julian **339**, 360
breast cancer 499, 509
breastfeeding 509
breathalyser **552**
breathing 515
   difficulties 496, 498, 503
Breathless 327
Brecht, Bertolt 33, *64*

Brecon Beacons 401, **402**
Brener, Marcel 156
Brer Rabbit **35**
bresaola **391**
Bresslaw, Bernard 312
Breton 432
Bretton Woods conference
   (1944) **225**
Brezhnev, Leonid **225**, 249
Brian Boru **225**
Briand, Aristide **225**
Bridal Veil Falls 447
Bride of Frankenstein, The
   317
Bride of Lammermoor, The
   53
bride price **172**
Brideshead Revisited **311**,
   319, 328, 403
bridge (architecture) **156**
Bridge of Sighs *414*, 460
Bridge on the River Kwai,
   The 319, 323, 457
Bridge Over Troubled Water
   358
Brie **391**
Brief Encounter **311**
Brief History of Time, A 533
Brigflatts, Cumbria *111*
Bright, John 196
Brighthelmstone **402**
Brighton **402**
   bomb 402
Brighton Rock 41, 309, 311
Bringing Up Baby 319, 320
Bring on the Empty Horses
   327
Brisbane 450, 461
Bristol **402**
Bristol Channel 402
Britain, Battle of **192**
Britannia Hospital 330
Britannia Royal Naval
   College, Dartmouth 405
British Broadcasting
   Corporation (BBC) **309**,
   327, 551, 561
British Empire **198**
British Expeditionary Force
   197
British Isles *see* individual
   place names
British Lions **365**, 382
British Museum 126
British National Party
   (BNP) 270
British Railways 565
British Telecom 304
British Union of Fascists
   207, 270
Britons **172**
Brittany **432**
Britten, Benjamin **339**, 343,
   356, 398
Broadlands, Hampshire 417
Broadmoor **402**
Broads, The **402**
Broadstairs **402**
Broadway Boogie-Woogie 137
Broadway **339**, 360,
brochette **391**
bromine *see* periodic table
   541
bronchi 515

bronchitis **498**, 508
Brontë, Anne **35**, 409
Brontë, Branwell 35
Brontë, Charlotte **35**, 409
Brontë, Emily **35**, 409
Bronx 446
Bronx Tale, A 314
Bronze Age 225
Brooke, Rupert **35**, 408
Brookhaven National
     Laboratory, USA *525*
Brooklyn 446
Brookner, Anita **35**
Brooks, Mel 327
Brooks, Ray 312
broom, seeds *490*
Broome, David 383
Brothers in Law 311
Brothers Karamazov, The **64**
Brown, George **192**
Brown, James **340**
Brown, John 216
Brown, Lancelot
     'Capability' **156**, 401,
       412, 415, 418, 420
Browne, Coral 33
Browning, Elizabeth
     Barrett **35**
Browning, Robert **35**, 86
Browning Version, The 51
Brownsea Island 415
Brown Shirts 225, 253
Brown Willy, Bodmin
     Moor 401
Bruant, Aristide 149
Brubeck, Dave **340**,
Bruce, Robert 189, **192**,
     398
Bruckner, Anton **340**
Bruegel, Jan 121
Bruegel, Pieter the Elder
     121
Bruegel, Pieter the Younger
     121
Bruges 430
Brunei **432**
Brunel, Isambard Kingdom
     156, 402, 421
Brunel, Sir Marc Isambard
     156
Brunelleschi, Filippo **156**
Brunhoff, Jean de 63
Brunhoff, Laurent de 63
Brünnhilde **78**
Bruno, Frank **365**
Brussels **432**
brut (Champagne) 396
Brute Force 323
Brutus **78**, 82, 240
bryophytes *489*
bubble chamber **525**
Bubbles (Millais) 136
bubonic plague 201, 224,
     498
Buchan, John **35**
Bucharest 226, **432**, 451
Buckingham, George
     Villiers, 1st Duke of **192**
Buckingham Palace *191*,
     402
Bucklers Hard 400
Budapest **432**
Budd, Zola **365**
Buddha **95**, 108

Buddhism **95**, 99, 108, 116,
     455, 457
Buddhist monasteries 443
Budesrat 262
Budget *264*, **291**
Buenos Aires 427, **432**
Buffalo Bill **225**
buffer (chemistry) **525**
Bugs Bunny **311**
Bugsy 309
buildings, listed **162**
building societies 290
built-in obsolescence **291**
bulb (plant) **480**
Bulgaria 223, **433**
Bulge, Battle of the **225**
bulgur wheat **391**, 395
bulimia **498**
bull **291**
Bull Durham 313
Bullets or Ballots 330
bullet train 565
bullfights 455
bullion **291**
Bullitt 324
bull market **291**
Bumble, Mr *38*
Bunbury, Sir Charles 369
Bundestag **262**, 431, 438
Bundy, Ted 185
Bunker Hill, Battle of **225**
Bunter, Billy 34
Bunyan, John **35**, 50, 400
Bure, River 402
Burgess, Anthony **35**, 312
Burgess, Guy 33, **192**
Burghley, Lord 403
Burghley House **403**
Burgundy **433**
Burgundy wine **396**
Burial of Count Orgaz, The
     (El Greco) 124
Burke, Edmund 17, **192**
Burke, Thomas 210
Burkina Faso 298
burlesque 64
Burlington, Lord **156**, 157
Burlington House 157, 415
Burma **433**
Burne-Jones, Sir Edward
     121
Burnet, Sir Alastair *327*
Burns, Robert **36**, 399
Burrell Collection **126**, 408
Burroughs, Edgar Rice 332
Burroughs, William 346
burs *491*
Burton, Richard **311**, *332*,
     334
Burton, Sir Richard
     (explorer) 62
Burundi 447
Bury St Edmunds **403**
Busby, Matt **365**
'Busby Babes' 365
Bush, President George
     239, **262**, 459
Bushmen 177, 180, 442
Busman's Honeymoon 53
Butch Cassidy and the
     Sundance Kid **311**, 327,
       329, 337
Buthelezi, Chief
     Mangosuthu 455

Butler, Samuel 36
Butterfield 8 332
butterfly, metamorphosis
     488
'butterfly effect' 526
butternut 395
buttress **156**
Buxton **403**
buyer's market **291**
bylaw **262**
Byron, Lord George
     Gordon **36**
byte **554**
Byzantine
     architecture **157**
     (art) **121**
Byzantine Empire **225**, 240
Byzantium 441

C

cabal **192**
Cabaret 314
Cabernet Franc (Bordeaux
     grape) 396
Cabernet Sauvignon **396**
cabinet government **263**
Cabinet-Maker and
     Upholsterer's Guide 127
cabinet secretary **263**
cables, fibre optic 556
Cabot, John and Sebastian
     226
Cabrera 455
Cadbury, George 401
Cadbury Castle 79
Cadbury chocolate 401
cadenza **350**
cadmium *see* periodic table
     541
Caedmon 48
Caesar **226**
Caesar, Julius 13, 228, **239**
Caesar and Cleopatra 323
Caesarean section **498**
caesium *see* periodic table
     541
Cage, John **340**
Cagliari 452
Cagney, James **311**, 312,
     317
Cahn, Sammy **340**
Caine, Michael **311**, 328
Caine Mutiny, The 310, 311
Cairngorms **403**
Cairns, Australia 450
Cairo **433**
Cakes and Ale 46
Calama, Chile 467
calamares (squid) 395
calciferol 520
calcium **528**
     see also periodic table **541**
calculators, pocket 563
calculus **525**
Calcutta **433**
Calder, Alexander **121**, 130

Calder Hall 418
Caledonian Canal 410
California **433**, *468*, 472
californium *see* periodic
     table **541**
Caligula **226**, 228
caliphs **226**, 246
Callaghan, James 205, 218,
     263
Callas, Maria **340**
Calliope 85
Calloway, Cab **340**
calorie **525**, 533
Calvary 97
Calvi, Roberto 100
Calvin, John **226**
Calvinism **95**, 226
calypso 457
calzone **391**
Cam, River 403, 408
Camargue **433**, 451
cambium 492
Cambodia 281, **433**
Cambridge 183, **403**
Camden Town Group 147
Camelford 79, 421
Camelot 79
Camelot 311
Camembert **391**
camera 535, **552**, 558
Camille 318
Camlann, Battle of 77
camouflage 480
Campaign for Nuclear
     Disarmament (CND)
     112, **265**, 267
Campbell, Colen **157**
Campbell, Donald **66**
Campbell, Sir Malcolm **366**
Campbell clan 200, 408
Camp David accords 223,
     226
Campese, David **366**
Camulodunum 404
Camus, Albert **64**
Canaan 92, 94, 100, 179
Canada **433**, *447*, 448
     gold rush 433
     Plains Indian tribes 183
     shield areas 466
Canadian Mounted Police,
     Royal 433
Canaletto, Antonio **121**,
     460
canals **157**, **192**
Canaries Current *471*
Canary Islands **433**, 455
Canary Wharf, Docklands
     405
Canberra **433**
cancer *90*, 548
cancer **499**, 506, 508
     breast 499, 506, 514
     cervical 499
     drugs 499
     in children 508
     prostate 515
     skin 472, 517, 547
     treatment 527
     uterus 506
Candide **64**, 105
candidiasis (thrush) 518
Cannae, Battle of **226**
Cannery Row 55

Cannes 435
Canning, George **192**
Cannock Chase 420
cantata **340**
Canterbury **403**
Canterbury, Archbishop of
     96, 189, 190, 196
Canterbury Tales, The **36**,
     59, 190
Cantinflas 63
Canton (Guangzhou) **433**
Cantos 51
Canute **192**
CAP (Common
     Agricultural Policy) **292**,
     296, 302, 303
capacitance 531
capacitor **552**
Cape Cod Bay 444
Cape Fear 314, 326, 330
Cape of Good Hope 231,
     434
Capet, Hugh 226
Capetians 226
Cape Town **434**, 454
Cap Gris-Nez 405
capillary *499*, *500*, **525**
capital **292**
capital gain **292**
capitalism **292**
Capitalism & Freedom **294**
capital letters **12**
capital punishment **263**
Capone, Al 249, 251, 330,
     435, 452
Cappadocia 458
Capra, Frank **312**, 331
Captains Courageous 333
Car
     technology **552**, 558
     industry 297
Caracas 459
Caractacus **193**
Caravaggio, Michelangelo
     121,
carbohydrates **480**, 491
carbon **525**, 539, *541*
     carbon-14 473
     dioxide (CO_2) 464, 469,
       489, 473, 525
     monoxide (CO) 525, 553
carbon fibre 552, **553**
Carboniferous period 466
cardiac arrest 505
Cardiff **403**
Cardigan, Lord **194**
cardiology 510
care in the community **172**
Carreras, José **340**
caret **12**
Caretaker, The 50
Carey, Peter **36**
Carib 461
Caribbean 469
caricature **121**
Carlton House, London
     416
Carlyle, Thomas 177
Carmen **353**
Carnac 432
Carnarvon, Lord 255
Carnival of the Animals 357
carob **391**

Caroline of Brunswick **193**
Carolingians **226**, 233
Caron, Leslie 64, 308, 319
carotene 520
Carothers, Wallace H. 560
Carousel 356, 411
carpaccio 391
Carpathian Mountains 451
carpel 486
Carpenter, Harry 365
Carpenter, Karen 340
Carpenter, Richard 340
Carpenters, The **340**
Carpenters 52
carpetbaggers **226**
Carpetbaggers, The 52
Carracci **121**
    Agostino 121,
    Annibale 121,
    Lodovico 121
Carrao, River 427
Carrara 458
Carregwastad Point 407
Carroll, Lewis 24, 32, **36**
Carry On (film series) **312**,
    334
Carson, Violet 313
carte blanche **12**
cartel **292**, 301
Carter, Angela **36**
Carter, Howard 255
Carter, Jimmy (James) 226,
    263
Carthage 80, 94, **226**, 237,
    249, 457
Cartier-Bresson, Henri **121**
cartilage **499**
Cartland, Barbara **36**
cartoon **121**
cartouche 127
Caruso, Enrico **340**
Casa Batlló 160
Casablanca 309, **312**
Casablanca 445
Casals, Pablo **340**
Casa Milá 160
case (language) **12**
Casement, Roger **193**
Cash, Johnny **340**
casino games **366**
Casino Royale 40
Caspian Sea 391, **434**
Cassandra **79**
Cassat, Mary **121**
casseroles *see* stews
cassis 391
cassoulet 391
Cast a Dark Shadow 323
caste system **172**
Castile 233
castle (architecture) **157**
Castle Combe **403**
Castle Howard **403**
Castlereagh, Viscount 192,
    193
Castle Rushen *412*
Castletown Bay *412*
Castro, Fidel 230, **263**
CAT (Computerised Axial
    Tomography) scan 516
catabolism 510
Çatal Hüyük 458
Catalonia 455
catalyst **525**, 526

catalytic converter 553
Cat and Mouse 67
Cat and the Canary, The 321
cataract 472, **499**
catastrophe theory **525**
Catch-22 12, **36**
Catcher in the Rye, The **36**
categorical imperative 104
caterpillar *488*
Catesby, Robert 201
Cathars **95**
cathedral (architecture) 157
Catherine de Valois 215
Catherine of Aragon **193**,
    202
Catherine the Great **226**,
    451
cathode **526**, 529
Catholic Church **96**
Catholic Emancipation
    193, 200, 208, 217
Catholicism *see* Roman
    Catholicism
Cathy Come Home **312**
Cat in the Hat, The 53
cation 534
Cato **226**
Cat on a Hot Tin Roof, A 59,
    327, 332
Cato Street conspiracy **193**
Cats 39, 349
cat's-eye 553
Catullus, Gaius Valerius 64
Caucasoid peoples 171,
    172, 185
cause and effect **96**
cause célèbre **12**
caustic soda 522, 524
Cautionary Tales 33
Cavalier poets **36**
Cavaliers 195
cave **465**
caveat emptor **292**
Cavendish, Lord Frederick
    210
Cavendish Laboratory 543
caviar 391
Cavour, Count Camillo
    Bensi di **226**
Cawley, Evonne 387
Caxton, William 47, **193**
Cayman Islands 305
CD (corps diplomatique)
    267
CD *see* compact discs
CDi, interactive CD *553*
CD-ROM **553**
CE (Common Era) 10
Ceausescu, Elena 451
Ceausescu, Nicolae **226**,
    432, 451
Cecil, 1st Earl of Salisbury,
    Robert 409
Cecil, Sir William **403**
Cedars of Lebanon 443
cedilla accent **12**
cell **480**, *481*, 485, *487*
cell division **480**, *481*, 484,
    486
Cellini, Benvenuto **121**
cellphone **553**, 564
cellulite **499**
cellulose 480, **481**, 541

Celsius, Anders 526
Celsius 524, **526**, 530, 534
Celtic Twilight **36**
Celts **193**, **227**, 432
    festival of Beltane 84
Cenotaph, The 162, 423
Cenozoic era *468*
censorship 173
census **173**
centaur **79**
centi- **12**
centi- 537
centigrade 526
centipedes 479
Central African Republic
    434
    see also Africa
central bank **292**, 300
central nervous system
    (CNS) 512
Central Park, New York
    434
centre of gravity **526**
centrifugal force 526
centripetal force **526**
cephalopods **481**
Cerberus **79**, 83
cerebellum 498
cerebral cortex 498
cerebral palsy **499**
cerebrum 498
Ceres **79**, 523
cerium *see* periodic table
    541
CERN *525*, *540*
Cerne Abbas Giant **403**
Cervantes, Miguel de **64**,
    71
cervical smear **499**
cetaceans **481**
Ceylon (Sri Lanka) 455
Cézanne, Paul **121**, 142,
    450
cf **12**
CFCs (chlorofluoro-
    carbons) **465**, 550, 562
Chablis 396
chacun à son goût **12**
Chad 455
Chagall, Marc **122**
Chain, Ernst 503, 514
'Chain Home' 192
chain reaction *539*, 547
Challenger space craft 563
Challenger Deep **434**, 449
Chamberlain, Austen **193**
Chamberlain, Joseph **193**
Chamberlain, Neville 188,
    194, 244
Chambord, Château *443*
chameleons 480
Champagne 391, **396**
Champion 315
Champs Élysées 81, 449
Chance 38
chancellor of the exchequer
    263, 291
Chancery Division 273
chancres 518
Chandler, Raymond **36**,
    310
Chanel, Gabrielle 'Coco'
    122, 130
Chaney, Lon **312**

Chaney, Lon Junior 312,
    315
Chang, Jung 59
Chang Jiang (Yangtze) **434**
    swimmers 405
Channel 4 **312**
Channel Islands **434**
Channel Tunnel **157**, 407
Chanukkah **96**
chaos theory **526**, 531, 546
chapatti 391
Chapel of Notre Dame du
    Haut *162*
Chaplin 309, 321
Chaplin, Sir Charles
    (Charlie) **312**
Chapman, Graham 326
Chappaquiddick incident
    227
Charade 319, 320
Chardin, Jean-Baptiste 148
Chardonnay (grape) **396**
Charge of the Light Brigade
    36, **194**, 317, 318, 327
Chariots of Fire 329, 362
charisma 186
charismatic movement 110
Charlemagne **227**, 238, 438
Charles I of England **194**,
    195, 214
Charles II of England 131,
    144, **194**, 201
Charles V of Spain 237,
    258
Charles VI, Holy Roman
    Emperor 222
Charles VII of France 165,
    239
Charles IX of France 251
Charles X of France 242
Charles, J.A.C. 560
Charles, Prince of Wales
    264, 380
Charles, Ray **340**
Charles Bridge, Prague 450
Charles Martel **227**
Charles River, Boston 431
Charleston **341**
charleston (dance) 341
*Charlie and the Chocolate
    Factory* 38
*Charlie and the Great Glass
    Elevator* 38
Charlotte, Queen 131
Charlton, Bobby **366**, 375
Charlton, Jack **366**
Charon **79**
Chartism **195**
Chartwell **403**
Charybdis whirlpool 476
Chatsworth 403
Chaucer, Geoffrey **37**, 65,
    72
Cheaper by the Dozen 324
Cheddar cheese **391**
Cheddar Gorge **403**
cheese 391, 455
    fondue 392
cheetahs 442
Chekhov, Anton Pavlovich
    64
Chelmsford 406
Chelsea **404**
    flower show 404

Pensioners 404
    Royal Hospital 404
Chelsea Girls, The 152
Cheltenham 401, **404**
    GCHQ 401
Cheltenham Gold Cup
    366, 404
chemical bond **524**, 547
chemical compounds *see*
    compound, chemical
chemical element 523, **530**,
    536, 537, 538, 540, *541*
chemical reaction **526**
chemistry **526**
chemotherapy **499**, 508
Chequers **404**
Cheriton 407
Chernenko, Konstantin 271
Chernobyl **227**, 458, 471,
    560
Cherry Orchard, The 64
chervil *393*
Cherwell, River 414
Cheshire, Leonard *178*
Cheshire cat **37**
chess 370
Chester 70, **404**
Chesterton, G. K. **37**
chest pains 495, 519
Chetham's library 413
Chevalier, Maurice **341**
Cheviot Hills **404**, 414
chèvre cheese 391
Chiang Kai-Shek **227**, 241,
    242, 456
Chibcha Indians 431
Chicago **434**, 531
    Symphony Orchestra 358
Chichester **404**
Chichester, Sir Francis 408
chickenpox **499**, 517, 520
chicory 391
Chicxulub crater 470
childbirth **499** *see also* birth
Childhood 67
Child of Our Time 360
children, mental
    development in 184
Children of Violence 45
Children's Friend, The 88
Child's Garden of Verses, A
    55
Chile 220, **435**, 467, 473
chilli pepper *393*
Chiltern Hundreds **264**
Chilterns **404**
chimera **79**
Chimes at Midnight 334
China 242, 267, 430, 433,
    435
    Communist Party 265
    Confucianism **96**
    Cultural Revolution **230**,
        282, 457
    economic policy 292
    Grand Canal 157, 160
    Hong Kong and 440
    Maoism in **278**
    Mongol conquest of 241
    opium wars and **246**
    People's Republic of 243
    Tiananmen Square
        massacre **254**
    Tibet and 457

china, Dresden 436
China Syndrome, The 317
Chinatown, Soho 419
Chinatown 327, 329
Chippendale, Thomas **122**
Chipping Campden, 161
Chirac, Jacques 271, 279
chiropractic 495, **499**, 510, 512
Chiswick House 156
Chitty-Chitty-Bang-Bang 40
chivalry **227**
chives *393*
chlorine *see* periodic table **541**
chlorofluorocarbons *see* CFCs
chloroform 495
chlorophyll 480, 487, 489
chloroplasts 480, 489
chocolate 391, 401, 455
cholera **499**, 504
cholesterol 496, **499**, 520
Chomsky, Noam **173**
Chopin, Frédéric 72, **341**, 450
chord 350
chordates 479
chorizo **391**
Chorley, Dave 79
chowder **391**
Christ 96, 103
    baptism of *94*
    birth of 190, 431
    crucifixion of *97*, 101
    Last Supper 83
    the Redeemer, statue *451*
    resurrection of 99
Christ Church, Oxford 414
Christian Democratic Party **264**
Christianity 82, **96**, 229,
Christian IV 448
Christian Science **96**
Christian Science Monitor 96
Christie, Dame Agatha **37**, 330, 333, 409
Christie, Linford **366**, *367*
Christmas **96**
Christmas Carol, A **37**, *38*
chromatography **526**
chromium *see* periodic table **541**
chromosomes 480, **481**, 484, 491
chromosphere 546
chronic illness **499**
Chronicles of Clovis, The 52
chrono-, chron- **12**
Chrysler Building *155*
Chrysomallus 82
Chump at Oxford, A 323
church **157**
Churchill, John *see* Marlborough, 1st Duke of
Churchill, Lady 148
Churchill, Winston 24, 54, 148, 192, **195**, 244, *255*, *258*, *268*, 401, 403
Church of Christ 96
Church of England **96**, 108, 109, 110, 196, 202

Church of Scotland 205
Church of the Holy Sepulchre 442
CIA (Central Intelligence Agency) 223, **264**, 284
ciabatta **391**
Ciboney peoples 461
Ciccone, Madonna Louise 350
Cicero, Marcus Tullius **64**
CID (Criminal Investigation Department) 281
Cid, El **227**
cigars, Havana 435
Cimabue **122**
Cinderella **64**
cinecamera 553
cinematography **553**
cinnamon *393*
Cinque Ports **195**
circadian rhythm **481**, 497
Circe 79
circle **526**, 527
circuit judge **264**
circulatory system 497, **499**
circum- **12**
circumcision **500**
circumference 526
circumflex **12**
circumlocution **12**
cirrhosis 494, **500**, 508
CIS (Commonwealth of Independent States) **264**
Citizen Kane 312, 333
Citizen's Charter 278
City Lights 312
City of London 201, 236, 298, **404**
    'Big Bang' 298
    see also Stock Exchange
City Technology Colleges **175**
civil court **264**
civil disobedience **264**
civil law **264**
Civil List **264**, 268
civil rights /civil rights movement **228**, 238, **264**
civil service 263, **264**
Civil War, English 194, **195**, 205, 211
clairvoyance 79
clams 480
Clapton, Eric **341**
claret (Bordeaux) 396
Clarissa **37**, 66
Clarke, Kenneth **264**
class **173**
Classical antiquity **228**
Classical architecture **157**
classical music **341**
Classical mythology 79
Classicism (art) **122**
Classicism (literature) **64**
Classics **366**
classification **481**
Claude, Georges 559
Claude, Lorrain **122**
Claudius **228**
Claudius the God 41, 228
clause **12**
    main 20
    relative 26

restrictive 26
subordinate 28
clause 28 **173**
clay 474
Clay, Marcellus Cassius **362**, 367
clay tablets, Mesopotamia *13*
Clayton, Jack 330
Cleese, John 316, 326
cleft palate 505
Cleland, John 40
Clemenceau, Georges **228**, 232
Clemens, Samuel Langhorne 58
Clement V, Pope 222
Cleopatra 32, 220, **228**
Cleopatra 311, *332*
Cleopatra's Needle 163, 434
cliché **12**
Clifton Suspension Bridge 156, 402
climate **465**
climatic change **465**
climax community (plant life) **481**
Clinton, Bill **265**
Clinton, Hillary 265
Clio 85
Cliveden **404**
Clive of India **195**, 197
clock 553
Clockwork Orange, A 35, **312**, 322
clone **481**, 490
Clontarf, Battle of 225
Clore Gallery 150
Close Encounters of the Third Kind 331
Clothe (goddess) 81
cloud **465**
Cloud-cuckoo-land **12**
Clouds, The **64**
Clough, Brian **366**
cloves *393*
Clovis, King 165
clubmosses **489**
Clwyd **404**
Clyde, Firth of 409
Clyde, River 407
Clytemnestra 76, 81
CN (Canadian National) Tower 457
coal **466**
    -mining 298, 416, 466
    trade 413
Coalbrookdale, Iron Gorge 410
'coals to Newcastle' 413
cobalamin 520
cobalt 535,
    see also periodic table **541**
Cobbett, William **195**
Cobden, Richard 196
cocaine 431, 435
Cochran, Eddie **341**
Cockerell, Christopher 557
cockneys 406
Cockney rhyming slang 26
cocktails
    Daiquiri 392
    Dry Martini 392

Harvey Wallbanger **393**
Kir, Kir Royale 391
Margarita **393**
Pina Colada 394
pink gin 390
Screwdriver 395
Singapore Sling 395, 454
cocoa 391
coconuts 491
cocoon **482**
coda **350**
Code Napoleon 245
cod's roe, smoked (taramasalata) 395
Cody, William F. 225
Coe, Sebastian **366**, 379
coelenterate *479*, **482**
coffee 431, 432, 441, 442
Coffin Texts 78
cognac **391**
Cohan, George M. 311
Colbert, Jean Baptiste 132
Colchester **404**
Colchis 82, 83
cold-blooded **482**
cold front 464, **466**, 471, 475, 476
cold fusion **526**
Colditz **228**
cold sores 505
cold war **228**, 229, 240, 244, 253, 255
Cole, George 326
Cole, Nat King **341**
Coleridge, Samuel Taylor **37**, 60, 416
Colette, Sidonie Gabrielle **64**
Coligny, Admiral de 251
collage 137, 47
collagen 490
collective unconscious **173**
Collector, The 40
Colleges of Further Education **175**
Colleges of Higher Education **175**
Collins, Jackie 53
Collins, Michael 550
Collins, Phil 344
colloid **526**, 530
colloquialism **12**
Colne, River 404
Cologne (Köln) 451, **435**
Colombia 431, **435**
Colombo 455
colon **12**
Colorado 451
    River *439*
coloratura soprano 359
Color of Money, The 313, 327, 330
Colosseum, Rome 154, 451
Colossus of Rhodes 451
colostomy **500**
colour blindness **500**, 599
Colt, Samuel 556
Columba, Saint 84, 410
Columbia space craft 459, 461, 563
Columbus, Christopher **229**, 453, 455, 518
columns and the Classical Orders 157

coma **500**, 520
Comaneci, Nadia **367**
combining form **12**
combustion 535, 540
Comedians, The 41
Comédie Humaine, La 63
comedy 63, **65**, 67
Comedy Man, The 326
'Come live with me and be my love' 37
comet **526**, *533*
comics 313
Coming Home 317
Coming of Age in Samoa 461
Comino 444
comma **12**
comme il faut **12**
Commentaries, Ghiberti's 126
Commission for Racial Equality, 185
commodity **292**, 295
Common Agricultural Policy (CAP) **292**, 296, 302, 303
common cold 520
Common Era, Before the (BCE) 11
Common Fisheries Policy 292
common law **265**
common noun **13**
Common Sense 109
Common Sense Book of Baby and Child Care 186
Commonwealth and Protectorate 196
Commonwealth Games, the 265
Commonwealth of Nations 198, 252, 261, 274
Communion, Holy **96**, 109
communism **265**
communism (as economic system) **292**
communism, collapse of 279
communism, principles of 229, **265**, 278, 285, **292**, 299
Communist Manifesto, The 99, 106, **229**, 265
community charge 277
Comorre the Cursed 78
compact disc (CD) *553*, **554**, 558
Companion of Honour 178, 284
comparative **13**
compass 470, **554**
complement **13**
complementarity 535
complementary medicine 495
complex number 539
complex sentence **13**
Composition (Mondrian) *137*
compos mentis **13**
compound, chemical **526**, 528, 530, 537
comprehensive schools **175**
Compton, Denis **367**
Compulsion 334

Computerised Axial Tomography (CAT; CT) 516
computer 524, 525, 550, 551, **554**, 557, 559, 566
computer program 544, **554**
Comte, Auguste **173**, 186
Conan, the Barbarian 330
concentration camp 222, **229**
  see also holocaust; names of individual camps
concordance **13**
Concorde 535, **554**
concrete **157**, 164, 165
concrete noun **13**
concussion **500**
condensation **526**
condenser 552
conditioning **173**
conditioning, operant 174, 185
conduction **527**, 533
Coney Island 319
Confederate States of America **229**
confession **96**
Confessions 94
confirmation **96**, 99
confit **391**
Confucianism **96**
Confucius 96
congenital **500**
  defects 500, 504, 505, 517, 518
Congo 288
Congregationalism **97**, 116
Congress, USA **266**, 274
Congress of Berlin 196
Congress of Vienna 193, **255**
Congreve, William 51
conic sections **527**, 530
conifers **482**, 486, *489*
conjunction **13**
conjunctivitis **500**, 505
Connecticut Yankee in King Arthur's Court, A 58
Connemara 441
Connery, Sean 70, *310*, **313**, 320
Connolly, Maureen **367**
connotation **13**
Conqueror, HMS 190
conquistadors, Spanish **229**
Conrad, Joseph **37**, 462
Conran, Shirley 53
Conran, Terence 127
consciousness, stream of 73
conservation, laws of **527**
conservation of energy, law of 546
Conservative Party 209, 215, **266**, 285
Consolation of Philosophy, The 95
consommé **391**
consonant **13**
Constable, John **122**, 418
Constable, Lionel 122
constant (physics) **527**
Constantine the Great 94, 108, **229**, 441

Constantinople 225, 229, 247, 250
constellation **527**, 548
constitution **266**
  USA 105, 261, 275, 285
constitutional monarchy **266**
consubstantiation **97**
consul 229
consumer credit **292**
consumption 519
contempt of court **266**
Contes du Temps 78
continent **466**
continental drift **466**, 471, 472
continental slope 471
contra- **13**
contraception 190, 214, **500**, 514, 520
contraction **13**
contralto **341**,
convection **527**, 533
convention **266**
convulsions 503
Conwy **404**
Conwy, River 401, 404
Coogan's Bluff 316
Cook, Beryl 139
Cook, Captain James **195**, 432, 457
Cook, Peter 33
Cooke, Sam 359
Cookson, Catherine 38
Cool Hand Luke 327
'cool jazz' movement 342
Cooper, Gary **313**
Cooper, Henry *362*, **367**
Co-operative movement **196**, 209, 416
coordinates **527**, 532
  geometry 528
coordination, physical 498
Copacabana 451
Copenhagen **435**
Copernican revolution 527
Copernicus, Nicolaus 450, 525, **527**
Copland, Aaron **341**
copper 462, 546
  see also periodic table **541**
Coppola, Francis Ford 308, 315, 319
Coptic Church **97**
coral 439, 466, 478
  reef 465, **466**
Coral Island, The 46
Coral Sea, Battle of **229**
Corcovado, Rio *451*
Cordoba, Great Mosque of 243
cordon bleu **392**
Corfu **435**
coriander *393*
Corinthian column **57**
Coriolis effect **466**, 471, 476
corm **482**
corn circles 79
cornea **500**, 503, 519
Corn Laws **196**, 213
cornmeal (polenta) 395
Cornwall **404**
  Duke of 264

corona 546
coronary thrombosis 518
Coronation Street **313**, 315
Corot, Jean Baptiste Camille **123**
corps de ballet **337**
Corsica **435**
Corsican Brothers, The 316
Cortés, Hernán **229**
cosmic background explorer (COBE) 527
cosmic background radiation 524, **527**
cosmic rays 522, 523, 524, **527**
cosmo- **13**
Cossacks **229**, 458
cost, real **303**
Costa Brava 455
Costa del Sol 455
Costa Rica **435**
Costner, Kevin **313**
cot death **500**
Côte Chalonnaise (Burgundy) 396
Côte d'Azur **435**
Côtes de Beaune (Burgundy) 396
Côtes de Nuits (Burgundy) 396
Côtes du Rhône (Syrah) 396
Cotswold Hills **404**
cottage cheese 391
Cotton, Billy **341**
Cotton Club, Harlem 340, 343
Coty 130
cotyledons **482**, 483, 488, 491
Coubertin, Baron Pierre de 379
coughing 498, 503, 519, 520
coulis **392**
Council of Europe **266**, 455
Council of Ministers **266**, 269
Council of Trent **97**, **254**
councils, county and district 276
Council Tax 277
Counter-Attack 53
Counterblast to Tobacco, A 204
counterpoint 337, **350**
Counter Reformation **97**, **229**
countertenor **341**
Countess from Hong Kong, A 312
count noun **13**
Count of Monte Cristo, The 66, 315
country and western **341**, 356
Country Girl, The 322
county court **266**
coup de grâce **13**
Court Jester, The 322
courtly love **65**, 72, 74
court martial **266**
Court of Session **266**

courts 260, 264, 266, 269, 273, 275, 277, 285, *286*, 414
courtship **482**
couscous **392**
Cousteau, Jacques 550
covalent bond 525
Covent Garden 162, **404**
  Royal Opera House 338, 358-9, 404
Coventry 82, 191, **404**
Coventry Cathedral 148, 404
Cover Girl 348
Coward, Sir Noël 311, 330, **341**
Cowes Week, 388, 405
Crab nebula 538
Cracow, Poland 450
Cram, Steve **367**
Cranford 40
Cranmer, Thomas **196**
Cratchit, Bob 38
Crathie Church 399
Crawford, Jack *380*
Crawford, Joan **313**
Crawford, Michael *349*
Crazy People 319
Cream (rock band) 341, 346
Creation of Adam, The (Michelangelo) 134-5
Crécy, Battle of **196**
credit cards 290, 557, 563
credit rating **292**
credit squeeze **292**
Credo 350
crème fraîche **392**
creole **13**, **392**
Creon, King 76
crescendo **350**
Cresta Run 365
Cretaceous Period *468*
Crete 77, **435**, 439
Creutzfeld Jakob Disease 509
Crick, Francis 484
cricket *363*, **368**, 371, 376, 377
Crickets, The 346
Crime and Punishment 65
Crimea **435**
Crimean War 194, **229**
Crimes of Passion 330
criminal court **266**
Criminal Investigation Department (CID) 281
  criminal law **266**
Cripplegate 404
Criss Cross 323
Critic, The 55
critical mass 539
Critique of Pure Reason, The 104
Croatia **435**, 462
Crockett, Davy **229**, 457
crocodile 490
croissant **392**
Crompton, Richmal 59
Cromwell, Oliver 47, 95, 194, 195, **196**, 208
Cromwell, Thomas **196**
croquet **368**
Crosby, Bing *321*, 330, **342**
Crosby, Mary 313

Crosland, Anthony 285
Crossfire 316, 326
crossing the Rubicon **13**
cross-reference **13**
Crow 43
Crowley, Aleister 90
Crown 266, 284
Crown Court 266
Crown Derby 405
Crown Jewels 468
Crown Prosecution Service (CPS) **266**, 267
Crow tribe *183*
cru 396
Crucible, The 47
crucifixion **97**, 101
crudités **392**
Cruise, Tom 113, **313**
crumple zones 553
Crusades 212, 224, **230**, 233, 251, 451
Crusade, Children's 230
Crusaders 456
crustacean *479*, **482**, 485
Cry in the Dark 332
cryogenics **527**
crystal 436, **527**
crystallography 548
Crystal Palace **158**, *201*, 557
CSE 177
CT (Computerised Axial Tomography) scan 516
Cuba 223, **435**, 461
  exiles in Miami 444
  missile crisis **230**, 459
  Revolution **230**, 236
Cuillin Hills, Skye 419
Cullinan diamond 468
Culloden, Battle of **196**
cult **174**
cultivar **483**
Cultural Revolution **230**, *282*, 457
culture **174**
culture shock 174
Cumberland and Westmoreland wrestling 388
cumin *393*
cummings e.e. **38**
cuneiform script **13**, 180, 244
Cunobelinus, King 404
Cupid *79*, 81, 87
Curie, Marie 450, **527**
Curie, Pierre *527*
curium *see* periodic table **541**
curling **368**
Curly Top 332
currencies 293, 294, 296
current (electricity) 554
currents, ocean 466, **471**
curriculum vitae **14**
Curse of Frankenstein, The 317
curtain wall **158**
Curtis, Tony 334
Curtiz, Michael 312
curvature of space 543
Curzon, Viceroy Lord *274*
Cushing, Peter 317

Cuthbert, St 158
cutting the Gordian Knot **14**
cuttlefish 481
Cutty Sark 408
cuvée **396**
Cuyp, Aelbert **123**
c.v. 14
Cyclades 426, 439
cycle racing 368, 386
  Tour de France *368*
cyclo-cross (cross country bicycling) 368
cyclone 466, 469, 471, 475
Cyclops 79
Cymbeline 54
Cyprus **436**
Cyrano de Bergerac 65, 314
Cyril, Saint 14
cyst **500**
cystic fibrosis **500**
cystitis **500**
cytoplasm 480, *481*
Czechoslovakia 249, **436**, 454
  Prague Spring, 232, **249**
  Soviet invasion of 232

D

Dachau 246
Dada **123**
Dad's Army 313
Daedalus 79, 83, 85
daffodil *489*
da Gama, Vasco **234**, 450
Daguerre, Louis 552
daguerreotype 552
Dahl, Roald **38**
Dahmer, Jeffrey 185
Daily Express **328**
Daily Mail **328**
Daily Mirror **328**
Daily Record **328**
Daily Telegraph, The **328**
Daimler, Gottlieb 552
Daiquiri **392**
Dalai Lama **97**, 457
Dalglish, Kenny **368**
Dali, Salvador **123**, 132, 320
Dallas **436**, 457
Dallas **313**
Dalmatia 435
Dalmatian coast 462
Dalton, John 523, **528**
Dalton, Timothy 311
Daltrey Roger 360
damages (legal) **267**
Damascus **436**, 456
Damask cloth 436
Dambuster raid **196**
Dame aux Camelias, La 66
damnation **97**
Damocles, sword of 29, **79**
dams **158**
Dance, Matisse 133

Dance of the Hours 316
Dancer, John Benjamin 559
Dances with Wolves 313
Dance to the Music of Time, A 51
dandelion seeds *490*, *491*
Dandy, The 313
Danelaw **196**
Dangerous 313
dangling participle **14**
Daniel, Book of 16
Danish Vikings 216
Dante Alighieri **65**, 85
Danton, Georges **230**
Danube, River 431, **436**
Darby, Abraham 410, 552
Dardanelles 458
Dar es Salaam 456
Darius 247
Dark Ages **231**
dark horse **14**
dark matter **528**
Dark Side Of The Moon 355
Darling, Grace 399
Darlington **405**
Darnley, Lord 207
Dart, River **405**
Dartmoor **405**
Dartmouth **405**
darts **369**
Darwin, Charles Robert 465, 478, **483**, 484, 485
dash **14**
'Das Kapital' 106
Daudet, Alphonse 339
Daumier, Honoré *66*, 121
dauphinoise **392**
David (sculpture) **97**, **123**,
David, Hal 337
David, Jacques-Louis **123**
David and Goliath **97**
David Copperfield **38**, 402
Davidian sect 174
da Vinci, Leonardo *see* Leonardo da Vinci
Davis, Bette **313**
Davis, Dwight 369
Davis, Fred 369
Davis, Jefferson 229
Davis, Joe **369**
Davis, Miles **342**
Davis, Steve **369**
Davis Cup **369**
Davison, Emily 215
Davy, Sir Humphry **528**
dawn raid 292
Day, Sir Robin **314**
Day at the Races, A 325
Day-Lewis, Daniel 330
Day of Atonement **116**
Day of Judgment 93, **97**
Day of the Jackal, The **40**, 334
Day of Yahweh 97
Days of Glory 328
Days of Wine and Roses 323
dB *see* decibel
DC *see* direct current
D-Day 230, **231**
DDT **466**
Dead Again 311
'Dead Parrot, The' 326
Dead Pool, The 315
Dead Sea *428*, **436**, 473

Dead Sea Scrolls **98**
Dean, Christopher *387*
Dean, James **314**
De Architectura 157
Death in the Afternoon 42
Death in Venice 69, **314**,
Death of a Salesman 47
Death of Ivan Ilyich, The 74
Death on the Nile 37, 333
death penalty 263
Death Shall Have No Dominion 57
Death Valley **436**
debt 297
  bad **290**
Debussy, Claude 69, **342**
debutante **174**
deca- 537
Decameron **65**, 71
decathlon **369**
decibel **528**, 551
deciduous **483**, 487
deci- **14**, 537
decimal system 524, **528**
Declaration of Independence **231**, 233
Declaration of the Rights of Man 234
declarative sentence **14**
Decline and Fall 59
Decline and Fall of the Roman Empire, History of the 233
deconstruction, theory of 98
Decorated style **158**
decree absolute and *nisi* 174
de'Dondi, Giovanni *553*
deductive reasoning **98**
Dee, Kiki 347
Dee, River 398, **405**
Deep Blue Sea, The 51, 323, 326
Deer Hunter, The 314, 332
de facto **14**
defence mechanism **174**
Defiant Ones, The 329
defining clause **15**
definite article **15**,
deflation **292**
Defoe, Daniel **39**,
deforestation **466**
Degas, Edgar **123**, 140
de Gaulle, Charles **231**, 271, 438, 449
degree **528**
de Groot, Jan 410
Deimos 536
deism **98**
déjà vu **15**
Déjeuner sur l'Herbe (Manet) *133*
de jure **15**
De Klerk, F.W. **267**
Delacroix, Eugène **123**
Delaunay 123
Delhi **436**
Delius, Frederick **342**
Delors, Jacques **267**
Delphic Oracle 76, **79**, 85
delta 474
dementia **501**, 510, 512
Demeter **79**, 108
demi- **15**

De Mille, Cecil B. **314**, 321, 332
demi sec (Champagne) 396
democracy 235, /b 267
Democratic Party **267**
Democritus 523
demonstrative pronoun **15**
Demosthenes **231**
Dench, Dame Judi **314**, 334
Deng Xiaoping **267**
De Niro, Robert **314**, 319, 330
Denmark **436**
Denning, Lord **267**
Dennis, John 28
denotation **15**
dénouement **65**
density 523, **528**
dentistry **501**
Depardieu, Gérard 65, **314**, 318
Depression, The **231**
  American 246, 256, 459
depression (economic) **292**, *293*, 303
depression (medical) **501**, 509, 514, 515, 517
Derby **405**
Derby (horse race) **369**, 406
Derby, Lord 369
Derbyshire **405**
Derek and the Dominoes 341
Der Fliegende Holländer 81
de rigueur **145**
derivative **15**
dermatitis (eczema) **502**
dermis 517
Derrida, Jacques **98**
Der Ring des Nibelungen **353**
Derwent Water *411*
Descartes, René 93, **98**, 113, **528**
Descent of Man, The 483
desert 443, **446**, **467**
Desert Fox 325
Desert Island Discs 314, 358
Desert Orchid **369**
Desert Rats **196**
De Sica, Vittorio 310, **314**, 324
Desire Under the Elms 324
Desk Set, The 320
desk-top publishing 561
Desmond, Paul 340
Destry Rides Again 331
detached retina **501**
detente **267**
determiner **15**
determinism **98**, 547
de trop **15**
Dettingen, Battle of 200
deus ex machina **15**
deuterium 533, 539
Dev, Kapil 373
De Valera, Eamon 197, **231**
de Valois, Dame Ninette **342**
devaluation **293**
developing nation **293**
devil 79, **98** 103, 113
Devils, The 330

Devil's Dyke **405**
Devil's Gallop, The 315
Devil's Island 436
devil to pay **15**
devolution 267, 285
Devon **405**, 412
Devonshire, Dukes of 403
dew 526
dhal **392**
dharma 102
diabetes **501**, 507
diacritical marks **15**
diaeresis **15**
Diaghilev Serge **342**, 355, 357
dialectic **98**
dialectical materialism 98
Dial M for Murder 322
dialysis **501**, 507
diameter 526
Diamond as Big as the Ritz, The 40
diamonds 446, 525
Diana (goddess) **79**
Diana, Princess of Wales 398
Dianetics 113
diaphragm 515
diarrhoea **501**
Diary of a Nobody 41
Dias, Bartolomeu **231**, 434, 450
Diaspora **98**
Dick Barton **315**
Dickens, Charles **39**, 48, 417
Dickens Festival 402
Dick Tracy 309, 328
dicotyledons 482, **483**, *489*
Dictes or Sayengis of the Philosophres 193
Dictionary of the English Language 43
Diddley, Bo 357
Diderot, Denis **231**
didgeridoo *170*
Dido, Queen 76, **80**
Die Brucke Group 124
Dien Bien Phu 232
diesel locomotive 565
diet 499
  macrobiotic **393**
Dietrich, Marlene **315**, 319, 331
diffraction **528**, 535, 548
diffusion **528**
digestion **501**, 513
digestive complaints 505
digital recording 554
dill *393*
DiMaggio, Joe 364, **369**
diminishing returns **293**
diminutive **15**
Dimples 332
Dinesen, Isak *see* Blixen, Karen **63**
'dinkys' (Double Income No Kids) 186
dinosaurs 470, 480, *482-3*, **483**
Dinsamo, Belayneh 377
diode **554**
Dionysus 76, 78, **80**, 84, 88
Dior, Christian **123**

diphtheria **502**, 507
diphthong **15**
Diplodocus 482
diplomacy **267**
diptych **123**, 149
direct current (DC) **528**, 554, 555
direct object **15**
Director of Public Prosecutions (DPP) **267**
direct rule (Northern Ireland) 267
direct speech **15**
Dirty Harry **315**
disarmament **267**
Discourse on Method 98
Discovery, American space shuttle *562*
discrimination **174**
discs (of spine) 497
discus *379*
disks, computer 554
Disney, Walt **315**, 316, 331
Disneyland, Los Angeles 443
Disney World 438
disposable income **293**
Disraeli, Benjamin **196**
Dissenters 108
dissolution (parliament) **268**
Dissolution of the Monasteries **197**
distillation **528**
district court **268**
diva **342**
divers and diving 550
diversification **293**
divertissement (ballet) **337**
dividend **293**, 306
divination **80**
Divine Comedy, The 53, 62, **65**
divine right of kings 194, 204, **232**
diving 369
divorce **174**
Dix, Otto **123**
DNA 480, 481, **484**, 486, 488, 490, 520, 556, 557
'D-notice' 280
Dobson, Anita 315
Docklands **405**
Doctor Dolittle **39**, 403
Doctor in the House 310, 326
Doctor Who **315**
Doctor Zhivago 72
Dodecanese 426, 439, 451
Dodgson, Charles Lutwidge (Lewis Caroll) 24, 32, **36**
dodo **484**
Dodoma 456
Dog Day Afternoon 328
Doges' Palace, Venice 460
dogma **99**
Dog Years 67
Dolby, Ray M. 555
Dolby system **555**
doldrums 476
Doll's House, A **65**
dolmades **392**
dolphins 481, **484**

Dome of the Rock 161, 163, 246, 442
Domesday Book 173, **197**
Domingo, Placido **342**
Dominican Republic 439, 461
Domino, Fats **342**
Don, River 418
Dona Isabel de Porcel (Goya) *127*
Donat, Robert **315**
Donatello **123**
Don Carlos 353
Donegan, Lonnie **342**
Don Giovanni 323
Donizetti, Gaetano 350, 359
Don Juan **36**
Donne, John 37, **39**, 40, 47
Don Quixote 64, **66**, 71
'Don't look a gift horse in the mouth' **15**
'Don't spoil the ship for a ha'p'orth of tar' 15
Doors, The **342**
dopamine 513
Doppler effect **528**, 543
Dorchester 405
Doric column **157**
dormancy 478, **484**
Dorset **405**
Dorsey, Thomas A. 345
Dostoyevsky, Fyodor Mikhailovich **66**
double entendre **15**
Double Indemnity 317, 330, 334
double negative **15**
double star *see* binary star
Doubting Thomas 100
Dougall, Robert *327*
Douglas, Isle of Man 412
Douglas, James 'Buster' 387
Douglas, Kirk **315**, 323, 334
Douglas, Michael **315**
Douro, River 448
doux (Champagne) 396
Dove Cottage, Grasmere 408
Dover **405**, 490
Dover Beach 32
Dow Jones Index **293**
Down, Northern Ireland 447
Down and Out in Paris and London 48
Downing Street 288, 423
Declaration 260
Down's syndrome 481, 495, **502**
Down with Skool 47
Doyle, Sir Arthur Conan **39**, 399, 459
D'Oyly Carte, Richard 344
Dozmary Pool 401
Drabble, Margaret **39**
Dracula 55, **80**, 321, 451
Dracula films **315**
dragon **80**
Dragon Hill, Oxon 423
drag racing 378
Drake, Sir Francis 189, **197**, 415

Drakensberg Mountains 455
Drake's Drum 197
dramatis personae **66**
Dream of Gerontius, The 343
dreams **502**, 517
Dresden 436
dressage 369
Dreyfus, Alfred 74, 232
Dreyfus affair **232**
Dr Faustus **39**, 46, 81
drift (soil) 474
drink and driving 552
Dr Jekyll and Mr Hyde 39, 311
Dr No 311
Dr Strangelove 322, 330
drug **502**
addiction **502**, 503
medical 431, 503
Druids 80, 88, 398
drunkometer 552
Druze (religion) **99**
Dryden, John **39**
Dry Martini **392**
Dr Zhivago 323, 329
DTs (Delirium Tremens) 494
dualism **99**
Dubai 458
Dubček, Alexander **232**, 249
Dublin **436**
Dubliners 44
Dubrovnik 462
Duccio di Buoninsegna **123**
Duchamp, Marcel 123
Duchess of Malfi, The 51, 59
Duck Soup 325
Dudevant, Baron 72
Duel 331
Dufy, Raoul **123**,
dugongs *84*
Duke Bluebeard's Castle 337
Duke of Wellington 247
Dulac, Edmund *71*
Duma (parliament) 451
Dumas, Alexandre (père) **66**
Dumas, Alexandre (fils) 66
du Maurier, Daphne **39**, 401
Dumbo 315
dumping **293**
dumpling (quenelle) 395
Dunaway, Faye, 311
Duncan, Isadora **342**
Dundee **405**
Dunkirk **197**, 257
Dunlop, John Boyd 566
Dunn, Clive 313
Dunnet Head 410
Dunvegan Castle **406**
du Pré, Jaqueline **343**
Dürer, Albrecht **124**, 133
Durham **406**
Durham Cathedral **158**
Durkheim, Emile **174**, 186
Dust Bowl, Oklahoma 474
Duvalier, Dr François 'Papa Doc' 439
Duvalier, 'Baby Doc' 439
Dvořák, Antonin **343**
Dyer, General 426
dykes **158**

Dylan, Bob **343**
dynamics *see* mechanics **536**
dynamo 531
dys- **15**
dysentery **502**
dyslexia **502**
dysprosium *see* periodic table *541*
dzongs (monasteries) 431

E

$E=mc^2$ **528**
Eagle 550
Eagle Has Landed, The 311
Ealing comedies **315**
ear **502**
Earhart, Amelia **232**
Earls Barton Tower 154
Early Bird satellite 562
Early English (architecture) **158**
Earth **467**, **528**, *544*
earthquake 452, **467**, 468, 472, 473, 474, 475, 558
earthworm 479
East Anglia 402, **406**
University of 414
East Australian Current *471*
East End **406**
EastEnders **315**
Easter **99**
Easter Island **436**, 450
Eastern Orthodox Church *see* Orthodox Church
Eastern Question **232**
Easter Parade 318
Easter Rising 193, **197**, 436, 441
East India Company, British 192, **197**, 201, 225, 433, 440, 446, 454
East Indies 461
Eastman, George 552, **555**
East of Eden 55, 314
East River 446
East Timor **436**
Eastwood, Clint 313, **315**
Easy Rider **316**
eating disorders 495, 498
eating humble pie **15**
Eboracum (York) 424
Ecclesiastes **99**
Ecclesiastical History of the English People 190
ECG (electrocardiogram) 503
echinoderms *479*
echoes 543
echolocation **484**
eclipse **528**, *529*
Eclogues 74
Eco, Umberto 70
economics **293**
Economist, The **324**
ecosystem **467**, 488
ectopic pregnancy **502**

Dylan, Bob **343**
ECU (European Currency Unit) 293
Ecuador **437**, 449
ecumenism **99**
eczema **502**
Edam cheese 391
Eddie 'the Eagle' Edwards 383
Eddington, Paul 334
Eddy, Mary Baker 96
Eden, Sir Anthony **197**
Edict of Nantes 238
Edinburgh **406**, 417
Arthur's Seat **398**
Festival 406
Edinburgh, Duke of 264, 268
Edington, Battle of 216
Edison, Thomas Alva **555**, 559
Edmund, Saint 403
Edmund of Langley, Duke of York 218
Edrich, Bill 367
Educating Rita 311
education system, British **175**
examinations 170, 175, 177
national curriculum **182**
Edward I 192, **197**, 209
Edward II **198**, 400
Edward III 87, 196, **198**, 199, 238
Edward IV **198**
Edward V **198**
Edward VI **198**
Edward VII **198**, 216
Edward VIII *188*, **198**
Edward 'The Confessor' **197**
Edwardian period **198**
Edwards, Blake 308, 328
Edwards, Gareth 374
Edwin, King of Northumbria 406
EFTA (European Free Trade Association) 266
e.g. **16**
egg **484** *see also* sex cells
ego **175**
ego- **16**
Egypt 221, 245, 250, **437**
Camp David accords 226
Israel and 226, 253, 261
Six-Day War 245, **252**
Suez crisis 197, 428
Yom Kippur War **258**
Egypt, ancient **232**, 248, 254, 437
Egyptian art **124**, 127
Eichmann, Adolf **232**
Eiffel, Gustave 158
Eiffel Tower **158**, 449
8½ 316
18-certificate 334
Eighth Army, British 188, 196
84 Charing Cross Road 314
Eine Kleine Nachtmusik 351
Einstein, Albert **528**, *529*, 542, 543
einsteinium *see* periodic table *541*

Eisenhower, Dwight D. **232**
Eisenstein, Sergei Mikhailovich 309, **316**
Eiswein **396**
Ekland, Anders 365
elasticity **293**
Elba 245
El Cid 227
El Cid (film) 324
Eldorado **80**, 235
Eleanor of Aquitaine *411*
elections **268**, 270, 282
Electra 76
Electra (play) **66**
'Electra complex' 183
electric charge **529**, 545
electric current **529**, 543
electric generator **529**, 531, **555**, 561
electricity 522, **529**, 530, 561
electric lighting *555*
electric locomotive 565
electric motor **555**
electric shocks 522
electrocardiogram **503**
electrode 522, **529**, 526
electrolysis **529**, 531, 555
electromagnetic induction **529**, 530, 535, 555
electromagnetic radiation **529**, 531, 537, 544, 547, 548, 560
electromagnetism **529**, *530*, 536
electromotive force 541, 547
electron 522, *523*, **529**, 542, 546, 548, 551, 559
shells 522, 524, 525, 540
electronic circuits 562, 565
electron microscope 548, 559
electroplated nickel silver (EPNS) 555
electroplating 529, **555**
elegy **66**
Elegy Written in a Country Church-Yard 41
element 523, 528, **530**, 531, 534, 536, 537
table of the *541*
elementary particles *see* subatomic particles
Elements (Euclid) 530
elephants 442
élévation (ballet) **337**
Elgar, Sir Edward **343**, 351, 408
Elgin, Earl of 124
Elgin Marbles **124**
El Giza 4 33
El Greco **124**, 444
Elijah **99**
Eliot, George **39**
Eliot, T. S. **39**
elitism **175**
Elizabeth I 159, **198**, 207
Elizabeth II 118, 264, **268**, *269*
Elizabeth of York 213, 215
Elizabeth, Queen Mother *191*, 407

Elizabethan style (architecture) 159
Elizabethan style (art) **124**
Ellington, Duke **343**
Elliott, Herb 369
Elliott, Virgina 363, *386*
ellipse, 527, **530**
ellipsis **16**
Ellis, William Webb 382, 417
Elmer Gantry 323
El Niño **467**, 471
El Salvador **437**
Ely **406**
Cathedral **159**, *406*
Elysian Fields **80**
embargo **293**
embezzlement **294**
embolism **503**
embryo **484**, 504, 514
emergency debate **268**
emergency powers **268**
emetic **503**
emissions, toxic 553
Emma 33, **39**
Emma, Lady Hamilton 208
Emmenthal cheese 391, 455
Emmy **316**
emperor moth 489
Emperor's New Clothes, The 62
emphysema 498, **503**, 508
Empire (Warhol) 152
Empire, British **198**
Empire of the Sun 33
Empire State Building **159**
Empire Strikes Back, The 331
empiricism **99**,
empty-nest syndrome **175**
emulsion **530**
encephalitis **503**
enchilada **392**, 395
en croûte **392**
Encyclopédie 231
endemic **503**, 513
endive 391
endocrine system **503**, 513, 514
endocrinology 510
endogamy **175**
endorphins **503**
endoscope **503**, 556
endowment policy **294**
Endymion 32, 44
Enemy of the People, An 325
energy **530**, 534, 535, 543
Enewetak atoll 444
enfant terrible **16**
Enforcer, The 315
Engels, Friedrich **99**, 278
'England expects that every man will do his duty' 198
Englishman Abroad, An 33
English National Opera **343**, *344*
engraving **124**
Enigma **232**, 258, 401
Enigma Variations 343
Enlightened One 95
enlightenment **99**
Enlightenment (movement) **99**
en papillote **392**
en primeur **396**

England 216 *see also* individual place names
Entebbe, Uganda 458
Entente Cordiale 198, 214, **232**
enterprise zones 298
Entertainer, The 328
Entertainer, The (ragtime) 347
Entertaining Mr Sloane 48
entrechat (ballet) **337**
entremets 392
entropy **530**, 546
environment **467**
protection movements 272, 467
enzyme 480, **484**, 490, 525
EOKA movement 436
Epcot Center 438
ephemeral **484**
Ephesus 458
Ephraimites 27
epic **66**
Epicureanism **99**
Epicurus 99
epidemic **503**, 513
epidemiology 510
epidermis **484**
epiglottis 507
epigram **16**
epilepsy **503**
Epiphany **99**
epiphyte **484**
episcopacy **99**
Episcopalian Churches 99
epistemology **99**
Epistles 110
epistolary novel **66**
epitaph **16**
Epithalamion 55
epithet **16**
EPNS (electroplated nickel silver) 555
eponymous **16**
Epsom **406**
Epsom salts 406
Epstein, Sir Jacob **124**
equality **175**
Equal Opportunities Commission 175
equation, chemical 526
equation, mathematical **530**
Equator 467, 476, 530
Equatorial Current *471*
equestrian sport 369, 373, 386
equilibrium **530**
equinox **530**
equity **294**, 304, 305
Equus 53
Erasmus, Desiderius **99**
Erato 85
erbium *see* periodic table **541**
Erebus, Mount *427*
Erewhon 36
ergonomics **555**
Ericsson, Leif **232**
Eric the Red **232**
Erie, Lake 439
Erinyes **81**
Eritrea 455
ERNIE *302*
Ernst, Max **124**, 137

Eros 76, 79, **81**
Eros (statue) 415
erosion **467**
ersatz **16**
escalator **555**
Escoffier, Auguste **392**
Eskimos **175**, 179
ESP **81**
Esperanto **16**
esprit de corps **16**
esprit d'escalier **16**
Essay on Criticism, An 50
Essay on Man, An 50
Essay on Women 217
Essenes 98
Essex **406**
'Essex Man' 406
Establishment **175**
Estates-General, French 284
Estates of the Realm **16**
Esterhazy, Major 232
Estonia 459
E.T. - The Extra-Terrestrial **316**, *331*
ETA (Basque separatists) 455
Eteocles 76
ethanol (ethyl alcohol) 522
Ethelbert of Kent, King 189
Ethelred the Unready 192
ether, the *see* Michelson-Morley experiment 537
ethics **99**
Ethiopia 87, 237, **437**
ethnic cleansing **175**
ethnicity **175**
ethno- **16**
ethnocentrism **175**
Eton **406**
College *184*, 202, 406
Etruscans **232**, 441
etymology **16**
eu- **16**
Eucharist 92, **99**
Euclid *523*, **530**
Euclidean geometry 523, 532
Eugene Onegin 72
eugenics **176**
eulogy **66**
euphemism **16**
Euphrates 233, **437**, 453, 457
Euphrosyne 82
Eureka! 522
Euripides **66**
euro-bond 291
eurocurrency **294**
Europe (Blake) 34
Europe, map of *437 see also* individual countries
Europe, Council of **266**, 455
European
Atomic Energy Community (Euratom) 269
Coal and Steel Community (ECSC) 269
Commission 268-9, **268**
Commission on Human Rights 275

Common Agricultural Policy (CAP) **292**
Community (EC) 269
Convention on Human Rights 269
Court of Justice 269, 443
Court of Human Rights **269**
Currency Unit (ECU) **294**
Economic Community (EEC) 250, 269
Exchange Rate Mechanism (ERM) 277, **294**, 303
Monetary System (EMS) **294**
Monetary Union (EMU) 277, **294**
Parliament 269, 455
Recovery Program (Marshall Aid) 243
European Union (EU) 250, **269**, 277, 295, 304
law 260, 285
europium *see* periodic table **541**
Euryale 82
Eurystheus 83
euthanasia **176**
eutrophication **468**
evangelist **100**, 101
Evans, Dame Edith **316**
Evans, Sir Geraint **343**
evaporation **530**
Evelyn, John 160
Everest, Sir George 445
Everglades, Florida 438
evergreen 482, **484**, 487
Evert, Chris 378
Everyman 39
Every Man in his Humour 43
Every Man out of his Humour 44
Every Which Way But Loose **316**, *331*
evil **100**
Evil Under the Sun 333
Evita 247, 349
evolution **484**
evolution, human **181**
Ewell, Tom *326*
Excalibur 77, **81**
Excellent Women 51
exchange rate 294, 296
Exchange Rate Mechanism (ERM) 277, **294**, 303
excise **294**
exclamation mark **16**
exclusion order **269**
excommunication **100**
Exe, River 406,
executive **269**
Exeter **406**
ex gratia **16**
Exile on Main Street 357
existentialism **100**
Exmoor **406**
exocrine gland 504
Exodus **100**, 109
exogamy **176**
exorcism **100**
exoskeleton **485**
expletive **16**

exponential growth **530**
exports 290
Exposition Internationale des Arts Décoratifs 118
Expressionism **124**
Express Newspapers 328
extinction 470, 483, **485**
extradition **269**
extraordinary general meeting **294**
extra-sensory perception (ESP) **81**
extraterrestrial life 544
extrovert **176**, 180
Exxon Valdez disaster 426
eye **503**
    cornea 500, 503, 519
Eysenck, Hans Jurgen **176**

F

Fabergé, (Peter) Carl **124**, 452
Fabian Society **270**
Façade 55, 336
Faces, The 359
Factor VIII 504
FA Cup **370**
Faerie Queen, The **40**, 198
Fahrenheit 526, **530**
Fahrenheit, Gabriel 530
Fail Safe 317
fainting 497, **503**
Fairbanks, Douglas **316**
Fairbanks, Douglas Junior 316
Fairfax, Thomas 208
fairies **81**
Fair Isle **407**
Fairy Glen, Snowdonia 401
fait accompli **16**
faith **100**
Falange **232**
Faldo, Nick **370**
Falkland Islands 198
Falklands War 190, **198**, 268, 428
Fall and Rise of Reginald Perrin, The 330
Fallen Idol, The 329
Fall of Man 92, 94, **100**, 109
Fall of Rome **233**
Fall of the House of Usher, The **40**
Fall of the Roman Empire, The 324
Fallopian tubes 502, 507, 512, 515
Falls Road, Belfast 430
false colours 30
Falstaff **40**, 42
Family Plot 320
Family Reunion, The 330
Fancy Pants 321
Fanfare for the Common Man 341

Fangio, Juan Manuel **370**
Fanny and Alexander 309
Fanny by Gaslight 325
Fanny Hill **40**
Fantasia 315, **316**
Fantasia on a Theme of Thomas Tallis 360
farad 531
Faraday, Michael **530**, 555
farce **66**
Farewell, My Lovely 36, 326
Farewell to Arms, A 42
Far from the Madding Crowd **40**
Farouk, King 245
Farquhar, George 51
Farrow, Mia 308
Far Side, The (Larson) 130
fasciitis, necrotising 495
fascism **270**
Fastnet Race 388
Fatal Attraction 315
Fates, The **81**
Father, The 73
Father Goose 319
Father of the Bride 332
Fathers and Sons 108
fatigue 509
fats *see* lipids **487**
fatwah **100**
Faulkner, William **40**
fault **468**
fauns 88
Fauré, Gabriel **343**
Faust 39, 67, **81**
Faustian bargain 81
Fauvism **124**
faux pas **16**
favrile glass 149
Fawkes, Guy **199**
Fawlty Towers **316**
fax **555**, 560
FBI (Federal Bureau of Investigation) **270**, 284
February Revolution **233**
federalism **270**
Federal Reserve System **294**
Fédération Internationale de l'Automobile (FIA) 370
feet of clay **16**
felafel **392**
Fellini, Federico **316**
feminism **176**, 182, 184
fencing **370**, 377
Fens, The **407**, 414
Feodorovna, Empress Alexandra *124*
Ferdinand and Isabella 229, **233**
Fermanagh 447
Fermat's last theorem **531**
Fermat, Pierre de 531
fermentation **485**
Fermi, Enrico **531**
fermium *see* periodic table **541**
'Fern Hill' 57
ferns 485, *489*
Ferrari 370, 385
Ferrer, José *65*
Ferrier, Kathleen **343**
fertile crescent **233**

fertilisation **485**, 490, 515
Fessenden, Reginald 561
Festival Hall, London 199
Festival of Britain **199**
feta cheese **391**
feudalism 233, 251, 255, 258
Feydeau, Georges 66
Fianna Fáil **270**
Fibonacci, Leonardo 531
Fibonacci sequence **531**
Fibreglass **556**
fibre optics 503, **556**
Fiddlers Three 322
Fielding, Henry **40**
Field of Dreams 313
Field of the Cloth of Gold **233**
Fields, Gracie **343**, 416
field sport **370**
Fifteen Discourses on the Rules of Art 145
'Fifteen' Rebellion **199**
Figaro 66
Fighting Téméraire, The, 150
figure of speech **16**
film noir **316**
filo pastry 390, 395
FIMBRA (Financial Intermediaries, Managers and Brokers) **294**
Final Solution **233** *see also* Holocaust
financial year **294**
FTSE-100 Index **295**
Financial Times 295, **328**
fin-de-siècle **66**
Fine Gael **270**
Fine Romance, A 314
Fingal's Cave **407**
fingerprinting **556**
Finland 251, **438**
Finlandia 358
Finnegans Wake 44, 73, 542
firearms **556**
fireflies 480
Fire Over England 323, 328
Firm, The 313
Firth of Forth **407**
fiscal policy **294**
Fischer, Bobby **370**
fish 479, 481, **485**, *492*
    see also fishing
Fishbourne Roman Palace 404, **407**
Fisher King **81**
Fishguard **407**
fishing 292 *see also* angling
fission, nuclear *see* nuclear fission
Fistful of Dollars, A 315, 331
fits 503
Fitt, Gerry 284
Fittipaldi, Emerson 432
Fitzgerald, Edward 71
Fitzgerald, Ella **344**
FitzGerald, F. Scott **40**
FitzGerald, Garrett 270
Fitzgerald, Zelda *40*
Fitzherbert, Maria 200

Fiumicino 13
Five Easy Pieces 327
Five Pillars of Faith 103
Five Towns 416
'flag of convenience' 443
Flamborough Head **407**
flamenco dancing 455
flamingos *446*
Flanders 430
flash in the pan **16**
Flatford Mill **407**
flatworms *479*
Flaubert, Gustave **66**
fleas 498, 519
Fleet, River 407
Fleet Street 328, **407**
Fleming, Alexander 495, **503**, *514*
Fleming, Ian **40**, 310
Fleming, Victor 334
Flesh and the Devil 318
'flesh-eating' disease 495
flight **485**, 522
Flight of the Bumble Bee 356
Flight of the Phoenix 331
flintlocks 556
Flodden, Battle of **199**
flood **468**
Florence 251, **438**, 458
Florentine (art) **124**
florentine (food) **392**
Florey, Howard 503, **514**
Florida **438**
Florrie Forde 239
flower **485**
Flowering Cherry 329
flower power 178, 452
flu 507
fluorescence **531**
fluoride 518
fluorine *see* periodic table **541**
fluting **159**
Flyer 566
Flying Down To Rio 336
Flying Dutchman **81**
'Flying Finn' 378
flying saucers *89*
Flynn, Errol **317**
flywheel 566
focaccia **392**
Focke, Heinrich 557
foetus 504, 515, 517, 520
fog 526
Fogg, Phileas 62
foie gras **392**
Fokine, Mikhail 337
fold (geology) **468**
    mountains 468, 471
folic acid 520
Folkard, Charles 62
Folkestone **407**
folk music 339, **344**
Follow the Fleet 336
folly (building) **159**
Fonda, Henry **317**
Fonda, Jane **317**
Fonda, Peter 316, 317
fondue **392**
Fontaine, Joan 319
fontanelles **504**
Fonteyn, Dame Margot 336, **344**, 346, *352*

food
    energy content of 525
    poisoning **504**
    preservation 558
Foot, Michael **270**
football 362, 370, 379, 388
Football Association (FA) **370**
For a Few Dollars More 315, 331
foraminifera 490
Forbidden City 430
force 531, 538
Ford, Anna *327*
Ford, Gerald 263
Ford, Harrison 310, **317**, 331
Ford, Henry 294, *295*, 552
Ford, John 317, 333
Ford Motor Company 294
forecasting, weather 465, **476**
foreign exchange **294**
Foreign Legion 426
foreign secretary 263
forest, rain *see* rain forest
Forester, C.S. 308
Forest of Dean **407**
Formby, George **317**
For Me and My Gal 318
Formentera 455
Formosa (Taiwan) 456
formula (chemical) **531**
Formula One **370**
Forster, E.M. **40**, 323, 325
Forsyte Saga, The **40**
Forsyth, Frederick **40**
Fort Apache 317
forte **350**
Forth, Firth of 159, 399, 407
    Rail Bridge **159**
    Road Bridge 407
Forth, River 407
fortissimo **350**
Fort Sumter 220
Fortune Cookie, The 323
Fort William 400
'Forty-five' Rebellion **199**
42nd Street 310, **317**
Forum, Rome 451
For Whom The Bell Tolls **40**, 313
Fosbury, Dick 370
Fosbury flop **370**
fossil 468, 469, **486**
fossil fuels 466, 471, 472
Foster, Sir George 214
Foster, Jodie **317**
Foster, Sir Norman **159**, 420
Fotheringhay Castle *207*
fouetté (ballet) **337**
Fountains Abbey 154, **407**, 416
Four Books of Architecture, The 163
four-colour theorem **531**
Four Horsemen of the Apocalypse, The 333
Four Hundred Blows, The 327, 333
Four-minute mile 363, 377

Four Quartets 39
Four Seasons, The 360
Fourth Estate **16**
Fowles, John **40**
Fox, Charles James **199**, 201, 217
Fox, George 111
Fox and the Grapes, The 62
Fox Broadcasting 300
foxhunting 370
Fra Bartolommeo *93*
fractal **531**
fraction 528, **531**
fractionation *see* distillation
fracture **504**
Fragonard, Jean Honore **124**
France **438**, 450
   Dreyfus affair **232**
   Entente Cordiale 198, 214, **232**
   Fifth Republic 231
   'Free French' 231
   Jacquerie 224
   metric system 234
   St Bartholomew's Day Massacre 251
   Vichy government **255**
   Vietnam and 460
   West Indies and 461
   wines of *396*
Francesca, Piero della *94*
franchise **199**, **294**
Franciscans 94, 100
Francis I 233
Francis of Assisi, St **100**
francium *see* periodic table **541**
Franco, General Francisco 232, **233**, 252, 455
Franco-Prussian War **233**, 247
Frank, Anne **233**
Frankenstein films **317**
Frankenstein **40**
Frankfurt Assembly 250
Franklin, Aretha 359
Franklin, Benjamin *231*, **233**, 470
Franks 227, **233**, 438
Franny and Zooey 52
Frantic 329
Franz Ferdinand, Archduke **233**, 452
Franz Josef **233**
Fraser, Antonia 50
Fraser, George Macdonald 57
fraud, computer 557
Frazier, Joe *362*
freckles 517
Frederick I Barbarossa **233**
Frederick II **233**
Frederick the Great 222, **234**, 252
free association **176**
Free Churches 108
free enterprise **294**
Freedom space station 563
'Freedom' statue, Washington DC *461*
freemasons **100**
free trade 209, 298
free will **101**

freezing point **531**
French
   Academy 132
   National Assembly 279
   Resistance, (Maquis) 249
   Revolution 105, 223, 230, **234**, 438
   see also France
French Lieutenant's Woman, The 40, 50, 332
Frenchman's Creek 39
Frenzy 320
Freons 465, 562
frequency **531**, 533, 548, 561
fresco 118, **124**
Freshman, The 323
Freud, Lucian **124**
Freud, Sigmund 66, 70, 175, **176**, 179, 180
Freudian psychology 176, 181, 183, 184, 186
'Freudian slip' 177
Friar Tuck **81**
fricassée **392**
friction **531**
Friedan, Betty 176
Friedman, Milton (1912-) **294-5**, 300
Friendly Islands *see* Tonga
Friends of Eddie Coyle, The 326
Friends of the Earth 272
Frink, Dame Elizabeth **124**
frisée 391
Frobisher, Sir Martin **199**
Frobisher Bay 199
frog 478, 482
Frogs, The 62, **66**, 71
fromage frais **392**
From Here To Eternity 334, 358
Front Page, The 323, 334
fronts *see* cold front; warm front; occluded front
Frost, David 332
Frost, Robert **40**
fruit **486**, 489
Fry, Elizabeth **199**
Fry, Roger 34
FTSE-100 Index (Financial Times Stock Exchange-100 Index) **295**
Fuerteventura, Spain 433
Fugitive, The 317
fugue **344**
Fuji, Mount 441
Fuller, Richard Buckminster **159**
Fullmer, Gene 381
Full Metal Jacket 322
full stop **17**
Funchal, Madeira 444
functionalism, theory of 181
fundamentalism **101**, 108
Funeral in Berlin 311
fungi **486**, 487
   toxins 519
Funny Girl 359
Funny Thing Happened on the Way to the Forum, A 327, 358
Furies, The **81**

Furness Abbey 399
furniture, styles of 119, 125, 143, 144
fusion, nuclear *see* nuclear fusion
futures 295, 296
future shock **177**
fuzzy logic **101**

G

G7 295
gabbro 474
gable **160**
Gable, Clark 311, **317**, 319
Gabor, Denis 557
Gabriel, Angel 92, 104, 108, 111
Gabriel, Peter 344
Gachet, Dr 151
Gaddafi, Muammar **270-1**
gadolinium *see* periodic table **541**
Gagarin, Yuri 234
Gagnan, Emile 550
Gaia 81, **82**
Gaia hypothesis **468**
Gainsborough, Thomas **125**
Gaitskell, Hugh **199**, 270
Galahad, Sir **82**
Galápagos Islands 437, 483
galaxy **532**, 537
Galbraith, John Kenneth **295**, 304
Galen 504, 505, 513
Galerie des Glaces, Versailles 131, 168
Galicia 455
Galilee, Sea of 441
Galileo (Galileo Galilei) 238, 450, 527, **532**, 553, 565
gall bladder **504**
galleries and museums of the world **126**
gallery (architecture) **160**
Galliano liqueur 393
Gallipoli **234**, 458
gallium *see* periodic table **541**
gallstones **504**
Gallup, George 280
Galsworthy, John 40
Galton, Sir Francis 176, 556
Gamay (grape) 396
Games, Abram *199*
gamete 480, **486**
   see also sex cells
gamma radiation 529, **532**, 542, 558
Gandhi 235, 309
Gandhi, Indira **234**
Gandhi, Rajiv 234
Gandhi, Mahatma *234*, **235**, 239, 246, 440

Gang of Four, Britain 284
Gang of Four, China 243
Ganges, River **438**, 440
gangrene **504**
Garbo, Greta 309, **318**
Garden of Earthly Delights', The (Bosch) *120*
Garden of Eden 92, 109
Garden Party, The 46
Garden Route, South Africa 455
Gardner, Ava 317
Gardner, Gerald 90
Garfunkel, Art 358
Gargantua 72
gargoyle **160**
Garibaldi, Giuseppe 226, **235**
Garland, Judy **318**, 334
Garrick, David 152
Garter, Order of the 87, 178, **199**, 284
Garvey, Marcus 111
gas **532**, 535, 547
gas chromatography 526
Gascoigne, Paul **371**
Gaskell, Mrs Elizabeth **40**
gas laws 532
Gaslight 309
gas lighting 559
gastroenteritis **504**
gastropod **486**
Gate of Hell (Rodin) 145
'Gather ye rosebuds while ye may' 41
GATT (General Agreement on Tarriffs and Trade) **295**
Gaudí, Antonio **160**, 429
Gauguin, Paul 46, **125**, 139, 142, 456
Gaul 438
Gaullism **271**
Gaultier, Jean Paul **125**, *350*
Gautama Siddhartha 95
Gaveston, Piers 198
Gawain, Sir **82**
Gay, John 33
Gay Divorcee, The 355
Gaye, Marvin 351, 359
gay rights **177**
Gaza Strip 261, **438**
gazpacho **392**
GCHQ (Government Communications Headquarters) 284, 401
GCSE **177**
Gdansk, Poland 450
GDP (Gross Domestic Product) **295**
gears **556**
GEC-Marconi Ltd 559
Gehenna 102
geisha **177**, 442
Gell-Mann, Murray 542
Gemini *90*, 548
gemsboks 442
gemstones **468**
General Agreement on Tarriffs and Trades (GATT) **295**
gender **17**

gender roles **177**, 182
gene 481, 484, **486**, 487, 490, 506
General, The 322
general elections, British **268**
generalisation **17**
General Strike 195, **200**, 287
general theory of relativity 543
Genesis (pop group) **344**
Genesis, Book of **101**
genetic code 484
genetic fingerprinting **557**
genetic engineering 176, 500, **556**
Geneva **438**, 455
   Lake 438, 451
Geneva Conventions **271**
Genevieve **318**, 322
Genghis Khan **235**
Genji, The Tale of 66
genocide **177**
genre 67
Gentleman and Cabinet Maker's Director, The 122
Gentleman Jim 317
Gentlemen Prefer Blondes 326
Gentlemen's Agreement 328
genus 481
geo- 16, **17**
Geoffrey of Anjou 210
Geoffrey of Monmouth 78, 88
geological time scale **468**
geometric progression **532**
geometry 530, **532**
'Geordie' 413
George, Saint 87
George Cross *178*, 444
George I **200**
George II **200**, 345
George III **200**, 217
George IV 143, 163, **200**, 212
George V **200**, 401, 405
George VI *191*, **200**
George in Civvy Street 317
Georgia 428, 459
Georgian style (architecture) **160**
Georgian style (art) **125**
Georgics 74
Georgy Girl 325
geothermal energy **469**
Gere, Richard **318**
germanium *see* periodic table **541**
German measles **504**
German Opera, Prague 348
Germany 430, **438**
   inflation *297*
   Parliament 262
   Poland and 450
   reunification 275
   Warsaw and 461
   Weimar Republic 237, 245, **257**
Germany, Year Zero 330
germination **486**, 491
germs **504**, 513
Gerry, Eldridge 271
gerrymandering 271

Gers, France 390
Gershwin, George 308, **344**
Gershwin, Ira 344
gerund 17
Gesang der Jünglinge 359
gestalt 177
Gestapo **235**
Getaway, The 325
Get Carter 311
Get Cracking 317
Getty, Jean Paul **295**
Getty III, John Paul 295
Getty Museum 126, 295
Gettysburg, Battle of **235**
Gettysburg Address **235**
Getz, Stan 342
Gewürztraminer grape **396**
geysers 447, 462
Ghana **439**
ghee **392**
Ghent 125, 430
Ghent Altarpiece, The **125**
ghetto **177**
Ghiberti, Lorenzo **125**
Ghost Breakers, The 321
Ghosts 68
Giacometti, Alberto **126**
Giant 314
giants 79, **82**
Giant's Causeway 407, 447, *474*
Giap, General 232
Giazotto, Remo 336
Gibberd, Sir Frederick 162
Gibbon, Edward 233
Gibbons, Grinling **160**, 415
Gibbs, James **160**
Gibraltar **439**
    Strait of 444
Gibson, Wing-Commander Guy *178*, 196
Gibson, Mel **318**, 334
Gide, André 67
Gielgud, Sir John 308, 311, **318**
giga- 537
Gigi 64, *119*, 341
Gigli, Beniamino 340
Gilbert, Sir William Schwenk 344
Gilbert and Sullivan **344**
gilding the lily 17
Gileadites 27
Gill, Eric **126**
Gillespie, Dizzy 338, **344**
Gilliam, Terry 326
Gillray, James 121, **126**, *291*
gills **486**
Gill Sans Serif 126
gilts **295**
ginger *393*
'gingerbread man' (fractals) *531*
gingivitis **504**, 505, 518
Giorgione **126**, 460
Giotto 124, **126**
Giotto space probe *533*
Gipsy Moth IV 408
giraffes 442
Girl Guides 189
Girl in Every Port, A 325
Girl Shy 323

Girton College, Cambridge 183
Giscard D'Estaing, Valéry 271, 434
Giverny 137
Giza, pyramids 164, 165, *251*
gizzard **486**
glaciation **469**, 470
glaciers *see* ice ages
gladiators 451
Gladstone, William Ewart **200**, 203, 210, 291
Gladstone bag 200
Glamis **407**
glands **504**, 518
glandular fever **504**
Glaser, Milton 127
Glasgow **407**
    football clubs 408
glasnost **271**, 458
glass 460, **557**, 562
Glass Menagerie, The 59
Glass of Blessings, A 51
Glastonbury 78, **82**
glaucoma **504**
Glen Coe **408**
    Massacre of **200**
Glevum (Gloucester) 408
gliding **371**
glima (Icelandic wrestling) 388
Glitter, Gary 349
global village **177**
global warming 465, **469**, 473, 474, 476
globe artichokes 390
Globe Theatre **41**
Gloria 350
Glorious Revolution **200**
glossary 17
Gloster Meteor 558
Gloucester **408**
glow worms 480
glucose **486**, 539
glue ear **504**
Glyme, River 401
Glyndebourne **344**
gnocchi **392**
Gnostics **101**
GNP (Gross National Product) **296**
Goat Fell, Arran 398
gobbledegook **17**
Gobelins factory 131, 148
Go-Between, The 324
Gobi Desert 445, 467
God **101**
Godard, Jean-Luc 327
Goddard, Robert Hutchings 562
Gödel, Kurt **532**
Gödel's theorem **532**
Godfather, The and sequels 311, 314, *319*, 328
Godiva, Lady **82**
Godse, Nathuram 235
Godwin, William 54
Godwin Austen (K2 peak) 442

Gogol 73
Going Gently 334
goitre 518
Golan Heights 252, **439**, 456
gold 235, 433, 442, 546
    see also periodic table **541**
Gold, Thomas 546
Gold Diggers, The 310
Golden Age 88
Golden Fleece **82**, 84
Golden Gate Bridge **160**, *452*
'Golden Hind' 197
Golden Horn 441
Golden Notebook, The 45
golden section **160**
Golden Temple, Amritsar 426, 450
'Golden Triangle' 433
Golding, William **41**
gold rush 235
Gold Rush, The 312
Goldsmith, Oliver **41**
gold standard **295**
Goldwyn, Samuel **319**
Goldwyn Pictures 319
golf 371, 382, 417
gondolas 460
Gondwanaland 466
Gone with the Wind 317, **319**, 323
gonorrhoea 520
Gonzales Pancho **371**
Gooch Graham **371**
Good, the Bad and the Ugly, The 315, 331
Goodbye Mr Chips 315
Goodbye to All That 41
Goodbye to Berlin 43
Goodfellas 314, 330
Good Housekeeping **324**
Goodman, Benny **345**, 346, 348
Good Old Days, The 411
Good Queen Bess 198
Good Samaritan **101**
goodwill **296**
Goolagong, Evonne 387
Goon Show, The **319**, 326, 330
Gorbachev, Mikhail 228, 251, **271**, 288
Gorbals 407
Gordian knot **17**, 220
Gordius, King of Phyrgia 14
Gordon, Charles **200**, 442
Gordon, Lord George 200
Gordon Riots **200**
Gordy, Berry 351
Gore, A.W. 380
Gorgons, **82**
Gorgonzola cheese **391**
Göring, Hermann **235**
Gorky, Maxim 67
gorse 491
Goscinny, René 63
gospel music **345**, 356
Gospel of Truth 90
Gospels **101**
Gothic architecture **160**
Gothic novel **67**

Goths **235**
Gouda cheese 391
goulash **392**
gourds 395
gout **504**
Government Communications Headquarters (GCHQ) 284, 401
governor **271**
Gower, David **371**
'Go west, young man' **236**
Goya, Francisco de **127**, 444
Gozo, Malta 444
Grable, Betty **319**
grace **101**
Grace, W.G. **371**
grace-and-favour 101
Graceland 444
Graces, Three **82**
gradable objective **17**
Graduate, The **320**, 369
Graff, Steffi **372**, 382
Graham, Billy **101**
Grahame, Gloria 317
Grahame, Kenneth 60
-gram **17**
gram *see* kilogram **534**
grammar **17**
grammar schools **175**
Grampian Mountains **408**
Gran Canaria 433
Gran Chaco 449
Grand Alliance 193
Grand Bahama 429
Grand Canal, China 157, **160**
Grand Canal, Venice 460
Grand Canyon **439**
Grande Jatte, La (Seurat) *147*
Grand Hotel 318
Grand Hotel, Brighton 402
grand mal 503
Grandma Moses **127**
Grand National **372**
grand prix 370, 388, 445
grand slam **372**
Grand Tour **127**
grand unified theory (GUT) **547**
granite 474
Grant, Cary **319**
Grant, Duncan 34
Grant, Ulysses S. *220*, **236**
Grantchester **408**
Grantham **408**
Grantham, Leslie 315
Grapes of Wrath, The 55, 317, 448
grape varieties 396
-graph- **17**
graph **532**
graphic arts **127**
graphite 525
graphology 17
grappa **392**
Grasmere **408**
Grass, Gunter 67
grasses **486**
Grass is Singing, The 45
gratin dauphinoise 392
gravad lax **392**

grave (music) **350**
grave accent **17**
Graves (wine) 396
Graves, Robert **41**
gravitation **532**, 547
graviton 528, 547
gravity 524, 526, *532*, 543
    acceleration due to 522
    tides and 475
gravure 561
Gray, Thomas 41
Gray's Elegy 40, **41**
Gray's Inn 274
Great Barrier Reef **439**, 450, 466
Great Britain, SS 156, 402
Great Dictator, The 312
Great Dividing Range, Australia 439
Great Eastern (liner) 156
Great Escape, The 325
Greatest Show on Earth, The 314, 320
Great Exhibition (1851) 188, 199, **201**
Great Expectations **41**, 323
Great Fire of London **201**
Great Gatsby, The 40, 329
Great Glen 409, 468
Great Lakes **439**
Great Malvern **408**
great man theory **177**
Great Ouse 414
Great Plague **201**, 412
Great Plains 448, 475
Great Pyramid of King Cheops, 164
Great Red Spot, Jupiter *534*
Great Salt Lake 459
Great Train Robbery, The **319**
Great Trek 191, **236**, 455
Great Wall of China **161**
Great Western (liner) 156
Great Western Railway 156, 421
Great Zimbabwe 462
Greaves, Jimmy **372**
Greece 428, **439**
Greece, Ancient **236**, 251, 377, 428
    see also Olympic Games 363, 369, 377, 379
Greek alphabet 236
Greek Myths 41
Greek Orthodox Church **109**, 225
Greeley, Horace 236
Green, Lucinda 363
Green Berets, The 333
Green Card 314
Greene, Graham **41**, 309, 460
greengrocer's apostrophe 11
greenhouse effect 272, **469**
Green Knight 82
Greenland 232, 469, 470
Green Man **82**
Greenmantle 35
green paper 272
Greenpeace *272*
green pound **296**
Greens (environmental protection) 272, 467

Greenwich **408**
  Mean Time 408
  Royal Observatory 408
Greenwich Village,
  Manhattan 446
Greer, Germaine 176
Gregorian chant 236, **345**
Gregory the Great, Pope
  236, 345
Gregson, John 318
gremlins **82**
gremolata 394
Grenada 283, 461
Gresham, Sir Thomas 296
Gresham's law **296**
Gretna Green **408**
Grey, Earl (Charles Grey)
  201
Grey, Lady Jane **201**
greyhound racing **372**
Greystoke 332
Grieg, Edvard **345**
Griffith, Arthur 285
Griffith, D.W. 310, **319**
Grimaldi family 445
Grimm, The Brothers **67**
Grimmond, Jo *268*
Grimm's Fairy Tales 67, 69,
  331
Grim Reaper **82**
Gris, Juan **127**
grisaille 137
grist to the mill **17**
Gromyko, Andrei 244
Groonfontein, Namibia 470
Gropius, Walter *156*, **161**
Gross Domestic Product
  (GDP) **296**
Grossmith, George and
  Weedon **41**
Gross National Product
  (GNP) **296**
Grosvenor Square 413
groundnuts scheme 456
grouper fish, symbiosis *492*
group therapy **177**
growth (in living things)
  486
Grundy, Mother 21
Gruyère cheese **391**, 455
guacamole **392**
Guangzhou *see* Canton
Guardi, Francisco **127**
Guardi, Giovanni 127
Guardian, The **328**, 413
Guardians of the Secret
  (Pollock) *142*
Guernica (Spain) **236**, 252
Guernica (Picasso) *141*, 236
Guernsey 434
*Guess Who's Coming to
  Dinner* 320, 329, 333
Guevara, Che **236**, 263
Guggenheim Museum 126,
  168
Guiana Highlands 459
guilds **236**
Guilin Hills 434
Guillotin, Dr Ignace 272
guillotine **272**
guilt and shame cultures
  177
Guimard, Hector *155*
Guinea Current *471*

Guinevere **82**
Guinness, Sir Alec *315*,
  319, 322, 333, 331
Gulag Archipelago, The 73
Gulf of Aqaba 473
Gulf of Mexico 475
Gulf Stream 447, **469**, *471*
Gulf War **236**, *237*, 429,
  442, 557, 564
Gulliver's Travels *41*, *56*
gumbo **392**
Gunfight at the OK Corral
  315, 323
Gunga Din 44, *316*
Gung Ho 326
Gunnell, Sally **373**
Gunpowder Plot 199, **201**
guns, submachine 556
Guns of Navarone, The 46,
  327
Gurkhas 446
Gurnemanz 86
guru **101**
Guru Nanak 114
Gustavus Adolphus, King
  253
Gutenberg, Johann 67, **236**,
  561
Gutenberg Bible **67**, 236
Guthrie, Woody **345**
guttural **17**
Guys and Dolls 311, 319
Gwyn, Nell 195, **201**
gymnastics 367,**373**, 374
gymnosperms 482, **486**,
  492
gynaecology 510
Gypsies **178**
gyrocompasses 554
gyroscope 537, 541, **557**

H

habeas corpus **272**
Habitat **127**
Habsburg, House of 222,
  236, 238, 252, 253, 429,
  440, 462
Habsburg jaw and lip 237
Habyarimana, President
  Juvenal 185, 451
hacker **557**
Hades **82**, 86, 88
Hadlee, Sir Richard **373**
Hadrian, Emperor 164
Hadrian's Wall *408*, **409**
hadrons 546
hadrosaurs 483
haematology, 510
haemo-, haem- **18**
haemoglobin 497, **504**
haemophilia 249, **504**
haemorrhoids **505**, 520
hafnium *see* periodic table
  541
haggis **392**
Hagia Sofia **161**, 240

Hagman, Larry 313
Hague 446
hahnium *see* periodic table
  541
hail **469**
Haile Selassie 111, **237**
Hailsham, Lord (Quintin
  Hogg) **272**
hair **505**
Hair 345
Haiti **439**, 461
Hakim 99
Haley, Bill **345**, 356
Haley, Jack 334
half-life **533**
Halicarnassus 431
halitosis **505**
Hallé Orchestra,
  Manchester 413
Halley, Edmond **533**
Halley's comet 190, 526,
  533
Hallowe'en **82**
Hals, Frans **127**, 446
halva **393**
Hamburg 438
Hamer, Robert 322
Hamilton, Charles 34
Hamilton, Great Bermuda
  431
Hamlet **42**, 45, 51, 57, 311,
  314, 318, 328, 330, 334
Hammer Films 317
Hammerstein II, Oscar **345**
Hammett, Dashiel 310
Hammurabi 223, **237**, 244
Hamnett, Katherine **127**
Hampstead **409**
Hampton, Lionel 345
Hampton Court Palace
  167, **409**
Han (Chinese) 435
Hancock, Tony **319**
Hancock's Half-Hour 319,
  334
Handel, George Frideric
  345
handfasting ceremony 171
Handful of Dust, A 59
Handley, Tommy 321
handwriting **17**
Hanging Gardens of
  Babylon 246
'Hanging Judge' 191
Hanna, William 332
Hanoi 460
Hanover, House of **201**
Hansard **272**
Hansard, Luke 272
Hans Christian Andersen
  319, 322
Hanseatic League **237**
Hansel and Gretel **68**
Hanson plc 293
Hanukkah **96**
Happy Prince, The 59
hara-kiri **178**
Harald V 447
Harare 462
hard currency **296**
Hardie, Keir **201**

Hardy, Captain Thomas
  208
Hardy, Oliver *323*
Hardy, Thomas **42**, 401,
  405
Hare Krishna movement
  102
harelip **505**
Harger, Rolla N. 552
Hargreaves, James 203
harijans ('untouchables')
  172
Harland and Wolff 430
Harlem 446, 447
Harlem Globetrotters 364
Harold, King *189*, 190, 201
Harold II 197
*Harold Lloyd's Funny Side of
  Life* 323
*Harold Lloyd's World of
  Comedy* 323
Harpies **82**
Harris, Joel Chandler 35
Harrisburg 449
Harrison, George 338, 343
Harrison, Rex *54*, 352
Harrogate **409**
Harrow **409**
Harrow School 409
Hart, Lorenz 356
Hartnell, William 315
Harvard 431
harvestmen 479
Harvey 331
Harvey, Laurence 330
Harvey, William **505**
Harvey Wallbanger **393**
Hastings **409**
Hastings, Battle of 189,
  190, **201**, 409
Hastings, Warren **201**
Hatfield House *161*, **409**
hatha yoga 116
Hattersley, Roy **272**
Hatton, Derek 279
Haughey, Charles 270
Haussmann, Baron Georges
  449
Havana 329, 435
Havel, Vaclav **272**
Hawaii **439**, 473, *475*
Haw Haw, Lord 206
Hawking, Stephen 511, **533**
Hawkins, Jack 323
Hawksmoor, Nicholas **127**
Haworth **409**, 423
Hawthorne, Nathaniel **42**
Hawthorne, Nigel 334
Hawtrey, Charles 312
Haydn, Joseph **345**, 351
hay fever 495, **505**
Hay-on-Wye **409**
Hay Wain, The (Constable)
  122
headache 510
Headingley 368
head of state **272**
Healey, Denis (Lord
  Healey) **272**
Heaney, Seamus **42**
hearing 491 *see also* ear
Hearst, William Randolph
  296, 312

heart 495, **505**
  attack **505**
  disease and disorders
    495, 505, 518
  electrical impulses 503
  failure **505**
  rate 497, 513
  rhythm 505
  transplant 505, 519
Heartbreak House 54
heartburn **505**
Heart of Darkness **42**, 71,
  462
Heart of the Matter, The 41
heartwood 492
heat 530, **533**, 546
heat capacity 533
'heat death of the Universe'
  530
Heath, Sir Edward 268,
  273, 288
Heathrow **409**
Heaven Can Wait 309
Heavens Above 311
heavy metal **346**, 348
heavy water **533**
Hebrew Bible 95
Hebrew language185
Hebrew scripture 96, 108
Hebrides **409**
hecto- 537
Hector 76, **82**
Hedda Gabler 68
hedging **296**, 301
Heep, Uriah **38**
Hegel, Georg Wilhelm
  Friedrich 98, **102**
Hegira, the 108
Heidi **68**
Heisenberg, Werner 547
Helen of Troy **82**, 83
helicopter 132, **557**
helio- 18
Helios (sun god) 451
helium 526, **533**, 538, 545,
  546 *see also* periodic
  table **541**
helix **533**
Hell **82**, **102**
Heller, Joseph 36
Hellespont 258
Hello! 324
Hello, Dolly! 336, 348
Hell's Angels 179
Helmer, Nora 65
Helpmann, Sir Robert **346**
Helsinki 438
Hemingway, Ernest 40, **42**,
  313
hemiplegia 513
Hemlock and After 60
Hendrix, Jimi **346**
Hendry, Stephen **373**
Henley Regatta **373**, 409
Henley-on-Thames **409**
Henreid, Paul 312
Henry I **201**
Henry II 190, **202**
Henry III **202**, 203
Henry IV **202**, 245
Henry IV, Parts 1 and 2, **42**,
Henry V 188, **202**
Henry V **43**, 311, 328
Henry VI 198, **202**, 213

Henry VI 53
Henry VII (Henry Tudor) 168, **202**, 213
Henry VIII 191, 193, 196, **202**, 207, 212, 233
Henry VIII 54
Henry the Navigator, Prince 450
Henry, Edward 556
hepatitis **505**, 508
Hepburn, Audrey *54*, **320**
Hepburn, Katharine 49, *308*, 317, **320**, 323, 333
Hephaestus **82**, 86, 87
Hepplewhite, George **127**
Heptarchy 188
Hepworth, Dame Barbara **127**
Hera 76, **83**
Heracles 83
Heraklion, Crete 435
herbal medicine **505**
Herbert, St 411
herbes de Provence *393*
herbs *393*
Herculaneum 460
herculean task 83
Hercules **83**, 87, 550
hereditary **505**
Hereford **409**
heresy **102**
Hereward the Wake **203**, 406
Herge 74
hermaphrodites 480
hermaphroditism 170
Hermes **83**, 84
Hermitage Museum 126, 452
hernia **505**
Herodotus 86, **237**
heroin 502
herpes **505**, 520
Herrick, Robert 36, 41
Herschel, William 547, 556
Hertford College, Oxford *414*
hertz 531, **533**
Hertz, Heinrich 533
Herzl, Theodor 288
Herzog 33
Heseltine, Michael **273**
Hess, Rudolf **237**
Hesse, Hermann **68**
Hestia 83
Heston, Charlton **320**, 329
hetero- **18**
heterosexuality 170
heterotroph **486**
hiatus hernia 505
Hiawatha, The Song of 43
hibernation **486**
Hicks, David **127**
hiding one's light under a bushel **18**
hieratics 127
hieroglyphs **18**, **127**
Hieronymus Bosch 114
Higgins, Alex **373**
High and the Mighty, The 333
High Court of Justiciary **273**
High Court of Justice 264, 266, **273**

Highlands, Scottish **409**, 468
High Noon 313, 322, 334
High Plains Drifter 316
High Sierra 310
High Society 322, 336, 355
high-tech **161**
hijack, airliner 458
Hill, Damon **373**
Hill, George Roy 311
Hill, Graham **373**
Hill, Rowland 209
Hillary, Edmund 445
Hilliard, Nicholas, **128**, *212*
Himalayas **440**, 446, *468*, 471
Himmler, Heinrich **237**
Hindenburg, airship 237, 566
Hindenburg, Paul von **237**, 438
Hindi language 440
Hinduism 95, 99, **102**, 172, 440
Hindu Kush range 426
Hindus 455
Hipparchus 535
hippies **178**, 442, 452
hippocampus 510
Hippocrates **506**, 513
Hippocratic oath 506
Hippocrene 86
Hippolyta 76
Hippolytus 76
hire purchase **296**
Hirohito **237**, 441
Hiroshima 221, 441, 560
Hiroshima Mon Amour 327
His Master's Voice 29
Hispaniola 439, 450, 461
histamine **506**
histogram 532
History of Mr. Polly, The 59, 326
History of the Decline and Fall of the Roman Empire, The 233
History of the English-Speaking Peoples, A 195
History of the Kings of Britain 78
History of Western Philosophy 112
Hitchcock, Sir Alfred 39, 313, 315, 319, **320**, 323, 324, 329
Hitler, Adolf 225, **237**, 244, *245*, 253, 255, 257, 379
  see also World War II
HIV 494, **506**, 513
hives **506**
Hoare, Henry 420
Hobart 456
Hobbes, Thomas **102**
Hobbit, The 46, 57
Hobbs, Sir Jack **373**
Hobson's Choice **18**, 323, 326
Ho Chi Minh **238**, 256
Ho Chi Minh City 238, 460
Hock **396**
hockey **373**
Hockney, David **128**
hocus-pocus **18**
Hodgkin's disease **506**

Hofburg Palace, Vienna 460
Hoffman, Dustin **320**
Hogarth, William 121, **129**
hoi polloi **18**
hoist with one's own petard **18**
Hokkaido, Japan 441
Hokusai 129
Holbein, Hans *202*
Holbein the Elder, Hans **129**
Holbein the Younger, Hans **129**
Holden, William 332
Holiday, Billie **346**
holism **102**
holistic medicine 102, 499, **506**
Holland, John 564
hollandaise *393*
Holloway, Stanley 352
Holly, Buddy **346**
Hollywood **321**, 355, 443
Hollywood Wives 53
Holmes, Andy 381
Holmes, Sherlock **43**
holmium *see* periodic table 541
Holocaust 170, 177, 179, 222, 229, 232, 233, 235, **238**
Holocene epoch *468*
hologram **557**
holography 534, 557
Holst, Gustav **346**
Holy Communion *see* Eucharist 99
Holy Father 110
Holy Ghost *see* Holy Spirit **102**
Holy Grail 82, **83**
Holy Island (Lindisfarne) 398, **409**
Holy Mosque, Mecca 163
Holy Roman Empire **238**
Holyroodhouse, Palace of **410**
Holy Spirit 92, **102**, 110
Holy Trinity **115**
Homage to Catalonia 48, 252
Home 329
Home, Alec Douglas 281
Home Counties **410**
Home Office 282
Homer 68, 80, 85
Home Rule **203**
Home Secretary 263
Hominoidae 181, 481
homo- **18**
Homo habilis 181
homoeopathy 495, **506**
homo erectus 181
homograph **18**
homonyms **18**
homophone **18**
Homo sapiens 181, 481
homosexuality 170, 173, 177, **178**
Honecker, Erich 439
Hong Kong 246, **440**
Honolulu 439
Honorary Consul, The 41

Honourable Schoolboy, The 45
honours and titles **178**, 241
Honshu, Japan 441
Hood, Robin **87**, 212, 414, 419
Hook 321, 331
Hooke, Robert 533
Hooke's Law **533**
Hoover, Herbert **238**
Hoover, J. Edgar **270**
Hoover Dam 246
Hope, Bob **321**, 330
Hopkins, Sir Anthony 317, **321**, 325
Hopkins, Gerard Manley **43**
Hopkins, Matthew 90
Hopkins, Miriam 309
Hopper, Dennis 316
Hopper, Edward **129**
Hoppy Serves a Writ 326
Horace **68**, 73
hormones **506**, 515, 517, 518
hormone replacement therapy (HRT) 506, 510
Horne, Janet 90
Hors d'Age 390
hors d'oeuvre 394, 395
Horse Feathers 325
horsepower 548, 566
horse racing 366, 369, *372*, **373**, 378, 413
Horseshoe Falls, Canada 447
horsetails 489
horse-trials, Badminton **363**
hostages 263
hot-air balloon *560*
hot cross buns 101
Hôtel du Lac 35
'hotspots' 473
hot springs 447, 462, 469
Hounds of the Baskervilles, The 39, 405
House at Pooh Corner, The 47
House for Mr Biswas, A 47
House of Bernarda Alba, The 69
House of Commons **203**, 273
  Chiltern Hundreds 404
  debating chamber *273*
  Northern Irish seats 288
  parliamentary committee **280**
House of Life, The 52
House of Lords 178, **203**, 205, **273**
House of Representatives **274**
House of Usher, The 329
House of Wax 329
Houses of Parliament 164
Housman, A.E. **43**, 419
Houston 457
hovercraft **557**
Howard, Catherine 202
Howard, Thomas, Earl of Surrey 199
Howard, Trevor 311
Howard of Effingham, Lord 189
Howard's End 40, 321, 325

Howarth, Jack 313
Howe, Elias 562
Howe, Geoffrey (Lord Howe) **274**, 287
How Green Was My Valley 317
How to Marry a Millionaire 326
Hoyle, Sir Fred 546
Huang He **440**
Hubbard, L. Ron 113
Hubble, Edwin **533**, 543
Hubble's constant 533
Hubble space telescope *564*, 565
Huckleberry Finn, The Adventures of **43**
Hud 327
Hughes, Howard **296**
Hughes, Ted **43**
Hughes, Thomas, 57
Hugo, Victor **68**
Huguenots **238**, 245, 251
Hulanicki, Barbara 119
Hulce, Tom 308
Hull **410**
Human Genome Project **506**
humanism 99, **102**
human rights 260, 269, **274**-5
Humber Bridge **161**
Humber estuary 414
Humboldt Current *471*
Hume, David 96, **102**
Hume, John 284
humidity 469
hummingbird 480, 485
hummous **393**, 395
humours **178**, 504
Humpty Dumpty 24
Hunchback of Notre Dame, The 67, **68**, 312
Hundred Years' War 188, 191, 196, 202, **238**, 239, 438
Hungarian Uprising **238**
Hungary 233, **440**
  Soviet Union and 238
hung parliament **274**
Huns **238**
Hunt, James **373**
Hunt, Rex 198
Hunt, William Holman **129**
Hunter, The 325
hunter-gatherers 177, **178**, 180, 185
hunting 370
Hunting of the Snark, The **43**
Hurd, Douglas **274**
Huron, Lake 439
hurricane 465, **469**, 475
Hurricane (aircraft) 192
Hush, Hush, Sweet Charlotte 313
Huss, John **238**
Hussein, King 442, 461
Hussein, Saddam 236, 239, **284**, 441, 442
Husserl, Edmund 110
Hussey, Olivia 334
Hussites 238

Hustler, The 327
Huston, Anjelica 321
Huston, John 308, 316, **321**
Huston, Walter 321
Hutton, Sir Len **373**, 384
Hutus 451, 452
Huxley, Aldous 35
Huxley, Thomas 92
Huygens, Christiaan 553
hybrid **486**
Hyde Park *354*, **410**
Hydra **83**
hydraulics 535, 542, **558**
hydro-, hydr- **18**
hydrocarbons 472, **533**, 553, 561
hydrofoil 551, **558**
hydrogen 524, **533**, 537, 538, 539, 545, 546
  sulphide 464
  see also periodic table **541**
hydrogen bomb 539, 560
hydrogen bonding 548
hydrologic cycle **469**
hydrophobia 515
hydrothermal vents 472
hydroxyl ions 524
Hyksos 232
Hymn of Creation 48
hyper- **18**
hyperactivity **506**
hyperbola *527*
hyperbole **18**
Hyperion 44
hypermetropia (long sight) 503
hypertension 497
hyperventilation **506**, 520
hyphen **18**
hypno- **18**
hypnosis **506**
hypo- **18**
hypotension 497
hypothalamus 498, 503, 514
hypothermia **506**, 518
hypothesis **103**
hypothyroidism 519
hysterectomy **506**
hysteria 506

I

Iberian Peninsula 450, 455
ibid. **18**
Ibiza 455
Iblis (devil) 98, 100, **103**
Ibn Saud 453
Ibsen, Henrik **68**, 329, 345
Icarus 79, **83**
ice ages 465, **469**, 474
iceberg **470**
Ice Cold in Alex 326
ice-dancing 386, *387*
ice hockey **374**
Iceland **440**, 450, 472
Iceman Cometh, The 48
ice sheets 469

Ice Station Zebra 46
I-Ching **103**
Ickx Jacky 375
I Claudius 41, 228
icon *109*, 121, **129**
iconoclasm **103**
iconoclasts 129
iconoscope 566
id **179**
Ideal Husband, An 59
idealism **103**
idée fixe **18**
idem **18**
ideogram 18
Ides of March 240
I Didn't Do It 317
idiolect **18**
idiom **18**
Idle, Eric 326
idolatry **103**
Idylls of the King 57
i.e. **18**
Iglesias, Julio **346**
Ignatius of Loyola, St **103**
igneous rock *see* rock
iguanodons 483
Iguazú Falls 432, **440**, *441*
'I have a dream' **238**, 241
Iliad **68**, 183, 245
Ilkley Moor **410**
illiteracy **18**
illness, acute **494**
imagery **69**
imaginary number 539
imago 488
I'm All Right Jack 311, 330
imam **103**
Immaculate Conception **103**
immune system 496, **507**, 515, 519, 520
immunisation 496, **507**, 509, 513, 520
immunology 510
impeachment **274**
imperative **18**
imperialism **274**
Imperial Palace, Tokyo 457
Imperial Russian Ballet 348, 354
impersonal verb **18**
Importance of Being Earnest, The 59, 316, 330, 331
imports 290
Impression, Sunrise (Manet) 129
Impressionism **129**, 138
Impressionists 142, 450
Imran Khan **374**
In a German Pension 46
in-breeding 179
in camera **18**
Incas **238**, 427, 457
incest **179**
Inchcape Rock, The 55
income, real **303**
income distribution **297**
income support 172
income tax 210, **297**
incubation period **507**
Indecent Proposal 329
indefinite article **18**
indefinite pronoun **19**
independence *see* countries

Independent, The **328**
independent clause **19**
Independent Labour Party 201
Independent Republicans, France 271
independent schools 175, 185
index-linked **297**
India **440**
  caste system 172, 235
  da Gama's sea route to 443
  film industry 431
  language 440
  Mughal rule in 244
  'untouchables' *172*
  see also Bangladesh; Indian; Pakistan
Indiana Jones and the Last Crusade 313, 317
Indiana Jones and the Temple of Doom 317, 331
Indianapolis **374**
Indian Mutiny **203**, 440
Indian Ocean 430, **440**, 471
indicative **19**
indirect object **19**
indirect speech **19**
indium *see* periodic table **541**
individualism 186
Indo-European **19**
Indonesia 429, 431, **440**
  invasion of East Timor 436-7
inductive reasoning **103**
indulgence **103**
Induráin, Miguel *368*
Indus, River 449
industrial
industrial relations **297**
Industrial Revolution **203** 410, 466
industrial tribunal **274**
Indy car series 374
inertia **534**, 536
in extremis **19**
infallibility **103**
infant mortality 500, 509
infectious diseases, childhood 504
infertility treatment **507**, 515
infinitive **19**
in flagrante delicto **19**
inflation **297**, 300
inflection **19**
influenza **507**, 520
Informer, The 317
infra dig **19**
  device 551, **558**
  radiation 529, **534**, 558
infrastructure **297**
Ingres, Jean **129**
Inherit the Wind 333
initialism **19**
initiation **179**
injunction **274**
Inkatha Freedom Party 455
inkblot test 176, **179**
Inland Revenue 290
in loco parentis **19**
In Memoriam 57

Inner Temple 274
Innocence of Father Brown, The 37
Innocent III, Pope 220
Innocents Abroad, The 58
Inn of the Sixth Happiness 315
Inns of Court **274**
innuendo **19**
Inquiry into the Nature and Causes of the Wealth of Nations, An 304
Inquisition 151, **238**, 532
insects 479, **486**, 491
  metamorphosis **488**
insemination, artificial 507
insider dealing **297**
In Society 308
insolvency **297**
Inspector Calls, An 51
instinct **486**
Institutes of the Christian Religion 226
institutional investors 297
insulin 501, 507, 513
insurance 290, 297, 299, 301, 306
intelligence 550
  artificial **550**
Intelligence Men, The 327
intelligence quotient (IQ) 176, 179
intelligence tests 179
Intelligent Woman's Guide to Socialism and Capitalism, The 54
Intelsat 6 satellite 562
inter- **19**
inter alia **19**
inter alios **19**
Intercontinental ballistic missiles (ICBMs) 560
interest **297**, 300
interference 528, 534, 535, 548
interferon 520
Inter-governmental Maritime Consultative Organisation 275
Interiors 308
interjection **19**
Intermezzo 309
Internal Affairs 318
internal market 297
internal-combustion engine 558
International Bank for Reconstruction and Development 306
International Bureau of Weights and Measures 534
International Convention Centre (ICC), Birmingham 401
International Court of Justice 275
International Development Association (IDA) 298
International Labour Organisation 275
international law 275
international modern style (architecture) 161

International Monetary Fund (IMF) 225, 298
International Red Cross 271
International Society for Krishna Consciousness 102
Internet, The 554
internment (Northern Ireland) 272
interrogative **19**
interventionism 298
intestine 500, 501, 502
in the doldrums **19**
In the Heat of the Night 329
In the World 67
Intimations of Immortality 60
Intolerance 319
in toto **19**
intra- **19**
intransitive verb **19**
intravenous 507
introvert 179, 180
Inuit 179
Inverewe 410
Inverness 410
inverse square law 532
invertebrate *479*, **487**
inverted commas **19**
investment trust 298
in vino veritas **19**
Invisible Man, The 59
invisibles 298
in vitro fertilisation 507
In Which We Serve 326
iodine 518, *see also* periodic table 541
ion 529, 534
Iona 410
Ionesco, Eugène 69, 74
Ionian Islands 435, 439
ionic bond 525
Ionic column 157
ionosphere 464, 470
Ipanema 451
Ipcress File, The 311
ipso facto **19**
Ipswich 421
IRA (Irish Republican Army) 191, 203, 208, 275, 285
Iran 108, 284, 440
  American hostages 263
  Iran-Contra affair 238, 283
  Iraq, war with 239, 440, 441, 453
  mullahs 108
  Shah of 240, 244
Iraq 429, **441**
  Gulf War 236
  Marsh Arabs 177, 284
  nuclear weapons 284
Ireland, Northern **447**
  Anglo-Irish Agreement **260**
· Belfast **430**
  Boyne, Battle of the **192**
  Democratic Unionist Party 288
  Devolution 267
  IRA 191, 203, 208, **275**, 285
  loyalist **277**

Orangemen 192, **208**
politics 288
Sinn Féin 260, 275, **285**
Ulster unionists **288**
see also IRA
Ireland, Republic of **441**
Anglo Irish Agreement **260**, 270
Anglo-Irish Treaty 285
Brian Boru **225**
Easter Rising **197**
Fianna Fáil **270**
Fine Gail **270**
potato famine **211**
World War II and 231
see also Irish; Ulster
iridium *see* periodic table **541**
Irish Free State 191, **203**, 270
Irish Home Rule 193, 197, **203**, 206, 209, 210
Irish Republican Army *see* IRA
Irish Republican Brotherhood 197
Irish 'Invincibles' 210
iron 535, 539, 546 *see also* periodic table **541**
Iron Age **239**
Ironbridge Gorge **410**
'Iron Chancellor' 224
'iron curtain' 224, 235
Irons, Jeremy 311
Ironweed 327
irony **19**
irradiation **558**
irrational number 539, 540
Irrawaddy river 433
irregular verb **19**
irrigation **470**
irritable bowel syndrome **507**
Irwell, River 412
Isaac 92
Isabel de Porcel, Dona 127
Isabella of France 198
Isadora 329
Isherwood, Christopher 32, **43**
Isis, River 421
Islam 92, **103**, 440
Islamic
architecture **161**, 431
art 431
banks and money-lending 306
religion 108, 115
Island of Doctor Moreau, The 59
Isle of Dogs 405
Isle of Man TT 378, 412
Isle of Skye 406, **419**
Isle of Wight **423**
Ismailis 114
isobars 465
isobutanes 465, 550
isolationism **275**
isomers 531, **534**
isotopes **534**, 547
Israel 180, 261, **441**
Arabs, conflict with 228, 236, 244, 258, 261, 442, 454

Camp David accords 226
economy 180
Entebbe, hostages 458
formation of 179, 449
kibbutz 180
Parliament 275
PLO and 281
Six-Day War **245**, 252, 461
Suez crisis 253
Yom Kippur War **258**
Israelites 93, 97, 107, 115, 454
Issigonis, Sir Alec **129**
Istanbul 225, **441**
italics **19**
Italy **441**
unification of 226, 250
Itchen, River 424
It Happened One Night 311, 317
ITN 327
It's a Wonderful Life 312, 331
It's That Man Again (ITMA) **321**
ITV **321**
Ivan III 'the Great' 162, **239**, 451
Ivan IV 'the Terrible' **239**, 451
Ivan, Grand Prince 451
Ivanhoe 53
Ivanov, Eugene 211
Ivory, James 325
ivory tower **20**
'I wandered lonely as a cloud' **43**

J

Jabberwock **43**
jacaranda trees 450
Jack-in-the-Green 82
Jacklin, Tony **374**
Jackson, Mahalia 345
Jackson, Michael 330, 340, **347**
Jackson Five 347
Jack the Ripper 185, **203**
Jack the Ripper 311
Jacobean **161**
Jacobins **239**
Jacobites 191, 199, **204**
Jacques, Hattie 312
Jagger, Mick 356
Jahan, Shah 436
jai-alai 379
Jainism **103**, 440
Jaïrzinho 432
Jakarta, Indonesia 440
Jamaica 170, **441**
Jamaica Inn 39, 401
Jamaican reggae 356
James I (VI of Scotland) **204**, 216

James II **204**, 206
James IV of Scotland 199, 215
James, Henry **43**
James, P.D. **43**
James, Sid 312, 319
Jameson, Dr Leander Starr 204
Jameson Raid **204**
Jamestown 459
Janacek, Leos **347**
Jane Eyre **43**
Japan 114, 237, 251, **441**, 457
balance of payments surplus 290
geisha 177
Mongols and 241
Nikkei Index **301**
Pearl Harbor attack and **247**
'purple codes' 258
ritual suicide 178
Samurai warriors 116
World War II and 229, 256
Japanese spider crab 482
japonism **129**, 137
jargon **20**
Jarlsberg cheese **391**
Jarlshof, Shetland 419
Jarrow March **204**
Jason **83**, 84
Jassy 323
jaundice 505, **507**
Java 475
Java man **181**
Jaws 33, **321**, 331
Jay, Douglas 285
jazz 338, 342, 345, **347**, 354, 359, 446
Jazz Singer, The **321**, *347*
Jean de Florette 314
Jeanne Hebuterne (Modigliani) *136*
Jean Paul II, Pope 105
Jeeves 60
Jefferson, Thomas *231*, **239**
Jeffrey Bernard is Unwell 328
Jeffreys, Judge 191
Jehovah **103**
Jehovah's Witnesses **103**
Jekyll, Gertrude **161**, 162
jellyfish *479*, 482
je ne sais quoi **20**
Jenkins, Captain Robert 239
Jenkins, Roy (Lord Jenkins) **275**
Jenkins' Ear, War of **239**
Jenner, Edward **507**, 513
Jericho 261, 281
jeroboam (bottle) 396
Jerome, Jerome K. **43**
Jerome, St 74
Jersey 434
Jerusalem 246, **442**
Jerusalem (Blake) 34
Jerusalem artichokes 390
Jerusalem, Temple of 93, 96, 98, 104, **115**
Jesuits **103**
Jesus Christ 82, **103**, 106, 109; *see also* Christ **96**

Jesus Christ Superstar 349
Jesus of Nazareth 334
jeté (ballet) **337**
jet engine **558**
jet fighters 558
jet lag 497
Jewish calendar 104
Jew of Malta, The 46, 51
Jews 93, 98, 104, 115, **179**, 222, 229, 238
captivity in Egypt 232
culture 104
Day of Atonement 116
Diaspora 98, 179
expulsion from England 179
food (kosher) 104, 110
genocide of 233
ghetto, Warsaw 461
ghettoes 177
laws 105
ostracism and 183
Passover **109**
persecution of 98, 170
Polish 450
settlements, West Bank 461
synagogue 93
taboos 186
see also concentration camps; holocaust; Israel; Judaism; World War II
Jezebel 313
Jezebel, Queen 99
JFK 313
Jiang Qing 243
Jinnah, Mohammed Ali **239**
Joan of Arc **239**
Joan of Arc 309
jobber **298**
Jocasta 86
Jockey Club, Newmarket 413
Johannesburg **442**, 454
John (King of England) **204**, 206, 417, 424
John, Augustus 57, **129**, 205
John, Barry **374**
John, Elton **347**, 349
John, Gwen **129**
'John Anderson, My Jo' 36
John of Gaunt 37, 202, **204**, 218
John O'Groats **410**
John Paul, Pope 450
Johns, Captain W.E. 34
Johns, Jasper **129**
Johns, Stratford 334
Johnson, Amy **204**
Johnson, Ben 375
Johnson, Celia 311
Johnson, Earvin 'Magic' *364*
Johnson, Katie *315*
Johnson, Lyndon **239**
Johnson, Samuel 34, **43**, 94
John the Baptist 104
joie de vivre **20**
joint 496, 499
pain 516
Jolson, Al 321, **347**
Jones, Brian 356

Jones, Inigo **162**, 404, 408, 423
Jones, Reverend Jim 174
Jones, Tom **347**
Jonson, Ben **43**
Joplin, Janice **347**
Joplin, Scott **347**, 356
Jordan **442**
Six-Day War 252
Jordan, River 442, 461, 473
Jorvik Viking Centre, York 424
Joseph 116
Joseph, Keith (Lord Joseph) **275**
Joseph and the Amazing Technicolor Dreamcoat 349
Joseph II 353
Joseph of Arimathea 82
Josephine **239**
joule 530, **534**, 541, 548
Joule, James Prescott 534
Journal of the Plague Year, A 39
Journey to the Centre of the Earth 74
Joyce, James **44**, 73, 542
Joyce, William *see* Haw Haw, Lord
Juan Carlos, King 455
Judaism 96, 98, **104**, 106, 107, 110, 115
Judas Iscariot 93
Jude the Obscure 42
Judge(s) 262, 264, 276, 277, 278, 283, *286*
Judgment of Paris 76, **83**
Judgment of Solomon 114
judicial review 275, 286
judo **374**, 377
ju-jitsu 374
Jules Rimet Trophy 388
Julia 329, 334
Julian Alps 454
Julian of Norwich 108
julienne **393**
Julius Caesar 13, 228, **239**
Julius Caesar **44**, 318, 325, 345
Julius II, Pope 134
Jumblies, The 45
Jumpers 56
Juneau 426
Jung, Carl Gustav 173, **180**, 186
Jungfrau peak 455
Jungian psychotherapy 180
Jungle Book, The **44**, 315
Jungle - Tiger Attacking a Buffalo, The 146
junk bond **298**
Juno **83**
Juno and the Paycock 48
Jupiter (god) **83**, 87, 90
Jupiter (planet) **534**, *544*, 563, 565
Jurassic Park **321**, 331, 483
Jurassic period *468*
justice 279
Justice, USA Department of 270
Justinian **240**

Just So Stories 44
Jutland, Battle of **204**
Juvenal **69**, 73
juvenile court **275**
juvenile delinquency 186

K

Kabuki theatre 442
Kabul 426, **442**
Kafka, Franz **69**
'Kaiser Bill' 257
Kalahari desert **442**
Kalashnikov, Mikhail 556
Kalashnikov AK 47 556
Kamasutra **180**, 412
kamikaze **240**
Kampala, Uganda 458
Kandinsky, Wassily **130**
Kansas meteorite 470
Kant, Immanuel 96, **104**
Karajan, Herbert von **347**
Karakoram **442**
karate **374**, 377
Karloff, Boris 317
Karlovy Vary (Carlsbad) 436
karma **104**
Karpov, Anatoly 370
Karr, Alphonse 24
Karsh, Yousouf **130**
Kathmandu **442**
Katyn massacre **240**, 450
Kaunda, Kenneth 462
Kaye, Danny 277, **321**
Kazakhstan **442**
Kazantzakis, Nikos **69**
Keating, Paul **275**
Keaton, Buster **322**, 332
Keaton, Diane, 308
Keaton, Michael **309**
Keats, John 32, **44**, 48, 229
kebab 391, **393**
kedgeree 393
Keeler, Christine *211*
Keep the Aspidistra Flying 48
Kekulé von Stradonitz, Friedrich August 524
Kellogg-Briand pact (1928) 225
Kelly, Gene 308, **348**
Kelly, Grace 319, **322**, 445
Kelmscott Press 138
Kelvin 522, **534**
Kelvin, William Thomson, 1st Baron 534
Kempis, Thomas à 108
Kendal **410**
   mint cake 410
Kendall, Kay 318, **322**
Kendall, Kenneth *327*
Keneally, T.M. 44
Kenneally, Thomas Michael **44**
Kennedy, Senator Edward 227
Kennedy, Jackie 240, 301

Kennedy, John F. 223, 230, 239, **240**, 246, 247, 459
Kennedy, Nigel **348**
Kennedy, Robert **240**
Kennet, River 413
Kensington **410**
   Gardens 410
   Palace 410
Kent, Bruce 265
Kent, River 410
Kent, William 420
Kenwood House 154, 409
Kenya 240, 279, **442**
   Mau Mau 240, **243** 442
Kenyatta, Jomo **240**, 442
Kepler, Johannes 525, 527, **534**
keratin 490, 517
Kerensky, Alexander 251
Kern, Jerome 345, **348**
Kerry, Ireland 441
Kew **410**
Key Largo 321, 330
Keynes, John Maynard **298**
Keynesian economics **298**
Keystone Cops, The **322**
Key West 438
Khama, Sir Seretse 432
Khan, Genghis **235**, 241, 244
Khan, Kublai **241**, 244
Khan, Imran *374*
Khartoum 320
Khartoum 200, **442**
Khmer Rouge 281, 433
Khoihkoi 180
Khoisan **180**
Khomeini, Ayatollah 94, 100, **240**, 244, 440
Khrushchev, Nikita 230, **240**, 244, 253
Khyber Pass **442**
kibbutz **180**
Kid, The 312
Kid Brother, The 323
Kid from Brooklyn, The 322
Kidnapped 55
kidneys 501, **507**, 519
kidney stones 507
Kielder Forest **410**
Kierkegaard, Soren **104**
Kiev **442**
Kilauea *475*
Kilimanjaro **442**, 456
Killers, The 317, 323
killers, serial **185**
Killing Fields, The 329
kilo- 537
kilogram **534**
kilowatt hour 548
Kim 44
Kind Hearts and Coronets 319, **322**
kinetic art **130**
kinetic energy **534**
kinetic theory of gases 532
King, Ben E. 359
King, Billie Jean **374**
King, Martin Luther 228, 238, **241**, 444
King and Country 324

King in New York, A 312
King James Bible **44**, 204
King Kong 322
King Lear **44**, 321, 328, 330
King of Kings 314
kings, divine right of 194, 204, **232**
King's College, Cambridge 167, 202, 403
Kingsley, Charles 59, 423
King's Road, Chelsea 404
Kingston, Jamaica 441
Kingston upon Hull **410**
Kinnock, Neil **275**, 276, 279
Kinsey, Alfred **180**
Kinsey Reports 180
Kinshasa 462
kinship **180**, 186
Kinski, Klaus 315
Kipling, Rudyard **44**, 433, 454
kir, kir royale 391
Kiribati 450
Kirklees Hall, Yorks 87
Kirkwall 414
Kirov Ballet **348**, 352, 452
Kiss, Kiss 38
Kiss, The (Klimt) 130
Kiss Me Kate 56, 355
Kiss of Death 334
Kiss Tomorrow Goodbye 311
'Kit Cat series' (Kneller) 130
Kitchener, Lord **205**, 442
Kiwis 447
Klee, Paul **130**
Klein, Calvin **130**
Klemperer, Otto **348**
Klerk, F.W. de **267**, 278
Klimt, Gustav **130**
Klondike River, gold rush 433
Klute 317
Kneller, Sir Godfrey **130**
Knesset **275**, 442
Knife in the Water 329
knight **241**
Knights of St John 444
Knights of the Round Table 77, 82, **87**
Knight's Tale, The 36
Knole **410**
Knossos **241**, 435
knowledge **104**
Know Your Own IQ 176
Knox, John **205**, 415
Köchel (K) number 351
Kodak *552*, 555
Kohl, Helmut **275**, 439
Kokoschka, Oskar **130**
Komodo dragon 490
Konishiki ('Dump Truck') *385*
Kon-Tiki expedition 448
Kopechne, Mary Jo 227
Koran **104**, *105*, 106, 108
Korbut, Olga **374**, *375*
Korea
   Japanese in 441
   North **447**
   South 447, 453, **455**
Korean War 232, **241**, 254, 453, 455

Koresh, David 174
Korn, Arthur 556
kosher food 104, 110
Kosko, Bart 101
Koussevitzky, Serge 337
Kowloon, Hong Kong 440
Krakatoa 440, 476
Krak des Chevalier 456
Kramer vs. Kramer 320, 332
Krantz, Judith 53
Kray, Ronnie 402
Kremlin **162**, 239, 445
Kretzmer, Herbert 348
Krishna 94, **104**
Kristiansen, Ingrid 377
Kronos 81, **83**, 90
Kruger, Paul **241**
krugerrand 241
Krupa, Gene 345
krypton 538, *see also* periodic table **541**
Kuala Lumpur 444
Kublai Khan **241**, 430
Kubla Khan **45**
Kubrick, Stanley 312, **322**, 330
Ku Klux Klan 310
kung fu 377
Kuomintang 227, **241**, 456
Kurdistan **442**
Kurds 177, 239, **442**
Kuroshio Current *471*
Kuwait **442**
   Gulf War 236, **442**
Kwai, River 457
Kwa Zulu 186
Kyd, Thomas **45**, 51
Kyoto 457
Kyrie 350
Kyshu, Japan 441

L

La Bohème **353**
labour **298**
Labour Organisation, International 275
Labour Party 199, 201, 265, 270, **276**
   shadow cabinet 285
   social democracy and 285
   unilateralism and 288
Labours of Hercules 78, 83
Labrador Current *471*
Labyrinth 83, 85
Labyrinths 64
Lace 53
Lachesis 81
Lacock **410**
Laconia 253
Laconians 20, 252
laconic **20**
lacrosse **374**
ladies' fingers (okra) 394
La Dolce Vita 316
Lady and the Tramp, The 315, 348

Lady at the Virginals with a Gentleman, A 151
Lady Chatterley's Lover **45**, 330
Lady from Shanghai, The 334
Lady from the Sea, The 329
Ladykillers, The 315, 319, 330
'Lady of Shalott, The' **45**
Lady of the Lake 77, 81
Lady Vanishes, The 320, 323
Lady Windermere's Fan 59, 205
La Fontaine, Jean de **69**, 148
Lagan, River 430
Lagerfeld, Karl **130**
Lagos 447
Lahr, Bert 334
Laing, R. D. **180**
Laissez-faire 294, **298**, 305
Laius, King 85
Lake at Annecy, The (Cezanne) *121*
Lake District 408, **410**
Lake Nyasa 205
Lake poets **45**, 410
Laker, Jim **374**
Lake Shore Drive Apartments, Chicago 163
Lalique, René **130**
Lamarck, Jean Baptiste 478, 484
lamb (noisette) 394
Lamb, Lady Caroline 36, 207
Lamb, Charles **45**
'Lamb, The' (Blake) 34
Lambeth Conference 92
lamb's lettuce 393
lame duck **298**
Lamont, Norman 264
Lamour, Dorothy 321, 330
lamprey 485
lamps 559
Lancaster, Burt 317, **323**, 386
Lancaster, House of **205**, 213
Lancelot, Sir 82, **83**
Land, Edwin 552
Landau, Jon 359
Landseer, Sir Edwin **130**, 422
Land's End, 404, **411**, 418
land speed record 366, **374**
Lang, Fritz 325
Langland, William **45**
langlaufing 383
Langtry, Lillie **205**
language 173, **180**
Languedoc 396
lantern **162**
lanthanide series 540, *541*
lanthanum *see* periodic table **541**
Lanzarote 433
Laocoon 89
Laos **442**
Lao-Tzu (also Lao Zi or Lao Tan) **104**, 115
La Paz 431
Lappland 438

Lara, Brian **375**
Large Electron-Positron (LEP) collider *540*
largo **350**
La Rioja 455
Larkin, Philip **45**, 410
Larson, Gary **130**
larva **487**
metamorphosis *488*
laryngitis **507**
larynx **507**
La Scala *353*, 360, 444
laser 557, **558**, 560
Las Malvinas *see* Falkland Islands
Lassie Come Home 332
Last, James **348**
Last Detail, The 327
Last Emperor, The 328
La Strada 316
Last Supper 106
Last Supper, The (Leonardo da Vinci) **131**
Last Tango in Paris 311
Last Temptation of Christ, The 69, 330
Las Vegas **443**
Late Extra 325
latent heat 533, **535**, 536
Latimer, Hugh **205**
Latin tags 64
Latvia 459
Laud, William **205**
Lauda, Niki **375**
Laughter in Paradise 320
Laughton, Charles 67
Laurasia *466*
Laurel, Stan *323*
Laurel and Hardy **323**
Lauren, Ralph **131**
Laurie, John 313
lava *470*, 474, 475, 476
Lavender Hill Mob, The 315, 319, 320
Lavenham 421
Laver, Rod **375**
Lavoisier, Antoine **535**
Law *see* individual entries
Lawley, Sue 314
Law Lords 273, **276**
Law of Universal Gravitation, The 532
Lawrence, D.H. **45**, 60, 173, 330
Lawrence, Sir Thomas **131**
Lawrence of Arabia **323**, 328, *329*
Lawrence of Arabia, **205**, 323, 453
lawrencium *see* periodic table **541**
Lay of the Last Minstrel, The 53
Lazenby, George 311
LCD (Liquid Crystal Display) **558**
L-dopa 513
Leach, Bernard **131**
lead *see* periodic table **541**
leader of the House **276**
leaf **487**
League of Nations 225, **241**, 252, 257
Leakey, Louis **181**

Leakey, Mary 181
Leakey, Richard 181
Lean, Sir David 49, 311, 319, **323**, 328
Leaning Tower of Pisa **162** *450*, 532
Lear, Edward **45**, 49
learning difficulties 514
Leaud, Jean-Pierre 333
Leaves of Grass 59
Lebanon 430, **443**
Le Brun, Charles **131**, 142
Le Carré, John **45**, 229
Le Corbusier **162**
LED (Light Emitting Diode) **558**
Leda and the Swan 83
Led Zeppelin **348**
Lee, Ann 113
Lee, Christopher 80, 315, 317
Lee, Peggy **348**
Lee, Robert E. 220
leech 479
Leeds **411**
Leeds Castle **411**, *411*
left wing **276**
legato 350
Léger 123
legionnaires' disease **507**
Lehár, Franz **348**
Leibniz, Gottfried 64, **105**, 525
Leigh, Janet 329
Leigh, Vivien 319, **323**, 326, 328
Leipzig **443**
Leith, Edinburgh 407
leitmotif **350**, 360
Lely, Sir Peter **131**
Le Mans **375**
Le Mesurier, John 313
Lemmon, Jack **323**, 334
lemurs 444
Len, River 411
Lend-Lease system 250
Leng, Virginia *see* Elliot, Virginia 386
Lenglen, Suzanne **375**
Lenin, Vladimir Ilyich **241**, 254, 276
Leninism **276**
Lennon, John 338, 342
lens **535**, 543, 552
Lent 99
lentigo **507**
Leo (zodiac) 90, 548
Leofric of Mercia, Earl 82
Leonardo da Vinci 121, **131**, 136, 147, 444, 557
Leone, Sergio 331
leopards 480
Leopold II of Belgium 462
Leo X, Pope 143
LEP (Large Electron Positron) collider *540*
leprechauns 83
Le Prince, Augustin 553
leprosy **507**, 508
Leptis Magna, Libya 443
leptons 546
Lerner, Alan Jay 352
Lerwick, Shetland 419
lesbianism 177, 178

Les Fauves 124
Les Liaisons Dangereuses 66
Les Misérables 68, **348**
Les Rougon-Macquart 74
less developed country **298**
Lesseps, Ferdinand de 163, 166
Lessing, Doris **45**
Less Than Angels 51
Let George Do It 317
Lethal Weapon 318
Lethe, River 82
Letter, The 313
letterpress 561
Lettice and Lovage 331
'Let us go then, you and I' **45**
Leucippus 523
leukaemia 499, **508**
Levellers 205
Leviathan 102
Levi-Strauss, Claude 179, **181**, 186
Lewes, G.H. 39
Lewis, Carl **375**
Lewis and Harris, Outer Hebrides 409
lexicon 20
Lexington and Concord, Battle of 220, 249
Lhasa **443**, 457
liability **298**
Liberace 348
Liberal Democratic Party 267, 270, **276**
liberalism **276**
Liberal Party 205
liberation theology **105**
Liberia **443**
Liberty, Sir Arthur Lasenby **132**
libido **181**
Lib-Lab Pact 205
Libra 90, 548
Library of Alexandria 426
Library of Congress 461
libretto **349**
Libya **443**
terrorism 271
USA and 271, 283
lice 508, 519
lichen **487**, 492
Lichtenstein, Roy **132**
Liddell, Alice 32
Liddell, Alvar 327
Liddell, Eric 362
Liechtenstein 305, **443**
life assurance 294, **298**
Liffey, River 436
lift **558**
ligament **508**, 518
light 528, 529, 530, **535**, 540, 543, 544, 547, 548
polarised **541**
speed of 527, 529, 535, 537, 543, **545**
wave-particle duality 535, 548
light bulb 555, 559
lighting **559**
Light My Fire 342
lightning 78, **470**, 475, 540, 545
light year **535**

Lilies of the Field 329
Lillee, Dennis **375**
Lilliputians 56
Limelight 312
limerick **45**
Limerick, Ireland 441
limestone, Portland 415
limited company **298**
limpets 486
Lincoln **411**
Lincoln, Abraham 236, **242**, 252, 445
Lincoln green 411
Lincoln Memorial 242
Lindbergh, Charles A. **242**
Linde, Karl von 562
Lindisfarne (Holy Island) **409**
Lindisfarne Gospels 409
Lindow Moss, Cheshire, Iron Age man 465
Lineker, Gary **375**
lingua franca **20**
linguistics **20**
Linnaeus, Carolus 481
Lion in Winter, The 320, 321, 328
Lion of Pakistan, The 374
lions 442, *479*
lipids **487**
Lipizzaner horses 460
Lippershey, Hans 565
Lipstick on Your Collar 329
liqueur
blackcurrant 391
Galliano 393
liquid **535**, 547
liquid asset **298**
liquidation 290, 297
liquidity **299**
Lisbon **443**, 450
listed buildings **162**
Lister, Joseph **508**
listeria 504, **508**
Liston, Sonny 362
Liszt, Cosima 349
Liszt, Franz **349**
lithium *see* periodic table **541**
litho-, -lith- **20**
Lithuania 459
litmus paper 522, 524, **535**
litotes **20**
Little Big Man 320
Little Caesar 330
Little Drummer Girl, The 45
Little Girl Who Lives Down the Lane, The 317
Little John 83
Little Man Tate 317
Little Men 32
Little Miss Marker 332
Little Nell 38
Little Night Music, A see Eine Kleine Nachtmusik 351
Little Night Music, A (film) 332
Little Night Music, A (Sondheim) 358
Little Princess, The 332
Little Red Book 243, *282*
Little Red Cap 69
Little Red Riding-Hood 69

Little Women 45
Live Aid charity concert 1985 348
Live and Let Die 311
liver 508, 519
damage and disease 500, 505, 507
Liver birds 411
Liverpool **411**
Football Club 411
Liverpool and Manchester Railway 166, 412
Liverpool Catholic Cathedral **162**
Liverpool City Council 279
Liverpool Football Club 369
Liverpool Metropolitan Cathedral **162**
liverworts **489**
Lives of the Most Eminent Italian Painters, Sculptors and Architects 151
Living Daylights, The 311
Livingstone, David **205**, 460
lizard 482, 490
Lizard Point **411**
Ljubljana 454
Llanfair PG **411**
Lloyd, Harold **323**
Lloyd, Marie 349
Lloyd George, David 178, 189, **205**
Lloyd's Building **162**, *165*, *299*
Lutine Bell 299
Lloyd's of London **299**
Lutine Bell 299
'names' 299
Register of Shipping 299
Lloyd Webber, Sir Andrew 39, **349**, 354
Llŷn Peninsula **412**
Loach, Ken 312
loam 474
lobby **276**
lobbying 276
lobster 479, 482-3
bisque 390
Local Education Authority (LEA) 175
local government **276**
local group (astronomy) 532
Local Hero 323, 329
Locarno Pact 193
loc. cit **20**
Loch Lomond **412**
Loch Ness **412**
Loch Ness Monster **84**, 412
Locke, John **105**, 279
Lockheed F-117 stealth plane *563*, 564
lockjaw 518
Lockwood, Margaret **323**
Locomotion (steam engine) 166, 405, 565
locomotives 565
loess 474
Loewe, Frederick 352
Lofting, Hugh 39
logarithms **535**, 541
logic **105**, 523

logical positivism **105**
logo **20**
Loire *443*
Lolita 45, 325, 330
Lollards **206**
Lombard-RAC Rally 380
Londinium 404, 412
London 412
Londonderry 447
Londonderry, Siege of **206**
London Olympics (1908) 243
London Philharmonia Orchestra 348
London Pride 341
London's Metropolitan Railway 167
London Zoo 416
Lonely Passion of Judith Hearne, The 330
Long Day's Journey into Night, A 48
Longest Day, The 231
Longfellow, Henry Wadsworth **45**
Long Goodbye, The 36
Long Island 446
long jump **376**
Longleat **412**
Long March **242**
long-sightedness 503
Longstone Island 399
Look Back in Anger 32, 48
Loot 48, 63, 330
Lorca, Frederico Garcìa **69**
Lord Advocate **277**
Lord Chancellor **277**
Lord Chief Justice **277**
Lord Haw Haw **206**
Lord Jim 38, 328
lord lieutenant 285
Lord Mayor of London 209, 404
Lord of the Flies 41, **45**
Lord of the Rings, The **46**
Lord President of the Council **277**
Lord Privy Seal **277**
Lord, Thomas 376
Lord's 363, 368, **376**
Lords of Appeal in Ordinary 276
Lorelei rock, River Rhine 451
Loren, Sophia 312, 314, **324**
Lorna Doone 406
Lorraine 233
Los Angeles **443**
  earthquake 473
Losey, Joseph **324**
loss leader **299**
Lost Weekend, The 334
Lost World, The 459
Lost World of the Kalahari, The 442
Louganis, Greg 369
Lough Neagh 447
Louis XIII 250
Louis XIV **242**, 245, 253, 337
Louis Quatorze style 131, **132**

Louis XV 248
Louis Quinze style **132**
Louis XVI 234, **242**
Louis Seize style **132**
Louis Philippe, King 163, **242**, 250
Louis, Joe **376**
Louisiana **443**
Louisiana Purchase 239
Lourdes **443**
Louvre 126, 449
Love 318
Loved One, The 59
Love for Three Oranges, The 355
Lovelace, Richard 36
Lovelock, James 468
Love on the Run 333
Love Song of J. Alfred Prufrock, The 45
Low, David 33
Lowe, Arthur 313
lower case **20**
Lowestoft 421
Lowry, L.S. **132**
Loy, Myrna **324**
loyalist **277**
Luanda, Angola 427
Lucas, George 331
Luciano, Charles 'Lucky' *181*
Lucifer 79, 113
Lucky Jim 32, 311
'Lucy' **181**
Luddites **206**
Ludlow **412**
Ludwig II *430*
Luftwaffe 191, 192, 235, 252
Lugosi, Bela 315
Lumière Brothers **324**
Lumley, Joanna 309
Luna1 space probe 563
lunar eclipse *529*
lunar rover 550
Lundy **412**
lungfish, aestivation 478
lungs 503, **508**, 514, 515, 519
Lusaka, Zambia 462
Lust for Life 315
lutetium *see* periodic table **541**
Luther, Martin 100, 101, **105**, 258, 443
Lutheran Church **105**
Lutherans 99
Lutine, HMS 299
Lutine Bell 299
Lutyens, Sir Edwin Landseer *162*, 436
Luxe, Calme et Volupte (Matisse) 133
Luxembourg **443**
Luxor, Egypt 437
lych gate **162**
Lycidas 47, 66
lymphatic system 504, **508**, 518, 519
lymph nodes 504
lymphocytes 507
Lynn, Dame Vera **349**
Lyonesse, lost kingdom of 418

lyric **69**
Lyrical Ballads 60
Lysistrata **69**
Lytell Geste of Robyn Hode, A 87

M

Ma Cuisine 392
Mabinogion, The **69**
McAdam, John Loudon **162**
MacArthur, Douglas 241, **242**
Macau **444**
Macbeth 28, 46, 329, 334
Macbeth, Thane of Glamis 407
McCarthyism **277**, 312
McCartney, Linda 338
McCartney, Paul 338
MacCool, Finn 407
McCormack, Count John **349**
MacCormick, John 285
McCoy, Charles 'Kid' 365
MacDermot, Galt 345
Macdonald, Flora 191, **206**, 419
Macdonald, Ramsey **206**, 218
McDonald, Trevor *327*
Macdonald clan 200, 408
McDowell, Malcolm 312
Macedonia 223, 462
McEnroe, John **376**
McGoohan, Patrick 329
Mach, Ernest 535
Machiavelli, Niccolo **105**
machine **535**
Mach number **535**
Machu Picchu 427, **444**
McKenzie, Robert *280*
McKern, Leo 330
Mackintosh, Charles Rennie **132**, *163*, 407
MacLaine, Shirley 309, *323*, **324**, 334
McLaren (cars) 373, 380
Maclean, Alistair **46**
Maclean, Donald **206**
Maclehose, Agnes 36
MacLeod, clan 406
McLuhan, Marshall 177
Macmillan, Harold **206**, 257, *302*
Macmillan, Kirkpatrick 551
MacMillan, Sir Kenneth **349**
McMurdo Sound *427*
MacNee, Patrick 309
MacNiece, Louis **46**
Mâconnais 396
McQueen, Steve **324**, *325*
macro- **20**
macro-economics **299**
macrobiotic 393

Madagascar **444**
Madame Bovary **69**
Madame Butterfly 178, **353**
Madame Gautrean 146
mad cow disease **509**
Madeira **444**
Madigan 334
Mad Max 318
Madonna 125
Madonna (singer) **350**
Madrid **444**, 455
Maestà 123
Mafeking 204
Mafia 11, **181**, 247, 249, 453
magazines 324
Magellan, Ferdinand **242**, 449, 457, 535
Magellanic clouds 242, **535**
Magi 99, 116
Magic 321
Magician of Lublin, The 73
'Magic' Johnson *364*
Magic Mountain, The **69**
Magic Realism 52, **69**
Magic Roundabout, The **325**
Maginot Line **242**
magistrate **277**
maglev trains 565
magma 474, 475
Magna Carta **206**, 417
magnesium *see* periodic table **541**
Magnet 34
magnetic tape **559**, 566
magnetic poles, Earth's *464*, **470**, 544, 554
Magnetic Resonance Imaging (MRI) 516
magnetism 529, 530, **535**
  terrestrial 464, 470, 544, 546, 554
Magnificent Ambersons 334
Magnificent Seven, The 324
Magnificent Two, The 327
magnitude **535**
magnum (bottle) 396
Magnum Force 315
magnum opus **20**
Magnusson, Magnus 325
Magritte, René **132**
Magus, The 40
Magyars 440
Mahabharata 94
Mahayana Buddhism 95
Mahdi 442
Mahé, Seychelles 453
Mahler, Gustav 348, **350**
mahogany 492
Maiden Castle **412**
Maid Marian 87
'Maid of Orléans' 239
Maiman, Theodore H. 558
Major, John **278**, 293
Major, Norma *278*
Major Barbara 54
Majorca 455
Makarios, Archbishop 436
Makarova, Natalia 348
Malaprop, Mrs 20
malapropism **20**
malaria **509**
Malawi **444**
  Lake 444, 456

Malayan Trilogy, The 35
Malaysia **444**, 454
Malcolm X *171*, **242**
Maldives 440, **444**
male-, mal- (prefix) **20**
Malé, Maldives 444
male bonding 172
male-voice choir, Welsh 416
Mali 457
malignant **509**
Malinowski, Bronislaw **181**
Mallard (locomotive) 565
Mallarmé, Stephane, **69**
malnutrition 495, **509**
Malory, Sir Thomas **46**
Malta **444**
Maltese Falcon, The 310, 321
Malthus, Thomas 184, **299**
Malvern Hills 408
mammals *479*, 481, **487**
mammogram 516
Mammoth Cave National Park, Kentucky 465
Managua 447
Man and Superman 54
Manchester Guardian, The 328, 413
Manchester **412**
  Ship Canal 412
Manchuria 441
Mancini, Henry **350**
Mancunium 412
Mandalay 44, 433
Mandarins 63
Mandela, Nelson 260, **278**, 455
Mandela, Winnie 278
Mandelbrot set 531
Manderley 39
mandrake **84**
Manet, Édouard *74*, **132**, *133*
Manet, Eugène 138
Man For All Seasons, A **46**, 207, 330, 334
manganese *see* periodic table **541**
Manhattan 308, 332, Manhattan 446
Manhattan Murder Mystery 308
Manhattan Project **242**
manic depression **509**, 513
Manichean religion 94
Manilow, Barry **350**
Man in Grey, The 323, 325
Man in the White Suit, The 315, 319
mankind **181**
mankind, evolution of **181**
Mann, Thomas **69**, 314
Mannerheim, Marshal 438
Mannerism **132**
Man of a Thousand Faces 312
Manor of Northstead, Yorkshire 264
Mansell, Nigel **376**
Mansfield, Katherine **46**
Mansion House, City of London 404
Mantegna, Andrea **133**, 149
Mantovani, Annunzio Paolo **350**

Man Who Fell To Earth, The
339
Man Who Knew Too Much,
The 331
Man Who Shot Liberty
Valance, The 317
Man Who Was Thursday,
The 37
Manx cat 412
Maoism **278**
Maori 181, 256, 447
Mao Zedong 96, 227, 230,
241, **243**, 258, 265, 278,
430
Mappa Mundi 409
Maputo 445
Maracaibo, Lake 459
Maradona, Diego **377**
Marathon, Battle of **243**
marathon (race) 243, **377**
Mara (Buddhist devil) 98
marble *474*
Marble Arch **413**
Marchant, Catherine 38
March of Time, The **325**
Marciano, Rocky **377**
Marconi, Guglielmo *558*,
559, 561
Marcuse, Herbert **106**
Mardi Gras, New Orleans
446
Margaret, Princess 407
Margaret Tudor 215
Margarita **393**
Marianas Trench 434, 471
Mariánske Lázne
(Marienbad) 436
Maria Theresa of Austria
222, 243
Marib 462
Marie Antoinette **243**
Maritime Consultative
Organisation, Inter-
governmental 275
marjoram *393*
Mark Antony 32
market economy **299**
market research **299**
Mark of Cornwall, King
89
Mark of Zorro, The 316
Markova, Dame Alicia 342
Marks & Spencer 299
Marks, Michael 299
Marks, Simon **299**
Marlborough 88, **413**
Marlborough, 1st Duke of
206, 224, 401
Marley, Bob **350**, 356
Marley, Jacob 37
Marlowe, Christopher **46**,
51, 54, 81, 82
Marmara, Sea of 458
Marmaris, Turkey 458
Marnie 313, 320
Marple, Miss **46**
Márquez, Gabriel García
69
Marrakech, Morocco 445
marriage 171, **182**
Marriage à la Mode 39
Marriage Italian Style 314,
324
Marriage of Figaro, The **353**

Married Love and Wise
Parenthood 214
marrow 395
Mars (god) **84**, 87
Mars (planet) **536**, 544
Marsala 396
'Marseillaise' 359
Marshall, General George
C. 243
Marshall Aid 225, **243**, 254
Marshall Islands **444**, 450
Marston Moor, Battle of
195
marsupials **487**
Martel, Charles 226
martial arts **377**
martial law **278**
Martini, Simone **133**
Marvell, Andrew **46**
Marvin, Hank 356
Marx, Karl **106**, 170, 265,
278, 285, **299-300**, *299*
Marx Brothers **325**
Marxism **106**, 276, **278**,
299-300
Mary I 95, 205, **206**
Mary II *see* William and
Mary
Mary, Queen of Scots 205,
207, 364, 410
Mary, Virgin *see* Virgin
Mary
Mary Barton 40
Mary Magdalene, St **106**
Mary Poppins 308, 315
Mary Rose 416
Masaccio **133**
Masai **182**
Maserati 370
*M*A*S*H* **324**
Masina, Guilietta 316
Mask of Anarchy, The 54
Mason, James 318, **325**
masque **69**
Masque of the Red Death,
The 329
Mass 99, **106**, **350**
mass (physics) 531, 534,
536, 537, 538, 543, 548
Massachusetts 431, **444**
Massachusetts Institute of
Technology 431
mass-energy equation 528,
530, 536, 539, 543
Massif Central 443
mass production 290
mastectomy **509**
Mastermind **325**
Master of the Rolls **278**
Mastersinger of Nuremburg,
The 343, 360
mastitis **509**
Mastroianni, Marcello 324
Mata Hari **243**
materialism **106**,108
Matilda (Henry I's
daughter) 214
Matisse, Henri **133**,
Matra 384
matriarchy **182**
matter **536**
Matterhorn **444**, 455
Matter of Life and Death, A
327

Matthau, Walter 323, 334
Matthews, Sir Stanley **377**
Maugham, (William)
Somerset **46**, 48, 454
Mau Mau 240, **243**, 442
Mauna Kea 473
Maundy Thursday 99
Maupassant, Guy de **69**
Mauritius 440
Mausoleum of
Halicarnassus 431
maxim **20**
Maxwell's equations 535,
536
Maxwell, James Clark 529,
536
Maxwell, Robert **294**, **300**
Maya **243**, 444
May Day **84**
Mayer, Louis B. 319
Mayfair **413**
Mayflower **243**, 415, 419,
444
Mayor of Casterbridge, The
42
Mazzini, Guiseppe 235
MCC (Marylebone Cricket
Club) 363, 376, **377**
ME (myalgic
encephalomyelitis) **509**
Mead, Margaret **182**, 461
Mead of Inspiration 85
mean, median and mode
536
Mean Streets 330
measles 503, **509**, 514
Measure for Measure 53,
Mecca **106**, 453
mechanics **536**
Medea 83, **84**
Medellin, Colombia 435
median *see* mean, median
and mode
medical ethics 506
Medici, Catherine de 244,
251
Medici, Marie 244
Medici, the 120, 124, **243**,
251, 438
medicine, alternative 495,
506
Medina 108
Medina, River 405
meditation 116
Mediterranean Sea 426,
444, *466*
medium **134**
Médoc (Bordeaux) 396
Medusa **84**
Medway, River 417
Meeting Houses, Quaker
111
Meet Me in St Louis 318
mega- **20**
mega- 537
Megaera 81
Meinhof, Ulrike 222
Mein Kampf 237, **244**
meiosis 480-1
Meir, Golda **244**
Meissen porcelain 436
Meistersinger von Nürnberg,
Die 343, 360
Melanesia 449-50

melanin **510**, 517
melanoma, malignant 517
Melba, Dame Nellie **350**,
394
Melbourne 429,
Melbourne, Viscount **207**
Melpomene 85
melting point **536**
Melville, Herman **46**
Member of Parliament (M)
261. 273. 281
membrane 480, 511, 519,
540
memento mori 148
Memling, Hans **134**
Memoirs of a Fox-Hunting
Man 53
Memoirs of a Woman of
Pleasure 40
memory 501, **510**
Memphis **444**
Men, The 311
Menai Strait 166, 167, 398
Mendel, Gregor (1822-84)
485, **487**
Mendeleev, Dmitri
Ivanovich **536**, *541*
mendelevium *see* periodic
table **541**
Mendelssohn, Jacob Felix
337, **351**, 407, 443
Mending Wall 40
Mendips **413**
Menelaus, King 82
Mengele, Josef 449
Meninas, Las 151
meningitis **510**
menopause 506, **510**, 512
Mensheviks 224
menstruation **510**, 512,
515, 520
mental health and illness
501, 509, 515
Menuhin, Sir Yehudi **351**
Men without Women 42
MEPs (Members of the
European Parliament)
269
Mercalli scale 467
mercantilism **300**
Mercedes 370
Merced, River *462*
Merchant, Ismail 325
Merchant-Ivory **325**
Merchant of Venice, The **46**,
319
Mercia 408, 414
Mercury, Freddie 355
mercury (element) *see*
periodic table **541**
Mercury (god) **84**
Mercury (planet) **84**, **537**,
544
Mereworth Castle 157
Merlin **84**, 88
Merlot (grape) 396
mermaid **84**
'mermaid's purse' 485
Merovingians 226, 233
Merry Christmas Mr
Lawrence 339
Merry Widow, The 348
Merry Wives of Windsor, The
40

Mersey, River 411, **413**
'Mersey beat' 338
Merz 147
Merzbau 147
mesons 546
Mesopotamia **244**, 437,
441, 457
mesosphere 464
Mesozoic era *468*
Messerschmitt (Me-262)
558
Messiah 104, **106**
Messiah (Handel) 345
Mestral, Georges de 565
metabolism 503, **510**,
518,
metal 537, 540, *541*
metamorphic rock *see* rock
Metamorphoses (Ovid) 70
metamorphosis 478, 482,
488
Metamorphosis, The **70**
metaphor **20**
Metaphysical poets **47**
metaphysics **106**
metastases 519
meteor **537**
meteorite 470
meteorology *see* weather;
climate
Meteosat satellite 562
meter **70**
methane 469, 471
methanol (methyl alcohol)
522
method acting 311
Methodism **106**
Methuselah (bottle) 396
metonymy **20**
metre **537**
metric system 234, **537**
Metro-Goldwyn-Mayer 319
Metropolis **325**
Metropolitan Museum of
Art 126
Metropolitan Opera, New
York 360
Metropolitan Police,
London 209, 281
-metry **20**
Metternich, Prince
Clemens von **244**, 255
Mexican yam 505
Mexico 243, **444**
Mexico City **444**
meze **394**
mezzo-soprano 358
MGM 319
MI5 284
MI6 284
Miami 438, **444**
Miandad, Javed 375
Michael, George **351**
Michaux, Pierre and Ernest
551
Michelangelo, Buonarroti
126, **134**, 149
Michelin 566
Michelson-Morley
experiment **537**
Michigan, Lake 439
micro- **20**, 537
microchip 552, 554, **559**,
565

micro-economics **300**
microfilm **559**
Micronesia 449-50
microprocessors 559
microscope(s) 533, 535, **559**, 566
microsurgery **510**, 556
microwave oven 537, **560**
microwaves 527, 529, **537**
Midas **84**
'Midas touch' 84
Mid-Atlantic Ridge 472
Middle Ages **244**
Middle East 261
　see also individual countries
Middle English **47**
Middlemarch 39
Middle Temple 274
Midler, Bette 350
Midnight Cowboy 320
Midnight's Children 52
Midsummer Eve **84**
Midsummer Night's Dream, A **47**, 81
migraine **510**
migration **488**
Mikado, The **344**
Milan **444**
　Conservatory 360
　La Scala *353*, 360, 444
Mildred Pierce 313
mile **377**
Milestone, Lewis 308
Militant 279
Militant Tendency **278-9**
Milky Way 532, **537**
Mill, John Stuart 94, **106**
Millais, Sir John Everett **135**
Milland, Ray 334
millennium **106**
Miller, Arthur **47**, 326, 329
Miller, Glenn **351**
Miller, Jonathan 33
Miller's Tale, The 36
Millet, Jean François **136**
Millet, Kate 176
milli- 537
Milligan, Spike 319, **326**
Millionairess, The 324
millipedes 479
Mill on the Floss, The 39
Mills, Barbara 267
Mills, Hayley 326
Mills, Sir John **326**
Mills, Juliet 326
Milne A.A **47**, *60*
Milton, John **47**, 49
Milton Keynes **413**
Milvian Bridge, Battle of 229
minaret **163**
Minder **326**
minerals 468, 472, 474, 527
miner's safety lamp 528
Minerva **85**
Mini car 129
minimum lending rate **300**
miniskirt 142
minister of state **279**
minister of the Crown **279**
Minnelli, Liza 318
Minnelli, Vincente 308

Minoan civilisation 77, 241, 435, 444
Minorca 455
Minos, King 79, 85
Minotaur 83, **85**, 241
mint *393*
Mintoff, Dom 444
Miracle in Milan 314
miracle play **70**
miracles 102
Miró, Joan **136**
Mirror Crack'd, The 332
Mirror Group Newspapers 294, 300, 328
Mir space station 563
Misanthrope, The **70**
misrelated construction **20**
missiles **560**
　crisis, Cuban 459
Missing 323
Mission, The 314, 329
Mississippi **445**, 468
Miss Julie 73
Miss Saigon 348
Mister Roberts 317
mistral 476
Mitchell, Margaret 319
Mitchum, Robert 317, **326**
mites 479, 519
Mitford, Diana 207
Mithraism **106**
Mithras 107
mitochondria 480
mitosis 480, *481*
Mitterand, François **279**
Mitty, Walter **47**
mixed economy **300**
Miyake, Issey **136**
mnemonic **21**
Moby Dick **47**, 334
mock-heroic **70**
mode *see* mean, median and mode
Model T Ford **294**, *295*, 552
modem 554, 555, 557, **560**
modern art **136**
modernism 51, **70**, 72, 126
Modern Times 312
Modest Proposal, A **47**
modifier **21**
Modigliani, Amedeo **136**
Modred 77, 82
mods and rockers **182**
modus operandi **21**
modus vivendi **21**
Moeketsi, Stompie 278
Mogadishu, Somalia 454
Mohammed *see* Muhammad
Mohammed Ali pasha 163
Mohammed Reza Pahlavi **244**
Mohenjo Daro, Pakistan 449
Moi, Daniel **279**
Mold, Clwyd 404
Moldavia 451
Moldova 459
molecule 531, **537**
moles, skin 517
Molesworth, Nigel **47**
Molière **70**

mollusc *479*, 480, 481, 486, **488**
Molotov, Vyacheslav **244**
Molotov cocktail 244
molybdenum *see* periodic table 541
Molyneux, James 288
Mombasa, Kenya 442
momentum **537**, 542
Monaco **445**
Monadhliath Mountains 399
Mona Lisa (La Gioconda) **136**
Monarch of the Glen, The 130
monarchy 96, 284
　absolute 232, 242, **260**
　and Parliament 190
monasteries 154, 163, 451
　Dissolution of **197**
monasticism **107**
Mondrian, Piet **137**
Monera, kingdom 479
Monet, Claude 129, **137**
monetarism **300**
money laundering **300**
moneylenders *306*
money supply **300**
Mongol Empire **244**
Mongolia 97, **445**, 467
Mongoloid **182**
monism **107**, 110
monkey *479*, 490
Monkey Business 325
Monmouth Rebellion 206, **207**
mono- **21**
monochrome **137**
monocotyledons 482, 483, **488**, *489*
monogamy 182
monomer 541
Monophysite doctrine 97
monopoly (business) **300**
Monopolies Commission 298, 300
Monopoly (game) **378**
monotheism 110
monotremes 487
Monroe, Marilyn 47, *152*, 240, 317, 321, **326**, 334, 369
Monroe, President James 244
Monroe Doctrine **244**
Monrovia, Liberia 443
Monsieur Verdoux 312
monsoon 440, **470**, 473, 476
montage **137**
Montagu, Lord 400
Mont Blanc **445**
Monte Carlo 435, 445
　Rally 380
Montenegro 223, 453, 462
Montesquieu, Charles **107**
Montessori, Maria **182**
Monteverdi, Claudio **351**
Montezuma II **244**
Montfort, Simon de 202, 203, 220
Montgolfier brothers **560**

Montgomery, Bernard (Viscount Montgomery of Alamein) 188, 196, **207**
Montgomery, L.M. 32
Montmartre 449
Montolieu, Mme de 73
Montreal **445**
Monty Python and the Holy Grail 326
Monty Python's Flying Circus **326**
Monty Python's Life of Brian 326
Monument Valley 459
mood **21**
mood swings 509
Moody, Ron 352
Moon 528, **537**, 565
　eclipse of *529*
　man on 240, 550
　tides and 475
Moon, Keith 360
Moon and Sixpence, The 46, 125
Moonies **107**
Moonlight 50
Moon's a Balloon, The 327
Moore, Bobby **378**, *388*
Moore, Dr Clement Clarke 88
Moore, Dudley 33
Moore, Henry **138**
Moore, Roger 311
Moors **244**
Moot Hill, Scone 418
Moran, 'Bugs' 251
Moray Firth 410
Morceli, Nouredine 377
More, Kenneth 318, **326**
More, Thomas 46, **207**, 330
Moreau, Gustave **138**
Morecambe **413**
Morecambe and Wise **326**
Morgan – A Suitable Case for Treatment 329
Morgan le Fay 78
Morisot, Berthe **138**
Mormons **107**
Morning After, The 317
Morning Cloud 273
Morning Glory 320
Morocco **445**
-morph- **21**
Morpheus **85**
morphine 85, 503
Morris (car) 129
Morris, Desmond 172
Morris, Jane *145*
Morris, William **138**, 155
Morrison, Jim 342
Morrison, Toni **47**
Morse, Samuel **560**
Morse code 560
mortal sin **107**
Morte d'Arthur, Le **47**, 83
mortgage 294, **300**
Mortimer, John 330
Mortimer, Roger 198
Morton, Jelly Roll 347
Morton, Thomas 21
mosaic **139**
Mosaic law **107**

Moscow **445**, 451
　Olympic Games 263
Moses 94, 100, 104, **107**
Moses, Grandma **127**
Mosley, Sir Oswald **207**, 270
mosque **107**, 163
mosque (architecture) **163**
mosquitoes 520
moss 488, *489*
Moss, Stirling **378**
Mostel, Zero **327**
Mother Courage 64
Mother Teresa 433
Mother Wore Tights 319
motion, Newton's laws of 522, 536, **538**
motion pictures 553
　see also films
mot juste **21**
motocross 378
motorcycle racing 378, *412*
motor neuron disease (MND) **511**, 512, 513
motor racing 372, 375, 380, 388, 432, 445
　see also names of drivers
Motown **351**
motto **21**
moulds *see* fungi
mountain building 468, **471**, 472
mountains *see* individual names
Mountbatten, Lord Louis **208**, 417
Mount Elbert 451
Mount Etna 453
Mount Everest *428*, 440, **445**
Mount Fuji 475
Mount Helicon 86
Mounties, The 433
Mount McKinley 426
Mount Olympus 82, 86, 90
Mount Parnassus 79, 86
Mount Pinatubo 476
Mount Rushmore **445**
Mount St Helens **445**, 476
Mount Vernon, Virginia 460
Mount Vesuvius 248, 446, 460
Mourning Becomes Electra 48
Mousehole **413**
Mousetrap, The 37
Mouse Trouble 333
Mowgli (*Jungle Book*) 44
Mozambique **445**
Mozart, Wolfgang Amadeus 53, 308, **351**, 358, 364, 452
Mozzarella **391**
MPs (Members of Parliament) 261, 273, 281
Mr and Mrs Andrews (Gainsborough) *125*
Mr and Mrs Bridge 327
Mr Blandings Builds His Dream House 319, 324
Mr Deeds Goes to Town 312, 313

Mr Norris Changes Trains 43
Mrs Dalloway 60
Mr Skeffington 313
Mr Smith Goes to Washington 312, 331
Mucha, Alfonse *118*
Much Ado About Nothing 53, 311
mucous membrane **511**, 519
Mugabe, Robert **279**, 462
Mughal Empire 440, 442
Muhammad **107**, 442, 453
Muir, Jean **139**
mule 486
Mull *413*
mullah **108**
multi- **21**
multiculturalism **182**
multinational **300**
multiple pregnancy **511**
multiple sclerosis (MS) **511**, 512
Muluzi, Bakili 444
Mumbles, The *413*
mumps 503,**511**
Mumtaz Mahal 167
Munch, Edvard **139**, 448
Munich **445**
Munich Agreement 188, 194, **244**
Munnings, Sir Alfred **139**
Munro, Hector Hugh 52
Munstead Wood, Surrey 162
Murasaki, Shikibu 67
murder 185, 266
Murder in the Cathedral 39, 190
Murder Must Advertise 53
Murder on the Orient Express 37, 309, 318
Murder She Said 330
Murdoch, Iris **47**
Murdoch, Rupert **300**, 328
Murillo, Bartolomé **139**
'Murphy Himself' *386*
Murphy's law **21**
Murray, Sir George 449
Muscat, Oman 448
Muscat (wine) **396**
muscles **511**
    diagram of *511*
muscular dystrophy **512**, 513
Musée d'Orsay 126
Musée Rodin 145
Muses **85**, 86
Museum of La Villette 557
Museum of Modern Art (MOMA), New York 126
museums of the world, 126
mushrooms **394** *see also* fungi
Music Box, The 323
Music Lovers, The 330
music terms **350**
muskets 556
Muslim **108**, 451, 459, 462
    League 239
    prohibitions 186, 453
    religion 96, 100, 104, 108, 109
    taboos 186

mussels 480
Musset, Alfred de 72
Mussolini, Benito 224, **244**, 441
Mussorgsky, Modest Petrovich **352**
mutation 470, **488**
Mutiny on the Bounty 317
Mycenae **245**
    civilisation 236, 444
My Cousin Rachel 311
My Darling Clementine 317
My Fair Lady 51, 54, 119, 308, 320, **352**
My Favourite Blonde 321
My Favourite Brunette 321
My Favourite Year 328
My Last Duchess 35
myopia (short sight) 503
Myrddin 84
mystery plays 70
mystery religions **108**
mysticism **108**
Mytens, David **139**
My Universities 67

N

Nabis **139**
Nabokov, Vladimir **70**
Nadir, Asil 261
Nagasaki 221, 441, 560
Nagorno-Karabakh 429
Nagy, Imre 238
nailing one's colours to the mast (phrase) **21**
Naipaul, Sir V.S. **47**
Nairobi, Kenya 442
naive art **139**, *146*
Naked Lunch 346
Name of the Rose, The **70**, 313
Namib Desert *446*
Namibia 442, **446**
nan **394**
Nanak, Guru 114
nano- **537**
Nantes 443
Nantes, Edict of **245**
napalm **560**
Napa Valley 433
Napier, Sir Charles 197
Naples **446**
Napoleon I (Bonaparte) 208, 215, 234, 239, **245**
Napoleonic Wars **245**, 407
narcissism 85
Narcissus **85**
narcotics 518
narrative **70**
narrator **70**
Naruto Strait whirlpools 476
NASA 457, 563
Naseby, Battle of 195, **208**
Nash, John **163**, 413, 416, 422

Nash, Ogden **48**
Nash, Paul **139**
Nash, Richard 'Beau' 400
Nassau, Bahamas 429
Nasser, Gamal Abdel **245**, 253, 428
Nasser, Lake 428
Nast, Thomas 283
National Conservatory, New York 343
national curriculum **182**
national debt **300**, 303
National Exhibition Centre (NEC), Birmingham 401
National Front 270
National Gallery, London 126, 422
National Geographic Magazine **324**
national grid 561
National Health Service (NHS) 189, 190, 288
    NHS ombudsman 280
National Hunt racing **378**
national insurance **301**
nationalisation **301**
nationalism **279**
National Maritime Museum, Greenwich 408
National Motor Museum, Beaulieu 400
National Railway Museum, York 424
National Stud, Newmarket 413
National Theatre 328
National Velvet 332
'nation of shopkeepers' **208**
Native Americans **182**
NATO (North Atlantic Treaty Organisation) 267, **279**, 432
natural monopoly **301**
natural gas **471**
naturalism **108**
naturalism (art) **140**
natural justice 206, **279**
natural law **279**
natural selection 478, 484, 485, 488
natural theology **108**
nature-nurture debate **183**, 505
nausea 516
Navigator, The 322
Navratilova, Martina 372, **378**
Nazism 222, 229, 233, 235, 237, 238, **245**
    eugenics programmes 176
    Nazi-Soviet Pact 244, **246**, 253
    propaganda **282**
    war criminals 235, 237, **246**, 248, 430
n.b. (*nota bene*) **21**
Neanderthal man **181**
Neave, Airey **208**
nebuchadnezzar (bottle) 246, 396
Nebuchadnezzar II, King **246**
nebula **537**

nectar 489
Necton Guild athletics club 363
needlepoint 148
negative equity 294
negative reinforcement 185
Negev 441
Negroid **183**
Nehru, Jawaharlal 234, **246**
Nelson, Horatio 198, **208**, 215, 416, 422
Nelson's Column 422
Nemesis **85**
neo- **21**
neo-fascist movements 270
neo-Classicism (architecture) **163**
neo-Classicism (art) **140**
neodymium *see* periodic table **541**
neo-Gothic **163**
neologism **21**
neon **538**, *see also* periodic table **541**
neon lighting 538
Neoptolemus 87
Nepal **446**
nephritis 507
Neptune (god) **85**, 87
Neptune (planet) 85, **538**, 541, *544*, 563
neptunium *see* periodic table **541**
Nero 73, 110, **246**
nervous system **512**, 513, 518, 520
Nesfield, W.E. 165
Nessun Dorma 354
Nestlé 296
netball **378**
Netherlands **446**
    and West Indies 461
Nether Stowey 416
nettle rash 506
neuralgia **512**
neurology 510
neurons 518
neurosis **512**
neuro transmitter 518
Neuschwanstein Castle 430
neutrino **538**, 546
neutron *523*, 534, **538**, 542, 546
neutron bombs 560
neutron star **538**, 545
Neva, River 452
Nevada 443
Never Love a Stranger 52
Never Say Never Again 311
Nevsky Prospekt 452
New Age 82, 180, **183**
'New Age travellers' 183
New Avengers, The 309
Newcastle upon Tyne **413**
Newcomen, Thomas 211, 564
'New Deal' 231, **246**
New Delhi 162
New Forest **413**
Newfoundland 232
New Guinea 440, 449-50
New Industrial State, The 295

'new man' 177
Newman, John Henry **108**, 109
Newman, Paul 327
Newmarket **413**
New Model Army 195, 196, **208**
New Orleans 443, **446**
Newport, Isle of Wight 423
New Providence, Bahamas 429
New Right **279**
New Scotland Yard 166, 281
News of the World, The 300
New South Wales 456
newspapers 328
Newspeak **21**, 48
newsreaders 327
newt 478
New Territories 440
New Testament 79, 92, 94, 101, 103, 106, **108**, 109
newton (unit of force) 531
Newton, Sir Isaac 525, *532*, 535, **538**, *543*, 565
Newton, Robert 327
Newton's Laws of Motion 522, 531, 536, **538**, 543
New Wave 327
New World **246**, 518
    trade with 407
    wines of **396**
New World, From the 343
New York 159, **446**
    Central Park **434**
    Theatre District 339
New Yorker 57, 308
New Zealand 256, **447**
niacin 520
Niagara Falls 439, **447**
Nibelungenlied **70**
Nicaragua 283, **447**
Nice, France 394, *435*
Nicene Creed **108**
niche 467
Nicholas, St 87
Nicholas II 124, **246**, 249, 251, 451
Nicholas Nickleby **48**
Nicholson, Ben **140**
Nicholson, Jack *309*, 316, 322, 324, **327**
nickel 535, 546, *see also* periodic table **541**
nicknames (1980s) 186
niçoise *394*
Nicolson, Harold 52, 419
Nicosia 436
Nietzsche, Friedrich **108**
Niger, River 447, 457
Nigeria 224, **447**
Night and the City 334
Night at the Opera, A 325
Night in Casablanca, A 325
Nightingale, Florence **208**
Night of the Generals 328
Night of the Hunter 326
Night of the Iguana, The 311, 321
'Night of the Long Knives' 225
Night Watch, The 143

nihilism 108
Nijinsky, Vaslav 69, **352**
Nikkei Index **301**
Nile, River 428, 434, **447**
Nile, Battle of 208
Nile Valley 233
Nilsen, Dennis 185
nimby (acronym) **183**
Nimoy, Leonard 331
Nine Tailors, The 53
Nineteen Eighty-four 34, **48**
1922 Committee 261
Nineveh 457
Ninotchka 318
niobium *see periodic table*
  541
Nirvana **108**
nitrates 488
nitric acid 464
nitrogen 464, **538**
  oxides 464
  see also periodic table
  541
nitrogen cycle **488**
nitrogen fixation 488
Niven, David 63, **327**
Nixon, Richard 241, **246**,
  256, 274, 459
Nkrumah, Kwame **246**,
  439
Noah 101, 427
Noakes, John 310
Nobel, Alfred Bernhard
  455, **560**
nobelium *see periodic table*
  541
Nobel prizes 560
  chemistry 527
  economics 560
  literature 32, 40, 42, 48
    54, 60, 63, 64, 67, 69,
    72, 73, 112, 195
  peace 193, 225, 241, 250,
    251, 433
  physics 524, 527
Noble, Richard 375
noble gases **538**
noble rot 396
noblesse oblige 21
no-claims bonus **301**
national savings **301**
Noddy **48**
noisette 394
No Man's Land 329
nom de plume **21**
non-alignment 246
nonce word **21**
Nonconformists **108**
non-Euclidean geometry
  530, 532
nonmetal 540, *541*
Nonnberg Abbey, Salzburg
  452
nonrestrictive clause **21**
nonsense verse **70**
non sequitur **21**
non-specific urethritis
  (NSU) 520
non-vintage **396**
Nordic ski racing 383
Norfolk **413**
Norgay, Tenzing 445
Noriega, General Manuel
  449

normal distribution curve
  538, 546
Norman, Greg 370
Norman, Jessye **352**
Norman architecture **163**
Norman Conquest 203,
  208
Normandy 256
Normandy, Duke of 438
Norse mythology **85**, 90
North, Oliver *239*
North America, map of **447**
  see also America, North
Northanger Abbey 33
North Atlantic Treaty
  Organisation (NATO)
  267, **279**, 432
North Briton 217
North By Northwest 319, 320
North Downs **414**
Northern Ireland *see*
  Ireland, Northern
North Island, New Zealand
  447
North Korea **447**
North Pole 427, 523
North Sea oil industry 447
Northumberland **414**
Northumberland, Dukes of
  398
Norway **447**
  Germany and 249
Norwich **414**
Nostradamus **85**
Notes of a Painter 133
Notorious 309, 319, 320
Nôtredam, Michel de **85**
Notre Dame Cathedral
  163, 449
Nottingham **414**
Notting Hill Carnival 170
noun **21**
  abstract 10
  collective 12
  common 13
  concrete 13
  count 13
  mass 20
  proper 24
nouveau riche **22**
nova **538**
novel **70**
novella **71**
Novello, Ivor **352**
No Way Out 313, 329
Now Voyager 313
Now We are Six 47
nuance **22**
nuclear
  deterrence 267
  disarmament 265, 267
nuclear energy 523, 528,
  530, **539**
nuclear family **183**
nuclear fission 533, **539**,
  547, 560
nuclear fusion 526, 533,
  539, 541, 545, 546, 560
nuclear power stations 418,
  471, **539**
nuclear reactor 531, 533,
  539, **560**
nuclear submarines 399,
  564

nuclear waste **471**, 473, **539**
nuclear weapon 221, 261,
  267, 288, 444, 529, **560**
nucleotides 484
nucleus, atomic 523, 538,
  539
nucleus, cell 480, *481*
number (grammar) **22**
number (mathematics) 535,
  539
numerals 522, 543
Nun's Story, The 320, 334
Nuremberg rallies 235, *245*,
  246
Nuremberg trials 235, 237,
  246, 248, 430
Nureyev, Rudolph 344,
  348, **352**
Nurmi, Paavo **378**
Nutcracker, The 359
nutmeg *393*
Nyasa, Lake 205
Nyerere, Julius 456
nylon **560**
nymph (zoology) **488**
Nymphs (mythology) **85**,

O

Oahu, Hawaii 439
OAS (Organisation of
  American States) **280**
oasis **471**
Oates, Captain Lawrence
  208, 213
Oates, Titus 210
OAU (Organisation of
  African Unity) **280**
obelisk **163**
Oberammergau 70, **448**
obesity **512**, 520
object **22**
Obote, Milton 221
Obree, Graeme *551*
obsessive-compulsive
  disorders **512**
obsidian 474
obsolescence, built-in **291**
obstetrics 510
O'Casey, Sean **48**
occluded front **471**, 476
ocean currents 466, 467,
  469, **471**
ocean depths **471**
ocean ridges 467, **471**, 472,
  474
Ockham (or Occam),
  William of **108**
'Ockham's razor' 108
O'Connell, Daniel 203, **208**
octane **539**
Octavian 220, 250
October 316
October Revolution **246**,
  251
octopus *479*, 481
Odd Couple, The 323

Odd Man Out 325, 327, 329
ode **71**
'Ode on a Grecian Urn' 48
Odessa File, The 40
Odin **85**
Odo, Bishop of Bayeux 190
Odyssey **71**, 89, 183
Odysseus **85**, 88
OECD (Organisation for
  Economic Cooperation
  and Development) **301**
Oedipus 76, **85**, 88, 359
Oedipus complex 86, 176,
  183
Oedipus **71**, 76, **85**
oesophagus 505
oestrogens 506, 510, **512**,
  514, 515
Offa, king 211, 414
Offa's Dyke **414**
Offenbach, Jacques **352**
Office of Fair Trading **301**
Officer and a Gentleman, An,
  318
Official Secrets Acts **280**
Of Human Bondage 46
Of Mice And Men 55, 312
Ohain, Hans von 558
Ohm, Georg Simon 539
ohm **539**, 543
Ohm's law 539
Oh! What a Lovely War 309
oil 301, 429, **472**
oil refining **561**
Okavango 432, **448**
O'Keeffe, Georgia **140**
Oklahoma **448**, 475
Oklahoma! 356
okra **394**
Oktoberfest 445
Olav V 447
Old Bailey 266, 330, **414**
'old boy network' 185
Old Curiosity Shop, The 38
Old English **48**
Old Faithful (geyser) 462
Old Gringo 317
Old Huntsman, The 53
'Old King Cole' 404
Oldman, Gary 315
Old Man and the Sea, The 42
Old Man of Hoy **414**
*Old Possum's Book of Practical
  Cats* 39, 349
Old Pretender **208**
Old Sarum, Salisbury 199,
  418
'old school tie' 185
Old Testament 79, 92, 99,
  100, 101, 107, **108**, 173,
  232, 246
Old Trafford 368
Old Vic, Bristol 402
'Old Vicarage, Granchester,
  The' 408
Old Wives' Tales, The 33
oligarchy **280**
oligopoly **301**
Oliver! 48, 329, 330, **352**
Oliver, Dr William 400
Oliver Twist 48, 319, 323,
  327
olives, purée of (tapenade)
  395

Odd Man Out 325, 327, 329
Olivier, Lord (Laurence)
  42, 311, 323, **328**
Olympians 83, 86
Olympic Games **379**, 388
  Ancient Greek 236, 363,
    369, 377
  (1896) Athens 377
  (1908) London 243
  (1912) Stockholm 377
  (1924) Paris 362
  (1924) Chamonix 383
  (1928/48) San Moritz
    452
  (1936) Berlin 379
  (1948) London
  (1960) Rome 369
  (1968) Mexico 370, 444
  (1972) Munich 374, 384,
    445
  (1976) Montreal 367
  (1980) Moscow 379
  (1984) Los Angeles 365,
    375
  (1984) Sarajevo 452
  (1988) Seoul 375, 453
  (1992) Barcelona 379
  (1996) Atlanta 379
  (2000) Sydney 456, 379
Olympus, Mount **86**
Olympus Mons 536
Oman 260, **448**, 449
Omar Khayyám **71**
Omayyads 226, **246**
ombudsman **280**
Omen, The 328
Omeros 58
omni- **22**
Onassis, Aristotle 240, **301**,
  340
Onassis, Jacqueline 240
*Once Upon a Time in the
  West* 317
oncology 510
One, Two, Three 311
*One Day in the Life of Ivan
  Denisovich* 73, 453
*One Flew Over the Cuckoo's
  Nest* 327
*One Hundred and One
  Dalmatians* 315
100 Cans of Campbell's Soup
  142
*One Hundred Years of
  Solitude* 69
O'Neil, Eugene **48**, 312
O'Neil, Oona 312
one-parent family **183**
On Golden Pond 317, 320
*On Her Majesty's Secret
  Service* 311
On Ilkla Moor baht 'at 410
onions 480
On Liberty (John Stuart
  Mill) 106
Only Two Can Play 330
onomatopoeia **22**
Ono, Yoko 338
Ontario **448**, 457
  Lake 439, 457
on tenterhooks **22**
'on the nail' 402
On The Waterfront 311,
  339
Op Art **140**, 151

OPEC (Organisation of Petroleum Exporting Countries) 292, **301**
Open Championship **379**
Open City 330
Open University **175**, 413
opera, plots **353**
operant conditioning 174, 185
Operation Crossbow 324
Operation Gold 264
'Operation Overlord' 231
operetta **352**
ophthalmology 510
opinion polls **280**, 538
Opium Wars **246**, 433
Oporto (Porto) **448**
Oppenheimer, Robert 560
opposition **280**
optical fibres 543
optical instruments 535
opting out (schools) 175
option 296, **301**
Opus Dei **109**
oracle **86**
oral contraception 514
oral tradition 171, **183**
Orangemen 192, **208**
Orbison, Roy 343, **354**
orbit **539**, 562
Orchestra
  Berlin Philharmonic 347
  Chicago Symphony 358
  City of Birmingham Symphony 356
  London Philharmonia 348
  London Philharmonic 338
  New York Philharmonic 339, 360
  Philadelphia 316
  Royal Philharmonic 336, 338
  Vienna Philharmonic 460
orchid 484, *489*
'orchids' (acromym) 186
Ordeal of Gilbert Pinfold, The 59
Order of the Garter 87, 178, **199**, 284
Ordinary People 329
ordination **109**
ore *472*
oregano *393*
Oresteia **71**
Orestes 76, 81
organic chemistry **539**
Organization of African Unity (OAU) **280**
Organisaiton of American States (OAS) **280**
Organisation for European Co-operation and Development (OECD) **301**
orienteering **379**
original sin 94, **109**
origin of life 486, **488**
Origin of Species by Means of Natural Selection, On The 483
Orion Nebula *564*
Orkney **414**

Orlando 52, 60
Orlando 438
Orléans, siege of 239
ornithischia 483
Orpheus and Eurydice **86**
Orpheus Descending 329
Orphism **140**
Orthodox Church 99, **103**, **109**, 121
orthopaedics 510
Orton, Joe **48**, 330
Orwell, George 21, 48, 252
Osborne, John 32, **48**, 328
Osborne House, Isle of Wight 423
Oscar (film, music, song and dance) **328**, 337, 348, 350, 352, 358, 359
oscillating Universe theory 524
Oslo 447, **448**, 455
osmium *see* periodic table **541**
osmosis **539**
osso bucco **394**
osteoarthritis 496
osteopathy 495, 510, **512**
osteoporosis **512**
ostracism **183**
ostrich 390, 480
Oswald, Lee Harvey 240, **246**
Otello 360
Othello **48**, 308, 328, 330, 334
Other Stories 46
Otis, Elisha 558
O'Toole, Peter 323, **328**
Ottawa **448**
otter hunting 370
Otto, Nikolaus, August 558
Ottoman Empire 223, 229, 232, **247**
Our American Cousin 242
Our Hospitality 322
Our Man in Havana 41, 329
Ouse, River **414**
Outcast of the Islands 329
Outlaw, The 296
Out of Africa 63, 329, 332
'out-of-body experience' 77
Out of the Past 326
Outsider, The 64
ouzo **394**
Oval, The 368, 370
ovarian cyst 512-13
ovaries 486, **488**, **512**
'Over the Rainbow' 318, 334
Ovett, Steve **379**
Ovid **71**
ovulation 512
ovule 485, 491
ovum 492
Owen, David (Lord Owen) **280**
Owen, Robert **209**
Owen, Wilfred **48**, 68
Owens, Jesse **379**
Owl and the Pussy-Cat, The **49**
oxbow lake 474
Oxbridge **183**
Oxford **414**

Oxford and Cambridge Boat Race 421
Oxford English Dictionary **22**, 43
Oxford Movement **109**
oxidation **539**, 543
oxides 540
oxygen 524, **539**, 540
  atmospheric 464, 539
  in living things 489, 490, 499
  see also periodic table **541**
oxymoron **22**
Oyashio Current *471*
oyster(s) 480
oyster mushrooms 394
ozone *472*, **540**
ozone layer *464*, 465, **472**, 517, 540, 550, 562, *Ozymandias* 54

P

pace **22**
pacemaker **513**
Pacifico, Don 209
Pacific Ocean 242, 441, **449**, 471, 472
  war in the 258
pacifism **280**
Pacino, Al 319, **328**
Pactolus, River 84
Paderewski, Ignacy Jan **354**
paediatrics 510
paella **394**, 455
Paganini, Nicolo **354**
paganism **109**
Page, Jimmy 348
Paine, Thomas **109**
Paisa 330
Paisley, Reverend Ian 280, 288, **414**
Pakistan 224, 239, **449**
  cricket 374
  People's Party 262
Pale Rider 316
Palace at 4am, The 126
Palace of Westminster 155
Palace Pier, Brighton *402*
palaeo-, paleo- **22**
Palaeozoic era *468*
Palazzo Pubblico, Siena 453
Paleface, The 321
Pale Fire 70
Palermo, Sicily 453
Palestine **449**
  and West Bank 461
Palestine Liberation Organisation (PLO) 261, **281**, 449
Palestinians 185
Palin, Michael 326
palindrome **22**
Palio horse race, Siena 453
Pal Joey 356, 358
Palladian **163**
Palladio, Andrea **163**

palladium *see* periodic table **541**
Palliser novels 58
Palm Beach **449**, *469*
Palmer, Arnold 378, **379**
Palmer, Samuel **140**
Palmerston, Viscount **209**
Palm Springs **449**
Palm Sunday 99
Palmyra 456
Palo Alto 454
pan- **22**
Pan 83, **86**
Pan African Congress 271
Panama **449**, 520
Panama Canal **163**, 449
pancake 390, 392, 395
pancreas 501, **513**
pandemic **513**
Pandora **86**, 87
Pandora's box 86
panettone 394
Pangaea *466*
Pankhurst, Christabel 215
Pankhurst, Emmeline *215*
Pankhurst, Sylvia 215
Panorama 314, 325
Panthalassa *466*
pantheism **109**
Pantheon, Rome *164*, 451
Pantiles, The (Tunbridge Wells) 422
pantothenic acid 520
Papeete 456
paper **561**
Papillon 324
Papua New Guinea **449**
parabola *527*, **540**
Paracelsus 504, **513**
Parade 357
paradigm **109**
paradise **109**
Paradise Lost 47, **49**, 66, 79
Paradise Regained 47
paradox **22**
paragraph **22**
Paraguay 177, **449**
parallax **540**
parallelogram of forces 547
Paralympics 379
paralysis **513**, 518
paranoia **513**
paraphrase **22**
paraplegia 513
parasite 479, **488**
parasitic insects 508
parchment 561
parentheses **22**
parenthesis **22**
par excellence **22**
pargetting **164**
Paris **449**
  Métro *155*
  and World War II 449
Paris (Greek legend) 76, 83, **86**, 87
Paris Commune **247**
Parker, Charlie 338, **354**
Parker, Dorothy **49**
Parkinson, C. Northcote 301
Parkinson, Michael 314
Parkinson, Norman **140**

Parkinson's disease **513**
Parkinson's Law **301**
Parks, Rosa 228
parliament 202, **209**, 212, 218, **280**, 286
  Bill 272
  dissolution of **268**
  European 269
  hung 274
  sovereignty of 285
  State Opening of **286**
  see also House of Commons; House of Lords
parliamentary committee **280**
parliamentary privilege **280**
Parma ham 395
Parmesan cheese **391**
Parmigianino, Francesco **140**
Parmigiano Reggiano 391
Parnell, Charles Stewart 203, **209**, 210
parody **71**
Parr, Catherine 202
Parrott, John 369
parsec 535
Parsees **109**
Parsifal 81, **86**
parsing **22**
parsley *393*
Parthenon 77, 124, **164**
participle, present **22**, 24
particle accelerator 522, 523, *525*, **540**
parting shot **22**
part of speech **22**
Parton, Dolly 341
Party, The 330
pas (ballet) **337**
Pasarell, Charlie 371
pascal (unit of pressure) 542
Pascal, Blaise 542
Pasiphae, Queen 85
Passage to India, A **49**, 308, 323
Passchendaele 258, 430
passe **22**
passim **23**
Passionate Shepherd to His Love 37, 46
Passover (or Pesach) **109**
Passport to Pimlico 315
pasta *394*, 431
  al dente 390
pastels **140**
Pasternak, Boris **72**
Pasteur, Louis 504, 508, **513**, 515
Pasteur Institute 513
pasteurisation **513**
pastiche **141**
pastis 390
pastoral **72**
past participle **23**
past perfect **23**
pastrami 394
past tense **23**
Patagonia **449**
Pat and Mike 320
paternalism **184**
-path- **23**
pathology 510

patina **141**
patois **23**
patriarchy 182, **184**
Patten, Chris 440
Patton, George **247**
Paul, St 93, **110**, 246
Paul Revere, The Midnight Ride of 249
Pavarotti, Luciano **354**
Pavlov, Ivan 171, 174
Pavlova, Anna **354**, 452
Paxton, Sir Joseph 158
'pay on the nail' 402
peach melba 350, 392, **394**
Peak District **414**
peanuts *see* groundnuts
peanut sauce (satay) 395
Pearl Harbor **247**, 439
Pearly kings and queens *26*
Pears, Sir Peter 339
Pears Ltd, A. & F. 136
Pearson Longman 328
Peary, Robert 427
Peasants' Revolt 204, **209**, 224
peat 466
Peck, Gregory 320, **328**
pecking order **23**
pediculosis 508
pediment **164**
Peekshill, meteorite 470
Peel, Robert 196, **209**, 266, 281
Peeping Tom 82
peerage 178
Pegasus 84, **86**
Peking man **181**
Pelé **379**, 432
Pelias, King 83
Pelléas and Mélisande 342
Peloponnesian Wars **247**, 253
pelota **379**
penalty shoot-out **379**
penance 92, **110**
pendulum 532
Penelope **86**
penicillin 495, 503, **514**
Peninsular War 192, 197, **247**
Penn, Arthur 311
Penn, William **247**, 449
Pennies from Heaven 329
Pennines **414**
Pennine Way 414
Pennsylvania 247, **449**
Penny Black *209*
penny-farthing *551*, 552
penny post **209**
pensions 301, 304
pentathlon, modern **377**
Pentecost **110**
Pentecostalism **110**
Pentland Firth 414
Penzance **415**
People, The 300
People's Democratic Republic of Yemen 462
PEP (Personal Equity Plan) **301**
Pepin the Short 227
pepsin 501
Pepys, Samuel **49**, 201
per capita **23**

Perceval, Spencer **209**
Percy family (Dukes of Northumberland) 398
peregrine falcon, and DDT 466
perennial **489**
perestroika 271
perfect (grammar) **23**
perfect competition **301**
Perfect Wagnerite, The 54
Perfect World, A 313
Pergamon Press 300
Pergamum 458
Pericles 54
periodic sentence **23**
periodic table **540**, *541*
peritonitis 496
Perkins, Anthony 329
permissive society 180,**184**
Perón, Eva 247, 349, 427
Perón, Juan **247**, 427
Perpendicular **164**
Perrault, Charles 78
Perry, Commodore 441
Perry, Fred **380**
per se **23**
Persephone **86**
Perseus 78, **86**
Persian Gulf **449**
    Gulf emirates 458
Persian Empire **247**, 251
person **23**
personal pronoun **23**
persona non grata **23**
personification **72**
perspective **141**
Perth 415, **449**, 461
Pertwee, Jon 315
Peru 238, **449**
Peru Current *471*
Perugino **141**
pesticide **23**
pesto **394**
Petacci, Clara 244
Pétain, Philippe **247**, 255
petal *485*
Peter, St 93, **110**, 246
Peter and Paul fortress 452
Peterloo Massacre **209**
Peter III of Russia 226
Peter Pan 49
Peter's Friends 311
Peter the Great **247**, 451
pétillant 396
petit mal 503
Petra 442, **449**
Petrarch **72**
Petrified Forest, The 310
petro-, petr- **23**
petrodollars **301**
petrol, unleaded 553
petroleum 539, 561
Petronius 73
Petticoat Lane **415**
Petty, Tom 343
Petworth House 160, **415**
Peugeot 566
Pfeiffer, Michelle 330
pH 525, 535, **540**
    soil 474
phagocyte 507
Phantom of the Opera, The 312, *349*
pharaohs **248**

Pharos (lighthouse) 426
Pheidippides 377
phenols 524
phenomenology **110**
pheromone **489**, 491
Philadelphia 449
Philadelphia Story, The 320, 331
Philby, Kim **210**
-philia **23**
Philip II of Spain 189, 198, 206, **248**
Philip V of Spain 222
Philip of Macedon 231, 236
Philippines **449**
Philips 554, 559
Philosophical Dictionary 74
Phineus, King 82
phloem *485*, **489**, 492
phlogiston 535, **540**
Phnom Penh 433
-phobia **23**
phobias 506, 512
Phobos 536
Phoenicia **248**
Phoenicians 94, 443, 456
Phoenix, Pat 313
phoenix **86**
Phoenix Park Murders **210**
phon- **23**
phonetic alphabet **23**
phonetics **23**
phoney war 257
phonograph 555
phosphorescence 531
phosphorus *534 see also* periodic table **541**
photochemical smog *see* smog
photocopier **561**
photoelectric effect 540
photoelectricity **540**
photomontage 137
photon 535, **540**, 542, 546
photophone 551
photosphere 546
photosynthesis 478, 479, 480, 487, **489**
phrase **23**
Phuket, Thailand 457
phylum *479*, 481
physics 98, **540**, 541, 543
physiotherapy, **514**
pi (π) 526, **540**
Pia de Tolomei, La (Rossetti) *145*
Piaf, Edith **354**
Piaget, Jean **184**
pianissimo **350**
piano **350**
Piano, Renzo 164
Piazza del Campo, Sienna 453
Piazza San Marco 460
Picasso, Pablo **141**, 236
Piccadilly **415**
'piccadils' 415
Pickett, Wilson 359
Pickwick, Mr *38*
Pickwick Papers *38*, **49**
pico- *537*
Pico de Teide, Tenerife 433

pictogram **23**
Picts **210**
Picture of Dorian Gray, The 59
Picture Post **324**
Picturesque **164**
pidgin **23**
pie chart 532
Pied Beauty 43
Pied Piper of Hamelin, The (Browning) 35
Pied Piper of Hamelin **86**, 230
Piero della Francesca *94*, *141*
Pierrepoint, Albert *263*
Piers Plowman **49**, 87
pieta **141**
Piggott, Lester **380**
pig in a poke **23**
pilaf, pilau **394**
Pilbara, marble *474*
piles 505
Pilgrim Fathers 243, 415, 419, 444, 459
Pilgrim's Progress, The **50**, 400
pill, the **514**
Piltdown Man **210**
Pina Colada **394**
Pincher Martin 41
pine 482, **489**, 492
Pink Floyd **355**
Pink Panther, The 327, **328**, *330*, 350
Pinocchio 315
Pinochet, General Augusto 220, 435
Pinot Noir (grape) **396**
Pinsent, Matthew 381
Pinter, Harold **50**, 329
Piper, John **141**
Piquet, Nelson 432
Pirandello, Luigi **72**
Pirate Coast 458
pirouette (ballet) **337**
Pisa 162, **450**, 532
Pisces *90*, 548
Pissarro, Camille **142**
pistol shooting 377, 556
pistou **394**
Pitt, William, the Elder (1st Earl of Chatham) **210**
pitta **395**
Pitt the Younger, William 200, **210**, 222, *291*
pituitary gland 498, 503, **514**
Pizarro, Francisco 238, **248**
pizzicato **350**
placebo **514**
Place de la Concorde 163
placenta 499, 512, **514**
plague 201, 224, 448, 498
Plague, The 64
Plaid Cymru **281**
Plains Indian Tribes 183
Plains of Abraham 218
plainsong 345, 350, **355**
Planck's constant 527, **540**
Planck, Max 535, 540, 541
planes, early 550
planet 528, 531, 536, 538, 539, **541**, *544*, 547

Planet of the Apes 320, **329**
planetoids 523
plankton **489**
planned economy **301-2**
Plant, Robert 348
plant kingdom **489**
Plantagenets 202, 205, **210**, 213
plant hormones **489**
plant tissues **489**
plaque **514**
plasma 497, 539, **541**
plastics 541, 551, **561**, 564
Plate, River 432
platelets 497
plate tectonics 466, 467, 471, **472**, 475
Plath, Sylvia **50**
plating, gold and silver 551
platinum *see* periodic table **541**
Plato 77, **110**, 523
platypus, duckbilled 487
Playboy of the Western World, The 56
Playing for Time 329
Play Misty For Me 316
Pleistocene epoch *468*, 469-70
pleonasm **23**
plesiosaurs 483
plié (ballet) **337**
PLO (Palestine Liberation Organisation) 261, **281**, 449
Plomley, Roy 314
Plough and the Stars, The 48
Plowright, Joan 328
plural **23**
pluralism **110**, 281
plus ca change, plus c'est la meme chose **24**
Pluto (god) **86**
Pluto (planet) 86, 541, *544*
plutonium 471, 539, 547
see also periodic table **541**
Plym estuary 415
Plymouth, England **415**
Plymouth, Massachusetts 444, 458
Plymouth Brethren **110**
Plzen 436
pneumatic tyres 566
pneumonia **514**
peripheral nervous system (PNS) 512
Po, River 457
Pobble Who Has No Toes, The 45
Poe, Edgar Allan **50**, 73
Poema del Cid 227
Poem in October 57
Poems and Ballads 56
poet laureate **50**
poetry **72**
Poet's Corner 168
pointillism **142**, 147
Poirot, Hercule **50**
Poitier, Sidney **329**
Poitiers, Battle of 227
Poland 248, 354, **450**
    Gdansk shipyard, 285
    see also place names
Polanski, Roman **329**

Polar easterlies 476
Polar ice caps 470
Polaris system 267
polarised light **541**
polenta **395**
Poles *see* North Pole; South Pole
police **281**
polio 507, **514**
political correctness **184**
political equality 175
pollen 485, **489**, 505
pollination 485, **489**
Pollock, Jackson **142**
poll tax 209, **210**, 287
pollution 467, *472*, **473**, 475, 508
Polo, Marco 241, **248**
Polo (fashion) 131
polo **380**
polonium 527 *see also* periodic table **541**
Polperro **415**
Pol Pot 229, **281**, 433
poltergeist **87**
poly- **24**
polyandry 182
polygamy 107, 182
Polyhmnia 85
polymer 537, **541**
polymerisation 561
Polynesia 447, 449, **450**, 456
Polynices 76
Polyphemus 79
polyptych 149
polytheism **110**
Pomerol (wine) 396
Pompadour, Madame de **248**
Pomp and Circumstance marches 343
Pompeii **248**, 460
Pompey 240
Pompidou, Georges 164
Pompidou Centre **164**, 449
Pond, The (Lowry) *133*
Pont du Gard *154*
Ponte Vecchio *438*
Pontius Pilate 104
pool (game) **380**
Poole **415**
poor law **210**, 218
pop art 120, 129, **142**
Pope, Alexander 33, **50**
pope, the 93, **110**, 112
Popish Plot 204, **210**
Popper, Sir Karl **110**
poppy, seed dispersal *490*
population **184**, 299, 303, 530
Poquelin, Jean-Baptiste *see* Molière **70**
porcelain 435-6
Porgy and Bess 319, 344
porpoises 481
Port Arthur 456
Port-au-Prince 439
Porter, Cole **355**
Porter, Edwin S. 319
portico **164**
Portinari, Beatrice 85
Port Jackson 432

Portland, Isle of **415**
Portland Bill 415
portmanteau word **24**
Portmeirion 329, **415**
Port Moresby 449
Portobello Road **416**
Port of Spain, Trinidad 457
Portrait of a Lady, The 43
Portrait of the Artist as a Young Man, A 44
Portree, Skye 419
Portsmouth **416**
Portugal 251, **450**
　　see also Peninsular War; Seven Years' War; War of Spanish Succession
Poseidon 79, 83, 85, **87**
positive discrimination 174
positive reinforcement 185
positivism **110**
positron 522
possessive **24**
possessive case 24
possessive noun 21
post- **24**
post-Impressionism **142**, 151
post-Modernism **164**, 168
post-natal depression **514**
post-traumatic stress syndrome **514**, 519
Potala Palace 443
potash **24**
potassium 528 *see also* periodic table **541**
potassium-argon dating 469, 473, 474
potatoes 491, 492
potato famine **211** 441
pot-au-feu **395**
potential difference 539, **541**, 543, 547
Potomac River 461
Potsdam **450**
Potsdam Conference (1945) **248**, 450
Potter, Beatrix **50**
Potter, Dennis **329**
Potteries **416**, 420
pottery 416, 420
Pottle, Pat 191
Poulsen, Valdemar 559
pound (weight) *see* Kilogram
Pound, Ezra **50**, 51
pounds, shillings and pence **211**
Poussin, Nicolas **142**
poverty level **302**
Powell, Anthony **51**
Powell, Enoch **281**
Powell, Mike 375, *376*
Powell, Robert 334
Powell, William 324
power (mathematics) 535, **541**
power (physics) **541**, 548
　　of tide 475
　　of wind 476
power station 539, **561**
Powers, Gary 255
Prado, Madrid 126, 444
pragmatic theory 116

Prague **450**
　　defenestration of 253
Prague Spring 232, **249**
prairies 481
praseodymium *see* periodic table **541**
pre- **24**
Precambrian era *468*
precedent **281**
precession **541**, 548
predation **490**
Predator 330
predestination doctrine 94, 95
predicate **24**
prefabrication **164**
prefix **24**
pregnancy 494, 495, 497, 502, 504, 511, **514**, 516, 520
Prelude, The 60
Prelude à l'après-midi d'un faune 342
premenstrual syndrome (PMS) **515**
premier cru wines 396
premise **110**
premium bond 301, **302**
preposition **24**
prep schools 175
Pre-Raphaelite Brotherhood 47, **51**, 62, 121, 129, 135, **142**, 145
Presbyterian Church 110, 116
Presbyterianism **110**
present participle **24**
Prescelly Mountains 88
present tense **24**
Presley, Elvis 345, *354*, **355**, 356, 444
Presley, Lisa Marie 113, 347
pressure 525, **542**
pressurised water reactor (PWR) 560
Prester, John **87**
presto 24
Preston, Battle of (1648) 195
Preston, Battle of (1715) 199
prestressed concrete **164**
preterite **24**
Pretoria 434, **450**, 454
Pretty Woman 318
pretzel **395**
Priam 79, 82, **87**
Price, Dennis 322
Price, Vincent **329**
price control **302**
price-earnings ratio (PE ratio) **302**
Pride, Colonel Thomas 211
Pride and Prejudice 33, **51**, 328
Pride and the Passion, The 324
Pride's Purge **211**
Pride Trust 177
Priestley, J.B. **51**
prima facie **24**
primary school teaching methods 184

primary sector **302**
primate 181, **490**
prime minister 263, **281**
prime number **542**
Prime of Miss Jean Brodie, The 55, 330
primitive art **142**
Prince 355
Prince, The 105, 224
Prince of Wales 198
'Princes in the Tower' 198, **211**, 217, 422
Princess Daisy 53
Princes Street, Edinburgh **416**
Princetown, Dartmoor 405
Princip, Gavrilo 233
Principia Mathematica 112
printing 236, **561**
prism *543*
Prison 281
Prisoner, The **329**
Prisoner of Zenda, The 316
Prisoners, The 415
Private Dancer 360
Private Eye **324**
Private Lives of Elizabeth and Essex, The 313
private member's bill 273, **282**
Private's Progress 311
private sector **302**
privatisation 300, **302**
Privy Council 261, **282**
Prizzi's Honor 321, 327
pro- **24**
proactive **24**
probability **542**
procurator fiscal **282**
Producers, The 327
professional foul **380**
profit **302**
Profumo Affair **211**, 267, 404
progesterone 510, **515**
progressive **24**
Progressive Democrats 270
Prohibition **249**, 251, 257, 435
Prokofiev, Sergei 64, **355**
Prometheus **87**
Prometheus Bound 87
Prometheus Unbound 54, 87
promethium *see* periodic table **541**
Promised Land (Canaan) 107, 179
Proms, the **355**, 356
pronoun **24**
　　demonstrative 15
　　indefinite 19
　　personal 23
　　possessive 24
　　reflexive 25
　　relative 26
propaganda **282**
propane 471
proper noun **24**
property prices 294
prophet **110**
proportional representation (PR) 270, **282**
proposition **111**
pro rata **24**

prosciutto **395**
Prospero's Books 318
Prost, Alain 380
prostate gland **515**
protactinium *see* periodic table **541**
protectionism **302**
proteins 478, 484, **490**, 537, 541
Protestantism **111**, 186
'protestant work ethic' 186
Protista 478, **490**
protists **490**
proton 522, *523*, **542**
protozoa 478, **490**
Proust, Marcel 72
proverb **24**
Prussia 224, 233, 234, **249**, 252
Pryderi 69
pseudo- **24**
pseudonym **24**
psoriasis **515**
Psyche 79, **87**
psychiatry 180, 184, 510, **515**
Psycho 320, **329**
psychoanalysis 176, 183, **184**
psychology **184**
psychosis **515**
psychosomatic disorder 515
psychotherapy **184**
pterosaurs 483
Ptolemy 527, **542**
puberty **515**, 518
Public Enemy, The 311
public expenditure **302**
public goods **302**
public inquiry **282**
Public Limited Companies (plc) **298**
public schools **175**, **185**
Public Sector Borrowing Requirement (PSBR) **303**
Puccini, Giacomo 353, **355**
Puerto Rico **450**, 461
Pugin, Augustus, W.N. **164**
pulling out all the stops **24**
pulsar 527, 538, **542**
pulse (heartbeat) 498, 519
Pumping Iron 330
pumpkin **395**
pun **24**
Punch 14, 41, 224, **324**
Punch and Judy Man, The 319
Punic Wars 226, 237, **249**
Punjab, India **450**
Punjab, Pakistan **450**
punk rock 355
Punta Arenas 449
pupa *488*
Purcell, Henry **355**
purdah **185**
purgatory **111**
Puritanism **111**
Puritans 195, **211**, 431
purple passage **25**
Purves, Peter 310
Pushkin, Alexandr 72
Puttnam, David **329**
Puzo, Mario 319

Pygmalion **87**
Pygmalion **51**, 54, 64, 87, 352
Pygmies 179, **185**
Pym, Barbara **51**
Pyongyang 447
pyramids **164**, *251*
Pyramid Texts 78
Pyrenees **450**, 455, 471
pyridoxine 520
Pyrrhic victory **25**
Pyrrhus, King **25**
Pythagoras's theorem 522, **542**

Q

Qatar 260
Qattara Depression 452
QC (Queen's Counsel) **282**
Q.E.D. **25**
Qin Shi Huangdi 161
qua **25**
quadriplegia 513
Quakers **111**, 280
quango 282-3
Quant, Mary **142**
Quantock Hills **416**
quantum mechanics 529, 535, 540, **542**, 547, 548
quarantine 515
quarks *523*, **542**, 546
quartz 544
quasar **542**
quasi- **25**
Quasimodo 67
quattrocento **143**
Quebec **450**
Queen **355**
'Queen Anne style' **165**
Queen Christina 318
Queen Mab 54
Queensberry Rules **380**
Queen's House, Greenwich 162, 408
Queensland **450**
Queen's Speech 286
quenelle **395**
question mark **25**
Question Time 273, **283**
Question Time 314
Quick, Diana 311
quicklime 524
quid pro quo **25**
Quiet American, The 41
Quiet Man, The 317, 333
Quinn, Anthony 323
Quisling, Vidkun **249**
Quito, Ecuador 437
quixotic **25**
Qumran 98
quotas 302, **303**
quotation marks **25**
Quotations of Chairman Mao 243
q.v. **25**

R

R101 airship 566
Rabat, Morocco 445
rabbi **111**
Rabelais, Francois **72**
rabies **515**, 520
Rabin, Yitzhak 261
race **185**
Rachel, Rachel 327
Rachmaninov, Sergei **356**
racism **185**, 228, 260
Rackham, Arthur *69*
Raclette 392
radar 550, 560, **561**
Radcliffe Library 160
Radiant Way, The 39
radiation **542**, 560
  alpha 542
  beta 542
  gamma 529, **532**, 542, 558
radiation sickness **515**
radicals **211**
radicchio 391
radio **561**, 565
radioactive waste *see* nuclear waste
radioactivity 523, 527, 533, **542**
radiocarbon dating **473**
radioisotopes 542
radiotherapy 508, **515**
Radio Times 324
radio waves 522, 529, 533, **542**, 561
radium 527, *see also* periodic table **541**
radius 526
Rado, James 345
radon 538, *see also* periodic table **541**
RAF *192*, 196
Raffles, Sir Stamford 454
Raffles Hotel 454
Raging Bull 314, 330
Raglan, Lord 194
Ragni, Gerome 345
Ragtime 311
ragtime 347, **356**
ragworms 479
Raiders of the Lost Ark 317, 331
railways 192, **211**, 565
Rain, Steam and Speed (Turner) *150*
rainbow **473**, 543
Rainbow, The 45
Rainbow Warrior 272
rainfall see cloud; flood; hydrologic cycle; weather
rain forest 426, 432, 466, 469, **473**, 481, 485
Rainier III, Prince 445
Rain Man 313, 321
Rains, Claude 312
Rais, Gilles de 78
Raise High the Roof-Beam 52
raison d'être **25**
Raj, the 274
Rake's Progress, The (Hogarth) 129

Raleigh (cycle) *551*, 552
Raleigh, Sir Walter 80, 204, **212**
rallentando **350**
rally (motor racing) **380**
Rama **111**
Ramadan **111**
Rameses II 179, 248
Ramsey, Sir Alf **381**
Rance, River 475
Ransome, Arthur 56
Raphael **143**, 438
rapid pulse 519
rap music 340, **356**
rare earths 540, *541*
Rasputin, Grigory **249**
rassemblement pour la République (RPR) 271
Rastafarianism **111**, 237, 356
ratification **283**
rationalism 98, 99, **112**
rational number 539
rat-race **25**
Rattigan, Sir Terence **51**
Rattle, Sir Simon, **356**
Ravel, Maurice 352, **356**
Raven, The 50
Rawhide 315
Ray, James Earl 241
Ray, Man **143**
ray (fish) 479, 485
Razin, Stepan 461
RCA 565
re **25**
Reach for the Sky 326
Reader's Digest **324**
Reagan, Ronald 228, 239, **283**
real cost **303**
real income **303**
realism (art) **143**
realism (literature) **72**
realism (philosophy) **112**
reality, virtual 566
'real McCoy', the 365
Reardon, Ray 373
Rear Window 320, 322, 331
Rebecca 39, 320, 328
Rebecca of Sunnybrook Farm 332
Rebel, The 319
Rebel Without A Cause 314
receiver 290, **303**
recession **303**
Recherche du Temps Perdu, A la 72
recitative **350**
recorder **283**
recorder, magnetic tape 559
Recuyell of the Historyes of Troye, The 193
recycling **561**
Red, Red Rose, A 36
Red Army 250, 254
'Red Baron', the 250
Red Cross 271, 438
Redding, Otis **356**
Redford, Robert 311, **329**
Red Fort, Delhi 436

red giant **543**, 545, 546, 548
Redgrave, Corin 329
Redgrave, Lynn 329
Redgrave, Sir Michael 329
Redgrave, Steve 381
Redgrave, Vanessa **329**
Red Guards (Chinese) *243*
red-handed (phrase) 19
red herring **25**
'Red' Indians 170, 182
redox reaction 543
red planet 536
Red River 333
Red Rum *372*
Reds 309
Red Sea 100, **450**
red shift 524, 528, 533, **543**
Red Shoes, The 346
Red Square *445*
reduction 539, **543**
reductionism **112**
redundancy **25**
Reed, Sir Carol **329**
Reed, Oliver 60
referendum **283**
reflation **303**
reflection 535, **543**, 548
Reflections on the Revolution in France 192
reflex **515**
reflexive pronoun **25**
reflexive verb **25**
reforestation **473**
Reform Acts 201, **212**
Reformation 101, 105, **112**
  Counter **229**, 248, 254
  English 202, 205, 206, **212**
  European 238, **249**
  Scottish 205, 415
Reformed Churches 99, 110, 114
refraction 473, 535, **543**, 548
refrigerator **562**
refugees 174, **185**
Regatta, Henley *373*, 409
Regency **212**
Regency (architecture) **165**
Regency style **143**
Regent's Park, London 165, **416**
Regent Street, London **416**
reggae 350, **356**
Reginald 52
Register of Shipping (Lloyd's) 299
regular verb **25**
Rehearsal, The (Degas) *123*
Reign of Terror 234, 239
reincarnation *95*, **112**
reinforced concrete **165**
Reinhardt, Django **356**
relative clause **26**
relative pronoun **26**
relativity, theory of 528, 532, 536, 537, **543**, 544, 547
relevé (ballet) 337
Reluctant Debutante, The 322
REM (rapid eye movement) 502, 517

Remains of the Day, The 321, 325
remand 283
Remarque, Erich Maria 62, 308
Rembrandt van Rijn **143**, 446
Remedia Amoris 71
Remembrance of Things Past 72
Remembrance Sunday 257
Remi, Georges 74
Renaissance architecture 165
Renaissance art **144**
Reno, Jesse W. 555
Renoir, Pierre Auguste **144**
repetitive strain injury **515**, 518
reported speech **26**
reprise **350**
reproduction 478, **490**
  asexual 481 *see also* spores
  sexual 480, 485
  see also spore **491**
reproductive system 512, **515**, 520
reptiles 479, 483, **490**
Repton, Humphry **165**
Republic 110
Republican Party 283
Repulsion 329
requiem **356**
resale price maintenance 303
rescheduling **303**
reserves 303
resistance (electrical) **543**
Resistance (patriotic) **249**
resistor **562**
Resnais, Alain 327
Resolution and Independence 60
resonance **543**
respiration 480, **490**, 539
respiratory system 508, **515**
resting on one's laurels **26**
Restoration **212**
Restoration comedy **51**
Restoration furniture **144**
restrictive clause **26**
Resurrection Cookham (Spencer) *148*
RPI (Retail Price Index) 297, **303-4**
retina, detached **501**
retinol 520
Return of Martin Guerre, The 314, 318
Return of the Jedi, The 331
revenge tragedy **51**
Revere, Paul **249**
reverse takeover **303**
Revolutionary Committee Movement 271
Revolutions of 1848 **250**
revolver 556
Reykjavik 440, **450**
Reynolds, Albert **283**
Reynolds, Sir Joshua 125, **145**
Rhea Sylvia 87
Rheims Cathedral **165**, 167

rhenium *see* periodic table **541**
Rhesus factor 497
rhetoric **26**
rhetorical question **26**
rheumatic fever **515**, 516
rheumatism **516**
rheumatoid arthritis 518
rheumatology 510
Rhine, River 431, **450**
Rhinoceros 69
rhizome **490**
Rhodes 251, **451**
Rhodes, Cecil **212**
Rhodesia 284, 462
  see also Africa, South;
  Zambia; Zimbabwe
Rhodes Scholarships 212
rhodium *see* periodic table
  541
Rhondda Valley **416**
Rhône **451**
rhyme **72**
rhyming slang **26**
rhythm and blues 342, **356**
Rialto Bridge 460
riboflavin 520
ribosome 480, **490**
Ricardo, David 293, **303**
Riccio, David 207
rice 394, 470
  risotto **395**
  wild **396**
Rice, Tim 349
Rice-Davies, Mandy *211*
Riceyman Steps 33
Richard I 'The Lionheart'
  212, *230*, 251
Richard II 209, **212**
Richard II 53
Richard III 202, **212**, 422
Richard III **51**, 328, 422
Richard, Cliff **356**
Richard, Duke of
  Gloucester 198
Richard, Duke of York 202
Richard, Prince 211
Richards, Sir Gordon **381**
Richards, Keith 356
Richards, Vivian **381**
Richardson, Samuel 37
Richardson, Sir Ralph **329**
Richardson, Tony 329
Richelieu, Cardinal **250**
Richmond Castle *416*
Richmond Park 416
Richmond, Virginia 460
Richmond, Yorkshire **416**
Richmond-upon-Thames
  416
Richter, C.F. 473
Richter scale 467, **473**, 535
Richthofen, Manfred von
  250
rickets **516**
rickettsia 519
Ricotta cheese **391**
'Ride a cock horse, to
  Banbury Cross' 399
Ride of the Valkyries, The 308
Ridgely, Andrew 351
Ridley, Nicholas (MP) 183
Ridley, Nicholas (preacher)
  205

Riesling 396
rifle 383, 556
rift valley **473**
Rigg, Diana 309
right wing (political) **283**
Rights, Bill of (US) **224**
Rights, Bill of (British)
  1689 **190**
Rights of Man, The 109
Rijksmuseum 126
Riley, Bridget 140
rillettes **395**
Rimbaud 73
*Rime of the Ancient Mariner,
  The* 52
Rimsky-Korsakov, Nicolai
  356
'Ring a Ring O' Roses' **52**,
  201
Ring cycle (Wagner) 353
ringing the changes 26
ringworm **516**
Rio Bravo 333
Rio de Janeiro 432, **451**
Ripon **416**
Rippon, Angela *327*
Rising Damp 330
risk **303**
Risorgimento 235, **250**, 441
risotto **395**
risqué **26**
Rite of Spring 352
rites of passage 179, **185**
Rites of Passage 41
Rivals, The 20, 55
river **473**
Rivera, Diego 124, **145**
River Runs Through It, A
  329
Riyadh 453
RNA 484, **490**
Roache, William 313
Road films 321, **330**
Road House 334
Road not Taken, The 40
Road to Wigan Pier, The 48
Road to Zanzibar, The 321
Roaring Twenties, The 310
Robben Island jail 278
robbing Peter to pay Paul
  26
Robbins, Harold **52**
Robeson, Paul 308, **356**,
  359
Robespierre, Maximilien de
  230, 234, **250**
Robin and Marian 313, 320
Robin Hood **87**
Robin Hood, Prince of Thieves
  313
*Robin Hood, The Adventures
  of* 317
Robin Hood 316
Robinson, Edward G. 321,
  330
Robinson, Jackie *364*
Robinson, Sugar Ray **381**
Robinson Crusoe **52**, 73
robots **562**
Rob Roy **212**
Rob Roy 53, 212
Rochdale **416**
Rochdale Pioneers 196, 416
Rochester **417**

rock (geology) 468, 469,
  470, **474**
rock cycle 474
Rockall **417**
Rockefeller, John D. **303**
Rockefeller Center 303
rocket 552, **562**
rocket bomb 560
Rocket, The 166, 565
rocket (salad) **395**
rock'n'roll 339, *345*, 355,
  356
Rock of Gibraltar 439
Rockwell, Norman 145
Rocky 331
Rocky Mountains 443, **451**,
  468, 475
rococo (architecture) **165**
rococo (art) 125, **145**
rodeo **381**
Rodgers, Jimmie 341
Rodgers, Richard **356**
Rodgers, William 284
Rodin, Auguste 145
Roentgen, Wilhelm *548*
Rogers, Ginger *336*
Rogers, Sir Richard **165**
Rogers, Roy 341
Roget, Peter Mark 29
Rohe, Ludwig Mies van der
  163
Rolling Stones **356**, *357*
Roman Britain **212**, 409
Roman Catholic Church
  103, 105, 110, **112**, 116,
  238
Romance languages **26**
romance literature 65, **72**
Romance of the Rose 72
Romancing the Stone 315
Roman Empire 228, 229,
  236, **250**, 254
  architecture of 400, 407
    409, 417
  collapse of 233
  Garland 438
  Vandals and 233, 255
Romanesque architecture
  165
Roman Holiday 320
Romania 226, 429, **451**
Roman law 240
Roman numerals **543**
Romanoff and Juliet 333
Romanovs **250**
Roman roads **165**
Romansch language 455
*Roman Spring of Mrs Stone,
  The* 323
Romantic **357**
romanticism **145**, 150
  in literature 36, 37, 44,
    54, 60, 64, **72**
Romany language 178
Rome **451**
  founding of 87
  Rome, Treaty of **250**
Romeo and Juliet **52**, 53,
  308, 323, 349
  ballet 355
  film 334
Rommel, Field Marshal
  188, **250**
Romney Marsh **417**

Romsey **417**
Romulus and Remus **87**,
  451
Romulus Augustulus 233
Rondanini Pietà
  (Michelangelo) 135
Ronsard 73
Room at the Top **330**
Room of One's Own, A 60
Room with a View, A 40,
  314, 325, 330
Rooney, Mickey 318
Roosevelt, Franklin D. 231,
  246, 247, **250**, *258*, 267,
  529
Roosevelt, Theodore **250**,
  445
root (language) **26**
root (plant) **490**
Roquefort cheese **391**
Rorschach, Hermann 179
rose oil 433
rosé 396
rose hips 491
rosemary *393*
Rosemary's Baby 329
*Rosencrantz and Guildenstern
  are Dead* 56
Roses, Wars of the 192,
  198, 202, **213**
Rosetta Stone **250**
Rosmersholm 59
Ross, Diana **357**
Ross, Sir James *427*
Rossellini, Isabella 330
Rossellini, Roberto **330**
Rossetti, Dante Gabriel 51,
  52, 145
Rossetti, Michael 142
Ross Ice Shelf 470
Rossini, Gioacchino 64,
  357
Rossiter, Leonard **330**
Ross-on-Wye **417**
Rostand, Edmond 65
Rosyth naval base 407
Rotherhithe Tunnel 156
Rothko, Mark **45**
Rothschild **303**
Rotorua 447
Rotten Row, Hyde Park
  410
Rotterdam 446
Rouge et Le Noir, Le 73
'Rough Riders' 250
Rougon-Macquart, Les 74
roulette **381**
Round the Horne 334
rounders **381**
Roundheads 195
Round Table, Knights of
  the 77, 82, **87**
roundworms *479*
Rousseau, Henri **146**
Rousseau, Jean-Jacques **112**
Rover (safety cycle) 552
rowing 373, **381**
Rowntrees 296
Royal Academy of Arts 125,
  136, 139, 415
Royal Albert Hall 188, 355

Royal and Ancient Golf
  Club 417
Royal Artillery, Woolwich
  424
royal assent **284**, 288
Royal Ballet 336, 342, 349,
  352, **357**
Royal Botanic Gardens,
  Kew 410
Royal Courts of Justice 273
Royal Crescent, Bath *400*
Royal Highland Gathering
  402
Royal Hunt of the Sun, The
  53
Royal Institution laboratory
  530
Royal Liver Building 411
Royal Mile, The **417**
Royal Military Academy,
  Sandhurst *418*
Royal National Theatre,
  London 328
Royal Naval College,
  Greenwich 408
Royal Pavilion, Brighton
  163, 165, *402*
Royal Philharmonic
  Orchestra 336, 338
royal prerogative **284**
Royal Shakespeare
  Company 421
Royal Society 212
Royal Society for the
  Prevention of Cruelty to
  Animals (RSPCA) 170
Royal Tank Regiment 207
Royal Worcester Porcelain
  Works 424
RP (received
  pronunciation) **26**
RPI (Retail Price Index)
  303
R.S.V.P. **27**
Rubáiyát 71
Rub al-Khali 451
rubber 440, 444
'rubber sheet' geometry 546
rubella 516
Rubens, Sir Peter Paul **146**
Rubicon, crossing the **13**,
  239
rubidium *see* periodic table
  541
Ruby, Jack 246, 247
rugby 365, 374, 417, 461
  league **381**
  union **382**
  'World In Union' theme
    song 360
Rugby, Warwickshire 417
Rugby School 185, 382
rule of law **284**
ruminants **490**
Rumpelstiltskin 67
Rumpole of the Bailey **330**
'Rump Parliament' 211
Runes **27**
running the gamut **27**
running the gauntlet **27**
Runnin' Wild 341
Runnymede **417**
run-on sentence **27**
Run Silent, Run Deep 317

Rural Rides 195
Rushdie, Salman **52**, 69, 100
Ruskin, John 142, **146**, 152
Russell, Bertrand **112**, 116, 532
Russell, Charles Taze 103
Russell, Jane 296
Russell, Lord John **213**
Russell, Ken **330**, 360
Russia 226, 247, **451**
  language of 451
  tsars of 254
  see also CIS; USSR
Russian Civil War **250**
Russian Revolution 224, 233, 249, **251**, 257, 452
Russo-Japanese War 250, **251**
Russo-Turkish War 223
rusting 539
rusts *see* fungi
Ruth, Babe (George Herman) *364*, **382**
ruthenium *see* periodic table **541**
Rutherford, Sir Ernest 523, 542, **543**
Rutherford, Dame Margaret **330**
rutherfordium *see* periodic table **541**
Rwanda 185, **451**-2
Ryan, Robert 317
Ryan's Daughter 323, 326
Ryder, Samuel 382
Ryder Cup **382**
Rye **417**

S

SA (Brown Shirts) **225**, 253
Sabah 431, 444
Sabbath **113**
Sabin, Albert Bruce 514
Sabotage 320
Sabrina 320
Sachs, Andrew 316
Sacks, Dr Oliver 513
Sackville-West, Vita **52**, 60, 419
sacrament **113**
Sacré-Coeur 449
sacred cow 27
Sacramento 433
Sadat, Anwar 223, **251**
Saddam Hussein **284**
Sadlers Wells Ballet 342, 346, 357
Sadler's Wells Opera 343
Safety Last 323
saffron **393**, 417
Saffron Walden **417**
sagas 72
sage *393*
Sagittarius *90*, 548

Sagrada Familia, Barcelona *160*
Sahara 426, 443, **452**, 457, 467
Sahel 467
Sailing to Byzantium 60
sailing under false colours 27
saint **113**
Saint, Eva Marie 319
St Albans **417**
St Andrews **417**
St Bartholemew's Day Massacre **251**
St Bartholomew's Hospital 419
St Basil's Cathedral 445
St Emilion (wine) 396
St George **87**, 423
St Gotthard Pass 167
St Helena 245, **452**, 457
St Ives 127, 131, **417**
Saint Joan 54, 239
St John, Knights of 451
St Laurence's Church, Ludlow 412
St Laurent, Yves **146**
St Lawrence River 450
St Lawrence Seaway 433
St Louis 445
St Lucia, West Indies 461
St Mark's, Venice 351, 460
St Martin-in-the-Fields, London 160
St Mary-le-Bow 406
St Mary-le-Strand 160
St Michael's Mount **417**
St Moritz 365, **452**
St Pancras Station 166
St Paul's Cathedral **165**, *168*
St Peter's Basilica 110, 135, 143, **166**, 451, 459
St Petersburg 248, 451, **452**
St Swithin's Day 424
St Valentine's Day Massacre **251**
St Vincent 461
Saint-Saëns, Camille **357**
Sakharov, Andrei **251**
Saki **52**
Saladin **251**
salamander 478
Salamis, Battle of **251**
Salazar, Antonio de Oliviera **251**
Salem 444
Salieri, Antonio 53, 308, 351
Salinger, J.D. **52**
Salisbury, Countess of 199
Salisbury, Marquess of **213**, 214
Salisbury **418**
Salisbury Cathedral **166**, *418*
Salisbury Plain **418**
salivary glands **516**
Salk, Jonas E. 514
Sally in Our Alley 343
salmon 491
salmonella 504, **516**
Salò, Lake Garda 244
Salomé 59

Salote, Queen 457
SALT (Strategic Arms Limitation Treaties) 267
salt 524, 525, **544**
Saltaire **418**
Salt Lake City 107, 459
salvation **113**
Salvation Army **113**, 191
Salyut I space station 563
Salzburg 437, **452**
Samaritans 101
samarium *see* periodic table **541**
Samarkand 459
Samhain Eve 82
Samoa 450, 461
samosa **395**
sample (statistics) 538
Samson Agonistes 47
Samson and Delilah 314, 357
samurai 441
San'a 462
San Andreas fault 433, 452, *468*
San Antonio 457
sanctions **284**
Sanctus 350
sand 474
Sand, George **72**, 341
Sandhurst **418**
Sandinistas 447
Sandringham **418**
Sands of Iwo Jima 333
Sandwich, Kent **418**
sandwich **418**
San Francisco 317
San Francisco **452**
  earthquake *467*
sang-froid 27
sanitation 519
San Jose 454
San Juan 450
San Marino **452**
San Romano, Battle of 150
San Salvador 437
Sans Souci Palace, Potsdam 450
Santa Claus **87**
Santa Maria delle Grazie 444
Santiago, Chile 435
Santorini, island of 77
San (Bushmen) 180
São Paulo 432, **452**
Sappho **72**
saprotroph 479, 486, **491**
sapwood 492
Sarajevo 233, 431, **452**
Sarawak 431, 444
Sardinia **452**
Sargasso Sea **452**
Sargent, John Singer **146**
Sargent, Sir Malcolm 355
Sark 434
Sartre, Jean-Paul 63, 100, **113**
sashimi **395**
Sassoon, Siegfried **52**
Satan **113**
Satanic Verses, The **52**, 100
satay **395**
satellite 552, **562**
Satie, Erik **357**
satire **73**

Saturn (god) **88**
Saturn (planet) **544**
Saturnalia 88
Satyricon **73**
satyrs 85, **88**
sauces
  béarnaise 390
  béchamel 390
  caper, tuna and anchovy 396
  hollandaise 393
  pesto, *pistou* 394
Sauchiehall Street, Glasgow 407
Saudi Arabia **453**
sauerkraut **395**
sauna 438
saurischia 483
sausages
  boudin blanc **390**
  boudin noir **391**
  chorizo **391**
Saussure, Ferdinand de 186
Sauternes 396
Sauvignon Blanc **396**
Sava, River 430
savannah 481
Savernake Forest **418**
Save the Tiger 323
savoir-faire 27
Savonarola, Girolamo **251**
Savoy Operas 344
Savoy Theatre 344
Saxe-Coburg-Gotha 201, 424
Saxon *see* Anglo-Saxon(s)
Sayers, Dorothy L. **53**
Scafell Pike 410
Scales, Prunella 316
scandium *see* periodic table **541**
scans **516**
Scapa Flow 414
scapegoat 27, 30
Scarborough **418**
scarcity **304**
scarlet fever **516**
Scarlet Letter, The 42
Scent of a Woman 328
scepticism **113**
Schiele, Egon **146**
Schiller, Friedrich von **73**
Schindler's List 44, 331
schistosomiasis (bilharzia) 497
schizophrenia 180, 513, **516**
Schliemann, Heinrich 89
schnapps **395**
Schoenberg, Arnold **357**
Scholar Gypsy, The 32
Schönberg, Claude-Michel 348
School for Scandal, The 55
schools, British **175**, 185
Schubert, Franz **357**
Schubertians 357
Schumann, Robert **358**
Schwarzenegger, Arnold **330**
Schwarzkopf, Elisabeth **358**
Schwarzkopf, General Norman *237*
Schwitters, Kurt **146**

sciatica 512, **516**
Science Museum, London 551
Scientology **113**, 174
Scilly, Isles of **418**
Scofield, Paul **330**
Scone, Stone of **213**
Scone Palace **418**
Scoop 29, 59
Scorpio 90, 548
Scorpio 330
scorpions 479
Scorsese, Martin 314, 317, **330**
Scotland 216
  Book of Common Prayer and 194
  Church of 205
  devolution 285
  Forty-Five Rebellion 200
  Glencoe Massacre 200
  independence 189, 285
  national flag 417
  see also individual topics and place names
Scotland Yard 556
Scotsman, The 328
Scott, George C. 247
Scott, Sir George Gilbert **166**
Scott, Gordon 332
Scott, James, Duke of Monmouth 207
Scott, Sir Peter 400
Scott, Ridley 310
Scott, Robert Falcon 208, **213**, 427
Scott, Sir Walter **53**, *423*
Scottish National Party (SNP) **285**
Scott of the Antarctic 326
Scouting Association 189
Scrabble **382**
Screwdriver (cocktail) **395**
Scrooge, Ebenezer 37, *38*
'scrumpy' 419
scuba 550
scurvy **516**-17
Scylla and Charybdis 88
SDLP (Social Democratic and Labour Party) **284**
SDP (Social Democratic Party) 205, 275, **284**
Sea, The 47
sea-floor spreading 470, 472, **474**
Seagram Building 163
Seagull, The 64
Sea Hawk, The 317
sea level 470, **474**
Sea of Love 328
Searchers, The 317, 333
Searle, Ronald 47
Sears Tower **166**, 434
seasonal adjustment **304**
seasonal affective disorder **517**
seasonal unemployment **304**
Sebastopol 229
Secombe, Harry 319
secondary schools, British 175
secondary sector **304**

Second Coming, 60, 104, **113**
Second Jungle Book, The 44
Second Sex, The 63
Second World War, The 195
Secret Agent 320
secretary of state **284**
Secret Diary of Adrian Mole, aged 13¾, 57
Secret Garden, The 330
Secret Life of Walter Mitty, The 47, 322
Secret Seven 34
securities 295, **304**
security, breaches of 557
security services **284**, 286
Sedgemoor, Battle of 207
sedimentary rock *see* rock
seed 486, **491**
seed dispersal **491**
Seikan rail tunnel 167
Seine, River 449
seismic wave 467, **474**
Selassie, Haile 111, **237**
select committee **284**
selective reproduction 176
selenium *see* periodic table **541**
Seles, Monica **382**
Selfridge, Harry Gordon **304**
Selfridge's department store 304
Selkirk, Alexander 52
Sellafield **418**, 471
Sellers, Peter 319, *324*, 328, **330**
sellers' market **304**
Selznick, David O. 319
semantics **27**
semi- **27**
semicolon **27**
semiconductor 542, 544, 554, 558, 559, **562**, 565
Sémillon grapes 396
semipermeable membrane 539
Semitic peoples 171, **185**
Senate **285**
Seneca **73**
Senna, Ayrton **382**, 432
Sennett, Mack 322
senses **491**
sentence **27**
   complex 13
   compound 13
   periodic 23
   simple 27
   topic 29
Sentimental Journey, A 55
'sent to Coventry' 404
Seoul **453**
Separate Tables 327
separation of powers **285**
sepia **147**
September 308
sequoia (tree) 482
Sequoia National Park 454
Serbia 223, 430, **453**, 462
   ethnic cleansing 175
Serengeti Plain **453**
serf **251**
Sergeant Pepper's Lonely Hearts Club Band 338

Sergeant York 313
serial killer **185**
Sermon on the Mount 18
Serpico 328
SERPS (State Earnings Related Pension Scheme) **304**
Servant, The 50, 310, 324
service industry **304**
set theory 525, **544**, 547
'Setting the Watch' (Ripon) 416
Seurat, Georges **147**
Seuss, Dr 53
Seven Pillars of Wisdom, The 205
Seventh Day Adventists **113**
Seventh Seal, The 309
Seventh Veil, The 325
Seven Wonders of the World **251**, 431, 451
Seven Year Itch, The 326
Seven Years' War 218, 222, 234, 248, **252**
Severed Head, A 47
Severn, River **418**
   estuary 418, 475
   Road Bridge 418
Seville **453**, 455
Sèvres, porcelain 248
Sewell, Anna 34
sewing machine **562**
sex-and-shopping novels **53**
sex cells 480, 481, 485, 486
sex discrimination 174
sexism **185**
Sex Pistols 355
sexual development 176
   intercourse 520, 515
   reproduction 480, 490
sexually transmitted disease 518, 520
Seychelles 440, **453**
Seymour, Jane 202
Seymour: an Introduction 52
Seyss-Inquart, Arthur 221
sfumato 132, **147**
shadow cabinet **285**
Shadow of a Doubt 320
Shadows, The 356
Shaffer, Peter **53**, 308
Shah, Eddie 328
Shah, Mohammed Reza Pahlavi 240, **244**
Shah Jahan, Mughal Emperor 167, 244
Shaka, Chief 186
Shakers **113**
Shakespeare, William **53**, 73, 189, 202, 420
'Shall I compare thee to a summer's day?' **54**
shame cultures 178
Shampoo 309
Shanghai **453**
Shankill Road, Belfast 430
Shankly, Bill **383**
Shannon, River 441
shares 294, **304**
Shari'a 103, 104
shark *479*, 485
Sharp, Becky (*Vanity Fair*) *58*

Sharples, Ena *313*
Shatner, William 331
Shatt al-Arab 239, **453**, 457
Shaw, George Bernard **54**
Shaw, Norman **166**
Shaw, Percy 553
Sheba, Queen of 462
She Done Him Wrong 319, 334
Sheen, Martin 308
Sheffield **418**
   plate 418, 555
Sheik, The 333
Shelley, Mary 40, 54, 317
Shelley, Percy Bysshe **54**, 87
Shem (Noah's son) 185
Shenandoah 331
Shenandoah Valley 460
Shepard, E.H 60
Shephearde's Calendar 55
Sher, Antony *51*
Sheraton 125
Shere Khan (*Jungle Book*) *44*
Sheridan, Dinah 318
Sheridan, Richard Brinsley **55**
sheriff **285**
sheriff court 264, 266, **285**
Sherman, General William 428, **454**
Sherpas 446
Sheriffmuir, Battle of 199
Sherwood Forest 87, **419**
She Stoops to Conquer 41
Shetland 407, **419**
   ponies 419
She Wore a Yellow Ribbon 317, 333
Shi'a (Shi'ite) 94, 103, 108, **114**
shibboleth **27**
Shikoku, Japan 441
Shilton, Peter *377*, **383**
shingles 499, **517**
Shining, The 322, 327
Shinto **114**
Ship of Fools 323
shipping forecasts 476
Shiraz 396
Shiva **114**
shivering 518
shock **517**, 519
Shoemaker-Levy comet 526, 534
Shoeshine 314
shoguns **252**, 441
Shona-Karanga civilisation 462
shooting 370, **383**
   clay pigeon 383
Shooting Party, The 325
shooting star *464*, 537
Shootist, The 333
short shrift **27**
short-sightedness 503
short story **73**
Shostakovich, Dmitri **358**
shotguns 556
Shottery, Stratford-upon-Avon 421
Shoulder Arms 312
Showboat 345, 348, 356

show jumping **383**
Shrewsbury **419**
Shrewsbury, Earls of 398
Shrimpton, Jean 119, 215
Shropshire **419**
Shropshire Lad, A 43, 419
Shute, Nevil 426
Shylock 46, **55**
Sibelius, Jean **358**, 438
Siberia 451, **453**
sibilant **27**
sic **27**
Sicily 441, **453**
sick building syndrome **517**
Sickert, Walter Richard **147**
sickle cell anaemia 495, **517**
Siddhartha Gautama 95
siderites (meteorites) 470
Sidney, Sir Philip **55**, **213**
Sidon 443
Sieff, Israel 299
Siegel, Don 315
Siegfried 353
Siena 147, **453**
Sienese **147**
Sierra Nevada 433, **454**, 462
sight 491 *see also* eye
Signac, Paul **147**
Sign of the Cross 314
Signoret, Simone 330
Sigurd 78
Sikhism 101, **114**, 426, 440, 450
Sikorsky, Igor 557
Silas Marner 39
Silbury Hill 399
Silence of the Lambs, The 317, 321
Silesia 222, 234
silicate minerals 544
silicon **544**
   chip 454, 559
   see also periodic table **541**
'Silicon Valley' **454**
silk moth 482
Silk Road 459
silver 546, *see also* periodic table **541**
Silverstone 388
Simenon, Georges **73**
simile **27**
Simnel, Lambert **213**
Simon, Neil 323
Simon, Paul 358, 369
Simon and Garfunkel **358**
Simon and Laura 322
simple sentence **27**
Simpson, Mrs Wallis 188, 198
Sims, Joan 312
simulator system 566
sin **114**
   mortal **107**
   original 94, **109**
   Seven Deadly **114**
   venial **116**
Sinai **454**
Sinatra, Frank **358**
Sinbad the Sailor 316
sine qua non **27**
Singapore **454**, 469
Singapore Sling **395**, 454

Singer, Isaac ((inventor) 562
Singer, Isaac Bashevis (novelist) **73**
Singh (Sikh surname) 114
Singin' in the Rain 348
Singing Detective, The 329
single currency, ECU 293
single European market **304**, 306
Singleton, Valerie 310
singular **27**
'singularity' (physics) 524
Sink the Bismarck 326
Sinn Féin 193, 260, 275, **285**
Sin of Harold Diddlebock, The 323
siren(s) 84, **88**
Sir Gawain and the Green Knight **55**, 82
Sirhan, Sirhan 240
sirocco 476
SIS (Secret Intelligence Service, MI6) 284
Sisley, Alfred **147**
Sissinghurst Castle Garden **419**
Sissons, Peter *327*
Sistine Chapel 133, *135*, 459
Sisulu, Walter 260
Sisyphus **88**
Sita 111
Sitwell, Dame Edith 55
SI units **544**
Siva **114**
Six-Day War **252**, 461
Sixth Form Colleges **175**
skeleton *516*, **517**
Skeleton Coast 446
Skelton, Nick **383**
skiffle 342, **358**
skiing 399
ski-jumping **383**
Ski Club of Great Britain 383
ski racing **383**
skin 427, 494, 495, 510, **517**, 520
skin cancer **517**
Skinner, B.F. 171, 174, **185**
Skinner, Dennis 274
Skorzeny, Otto 244
Skye, Isle of **419**
'Skye Boat Song' 191, 419
Skylab space station 563
Sky satellite television 300
skyscrapers 158, 559
Slaney, Mary 365
slang **28**
   Cockney rhyming **26**
slavery 28, 183, 186, 199, 201, 217, 459, 461
Slaves (Michelangelo) 135
slave trade **252**
   see also slavery
Slavic script 14
Slavs **185**
Sledge, Percy 359
Sleep 152
sleep **517**
Sleeping Beauty, The **73**, 359
sleeping sickness **517**

Sleuth 311, 328
Slimbridge Wildfowl and
    Wetlands Trust 400
slipped disc 497, **517**
slogan **28**
Slough 34, 400
Slovakia **454**
Slovenia **454**, 462
smallpox 507, **517**
smart card **563**
smell 491, **517**, 518
smelting 552
Smiles of a Summer Night
    309
Smiley, George 45
Smiley's People 45, 319
Smith, Adam **304-5**
Smith, Bessie 339
Smith, Harvey 383
Smith, Ian 462
Smith, John 276, 410
Smith, Joseph 107
Smith, Dame Maggie **330**
Smith, Margaret 374
Smith, Paul **147**
Smithfield **419**
Smithsonian Institution 461
smog 473, **474**, 475, 540
smoking 503, 508, 519
smörgåsbord **395**, 455
Smuts, Jan **252**
Smythe, Pat 383
snail *479*, 486
snake *479*, 490
sneezing 519
Snodgrass, Mr (*Pickwick
    Papers*) 38
snooker **383**
snoring **517**
Snowdon, Wales 419
Snowdonia 419
*Snow White and the Seven
    Dwarfs* 67, 315, **331**
SNP (Scottish National
    Party) **285**
Sobers, Sir Gary (Garfield)
    381, **384**
social cost **305**
social democracy **285**
social equality 285
Social Democratic and
    Labour Party (SDLP)
    284
Social Democratic Party
    (SDP), British 205, 275,
    284-6
social insects **491**
socialism 278, **285**, 301
social welfare 285
social security 288
society, human **169-86**
Society of Friends 111
Society of Jesus (SJ) 103
sociology 174, **186**
Socrates 98, 110, **114**, *115*
Sócrates (footballer) 432
sodium 528, *see also* periodic
    table **541**
Sofia 433
Softly, Softly 334
Soho **419**
soil **474**
solar cell **563**
solar eclipse 528, *529*

solar flares 544
solar panels 563
Solar System 526, 538, 541,
    544, 546, 547
solar wind 470, 526, **544**
sold down the river **28**
Soldier, The 35
solecism **28**
Solent **419**
solicitor **285**
Solicitor General 261
solid 535
Solidarity (Solidarność)
    285, 450
soliloquy **73**
Solomon 99, **114**, 443, 462
Solomon Islands 450
solstice **544**
Solti, Sir Georg **358**
Solzhenitsyn, Alexandr **73**
Somalia **454**
Somebody Up There Likes Me
    327
Some Like It Hot 326, 334
Somerset **419**
Something's Got to Give 326
Somme, Battle of the **214**
Sommersby 318
Somoza, President 447
sonar (Sound Navigation
    and Ranging) **563**
Sondheim, Stephen 147,
    358
Song of Solomon, The 114
Song of the Lord (Sanskrit
    poem) 94
Songs of Experience 58
sonic boom 544
sonnet **73**
Sonnets from the Portuguese
    35
Son of Frankenstein 317
Sonoma Valley 433
Sons and Lovers 45
Sophie's Choice 332
sophists **114**
Sophocles **73**
soprano **358**
Sorcerer's Apprentice, The
    316
*Sorrows of Young Werther,
    The* 67
SOS (distress call) 560
sotto voce **28**
Soubirous, Marie-Bernarde
    443
soul music 340, 357, **359**
sound 528, 531, 535, 542,
    543, **544**, 548
    intensity of (dB) 528
    speed of 535, 544
Sound and the Fury, The 40
sound barrier 544
Sound of Music, The 308,
    356, 452
soups
    bisque **390**
    borscht **390**
    bouillabaisse **391**
    chowder **391**
    consommé **391**
    gazpacho **392**
    gumbo **392**
    vichyssoise **395**

soutenu (ballet) **337**
South Africa **454**
South America, map of *454*
Southampton **419**
South Downs **419**
Southend-on-Sea **419**
Southey, Robert **55**
South Island, New Zealand
    447
South Korea **455**
South Pacific 356
South Pole *213*, 427, 523
South Sea Bubble **214**
South-West Africa People's
    Organisation (SWAPO)
    446
sovereignty of parliament
    285
Soviet Union *see* USSR
Soweto 442
soya beans (tofu) 395
Space Center, John F.
    Kennedy 438
Space programme 240, 550
    craft 563
    probe 547, **563**
    shuttle, US *562*, **563**
    station 563
    telescope *564*, 565
space-time **544**
Spaghetti Westerns 315,
    331
Spain 429, **455**
    Conquistadors 229, 455
    Falange 232
    Muslim architecture 244
    West Indies and 461
Spalding **420**
Spandau prison, Berlin 237
Spanish-American Fair
    (1929) *453*
Spanish Armada **189**, 197,
    199, 455
Spanish Civil War 236, 244,
    252, 455
Spanish Inquisition **238**
Spanish Riding School 460
Spanish Succession, War of
    224, **252**
Spanish Tragedy, The 45, 51
Spare a Copper 317
Spark, Muriel **55**, 330
Sparta 247, **252**
Spartacus **253**, 315, 333
Spartans 20, **253**
Spassky, Boris 370
spatial skills 498
Speaker,
    House Of Commons
        262, 268, **286**
    House of Lords 277
Speakers' Corner, Hyde
    Park 410
Special Branch (British
    police) 281, 284, **286**
special theory of relativity
    543
species 483, **491**
specific gravity 528
specific heat 533
Spectator, The 32, **324**
spectroscopy 528, **544**
spectrum 473, 538, *543*,
    544

speculator 305
speech, part of 22
speed **545**
speed limit 553
speed of light 529, 535,
    537, 543, **545**
speed of sound 535, 544
Speed the Plough 21
speedway 378
Speedy 323
Speer, Albert 246
Speke, John 460
Spellbound 320
Spencer, Stanley **148**
Spencer family (Althorp)
    398
Spender, Stephen **55**
Spenser, Edmund **55**
sperm 480, **491**, 515, 518
    see also sex cells
Spey, River **420**
Sphinx **88**
spices *393*, 440, 446
spiders 479
Spielberg, Steven 44, 316,
    321, **331**, 483
spina bifida **517**
spinal cord **517**
spine 516
Spinks, Leon 362
Spinoza, Benedict de **114**
*Spinoza of Market Street,
    The* 73
Spirit of Laws, The 107
Spirit of St Louis 242
spirits (alcohol)
    aquavit **390**
    Armagnac **390**
    Bourbon **396**
    brandy 390, 391
    cognac **391**
    fine champagne 391
    grappa **392**
    ouzo **394**
    pastis (anise) **390**
    rye **396**
    schnapps **395**
    tequila **395**
    whisky **396**
spiritual 356, **359**
Spitfire 192
Spithead channel 423
Spitz, Mark **384**
spleen **517**
splendid isolation (foreign
    policy) **214**, 275
split infinitive **28**
Spock, Benjamin, **186**
sponges *479*
Spooner, William **28**
Spoonerism **28**
Sporades 426, 439
spore **491**
Sporting Times, The 363
Spring, Dick 283
springboks 442
Springsteen, Bruce **359**
Spruce Goose 296
spumante 396
Sputnik I 562
Spycatcher case 263
Spyri, Johanna 68
*Spy Who Came in from the
    Cold, The* 45, 311

squamous cell carcinoma
    517
square brackets **28**
Square Mile, the 404
squash (food) **395**
squash (sport) **384**
Squaw Man, The 314, 321
squid 481
Sri Lanka 444, **455**
SS (Schutzstaffel) 224, 237,
    253
staccato **350**
Stael, Nicholas de **148**
Staffa 413
Stafford 420
Staffordshire **420**
stag 305
Stagecoach 317, 333, 459
stagflation **305**
Staircase 330
stalactites **475**
stalagmites **475**
Stalin, Joseph 229, **253**,
    254, *258*, 265, 286, 287
Stalingrad 253
    Battle of 461
Stalinism 253, **286**
Stallone, Sylvester **331**
Stamboul Train 41
stamen 486
Stamp Act **253**
stamp duty **305**
stamp, first postage *209*
standard deviation **545**
Standard Oil Company 303
Stanley, Henry Morton 205
Stansted Airport *159*, **420**
star 524, 537, 538, 542,
    544, **545**, 546
    magnitude **535**
    shooting 470
star anise **390**
starch **491**
Star Chamber **214**
Stargazy Pie 413
Star is Born, A 318, 325
Starley, John 552
Starr, Ringo 338
Starry Night 151
START (Strategic Arms
    Reduction Treaties) 267
Star Trek **331**
Star Wars **286**, **331**
State Department **286**
Staten Island 446
State Opening of
    Parliament **286**
states of matter *see* gas;
    liquid; plasma; solid
static electricity 529, **545**
statics *see* mechanics
statistics 538, **545**
Statue of Liberty 446
status, social 173
status quo **28**
status quo ante **28**
statute law **286**
steady-state theory **546**
stealing someone's thunder
    28
stealth aircraft **563**
Steamboat Willie 315
steam engine 203, **564**
steam locomotive 565

steam train 564
Steaming 329
steel 522, 552, **564**, 561
Steel, Sir David 205, **286**
steel bands 457
Steele, Tommy 356
steeplechase (horse racing) 372, 378
stegosaurus 483
Stein, Jock **384**
Steinbeck, John **55**, 314, 448
Stella 55
stem **28**
Stendhal 73
Stephen, King 202, **214**
Stephens, Frederic 142
Stephenson, George 166, 211, 405, 413, 416, **564**
Stephenson, Robert **166**, 413, 565
Steppenwolf 346
Stern, Irma **148**
Sternberg, Joseph Von 315
Sterne, Laurence **55**
steroid **517**
stet **28**
Stevenson, Robert Louis **55**, 461
Stewart, Jackie **384**
Stewart, James 317, **331**
Stewart, Rod **359**
stews and casseroles
  blanquette **390**
  bouillabaise **391**
  bourguignon **391**
  cassoulet **391**
  chowder **391**
  fricassée **392**
  goulash **392**
  osso bucco **394**
  pot-au-feu **395**
Stheno 82
Stieglitz, Alfred **148**
stigma (botany) *485*, 489
Still Falls the Rain 55
still life **148**
still waters run deep **28**
Stilton cheese **391**
Sting, The 329, 347
Stirling **420**
Stirling Bridge, Battle of 216
stock **305**
stock exchange **305**
  big bang **291**
  Dow Jones Index **293**
  FTSE-100 Index **295**
  jobbers **298**
  Nikkei Index **301**
  Wall Street **306**
Stockhausen, Karlheinz **359**
Stockholm **455**, 474
Stockton and Darlington railway 166
Stockton-on-Tees **420**
Stoics 73, **115**
Stoke, Battle of 213
Stoke-on-Trent 416, **420**
Stoker, Bram (Abraham) **55**, 80
Stokowski, Leopold 316
Stolen Kisses 333
stomach 501, 504

stomata 487
Stone Age **253**
Stonehenge *80*, 84, **88**, **420**
Stone of Scone **213**, 418
Stopes, Marie **214**
Stoppard, Tom **56**
Stopping by Woods on a Snowy Evening 40
Stormont 203, 267
storms 465, **475**
Story of Esther Costello, The 313
Story of G.I. Joe, The 326
Stour, River 407, 420
Stourhead **420**
Stove, Betty 387
Stowe, Harriet Beecher 58
Stowe **420**
Strachey, Lytton 34
Stradivari Antonio *359*
Stradivarius **359**
Strafford, Thomas Wentworth, Earl of **214**
strain *see* stress and strain
Strait of Hormuz 448, 449
Strait of Magellan 242
Stranger, The 334
Strangers on a Train 320
Strasbourg **455**
Strategic Arms Limitation Treaties (SALT) 267
Stratford-upon-Avon **420**
stratosphere 464
Strauss I, Johann 460
Strauss II, Johann 358, **359**, 460
Strauss, Richard 59, **359**
Stravinsky, Igor 337, 352, **359**-60
Straw, Jack 209
stream of conciousness 73
Streep, Meryl **332**
Streetcar Named Desire, A **56**, 59, 311, 323
Streets of San Francisco, The 315
Streisand, Barbra **359**
Streptococcus 495
stress 507, **518**, 519
stress and strain **546**
Stribling, Melissa *80*
strikes 297 *see also* industrial action
Strike Up the Band 318
Strindberg, August **73**
Stroessner, General 449
Stroheim, Erich Von 332
stroke 513, **518**
Stromboli 330
Stromboli 475
Strong Poison 53
strong verb **28**
strontium *see* periodic table **541**
structuralism **186**
Struggle, The 319
Stuart, House of 199, 208, **214**
Stuart, Moira *327*
Stubbs, George **148**
stucco **166**
Studley Royal, North Yorkshire 407
Study in Scarlet, A 39

Stunt Man, The 328
sturgeon 391
Sturmabteilungen (SA) 225, 253
Sturm und Drang **73**
style (botany) *485*
Styx 76, 79, **88**
sub- **28**
Subaltern's Love-song, A 34
subatomic particles 522, 523, *525*, 529, 540, 542, **546**
subject **28**
sub judice 28, **286**
subjunctive **28**
sublimation 181
submarine **564**
subordinate clause **28**
subsistence **305**
substantive **28**
Sudan 97, **455**
Sudden Impact 315
Sudden Infant Death Syndrome (SIDS) 500
Suddenly Last Summer 320, 332
Sudetenland 244
Suez Canal **166**, 196
Suez crisis 197, **253**, 428
suffix **28**
Suffolk **421**
suffragettes **215**
Sufism **115**
sugar 441
Sugar Loaf mountain 451
sui generis **28**
Sulawesi 440
Suleiman the Magnificent 247, **253**
Sullivan, Sir Arthur Seymour 344
sulphur *see* periodic table **541**
  dioxide 464
sulphuric acid 464, 522
Sumatra 440
Sumer civilisation 441
Sumeria **253**
Sumer is icumen in **56**
Summer Birdcage, A 39
Summer Holiday 356
Summer Madness 323
sumo wrestling **384**, *385*
Sun 543, *544*, **546** *see also* star, solar system
  equinox 530
  solar eclipses *529*
  tides and 475
Sun, The 263, 267, 300, **328**
Sun Also Rises, The 42
Sunday in the Park with George 147
Sunday Mail 300
Sunday Mirror 300
Sunday Times, The 300
Sundowners, The 326
Sunflowers 151
'Sun King', the 242, **253**
Sun Myung Moon 107
Sunni **115**
Sunset Boulevard **332**, 334, 349
sunspot **546**
suntan 510

Sun Yat-Sen 227, 241
Super Bowl **384**
superconductivity 527, 542, **546**
superego **186**
superfluidity 526, 527, 533
Superglue **564**
Superior, Lake 439
superlative **29**
'Superman' ideal 108
supernova 524, 527, 538, 545, **546**
'superstrings' 547
supply and demand 293, **305**
supply side economics **305**
Supreme Court (Britain) **286**
Supreme Court of Judicature (USA) **286**
Supremes, the 357
surface tension **546**
surfing **384**
surgery 519
surrealism 123, 132, **148**
Surrey, Henry 72
Surtees, John **384**
Suryavarman II, King 154
Susann, Jacqueline 53
sushi **395**
Suspicion 319
Sutcliffe, Peter 185, 513
Sutcliffe, Stuart 338
Sutherland, Graham **148**, 404
Sutherland, Dame Joan **359**
Swale, River 416
Swaledale 416, *424*
Swallows and Amazons **56**
swamps 466
swan, aggression in *478*
Swan, Joseph 555, 559
Swan Lake **359**
Swansea **421**
Swanson, Gloria 332
SWAPO (South-West Africa People's Organisation) 446
sweat glands **518**
Sweden **455**
sweetbreads **395**
Sweet Charity 324
Sweet Smell of Success 323
Swift, Jonathan 32, 33, **56**
swimming **385**
Swinburne, Algernon Charles **56**
Swindon **421**
swing 347, **359**
Swing, The (Fragonard) 124
swinging sixties 119, 142, **215**
Swiss Family Robinson, The **73**
Switzerland 431, **455**
  independence 89
Sword in the Stone, The 47
sword of Damocles **29**
Sword of Honour 59
sycamore, seed dispersal 490, 491
Sydney **456**
Sydney Harbour Bridge **166**, 432, 456

Sydney Opera House **167**, 456
syllable **29**
syllepsis **29**
syllogism **115**, 523
sym-, syn- **29**
symbiosis **492**
symbolism **148**
Symbolists **73**
Symond's Yat Rock 424
symphonic poem 348
synapse 512, **518**
syncopation **350**
synecdoche **29**
Synge, John Millington **56**
synonym **29**
synopsis **29**
syntax **29**
synthetic fibres 541
Syon House 154, **421**
syphilis **518**, 520
Syrah grape 396
Syria 261, 437, **456**, 457
  Six-Day War 252
  Yom Kippur War 258

T

tabbouleh **395**
Table Mountain 434
table tennis **385**
taboo **186**
taco **395**
tadpole 488
Taff, River 403
Tagus, River 443
tahini **395**
Tahiti 450, **456**
T'ai-pei, Taiwan 456
Taiwan 227, **456**
Tajikstan 459
Taj Mahal **167**, 244
Take Five 340
takeover 303, **305**
  asset stripping 290
  Panel 305
  reverse 303
Talbot, Henry Fox 410, 552
Tale of a Tub, A 56
Tales from Shakespeare 45
Tales of Beatrix Potter 336
Tales of Hoffman 352
talkies, early 553
Talking Heads 33
Talmud **115**
Tamar, River 404, 413
Tamburlaine the Great 46
Tamerlane 244, 459
Tamils 455
Taming of the Shrew, The **56**, 334
Tam O'Shanter museum (Ayr) 399
Tamworth Manifesto 209, 266
Tanganyika, Lake 456
Tanglewood Tales 42

tantalum *see* periodic table **541**
Tantalus **88**
Tanzania 181, 453, **456**
Taoiseach **287**
Taoism 105, **115**
Tao Te Ching 105, 115
tapas **395**
tape cassettes 559
tapenade **395**
tapestry **148**
tapeworm 479, **518**
taramasalata **395**
Taranenko, Leonid 387
tarot cards **88**
tarragon *393*
Tarzan 332
Tarzan of the Apes 332
Tashkent, Uzbekistan 459
Tasman, Abel 456
Tasmania **456**
Tassi, Agostino 122
taste 491, **518**
Tatars 451
Tate Gallery 126, 150, 411
Tatler, The 32
Tatras, High 454
Tauber, Richard 348
Taunton 419
Taupin, Bernie 347
Taurus *90*, 548
tautology **29**
Tawe, River 421
tax 292, 297, 305
  capital gains 292
  exiles 305
  haven 305
  income 297
  VAT 305, **306**
taxation **305**
tax avoidance **305**
Tax Exempt Special Savings
  Account (TESSA) **306**
Taxi Driver 314, 317, 330
Tay, River **421**
Taylor, Elizabeth 311, **332**,
  334
TB (tuberculosis) **519**
TCCB (Test and County
  Cricket Board) 376
Tchaikovsky, Peter Ilyich
  359, 452
teak 492
Tea Party, Boston **225**
Tebbit, Norman (Lord
  Tebbit) **287**
technetium *see* periodic
  table **541**
tectonic plates *see* plate
  tectonics
teddy bear 250
Teddy boys **186**
Tees, River **421**
Teesdale 421
teeth **518**
Teflon **564**
Tehran 440
Te Kanawa, Dame Kiri
  359
Tel Aviv-Jaffa 441, **456**
Tel Aviv opera company
  342
telegraph 560

telegraphese **29**
telepathy 81
telephone 551, 553, 555,
  556, **564**
telescopes 532, 535, *538*,
  540, 547, *564*, **565**
television 551, 562, **565**
Telford **421**
Telford, Thomas **167**, 421
Tell, William **89**
tellurium *see* periodic table
  541
Telstar satellite 562
Tême, River 412
tempera **148**
temperature 565
  atmospheric 464
  conversion 526
  global 465, 469
temperature, body **518**
temperature inversion 464,
  474, **475**
temperature scale 526, 530
Tempest, The 35, 36, **56**, 72,
  319
Tempest, The (Giorgione)
  126
Temple, Shirley **332**
Temple of Apollo 79
Temple of Jerusalem 93, 96,
  98, 104
tempo 350
Tenant of Wildfell Hall, The
  35
Ten Commandments 93,
  107, **115**, 454
Ten Commandments, The
  314, 320
tendon **518**
Tenerife 433
Tenniel, Sir John 37, **148**
tennis 369, 372, **385**
tennis elbow 518
Tennyson, Alfred, Lord **57**,
  194
tenor **360**
tenpin bowling **386**
tense **29**
tequila 393, **395**
tera- 537
terbium *see* periodic table
  541
Ter Borch, Gerard **148**
Terence (poet) 12
Tereshkova, Valentina **253**
teriyaki **395**
Terminator, The 330
termite colonies 489, 491
Terms of Endearment 324,
  327
tern, Arctic 488
Terpischore 85
terra firma **29**
terrine **395**
territory 478, **492**
terrorism 266, 271, 277,
  281 *see also* Ireland, IRA
Tertiary period 468
TESSA (tax exempt special
  savings account) **306**
Tess of the D'Urbervilles 42
Test, River 417
Test Act 1673 **215**
Testament, Le 74

testes 515, **518**, 520
testosterone 506, 515, 518
tetanus 507, **518**, 519
tête-à-tête **29**
Tethys Sea *466*
Tewkesbury **421**
Texas **456**
TGV *Train à Grande Vitesse*
  565
Thackeray, William
  Makepeace **57**, 309
Thailand 429, **457**
Thalia 82
thalidomide **518**
thallium *see* periodic table
  541
Thames, River **421**, *422*
  Barrier 421, 468
  'frost fairs' 465
Thanks for the Memory 321
Thatcher, Margaret (Lady
  Thatcher) 260, **287**
That Hamilton Woman 323,
  328
That Riviera Touch 326
That's Life 308
That Touch of Mink 319
*That Was The Week That
  Was* 332
Theatre of Blood 329
theatre of the absurd 63,
  69, **74**
Theatre Royal, Bristol 416
Theatre Royal, Richmond
  416
Thebes 85, 88
theism **115**
'The Lanes', Brighton 402
Theodoric, King 95
Theosophical Society **115**
Theotocopoulos,
  Domenicos *see* El Greco
  124
therapy, group 180
Theravada 95
There's a Girl in My Soup
  330
Thermal Oxide
  Reprocessing Plant
  (THORP) 471
thermodynamics 533, **546**
Thermopylae 258
thermostat **565**
thesaurus **29**
Theseus 76, 83, **89**
*They Died With Their Boots
  On* 317
*They Shoot Horses, Don't
  They?* 317
thiamin 520
Thief of Baghdad, The 316
Things are Looking Up 323
Thin Man, The 324
Third Man, The 41, 329,
  334, 460
Third World countries 298
Thirty-Nine Steps, The 35,
  308, 315, 320
Thirty Years' War **253**
This Happy Breed 323
This Side of Paradise 40
Thistlewood, Arthur 193
Thomas, Dylan 21, **57**, 311,
  343, 421

Thomas, the Tank Engine **57**
Thomas Aquinas, St *93*,
  108
Thompson, Daley **386**
Thompson, Emma 311,
  321, 325
Thompson, Eric 325
Thomson, Robert 566
Thomson Corporation 328
Thor **89**
thorium *see* periodic table
  541
Thornhill, Sir James **149**
THORP (Thermal Oxide
  Reprocessing Plant) 471
Thorpe, Jeremy 286
Thorpe, Jim **386**
Thorson, Linda 309
Thrace 458
Threadneedle Street 290
three-day event **386**
three-day week **215**
Three Flags (Johns) *129*
Three for the Show 319
Three Little Pigs, The 315
Three Men in a Boat 43
Three-Mile Island 560
Three Musketeers, The 66,
  316
Threepenny Opera, The 33,
  64
Three Sisters 64
Through a Glass Darkly 309
Through the Looking-Glass
  24, *32*, 43, **57**
throwing down the
  gauntlet **29**
thrush **518**
Thucydides **253**
thulium *see* periodic table
  541
thunderstorm 465, **475**
Thurber, James 47, **57**
Thus Spake Zarathustra 359
thyme *393*
thymus **518**
thyroid gland **518**
Tiahuanaco 457
Tiananmen Square 430
  Massacre **254**, 267
Tiber, River 451
Tibesti mountain 452
Tibet 97, 177, 443, **457**
ticks 479, 519
tidal power **475**
tidal wave **475**
tide **475**
Tiepolo, Giovanni Battista
  (Giambattista) 124, 127,
  149
Tierra del Fuego **457**
Tiffany, Louis Comfort
  149
tiger, territorial behaviour
  492
Tiger Bay 326
Tigris 429, 453, **457**
tilde **29**
Timbuktu **457**
Time (magazine) **324**, 325
time 543, 544
Time Machine, The 59
Times, The 300, **328**

Times Square, New York
  446
Timisoara, Romania 451
Timor, East 177
tin *see* periodic table **541**
Tin Drum, The 67
Tinker, Tailor, Soldier, Spy
  45, 319
tinkers 178
tinnitus **519**
Tin Pan Alley 319
Tintagel **421**
Tintern Abbey **421**
Tintern Abbey (poem) **57**
Tintin **74**
Tintoretto 124, **149**
Tiny Tim *38*
Tippett, Sir Michael **360**
tiramisu **395**
Tiranë, Albania 426
Tirel, Walter 218
Tisiphone 81
tissue **492** *see also* plant
  tissues
Titan (moon) 544
Titanic **215**, 470
titanium *see* periodic table
  541
Titans 83, **89**, 90
Titfield Thunderbolt, The 315
tithe **215**
Titian, Tiziano Vecellio
  149
Titicaca, Lake 431, **457**
titles and honours **178**
Tito, Marshal **254**, 462
Tivoli Gardens,
  Copenhagen 435
toad 478, 480, 482
Toad of Toad Hall 60
toadstools *see* fungi
To a Mouse 36
To a Skylark 54
'To be, or not to be' 42, **57**
Tobermory, Mull 413
To Catch a Thief 319, 322
tocopherol 520
Today 300, **328**
Toffler, Alvin 177
tofu **395**
To Have and Have Not 310
Toilet of Venus 151
To Kill a Mocking Bird 328
Tokyo **457**
  Stock Exchange 301
Tolkien, J.R.R. **57**
Tolpuddle martyrs **215**
Tolstoy, Count Leo **74**
Tom and Jerry **332**
Tomba, Alberto (La
  Bomba) *383*
Tom Brown's Schooldays **57**,
  185, 327, 417
Tom Horn 325
Tom Jones **57**
Tommy 330, 360
*Tom Sawyer, The Adventures
  of* **57**
tone **149**
Tonga 450, **457**
tonsillitis 514, 519
tonsils **519**
Tontons Macoutes 439
'Toot, Toot, Tootsie' 321

tooth decay 518
Topaz 320
Top Hat 336, 338
topic sentence **29**
Topkapi 333
topology **546**
torah 93, 104, **115**
Torbay **422**
torches 551
Tories **215**, 266 *see also*
    Conservative Party
tornado **475**
Tornado Alley 475
Torn Curtain 308, 320
Toronto, **457**
torque 541, **546**
Torrent, The 318
tort **287**
tortilla 392, **395**
Torvill, Jayne and
    Christopher Dean **386**,
    387
Tosca 353
Toscanini, Arturo **360**
To Sir with Love 329
tostadas 395
totalitarianism 184, **287**
Total Recall 330
Totes Meer (Nash) 139
To the Lighthouse 60
*To the Virgins, to Make Much
    of Time* 41
touch 491, **519**
Touch of Evil 334
Tough Guys 323
Toulouse-Lautrec, Henri de
    149
tour de force **29**
Tour de France *368*, **386**
Tower, The 60
Tower Bridge **422**
Towering Inferno, The 324,
    327
Tower of Babel 168
Tower of London **422**
Town of Giants, Llŷn
    Peninsula 412
Townsend, Sue **57**
Townshend, Pete 360
toxic emissions 553
toxins **519**
tracery **167**
trachea 507
Tract (90) 108
Tracy, Spencer 320, **333**
trade
    barrier **306**
    cycle **306**
    embargo **293**
    invisible 290
    visible 290
trademark **29**
trades unions 273, **287**
trade winds **476**
Trafalgar, Battle of 198,
    208, **215**
Trafalgar Square 130, **422**
tragedy 51, **74**
*Tragical History of Dr
    Faustus, The* 39
tragi-comedy **74**
Trail of the Pink Panther 330
Train, The 330
train **565**

Traitor's Gate 422
Trajan **254**
trans- **29**
transformer 522, 529
transistor 562, **565**
transition elements 540,
    541, **546**
transitive verb **29**
transliteration **30**
transpiration **492**
transplant surgery 505, 507,
    519
Transport & General
    Workers Union 190
Trans-Siberian Railway **167**
transubstantiation **115**
transuranic elements 530
Trans World Airlines
    (TWA) 296
Trapeze 323, 329
Trapp, Maria Von 452
trauma **519**
travellers 178
Traveling Wilburys, The 343,
    354
Travels with my Aunt 41,
    330
Travesties 56
Traviata, La **353**
Travolta, John 113
treason 263
Treasure Island **57**, 327
*Treasure of the Sierra Madre,
    The* 321
Treasury **287**
    First Lord of the 287
treasury bills **306**
Treatise of Human Nature
    102
Treaty:
    Anglo-Irish 285
    Antarctic 427
    of Maastricht **277**, 294
    of Paris 220
    of Rome **250**, 269
    of Tordesillas 432
    USA/Soviet disarmament
        228
    of Versailles 206, 221,
        228, 237, 241, **255**, 257
    of Waitangi **256**
    of Westphalia 253
Treblinka 229
tree 482, 483, 484, 489, **492**
Tree of Knowledge 92, *109*
trench warfare 257
Trent, Council of **254**
Trent, River 414
Tresco *418*
Trevithick, Richard 211,
    565
Trial, The 69
Trial by Jury 344
triangle **546**
Triano, Rodrigo de 380
Triassic period *468*
tribunal **287**
Trident II 267
trigonometry **547**
Trinder, Tommy 322
Trinidad 461
Trinidad and Tobago **457**
Trinity, Holy **115**
Trinity College, Dublin 436

Tripoli, Libya 443
triptych **149**
Tristan and Iseult **89**
Tristan da Cunha 452, **457**
Tristram Shandy **58**
tritium 533, 539
Triumph of Time, The 56
Troilus and Cressida 53
Trojan horse **89**
Trojans, The 339
Trojan War 68, 76, 77, 83,
    85, **89**
Trollope, Anthony **58**
trolls **89**
trompe l'oeil **149**
Tropic of Cancer 544
Tropic of Capricorn 544
tropism 489, **492**
tropopause 464, 475
troposphere 464
Trotsky, Leon *241*, **254**
troubadours **74**
Trouble in Store 334
Trouble with Harry, The 324
Troughton, Patrick 315
trout 491
Trowbridge 424
Troy **89**, 245
Trubshaw, Brian 554
Trucial Coast 458
True Grit 333
Trueman, Fred **386**
truffles 394, **395**
Truman, Harry S 242, **254**
Truro 404
truth **116**
trypanosomiasis (sleeping
    sickness) 517
tsars **254**
tsetse fly 517
tsunami 474, **475**
Tuareg 452
tuber **492**
tuberculosis (TB) **519**
Tuck, Friar 81
Tudor (architecture) **167**
Tudor, House of 204, **215**
Tudor Rose 202
tulips 480
Tull, Jethro 188, **215**
tumour 497, 499, **519**
Tunbridge Ware 422
Tunbridge Wells **422**
Tunes of Glory 326
tungsten *see* periodic table
    541
Tunisia **457**
tunnels **167**
Turandot 353
turbines 561
turbochargers 558
turbogenerators 561
Turgenev, Ivan **74**, 108
Turin **457**
    Shroud 457
Turing, Alan 232
Turkana, Lake 442
Turkey 221, 437, 441, 442,
    458
    and Pakistan 449
    and Saudi Arabia 453
Turkmenistan 459
Turned Out Nice Again 317

Turner, Ike 360
Turner, J.M.W. **150**, 415
Turner, Tina **360**
Turn of the Screw, The 43,
    339
turnpike trusts **216**
Turpin, Randolph 381
turtles 490
Tuscany 453, **458**
'Tut, King' 255
Tutankhamun 248, **254**
Tutsi 451-2
tutti 350
TWA (Trans World
    Airlines) 296
Twain, Mark **58**, 445
Tweed, River 401
Twelfth Night **58**
Twelve Angry Men 317
Twelve O'Clock High 328
Twentieth Century Fox 300
*Twenty Thousand Leagues
    Under the Sea* 74
Twiggy 215
twin paradox **547**
twins 511
Twist, Oliver **38**
Two-Faced Woman 318
Two Jakes, The 327
2001, A Space Odyssey 359
Two Women 314, 324
Tycho Brahe *see* Brahe,
    Tycho
Tyger, The **58**
Tyler, Wat *209*, 401
Tyne and Wear **422**
Tyne River 409, 413
Tyneside 413
Tynwald 412
typhoid **519**
typhoon 469
typhus **519**
Tyrannosaurus rex *482*, 483
Tyre 443
tyres 552, 566
Tyrone 447
Tyson, Mike 365, **386**
tzatziki **395**

U

U-2 240, **255**
U-boat *Unterseeboot* 564
Uccello, Paolo **150**
Üçhisar, Cappadocia *458*
Uderzo, Albert 63
Uffington Castle 423
Uffizi 126, 151
UFOs **89**
Uganda 220, **458**
Ugly Duckling, The 62
UHF 470
Uist 400
Ukraine **458**
Ulan Bator 445
ulcer 518, **519**
ullage 396

Ulster Freedom Fighters
    (UFF) 277
Ulster unionist **288**
    apprentice boys' march
    206
Ulster Volunteer Force
    (UVF) 277
ultra- **30**
ultrasound 507, 516
ultraviolet radiation 472,
    510, 529, 540, **547**
Ulyanov, Vladimir Ilyich
    (Lenin) **241**
Ulysses **89**
Ulysses **58**, 73
Umberto D 314
Umbrellas, The 144
umlaut **30**
uncertainty principle 542,
    547
Uncle Tom's Cabin **58**
Uncle Vanya 64, 330
unconcious mind **186**
uncountable noun **30**
underground railways **167**
Under Milk Wood 21, **58**,
    311, 407
understatement **30**
Under the Net 47
underwriting **306**
unemployment 304, 305,
    306
UNESCO **288**
Unforgiven 316
unicorn **89**
Unidentified Flying Objects
    (UFO) 89
Unification Church
    (Moonies) 107, 174
unified field theories 523,
    529, 546, **547**
unilateralism 265, 267,
    288
Union, Acts of **216**
Union Carbide 224
Union for French
    Democracy 271
Union Jack 188, 216
UNITA 427
Unitarians **116**
United Arab Emirates **458**
Unité d'Habitation,
    Marseilles 162
United Kingdom 216
    see also individual topics
    and place names
United Nations (UN) 236,
    241, 258, 274, 275, **288**,
    455
    Educational, Scientific
    and Cultural
    Organisation 288
    General Assembly and
    Security Council 275,
    288
United Reformed Church
    110, **116**
United Society for Believers
    in Christ's Second
    Appearing 113
United States of America
    (USA) 220, 223, 439,
    444, 458, **458**, 461, 554
    Air Force 560

business and economics
294 *see also* Wall Street
civil rights movement
228, 241
Constitution of 224
Cuban missile crisis and
230
Depression, The **231**
flag 459
formation of 458-9
Founding Fathers 107
Iran-Contra scandal
238
Manhattan project 242
Monroe doctrine 244
'New Deal' 231, **246**,
459
nuclear weapons and 261,
286
Prohibition **249**
secret services *see also*
CIA 247
and Soviet Union
disarmament treaty
228
Strategic Defence
Initiative (SDI) 286
'Truman doctrine' 254
war with Japan 247
Watergate scandal 246,
256
wine and spirits 396
see also America, North;
Cold War
unit trust **306**
universe, origin of 524, 528,
546
universities **175**
Unknown Warrior,
tomb of 257
Unst 410
Unter den Linden 430
Untouchables, The 313
Up in Arms 322
upper case **30**
Ur 437
Ural Mountains 451
Urania 85
uranium **547**, 539, 560
see also periodic table **541**
Uranus *544*, **547**, 563
urea 539
ureter 507, 519
urethra 501, 520
urine 501, **519**, 520
urine tests 520
urology 510
Urquhart Castle, Loch
Ness 412
urticaria 506
Uru people 457
Usk, River 398
USSR (Union of Soviet
Socialist Republics) 240,
241, 246, 251, 253, **459**,
451, **459**
Communism, collapse of
265
Communist Party 265
coup d'etat 1991 271
Cuban missile crisis 230
disarmament treaty
(1989) 228
glasnost **271**, 458

Hungary and 238
Kremlin 239, 445
nuclear weapons and 261
perestroika 271, 458
Poland and 246
Warsaw Pact and 225,
238, 279
Yugoslavia and 462
see also CIS; Russia
Ustinov, Sir Peter **333**
usury **306**
Utah 459
Utahraptor 484
uterus **520**, 506
Utilitarianism 94, 106,
116
Utrillo, Maurice 150
Utzon, Jørn 167
Uzbekistan **459**

V2 (rocket bomb) 560
vaccination **520**
vaccines 507, 515, 520
vacuum **547**
Vadim, Roger 309
Vaduz, Liechtenstein 443
*Valediction Forbidding
Mourning, A* 39
valence **547**
Valencia 455
Valentino, Rudolph **333**
Valera, Eamon de **231**, 270,
285
Valhalla 85, 90
Valkyries **90**
Valles Marineris canyon
536
Valletta, Malta 444
Valley of the Dolls, The 53
Valley of the Kings 232
Valois, House of **255**
vampire bats 90
vampires **90**
vanadium *see* periodic table
541
Vanbrugh, Sir John **167**,
401, 403
Vancouver 433
Vandals 233, **255**
Van der Beek, Harmsen 48
Van der Post, Laurens 442
Van Diemen's Land 456
Van Dyck, Sir Antony 125,
131, **150**
Vane, Harriet 53
Van Eyck, Hubert 125
Van Eyck, Jan 125, **150**,
446
Van Gogh, Theo 151
Van Gogh, Vincent **151**,
315, 446
Vanity Fair **58**, 309
variable stars 524
varicose veins **520**
Vasarely, Victor **151**

Vasari, Giorgio **151**
vasectomy **520**
Vasco da Gama **234**
vassal 233, **255**
VAT (value added tax) **306**
Vatican City 143, 451, **459**
Vatican Council 103
Vaughan Williams, Ralph
360
vault **167**
veal 394, 396
vector **547**
V-E Day **255**
vegetative reproduction 490
veins 498, *499*, 520
Velásquez, Diego
Rodriguez da Silva *97*,
151
Velcro **565**
vellum 561
Velociraptor 483
velocity 537, **547**
Venables, Terry **387**
venereal disease **520**
Venezuela **459**
venial sin **116**
Venice **460**
venison 390
Venn diagram 544, **547**
Venturi, Robert **168**
Venus (Aphrodite) 76, 87,
90
Venus (planet) *544*, **547**,
561, 565
Venus and Adonis 53
Venus de Milo **151**
Ver, River 417
verb **30**
    auxiliary 11
    impersonal 18
    intransitive 19
    irregular 19
    reflexive 25
    regular 25
    transitive 29
    weak 30
verbatim **30**
Verdi, Giuseppe 357, **360**
Verdict, The 325, 327
Verlaine, Paul 73
Vermeer, Jan **151**, 446
vermouth 392
vernacular **395**
Verne, Jules **74**
Verona **460**
Veronese. Paolo **151**
Verrazano Narrows Bridge
160
verruca **520**
Versace, Gianni **151**
Versailles, Palace of 131,
168, 242
Versailles, Treaty of **255**
verse, blank 34
vertebrae 517
vertebrate *479*, **492**
vertigo 520
Vertigo 331
Verulamium 417
Verwoerd, Hendrik **255**
Vespucci, Amerigo **255**, 459
Vesta, sacred flame of 90
Vestal Virgins **90**
Vesuvius **460**

veto **288**
VHF 470
vibrato **350**
Vicar of Wakefield, The 41
Viceroy House, New Delhi
162
vice versa **30**
Vichy government **255**
vichyssoise **395**
Victim 310
Victor Emmanuel II 235,
250
Victoria, Lake 458, **460**
Victoria, Queen 32, 188,
196,201, 207, **216**, 400
Victoria and Albert
Museum 126, 188
Victoria Cross 178
Victoria Embankment 434
Victoria Falls 205, **460**
Victorian period 168, **216**
Victorian style
(architecture) **168**
Victorian style (art) 151
Victory, HMS 198, *208*,
416
Vic-Wells Ballet 357
Vidal, Gore **58**
video camcorders **566**
video cassette recorder
(VCR) 551, 566
videophones **565**
video tapes 559
Vienna **460**
    Art Museum 126
    Boys Choir 460
    Congress of 244, **255**
Vienna Sezession 130
Vientiane, Laos 443
Vietcong guerrillas 256
Vietnam 256, **460**
Vietnam War 225, 239,
246, **256**
View of Delft 151
Viking space probes *536*,
563
Vikings **216**, 225, 232, **256**
Village Blacksmith, The 45
Villa Rotonda, Italy 156
Villiers de L'Isle, Adam 62
Villon, François **74**
vinaigrette 395
vinegar **395**
    balsamic 395
vineyards, 396, 458
Vinland 232
VIPs, The 330
viral infections **520**
Virgil 62, **74**
Virgin Birth 103, **116**
Virginia **460-1**
Virginian, The 313
Virgin Islands **461**
Virgin Mary 92, 103, **116**
443
'virgin queen'
    see Elizabeth I
Virgo **90**, 548
virtual reality **566**
virus **492**, 504
virus, computer **566**
vis-à-vis **30**
Visconti, Luchino 314
viscosity **547**

Vishnu **116**
Vision of Piers Plowman, The
49, 87
Visit of St Nicholas, The 88
Vistula, River 450, 461
visual display unit (VDU)
554, 566
vitamins **520**
Vita Nuova, La 65
vitello tonnato **396**
Vitruvius Britannicus 157
vivace **350**
Vivaldi, Antonio **360**
viviparity 484
viz. **30**
V-J day **256**
Vlaminck, Maurice 124
Vltava, River, 450
vocal chords 507
Vogue 324
vogue word **30**
voice **30**
voice box 507
Vojvodina, Serbia 450
volcanic islands 473
volcano 447, 464, 471, 472,
475, 476
Volga **461**
Volga Boat Song 461
Volgograd 461
volleyball **387**
Volpone 44
volt 529, 541, **547**, 551
Volta, Alessandro 547, 551
Voltaire, François **74**, 238
volte-face **30**
Voluntary Euthanasia
Society 176
vomiting 498, 503
voodoo **116**
VO (brandy) 390
Vostok spaceships 234, 253
voting 270, 282
vowel **30**
Voyage Round My Father, A
328
Voyager space probes 536,
538, 547, 563
Voysey, Charles **168**
VSOP (brandy) 390, 391
Vuillard, Édouard 139
Vulcan 82, **90**
Vulgate **74**

Wace, Robert 87
Wade, Virginia **387**
Waffen SS 253
Wagner, Richard 54, 70, 73,
78, 81, 349, 353, **360**
Wailing Wall *104*, 115, 442
Waitangi, Treaty of **256**
Waiting for Godot 63, **74**
Wakeham, John 402
Walcott, Derek **58**
Walcott, Jersey Joe 377

Wales 216
  devolution 267
  National Library of 398
  Prince of 198
  University of 398
  see also individual topics
    and place names
Walesa, Lech 285, 450
Walker, John 377
Wallabies (rugby team)429
Wallace, A.E. 484
Wallace, Sir William **216**
Waller, Fats **360**
Wallis, Barnes 196
Wall Street 256, 293, **306**,
  315, 446
Wall Street Crash 231, **256**,
  306, 459
Walpole, Horace 455
Walpole, Sir Robert 214,
  217
Walrus and the Carpenter,
  The 70
Walton, Sir William 55
waltz, the *358*
Walworth, William *209*
War and Peace **74**, 320
War and Remembrance 326
Warbeck, Perkin **217**
War Cry, The 113
Ward, Burt 309
Ward, Stephen *211*
Warden, The 58
warfare, rules of 271
Warhol, Andy 142, **152**
warm-blooded **492**
warm front 464, 471, 475,
  476
War of the Worlds, The 59,
  333
Warsaw **461**
Warsaw Pact 225, 238, **256**,
  279
Warspite, HMS 564
wart **520**
Warwick **423**
  Castle *423*
  Earl of **217**
Wash, The **423**
Washington DC 459, **461**
Washington, George **256**,
  445, 460
Washington Post 256
Washington Square 43
Washkansky, Louis *519*
wasps 491
Wassily chair *156*
Waste Isolation Pilot Plant
  471
Waste Land, The 51, **58**
watchmaking, Swiss 455
Watchtower, The 103
water **547**
waterpolo **387**
water purification **566**
water speed record 366
Water Babies, The **59**
waterfall 447, 459-60, 462
  world's highest 427
Watergate 246, **256**, 459
Waterhouse, Keith 34
Waterlilies 137
Waterloo, Battle of **257**,
  430

Waterman, Dennis 326
Waters, Muddy **360**
waterspout **476**
water table 469, **476**
Watson, James 484
Watson, J.B. 171
Watson, Dr John 43
Watson, Thomas 551
watt **548**
Watt, James 203, 211, 548,
  564, **566**
Watteau, Jean-Antoine **152**
wattle-and-daub 168
Watts, Charlie 357
Waugh, Evelyn 29, **59**, 311
wave **548**, 534
  amplitude **522**
  electromagnetic *see*
    electromagnetic
    radiation
  frequency **531**
  sound 528, 531, 543, 544,
    548
  wave-particle duality 535,
    543, 548
wavelength 529, 531, **548**
Waveney, River 402
Waverley 53
Waves, The 60
Way Ahead, The 327
Wayne, John 317, **333**
Way Out West 323
'We few, we happy few, we
  band of brothers' **59**
weak verb 30
Weald, The 414
Wealth of Nations 304
weasel words 30
weather 464, 471, 527
weather forecasting 465,
  476
weather satellites 562
Webb, Beatrice 270
Webb, Captain 405
Webb, Sidney 270
Webb Ellis, William 382
Weber, Max **186**
Webster, Gary 326
Webster, John 51, **59**
wedding customs and
  dowry 172
Wedgwood, Josiah **152**
Weekley, Frieda 45
Weekly Political Register 195
Wegener, Alfred 466
weight 536, **548**
weightlifting **387**
Weill, Kurt 33
Weimar Republic *see*
  Germany **257**
Weir of Hermiston 55
Weissmuller, Johnny 332
welfare state 190, 276, **288**,
  301
Welland, River 420
Welles, Orson 312, **333**
Wellington, Duke of **217**
Wellington, New Zealand
  447
Wellington boot 217
Wellingtonia 217
Wells **423**
Wells Cathedral 158, 160,
  423

Wells, H.G. **59**
Welsh nationalism 281
Wembley Stadium 370
Wenceslas I (Saint) 436,
  450
Wenceslas Square 450
Wensum, River 414
werewolves **90**
Wesley, Charles 106, 116
Wesley, John 106, **116**
Wessex 188, 196, 424
West, Adam 309
West, Mae 319, **334**
West, Dame Rebecca **59**
West Bank 261, 442, **461**
Westbrook, Harriet 54
westerlies **476**
Western Australia **461**
Westerner, The 319
Western Isles 409
Westerns, spaghetti *315*,
  331
Western Samoa **461**
West India Dock 401
West Indies **461**
Westland Affair 273
Westminster Abbey **168**,
  276, 423
Westminster, City of **423**
Westminster, Palace of 155,
  214
Weston-super-Mare **423**
West Side Story 52, *339*,
  358
Westward Ho! **423**
West Wind Drift *471*
Westwood, Vivienne **152**
West Yorkshire **423**
Wetherell, Marmaduke 84
whale 478, 481, 487
Wham! 351
Whatever Happened to Baby
  Jane? 313
What Maisie Knew 43
What's Up Doc 311
What the Butler Saw 48, 329
wheel **566**
whelks 486
When the Whales Came 330
When We Are Married 51
When We Were Very Young
  47
Where Danger Lives 326
Where Eagles Dare 46, 316
Whigs **217**
Whip (politics) **288**
whipping boy 30
whirlpool **476**
whisky **396**
Whisky Galore 315
Whistler, James Abbott
  McNeill **152**
Whistler, Rex *33*
Whitaker, John 383
Whitaker, Michael 383
White, Carol 312
White, Jimmy 373
white-collar **186**
White Devil, The 59
white dwarf 539, 543, 545,
  546, **548**
white elephant 30
White Goddess, The 41
White Heat 311

White Horse Hill **423**
White House, Washington
  DC 461
White Hunter, Black Heart
  316
white knight **306**
white paper **288**
Whitehall **423**
Whitehead, A.N. 112
Whiting, Leonard 334
Whitman, Walt **59**
Whitney, Mount 454
Whitsun 110
Whittington, Dick **217**
Whittle, Sir Frank 558
Whizz for Atomms 47
WHO (World Health
  Organisation) **288**, 507,
  514
Who, The **360**
whooping cough **520**
Whore 330
Who's Afraid of Virginia
  Woolf? **59**, 311, 332
Whymper, Edward *444*
'Wicca' **90**
'Wicked Bible' 95
Wicked Lady, The 323, 325
Wicked Stepmother, The 313
Wicken Fen 407
Widmark, Richard **334**
Wieck, Clara 358
Wife of Bath 36, **59**
Wight, Isle of **423**
Wilberforce, William **217**,
  252, 410
Wilde, Oscar **59**, 152, 316,
  330, 331
Wilder, Billy 316, 323, 326,
  332, **334**, 349
Wild One, The 311
wild rice **396**
Wild Strawberries 309
Wild Swans **59**
Wilhelm I, Kaiser *196*
Wilhelm II, Kaiser 224,
  257, 438
Wilkes, John **217**
Wilkins, Maurice 484
Willans, Geoffrey 47
William I (the Conqueror)
  197, 201, **217**, 438
William II ('Rufus') 201,
  218, 413
William III *see* William and
  Mary
William IV **218**
William and Mary 190,
  200, 206, **218**
'William' books **59**
William of Orange *see*
  William and Mary
William of Wykeham 424
Williams, Hank 341
Williams, John **360**
Williams, Kenneth 312,
  334
Williams, Marcia (Lady
  Falkender) 288
Williams, Michael 314
Williams, Shirley 284
Williams, Ted *364*
Williams, Tennessee **59**,
  329

Williamsburg, Virginia 460
Williams-Ellis, Clough *415*
Williams-Renault 377
Williams (motor racing)
  376
William Tell 357
Will o' the Wisps **90**
'willow pattern' china 453
Wilson, Sir Angus **60**
Wilson, Harold (Lord
  Wilson) **268**, **288**, 293,
  297
Wilson R.K. 84
Wilson, Teddy 345
Wilson, Woodrow **257**, 259
Wilton **423**
Wilton House 423
Wiltshire **423**
Wiltshire, Stephen *496*
Wimbledon **424**
  Common 424
Wimbledon (tennis) **387**
Wimsey, Lord Peter 53
Winchester **424**
wind 466, 469, 470, 471,
  527, **476**
  Beaufort scale **465**
wind-chill **476**
Windermere, Lake 410
Windhoek 446
Windhover, The 43
Wind in the Willows, The
  60
'wind of change' **257**
Windscale 418
Winds of War, The 326
Windsor **424**
  Castle 402, 424
  House of **218**
Windsor, Barbara 312
Windsor, Duke of 198
Windsor, Frank 334
windsurfing **387**
wind turbines 476
wine **396**, 438, 443-4,
  448, 450-1, 455, 485
  corked **396**
wine, New World **396**
Wings 338
Winnie-the-Pooh **60**
Winslow Boy, The 51
winter of discontent **218**,
  263
Winter Olympics **388**
Winter Palace, St
  Petersburg 452
Winter's Tale, The 54, 72
Wireless Telegraph and
  Signal Company 559
Wisdom, Norman **334**
witan **218**
witchcraft **90**, 116, 444
Witchcraft Today 90
witches **90**
Witches of Eastwick, The 327
Witham, River 411
Wittenberg 105,
Wittgenstein, Ludwig **116**
Witwatersrand 442
'Wizard of Dribble', the
  377
Wizard of Oz, The 318, **334**
Woburn Abbey **424**
Wodehouse, Sir P.G. **60**

Woden 85
Wöhler, Friedrich 539
Wojtyla, Cardinal 450
wok **396**
Wolds, the 411
Wolf 327
Wolfe, James **218**
Wollstonecraft Godwin,
    Mary 54
Wolsey, Cardinal Thomas
    202, **218**, 409
Wolverhampton 401
Woman of Affairs, A 318
Woman of the Year 320
Woman's Face, A 313
Woman's Own **324**
womb 520
Wombles, The 424
Women in Love 45, **60**, 330
women's liberation 176 see
    also feminism
women's ordination 109
Wonder, Stevie **360**
*Wonderful Wizard of Oz,
    The* 334
Wonder Man 322
wood **492**
Wood, Sir Henry 355
wood avens *490*
woodcut **152**
woodlice 482
Woodstock, Oxfordshire,
    401
Woodstock rock concerts
    178
Wood the Elder, John 400
Wood the Younger, John
    400
Woodward, Bob 256
Woodward, Joanne 327
Wookey Hole **424**
Woolf, Leonard 60
Woolf, Virginia 34, 52, **60**,
    73
Woolner, Thomas 142
Woolwich **424**
Woolworth, Frank Winfield
    306
Woolworth building 306
Wooster, Bertie 60
Worcester **424**
Worcestershire sauce 424
word processor **566**
Words and Music 341
Wordsworth, Dorothy 37
Wordsworth, William 37,
    43, 57, **60**, 408
work 534, 535, **548**
workhouses **218**
World Bank 225, **306**

World Council of Churches
    99
World Cup **388**
world drivers'
    championship **388**
World Health Organisation
    (WHO) 288, 507, 514
World in Action 325
World Trade Center **168**,
    446
World Tree 85, **90**
World War I 214, 255, **257**,
    258, 445, 446, 452, 566
World War II 229, 231,
    232, 240, 246, 247, **257**,
    258, 430, 432, 436, 444,
    450, 451, 461, 552, 558,
    560
worms 479, 497
Worms, Diet of 258
Wray, Fay 322
Wren, Sir Christopher 160,
    168
Wren, P.C. 426
wrestling **388**
Wright brothers (Orville
    and Wilbur) 550, **566**
Wright, Elsie *81*
Wright, Frank Lloyd **168**,
    434
Würzburg Palace 149
Wuthering Heights **60**, 319,
    328
Wyatt, Thomas 72
Wycherly, William 51
Wycliffe, John 206, **218**,
    238
Wye, River **424**
Wykehamists 424
Wylye, River 418
Wyman, Bill 357
Wynette, Tammy **360**
Wyoming 426
Wyss, Johann David 73

X-certificate **334**
X chromosome 481
xenon 538, *see also* periodic
    table **541**
xerography 561
Xerxes 251, **258**

Xhosa **186**
Xizang Autonomous
    Region 443, 457
X-rays 516, 529, **548**
xylem *485*, 489, 492

Y

yacht racing 362-3, **388**
yagli (Turkish wrestling)
    388
Yahweh 103, **116**
Yakut region 453
Yalta Conference **258**, 435
Yamasaki, Minoru 168
Yankee Doodle Dandy 311
Yathrib (Medina) 108
Y chromosome 481
yeast 485, 486, **492**
Yeats, William Butler **60**,
    83
Yellowbeard 326
yellow fever **520**
Yellowstone National Park
    451, **462**
Yeltsin, Boris 271, **288**
Yemen **462**
Yentl 359
yeoman warder 422
Yes, Minister **334**
*Yesterday, Today and
    Tomorrow* 314, 324
Yeti 76
Yggdrasil 90
yield **306**
yin and yang **116**, 393
yoga **116**
Yom Kippur **116**
Yom Kippur War **258**
York **424**
    Archbishop of 96
    Minster 424
York, House of **218**
    see also Roses, Wars of the
York Minster **168**, 424
Yorkshire Dales **424**
    National Park 424
Yorkshire Ripper, the 185,
    513
Yorktown, Battle of 220
Yosemite National Park
    118, 454, **462**
You Bet Your Life 325

You Can't Take It With You
    312, 331
Young, Brigham 107, 459
Young, Thomas 535
Young Girl, The (Klimt) *130*
'Young Italy' movement
    235
Young Mr Lincoln, The 317
Young Ones, The 356
*Young Person's Guide to the
    Orchestra* 339
Young Pretender **218**
Young Winston 309, 321
Ypres **258**, 430
    Battles of **258**
ytterbium *see* periodic table
    541
yttrium *see* periodic table
    541
Yucatán peninsula 444
Yugoslavia 117, 185, 254,
    429, 430, 431, 452, 453,
    454, **462**
    break-up of 453
    Civil War (1991) 254
Yukon Territory 433
Yule 96
yuppy **186**

Z

zabaglione **396**
Zagreb 435
Zaharias, Mildred 'Babe'
    388
Zaire **462**
Zambezi River 205, 460,
    462
Zambia **462**
Zamenhof, Dr Ludwig
    Lazarus 16
Zanu 279
Zapu 279
Zarathustra 116
Zatopek, Emil **388**
Z Cars **334**
Zealand, Denmark 436
Zeffirelli, Franco 318, **334**
Zeitgeist **186**
Zele, Margarete Getrude
    (Mata Hari) 243
Zen Buddhism **116**, 393
Zeno of Elea 115, 548

Zeno's paradoxes **548**
Zeppelin, Count
    Ferdinand von **566**
zeppelins 566
zeugma 30
Zeus 76, 77, 83, 85, 87,
    89, **90**
Zhou dynasty **258**
Zhou En-lai *243*, **258**
Zia ul-Haq, General 224,
    262
ziggurat **168**
Ziggy Stardust 339
Zimbabwe **462**
zinc 546, *see also* periodic
    table **541**
Zinfandel (grape) 396
Zinnemann, Fred **334**
Zinoviev letter **218**
Zionism **288**
zirconium *see* periodic
    table **541**
Zodiac 77, **90**, 527, **548**
Zoffany, Johan **152**
Zola, Emile **74**, 232
zombies 116
Zorba the Greek 69
Zoroaster 116
Zoroastrianism 109, **116**
zucchini 396
Zugspitze 430
Zuleika Dobson 33
Zulu 311
Zulus **186**, 454,
    Inkatha 260
Zululand 186
Zurich, bullion market 291
Zworykin, Vladimir **566**
zygote 484, 485, 486, 490,
    492

ACKNOWLEDGMENTS

The sources for the photographs are listed below. The following short forms have been used: Bettmann Newsphotos = BN; The Bridgeman Art Library = BAL; Bruce Coleman Ltd = BC; Mary Evans Picture Library = MEPL; The Ronald Grant Archive = RGA; Michael Holford = MH; The Hulton Deutsch Collection = HDC; The Image Bank = IB; The Kobal Collection = KC; The Mansell Collection = MC; National Portrait Gallery, London = NPG; Rex Features Ltd = Rex; Science Photo Library = SPL. Abbreviations: T = top; TL = top left; TC = top centre; TR = top right; C = centre; CL = centre left; CR = centre right; B = bottom; BL = bottom left; BC = bottom centre; BR = bottom right.

1 (Parthenon) BC/Norman Owen Tomalin (Marilyn) Movie Stills Archives (Penny Black) National Postal Museum, London (Sunflowers) BAL/The National Gallery, London/Index (Atom) SPL/Michael Gilbert 4 (Embryo) SPL/Petit Format/Nestlé (Gandhi) Camera Press (Aphrodite) MH (Wolsey) NPG (Brighton Rock) The Penguin Group (Leeds Castle) Robert Harding Picture Library/Adam Woolfitt (Kennedy) Camera Press/F. Bachrach 5 TR Bildarchiv Preussischer Kulturbesitz (Rocket) The Science Museum, London (Einstein) SPL/US Library of Congress (Madonna) MH (Superbowl) All-Sport (UK)/Mike Powell (Mandela) Rex (Sumo) All-Sport (UK)/Chris Cole (Volcano) Explorer/K. Krafft (C. Eastwood) British Film Institute (Pisa) ZEFA 9 BR MEPL/Explorer 13 BR Permission of the Trustees of the British Museum 14 TL MEPL CR Designed by Julian Rothenstein/from 'Alphabets & Other Signs' B MEPL/Explorer 25 MEPL 26 CR HDC 28 MEPL 29 EMI Archives 30 ET Archive 31 L Courtesy of the Trustees of the Victoria & Albert Museum, London BR Sotheby's 32 From the collections of the Theatre Museum by courtesy of the Trustees of the Victoria & Albert Museum 33 T BAL BR MEPL 34 C ET Archive BR Robert Opie 35 NPG 36 TL Burns National Library of Scotland, Edinburgh CL NPG B © Glasgow Museum & Art Galleries 37 L MEPL R Popperfoto 39 Popperfoto 40 UPI/BN 41 (Background) British Film Institute BL NPG BR The Penguin Group 42 KC 44 B NPG 48 Popperfoto 49 TL MC CR KC/Colombia Pictures 50 B HDC 51 Donald Cooper 52 MC 53 BL Courtesy of the Trustees of the Victoria & Albert Museum, London BR Pat Hodgson 54 TL KC BR Popperfoto 55 Sotheby's/Cecil Beaton 56 MC 57 BAL/National Museum of Wales, Cardiff/By Permission of Mrs Vivian White 58 Popperfoto 59 NPG 60 CL Popperfoto B ET Archive 61 TC Roger-Viollet CL Bildarchiv Preussischer Kulturbesitz CR Novosti 62 L MEPL Ullstein CR RGA 63 T RGA BL Jakob Skou-Hansen BR Royal Library, Copenhagen 64 T Novosti 64 B Roger-Viollet 65 T Scala B RGA 66 Artothek Joachim Blauel, Neue Pinakothek 67 TL RGA BR Bildarchiv Preussischer Kulturbesitz 68 T MH BL Tromsö Museum BR HDC 69 BAL 70 BAL/Musée Condé Chantilly 71 The Estate of Edmund Dulac (The Publishers have been unable to trace the copyright holder) 73 Statens Konstmuseer, Stockholm 74 T Novosti B BAL/Musée D'Orsay, Paris 75 T Rex BR MEPL 76 T MEPL B MH 77 C MEPL B Bibliothèque Nationale, Paris (Ms. Fr. 343 f. 3) 78 MH 80 C Rex BR KC 81 R MEPL 84 T Popperfoto BL MEPL BR MC 85 MC 86 MEPL 87 T MEPL B MEPL 88 MEPL 89 MEPL 91 TL MEPL/Ida Kar TR MH BL Frank Spooner BR Archiv für Kunst und Geschichte, Berlin B BAL/Galleria Degli Uffizi, Florence BL Lucian Niemeyer - LNS Arts 93 BAL 94 BAL/National Gallery, London 95 TL Permission of the Trustees of the British Museum TC Giraudon TR Frank Spooner 96 BAL/Bibliothèque Nationale, Paris 97 MH/Prado, Madrid 98 TL The Israel Museum, Jerusalem TC Robert Harding Picture Library/Christina Gascoigne B MEPL 100 T Board of General Purposes of the United Grand Lodge of England CR BAL/Giraudon 101 Black Star, New York/St Louis Post Dispatch 102 BL Magnum/Philip Jones Griffiths BC MH 104 Magnum/F. Mayer 105 Archiv für Kunst und Geschichte, Berlin/Munchen, Bayerische Staatsbibliothek (cod. arab. 1113 fol. 4v) 106 Frank Spooner/Mohamed Lounes 107 C Courtesy of the Museum of Art at Brigham Young University. All Rights reserved. Artist, C.C.A. Christensen 'Pioneers Crossing the Plains of Nebraska' 108 MEPL 109 TC MH BL BAL/Courtauld Institute Galleries 111 C The Quaker Tapestry Scheme BR Religious Society of Friends 112 TL MEPL BR MEPL/Ida Kar 113 BR Rex BR The Salvation Army 114 Museo del Prado Madrid 115 Metropolitan Museum of Art/Wolfe Fund, 1931. Catherine Lorillard Wolfe Collection (31.45) 116 MH 117 BAL/John Hay Whitney Collection, New York 118 TL Emporio Armani TR BAL/By courtesy of the Board of Trustees of the Victoria & Albert Museum, London BR Angelo Hornak 119 BL MH BR HDC 120 BAL/Prado, Madrid 121 Courtauld Institute of Art 122 BAL/By courtesy of the Trustees of the Victoria & Albert Museum, London 123 BAL/Metropolitan Museum of Art, New York 124 MH 125 BAL 127 BL The National Gallery, London BAL/Tate Gallery/© David Hockney 129 BAL/© Jasper Johns/DACS, London/VAGA, New York 1995 130 TL Archiv für Kunst und Geschichte, Berlin/Erich Lessing/Nationalgalerie, Prague BR FAR SIDE copyright FARWORKS, INC. /Dist. by Universal Press Syndicate 131 C Christie's Colour Library B BAL 132 National Trust for Scotland 133 TL Tate Gallery, London BR Reunion des Musées Nationaux 134-5 BAL/Vatican Museums & Galleries, Rome 136 Corporate Art Collection, The Reader's Digest Association, Inc. 137 TL © 1994 ABC/Mondrian Estate/Holtzman Trust. Licensed by ILP/Photo: Martin Buhler & Corporate Art Collection, The Reader's Digest Association, Inc. 138 Tate Gallery, London BL The William Morris Gallery, Walthamstow, London BR BAL 139 BAL/© The Munch Museum/The Munch-Ellingsen Group/DACS 1995 140 L Courtauld Institute of Art/Hunter Bequest 1982/By Permission of Angela Verren-Taunt R Norman

Parkinson 141 BAL/Prado, Madrid/© DACS 1995 142 BL San Francisco Museum of Modern Art Albert M. Bender Collection, Albert M. Bender Bequest Fund Purchase/© ARS, NY and DACS, London 1995 BR HDC 143 TR BAL/Kenwood House BL © TMR/ADAGP, Paris, 1993, Collection L. Treillard 144 BAL/John Hay Whitney Collection, New York 145 TL Studio Des Grands Augustins/Photographer, J. F. Chavannes BR Spencer Museum of Art, The University of Kansas, Lawrence, Kansas 146 TR The Cleveland Museum of Art, Gift of the Hanna Fund, 49. 186 BL BAL/Prado, Madrid 147 BAL/Art Institute of Chicago 148 BAL/Tate Gallery, London 149 BL Christie's Colour Library BR BAL/By Courtesy of the Board of Trustees of the Victoria & Albert Museum 150 BAL/National Gallery, London 151 BAL/National Gallery, London/Index 152 T BAL/Giraudon/Louvre, Paris B BAL/© 1995 Andy Warhol Foundation for the Visual Arts/ARS, New York 153 T BCB/Norman Owen Tomalin BL BAL/Fitzwilliam Museum, University of Cambridge BR Arcaid/Scott Frances/ESTO 154 MH 155 TC IB/Steve Krongard BR RETORIA: Y. Futagawa & Associated Photographers 156 TL Christie's Colour Library TC Ullstein BR HDC 158 TL BAL/Fitzwilliam Museum, University of Cambridge B Giraudon/Lauros 159 T IB B Giraudon/Lauros 160 L IB/Jeff Hunter R The National Trust/Nicolas Sapieha 161 TL IB/Joe McNally C Robert Harding Picture Library 162 T Arcaid/Stephen Couturier B Magnum/René Burri 163 IB/Derik Berwin 164 BC/Norman Owen Tomalin 165 IB/P & G Bowater 166 IB/Robbi Newman 167 IB/Thomas Rampy 168 T Arcaid/Scott Frances/Esto B IB/David Gould 169 TL Popperfoto TR Camera Press BR The Hutchison Picture Library/John Hatt 170 Colorific/Penny Tweedie 171 Magnum/Eve Arnold 172 Colorific/Dilip Mehta/Contact 173 TL Topham Picture Library C The Penguin Group 174 HDC 176 TC Camera Press TR The Freud Museum 177 The Hutchison Picture Library/Michael MacIntyre 178 TR Spink & Son Ltd BL Imperial War Museum BC Imperial War Museum BR Spink & Son Ltd 179 Bryan & Cherry Alexander 180 TL Camera Press/Karsh of Ottawa BR Courtesy of the Trustees of the Victoria & Albert Museum, London 181 UPI/BN 182 TL The Hutchison Picture Library/John Hatt BC Colorific/Terence Spencer BR Colorific Terence Spencer 183 Magnum/Ernst Haas 184 Popperfoto 185 Colorific/Christopher Morris/Black Star 186 HDC 187 TL NPG TC Imperial War Museum TR HDC BR HDC 188 TL HDC TC HDC 189 MH 190 BAL 191 Rex 192 HDC 193 T HDC C Permission of the Board of the British Library BL © The Pierpont Morgan Library 1994 (PML 18386, f. 1, ch L 1760) 194 T MEPL B Topham Picture Source 195 BC Topham Picture Library BR HDC 196 T NPG BL MEPL 197 The Associated Press 199 TL MC CL Ashmolean Museum, Oxford BR Robert Opie 200 T MEPL TC TUC Library 201 Windsor Castle, Royal Library. © 1989 Her Majesty The Queen 202 NPG 203 BR BAL 204 BR HDC 205 TL Imperial War Museum TR NPG BC HDC 206 Popperfoto 207 BR 'Execution of Mary Queen of Scots' Scottish National Portrait Gallery BR 'Mary Queen of Scots' after Clouet. Scottish National Portrait Gallery BR HDC 208 TL Imperial War Museum BL BAL/National Maritime Museum, London BC HDC 209 TR National Postal Museum, London BR Permission of the Board of the British Library 210 HDC 211 TL HDC TC Popperfoto 212 L MC TR NPG 213 T Popperfoto CR Permission of the Board of the British Library 214 T Imperial War Museum BR Harry Roe-Stokes 215 TC Popperfoto TR MEPL BR John Frost Historical Newspaper Service 216 MC 217 TL BAL/By courtesy of the Board of Trustees of the Victoria & Albert Museum/Stapleton Collection BR ET Archive 218 NPG 219 TL Robert Harding Picture Library TR The Granger Collection BL Rex 220 The Granger Collection 221 TL Culver Pictures, New York CL Popperfoto 222 TL Wiener Library C Popperfoto BR Scala 223 C Popperfoto BR Rex/Witt/Sipa Press 226 UPI/BN 227 TL The Associated Press TR Stiftsbibliothek St Gallen (Cod. Sang. 22.S. 141) BC Bibliothek des Domstifs Merseburg (Ms.136 f.16) 228 TR Camera Press 230 TL Bibliothèque Nationale, Paris BR Private Collection 231 T Popperfoto BR Peter Newark's Pictures 233 Jean-Loup Charmet 234 TL BAL/Musée Carnavalet, Paris BR Camera Press 235 T HDC 236 Rex/© Sipa-Press 237 C Rex/© Sipa-Press B Rex/©Sipa-Press 238 Lee Boltin Picture Library 239 TL Rex 240 TC Camera Press BR Camera Press B Camera Press/F. Bachrach 241 T Rex BR Rex 242 T Popperfoto TR Bulloz, Paris 243 TR Magnum/Collection J.A.F. /Paris BR Popperfoto 245 TR Tate Gallery, London B Rex 246 T Camera Press/Robert Jackson/Dallas Times Herald 247 BR ET Archive 248 TL Scala TR Archivi Alinari/Giacomo Brogi 249 TR HDC CR Underwood & Underwood 251 Aspect/Kelly Langley 252 CR Magnum/Robert Capa 253 Sonia Halliday 254 TL Magnum/Stuart Franklin C Frank Spooner/Chip Hires BR Robert Harding Picture Library/F L. Kenett 255 BC Topham Picture Library BR John Frost Historical Newspaper Service 256 TL The Associated Press/Nguyen Kong (Nick Ut) BR John Frost Historical Newspaper Service 258 Private Collection/US Army 259 CR Central Office of Information/Terry Moore 259 TL Rex BR Rex 260 BC Sygma/W. Campbell BR Impact/Billy Paddock 261 Rex/Sipa 262 Frank Spooner/Gamma 263 TR John Frost Historical Newspaper Service TR Popperfoto BL HDC 264 Rex/Tim Rooke 265 TL Rex BR Topham Picture Library 268 (Conservative) The Bodleian Library (Liberal) The Bodleian Library (Labour) The Bodleian Library (Ballot box) HDC 269 BBC 270 CL UPI/BN BR Frank Spooner /Gamma/Sebah 271 TC UPI/BN BC Colorific/Peter Turnley/Black Star 272 C Rex/Today BR Rex/Sipa-Press 273 Central Office of Information/Terry Moore 274 TL MC TR ET Archive 276 Universal Pictorial Press and Agency 277 TL UPI/BNI C Popperfoto 278 TC Rex/The Times BL Rex 279 Rex/Sipa-Press 280 BBC 281 TC HDC TR Rex/Tim